September 25–27, 2013
Boston, Massachusetts, USA

Association for
Computing Machinery

Advancing Computing as a Science & Profession

ICFP'13

Proceedings of the 2013 ACM SIGPLAN
International Conference on Functional Programming

Sponsored by:

ACM SIGPLAN

Supported by:

Jane Street, FPComplete, Microsoft Research, NSF, ORACLE LABS, Standard Chartered, Credit Suisse, Erlang Solutions, Galois, Google, INRIA, Twitter, Northwestern University, IntelliFactory, & QuviQ

Association for
Computing Machinery

Advancing Computing as a Science & Profession

The Association for Computing Machinery
2 Penn Plaza, Suite 701
New York, New York 10121-0701

ISBN: 978-1-4503-2326-0

Additional copies may be ordered prepaid from:

ACM Order Department
PO Box 30777
New York, NY 10087-0777, USA

Phone: 1-800-342-6626 (USA and Canada)
+1-212-626-0500 (Global)
Fax: +1-212-944-1318
E-mail: acmhelp@acm.org
Hours of Operation: 8:30 am – 4:30 pm ET

Printed in the USA

"Cover photo by Werner Kunz; used with the author's permission."

Foreword

It is my great pleasure to welcome you to the *18th ACM SIGPLAN International Conference on Functional Programming, ICFP '13*, in Boston, Massachusetts, USA.

ICFP is a forum for researchers and practitioners to hear about the latest developments in the art and science of functional programming. The conference covers the entire spectrum of work, from theory to practice.

This year's call for papers attracted 133 submissions, which is an all-time record for ICFP: 115 regular research papers, 11 functional pearls and 7 experience reports. From those, the Program Committee selected 40 papers--33 regular papers, 4 functional pearls and 3 experience reports–for presentation at the conference and inclusion in the proceedings. One paper submitted as a regular research paper was recategorized to an experience report, one experience report to a functional pearl, yielding 32 regular papers, 5 functional pearls and 3 experience reports.

Each submission was reviewed by at least 3 people (either PC members or external reviewers). After initial online discussion in the PC, the reviews were communicated to the authors, who then had three days to comment back. Following updating of the reviews and, in several cases, addition of new reviews, as well as further online discussion, the PC met in Munich, Germany, for two days for final decisions. All but two PC members attended the meeting in person. One of them could not make it for personal reasons, the other had his transatlantic flight canceled; they took part by phone. The competition was tough and the PC had to reject many good papers.

Submission by PC members was allowed. There were 7 such submissions. Those were scrutinized against a higher standard; 2 of them were accepted.

Authors had the possibility to submit additional material (such as code or proofs) with their papers, on the understanding that reviewers may choose not to look at it. This was used by the authors of 27 submissions. Authors of papers previously rejected from another conference were given the option to attach the reviews of their previous submission, with their explanations about how they have addressed the criticisms raised. These reviews and comments would be communicated by the Program Chair only to reviewers who identify themselves as reviewers of the earlier version. This option was used by the authors of 5 submissions.

As keynote speakers we are privileged to hear Ulf Norell (Chalmers University of Technology, Sweden) and Simon Peyton Jones (Microsoft Research, Cambridge, UK) at ICFP '13.

I felt enormously honored to be asked to serve as this year's Program Chair. I am most grateful to the many people that assisted me, first of all the ICFP '13 General Chair, Greg Morrisett, and the members of the Steering Committee. Thanks to all authors, both accepted and rejected, for submitting, for choosing ICFP. The Program Committee did a tremendous job, as did the 166 external reviewers who we engaged for their expertise. As PC software we used the EasyChair system of Cool Press. The PC meeting in Munich was made possible by Martin Hofmann and Sigrid Roden of Ludwig-Maximilians-Universität München. To Lisa Tolles at Sheridan Communications I owe thanks for coordinating the production of this proceedings volume.

Tarmo Uustalu
ICFP '13 Program Chair
Institute of Cybernetics at TUT, Estonia

Table of Contents

Session 5: Handling Effects

Keynote 2

Session 6: Concurrency

Session 7: (Co-)Recursion

Session 8: Functional Reactive Programming and More

Session 9: Lambda-Calculus

Session 10: Monads

Session 11: Modular Meta-Theory

Session 12: Experience

Session 13: Program Logics

Session 14: Language Design

Session 15: Analysis and Optimization

ICFP 2013 Organization

General Chair: Greg Morrisett *(Harvard University, USA)*

Program Chair: Tarmo Uustalu *(Institute of Cybernetics at TUT, Estonia)*

Workshop Co-Chairs: Patrik Jansson *(Chalmers University of Technology, Sweden)*
Sam Tobin-Hochstadt *(Northeastern University, USA)*

Programming Contest Co-Chairs: Peli de Halleux *(Microsoft Research, Redmond, USA)*
Michal Moskal *(Microsoft Research, Redmond, USA)*
Nikhil Swamy *(Microsoft Research, Redmond, USA)*
Nikolai Tillmann *(Microsoft Research, Redmond, USA)*

Industrial Relations Chair: Andy Adams-Moran *(Standard Chartered Bank, UK)*

Publicity Chair: David Van Horn *(Northeastern University, USA)*

Treasurer: Jean-Baptiste Tristan *(Oracle Labs, USA)*

Conference Coordinator: Annabel Satin

Steering Committee Co-Chairs: Manuel Chakravarty *(University of New South Wales, Australia)*
Zhenjiang Hu *(National Institute of Informatics, Japan)*

Steering Committee: Olivier Danvy *(Aarhus University, Denmark)*
Robby Findler *(Northwestern University, USA)*
Jeremy Gibbons *(University of Oxford, UK)*
Fritz Henglein *(University of Copenhagen, Denmark)*
David Van Horn *(Northeastern University, USA)*
Johan Jeuring *(Universiteit Utrecht, The Netherlands)*
Gabriele Keller *(University of New South Wales, Australia)*
John Launchbury *(Galois, USA)*
Yaron Minsky *(Jane Street Capital, USA)*
Greg Morrisett *(Harvard University, USA)*
Peter Thiemann *(Universität Freiburg, Germany)*
Tarmo Uustalu *(Institute of Cybernetics at TUT, Estonia)*
Jan Vitek *(Purdue University, USA)*

Program Committee:

Thorsten Altenkirch *(University of Nottingham, UK)*
Olaf Chitil *(University of Kent, UK)*
Silvia Ghilezan *(University of Novi Sad, Serbia)*
Michael Hanus *(Christian-Albrechts-Universität zu Kiel, Germany)*
Fritz Henglein *(University of Copenhagen, Denmark)*
Mauro Jaskelioff *(Universidad Nacional de Rosario, Argentina)*
Alan Jeffrey *(Alcatel-Lucent Bell Labs, USA)*
Shin-ya Katsumata *(Kyoto University, Japan)*
Shriram Krishnamurthi *(Brown University, USA)*
John Launchbury *(Galois, USA)*
Ryan Newton *(Indiana University, USA)*
Sungwoo Park *(Pohang University of Science and Technology, Korea)*
Sam Staton *(University of Cambridge, UK)*
Nikhil Swamy *(Microsoft Research, Redmond, USA)*
Dimitrios Vytiniotis *(Microsoft Research, Cambridge, UK)*

Additional reviewers:

Andreas Abel
Umut Acar
Michael D. Adams
Danel Ahman
Amal Ahmed
Edward Amsden
David Archer
Kazuyuki Asada
Robert Atkey
Patrick Bahr
Stefano Berardi
Martin Berger
Lars Bergstrom
Jost Berthold
Malgorzata Biernacka
Regis Blanc
Eerke Boiten
Johannes Borgström
Edwin Brady
Chris Brown
Neil Brown
Pablo Buiras
Venanzio Capretta
Manuel Chakravarty
Stephen Chang
James Chapman
Arthur Charguéraud
Juan Chen
James Cheney
Adam Chlipala
Tristan Crolard
Pierre-Evariste Dagand
Jason Dagit
Germán Andrés Delbianco
Pietro Di Gianantonio
Iavor Diatchki
Christos Dimoulas
Tim Disney
Mike Dodds
Gergely Dévai
Trevor Elliott
Martin Elsman
Martin Erwig
Manuel Fähndrich
Andrzej Filinski
Sebastian Fischer
Adam Foltzer
Ronald Garcia
Tony Garnock-Jones
Giorgio Ghelli
George Giorgidze
Neal Glew
Alwyn Goodloe
Sergei Gorlatch

Additional reviewers (continued):

Niels Bjørn Bugge Grathwohl
Kathryn E. Gray
Torsten Grust
Arjun Guha
Kenji Hashimoto
Hugo Herbelin
Maurice Herlihy
David Herman
Pat Hickey
Naohiko Hoshino
Frank Huch
Brian Huffman
Atsushi Igarashi
Hyeonseung Im
Jelena Ivetić
Svetlana Jakšić
Roshan James
Wolfgang Jeltsch
Richard Jones
Stefan Kahrs
Yoshihiko Kakutani
Yukiyoshi Kameyama
Ohad Kammar
Jerzy Karczmarczuk
Zurab Khasidashvili
Andy King
Oleg Kiselyov
Nils Klarlund
Jael Kriener
Neelakantan Krishnaswami
Lindsey Kuper
Peeter Laud
Gyesik Lee
Daan Leijen
Benjamin S. Lerner
Xavier Leroy
Pierre Lescanne
Huiqing Li
Silvia Likavec
Sam Lindley
Hans-Wolfgang Loidl
Zhaohui Luo
Geoffrey Mainland
Simon Marlow
Kazutaka Matsuda
Kiminori Matsuzaki
Ralph Matthes
Conor McBride
Jay McCarthy
Jan Midtgaard
Yasuhiko Minamide
Sasa Misailovic
Neil Mitchell
Akimasa Morihata
Todd Mytkowicz
Peter Müller
Keiko Nakata
Timothy Nelson
Susumu Nishimura
Cosmin E. Oancea
Christopher Okasaki
Luke Ong
Dominic Orchard
Scott Owens
Alberto Pardo
Hyungchul Park
Björn Peemöller
Simon Peyton Jones
Frank Pfenning
Lee Pike
Joe Gibbs Politz
Matija Pretnar
Ulrik Terp Rasmussen
Fabian Reck
Jakob Rehof
Ezequiel Rivas
Alejandro Russo
Ondřej Rypáček
Sukyoung Ryu
Guido Salvaneschi
Alexis Saurin
Sven-Bodo Scholtz
Neil Sculthorpe
Peter Sestoft
Jeremy Siek

Additional reviewers (continued):

Alexandra Silva
Axel Simon
Connor Smith
Paul Steckler
Pierre-Yves Strub
Kohei Suenaga
Josef Svenningsson
Doaitse Swierstra
Wouter Swierstra
Peter Thiemann
Mikkel Thorup
Aaron Todd
Takeshi Tsukada
Kanae Tsushima
Hiroshi Unno
Viktor Vafeiadis
Bas van Gijzel
Varmo Vene
Germán Vidal
Janis Voigtländer
Philip Wadler
Daniel Wagner
David Wakeling
Igor Wałukiewicz
Simon Winwood
Na Xu
Steve Zdancewic

ICFP 2013 Sponsor & Supporters

Sponsor:

Platinum partner:

Gold partners:

Silver partners:

Bronze partners:

Interactive Programming with Dependent Types

Ulf Norell
University of Gothenburg
ulf.norell@cse.gu.se

Abstract

In dependently typed languages run-time values can appear in types, making it possible to give programs more precise types than in languages without dependent types. This can range from keeping track of simple invariants like the length of a list, to full functional correctness. In addition to having some correctness guarantees on the final program, assigning more precise types to programs means that you can get more assistance from the type checker while writing them. This is what I focus on here, demonstrating how the programming environment of AGDA can help you when developing dependently typed programs.

Categories and Subject Descriptors D.1.1 [*Programming Techniques*]: Applicative (Functional) Programming; D.2.2 [*Software Engineering*]: Design Tools and Techniques

General Terms Design, Languages, Theory

Keywords Dependent types

1. Introduction

Dependent type systems blur the line between the expression language and the type language, allowing types to talk about run-time values as well as allowing types to be defined by computation. Dependent types are used heavily in the theorem proving community, most notably in COQ, where the 'propositions-as-types' paradigm lets types act as predicates on values. In recent years, however, there has been an increasing interest in using dependent types for programming with languages such as AGDA [3], IDRIS [1] and EPIGRAM [2], as well as COQ [6], exploring the notion of a dependently typed program in contrast to a simply typed program with associated dependently typed properties.

We have also seen dependent types making their way into languages like HASKELL with the introduction of GADTs [4], type families [5] and data kinds [7], which, while not offering full dependent types, still provides rich opportunities for dependently typed programming.

2. Interacting with the Type Checker

With dependent types we can no longer expect the machine to infer types for us, instead it becomes an important design decision to decide what properties of a program to track in its type. This does not mean that programs are cluttered with type annotations everywhere—once the top-level type of a function is given, type information can routinely be pushed inwards resulting in implementations as short as the corresponding simply typed function.

Having written down a precise type before implementing a function means that the type checker knows what it is you are trying to do. This opens up a wide range of opportunities for the type checker to assist in the implementation. Some of these opportunities are taken advantage of by the programming environment of AGDA.

The central notion of AGDA's interactive programming model is that of a *hole*. A hole is an unfinished part of the program and a program under development can contain any number of holes. For each hole the type checker can answer a number of questions, such as, what is the type of the expression expected in the hole, what are the types of the variables in scope of the hole, etc. In addition to providing this information the type checker can also help you fill the hole in various ways. For instance, filling in the appropriate data type constructor with holes as arguments when there is only one choice, or introducing a case split on a given term.

3. What is Missing?

The main feature that is missing in the AGDA environment is support for refactoring. A larger design space for types means that there are more opportunities for making mistakes and having to go back and revise previous definitions. This is a situation where having more precise types would help as well–with more precise information, the machine can make more precise changes.

References

[1] E. Brady. Idris—systems programming meets full dependent types. In *Proc. of 5th ACM Workshop on Programming Languages Meets Program Verification, PLPV '11*, pp. 1–2. ACM, 2011.

[2] C. McBride and J. McKinna. The view from the left. *J. of Funct. Program.*, 14(1):69–111, 2004.

[3] U. Norell. *Towards a practical programming language based on dependent type theory*. PhD thesis, Chalmers U. of Techn., 2007.

[4] S. Peyton Jones, D. Vytiniotis, S. Weirich, and G. Washburn. Simple unification-based type inference for GADTs. In *Proc. of 11th ACM SIGPLAN Int. Conf. on Functional Programming, ICFP '06*, pp. 50–61. ACM, 2006.

[5] T. Schrijvers, S. Peyton Jones, M. Chakravarty, and M. Sulzmann. Type checking with open type functions. In *Proc. of 13th ACM SIGPLAN Int. Conf. on Functional Programming, ICFP '08*, pp. 51–62. ACM, 2008.

[6] M. Sozeau. PROGRAM-ing finger trees in Coq. In *Proc. of 12th ACM SIGPLAN Int. Conf. on Functional Programming, ICFP '07*, pp. 13–24. ACM, 2007.

[7] B. A. Yorgey, S. Weirich, J. Cretin, S. Peyton Jones, D. Vytiniotis, and J. P. Magalhães. Giving Haskell a promotion. In *Proc. of 8th ACM SIGPLAN Workshop on Types in Language Design and Implementation, TLDI '12*, pp. 53–66. ACM, 2012.

ICFP '13, September 25–27, 2013, Boston, MA, USA.
ACM 978-1-4503-2326-0/13/09.
http://dx.doi.org/10.1145/2500365.2500609

Verified Decision Procedures for MSO on Words Based on Derivatives of Regular Expressions

Dmitriy Traytel   Tobias Nipkow
Technische Universität München, Germany
traytel@in.tum.de   www.in.tum.de/~nipkow

Abstract

Monadic second-order logic on finite words (MSO) is a decidable yet expressive logic into which many decision problems can be encoded. Since MSO formulas correspond to regular languages, equivalence of MSO formulas can be reduced to the equivalence of some regular structures (e.g. automata). This paper presents a verified functional decision procedure for MSO formulas that is not based on automata but on regular expressions. Functional languages are ideally suited for this task: regular expressions are data types and functions on them are defined by pattern matching and recursion and are verified by structural induction.

Decision procedures for regular expression equivalence have been formalized before, usually based on Brzozowski derivatives. Yet, for a straightforward embedding of MSO formulas into regular expressions an extension of regular expressions with a projection operation is required. We prove total correctness and completeness of an equivalence checker for regular expressions extended in that way. We also define a language-preserving translation of formulas into regular expressions with respect to two different semantics of MSO. Our results have been formalized and verified in the theorem prover Isabelle. Using Isabelle's code generation facility, this yields purely functional, formally verified programs that decide equivalence of MSO formulas.

Categories and Subject Descriptors F.4.3 [*Mathematical Logic And Formal Languages*]: Formal Languages—Decision problems; F.3.1 [*Mathematical Logic And Formal Languages*]: Specifying and Verifying and Reasoning about Programs

General Terms Algorithms, Theory, Verification

Keywords MSO; WS1S; decision procedure; regular expressions; Brzozowski derivatives; interactive theorem proving; Isabelle

1. Introduction

Many decision procedures for logical theories are based on the famous logic-automaton connection. That is, they reduce the decision problem for some logical theory to a decidable question about some class of automata. Automata are usually implemented with the help of imperative data structures for efficiency reasons.

ICFP '13, September 25–27, 2013, Boston, MA, USA.

ACM 978-1-4503-2326-0/13/09... $15.00.
http://dx.doi.org/10.1145/2500365.2500612

In functional languages, automata are not an ideal abstraction because they are graphs rather than trees. In contrast, regular expressions are perfect for functional languages and they are equally expressive. In fact, Brzozowski [8] showed how automata-based algorithms can be recast as recursive algebraic manipulations of regular expressions. His *derivatives* can be seen as a way of simulating automaton states with regular expressions and computing the next-state function symbolically.

Recently Brzozowski's derivatives were discovered by functional programmers and theorem provers. Owens *et al.* [23] realized that regular expressions and their derivatives fit perfectly with data types and recursive functions. Their paper explores regular expression matching based directly on regular expressions rather than automata. Fischer *et al.* [13] also explore regular expression matching, but by means of marked regular expressions rather than derivatives. Slightly later, the interactive theorem proving community woke up to the beauty of derivatives, too. This resulted in four papers about verified decision procedures for the equivalence of regular expressions based on derivatives and on marked regular expressions (see Related Work below). In one of these four papers, Coquand and Siles [10] state that "A more ambitious project will be to use this work for writing a decision procedure for WS1S", a monadic second-order logic. Our paper does just that (and more).

Monadic second-order logic on finite words (MSO) is a decidable yet expressive logic into which many decision problems can be encoded [26]. MSO allows only monadic predicates but quantification both over numbers and finite sets of numbers. Two closely related but subtly different semantics can be found in the literature. One of the two, WS1S—the Weak monadic Second-order logic of 1 Successor, is based on arithmetic. The other, M2L(Str) [16], is more closely related to formal languages. There seems to be some disagreement as to which semantics is the more appropriate one for verification purposes [3, 17]. Hence we cover both.

Essentially, MSO formulas describe regular languages. Therefore MSO formulas can be decided by translating them into automata. This is the basis of the highly successful MONA tool [12] for deciding WS1S. MONA's success is due to its (in practical terms) highly efficient implementation and to the ease with which very different verification problems can be encoded in monadic second-order logic, for example Presburger arithmetic and Hoare logic for pointer programs.

The contribution of this paper is the presentation of the first purely functional decision procedures for two interpretations of MSO based on derivatives of regular expressions. These decision procedures have been verified in Isabelle/HOL and we sketch their correctness proofs. We are not aware of any previous decision procedure for MSO based on regular expressions (as opposed to automata), let alone a verified program.

It is instructive to compare our decision procedure for WS1S with MONA. MONA is a highly tuned implementation using cache-conscious data structures including a BDD-based automaton representation. Ours is a (by comparison tiny) purely functional program that operates on regular expressions and can only cope with small examples. MONA is not verified (and the prospect of doing so is daunting), whereas our code is.

In this paper we distinguish ordinary regular expressions that contain only concatenation, union, and iteration from *extended* regular expressions that also provide complement and intersection.

The rest of the paper is organized as follows. Section 2 gives an overview of related work. Section 3 introduces some basic notations. Sections 4 and 5 constitute the main contribution of our paper—the first shows how to decide equivalence of extended regular expressions with an additional projection operation, the second reduces equivalence of MSO formulas to equivalence of exactly those regular expressions with respect to both semantics, M2L and WS1S. In total this yields a decision procedure for MSO on words. A short case study of the decision procedure is given in Section 6.

2. Related Work

Brzozowski [8] introduced derivatives of extended regular expressions. Antimirov [1] introduced partial derivatives of regular expressions. Caron *et al.* [9] extended Antimirov to extended regular expressions. The concept of derivatives as means to compute the next state symbolically goes beyond regular expressions—as witnessed by libraries for parsing developed by Danielsson [11] in Agda and by Might *et al.* [19] in Lisp using lazily evaluated variations of Brzozowski derivatives for parser combinators.

MONA was linked to Isabelle by Basin and Friedrich [5] and to PVS by Owre and Rueß [24]. In both cases, MONA is used as an oracle for deciding formulas in the respective theorem prover.

Now we discuss work on verified decision procedures for regular expressions. The first verified equivalence checker for regular expressions was published by Braibant and Pous [7]. They worked with automata, not regular expressions, their theory was large and their algorithm efficient. In response, Krauss and Nipkow [18] gave a much simpler partial correctness proof for an equivalence checker for regular expressions based on derivatives. Coquand and Siles [10] showed total correctness of their equivalence checker for extended regular expressions based on derivatives. Asperti [2] presented an equivalence checker for regular expressions via marked regular expressions (as previously used by [13]) and showed total correctness. Moreira *et al.* [20] presented an equivalence checker for regular expressions based on partial derivatives and showed its total correctness. Berghofer and Reiter [6] formalized a decision procedure for Presburger arithmetic via automata in Isabelle/HOL.

Outside of the application area of equivalence checking, Wu *et al.* [28] benefited from the inductive structure of regular expressions to formally verify the Myhill-Nerode theorem.

3. Preliminaries

Although we formalized everything in this paper in the theorem prover Isabelle/HOL [21, 22], no knowledge of theorem provers or Isabelle/HOL is required because we employ mostly ordinary mathematical notation in our presentation. Some specific notations are summarized below.

The symbol $\mathbb{B}$ represents the type of Booleans, where $\top$ and $\bot$ represent true and false. The type of sets and the type of lists over some type τ are written $\tau\,\mathsf{set}$ and $\tau\,\mathsf{list}$. In general, type constructors follow their arguments. The letters α and β represent type variables. The notation $t :: \tau$ means that term t has type τ.

Many of our functions are curried. In some cases we write the first argument as an index: instead of $f\ a\ b$ we write $f_a(b)$ (in preference to just $f_a\ b$). The projection functions on pairs are called fst and snd. The image of a function f over a set S is written $f \bullet S$.

Lists are built up from the empty list $[\,]$ via the infix # operator that prepends an element x to a list xs: $x \# xs$. Two lists are concatenated with the infix @ operator. Accessing the nth element of a list xs is denoted by $xs[n]$; the indexing is zero-based. The length of the list xs is written $|xs|$.

Finite words as in formal language theory are modelled as finite lists, i.e. type $\alpha\,\mathsf{list}$. The empty word is the empty list. As is customary, concatenation of two words u and v is denoted by their juxtaposition uv; similarly for a single letter a of the alphabet and a word w: aw. That is, the operators # and @ remain implicit (for words, not for arbitrary lists).

4. Extended Regular Expressions

In Section 5, MSO formulas are translated into regular expressions such that encodings of models of a formula correspond exactly to words in the regular language. Thereby, equivalence of formulas is reduced to the equivalence of regular expressions.

Decision procedures for equivalence of regular expression have been formalized earlier in theorem provers. Here, we extend the existing formalization and the soundness proof in Isabelle/HOL by Krauss and Nipkow [18] with negation and intersection operation on regular expressions, as well as with a nonstandard projection operation. Additionally, we provide proofs of termination and completeness.

4.1 Syntax and Semantics

Regular expressions extended with intersection and complement allow us to encode Boolean operators on formulas in a straightforward fashion. A further operation—the *projection* Π—plays the crucial role of encoding existential quantifiers. These Π*-extended* regular expressions (to distinguish them from mere extended regular expressions) are defined as a recursive data type $\alpha\,\mathsf{RE}$, where α is the type of the underlying alphabet. In conventional concrete syntax, $\alpha\,\mathsf{RE}$ is defined by the grammar

$$\begin{array}{rcccccc} r & = & \mathbf{0} & \mid & \mathbf{1} & \mid & a \\ & \mid & r+s & \mid & r \cdot s & \mid & r^* \\ & \mid & r \cap s & \mid & \neg r & \mid & \Pi r \end{array}$$

where $r, s :: \alpha\,\mathsf{RE}$ and $a :: \alpha$. Note that much of the time we will omit the "Π-extended" and simply speak of regular expressions if there is no danger of confusion.

We assume that type α is partitioned into a family of alphabets Σ_n that depend on a natural number n. In our application, n will represent the number of free variables of the translated MSO formula. For now Σ_n is just a parameter of our setup.

We focus on wellformed regular expressions where all atoms come from the same alphabet Σ_n. This will guarantee that the language of such a wellformed expression is a subset of Σ_n^*. The projection operation complicates wellformedness a little. Because projection is meant to encode existential quantifiers, projection should transform a regular expression over Σ_{n+1} into a regular expression over Σ_n, just as the existential quantifier transforms a formula with $n+1$ free variables into a formula with n free variables. Thus projection changes the alphabet. Wellformedness is defined as the recursive predicate $\mathsf{wf} :: \mathbb{N} \to \alpha\,\mathsf{RE} \to \mathbb{B}$.

$$\begin{array}{llll} \mathsf{wf}_n(\mathbf{0}) & = \top & \mathsf{wf}_n(\mathbf{1}) & = \top \\ \mathsf{wf}_n(a) & = a \in \Sigma_n & \mathsf{wf}_n(r+s) & = \mathsf{wf}_n(r) \wedge \mathsf{wf}_n(s) \\ \mathsf{wf}_n(r \cdot s) & = \mathsf{wf}_n(r) \wedge \mathsf{wf}_n(s) & \mathsf{wf}_n(r^*) & = \mathsf{wf}_n(r) \\ \mathsf{wf}_n(r \cap s) & = \mathsf{wf}_n(r) \wedge \mathsf{wf}_n(s) & \mathsf{wf}_n(\neg r) & = \mathsf{wf}_n(r) \\ \mathsf{wf}_n(\Pi r) & = \mathsf{wf}_{n+1}(r) & & \end{array}$$

We call a regular expression r *n-wellformed* if $\mathsf{wf}_n(r)$ holds.

The *language* $\mathcal{L} :: \mathbb{N} \to \alpha\,\mathsf{RE} \to (\alpha\,\mathsf{list})\,\mathsf{set}$ of a regular expression is defined as usual, except for the equations for complement and projection. For an n-wellformed regular expression the definition yields a subset of Σ_n^*.

$$\begin{array}{llll} \mathcal{L}_n(\mathbf{0}) & = \{\} & \mathcal{L}_n(\mathbf{1}) & = \{[\,]\} \\ \mathcal{L}_n(a) & = \{a\} & \mathcal{L}_n(r+s) & = \mathcal{L}_n(r) \cup \mathcal{L}_n(s) \\ \mathcal{L}_n(r \cdot s) & = \mathcal{L}_n(r) \cdot \mathcal{L}_n(s) & \mathcal{L}_n(r^*) & = \mathcal{L}_n(r)^* \\ \mathcal{L}_n(r \cap s) & = \mathcal{L}_n(r) \cap \mathcal{L}_n(s) & \mathcal{L}_n(\neg r) & = \Sigma_n^* \setminus \mathcal{L}_n(r) \\ \mathcal{L}_n(\Pi r) & = (\mathsf{map}\,\pi) \bullet \mathcal{L}_{n+1}(r) & & \end{array}$$

The first unusual point is the parametrization with n. It expresses that we expect a regular expression over Σ_n and is necessary for the definition $\mathcal{L}_n(\neg r) = \Sigma_n^* \setminus \mathcal{L}_n(r)$.

The definition $\mathcal{L}_n(\Pi r) = \mathsf{map}\,\pi \bullet \mathcal{L}_{n+1}(r)$ is parameterized by a function $\pi :: \Sigma_{n+1} \to \Sigma_n$[1]. The projection Π denotes the homomorphic image under this fixed π. In more detail: map lifts π homomorphically to words (lists), and $\bullet$ lifts it to sets of words. Therefore Π transforms a language over Σ_{n+1} into a language over Σ_n.

To understand the "projection" terminology, it is helpful to think of elements of Σ_n as lists of fixed length n over some alphabet Σ and of π as the tail function on lists that drops the first element of the list. A word over Σ_n is then a list of lists. Though this is a good intuition, the actual encoding of formulas later on will be slightly more complicated. Fortunately we can ignore these complications for now by working with arbitrary but fixed Σ_n and π in the current section. Specific instantiations for them are given in Section 5.

4.2 Deciding Language Equivalence

Now we turn our attention to deciding equivalence of Π-extended regular expressions. The key concepts required for this are finality and derivatives. We call a regular expression *final* if its language contains the empty word $[\,]$. Finality can be easily checked syntactically by the following recursive function $\varepsilon :: \alpha\,\mathsf{RE} \to \mathbb{B}$.

$$\begin{array}{llll} \varepsilon(\mathbf{0}) & = \bot & \varepsilon(\mathbf{1}) & = \top \\ \varepsilon(a) & = \bot & \varepsilon(r+s) & = \varepsilon(r) \vee \varepsilon(s) \\ \varepsilon(r \cdot s) & = \varepsilon(r) \wedge \varepsilon(s) & \varepsilon(r^*) & = \top \\ \varepsilon(r \cap s) & = \varepsilon(r) \wedge \varepsilon(s) & \varepsilon(\neg r) & = \neg \varepsilon(r) \\ \varepsilon(\Pi r) & = \varepsilon(r) & & \end{array}$$

The characteristic property—$\varepsilon(r)$ iff $[\,] \in \mathcal{L}_n(r)$ for any regular expression r and $n \in \mathbb{N}$—follows by structural induction on r.

The second key concept—the *derivative* of a regular expression $\mathcal{D} :: \alpha \to \alpha\,\mathsf{RE} \to \alpha\,\mathsf{RE}$ and its lifting to words $\mathcal{D}^* :: \alpha\,\mathsf{list} \to \alpha\,\mathsf{RE} \to \alpha\,\mathsf{RE}$—semantically corresponds to left quotients of regular languages with respect to a fixed letter or word. Just as before, the recursive definition is purely syntactic and the semantic correspondence is established by induction.

$$\begin{array}{llll} \mathcal{D}_b(\mathbf{0}) & = \mathbf{0} & \mathcal{D}_b(\mathbf{1}) & = \mathbf{0} \\ \mathcal{D}_b(a) & = \textbf{if } a = b \textbf{ then } \mathbf{1} \textbf{ else } \mathbf{0} & \mathcal{D}_b(r+s) & = \mathcal{D}_b(r) + \mathcal{D}_b(s) \\ \mathcal{D}_b(r \cdot s) & = & \mathcal{D}_b(r^*) & = \mathcal{D}_b(r) \cdot r^* \\ \multicolumn{4}{l}{\quad \textbf{if } \varepsilon(r) \textbf{ then } \mathcal{D}_b(r) \cdot s + \mathcal{D}_b(s)} \\ \multicolumn{4}{l}{\quad \textbf{else } \mathcal{D}_b(r) \cdot s} \\ \mathcal{D}_b(r \cap s) & = \mathcal{D}_b(r) \cap \mathcal{D}_b(s) & \mathcal{D}_b(\neg r) & = \neg \mathcal{D}_b(r) \\ \mathcal{D}_b(\Pi r) & = \Pi\left(\bigoplus_{c \in \pi^- b} \mathcal{D}_c(r)\right) & & \\ \mathcal{D}^*_{[\,]}(r) & = r & \mathcal{D}^*_{bw}(r) & = \mathcal{D}^*_w(\mathcal{D}_b(r)) \end{array}$$

[1] Due to Isabelle's lack of dependent types the actual type of π is $\alpha \to \alpha$. The more refined dependent type $\Sigma_{n+1} \to \Sigma_n$ is realized via Isabelle's tool for modeling parameterized systems with additional assumptions: locales [4]. A locale fixes parameters and states assumptions about them. Hence, we use the locale assumption $\pi \bullet \Sigma_{n+1} \subseteq \Sigma_n$ to relate locale parameters π and Σ.

Lemma 1. *Assume $b \in \Sigma_n$, $v \in \Sigma_n^*$ and let r be an n-wellformed regular expression. Then $\mathcal{L}_n(\mathcal{D}_b(r)) = \{w \mid bw \in \mathcal{L}_n(r)\}$ and $\mathsf{wf}_n(\mathcal{D}_b(r))$, and consequently $\mathcal{L}_n(\mathcal{D}^*_v(r)) = \{w \mid vw \in \mathcal{L}_n(r)\}$ and $\mathsf{wf}_n(\mathcal{D}^*_v(r))$.*

The projection case introduced some new syntax that deserves some explanation. The preimage π^- applied to a letter $b \in \Sigma_n$ denotes the set $\{c \in \Sigma_{n+1} \mid \pi\, c = b\}$. Our alphabets Σ_n are finite for each n, hence so is the preimage of a letter. The summation $\bigoplus$ over a finite set denotes the iterated application of the $+$-constructor of regular expressions. Summation over the empty set is defined as $\mathbf{0}$.

Derivatives of extended regular expressions were introduced by Brzozowski [8] almost fifty years ago. Our contribution is the extension of the concept to handle the projection operation. Since the projection acts homomorphically on words, it is clear that the derivative of Πr with respect to a letter b can be expressed as a projection of derivatives of r. The concrete definition is a consequence of the following identity of left quotients for $b \in \Sigma_n$ and $A \subseteq \Sigma_{n+1}^*$:

$$\{w \mid bw \in \mathsf{map}\,\pi \bullet A\} = \mathsf{map}\,\pi \bullet \bigcup_{c \in \pi^- b} \{w \mid cw \in A\}$$

Although we completely avoid automata in the formalization, a derivative with respect to the letter b can be seen as a transition labelled by b in a deterministic automaton, the states of which are labelled by regular expressions. The automaton accepting the language of a regular expression r can be thus constructed iteratively by exploring all derivatives of r and defining exactly those states as accepting, which are labelled by a final regular expression. However, the set $\{\mathcal{D}^*_w(r) \mid w :: \alpha\,\mathsf{list}\}$ of states reachable in this manner is infinite in general. To obtain a finite automaton, the states must be partitioned into classes of regular expressions that are *ACI-equivalent*, i.e. syntactically equal modulo associativity, commutativity and idempotence of the $+$-constructor. Brzozowski showed that the number of such classes for a fixed regular expression r is finite by structural induction on r. The inductive steps require proving finiteness by representing equivalence classes of derivatives of the expression in terms of equivalence classes of derivatives of subexpressions. This is technically complicated, especially for concatenation, iteration and projection, since it requires a careful choice representatives of equivalence classes to reason about them, and Isabelle's automation can not help much with the finiteness arguments—indeed the verification of Theorem 2 constitutes the most intricate proof in the present work.

Theorem 2. *$\{\langle\!\langle \mathcal{D}^*_w(r) \rangle\!\rangle \mid w :: \alpha\,\mathsf{list}\}$ is finite for any regular expression r.*

The function $\langle\!\langle - \rangle\!\rangle :: \alpha\,\mathsf{RE} \to \alpha\,\mathsf{RE}$ is the ACI normalization function, which maps ACI-equivalent regular expressions to the same representative. It is defined by means of a normalizing constructor $\oplus :: \alpha\,\mathsf{RE} \to \alpha\,\mathsf{RE} \to \alpha\,\mathsf{RE}$ and an arbitrary linear order $\preceq$ on regular expressions. The equations for $\oplus$ are matched sequentially.

$$\begin{array}{llll} \langle\!\langle \mathbf{0} \rangle\!\rangle & = \mathbf{0} & \langle\!\langle \mathbf{1} \rangle\!\rangle & = \mathbf{1} \\ \langle\!\langle a \rangle\!\rangle & = a & \langle\!\langle r+s \rangle\!\rangle & = \langle\!\langle r \rangle\!\rangle \oplus \langle\!\langle s \rangle\!\rangle \\ \langle\!\langle r \cdot s \rangle\!\rangle & = \langle\!\langle r \rangle\!\rangle \cdot \langle\!\langle s \rangle\!\rangle & \langle\!\langle r^* \rangle\!\rangle & = \langle\!\langle r \rangle\!\rangle^* \\ \langle\!\langle r \cap s \rangle\!\rangle & = \langle\!\langle r \rangle\!\rangle \cap \langle\!\langle s \rangle\!\rangle & \langle\!\langle \neg r \rangle\!\rangle & = \neg \langle\!\langle r \rangle\!\rangle \\ \langle\!\langle \Pi r \rangle\!\rangle & = \Pi \langle\!\langle r \rangle\!\rangle & & \end{array}$$

$$\begin{array}{lll} (r+s) \oplus t & = & r \oplus (s \oplus t) \\ r \oplus (s+t) & = & \textbf{if } r = s \textbf{ then } s + t \\ & & \textbf{else if } r \preceq s \textbf{ then } r + (s+t) \\ & & \qquad \textbf{else } s + (r \oplus t) \\ r \oplus s & = & \textbf{if } r = s \textbf{ then } r \\ & & \textbf{else if } r \preceq s \textbf{ then } r + s \\ & & \qquad \textbf{else } s + r \end{array}$$

After the application of $\langle\!\langle - \rangle\!\rangle$ all sums in the expression are associated to the right and the summands are sorted with respect to $\leq$ and duplicated summands are removed. From this, further later on useful properties of $\langle\!\langle - \rangle\!\rangle$ can be derived:

Lemma 3. *Let r be a regular expression, $n \in \mathbb{N}$ and $b \in \Sigma_n$. Then $\mathcal{L}_n \langle\!\langle r \rangle\!\rangle = \mathcal{L}_n(r)$, $\langle\!\langle \langle\!\langle r \rangle\!\rangle \rangle\!\rangle = \langle\!\langle r \rangle\!\rangle$ and $\langle\!\langle \mathcal{D}_b \langle\!\langle r \rangle\!\rangle \rangle\!\rangle = \langle\!\langle \mathcal{D}_b(r) \rangle\!\rangle$.*

So far, ACI normalization only connects Brzozowski derivatives to deterministic finite automata. Furthermore, it will ensure termination of our decision procedure even without ever entering the world of automata. Instead we follow Rutten [25], who gives an alternative view on deterministic automata as coalgebras. In the coalgebraic setting the function $\lambda r.\ (\varepsilon(r), \lambda b.\ \mathcal{D}_b(r)) :: \alpha\,\mathsf{RE} \to \mathbb{B} \times (\alpha \to \alpha\,\mathsf{RE})$ is a D-coalgebra for the functor $D(S) = \mathbb{B} \times (\alpha \to S)$. The final coalgebra of D exists and corresponds exactly to the set of all languages. Therefore, we obtain the powerful coinduction principle, reducing language equality to bisimilarity. We phrase this general theorem instantiated to our concrete setting. The formalized proof itself does not require any category theory; it resembles the reasoning in Rutten [25, §4].

Theorem 4 (Coinduction). *Let $R :: (\alpha\,\mathsf{RE} \times \alpha\,\mathsf{RE})\,\mathsf{set}$ be a relation, such that for all $(r, s) \in R$ we have:*

1. $\mathsf{wf}_n(r) \wedge \mathsf{wf}_n(s)$;
2. $\varepsilon(r) \leftrightarrow \varepsilon(s)$;
3. $(\langle\!\langle \mathcal{D}_b(r) \rangle\!\rangle, \langle\!\langle \mathcal{D}_b(s) \rangle\!\rangle) \in R$ *for all* $b \in \Sigma_n$.

Then for all $(r, s) \in R$, $\mathcal{L}_n(r) = \mathcal{L}_n(s)$ holds.

From Lemma 1 and Lemma 3, we know that the relation

$$\mathcal{B} = \{(\langle\!\langle \mathcal{D}^*_w(r) \rangle\!\rangle, \langle\!\langle \mathcal{D}^*_w(s) \rangle\!\rangle) \mid w \in \Sigma^*_n\}$$

contains $(\langle\!\langle r \rangle\!\rangle, \langle\!\langle s \rangle\!\rangle)$ and fulfils the assumptions 1 and 3 of the coinduction theorem, assuming that r and s are both n-wellformed. Moreover, using Theorem 2 it follows that this relation is finite. Thus, checking assumption 2 for every pair of this finite relation is sufficient to prove language equality of r and s by coinduction. We obtain the following abstract specification of a language equivalence checking algorithm.

Theorem 5. *Let r and s be n-wellformed regular expressions. Then $\mathcal{L}_n(r) = \mathcal{L}_n(s)$ iff we have $\varepsilon(r') \leftrightarrow \varepsilon(s')$ for all $(r', s') \in \mathcal{B}$.*

4.3 Executable Algorithm from a Theorem

Our goal is not only to prove some abstract theorems about a decision procedure, but also to extract executable code in some functional programming language (e.g. Standard ML, Haskell, OCaml) using the code generation facility of Isabelle/HOL [15]. Theorem 5 is not enough to do so: it contains a set comprehension ranging over the infinite set Σ^*_n, which is not executable as such. We need to instruct the system how to enumerate $\mathcal{B}$.

We start with the pair $(\langle\!\langle r \rangle\!\rangle, \langle\!\langle s \rangle\!\rangle)$ and compute its pairwise derivatives for all letters of the alphabet. For the computed pairs of regular expressions we proceed by computing their derivatives and so on. This of course does not terminate. However, if we stop our exploration at pairs that we have seen before it does, since we are exploring a finite set.

In more detail, we use a worklist algorithm that iteratively adds not yet inspected pairs of regular expressions while exhausting words of increasing length until no new pairs are generated. Saturation is reached by means of the executable combinator $\mathsf{while} :: (\alpha \to \mathbb{B}) \to (\alpha \to \alpha) \to \alpha \to \alpha\,\mathsf{option}$ from the Isabelle/HOL library. The option type $\alpha\,\mathsf{option}$ has two constructors $\mathsf{None} :: \alpha\,\mathsf{option}$ and $\mathsf{Some} :: \alpha \to \alpha\,\mathsf{option}$. Some lifts elements from the base type α to the option type, while None is usually used to indicate some exceptional behaviour. The definition of while

$$\mathsf{while}\ b\ c\ s = \textbf{if}\ \exists k. \neg b(c^k(s))\ \textbf{then}\ \mathsf{Some}\ (c^{\mathsf{Least}\ k. \neg b(c^k(s))}(s))\ \textbf{else}\ \mathsf{None}$$

is not executable, but the following key lemma is:

$$\mathsf{while}\ b\ c\ s\ =\ \textbf{if}\ b\,s\ \textbf{then}\ \mathsf{while}\ b\ c\ (c\ s)\ \textbf{else}\ \mathsf{Some}\ s$$

The code generated from this recursive equation will return $\mathsf{Some}\ s$ in case the definition of while says so, but instead of returning None, it will not terminate. Thus we can prove termination if we can show that the result is $\neq$ None.

In our algorithm, the state s of the while loop consists of a worklist $ws :: (\alpha\,\mathsf{RE} \times \alpha\,\mathsf{RE})\,\mathsf{list}$ of unprocessed pairs of regular expressions together with a set $N :: (\gamma \times \gamma)\,\mathsf{set}$ of already seen pairs modulo a normalization function $\mathsf{norm} :: \alpha\,\mathsf{RE} \to \gamma$. This normalization function (which is a parameter of our setup) is applied to already ACI-normalized expressions, to syntactically identify further language equivalent expressions. This makes the bisimulation relation that must be exhausted smaller, thus saturation is reached faster. The range type of the normalization is not fixed, but we require a notion of languages $\mathcal{L}^\gamma :: \mathbb{N} \to \gamma \to (\alpha\,\mathsf{list})\,\mathsf{set}$ to be available for it, such that $\mathcal{L}^\gamma_n(\mathsf{norm}\ r) = \mathcal{L}_n(r)$ holds. In the simplest case norm can be the identity function and $\mathcal{L}^\gamma = \mathcal{L}$. More interesting is a function on regular expressions that eliminates $\mathbf{0}$ from unions, concatenations and intersections and $\mathbf{1}$ from concatenations. Not fixing the range type allows us to use different regular structures such as automata or different types of regular expressions, on which further simplifications might be easier.

Finally, the functions $\mathsf{b} :: (\alpha\,\mathsf{RE} \times \alpha\,\mathsf{RE})\,\mathsf{list} \times (\gamma \times \gamma)\,\mathsf{set} \to \mathbb{B}$ and $\mathsf{c} :: \mathbb{N} \to (\alpha\,\mathsf{RE} \times \alpha\,\mathsf{RE})\,\mathsf{list} \times (\gamma \times \gamma)\,\mathsf{set} \to (\alpha\,\mathsf{RE} \times \alpha\,\mathsf{RE})\,\mathsf{list} \times (\gamma \times \gamma)\,\mathsf{set}$ defined below are given as arguments to while. A wellformedness check completes the now executable algorithm $\mathsf{eqv}^{\mathsf{RE}} :: \mathbb{N} \to \alpha\,\mathsf{RE} \to \alpha\,\mathsf{RE} \to \mathbb{B}$.

$$\begin{array}{l}
\mathsf{b}\ ([\,], _) \qquad\quad\ = \bot \\
\mathsf{b}\ ((r,s)\ \#\ _, _)\ =\ \varepsilon(r) \leftrightarrow \varepsilon(s)
\end{array}$$

$$\begin{array}{l}
\mathsf{c}_n\ ((r,s)\ \#\ ws, N)\ = \\
\quad \textbf{let} \\
\qquad succs = \mathsf{map}\ (\lambda b. \\
\qquad\quad \textbf{let} \\
\qquad\qquad r' = \langle\!\langle \mathcal{D}_b(r) \rangle\!\rangle \\
\qquad\qquad s' = \langle\!\langle \mathcal{D}_b(s) \rangle\!\rangle \\
\qquad\quad \textbf{in}\ ((r', s'), (\mathsf{norm}\ r', \mathsf{norm}\ s')))\ \Sigma_n \\
\qquad new = \mathsf{remdups\ snd}\ (\mathsf{filter}\ (\lambda(_, rs).\ rs \notin N)\ succs) \\
\quad \textbf{in}\ (ws\ @\ \mathsf{map\ fst}\ new, \mathsf{set}\ (\mathsf{map\ snd}\ new) \cup N)
\end{array}$$

$$\begin{array}{l}
\mathsf{eqv}^{\mathsf{RE}}_n\ r\ s\ = \\
\quad \mathsf{wf}_n(r) \wedge \mathsf{wf}_n(s) \wedge \\
\quad (\textbf{case}\ \mathsf{while\ b}\ \mathsf{c}_n\ ([(\langle\!\langle r \rangle\!\rangle, \langle\!\langle s \rangle\!\rangle)], \{(\mathsf{norm}\langle\!\langle r \rangle\!\rangle, \mathsf{norm}\langle\!\langle s \rangle\!\rangle)\})\ \textbf{of} \\
\qquad\quad ([\,], _) \Rightarrow \top \\
\quad\ \mid\ \ (_\ \#\ _, _) \Rightarrow \bot)
\end{array}$$

The function $\mathsf{set} :: \alpha\,\mathsf{list} \to \alpha\,\mathsf{set}$ maps a list to the set of its elements, $\mathsf{filter} :: (\alpha \to \mathbb{B}) \to \alpha\,\mathsf{list} \to \alpha\,\mathsf{list}$ removes elements that do not fulfil the given predicate, while $\mathsf{remdups} :: (\alpha \to \beta) \to \alpha\,\mathsf{list} \to \alpha\,\mathsf{list}$ is used to keep the worklist as small as possible. $\mathsf{remdups}\ f\ xs$ removes duplicates from xs modulo the function f, e.g. $\mathsf{remdups\ snd}\ [(\mathbf{0}, \mathbf{0}), (\mathbf{1}, \mathbf{0})] = [(\mathbf{1}, \mathbf{0})]$ (which element is actually kept is irrelevant; the result $[(\mathbf{0}, \mathbf{0})]$ would also be valid).

The termination of $\mathsf{eqv}^{\mathsf{RE}}$ for any input is guaranteed by two facts: (1) all recursively defined functions in Isabelle/HOL terminate by their definitional principle (either primitive or wellfounded recursion) and (2) the termination of while follows from Theorem 2 and the fact that the set N of already seen pairs in the state is a subset of $\mathsf{norm} \bullet \{(\langle\!\langle \mathcal{D}^*_w(r) \rangle\!\rangle, \langle\!\langle \mathcal{D}^*_w(s) \rangle\!\rangle) \mid w \in \Sigma^*_n\}$.

Theorem 6 (Termination). *Let r and s be n-wellformed regular expressions. Then*

$$\text{while b } c_n\,([(\langle\!\langle r\rangle\!\rangle, \langle\!\langle s\rangle\!\rangle)], \{(\text{norm}\langle\!\langle r\rangle\!\rangle, \text{norm}\langle\!\langle s\rangle\!\rangle)\}) \neq \text{None}.$$

Function eqv^{RE} deserves the name decision procedure since it constitutes the refinement of the algorithm abstractly stated in Theorem 5, and is therefore sound and complete.

Theorem 7 (Soundness). *Let r and s be regular expressions such that* $\text{eqv}_n^{\text{RE}}\ r\ s$. *Then* $\mathcal{L}_n(r) = \mathcal{L}_n(s)$.

Theorem 8 (Completeness). *Let r and s be n-wellformed regular expressions such that* $\mathcal{L}_n(r) = \mathcal{L}_n(s)$. *Then* $\text{eqv}_n^{\text{RE}}\ r\ s$.

Let us observe the decision procedure at work by looking at the regular expressions a^* and $\mathbf{1} + a \cdot a^*$ for some $a \in \Sigma_n = \{a,b\}$ for some n. For presentation purposes, the correspondence of derivatives to automata is useful. Figure 1 shows two automata, the states of which are equivalence classes of pairs of regular expressions indicated by a dashed fringe (which is omitted for singleton classes). The equivalence classes of automaton (a) are modulo plain ACI normalization, while those of automaton (b) are modulo a stronger normalization function, making the automaton smaller. Transitions correspond to pairwise derivatives and doubled margins denote states for which the associated pairs of regular expressions are pairwise final. Both automata are the result of our decision procedure performing a breadth-first exploration starting with the initially given pair and ignoring states that are in the equivalence class of already visited states. The absence of pairs (r, s) for which r is final and s is not final (or vice versa) proves the equivalence of all pairs in the automaton, including the pair $(a^*, \mathbf{1} + a \cdot a^*)$.

5. MSO on Finite Words

Logics on finite words consider formulas in the context of a formal word, with variables representing positions in the word. In the first-order logic on words a variable always denotes a single position, while in monadic second-order logic (MSO) variables come in two flavours: first-order variables for single positions and second-order variables for finite sets of positions.

In the next subsections we first define the syntax of formulas and give them a semantics that is related to formal languages: M2L(Str). The second semantics, WS1S, is then introduced as a relaxation of M2L (we drop the "(Str)" from now on). Both semantics are equally expressive and deciding both is of nonelementary complexity. The benefits and drawbacks of the two semantics are discussed elsewhere [3, 17].

5.1 Syntax and M2L Semantics

MSO formulas are syntactically represented by the recursive data type $\alpha\,\Phi$ using de Bruijn indices for variable bindings. Terms of $\alpha\,\Phi$ are generated by the grammar

$$\begin{array}{rcl|c|c} \varphi & = & \mathsf{Q}\,a\,m & m_1 < m_2 & m \in M \\ & | & \varphi \wedge \psi & \varphi \vee \psi & \neg \varphi \\ & | & \exists \varphi & \boldsymbol{\exists} \varphi & \end{array}$$

where $\varphi, \psi :: \alpha\,\Phi$, $m, m_1, m_2, M \in \mathbb{N}$ and $a \in \alpha$. Lower-case variables m, m_1, m_2 denote first-order variables, M denotes a second order variable. The atomic formula $\mathsf{Q}\,a\,m$ requires the letter of the word at the position represented by variable m to be a; the constructors $<$ and $\in$ compare positions; Boolean operators are interpreted as usual.

The bold existential quantifier $\boldsymbol{\exists}$ binds second-order variables, $\exists$ binds first-order variables. Occurrences of bound variables represented as de Bruijn indices refer to their binders by counting the number of nested existential quantifier between the binder and the occurrence. For example, the formula $\exists (\mathsf{Q}\,a\,0 \wedge (\boldsymbol{\exists}\, 1 \in 0))$ corresponds to $\exists x. (\mathsf{Q}\,a\,x \wedge (\exists X.\, x \in X))$ when using names. The first 0 in the nameless formula refers to the outermost first-order quantifier. Inside of the inner second-order quantifier, index 1 refers to the outermost quantifier and index 0 to the inner quantifier. The nameless representation simplifies reasoning by implicitly capturing α-equivalence of formulas. On the downside, de Bruijn indices are less readable and must be manipulated with care.

Formulas may have free variables. The functions $\mathcal{V}_1 :: \alpha\,\Phi \to \mathbb{N}\,\text{set}$ and $\mathcal{V}_2 :: \alpha\,\Phi \to \mathbb{N}\,\text{set}$ collect the free first-order and second-order variables:

$$\begin{array}{llll}
\mathcal{V}_1(\mathsf{Q}\,a\,m) & = \{m\} & \mathcal{V}_2(\mathsf{Q}\,a\,m) & = \{\} \\
\mathcal{V}_1(m_1 < m_2) & = \{m_1, m_2\} & \mathcal{V}_2(m_1 < m_2) & = \{\} \\
\mathcal{V}_1(m \in M) & = \{m\} & \mathcal{V}_2(m \in M) & = \{M\} \\
\mathcal{V}_1(\varphi \wedge \psi) & = \mathcal{V}_1(\varphi) \cup \mathcal{V}_1(\psi) & \mathcal{V}_2(\varphi \wedge \psi) & = \mathcal{V}_2(\varphi) \cup \mathcal{V}_2(\psi) \\
\mathcal{V}_1(\varphi \vee \psi) & = \mathcal{V}_1(\varphi) \cup \mathcal{V}_1(\psi) & \mathcal{V}_2(\varphi \vee \psi) & = \mathcal{V}_2(\varphi) \cup \mathcal{V}_2(\psi) \\
\mathcal{V}_1(\neg \varphi) & = \mathcal{V}_1(\varphi) & \mathcal{V}_2(\neg \varphi) & = \mathcal{V}_2(\varphi) \\
\mathcal{V}_1(\exists \varphi) & = \lfloor \mathcal{V}_1(\varphi) \setminus \{0\} \rfloor & \mathcal{V}_2(\exists \varphi) & = \lfloor \mathcal{V}_2(\varphi) \rfloor \\
\mathcal{V}_1(\boldsymbol{\exists} \varphi) & = \lfloor \mathcal{V}_1(\varphi) \rfloor & \mathcal{V}_2(\boldsymbol{\exists} \varphi) & = \lfloor \mathcal{V}_2(\varphi) \setminus \{0\} \rfloor
\end{array}$$

The notation $\lfloor X \rfloor$ is shorthand for $(\lambda x.\, x - 1) \bullet X$, which reverts the increasing effect of an existential quantifier on previously bound or free variables. To obtain only free variables, bound variables are removed when their quantifier is processed, at which point the bound variable has index 0.

Just as for Π-extended regular expressions, not all formulas in $\alpha\,\Phi$ are meaningful. Consider $0 \in 0$, where 0 is both a first-order and a second-order variable. To exclude such formulas, we define the predicate $\text{wf}^{\Phi} :: \mathbb{N} \to \alpha\,\Phi \to \mathbb{B}$ as $\text{wf}_n^{\Phi}(\varphi) = (\mathcal{V}_1(\varphi) \cap \mathcal{V}_2(\varphi) = \{\}) \wedge \text{pre\_wf}_n^{\Phi}(\varphi)$ and call a formula φ *n-wellformed* if $\text{wf}_n^{\Phi}(\varphi)$ holds. The recursively defined predicate $\text{pre\_wf}^{\Phi} :: \mathbb{N} \to \alpha\,\Phi \to \mathbb{B}$ is used for further assumptions on the structure of n-wellformed formulas, which will simplify our proofs:

$$\begin{array}{ll}
\text{pre_wf}_n^{\Phi}(\mathsf{Q}\,a\,m) & = a \in \Sigma \wedge m < n \\
\text{pre_wf}_n^{\Phi}(m_1 < m_2) & = m_1 < n \wedge m_2 < n \\
\text{pre_wf}_n^{\Phi}(m \in M) & = m < n \wedge M < n \\
\text{pre_wf}_n^{\Phi}(\varphi \wedge \psi) & = \text{pre_wf}_n^{\Phi}(\varphi) \wedge \text{pre_wf}_n^{\Phi}(\psi) \\
\text{pre_wf}_n^{\Phi}(\varphi \vee \psi) & = \text{pre_wf}_n^{\Phi}(\varphi) \wedge \text{pre_wf}_n^{\Phi}(\psi) \\
\text{pre_wf}_n^{\Phi}(\neg \varphi) & = \text{pre_wf}_n^{\Phi}(\varphi) \\
\text{pre_wf}_n^{\Phi}(\exists \varphi) & = \text{pre_wf}_{n+1}^{\Phi}(\varphi) \wedge 0 \in \mathcal{V}_1(\varphi) \wedge 0 \notin \mathcal{V}_2(\varphi) \\
\text{pre_wf}_n^{\Phi}(\boldsymbol{\exists} \varphi) & = \text{pre_wf}_{n+1}^{\Phi}(\varphi) \wedge 0 \notin \mathcal{V}_1(\varphi) \wedge 0 \in \mathcal{V}_2(\varphi)
\end{array}$$

$\text{pre\_wf}_n^{\Phi}(\varphi)$ ensures that the index of every free variable in φ is below n and the values of type α come from a fixed alphabet Σ. Note that Σ is really just a fixed set of letters of type α, independent of any n and is a parameter of our setup. Moreover, pre_wf^{Φ} checks that bound variables are correctly used as first-order or second-order with respect to their binders and excludes formulas with unused binders; unused binders are obviously superfluous.

An *interpretation* of an MSO formula is a pair of a word $w :: \alpha\,\text{list}$ from Σ^* and an assignment $\mathcal{I} :: (\mathbb{N} + \mathbb{N}\,\text{set})\,\text{list}$ for free variables. The latter essentially consists of two functions with finite domain: one from first-order variables to positions and the other from second-order variables to sets of positions. We represent those two functions by a list, once again benefiting from de Bruijn indices—the value lookup for a variable with de Bruijn index i corresponds to inspecting the assignment $\mathcal{I}$ at position i, i.e. $\mathcal{I}[i]$. The range of $\mathcal{I}$ is a sum type, denoting the disjoint union of its two argument types. The sum type has two constructors $\text{Inl} :: \alpha \to \alpha + \beta$ and $\text{Inr} :: \beta \to \alpha + \beta$, such that for a first-order variable m there is a position p with $\mathcal{I}[m] = \text{Inl}\ p$ and for a second-order variable M there is a finite set of positions P with $\mathcal{I}[M] = \text{Inr}\ P$.

An interpretation that *satisfies* a formula is called a model. Satisfiability for M2L, denoted by infix $\models :: \alpha\,\text{list} \times (\mathbb{N} + \mathbb{N}\,\text{set})\,\text{list} \to$

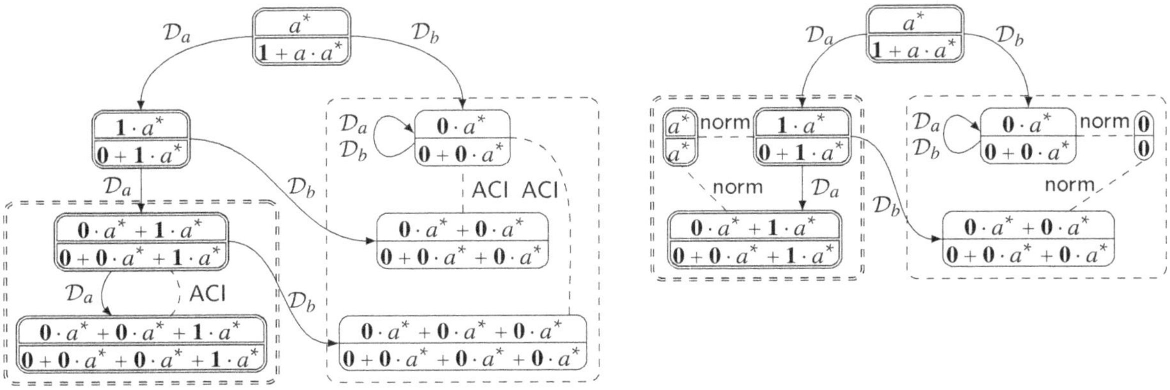

(a) norm is identity function

(b) norm unfolds $\mathbf{0} + r = r$, $\mathbf{0} \cdot r = \mathbf{0}$ and $\mathbf{1} \cdot r = r$

Figure 1. Checking the equivalence of a^* and $\mathbf{1} + a \cdot a^*$ for $\Sigma_n = \{a,b\}$

$\alpha\,\Phi \to \mathbb{B}$, is defined recursively on $\alpha\,\Phi$. To simplify the notation, the sum constructors Inl and Inr are stripped implicitly in the definition.

$$\begin{aligned}
(w,\mathcal{I}) &\models \mathsf{Q}\,a\,m &&\leftrightarrow w[\mathcal{I}[m]] = a\\
(w,\mathcal{I}) &\models m_1 < m_2 &&\leftrightarrow \mathcal{I}[m_1] < \mathcal{I}[m_2]\\
(w,\mathcal{I}) &\models m \in M &&\leftrightarrow \mathcal{I}[m] \in \mathcal{I}[M]\\
(w,\mathcal{I}) &\models \varphi \wedge \psi &&\leftrightarrow (w,\mathcal{I}) \models \varphi \wedge (w,\mathcal{I}) \models \psi\\
(w,\mathcal{I}) &\models \varphi \vee \psi &&\leftrightarrow (w,\mathcal{I}) \models \varphi \vee (w,\mathcal{I}) \models \psi\\
(w,\mathcal{I}) &\models \neg\varphi &&\leftrightarrow (w,\mathcal{I}) \not\models \varphi\\
(w,\mathcal{I}) &\models \exists\varphi &&\leftrightarrow \exists p \in \{0,\dots,|w|-1\}.\ (w, \mathsf{Inl}\ p\ \#\ \mathcal{I}) \models \varphi\\
(w,\mathcal{I}) &\models \boldsymbol{\exists}\varphi &&\leftrightarrow \exists P \subseteq \{0,\dots,|w|-1\}.\ (w, \mathsf{Inr}\ P\ \#\ \mathcal{I}) \models \varphi
\end{aligned}$$

For the definition to make sense, $\mathcal{I}$ must correctly map first-order variables to positions (i.e. $\mathcal{I}[m] = \mathsf{Inl}\ p$) and second-order variables to sets of positions (i.e. $\mathcal{I}[M] = \mathsf{Inr}\ P$). Furthermore, all positions in $\mathcal{I}$ should be below the length of the word, and for technical reasons the word should not be empty. We formalize these assumptions by the predicate $\mathsf{wf}^{\mathsf{M2L}} :: \alpha\,\Phi \to \alpha\ \mathsf{list} \times (\mathbb{N} + \mathbb{N}\,\mathsf{set})\ \mathsf{list} \to \mathbb{B}$ and call an interpretation *M2L-wellformed* for φ if $\mathsf{wf}^{\mathsf{M2L}}_\varphi(w,\mathcal{I})$ holds:

$$\begin{aligned}
&\mathsf{wf}^{\mathsf{M2L}}_\varphi(w,\mathcal{I}) =\\
&\quad w \neq [\,] \wedge w \in \Sigma^* \wedge\\
&\quad \forall\,\mathsf{Inl}\ p \in \mathsf{set}\ \mathcal{I}.\ p < |w| \wedge\\
&\quad \forall\,\mathsf{Inr}\ P \in \mathsf{set}\ \mathcal{I}.\ (\forall p \in P.\ p < |w|) \wedge\\
&\quad \forall m \in \mathcal{V}_1(\varphi)\ (\exists p.\ \mathcal{I}[m] = \mathsf{Inl}\ p) \wedge\\
&\quad \forall M \in \mathcal{V}_2(\varphi)\ (\exists P.\ \mathcal{I}[M] = \mathsf{Inr}\ P)
\end{aligned}$$

5.2 WS1S Semantics

In an M2L-wellformed model, positions are restricted by the length of the word. This is the key difference compared to WS1S. In WS1S no a priori restrictions on the variable ranges are made, although all second-order variables still represent finite sets. The subtle difference is illustrated by the formula $\boldsymbol{\exists}\,(\forall\,0 \in 1)$ (with names: $\exists X.\,\forall x.\ x \in X$), where $\forall\,\varphi$ is just an abbreviation for $\neg\,\exists\,\neg\,\varphi$. In the M2L semantics $\boldsymbol{\exists}\,(\forall\,0 \in 1)$ is satisfied by all wellformed interpretations—the witness set for the outer existential quantifier is for a wellformed interpretation $(w,\mathcal{I})$ just the set $\{0,\dots,|w|-1\}$. In contrast, in WS1S, there is no finite set which contains all arbitrarily large positions, thus $\boldsymbol{\exists}\,(\forall\,0 \in 1)$ is unsatisfiable.

Formally, satisfiability for WS1S, denoted by infix $\overset{\circ}{\models} :: \alpha\ \mathsf{list} \times (\mathbb{N} + \mathbb{N}\,\mathsf{set})\ \mathsf{list} \to \alpha\,\Phi \to \mathbb{B}$, is defined just as for M2L (replacing $\models$ by $\overset{\circ}{\models}$) except for the following equations.

$$\begin{aligned}
(w,\mathcal{I}) &\overset{\circ}{\models} \mathsf{Q}\,a\,m &&\leftrightarrow (\mathbf{if}\ \mathcal{I}[m] < |w|\ \mathbf{then}\ w[\mathcal{I}[m]]\ \mathbf{else}\ \mathsf{z}) = a\\
(w,\mathcal{I}) &\overset{\circ}{\models} \exists\varphi &&\leftrightarrow \exists p.\ (w, \mathsf{Inl}\ p\ \#\ \mathcal{I}) \overset{\circ}{\models} \varphi\\
(w,\mathcal{I}) &\overset{\circ}{\models} \boldsymbol{\exists}\varphi &&\leftrightarrow \exists P.\ (w, \mathsf{Inr}\ P\ \#\ \mathcal{I}) \overset{\circ}{\models} \varphi \wedge \mathsf{finite}\ P
\end{aligned}$$

Here, z is a distinguished letter from Σ. WS1S as defined in the literature does not handle the $\mathsf{Q}\,a\,m$ case at all, usually interpreting formulas only with respect to the assignment $\mathcal{I}$. In order to be able to use the same syntax and the same type of interpretations for both semantics, we have made the above choice. This also allows us to translate $\mathsf{Q}\,a\,m$ into the same regular expression irrespective of the intended semantics.

Besides the mentioned relaxation of *WS1S-wellformedness* with respect to variable ranges, the empty word does not impose technical complications as in M2L. Therefore, the predicate $\mathsf{wf}^{\mathsf{WS1S}} :: \alpha\,\Phi \to \alpha\ \mathsf{list} \times (\mathbb{N} + \mathbb{N}\,\mathsf{set})\ \mathsf{list} \to \mathbb{B}$ is defined as follows.

$$\begin{aligned}
&\mathsf{wf}^{\mathsf{WS1S}}_\varphi(w,\mathcal{I}) =\\
&\quad w \in \Sigma^* \wedge\\
&\quad \forall\,\mathsf{Inr}\ P \in \mathsf{set}\ \mathcal{I}.\ \mathsf{finite}\ P \wedge\\
&\quad \forall m \in \mathcal{V}_1(\varphi)\ (\exists p.\ \mathcal{I}[m] = \mathsf{Inl}\ p) \wedge\\
&\quad \forall M \in \mathcal{V}_2(\varphi)\ (\exists P.\ \mathcal{I}[M] = \mathsf{Inr}\ P)
\end{aligned}$$

5.3 Encoding Interpretations as Words

Formulas are equivalent if they have the same set of wellformed models. To relate equivalent formulas with language equivalent regular expressions, the set of wellformed models must be represented as a formal language by encoding interpretations as words. As before, we cover the encoding of the M2L semantics first.

To simplify the formalization, we choose a very simple encoding using Boolean vectors. For an interpretation $(w,\mathcal{I})$, we associate with every position p in the word w a Boolean vector bs of length $|\mathcal{I}|$, such that $bs[m] = \top$ iff the mth variable in $\mathcal{I}$ is first-order and its value is p or it is second-order and its value contains p. For example, for $\Sigma = \{a,b\}$ the interpretation $(w,\mathcal{I}) = (aba, \mathsf{Inl}\ 0\ \#\ \mathsf{Inr}\ \{1,2\}\ \#\ \mathsf{Inl}\ 2\ \#\ [\,])$ can be written in two dimensions as follows:

	a	b	a
Inl 0	$\top$	$\bot$	$\bot$
Inr $\{1,2\}$	$\bot$	$\top$	$\top$
Inl 2	$\bot$	$\bot$	$\top$

In the first row, the value $\top$ is placed only in the first column because the first variable of $\mathcal{I}$ is the first-order position 0. In general, the columns correspond to the Boolean vectors associated with positions in the word, while every row corresponds to one variable. For first-order variables there must be exactly one $\top$ per row. The first row encodes the value of the most recently bound variable. Now, we consider every column as a letter of a new alphabet, which is the underlying alphabet $\Sigma_n = \Sigma \times \mathbb{B}^n$ of regular expressions of Section 4. This transformation of interpretations into words over Σ_n is performed by the function $\mathsf{enc}^{\mathsf{M2L}} :: \alpha\ \mathsf{list} \times (\mathbb{N} + \mathbb{N}\,\mathsf{set})\ \mathsf{list} \to (\alpha \times \mathbb{B}\,\mathsf{list})\ \mathsf{list}$; we omit its obvious definition.

Furthermore, the second parameter $\pi :: \Sigma_{n+1} \to \Sigma_n$ of our decision procedure for regular expressions can now be instantiated as the function that maps $(a, b \# bs)$ to (a, bs). Thus, the projection Π operates on words by removing the first row from words in the language of the body expression, reflecting the semantics of an existential quantifier.

Below we use a more visually appealing notation for elements of Σ_n. E.g. $(a, \top \# \bot \# \bot \# [\,])$ is written as

$$\begin{pmatrix} a \\ \top\bot\bot \end{pmatrix}.$$

Finally, the *M2L-language* $\mathcal{L}^{\mathsf{M2L}} :: \mathbb{N} \to \alpha\,\Phi \to (\alpha \times \mathbb{B}\,\mathsf{list})\ \mathsf{set}$ of an MSO formula is the set of encodings of its wellformed models, i.e. $\mathcal{L}_n^{\mathsf{M2L}}(\varphi) = \{\mathsf{enc}^{\mathsf{M2L}}(w,\mathcal{I}) \mid \mathsf{wf}_\varphi^{\mathsf{M2L}}(w,\mathcal{I}) \wedge |\mathcal{I}| = n \wedge (w,\mathcal{I}) \models \varphi\}$.

Concerning WS1S, the encoding is slightly more complicated due to the following observation: Interpretations $(w,\mathcal{I})$ and $(w\mathsf{z}^n,\mathcal{I})$ for all $n \in \mathbb{N}$ behave the same when considering satisfiability and wellformedness with respect to a formula (z^n denotes n-fold repetition of the letter z as a word). That suggests that the example interpretation $(w,\mathcal{I}) = (aba, \mathsf{Inl}\,0 \# \mathsf{Inr}\,\{1,2\} \# \mathsf{Inl}\,2 \# [\,])$ from above can be encoded as

	a	b	a	z^m
$\mathsf{Inl}\,0$	$\top$	$\bot$	$\bot$	$\bot^m$
$\mathsf{Inr}\,\{1,2\}$	$\bot$	$\top$	$\top$	$\bot^m$
$\mathsf{Inl}\,2$	$\bot$	$\bot$	$\top$	$\bot^m$

for every $m \in \mathbb{N}$. Hence, the a single WS1S interpretation is translated into a countably infinite set of words by a function $\mathsf{enc}^{\mathsf{WS1S}} :: \alpha\ \mathsf{list} \times (\mathbb{N} + \mathbb{N}\,\mathsf{set})\ \mathsf{list} \to (\alpha \times \mathbb{B}\,\mathsf{list})\ \mathsf{list}\ \mathsf{set}$; we again omit its formal definition. Accordingly, the *WS1S-language* $\mathcal{L}^{\mathsf{WS1S}} :: \mathbb{N} \to \alpha\,\Phi \to (\alpha \times \mathbb{B}\,\mathsf{list})\ \mathsf{set}$ of an MSO formula is defined by taking the union of all encodings of its wellformed models: $\mathcal{L}_n^{\mathsf{WS1S}}(\varphi) = \bigcup\{\mathsf{enc}^{\mathsf{M2L}}(w,\mathcal{I}) \mid \mathsf{wf}_\varphi^{\mathsf{WS1S}}(w,\mathcal{I}) \wedge |\mathcal{I}| = n \wedge (w,\mathcal{I}) \models \varphi\}$.

5.4 From Formulas to Regular Expressions

MSO formulas interpreted in M2L are translated into regular expressions by means of the primitive recursive function $\mathsf{mkRE}^{\mathsf{M2L}} :: \mathbb{N} \to \alpha\,\Phi \to \alpha\,\mathsf{RE}$ (see Figure 2). The natural number parameter of $\mathsf{mkRE}^{\mathsf{M2L}}$ indicates the number for free variables for the processed formula. The parameter is increased when entering recursively the scope of an existential quantifier. In general, the abbreviation

$$\begin{pmatrix} X \\ \underbrace{\bot/\top \cdots \bot/\top}_{m}\ \top\ \underbrace{\bot/\top \cdots \bot/\top}_{n-m-1} \end{pmatrix}$$

actually denotes the huge summation

$$\bigoplus_{\substack{a \in X \\ b_i \in \{\top,\bot\} \\ i \in \{0,\ldots,m-1,m+1,\ldots,n-1\}}} \begin{pmatrix} a \\ b_0 \cdots b_{m-1}\ \top\ b_{m+1} \cdots b_{n-1} \end{pmatrix}.$$

The intuition behind the translation is demonstrated by the case $\mathsf{Q}\,a\,m$. We fix a wellformed model $(w,\mathcal{I})$ of $\mathsf{Q}\,a\,m$. $(w,\mathcal{I})$ must satisfy $w[\mathcal{I}[m]] = a$, or equivalently the fact that there exists a Boolean vector bs of length n such that $\mathsf{enc}^{\mathsf{M2L}}(w,\mathcal{I})[\mathcal{I}[m]] = (a, bs)$ and $bs[m] = \top$. Therefore, the letter at position $\mathcal{I}[m]$ of $\mathsf{enc}^{\mathsf{M2L}}(w,\mathcal{I})$ is matched by the "middle" part of $\mathsf{mkRE}_n^{\mathsf{M2L}}(\mathsf{Q}\,a\,m)$, while the subexpressions $\neg\,\mathbf{0}$ (which denotes Σ_n^*) match the first $\mathcal{I}[m]$ and the last $n - \mathcal{I}[m]$ letters of $\mathsf{enc}^{\mathsf{M2L}}(w,\mathcal{I})$.

Conversely, if we fix a word from $\mathsf{mkRE}_n^{\mathsf{M2L}}(\mathsf{Q}\,a\,m)$, it will be equal to an encoding of an interpretation that satisfies $\mathsf{Q}\,a\,m$ by a similar argument. However, the interpretation might be not wellformed for $\mathsf{Q}\,a\,m$. This happens because the regular expression $\mathsf{mkRE}_n^{\mathsf{M2L}}(\mathsf{Q}\,a\,m)$ does not capture the distinction between first-order and second-order variables, such that it accepts encodings of interpretations that have the value $\top$ more than once at different positions representing the same first-order variable. This indicates that the subexpressions $\neg\,\mathbf{0}$ in the base cases are not precise enough, but also in the case of Boolean operators similar issues arise. So instead of tinkering with the base cases, it is better to separate the generation a regular expression that encodes models from the one that encodes wellformed interpretations.

To rule out not wellformed interpretations is exactly the purpose of the $\mathsf{WF} :: \mathbb{N} \to \alpha\,\Phi \to \alpha\,\mathsf{RE}$ function. The regular expression $\mathsf{WF}_n(\varphi)$ (see Figure 2) accepts exactly the encodings of wellformed interpretations (both models and non-models) for φ by ensuring that first-order variables are encoded correctly.

Lemma 9. *Let φ be an n-wellformed formula. Then*

- $\mathcal{L}_n(\mathsf{WF}_n(\varphi)) = \{\mathsf{enc}^{\mathsf{WS1S}}(w,\mathcal{I}) \mid \mathsf{wf}_\varphi^{\mathsf{WS1S}}(w,\mathcal{I}) \wedge |\mathcal{I}| = n\}$, *and*
- $\mathcal{L}_n(\mathsf{WF}_n(\varphi)) \setminus \{[\,]\} = \{\mathsf{enc}^{\mathsf{M2L}}(w,\mathcal{I}) \mid \mathsf{wf}_\varphi^{\mathsf{M2L}}(w,\mathcal{I}) \wedge |\mathcal{I}| = n\}$.

Using WF in every case of the recursive definition of $\mathsf{mkRE}^{\mathsf{M2L}}$ is very redundant—it is enough to perform the intersection once globally for the entire formula and additionally for every existential quantifier.

MSO formulas interpreted in WS1S are translated into regular expressions by means of the function $\mathsf{mkRE}^{\mathsf{WS1S}} :: \mathbb{N} \to \alpha\,\Phi \to \alpha\,\mathsf{RE}$.

The definition of $\mathsf{mkRE}^{\mathsf{WS1S}}$ coincides with the one of $\mathsf{mkRE}^{\mathsf{M2L}}$ except for the existential quantifier cases:

$$\mathsf{mkRE}_n^{\mathsf{WS1S}}(\exists\varphi) = \mathcal{Q}\begin{pmatrix} \mathsf{z} \\ \bot^n \end{pmatrix}\left(\Pi\left(\mathsf{mkRE}_{n+1}^{\mathsf{WS1S}}(\varphi) \cap \mathsf{WF}_{n+1}(\varphi)\right)\right)$$

$$\mathsf{mkRE}_n^{\mathsf{WS1S}}(\exists\varphi) = \mathcal{Q}\begin{pmatrix} \mathsf{z} \\ \bot^n \end{pmatrix}\left(\Pi\left(\mathsf{mkRE}_{n+1}^{\mathsf{WS1S}}(\varphi) \cap \mathsf{WF}_{n+1}(\varphi)\right)\right)$$

The regular operation $\mathcal{Q} :: \alpha \times \mathbb{B}\,\mathsf{list} \to \alpha\,\mathsf{RE} \to \alpha\,\mathsf{RE}$ reestablishes the invariant of having all words terminated with a suffix $\begin{pmatrix} \mathsf{z} \\ \bot^n \end{pmatrix}^m$ for every $m \in \mathbb{N}$ in the WS1S language encoding of a formula as required by definition of $\mathsf{enc}^{\mathsf{WS1S}}$ (this invariant might be violated by the projection). More precisely, the following language identity holds for an n-wellformed regular expression r:

$$\mathcal{L}_n(\mathcal{Q}\,a\,r) = \left\{xa^m \mid m \in \mathbb{N} \wedge \exists l.\ xa^l \in \mathcal{L}_n(r)\right\}$$

We do not show the concrete executable definition of $\mathcal{Q}$ which can be found in our formalization. On a high-level, $\mathcal{Q}$ is computed by repeatedly deriving from the right by a (dual to $\mathcal{D}_a$ which derives from the left). The termination of the repeated derivation is established by the dual of Theorem 2 for ACI-equivalent "right derivatives".

Finally, we can establish the language correspondence between formulas and generated regular expressions.

Theorem 10. *Let φ be an n-wellformed formula. Then*

- $\mathcal{L}_n^{\mathsf{WS1S}}(\varphi) = \mathcal{L}_n(\mathsf{mkRE}_n^{\mathsf{WS1S}}(\varphi) \cap \mathsf{WF}_n(\varphi))$, *and*
- $\mathcal{L}_n^{\mathsf{M2L}}(\varphi) = \mathcal{L}_n(\mathsf{mkRE}_n^{\mathsf{M2L}}(\varphi) \cap \mathsf{WF}_n(\varphi)) \setminus \{[\,]\}$.

The proof is by structural induction on φ. Above we have seen the argument for the base case $\mathsf{Q}\,a\,m$, other base cases follow similarly. The cases $\exists\varphi$ and $\exists\varphi$ follow easily from the semantics of Π given by our concrete instantiation for π and Σ_n and the induc-

$$
\begin{aligned}
\mathsf{mkRE}_n^{\mathsf{M2L}}(\mathsf{Q}\,a\,m) &= \neg\mathbf{0}\cdot\left(\begin{matrix}\{a\}\\ \underbrace{\bot/\top\cdots\bot/\top}_{m}\ \top\ \underbrace{\bot/\top\cdots\bot/\top}_{n-m-1}\end{matrix}\right)\cdot\neg\mathbf{0}\\
\mathsf{mkRE}_n^{\mathsf{M2L}}(m_1<m_2) &= \neg\mathbf{0}\cdot\left(\begin{matrix}\Sigma\\ \underbrace{\bot/\top\cdots\bot/\top}_{m_1}\ \top\ \underbrace{\bot/\top\cdots\bot/\top}_{n-m_1-1}\end{matrix}\right)\cdot\neg\mathbf{0}\cdot\left(\begin{matrix}\Sigma\\ \underbrace{\bot/\top\cdots\bot/\top}_{m_2}\ \top\ \underbrace{\bot/\top\cdots\bot/\top}_{n-m_2-1}\end{matrix}\right)\cdot\neg\mathbf{0}\\
\mathsf{mkRE}_n^{\mathsf{M2L}}(m\in M) &= \neg\mathbf{0}\cdot\left(\begin{matrix}\Sigma\\ \underbrace{\bot/\top\cdots\bot/\top}_{\min m M}\ \top\ \underbrace{\bot/\top\cdots\bot/\top}_{\max m M-\min m M-1}\ \top\ \underbrace{\bot/\top\cdots\bot/\top}_{n-\max m M-1}\end{matrix}\right)\cdot\neg\mathbf{0}\\
\mathsf{mkRE}_n^{\mathsf{M2L}}(\varphi\wedge\psi) &= \mathsf{mkRE}_n^{\mathsf{M2L}}(\varphi)\cap\mathsf{mkRE}_n^{\mathsf{M2L}}(\psi)\\
\mathsf{mkRE}_n^{\mathsf{M2L}}(\varphi\vee\psi) &= \mathsf{mkRE}_n^{\mathsf{M2L}}(\varphi)+\mathsf{mkRE}_n^{\mathsf{M2L}}(\psi)\\
\mathsf{mkRE}_n^{\mathsf{M2L}}(\neg\varphi) &= \neg\,\mathsf{mkRE}_n^{\mathsf{M2L}}(r)\\
\mathsf{mkRE}_n^{\mathsf{M2L}}(\exists\,\varphi) &= \Pi\left(\mathsf{mkRE}_{n+1}^{\mathsf{M2L}}(\varphi)\cap\mathsf{WF}_{n+1}(\varphi)\right)\\
\mathsf{mkRE}_n^{\mathsf{M2L}}(\boldsymbol{\exists}\,\varphi) &= \Pi\left(\mathsf{mkRE}_{n+1}^{\mathsf{M2L}}(\varphi)\cap\mathsf{WF}_{n+1}(\varphi)\right)
\end{aligned}
$$

$$
\mathsf{WF}_n(\varphi) = \bigcap_{m\in\mathcal{V}_1(\varphi)}\left(\begin{matrix}\Sigma\\ \underbrace{\bot/\top\cdots\bot/\top}_{m}\ \bot\ \underbrace{\bot/\top\cdots\bot/\top}_{n-m-1}\end{matrix}\right)^*\cdot\left(\begin{matrix}\Sigma\\ \underbrace{\bot/\top\cdots\bot/\top}_{m}\ \top\ \underbrace{\bot/\top\cdots\bot/\top}_{n-m-1}\end{matrix}\right)\cdot\left(\begin{matrix}\Sigma\\ \underbrace{\bot/\top\cdots\bot/\top}_{m}\ \bot\ \underbrace{\bot/\top\cdots\bot/\top}_{n-m-1}\end{matrix}\right)^*
$$

Figure 2. Definition of $\mathsf{mkRE}^{\mathsf{M2L}}$ and WF

tion hypothesis. The most interesting cases are, somehow unexpectedly, those for Boolean operators. Although the definitions are purely structural, sets of encodings of models must be composed or, even worse, complemented in the inductive steps. The key property required here is that $\mathsf{enc}^{\mathsf{M2L}}$ (and $\mathsf{enc}^{\mathsf{WS1S}}$) do not collapse models and non-models: two different wellformed interpretations for a formula—one being a model, the other being a non-model—are encoded into different words (sets of words). This is again established by structural induction on formulas for both semantics.

Lemma 11. *Let $(w_1,\mathcal{I}_1)$ and $(w_2,\mathcal{I}_2)$ be two M2L-wellformed interpretations for φ such that $\mathsf{enc}^{\mathsf{M2L}}(w_1,\mathcal{I}_1)=\mathsf{enc}^{\mathsf{M2L}}(w_2,\mathcal{I}_2)$. Then $(w_1,\mathcal{I}_1)\models\varphi\leftrightarrow(w_2,\mathcal{I}_2)\models\varphi$.*

Lemma 12. *Let $(w_1,\mathcal{I}_1)$ and $(w_2,\mathcal{I}_2)$ be two WS1S-wellformed interpretations for φ such that $\mathsf{enc}^{\mathsf{WS1S}}(w_1,\mathcal{I}_1)=\mathsf{enc}^{\mathsf{WS1S}}(w_2,\mathcal{I}_2)$. Then $(w_1,\mathcal{I}_1)\stackrel{\circ}{\models}\varphi\leftrightarrow(w_2,\mathcal{I}_2)\stackrel{\circ}{\models}\varphi$.*

5.5 Deciding Language Equivalence of Formulas

The algorithms $\mathsf{eqv}^{\mathsf{M2L}}::\mathbb{N}\to\alpha\,\Phi\to\alpha\,\Phi\to\mathbb{B}$ and $\mathsf{eqv}^{\mathsf{WS1S}}::\mathbb{N}\to\alpha\,\Phi\to\alpha\,\Phi\to\mathbb{B}$ that decide language equivalence of MSO formulas check wellformedness of the input formulas, translate the formulas into regular expressions and let $\mathsf{eqv}^{\mathsf{RE}}$ do the work:

$$
\begin{aligned}
&\mathsf{eqv}_n^{\mathsf{M2L}}\,\varphi\,\psi =\\
&\quad \mathsf{wf}_n^{\Phi}(\varphi\vee\psi)\wedge\\
&\quad \mathsf{eqv}_n^{\mathsf{RE}}\,(\mathsf{mkRE}_n^{\mathsf{M2L}}(\varphi)+\mathbf{1})\;(\mathsf{mkRE}_n^{\mathsf{M2L}}(\psi)+\mathbf{1})
\end{aligned}
$$

$$
\begin{aligned}
&\mathsf{eqv}_n^{\mathsf{WS1S}}\,\varphi\,\psi =\\
&\quad \mathsf{wf}_n^{\Phi}(\varphi\vee\psi)\wedge\\
&\quad \mathsf{eqv}_n^{\mathsf{RE}}\,(\mathsf{mkRE}_n^{\mathsf{WS1S}}(\varphi))\;(\mathsf{mkRE}_n^{\mathsf{WS1S}}(\psi))
\end{aligned}
$$

Note that wellformedness is checked on the disjunction of both formulas to ensure that they agree on free variables (i.e. no first-order free variable of φ is used as a second-order free variable in ψ and vice versa). Further, we add the empty word into both regular expression when working with the M2L semantics. This is allowed, since [] is not a valid encoding of an interpretation, and necessary because Theorem 10 does not give us any information whether the empty word is contained in the output of $\mathsf{mkRE}^{\mathsf{M2L}}$ or not.

Termination of $\mathsf{eqv}^{\mathsf{RE}}$ is ensured by Theorem 6 and the definition principle of primitive recursion for wf^{Φ}, $\mathsf{mkRE}^{\mathsf{M2L}}$ and $\mathsf{mkRE}^{\mathsf{WS1S}}$. Soundness and completeness follow easily from Theorems 7, 8 and 10.

Theorem 13 (Soundness)**.** *Let φ and ψ be MSO formulas.*

- *If $\mathsf{eqv}_n^{\mathsf{M2L}}\,\varphi\,\psi$, then $\mathcal{L}_n^{\mathsf{M2L}}(\varphi)=\mathcal{L}_n^{\mathsf{M2L}}(\psi)$.*
- *If $\mathsf{eqv}_n^{\mathsf{WS1S}}\,\varphi\,\psi$, then $\mathcal{L}_n^{\mathsf{WS1S}}(\varphi)=\mathcal{L}_n^{\mathsf{WS1S}}(\psi)$.*

Theorem 14 (Completeness)**.** *Let $\varphi\vee\psi$ be an n-wellformed MSO formula.*

- *If $\mathcal{L}_n^{\mathsf{M2L}}(\varphi)=\mathcal{L}_n^{\mathsf{M2L}}(\psi)$, then $\mathsf{eqv}_n^{\mathsf{M2L}}\,\varphi\,\psi$.*
- *If $\mathcal{L}_n^{\mathsf{WS1S}}(\varphi)=\mathcal{L}_n^{\mathsf{WS1S}}(\psi)$, then $\mathsf{eqv}_n^{\mathsf{WS1S}}\,\varphi\,\psi$.*

6. Application: Finite-Word LTL

We want to execute the code generated by Isabelle/HOL for our decision procedures on some larger examples. For simplicity, we focus on M2L.

In order to create larger formulas, it is helpful to introduce some syntactic abbreviations. We define the unsatisfiable formula $\bot$ as $\exists\,0<0$ and the valid formula $\top$ as $\neg\bot$. Now, checking that a formula is valid amounts to checking its equivalence to $\top$. Implication $\varphi\to\psi$ is defined as $(\neg\varphi)\vee\psi$ and universal quantification $\forall\,\varphi$ as before as $\neg\exists\neg\varphi$. Next, we introduce temporal logical operators *always* $\Box P::\mathbb{N}\to\alpha\,\Phi$ and *eventually* $\Diamond P::\mathbb{N}\to\alpha\,\Phi$ depending on $P::\mathbb{N}\to\alpha\,\Phi$—a formula parameterized by a single variable indicating the time. The operators have their usual meaning except that with the given M2L semantics the time variable ranges over a fixed set determined by the interpretation. Additionally, we lift the disjunction and implication to time-parameterized formulas.

$$
\begin{array}{lcl}
\Box P\,t & = & \forall(\neg\, t+1<0 \rightarrow P\,0) \\
\Diamond P\,t & = & \exists(\neg\, t+1<0 \wedge P\,0) \\
(P \Rightarrow Q)\,t & = & P\,t \rightarrow Q\,t \\
(P \ovee Q)\,t & = & P\,t \vee Q\,t
\end{array}
$$

Note that $t+1$ has nothing to do with the next time step. It is just the lifting of the de Bruijn index under a single quantifier.

Further, formulas of linear temporal logic contain atomic predicates for which the interpretation must specify at which points in time they are true. This information can be encoded in two ways, which we compare in the following.

The first possibility is to encode atomic predicates in the word of the interpretation. This is done by identifying Σ with the powerset $\mathcal{P}$ of atomic predicates. For every point in time, that is for every position in the word, the letter is the set of predicates that are true at this point. Using this encoding we can prove the validity of the following closed formulas over the alphabet $\mathcal{P}\{P\} = \{\{P\},\{\}\}$ automatically within a few milliseconds.

$$
\begin{array}{c}
\forall(\Box(\mathsf{Q}\{P\}) \Rightarrow \Diamond(\mathsf{Q}\{P\}))\ 0 \\
\forall(\Box(\mathsf{Q}\{P\}) \Rightarrow \Box\Diamond(\mathsf{Q}\{P\}))\ 0
\end{array}
$$

Alternatively, a free second-order variable can be used to encode an atomic predicate directly. The variable denotes the set of points in time for which the atomic predicate holds. The alphabet Σ can then be trivial, i.e. $\Sigma = \{a\}$ for an arbitrary a. Using this encoding the above two formulas correspond to

$$
\begin{array}{c}
\forall(\Box(\lambda t.\, t\in 2) \Rightarrow \Diamond(\lambda t.\, t\in 2))\ 0 \\
\forall(\Box(\lambda t.\, t\in 2) \Rightarrow \Box\Diamond(\lambda t.\, t\in 3))\ 0
\end{array}
$$

Both formulas have one free second-order variable 0 that is lifted when passing two or three quantifiers. The generated algorithm shows the equivalence to $\top$ again within milliseconds.

In order to explore the limits of our decision procedure, formulas over more atomic predicates are required. Therefore, we consider the distributivity theorems of $\Box$ over implication for both representations of atomic predicates as shown in Figure 3. When the number of predicates n is increased, the size of φ_n grows exponentially: to express that a predicate P holds at some position we need the disjunction of all atoms containing P. In contrast, the size of ψ_n grows linearly. The complexity of ψ_n is hidden in its encoding—the latter also grows exponentially with increasing n. The running times of the decision procedure are summarized in Figure 4. Thereby, ψ_1, ψ_2 and ψ_3 were processed over $\Sigma = \{a\}$, φ_1 was processed over $\Sigma = \mathcal{P}\{P\}$, φ_2 over $\Sigma = \mathcal{P}\{P_1,P_2\}$ and finally φ_3 over $\Sigma = \mathcal{P}\{P_1,P_2,P_3\}$. Figure 4 also shows the sizes of the generated regular expressions. Both size and $\mathsf{size}_{\mathsf{len}}$ count the constructors in a regular expression. The difference is that the size of an atom is 1 whereas the $\mathsf{size}_{\mathsf{len}}$ of an atom is the length of its Boolean vector.

The attentive reader will have noticed that we have said nothing about how sets are represented in the code generated from our mathematical definitions. We have chosen an existing verified red-black tree implementation for our measurements. Isabelle's code generator supports the transparent replacement of sets by some verified implementation [14].

The performance of our automatically generated code may appear disappointing but that would be a misunderstanding of our intentions. We see our work primarily as a succinct and elegant functional program that may pave the way towards verified and efficient decision procedures. As a bonus, the generated code is applicable to small examples. In the context of interactive theorem proving, this is primarily what one encounters: small formulas. Any automation is welcome here because it saves the user time and effort. Automatic verification of larger systems is the domain of highly tuned implementations such as MONA.

7. Conclusion

We have presented functional programs that decide equivalence of MSO formulas for two different semantics in Isabelle/HOL. They come with formal proofs of termination, soundness and completeness. The programs operate by translating formulas into Π-extended regular expressions and deciding the language equivalence of the latter using Brzozowski derivatives. Although formalized in Isabelle/HOL's functional programming language, we can automatically generate code from them in different functional target languages. The development amounts to roughly 350 lines of functional programs and 5000 lines of proofs, of which 2100 lines are devoted to deciding equivalence of Π-extended regular expressions. For M2L, the program is completely contained in this paper. The Isabelle scripts are publicly available [27].

Our work can be continued in two dimensions. First, the algorithm is not optimized. Especially the encoding of interpretations as Boolean vectors leaves room for improvement.

Second, several related decidable logics can be formalized and verified using similar technology. A related logic is MSO on infinite words (also called S1S). S1S formulas can be translated into ω-regular expressions representing ω-regular languages. A verified decision procedure for deciding equivalence of ω-regular expressions without constructing ω-automata is an interesting challenge. An even more distant goal is to move from words to trees (or even from ω-words to ω-trees) and decide equivalence of MSO formulas on (in)finite trees (or alternatively (W)S2S formulas) by translating them into (ω-)regular tree expressions.

Acknowledgments

We thank Alexander Krauss for inspiring discussions and Jasmin Christian Blanchette for numerous comments on the presentation. Comments and questions of four anonymous reviewers helped to clarify certain fine points. The first author's research is supported by the doctorate program 1480 (PUMA) of the Deutsche Forschungsgemeinschaft (DFG).

References

[1] V. Antimirov. Partial derivatives of regular expressions and finite automaton constructions. *Theor. Comput. Sci.*, 155(2):291–319, Mar. 1996.

[2] A. Asperti. A compact proof of decidability for regular expression equivalence. In L. Beringer and A. Felty, eds., *Interactive Theorem Proving, ITP 2012*, vol. 7406 of *LNCS*, pp. 283–298. Springer, 2012.

[3] A. Ayari and D. Basin. Bounded model construction for monadic second-order logics. In E. A. Emerson and A. P. Sistla, eds., *Proc. Int. Conf. Computer Aided Verification, CAV 2000*, vol. 1855 of *LNCS*, pp. 99–112. Springer, 2000.

[4] C. Ballarin. Interpretation of locales in Isabelle: Theories and proof contexts. In J. M. Borwein and W. M. Farmer, eds., *Mathematical Knowledge Management, MKM 2006*, vol. 4108 of *LNCS*, pp. 31–43. Springer, 2006.

[5] D. Basin and S. Friedrich. Combining WS1S and HOL. In D. Gabbay and M. de Rijke, eds., *Frontiers of Combining Systems 2*, vol. 7 of *Studies in Logic and Computation*, pp. 39–56. Research Studies Press/Wiley, 2000.

[6] S. Berghofer and M. Reiter. Formalizing the logic-automaton connection. In S. Berghofer, T. Nipkow, C. Urban, and M. Wenzel, eds., *Theorem Proving in Higher Order Logics, TPHOLs 2009*, vol. 5674 of *LNCS*, pp. 147–163. Springer, 2009.

$$
\begin{aligned}
\varphi_1 &= \forall\,(\square(\mathsf{Q}\{P\}) \Rightarrow \square(\mathsf{Q}\{P\}))\ 0\\
\varphi_2 &= \forall\,(\square(\mathsf{Q}\{P_1\} \circledvee \mathsf{Q}\{P_1,P_2\} \Rightarrow \mathsf{Q}\{P_2\} \circledvee \mathsf{Q}\{P_1,P_2\}) \Rightarrow \square(\mathsf{Q}\{P_1\} \circledvee \mathsf{Q}\{P_1,P_2\}) \Rightarrow \square(\mathsf{Q}\{P_2\} \circledvee \mathsf{Q}\{P_1,P_2\}))\ 0\\
\varphi_3 &= \forall\,(\square(\mathsf{Q}\{P_1\} \circledvee \mathsf{Q}\{P_1,P_2\} \circledvee \mathsf{Q}\{P_1,P_3\} \circledvee \mathsf{Q}\{P_1,P_2,P_3\} \Rightarrow\\
&\qquad\qquad \mathsf{Q}\{P_2\} \circledvee \mathsf{Q}\{P_1,P_2\} \circledvee \mathsf{Q}\{P_2,P_3\} \circledvee \mathsf{Q}\{P_1,P_2,P_3\} \Rightarrow \mathsf{Q}\{P_3\} \circledvee \mathsf{Q}\{P_1,P_3\} \circledvee \mathsf{Q}\{P_2,P_3\} \circledvee \mathsf{Q}\{P_1,P_2,P_3\}) \Rightarrow\\
&\qquad \square(\mathsf{Q}\{P_1\} \circledvee \mathsf{Q}\{P_1,P_2\} \circledvee \mathsf{Q}\{P_1,P_3\} \circledvee \mathsf{Q}\{P_1,P_2,P_3\}) \Rightarrow\\
&\qquad \square(\mathsf{Q}\{P_2\} \circledvee \mathsf{Q}\{P_1,P_2\} \circledvee \mathsf{Q}\{P_2,P_3\} \circledvee \mathsf{Q}\{P_1,P_2,P_3\}) \Rightarrow\\
&\qquad \square(\mathsf{Q}\{P_3\} \circledvee \mathsf{Q}\{P_1,P_3\} \circledvee \mathsf{Q}\{P_2,P_3\} \circledvee \mathsf{Q}\{P_1,P_2,P_3\}))\ 0\\
\psi_1 &= \forall\,(\square(\lambda t.\,t \in 2) \Rightarrow \square(\lambda t.\,t \in 2))\ 0\\
\psi_2 &= \forall\,(\square(\lambda t.\,t \in 2 \rightarrow t \in 3) \Rightarrow \square(\lambda t.\,t \in 2) \Rightarrow \square(\lambda t.\,t \in 3))\ 0\\
\psi_3 &= \forall\,(\square(\lambda t.\,t \in 2 \rightarrow t \in 3 \rightarrow t \in 4) \Rightarrow \square(\lambda t.\,t \in 2) \Rightarrow \square(\lambda t.\,t \in 3) \Rightarrow \square(\lambda t.\,t \in 4))\ 0
\end{aligned}
$$

Figure 3. Definition of φ_n and ψ_n

	Time to prove φ_n	Time to prove ψ_n	$\mathsf{size}\,(\mathsf{mkRE}_0^{\mathsf{M2L}}(\varphi_n))$	$\mathsf{size}\,(\mathsf{mkRE}_n^{\mathsf{M2L}}(\psi_n))$	$\mathsf{size}_{\mathsf{len}}\,(\mathsf{mkRE}_0^{\mathsf{M2L}}(\varphi_n))$	$\mathsf{size}_{\mathsf{len}}\,(\mathsf{mkRE}_n^{\mathsf{M2L}}(\psi_n))$
n=1	2ms	2ms	262	262	330	404
n=2	2s	2s	741	960	949	1370
n=3	81min	44min	1920	1836	2480	4148

Figure 4. Comparison of φ_n and ψ_n in the M2L semantics

[7] T. Braibant and D. Pous. An efficient Coq tactic for deciding Kleene algebras. In M. Kaufmann and L. Paulson, eds., *Interactive Theorem Proving, ITP 2010*, vol. 6172 of *LNCS*, pp. 163–178. Springer, 2010.

[8] J. A. Brzozowski. Derivatives of regular expressions. *J. ACM*, 11(4):481–494, Oct. 1964.

[9] P. Caron, J.-M. Champarnaud, and L. Mignot. Partial derivatives of an extended regular expression. In A.-H. Dediu, S. Inenaga, and C. Martín-Vide, eds., *Proc. Int. Conf. Language and Automata Theory and Applications, LATA 2011*, vol. 6638 of *LNCS*, pp. 179–191. Springer, 2011.

[10] T. Coquand and V. Siles. A decision procedure for regular expression equivalence in type theory. In J.-P. Jouannaud and Z. Shao, eds., *Proc. Int. Conf. Certified Programs and Proofs, CPP 2011*, vol. 7086 of *LNCS*, pp. 119–134. Springer, 2011.

[11] N. A. Danielsson. Total parser combinators. In P. Hudak and S. Weirich, eds., *Proc. Int. Conf. Functional Programming, ICFP 2010*, pp. 285–296. ACM, 2010.

[12] J. Elgaard, N. Klarlund, and A. Møller. MONA 1.x: new techniques for WS1S and WS2S. In A. J. Hu and M. Y. Vardi, eds., *Proc. Int. Conf. Computer Aided Verification, CAV 1998*, vol. 1427 of *LNCS*, pp. 516–520. Springer, 1998.

[13] S. Fischer, F. Huch, and T. Wilke. A play on regular expressions: functional pearl. In P. Hudak and S. Weirich, eds., *Proc. Int. Conf. Functional Programming, ICFP 2010*, pp. 357–368. ACM, 2010.

[14] F. Haftmann, A. Krauss, O. Kunčar, and T. Nipkow. Data refinement in Isabelle/HOL. In S. Blazy, C. Paulin-Mohring, and D. Pichardie, eds., *Interactive Theorem Proving, ITP 2013*, vol. 7998 of *LNCS*, pp. 100–115. Springer, 2013.

[15] F. Haftmann and T. Nipkow. Code generation via higher-order rewrite systems. In M. Blume, N. Kobayashi, and G. Vidal, eds., *Functional and Logic Programming, FLOPS 2010*, vol. 6009 of *LNCS*, pp. 103–117. Springer, 2010.

[16] J. G. Henriksen, J. L. Jensen, M. E. Jørgensen, N. Klarlund, R. Paige, T. Rauhe, and A. Sandholm. MONA: Monadic second-order logic in practice. In E. Brinksma, R. Cleaveland, K. Larsen, T. Margaria, and B. Steffen, eds., *Tools and Algorithms for the Construction and Analysis of Systems, TACAS 1995*, vol. 1019 of *LNCS*, pp. 89–110. Springer, 1995.

[17] N. Klarlund. A theory of restrictions for logics and automata. In N. Halbwachs and D. Peled, eds., *Proc. Int. Conf. Computer Aided Verification, CAV 1999*, vol. 1633 of *LNCS*, pp. 406–417. Springer, 1999.

[18] A. Krauss and T. Nipkow. Proof pearl: Regular expression equivalence and relation algebra. *J. Automated Reasoning*, 49:95–106, 2012. published online March 2011.

[19] M. Might, D. Darais, and D. Spiewak. Parsing with derivatives: A functional pearl. In M. M. T. Chakravarty, Z. Hu, and O. Danvy, eds., *Proc. Int. Conf. Functional Programming, ICFP 2011*, pp. 189–195. ACM, 2011.

[20] N. Moreira, D. Pereira, and S. M. de Sousa. Deciding regular expressions (in-)equivalence in Coq. In W. Kahl and T. Griffin, eds., *Relational and Algebraic Methods in Computer Science, RAMiCS 2012*, vol. 7560 of *LNCS*, pp. 98–113. Springer, 2012.

[21] T. Nipkow. Programming and proving in Isabelle/HOL. `http://isabelle.in.tum.de/doc/prog-prove.pdf`.

[22] T. Nipkow, L. Paulson, and M. Wenzel. *Isabelle/HOL — A Proof Assistant for Higher-Order Logic*, vol. 2283 of *LNCS*. Springer, 2002.

[23] S. Owens, J. H. Reppy, and A. Turon. Regular-expression derivatives re-examined. *J. Funct. Program.*, 19(2):173–190, 2009.

[24] S. Owre and H. Rueß. Integrating WS1S with PVS. In E. A. Emerson and A. P. Sistla, eds., *Proc. Int. Conf. Computer Aided Verification, CAV 2000*, vol. 1855 of *LNCS*, pp. 548–551. Springer, 2000.

[25] J. J. M. M. Rutten. Automata and coinduction (an exercise in coalgebra). In D. Sangiorgi and R. de Simone, eds., *Proc. Int. Conf. Concurrency Theory, CONCUR 1998*, vol. 1466 of *LNCS*, pp. 194–218. Springer, 1998.

[26] W. Thomas. Languages, automata, and logic. In G. Rozenberg and A. Salomaa, eds., *Handbook of Formal Languages*, pp. 389–455. Springer, 1997.

[27] D. Traytel and T. Nipkow. Formal development associated with this paper. `http://www21.in.tum.de/~traytel/icfp13_mso.tar.gz`.

[28] C. Wu, X. Zhang, and C. Urban. A formalisation of the Myhill-Nerode theorem based on regular expressions (Proof pearl). In M. Eekelen, H. Geuvers, J. Schmaltz, and F. Wiedijk, eds., *Interactive Theorem Proving, ITP 2011*, vol. 6898 of *LNCS*, pp. 341–356. Springer, 2011.

C-SHORe

A Collapsible Approach to Verifying Higher-Order Programs

Christopher Broadbent

LIAFA, Université Paris Diderot – Paris 7 & CNRS & University of Tokyo & Technische Universität München

broadben@in.tum.de

Arnaud Carayol

LIGM, Université Paris-Est & CNRS

arnaud.carayol@univ-mlv.fr

Matthew Hague

Royal Holloway University of London & LIGM, Université Paris-Est & LIAFA, Université Paris Diderot – Paris 7 & CNRS

matthew.hague@rhul.ac.uk

Olivier Serre

LIAFA, Université Paris Diderot – Paris 7 & CNRS

olivier.serre@liafa.univ-paris-diderot.fr

Abstract

Higher-order recursion schemes (HORS) have recently received much attention as a useful abstraction of higher-order functional programs with a number of new verification techniques employing HORS model-checking as their centrepiece. This paper contributes to the ongoing quest for a truly scalable model-checker for HORS by offering a different, automata theoretic perspective. We introduce the first practical model-checking algorithm that acts on a generalisation of pushdown automata equi-expressive with HORS called *collapsible pushdown systems* (CPDS). At its core is a substantial modification of a recently studied saturation algorithm for CPDS. In particular it is able to use information gathered from an approximate forward reachability analysis to guide its backward search. Moreover, we introduce an algorithm that prunes the CPDS prior to model-checking and a method for extracting counter-examples in negative instances. We compare our tool with the state-of-the-art verification tools for HORS and obtain encouraging results. In contrast to some of the main competition tackling the same problem, our algorithm is fixed-parameter tractable, and we also offer significantly improved performance over the only previously published tool of which we are aware that also enjoys this property. The tool and additional material are available from `http://cshore.cs.rhul.ac.uk`.

Categories and Subject Descriptors F.1.1 [*Models of Computation*]: Automata

Keywords Higher-Order; Verification; Model-Checking; Recursion Schemes; Collapsible Pushdown Systems

ICFP '13, September 25 - 27 2013, Boston, MA, USA.

ACM 978-1-4503-2326-0/13/09... $15.00.

http://dx.doi.org/10.1145/2500365.2500589

1. Introduction

Functional languages such as Haskell, OCaML and Scala strongly encourage the use of higher-order functions. This represents a challenge for software verification, which usually does not model recursion accurately, or models only first-order calls (e.g. SLAM [2] and Moped [33]). However, there has recently been much interest in a model called *higher-order recursion schemes (HORS)* (see e.g. [29]), which offers a way of abstracting functional programs in a manner that precisely models higher-order control-flow.

The execution trees of HORS enjoy decidable μ-calculus theories [29], which testifies to the good algorithmic properties of the model. Even 'reachability' properties (subsumed by the μ-calculus) are very useful in practice. As a simple example, the safety of incomplete pattern matching clauses could be checked by asking whether the program can 'reach a state' where a pattern match failure occurs. More complex 'reachability' properties can be expressed using a finite automaton and could, for example, specify that the program respects a certain discipline when accessing a particular resource (see [22]). Despite even reachability being $(n-1)$-EXPTIME complete, recent research has revealed that useful properties of HORS can be checked in practice.

Kobayashi's TRecS [23] tool, which checks properties expressible by a deterministic trivial Büchi automaton (all states accepting), was the first to achieve this. It works by determining whether a HORS is typable in an intersection-type system characterising the property to be checked [22]. In a bid to improve scalability, a number of other algorithms have subsequently been designed and implemented such as Kobayashi *et al.*'s GTRecS(2) [25, 26] and Neatherway *et al.*'s TravMC [28] tools (appearing in ICFP 2012), all of which remain based on intersection type inference.

This work is the basis of various techniques for verifying functional programs. Kobayashi *et al.* have developed MoCHi [27] that checks safety properties of (OCaML) programs, and EHMTT Verifier [38] for tree processing programs. Both use a model-checker for recursion schemes as a central component. Similarly, Ramsay and Ong [30] provide a verification procedure for programs with pattern matching employing recursion schemes as an abstraction.

Despite much progress, even the state-of-the-art TRecS does not scale to recursion schemes big enough to model realistically sized programs; achieving scalability while accurately tracking higher-order control-flow is a challenging problem. This paper offers an automata-theoretic perspective on this challenge, providing a fresh set of tools that contrast with previous intersection-type approaches. Techniques based on pushdown automata have previously visited ICFP, such as the approximate higher-order control-flow analysis CFA2 [40], but our aims are a bit different in that we wish to match the expressivity of HORS. Consequently we require a more sophisticated notion of pushdown automaton.

Collapsible pushdown systems (CPDS) [16] are an alternative representation of the class of execution trees that can be generated by recursion schemes (with linear-time mutual-translations between the two formalisms [10, 16]). While pushdown systems augment a finite-state machine with a stack and provide an ideal model for first-order programs [20], collapsible pushdown systems model higher-order programs by extending the stack of a pushdown system to a nested "stack-of-stacks" structure. The nested stack structure enables one to represent closures. Indeed the reader might find it helpful to view a CPDS as being Krivine's Abstract Machine in a guise making it amenable to the generalisation of techniques for pushdown model-checking. Salvati and Walukiewicz have studied in detail the connection with the Krivine abstract machine [32].

For ordinary ('order-1') pushdown systems, a model-checking approach called *saturation* has been successfully implemented by tools such as Moped [33] and PDSolver [15]. Given a regular set of configurations of the pushdown system (represented by a finite automaton A acting on stacks), saturation can solve the 'backward reachability problem' by computing another finite automaton recognising a set of configurations from which a configuration in $\mathcal{L}(A)$ can be reached. This is a fixed-point computation that gradually adds transitions to A until it is 'saturated'. If A recognises a set of error configurations, one can determine whether the pushdown system is 'safe' by checking if its initial configuration is recognised by the automaton computed by saturation.

We recently extended the saturation method to a backward reachability analysis of collapsible pushdown systems [7]. This runs in PTIME when the number of control states is bounded. Crucially, this condition is satisfied when translating from recursion schemes of bounded arity with properties represented by automata of bounded size [16]. Whilst the HORS/intersection-type based tool GTRecS(2) also enjoys this fixed-parameter tractability (others do not), it times out on many benchmarks that our tool solves quickly.

Motivated by these facts, we revisit the foundations of higher-order verification tools and introduce C-SHORe — the first model-checking tool for the (direct) analysis of collapsible pushdown systems. Whilst the tool is based on the ICALP 2012 result, some substantial modifications and additions are made to the algorithm, leading to several novel practical and theoretical contributions:

1. An approximate *forward* reachability algorithm providing data
   (a) ...allowing for the CPDS to be pruned so that saturation receives a smaller input.
   (b) ...employed by a modified saturation algorithm to guide its *backward* search.

   This is essential for termination on most of our benchmarks.
2. A method for extracting witnesses to reachability.
3. A complete reworking of the saturation algorithm that speeds up the fixed-point computation.
4. Experimental results showing our approach compares well with TRecS, GTRecS(2) and TravMC.

It is worth remarking that the other type-based tools mentioned above all work by propagating information in a forward direction with respect to the evaluation of the model. In contrast, the raw saturation algorithm works backwards, but we also show here how forward and backward propagation can be combined.

In Sections 5 to 8 we describe the original contributions of this paper. These sections can be understood independently of one another, and hence the reader does not need to fully grasp each section before continuing to the next. The remaining sections describe the background, related work and conclusions.

In Section 3 we recall the basic structures used in the paper as well as recapping the ICALP 2012 algorithm. In Section 5 we describe the approximate forwards-reachability analysis and how it is exploited. In Section 6 we show how to generate witnesses to reachability. In Section 7, we then consider how to restructure the saturation algorithm to more efficiently compute the fixed-point. We provide experimental results in Section 8. Note that we do not discuss in formal detail the translation from HORS model-checking to reachability for CPDS, which essentially follows [10]. However, we do give an informal overview in Section 2, which we hope serves to demonstrate how closures can be accurately modelled.

The tool is available at `http://cshore.cs.rhul.ac.uk`. An appendix containing additional material appears in the long version of this paper, available from the same URL.

2. Modelling Higher-Order Programs

In this section we give an informal introduction to the process of modelling higher-order programs for verification. In particular, we show how a simple example program can be modelled using a higher-order recursion scheme, and then we show how this scheme is evaluated using a collapsible pushdown system. For a more systematic approach to modelling higher-order programs with recursion schemes, we refer the reader to work by Kobayashi *et al.* [27]. This section is for background only, and can be safely skipped.

For this section, consider the toy example below.

```
Main = MakeReport Nil
MakeReport x = if * (Commit x)
               else (AddData x MakeReport)
AddData y f = if * (f Error) else (f Cons(_, y))
```

In this example, * represents a non-deterministic choice (that may, for example, be a result of some input by the user). Execution begins at the `Main` function whose aim is to make a report which is a list. We begin with an empty report and send it to `MakeReport`. Either `MakeReport` indicates the report is finished and commits the report somehow, or it adds an item to the head of the list, using the `AddData` function, which takes the report so far, and a continuation. `AddData` either detects a problem with the new data (maybe it is inconsistent with the rest of the report) and flags an error by passing `Error` to the continuation, or extends the report with some item. In this case, the programmer has not provided error handling as part of the `MakeReport` function, and so an `Error` may be committed.

2.1 Higher-Order Recursion Schemes

As a first step in modelling this program, we introduce, informally, higher-order recursion schemes. These are rewrite systems that generate the computation tree of a functional program. A rewrite rule takes the form

$$N\ \phi\ x\ \hookrightarrow\ t$$

where N is a typed non-terminal with (possibly higher-order) arguments ϕ and x. A term $N\ t_\phi\ t_x$ rewrites to t with t_ϕ substituted for ϕ and t_x substituted for x. Note that recursion schemes require t to be of ground type. We will illustrate the behaviour of a recursion scheme and its use in analysis using the toy example from above.

We can directly model our example with the scheme

$$\begin{array}{rcl} main & \hookrightarrow & M\ nil \\ M\ x & \hookrightarrow & or\ (commit\ x)\ (A\ x\ M) \\ A\ y\ \phi & \hookrightarrow & or\ (\phi\ error)\ (\phi\ (cons\ y)) \end{array}$$

where M is the non-terminal associated with the MakeReport function, and A is the non-terminal associated with the AddData function; nil, or, $commit$, $error$ and $cons$ are terminal symbols of arity 0, 2, 1, 0 and 1 respectively (e.g. in the second rule, or takes the two arguments ($commit\ x$) and ($A\ x\ M$)). The scheme above begins with the non-terminal $main$ and, through a sequence of rewrite steps, generates a tree representation of the evolution of the program. Figure 1, described below, shows such a sequence.

Beginning with the non-terminal $main$, we apply the first rewrite rule to obtain the tree representing the term ($A\ nil$). We then apply the second rewrite rule, instantiating x with nil to obtain the next tree in the sequence. This continues *ad infinitum* to produce a possibly infinite tree labelled only by terminals.

We are interested in ensuring the correctness of the program. In our case, this means ensuring that the program never attempts to $commit$ an $error$. By inspecting the rightmost tree in Figure 1, we can identify a branch labelled $or, or, or, commit, error$. This is an error situation because $commit$ is being called with an $error$ report. In general we can define the regular language $\mathcal{L}_{err} = or^* commit\ or^* error$. If the tree generated by the recursion scheme contains a branch labelled by a word appearing in $\mathcal{L}_{err}$, then we have identified an error in the program.

2.2 Collapsible Pushdown Automata

Previous research into the verification of recursion schemes has used an approach based on *intersection types* (e.g. [24, 28]). In this work we investigate a radically different approach exploiting the connection between higher-order recursion schemes and an automata model called *collapsible pushdown automata* (CPDA). These two formalisms are, in fact, equivalent.

Theorem 2.1 (Equi-expressivity [16]). *For each order-n recursion scheme, there is an order-n collapsible pushdown automaton generating the same tree, and vice-versa. Furthermore, the translations in both directions are linear.*

We describe at a high level the structure of a CPDA and how they can be used to evaluate recursion schemes. In our case, this means outputting a sequence of non-terminals representing each path in the tree. More formal definitions are given in Section 3. At any moment, a CPDA is in a *configuration* $\langle p, w \rangle$, where p is a control state taken from a finite set $\mathcal{P}$, and w is a higher-order collapsible stack. In the following we will focus on the stack. Control states are only needed to ensure that sequences of stack operations occur in the correct order and are thus elided for clarity.

In the case of our toy example, we have an order-2 recursion scheme and hence an order-2 stack. An order-1 stack is a stack of characters a from a finite alphabet Σ. An order-2 stack is a stack of order-1 stacks. Thus we can write $[[main]]$ to denote the order-2 stack containing only the order-1 stack $[main]$; $[main]$ is an order-1 stack containing only the character $main$. In general Σ will contain all subterms appearing in the original statement of our toy example recursion scheme. The evolution of the CPDA stack is given in Figure 2 and explained below.

The first step is to rewrite $main$ using $main \hookrightarrow M\ nil$. Since $(M\ nil)$ is a subterm of our recursion scheme, we have $(M\ nil) \in \Sigma$ and we simply rewrite the stack $[[main]]$ to $[[M\ nil]]$.

The next step is to call the function M. As is typical in the execution of programs, a function call necessitates a new stack frame. In particular, this means pushing the body of M (that is $(or\ (commit\ x)\ (A\ x\ M))$) onto the stack, resulting in the third stack in Figure 2. Note that we do not instantiate the variable x, hence we use only the subterms appearing in the recursion scheme.

Recall that we want to obtain a CPDA that outputs a sequence of terminals representing each path in the tree. To evaluate the term $or\ (\cdots)\ (\cdots)$ we have to output the terminal or and then (non-deterministically) choose a branch of the tree to follow. Let us choose ($A\ x\ M$). Hence, the CPDA outputs the terminal or and rewrites the top term to ($A\ x\ M$). Next we make a call to the A function, pushing its body on to the stack, and then pick out the ($\phi\ error$) branch of the or terminal. This takes us to the beginning of the second row of Figure 2.

To proceed, we have to evaluate ($\phi\ error$). To be able to do this, we have to know the value of ϕ. We can obtain this information by inspecting the stack and seeing that the second argument of the call of A is M. However, since we can only see the top of a stack, we would have to remove the character ($\phi\ error$) to be able to determine that $\phi = M$, thus losing our place in the computation.

This is where we use the power of order-2 stacks. An order-2 stack is able — via a $push_2$ operation — to create a copy of its topmost order-1 stack. Hence, we perform this copy (note that the top of the stack is written on the left) and delve into the copy of the stack to ascertain the value of ϕ. While doing this we also create a *collapse link*, pictured as an arrow from M to the term ($\phi\ error$). This collapse link is a pointer from M to the context in which M will be evaluated. In particular, if we need to know the value of x in the body of M, we will need to know that M was called with the $error$ argument, within the term ($\phi\ error$); the collapse link provides a pointer to this information (in other words we have encoded a closure in the stack). We can access this information via a *collapse* operation. These are the two main features of a higher-order collapsible stack, described formally in the next section.

To continue the execution, we push the body of M on to the stack, output the or symbol and choose the ($commit\ x$) branch. Since $commit$ is a terminal, we output it and pick out x for evaluation. To know the value of x, we have to look into the stack and follow the collapse link from M to ($\phi\ error$) Note that we do not need to create a copy of the stack here because x is an order-0 variable and thus represents a self-contained execution. Since $error$ is the value of the argument we are considering, we pick it out and then output it before terminating. This completes the execution corresponding to the error branch identified in Figure 1.

2.3 Collapsible Pushdown Systems

The CPDA output $or, or, or, commit, error$ in the execution above. This is an error sequence in $\mathcal{L}_{err}$ and should be flagged. In general, we take the finite automaton A representing the regular language $\mathcal{L}_{err}$ and form a product with the CPDA described above. This results in a CPDA that does not output any symbols, but instead keeps in its control state the progression of A. Thus we are interested in whether the CPDA is able to reach an accepting state of A, not the language it generates. We call a CPDA without output symbols a *collapsible pushdown system* (CPDS), and the question of whether a CPDS can reach a given state is the reachability problem. This is the subject of the remainder of the paper.

3. Preliminaries

3.1 Collapsible Pushdown Systems

We first introduce higher-order collapsible stacks and their operations, before giving the definition of collapsible pushdown systems.

3.1.1 Higher-Order Collapsible Stacks and Their Operations

Higher-order collapsible stacks are built from a stack alphabet Σ and form a nested "stack-of-stacks" structure. Using an idea from *panic automata* [21], each stack character contains a pointer — called a "link" — to a position lower down in the stack. Operations updating stacks (defined below) may create copies of sub-stacks. The link is intuitively a pointer to the context in which the stack character was first created. In the sequel, we fix the maximal order to n, and use k to range between 1 and n. In the definition below, we defer the meaning of *collapse link* to Definition 3.2.

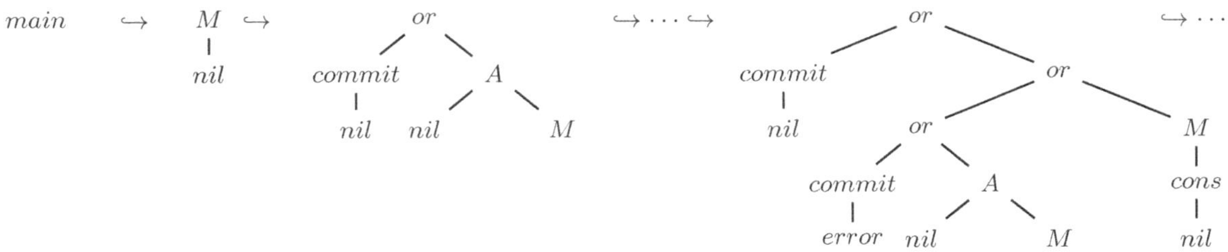

Figure 1: The behaviour of a toy recursion scheme.

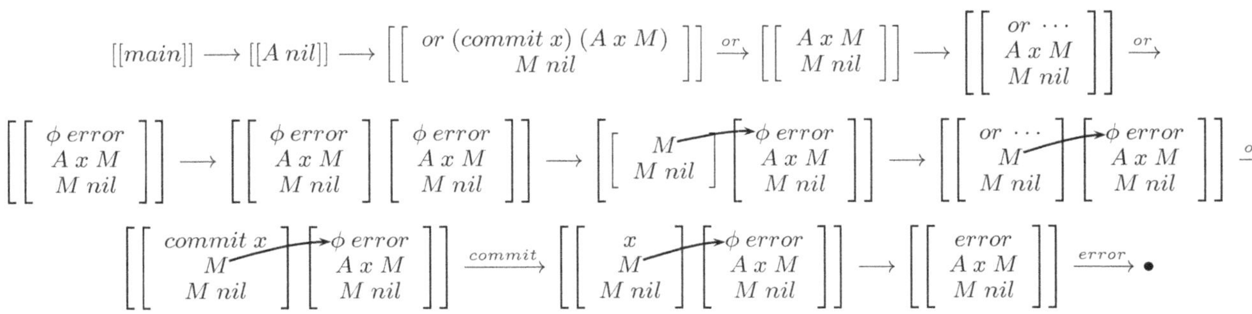
Figure 2: A stack evaluating the toy example.

Definition 3.1 (Order-n Collapsible Stacks). *Given a finite set of stack characters Σ, an* order-0 stack *is simply a character $a \in \Sigma$. An* order-n stack *is a sequence $w = [w_\ell \dots w_1]_n$ such that each w_i is an order-$(n-1)$ stack and each character a on the stack is augmented with a collapse link. The top-most stack is w_ℓ. Let $Stacks_n$ denote the set of order-n stacks.*

Collapse links point to positions in the stack. Before describing them formally, we give an informal description and some basic definitions. An order-n stack can be represented naturally as an edge-labelled word-graph over the alphabet $\{[_{n-1}, \dots, [_1,]_1, \dots,]_{n-1}\} \uplus \Sigma$, with additional collapse-links pointing from a stack character in Σ to the beginning of the graph representing the target of the link. For technical convenience we do not use $[_n$ or $]_n$ symbols (these appear uniquely at the beginning and end of the stack). An example order-3 stack is given in Figure 3, with only a few collapse links shown, ranging from order-3 to order-1 respectively.

Stacks are written with the top on the left. Given an order-n stack $[w_\ell \dots w_1]_n$, we define

$$\begin{array}{rcll} top_{n+1}([w_\ell \dots w_1]_n) & = & [w_\ell \dots w_1]_n & \\ top_n([w_\ell \dots w_1]_n) & = & w_\ell & \text{if } \ell > 0 \\ top_n([\,]_n) & = & [\,]_{n-1} & \text{otherwise} \\ top_k([w_\ell \dots w_1]_n) & = & top_k(w_\ell) & \text{if } k < n \text{ and } \ell > 0 \end{array}$$

noting that $top_k(w)$ is undefined if $top_{k'}(w)$ is empty for any $k' > k$. We also remove the top portion of a top_k stack using

$$bot^i_n([w_\ell \dots w_1]_n) = [w_i \dots w_1]_n$$

when $i \leq \ell$ and $\ell > 0$, and

$$bot^i_k([w_\ell \dots w_1]_n) = [bot^i_k(w_\ell) w_{\ell-1} \dots w_1]_n$$

when $k < n$ and $\ell > 0$. We are now ready to define collapse links.

Definition 3.2 (Collapse Links). *An* order-k collapse link *is a pair (k, i) where $1 \leq k \leq n$ and $i > 0$.*

For $top_1(w) = a$ where a has the link (k, i), the destination of the link is $bot^i_k(w)$. We disallow collapse links where bot^i_k does not lead to a valid stack. The example stack in Figure 3 is thus $[[[a^{(3,1)}b]_1]_2[[c^{(2,1)}]_1[d^{(1,1)}e]_1]_2]_3$, where collapse links are denoted as superscripts. Often (as we have done for the stack characters b and e) we will omit these superscripts for readability.

Finally the following notation appends a stack on top of another. Given an order-k stack $v = [v_\ell \dots v_1]_k$ and an order-$(k'-1)$ stack u (with $k' \leq k$), we define $u :_{k'} v = [u\, v_\ell \dots v_1]_k$ if $k' = k$ and $u :_{k'} v = [(u :_{k'} v_\ell) \dots v_1]_k$ if $k' < k$.

The following operations apply to an order-n collapsible stack.

$$\begin{array}{rcl} \mathcal{O}_n & = & \{pop_1, \dots, pop_n\} \cup \{push_2, \dots, push_n\} \cup \\ & & \{collapse_2, \dots, collapse_n\} \cup \\ & & \{push^2_a, \dots, push^n_a, rew_a \mid a \in \Sigma\} \end{array}$$

We define each stack operation for an order-n stack w. Collapse links are created by $push^k_a$, which add a character to the top of a given stack w with a link pointing to $top_{k+1}(pop_k(w))$. This gives a access to the context in which it was created. We set

1. $pop_k(u :_k v) = v$,
2. $push_k(u :_k v) = u :_k (u :_k v)$,
3. $collapse_k(w) = bot^i_k(w)$ where $top_1(w) = a^{(k,i)}$ for some i,
4. $push^k_b(w) = b^{(k,\ell-1)} :_1 w$ where $top_{k+1}(w) = [w_\ell \dots w_1]_k$,
5. $rew_b\left(a^{(k,i)} :_1 v\right) = b^{(k,i)} :_1 v$.

Note that, for a $push_k$ operation, links outside of $u = top_k(w)$ point to the same destination in both copies of u, while links pointing within u point within the respective copies of u. Since $collapse_1$ would always be equivalent to pop_1, we neither create nor follow order-1 links. (Often in examples we do not illustrate links that are never used.) For a more detailed introduction see [10].

3.1.2 Collapsible Pushdown Systems

We are now ready to define collapsible pushdown systems.

Definition 3.3 (Collapsible Pushdown Systems). *An order-n collapsible pushdown system (n-CPDS) is a tuple $\mathcal{C} = (\mathcal{P}, \Sigma, \mathcal{R})$ where $\mathcal{P}$ is a finite set of control states, Σ is a finite stack alphabet, and $\mathcal{R} \subseteq \mathcal{P} \times \Sigma \times \mathcal{O}_n \times \mathcal{P}$ is a set of rules.*

A *configuration* of a CPDS is a pair $\langle p, w \rangle$ where $p \in \mathcal{P}$ and $w \in Stacks_n$. We denote by $\langle p, w \rangle \longrightarrow \langle p', w' \rangle$ a transition from a rule (p, a, o, p') with $top_1(w) = a$ and $w' = o(w)$. A run of a CPDS is a finite sequence $\langle p_0, w_0 \rangle \longrightarrow \cdots \longrightarrow \langle p_\ell, w_\ell \rangle$.

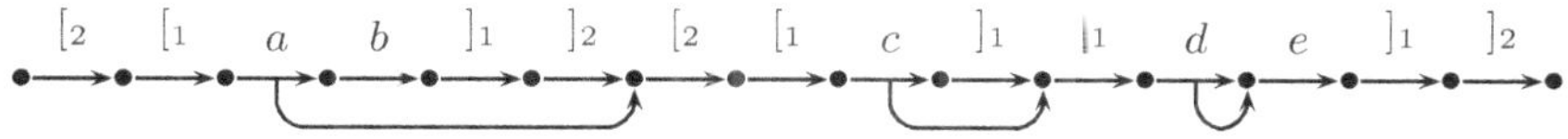

Figure 3: A graph representation of a stack.

3.2 Representing Sets of Stacks

Our algorithm represents sets of configurations using order-n stack automata. These are a kind of alternating automata with a nested structure that mimics the nesting in a higher-order collapsible stack. We recall the definition below.

Definition 3.4 (Order-n Stack Automata). *An order-n stack automaton $A = (\mathbb{Q}_n, \ldots, \mathbb{Q}_1, \Sigma, \Delta_n, \ldots, \Delta_1, \mathcal{F}_n, \ldots, \mathcal{F}_1)$ is a tuple where Σ is a finite stack alphabet, and*

1. *for all $n \geq k \geq 2$, we have $\mathbb{Q}_k$ is a finite set of states, $\mathcal{F}_k \subseteq \mathbb{Q}_k$ is a set of accepting states, and $\Delta_k \subseteq \mathbb{Q}_k \times \mathbb{Q}_{k-1} \times 2^{\mathbb{Q}_k}$ is a transition relation such that for all q and Q there is* at most one *q' with $(q, q', Q) \in \Delta_k$, and*
2. *$\mathbb{Q}_1$ is a finite set of states, $\mathcal{F}_1 \subseteq \mathbb{Q}_1$ a set of accepting states, and $\Delta_1 \subseteq \bigcup_{2 \leq k \leq n} \left(\mathbb{Q}_1 \times \Sigma \times 2^{\mathbb{Q}_k} \times 2^{\mathbb{Q}_1}\right)$ a transition relation.*

The sets $\mathbb{Q}_k$ are disjoint and their states recognise order-k stacks. Stacks are read from "top to bottom". A transition $(q, q', Q) \in \Delta_k$, written $q \xrightarrow{q'} Q$, from q to Q for some $k > 1$ requires that the top_{k-1} stack is accepted from $q' \in \mathbb{Q}_{(k-1)}$ and the rest of the stack is accepted from each state in Q. At order-1, a transition (q, a, Q_{col}, Q) has the additional requirement that the stack linked to by a is accepted from Q_{col}. A stack is accepted if a subset of $\mathcal{F}_k$ is reached at the end of each order-k stack. We write $w \in \mathcal{L}_q(A)$ to denote the set of all w accepted from q. Note that a transition to the empty set is distinct from having no transition. Figure 4 shows part of a run over the stack in Figure 3 where each node in the graph is labelled by the states from which the remainder of the stack containing it (as well as the stacks linked to) must be accepted. Note, e.g., that since Q_2 appears at the bottom of an order-2 stack, we must have $Q_2 \subseteq \mathcal{F}_2$ for the run to be accepting. The transitions used are $q_3 \xrightarrow{q_2} Q_3 \in \Delta_3$, $q_2 \xrightarrow{q_1} Q_2 \in \Delta_2$, and $q_1 \xrightarrow[Q_{col}]{a} Q_1 \in \Delta_1$. See Section 4 for further examples.

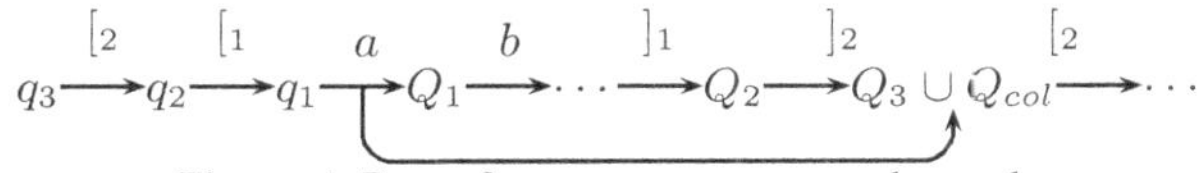

Figure 4: Part of a run over an example stack.

3.2.1 Representing Transitions and States

We use a *long-form* notation (defined below) that captures nested sequences of transitions. For example, we may write $q_3 \xrightarrow[Q_{col}]{a} (Q_1, Q_2, Q_3)$ to capture the transitions shown in Figure 4. Together, these indicate that after starting from the beginning of the stack and reading only the topmost stack character, the remainder of the stack must be accepted by Q_{col}, Q_1, Q_2, and Q_3. More generally, we may also use $q_3 \xrightarrow{q_1} (Q_2, Q_3)$, and $q_3 \xrightarrow{q_2} (Q_3)$.

Formally, when $q \in \mathbb{Q}_k$, $q' \in \mathbb{Q}_{k'}$, $Q_i \subseteq \mathbb{Q}_i$ for all $k \geq i \geq 1$, and there is some i with $Q_{col} \subseteq \mathbb{Q}_i$, we write

$$q \xrightarrow[Q_{col}]{a} (Q_1, \ldots, Q_k) \text{ and } q \xrightarrow{q'} (Q_{k'+1}, \ldots, Q_k).$$

In the first case, there exist $q_{k-1}, \ldots, q_1$ such that $q \xrightarrow{q_{k-1}} Q_k \in \Delta_k, q_{k-1} \xrightarrow{q_{k-2}} Q_{k-1} \in \Delta_{k-1}, \ldots, q_1 \xrightarrow[Q_{col}]{a} Q_1 \in \Delta_1$. In the second case there exist $q_{k-1}, \ldots, q_{k'+1}$ with $q \xrightarrow{q_{k-1}} Q_k \in \Delta_k, q_{k-1} \xrightarrow{q_{k-2}} Q_{k-1} \in \Delta_{k-1}, \ldots, q_{k'+2} \xrightarrow{q_{k'+1}} Q_{k'+2} \in \Delta_{k'+2}$ and $q_{k'+1} \xrightarrow{q'} Q_{k'+1} \in \Delta_{k'+1}$.

Remark 3.1. *We may also write $q_{Q_k, \ldots, Q_{k'+1}}$ for the q' above (which is uniquely determined by $Q_k, \ldots, Q_{k'+1}$).*

Note that our definitions mean that we have, e.g., $q \xrightarrow[Q_{col}]{a} (Q_1, Q_2, Q_3)$ if and only if we have $q_{Q_3, Q_2} \xrightarrow[Q_{col}]{a} Q_1$ in Δ_1.

3.2.2 Representing Sets of Transitions

Let Δ_k^S denote the set of all order-k *long-form* transitions $q \xrightarrow[Q_{col}]{a} (Q_1, \ldots, Q_k)$ of order-k. For a set $T = \{t_1, \ldots, t_\ell\} \subseteq \Delta_k^S$, we say T is of the form

$$Q \xrightarrow[Q_{col}]{a} (Q_1, \ldots, Q_k)$$

whenever $Q = \{q_1, \ldots, q_\ell\}$ and for all $1 \leq i \leq \ell$ we have $t_i = q_i \xrightarrow[Q_{col}^i]{a} (Q_1^i, \ldots, Q_k^i)$ and $Q_{col} = \bigcup_{1 \leq i \leq \ell} Q_{col}^i$ and for all $1 \leq k' \leq k$, $Q_{k'} = \bigcup_{1 \leq i \leq \ell} Q_{k'}^i$. Because a link can only be of one order, we insist that $Q_{col} \subseteq \mathbb{Q}_{k'}$ for some $1 \leq k' \leq n$.

3.3 Representing Sets of Configurations

We define a notion of $\mathcal{P}$-multi-automata [4] for representing sets of configurations of collapsible pushdown systems.

Definition 3.5 ($\mathcal{P}$-Multi Stack Automata). *Given an order-n CPDS with control states $\mathcal{P}$, a $\mathcal{P}$-multi stack automaton is an order-n stack automaton $A = (\mathbb{Q}_n, \ldots, \mathbb{Q}_1, \Sigma, \Delta_n, \ldots, \Delta_1, \mathcal{F}_n, \ldots, \mathcal{F}_1)$ such that for each $p \in \mathcal{P}$ there exists a state $q_p \in \mathbb{Q}_n$.*

A state is *initial* if it is of the form $q_p \in Q_n$ for some control state p or if it is a state $q_k \in Q_k$ for $k < n$ such that there exists a transition $q_{k+1} \xrightarrow{q_k} Q_{k+1}$ in Δ_{k+1}. The language of a $\mathcal{P}$-multi stack automaton A is the set $\mathcal{L}(A) = \{\langle p, w \rangle \mid w \in \mathcal{L}_{q_p}(A)\}$.

3.4 Basic Saturation Algorithm

Our algorithm computes the set $Pre^*_{\mathcal{C}}(A_0)$ of a collapsible pushdown system $\mathcal{C}$ and a $\mathcal{P}$-multi stack automaton A_0. We assume without loss of generality that initial states of A_0 do not have incoming transitions and are not final. To accept empty stacks from initial states, a bottom-of-stack symbol can be used.

Let $Pre^*_{\mathcal{C}}(A_0)$ be the smallest set with $Pre^*_{\mathcal{C}}(A_0) \supseteq \mathcal{L}(A_0)$, and $Pre^*_{\mathcal{C}}(A_0) \supseteq \{\langle p, w \rangle \mid \exists \langle p, w \rangle \longrightarrow \langle p', w' \rangle \in Pre^*_{\mathcal{C}}(A_0)\}$.

We begin with A_0 and iterate a saturation function Π — adding new transitions to A_0 — until a 'fixed point' is reached; that is, we cannot find any more transitions to add.

Notation for Adding Transitions During saturation we designate transitions $q_n \xrightarrow[Q_{col}]{a} (Q_1, \ldots, Q_n)$ to be added to the automaton. Recall this represents $q \xrightarrow{q_{n-1}} Q_n \in \Delta_n, q_{n-1} \xrightarrow{q_{n-2}} Q_{n-1} \in \Delta_{n-1}, \ldots, q_1 \xrightarrow[Q_{col}]{a} Q_1 \in \Delta_1$. Hence, we first, for each $n \geq k > 1$, add $q_k \xrightarrow{q_{k-1}} Q_k$ to Δ_k if it does not already exist. Then, we add $q_1 \xrightarrow[Q_{col}]{a} Q_1$ to Δ_1.

Justified Transitions In this paper, we extend the saturation function to add *justifications* to new transitions that indicate the provenance of each new transition. This permits counter example generation. To each $t = q \xrightarrow[Q_{col}]{a} (Q_1, \ldots, Q_n)$ we will define the justification $J(t)$ to be either 0 (indicating the transition is in A_0), a pair (r, i), a tuple (r, t', i) or a tuple (r, t', T, i) where r is a rule of the CPDS, i is the number of iterations of the saturation function required to introduce the transition, t' is a long-form transition and T is a set of such transitions. This information will be used in Section 6 for generating counter examples. Note that we apply J to the long-form notation. In reality, we associate each justification with the unique order-1 transition $q_1 \xrightarrow[Q_{col}]{a} Q_1$ associated to each t.

The Saturation Function We are now ready to recall the saturation function Π for a given $\mathcal{C} = (\mathcal{P}, \Sigma, \mathcal{R})$. As described above, we apply this function to A_0 until a fixed point is reached. First set $J(t) = 0$ for all transitions of A_0. The intuition behind the saturation rules can be quickly understood via a rewrite rule (p, a, rew_b, p') which leads to the addition of a transition $q_p \xrightarrow[Q_{col}]{a} (Q_1, \ldots, Q_n)$ whenever there already existed a transition $q_{p'} \xrightarrow[Q_{col}]{b} (Q_1, \ldots, Q_n)$. Because the rewrite can change the control state from p to p' and the top character from a to b, we must have an accepting run from q_p with a on top whenever we had an accepting run from $q_{p'}$ with b on top. We give examples and intuition of the more complex steps in Section 4, which may be read alongside the definition below.

Definition 3.6 (The Saturation Function Π)**.** *Given an order-n stack automaton A_i we define $A_{i+1} = \Pi(A_i)$. The state-sets of A_{i+1} are defined implicitly by the transitions which are those in A_i plus, for each $r = (p, a, o, p') \in \mathcal{R}$,*

1. *when $o = pop_k$, for each $q_{p'} \xrightarrow{q_k} (Q_{k+1}, \ldots, Q_n)$ in A_i, add $t = q_p \xrightarrow[\emptyset]{a} (\emptyset, \ldots, \emptyset, \{q_k\}, Q_{k+1}, \ldots, Q_n)$ to A_{i+1} and set $J(t) = (r, i+1)$ whenever t is not already in A_{i+1},*
2. *when $o = push_k$, for each $t = q_{p'} \xrightarrow[Q_{col}]{a} (Q_1, \ldots, Q_k, \ldots, Q_n)$ and T of the form $Q_k \xrightarrow[Q'_{col}]{a} (Q'_1, \ldots, Q'_k)$ in A_i, add to A_{i+1} the transition*
$$t' = q_p \xrightarrow[Q_{col} \cup Q'_{col}]{a} \begin{pmatrix} Q_1 \cup Q'_1, \ldots, Q_{k-1} \cup Q'_{k-1}, \\ Q'_k, \\ Q_{k+1}, \ldots, Q_n \end{pmatrix}$$
and set $J(t') = (r, t, T, i+1)$ if t' is not already in A_{i+1},
3. *when $o = collapse_k$, when $k = n$, add $t = q_p \xrightarrow[\{q_{p'}\}]{a} (\emptyset, \ldots, \emptyset)$ if it does not exist, and when $k < n$, for each transition $q_{p'} \xrightarrow{q_k} (Q_{k+1}, \ldots, Q_n)$ in A_i, add to A_{i+1} the transition $t = q_p \xrightarrow[\{q_k\}]{a} (\emptyset, \ldots, \emptyset, Q_{k+1}, \ldots, Q_n)$ if t does not already exist. In all cases, if t is added, set $J(t) = (r, i+1)$,*
4. *when $o = push^k_b$ for all transitions $t = q_{p'} \xrightarrow[Q_{col}]{b} (Q_1, \ldots, Q_n)$ and $T = Q_1 \xrightarrow[Q'_{col}]{a} Q'_1$ in A_i with $Q_{col} \subseteq \mathbb{Q}_k$, add to A_{i+1} the transition*
$$t' = q_p \xrightarrow[Q'_{col}]{a} \left(Q'_1, Q_2, \ldots, Q_k \cup Q_{col}, \ldots, Q_n\right) ,$$
and set $J(t') = (r, t, T, i+1)$ if t' is not already in A_{i+1},
5. *when $o = rew_b$ for each transition $t = q_{p'} \xrightarrow[Q_{col}]{b} (Q_1, \ldots, Q_n)$ in A_i, add to A_{i+1} the transition $t' = q_p \xrightarrow[Q_{col}]{a} (Q_1, \ldots, Q_n)$, setting $J(t') = (r, t, i)$ when t' is not already in A_{i+1}.*

From A_0, we iterate $A_{i+1} = \Pi(A_i)$ until $A_{i+1} = A_i$. Generally, we terminate in n-EXPTIME. When A_0 satisfies a "non-alternating" property (e.g. when we're only interested in reaching a designated control state), we can restrict Π to only add transitions where Q_n has at most one element, giving $(n-1)$-EXPTIME complexity. In all cases saturation is linear in the size of Σ.

4. Examples of Saturation

As an example of saturation, consider a CPDS with the run

$$\langle p_1, [b]\,[c]\,[d] \rangle \xrightarrow{push^2_a} \langle p_2, [ab]\,[c]\,[d] \rangle \xrightarrow{push_2}$$
$$\langle p_3, [ab]\,[ab]\,[c]\,[d] \rangle \xrightarrow{collapse_2} \langle p_4, [c]\,[d] \rangle \xrightarrow{pop_2} \langle p_5, [d] \rangle \ .$$

Figure 5 shows the sequence of saturation steps, beginning with an accepting run of $\langle p_5, [d] \rangle$ and finishing with an accepting run of $\langle p_1, [b]\,[c]\,[d] \rangle$. The individual steps are explained below.

Initial Automaton We begin at the top of Figure 5 with a stack automaton containing the transitions $q_{p_5} \xrightarrow{q_1} \emptyset$ and $q_1 \xrightarrow[\emptyset]{d} \emptyset$, which we write $q_{p_5} \xrightarrow[\emptyset]{d} (\emptyset, \emptyset)$. This gives the pictured run over $\langle p_5, [d] \rangle$.

Rule (p_4, c, pop_2, p_5) When the saturation step considers such a pop rule, it adds $q_{p_4} \xrightarrow[\emptyset]{c} (\emptyset, \{q_{p_5}\})$. We add such a transition because we only require the top order-1 stack (removed by pop_2) to have the top character c (hence $\emptyset$ is the next order-1 label), and after the pop_2 the remaining stack needs to be accepted from q_{p_5} (hence $\{q_{p_5}\}$ is the next order-2 label). This new transition allows us to construct the next run over $\langle p_4, [c]\,[d] \rangle$ in Figure 5.

Rule $(p_3, a, collapse_2, p_4)$ Similarly to the pop rule above, the saturation step adds the transition $q_{p_3} \xrightarrow[\{q_{p_4}\}]{a} (\emptyset, \emptyset)$. The addition of such a transition allows us to construct the pictured run over $\langle p_3, [ab]\,[ab]\,[c]\,[d] \rangle$ (collapse links omitted), recalling that $\emptyset \xrightarrow{\emptyset} \emptyset$, $\emptyset \xrightarrow[\emptyset]{a} \emptyset$ and $\emptyset \xrightarrow[\emptyset]{b} \emptyset$ transitions are always possible due to the empty initial set. Note that the labelling of $\{q_{p_4}\}$ in the run comes from the collapse link on the topmost a character on the stack.

Rule $(p_2, a, push_2, p_3)$ Consider the run from q_{p_3} in Figure 5. The initial transition of the run accepting the first order-1 stack is $q_{p_3} \xrightarrow[\{q_{p_4}\}]{a} (\emptyset, \emptyset)$. We also have $\emptyset \xrightarrow{\emptyset} \emptyset$ (trivially) accepting the second order-1 stack. Any $push_2$ predecessor of this stack must have a top order-1 stack that could have appeared twice at the top of the stack from q_{p_3}. Thus, the saturation step makes the intersection of the initial order-1 transitions of first two order-1 stacks. This results in the transition $q_{p_2} \xrightarrow[\{q_{p_4}\} \cup \emptyset]{a} (\emptyset \cup \emptyset, \emptyset)$, which is used to form the shown run over $\langle p_2, [ab]\,[c]\,[d] \rangle$ (collapse links omitted).

Rule $(p_1, b, push^2_a, p_2)$ The run from q_{p_2} in Figure 5 begins with $q_{p_2} \xrightarrow[\{q_{p_4}\}]{a} (\emptyset, \emptyset)$ and $\emptyset \xrightarrow[\emptyset]{b} \emptyset$. Note that the $push^2_a$ gives a stack with ab on top. Moreover, the collapse link on a should point to the order-1 stack just below the current top one. Since the transition from q_{p_2} requires that the linked-to stack is accepted from q_{p_4}, we need this requirement in the preceding stack (accepted from q_{p_1} and without the a on top). Thus, we move the target of the collapse link into the order-2 destination of the new transition. That is, the saturation step for $push^2_a$ rules creates $q_{p_1} \xrightarrow[\emptyset]{b} (\emptyset, \emptyset \cup \{q_{p_4}\})$. This can be used to construct an accepting run over $\langle p_1, [b]\,[c]\,[d] \rangle$.

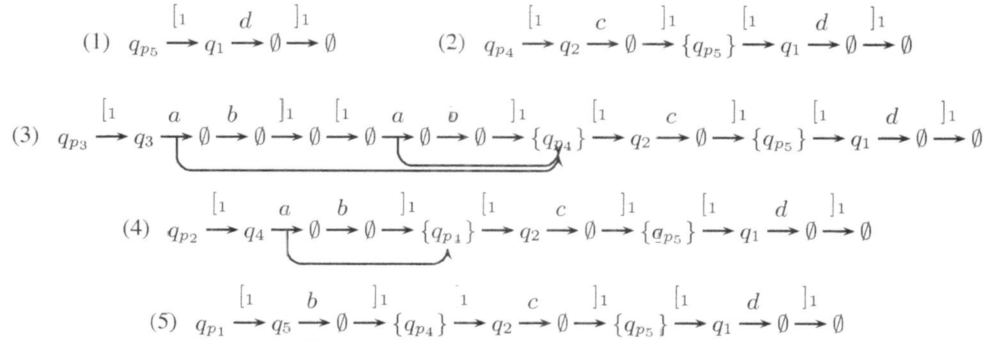

Figure 5: A sequence of saturation steps.

5. Initial Forward Analysis

In this section we distinguish an *error state* p_{err} and we are interested only in whether $\mathcal{C}$ can reach a configuration of the form $\langle p_{err}, w\rangle$ (hence our A_0 is "non-alternating"). This suffices to capture the same safety (reachability) properties of recursion schemes as TRecS. We fix a stack-automaton $\boldsymbol{\mathcal{E}}$ recognising all error configurations (those with the state p_{err}). We write $Post^*_{\mathcal{C}}$ for the set of configurations reachable by $\mathcal{C}$ from the initial configuration. This set cannot be represented precisely by a stack automaton [5] (for instance using $push_2$, we can create $[[a^n]_1[a^n]_1]_2$ from $[[a^n]_1]_2$ for any $n \geq 0$). We summarise our approach then give details in Sections 5.1, 5.2 and 5.3.

It is generally completely impractical to compute $Pre^*_{\mathcal{C}}(\boldsymbol{\mathcal{E}})$ in full (most non-trivial examples considered in our experiments would time-out). For our saturation algorithm to be usable in practice, it is therefore essential that the search space is restricted, which we achieve by means of an initial forward analysis of the CPDS. Ideally we would compute only $Pre^*_{\mathcal{C}}(\boldsymbol{\mathcal{E}}) \cap Post^*_{\mathcal{C}}$. Since this cannot be represented by an automaton, we instead compute a sufficient approximation T (ideally a *strict* subset of $Pre^*_{\mathcal{C}}(\boldsymbol{\mathcal{E}})$) where:

$$Pre^*_{\mathcal{C}}(\boldsymbol{\mathcal{E}}) \cap Post^*_{\mathcal{C}} \subseteq T \subseteq Pre^*_{\mathcal{C}}(\boldsymbol{\mathcal{E}}).$$

The initial configuration will belong to T iff it can reach a configuration recognised by $\boldsymbol{\mathcal{E}}$. Computing such a T is much more feasible.

We first compute an over-approximation of $Post^*_{\mathcal{C}}$. For this we use a *summary algorithm* [34] (that happens to be precise at order-1) from which we extract an over-approximation of the set of CPDS rules that may be used on a run to p_{err}. Let $\mathcal{C}'$ be the (smaller) CPDS containing only these rules. That is, we remove all rules that we know cannot appear on a run to p_{err}. We could thus take $T = Pre^*_{\mathcal{C}'}(\boldsymbol{\mathcal{E}})$ (computable by saturation for $\mathcal{C}'$) since it satisfies the conditions above. This is what we meant by *'pruning'* the CPDS (1a in the list on page 2)

However, we further improve performance by computing an even smaller T (1b in the list on page 2). We extract contextual information from our over-approximation of $Post^*_{\mathcal{C}}$ about how pops and collapses might be used during a run to p_{err}. Our $\mathcal{C}'$ is then restricted to a model $\mathcal{C}''$ that 'guards' its rules by these contextual constraints. Taking $T = Pre^*_{\mathcal{C}''}(\boldsymbol{\mathcal{E}})$ we have a T smaller than $Pre^*_{\mathcal{C}'}(\boldsymbol{\mathcal{E}})$, but still satisfying our sufficient conditions. In fact, $\mathcal{C}''$ will be a *'guarded CPDS'* (defined in the next subsection). We cannot compute $Pre^*_{\mathcal{C}''}(\boldsymbol{\mathcal{E}})$ precisely for a guarded CPDS, but we can adjust saturation to compute T such that $Pre^*_{\mathcal{C}''}(\boldsymbol{\mathcal{E}}) \subseteq T \subseteq Pre^*_{\mathcal{C}'}(\boldsymbol{\mathcal{E}})$. This set will thus also satisfy our sufficient conditions.

5.1 Guarded Destruction

An *order-n guarded CPDS (n-GCPDS)* is an n-CPDS where conventional pop_k and $collapse_k$ operations are replaced by *guarded operations* of the form pop^S_k and $collapse^S_k$ where $S \subseteq \Sigma$. These operations may only be fired if the resulting stack has a member of S on top. That is, for $o \in \{collapse_k, pop_k \mid 1 \leq k \leq n\}$:

$$o^S(u) := \begin{cases} o(u) & \text{if } o(u) \text{ defined and } top_1(o(u)) \in S \\ \text{undefined} & \text{otherwise}. \end{cases}$$

Note, we do not guard the other stack operations since these themselves guarantee the symbol on top of the new stack (e.g. when a transition $(p, a, push_2, p')$ fires it must always result in a stack with a on top, and $(p, a, push^b_k, p')$ produces a stack with b on top).

Given a GCPDS $\mathcal{C}$, we write $\mathsf{Triv}(\mathcal{C})$ for the ordinary CPDS that is the *trivialisation* of $\mathcal{C}$, obtained by replacing each pop^S_k (resp. $collapse^S_k$) in the rules of $\mathcal{C}$ with pop_k (resp. $collapse_k$).

We modify the saturation algorithm to use 'guarded' saturation steps for pop and collapse rules. Other saturation steps are unchanged. Non-trivial guards reduce the size of the stack-automaton constructed by avoiding certain additions that are only relevant for unreachable (and hence uninteresting) configurations in the pre-image. This thus improves performance.

1. when $o = pop^S_k$, for each $q_{p'} \xrightarrow{q_k} (Q_{k+1}, \dots, Q_n)$ in A such that there is a transition of the form $q_k \xrightarrow{b} (\_, \dots, \_)$ in A such that $b \in S$, add $q_p \xrightarrow[\emptyset]{a} (\emptyset, \dots, \emptyset, \{q_k\}, Q_{k+1}, \dots, Q_n)$ to A',

3. when $o = collapse^S_k$, for each $q_{p'} \xrightarrow{q_k} (Q_{k+1}, \dots, Q_n)$ in A such that there is a transition of the form $q_k \xrightarrow{b} (\_, \dots, \_)$ in A with $b \in S$, add $q_p \xrightarrow[\{q_k\}]{a} (\emptyset, \dots, \emptyset, Q_{k+1}, \dots, Q_n)$ to A'.

E.g., suppose that an ordinary (non-guarded) 2-CPDS has rules $(p_1, c, collapse_2, p)$ and $(p_2, d, collapse_2, p')$. The *original* saturation algorithm would process these rules to add the transitions:

$$q_{p_1} \xrightarrow[\{q_p\}]{c} (\emptyset, \emptyset) \quad \text{and} \quad q_{p_2} \xrightarrow[\{q_{p'}\}]{d} (\emptyset, \emptyset)$$

Now suppose that the saturation algorithm has produced two transitions of the form $q_p \xrightarrow{a} (\_, \_)$ and $q_{p'} \xrightarrow{b} (\_, \_)$. If a GCPDS had, for example, the rules $(p_1, c, collapse^{\{a\}}_2, p)$ and $(p_2, d, collapse^{\{b\}}_2, p')$, then these same two transitions would be added by the modified saturation algorithm. On the other hand, the rules $(p_1, c, collapse^{\{a\}}_2, p)$ and $(p_2, d, collapse^{\{a\}}_2, p')$ would only result in the first of the two transitions being added.

Lemma 5.1. *The revised saturation algorithm applied to $\boldsymbol{\mathcal{E}}$ (for a GCPDS $\mathcal{C}$) gives a stack automaton recognising T such that $Pre^*_{\mathcal{C}}(\boldsymbol{\mathcal{E}}) \subseteq T \subseteq Pre^*_{\mathsf{Triv}(\mathcal{C})}(\boldsymbol{\mathcal{E}})$*

Remark 5.1. *The algorithm may result in a stack-automaton recognising configurations that do not belong to $Pre^*_{\mathcal{C}}(\boldsymbol{\mathcal{E}})$ (although still in $Pre^*_{\mathsf{Triv}(\mathcal{C})}(\boldsymbol{\mathcal{E}})$). This is because a state q_k having a transition $q_k \xrightarrow{b} (\_, \dots, \_)$ may also have another transition*

$q_k \xrightarrow{b'} (\_, \ldots, \_)$ *with* $b \neq b'$ *(and so it might recognise a stack from which a* pop_k*, say, guarded by* b *cannot be performed).*

Remark 5.2. *The above modification to the naive saturation algorithm can also be easily incorporated into the efficient fixed point algorithm described in Section 7.*

5.2 Approximate Reachability Graphs

We now give an overview of the summary algorithm used to obtain an over-approximation of $Post^*_{\mathcal{C}}$ and thus compute the GCPDS $\mathcal{C}''$ mentioned previously. We refer the reader to the long version of this paper for details, including a formal account of the invariants on the graph maintained by the algorithm. For simplicity, we assume that a stack symbol uniquely determines the order of any link that it emits (which is the case for a CPDS obtained from a HORS).

An *approximate reachability graph* for $\mathcal{C}$ is a structure (H, E) describing an over-approximation of the reachable configurations of $\mathcal{C}$. The set of nodes of the graph H consists of *heads* of the CPDS, where a head is a pair $(p, a) \in \mathcal{P} \times \Sigma$ and describes configurations of the form $\langle p, u\rangle$ where $top_1(u) = a$. The set E contains directed edges $((p, a), r, (p', a'))$ labelled by rules of $\mathcal{C}$. Such edges over-approximate the transitions that $\mathcal{C}$ might make using a rule r from a configuration described by (p, a) to one described by (p', a'). For example, suppose that $\mathcal{C}$ is order-2 and has, amongst others, the rules $r_1 := (p_1, b, push_2, p_2)$, $r_2 := (p_2, b, push^2_c, p_3)$ and $r_3 := (p_3, c, pop_1, p_4)$ so that it can perform transitions:

$$\left\langle p_1, \left[\begin{bmatrix} b \\ a \end{bmatrix}\right]\right\rangle \xrightarrow{r_1} \left\langle p_2, \left[\begin{bmatrix} b \\ a \end{bmatrix}\begin{bmatrix} b \\ a \end{bmatrix}\right]\right\rangle$$

$$\xrightarrow{r_2} \left\langle p_3, \left[\begin{bmatrix} c \\ b \\ a \end{bmatrix}\begin{bmatrix} b \\ a \end{bmatrix}\right]\right\rangle \xrightarrow{r_3} \left\langle p_4, \left[\begin{bmatrix} b \\ a \end{bmatrix}\begin{bmatrix} b \\ a \end{bmatrix}\right]\right\rangle$$

where the first configuration mentioned here is reachable. We should then have edges $((p_1, b), r_1, (p_2, b))$, $((p_2, b), r_2, (p_3, c))$ and $((p_3, c), r_3, (p_4, b))$ in E. We denote the configurations above C_1, C_2, C_3 and C_4 respectively, with respective stacks s_1, s_2, s_3, s_4.

Such a graph can be computed using an *approximate summary algorithm*, which builds up an object (H, E, B, U) consisting of an approximate reachability graph together with two additional components. B is a map assigning each head h in the graph a set $B(h)$ of *stack descriptors*, which are $(n + 1)$-tuples $(h_n, \ldots, h_1, h_c)$ of heads. In the following, we refer to h_k as the order-k component and h_c the collapse component. Roughly speaking, h_k describes at which head the new top_k-stack resulting from a pop_k operation (applied to a configuration with head h) may have been created, and h_c does likewise for a *collapse* operation. (We will use $\perp$ in place of a head to indicate when pop_k or *collapse* is undefined.)

Consider $C_3 = \langle p_3, s_3\rangle$ from the example above. This has control-state p_3 and top stack symbol c and so is associated with the head (p_3, c). Thus $B((p_3, c))$ should contain the stack-descriptor $((p_1, b), (p_2, b), (p_1, b))$, which describes s_3. The first (order-2) component is because $top_2(s_3)$ was created by a $push_2$ operation from a configuration with head (p_1, b). The second (order-1) component is because the top symbol was created via an order-1 push from (p_2, b). Finally, the order-2 link from the top of s_3 points to a stack occurring on top of a configuration at the head (p_1, b), giving rise to the final (collapse) component describing the collapse link.

Tracking this information allows the summary algorithm to process the rule r_3 to obtain a description of C_4 from the description of C_3. Since this rule performs a pop_1, it can look at the order-1 component of the stack descriptor to see the head (p_2, b), telling us that pop_1 results in b being on top of the stack. Since the rule r_3 moves into control-state p_4, this tells us that the new head should be (p_4, b). It also tells us that certain pieces of information in $B((p_2, b))$ are relevant to the description of $top_2(s_4)$ contained in $B((p_4, b))$. First remark that this situation only occurs for the pop_k and $collapse_k$ operations. To keep track of these correlations, we use the component U of the graph.

The component U is a set of *approximate higher-order summary edges*. A summary edge describes how information contained in stack descriptors should be shared between heads. An *order-k summary edge* from a head h to a head h' is a triple of the form $(h, (h'_n, \ldots, h'_{k+1}), h')$ where each h'_i is a head. Such a summary edge is added when processing either a pop_k or a $collapse_k$ operation on an order-k link. Intuitively such a summary edge means that if $(h_n, \ldots, h_{k+1}, h_k, \ldots, h_1, h_c) \in B(h)$, then we should also have $(h'_n, \ldots, h'_{k+1}, h_k, \ldots, h_1, h_c) \in B(h')$. To continue our example, the r_3 rule (which performs a pop_1 operation) from C_3 to C_4 means U should contain an order-1 summary edge $((p_2, b), ((p_1, b)), (p_4, b))$. Since pop_1 is an order-1 operation, we have $pop_2(s_3) = pop_2(s_4)$. Hence (p_1, b) (the order-2 component of the stack descriptor for s_3) should also be the first component of a stack descriptor for s_4. However, since $top_1(s_4)$ was created at a configuration with head (p_2, b), the order-1 and collapse components of such a stack descriptor for s_4 should be inherited from a stack descriptor in $B((p_2, b))$. In general if we go from a configuration (p, s) with h to a configuration (p', s') with head h' by the pop_k operation or $collapse_k$ on an order-k link, we have that $pop_{k+1}(s) = pop_{k+1}(s')$ and hence we have a summary edge $(h, (h'_n, \ldots, h'_{k+1}), h')$

The construction of the approximate reachability graph is described in algorithms 7, 8, 9 and 10. The main work is done in the function ProcessHeadWithDescriptor. In particular, this is where summary edges are added for the pop_k and $collapse_k$ operations. A fully worked example is given in the long version.

5.3 Extracting the Guarded CPDA

Let $\mathcal{G} = (H, E)$ be an approximate reachability graph for $\mathcal{C}$. Let $\textsf{Heads}(\boldsymbol{\mathcal{E}})$ be the set of heads of error configurations, *i.e.* $\textsf{Heads}(\boldsymbol{\mathcal{E}}) := \{(p_{err}, a) \mid a \in \Sigma\}$. We do a simple backwards reachability computation on the finite graph $\mathcal{G}$ to compute the set $\textsf{BackRules}(\mathcal{G})$, which is defined to be the smallest set satisfying:

$$\textsf{BackRules}(\mathcal{G}) = \left\{ e \in E \;\middle|\; \begin{array}{l} e = (h, r, h') \in E \text{ for some} \\ h' \in \textsf{Heads}(\boldsymbol{\mathcal{E}}) \end{array} \right\}$$
$$\cup \left\{ e \in E \;\middle|\; \begin{array}{l} e = (h, r, h') \in E \text{ for some} \\ (h', \_, \_) \in \textsf{BackRules}(\mathcal{G}) \end{array} \right\}$$

The CPDS rules occurring in the triples in $\textsf{BackRules}(\mathcal{G})$ can be used to define a pruned CPDS $\mathcal{C}'$ that reaches an error state if and only if the original also does. However, the approximate reachability graph provides enough information to construct a guarded CPDS $\mathcal{C}''$ whose guards are non-trivial. It should be clear that the following set $\textsf{BackRulesG}(\mathcal{G})$ of *guarded* rules can be computed:

$$\left\{ (p, a, o', p') \;\middle|\; \begin{array}{l} (\_, (p, a, o, p'), \_) \in \textsf{BackRules}(\mathcal{G}) \text{ and} \\ o' = \begin{cases} o^S & \text{if } o \text{ is a pop or a collapse and } S \\ & = \left\{ b \;\middle|\; \begin{array}{l} ((p, a), r, (p', b)) \\ \in E \end{array} \right\} \\ & \text{with } r = (p, a, o, p') \\ o & \text{if } o \text{ is a rewrite or push} \end{cases} \end{array} \right\}$$

These rules define a GCPDS on which C-SHORe finally performs saturation.

Lemma 5.2. *The GCPDS* $\mathcal{C}''$ *defined using* $\textsf{BackRulesG}(\mathcal{G})$ *satisfies:* $Post^*_{\mathcal{C}} \cap Pre^*_{\mathcal{C}}(\boldsymbol{\mathcal{E}}) \subseteq Pre^*_{\mathcal{C}''}(\boldsymbol{\mathcal{E}}) \subseteq Pre^*_{\mathcal{C}}(\boldsymbol{\mathcal{E}})$

Algorithm 1 The Approximate Summary Algorithm

Require: An n-CPDS with rules $\mathcal{R}$ and heads $\mathcal{P} \times \Sigma$ and initial configuration $\langle p_0, [\cdots[a_0]_1 \cdots]_n\rangle$
Ensure: The creation of a structure (H, E, B, U) where (H, E) is an approximate reachability graph and U is a set of approximate higher-order summary edges.

Set $H := \{(p_0, a_0)\}$ and set E, B and U to be empty
Call AddStackDescriptor($(p_0, a_0), (\bot, \ldots, \bot, \bot)$)
return Done, (H, E, B, U) will now be as required

Algorithm 2 AddStackDescriptor($h, (h_n, \ldots, h_1, h_c)$)

Require: A head $h \in H$ and a stack descriptor $(h_n, \ldots, h_1, h_c)$
Ensure: $(h_n, \ldots, h_1, h_c) \in B(h)$ and all additions to $B(h')$ for all $h' \in H$ needed to respect summary edges are made.

if $(h_n, \ldots, h_1, h_c) \in B(h)$ **then**
  return Done (Nothing to do)
Add $(h_n, \ldots, h_1, h_c)$ to $B(h)$
Call ProcessHeadWithDescriptor($h, (h_n, \ldots, h_1, h_c)$)
for $h' \in H$ such that $(h, (h'_n, \ldots, h'_{k+1}), h') \in U$ **do**
  Call AddStackDescriptor($h', (h'_n, \ldots, h'_{k+1}, h_k, \ldots, h_1, h_c)$)
return Done

Algorithm 3 ProcessHeadWithDescriptor($h, (h_n, \ldots, h_1, h_c)$)

Require: A head $h := (p, a) \in H$ and a stack descriptor $(h_n, \ldots, h_1, h_c) \in B(h)$
Ensure: All necessary modifications to the graph are made so that it is consistent with $(h_n, \ldots, h_1, h_c) \in B(h)$. In particular this is the procedure that processes the CPDS rules from h (with respect to a stack described by h and the stack descriptor).

for o and p' such that $r = (p, a, o, p') \in \mathcal{R}$ **do**
  if $o = rew_b$ **then**
    Add (p', b) to H and $((p, a), r, (p', b))$ to E
    Call AddStackDescriptor($(p', b), (h_n, \ldots, h_1, h_c)$)
  else if $o = push_b^k$ **then**
    Add (p', b) to H and $((p, a), r, (p', b))$ to E
    Call AddStackDescriptor($(p', b), (h_n, \ldots, h_2, (p, a), h_k)$)
  else if $o = push_k$ **then**
    Add (p', a) to H and $((p, a), r, (p', a))$ to E
    Call AddStackDescriptor($(p', a), (h_n, \ldots, h_{k+1}, (p, a), h_{k-1}, \ldots, h_1, h_c)$)
  else if $o = pop_k$ with $h_k = (p_k, a_k)$ where $a_k \neq \bot$ **then**
    Add (p', a_k) to H and $((p, a), r, (p', a_k))$ to E
    Call AddSummary($(p_k, a_k), (h_n, \ldots, h_{k+1}), (p', a_k)$)
  else if $o = collapse_k$, $h_c = (p_c, a_c)$ and $a_c \neq \bot$ **then**
    Add (p_c, a_c) to H and $((p, a), r, (p', a_c))$ to E
    Call AddSummary($(p_c, a_c), (h_n, \ldots, h_{k+1}), (p', a_c)$)
return Done

6. Counter Example Generation

In this section, we describe an algorithm that given a CPDS $\mathcal{C}$ and a stack automaton A_0 such that a configuration $\langle p, w\rangle$ of $\mathcal{C}$ belongs $Pre^*_{\mathcal{C}}(A_0)$, constructs a sequence of rules of $\mathcal{C}$ which when applied from $\langle p, w\rangle$ leads to a configuration in $\mathcal{L}(A_0)$. In practice, we use the algorithm with A_0 accepting the set of all configurations starting with some error state p_{err}. The output is a counter-example showing how the CPDS can reach this error state.

The algorithm itself is a natural one and the full details are given in the full version of this paper. We describe it informally here by means of the example in Figure 5, described in Section 4.

To construct a trace from $\langle p_1, [b]\,[c]\,[d]\rangle$ to $\langle p_5, [d]\rangle$ we first note that, when adding the initial transition of the pictured run from q_{p_1}, the saturation step marked that the transition was added due to the

Algorithm 4 AddSummary($h, (h'_n, \ldots, h_{k+1}), h'$)

Require: An approximate higher-order summary edge $(h, (h'_n, \ldots, h_{k+1}), h')$
Ensure: $(h, (h'_n, \ldots, h'_{k+1}), h') \in U$ and that all necessary stack descriptors are added to the appropriate $B(h'')$ for $h'' \in H$ so that all summary edges (including the new one) are respected.

if $(h, (h'_n, \ldots, h'_{k+1}), h') \in U$ **then**
  return Done (Nothing to do)
Add $(h, (h'_n, \ldots, h'_{k+1}), h')$ to U
for $(h_n, \ldots, h_{k+1}, h_k, \ldots, h_1, h_c) \in B(h)$ **do**
  AddStackDescriptor($h', (h'_n, \ldots, h'_{k+1}, h_k, \ldots, h_1, h_c)$)
return Done

rule $(p_1, b, push^2_c, p_2)$. If we apply this rule to $\langle p_1, [b]\,[c]\,[d]\rangle$ we obtain $\langle p_2, [ab]\,[c]\,[d]\rangle$ (collapse links omitted). Furthermore, the justifications added during the saturation step tell us which transitions to use to construct the pictured run from q_{p_2}. Hence, we have completed the first step of counter example extraction and moved one step closer to the target configuration. To continue, we consider the initial transition of the run from q_{p_2}. Again, the justifications added during saturation tell us which CPDS rule to apply and which stack automaton transitions to use to build an accepting run of the next configuration. Thus, we follow the justifications back to a run of A_0, constructing a complete trace on the way.

The main technical difficulty lies in proving that the reasoning outlined above leads to a terminating algorithm. For example, we need to prove that following the justifications does not result us following a loop indefinitely. Since the stack may shrink and grow during a run, this is a non-trivial property. To prove it, we require a subtle relation on runs over higher-order collapsible stacks.

6.1 A Well-Founded Relation on Stack Automaton Runs

We aim to define a well-founded relation over runs of the stack automaton A constructed by saturation from $\mathcal{C}$ and A_0. To do this we represent a run over a stack as another stack of (sets of) transitions of A. This can be obtained by replacing each instance of a stack character with the set of order-1 transitions that read it. This is formally defined in the full version of the paper and described by example here. Consider the run over $[[b]\,[c]\,[d]]$ from q_{p_1} in Figure 5. We can represent this run as the stack $[[\{t_1\}]\,[\{t_2\}]\,[\{t_3\}]]$ where $t_1 = q_5 \xrightarrow[\emptyset]{b} \emptyset$, $t_2 = q_2 \xrightarrow[\emptyset]{c} \emptyset$ and $t_3 = q_1 \xrightarrow[\emptyset]{d} \emptyset$. Note that since q_5 uniquely labels the order-2 transition $q_{p_1} \xrightarrow{q_5} \{q_{p_4}\}$ (and similarly for the transitions from q_{p_4} and q_{p_5}) we do not need to explicitly store these transitions in our stack representation of runs.

Using this representation, we can define by induction a relation $\hookrightarrow_k$ on the order-k runs of A. Note that this is not an order relation as it is not always transitive. There are several cases to $\hookrightarrow_k$.

1. For $k = 1$, we say $w' \hookrightarrow_1 w$ if for some $i \geq 0$, w contains strictly fewer transitions in Δ_1 justified at step i than w' and that for all $j > i$ they both contain the same number of transitions in Δ_1 justified at step j.
2. For $k > 1$, we say $u = [u_\ell \ldots u_1]_k \hookrightarrow_k v = [v_{\ell'} \ldots v_1]_k$ if
   (a) $\ell' < \ell$ and $u_i = v_i$ for $i \in [1, \ell' - 1]$ and either $u_{\ell'} = v_{\ell'}$ or $u_{\ell'} \hookrightarrow_{k-1} v_{\ell'}$, or
   (b) $\ell' \geq \ell$ and $u_i = v_i$ for $i \in [1, \ell - 1]$ and $u_\ell \hookrightarrow_{k-1} v_i$ for all $i \in [\ell, \ell']$.

Lemma 6.1. *For all $k \in [1, n]$, the relation $\hookrightarrow_k$ is well-founded. Namely there is no infinite sequence $w_0 \hookrightarrow_k w_1 \hookrightarrow_k w_2 \hookrightarrow_k \cdots$.*

It is possible to show that by following the justifications, from stack w to a w', we always have $w \hookrightarrow_n w'$. Since this relation is well-founded, the witness generation algorithm always terminates.

7. Efficient Fixed Point Computation

We introduce an efficient method of computing the fixed point in Section 3, inspired by Schwoon *et al.*'s algorithm for alternating (order-1) pushdown systems [36]. Rather than checking all CPDS rules at each iteration, we fully process *all* consequences of each new transition at once. New transitions are kept in a set Δ_{new} (implemented as a stack), processed, then moved to a set Δ_{done}, which forms the transition relation of the final stack automaton. We assume w.l.o.g. that a character's link order is determined by the character. This is true of all CPDSs obtained from HORSs.

In most cases, new transitions only depend on a single existing transition, hence processing the consequences of a new transition is straightforward. The key difficulty is the push rules, which depend on *sets* of existing transitions. Given a rule $(p, a, push_k, p')$, processing $t = q_{p'} \xrightarrow[Q_{col}]{a} (Q_1, \ldots, Q_k, \ldots, Q_n)$ 'once and once only' must somehow include adding a new transition whenever there is a set of transitions of the form $Q_k \xrightarrow[Q'_{col}]{a} (Q'_1, \ldots, Q'_k)$ in A_i either now *or in the future*. When t is processed, we therefore create a *trip-wire*, consisting of a *source* and *target*. A *target* collects transitions from a given set of states (such as Q_k above), whilst a *source* describes how such a collection could be used to form a new transition according to a *push* saturation step.

Definition 7.1. *An* order-k source *for $k \geq 1$ is defined as a tuple (q_k, q_{k-1}, a, Q_k) in $\mathbb{Q}_k \times \mathbb{Q}_{k-1}^{\perp} \times \Sigma \times 2^{\mathbb{Q}_k}$ where $\mathbb{Q}_0^{\perp} := \{\perp\}$ and $\mathbb{Q}_i^{\perp} = \mathbb{Q}_i \cup \{\perp\}$ for $i \geq 1$. An* order-k target *is a tuple*

$$(Q_k, Q_k^C, Q_{lbl}, Q'_k) \in 2^{\mathbb{Q}_k} \times 2^{\mathbb{Q}_k} \times 2^{\mathbb{Q}_{k-1}} \times 2^{\mathbb{Q}_k}$$

if $k \geq 2$, and if $k = 1$

$$(Q_1, Q_1^C, a, Q_{col}, Q'_1) \in \bigcup_{k'=2}^{n} \left(2^{\mathbb{Q}_1} \times 2^{\mathbb{Q}_1} \times \Sigma \times 2^{\mathbb{Q}_{k'}} \times 2^{\mathbb{Q}_1}\right).$$

The set Q_k^C is a *countdown* containing states in Q_k still awaiting a transition. We always have $Q_k^C \subseteq Q_k$ and $(Q_k \setminus Q_k^C) \xrightarrow{Q_{lbl}} Q'_k$. Likewise, an order-1 target $(Q_1, Q_1^C, a, Q_{col}, Q_1)$ will satisfy $(Q_1 \setminus Q_1^C) \xrightarrow[Q_{col}]{a} Q'_1$. A target is *complete* if $Q_k^C = \emptyset$ or $Q_1^C = \emptyset$.

A *trip-wire* of order-k is an order-k source-target pair of the form $((\_, \_, \_, Q_k), (Q_k, \_, \_, \_))$ when $k \geq 2$ or $((\_, \_, a, Q_k), (Q_k, \_, a, \_, \_))$ when $k = 1$. When the target in a trip-wire is *complete*, the action specified by its source is triggered, which we now sketch.

An order-k *source* for $k \geq 2$ describes how an order-$(k-1)$ source should be created from a complete target, propagating the computation to the level below, and an order-1 source describes how a new long-form transition should be created from a complete target. That is, when we have $(q_k, \_, a, Q_k)$ (we hide the second component for simplicity of description) and $(Q_k, \emptyset, Q_{lbl}, Q'_k)$ this means we've found a set of transitions witnessing $Q_k \xrightarrow{Q_{lbl}} Q'_k$ and should now look for transitions from Q_{lbl}. Hence the algorithm creates a new source and target for the order-$(k-1)$ state-set Q_{lbl}. When this process reaches order-1, a new transition is created. This results in the construction of the t' from a *push* saturation step.

Algorithm 5 gives the main loop and introduces the global sets Δ_{done} and Δ_{new}, and two arrays $\mathcal{U}_{src}[k]$ and $\mathcal{U}_{targ}[k]$ containing sources and targets for each order. Omitted are loops processing pop_n and $collapse_n$ rules like the naive algorithm. Algorithm 6 gives the main steps processing a new transition. We present only two CPDS rule cases here. In most cases a new transition is created, however, for *push* rules we create a trip-wire. Remaining algorithms, definitions, justification handling, and proofs are given in the long version of this paper. We describe some informally below.

In create_trip_wire we create a trip-wire with a new target $(Q_k, Q_k, \emptyset, \emptyset)$. This is added using an add_target procedure which also checks Δ_{done} to create further targets. E.g., a new target $(Q_k, Q_k^C, Q_{lbl}, Q'_k)$ combines with an existing $q_k \xrightarrow{q_{k-1}} Q''_k$ to create a new target $(Q, Q_k^C \setminus \{q_k\}, Q_{lbl} \cup \{q_{k-1}\}, Q'_k \cup Q''_k)$. (This step corrects a bug in the algorithm of Schwoon *et al.*) Similarly update_trip_wires updates existing targets by new transitions. In all cases, when a source and matching complete target are created, we perform the propagations described above.

Proposition 7.1. *Given a CPDS $\mathcal{C}$ and stack automaton A_0, let A be the result of Algorithm 5. We have $\mathcal{L}(A) = Pre^*_{\mathcal{C}}(A_0)$.*

8. Experimental Results

We compared C-SHORe with the current state-of-the-art verification tools for higher-order recursion schemes (HORS): TRecS [23], GTRecS2 [26] (the successor of [25]), and TravMC [28]. Benchmarks are from the TRecS and TravMC benchmark suites, plus several larger examples provided by Kobayashi. The majority of the TravMC benchmarks were translated into HORS from an extended formalism, HORS with Case statements (HORSC), using a script by Kobayashi. For fairness, all tools in our experiments took a pure HORS as input. However, the authors of TravMC report that TravMC performs faster on the original HORSC examples than on their HORS translations.

In all cases, the benchmarks consist of a HORS (generating a computation tree) and a property automaton. In the case of C-SHORe, the property automaton is a regular automaton describing branches of the generated tree that are considered errors. Thus, following the intuition in Section 2, we can construct a reachability query over a CPDS, where the reachability of a control state p_{err} indicates an erroneous branch (see [10] for more details). All other tools check co-reachability properties of HORS and thus the property automaton describes only valid branches of the computation tree. In all cases, it was straightforward to translate between the co-reachability and reachability properties.

The experiments were run on a Dell Latitude e6320 laptop with 4Gb of RAM and four 2.7GHz Intel i7-2620M cores. We ran C-SHORe on OpenJDK 7.0 with IcedTea7 replacing binary plugs, using the argument "-Xmx" to limit RAM usage to 2.5Gb. As advised by the TravMC developers, we ran TravMC on the Mono JIT Compiler version 3.0.3 with no command line arguments. Finally TRecS (version 1.34) and GTRecS2 (version 3.17) were compiled with the OCaml version 4.00.1 compilers. On negative examples, GTRecS2 was run with its `-neg` argument. We used the "ulimit" command to limit memory usage to 2.5Gb and set a CPU timeout of 600 seconds (per benchmark). The given runtimes were reported by the respective tools and are the means of three separate runs on each example. Note that C-SHORe was run until the automaton was completely saturated.

Table 1 shows trials where at least one tool took over 1s. This is because virtual machine "warm-up" and HORS to CPDS conversion can skew the results on small benchmarks. Full results are in the full paper. Examples violating their property are marked "(bug)". The order (Ord) and size (Sz) of the schemes were reported by TRecS. We show reported times in seconds for TRecS (T), GTRecS2 (G), TravMC (TMC) and C-SHORe (C) where "—" means analysis failed. For C-SHORe, we report the times for HORS to CPDS translation (Ctran), CPDS analysis (Ccpds), and building the approximation graph (Capprox). Capprox is part of Ccpds, and the full time (C) is the sum of Ctran and Ccpds.

Of 26 benchmarks, C-SHORe performed best on 5 examples. In 6 cases, C-SHORe was the slowest. In particular, C-SHORe does not perform well on `exp4-1` and `exp4-5`. These belong to a class of benchmarks that stress higher-order model-checkers and indi-

Algorithm 5 Computing $Pre^*_{\mathcal{C}}(A_0)$

Let $\Delta_{done} = \emptyset$, $\Delta_{new} = \bigcup_{n \geq k \geq 1} \Delta_k$, $\mathcal{U}_{src}[k] = \emptyset$, $\mathcal{U}_{targ}[k] = \{(\emptyset, \emptyset, \emptyset, \emptyset)\}$ for each $n \geq k > 1$ and $\mathcal{U}_{targ}[1] = \{(\emptyset, \emptyset, a, \emptyset, \emptyset) \mid a \in \Sigma\}$.

...

while $\exists t \in \Delta_{new}$ **do**

  update_rules(t); update_trip_wires(t); move t from Δ_{new} to Δ_{done}

Algorithm 6 update_rules(t)

if t is an order-k transition for $2 \leq k \leq n$ of the form $q_{p' Q_n \cdots Q_{k+1}} \longrightarrow Q_k$ **then**

  for $p \in \mathcal{P}$ and $a \in \Sigma$ such that $r := (p, a, pop_k, p') \in \mathcal{R}$ **do**

    add_to_worklist$\left(q_p \xrightarrow[\mathbb{Q}_{col}]{a} (\emptyset, \ldots, \emptyset, \left\{q_{p' \mathbb{Q}_n \cdots \mathbb{Q}_{k+1}}\right\}, \mathbb{Q}_{k+1}, \ldots, \mathbb{Q}_n), r\right)$

  for $p \in \mathcal{P}$ and $a \in \Sigma$ such that $r := (p, a, push_k, p') \in \mathcal{R}$ **do**

    create_trip_wire$\left(q_{p, Q_n, \ldots, Q_{k+1}}, q_{p', Q_n, \ldots, Q_{k+1}, Q_k}, a, Q_k, (r, t)\right)$

...

Benchmark file	Ord	Sz	T	TMC	G	C	Ctran	Ccpds	Capprox	✓/✗
`order5`	5	52	0.007	0.039	—	**0.415**	0.057	0.358	0.205	
`order5-2`	5	40	0.022	0.084	—	**0.305**	0.050	0.255	0.157	
`order5-variant`	5	55	0.019	0.039	**1.519**	**0.427**	0.057	0.370	0.177	
`filepath`	2	5956	210.102	—	—	**0.397**	0.168	0.229	0.221	✓
`filter-nonzero` (bug)	5	484	0.006	0.115	**0.182**	**1.443**	0.100	1.344	1.006	✗
`filter-nonzero-1`	5	890	0.176	211.907	—	**4.492**	0.159	4.332	3.484	
`map-head-filter-1`	3	830	0.141	1.343	—	**0.400**	0.119	0.281	0.273	
`map-plusone-1`	5	459	0.030	0.736	—	**1.247**	0.119	1.128	0.908	
`map-plusone-2`	5	704	1.358	13.962	—	**2.634**	0.142	2.491	2.183	
`exp4-1`	4	31	—	0.047	**0.114**	—	0.039	—	0.240	✗
`exp4-5`	4	55	—	—	**0.818**	—	0.046	—	2.128	✗
`cfa-life2`	14	7648	—	—	—	—	0.479	—	—	
`cfa-matrix-1`	8	2944	16.937	—	—	**19.230**	0.332	18.898	18.892	
`cfa-psdes`	7	1819	17.654	—	—	**1.920**	0.273	1.647	1.640	✓
`dna`	2	411	0.031	0.263	**0.046**	**6.918**	0.175	6.743	6.206	✗
`fibstring`	4	29	—	74.569	**0.114**	—	0.042	—	0.256	✗
`fold_fun_list`	7	1346	0.519	—	—	**1.356**	0.202	1.154	1.147	
`fold_right`	5	1310	31.624	—	—	**1.255**	0.191	1.064	1.043	✓
`jwig-cal_main`	2	7627	0.062	0.052	**0.161**	**3.802**	3.739	0.063	0.057	✗
`l`	3	35	—	15.743	**0.010**	**0.248**	0.042	0.206	0.199	
`search-e-church` (bug)	6	837	0.012	0.258	—	**4.741**	0.155	4.586	1.760	
`specialize_cps_coerce1-c`	3	2731	—	—	—	**1.131**	0.293	0.838	0.830	✓
`tak` (bug)	8	451	—	3.945	—	**41.772**	0.136	41.636	34.855	
`xhtmlf-div-2` (bug)	2	3003	0.234	—	**39.961**	**2.743**	2.303	0.440	0.422	
`xhtmlf-m-church`	2	3027	0.238	—	**8.420**	**2.708**	2.319	0.389	0.382	
`zip`	4	2952	22.251	—	—	**3.356**	0.295	3.061	1.609	✓

Table 1: Comparison of model-checking tools. Shown in bold are the two fixed-parameter tractable algorithms, GTRecS2 and C-SHORe.

cate that our tool currently does not always scale well. However, C-SHORe seems to show a more promising capacity to scale on larger HORS produced by tools such as MoCHi [27], which are particularly pertinent in that they are generated by an actual software verification tool. We also note that C-SHORe timed out on the fewest examples despite not always terminating in the fastest time.

It is also very important to note that C-SHORe and GTRecS2 are the only implemented fixed-parameter tractable algorithms in the literature for HORS model-checking of which we are aware (both TRecS and TravMC have worst-case run-times non-elementary in the size of the recursion scheme). Moreover, C-SHORe generally performs much better than GTRecS2. Thus not only does C-SHORe's performance seem promising when compared to the competition, there is also theoretical reason to suggest that the approach could in principle be scalable, in contrast to some of the alternatives. Thus initial work justifies further investigation into saturation based algorithms for higher-order model-checking.

Finally, we remark that without the forwards analysis described in Section 5, all shown examples except `filepath` timed out. We also note that we did not implement a naive version of the saturation algorithm, where after each change to the stack automaton, each rule of the CPDS is checked for further updates. However, experience implementing PDSolver [15] (for order-1 pushdown systems) indicates that the naive approach is at least an order of magnitude slower than the techniques [36] we generalised in Section 7.

9. Related Work

The saturation technique has proved popular in the literature. It was introduced by Bouajjani *et al.* [4] and Finkel *et al.* [13] and based on a string rewriting algorithm by Benois [3]. It has since been extended to Büchi games [8], parity and μ-calculus conditions [15], and concurrent systems [1, 37], as well as weighted pushdown systems [31]. In addition to various implementations, efficient versions of these algorithms have also been developed [12, 36].

The saturation algorithm for CPDS that we introduced in [7], extending and improving [14] (and [5]), follows a number of papers solving parity games on the configuration graphs of higher-order automata [6, 9, 11, 16]. While only handling reachability, saturation lends itself well to implementation. This paper describes such a practical incarnation and a number of significant optimisations, such as using a forwards analysis to guide the backward search.

This latter point is an important way in which C-SHORe differs from previous model-checkers for HORS, which employ intersection types and propagate information purely in a forward direction.

This is related to the fact that the latter accept 'co-reachability properties' (represented by trivial Büchi automata) as input, expressing the complement of properties taken by C-SHORe.

Indeed it would be interesting to investigate in more detail how approximate forward and backward analyses of varying degrees of accuracy could be combined for efficiency. It would also be helpful to more closely analyse the relationship between CPDS and type-based algorithms allowing a transfer of ideas. In any case, this paper shows that saturation-based algorithms for HORS/CPDS perform sufficiently well in practice to warrant further study.

To finish, we briefly mention several approaches to analysing higher-order programs with differing aims to ours. In static analysis, k-CFA [35] and CFA2 [39] perform an over-approximative analysis of higher-order languages with at-most first-order granularity. Similarly Jhala *et al.* use refinement types to analyse OCaml programs by reducing the problem to first-order model-checking, which is thus incomplete [19]. Finally, Hopkins *et al.* have produced tools for equivalence checking fragments of ML and Idealized Algol up to order-3 [17, 18].

10. Conclusion

We have considered the problem of verifying safety properties of a model that can be used to precisely capture control-flow in the presence of higher-order recursion. Whilst previous approaches to such an analysis are based on higher-order recursion schemes and intersection types, our approach is based on automata and saturation techniques previously only applied in practice to the first-order case. At a more conceptual level, our algorithm works by propagating information backwards from error states towards the initial state. Moreover, it combines this with an approximate forward analysis to gather information that guides the backward search. In contrast, the preceding type-based algorithms all work by propagating information purely in a forward direction.

Our preliminary work brings new techniques to the table for tackling a problem, which in contrast to its first-order counterpart, has proven difficult to solve in a scalable manner. Our algorithm has the advantage that it accurately models higher-order recursion whilst also being fixed-parameter tractable, therefore giving a theoretical reason for hope that it could scale. In contrast TRecS and TravMC have worst-case run-times non-elementary in the size of the recursion scheme. Our tool also seems to work significantly better in practice than GTRecS2, the only other HORS model-checker in the literature that does enjoy fixed-parameter tractability.

We therefore believe that a C-SHORe-like approach shows much promise and warrants further investigation.

Acknowledgments

We are extremely to Robin Neatherway and Naoki Kobayashi for help with benchmarking, Łukasz Kaiser for web-hosting, and for discussions with Stefan Schwoon. Supported by Fond. Sci. Math. Paris, AMIS (ANR 2010 JCJC 0203 01 AMIS), FREC (ANR 2010 BLAN 0202 02 FREC), VAPF (Région IdF), and EPSRC (EP/K009907/1).

References

[1] M. F. Atig. Global model checking of ordered multi-pushdown systems. In *FSTTCS*, 2010.

[2] T. Ball and S. K. Rajamani. The SLAM project: Debugging system software via static analysis. In *POPL*, 2002.

[3] M. Benois. Parties rationnelles du groupe libre. *Comptes-Rendus de l'Acamdémie des Sciences de Paris, Série A*, 269:1188–1190, 1969.

[4] A. Bouajjani, J. Esparza, and O. Maler. Reachability analysis of pushdown automata: Application to model-checking. In *CONCUR*, 1997.

[5] A. Bouajjani and A. Meyer. Symbolic Reachability Analysis of Higher-Order Context-Free Processes. In *FSTTCS*, 2004.

[6] C. H. Broadbent, A. Carayol, C.-H. L. Ong, and O. Serre. Recursion schemes and logical reflection. In *LICS*, 2010.

[7] C. H. Broadbent, A. Carayol, M. Hague, and O. Serre. A saturation method for collapsible pushdown systems. In *ICALP*, 2012.

[8] T. Cachat. *Games on Pushdown Graphs and Extensions*. PhD thesis, RWTH Aachen, 2003.

[9] T. Cachat. Higher order pushdown automata, the Caucal hierarchy of graphs and parity games. In *ICALP*, 2003.

[10] A. Carayol and O. Serre. Collapsible pushdown automata and labeled recursion schemes: Equivalence, safety and effective selection. In *LICS*, 2012.

[11] A. Carayol, M. Hague, A. Meyer, C.-H. L. Ong, and O. Serre. Winning Regions of Higher-Order Pushdown Games. In *LICS*, 2008.

[12] J. Esparza, D. Hansel, P. Rossmanith, and S. Schwoon. Efficient algorithms for model checking pushdown systems. In *CAV*, 2000.

[13] A. Finkel, B. Willems, and P. Wolper. A direct symbolic approach to model checking pushdown systems. In *INFINITY*, 1997.

[14] M. Hague and C.-H. L. Ong. Symbolic backwards-reachability analysis for higher-order pushdown systems. *Logical Methods in Computer Science*, 4(4), 2008.

[15] M. Hague and C.-H. L. Ong. Analysing mu-calculus properties of pushdown systems. In *SPIN*, 2010.

[16] M. Hague, A. S. Murawski, C.-H. L. Ong, and O. Serre. Collapsible pushdown automata and recursion schemes. In *LICS*, 2008.

[17] D. Hopkins and C.-H. L. Ong. Homer: A higher-order observational equivalence model checker. In *CAV*, 2009.

[18] D. Hopkins, A. S. Murawski, and C.-H. L. Ong. Hector: An equivalence checker for a higher-order fragment of ml. In *CAV*, 2012.

[19] R. Jhala, R. Majumdar, and A. Rybalchenko. Hmc: Verifying functional programs using abstract interpreters. In *CAV*, 2011.

[20] N. D. Jones and S. S. Muchnick. Even simple programs are hard to analyze. *J. ACM*, 24:338–350, April 1977.

[21] T. Knapik, D. Niwinski, P. Urzyczyn, and I. Walukiewicz. Unsafe grammars and panic automata. In *ICALP*, 2005.

[22] N. Kobayashi. Types and higher-order recursion schemes for verification of higher-order programs. In *POPL*, 2009.

[23] N. Kobayashi. Model-checking higher-order functions. In *PPDP*, 2009.

[24] N. Kobayashi. Higher-order model checking: From theory to practice. In *LICS*, 2011.

[25] N. Kobayashi. A practical linear time algorithm for trivial automata model checking of higher-order recursion schemes. In *FOSSACS*, 2011.

[26] N. Kobayashi. GTRecS2: A model checker for recursion schemes based on games and types. A tool available at `http://www-kb.is.s.u-tokyo.ac.jp/~koba/gtrecs2/`, 2012.

[27] N. Kobayashi, R. Sato, and H. Unno. Predicate abstraction and cegar for higher-order model checking. In *PLDI*, 2011.

[28] R. P. Neatherway, S. J. Ramsay, and C.-H. L. Ong. A traversal-based algorithm for higher-order model checking. In *ICFP*, 2012.

[29] C.-H. L. Ong. On model-checking trees generated by higher-order recursion schemes. In *LICS*, 2006.

[30] C.-H. L. Ong and S. J. Ramsay. Verifying higher-order functional programs with pattern-matching algebraic data types. In *POPL*, 2011.

[31] T. W. Reps, S. Schwoon, S. Jha, and D. Melski. Weighted pushdown systems and their application to interprocedural dataflow analysis. *Sci. Comput. Program.*, 58(1-2):206–263, 2005.

[32] S. Salvati and I. Walukiewicz. Recursive schemes, krivine machines, and collapsible pushdown automata. In *RP*, 2012.

[33] S. Schwoon. *Model-checking Pushdown Systems*. PhD thesis, Technical University of Munich, 2002.

[34] M. Sharir and A. Pnueli. *Two approaches to interprocedural data flow analysis*, chapter 7, pages 189–234. Prentice-Hall, 1981.

[35] O. Shivers. *Control-Flow Analysis of Higher-Order Languages*. PhD thesis, Carnegie-Mellon University, 1991.

[36] D. Suwimonteerabuth, S. Schwoon, and J. Esparza. Efficient algorithms for alternating pushdown systems with an application to the computation of certificate chains. In *ATVA*, 2006.

[37] D. Suwimonteerabuth, J. Esparza, and S. Schwoon. Symbolic context-bounded analysis of multithreaded java programs. In *SPIN*, 2008.

[38] H. Unno, N. Tabuchi, and N. Kobayashi. Verification of tree-processing programs via higher-order model checking. In *APLAS*, 2010.

[39] D. Vardoulakis. *CFA2: Pushdown-Flow Analysis for Higher-Order Languages*. PhD thesis, Northeastern University, Boston, 2012.

[40] D. Vardoulakis and O. Shivers. Pushdown flow analysis of first-class control. In *ICFP*, 2011.

Automatic SIMD Vectorization for Haskell

Leaf Petersen
Intel Labs
leaf.petersen@intel.com

Dominic Orchard
Computer Laboratory
University of Cambridge
dominic.orchard@cl.cam.ac.uk

Neal Glew
Intel Labs
aglew@acm.org

Abstract

Expressing algorithms using immutable arrays greatly simplifies the challenges of automatic SIMD vectorization, since several important classes of dependency violations cannot occur. The Haskell programming language provides libraries for programming with immutable arrays, and compiler support for optimizing them to eliminate the overhead of intermediate temporary arrays. We describe an implementation of automatic SIMD vectorization in a Haskell compiler which gives substantial vector speedups for a range of programs written in a natural programming style. We compare performance with that of programs compiled by the Glasgow Haskell Compiler.

Categories and Subject Descriptors D.3.4 [*Programming Languages*]: Processors—Compilers; D.3.4 [*Programming Languages*]: Processors—Optimization; D.1.1 [*Programming Techniques*]: Applicative (Functional) Programming

Keywords Vectorization, SIMD, Compiler Optimization, Haskell, Functional Languages

1. Introduction

In the past decade, power has increasingly been recognized as the key limiting resource in micro-processors, in part due to the limited battery on mobile devices, but more fundamentally due to the non-linear scaling of power usage with frequency. This has forced micro-processor designs to explore (or re-explore) different avenues at both the micro-architectural and the architectural levels. One successful architectural trend has been the increasing emphasis on data parallelism in the form of single-instruction multiple-data (SIMD) instruction sets.

The key idea of data parallelism is that significant portions of many sequential computations consist of uniform (or almost uniform) operations over large collections of data. SIMD instruction sets exploit this at the machine instruction level by providing data paths for and operations on fixed-width vectors of data. Programmers (or preferably compilers) are then responsible for finding data parallel computations and expressing them in terms of fixed-width vectors. In the context of languages with loops (or compiled to loops), this corresponds to choosing loops for which multiple iterations can be computed simultaneously.

ICFP'13, September 25–27, 2013, Boston, USA.

ACM 978-1-4503-2326-0/13/09... $15.00.
http://dx.doi.org/10.1145/2500365.2500605

The task of automatically finding SIMD vectorizable code in the context of a compiler has been the subject of extensive study over the course of decades. For common imperative programming languages, such as C and Fortran, in which programs are structured as loops over mutable arrays of data, the task of rewriting loops in SIMD vector form is straightforward. However, the task of discovering which loops permit a valid rewriting (via dependency analysis) is in general undecidable, and has been the subject of extensive research (see e.g. [13] and overview in [15]). Even quite sophisticated compilers are often forced to rely on programmer annotations to *assert* that a given loop is a valid target of SIMD vectorization (for example, the `INDEPENDENT` keyword in HPF [7]).

A great deal of the difficulty in finding vectorizable loops simply goes away in the context of a functional language. In functional languages, the absence of mutation eliminates large classes of the more difficult kinds of dependence violations that block vectorization in compilers for imperative languages. In this sense, SIMD vectorization would seem to be quite low-hanging fruit for functional language compiler writers. In this paper, we describe the implementation of an automatic SIMD vectorization optimization pass in the Intel Labs Haskell Research Compiler (HRC). We argue that in a functional language context, this optimization is straightforward to implement and gives excellent results.

HRC was originally developed to compile programs written in an experimental strict functional language, and the vectorization optimization that we present here was developed in that context. However, the main bulk of our compiler infrastructure was designed to be fairly language agnostic, and we have more recently used it to build an experimental Haskell compiler using the Glasgow Haskell Compiler (GHC) as a front end. While Haskell is quite a complex language on the surface, the GHC front end reduces it to a relatively simple intermediate representation based on System F, which is fairly straightforward to compile using HRC. By intercepting the GHC intermediate representation (IR) after the main high-level optimization passes have run, we gain the benefit of the substantial and sophisticated optimization infrastructure built up in GHC, and in particular we benefit from its ability to optimize away temporary intermediate arrays.

We make the following three contributions:

- We design a core language with arrays and SIMD vector primitives (Section 3).
- We present a detailed compositional vectorization process over this language (Section 4).
- We evaluate our performance compared to GHC with the native and LLVM backends, showing significant scalar speedups over GHC and additional vector speedups of up to 6.5× over our own scalar compiler, on a selection of array processing benchmarks (Section 5).

We begin with a brief overview of HRC and its relationship to GHC.

2. Intel Labs Haskell Research Compiler

HRC provides an optimization platform aimed at producing high-performance executables from functional-style code. The core intermediate language of the compiler is a static single-assignment style, control-flow graph based intermediate representation (IR). It is strict and has explicit thunks to represent laziness. While the intermediate representation is largely language agnostic, it is not paradigm agnostic. The core technologies of the compiler are designed specifically around compiling functional-language programs. Most importantly for the purposes of this paper, the compiler relies on maintaining a distinction between mutable and immutable data, and focuses almost all of its optimization effort on the latter. The compiler is structured as a whole-program compiler—however, none of the optimizations in the compiler rely on this property in any essential way. In addition to the usual inlining-style optimizations, contification [5] is performed to turn many uses of (mutual) recursion into loops. This optimization is crucial for our purposes since we structure our SIMD-vectorization optimization as an optimization on loops. Many standard compiler optimizations have been implemented in the compiler, including loop-invariant code motion and a very general simplifier in the style of Appel and Jim [2]. The compiler also implements a number of interprocedural representation optimizations using a field-sensitive flow analysis [11].

The compiler generates output in a modified extension of the C language called *Pillar* [1]. Among other things, the Pillar language supports tail calls and second-class continuations. Most importantly, it also provides the necessary mechanisms to allow for accurate garbage collection of managed memory. While an early version of Pillar was implemented as a modification of a C compiler, Pillar is currently implemented as a source to source translation targeting standard C, which is then compiled using either the Intel C Compiler or GCC. Our garbage collector and a small runtime are linked in to produce the final executable.

2.1 Haskell and GHC

The Haskell language and the GHC extensions to it provide a large base of useful high-level libraries written in a very powerful programming language. These libraries are often written using a high-level functional-language style of programming, relying on excellent compiler technology to achieve good performance. While we wished to compile Haskell programs and take advantage of the many libraries, we had no interest in attempting the monumental task of duplicating all of the high-level compiler technology implemented in GHC. The approach we took therefore was to essentially use GHC as a Haskell frontend, thereby taking advantage of the existing type-checker and high-level optimizer.

GHC provides some support for writing its main System-F-style internal representation (called Core) out to files. While this code is not entirely maintained, we were able to easily modify it to support all the current Core features we require. We use this facility to build a Haskell compiler pipeline by first running GHC to perform type checking, desugaring, and all of its Core-level optimizations, and then writing out the Core IR immediately before it would otherwise be translated to the next-lower representation. HRC then reads in the serialized Core, and after several initial transformations and optimizations (including making thunks explicit), performs a closure-conversion pass and transforms it down to our main CFG based intermediate representation for subsequent optimization.

2.2 GHC Modifications

Using this approach, we are able to provide a fairly close to functionally complete implementation of the Haskell language as implemented by GHC. However, some of the choices of primitives used in GHC do not match up well with the needs of HRC, and so some modification of GHC itself was required. A notable example of this for the purposes of this paper is the treatment of arrays in the Data.Vector libraries.

The GHC libraries Data.Vector and REPA [6] provide clean high-level interfaces for generating immutable arrays. Programmers can use typical functional-language operations like maps, folds, and zips to compute arrays from other arrays. These operations are naturally data parallel and amenable to SIMD vectorization by HRC. For example, consider a map operation over an immutable array represented with the Data.Vector library. Such arrays are represented internally to the libraries using streams, and so map first turns the source array into a stream, applies the map operation to the stream, and then unstreams that back into the final array. Unstreaming is implemented by running a monadic computation that first creates a mutable array of the appropriate size, then initializes the elements of the array using array update, and finally does an unsafe freeze of the mutable array to an immutable array type [8]. GHC has optimizations which usually eliminate all of the intermediate streaming, mapping, and unstreaming operations. The result of this optimization is a piece of code that sequences the array creation, the calling of a tail-recursive function that initializes the array elements, and the unsafe freeze. After translation into our internal representation, HRC can then contify the tail-recursive function into a loop, resulting in a natural piece of code that can be effectively optimized using standard loop-based optimizations adapted to leverage the benefits of immutability.

Unfortunately, observe that as described in the previous paragraph we do not actually get the benefits of immutability with an unmodified GHC. Instead, we end up with code that creates a mutable array and then initializes it with general array update operations—a style of code that we argue is drastically harder to optimize well in general, and to perform SIMD vectorization on in particular. As we discuss in Section 4.7, immutable arrays make determining when a loop can be SIMD vectorized much easier. For our purposes then, what we would like GHC to generate instead of the code described above is code that creates a new uninitialized immutable array and then uses *initializing writes* to initialize the array. The two invariants of initializing writes are that reading an array element must always follow the initializing write of that element, and that any element can only be initialized once. This style of write preserves the benefits of immutability from the compiler standpoint, since any initializing write to an element is the unique definition of that element. Initializing writes are key to representing the initialization of an immutable array using the usual loop code, while preserving the ability to leverage immutability.

In order to get immutable code written in this style from GHC and the libraries discussed above, we modified GHC with new primitive immutable array types[1] and primitive operations on them. The additional operations include creation of a new uninitialized array, initializing writes, and a subscript operation. We also modified the Data.Vector library and a small part of the REPA library to use these immutable arrays instead of mutable arrays and unsafe freeze (of course, as with the standard GHC primitives, correctness requires that the library writer use the primitives correctly). With these modifications, the code produced by GHC is suitable for optimization by HRC, including in many cases SIMD vectorization.

2.3 Vectorization in HRC

SIMD vectorization in HRC targets loops for which the compiler can show that executing several iterations in parallel is semantics preserving, rewriting them to use SIMD vector instructions. Usually these loops serve to initialize immutable arrays, or to per-

[1] GHC does already have some such types—however, we added new ones to avoid compatibility issues

Register kind	k	$::=$	$s \mid v$
Variables	$x^k, y^k, z^k, \ldots$		
Constants	c	$::=$	$-2^{31}, \ldots, (2^{31}-1)$
Operations	op	$::=$	$+, -, *, /, \ldots$
Instruction	I	$::=$	$z^s = c$
		$\mid$	$z^v = \langle x_0^s, \ldots, x_7^s \rangle$
		$\mid$	$z^s = x^v!i$
		$\mid$	$z^s = op(x_0^s, \ldots, x_n^s)$
		$\mid$	$z^v = \langle op \rangle(x_0^v, \ldots, x_n^v)$
		$\mid$	$z^s = \texttt{new}[x^s]$
		$\mid$	$z^s = x^s[y^s]$
		$\mid$	$z^v = x^s[\langle y^v \rangle]$
		$\mid$	$z^v = \langle x^v \rangle[y^s]$
		$\mid$	$z^v = \langle x^v \rangle[\langle y^v \rangle]$
		$\mid$	$x^s[y^s] \leftarrow z^s$
		$\mid$	$x^s[\langle y^v \rangle] \leftarrow z^v$
		$\mid$	$\langle x^v \rangle[y^s] \leftarrow z^v$
		$\mid$	$\langle x^v \rangle[\langle y^v \rangle] \leftarrow z^v$
Comparisons	cmp	$::=$	$x^s < y^s \mid x^s \leq y^s \mid x^s = y^s$
Labels	L	$::=$	$\texttt{L}^0, \texttt{L}^1, \ldots$
Transfers	t	$::=$	$\texttt{goto}\ L(x_0^k, \ldots, x_n^k)$
		$\mid$	$\texttt{if}\ (cmp)\ \texttt{goto}\ L_0(x_0^k, \ldots, x_n^k)$ $\texttt{else goto}\ L_1(y_0^k, \ldots, y_m^k)$
		$\mid$	$\texttt{halt}$
Blocks	B	$::=$	$L(x_0^k, \ldots, x_n^k)$: I_0 ... I_m t
Control Flow Graph		$::=$	$\texttt{Entry}\ L\ \texttt{in}\ \{B_0, \ldots, B_n\}$

Figure 1. Syntax

form reductions over immutable arrays. The compiler generates the SIMD loops and all of the related control logic simply as code in our intermediate language. Rather than requiring the compiler to generate only the SIMD instructions provided by the target machine, we provide a more uniform SIMD instruction set that may be a superset of the machine-supported instructions. Our small runtime provides a library of impedance-matching macros that implements the uniform SIMD instructions in terms of SIMD intrisics understood by the underlying C compiler. The C compiler is then responsible for low-level optimizations including register allocation and instruction selection.

In the next section we define a vector core language with which to discuss the vectorization process. This core language is clean, uniform, and is almost exactly faithful to (a small subset of) our actual intermediate representation.

3. Vector Core language

We define here a small core language in which to present the vectorization optimization. We restrict ourselves to an intra-procedural fragment only, since for our purposes here we are not interested in inter-procedural control flow. Programs in the language are given as control-flow graphs written in a variant of static single-assignment (SSA) form. To keep things concrete, our language is based on a 32-bit machine with vector registers that are 256-bits wide; handling other register and vector widths is a straightforward extension.

3.1 Objects

The primitive objects of the vector core language consist of heap objects and register values. Heap objects are variable-length immutable arrays subscripted by 32-bit integers. The elements contained in the fields of heap objects are constrained to be 32-bit register values. Register values are small values that may be bound to variables and are implicitly represented at the machine level via registers or spill slots. The register values consist of 32-bit integers, 32-bit pointers to heap values, and 256-bit SIMD vectors each consisting of eight 32-bit register values. Adding additional primitive register values such as floating-pointer numbers, booleans, etc. is straightforward and adds nothing essential to the presentation.

3.2 Variables

Variables are divided into two classes according to size: scalar variables x^s that may only be bound to 32-bit register values and vector variables x^v that may only be bound to 256-bit vector values. In practice of course, a real intermediate language will also have additional variable sizes: 64-bit variables for doubles and 64-bit integers, and a range of vector widths possibly including 128- and 512-bit vectors. Note that the variables x^s and x^v are considered to be distinct variables. Informally, we will sometimes use x^v to denote the variable containing a vectorized version of an original program variable x^s—however, this is intended to be suggestive only and has no semantic significance.

3.3 Instructions

The instructions of the vector language serve to introduce and operate on the primitive objects of the language. Most of the instructions bind a new variable of the appropriate register kind, with the exception of the array-initialization instructions which write values into uninitialized array elements. The move instruction $z^s = c$ binds a variable to the 32-bit integer constant c. The vector introduction instruction $z^v = \langle x_0^s, \ldots, x_7^s \rangle$ binds the vector variable z^v to a vector composed of the contents of the eight listed 32-bit variables. We use the derived syntax $z^v = \langle c_0^s, \ldots, c_7^s \rangle$ to introduce a vector of constants—this may be derived in the obvious way by first binding each of the constants to a fresh 32-bit variable. A component of a vector may be selected out using the select instruction $z^s = x^v!i$, which binds z^s to the ith component of the vector in x^v (where i must be in the range $0 \ldots 7$).

The instruction $z^s = op(x_0^s, \ldots, x_n^s)$ corresponds to a family of instructions operating on primitive 32-bit integers, indexed by the operation op (e.g. addition, subtraction, negation etc.). Primitive operations must be fully saturated—that is, the number of operands provided must equal the arity of the given operation. We lift the primitive operations on integers to pointwise primitive operations on vectors with the $z^v = \langle op \rangle(x_0^v, \ldots, x_n^v)$ instruction, which applies op pointwise across the vectors. That is, semantically $z^v = \langle op \rangle(x_0^v, \ldots, x_n^v)$ behaves identically to a sequence of instructions performing the scalar version of op to each of the corresponding elements of the argument vectors, and then packaging up the result as the final result vector.

Array objects in the vector language are immutable sequences of 32-bit data allocated in the heap. New uninitialized array objects are allocated via the $z^s = \texttt{new}[x^s]$ instruction which allocates a new array of length x^s (where x^s must contain a 32-bit integer) and binds z^s to a pointer to the array. The initial contents of the array are undefined, and every element must be initialized before being read. It is an unchecked invariant of the language that every element of the array is initialized before it is read, and that every element of the array is initialized at most once. It is in this sense that the arrays are immutable—the write operation on arrays serves only as an initializing write but does not provide for mutation. Ordinary scalar element initialization is performed via the $x^s[y^s] \leftarrow z^s$ operation which initializes the element of array x^s at offset y^s to z^s. Scalar reads from the array are performed using the $z^s = x^s[y^s]$

instruction, which reads a single element from the array x^s at offset y^s and binds z^s to it.

In order to support SIMD vectorization, the vector language also provides a general set of vector subscript and initialization operations permitting vectors of elements to be read from and written to arrays (or vectors of arrays) in a single instruction. The set of instructions we provide are more general than what is supported by most existing machine architectures. This is done intentionally since it is often beneficial to vectorize a loop even if some instructions must be emulated via translation to scalar operations. Moreover, we believe it is useful to present the language in its most general form—it is always possible to restrict the set of generated instructions as desired. We defer discussion of the situations in which these various styles of loads and stores arise to subsequent sections on the actual vectorization operation.

The simplest vector array loads and stores are the operations that read multiple elements directly from a single array into a vector variable, or initialize multiple elements of a single array with elements contained in a vector variable. The instruction $z^v = x^s[\langle y^v \rangle]$ takes a single array x^s and a vector of offsets y^v and binds z^v to a vector containing the elements of x^s from the given offsets. That is, semantically we may treat the instruction $z^v = x^s[\langle y^v \rangle]$ as equivalent to the following list of instructions:

$$\begin{array}{ll} y_0^s & = y^v!0 \\ z_0^s & = x^s[y_0^s] \\ \ldots & \\ y_7^s & = y^v!7 \\ z_7^s & = x^s[y_7^s] \\ z^v & = \langle z_0^s, \ldots, z_7^s \rangle \end{array}$$

This instruction is commonly known as a "gather" instruction. The initializing store $x^s[\langle y^v \rangle] \leftarrow z^v$, commonly known as the "scatter" instruction, writes the elements of the vector z^v to the fields of x^s at offsets given by the vector y^v.

There are several interesting special cases of scatters and gathers that are worth further discussion. A common idiom that arises in SIMD vectorization consists of array loads and stores such that the index vector is constructed by adding multiples of a constant stride to a scalar index. We choose to introduce this idiom as derived syntax as follows, where i is a constant valued stride:

$$\begin{array}{c} z^v = x^s[\langle y^s{:}i \rangle] \stackrel{\text{def}}{=} z^v = x^s[\langle y^v \rangle] \\ x^s[\langle y^s{:}i \rangle] \leftarrow z^v \stackrel{\text{def}}{=} x^s[\langle y^v \rangle] \leftarrow z^v \\ \text{where} \quad \left\{ \begin{array}{l} y_l^v = \langle y^s, \ldots, y^s \rangle \\ y_b^v = \langle 0, \ldots, 7 * i \rangle \\ y^v = \langle + \rangle (y_l^v, y_b^v) \end{array} \right. \end{array}$$

Note that the stride multiplications (e.g. $7 * i$) are meta-level operations. We also provide derived syntax for the further special case in which the stride is known to be one:

$$\begin{array}{c} z^v = x^s[\langle y^s{:} \rangle] \stackrel{\text{def}}{=} z^v = x^s[\langle y^s{:}1 \rangle] \\ x^s[\langle y^s{:} \rangle] \leftarrow z^v \stackrel{\text{def}}{=} x^s[\langle y^s{:}1 \rangle] \leftarrow z^v \end{array}$$

For the purposes of simplicity of the vector language, we have left these as derived forms. However, it is worth noting that many architectures provide support for these idioms directly (and in fact may provide support *only* for these idioms) and hence from a pragmatic standpoint it can be important to provide primitive support for these addressing modes.

A second mode of addressing for array loads and stores covers the case where a vector of arrays is indexed pointwise by a single fixed scalar offset. The $z^v = \langle x^v \rangle [y^s]$ instruction produces a vector z^v such that the ith element of z^v is produced by indexing the ith array from the vector of arrays x^v, using offset y^s. Similarly, the $\langle x^v \rangle [y^s] \leftarrow z^v$ instruction sets the element of the ith array in the vector x^v at offset y^s to the value in the ith position of z^v.

The final mode of addressing for array loads and stores covers the case in which a vector of arrays is indexed pointwise using a vector of offsets. The $z^v = \langle x^v \rangle [\langle y^v \rangle]$ instruction produces a vector z^v such that the ith element is produced by indexing the ith array from the vector of arrays x^v using the ith offset from the vector of offsets y^v. Similarly, the $\langle x^v \rangle [\langle y^v \rangle] \leftarrow z^v$ instruction sets the element of the ith array in the vector x^v at the offset given by the ith element of the vector of offsets y^v to the value in the ith position of z^v.

3.4 Basic Blocks

Instructions are grouped into basic blocks consisting of a labeled entry, a sequence of instructions, and a transfer which terminates the block and either transfers control to another block or terminates the program. We assume an infinite supply of distinct program labels ranged over by metavariable L used to label basic blocks that we distinguish by numbering distinct labels with distinct integers (as $\mathtt{L}^0$, $\mathtt{L}^1$, etc.).

Basic block headers consist of the label of the block and a list of entry variables which are defined on entry to the block. The entry variables are given their defining values by the transfer which transfers control to the block. Block entry variables may have scalar or vector kind.

Transfers terminate basic blocks, and serve to transfer control within a program. The $\mathtt{goto}\ L(x_0^k, \ldots, x_n^k)$ transfer shifts control to the block labeled with L. Well-formed programs must have matching arities on transfers and the block headers which they target, that is, the block labeled with L must have entry variables $z_0^k, \ldots, z_n^k$. The transfer of control effected by $\mathtt{goto}\ L(x_0^k, \ldots, x_n^k)$ also defines the entry variables $z_0^k, \ldots, z_n^k$ to be the values of $x_0^k, \ldots, x_n^k$.

The conditional control transfer

$$\mathtt{if}\ (cmp)\ \mathtt{goto}\ L_0(x_0^k, \ldots, x_n^k)\ \mathtt{else\ goto}\ L_1(y_0^k, \ldots, y_m^k)$$

behaves as $\mathtt{goto}\ L_0(x_0^k, \ldots, x_n^k)$ if the comparison holds, and as $\mathtt{goto}\ L_1(y_0^k, \ldots, y_m^k)$ if the comparison does not hold. Note that the targets of the two different arms of the conditional are not required to be distinct.

The `halt` transfer terminates the program. We do not consider inter-procedural control-flow in this core language since it is not relevant to the vectorization optimization—however it is straightforward to add additional transfers to account for this if desired.

3.5 Programs

Programs in the core language consist of a single control flow graph. A control flow graph consists of a designated entry label L and set of associated basic blocks, each with a distinct label, one of which (the entry block) is labeled with the entry label L. The entry block must expect no entry variables. Program execution proceeds by starting at the designated entry block and executing block instructions and transfers until a `halt` instruction is reached (if ever). Well-formed programs must not contain transfers whose target label is not in the control-flow graph, and every block in the control-flow graph must be labeled with a distinct label. As usual with static single-assignment form, variables may only be defined once, must be defined before their first use, and have scope given by the dominator tree of the control-flow graph rooted at the entry label. The style of static single-assignment form used in this core language is similar to that used in compilers such as the MLton compiler [16].

4. Vectorization

The SIMD-vectorization optimization attempts to rewrite a loop to a new loop that executes multiple iterations of the original loop on each iteration using SIMD instructions and registers. While the core idea is quite simple, there are a number of issues that must be addressed in order to preserve the semantics of the original program. In the first part of this section we introduce the key issues using a series of examples. Before doing so, we first review some preliminary concepts.

4.1 Loops

We have informally described our vectorization efforts as focusing on loops. Loops tend to account for a high proportion of executed instructions in programs, and as such are natural targets for introducing SIMD-vector code. We define loops using the standard notion of a natural loop, merging loops with shared headers in the usual way to ensure that the nesting structure of loops form a tree. We do not assume a reducible control-flow graph (since in general the translation of mutually-recursive functions into loops may introduce irreducible control flow). We focus our vectorization efforts more specifically on the innermost loops that make up the leaves of the loop forest of the control-flow graph. For simplicity, we only target bottom-test loops. A separate optimization pass inverts top-test loops to form bottom-test loops, both to enable vectorization and loop-invariant code motion.

4.2 Induction variables

Our notion of induction variable is standard, but we review it in some detail here since induction variables play a critical role in our algorithm. We define the *base* induction variables of a loop to be the entry variables of the entry block of the loop such that the definition of that variable provided on the loop back edge is produced by adding a constant to the variable itself, and where the initial value passed into the loop is a compile-time constant. The *step* of a base induction variable is the constant added each time around the loop. The full set of induction variables is the least set of variables satisfying:

- A base induction variable is an induction variable.
- A variable defined by $x^s = +(y^s, z^s)$, where y^s is an induction variable and z^s is a constant (defined by $z^s = c$), is an induction variable.
- A variable defined by $x^s = *(y^s, z^s)$, where y^s is an induction variable and z^s is a constant, is an induction variable.

Our implementation also deals with the symmetric versions of the last two cases, and also considers operations such as subtraction and negation. Arbitrary initial values can be allowed for base induction variables and loop invariants can be allowed in place of constants at the cost of some additional complexity as discussed below, but we do not currently support this.

Induction variables can be characterized as affine functions of the iteration count of the loop. The characteristic function for an induction variable i^s is an equation of the form $i^s = p*\#+d$ where p is a constant (the step of the induction variable), and d is also a constant (the initial value of the induction variable). The symbol $\#$ stands for the iteration number: the value of the induction variable i^s for iteration j can be computed directly from its characteristic function simply by replacing $\#$ with j.

The characteristic function for an induction variable is derived as follows:

- The characteristic function of a base induction variable is $p * \# + d$ where p is the step of the base induction variable as defined above, and d is the constant initial value of the induction variable.
- The characteristic function of an induction variable defined by $x^s = +(y^s, z^s)$ is $p*\#+d+c$ where z^s is a constant (defined by $z^s = c$), and $p * \# + d$ is the characteristic function of y^s.
- The characteristic function of an induction variable defined by $x^s = *(y^s, z^s)$ is $c*p*\#+c*d$ where z^s is a constant (defined by $z^s = c$), and $p * \# + d$ is the characteristic function of y^s.

A subtle but important point is that in these computations the compiler must ensure that the overflow semantics of the underlying numeric type are respected to avoid introducing or eliminating numeric overflow. It is possible to extend the definition of characteristic functions to allow loop invariants to take the place of the constants in the above definition at the expense of representing the characteristic function symbolically, thereby somewhat complicating code generation and overflow avoidance as discussed below.

4.3 Vectorization by example

Consider the following simple program which computes the pointwise sum of two arrays b^s and c^s, each of length l^s.

$$
\begin{array}{ll}
\texttt{L}^0(): & \texttt{L}^1(i^s): \\
\quad a^s = \texttt{new}[l^s] & \quad x^s = b^s[i^s] \\
\quad i_0^s = 0 & \quad y^s = c^s[i^s] \\
\quad \texttt{goto L}^1(i_0^s) & \quad z^s = +(x^s, y^s) \\
 & \quad a^s[i^s] \leftarrow z^s \\
 & \quad i_1^s = +(i^s, 1) \\
 & \quad \texttt{if } (i_1^s < l^s) \texttt{ goto L}^1(i_1^s) \\
 & \qquad\qquad \texttt{else goto L}^{\text{exit}}(i_1^s)
\end{array} \tag{1}
$$

Ignoring the crucial issue of whether or not it is in fact *valid* to vectorize this loop, there are a number of issues that need to be addressed in order to produce a vector version of this program.

4.3.1 The vector loop

The core of the vectorization optimization is to produce an inner loop, each iteration of which executes multiple iterations of the original loop. For Example 1, this corresponds to generating code to vector-load eight elements of the arrays b and c at appropriate offsets, perform a pointwise vector addition of the loaded elements, and to perform a vector write of the eight result elements into the new array a. The comparison which controls the exit test at the bottom of the loop must also be adjusted appropriately to account for the fact that multiple iterations are being performed. Finally, on the exit edge of the loop, the use of the last value of the induction variable i_1^s must also be accounted for.

To motivate the general treatment of the vectorization optimization, we first consider the individual instructions of Example 1, beginning with the load instruction $x^s = b^s[i^s]$. Executing this instruction during iteration j of the loop loads a single element from the array b^s at an offset given by the value of i^s. In the vector loop, we wish to perform iterations $j, j+1, \ldots, j+7$ simultaneously. The vector version of this instruction then must load eight elements from b^s at offsets given by the values of i^s at iteration $j, j+1, \ldots, j+7$ A natural first attempt at vectorization might be to simply assume that vector versions of all variables are available, and to then generate the corresponding vector instruction using the vector variables. In this case, if we assume the existence of variables b^v and i^v containing the values of b^s and i^s for iterations $j, \ldots, j+7$ then the vector instruction $x^v = \langle b^v \rangle [\langle i^v \rangle]$ puts into x^v the appropriate values of x^s for iterations $j, \ldots, j+7$.

While this approach is correct (and in the most general case is sometimes necessary) a key insight in SIMD vectorization is that it is often possible to do much better by using knowledge of loop invariants and induction variables. In this case, the variable b^s is loop invariant, and consequently b^v will consist simply of eight copies of the same value. Semantically then, we can replace our use of the general vector load instruction with the simpler gather instruction $x^v = b^s[\langle i^v \rangle]$, which does not require us to produce the vector version of b^s and which may also have a more efficient implementation. More importantly, the variable i^s here is a base induction variable with step 1. It is consequently possible to predict the value of i^s at each of the next eight iterations: that is, the value of i^v will always be $\langle i^s, i^s{+}1, \ldots, i^s{+}7 \rangle$. The vector load can then be seen to be a load of eight contiguous elements from b^s, for which we have provided the derived instruction $x^v = b^s[\langle i^s{:}\rangle]$, which performs a contiguous load of eight elements, as desired. Since this form of load is generally well supported in vector hardware, generating this specialized form in preference to the general form is highly desirable.

The second load instruction can then be vectorized in an exactly analogous fashion, resulting in two vector variables x^v and y^v. The addition instruction $z^s = +(x^s, y^s)$ can then be computed using vector addition on the vector variables, as $z^v = \langle + \rangle(x^v, y^v)$. To produce a vector version of the instruction $a^s[i^s] \leftarrow z^s$ which writes the computed value to the new array we follow a similar argument to that above for the loads to produce the $a^s[\langle i^s{:}\rangle] \leftarrow z^v$ instruction which performs a contiguous write of the values in z^v into the array a^s starting at offset i^s.

The last instruction of the loop, $i_1^s = +(i^s, 1)$, is the induction variable computation, and as such requires special treatment. The result of this instruction is used for three purposes: in the computation of the test to decide whether to proceed with another iteration, to provide a new value for the induction variable in the next iteration, and to provide the value passed out on the exit edge.

For the latter two uses, the required value is easy to see. Each iteration of the vector loop corresponds to eight iterations of the scalar loop, and we require on entry to the loop that the induction variable i^s contain the value appropriate for the first of the eight iterations. Given the value of i^s for iteration j then, the back edge of the loop requires the value of i_1^s for iteration $j+7$, which is one plus the value of i^s on iteration $j+7$. Similarly, the exit edge of the loop requires the value of i_1^s at iteration $j{+}7$. Since the computation of the value of i^s for each iteration depends on the value of itself in the previous iteration, we might imagine ourselves to be stuck. However, the nature of induction variables as affine transformations means that we can compute the value of i_1^s at iteration $j{+}7$ directly: each iteration adds 1 to the original value, hence the value of i^s at iteration $j+7$ is given by $i^s + 7$, and the value of i_1^s at iteration $j+7$ is $i^s + 7 + 1$. Hence we can compute the appropriate value of i_1^s for both the back and the exit edge as $i^s + 8$.

The remaining use of the induction variable i_1^s is to compute the loop exit test. The key insight is that it is no longer sufficient to check that there is at least one iteration remaining: in order to execute the vector loop again, we must have at least eight remaining iterations. Upon completion of a vector iteration computing scalar iterations $j, \ldots, j+7$, the question that must be answered is whether the scalar loop would always execute iterations $j+8, \ldots, j+15$. Because of the monotonic nature of the induction variable computation this in turn can be reduced to the question of whether or not the value of i_1^s at iteration $j+14$ is less than l^s. Since i_1^s is an induction variable which is incremented by 1 on each iteration, this corresponds to changing the exit test to ask whether $i^s + 15 < l^s$.

4.3.2 Entry and exit code

Using the ideas from previous section, it is straightforward to write a vector version of the core loop. In addition to the issues touched on above, vectorizing this example also requires accounting for the possibility that there may be insufficient iterations to allow use of the vector loop, and also for the possibility that there may be extra iterations left over if the exit test succeeds with fewer than eight but more than zero iterations left. To account for these we keep around the original scalar loop, and use it to perform any iterations that cannot be computed with the vector loop. A preliminary test is inserted before the loop choosing either to target the scalar loop (if less than eight total iterations will be performed) or the vector loop (otherwise). Similarly, after the vector loop exits, a check is done for the presence of extra iterations, which if required are again performed using the scalar loop.

Using these transformations, we arrive at the final desired vectorized program.

$$
\begin{array}{ll}
\mathtt{L}^0(): & \mathtt{L}^{\text{check}}(): \\
\quad a^s = \mathtt{new}[l^s] & \\
\quad i_0^s = 0 & \quad \mathtt{if}\ (i_3^s < l^s)\ \mathtt{goto}\ \mathtt{L}^1(i_3^s) \\
\quad \mathtt{if}\ (7 < l^s)\ \mathtt{goto}\ \mathtt{L}^2(i_0^s) & \qquad \mathtt{else\ goto}\ \mathtt{L}^{\text{exit}}(i_3^s) \\
\qquad \mathtt{else\ goto}\ \mathtt{L}^1(i_0^s) & \\
 & \\
\mathtt{L}^2(i_2^s): & \mathtt{L}^1(i^s): \\
\quad x^v = b^s[\langle i_2^s{:}\rangle] & \quad x^s = b^s[i^s] \\
\quad y^v = c^s[\langle i_2^s{:}\rangle] & \quad y^s = c^s[i^s] \\
\quad z^v = \langle + \rangle(x^v, y^v) & \quad z^s = +(x^s, y^s) \\
\quad a^s[\langle i_2^s{:}\rangle] \leftarrow z^v & \quad a^s[i^s] \leftarrow z^s \\
\quad i_3^s = +(i_2^s, 8) & \quad i_1^s = +(i^s, 1) \\
\quad i_4^s = +(i_2^s, 15) & \quad \mathtt{if}\ (i_1^s < l^s)\ \mathtt{goto}\ \mathtt{L}^1(i_1^s) \\
\quad \mathtt{if}\ (i_4^s < l^s)\ \mathtt{goto}\ \mathtt{L}^2(i_3^s) & \qquad \mathtt{else\ goto}\ \mathtt{L}^{\text{exit}}(i_1^s) \\
\qquad \mathtt{else\ goto}\ \mathtt{L}^{\text{check}}() &
\end{array}
\qquad (2)
$$

4.4 Automatic vectorization

The reasoning of the previous section leads us to the desired result, but seems completely ad hoc and unsuitable to implementation in a compiler. Fortunately, it is possible to derive a simple compositional transformation which accomplishes the same thing in a general manner.

The essential design principles that guide the design of the optimization are those of orthogonality and compositionality. As we will see, while the local transformation of instructions produces specialized code depending on the particulars of the instruction, each instruction is nonetheless translated in a compositional fashion in the sense that the translation does not depend on how the result is used. A consequence of this choice is that the compositional translation may produce numerous extraneous, redundant, or loop-invariant instructions, which could be avoided in a less compositional approach. The principle that we follow is that the elimination of extraneous, redundant, and loop-invariant instructions is an orthogonal issue, which is already addressed by dead-code elimination, common sub-expression elimination, and loop-invariant code motion respectively. So long as the vectorization transformation is defined appropriately, we can safely rely on these optimizations to sweep away the chaff, leaving behind only the essential bits.

The core of the vector transformation works by translating each scalar instruction into a sequence of instructions which compute three separate values: the scalar value, the vector value, and the last value. For a vector loop computing iterations $j, \ldots, j+7$ of a scalar loop, the scalar value of a variable x is the value computed at iteration j, the last value is the value computed at iteration $j{+}7$, and the vector value is the vector containing the computed values for all of the iterations. While it is clear that there is always a degenerate implementation that simply computes the vector variable and then computes the scalar and last values by projecting out the first and last iteration value, we often compute the scalar and last values separately. This is crucial for a number of reasons: in the first place, we may be able to compute the vector variable more efficiently as a direct function of the scalar value; but more importantly, it will frequently be the case that the vector variable (or similarly the last value) will be unused. It is therefore important not to introduce a data-dependence of the scalar (or last) value on the vector value lest we keep an expensive-to-compute vector value live unnecessarily.

For clarity in the translation, we define meta-operators for producing fresh variables from existing scalar variables. For a variable x^s, we take ${}^{\mathsf{fv}}x^s$ to be a fresh scalar variable, which by convention will contain the scalar value of x^s in the vector loop. Similarly, we take ${}^{\mathsf{lv}}x^s$ to be a fresh scalar variable, which by convention will contain the last value of x^s; and we take ${}^{\mathsf{vv}}x^v$ to be a fresh vector variable, which by convention will contain the vector value of x^s.

Induction variables require a small amount of additional mechanism. For every base induction variable i^s with step s, we say that the *affine basis* of i^s is the vector $\langle 0*s, 1*s, \ldots, 7*s\rangle$ (the multiplications here are at the meta-level). Note that for a base induction variable i^s, adding i^s to each of the elements of its affine basis gives the values of i^s for each of the next eight iterations. Other (non-base) induction variables also have affine bases, which are computed by code emitted as part of the transformation described below, starting from the bases of the base induction variables. We use the notation ${}^{\mathsf{bv}}i^v$ to denote a fresh variable which by convention holds the affine basis for the scalar induction variable i^s.

It is occasionally necessary to introduce a *promoted* version of a variable: that is, for a variable x^s, to produce a vector variable containing the vector $\langle x^s, \ldots, x^s\rangle$. By convention, we use ${}^{\mathsf{pv}}x^v$ to denote a fresh variable containing the promoted version of x^s.

In order to simplify the algorithm, it is convenient to apply it only to loops for which all variables defined in the loop and used outside of the loop (that is, live out from the loop) are explicitly passed as parameters on the exit edge. This is in no way necessary, but avoids the need to rename variables throughout the rest of the program to preserve the SSA property. This does not restrict the generality of the algorithm since it is always possible to transform loops into this form.

The algorithm applies to single block loops of the form

$$
\begin{array}{l}
L(i_0^s, \ldots, i_n^s):\\
\quad I_0\\
\quad \ldots\\
\quad I_m\\
\quad \texttt{if } (i^s < l^s) \texttt{ goto } L(i_{01}^s, \ldots, i_{n1}^s)\\
\qquad\qquad \texttt{else goto } L^{\text{exit}}(x_0^s, \ldots, x_p^s)
\end{array}
$$

where the variables $i_0^s, \ldots, i_n^s$ are base induction variables, i^s is an induction variable with a positive step (the case where the step is zero or negative make no sense), and the variables $x_0^s, \ldots, x_p^s$ are the live out variables of the loop. All the instructions $I_0, \ldots, I_m$ must be scalar instructions (and thus define scalar variables), and cannot create new arrays. It is straightforward to support exit tests of the form $i^s \le l^s$ as well. In all cases, the variable l^s must be defined outside of the loop (and hence be loop invariant).

We assume the loop has a preheader,[2] that is a block that ends with $\texttt{goto } L(ii_0^s, \ldots, ii_n^s)$ and that only this block and the loop transfer to L.

As suggested by the ad hoc development from the previous section, the vectorization transformation must produce three new pieces of code: an entry test that decides whether there are sufficient iterations to enter the vector loop; the core vector loop itself that performs the SIMD iterations; and a cleanup test that checks if there are any iterations remaining after the SIMD loop has finished, which must be processed by the original scalar loop which remains in the program unchanged. By convention we take L^{vec} and L^{check} to be fresh labels for the new vector loop and cleanup test respectively.

[2] Assuming preheaders does not restrict our algorithm - transforming a program into an equivalent one where all loops have preheaders is a standard technique.

4.4.1 Entry tests

The job of the entry test is to determine if there are sufficient iterations to execute the vector loop, and if not to go straight to the original scalar loop. It also needs to set up some initial values for use in the vector loop. In particular, any variables used in the loop but not defined in the loop must have scalar, last value, and vector versions for use by the instructions in the vector loop.

First, for each variable y^s used in the loop but not defined in it (and not an entry variable), we add the following instructions to the end of the instructions of the preheader:

$$
\begin{array}{l}
{}^{\mathsf{fv}}y^s = y^s\\
{}^{\mathsf{lv}}y^s = y^s\\
{}^{\mathsf{vv}}y^v = \langle y^s, \ldots, y^s\rangle
\end{array}
$$

Next, we must determine whether the vector loop should be entered at all. The desired property of the entry test is that the vector loop should only be entered if there are at least 8 iterations to be performed. The monotonic nature of induction variables means that this question is equivalent to asking whether at least one more iteration remains after performing the first 7 iterations: that is, we wish to know the result of the exit test of the original loop on the 7th iteration. If the characteristic function for i^s is $s * \# + d$, then the value of i^s on the 7th iteration can be obtained by replacing $\#$ with 6 and calculating the result statically. The appropriate entry test is then of the form $ii^s < l^s$ where ii^s is defined as $ii^s = s * 6 + d$.

The value $s * 6 + c$ is a compiler computed constant, and the compiler can statically determine that this does not overflow. If we generalize the notion of characteristic function to include loop-invariants in addition to constants this test may require generating multiplication and addition instructions, and code must also be emitted to fall back to the scalar code if there is a possibility that the additional arithmetic might overflow.

4.4.2 Vector loop

To generate code for the main vector loop, we perform three operations. We first generate the last value and vector versions of base induction variables, using their steps to produce these directly from the scalar values. For each of the original instructions of the loop we then generate instructions to compute the scalar, vector, and last value versions of the instruction. Finally, we adjust the exit test.

For each entry variable i_j^s for $0 \le j \le n$, which is a base induction variable of step s_j, we produce the vector, basis, promoted, and last value versions of the induction variable as follows. The basis variable and promoted variables ${}^{\mathsf{bv}}i_j^v$ and ${}^{\mathsf{pv}}i_j^v$ are defined as

$$
\begin{array}{l}
{}^{\mathsf{bv}}i_j^v = \langle 0 * s_j, \ldots, 7 * s_j\rangle\\
{}^{\mathsf{pv}}i_j^v = \langle {}^{\mathsf{fv}}i_j^s, \ldots, {}^{\mathsf{fv}}i_j^s\rangle
\end{array}
$$

The vector version of i_j^s can then be defined directly as follows and the last value ${}^{\mathsf{lv}}i_j^s$ can be defined directly using the step.

$$
\begin{array}{l}
{}^{\mathsf{vv}}i_j^v = \langle + \rangle({}^{\mathsf{bv}}i_j^v, {}^{\mathsf{pv}}i_j^v)\\
{}^{\mathsf{lv}}i_j^s = +({}^{\mathsf{fv}}i_j^s, 7 * s_j)
\end{array}
$$

This initial step defines vector and last value variables for each base induction variable of the loop, as well as basis and promoted variables. The translation of each instruction then proceeds compositionally, with the translated version of each instruction making use of the vector and last value variables produced by the translation of all of the previous instructions. In addition, each induction variable makes use of the previously defined basis variables to produce its own vector, last value, basis, and promoted variables directly. The complete definition of this translation is given in Figure 2.

Adjusting the exit test of the loop is again straightforward using the step information. The desired new exit test must check whether

Instruction	Vector translation	Side conditions
$z^s = c$	${}^{\mathsf{fv}}z^s = c$ ${}^{\mathsf{vv}}z^v = \langle {}^{\mathsf{fv}}z^s, \ldots, {}^{\mathsf{fv}}z^s \rangle$ ${}^{\mathsf{lv}}z^s = {}^{\mathsf{fv}}z^s$	
$z^s = +(x^s, y^s)$	${}^{\mathsf{fv}}z^s = +({}^{\mathsf{fv}}x^s, {}^{\mathsf{fv}}y^s)$ ${}^{\mathsf{bv}}z^v = {}^{\mathsf{bv}}x^v$ ${}^{\mathsf{pv}}z^v = \langle {}^{\mathsf{fv}}z^s, \ldots, {}^{\mathsf{fv}}z^s \rangle$ ${}^{\mathsf{vv}}z^v = \langle + \rangle ({}^{\mathsf{bv}}z^v, {}^{\mathsf{pv}}z^v)$ ${}^{\mathsf{lv}}z^s = +({}^{\mathsf{lv}}x^s, {}^{\mathsf{fv}}y^s)$	If z^s and x^s are induction variables.
$z^s = *(x^s, y^s)$	${}^{\mathsf{fv}}z^s = *({}^{\mathsf{fv}}x^s, {}^{\mathsf{fv}}y^s)$ ${}^{\mathsf{bv}}z^v = \langle * \rangle ({}^{\mathsf{bv}}x^v, {}^{\mathsf{vv}}y^v)$ ${}^{\mathsf{pv}}z^v = \langle {}^{\mathsf{fv}}z^s, \ldots, {}^{\mathsf{fv}}z^s \rangle$ ${}^{\mathsf{vv}}z^v = \langle + \rangle ({}^{\mathsf{bv}}z^v, {}^{\mathsf{pv}}z^v)$ ${}^{\mathsf{lv}}z^s = *({}^{\mathsf{lv}}x^s, {}^{\mathsf{fv}}y^s)$	If z^s and x^s are induction variables.
$z^s = op(x_0^s, \ldots, x_n^s)$	${}^{\mathsf{fv}}z^s = op({}^{\mathsf{fv}}x_0^s, \ldots, {}^{\mathsf{fv}}x_n^s)$ ${}^{\mathsf{vv}}z^v = \langle op \rangle ({}^{\mathsf{vv}}x_0^v, \ldots, {}^{\mathsf{vv}}x_n^v)$ ${}^{\mathsf{lv}}z^s = op({}^{\mathsf{lv}}x_0^s, \ldots, {}^{\mathsf{lv}}x_n^s)$	If z^s is not an induction variable.
$z^s = x^s[y^s]$	${}^{\mathsf{fv}}z^s = {}^{\mathsf{fv}}x^s[{}^{\mathsf{fv}}y^s]$ ${}^{\mathsf{vv}}z^v = {}^{\mathsf{fv}}x^s[\langle {}^{\mathsf{fv}}y^s{:}\rangle]$ ${}^{\mathsf{lv}}z^s = {}^{\mathsf{fv}}x^s[{}^{\mathsf{lv}}y^s]$	If x^s is loop invariant, and y^s is an induction variable with step 1.
$z^s = x^s[y^s]$	${}^{\mathsf{fv}}z^s = {}^{\mathsf{fv}}x^s[{}^{\mathsf{fv}}y^s]$ ${}^{\mathsf{vv}}z^v = {}^{\mathsf{fv}}x^s[\langle {}^{\mathsf{fv}}y^s{:}i\rangle]$ ${}^{\mathsf{lv}}z^s = {}^{\mathsf{fv}}x^s[{}^{\mathsf{lv}}y^s]$	If x^s is loop invariant, and y^s is affine with step i
$z^s = x^s[y^s]$	${}^{\mathsf{fv}}z^s = {}^{\mathsf{fv}}x^s[{}^{\mathsf{fv}}y^s]$ ${}^{\mathsf{vv}}z^v = {}^{\mathsf{fv}}x^s[\langle {}^{\mathsf{vv}}y^v\rangle]$ ${}^{\mathsf{lv}}z^s = {}^{\mathsf{fv}}x^s[{}^{\mathsf{lv}}y^s]$	If x^s is loop invariant, and y^s is not an induction variable.
$z^s = x^s[y^s]$	${}^{\mathsf{fv}}z^s = {}^{\mathsf{fv}}x^s[{}^{\mathsf{fv}}y^s]$ ${}^{\mathsf{vv}}z^v = \langle {}^{\mathsf{vv}}x^v\rangle[{}^{\mathsf{fv}}y^s]$ ${}^{\mathsf{lv}}z^s = {}^{\mathsf{lv}}x^s[{}^{\mathsf{fv}}y^s]$	If x^s is not loop invariant, and y^s is loop invariant.
$z^s = x^s[y^s]$	${}^{\mathsf{fv}}z^s = {}^{\mathsf{fv}}x^s[{}^{\mathsf{fv}}y^s]$ ${}^{\mathsf{vv}}z^v = \langle {}^{\mathsf{vv}}x^v\rangle[\langle {}^{\mathsf{vv}}y^v\rangle]$ ${}^{\mathsf{lv}}z^s = {}^{\mathsf{lv}}x^s[{}^{\mathsf{lv}}y^s]$	If both x^s and y^s are not loop invariant.
$x^s[y^s] \leftarrow z^s$	${}^{\mathsf{fv}}x^s[\langle {}^{\mathsf{fv}}y^s{:}\rangle] \leftarrow {}^{\mathsf{vv}}z^v$	If x^s is loop invariant, and y^s is an induction variable with step 1.
$x^s[y^s] \leftarrow z^s$	${}^{\mathsf{fv}}x^s[\langle {}^{\mathsf{fv}}y^s{:}i\rangle] \leftarrow {}^{\mathsf{vv}}z^v$	If x^s is loop invariant, and y^s is an induction variable with step i.
$x^s[y^s] \leftarrow z^s$	${}^{\mathsf{fv}}x^s[\langle {}^{\mathsf{vv}}y^v\rangle] \leftarrow {}^{\mathsf{vv}}z^v$	If x^s is loop invariant, and y^s is not an induction variable.
$x^s[y^s] \leftarrow z^s$	$\langle {}^{\mathsf{vv}}x^v\rangle[{}^{\mathsf{fv}}y^s] \leftarrow {}^{\mathsf{vv}}z^v$	If x^s is not loop invariant, and y^s is loop invariant.
$x^s[y^s] \leftarrow z^s$	$\langle {}^{\mathsf{vv}}x^v\rangle[\langle {}^{\mathsf{vv}}y^v\rangle] \leftarrow {}^{\mathsf{vv}}z^v$	If both x^s and y^s are not loop invariant.

Figure 2. Vector Block Instruction Translation

$i^s < l^s$ would succeed for at least eight more iterations. Since i^s is an induction variable, letting s be its step, it increases by s on each iteration. Thus the value of i^s on the next eight iterations will be ${}^{\mathsf{lv}}i^s + 0 * s, \ldots, {}^{\mathsf{lv}}i^s + 7 * s$. These will all be less than l^s if the last of them is less than l^s (recall that l^s is loop invariant). Thus the desired new exit condition is ${}^{\mathsf{lv}}i^s + 7 * s < l^s$.

Putting this all together the vector loop will be as follows, where i'^s is a fresh variable:

$L^{\text{vec}}({}^{\mathsf{fv}}i_0^s, \ldots, {}^{\mathsf{fv}}i_n^s)$:
  Instructions for base induction variables
  Transformed $I_0, \ldots, I_m$
  $i'^s = +({}^{\mathsf{lv}}i^s, 7 * s)$
  if $(i'^s < l^s)$ **goto** $L^{\text{vec}}({}^{\mathsf{lv}}i_{01}^s, \ldots, {}^{\mathsf{lv}}i_{n1}^s)$
    else goto $L^{\text{check}}()$

Note that the back edge targets the vector loop, the exit edge targets the cleanup check, and the last values of the base induction variables are passed on the back edge.

4.4.3 On the subject of overflow

For the most part, the vectorization transformation here is careful to only compute the same values computed in the original program. Generating entry and exit tests violate this property. As mentioned in Section 4.4.1, the compiler can check statically that overflow does not occur when computing constants for the initial entry test. For the exit test, it is sufficient to check before entry to the vector loop that $l^s < \mathrm{MI} - 7 * s$ where MI is the largest representable integer and s is the step of i^s. For signed types, this check must be adjusted in the obvious way when loop bounds or steps are negative. In all cases, if the checks fail then the original scalar loop is used to perform the calculation using the original code.

4.4.4 Cleanup check

The cleanup check is responsible for determining if scalar iterations remain to be performed after the vector loop has exited. This is done simply by performing the original loop exit test. Scalar iterations remain to be performed exactly when ${}^{\mathsf{lv}}i^s < l^s$, where ${}^{\mathsf{lv}}i^s$ is the last value for i^s computed in the vector loop (since this represents the

Entry test	Vector loop	Cleanup check	Optimized result
$\mathtt{L}^0()$: $a^s = \mathtt{new}[l^s]$ $i_0^s = 0$ ${}^{\mathsf{fv}}a^s = a^s$ ${}^{\mathsf{vv}}a^v = \langle a^s, \ldots, a^s \rangle$ ${}^{\mathsf{lv}}a^s = a^s$ ${}^{\mathsf{fv}}b^s = b^s$ ${}^{\mathsf{vv}}b^v = \langle b^s, \ldots, b^s \rangle$ ${}^{\mathsf{lv}}b^s = b^s$ ${}^{\mathsf{fv}}c^s = c^s$ ${}^{\mathsf{vv}}c^v = \langle c^s, \ldots, c^s \rangle$ ${}^{\mathsf{lv}}c^s = c^s$ ${}^{\mathsf{fv}}l^s = l^s$ ${}^{\mathsf{vv}}l^v = \langle l^s, \ldots, l^s \rangle$ ${}^{\mathsf{lv}}l^s = l^s$ $ii^s = 6 * 1 + 1$ $\mathtt{if}\ (ii^s < l^s)\ \mathtt{goto}\ \mathtt{L}^2(i_0^s)$ $\mathtt{else\ goto}\ \mathtt{L}^1(i_0^s)$	$\mathtt{L}^2({}^{\mathsf{fv}}i^s)$: ${}^{\mathsf{bv}}i^v = \langle 0 * 1, \ldots, 7 * 1 \rangle$ ${}^{\mathsf{pv}}i^v = \langle {}^{\mathsf{fv}}i^s, \ldots, {}^{\mathsf{fv}}i^s \rangle$ ${}^{\mathsf{vv}}i^v = \langle + \rangle({}^{\mathsf{bv}}i^v, {}^{\mathsf{pv}}i^v)$ ${}^{\mathsf{lv}}i^s = +({}^{\mathsf{fv}}i^s, 7 * 1)$ ${}^{\mathsf{fv}}x^s = {}^{\mathsf{fv}}b^s[{}^{\mathsf{fv}}i^s]$ ${}^{\mathsf{vv}}x^v = {}^{\mathsf{fv}}b^s[\langle {}^{\mathsf{fv}}i^s : \rangle]$ ${}^{\mathsf{lv}}x^s = {}^{\mathsf{fv}}b^s[{}^{\mathsf{lv}}i^s]$ ${}^{\mathsf{fv}}y^s = {}^{\mathsf{fv}}c^s[{}^{\mathsf{fv}}i^s]$ ${}^{\mathsf{vv}}y^v = {}^{\mathsf{fv}}c^s[\langle {}^{\mathsf{fv}}i^s : \rangle]$ ${}^{\mathsf{lv}}y^s = {}^{\mathsf{fv}}c^s[{}^{\mathsf{lv}}i^s]$ ${}^{\mathsf{fv}}z^s = +({}^{\mathsf{fv}}x^s, {}^{\mathsf{fv}}y^s)$ ${}^{\mathsf{vv}}z^v = \langle + \rangle({}^{\mathsf{vv}}x^v, {}^{\mathsf{vv}}y^v)$ ${}^{\mathsf{lv}}z^s = +({}^{\mathsf{lv}}x^s, {}^{\mathsf{lv}}y^s)$ ${}^{\mathsf{fv}}a^s[\langle {}^{\mathsf{fv}}i^s : \rangle] \leftarrow {}^{\mathsf{vv}}z^v$ ${}^{\mathsf{fv}}i_1^s = +({}^{\mathsf{fv}}i^s, 1)$ ${}^{\mathsf{bv}}i_1^v = {}^{\mathsf{bv}}i^v$ ${}^{\mathsf{pv}}i_1^v = \langle {}^{\mathsf{fv}}i_1^s, \ldots, {}^{\mathsf{fv}}i_1^s \rangle$ ${}^{\mathsf{vv}}i_1^v = \langle + \rangle({}^{\mathsf{bv}}i_1^v, {}^{\mathsf{pv}}i_1^v)$ ${}^{\mathsf{lv}}i_1^s = +({}^{\mathsf{lv}}i^s, 1)$ $i_1'^s = +({}^{\mathsf{lv}}i_1^s, 7 * 1)$ $\mathtt{if}\ (i_1'^s < l^s)\ \mathtt{goto}\ \mathtt{L}^2({}^{\mathsf{lv}}i_1^s)$ $\mathtt{else\ goto}\ \mathtt{L}^{\mathrm{check}}()$	$\mathtt{L}^{\mathrm{check}}()$: $i_2^s = +({}^{\mathsf{fv}}i^s, 7 * 1)$ $i_3^s = +(i_2^s, 1)$ $\mathtt{if}\ (i_3^s < l^s)\ \mathtt{goto}\ \mathtt{L}^1(i_3^s)$ $\mathtt{else\ goto}\ \mathtt{L}^{\mathrm{exit}}(i_3^s)$	$\mathtt{L}^0()$: $a^s = \mathtt{new}[l^s]$ $i_0^s = 0$ $ii^s = 7$ $\mathtt{if}\ (ii^s < l^s)\ \mathtt{goto}\ \mathtt{L}^2(i_0^s)$ $\mathtt{else\ goto}\ \mathtt{L}^1(i_0^s)$ $\mathtt{L}^2({}^{\mathsf{fv}}i^s)$: ${}^{\mathsf{lv}}i^s = +({}^{\mathsf{fv}}i^s, 7)$ ${}^{\mathsf{vv}}x^v = b^s[\langle {}^{\mathsf{fv}}i^s : \rangle]$ ${}^{\mathsf{vv}}y^v = c^s[\langle {}^{\mathsf{fv}}i^s : \rangle]$ ${}^{\mathsf{vv}}z^v = \langle + \rangle({}^{\mathsf{vv}}x^v, {}^{\mathsf{vv}}y^v)$ $a^s[\langle {}^{\mathsf{fv}}i^s : \rangle] \leftarrow {}^{\mathsf{vv}}z^v$ ${}^{\mathsf{lv}}i_1^s = +({}^{\mathsf{lv}}i^s, 1)$ $i_1'^s = +({}^{\mathsf{lv}}i_1^s, 7)$ $\mathtt{if}\ (i_1'^s < l^s)\ \mathtt{goto}\ \mathtt{L}^2({}^{\mathsf{lv}}i_1^s)$ $\mathtt{else\ goto}\ \mathtt{L}^{\mathrm{check}}()$ $\mathtt{L}^{\mathrm{check}}()$: $i_2^s = +({}^{\mathsf{fv}}i^s, 7)$ $i_3^s = +(i_2^s, 1)$ $\mathtt{if}\ (i_3^s < l^s)\ \mathtt{goto}\ \mathtt{L}^1(i_3^s)$ $\mathtt{else\ goto}\ \mathtt{L}^{\mathrm{exit}}(i_3^s)$

Figure 3. Vectorized version of Example 1

value of i^s from the last completed iteration). Since the vector loop dominates the cleanup check, all its entry variables and variables it defines are in scope, so the cleanup check could be formed as:

$$
\begin{aligned}
&L^{\mathrm{check}}():\\
&\quad \mathtt{if}\ ({}^{\mathsf{lv}}i^s < l^s)\ \mathtt{goto}\ L({}^{\mathsf{lv}}i_{01}^s, \ldots, {}^{\mathsf{lv}}i_{n1}^s)\\
&\qquad\qquad \mathtt{else\ goto}\ L^{\mathrm{exit}}({}^{\mathsf{lv}}x_0^s, \ldots, {}^{\mathsf{lv}}x_p^s)
\end{aligned}
$$

Note that the last values of the base induction variables are passed to the scalar loop and the last values of the live-out variables $(x_0^s, \ldots, x_p^s)$ are passed to the exit label.

However, instead of using the last values computed in the vector loop, it is better to recompute them in order to avoid introducing data dependencies that may keep instructions live in the loop which could otherwise be eliminated. This turns out to be straightforward: the portion of the translation in Figure 2 that computes last values can simply be repeated. This results in a complete calculation of all of the last values, including ${}^{\mathsf{lv}}i^s$. While most of these instructions will turn out to be unnecessary, a single pass of dead code elimination is sufficient to eliminate them.

4.5 Transformed example

The actual process of producing SIMD vector versions of loops seems at first quite ad hoc and difficult to do cleanly, but turns out to be amenable to a simple and straightforward translation which systematically produces vector versions of scalar instructions, relying on orthogonal optimizations to clean up unnecessary generated code. To illustrate the results of this process, Figure 3 shows the results of applying the algorithm to Example 1. First note that the base induction variables are just i^s of step 1, and the only other induction variable is i_1^s also of step 1. The variables a^s, b^s, c^s, and l^s are used in the loop but not defined by it. Block $\mathtt{L}^0$ is the preheader for the loop. We first transform the preheader to define variables used by but not defined by the loop and to do the entry test. This results in Figure 3 under the header "Entry test". Next we generate the instructions for the base induction variable, transformed instructions of the loop, and adjusted exit condition to form the vector loop. The result of this appears under the header "Vector loop". Finally we form the cleanup check by regenerating the last-value computations and using the original loop-exit condition. For simplicity we just show enough instructions to compute the last value of i_1^s, the only needed last value. This block appears under the header "Cleanup check".

This code, as expected, is terribly verbose. However, by applying copy propagation followed by dead-code elimination, the extraneous parts disappear, yielding the code shown under the header "Optimized result". By applying common sub-expression elimination this code can be further improved by eliminating the calculation of i_2^s in favor of ${}^{\mathsf{lv}}i^s$, and i_3^s in favor of ${}^{\mathsf{lv}}i_1^s$. Finally, simplifying the chained arithmetic expressions yields the same vectorized loop as derived by the initial ad hoc vectorization shown in Section 4.3.

4.6 Reductions

The SIMD vectorization process defined so far primarily applies to loops which serve to create new arrays. An additional idiom that is important to handle in vectorization is that of loops which serve (in total or in part) to compute a reduction using a binary operator. That is, instead of, or in addition to, initializing a new array, each iteration of the loop accumulates a value into an accumulator parameter as a function of the value from the last iteration. For example, the innermost dot product of a matrix multiply routine generally takes the form of a reduction.

Adding support for reductions to the vectorization transformation is not difficult. In the same manner that we identify certain variables as induction variables and treat them specially, we identify variables that fit the pattern of reductions and add additional cases to the vectorization transformation to handle them differently. Specifically, we say that a variable x^s is a reduction variable if it is a parameter to the loop that is not an induction variable, and which is defined on the back edge of the loop by the application of an associative, commutative binary operator applied to x^s and some distinct variable. All uses of x^s and its associated back edge variable must be in reductions. For example, the loop:

$$
\begin{array}{ll}
\texttt{L}^0(): & \texttt{L}^1(i^s, x^s): \\
\quad x_0^s = 1 & \quad y^s = c^s[i^s] \\
\quad i_0^s = 0 & \quad x_1^s = +(x^s, y^s) \\
\quad \texttt{goto L}^1(i_0^s, x_0^s) & \quad i_1^s = +(i^s, 1) \\
 & \quad \texttt{if } (i_1^s < l^s) \texttt{ goto L}^1(i_1^s, x_1^s) \\
 & \qquad\qquad \texttt{else goto L}^{\text{exit}}(x_1^s)
\end{array} \tag{3}
$$

computes one more than the sum of the elements of the array c^s via a reduction (assuming that l^s is the length of c^s) and passes out the result on the exit edge as x_1^s. We say that x^s and x_1^s are reduction variables in this loop, with initial value 1.

The general strategy for SIMD vectorization of reductions is to pass a vector variable around the loop, each element of which contains a partial reduction. Implicitly, we re-associate the reduction so that element i of the vector variable contains the partial reduction of all of the values of the iterations which are congruent to i modulo the vector width (8 here). After exiting the vector loop, performing a horizontal reduction on the vector variable itself results in the full reduction of all the iterations (albeit performed in a different order, hence the requirement of associativity and commutativity).

More concretely, to vectorize a reduction variable x^s, we simply promote x^s to a vector variable x^v. In the preheader of the loop, we lift the definition of the initial value for the reduction variable to contain the original initial value in element 0, and the unit for the reduction operation in all other elements. In Example 3 this corresponds to defining the initial value as $x_0^v = \langle 1, 0, \ldots, 0 \rangle$ (since 0 is unit for addition). The reduction operation in the loop is lifted to perform the same vector operation pointwise, hence $x_1^v = \langle + \rangle(x^v, y^v)$ for the example. Finally, in the cleanup check block, the lifted reduction variable x_1^v is itself reduced to produce the final scalar result of the portion of the reduction performed by the vector loop (which is then passed in as the initial value to the scalar loop if subsequent iterations remain to be computed). This final reduction may be performed using scalar operations. It is possible to maintain last value and scalar values for reduction variables within the vector loop as well as the vector value, but doing so requires performing a reduction on the vector value on each iteration which is potentially expensive enough to make SIMD vectorization a poor idea. Consequently, we simply choose to reject SIMD vectorization of loops which would require the calculation of scalar or last values for reduction variables.

Unfortunately, the associativity requirement for binary operations used in reductions can be problematic since most floating point operations (e.g. addition and multiplication) are not fully associative. In practice, reductions over floating point operators are important idioms. By default, HRC does not re-associate floating point operations, and hence refuses to vectorize loops which perform reductions over floating point data. We provide a flag which permits the compiler to re-associate floating point operations only for SIMD vectorization (but not other optimizations) which allows such loops to be vectorized at the expense of occasionally producing slightly different results from the sequential version.

4.7 Dependence Analysis

At this point, one might be concerned that we have left aside a critical point in our development. While we have shown *how* to vectorize a loop, we have said nothing about when (or why) it might be valid to do so. The crux of any kind of automatic vectorization lies in determining when it is semantics preserving to execute multiple iterations of a scalar loop in parallel. In the most general case this can be a tremendously hard problem to solve, and there is a vast literature on techniques for showing that particular loops can validly be vectorized (see for example Bik [3] for an overview). For the particular case of immutable arrays however, the problem becomes drastically easier. In this section we give a brief overview of why this is the case.

We say that an instruction I_2 is dependent on an instruction I_1 if I_2 must causally follow I_1. There are a number of different reasons that this ordering might be required, each inducing a different kind of dependence. Flow dependence (or data-dependence) is a standard dataflow dependence induced by a read of the value of a variable or location which was written at an earlier point in the program execution. This is sometimes known as a read-after-write dependence. An anti-dependence on the other hand is induced by a write after a read: that is, a location or variable is updated with a new value after an old value has been read, and therefore the write must happen after the read to avoid changing the value seen by the read. Finally, output dependence is dependence induced by a write after a write: that is, a location or variable is updated with a new value which overwrites an old value written by a previous statement (and hence the writes cannot be re-ordered without affecting the final value of the written to location or variable).

The key insight for automatic vectorization of immutable arrays is that neither anti-dependence nor output dependence can occur. This is obvious by construction, since the nature of immutability is such that the only writes are initializing writes. Therefore, there cannot be a write after a read (since this would imply a read of uninitialized data), nor can there be a write after a write (since this would imply mutation). The only remaining dependence then is flow-dependence. Flow-dependences which are carried by variable definitions and uses are straightforward to account for, and do not generally cause unusual trouble. In general, it is possible for loop-carried flow-dependences to block vectorization, however. For example, consider the following simple program:

$$
\begin{array}{ll}
\texttt{L}^0(): & \texttt{L}^1(i^s): \\
\quad a^s = \texttt{new}[l^s] & \quad a^s[i^s] \leftarrow i^s \\
\quad a^s[0] \leftarrow 0 & \quad x^s = a^s[i^s - 1] \\
\quad \texttt{goto L}^1(1) & \quad \texttt{if } (i^s < l^s) \texttt{ goto L}^1(i^s + 1) \\
 & \qquad\qquad \texttt{else goto L}^{\text{exit}}(x^s)
\end{array}
$$

While this program uses only initializing writes, it nonetheless incurs a loop-carried dependence in which a read in one iteration depends on a write in a previous iteration. Clearly then, the problem of dependence analysis is not completely trivial even for functional programs even after eliminating the problems of anti-dependences and output-dependences. Note that while this example reads and writes a^s through the same variable name, there is nothing preventing the binding of a^s to a different variable name, and hence allowing array accesses (reads or initializing writes) via an alias.

In practice however, all programs that we have considered (and indeed, based on the way that immutable arrays are produced, all programs that we are at all likely to consider) have the very useful property that they are allocated and initialized in the same lexical scope. The implication of this is that it is usually trivially easy to conservatively determine that an initializing write in a loop does not alias with any of the reads in the loop simply by checking that no aliases for the newly allocated array are introduced before the loop. As a result, a very naive analysis is quite successful at breaking read after write dependences in this style of loops.

5. Benchmarks

We show performance results for eight benchmarks, measured on an Intel Xeon E5-4650 (Sandybridge) processor implementing the AVX SIMD instruction set. For each benchmark, the best time out of five runs was recorded. Three of the benchmarks are small

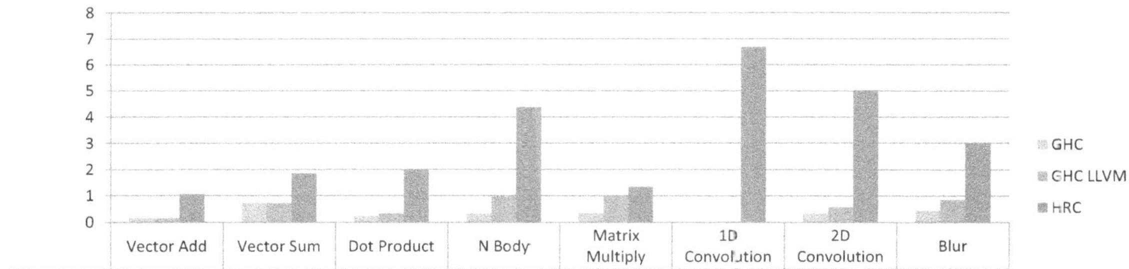

	Vector Add	Vector Sum	Dot Product	N Body	Matrix Multiply	1D Convolution	2D Convolution	Blur
GHC	0.15	0.72	0.24	0.34	0.35	0.02	0.34	0.45
GHC LLVM	0.15	0.73	0.35	0.97	0.98	0.02	0.58	0.86
HRC	1.05	1.84	2.00	4.37	1.34	6.68	5.03	3.02

Figure 4. Speedup over HRC Scalar (HRC Scalar=1).

synthetic benchmarks. The first computes the pointwise sum of two arrays of 32-bit floating point numbers using the following code:

```
addV v1 v2 = zipWith (+) v1 v2
```

The second computes the horizontal sum of an array of 32-bit floating point numbers using the following code:

```
sumV v = foldl (+) 0 v
```

Both of the kernels use the operations from our modified version of the Data.Vector.Unboxed library. The third kernel computes a dot product, implemented precisely as the composition of the two previous kernels above. These code snippets are each run in a benchmark harness which generates test data and repeatedly runs the same kernel a number of times in order to increase the runtime to reasonable lengths for benchmarking.

The fourth benchmark is an n-body simulation kernel which uses the naive quadratic algorithm to calculate accelerations for n gravitational bodies, represented as quadruples of 32-bit floating point numbers (three dimensions plus mass). For our measurements, one time step is computed for 100,000 bodies. The code is written in an straightforward manner using the REPA array library.

The fifth benchmark is the matrix-matrix multiply routine included in the REPA array library. The matrix elements are double precision (64-bit) floating point numbers. The program generates random arrays, performs a single multiplication, computes a checksum, and writes the result out to a file. The portion of the program that is timed and reported here is the matrix multiplication and the checksum computation. The measurements were taken using a 3000 by 3000 element array.

The sixth benchmark is a two dimensional five-by-five stencil convolution written using the REPA stencil libraries [9]. The convolution is repeatedly performed 4000 consecutive times on a 1000 by 1000 element array of 32-bit floating point numbers.

The seventh benchmark is a one dimensional convolution of an 8192 element floating-point stencil applied to an array of complex numbers represented as pairs of 32-bit floats. The REPA stencil libraries could not be applied to this problem, but an elegant and simple solution was arrived at which extracts a slice of the complex array, zips it with the stencil array, and then reduces with a fold.

The final benchmark is the "blur" image processing example included with the REPA distribution. The benchmark was modified slightly to match our benchmark harness requirements, with timing code inserted around the kernel of the computation to avoid including file input/output times in the measurements. No changes to the code implementing the algorithm itself were made. The timings presented measure the result of performing twenty successive blurrings on a 4592x3056 pixel image.

The performance of these eight benchmarks is given in Figure 4. Each bar shows speedup over our standard scalar compiler without vectorization, since the primary goal is to demonstrate the performance increase obtained from SIMD vectorization Speedup for a given build is computed by dividing the HRC Scalar runtime by the runtime for that build: thus HRC Scalar is always at 1, and higher numbers indicate better performance. We also show the performance of unmodified GHC 7.6.1 using both the standard back end and the new LLVM backend [14]. This is intended primarily to demonstrate that the scalar code from which we begin is suitably optimized. Both the unmodified and our modified version of GHC were run with optimization flags "–O2", "–msse2". Various combinations of the flags "–fno-liberate-case", "–funfolding-use-threshold", and "–funfolding-keeness-factor" were also used following the documentation of the REPA libraries, and based on some limited experimentation as to which arguments gave better performance. HRC was run with flags requiring it to preserve floating point value semantics and requiring the backend C compiler to do the same. The only exception was that the flag discussed in Section 4 to permit the re-association of floating point operations during vectorization of reductions was used. For some benchmarks, this caused small perturbations in the results.

For the vector-vector addition benchmark, our baseline compiler gives large speedups over both the standard GHC backend and the LLVM backend. Unfortunately this benchmark is poorly structured for measuring floating point performance. Performance analysis shows that the run time is almost entirely dominated by memory costs associated with initializing the new arrays allocated on each iteration. The vector sum benchmark on the other hand performs a reduction over the input vector producing only a scalar result. Consequently memory latency issues are less important since the input vectors are in cache, and SIMD vectorization gives 1.8× speedup. For the dot product kernel, the GHC frontend successfully eliminates the intermediate array, and further optimization by HRC results in a vectorizable loop for a 2× speedup.

The N-Body simulation benchmark benefits significantly from SIMD vectorization, since the core of the inner loop does a substantial amount of floating point work on each iteration. While our baseline compiler gives only slightly better performance than the LLVM backend on the benchmark, the SIMD vectorized version gets a 4.4× speedup over the scalar version.

The matrix multiplication routine gets some limited benefit from SIMD vectorization (1.3×). This benchmark uses double precision which reduces the expected speedup, and more work is done outside of the core inner (vectorizable) loop. Memory latency is also a factor in this benchmark.

The one dimensional convolution benchmark gets an excellent SIMD vector speedup of $6.7\times$. Good cache locality makes this benchmark largely compute bound. Unfortunately, while GHC and REPA do an excellent job of fusing away the implied intermediate arrays, GHC is unable to eliminate all of the allocation in the inner loop and so performs extremely poorly on this benchmark. HRC is able to eliminate all of the remaining allocation and so achieves significantly better baseline performance.

Both the two dimensional convolution and blur benchmarks suffered originally from a sequential optimization of the REPA libraries in which the inner loop was unrolled four times[3] [9]. While this gave substantial speedup on the scalar builds, it limited the vector speedup because the generated code used non unit-stride vector loads which are not supported natively on the measurement hardware. To address this, we modified our version of the REPA library to eliminate the unrolling. This penalizes our scalar build substantially, but greatly benefits the vector build since contiguous vector loads can be emitted. The GHC builds were measured using the original REPA optimizations. The 2D convolution benchmark gets a $5\times$ speedup, and the blur benchmark gets a $3\times$ speedup.

Of particular importance to note with respect to all of the benchmarks but most especially for the last two is that the timings presented here are not for the vectorized loops alone, but for the entire kernel of the program (essentially everything except the input (or input generation) and output).

6. Related and Future Work, Conclusions

There is a vast and rich literature on automatic SIMD vectorization in compilers. Bik [3] provides an excellent overview of the essential ideas and techniques in a modern setting. Many standard compiler textbooks also provide at least some rudimentary introduction to SIMD vectorization. The NESL programming language [4] pioneered the idea of writing nested data parallel programs in a functional language, an idea which has more recently been picked up by the Data Parallel Haskell project [12]. A related project focusing on regular arrays [6] (REPA) has had good success in getting array computations to scale on multi-processor machines. Programs written using the REPA libraries are promising targets for SIMD vectorization, either automatic as in this work, or via explicit language constructs in the library implementation. Mainland et al. [10] have pursued this latter approach. They implement primitives in GHC that correspond to SIMD instructions and modify the stream fusion used in the Data.Vector library to generate these SIMD primitives. In this way, they achieve SIMD vectorization in the library, where we achieve SIMD vectorization in the compiler. Two different, possibly complimentary, ways to achieve the same ends.

Our initial implementation of SIMD vectorization targets only simple loops with no conditional tests. An obvious extension to this work would be to incorporate support for predicated instructions to allow more loops to be SIMD vectorized. However, hardware support for this is somewhat limited in current processors, and the performance effects of generating predicated code are harder to predict. A more limited effort to target the special case of conditionals performing array bounds checks seems like a promising area for investigation. As functional languages tend to allocate heavily, supporting allocation of heap objects inside vectorized loops could be important. A vector allocation instruction allocates 8 objects and places pointers to them in a vector variable. Implementing this operation for fixed-size objects is straightforward and should be quick—a single limit check, vector instructions to compute the pointers, and a scatter to initialize the object meta-data used by the garbage collector. Implementing vectorized allocation of variable-length arrays should also be straightforward. A special-case instruction for when the length is loop-invariant would likely have a faster implementation.

To summarize, we have utilized the naturally data-parallel typical functional-language operations on immutable arrays such as maps, folds, zips, etc., utilized the large body of work on eliminating intermediate arrays, and utilized our own internal operations on immutable arrays to produce nice loops amenable to SIMD vectorization. Implementing that SIMD vectorization automatically is a surprisingly straightforward process, and one that we have shown can produce excellent speedups on functional language workloads. A key part of this simplicity is the use of immutable objects and operations on them, and in particular our use of initializing writes. As utilizing SIMD instruction sets is important on modern architectures, these techniques are an important and low-hanging fruit for functional-language implementations.

[3] Thanks to an anonymous reviewer for pointing out the source of this unrolling which we had embarrassingly missed.

References

[1] T. Anderson, N. Glew, P. Guo, B. T. Lewis, W. Liu, Z. Liu, L. Petersen, M. Rajagopalan, J. M. Stichnoth, G. Wu, and D. Zhang. Pillar: A parallel implementation language. In V. Adve, M. J. Garzarán, and P. Petersen, editors, *Languages and Compilers for Parallel Computing*, pages 141–155. Springer-Verlag, Berlin, Heidelberg, 2008.

[2] A. Appel and T. Jim. Shrinking lambda expressions in linear time. *Journal of Functional Programming*, 7(5), Sept. 1997.

[3] A. J. C. Bik. *The Software Vectorization Handbook*. Intel Press, 2004.

[4] G. E. Blelloch. Programming parallel algorithms. *Communications of the ACM*, 39(3):85–97, Mar. 1996. ISSN 0001-0782.

[5] M. Fluet and S. Weeks. Contification using dominators. In *International Conference on Functional Programming*, pages 2–13, Florence, Italy, 2001. ACM.

[6] G. Keller, M. M. Chakravarty, R. Leshchinskiy, S. Peyton Jones, and B. Lippmeier. Regular, shape-polymorphic, parallel arrays in Haskell. In *International Conference on Functional Programming*, pages 261–272, Baltimore, Maryland, USA, 2010. ACM.

[7] K. Kennedy, C. Koelbel, and H. Zima. The rise and fall of High Performance Fortran: an historical object lesson. In *History of Programming Languages*, pages 1–22. ACM, 2007.

[8] R. Leshchinskiy. Recycle your arrays! In *Practical Aspects of Declarative Languages*, pages 209–223. Springer, 2009.

[9] B. Lippmeier and G. Keller. Efficient parallel stencil convolution in haskell. In *Haskell Symposium*, pages 59–70. ACM, 2011.

[10] G. Mainland, R. Leshchinskiy, and S. Peyton Jones. Exploiting Vector Instructions with Generalized Stream Fusion. In *International Conference on Functional Programming*. ACM, 2013.

[11] L. Petersen and N. Glew. GC-safe interprocedural unboxing. In *Compiler Construction*, pages 165–184, Tallinn, Estonia, 2012. Springer-Verlag.

[12] S. Peyton Jones. Harnessing the multicores: Nested data parallelism in Haskell. In *Asian Symposium on Programming Languages and Systems*, pages 138–138, Bangalore, India, 2008. Springer-Verlag.

[13] W. Pugh. A practical algorithm for exact array dependence analysis. *Communications of the ACM*, 35(8):102–114, 1992.

[14] D. A. Terei and M. M. Chakravarty. An LLVM backend for GHC. *SIGPLAN Notices*, 45(11):109–120, 2010.

[15] N. Vasilache, C. Bastoul, A. Cohen, and S. Girbal. Violated dependence analysis. In *International Conference on Supercomputing*, pages 335–344. ACM, 2006.

[16] S. Weeks. Whole-program compilation in MLton. In *Workshop on ML*, pages 1–1, Portland, Oregon, USA, 2006. ACM.

Exploiting Vector Instructions with Generalized Stream Fusion

Geoffrey Mainland
Microsoft Research Ltd
Cambridge, England
gmainlan@microsoft.com

Roman Leshchinskiy
rl@cse.unsw.edu.au

Simon Peyton Jones
Microsoft Research Ltd
Cambridge, England
simonpj@microsoft.com

Abstract

Stream fusion [6] is a powerful technique for automatically transforming high-level sequence-processing functions into efficient implementations. It has been used to great effect in Haskell libraries for manipulating byte arrays, Unicode text, and unboxed vectors. However, some operations, like vector append, still do not perform well within the standard stream fusion framework. Others, like SIMD computation using the SSE and AVX instructions available on modern x86 chips, do not seem to fit in the framework at all.

In this paper we introduce generalized stream fusion, which solves these issues. The key insight is to *bundle* together multiple stream representations, each tuned for a particular class of stream consumer. We also describe a stream representation suited for efficient computation with SSE instructions. Our ideas are implemented in modified versions of the GHC compiler and `vector` library. Benchmarks show that high-level Haskell code written using our compiler and libraries can produce code that is faster than both compiler- and hand-vectorized C.

Categories and Subject Descriptors D.3.3 [*Software*]: Programming Languages

Keywords Haskell; vectorization; SIMD; stream fusion

1. Introduction

It seems unreasonable to ask a compiler to be able to turn numeric algorithms expressed as high-level Haskell code into tight machine code. The compiler must cope with boxed numeric types, handle lazy evaluation, and eliminate intermediate data structures. However, the Glasgow Haskell Compiler has become "sufficiently smart" that Haskell libraries for expressing numerical computations, such as Repa [17, 21], no longer have to sacrifice speed at the altar of abstraction.

The key development that made this sacrifice unnecessary is *stream fusion* [6]. Algorithms over sequences—whether they are lists or vectors (arrays)—are expressed naturally in a functional language using operations such as folds, maps, and zips. Although highly modular, these operations produce unnecessary intermediate structures that lead to inefficient code. Eliminating these intermediate structures is termed deforestation, or fusion. Equational laws, such as $\mathsf{map}\ f \circ \mathsf{map}\ g \equiv \mathsf{map}\ (f \circ g)$, allow some of these intermediate structures to be eliminated; finding more general rules has been the subject of a great deal of research [8, 12, 15, 23, 29, 30, 34]. Stream fusion [6], based on the observation that recursive structures can be transformed into non-recursive co-structures for which fusion is relatively straightforward, was the first truly general solution.

Instead of working directly with lists or vectors, stream fusion works by re-expressing these functions as operations over streams, each represented as a state and a step function that transforms the state while potentially yielding a single value. Alas, different operations need different stream representations, and no single representation works well for all operations (§2.3). Furthermore, for many operations it is not obvious what the choice of representation should be.

In this paper we solve this problem with a new *generalized stream fusion* framework where the primary abstraction over which operations on vectors are expressed is a *bundle* of streams. The streams are chosen so that for any given high-level vector operation there is a stream in the bundle whose representation leads to an efficient implementation. The bundle abstraction has no run-time cost because standard compiler optimizations eliminate intermediate bundle structures. In addition, we describe several optimized stream representations. Our contributions are as follows:

- We describe a generalization of stream fusion that bundles together multiple, alternate representations of a stream. This allows the stream consumer to choose the representation that is most efficient for its use case (Section 3.1).
- We show in Section 3.2 how generalized stream fusion enables the use of bulk memory operations, such as `memcpy` and `memset`, for manipulating vectors.
- Generalized stream fusion opens up entirely new opportunities for optimization. We exploit this opportunity in Section 3.3 by crafting a stream representation well-suited for SIMD-style vector operations (SSE, AVX etc). The result is a massive performance gain (up to a factor of more than three) at a much lower programming cost than using conventional approaches (Section 5).
- Using generalized stream fusion, we describe in Section 3.5 how to modify Data Parallel Haskell [4] so that DPH programs can automatically take advantage of SIMD operations without requiring any code modification.

Everything we describe is fully implemented in GHC and its libraries (Section 4). Our benchmarks compare to the very best C and C++ compilers and libraries that we could find. Remarkably, our benchmarks show that choosing the proper stream representations can result in machine code that beats compiler-vectorized C, and that is competitive with hand-tuned assembly. Moreover, using DPH, programs can easily exploit SIMD instructions *and* automatically parallelize to take advantage of multiple cores.

ICFP '13, September 25–27, 2013, Boston, MA, USA.

ACM 978-1-4503-2326-0/13/09...$15.00.
http://dx.doi.org/10.1145/2500365.2500601

2. Stream Fusion Background

We begin by providing the background necessary for understanding stream fusion. There is no new material here—it is all derived from Coutts et al. [6]. However, we describe fusion for functions of *vectors* of unboxed values, as implemented in the `vector` [19] library, rather than fusion for functions over *lists*. Some of the implementation details are elided, but the essential aspects of stream fusion as we describe them are faithful to the implementation.

2.1 The key insight

The big idea behind stream fusion is to rewrite recursive functions, which are difficult for a compiler to automatically optimize, as non-recursive functions. The abstraction that accomplishes this is the Stream data type:

```
data Stream a where
  Stream :: (s → Step s a) → s → Int → Stream a

data Step s a = Yield a s
              | Skip s
              | Done
```

A stream is a triple of values: an existentially-quantified state, represented by the type variable s in the above definition, a size, and a step function that, when given a state, produces a Step. A Step may be Done, indicating that there are no more values in the Stream, it may Yield a value and a new state, or it may produce a new state but Skip producing a value. The presence of Skip allows us to easily express functions like filter within the stream fusion framework.

To see concretely how this helps us avoid recursive functions, let us write map for vectors using streams

```
map :: (a → b) → Vector a → Vector b
map f = unstream ∘ map_s f ∘ stream
```

The functions stream and unstream convert a Vector to and from a stream. A Vector is converted to a stream whose state is an integer index and whose step function yields the value at the current index, which is incremented at each step. To convert a stream back into a Vector, unstream allocates memory for a new vector and writes each element to the vector as it is yielded by the stream—unstream embodies a recursive loop. Though imperative, the allocation and writing of the vector are safely embedded in pure Haskell using the ST monad [18].

The real work is done by $\mathsf{map_s}$, which is happily non-recursive.

```
map_s :: (a → b) → Stream a → Stream b
map_s f (Stream step s) = Stream step′ s
  where
    step′ s = case step s of
      Yield x s′ → Yield (f x) s′
      Skip s′    → Skip s′
      Done       → Done
```

With this definition, the equational rule mentioned in the Introduction, map f ∘ map g ≡ map (f ∘ g), falls out automatically. To see this, let us first inline our new definition of map in the expression map f ∘ map g.

```
map f ∘ map g ≡
  unstream ∘ map_s f ∘ stream ∘ unstream ∘ map_s g ∘ stream
```

Given this form, we can immediately spot where an intermediate structure is formed—by the composition stream ∘ unstream. This composition is morally the identity function [7, §3.7-3.8], so we should be able to eliminate it entirely. Rewrite rules [28] enable programmers to express algebraic identities such as stream ∘ unstream = id in a form that GHC can understand and automatically apply. Stream fusion relies *critically* on this ability, and the `vector` library includes exactly this rule. With the rule in place, GHC transforms our original composition of maps into

```
map f ∘ map g ≡
  unstream ∘ map_s f ∘ map_s g ∘ stream
```

Conceptually, stream fusion pushes all recursive loops into the final consumer. The two composed invocations of map become a composition of two *non-recursive* calls to $\mathsf{map_s}$. The inliner is now perfectly capable of combining $\mathsf{map_s}$ f ∘ $\mathsf{map_s}$ g into a single Stream function. Stream fusion gives us the equational rule map f ∘ map g ≡ map (f ∘ g) *for free*.

2.2 Fusing the vector dot product

The motivating example we will use for the rest of the paper is the vector dot product. A high-level implementation of this function in Haskell might be written as follows:

```
dotp :: Vector Double → Vector Double → Double
dotp v w = sum (zipWith (*) v w)
```

It seems that this implementation will suffer from severe inefficiency—the call to zipWith produces an unnecessary intermediate vector that is immediately consumed by the function sum. In expressing dotp as a composition of collective operations, we have perhaps gained a bit of algorithmic clarity but in turn we have incurred a performance hit.

We have already seen how stream fusion eliminates intermediate structures in the case of a composition of two calls to map. Previous fusion frameworks could handle that example, but were stymied by the presence of a zipWith. However, stream fusion has no problem fusing zipWith, which we can see by applying the transformations we saw in Section 2.1 to dotp.

The first step is to re-express each Vector operation as the composition of a Stream operation and appropriate conversions between Vectors and Streams at the boundaries. The functions zipWith and sum are expressed in this form as follows.

```
zipWith :: (a → b → c) → Vector a → Vector b → Vector c
zipWith f v w = unstream (zipWith_s f (stream v) (stream w))

sum :: Num a ⇒ Vector a → a
sum v = foldl′_s 0 (+) (stream v)
```

It is now relatively straightforward to transform dotp to eliminate the intermediate structure.

```
dotp :: Vector Double → Vector Double → Double
dotp v w ≡ sum (zipWith (*) v w)
         ≡ foldl′_s 0 (+) (stream (unstream
               (zipWith_s (*) (stream v) (stream w))))
         ≡ foldl′_s 0 (+)
               (zipWith_s (*) (stream v) (stream w))
```

This transformation again consists of inlining a few definitions, something that GHC can easily perform, and rewriting the composition stream ∘ unstream to the identity function. After this transformation, the production (by zipWith) and following consumption (by sum) of an intermediate Vector becomes the composition of non-recursive functions on streams.

We can see how iteration is once again pushed into the final consumer by looking at the implementations of $\mathsf{foldl'_s}$ and $\mathsf{zipWith_s}$. The final consumer in dotp is $\mathsf{foldl'_s}$, which is implemented by an explicit loop that consumes stream values and combines the yielded values with the accumulator z using the function f (the call to seq guarantees that the accumulator is strictly evaluated).

```
foldl's :: (a → b → a) → a → Stream b → a
foldl's f z (Stream step s) = loop z s
  where
    loop z s = z `seq`
      case step s of
        Yield x s' → loop (f z x) s'
        Skip s'    → loop z s'
        Done       → z
```

However, in $\mathsf{zipWith}_s$ there is no loop—the two input streams are consumed until either both streams yield a value, in which case a value is yielded on the output stream, or until one of the input streams is done producing values. The internal state of the stream associated with $\mathsf{zipWith}_s$ contains the state of the two input streams and a one-item buffer for the value produced by the first input stream.

```
zipWiths :: (a → b → c) → Stream a → Stream b → Stream c
zipWiths f (Stream stepa sa na) (Stream stepb sb nb) =
    Stream step (sa, sb, Nothing) (min na nb)
  where
    step (sa, sb, Nothing) =
      case stepa sa of
        Yield x sa' → Skip (sa', sb, Just x)
        Skip sa'    → Skip (sa', sb, Nothing)
        Done        → Done
    step (sa, sb, Just x) =
      case stepb sb of
        Yield y sb' → Yield (f x y) (sa, sb', Nothing)
        Skip sb'    → Skip (sa, sb', Just x)
        Done        → Done
```

Given these definitions, call-pattern specialization [24] in concert with the standard GHC inliner suffice to transform dotp into a single loop that does not produce an intermediate structure, and the moral result is shown here, where !! is infix byte array indexing.

```
dotp (Vector n u) (Vector m v) = loop 0.0 0 0
  where
    loop z i j
      | i < n ∧ j < m = loop (z + u !! i ∗ v !! j) (i + 1) (j + 1)
      | otherwise     = z
```

If there is any doubt that this results in efficient machine code, we give the actual assembly language inner loop output by GHC using the LLVM back end [31]. Stream fusion preserves the ability to write compositionally without sacrificing performance.

```
.LBB2_3:
    movsd (%rcx), %xmm0
    mulsd (%rdx), %xmm0
    addsd %xmm0, %xmm1
    addq  $8, %rcx
    addq  $8, %rdx
    decq  %rax
    jne .LBB2_3
```

2.3 Stream fusion inefficiencies

Unfortunately, while stream fusion does well for the examples we have shown, it still does not produce efficient implementations for many other operations one might want to perform on vectors. We next give examples of two classes of operations that are either inefficient or impossible to handle in the stream fusion framework. As we describe in Section 3, generalized stream fusion can implement both of these classes of operations efficiently.

2.3.1 Bulk memory operations

Appending two vectors is a simple operation for which an obvious, efficient implementation exists—a vector large enough to hold the result is allocated, and the two vectors being appended are copied, one after the other, to the destination using an optimized `memcpy`. Similarly, replicating a scalar across a vector should be implemented by a call to `memset`. In other words, we would like to be able to take advantage of highly optimized bulk memory operations like `memcpy` and `memset` in our vector library. Unfortunately, this is far from straightforward. To see why, let us look at how we might implement vector append using stream fusion.

In this framework, vector append is first rewritten in terms of stream, unstream, and a worker function append_s.

```
append :: Vector a → Vector a → Vector a
append u v = unstream (appends (stream u) (stream v))

appends :: Stream a → Stream a → Stream a
appends (Stream stepa sa na) (Stream stepb sb nb) =
    Stream step (Left sa) (na + nb)
  where
    step (Left sa) =
      case stepa sa of
        Yield x sa' → Yield x (Left sa')
        Skip sa'    → Skip    (Left sa')
        Done        → Skip    (Right sb)
    step (Right sb) =
      case stepb sb of
        Yield x sb' → Yield x (Right sb')
        Skip sb'    → Skip    (Right sb')
        Done        → Done
```

The function append_s appends two streams by first yielding all the values produced by the first stream and then those values produced by the second stream. When passed to unstream, this results in two loops, one executed after the other, that write elements one by one into a newly allocated vector. Similarly, replication compiles to a loop that writes, one by one, a constant to each element of a newly allocated vector. While it is theoretically possible for a compiler to transform this into code equivalent to `memcpy` and `memset`, this requires significant low-level optimization capabilities and is currently beyond the reach of GHC.

How could we possibly rewrite append_s into two calls to `memcpy`? We cannot. The difficulty is that a Stream produces a single value at a time. To take advantage of `memcpy`, it seems we need a stream that produces *entire vectors*, one at a time. However, this latter representation, though ideal for vector append, would be a dismal failure if we wished to calculate a dot product!

2.3.2 SIMD computation with vectors

The inadequacy of the single-value-at-a-time nature of streams becomes even more apparent when attempting to opportunistically utilize the SIMD instructions available on many current architectures, e.g., SSE on x86 and NEON on ARM. These instructions operate in parallel on data values that contains two (or four or eight, depending on the hardware architecture) floating point numbers. To avoid notational confusion, we call these *multi-values*, or sometimes just *multis*.

To enable sum to use SIMD instructions, we would like a stream representation that yields multi-values (rather than scalars), with perhaps a bit of scalar "dribble" at the end of the stream when the number of scalar values is not divisible by the size of a multi.

A stream of scalar values is useless for SIMD computation. However, a stream of multi-values isn't quite right either, because of the "dribble" problem. Perhaps we could get away with a stream

```
newMVector    :: Int → ST s (MutableVector s a)
sliceMVector  :: MutableVector s a → Int → Int
              → MutableVector s a
readMVector   :: MutableVector s a → Int → ST s a
writeMVector  :: MutableVector s a → Int → a → ST s ()
copyMVector   :: Vector a → MutableVector s a → ST s ()
freezeMVector :: MutableVector s a → ST s (Vector a)
```

Figure 1: **Operations on mutable vectors.**

that yielded *either* a scalar or a multi at each step, but this would force all scalar-only operations to handle an extra case, complicating the implementations of *all* operations and making them less efficient. There is a better way!

3. Generalized Stream Fusion

We saw in the previous Section that different stream operations work best with different stream representations. In this Section, we describe new stream representations that take advantage of bulk memory operations (§3.2) and enable SIMD computation with vectors (§3.3). Finally, we show how to use our framework to transparently take advantage of SIMD instructions in Data Parallel Haskell programs (§3.5).

3.1 Bundles of streams

The idea underlying generalized stream fusion is straightforward but its effects are wide-ranging: instead of transforming a function over vectors into a function over streams, transform it into a function over a *bundle* of streams. A bundle is simply a collection of streams, each semantically identical but with a different cost model. Individual stream operations can therefore choose to work with the most advantageous stream representation in the bundle. We give a simplified version of the Bundle data type here.

```
data Bundle a = Bundle
  {sSize   :: Size
  , sElems  :: Stream a
  , sChunks :: Stream (Chunk a)
  , sMultis :: Multis a
  }
```

The sElems field of the Bundle data type contains the familiar stream of scalar values that we saw in Section 2. In Section 3.3 we describe the representation contained in the sMultis field of the record, which enables the efficient use of SSE instructions. As we show next, the stream of Chunks contained in the sChunks field of the record enables the use of bulk memory operations.

3.2 Taking advantage of bulk memory operations with Chunks

We observed in Section 2.3.1 that append could take advantage of `memcpy` if a stream could produce whole vectors rather than single scalar values in one step. The mechanism we use is slightly more general: a Chunk is a computation that destructively initializes a vector slice of a particular length:

```
data Chunk a = Chunk Int (∀s.MutableVector s a → ST s ())
```

A MutableVector s a is the mutable cousin of a Vector a. The extra type variable s is the state token that allows us to safely embed imperative code in pure computations using the ST monad [18]. Some of the operations on mutable vectors are given in Figure 1. These include operations such as copyMVector which ultimately uses a variant of `memcpy`. A producer can use these to generate Chunks which initialize large parts of a vector in one step:

```
stream :: Vector a → Bundle a
stream v = Bundle {...sChunks = singleton chunk...}
  where
    chunk = Chunk (length v) (copyMVector v)
```

Here, stream produces only one Chunk which copies the entire vector in one efficient bulk operation. To convert a Bundle to a vector, we now simply allocate a single mutable vector of sufficient size and initialize it by applying each Chunk to the appropriate slice:

```
unstream :: Bundle a → Vector a
unstream (Bundle {sChunks = Stream step s n}) =
    runST $ do mvec ← newMVector n
               loop mvec 0 s
  where
    loop mvec i s =
      case step s of
        Yield (Chunk k fill) s′ → do
          fill (sliceMVector mvec i k)
          loop mvec (i + k) s′
        Skip s′ → loop mvec i s′
        Done   → freezeMVector mvec
```

This representation is ideal for both append and replicate. The former appends the sChunks components of the two bundles using the version of append_s from Section 2.3.1. When unstream uses the resulting stream of chunks to manifest the vector, it automatically takes advantage of bulk memory operations. Similarly to stream, replicate produces only one Chunk that ultimately invokes `memset`. Thus, if we append a vector produced by stream and a vector produced by replicate, we will perform one `memcpy` followed by one `memset` which is as efficient as possible.

Though ideal for appending vectors efficiently, streams of chunks are not a useful representation for operations like zipWith or fold. This is not a problem, however, since the stream-of-values representation is still available in the sElems component of the Bundle. In general, each consumer will choose the best representation for the particular operation.

What happens when we append two streams that resulted from separate map_s operations? There is a natural conversion from a stream of scalar values to a stream of chunks—each scalar value becomes a chunk that writes a single value to a mutable vector. The result of map_s is therefore a Bundle that contains a degenerate stream of chunks in the sChunks field. There is not much we can do about this—mapping a function over each element in the two streams precludes us from using `memcpy` to append them. Fortunately, the degenerate stream of chunks produced by map_s does not in the end impose any overhead thanks to the optimizer. Furthermore, if we really are appending two vectors without first altering their contents, generalized stream fusion does not force us to give up an implementation in terms of efficient memory copies in order to gain fusion for other operations, like map. While a consumer chooses *one* representation, a producer outputs a bundle containing *all* representations, though some may be degenerate. The "degenerate" form—a stream of scalar values—results in no worse an implementation that non-generalized stream fusion. In other words, generalized stream fusion always produces code that is at least as good as that produced by stream fusion.

It might seem that maintaining a bundle of streams risks work duplication since the result is computed multiple times. Crucially, the stream representations are functions which only do work when applied by a consumer such as unstream and just like unstream, all consumers pick *exactly one* representation and discard all others so no work is ever duplicated. Standard optimizations are typically able to resolve this at compile time so that no code is duplicated,

```
class MultiType a where
  data Multi a   -- Associated type

    -- The number of elements of type a in a Multi a.
  multiplicity :: Multi a → Int

    -- A Multi a containing the values 0, 1 ...,
    -- multiplicity - 1.
  multienum :: Multi a

    -- Replicate a scalar across a Multi a.
  multireplicate :: a → Multi a

    -- Map a function over the elements of a Multi a.
  multimap :: (a → a) → Multi a → Multi a

    -- Fold a function over the elements of a Multi a.
  multifold :: (b → a → b) → b → Multi a → b

    -- Zip two Multi a's with a function.
  multizipWith :: (a → a → a)
                  → Multi a → Multi a → Multi a
```

Figure 2: **The** MultiType **type class and its associated type,** Multi.

either. The scheme does not rely on lazy evaluation and would work fine in a call-by-value language.

3.3 A stream representation fit for SIMD computation

Modifying the stream fusion framework to accommodate SIMD operations requires a more thoughtful choice of representation. However, proper SIMD support opens up the possibility of dramatically increased performance for a wide range of numerical algorithms. We focus on SIMD computations using 128-bit wide vectors and SSE instructions on x86 since that is what our current implementation supports, although the approach generalizes.

Our implementation represents SIMD values using the type family Multi. We have chosen the name to avoid confusion with the Vector type which represents arrays of arbitrary extent. In contrast, a value of type Multi a is a short vector containing a *fixed* number of elements—known as its *multiplicity*—of type a. On a given platform, Multi a has a multiplicity that is appropriate for the platform's SIMD instructions. For example, on x86, a Multi Double will have multiplicity 2 since SSE instructions operate on 128-bit wide vectors, whereas a Multi Float will have multiplicity 4. Multi is implemented as an associated type [3] in the MultiType type class; their definitions are shown in Figure 2. MultiType includes various operations over Multi values, such as replicating a scalar across a Multi and folding a function over the scalar elements of a Multi. These operations are defined in terms of new primitives we added to GHC that compile directly to SSE instructions.

Given a value of type Vector Double, how can we operate on it efficiently using SSE instructions within the generalized stream fusion framework? An obvious first attempt is to include a stream of Multi Doubles in the stream bundle. However, this representation is insufficient for a vector with an odd number of elements since we will have one Double not belonging to a Multi at the end. Let us instead try this instead: a stream that can contain *either* a scalar or a Multi. We call this stream a MultisP because the *producer* chooses what will be yielded at each step.

```
data Either a b = Left a | Right b
type MultisP a = Stream (Either a (Multi a))
```

Now we can implement summation using SIMD operations. Our strategy is to use two accumulating parameters, one for the sum of the Multi values yielded by the stream and one for the sum of the scalar values. Note that (+) is overloaded: we use *SIMD* (+) to add summ and y, and *scalar* (+) to add sum1 and x.

```
msumP_s :: (Num a, Num (Multi a)) ⇒ MultisP a → a
msumP_s (Stream step s _) = loop 0.0 0.0 s
  where
    loop summ sum1 s =
      case step s of
        Yield (Left x)  s' → loop summ       (sum1 + x) s'
        Yield (Right y) s' → loop (summ + y) sum1       s'
        Skip            s' → loop summ       sum1       s'
        Done               → multifold (+) sum1 summ
```

When the stream is done yielding values, we call the multifold member of the MultiType type class to fold the addition operator over the components of the Multi.

This implementation strategy works nicely for folds. However, if we try to implement the SIMD equivalent of zipWith_s, we hit a roadblock. A SIMD version of zipWith_s requires that at each step either *both* of its input streams yield a Multi or they *both* yield a scalar—if one were to yield a scalar while the other yielded a Multi, we would have to somehow buffer the components of the Multi. And if one stream yielded *only* scalars while the other yielded only Multis, we would be hard-pressed to cope.

Instead of a stream representation where the producer chooses what is yielded, let us instead choose a representation where the stream *consumer* is in control.

```
data MultisC a where
  MultisC :: (s → Step s (Multi a))
          → (s → Step s a)
          → s
          → MultisC a
```

The idea is for a MultisC a to be able to yield either a value of type Multi a or a value of type a—the stream consumer chooses which by calling one of the two step functions. Note that the existential state is quantified over both step functions, meaning that the same state can be used to yield either a single scalar or a Multi. If there is not a full Multi available, the first step function will return Done. The remaining scalars will then be yielded by the second step function. This representation allows us to implement a SIMD version of zipWith_s (not shown here) and to slightly improve summation:

```
msumC_s :: (Num a, Num (Multi a)) ⇒ MultisC a → a
msumC_s (Stream mstep sstep s _) = mloop 0.0 s
  where
    mloop summ s =
      case mstep s of
        Yield x s' → mloop (summ + x) (Left s')
        Skip    s' → mloop summ       (Left s')
        Done       → sloop  summ 0.0 s

    sloop summ sum1 s =
      case sstep s of
        Yield x s' → sloop summ (sum1 + x) s'
        Skip    s' → sloop summ sum1       s'
        Done       → multifold (+) sum1 summ
```

Regrettably, a MultisC *still* isn't quite what we need. Consider appending two vectors of Doubles, each of which contains 41 elements. We cannot assume that the two vectors are laid out consecutively in memory, so even though the stream that results from appending them together will contain 82 scalars, this stream is forced to yield a scalar in the middle of the stream. One might imagine an implementation that buffers and shifts partial Multi values, but this leads to very inefficient code. The alternative is for append_s to produce a stream in which either a scalar or a Multi is yielded at each step—but that was the original representation we selected and then discarded because it was not suitable for zips!

The final compromise is to allow either—but not both—of these two representations. We cannot allow both—hence there is only one new bundle member rather than two—because while we can easily convert a MultisC a into a MultisP a, the other direction is not efficiently implementable. The final definition of the Multis type alias is therefore

type Multis a = Either (MultisC a) (MultisP a)

Each stream function that can operate on Multi values consumes the Multis a in the sMultis field of the stream bundle. It must be prepared to accept either a MultisC or a "mixed" stream of scalars and Multi's, as this final definition of $\mathsf{msum_s}$ shows:

```
msum_s :: (Num a, Num (Multi a)) ⇒ Bundle a → a
msum_s (Bundle {sMultis = Left  s}) = msumC_s s
msum_s (Bundle {sMultis = Right t}) = msumP_s t
```

However, we always try to produce a MultisC and only fall back to a MultisP as a last resort. Even operations that can work with either representation are often worth specializing for the MultisC form. In the case of $\mathsf{msum_s}$ above, this allows us to gobble up as many Multi values as possible and only then switch to consuming scalars, thereby cutting the number of accumulating parameters in half and reducing register pressure.

One could imagine attempting a representation that somehow guarantees longer runs of Multis, but this would add complexity and we doubt it would have any advantage over the MultisC representation, which has a distinct "phase shift" between operations on Multi and operations on scalars. For operations like zip that operate on multiple streams, we would need to guarantee that *both* streams have the same structure—it simply does not do to have one stream in the pair yield a scalar while the other yields a Multi. The MultiC/MultiP distinction neatly captures this requirement by framing it in terms of who has control over what is yielded next, consumers or producers.

3.4 A SIMD version of dotp

With a stream representation for SIMD computation in hand, we can write a SIMD-ized version of the dot product from Section 2.

```
dotp_simd :: Vector Double → Vector Double → Double
dotp_simd v w = msum (mzipWith (*) v w)
```

The only difference with respect to the scalar implementation in Section 2.2 is that we use variants of foldl′ and zipWith specialized to take function arguments that operate on values that are members of the Num type class. While we could have used versions of these functions that take two function arguments (our library contains both varietals), one for scalars and one for Multis, the forms that use overloading to allow the function argument to be used at both the type a → a → a and Multi a → Multi a → Multi a are a convenient shorthand.

```
mfold′ :: (PackedVector Vector a, Num a, Num (Multi a))
       ⇒ (∀b.Num b ⇒ b → b → b)
       → a → Vector a → a
mzipWith :: (PackedVector Vector a, Num a, Num (Multi a))
         ⇒ (∀b.Num b ⇒ b → b → b)
         → Vector a → Vector a → Vector a
msum :: (PackedVector Vector a, Num a, Num (Multi a))
     ⇒ Vector a → a
msum = mfold′ (+) 0
```

The particular fold we use here, mfold′, maintains two accumulators (a scalar and a Multi) when given a MultisP a, and one accumulator when given a MultisC a. The initial value of the scalar accumulator is the third argument to mfold′, and the initial value of the Multi accumulator is formed by replicating this scalar argument across a Multi. The result of the fold is computed by combining the elements of the Multi accumulator and the scalar accumulator using the function multifold, just as our implementation of $\mathsf{msum_s}$. Note that the first argument to mfold′ must be associative and commutative. The PackedVector type class constraint on mfold′, mzipWith, and msum ensures that the type a is an instance of MultiType and that elements contained in the vector can be extracted a Multi a at a time.

The stream version of mfold′, $\mathsf{mfold'_s}$, can generate efficient code no matter what representation is contained in a Multis a. On the other hand, the stream version of mzipWith, $\mathsf{mzipWith_s}$, requires that both its vector arguments have a MultisC representation. Since there is no good way to zip two streams when one yields a scalar and the other a Multi, if either bundle argument to $\mathsf{mzipWith_s}$ does not have a MultisC representation available, $\mathsf{mzipWith_s}$ falls back to an implementation that uses only scalar operations.

3.5 Automatically parallelizing SIMD computations

Using SIMD instructions does not come entirely for free. Consider mapping over a vector represented using multis:

```
mmap :: (PackedVector Vector a)
     ⇒ (a → a)
     → (Multi a → Multi a)
     → Vector a → Vector a
```

To map efficiently over the vector it does not suffice to pass a function of type (a → a), because that does not work over multis. We must also pass a semantically equivalent multi-version of the function. For simple arithmetic, matters are not too bad:

```
foo :: Vector Float → Vector Float
foo v = mmap (λx y → x + y ∗ 2) (λx y → x + y ∗ 2) v
```

The two lambdas are at different types, but Haskell's overloading takes care of that. We could attempt to abstract this pattern like this:

```
mmap :: (PackedVector Vector a)
     ⇒ (∀a.Num a ⇒ a → a)
     → Vector a → Vector a
```

But that attempt fails if you want operations in class Floating, say, rather than Num. What we want is a way to *automatically multi-ize scalar functions* (such as (λx y → x + y ∗ 2) above), so that we get a pair of a scalar function and a multi function, which in turn can be passed to map.

There is another problem: mmap only takes a function of type (a → a) which is less general (and hence less useful) than usual. The reason for this is the limited range of functions that the hardware offers over Multis, which is reflected in the type of multimap in the MultiType class (Figure 2).

Happily, both problems are already solved by the vectorization transformation of Data Parallel Haskell [4, 25], itself based on the pioneering NESL [1]. Given a function f over scalars, DPH produces a function f′ which operates on *vectors* of scalars and is equivalent to map f, but uses only primitive collective operations rather than iteration. Of course, a Multi is a special case of a vector and MultiType includes enough functionality to provide the primitive collective operations that DPH needs which means we can use it to produce SIMD code. Better still, DPH allows us to take advantage of *multiple cores*, as well as the SIMD instruction in each core. There are many moving parts here, but in principle we can get the convenience of scalar `vector` code, and *automatically* exploit both SIMD instructions and multi-core.

We start with an advantage: DPH is already built on the stream abstraction provided by the `vector` library. We modified the DPH libraries to use our bundle abstraction instead. Because DPH programs are vectorized by the compiler so that all scalar operations are turned into operations over wide vectors, by implementing these wide vector operations using our new SIMD functions like msum, programs written using DPH automatically and transparently take advantage of SSE instructions—no code changes are required of the programmer.

3.6 How general is generalized stream fusion?

We do not mean to suggest that the representations we have chosen for our Bundle data type are complete in any sense except that they allows us to take advantage of bulk memory operations and SIMD instructions, which was our original goal. Generalized stream fusion is not "general" because we have finally hit upon the full set of representations one could possibly ever need, but because the frameworks we have put forth admit multiple new, specialized representations. The key features of generalized stream fusion are 1) the ability to add new specialized stream representations, notably without requiring the library writer to rewrite the entire library; 2) leveraging the compiler to statically eliminate all intermediate Bundle structures and leave behind the single representation that is actually necessary to perform the desired computation; and 3) not requiring the end user to know about the details of Bundles, or even that they exist.

Generalized stream fusion provides a representation and algebraic laws for rewriting operations over this representation whose usefulness extends beyond Haskell. Although we have implemented generalized stream fusion as a library, it could also be incorporated into a compiler as an intermediate language. This was not necessary in our implementation because GHC's generic optimizer is powerful enough to eliminate all intermediate structures created by generalized stream fusion. In other words, GHC is such a good partial evaluator that we were able to build generalized stream fusion as a library rather than incorporating it into the compiler itself. Writing high-level code without paying an abstraction tax is desirable in any language, and compilers other than GHC could also avoid this tax by using the ideas we outline in this paper, although perhaps only by paying a substantial one-time implementation cost.

4. Implementation

There are three substantial components of our implementation. We first modified GHC itself to add support for SSE instructions. This required changing GHC's register allocator to allow overlapping register classes. Previously, single- and double-precision registers could only be drawn from disjoint sets of registers even though on many platforms, including x86 (when using SSE) and x86-64, there is a single register class for both single- and double-precision floating point values. This change was also necessary to allow SSE vectors to be stored in registers. We then added support for primitive SIMD vector types and primitive operations over these types to GHC's dialect of Haskell. These primitives are fully unboxed [26]. The STG [22] and C-- [27] intermediate languages, as well as the LLVM code generator [31], were also extended to support compiling the new Haskell SIMD primitives. Boxed wrappers for the unboxed primitives and the MultiType type class and its associated Multi type complete the high-level support for working directly with basic SIMD data types. Because the SIMD support we added to GHC utilizes the LLVM back-end, it should be relatively straightforward to adapt our modifications for other CPU architectures, although at this time only x86-64 is supported.

Second, we implemented generalized stream fusion in a modified version of the `vector` library [19] for computing with efficient unboxed vectors in Haskell. We replaced the existing stream fusion implementation with an implementation that uses the Bundle representation and extended the existing API with functions such as mfold′ and mzipWith that enable using SIMD operations on the contents of vectors. The examples in this paper are somewhat simplified from the actual implementations. For example, the actual implementations are written in monadic form and involve type class constraints that we have elided. Vectors whose scalar elements can be accessed in SIMD-sized groups, i.e., vectors whose scalar elements are laid out consecutively in memory, are actually represented using a PackedVector type class. These details do not affect the essential design choices we have described, and the functions used in all examples are simply type-specialized instances of the true implementations.

Third, we modified the DPH libraries to take advantage of our new `vector` library. The DPH libraries are built on top of the stream representation from a previous version of the `vector` library, so we first updated DPH to use our bundle representation instead. We next re-implemented the primitive wide-vector operations in DPH in terms of our new SIMD operations on bundles. While we only provided SIMD implementation for operations on double-precision floating point values, this part of the implementation was quite small, consisting of approximately 20 lines of code not counting `#ifdefs`. Further extending SIMD support in DPH will be easy now that it is based on bundles rather than streams.

Our register allocation patch and our SIMD patches supporting SSE instructions have already been accepted into mainline GHC. Our modifications to the `vector` and DPH libraries are available in a public git repository. We expect these library modifications to also be adopted by their respective maintainers. Our branch of GHC also supports AVX instructions. We are working with all maintainers to ensure that the work we report on in this paper will be available in the GHC 7.8 release along with our support for AVX instructions. In the evaluation that follows, we focus on SSE instructions because the libraries we use for comparison do not yet support AVX.

```
double cddotp(double* u, double* v, int n)
{
    double s = 0.0;
    int    i;

    for (i = 0; i < n; ++i)
        s += u[i] * v[i];

    return s;
}
```

Figure 3: **C implementation of vector dot product using only scalar operations.**

5. Evaluation

Our original goal in modifying GHC and the `vector` library was to make efficient use of SSE instructions from high-level Haskell code. The inability to use SSE operations from Haskell and its impact on performance is a deficiency that was brought to our attention by Lippmeier and Keller [20]. The first step we took was to write a small number of simple C functions utilizing SSE intrinsics to serve as benchmarks. This gave us a very concrete goal—to generate machine code from Haskell that was competitive with these C implementations.

For comparison, we also implemented a C version of `ddotp` using only scalar operations, shown in Figure 3. The C implementation we use as a benchmark for double-precision dot product, to which we have added support for SSE by hand, is given in Figure 4. We repeat the definition of the Haskell implementation here.

```
#include <xmmintrin.h>

#define VECTOR_SIZE 2

typedef double v2sd __attribute__
  ((vector_size(sizeof(double)*
        VECTOR_SIZE)));

union d2v
{
  v2sd    v;
  double d[VECTOR_SIZE];
};

double ddotp(double* u, double* v, int n)
{
    union d2v d2s = {0.0, 0.0};
    double     s;
    int        i;
    int        m = n & (~VECTOR_SIZE);

    for (i = 0; i < m; i += VECTOR_SIZE)
        d2s.v += (*((v2sd*) (u+i)))*(*((v2sd*)
            (v+i)));

    s = d2s.d[0] + d2s.d[1];

    for (; i < n; ++i)
        s += u[i] * v[i];

    return s;
}
```

Figure 4: **C implementation of vector dot product using SSE intrinsics.**

ddotp :: Vector Double → Vector Double → Double
ddotp v w = mfold′ (+) 0 (mzipWith (∗) v w)

Though not exactly onerous, the C version with SSE support is already unpleasantly more complex than the scalar version. And surely the Haskell version, consisting of a single line of code (not including the optional type signature) is a good bit simpler. Also note that the Haskell programmer can think compositionally—it is natural to think of dot product as pair-wise multiplication followed by summation. The C programmer, on the other hand, must manually fuse the two loops into a single multiply-add. Furthermore, as well as being constructed compositionally, the Haskell implementation can itself be *used* compositionally. That is, if the input vectors to ddotp are themselves the results of vector computations, generalized stream fusion will potentially fuse all operations in the chain into a single loop. In contrast, the C programmer must manifest the input to the C implementation of ddotp as concrete vectors in memory—there is no potential for automatic fusion with other operations.

Figure 5 compares the single-threaded performance of several implementations of the dot product, including C and Haskell versions that only use scalar operations as well as the implementation provided by GotoBLAS2 1.13 [9, 10]. Times were measured on a 3.40GHz Intel i7-2600K processor, averaged over 100 runs. To make the relative performance of the various implementations clearer, we show the execution time of each implementation relative to the scalar C version (from Figure 4), which is normalized to 1.0, in Figure 6.

Surprisingly, both the naive scalar C implementation (Figure 3) and the version written using SSE intrinsics (Figure 4) perform approximately the same. This is because GCC in fact vectorizes the scalar implementation. However, the Haskell implementation is almost always faster than both C versions; it is 5-20% slower for very short vectors (those with fewer than about 16 elements) and 1-

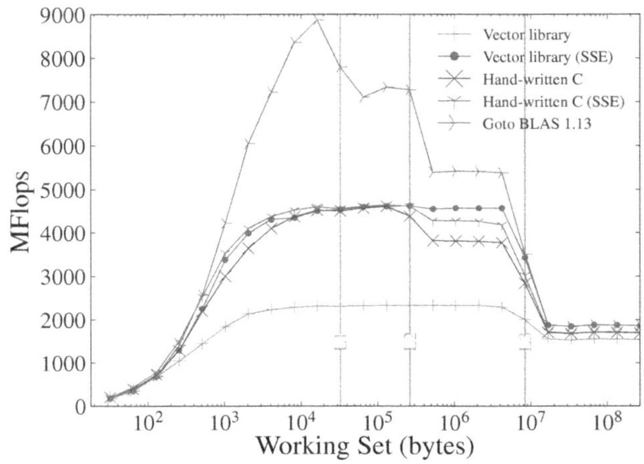

Figure 5: **Single-threaded performance of double-precision dot product implementations.** C implementations were compiled using GCC 4.8.1 and compiler options `-O3 -msse4.2 -ffast-math -ftree-vectorize -funroll-loops`. Sizes of the L1, L2, and L3 caches are marked.

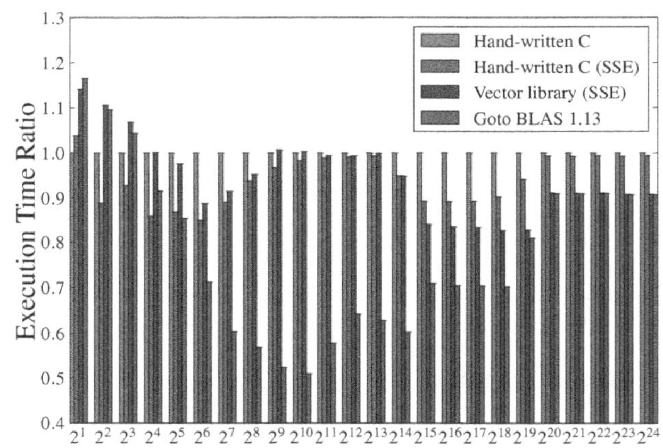

Figure 6: **Relative performance of single-threaded ddot implementations.** All times are normalized relative to the hand-written, compiler-vectorized, C implementation.

2% slower just when the working set size exceeds the capacity of the L1 cache. Not only does Haskell outperform C on this benchmark, but it outperforms GCC's vectorizer. Once the working set no longer fits in L3 cache, the Haskell implementation is even neck-and-neck with the implementation of ddotp from GotoBLAS, a collection of highly-tuned BLAS routines hand-written in assembly language that is generally considered to be one of the fastest BLAS implementation available. Unfortunately, at the time of publication we do not yet have a license for Intel's compiler. However, we note that anecdotally it performs a much better job vectorizing loops than GCC, especially for the simple loops shown here. We view this as future challenge for Haskell.

5.1 Prefetching and loop unrolling

Why is Haskell so fast? Because we have exploited the high-level stream-fusion framework to embody two additional optimizations: *loop unrolling* and *prefetching*.

The generalized stream fusion framework allowed us to implement the equivalent of loop unrolling by adding under 200 lines of code the to `vector` library. We changed the MultisC data type to incorporate a *leap*, which is a Step that contains multiple values of type Multi a. We chose Leap to contain four values—so loops are unrolled four times—since on x86-64 processors this tends not to put too much register pressure on the register allocator. Adding multiple Leaps of different sizes would also be possible. MultisC consumers may of course chose not to use the Leap stepping function, in which case loops will not be unrolled.

```
data Leap a = Leap a a a a
data MultisC a where
  MultisC :: (s → Step s (Leap (Multi a)))
             → (s → Step s (Multi a))
             → (s → Step s a)
             → s
             → MultisC a
```

Prefetch instructions on Intel processors allow the program to give the CPU a hint about memory access patterns, telling it to prefetch memory that the program plans to use in the future. In our library, these prefetch hints are implemented using prefetch primitives that we added to GHC. When converting a Vector to a MultisC, we know exactly what memory access pattern will be used—each element of the vector will be accessed in linear order. The function that performs this conversion, stream, takes advantage of this knowledge by executing prefetch instructions as it yields each Leap. Only consumers using Leaps will compile to loops containing prefetch instructions, and stream will only add prefetch instructions for vectors whose size is above a fixed threshold (currently 8192 elements), because for shorter vectors the extra instruction dispatch overhead is not amortized by the increase in memory throughput. Loop unrolling and prefetching produce an inner loop for our Haskell implementation of ddotp that is shown in Figure 7.

Not only can the client of our modified `vector` library write programs in terms of boxed values and directly compose vector operations instead of manually fusing operations without paying an abstraction penalty, but he or she can transparently benefit from low-level prefetch magic baked into the library. Of course the same prefetch magic could be expressed manually in the C version. However, the author who wrote the code in Figure 4 did not know about prefetch at the time of implementation. We suspect that many C programmers are in the same state of ignorance. In Haskell, this knowledge is embedded in a library, and clients benefit from it automatically.

```
.LBB4_12:
        prefetcht0 1600(%rsi,%rdx)
        movupd     64(%rsi,%rdx), %xmm3
        prefetcht0 1600(%rdi,%rdx)
        movupd     80(%rsi,%rdx), %xmm0
        movupd     80(%rdi,%rdx), %xmm2
        mulpd      %xmm0, %xmm2
        movupd     64(%rdi,%rdx), %xmm0
        mulpd      %xmm3, %xmm0
        addpd      %xmm1, %xmm0
        addpd      %xmm2, %xmm0
        movupd     96(%rsi,%rdx), %xmm3
        movupd     96(%rdi,%rdx), %xmm1
        movupd     112(%rsi,%rdx), %xmm4
        movupd     112(%rdi,%rdx), %xmm2
        mulpd      %xmm4, %xmm2
        mulpd      %xmm3, %xmm1
        addq       $64, %rdx
        leaq       8(%rax), %rcx
        addq       $16, %rax
        addpd      %xmm0, %xmm1
        cmpq       %r9, %rax
        addpd      %xmm2, %xmm1
        movq       %rcx, %rax
        jle        .LBB4_12
```

Figure 7: **Inner loop of Haskell** ddotp **function.**

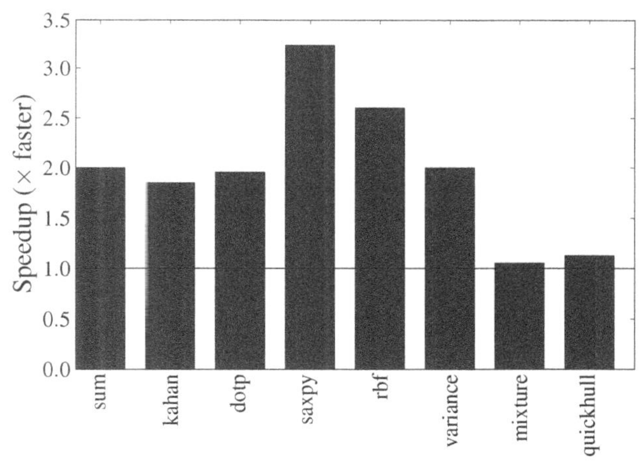

Figure 8: **Speedup of benchmarks from using modified** `vector`.

5.2 Speeding up Haskell

To see how easy it is to integrate SIMD instruction into existing programs, we rewrote a number of functions from various packages using our modified `vector` library. In all cases, we simply identified suitable operations (typically maps and folds) and replaced them by multi-enabled versions. We did *not* modify or refactor the algorithms. The speedup of the rewritten versions is shown in Figure 8. The 'sum', 'kahan', 'dotp', 'saxpy', and 'rbf' benchmarks are short programs that make heavy use of numerics ('kahan' implements Kahan summation [16]). One benchmark, 'variance', is adapted from the `statistics` [2] Haskell package. These first six benchmarks were run using vectors containing 2^{16} Doubles. The 'mixture' benchmark is adapted from the `StatisticalMethods` [5] Haskell package and implements the expectation-maximization (EM) algorithm for a mixture of two Gaussians [13, §8.5.1]. The final benchmark, 'quickhull', is adapated from the examples included with DPH.

The first six benchmarks consist almost entirely of numeric operations for which SSE version are available; correspondingly, they show a significant speedup, from more than 1.5× to more than 3×. The final two functions contain features that frustrated our efforts, such as use of non-numeric operations or data-dependent control flow, which is difficult to vectorize. One benchmark, 'mixture', has a run time that is exponential in the size of its input, so we could only run it on very small data sets. Nevertheless, we were able to gain at least a minimum of a few percentage points even on these difficult-to-vectorize benchmarks just by picking some low-hanging fruit. Notably, we were unable to improve the run time of

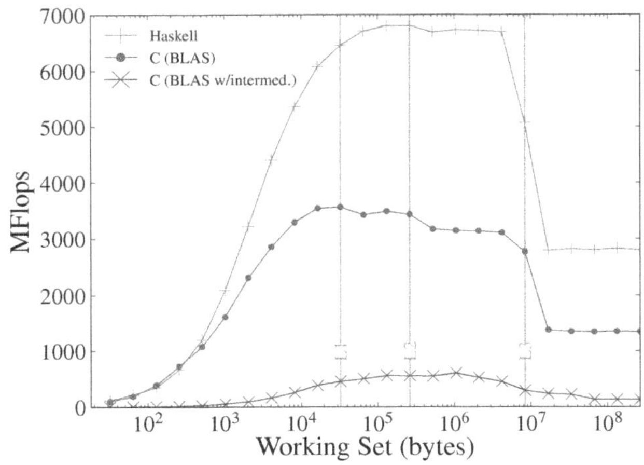

Figure 9: **Performance of Haskell and C Gaussian RBF implementations..**

benchmarks that made heavy use of operations like exponentiation for which we do not have vectorized versions. Using Intel's Math Kernel Library (MKL), which provides such primitives, would enable further speedups. Nonetheless, we expect that many Haskell programs that make some use of numerical operations on sequences will have at least a few opportunities for vectorization. Rewriting a small amount of code for a 5% performance improvement is worthwhile; rewriting a small amount of code for a 3× performance improvement is an unbelievably good deal.

5.3 Abstraction without cost

Using Haskell for implementing kernels such as `dotp` provides us with another significant advantage: these kernels can fuse with other vector operations! Fusion is not possible with BLAS routines but can dramatically increase performance. Consider the Gaussian radial basis function [13], defined as

$$K(\mathbf{x},\mathbf{y}) = e^{-\nu\|\mathbf{x}-\mathbf{y}\|^2}$$

A C programmer implementing this function could take advantage of high-performance BLAS routines in two possible ways. The first is to write $\mathbf{x}-\mathbf{y}$ to a temporary vector and then call BLAS. Of course this requires an intermediate structure, which is undesirable. The second possibility is to apply the identity $\|\mathbf{x}-\mathbf{y}\|^2 = \mathbf{x}\cdot\mathbf{x} - 2\mathbf{x}\cdot\mathbf{y} + \mathbf{y}\cdot\mathbf{y}$ and call into the BLAS three times without creating a temporary vector. This does not require an intermediate structure, but it requires making multiple passes over each input vector. It is also numerically unstable. The Haskell programmer, on the other hand, could straightforwardly write the following implementation

```
rbf :: Double → Vector Double → Vector Double → Double
rbf ν v w = exp (−ν ∗ msum (mzipWith norm v w))
  where
    norm x y = square (x − y)
    square x = x ∗ x
```

We show the performance of three implementations of the Gaussian RBF in Figure 9. The first is the Haskell function rbf whose definition we have just given. The second is the C version that uses the above identity to avoid temporary allocation, and the third allocates an intermediate value. The Haskell version with SSE support is the clear winner—due to fusion, it touches each element of the two vectors only once.

```
double norm2(VectorXd const& v)
{
    return v.dot(v);
}

double eigen_rbf(double nu, VectorXd const& u,
    VectorXd const& v)
{
    VectorXd temp = u - v;

    return exp(-nu*norm2(u-v));
}
```

Figure 10: **Poorly-performing C++ implementation of Gaussian radial basis function.**

5.4 The cost of abstraction in C++

C is a straw man when fusion of array operations becomes critical for performance—we know of no C compiler that can perform this kind of optimisation. An imperative programmer would not attack these sorts of problems with C in any case, but likely turn to C++, for which there are a number of libraries tailored to matrix computation that do perform fusion. These libraries all use expression templates [32], a technique pioneered by the Blitz++ [33] library.

We have implemented C++ versions of the Gaussian RBF using three different libraries: Blitz++ 0.10 [33], Boost uBLAS 1.53 [14], and Eigen 3.1.2 [11]. We give performance numbers for all three, but our discussion focuses on Eigen, which utilizes SSE instructions and is generally considered the most performant library in this class. Figure 10 shows the Gaussian RBF implemented using Eigen. Note that we have implemented the square of the L_2-norm ourselves, a point we return to later. In this specific case the Eigen library has the squared L_2-norm in its API, but in more complicated examples there might be no such built-in provision.

After writing the code in Figure 10, we decided to actually read the Eigen documentation. We reproduce a highly relevant note here [11]:

> To summarize, the implementation of functions taking non-writable (const referenced) objects is not a big issue and does not lead to problematic situations in terms of compiling and running your program. However, a naive implementation is likely to introduce unnecessary temporary objects in your code. In order to avoid evaluating parameters into temporaries, pass them as (const) references to MatrixBase or ArrayBase (so templatize your function).

Having read this, we realized our mistake and modified our code, producing the version in Figure 11. Avoiding temporary allocation in Eigen and other libraries can require some care because expression templates are not vectors or matrices, but represent *computations* that, when run, compute a matrix or vector. Programmer-written abstractions must be careful to abstract over *expression templates*, and not over matrices or vectors. Figure 12 shows the performance of the Haskell and C++ implementations of the Gaussian radial basis function. Our initial version using Eigen (from Figure 10, labeled "Eigen (bad norm2)") performs quite poorly but the modified one is the fastest by far. Interestingly, once the working set no longer fits in L3 cache, the Boost version, which does not use SSE instructions, outperforms all SSE-enabled variants except the fast Eigen version. We suspect that Boost and Eigen interact better with the processor's prefetch prediction than the other libraries.

Clearly "properly"-written C++ can outperform Haskell. The challenge is in figuring out what "proper" means. In the domain covered by vectorlib, a Haskell programmer can write straightfor-

```
template <typename Derived>
typename Derived::Scalar norm2(const
    MatrixBase<Derived>& v)
{
    return v.dot(v);
}

double eigen_rbf(double nu, VectorXd const& u,
    VectorXd const& v)
{
    VectorXd temp = u - v;

    return exp(-nu*norm2(u-v));
}
```

Figure 11: **Performant C++ implementation of Gaussian radial basis function.** This version is templatized, vastly improving its performance.

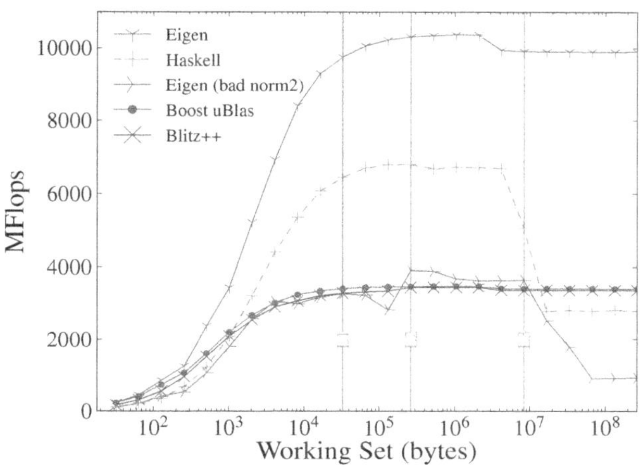

Figure 12: **Performance of Haskell and C++ Gaussian RBF implementations.**

ward, declarative code and expect the compiler to handle fusion. The C++ programmer must worry about the performance implications of abstraction.

Furthermore, unlike Eigen, our implementation is immature, and there are several straightforward changes that will further improve the absolute performance of Haskell code. There is room for improvement in our use of prefetching. More importantly, we currently cannot rely on memory allocated by GHC to be properly aligned for SSE move-aligned instructions, so all SSE move instructions are unaligned. Differentiating between unaligned and aligned memory will allow us to avoid the large performance hit incurred by our current implementation.

5.5 Generalized stream fusion in Data Parallel Haskell

As we described in Section 3.5, we have modified Data Parallel Haskell (DPH) to generate vectorized programs that work over bundles, and hence exploit both SSE and multi-core parallelism. Figure 13 shows the performance of several dot product implementations, including DPH implementations with and without our rewritten run-time. These measurements were taken on a 32-core (4×8) AMD Opteron 6128 running at 2GHz. In addition to transparently taking advantage of SSE instructions, our modified version of DPH transparently takes advantage of additional cores. Unfortunately, DPH does not scale particularly well on this benchmark. This is

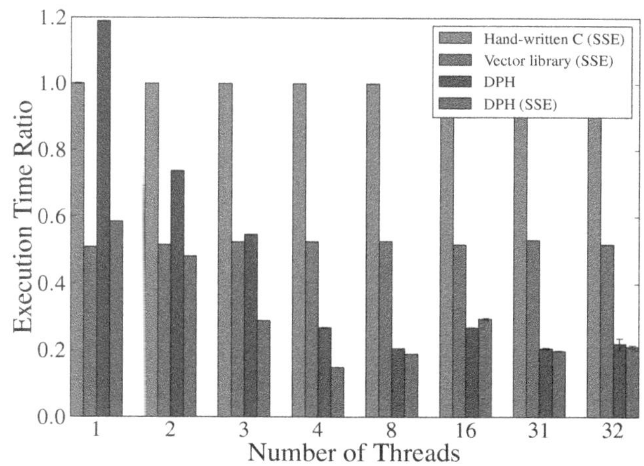

Figure 13: **Performance of double-precision dot product implementations.** The DPH implementations are multi-threaded, and the vector library and hand-written C implementations are single-threaded. Error bars show variance.

undoubtedly in part because we not only used a development version of DPH, but we also then performed substantial surgery to adapt it to our version of `vector`. We do not know why the scalar version outperformed the SSE-enabled version in the 16-core case.

6. Related Work

Wadler [34] introduced the problem of deforestation, that is, of eliminating intermediate structures in programs written as compositions of list transforming functions. A great deal of follow-on work [8, 12, 15, 23, 29, 30] attempted to improve the ability of compilers to automate deforestation through program transformations. Each of these approaches to fusion has severe limitations. For example, Gill et al. [8] cannot fuse left folds, such as that which arises in `sum`, or `zipWith`, and Svenningsson [29] cannot handle nested computations such as mapping a function over concatenated lists. Our work is based on the stream fusion framework described by Coutts et al. [6], which can fuse all of these use cases and more. The `vector` library uses stream fusion to fuse operations on vectors rather than lists, but the principles are the same.

7. Conclusion

Generalized stream fusion is a strict improvement on stream fusion; by re-casting stream fusion to operate on bundles of streams, each vector operation or class of operations can utilize a stream representation tailored to its particular pattern of computation. We describe two new stream representations, one supporting bulk memory operations, and one adapted for SIMD computation with short-vector instructions, e.g., SSE on x86. We have added support for low-level SSE instructions to GHC and incorporated generalized stream fusion into the `vector` library. Using our modified library, programmers can write compositional, high-level programs for manipulating vectors without loss of efficiency. Benchmarks show that these programs can perform competitively with hand-written C.

Although we implemented generalized stream fusion in a Haskell library, the bundled stream representation could be used as an intermediate language in another compiler. Vector operations would no longer be first class in such a formulation, but it would allow a language to take advantage of fusion without requiring implementations of the general purpose optimizations present in

GHC that allow it to eliminate the intermediate structures produced by generalized stream fusion.

Acknowledgments

The authors would like to thank Simon Marlow for his help debugging GHC's runtime system and code generator. We are also grateful for Andrew Fitzgibbon's many insightful comments.

References

[1] G. E. Blelloch, J. C. Hardwick, J. Sipelstein, M. Zagha, and S. Chatterjee. Implementation of a portable nested data-parallel language. *Journal of Parallel and Distributed Computing*, 21(1):4–14, 1994.

[2] Bryan O'Sullivan. statistics: A library of statistical types, data, and functions, aug 2012. URL `http://hackage.haskell.org/package/statistics`.

[3] M. M. T. Chakravarty, G. Keller, S. Peyton Jones, and S. Marlow. Associated types with class. In *Proceedings of the 32nd ACM SIGPLAN-SIGACT symposium on Principles of Programming Languages*, POPL '05, page 1–13, New York, NY, USA, 2005.

[4] M. M. T. Chakravarty, R. Leshchinskiy, S. Peyton Jones, G. Keller, and S. Marlow. Data Parallel Haskell: a status report. In *Proceedings of the 2007 workshop on Declarative Aspects of Multicore Programming*, DAMP '07, page 10–18, Nice, France, 2007.

[5] Christian Höner zu Siederdissen. StatisticalMethods: collection of useful statistical methods., aug 2011. URL `http://hackage.haskell.org/package/StatisticalMethods`.

[6] D. Coutts, R. Leshchinskiy, and D. Stewart. Stream fusion: from lists to streams to nothing at all. In *Proceedings of the 12th ACM SIGPLAN International Conference on Functional Programming*, pages 315–326, Freiburg, Germany, 2007.

[7] Duncun Coutts. *Stream Fusion: Practical shortcut fusion for coinductive sequence types*. PhD thesis, University of Oxford, 2010.

[8] A. Gill, J. Launchbury, and S. L. Peyton Jones. A short cut to deforestation. In *Proceedings of the conference on Functional Programming Languages and Computer Architecture*, FPCA '93, page 223–232, New York, NY, USA, 1993.

[9] K. Goto and R. v. d. Geijn. Anatomy of high-performance matrix multiplication. *ACM Trans. Math. Softw.*, 34(3):1–25, 2008.

[10] K. Goto and R. v. d. Geijn. High-performance implementation of the level-3 BLAS. *ACM Trans. Math. Softw.*, 35(1):1–14, 2008.

[11] G. Guennebaud, B. Jacob, and others. Eigen v3, 2010. URL `http://eigen.tuxfamily.org`.

[12] G. W. Hamilton. Extending higher-order deforestation: transforming programs to eliminate even more trees. In K. Hammond and S. Curtis, editors, *Proceedings of the Third Scottish Functional Programming Workshop*, page 25–36, Exeter, UK, UK, aug 2001.

[13] T. Hastie, R. Tibshirani, and J. Friedman. *The Elements of Statistical Learning*. 2 edition, 2009.

[14] Joerg Walter, Mathias Koch, Gunter Winkler, and David Bellot. Boost basic linear algebra - 1.53.0, 2010. URL `http://www.boost.org/doc/libs/1_53_0/libs/numeric/ublas/doc/index.htm`.

[15] P. Johann. Short cut fusion: proved and improved. In *Proceedings of the 2nd international conference on Semantics, applications, and implementation of program generation*, SAIG'01, page 47–71, Berlin, Heidelberg, 2001.

[16] W. Kahan. Pracniques: further remarks on reducing truncation errors. *Commun. ACM*, 8(1):40–, jan 1965.

[17] G. Keller, M. M. Chakravarty, R. Leshchinskiy, S. Peyton Jones, and B. Lippmeier. Regular, shape-polymorphic, parallel arrays in Haskell. In *Proceedings of the 15th ACM SIGPLAN International Conference on Functional Programming*, ICFP '10, page 261–272, New York, NY, USA, 2010.

[18] J. Launchbury and S. L. Peyton Jones. State in Haskell. *Lisp and Symbolic Computation*, 8(4):293–341, 1995.

[19] R. Leshchinskiy. vector: Efficient arrays, oct 2012. URL `http://hackage.haskell.org/package/vector`.

[20] B. Lippmeier and G. Keller. Efficient parallel stencil convolution in Haskell. In *Proceedings of the 4th ACM Symposium on Haskell*, Haskell '11, page 59–70, New York, NY, USA, 2011.

[21] B. Lippmeier, M. Chakravarty, G. Keller, and S. Peyton Jones. Guiding parallel array fusion with indexed types. In *Proceedings of the 2012 Symposium on Haskell*, Haskell '12, page 25–36, New York, NY, USA, 2012.

[22] S. Marlow and S. Peyton Jones. Making a fast curry: Push/Enter vs. Eval/Apply for higher-order languages. *Journal of Functional Programming*, 16(4-5):415–449, 2006.

[23] S. Marlow and P. Wadler. Deforestation for higher-order functions. In *Proceedings of the 1992 Glasgow Workshop on Functional Programming*, page 154–165, London, UK, UK, 1993.

[24] S. Peyton Jones. Call-pattern specialisation for Haskell programs. In *Proceedings of the 12th ACM SIGPLAN International Conference on Functional Programming*, ICFP '07, page 327–337, New York, NY, USA, 2007.

[25] S. Peyton Jones, R. Leshchinskiy, G. Keller, and M. Chakravarty. Harnessing the multicores: Nested data parallelism in Haskell. In *Programming Languages and Systems*, page 138. 2008.

[26] S. L. Peyton Jones and J. Launchbury. Unboxed values as first class citizens in a non-strict functional language. In *Proceedings of the 5th ACM Conference on Functional Programming Languages and Computer Architecture*, pages 636–666, 1991.

[27] S. L. Peyton Jones, N. Ramsey, and F. Reig. C--: a portable assembly language that supports garbage collection. In *International Conference on Principles and Practice of Declarative Programming*, sep 1999.

[28] S. L. Peyton Jones, T. Hoare, and A. Tolmach. Playing by the rules: rewriting as a practical optimisation technique. In *Proceedings of the 2001 ACM SIGPLAN Workshop on Haskell*, 2001.

[29] J. Svenningsson. Shortcut fusion for accumulating parameters & zip-like functions. In *Proceedings of the seventh ACM SIGPLAN International Conference on Functional Programming*, ICFP '02, page 124–132, New York, NY, USA, 2002.

[30] A. Takano and E. Meijer. Shortcut deforestation in calculational form. In *Proceedings of the seventh international conference on Functional Programming and Computer Architecture*, FPCA '95, page 306–313, New York, NY, USA, 1995.

[31] D. A. Terei and M. M. Chakravarty. An LLVM backend for GHC. In *Proceedings of the third ACM Symposium on Haskell*, Haskell '10, page 109–120, New York, NY, USA, 2010.

[32] T. Veldhuizen. Expression templates. *C++ Report*, 7(5):26–31, jun 1995.

[33] T. L. Veldhuizen. Arrays in Blitz++. In D. Caromel, R. R. Oldehoeft, and M. Tholburn, editors, *Computing in Object-Oriented Parallel Environments*, number 1505 in Lecture Notes in Computer Science, pages 223–230. jan 1998.

[34] P. Wadler. Deforestation: transforming programs to eliminate trees. *Theoretical Computer Science*, 73(2):231–248, jun 1990.

Optimising Purely Functional GPU Programs

Trevor L. McDonell Manuel M. T. Chakravarty Gabriele Keller Ben Lippmeier

University of New South Wales, Australia

{tmcdonell,chak,keller,benl}@cse.unsw.edu.au

Abstract

Purely functional, embedded array programs are a good match for SIMD hardware, such as GPUs. However, the naive compilation of such programs quickly leads to both code explosion and an excessive use of intermediate data structures. The resulting slowdown is not acceptable on target hardware that is usually chosen to achieve high performance.

In this paper, we discuss two optimisation techniques, *sharing recovery* and *array fusion*, that tackle code explosion and eliminate superfluous intermediate structures. Both techniques are well known from other contexts, but they present unique challenges for an embedded language compiled for execution on a GPU. We present novel methods for implementing sharing recovery and array fusion, and demonstrate their effectiveness on a set of benchmarks.

Categories and Subject Descriptors D.3.2 [*Programming Languages*]: Language Classification—Applicative (functional) languages; Concurrent, distributed, and parallel languages

Keywords Arrays; Data parallelism; Embedded language; Dynamic compilation; GPGPU; Haskell; Sharing recovery; Array fusion

1. Introduction

Recent work on stream fusion [12], the `vector` package [23], and the parallel array library Repa [17, 19, 20] has demonstrated that (1) the performance of purely functional array code in Haskell can be competitive with that of imperative programs and that (2) purely functional array code lends itself to an efficient parallel implementation on control-parallel multicore CPUs.

So far, the use of purely functional languages for programming data parallel SIMD hardware such as GPUs (Graphical Processing Units) has been less successful. Vertigo [13] was an early Haskell EDSL producing DirectX 9 shader code, though no runtime performance figures were reported. Nikola [22] produces code competitive with CUDA, but without supporting generative functions like `replicate` where the result size is not statically fixed. Obsidian [10] is additionally restricted to only processing arrays of a fixed, implementation dependent size. Additionally, both Nikola and Obsidian can only generate single GPU kernels at a time, so that in programs consisting of multiple kernels the intermediate data structures must be shuffled back and forth across the CPU-GPU bus.

We recently presented *Accelerate*, an EDSL and skeleton-based code generator targeting the CUDA GPU development environment [8]. In the present paper, we present novel methods for optimising the code using *sharing recovery* and *array fusion*.

Sharing recovery for embedded languages recovers the sharing of let-bound expressions that would otherwise be lost due to the embedding. Without sharing recovery, the value of a let-bound expression is recomputed for every use of the bound variable. In contrast to prior work [14] that decomposes expression trees into graphs and fails to be type preserving, our novel algorithm preserves both the tree structure and typing of a deeply embedded language. This enables our runtime compiler to be similarly type preserving and simplifies the backend by operating on a tree-based intermediate language.

Array fusion eliminates the intermediate values and additional GPU kernels that would otherwise be needed when successive bulk operators are applied to an array. Existing methods such as `foldr/build` fusion [15] and stream fusion [12] are not applicable to our setting as they produce tail-recursive loops, rather than the GPU kernels we need for Accelerate. The NDP2GPU system of [4] *does* produce fused GPU kernels, but is limited to simple map/map fusion. We present a fusion method partly inspired by Repa's *delayed arrays* [17] that fuses more general producers and consumers, while retaining the combinator based program representation that is essential for GPU code generation using skeletons.

With these techniques, we provide a high-level programming model that supports shape-polymorphic maps, generators, reductions, permutation and stencil-based operations, while maintaining performance that often approaches hand-written CUDA code.

In summary, we make the following contributions:

- We introduce a novel sharing recovery algorithm for type-safe ASTs, preserving the tree structure (Section 3).
- We introduce a novel approach to array fusion for embedded array languages (Section 4).
- We present benchmarks for several applications including Black-Scholes options pricing, Canny edge detection, and a fluid flow simulation, including a comparison with hand-optimised CPU and GPU code (Section 5).

This paper builds on our previous work on a skeleton-based CUDA code generator for Accelerate [8]. Although we motivate and evaluate our novel approaches to sharing recovery and array fusion in this context, our contribution is not limited to Accelerate. Specifically, our sharing recovery applies to any embedded language based on the typed lambda calculus and our array fusion applies to any dynamic compiler targeting bulk-parallel SIMD hardware.

We discuss related work in detail in Section 6. The source code for Accelerate including our benchmark code is available from `https://github.com/AccelerateHS/accelerate`.

ICFP '13, September 25–27, 2013, Boston, MA, USA.

ACM 978-1-4503-2326-0/13/09... $15.00.
http://dx.doi.org/10.1145/2500365.2500595

2. Optimising embedded array code

Accelerate is a *domain specific* language, consisting of a carefully selected set of array operators that we can produce efficient GPU code for. Accelerate is *embedded* in Haskell, meaning that we write Accelerate programs using Haskell syntax, but do not compile arbitrary Haskell programs to GPU machine code. Accelerate is stratified into *array computations*, wrapped in a type constructor `Acc`, and *scalar expressions*, represented by terms of type `Exp t`, where `t` is the type of value produced by the expression. This stratification is necessary due to the hardware architecture of GPUs and their reliance on SIMD parallelism, as we discussed in our previous work [8].

2.1 Too many kernels

For example, to compute a dot product, we use:

```
dotp :: Vector Float -> Vector Float
     -> Acc (Scalar Float)
dotp xs ys = let xs' = use xs
                 ys' = use ys
             in  fold (+) 0 (zipWith (*) xs' ys')
```

The function `dotp` consumes two one-dimensional arrays (`Vector`) of floating-point values and produces a single (`Scalar`) floating-point result. From the return type `Acc (Scalar Float)`, we see that `dotp` is an embedded Accelerate computation, rather than vanilla Haskell code.

The functions `zipWith` and `fold` are defined in our library `Data.Array.Accelerate`, and have *massively parallel* GPU implementations with the following type signatures:

```
zipWith :: (Shape sh, Elt a, Elt b, Elt c)
        => (Exp a -> Exp b -> Exp c)
        -> Acc (Array sh a)
        -> Acc (Array sh b)
        -> Acc (Array sh c)

fold    :: (Shape ix, Elt a)
        => (Exp a -> Exp a -> Exp a)
        -> Exp a
        -> Acc (Array (ix:.Int) a)
        -> Acc (Array ix a)
```

The type classes `Elt` and `Shape` indicate that a type is admissible as an array element and array shape, respectively. Array shapes are denoted by type-level lists formed from `Z` and `(:.)` — for example, `Z:.Int:.Int` is the shape of a two-dimensional array (see [8, 17] for details). The type signatures of `zipWith` and `fold` clearly show the stratification into scalar computations using the `Exp` type constructor, and array computations wrapped in `Acc`.

The arguments to `dotp` are of plain Haskell type `Vector Float`. To make these arguments available to the Accelerate computation they must be embedded with the `use` function:

```
use :: Arrays arrays => arrays -> Acc arrays
```

This function is overloaded so that it can accept entire tuples of `arrays`. Operationally, `use` copies array data from main memory to GPU memory, in preparation for processing by the GPU.

The above Haskell version of the GPU-accelerated dot product is certainly more compact than the corresponding CUDA C code. However, when compiled with the skeleton-based approach we described in previous work [8], it is also significantly slower. The CUDA C version executes in about half the time (see Table 2).

The slow-down is due to Accelerate generating one *GPU kernel function* for `zipWith` and another one for `fold`. In contrast, the CUDA C version only uses a single kernel. The use of two separate kernels requires an intermediate array to be constructed, and in a memory bound benchmark, such as `dotp`, this doubles the runtime. To eliminate this intermediate array we need to *fuse* the adjacent aggregate array computations. Although there is an existing body of work on array fusion, no existing method adequately deals with massively parallel GPU kernels. We present a suitable fusion framework as the first major contribution of this paper.

2.2 Too little sharing

As a second example, consider the pricing of European-style options using the Black-Scholes formula. The Accelerate program is in Figure 1. Given a vector of triples of underlying stock price, strike price, and time to maturity (in years), the Black-Scholes formula computes the price of a call and a put option. The function `callput` evaluates the Black-Scholes formula for a single triple, and `blackscholes` maps it over a vector of triples, such that all individual applications of the formula are executed in parallel.

If we compare the performance of the GPU code generated by Accelerate with that of an equivalent implementation in CUDA C, the Accelerate version is almost twenty times slower. As `blackscholes` includes only one aggregate array computation, the problem can't be a lack of fusion. Instead, as we noted previously [8], it is due to the embedding of Accelerate in Haskell.

The function `callput` includes a significant amount of sharing: the helper functions `cnd'`, and hence also `horner`, are used twice —for `d1` and `d2`— and its argument `d` is used multiple times in the body. Our embedded implementation of Accelerate reifies the abstract syntax of the (deeply) embedded language in Haskell. Consequently, each occurrence of a let-bound variable in the source program creates a separate unfolding of the bound expression in the compiled code.

This is a well known problem that has been solved elegantly by the *sharing recovery* algorithm of Gill [14], which makes use of stable names. Unfortunately, Gill's original approach (1) reifies the abstract syntax in *graph* form and (2) it assumes an *untyped* syntax representation. In contrast, Accelerate is based on a typed tree representation using GADTs and type families in conjunction with type-preserving compilation in most phases. In other words, we use Haskell's type checker to statically ensure many core properties of our Accelerate compiler. The fact that the compiler for the *embedded language* is type preserving, means that many bugs in the Accelerate compiler itself are caught by the Haskell compiler during development. This in turn reduces the number of Accelerate compiler bugs that the end-user might be exposed to.

As we require typed trees, where sharing is represented by let bindings rather than untyped graphs, we cannot directly use Gill's approach to sharing recovery. Instead, we have developed a novel sharing recovery algorithm, which like Gill's, uses stable names, but unlike Gill's, operates on typed abstract syntax. Our algorithm produces a typed abstract syntax *tree*, and we are able to recover exactly those let bindings used in the source program. This is the second major contribution of this paper.

2.3 Summary

In summary, a straightforward skeleton-based implementation of an embedded GPU language suffers from two major inefficiencies: *lack of sharing* and *lack of fusion*. Both sharing recovery in embedded languages, and array fusion in functional languages have received significant prior attention. However, we have found that none of the existing techniques are adequate for a *type-preserving* embedded language compiler targeting *massively parallel SIMD hardware*, such as GPUs.

3. Sharing recovery

Gill [14] proposed to use *stable names* [27] to recover the sharing of source terms in a deeply embedded language. The stable names

```
blackscholes :: Vector (Float, Float, Float)
             -> Acc (Vector (Float, Float))
blackscholes = map callput . use
  where
  callput x =
    let (price, strike, years) = unlift x
        r        = constant riskfree
        v        = constant volatility
        v_sqrtT  = v * sqrt years
        d1       = (log (price / strike) +
                   (r + 0.5 * v * v) * years) / v_sqrtT
        d2       = d1 - v_sqrtT
        cnd d    = let c = cnd' d in d >* 0 ? (1.0 - c, c)
        cndD1    = cnd d1
        cndD2    = cnd d2
        x_expRT  = strike * exp (-r * years)
    in
    lift ( price * cndD1 - x_expRT * cndD2
         , x_expRT * (1.0 - cndD2) - price * (1.0 - cndD1))
```

```
riskfree, volatility :: Float
riskfree   = 0.02
volatility = 0.30

horner :: Num a => [a] -> a -> a
horner coeff x = x * foldr1 madd coeff
  where
    madd a b = a + x*b

cnd' :: Floating a => a -> a
cnd' d =
  let poly      = horner coeff
      coeff     = [0.31938153, -0.356563782,
                   1.781477937, -1.821255978,
                   1.330274429]
      rsqrt2pi  = 0.39894228040143267793994605993438
      k         = 1.0 / (1.0 + 0.2316419 * abs d)
  in
  rsqrt2pi * exp (-0.5*d*d) * poly k
```

Figure 1. Black-Scholes option pricing in Accelerate

of two Haskell terms are equal only when the terms are represented by the same heap structure in memory. Likewise, when the abstract syntax trees (ASTs) of two terms of an embedded language have the same stable name, we know that they represent the same value. In this case we should combine them into one shared AST node. As the stable name of an expression is an intensional property, it can only be determined in Haskell's `IO` monad.

Accelerate's runtime compiler preserves source types throughout most of the compilation process [8]. In particular, it converts the source representation based on higher-order abstract syntax (HOAS) to a type-safe internal representation based on de Bruijn indices. Although developed independently, this conversion is like the *unembedding* of Atkey et al. [1]. Unembedding and sharing recovery necessarily need to go hand in hand for the following reasons. Sharing recovery must be performed on the source representation; otherwise, sharing will already have been lost. Nevertheless, we cannot perform sharing recovery on higher-order syntax as we need to traverse below the lambda abstractions used in the higher-order syntax representation. Hence, both need to go hand in hand.

As shown by Atkey et al. [1], the conversion of HOAS in Haskell can be implemented in a type-preserving manner with the exception of one untyped, but dynamically checked environment look up, using Haskell's `Typeable`. To preserve maximum type safety, we do not want any further operations that are not type preserving when adding sharing recovery. Hence, we cannot use Gill's algorithm. The variant of Gill's algorithm used in Syntactic [2] does not apply either: it (1) also generates a graph and (2) discards static type information in the process. In contrast, our novel algorithm performs simultaneous sharing recovery and conversion from HOAS to a typed de Bruijn representation, where the result of the conversion is a tree (not a graph) with sharing represented by let bindings. Moreover, it is a type-preserving conversion whose only dynamically checked operation is the same environment lookup deemed unavoidable by Atkey et al. [1].

In the following, we describe our algorithm using plain typed lambda terms. This avoids much of the clutter that we would incur by basing the discussion on the full Accelerate language. In addition to its implementation in Accelerate, a working Haskell implementation of our algorithm for the plain lambda calculus can be found at `https://github.com/mchakravarty/hoas-conv`.

3.1 Our approach to sharing recovery

Before we formalise our sharing recovery algorithm in the following subsections, we shall illustrate the main idea. Consider the following source term:

```
let    inc  = (+) 1
in let nine = let three = inc 2
              in
              (*) three three
in
(-) (inc nine) nine
```

This term's abstract syntax DAG is the leftmost diagram in Figure 2. It uses @ nodes to represent applications; as in this grammar:

$$
\begin{array}{llll}
T \to C & T^{\tau} \textbf{ where} & & \\
\quad \mid x & C^{\tau} & :: & T^{\tau} \\
\quad \mid \lambda x.\, T & x^{\tau} & :: & T^{\tau} \\
\quad \mid T_1 \mathbin{@} T_2 & \lambda x^{\tau_1}.T^{\tau_2} & :: & T^{\tau_1 \to \tau_2} \\
C \to \langle\text{constants}\rangle & T_1^{\tau_1 \to \tau_2} \mathbin{@} T_2^{\tau_1} & :: & T^{\tau_2}
\end{array}
$$

The left definition does not track types, whereas the right one does. We implement typed ASTs in Haskell with GADTs and work with typed representations henceforth. Typed HOAS conversion with sharing recover proceeds in three stages:

1. *Prune shared subterms:* A depth first traversal over the AST annotates each node with its unique stable name, where we build an occurrence map of how many times we've already visited each node. If we encounter a previously visited node, it represents a *shared subterm*, and we replace it by a placeholder containing its stable name. The second diagram in Figure 2 shows the outcome of this stage. Each node is labeled by a number that represents its stable name, and the dotted edges indicate where we encountered a previously visited, shared node. The placeholders are indicated by underlined stable names.

2. *Float shared terms:* All shared subterms float upwards in the tree to just above the lowest node that dominates all edges to the original position of that shared subterm — see the third diagram in Figure 2. Floated subterms are referenced by circled stable names located *above* the node that they floated to. If a node collects more than one shared subterm, the subterm whose origin is deeper in the original term goes on top — here, 9 on top of 5. Nested sharing leads to subterms floating up inside other floated subterms — here, 8 stays inside the subterm rooted in 5.

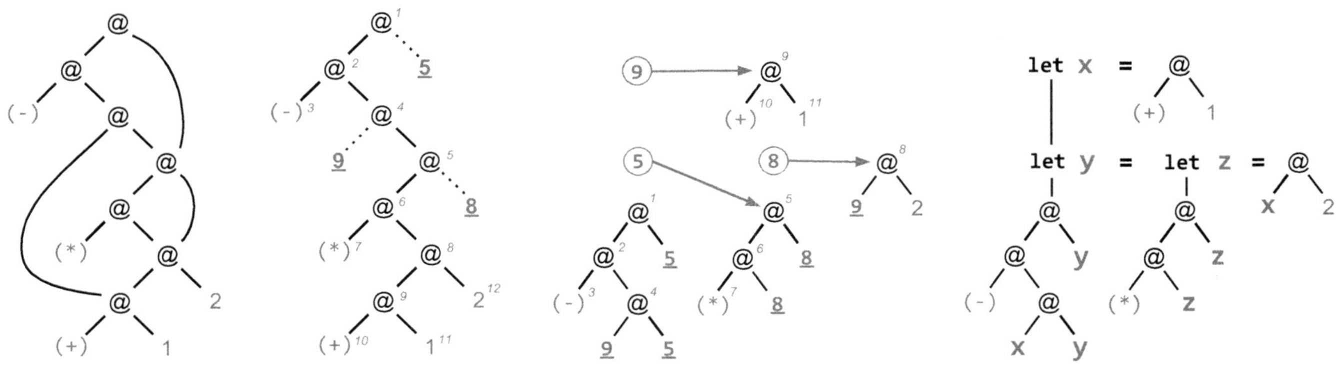

Figure 2. Recovering sharing in an example term

3. *Binder introduction:* Each floated subterm gets let-bound right above the node it floated to (rightmost diagram in Figure 2). While we use explicit, bound names in the figure, we introduce de Bruijn indices at the same time as introducing the lets.

3.2 Prune shared subterms

First, we identify and prune shared subtrees, producing a pruned tree of the following form (second diagram in Figure 2):

$$
\begin{array}{lll}
{}^{\circ}T^{\tau} \ \mathbf{where} & & \\
\quad \ell & :: {}^{\circ}T^{\tau} & \text{-- binder conversion level} \\
\quad \underline{\nu}^{\tau} & :: {}^{\circ}T^{\tau} & \text{-- pruned subtree (name)} \\
\quad C^{\tau} & :: {}^{\circ}T^{\tau} & \\
\quad \lambda\ell.{}^{\circ}T^{\tau_2} & :: {}^{\circ}T^{\tau_1 \to \tau_2} & \\
\quad {}^{\circ}T_1^{\tau_1 \to \tau_2} \ @ \ {}^{\circ}T_2^{\tau_1} & :: {}^{\circ}T^{\tau_2} &
\end{array}
$$

A stable name (here, of type *Name*) associates a unique name with each unique term node, so that two terms with the same stable name are identical, and are represented by the same data structure in memory. Here, we denote the stable name of a term as a superscript during pattern matching — e.g., 1^{ν} is a constant with stable name ν, just as in the second and third diagram in Figure 2.

An *occurrence map*, $\Omega :: Name \mapsto Int$, is a finite map that determines the number of occurrences of a *Name* that we encountered during a traversal. The expression $\Omega\nu$ yields the number of occurrences of the name ν, and we have $\nu \in \Omega \equiv (\Omega\nu > 0)$. To add an occurrence to Ω, we write $\nu \rhd \Omega$. We will see in the next subsection that we cannot simplify Ω to be merely a set of occurring names. We need the actual occurrence count to determine where shared subterms should be let-bound.

The identification and pruning of shared subtrees is formalised by the following function operating on *closed* terms from T^{τ}:

$$
\begin{array}{l}
prune :: Level \to (Name \mapsto Int) \to T^{\tau} \to ((Name \mapsto Int), {}^{\circ}T^{\tau}) \\
prune\ \ell\ \Omega\ e^{\nu} \mid \nu \in \Omega \qquad = (\nu \rhd \Omega,\ \underline{\nu}) \\
prune\ \ell\ \Omega\ e^{\nu} \mid otherwise = enter\ (\nu \rhd \Omega)\ e \\
\quad \mathbf{where} \\
\qquad enter\ \Omega\ c \qquad\quad = (\Omega,\ c) \\
\qquad enter\ \Omega\ (\lambda x.e) \quad = \mathbf{let} \\
\qquad\qquad\qquad\qquad\qquad (\Omega',\ e') = prune\ (\ell + 1)\ \Omega\ ([\ell/x]e) \\
\qquad\qquad\qquad\qquad\quad \mathbf{in} \\
\qquad\qquad\qquad\qquad\qquad (\Omega',\ \lambda\ell.e') \\
\qquad enter\ \Omega\ (e_1\ @\ e_2) = \mathbf{let} \\
\qquad\qquad\qquad\qquad\qquad (\Omega_1,\ e_1') = prune\ \ell\ \Omega\ e_1 \\
\qquad\qquad\qquad\qquad\qquad (\Omega_2,\ e_2') = prune\ \ell\ \Omega_1\ e_2 \\
\qquad\qquad\qquad\qquad\quad \mathbf{in} \\
\qquad\qquad\qquad\qquad\qquad (\Omega_2,\ e_1'\ @\ e_2')
\end{array}
$$

The first equation of $prune$ covers the case of a term's repeated occurrence. In that case, we prune sharing by replacing the term e^{ν} by a tag $\underline{\nu}$ containing its stable name — these are the dotted lines in the second diagram in Figure 2.

To interleave sharing recovery with the conversion from HOAS to typed de Bruijn indices, $prune$ tracks the nesting $Level$ of lambdas. Moreover, the lambda case of $enter$ replaces the HOAS binder x by the level ℓ at the binding and usage sites.

Why don't we separate computing occurrences from tree pruning? When computing occurrences, we must not traverse shared subtrees multiple times, so we can as well prune at the same time. Moreover, in the first line of $prune$, we cannot simply return e instead of $\underline{\nu}$ — e is of the wrong form as it has type T and not ${}^{\circ}T$!

As far as type-preservation is concerned, we do lose information due to replacing variables by levels ℓ. This is the inevitable loss described by Atkey et al. [1], which we make up for by a dynamic check in an environment lookup, as already discussed.

3.3 Float shared subterms

Second, we float all shared subtrees out to where they should be let-bound, represented by (see third diagram in Figure 2)

$$
\begin{array}{ll}
{}^{\uparrow}T^{\tau} \to \overline{\nu : {}^{\uparrow}T^{\tau'}} \succ {}^{\downarrow}T^{\tau} & \\
{}^{\downarrow}T^{\tau} \ \mathbf{where} & \\
\quad \underline{\nu}^{\tau} & :: {}^{\downarrow}T^{\tau} \\
\quad C^{\tau} & :: {}^{\downarrow}T^{\tau} \\
\quad \lambda\nu.{}^{\uparrow}T^{\tau_2} & :: {}^{\downarrow}T^{\tau_1 \to \tau_2} \\
\quad {}^{\uparrow}T_1^{\tau_1 \to \tau_2} \ @ \ {}^{\uparrow}T_2^{\tau_1} & :: {}^{\downarrow}T^{\tau_2}
\end{array}
$$

A term in ${}^{\uparrow}T$ comprises a sequence of floated-out subterms labelled by their stable name as well as a body term from ${}^{\downarrow}T$ from which the floated subterms where extracted. Moreover, the levels ℓ that replaced lambda binders in ${}^{\circ}T$ get replaced by the stable name of their term node. This simplifies a uniform introduction of de Bruijn indices for let and lambda bound variables.

We write $\overline{\nu : {}^{\uparrow}T}$ for a possibly empty sequence of items: $\nu_1 : {}^{\uparrow}T_1, \ldots, \nu_n : {}^{\uparrow}T_n$, where • denotes an empty sequence.

The floating function *float* maintains an auxiliary structure of floating terms and levels, defined as follows:

$$
\Gamma \to \nu \overset{i}{:} {}^{\uparrow}T^{\tau} \mid \nu \overset{i}{:} \cdot \mid \nu \overset{i}{:} \ell
$$

These are floated subtrees named ν of which we have collected i occurrences. The occurrence count indicates where a shared subterm gets let bound: namely at the node where it matches $\Omega\nu$. This is why $prune$ needed to collect the number of occurrences in Ω. When the occurrence count matches $\Omega\nu$, we call the floated term *saturated*. The following function determines saturated floated terms, which ought to be let bound:

$$
\begin{array}{lll}
\mathit{bind} :: (\mathit{Name} \mapsto \mathit{Int}) \to \overline{\Gamma} \to \overline{\exists\tau.\nu : {}^{\uparrow}T^{\tau}} & & \\
\mathit{bind}\ \Omega\ \bullet & = & \bullet \\
\mathit{bind}\ \Omega\ (\nu \overset{i}{:} e,\ \overline{\Gamma})\ \mid\ \Omega\nu\ ==\ i & = & \nu : e,\ \mathit{bind}\ \Omega\ \overline{\Gamma} \\
\mathit{bind}\ \Omega\ (\nu \overset{i}{:} \_,\ \overline{\Gamma}) & = & \mathit{bind}\ \Omega\ \overline{\Gamma}
\end{array}
$$

Note that Γ does not keep track of the type τ of a floated term ${}^{\uparrow}T^{\tau}$; hence, floated terms from *bind* come in an existential package. This does *not* introduce additional loss of type safety as we already lost the type of lambda bound variables in $\nu \overset{i}{:} \ell$. It merely means that let bound, just like lambda bound, variables require the dynamically checked environment look up we already discussed.

When floating the *first occurrence* of a shared tree (not pruned by *prune*), we use $\nu \overset{i}{:} {}^{\uparrow}T^{\tau}$. When floating *subsequent occurrences* (which were pruned), we use $\nu \overset{i}{:} \cdot$. Finally, when floating a level, to replace it by a stable name, we use $\nu \overset{i}{:} \ell$.

We define a partial ordering on floated terms: $\nu_1 \overset{i}{:} x\ <\ \nu_2 \overset{j}{:} y$ iff the direct path from ν_1 to the root of the AST is shorter than that of ν_2. We keep sequences of floated terms in *descending order* — so that the deepest subterm comes first. We write $\overline{\Gamma_1} \uplus \overline{\Gamma_2}$ to merge two sequences of floated terms. Merging respects the partial order, and it combines floated trees with the same stable name by adding their occurrence counts. To combine the first occurrence and a subsequent occurrence of a shared tree, we preserve the term of the first occurrence. We write $\overline{\Gamma} \setminus \overline{\nu}$ to delete elements of $\overline{\Gamma}$ that are tagged with a name that appears in the sequence $\overline{\nu}$.

We can now formalise the floating process as follows:

$$
\begin{array}{l}
\mathit{float} :: (\mathit{Name} \mapsto \mathit{Int}) \to {}^{\circ}T^{\tau} \to (\overline{\Gamma}, {}^{\uparrow}T^{\tau}) \\
\mathit{float}\ \Omega\ \ell^{\nu}\ =\ (\nu \overset{1}{:} \ell,\ \underline{\nu}) \\
\mathit{float}\ \Omega\ \underline{\nu}\ \ =\ (\nu \overset{1}{:} \cdot,\ \underline{\nu}) \\
\mathit{float}\ \Omega\ e^{\nu}\ =\ \mathbf{let} \\
\qquad\qquad (\overline{\Gamma},\ e') = \mathit{descend}\ e \\
\qquad\qquad \overline{\nu_b\ :\ e_b} = \mathit{bind}\ \Omega\ \overline{\Gamma} \\
\qquad\qquad d \qquad\ \ = \overline{\nu_b\ :\ e_b} \succ e' \\
\qquad\quad \mathbf{in} \\
\qquad\quad \mathbf{if}\ \Omega\nu\ ==\ 1\ \mathbf{then} \\
\qquad\qquad (\overline{\Gamma} \setminus \overline{\nu_b},\ d) \\
\qquad\quad \mathbf{else} \\
\qquad\qquad (\overline{\Gamma} \setminus \overline{\nu_b} \uplus \{\nu : d\},\ \underline{\nu}) \\
\ \ \mathbf{where} \\
\qquad \mathit{descend}\ ::\ {}^{\circ}T^{\tau}\ \to\ (\overline{\Gamma},\ {}^{\downarrow}T^{\tau}) \\
\qquad \mathit{descend}\ c \qquad\quad = (\bullet,\ c) \\
\qquad \mathit{descend}\ (\lambda\ell.e) \quad = \mathbf{let} \\
\qquad\qquad\qquad\qquad\quad (\overline{\Gamma},\ e') = \mathit{float}\ \Omega\ e \\
\qquad\qquad\qquad\qquad \mathbf{in} \\
\qquad\qquad\qquad\qquad \mathbf{if}\ \exists\,\nu'\ i.\ (\nu' \overset{i}{:} \ell) \in \overline{\Gamma}\ \mathbf{then} \\
\qquad\qquad\qquad\qquad\quad (\overline{\Gamma} \setminus \{\nu'\},\ \lambda\nu'.e') \\
\qquad\qquad\qquad\qquad \mathbf{else} \\
\qquad\qquad\qquad\qquad\quad (\overline{\Gamma},\ \lambda\_.e') \\
\qquad \mathit{descend}\ (e_1\ @\ e_2) = \mathbf{let} \\
\qquad\qquad\qquad\qquad\quad (\overline{\Gamma}_1,\ e_1') = \mathit{float}\ \Omega\ e_1 \\
\qquad\qquad\qquad\qquad\quad (\overline{\Gamma}_2,\ e_2') = \mathit{float}\ \Omega\ e_2 \\
\qquad\qquad\qquad\qquad \mathbf{in} \\
\qquad\qquad\qquad\qquad (\overline{\Gamma}_1 \uplus \overline{\Gamma}_2,\ e_1'\ @\ e_2')
\end{array}
$$

The first two cases of *float* ensure that the levels of lambda bound variables and the names of pruned shared subterms are floated regardless of how often they occur. In contrast, the third equation floats a term with name ν only if it is shared; i.e., $\Omega\nu$ is not 1. If it is shared, it is also pruned; i.e., replaced by its name $\underline{\nu}$ — just as in the third diagram of Figure 2.

Regardless of whether a term gets floated, all saturated floated terms, $\overline{\nu_b\ :\ e_b}$, must prefix the result, e', and be removed from $\overline{\Gamma}$.

When *descending* into a term, the only interesting case is for lambdas. For a lambda at level ℓ, we look for a floated level of the form $\nu' : \ell$. If that is available, ν' replaces ℓ as a binder and we remove $\nu' : \ell$ from $\overline{\Gamma}$. However, if $\nu' : \ell$ is not in $\overline{\Gamma}$, the binder introduced by the lambda doesn't get used in e. In this case, we pick an arbitrary new name; here symbolised by an underscore "_".

3.4 Binder introduction

Thirdly, we introduce typed de Bruijn indices to represent lambda and let binding structure (rightmost diagram in Figure 2):

$$
\begin{array}{lll}
{}^{env}T^{\tau}\ \mathbf{where} & & \\
\quad C^{\tau} & :: & {}^{env}T^{\tau} \\
\quad {}^{env}\iota^{\tau} & :: & {}^{env}T^{\tau} \\
\quad \lambda^{(\tau_1,\, env)}T^{\tau_2} & :: & {}^{env}T^{\tau_1 \to \tau_2} \\
\quad {}^{env}T_1^{\tau_1 \to \tau_2}\ @\ {}^{env}T_2^{\tau_1} & :: & {}^{env}T^{\tau_2} \\
\quad \mathtt{let}\ {}^{env}T_1^{\tau_1}\ \mathtt{in}\ {}^{(\tau_1,\, env)}T_2^{\tau_2} & :: & {}^{env}T^{\tau_2}
\end{array}
$$

With this type of terms, $e :: {}^{env}T^{\tau}$ means that e is a term representing a computation producing a value of type τ under the type environment env. Type environments are nested pair types, possibly terminated by a unit type (). For example, $(((),\ \tau_1),\ \tau_0)$ is a type environment, where de Bruijn index 0 represents a variable of type τ_0 and de Bruijn index 1 represents a variable of type τ_1.

We abbreviate $\mathtt{let}\ e_1\ \mathtt{in}\ \cdots\ \mathtt{let}\ e_n\ \mathtt{in}\ e_b$ as $\mathtt{let}\ \overline{e}\ \mathtt{in}\ e_b$. Both λ and `let` use de Bruijn indices ι instead of introducing explicit binders.

To replace the names of pruned subtrees and of lambda bound variables by de Bruijn indices, we need to construct a suitable type environment as well as an association of environment entries, their de Bruijn indices, and the stable names that they replace. We maintain the type environment with associated de Bruijn indices in the following *environment layout* structure:

$$
\begin{array}{lll}
{}^{env}\Delta^{env'}\ \mathbf{where} & & \\
\quad \circ & :: & {}^{env}\Delta^{()} \\
\quad {}^{env}\Delta^{env'}\ \ {}^{env}\iota^{\tau} & :: & {}^{env}\Delta^{(env',\, t)}
\end{array}
$$

Together with a layout, we use a sequence of names $\overline{\nu}$ of the same size as the layout, where corresponding entries represent the same variable. As this association between typed layout and untyped sequence of names is not validated by types, the lookup function $lyt \downarrow i$ getting the ith index of layout lyt makes use of a dynamic type check. It's signature is $(\downarrow)\ ::\ \mathbb{N} \to {}^{env}\Delta^{env'} \to {}^{env}\iota^{\tau}$.

Now we car introduces de Bruijn indices to body expressions:

$$
\begin{array}{lll}
\mathit{body} :: {}^{env}\Delta^{env} \to \overline{\nu} \to {}^{\downarrow}T^{\tau} \to {}^{env}T^{\tau} & & \\
\mathit{body}\ \mathit{lyt}\ (\nu_{\rho,0}, \ldots, \nu_{\rho,n})\ \underline{\nu} & & \\
\quad \mid\ \nu\ ==\ \nu_{\rho,i} & = & \mathit{lyt} \downarrow i \\
\mathit{body}\ \mathit{lyt}\ \overline{\nu_\rho}\ c & = & c \\
\mathit{body}\ \mathit{lyt}\ \overline{\nu_\rho}\ (\lambda\nu.e) & = & \lambda(\mathit{binders}\ \mathit{lyt}^{+}\ (\nu, \overline{\nu_\rho})\ e) \\
\mathit{body}\ \mathit{lyt}\ \overline{\nu_\rho}\ (e_1\ @\ e_2) & = & (\mathit{binders}\ \mathit{lyt}\ \overline{\nu_\rho}\ e_1)\ @\ (\mathit{binders}\ \mathit{lyt}\ \overline{\nu_\rho}\ e_2)
\end{array}
$$

The first equation performs a lookup in the environment layout at the same index where the stable name ν occurs in the name environment $\overline{\nu}$. The lookup is the same for lambda and let bound variables. It is the only place where we need a dynamic type check and that is already needed for lambda bound variables alone.

In the case of a lambda, we add a new binder by extending the layout, denoted lyt^{+}, with a new zeroth de Bruijn index and shifting all others one up. Keeping the name environment in sync, we add the stable name ν, which ${}^{\downarrow}T$ used as a binder.

In the same vein, we bind n floated terms $\overline{\nu : e}$ with `let` bindings in body expression e_b, by extending the type environment n times (*map* applies a function to each element of a sequence):

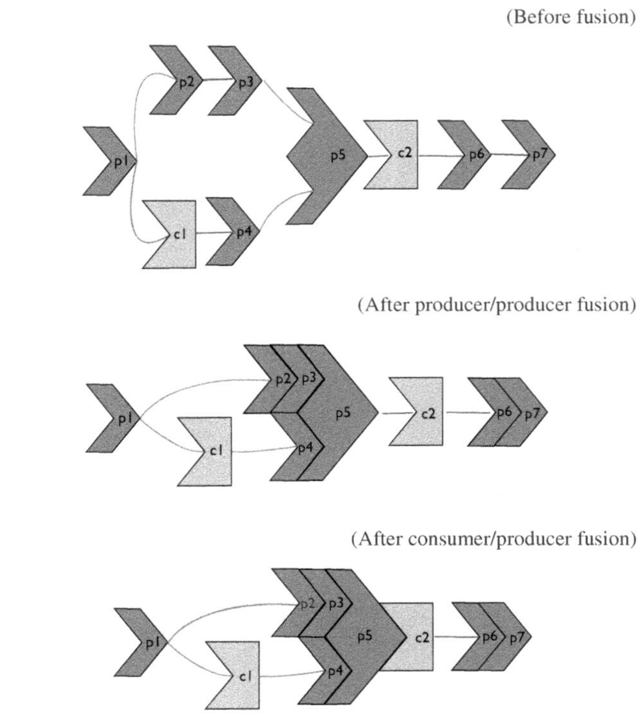

Figure 3. Produce/producer and consumer/producer fusion

$$
\begin{array}{l}
\mathit{binders} :: {}^{\mathit{env}}\Delta^{\mathit{env}} \to \overline{\nu} \to {}^{\uparrow}T^{\tau} \to {}^{\mathit{env}}T^{\tau} \\
\mathit{binders}\ \mathit{lyt}\ \overline{\nu_\rho}\ (\overline{\nu : e} \succ e_b) = \\
\quad \mathtt{let}\ \mathit{map}\ (\mathit{binders}\ \mathit{lyt}\ \overline{\nu_\rho})\ \overline{e}\ \mathtt{in}\ \mathit{body}\ \mathit{lyt}^{+n}\ (\overline{\nu}, \overline{\nu_\rho})\ e_b \\
\quad \mathbf{where}\ n = \mathit{length}\ (\overline{\nu : e})
\end{array}
$$

We tie the three stages together to convert from HOAS with sharing recovery producing let bindings and typed de Bruijn indices:

$$
\begin{array}{l}
\mathit{hoasSharing} :: T^{\tau} \to {}^{()}T^{\tau} \\
\mathit{hoasSharing}\ e = \mathbf{let} \\
\qquad (\Omega,\ e') = \mathit{prune}\ 0\ \bullet\ e \\
\qquad (\bullet,\ e'') = \mathit{float}\ \Omega\ e' \\
\quad \mathbf{in} \\
\qquad \mathit{binders} \circ \bullet\ e''
\end{array}
$$

4. Array fusion

Fusion in a massively data-parallel, embedded language for GPUs, such as Accelerate, requires a few uncommon considerations.

Parallelism. While fusing parallel collective operations, we must be careful not to lose information essential to parallel execution. For example, `foldr/build` fusion [15] is not applicable, because it produces sequential tail-recursive loops rather than massively parallel GPU kernels. Similarly, the `split/join` approach used in Data Parallel Haskell (DPH) [16] is not helpful, although fused operations are split into sequential and parallel subcomputations, as they assume an explicit parallel scheduler, which in DPH is written directly in Haskell. Accelerate compiles massively parallel array combinators to CUDA code via template skeleton instantiation, so any fusion system must preserve the combinator representation of the intermediate code.

Sharing. Existing fusion transforms rely on inlining to move producer and consumer expressions next to each other, which allows producer/consumer pairs to be detected. However, when let-bound variables are used multiple times in the body of an expression, unrestrained inlining can lead to duplication of work. Compilers such as GHC, handle this situation by only inlining the definitions of let-bound variables that have a single use site, or by relying on some heuristic about the size of the resulting code to decide what to inline [26]. However, in typical Accelerate programs, each array is used at least twice: once to access the shape information and once to access the array data; so, we must handle at least this case separately.

Filtering. General array fusion transforms must deal with filter-like operations, for which the size of the result structure depends on the *value* of the input structure, as well as its size. Accelerate does not encode filtering as a primitive operation, so we do not need to consider it further.[1]

Fusion at run-time. As the Accelerate language is embedded in Haskell, compilation of the Accelerate program happens at Haskell *runtime* rather than when compiling the Haskell program. For this reason, optimisations applied to an Accelerate program contribute to its overall runtime, so we must be mindful of the cost of analysis and code transformation. On the flip-side, runtime optimisations can make use of information that is only available at runtime.

Fusion on typed de Brujin terms. We fuse Accelerate programs by rewriting typed de Bruijn terms in a type preserving manner. However, maintaining type information adds complexity to the definitions and rules, which amounts to a partial proof of correctness checked by the type checker, but is not particularly exciting for the present exposition. Hence, in this section, we elide the steps necessary to maintain type information during fusion.

4.1 The Main Idea

All collective operations in Accelerate are array-to-array transformations. Reductions, such as `fold`, which reduce an array to a single element, yield a singleton array rather than a scalar expression. Hence, we can partition array operations into two categories:

1. Operations where each element of the result array depends on at most one element of each input array. Multiple elements of the output array may depend on a single input array element, but all output elements can be computed independently. We refer to these operations as *producers*.
2. Operations where each element of the result array depends on multiple elements of the input array. We call these functions *consumers*, in spite of the fact that they also produce an array.

Table 1 summarises the collective array operations that we support. In a parallel context, producers are more pleasant to deal with because independent element-wise operations have an obvious mapping to the GPU. Consumers are a different story, as we need to know exactly how the computations depend on each other to implement them efficiently. For example, a parallel fold (with an associative operator) can be implemented efficiently as a tree reduction, but a parallel scan requires two separate phases [9, 31]. Unfortunately, this sort of information is obfuscated by most fusion techniques. To support the different properties of producers and consumers, our fusion transform is split into two distinct phases:

- *Producer/producer:* fuse sequences of producers into a single producer. This is implemented as a source-to-source transformation on the AST.
- *Consumer/producer:* fuse producers followed by a consumer into the consumer. This happens during code generation, where we specialise the consumer skeleton with the producer code.

[1] `filter` is easily implemented as a combination of the core primitives, and is provided as part of the library.

	Producers	
`map`	`:: (Exp a -> Exp b) -> Acc (Array sh a) -> Acc (Array sh b)`	map a function over an array
`zipWith`	`:: (Exp a -> Exp b -> Exp c) -> Acc (Array sh a) -> Acc (Array sh b)`	apply funciton to...
	`-> Acc (Array sh c)`	...a pair of arrays
`backpermute`	`:: Exp sh' -> (Exp sh' -> Exp sh) -> Acc (Array sh a)`	backwards permutation
	`-> Acc (Array sh' e)`	
`replicate`	`:: Slice slix => Exp slix`	extend array across...
	`-> Acc (Array (SliceShape slix) e)`	...new dimensions
	`-> Acc (Array (FullShape slix) e)`	
`slice`	`:: Slice slix`	remove existing dimensions
	`=> Acc (Array (FullShape slix) e) -> Exp slix`	
	`-> Acc (Array (SliceShape slix) e)`	
`generate`	`:: Exp sh -> (Exp sh -> Exp a) -> Acc (Array sh a)`	array from index mapping
	Consumers	
`fold`	`:: (Exp a -> Exp a -> Exp a) -> Exp a -> Acc (Array (sh:.Int) a)`	tree reduction along...
	`-> Acc (Array sh a)`	...innermost dimension
`scan{l,r}`	`:: (Exp a -> Exp a -> Exp a) -> Exp a -> Acc (Vector a)`	left-to-right or right-to-left
	`-> Acc (Vector a)`	...vector pre-scan
`permute`	`:: (Exp a -> Exp a -> Exp a) -> Acc (Array sh' a)`	forward permutation
	`-> (Exp sh -> Exp sh') -> Acc (Array sh a) -> Acc (Array sh' a)`	
`stencil`	`:: Stencil sh a stencil => (stencil -> Exp b) -> Boundary a`	map a function with local...
	`-> Acc (Array sh a) -> Acc (Array sh b)`	...neighbourhood context

Table 1. Summary of Accelerate's core collective array operations, omitting `Shape` and `Elt` class constraints for brevity. In addition, there are other flavours of folds and scans as well as segmented versions of these.

Separating fusion into these two phases reduces the complexity of the task, though there is also a drawback: as all collective operations in Accelerate output arrays, we might wish to use the output of a consumer as an input to a producer as in `map g . fold f z`. Here, the `map` operation could be fused into the `fold` by applying the function `g` to each element produced by the reduction before storing the final result in memory. This is useful, as Accelerate works on multidimensional arrays, so the result of a `fold` can be a large array rather than just a singleton array. Our approach currently does not fuse producer/consumer pairs, only consumer/producer and producer/producer combinations.

Figure 3 illustrates how fusion affects the AST: blue boxes p_1 to p_7 represent producers, where p_5 is a producer like `zipWith` with two input arrays. The consumers are c_1 and c_2. Firstly, we fuse all producers, with the exception of p_1 whose result is used by both c_1 and p_2. Next, we plug the fused producers into consumers where possible. Again, p_1 is left as is. It would be straightforward to change our implementation such that it would fuse p_1 into both p_2 and c_1. This would duplicate the work of p_1 into both p_2 and c_1, which, despite reducing memory traffic, is not always advantageous. Our current implementation is conservative and never duplicates work; we plan to change this in future work as the restricted nature of Accelerate means that we can compute accurate cost estimates and make an informed decision. In contrast, producer/consumer fusion of c_1 into p_4 would require fundamental changes.

4.2 Producer/producer fusion for parallel arrays

The basic idea behind the representation of producer arrays in Accelerate is well known: simply represent an array by its shape and a function mapping indices to their corresponding values. We previously used it successfully to optimise purely functional array programs in Repa [17], but it was also used by others [11].

However, there are at least two reasons why it is not always beneficial to represent all array terms uniformly as functions. One is *sharing*: we must be able to represent some terms as manifest arrays so that a delayed-by-default representation can not lead to arbitrary loss of sharing. This is a well known problem in Repa. The other consideration is *efficiency*: since we are targeting an architecture designed for performance, we prefer more specific operations. An opaque indexing function is too general, conveying no information about the pattern in which the underlying array is accessed, and hence no opportunities for optimisation. We shall return to this point in Section 5, but already include a form of structured traversal over an array (`Step`) in the following definition:

```
data DelayedAcc a where
  Done  :: Acc a
        -> DelayedAcc a

  Yield :: (Shape sh, Elt e)
        => Exp sh
        -> Fun (sh -> e)
        -> DelayedAcc (Array sh e)

  Step  :: (Shape sh, Shape sh', Elt e, Elt e')
        => Exp sh'
        -> Fun (sh' -> sh)
        -> Fun (e -> e')
        -> Idx (Array sh e)
        -> DelayedAcc (Array sh' e')
```

We have three constructors: `Done` injects a manifest array into the type. `Yield` defines a delayed array in terms of its shape and a function which maps indices to elements. The third constructor, `Step`, encodes a special case of the more general `Yield` that represents the application of an index and/or value space transformation to the argument array. The type `Fun (sh -> e)` is that of a term representing a scalar function from shape to element type. The type `Idx (Array sh e)` is that of a de Bruijn index representing an array valued variable. Representing the argument array in this way means that both `Step` and `Yield` are non-recursive in `Acc` terms, and so they can always be expressed as scalar functions and embedded into consumers in the second phase of fusion.

We represent all array functions as constructors of the type `DelayedAcc`. Producer/producer fusion is achieved by tree contraction on the AST, merging sequences of producers into a single one. All array producing functions, such as `map` and `backpermute`, are expressed in terms of smart constructors for the `DelayedAcc` type. The smart constructors manage the integration with successive producers, as shown in the following definition of `mapD`, the delayed version of the `map` function:

```
mapD :: (Shape sh, Elt a, Elt b)
     => Fun (a -> b)
     -> DelayedAcc (Array sh a)
     -> DelayedAcc (Array sh b)
mapD f (Step  sh p g v) = Step  sh p (f . g) v
mapD f (Yield sh g)     = Yield sh   (f . g)
```

The function composition operator `(.)` is overloaded here to work on scalar function terms. With this definition we now have the well known fusion rule that reduces `mapD f . mapD g` sequences to `mapD (f . g)`. Similarly, the definition of delayed backpermute means that `backpermuteD sh p (backpermuteD _ q arr)` reduces to `backpermute sh (q . p) arr`:

```
backpermuteD
    :: (Shape sh, Shape sh', Elt e)
    => Exp        sh'
    -> Fun        (sh' -> sh)
    -> DelayedAcc (Array sh  e)
    -> DelayedAcc (Array sh' e)
backpermuteD sh' p acc = case acc of
  Step  _ ix f a  -> Step  sh' (ix . p) f a
  Yield _ f       -> Yield env sh' (f . p)
  Done    env a   -> Step  sh' p identity (toIdx a)
```

Of course, combinations of maps with backpermutes also reduce to a single producer.

As desired, this approach also works on producers which take their input from multiple arrays. This is in contrast to `foldr/build` [15], which can fuse one of the input arguments, but not both. The definition of `zipWithD` considers all possible combinations of constructors (only some of which we list here) and can therefore fuse producers of both arguments:

```
zipWithD :: (Shape sh, Elt a, Elt b, Elt c)
         => Fun (a -> b -> c)
         -> DelayedAcc (Array sh a)
         -> DelayedAcc (Array sh b)
         -> DelayedAcc (Array sh c)
zipWithD f (Yield sh1 g1) (Yield sh2 g2)
  = Yield (sh1 `intersect` sh2)
          (\sh -> f (g1 sh) (g2 sh))
zipWithD f (Yield sh1 g1) (Step  sh2 ix2 g2 a2)
  = Yield ...
```

In this manner, sequences of producers fuse into a single producer term; then, we turn them back into a manifest array using the function `compute`. It inspects the argument terms of the delayed array to identify special cases, such as maps or backpermutes, as shown in the following snippet of pseudo-code:

```
compute :: DelayedAcc a -> Acc a
compute (Done a)          = a
compute (Yield sh f)      = Generate sh f
compute (Step sh p f v)
  | sh == shape a, isId p, isId f
                          = a
  | sh == shape a, isId p = Map f a
  | isId f                = Backpermute sh p a
  | otherwise             = Transform sh p f a
  where a = Avar v
```

Since we operate directly on the AST of the program, we can inspect function arguments and specialise the code accordingly. For example, `isId :: Fun (a->b) -> Bool` checks whether a function term corresponds to the term $\lambda x.x$.

4.3 Consumer/Producer Fusion

Now that we have the story for producer/producer fusion, we discuss how to deal with consumers. We pass producers encoded in the `DelayedAcc` representation as arguments to consumers, so that the consumers can compute the elements they need on-the-fly. Consumers themselves have no `DelayedAcc` representation, however.

Consumers such as `stencil`, access elements of their argument array multiple times. These consumers are implemented carefully not to duplicate work. Indeed, even when the argument of such a consumer is a manifest array, the consumer should ensure that it caches already fetched elements, as GPUs impose a high performance penalty for repeated memory loads. Some consumers can be implemented more efficiently when given a producer expressed in terms of a function from a multi-dimensional array index to an element value. Other consumers prefer functions that map the flat linear index of the underling array to its value. Our consumer-friendly representation of delayed arrays therefore contains both versions:

```
data Embedded sh e
  =  (Shape sh, Elt e)
  => DelayedArray { extent      :: Exp sh
                  , index       :: Fun (sh  -> e)
                  , linearIndex :: Fun (Int -> e) }

embedAcc :: (Shape sh, Elt e)
         => Acc (Array sh e) -> Embedded sh e
embedAcc (Generate sh f)
  = DelayedArray sh f (f . (fromIndex sh))
embedAcc (Map f (AVar v))
  = DelayedArray (shape v) (indexArray v)
                           (linearIndexArray v)
embedAcc ...
```

The function `embedAcc` intelligently injects each producer into the `Embedded` type by inspection of the constructor, as shown in the code snippet above. In theory, `compute` and `embedAcc` could be combined to go directly from the delayed representation which is convenient for producer/producer fusion to the one for consumer/producer fusion. However, these two steps happen at different phases in the compilation, so we want to limit the visibility of each delayed representation to the current phase.

Producers are finally embedded into consumers during code generation. During code generation, the code for the embedded producers is plugged into the consumer template. The `codegenAcc` function inspects the consumer and generates code for the arguments of the consumer. It then passes these CUDA code snippets to a function specialised on generating code for this particular consumer (`mkFold` in the example below), which combines these snippets with the actual CUDA consumer code:

```
codegenAcc :: DeviceProperties -> OpenAcc arrs
           -> Gamma aenv -> CUTranslSkel arrs
codegenAcc dev (OpenAcc (Fold f z a)) aenv
  = mkFold dev  aenv (codeGenFun f) (codeGenExp z)
           (codegenDelayedAcc $ embedAcc a)
codegenAcc dev (OpenAcc (Scanl f z a)) aenv
  = ...
```

As a result, the code producing each element is integrated directly into the consumer, and no intermediate array needs to be created.

4.4 Exploiting all opportunities for fusion

As mentioned previously, we need to be careful about fusing shared array computations, to avoid duplicating work. However, *scalar* Accelerate computations that manipulate *array shapes*, as opposed to the bulk array data, can lead to terms that employ sharing, but can never duplicate work. Such terms are common in Accelerate code, and it is important to that they do not inhibit fusion.

Consider the following example that first reverses a vector with `backpermute` and then maps a function `f` over the result. Being a sequence of two producer operations, we would hope these are fused into a single operation:

```
reverseMap f a
  = map f
  $ backpermute (shape a) (\i->length a-i-1) a
```

Unfortunately, sharing recovery, using the algorithm from Section 3, causes a problem. The variable `a` is used three times in the arguments to `backpermute`; hence, sharing recovery will introduce a let binding at the lowest common meet point for all uses of the array. This places it between the `map` and `backpermute` functions:

```
reverseMap f a
  = map f
  $ let v = a
    in backpermute (shape v) (\i->length v-i-1) v
```

This binding, although trivial, prevents fusion of the two producers, and it does so unnecessarily. The argument array is used three times: twice to access shape information, but only once to access the array data — in the final argument to `backpermute`.

Fortunately, there is a simple work around. Recall that our delayed array constructors `Step` and `Yield` carry the shape of the arrays they represent. Hence, we can eliminate all uses of the array that *only access shape information*, leaving us with a single reference to the array's payload. That single reference enables us to remove the let binding and to re-enable fusion.

Similarly, we may float let bindings of manifest data out (across producer chains). This helps to expose further opportunities for producer/producer fusion. For example, we allow the binding of `xs` to float above the `map` so the two producers can be fused:

```
map g $ let xs = use (Array ...)
        in zipWith f xs xs
```

While floating let bindings opens up the potential for further optimisations, we are careful to not increase the lifetime of bound variables, as this would increase live memory usage.

5. Benchmarks

Benchmarks were conducted on a single Tesla T10 processor (compute capability 1.3, 30 multiprocessors = 240 cores at 1.3GHz, 4GB RAM) backed by two quad-core Xenon E5405 CPUs (64-bit, 2GHz, 8GB RAM) running GNU/Linux (Ubuntu 12.04 LTS). The reported GPU runtimes are averages of 100 runs.

5.1 Execution Overheads

Runtime program optimisation, code generation, kernel loading, data transfer, and so on can contribute significant overheads to short lived GPU computations. Accelerate mitigates these overheads via caching and memoisation. For example, the first time a particular expression is executed it is compiled to CUDA code, which is reused for subsequent invocations. In the remainder of this section we factor out the cost of runtime code generation, and the associated caching, by reporting just the runtimes of the GPU kernels — for our system as well as the others we compare against.

5.2 Dot product

Dot product uses the code from Section 2.1. Without fusion the intermediate array produced by `zipWith` is created in GPU memory before being read back by `fold`. This is a simple memory-bound benchmark; hence, fusion roughly doubles the performance.

The `Data.Vector` baseline is sequential code produced via stream fusion [12], running on the host CPU. The `Repa` version runs in parallel on all eight cores of the host CPU, using the fusion method reported in [17]. The `NDP2GPU` version [4] compiles NESL code [6] to CUDA. The performance of this version suffers because the `NDP2GPU` compiler uses the legacy NESL compiler for the front-end, which introduces redundant administrative operations that are not strictly needed when evaluating a dot product.

The Accelerate version is still slightly slower than CUBLAS. The fused code embeds a function of type `(sh -> a)` into the reduction. The extra arithmetic for converting the multidimentional `sh` index to a linear index is significant for this simple benchmark.

5.3 Black-Scholes options pricing

Black-Scholes uses the code from Figure 1. The source contains several let-bound variables that are used multiple times, and without sharing recovery the corresponding values are recomputed for each occurrence. The Accelerate version is faster than the reference CUDA version because the latter contains a common subexpression that is not eliminated by the CUDA compiler. The CUDA version is part of the official NVIDIA CUDA distribution. The common subexpression performs a single multiplication.

5.4 N-Body gravitational simulation

The n-body example simulates Newtonian gravitational forces on a set of massive bodies in 3D space, using the naive $O(n^2)$ algorithm. In a data-parallel setting, the natural implementation first computes the forces between every pair of bodies, before reducing the components applied to each body using a segmented sum. Without fusion this approach requires $O(n^2)$ space for the intermediate array of forces, which exhausts the memory of our device for more than about 5k bodies. With fusion, the reduction consumes each force value on-the-fly, so that the program only needs $O(n)$ space to store the final force values.

Even with fusion the hand-written CUDA version is over 10× faster, as it uses on-chip *shared memory* to reduce the memory bandwidth requirements of the program. The shared memory is essentially a software managed cache, and making automatic use of it remains an open research problem [21].

5.5 Mandelbrot fractal

The Mandelbrot set is generated by sampling values c in the complex plane, and determining whether under iteration of the complex quadratic polynomial $z_{n+1} = z_n^2 + c$ that $|z_n|$ remains bounded however large n gets. As recursion in Accelerate always proceeds through the host language, we define each step of the iteration as a collective operation and unfold the loop a fixed number of times.

Table 2 shows that without fusion performance is poor because storing each step of the iteration saturates the memory bus. The CUDA version is about 70% faster because it includes a custom software thread block scheduler to manage the unbalanced workload inherent to this benchmark.

5.6 Fluid Flow

Fluid flow implements Jos Stam's stable fluid algorithm [32], a fast approximate algorithm intended for animation and games, rather than accurate engineering simulation. The core of the algorithm is a finite time step simulation on a grid, implemented as a matrix relaxation involving the discrete Laplace operator (∇^2). Relaxation

Benchmark	Input Size	Contender (ms)		Accelerate full (ms)		Accelerate no fusion (ms)		Accelerate no sharing (ms)	
Black Scholes	20M	6.70	(CUDA)	6.19	(92%)	(not needed)		116	(1731%)
Canny	16M	50.6	(OpenCV)	78.4	(155%)	(not needed)		82.7	(164%)
Dot Product	20M	1.88	(CUBLAS)	2.35	(125%)	3.90	(207%)	(not needed)	
Fluid Flow	2M	5461	(Repa -N7)	107	(1.96%)	(not needed)		119	(2.18%)
Mandelbrot (limit)	2M	14.0	(CUDA)	24.0	(171%)	245	(1750%)	245	(1750%)
N-Body	32k	54.4	(CUDA)	607	(1116%)	(out of memory)		(out of memory)	
Radix sort	4M	780	(Nikola)	442	(56%)	657	(84%)	657	(84%)
SMVM (protein)	4M	0.641	(CUSP)	0.637	(99%)	32.8	(5115%)	(not needed)	

Table 2. Benchmark Summary

is performed by stencil convolution using the standard four-point Laplace kernel. The program is very memory intensive, performing approximately 160 convolutions of the grid per time step. The Repa version running on the host CPUs is described in [20]; it suffers from a lack of memory bandwidth compared with the GPU version.

5.7 Canny edge detection

Edge detection applies the Canny algorithm [7] to square images of various sizes. The algorithm consists of seven phases, the first six are naturally data parallel and performed on the GPU. The last phase uses a recursive algorithm to "connect" pixels that make up the output lines. In our implementation this phase is performed sequentially on a host CPU, which accounts for the non-linear slowdown visible with smaller images. We also show the runtime for just the first six data parallel phases.

The data parallel phases are slightly slower than the baseline OpenCV version. This is as our implementation of stencil convolution in Accelerate checks whether each access to the source array is out of bounds, and must have boundary conditions applied. To address this shortcoming we intend to separate computation of the border region which requires boundary checks, from the main internal region which does not [19], but we leave this to future work.

5.8 Radix sort

Radix sort implements the algorithm described in Blelloch [5] to sort an array of signed 32-bit integers. We compare our implementation against a Nikola [22] version.[2]

The Accelerate version is faster then Nikola because Nikola is limited to single kernel programs and must transfer intermediate results back to the host. Hand written CUDA implementations such as in the Thrust [29] library make use of on-chip shared memory and are approximately 10× faster. As mentioned earlier, automatically making use of GPU shared memory remains an open research problem [21].

5.9 Sparse-matrix vector multiplication (SMVM)

SMVM multiplies a sparse matrix in compressed row format (CSR) [9] with a dense vector. Table 3 compares Accelerate to the CUSP library [3], which is a special purpose library for sparse matrix operations. For test data we use a 14 matrix corpus derived from a variety of application domains [33].

Compared to our previous work [8] the fusion transformation converts the program to a single segmented reduction. The corresponding reduction in memory bandwidth puts Accelerate on par with CUSP for several test matrices. In a balanced machine SMVM should be limited by memory throughput, and a dense matrix in sparse format should provide an upper bound on performance.

[2] We repeat figures of [22] as Nikola no longer compiles with recent GHC versions. The figures from [22] were obtained using the same GPU as ours.

Name	Non-zeros (nnz/row)	CUSP	Accelerate	Accelerate no fusion
Dense	4M (2K)	14.48	14.62	3.41
Protein	4.3M (119)	13.55	13.65	0.26
FEM/Spheres	6M (72)	12.63	9.03	4.70
FEM/Cantilever	4M (65)	11.98	7.96	4.41
Wind Tunnel	11.6M (53)	11.98	7.33	4.62
FEM/Harbour	2.37M (50)	9.42	6.14	0.13
QCD	1.9M (39)	7.79	4.66	0.13
FEM/Ship	3.98 (28)	12.28	6.60	4.47
Economics	1.27M (6)	4.59	0.90	1.06
Epidemiology	1.27M (4)	6.42	0.59	0.91
FEM/Accelerator	2.62M (22)	5.41	3.08	2.92
Circuit	959k (6)	3.56	0.82	1.08
Webbase	3.1M (3)	2.11	0.47	0.74
LP	11.3M (2825)	5.22	5.04	2.41

Table 3. Overview of sparse matrices tested and results of the benchmark. Measurements are in GFLOPS/s (higher is better).

However, with matrices such as FEM/Spheres which contain only a few non-zeros per row ($\lesssim 2 \times$ warp size $= 64$), Accelerate is slightly slower than CUSP. We conjecture that this is due to the way our skeleton code vector read of each matrix row is coalesced and aligned to the warp boundary to maximise global memory throughput, but is then not able to amortise this extra startup cost over the row length.

Matrices with large vectors and few non-zeros per row (e.g., Epidemiology), exhibit low flop/byte ratio and poorly suit the CSR format, with all implementations performing well below peak.

6. Related work

Repa [17] is a Haskell library for parallel array programming on shared-memory SMP machines. Repa uses the delayed/manifest representation split on which our `DelayedAcc` type is based, though the idea of representing arrays as functions is folklore. With Repa the conversion between array representations is done manually and can cause shared expressions to be recomputed rather than stored. Such recomputation can improve runtime performance depending on the algorithm. In Accelerate the conversion is automatic and conservative, so that shared expressions are never recomputed.

Vertigo [13], Nikola [22] and Obsidian [10] are EDSLs in Haskell and were mentioned in Section 1. Vertigo is a first-order language for writing shaders, and does not provide higher-order combinators such as `map` and `fold`. Nikola uses an instance of Gill's approach [14] to sharing recovery, is limited to single GPU kernel programs, and performs no fusion.

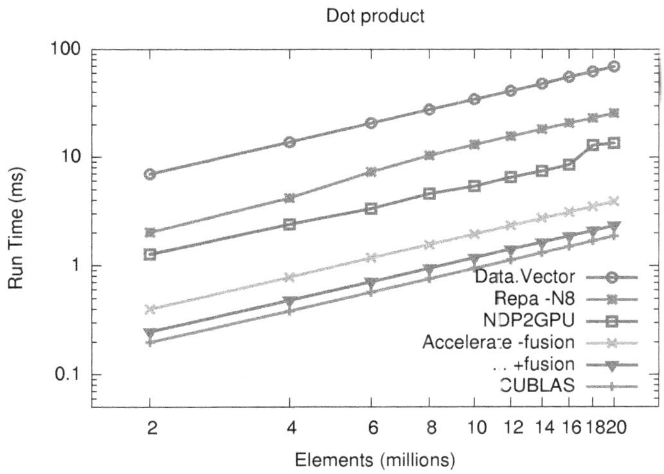
Dot product
Run Time (ms)
Elements (millions)
Data.Vector
Repa -N8
NDP2GPU
Accelerate -fusion
... +fusion
CUBLAS

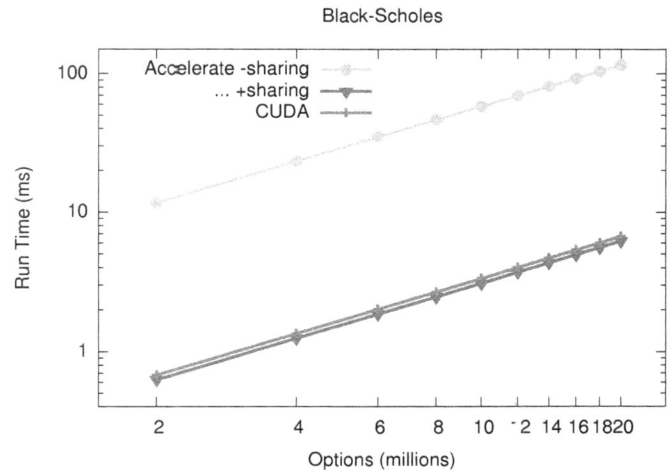
Black-Scholes
Run Time (ms)
Options (millions)
Accelerate -sharing
... +sharing
CUDA

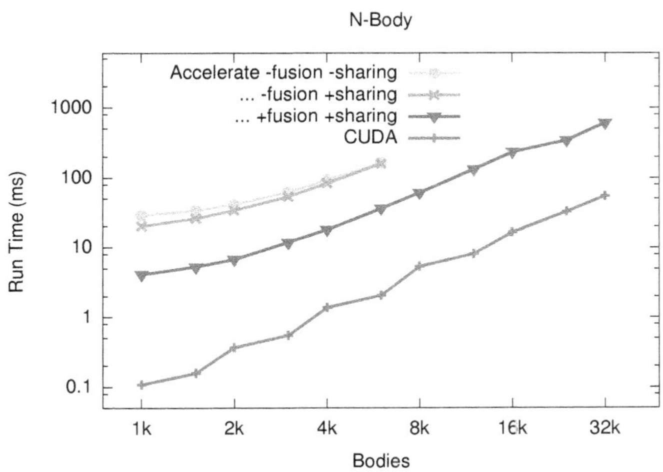
N-Body
Run Time (ms)
Bodies
Accelerate -fusion -sharing
... -fusion +sharing
... +fusion +sharing
CUDA

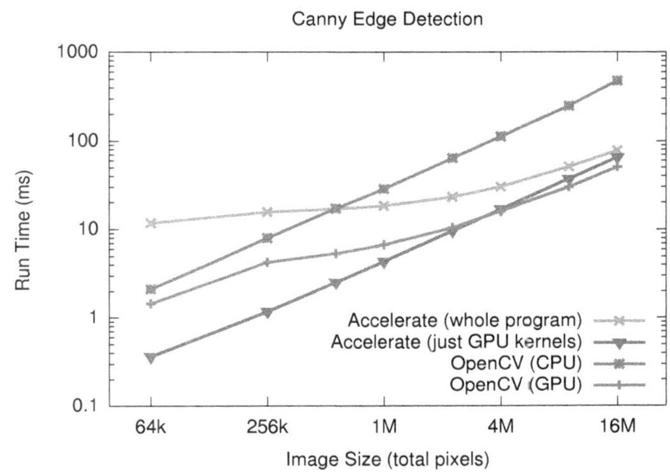
Canny Edge Detection
Run Time (ms)
Image Size (total pixels)
Accelerate (whole program)
Accelerate (just GPU kernels)
OpenCV (CPU)
OpenCV (GPU)

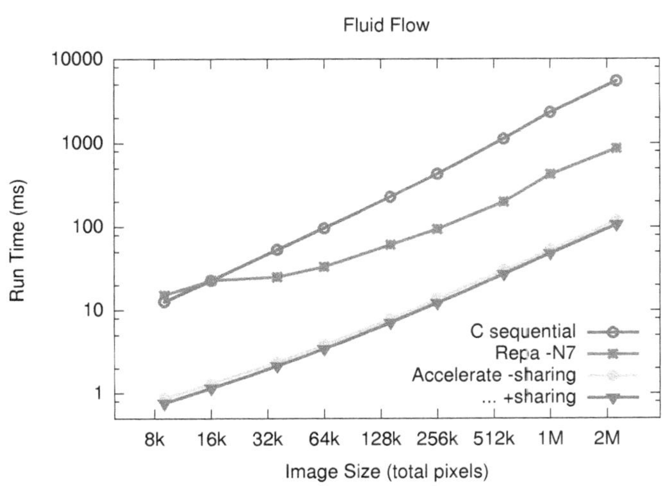
Fluid Flow
Run Time (ms)
Image Size (total pixels)
C sequential
Repa -N7
Accelerate -sharing
... +sharing

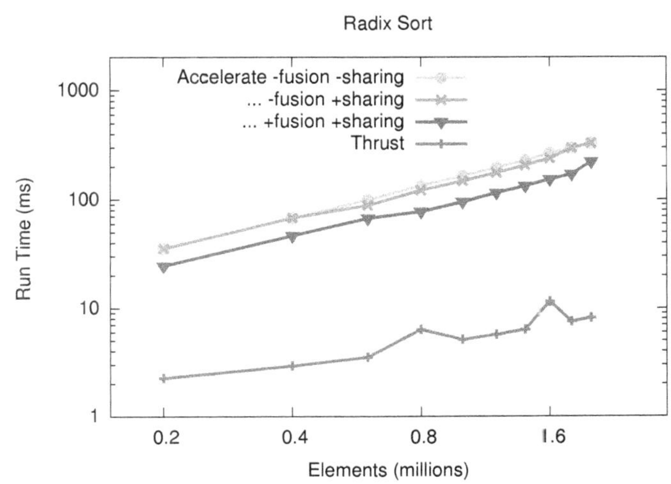
Radix Sort
Run Time (ms)
Elements (millions)
Accelerate -fusion -sharing
... -fusion +sharing
... +fusion +sharing
Thrust

Obsidian [10] is a lower level language where more details of the GPU hardware are exposed to the programmer. Recent versions of Obsidian [11] implement Repa-style delayed *pull arrays* as well as *push arrays*. Whereas a pull array represents a general producer, a push array represents a general consumer. Push arrays allow the intermediate program to be written in continuation passing style (CPS), and helps to compile (and fuse) append-like operations.

Baracuda [18] is another Haskell EDSL that produces CUDA GPU kernels, though is intended to be used offline, with the kernels being called directly from C++. The paper [18] mentions a fusion system that appears to be based on pull arrays, though the mechanism is not discussed in detail. Barracuda steps around the sharing problem by requiring let-bindings to be written using the AST node constructor, rather than using Haskell's native let-expressions.

Delite/LMS [28] is a parallelisation framework for DSLs in Scala that uses library-based multi-pass staging to specify complex optimisations in a modular manner. Delite supports loop fusion for DSLs targeting GPUs using rewrite rules on a graph-based IR.

NDP2GPU [4] compiles NESL code down to CUDA. As the source language is not embedded there is no need for sharing recovery. NDP2GPU performs `map/map` fusion but cannot fuse `maps` into reduction combinators.

Sato and Iwasaki [30] describe a C++ library for GPGPU programming that includes a fusion mechanism based on list homomorphisms [25]. The fusion transformation itself is implemented as a source to source translation. SkeTo [24] is a C++ library that provides parallel skeletons for CPUs. SkeTo's use of C++ templates provides a fusion system similar to delayed arrays, which could be equivalently implemented using CUDA templates. The authors of SkeTo note that the lack of type inference in C++ leads them to write their array code as nested expressions — to avoid intermediate variable bindings and their required type annotations.

Acknowledgements. This work was supported in part by the Australian Research Council under grant number LP0989507.

References

[1] R. Atkey, S. Lindley, and J. Yallop. Unembedding domain-specific languages. In *Haskell Symposium*, 2009.

[2] E. Axelsson. A generic abstract syntax model for embedded languages. In *ICFP: International Conference on Functional Programming*. ACM, 2012.

[3] N. Bell and M. Garland. Implementing sparse matrix-vector multiplication on throughput-oriented processors. In *Proc. of High Performance Computing Networking, Storage and Analysis*. ACM, 2009.

[4] L. Bergstrom and J. Reppy. Nested data-parallelism on the GPU. In *ICFP: International Conference on Functional Programming*. ACM, 2012.

[5] G. E. Blelloch. Prefix sums and their applications. Technical Report CMU-CS-90-190, Nov. 1990.

[6] G. E. Blelloch. NESL: A nested data-parallel language. Technical Report CMU-CS-95-170, Carnegie Mellon University, 1995.

[7] J. F. Canny. A Computational Approach to Edge Detection. *Pattern Analysis and Machine Intelligence*, (6), 1986.

[8] M. M. Chakravarty, G. Keller, S. Lee, T. L. McDonell, and V. Grover. Accelerating Haskell array codes with multicore GPUs. In *DAMP: Declarative Aspects of Multicore Programming*. ACM, 2011.

[9] S. Chatterjee, G. E. Blelloch, and M. Zagha. Scan primitives for vector computers. In *Proc. of Supercomputing*. IEEE Computer Society Press, 1990.

[10] K. Claessen, M. Sheeran, and J. Svensson. Obsidian: GPU programming in Haskell. In *IFL: Implementation and Application of Functional Languages*, 2008.

[11] K. Claessen, M. Sheeran, and B. J. Svensson. Expressive array constructs in an embedded GPU kernel programming language. In *DAMP: Declarative Aspects and Applications of Multicore Programming*. ACM, 2012.

[12] D. Coutts, R. Leshchinskiy, and D. Stewart. Stream fusion from lists to streams to nothing at all. In *ICFP: International Conference on Functional Programming*. ACM, 2007.

[13] C. Elliott. Programming graphics processors functionally. In *Haskell Workshop*. ACM Press, 2004.

[14] A. Gill. Type-Safe Observable Sharing in Haskell. In *Haskell Symposium*, 2009.

[15] A. Gill, J. Launchbury, and S. L. Peyton Jones. A short cut to deforestation. In *FPCA: Functional Programming Languages and Computer Architecture*. ACM, 1993.

[16] G. Keller and M. M. T. Chakravarty. On the distributed implementation of aggregate data structures by program transformation. In *Workshop on High-Level Parallel Programming Models and Supportive Environments*. Springer-Verlag, 1999.

[17] G. Keller, M. M. T. Chakravarty, R. Leshchinskiy, S. L. Peyton Jones, and B. Lippmeier. Regular, Shape-polymorphic, Parallel Arrays in Haskell. In *ICFP: International Conference on Functional Programming*. ACM, 2010.

[18] B. Larsen. Simple optimizations for an applicative array language for graphics processors. In *DAMP: Declarative Aspects of Multicore Programming*. ACM, 2011.

[19] B. Lippmeier and G. Keller. Efficient Parallel Stencil Convolution in Haskell. In *Haskell Symposium*. ACM, 2011.

[20] B. Lippmeier, M. Chakravarty, G. Keller, and S. Peyton Jones. Guiding parallel array fusion with indexed types. In *Haskell Symposium*. ACM, 2012.

[21] W. Ma and G. Agrawal. An integer programming framework for optimizing shared memory use on GPUs. In *PACT: Parallel Architectures and Compilation Techniques*. ACM, 2010.

[22] G. Mainland and G. Morrisett. Nikola: Embedding compiled GPU functions in Haskell. In *Haskell Symposium*. ACM, 2010.

[23] G. Mainland, R. Leshchinskiy, and S. Peyton Jones. Exploiting vector instructions with generalized stream fusion. In *ICFP: International Conference on Functional Programming*. ACM, 2013.

[24] K. Matsuzaki and K. Emoto. Implementing fusion-equipped parallel skeletons by expression templates. In *IFL: Implementation and Application of Functional Languages*. Springer-Verlag, 2010.

[25] E. Meijer, M. M. Fokkinga, and R. Paterson. Functional programming with bananas, lenses, envelopes and barbed wire. In *FPCA: Functional Programming and Computer Architecture*, 1991.

[26] S. Peyton Jones and S. Marlow. Secrets of the Glasgow Haskell Compiler inliner. *J. Funct. Program.*, 12(5), July 2002.

[27] S. Peyton Jones, S. Marlow, and C. Elliott. Stretching the Storage Manager: Weak Pointers and Stable Names in Haskell. In *IFL: Implementation of Functional Languages*. Springer Heidelberg, 2000.

[28] T. Rompf, A. K. Sujeeth, N. Amin, K. J. Brown, V. Jovanovic, H. Lee, M. Odersky, and K. Olukotun. Optimizing data structures in high-level programs: New directions for extensible compilers based on staging. In *POPL: Symposium on Principles of Programming Languages*. ACM, 2013.

[29] N. Satish, M. Harris, and M. Garland. Designing efficient sorting algorithms for manycore GPUs. In *IPDPS: Parallel and Distributed Processing*. IEEE Computer Society, 2009.

[30] S. Sato and H. Iwasaki. A skeletal parallel framework with fusion optimizer for GPGPU programming. In *APLAS: Asian Symposium on Programming Languages and Systems*. Springer-Verlag, 2009.

[31] S. Sengupta, M. Harris, Y. Zhang, and J. D. Owens. Scan primitives for GPU computing. In *SIGGRAPH/EUROGRAPHICS Symposium on Graphics Hardware*. Eurographics Association, 2007.

[32] J. Stam. Stable fluids. In *SIGGRAPH: Computer graphics and Interactive Techniques*. ACM Press, 1999.

[33] S. Williams, L. Oliker, R. Vuduc, J. Shalf, K. Yelick, and J. Demmel. Optimization of sparse matrix-vector multiplication on emerging multicore platforms. *Parallel Computing*, 35(3), 2009.

Type-Theory In Color

Jean-Philippe Bernardy Guilhem Moulin
Chalmers University of Technology and University of Gothenburg
{bernardy,mouling}@chalmers.se

Abstract

Dependent type-theory aims to become the standard way to formalize mathematics at the same time as displacing traditional platforms for high-assurance programming. However, current implementations of type theory are still lacking, in the sense that some obvious truths require explicit proofs, making type-theory awkward to use for many applications, both in formalization and programming. In particular, notions of erasure are poorly supported.

In this paper we propose an extension of type-theory with colored terms, color erasure and interpretation of colored types as predicates. The result is a more powerful type-theory: some definitions and proofs may be omitted as they become trivial, it becomes easier to program with precise types, and some parametricity results can be internalized.

Categories and Subject Descriptors F.4.1 [*Mathematical logic*]: Lambda calculus and related systems

Keywords type-theory, parametricity, erasure

1. Introduction

Intelligent use of color in a written argument can go a long way into conveying an idea. But how convincing can it really be? Consider the case of the computer scientist Philip Wadler, who is fond of using color in his papers. On multiple occasions, Wadler (2003, 2007, 2012) presents a programming language and its type-system, and shows that, by erasing the appropriate parts of the type-system, a logic appears. This is done by a straightforward but clever use of colors. Typically, in the presentation of a typing rule, the program parts are written in blue. The corresponding logic rule appears if one erases that color. As Wadler suggests, one can see the erasure simply by putting on blue glasses.

$$\frac{f :A \to B \qquad u :A}{f\ u :B} \qquad\qquad \frac{A \to B \qquad A}{B}$$

Typing rule for application After erasure: modus ponens

The relationship between the programming language and the logic is deep: for every aspect of the language, there is a "blue part" that can be erased away to obtain the corresponding logical concept. For example, a computation step on the programming side yields a cut-elimination step on the logic side. That is, Wadler does not play mindlessly with colors, he is consistent; he follows in fact a precise (however unwritten) logic of colors[1]. In fact, his "proofs by putting on glasses" are extremely compelling.

In this paper, we set-out to formalize this kind of reasoning with colors as an extension of dependent type-theory. The result is a more powerful type-theory: some definitions and proofs may be omitted as they become trivial; it becomes easier to program with precise types; and some propositions that were impossible to prove now become provable.

In Sec. 2 we demonstrate how one can program and reason with colors via a number of examples, and introduce the fundamental concepts of type-theory with color at the same time. In Sec. 3, we describe CCCC (the main technical contribution of this paper), a core calculus of constructions with colors, and prove meta-theoretical properties (subject-reduction, normalization). In Sec. 4, we discuss some possible extensions of CCCC. Related work is discussed in Sec. 5, and we conclude in Sec. 6.

ICFP '13, September 25–27, 2013, Boston, MA, USA.

ACM 978-1-4503-2326-0/13/09... $15.00.
http://dx.doi.org/10.1145/2500365.2500577

2. Programming And Reasoning With Colors

In this section we explain how we envision a full-featured type-theory with color (TTC) would be designed, in the form of a short tutorial. We assume familiarity with a proof assistant based on type-theory such as AGDA or COQ (Norell 2007; The Coq development team 2012).

2.1 Colored Lists

We start with an example similar in structure, but significantly simpler than those presented by Wadler. In the standard inductive definition of lists, the structure of the list does not depend on the elements it contains. Hence, it makes sense to color the elements: erasing that color yields a meaningful definition. In fact, the result is structurally equal to the usual unary representation of natural numbers:

$$\mathbb{N} = \lfloor \mathsf{List}\ a \rfloor_i$$

(In this section we assume a color i that we render in blue. Even though we strongly recommend reading the colored version, we index an i-tainted typing with i, so readers can make sense of what follows even if it is printed in black and white.)

$$\begin{array}{l}
\mathit{data}\ \mathsf{List}\ (a :_i \star) : \star \\
\quad \mathsf{stop} : \mathsf{List}\ a \\
\quad \mathsf{more} : (x :_i a) \to \mathsf{List}\ a \to \mathsf{List}\ a \\
\mathit{data}\ \mathsf{List} \qquad\qquad : \star \\
\quad \mathsf{stop} : \mathsf{List} \\
\quad \mathsf{more} : \qquad\qquad \mathsf{List} \quad \to \mathsf{List}
\end{array}$$

As in Wadler's examples, the relationship between colored objects and their erasure carries over everywhere. For example, erasing

[1] A meta-level logic, not to be confused with the object logics studied by Wadler.

color from a given list yields its length — and the typing relation is preserved.

$$\mathsf{more}\,{'b'}\,(\mathsf{more}\,{'l'}\,(\mathsf{more}\,{'u'}\,\mathsf{stop})) : \mathsf{List}\,\mathsf{Char}$$
$$\mathsf{more}\quad(\mathsf{more}\quad(\mathsf{more}\quad\mathsf{stop})) : \mathsf{List}$$

Concatenation yields addition; assuming $a :_i \star$:

$$\begin{array}{lllll} (+) : \mathsf{List}\,a & \to \mathsf{List}\,a & \to \mathsf{List}\,a & & \\ \mathsf{stop} & + & x_s & = & x_s \\ \mathsf{more}\,x\,x_s & + & y_s & = & \mathsf{more}\,x\,(x_s + y_s) \\ (+) : \mathsf{List} & \to \mathsf{List} & \to \mathsf{List} & & \\ \mathsf{stop} & + & x_s & = & x_s \\ \mathsf{more}\quad x_s & + & y_s & = & \mathsf{more}\quad(x_s + y_s) \end{array}$$

This structural relation is a benefit of abiding to color discipline: colorless parts shall never refer to tainted ones, and in return one gets some equalities for free. For example, the length of the concatenation is the addition of the lengths. This proposition requires a proof in AGDA or COQ, but thanks to colors, it holds by definition. Writing $\lfloor t \rfloor_i$ for the i-erasure of t:

$$\lfloor x_s + y_s \rfloor_i = \lfloor x_s \rfloor_i + \lfloor y_s \rfloor_i$$

In fact, TTC does not have a special purpose operator for erasure: the context determines whether variables refer to complete objects or to their erasures. For example in the following signature, the annotation $\not{i}$ indicates that type of the first argument of $<$ is any type which yields $\mathbb{N}$ after erasing i. (We will say that x_s is oblivious to i in the definition of $<$.)

$$(<) : (x_s :_{\not{i}} \mathbb{N}) \to (y : \mathbb{N}) \to \mathsf{Bool}$$

Hence, if $x_s : \mathsf{List}\,a$ then $x_s < 5$ is a valid expression[2]; and it tests whether x_s has less than 5 elements. The expression $3 < 5$ is also type-correct, because the erasure is idempotent. In general, it has no effect on terms which do not mention the erased color ($\lfloor \mathbb{N} \rfloor_i = \mathbb{N}$).

We note also already that substitution behaves specially on oblivious arguments. Consider again the expression $x_s < 5$. In it, one can substitute for x_s a concrete list containing information. The remarkable feature is that in the resulting term, the *erased* list will stand for x_s. For example:

$$\begin{aligned} &(x_s < 5)[\mathsf{more}\,{'b'}\,(\mathsf{more}\,{'l'}\,(\mathsf{more}\,{'u'}\,\mathsf{stop}))/x_s] \\ &= \mathsf{more}\quad(\mathsf{more}\quad(\mathsf{more}\quad\mathsf{stop})) < 5 \\ &= 3 < 5 \end{aligned}$$

2.2 Types as predicates

By using colored types, one effectively specifies structural invariants. For example, the type of the above concatenation operation constrains the length of its result. In our TTC it is possible to reveal these invariants explicitly by viewing types as predicates, and terms as proofs that the predicates are satisfied by the i-erasure. This is done by modulating the typing judgment. For example, under the modality i, the type of lists is seen as a predicate over $\mathbb{N}$. To indicate that the judgment is modulated, the typing operator (colon) is indexed with i.

$$\mathsf{List}\,(a :_i \star) \;:_i\; (x_s :_{\not{i}} \mathbb{N}) \to \star$$

Any typing can be so modulated. For example, a list $x_s : \mathsf{List}\,a$ becomes a proof that $\lfloor x_s \rfloor_i$ satisfies the $\mathsf{List}\,a$ seen as a predicate.

$$x_s :_i \mathsf{List}\,a \bullet_{\not{i}} x_s$$

(To avoid confusion we write predicate test using the $\bullet_{\not{i}}$ operator. Formally it is just the application corresponding to i-oblivious abstraction.) Likewise, the concatenation returns a list whose length is the sum of the lengths of its inputs.

$$(+) :_i (x_s : \mathsf{List}\,a) \to (y_s : \mathsf{List}\,a) \to \mathsf{List}\,a \bullet_{\not{i}} (x_s + y_s)$$

(To make sense of the above typings, recall that the second argument to List is a natural after erasing i; in general a variable $x_s :_i \mathsf{List}\,a \bullet_{\not{i}} n$ stands for a list of size n.)

Additionally, we remark that even though every type becomes a predicate, the computations (or data) that it represents do not essentially change. Taking our list example, the union of the types $\mathsf{List}\,a \bullet_{\not{i}} n$ for any $n : \mathbb{N}$ is isomorphic to $\mathsf{List}\,a$ seen as a type. Hence, assuming one has existential quantification, the type $A : \star$ remains available as a type under the modality i, as $\exists x.A\,x : \star$. Hence, one can continue to use types as types, even under a colored typing, referring implicitly to the above existential construction. We will take advantage of this shortcut in Sec. 2.4 for concision.

2.3 Colored Pairs

Another (dual) way to introduce colors is via pairs. A colored pair type, whose general form is written $(x : A) \times_i B$, is similar to the usual type $\Sigma(x : A)\,B$ (in particular x may occur in B). The difference is that B is tainted with the color i; and A is oblivious to i. Given $a : A$ and $b :_i B[a/x]$ one can construct an inhabitant of the pair type. As usual, colors must match: $a,_i b : (x : A) \times_i B$ is valid only if b is tainted and a is oblivious to i. Erasure extracts the first component of a pair, and interpreting a pair as a predicate yields its second component. The following example illustrates how colored pairs can be used to prove some parametricity properties. Assume the following (i-oblivious) context.

$$\begin{aligned} &f : (a : \star) \to a \to a \\ &b : \star \\ &y : b \end{aligned}$$

We then can define

$$\begin{aligned} &t : (x : b) \times_i (x \equiv y) \\ &t = f\,((x : b) \times_i (x \equiv y))\,(y,_i \mathsf{refl}) \end{aligned}$$

By definition of erasure:

$$\lfloor t \rfloor_i = f\,b\,y \tag{1}$$

The above equation can also be intuited by looking at t under i-glasses:

$$f\,((\quad b) \times_i (\lfloor x \rfloor_i \equiv y))\,(y \qquad)$$

In an i-modulated typing, one implicitly refers to the colored component of pairs, and therefore we have: $t :_i \lfloor t \rfloor_i \equiv y$. By (1) we obtain

$$t :_i f\,b\,y \equiv y$$

This result is normally obtained by a logical relation argument *outside* the theory, while it is internalized here — albeit via a judgment with an extra color. (A fully formal version of this example is presented in Sec. 4.) It may be worth stressing that, if one were to use a regular pair type, then, because f is abstract, the first component of t would *not* compute. In contrast, erasure is defined even on neutral terms.

2.4 Multiple Colors

We propose to support arbitrarily many colors. This feature is important for compositionality: it ensures that one can always mark a binding as tainted without corrupting interactions with the rest of the program. Indeed the other parts of the programs will use other, orthogonal colors. For example, the $\mathsf{List}\,a$ type described above is sufficient, there is no need to define a version without color. If one needs to access the elements of the list in a function, one simply

[2] We take the liberty to use decimal notation for unary naturals.

taints its typing with the color. For example, a summation function may be given the type $\mathsf{sum} :_i \mathsf{List}\,\mathbb{N} \to \mathbb{N}$. The taint will be transitively inherited by all functions using sum (and they can use other colors at will).

In fact, it is advisable to use colors even more effectively, and instead define sum by erasure. Assume the following definition of concat, where the nested lists use a different color j for the type a of elements, which we render in red. (In the type of concat, a occurs in an i-tainted context, so it is tainted both with i and j. We have $a :_{ij} \star$, and we render it with the combination of blue and red: magenta).

$$\begin{aligned}
&\mathsf{concat} :_i \mathsf{List}\,(\mathsf{List}\,a) \to \mathsf{List}\,a \\
&\mathsf{concat}\;\mathsf{stop} && = \mathsf{stop} \\
&\mathsf{concat}\,(\mathsf{more}\,x\,x_s) && = x + \mathsf{concat}\,x_s
\end{aligned}$$

Then one can obtain sum by erasing j from concat: ($\mathsf{sum} = \lfloor\mathsf{concat}\rfloor_j$). This would be impossible with a single color: attempting to erase the elements of the inner lists would erase the whole function.

Another use for multiple colors is to nest pairs. One cannot nest pairs which differentiate on the same given color, because this would break the rule that either side of an i-colored pair must respectively be oblivious to i or be tainted with it. However one can nest pairs which use different colors. The general form of j-colored pairs nested inside an i-colored one is the following:

$$(x : (w : A) \times_j B[w]) \times_i ((z : C[x]) \times_j D[x, z])$$

C can only refer to the j-oblivious part of x. C may not refer to the j-tainted part of w, since it does not carry that color itself. Looking at the above type successively with i and j glasses[3]:

$$\begin{aligned}
&(\quad\;\; (w : A) \times_j B[w]) \times_i ((z : C[x]) \times_j D[x, z]) \\
&(x : (\quad\;\; A) \times_j B[w]) \times_i ((\quad\;\; C[x]) \times_j D[x, z])
\end{aligned}$$

Using nested pairs is syntactically inconvenient, hence in the rest of the section we use a record-like syntax. Using record syntax, the above pair would be written

$$\{w :_{\not{i}\not{j}} A;\; y :_{\not{i}} B[w];\; z :_{\not{j}} C[w];\; D((w,_j y)\,,\, z)\}$$

The following example illustrates how multiple colors can be used to program with relations. Assume a definition of streams $\mathsf{Stream} : \star \to \star$. Stream is a functor as witnessed by $\mathsf{map} : (a : \star) \to (b : \star) \to (a \to b) \to \mathsf{Stream}\,a \to \mathsf{Stream}\,b$, with usual definitions. Assume furthermore the following abstract context:

$$\begin{aligned}
nth &: (a : \star) \to \mathsf{Stream}\,a \to \mathbb{N} \to a \\
a &: \star \\
b &: \star \\
f &: a \to b \\
x_s &: \mathsf{Stream}\,a \\
n &: \mathbb{N}
\end{aligned}$$

We define:

$$\begin{aligned}
r &: \star \\
r &= \{x :_{\not{i}} a;\; y :_{\not{j}} b;\; f\,x \equiv y\} \\
u &: a \to r \\
u &= \lambda z.\{x = z;\; y = f\,z;\; \mathsf{refl}\} \\
t &: r \\
t &= nth\,r\,(\mathsf{map}\,u\,x_s)\,n \\
&= nth\,\{x :_{\not{i}} a;\; y :_{\not{j}} b;\; f\,x \equiv y\} \\
&\qquad\quad (\mathsf{map}\,(\lambda z.\{x = z;\; y = f\,z;\; \mathsf{refl}\})\,x_s) \\
&\qquad\quad n
\end{aligned}$$

Erasing colors from t yields:

$$\begin{aligned}
\lfloor t\rfloor_i &= nth\,a\,(\mathsf{map}\,\mathsf{id}_a\,x_s)\,n = nth\,a\,x_s\,n \\
\lfloor t\rfloor_j &= nth\,b\,(\mathsf{map}\,f\,x_s)\,n
\end{aligned}$$

Indeed, looking at t respectively under i-colored and j-colored glasses:

$$\begin{aligned}
&nth\,\{\quad a \qquad\qquad\quad\;\; \}\,(\mathsf{map}\,(\lambda z.\{\quad z \qquad\qquad\quad \})\,x_s)\,n \\
&nth\,\{\qquad\qquad b \qquad\quad \}\,(\mathsf{map}\,(\lambda z.\{\qquad\qquad f\,z \quad\;\; \})\,x_s)\,n
\end{aligned}$$

Now, viewing t under the i then $\{i, j\}$-modalities:

$$\begin{aligned}
&t : r \\
&t :_i r\,\lfloor t\rfloor_i \\
&t :_{i,j} r\,\lfloor t\rfloor_i\,\lfloor t\rfloor_j \\
&t :_{i,j} f\,\lfloor t\rfloor_i \equiv \lfloor t\rfloor_j \\
&t :_{i,j} f(nth\,a\,x_s\,n) \equiv nth\,b\,(\mathsf{map}\,f\,x_s)\,n
\end{aligned}$$

Hence writing $nth\,a\,x_s\,n$ as $x_s\,!!\,n$, we obtain the expected commuting law

$$f(x_s\,!!\,n) \equiv \mathsf{map}\,f\,x_s\,!!\,n.$$

2.5 Conclusion

A motto of programming with dependent types is to use more and more types to express one's intentions more and more precisely. However, there is a drawback to precise types: hard work to convince a type-checker that programs inhabit them. We observe that the use of colors is a way to specify invariants in types which does not complicate user code. For instance we have seen that it is just as easy to program with colored lists as with regular ones, and length invariants are captured. Furthermore, the system can automatically discover equations which would require a proof without the use of colors.

One cannot "go wrong" by using more colors in a library. In the worst case, colors can simply be ignored by the users of the library. In the best case, they serve to specify invariants concisely, facilitate reasoning, and provide a variant of the library to the user for each possible erasure combination.

We have implemented a prototype of TTC as an extension of the AGDA system. The prototype, in its current version at the time of writing, features colored bindings and abstraction over colors, but is still lacking erasure, oblivious bindings and colored pairs. The prototype, together with a short tutorial for it, can be obtained online: `http://www.cse.chalmers.se/~mouling/Parametricity/TTC.html`.

3. CCCC: A Core Calculus of Colored Constructions

In this section we present CCCC (the Core Calculus of Colored Constructions) which is the formal core of the TTC we envision.

[3] The analogy to perceptual colors still holds here: magenta both appears blue under blue glasses and red under red glasses. (i.e. it fades into the background in both cases.) The analogy breaks only when one uses too many colors: most humans can only perceive three primary colors, while we allow an unbounded number of colors in TTC.

Technically, CCCC is an extension of CC (the plain Calculus of Constructions (Coquand and Huet 1986)) with the notion of color informally introduced in the previous section. Even though we use CC as a base, we do not rely on its specifics. Along the lines presented here, it is conceivable to construct a variant of any type-system with colors, including intuitionistic type-theory (Martin-Löf 1984).

The rest of the section describes the main features of CCCC in pedagogical order. A summary is shown in appendix for reference. We emphasize that we describe only on the core features of TTC. Some features used in the previous section will not be included here, even though it is conceivable to integrate them with limited effort.

Even though we continue to render some expressions in color as a visual aid, the formal system does not rely on them in any way. This section can be read in black and white without any loss in precision.

3.1 CC as a PTS

We use CC as a base, so we recall briefly its definition, using a pure type system (Barendregt 1992) presentation. The typing rules are as follows:

$$\textsc{Conv}\ \frac{\Gamma \vdash a : A \qquad A =_\beta A'}{\Gamma \vdash a : A'} \qquad \textsc{Axiom}\ \frac{\vdash \Gamma}{\Gamma \vdash \star : \Box} \qquad \textsc{Var}\ \frac{\vdash \Gamma \qquad x : A \in \Gamma}{\Gamma \vdash x : A}$$

$$\textsc{Prod}\ \frac{\Gamma, x : A \vdash B : s}{\Gamma \vdash (x : A) \to B : s} \qquad \textsc{Abs}\ \frac{\Gamma, x : A \vdash b : B}{\Gamma \vdash \lambda x : A.b : (x : A) \to B}$$

$$\textsc{App}\ \frac{\Gamma \vdash F : (x : A) \to B \qquad \Gamma \vdash u : A}{\Gamma \vdash F \bullet u : B[u/x]}$$

To limit clutter we omit the well-formedness conditions of types A and B in the rule ABS. The product $(x : A) \to B$ may be also written $A \to B$ when x does not occur free in B, and we generally omit the application operator $\bullet$. The metasyntactic variable s ranges over the sorts $\star$ and $\Box$. The context-lookup relation $(x : A \in \Gamma)$ is straightforward, and the context-formation rules are:

$$\textsc{Empty}\ \frac{}{\vdash -} \qquad \textsc{Bind}\ \frac{\vdash \Gamma \qquad \Gamma \vdash A : s}{\vdash \Gamma, x : A}$$

Traditional presentations of PTSs, including that of Barendregt (1992), use another formulation, which integrates the context-lookup, context-formation and typing rules. Instead of the VAR rule, one has the following WEAKENING and START rules, and axioms can only be used in the empty context.

$$\textsc{Start}\ \frac{\Gamma \vdash A : s}{\Gamma, x : A \vdash x : A} \qquad \textsc{Weakening}\ \frac{\Gamma \vdash A : B \qquad \Gamma \vdash C : s}{\Gamma, x : C \vdash A : B}$$

While the presentation of Barendregt economizes a couple derivation rules, it has the disadvantage to conflate separate concepts in a single definition. Consequently, is it harder to extend, and modern presentations tend to use separate context-lookup and context-formation relations.

3.2 Colors, Taints and Modalities

We assume an infinite supply of color names; the metasyntactic variables i and j stand for them in the remainder. We call an ordered set of such color names a *taint* and use θ or ι to range over taints. A color may be introduced in the context by its name. After such a mention, terms may contain i-tainted parts, but also non i-tainted parts. In contrast, before the mention of i, terms are i-oblivious: they cannot depend on i in any way.

Our typing judgment $\Gamma \vdash A :_\theta B$ is indexed by a taint θ, which must be a subset of the colors present in Γ. The presence of a given color i in θ indicates how i can be used in A and B.

- $i \notin \theta$ indicates that A is not tainted with i. A term A typed in such a taint may still mention the color i. For example $\lambda(x :_i T) \to a$ is allowed. However, the usage of i-tainted variables is forbidden in the target (a) of the term. For example $\lambda(x :_i T) \to x$ is forbidden.
- $i \in \theta$ indicates that the term A is tainted with i. In such a judgment, using i-tainted variables is allowed in the targets of terms and types. *Remark*: It does not make sense to erase i from a judgment using this taint; conceptually the whole typing is tainted, so it would be entirely removed.

For each taint θ we have two sorts $\star_\theta$ and $\Box_\theta$, with the axiom $\star_\theta : \Box_\theta$. The conversion rule merely preserves taints.

$$\textsc{Conv}\ \frac{\Gamma \vdash a :_\theta A \qquad A =_\beta A'}{\Gamma \vdash a :_\theta A'} \qquad \textsc{Axiom}\ \frac{\vdash \Gamma}{\Gamma \vdash \star_\theta :_\theta \Box_\theta}$$

A variable binding $x :_\psi A$ does not only carry a taint, but also a *modality*. (ψ and φ range over modalities.) A modality is composed of two disjoint sets of colors (say $\psi = (\theta, \iota)$ with $\theta \cap \iota = \varnothing$) that constrain what kind of a term u can be substituted for x. The first set θ is the taint of u. The second set ι is an "anti-taint": a set of colors which u must be oblivious to. We often use the compact notation $i_1 \ldots i_n, \not{j_1} \ldots \not{j_n}$ for the modality $(\{i_1 \ldots i_n\}, \{j_1 \ldots j_n\})$. Similarly we will write $\not{j} \in \psi$ to mean that j is found in the second set. Using this notation, the following two contexts are equivalent (one can substitute one for another without changing the provability of a judgment):

$$\Gamma, x : A, i, \Delta$$
$$\Gamma, i, x :_{\not{i}} A, \Delta$$

That is, declaring a variable before i, or declaring it i-oblivious explicitly are equivalent. The product and abstraction rules can change the modality of the type quantified over; the application rule behaves correspondingly.

$$\textsc{Prod}\ \frac{\Gamma, x :_\psi A \vdash B :_\theta s}{\Gamma \vdash (x :_\psi A) \to B :_\theta s} \qquad \textsc{Abs}\ \frac{\Gamma, x :_\psi A \vdash b :_\theta B}{\Gamma \vdash (\lambda x :_\psi A.b) :_\theta (x :_\psi A) \to B}$$

$$\textsc{App}\ \frac{\Gamma \vdash F :_\theta (x :_\psi A) \to B \qquad \Gamma \vdash u :_\psi A}{\Gamma \vdash F \bullet_\psi u :_\theta B[u/x]}$$

(where the metasyntactic variable s now ranges over the sorts $\star_\iota$ or $\Box_\iota$, for any ι.) To be able to merely forward modalities, we need to extend the judgment to support arbitrary modalities φ, not just taints θ, as we do at the beginning of the next section.

We generally omit the modality annotation on applications, because they are easily inferred from the context. One can embed any derivation from CC into CCCC simply by using the empty taint everywhere.

3.3 Obliviousness and variable lookup

We extend the typing judgment to support any modality ψ (not just a taint) as follows:

Definition 1 (Oblivious judgment)**.**

$$\textit{If } \psi = (\theta, \iota) \textit{ then } \Gamma \vdash A :_\psi B \triangleq \lfloor \Gamma \rfloor_\iota \vdash A :_\theta B$$

This captures the intuition that A and B are oblivious to every color in ι. Indeed, the erasure removes all mentions of i from the context Γ for every $i \in \iota$ (a complete definition and justification of erasure is given in the following section). In particular, if $x : A \in \Gamma$, then $\Gamma \vdash x :_{\not{i}} \lfloor A \rfloor_i$; in words, referencing a variable from an i-oblivious judgment yields only a witness of the i-erased type.

Hence, variable lookup requires equality of taints, not merely inclusion:

$$\textsc{Var}\ \frac{\vdash \Gamma \qquad x :_\theta A \in \Gamma}{\Gamma \vdash x :_\theta A}$$

There are two ways to access an i-oblivious variable x. First, it is accessible in an i-oblivious judgment, as can be seen by expanding Def. 1:

$$\Gamma, x :_{\not{i}} A, \Delta \vdash x :_{\not{i}} A \;\triangleq\; \lfloor \Gamma \rfloor_i, x : A, \lfloor \Delta \rfloor_i \vdash x : A$$

Second, it can be accessed from an i-aware judgment, as formalized in the context-lookup rules:

$$\textsc{Start}\ \frac{}{x :_\theta A \in \Gamma, x :_{(\theta,\iota)} A} \qquad \textsc{Col. Wk}\ \frac{x :_\theta A \in \Gamma \qquad i \notin \theta}{x :_\theta A \in \Gamma, i}$$

$$\textsc{Wk}\ \frac{x :_\theta A \in \Gamma}{x :_\theta A \in \Gamma, y :_\psi B}$$

The Col. Wk rule ensures that x is accessible from an i-aware context (but not an i-tainted one), even if it is declared before the introduction the color i. The Start rule plays a similar role: x can be explicitly oblivious to any set of colors, it does not change its accessibility.

Consider as an example the following definition, a variant of Leibniz equality.

$$x \equiv_a^i y \;\triangleq\; (P :_i (z :_{\not{i}} a) \to \star_i) \to P\,x \to P\,y$$

One can verify that it is a well-colored type as follows. Let $\Delta = a : \star, x : a, y : a$:

$$\textsc{Prod}\ \dfrac{\textsc{App}\ \dfrac{\vdots \qquad \text{Def. 1}\ \dfrac{\Delta \vdash y : a}{\Delta, i, \ldots \vdash y :_{\not{i}} a}}{\Delta, i, P :_i (z :_{\not{i}} a) \to \star_i, q :_i P\,x \vdash P\,y : \star_i}}{\Delta, i \vdash x \equiv_a^i y :_i \star_i}$$

With $\mathsf{refl}^i \triangleq \lambda(P :_i \star).\lambda(q :_i P).q$, one can also derive $a : \star, x : a, i \vdash \mathsf{refl}^i :_i x \equiv_a^i x$.

In order to use $\equiv$ as an equality, we need to access oblivious variables from non-oblivious contexts, as we explain in this paragraph. The key difference between $\equiv$ as defined above and the usual Leibniz equality here is that we use propositions P of type $(x :_{\not{i}} a) \to \star_i$; that is, the parameter of P is i-oblivious.

Thanks to the context lookup rules, a variable $x :_{\not{i}} \mathsf{Bool}$ may be used even in an i-aware context, so one can construct a proposition Q^i of the right type which returns truth if the Boolean is true and falsity otherwise. Then one can obtain falsity from true $\equiv_{\mathsf{Bool}}$ false by substituting Q^i for P. Assuming a definition $\mathsf{Test} :_i \mathsf{Bool} \to \star_i$ which does the adequate case analysis on booleans, one has:

$$\text{Def.}\ \dfrac{\textsc{Abs}\ \dfrac{\textsc{App}\ \dfrac{\vdots \qquad \dfrac{x : \mathsf{Bool} \in i, x :_{\not{i}} \mathsf{Bool}}{i, x :_{\not{i}} \mathsf{Bool} \vdash x : \mathsf{Bool}}\ \textsc{Var}}{i, x :_{\not{i}} \mathsf{Bool} \vdash \mathsf{Test}\,x :_i \star_i}}{i \vdash \lambda(x :_{\not{i}} \mathsf{Bool}).\mathsf{Test}\,x :_i (x :_{\not{i}} \mathsf{Bool}) \to \star_i}}{i \vdash Q^i :_i (x :_{\not{i}} \mathsf{Bool}) \to \star_i}$$

3.4 Erasure

Color erasure is defined by structural induction on terms. The effect on each modality is the following. Applying i-erasure on an i-tainted binding removes it. The i-erasure of a non i-tainted binding is the binding of the erasure. Erasing i from an i-oblivious binding has no effect besides removing the mention of $\not{i}$.

Erasure of product, abstraction and application follows directly from the behavior on bindings. Erasure preserves all variable occurrences, as well as sorts. In the following table we sum up all cases. The erasure of terms which do not mention a modality are show in the first column For terms which mention a modality, we show the various cases in various columns. The first column shows the case where the color occurs nowhere in the modality. The second one shows the case where i occurs as a taint. The third one shows the case where the i occurs as an anti-taint.

$i \notin \psi$	$i \in \psi$	$\psi = \varphi, \not{i}$
$\lfloor x \rfloor_i = x$		
$\lfloor s \rfloor_i = s$		
$\lfloor (x :_\psi A) \to B \rfloor_i = (x :_\psi \lfloor A \rfloor_i) \to \lfloor B \rfloor_i$	$\lfloor B \rfloor_i$	$(x :_\varphi A) \to \lfloor B \rfloor_i$
$\lfloor \lambda x :_\psi A.b \rfloor_i = \lambda x :_\psi \lfloor A \rfloor_i.\lfloor b \rfloor_i$	$\lfloor b \rfloor_i$	$\lambda x :_\varphi A.\lfloor b \rfloor_i$
$\lfloor F \bullet_\psi a \rfloor_i = (\lfloor F \rfloor_i) \bullet_\psi \lfloor a \rfloor_i$	$\lfloor F \rfloor_i$	$(\lfloor F \rfloor_i) \bullet_\varphi a$
$\lfloor \Gamma, x :_\psi A \rfloor_i = \lfloor \Gamma \rfloor_i, x :_\psi \lfloor A \rfloor_i$	$\lfloor \Gamma \rfloor_i$	$\lfloor \Gamma \rfloor_i, x :_\varphi A$
$\lfloor \Gamma, j \rfloor_i = \lfloor \Gamma \rfloor_i, j$		
$\lfloor \Gamma, i \rfloor_i = \Gamma$		

Lemma 1 (Erasure preserves typing). *If $\Gamma \vdash A :_\theta B$ and $i \notin \theta$ then $\lfloor \Gamma \rfloor_i \vdash \lfloor A \rfloor_i :_\theta \lfloor B \rfloor_i$.*

Proof. By induction on the derivation. The proof relies on the color-discipline enforced by the typing rules. □

This lemma means that erasure makes sense as a meta-level definition. The precondition is important: erasing i makes no sense on an i-tainted term; conceptually the whole term would be erased in that case. This justifies for example the case for sorts in the definition: the precondition guarantees that erasure will not be applied to a sort $\star_i$. In the system, we use erasure only in situations where this precondition is satisfied.

Erasure is used in the definition of substitution (whose full definition is given in Sec. 6): when substituting in an oblivious argument, or in the type of an oblivious parameter, one needs to erase the substitutee. For example:

$$(f \bullet_{\not{i}} u)[t/x] = f[t/x] \bullet_{\not{i}} u[\lfloor t \rfloor_i/x]$$

Note that if x is i-tainted, the type-system prevents any occurrence of x in u, ensuring that the precondition of Lem. 1 is respected.

We have not yet defined how to reduce terms in CCCC, but it is worth mentioning already that erasure preserves computation. A proof is given latter in Lem. ??.

$$\text{if } A \longrightarrow^\star B, \text{ then } \lfloor A \rfloor_i \longrightarrow^\star \lfloor B \rfloor_i, \text{ for any color } i.$$

3.5 Types as Predicates

By modulating a judgment with a color i, a type B becomes a predicate over $\lfloor B \rfloor_i$ [4]. The erasure of a term A of type B satisfies the type B seen as a predicate.

The parametric interpretation defined by Bernardy et al. (2010), can be extented to our theory with colors:

[4] With the exception of terms which are sorted in under that color. For example, $\star_i :_i \Box_i$ and not $\star_i :_i \star_i \to \Box_i$. This feature prevents an "infinite descent" into deeper and deeper predicates.

$$
\begin{aligned}
[\![x]\!]^i &= x^i \\
[\![\lambda x :_\psi A.b]\!]^i &= \lambda x :_\psi A.\lambda x^i :_{\psi,i} x \in_\psi [\![A]\!]^i.[\![b]\!]^i && \text{if } i \notin \psi \\
&= [\![b]\!]^i && \text{if } i \in \psi \\
&= \lambda x :_\varphi A.[\![b]\!]^i && \text{if } \psi = \varphi, \dot{\imath} \\
[\![F \bullet_\psi a]\!]^i &= [\![F]\!]^i \bullet_\psi a \bullet_{\psi,i} [\![a]\!]^i && \text{if } i \notin \psi \\
&= [\![F]\!]^i && \text{if } i \in \psi \\
&= [\![F]\!]^i \bullet_\varphi a && \text{if } \psi = \varphi, \dot{\imath} \\
[\![T]\!]^i &= \lambda x :_i T.x \in [\![T]\!]^i && \text{if } T \text{ is a type}
\end{aligned}
$$

$$
\begin{aligned}
C \in_\psi [\![s]\!]^i &= (x :_{\psi,\dot{\imath}} C) \to s && \text{if } i \notin \psi \\
&= s && \text{if } i \in \psi \\
&= (x :_\varphi C) \to s && \text{if } \psi = \varphi, \dot{\imath} \\
C \in_\psi [\![(x :_i A) \to B]\!]^i &= \\
(x :_\psi A) \to (x^i :_{\psi,i} x \in_\psi [\![A]\!]^i) &\to (C \bullet_\psi x) \in_\psi [\![B]\!]^i && \text{if } i \notin \psi \\
&= C \in_\psi [\![B]\!]^i && \text{if } i \in \psi \\
&= (x :_\varphi A) \to (C \bullet_\varphi x) \in_\varphi [\![B]\!]^i && \text{if } \psi = \varphi, \dot{\imath} \\
C \in_\psi [\![T]\!]^i &= [\![T]\!]^i \bullet_{\psi,\dot{\imath}} \lfloor T \rfloor_i && \text{if } T \text{ is not a type}
\end{aligned}
$$

Theorem 1 (Parametricity of closed terms). *If* $\vdash A :_\theta B$ *and* $i \notin \theta$, *then*

$$\vdash [\![A]\!]^i :_{\theta,i} [\![B]\!]^i \bullet_{\theta,\dot{\imath}} \lfloor A \rfloor_i$$

Proof. The proof uses the standard techniques of logical relations, extended to dependent types by Bernardy et al. (2010). □

We wish however not to be limited to closed terms, and want parametricity even on open terms. The presence of colors allows[5] to add the following rule, which internalizes the reinterpretation of terms as predicates and proofs.

$$\textsc{Param}\ \frac{\Gamma \vdash A :_\theta B \qquad i \notin \theta}{\Gamma \vdash A :_{\theta,i} B \bullet_{\theta,\dot{\imath}} \lfloor A \rfloor_i}$$

This rule is a generalization of Th. 1 and it allows to deduce, within the calculus, theorems which could only be obtained meta-theoretically without it. However, in this paper, the treatment of logical relations differs from the usual one: a type is not *interpreted* as a predicate (via the above transformation of terms and types $[\![\cdot]\!]$), but is directly *used* as such in an i-modulated judgment.

In order to use T as a predicate we extend reduction rules as follows, where we recall that s ranges over sorts, while t ranges over terms.

$$s_\theta \bullet_\varphi t \longrightarrow (z :_\varphi t) \to s_{\theta \cup \iota} \quad \text{where } \varphi = (\theta, \iota) \tag{1}$$

$$((x :_\psi A) \to B) \bullet_\varphi t \longrightarrow (x :_\psi A) \to (B \bullet_\varphi t) \quad \text{if } \exists i \text{ such that } i \in \psi \text{ and } \dot{\imath} \in \varphi \tag{2}$$

$$((x :_\psi A) \to B) \bullet_\varphi t \longrightarrow (x :_\psi A) \to (B \bullet_\varphi (t \bullet_\psi x)) \quad \text{otherwise} \tag{3}$$

$$(\lambda x :_\psi A.b) \bullet_\psi t \longrightarrow b[t/x] \tag{4}$$

- (1): Since a type becomes a predicate, a type of types (a sort) becomes a type of predicates. The target sort of the predicate type is adjusted, in order to obtain a type (and not again a predicate — see footnote 4).
- (2) and (3): A function t satisfies the predicate of a function type if an argument x (which implicitly satisfies the predicate of the domain A) is mapped by the function t to a value satisfying the codomain B. In the case of (2), the modality φ mandates erasure of the domain A, therefore x is not given as an argument to t.
- (4): The β-reduction is trivially amended to account for colors. The rules (1,2,3) do not interfere with β, because they concern other syntactic forms.

[5] The issues that one faces when attempting to internalize parametricity in a theory without colors are detailed by Bernardy and Moulin (2012).

The cases (1,2,3) agree with the standard interpretation of types as predicates. Bernardy and Moulin (2012); Bernardy et al. (2012) give a detailed account of logical relations in the presence of dependent types. As an example, one can check that reduction behaves as expected for the list concatenation type:

$$
\begin{aligned}
&((x_s : \mathsf{List}\, a) \to (y_s : \mathsf{List}\, a) \to \mathsf{List}\, a) \bullet_{\dot{\imath}} c \\
\longrightarrow\ &(x_s : \mathsf{List}\, a) \to ((y_s : \mathsf{List}\, a) \to \mathsf{List}\, a) \bullet_{\dot{\imath}} (c\, x_s) \\
\longrightarrow\ &(x_s : \mathsf{List}\, a) \to (y_s : \mathsf{List}\, a) \to \mathsf{List}\, a \bullet_{\dot{\imath}} (c\, x_s\, y_s)
\end{aligned}
$$

3.6 Example

Assume the colors i and j as well as the context

$$
\begin{aligned}
\mathsf{List}_i &: (a :_i \star_i) \to \star \\
\mathsf{List}_j &: (b :_j \star_j) \to \star \\
\mathsf{fold} &: (a :_i \star_i) \to (b : \star) \to \\
&\quad (a \to b \to b) \to b \to \mathsf{List}_i\, a \to b
\end{aligned}
$$

One can define a variant of the ubiquitous *map* function as follows:

$$
\begin{aligned}
map &: (a :_i \star_i) \to (b :_j \star_j) \to \\
&\quad (f :_j (x :_i a) \to b) \to \mathsf{List}_i\, a \to \mathsf{List}_j\, b \\
map &= \lambda f.\mathsf{fold}\, a\, (\mathsf{List}_j\, b)\, (\lambda\, x\, x_s.\mathsf{more}\, (f\, x)\, x_s)\, \mathsf{stop}
\end{aligned}
$$

This version of map is versatile. After erasing j, the f argument disappears and map becomes a function returning the length of its input. After erasing i, f becomes a constant of type b, the input "list" becomes a natural number (n), and map returns a list containing n copies of f.

3.7 Analysis

In this section we state and prove a number of standard meta-theoretical results for our calculus. Details can be found in the appendix.

Corollary 1 (Confluence). *CCCC has the confluence property.*

Proof. A direct consequence of Th. **??** and $\longrightarrow^\star = \rhd^\star$. □

Lemma 2 (Thinning). *Let* Γ *and* Δ *be legal contexts such that* $\Gamma \subseteq \Delta$. *Then* $\Gamma \vdash A :_\theta B \Longrightarrow \Delta \vdash A :_\theta B$.

Proof. As in (Barendregt 1992, lem. 5.2.12). □

The generation lemma for PTS can be extended to colored bindings. The only difficulty is the following. In (Barendregt 1992), the generation lemma includes a case for applications. This case is difficult to extend to our calculus, since application can be done not only on lambda abstractions, but also on types, when they are used as predicates. Fortunately, that case is not used in the subject reduction lemma, and therefore we can omit it from our version of the generation lemma.

Lemma 3 (Generation). *The statement is similar to that of (Barendregt 1992, lem. 5.2.13). Points 1. to 4. (constant, variable, product, abstraction) are adapted in a straightforward manner to colored binding. Point 5. (application) is removed. The following two points are added.*

- *If* $\Gamma \vdash (s_{\theta,i} \bullet_{\theta,\dot{\imath}} t) :_{\theta,i} C$, *then*

$$\Gamma \vdash t :_{\theta,\dot{\imath}} s_\theta \text{ and } C \equiv_\beta s'_\theta \text{ with } (s, s') \in \mathcal{A}$$

- *If* $\Gamma \vdash ((x :_\varphi A) \to B) \bullet_{\theta,\dot{\imath}} t :_{\theta,i} C$, *then*

$$\Gamma \vdash t :_{\theta,\dot{\imath}} \lfloor (x :_\varphi A) \to B \rfloor_i \text{ and } C \equiv_\beta s'_\theta \text{ with}$$
$$\Gamma \vdash (x :_\varphi A) \to B :_\theta s_\theta$$

Proof. As in (Barendregt 1992): we follow the derivations until $s_{\theta,i}$ (resp. $(x :_\varphi A) \to B$) is introduced. It can only be done by the PARAM rule, and the conclusion follows from a use of the Thinning Lemma. (An example of such derivations can be found in Fig. 1.) □

Theorem 2 (Subject reduction). *If* $A \longrightarrow A'$ *and* $\Gamma \vdash A : T$, *then* $\Gamma \vdash A' : T$.

Proof. Most of the technicalities of the proof of subject reduction for PTSs (Barendregt 1992) concern β-reduction, and are not changed by the addition of colors.

Hence we discuss here only the handling of reduction rules (1) to (3). We treat first the case of sorts (1):

$$s_\theta \bullet_\varphi t \longrightarrow (z :_\varphi t) \to s_{\theta \cup \iota} \qquad (1)$$
$$\text{where } \varphi = (\theta, \iota)$$

In this case, the Generation Lemma indicates that the derivation tree must end with an APP rule and contain a chain PARAM-AX on the left-hand side of the derivation. A template for such a tree is shown in Fig. 1. One can then construct a typing derivation for the reduct, which ends with the PROD rule, and does not mention PARAM nor APP. The template for typing the reduct is also shown in Fig. 1.

Second we treat the case of products (2) and (3).

$$((x :_\psi A) \to B) \bullet_\varphi t \longrightarrow (x :_\psi A) \to (B \bullet_\varphi t) \qquad (2)$$
$$\text{if } \exists i \text{ such that } i \in \psi \text{ and } \dot{\imath} \in \varphi$$
$$((x :_\psi A) \to B) \bullet_\varphi t \longrightarrow (x :_\psi A) \to (B \bullet_\varphi (t \bullet_\psi x)) \qquad (3)$$
$$\text{otherwise}$$

Again we can use the Generation Lemma to obtain the shape of a derivation tree of the reducible expression, and obtain a valid typing for the reduct (also shown in Fig. 1. In this case the typing of the source involves the chain of rules PARAM-PROD on the left-hand side of APP. The typing of the reduct ends with PROD. □

We have taken the view in our presentation that the reduction rules are untyped, and therefore subject reduction must recover typings using the Generation Lemma. An alternative would be to have a typed reduction relation (this relation usually goes by the name of "judgmental equality"). In this case the reduction of proof trees shown in Fig. 1 would be part of the definition of reduction. The two approaches have been proved equivalent for arbitrary PTSs by Siles (2010).

Theorem 3 (Normalization). *CCCC is strongly normalizing: every sequence of reductions eventually terminates.*

Proof. The new reduction rules, involving PARAM, are much easier to handle than β-reduction (rule 4). Indeed, the argument to the application is not duplicated by these reduction rules.

Hence, one can adapt the proofs of termination of CC to CCCC. At a high-level, the argument goes as follows. Consider reduction rules (1) to (3), that we collectively call PARAM-reductions below. Their effect is to make the left-hand-side of the $\bullet_\psi$ operator smaller. This can also be seen by examining the corresponding typing derivations: the reductions strictly decrease the size of the tree above the PARAM rule involved.

Consequently, between each β-reduction step there can be only a finite number of PARAM-reductions. The question is now: do these PARAM-reductions create β-redexes? The reductions (1) and (2) do not, but (3) does. However, the new redex is harmless: it lies in an i-oblivious context, and therefore there is no risk of an (i-aware) PARAM-reduction to be created by that redex.

The situation is then that, by importing the proof techniques developed for CC, one can bound the chains of β-reductions, and use the above argument to finitely-bound the PARAM-reductions occurring between β-reduction steps. □

The above proof is an alternative to that done in earlier work (Bernardy and Moulin 2012), which works by construction a model by translation into CC. Even though the earlier proof can be adapted to the present system, we find the above proof more modular, and thus easier to grasp.

3.8 Type-Checking With Colors

The rules PARAM and the definition of and oblivious judgment Def. 1 are not syntax-directed, therefore it may be non-obvious how they should be used in type-checking. In this subsection we sketch a possible type-checking algorithm and briefly argue for its soundness. A full description of the algorithm, together with a completeness proof, is left for future work.

We assume that the user supplies a term t, a type T, a modality φ and a context Γ. The task is to reconstruct a derivation of $\Gamma \vdash t :_\varphi T$.

Most of the implementation of the new rules is realized at the point of checking a variable ($t = x$). Let us assume that looking up x in the context Γ yields $x :_\psi A$.

For each color $i \in \Gamma$ we have to take into account its status in φ and ψ. For simplicity we assume that φ and ψ contain at most one color; a full implementation will do the same task for each color independently.

1. $\dot{\imath} \in \varphi$. If i is not mentioned in ψ, then the derivation is the following.

$$\text{Def. 1}\ \dfrac{\text{Lem. 1}\ \dfrac{\text{VAR}\ \dfrac{x : A \in \Gamma}{\Gamma \vdash x : A}}{\lfloor \Gamma \rfloor_i \vdash x : \lfloor A \rfloor_i}}{\Gamma \vdash x :_{\dot{\imath}} \lfloor A \rfloor_i}$$

   Hence we simply check that $T = \lfloor A \rfloor_i$. For $i \in \psi$, then x is not accessible and type-checking reports failure. For $\dot{\imath} \in \psi$ one needs only to check $T = A$.

2. If the judgment is i-aware ($\varphi = \varnothing$), we have three cases. If $i \in \psi$, then x is not accessible and type-checking reports failure. Otherwise, then modalities match and we only need to check $T = A$. Notably, if $\dot{\imath} \in \psi$, x is more oblivious than required, but this is accepted by the START rule, which allows arbitrary extra anti-taints in the binding of the looked-up variable.

3. If $i \in \varphi$, we have two cases. If $i \in \psi$, then one simply checks $T = A$. Otherwise, one must take into account PARAM, that is, check $T = A \bullet_{\dot{\imath}} x$ instead of $T = A$.

Lastly, when checking a type used as a predicate, that is a term t of the form $(\Delta \to B) \bullet_\psi u$ (for any telescope Δ) or $s \bullet_\psi u$, we reduce the term t before checking it. The number of reduction steps is at most $|\Delta| + 1$ in the first case or 1 in the second case: the performance hit is minimal.

As usual in type-checking algorithms, all the equality-tests mentioned above have to be performed up-to the reduction relation, in order to take into account the CONV rule. This is done using standard means, for example normalizing terms before comparison, which is possible thanks to Th. 3.

$$\text{App}\ \dfrac{\text{Conv}\ \dfrac{\text{Param}\ \dfrac{\text{Ax}\ \dfrac{\vdash \Gamma}{\Gamma \vdash \star : \Box}}{\Gamma \vdash \star :_i \Box \bullet_{\not{i}} \star}}{\Gamma \vdash \star :_i (x :_{\not{i}} \star) \to \Box_i} \qquad \Gamma \vdash t :_{\not{i}} \star}{\Gamma \vdash \star \bullet_{\not{i}} t :_i \Box_i} \quad \Longrightarrow \quad \text{Prod}\ \dfrac{\text{Ax}\ \dfrac{\text{Bind}\ \dfrac{\vdash \Gamma \qquad \Gamma \vdash t :_{\not{i}} \star}{\vdash \Gamma, x :_{\not{i}} t}}{\Gamma, x :_{\not{i}} t \vdash \star_i :_i \Box_i}}{\Gamma \vdash (x :_{\not{i}} t) \to \star_i :_i \Box_i}$$

$$\text{App}\ \dfrac{\text{Conv}\ \dfrac{\text{Param}\ \dfrac{\text{Prod}\ \dfrac{\Gamma, x : A \vdash B : \star}{\Gamma \vdash (x : A) \to B : \star}}{\Gamma \vdash (x : A) \to B :_i \star \bullet_{\not{i}} \lfloor (x : A) \to B \rfloor_i}}{\Gamma \vdash (x : A) \to B :_i \lfloor (x : A) \to B \rfloor_i \to \star_i} \qquad \Gamma \vdash t :_{\not{i}} \lfloor (x : A) \to B \rfloor_i}{\Gamma \vdash ((x : A) \to B) \bullet_{\not{i}} t :_i \star_i} \quad \Longrightarrow$$

$$\text{Prod}\ \dfrac{\text{App}\ \dfrac{\text{Param}\ \dfrac{\Gamma, x : A \vdash B : \star}{\Gamma, x : A \vdash B :_i \lfloor B \rfloor_i \to \star_i} \qquad \text{App}\ \dfrac{\Gamma \vdash t :_{\not{i}} \lfloor (x : A) \to B \rfloor_i}{\Gamma, x : A \vdash t\, x :_{\not{i}} B}}{\Gamma, x : A \vdash B \bullet_{\not{i}} (t\, x) :_i \star_i}}{\Gamma \vdash (x : A) \to B \bullet_{\not{i}} (t\, x) :_i \star_i}$$

Figure 1. Proof-reduction templates corresponding to the term-reductions (1) and (3). The sorts and taint annotations are specialized to the simplest case to reduce clutter; generalization to arbitrary taints and sorts is straightforward.

4. Extensions

4.1 Inductive Definitions

The definitions presented in the previous section can be extended to work on inductive types in a straightforward manner, merely recursively applying the definitions on the types of each component of the inductive type, as we have done in the examples in Sec. 2. The extension of a similar system to inductive definitions is described in full detail by Bernardy et al. (2012). We conjecture that the addition of inductive definitions does not compromise any meta-theoretical property.

4.2 Colored Pairs

In this section we formally introduce colored pairs, and formalize a example presented in Sec. 2: inhabitants of the type $(a : \star) \to a \to a$ must be the identity function.

The formation and introduction rules (SUM, PAIR) are similar to the usual rules for dependent pairs, with the difference that the modalities track that the first component is oblivious to the color while the second component is tainted.

$$\text{Sum}\ \dfrac{\Gamma, x :_{\not{i}} A \vdash B :_i s}{\Gamma \vdash (x : A) \times_i B : s} \qquad \text{Pair}\ \dfrac{\Gamma \vdash a :_{\not{i}} A \qquad \Gamma \vdash b :_i B[a/x]}{\Gamma \vdash a,_i b : (x : A) \times_i B}$$

We do not provide special elimination rules for colored pairs. Instead, erasure and PARAM play this role. The erasure of a pair yields its first component if colors match, otherwise it acts structurally.

$$\begin{aligned} \lfloor (x : A) \times_i B \rfloor_i &= A \\ \lfloor (x : A) \times_j B \rfloor_i &= (x : \lfloor A \rfloor_i) \times_j \lfloor B \rfloor_i \\ \lfloor a,_i b \rfloor_i &= a \\ \lfloor a,_j b \rfloor_i &= \lfloor a \rfloor_i,_j \lfloor b \rfloor_i \end{aligned}$$

We remark that the property that erasure preserves typing is conserved. In particular:

$$\text{if } \Gamma \vdash p : (x : A) \times_i B \text{ then } \lfloor \Gamma \rfloor_i \vdash \lfloor p \rfloor_i : A$$

Interpreting a pair as a predicate yields the second component if colors match, otherwise it acts structurally:

$$\begin{aligned} ((x : A) \times_i B) \bullet_{\psi, \not{i}} t &= B[t/x] \\ ((x : A) \times_j B) \bullet_{\psi} t &= (x : A \bullet_{\psi} \lfloor t \rfloor_j) \times_j (B \bullet_{\psi} t) \end{aligned}$$

We can now explain fully formally how one can derive that any function of type $(a : \star) \to a \to a$ is indeed an identity function. Let

$$\begin{aligned} \Gamma &\triangleq f : (a : \star) \to a \to a, \quad b : \star, \quad y : b \\ x \equiv_a y &\triangleq (P : a \to \star) \to P\, x \to P\, y \\ t &\triangleq f\, ((x : b) \times_i (x \equiv_b y))\, (y,_i \mathsf{refl}^i) \end{aligned}$$

Where $\equiv$ refers to the definition of the previous section. We first check that $(x : b) \times_i (x \equiv_b y)$ is well-colored (and well-sorted):

$$\text{Sum}\ \dfrac{\text{Def. 1}\ \dfrac{\text{Erasure Def.}\ \dfrac{\Gamma \vdash b : \star}{\lfloor \Gamma, i \rfloor_i \vdash b : \star}}{\Gamma, i \vdash b :_{\not{i}} \star} \qquad \dfrac{\Gamma, i, x :_{\not{i}} b \vdash x :_{\not{i}} b}{\Gamma, i, x :_{\not{i}} b \vdash (x \equiv_b y) :_i \star_i}}{\Gamma, i \vdash (x : b) \times_i (x \equiv_b y) : \star}$$

And proceed with the main result:

$$\text{Erasure Def.}\ \dfrac{\text{Param}\ \dfrac{\text{Def.}\ \dfrac{\text{App}\ \dfrac{\vdots \qquad \text{Pair}\ \dfrac{\Gamma \vdash y : b \qquad \Gamma, i \vdash \mathsf{refl}^i :_i (y \equiv_b y)}{\Gamma, i \vdash (y,_i \mathsf{refl}^i) : (x : b) \times_i (x \equiv_b y)}}{\Gamma, i \vdash f\, ((x : b) \times_i (x \equiv_b y))\, (y,_i \mathsf{refl}^i) : ((x : b) \times_i (x \equiv_b y))}}{\Gamma, i \vdash t : (x : b) \times_i (x \equiv_b y)}}{\Gamma, i \vdash t :_i (\lfloor t \rfloor_i \equiv_b y)}}{\Gamma, i \vdash t :_i f\, b\, y \equiv_b y}$$

An essential component of the trick is that f is i-oblivious. Hence it cannot distinguish in any way between i-tainted and non i-tainted terms, thus we can pass it a colored pair as its type argument.

The trick generalizes: one is able to derive useful properties about a polymorphic term q of type A by construction of an adequate term p of type $(x : A) \times_i B$ such that $\lfloor p \rfloor_i = q$. The construction of q involves specializing a type parameter to a colored pair type involving the property of interest.

In fact, by pairing a type A with a predicate $B[x]$, colored pair type allows to override the default predicate interpretation of the type A with $B[x]$, for a given specific color.

4.3 Abstraction Over Colors

So far we have assumed that colors were available in the context. In a complete TTC, a mechanism to abstract over colors should be provided. At this stage we have thought of colors only as a first-order concept, that is, we propose only first-order quantification over colors.

As such, color abstraction is a relatively modest, straightforward addition. We need new syntax for abstraction, quantification, and application, as well as a constant color (written 0 in the following) used for erasure. A notable feature is that one cannot abstract over a color which is present in the modality; otherwise the color would escape the scope where it is introduced. Using k to range over color names or 0, the typing rules are as follows:

$$\textsc{Col. Abs}\ \frac{\Gamma, i \vdash A :_\theta B \qquad i \notin \theta}{\Gamma \vdash \lambda i.A :_\theta \forall i.B} \qquad \textsc{Col. App}\ \frac{\Gamma \vdash A :_\theta \forall i.B}{\Gamma, k \vdash A\, k :_\theta B[k/i]}$$

and the reduction rules:

$$\begin{aligned}(\forall i.T) \bullet_\psi t &\longrightarrow \forall i.T \bullet_\psi (t\, i)\\ (\lambda i.t)\, 0 &\longrightarrow \lfloor t \rfloor_i\\ (\lambda i.t)\, j &\longrightarrow t[j/i]\end{aligned}$$

Erasure must be extended as well to substitute occurrences of colors as arguments:

$$\begin{aligned}\lfloor t\, i \rfloor_i &= \lfloor t \rfloor_i\, 0\\ \lfloor t\, i \rfloor_j &= \lfloor t \rfloor_j\, i\\ \lfloor t\, 0 \rfloor_i &= \lfloor t \rfloor_i\, 0\\ \lfloor \lambda i.\, t \rfloor_j &= \lambda i. \lfloor t \rfloor_j\end{aligned}$$

With this extension, the subject reduction property depends on Lem. 1.

5. Discussion and Related Work

Coq-*style erasure* Thanks to Paulin-Mohring (1989), Coq features *program extraction*, which is an erasure of proofs to obtain programs. Such programs are external entities, that is, they cannot be referred to as an erasure from the Coq script they originate. This shortcoming is remedied in TTC. For the purpose of extraction, Coq separates types from propositions, using different sorts for each, and allows types to depend on the existence of proofs (but not their structure). In contrast, in the system we present here, untainted terms cannot even depend on the existence of a tainted term. It is likely that the two notions of erasure can be combined in a single system, but we leave the study of that combination to future work.

Agda-*style erasure* A number of systems with modalities for erasure have been proposed (Pfenning 2001; Mishra-Linger and Sheard 2008; Abel and Scherer 2012), with the interpretation of *irrelevance*: types marked with a special modality (usually written $x \div A$) are understood as proofs, whose inhabitants are irrelevant for the execution of the programs.

The system presented here bears some similarity to such systems, but also presents important differences:

- Our binding form $x :_i A$ corresponds to the irrelevant binding $x \div A$.
- We have, in addition to irrelevant bindings, the complementary notion (written $x :_{\not i} A$). This allows us to mix erased terms with non-erased ones, and choose arbitrarily which version we mean. In contrast, systems with erasure usually fix a specific view on which parts of a term is accessible.
- We support an arbitrary number of colors instead of a single one, which is essential for compositionality and to support n-ary parametricity.
- We focus on erasure instead of irrelevance. Previous authors usually allow the use of the *ex falso quod libet* principle on irrelevant assumptions, while we forbid any use of a tainted variable in a non-tainted context.

Types for language-based security Our notion of taint is reminiscent of that used in language-based security. More precisely, our tainted variables would correspond to variables at high security levels: tainted variables may be used only in tainted contexts. The present work can be seen as a generalization of (Abadi et al. 1999) to dependent types. A difference is that we use modalities instead of a different type former for security levels. As a consequence, we do not need a monad to relate security levels. To our knowledge, the combination of dependent types and security-levels in a type-system has not been realized before.

Ornaments Relating variants of dependently-typed programs have been a concern for a long time. The idea of ornamenting inductive structures have been proposed to remedy this problem (Dagand and McBride 2012). Here, we instead focus on erasure (let the user specify an ornamented type and recover the relation with its erasure) instead of specifying ornamentation of already existing types. This is not much of a difference in practice, because ornaments typically can only be applied to a single type. An advantage of colors over ornaments is that colors integrate natively with existing type-theories, while ornamentation relies on encodings; additionally we get free equalities when working with erasures, and colored pairs reveal parametricity properties. The chief advantage of ornaments is that any algebra can be used to ornament datatypes, while we are limited to structural relations.

? have shown how to compose ornaments. Composition is lacking from the system presented here, but we plan to support it in future extensions of TTC. Indeed, if two terms A and B share an erasure (for example $C = \lfloor A \rfloor_i = \lfloor B \rfloor_j$), it means that A and B are to versions of C ornamented differently. Under the same assumption, it is possible to automatically construct a term D such that $\lfloor D \rfloor_j = A$, $\lfloor D \rfloor_i = B$, and $\lfloor D \rfloor_{ij} = C$. That is, D contains both the ornamentations coming from A and B.

Parametricity Bernardy and Moulin (2012) have described a calculus which internalizes parametricity, and have shown that higher dimensions are necessary to nest parametricity. The present work has the same model as the previous one (colors are dimensions under another name). Besides re-framing dimensions as colors, which we find allows an easier grasp of intuitions, the present system features a number of technical simplifications:

1. In the system of Bernardy and Moulin (2012), one has to be explicit about the number of dimensions that a term has. In contrast, here, the dimensionality of a term is implicit. Indeed, contexts can be extended with an arbitrary number of dimensions. This means that a term can always be used in a context which has more (distinct) colors, whereas previously an explicit conversion had to take place. In other words, terms can be seen as infinitely-dimensional; but if they do not mention a dimension explicitly they behave uniformly over it. In particular, usual λ-terms are uniform, and parametricity is a consequence of this uniformity.
2. In this paper, we name dimensions, whereas they are numbered in (Bernardy and Moulin 2012). The situation is analogous to the issue of the representation of variables in lambda-calculi.

One can either use explicit names or De Brujin indices, and using names is usually more convenient.

It is worth underlining that the notion of erasure we employ here is not the same as that of (Bernardy and Lasson 2011). Here, we erase the colored component; whereas Bernardy and Lasson (2011) erase the oblivious components.

Parametricity has more "standard consequences" such as the deduction of induction principles. Unfortunately, many of these consequence also require extensionality (Wadler (2007) gives a complete development). Since extensionality is not well integrated to type-theory (let alone TTC) at the moment, we cannot derive such constructions, at least not without postulating extensionality.

Higher-dimensional Equality Recent work on the interpretation of the equality-type in intensional type theory suggests that it should be modeled using higher-dimensional structures (Licata and Harper 2012). In the present work we support the definition of higher-dimensional structures via dependencies on colors. In future work we wish to investigate whether the presence of colors can help encoding the higher-dimensional structure of equality.

A potential difficulty is that the structure of equality is simplectic, while we have here a cubic structure (colors are orthogonal). A simplex is however easily embedded in a cube, so there are grounds to believe that the two aspects can eventually be integrated.

6. Conclusion and Future Work

We have described an extension of type-theory with colored terms, a notion of color erasure, and a way to interpret colored types as predicates. We have shown how that extension provides a new kind of genericity, and how the coloring discipline enforces invariants when writing programs. We also shown how to reveal these invariants (by typing the judgment in another modality) and internalize some parametricity results.

We detailed extensively a core version of that colored type-theory, namely CCCC. In particular, we proved fundamental properties for that system, such as Church-Rosser's, subject-reduction, and strong normalization. We also implemented some features of CCCC in a prototype we aim to merge into the main stream AGDA proof assistant.

Future work chiefly involves unifying colors as presented here with previous similar notions. On the implementation side, we aim to complete our prototype with all the features presented in this paper. Besides, we would like to investigate the feasibility of inference of color annotations before merging our implementation of TTC into the main branch of AGDA. We will then be able to assess the practical power of TTC. A first step in this direction is the retrofitting of the AGDA standard library to use colors.

Acknowledgments

Many ideas underlying this paper have germinated and matured in discussions with Thierry Coquand, Simon Huber and Patrik Jansson. We thank Peter Dybjer, Cezar Ionescu, Nicolas Pouillard and Philip Wadler as well as anonymous reviewers for useful feedback.

This work has been partially funded by the Swedish Foundation for Strategic Research, under grant RAWFP.

References

M. Abadi, A. Banerjee, N. Heintze, and J. Riecke. A core calculus of dependency. In *POPL'99*, pages 147–160. ACM, 1999.

A. Abel and G. Scherer. On irrelevance and algorithmic equality in predicative type theory. *Logical Methods in Comp. Sci.*, 8(1):1–36, 2012. TYPES'10 special issue.

H. P. Barendregt. Lambda calculi with types. *Handbook of logic in computer science*, 2:117–309, 1992. .

J.-P. Bernardy and M. Lasson. Realizability and parametricity in pure type systems. In M. Hofmann, editor, *FoSSaCS*, volume 6604 of *LNCS*, pages 108–122. Springer, 2011.

J.-P. Bernardy and G. Moulin. A computational interpretation of parametricity. In *Proc. of the Symposium on Logic in Comp. Sci.* IEEE, 2012.

J.-P. Bernardy, P. Jansson, and R. Paterson. Parametricity and dependent types. In *Proc. of ICFP 2010*, pages 345–356, Baltimore, Maryland, 2010. ACM.

J.-P. Bernardy, P. Jansson, and R. Paterson. Proofs for free — parametricity for dependent types. *J. Funct. Program.*, 22(02):107–152, 2012. .

T. Coquand and G. Huet. The calculus of constructions. Technical report, INRIA, 1986.

P.-E. Dagand and C. McBride. Transporting functions across ornaments. In *Proc. of ICFP 2012*, ICFP '12, New York, NY, USA, 2012. ACM.

D. Licata and R. Harper. Canonicity for 2-dimensional type theory. In *Proc. of POPL 2012*. ACM, 2012.

P. Martin-Löf. *Intuitionistic type theory*. Bibliopolis, 1984.

N. Mishra-Linger and T. Sheard. Erasure and polymorphism in pure type systems. In *FoSSaCS 2008*, pages 350–364. Springer-Verlag, 2008.

U. Norell. *Towards a practical programming language based on dependent type theory*. PhD thesis, Chalmers Tekniska Högskola, 2007. URL `http://publications.lib.chalmers.se/cpl/record/index.xsql?pubid=46311`.

C. Paulin-Mohring. Extracting Fω's programs from proofs in the calculus of constructions. In *POPL'89*, pages 89–104. ACM, 1989. ISBN 0-89791-294-2. .

F. Pfenning. Intensionality, extensionality, and proof irrelevance in modal type theory. In *Proc. 16th Annual IEEE Symposium on Logic in Comp. Sci.*, pages 221–230. IEEE, 2001. ISBN 0-7695-1281-X. . URL `http://ieeexplore.ieee.org/lpdocs/epic03/wrapper.htm?arnumber=932499`.

V. Siles. *Investigation on the typing of equality in type systems*. Phd thesis, École Polytechnique, 2010.

The Coq development team. The Coq proof assistant, 2012. URL `http://coq.inria.fr`.

P. Wadler. Call-by-value is dual to call-by-name. In *Proc. of ICFP 2003*, ICFP '03, pages 189–201, New York, NY, USA, 2003. ACM. ISBN 1-58113-756-7. . URL `http://doi.acm.org/10.1145/944705.944723`.

P. Wadler. The Girard–Reynolds isomorphism (second edition). *Theor. Comp. Sci.*, 375(1–3):201–226, 2007.

P. Wadler. Propositions as sessions. In *Proc. of ICFP 2012*, ICFP '12, pages 273–286, New York, NY, USA, 2012. ACM.

Appendix A: Definition of CCCC

Definition 2 (Syntax).

Variable	$\ni x, y, z$			
Color	$\ni i, j$			
Sort	$\ni s$	$::=$	$\star_\theta \mid \Box_\theta$	
Taint	$\ni \theta, \iota$	$::=$	$\varnothing$	*empty*
		$\mid$	θ, i	*tainted*
Modality	$\ni \psi, \varphi$	$::=$	(θ, ι)	
Term	$\ni A, \ldots, Z$	$::=$	x	*variable*
	a, b, c, t, u	$\mid$	s	*sort*
		$\mid$	$(x :_\psi A) \to B$	*product*
		$\mid$	$\lambda x :_\psi A.b$	*abstraction*
		$\mid$	$F \bullet_\psi a$	*application*
Context	$\ni \Gamma, \Delta$	$::=$	$-$	*empty*
		$\mid$	$\Gamma, x :_\psi A$	*binding*
		$\mid$	Γ, i	*color*

Definition 3 (Typing rules $\boxed{\Gamma \vdash A :_\theta B}$).
$\Gamma \vdash A :_\theta B$ is well-formed only if $i \in \Gamma$ for ecch $i \in \theta$.

CONV
$$\frac{\Gamma \vdash a :_\theta A \qquad A =_\beta A'}{\Gamma \vdash a :_\theta A'}$$

AXIOM
$$\frac{\vdash \Gamma}{\Gamma \vdash \star_\theta :_\theta \Box_\theta}$$

VAR
$$\frac{\vdash \Gamma \qquad x :_\theta A \in \Gamma}{\Gamma \vdash x :_\theta A}$$

PROD
$$\frac{\Gamma, x :_\psi A \vdash B :_\theta s}{\Gamma \vdash (x :_\psi A) \to B :_\theta s}$$

ABS
$$\frac{\Gamma, x :_\psi A \vdash b :_\theta B}{\Gamma \vdash (\lambda x :_\psi A.b) :_\theta (x :_\psi A) \to B}$$

APP
$$\frac{\Gamma \vdash F :_\theta (x :_\psi A) \to B \qquad \Gamma \vdash u :_\psi A}{\Gamma \vdash F \bullet_\psi u :_\theta B[u/x]}$$

PARAM
$$\frac{\Gamma \vdash A :_\theta B \qquad i \notin \theta}{\Gamma \vdash A :_{\theta,i} B \bullet_{\theta,\not{i}} \lfloor A \rfloor_i}$$

(To limit clutter we omit the well-sorted conditions of types A and B in the rule ABS*.) We also have*

$$\textit{If } \psi = (\theta, \iota) \textit{ then } \Gamma \vdash A :_\psi B \;\triangleq\; \lfloor \Gamma \rfloor_\iota \vdash A :_\theta B$$

Definition 4 (Accessible variable $\boxed{x :_\theta A \in \Gamma}$).

START
$$\frac{}{x :_\theta A \in \Gamma, x :_{(\theta,\iota)} A}$$

COL. WK
$$\frac{x :_\theta A \in \Gamma \qquad i \notin \theta}{x :_\theta A \in \Gamma, i}$$

WK
$$\frac{x :_\theta A \in \Gamma}{x :_\theta A \in \Gamma, y :_\psi B}$$

Definition 5 (Well-formed contexts $\boxed{\vdash \Gamma}$).

EMPTY
$$\frac{}{\vdash -}$$

COLOR
$$\frac{\vdash \Gamma}{\vdash \Gamma, i}$$

BIND
$$\frac{\vdash \Gamma \qquad \Gamma \vdash A :_\psi s}{\vdash \Gamma, x :_\psi A}$$

Definition 6 (erasure $\boxed{\lfloor T \rfloor_i}$). *The definition of erasure depends on the actual modality used. We write all the cases on the same line; the condition is written above each column.*

$i \notin \psi$	$i \in \psi$	$\psi = \varphi, \not{i}$
$\lfloor x \rfloor_i = x$		
$\lfloor s \rfloor_i = s$		
$\lfloor (x :_\psi A) \to B \rfloor_i = (x :_\psi \lfloor A \rfloor_i) \to \lfloor B \rfloor_i$	$\lfloor B \rfloor_i$	$(x :_\varphi A) \to \lfloor B \rfloor_i$
$\lfloor \lambda x :_\psi A.b \rfloor_i = \lambda x :_\psi \lfloor A \rfloor_i . \lfloor b \rfloor_i$	$\lfloor b \rfloor_i$	$\lambda x :_\varphi A.\lfloor b \rfloor_i$
$\lfloor F \bullet_\psi a \rfloor_i = (\lfloor F \rfloor_i) \bullet_\psi \lfloor a \rfloor_i$	$\lfloor F \rfloor_i$	$(\lfloor F \rfloor_i) \bullet_\varphi a$
$\lfloor \Gamma, x :_\psi A \rfloor_i = \lfloor \Gamma \rfloor_i, x :_\psi \lfloor A \rfloor_i$	$\lfloor \Gamma \rfloor_i$	$\lfloor \Gamma \rfloor_i, x :_\varphi A$
$\lfloor \Gamma, j \rfloor_i = \lfloor \Gamma \rfloor_i, j$		
$\lfloor \Gamma, i \rfloor_i = \Gamma$		

Erasure is extended to taints as follows:

Definition 7 (erasure $\boxed{\lfloor T \rfloor_\iota}$).

$$\lfloor T \rfloor_\varnothing = T$$
$$\lfloor T \rfloor_{\iota,i} = \lfloor \lfloor T \rfloor_i \rfloor_\iota$$

Definition 8 (Reduction $\boxed{t \longrightarrow u}$).

$$s_\theta \bullet_\varphi t \longrightarrow (z :_\varphi t) \to s_{\theta \cup \iota} \tag{1}$$
where $\varphi = (\theta, \iota)$
$$((x :_\psi A) \to B) \bullet_\varphi t \longrightarrow (x :_\psi A) \to (B \bullet_\varphi \not{t}) \tag{2}$$
if $\exists i$ such that $i \in \psi$ and $\not{i} \in \varphi$
$$((x :_\psi A) \to B) \bullet_\varphi t \longrightarrow (x :_\psi A) \to (B \bullet_\varphi (t \bullet_\psi x)) \tag{3}$$
otherwise
$$(\lambda x :_\psi A.b) \bullet_\psi t \longrightarrow b[t/x] \tag{4}$$

and congruences.

Definition 9 (Substitution). *The substitution of variables in i-oblivious contexts erases i from the substitutees.*

$$(F \bullet_\psi a)[u/x] = F[u/x] \bullet_\psi a[u\{\psi\}/x]$$
$$((y :_\psi A) \to B)[u/x] = (y :_\psi A[u\{\psi\}/x]) \to B[u/x]$$
$$(\lambda y :_\psi A.b)[u/x] = \lambda y :_\psi A[u\{\psi\}/x].b[u/x]$$

Where

$$u\{(\theta, \iota)\} = \lfloor u \rfloor_\iota$$

Typed Syntactic Meta-programming

Dominique Devriese Frank Piessens
iMinds – DistriNet, KU Leuven
firstname.lastname@cs.kuleuven.be

Abstract

We present a novel set of meta-programming primitives for use in a dependently-typed functional language. The types of our meta-programs provide strong and precise guarantees about their termination, correctness and completeness. Our system supports type-safe construction and analysis of terms, types and typing contexts. Unlike alternative approaches, they are written in the same style as normal programs and use the language's standard functional computational model. We formalise the new meta-programming primitives, implement them as an extension of Agda, and provide evidence of usefulness by means of two compelling applications in the fields of datatype-generic programming and proof tactics.

Categories and Subject Descriptors D3.3 [*Programming Languages*]: Language Constructs and Features: Data types and structures; F3.1 [*Logics and Meanings of Programs*]: Specifying and Verifying and Reasoning about Programs: Specification Techniques; F4.1 [*Mathematical Logic*]: Lambda Calculus and Related Systems

Keywords meta-programming; dependent types; datatype-generic programming; tactics.

1. Introduction

Meta-programming means writing programs that write or manipulate other programs. It is an important software engineering technique that is widely used in practice. The term covers a wide variety of techniques and applications, including parser generators [29], reflection and byte-code generation in Java-like languages [8, 40], macro's in Lisp-like languages [53], eval primitives in languages like JavaScript [45], special-purpose meta-programming or generic programming primitives [6, 11, 13, 26, 33, 48, 52], tactics in proof assistants [20, 50, 51] and term representations in advanced type systems [9, 15, 23, 38]. Meta-programming jargon distinguishes between the *meta-language*, that meta-programs are written in, and the *object language*, that the programs being manipulated are in.

Meta-programming can often be used to implement features in a library that would otherwise require ad hoc compiler support. This ranges from meta-programs that generate small amounts of boilerplate code to give libraries a more native feel (e.g. [31, 34, 46]) to languages built from the ground up using meta-programming [53].

ICFP '13, September 25–27, 2013, Boston, MA, USA.

http://dx.doi.org/10.1145/2500365.2500575

In many applications, meta-programs must not only be able to produce new code but also analyse existing terms, types or type contexts. Applications in e.g. datatype-generic programming or tactics for proof assistants involve meta-programs that analyse the syntactic structure of object language data types [13, 33], types [26, 50], types and contexts [20]. Some systems allow analysing terms [11], terms and types [48] or all three [9, 15, 38, 51].

Type-safety in the context of meta-programming can mean different things. In some approaches, generated code is type-checked upon completion of the meta-program, either at compile-time or run-time [8, 20, 48]. This can be sufficient to guarantee type-correctness of the resulting program. In this text, we are interested in a stronger form of type-safety, in which a meta-program's type can guarantee type-correctness of all programs it will ever generate [11, 26, 33, 50–52]. This stronger form of type-safety provides meta-program authors and users with greater correctness assurance. Sometimes, it also enables additional applications. For example, MetaML runs meta-programs and compiles the generated code at run-time, but type errors during this run-time compilation are ruled out by its strong type-safety [52]. In the context of a dependently-typed proof assistant, where proofs and programs are equated, Chlipala argues that the stronger form of type-safety has a performance advantage because proofs generated by meta-programs do not need to be calculated as long as they can be trusted to exist [14]. Note that for this last application, the meta-program must be guaranteed to terminate, as well as produce well-typed code.

However, this stronger form of type-safety puts a high demand on representations of object code and the meta-language type system, especially for object languages with strong (e.g. dependent) type systems and if meta-programs can construct and analyse both terms, types and typing contexts. Most approaches use an explicit syntactic representation of object language terms and/or types. To achieve strong type safety, they employ advanced type-system features of the meta-language, including GADTs [11, 52], strong type systems with powerful type-level languages [13, 23, 50, 51] and an advanced feature of dependent type systems called induction-recursion [9, 15, 38]. However, even the most powerful approaches have to make certain compromises, simplifying the resulting system at the cost of expressivity. For example, many approaches provide syntactic models of only types [33] or only terms [11, 52] or types and terms but not typing contexts [50].

Particularly technically ambitious are those meta-programming systems that use a syntactic model of a dependently-typed language within another one [9, 15, 38]. Their term encoding represents type-correctness *internally*, i.e. only well-typed terms are represented. To support this, they require an advanced dependent type system with support for induction-recursion in the meta-language and even then have trouble fitting the interpretation function in it [9, 15]. McBride presents a model that is accepted by Agda but has to significantly limit the dependent nature of the object language's type system in the process [38]. The objective in this work is generally to prove meta-theory for the object language and the authors work hard to fit their encodings into the advanced, but general and previously studied schema of inductive-recursive definitions.

However, beside their meta-theoretical value, syntactic models of a typed object language with a well-typed interpretation function are also promising for meta-programming applications. Unfortunately, the full potential of this has not been explored or demonstrated so far because researchers have not yet managed to build syntactic models of dependently-typed programming languages that support a big enough subset of a dependently-typed language and still have provably sound interpretation functions. In this paper, we ignore the aim of building meta-theory for dependent type theories within themselves and instead focus on applying such techniques to meta-programming. We will show that this approach has some very compelling qualities.

We use Agda [39], a pure functional dependently-typed language, as both the meta- and object language and we start from a conventional representation of the object language based on de Bruijn-encoded lambda terms and an external typing judgement. We make an interpretation function available as a new meta-programming primitive. This puts us on shakier ground, because the soundness of the primitive is not guaranteed by existing meta-theory, but it allows us to side-step the unsolved problem of syntactically representing a dependent type theory within itself with a provably sound interpretation function. As such, we gain the ability to explore and demonstrate our approach's potential for meta-programming and present novel techniques for it.

Our choice to keep the meta- and object language the same (known as *homogeneous* meta-programming [48, 52]) contrasts with systems where meta-programs use a different computational model than object programs. Often this is an imperative model [20, 48, 50, 51], but some systems even use a logic programming-like model derived from the meta-programs' interaction with type inference [26, 33]. Our meta-programs use the same functional model as normal programs and dependent pattern matching [25] for syntactically analysing terms, types and typing contexts. This choice keeps the system smaller, makes techniques, tools and knowledge for normal programming directly reusable in meta-programs and it allows meta-programs to use other meta-programs to do their work. It does not exclude imperative, generally recursive, non-deterministic or unification-based reasoning in meta-programs. Research has demonstrated functional models of such algorithms [16, 30, 32] and such ideas could be combined with our work.

In the dependently typed meta-language, meta-programs have strong and precise types that guarantee termination and correctness. Termination is standard for Agda functions (Agda is total). For strong type safety, our primitives require meta-programs to provide type-correctness proofs together with generated code and they can exploit type-correctness proofs for the code they analyse.

Some homogeneous meta-programming systems couple meta-programming with *multi-stage programming* [6, 48, 52], which allows object code programs to explicitly invoke meta-programs and use the generated expressions as if they were hand-written (*unquoting*) and allows meta-programs to include references to existing terms in generated code (*quoting*). A linear hierarchy of staging levels exists when meta-programs may unquote expressions generated by other meta-programs. The bottom stage is the program executed at run-time, while other stages execute at compile-time or run-time, depending on the system. Our interpretation function for encoded terms is analogous to an unquoting primitive and we will demonstrate how object-level terms can be referenced in generated code. The question of when meta-programs are executed becomes a matter of choice and a special case of partial evaluation.

We demonstrate the properties of our system by applying it to two important application domains: *datatype-generic programming* and *proof tactics*. For the first, we define a syntactic representation $\mathit{SimpleDT}$ of inductive data types that can be used to write general datatype-generic meta-programs. As proof-of-concept, we present a meta-program $\mathit{deriveShow}$ that syntactically derives a serialisation function $\mathit{show} : A \rightarrow \mathit{String}$ for a data type A.

$$\mathit{deriveShow} : (A : \mathit{Set}) \rightarrow \mathit{SimpleDT}\ A \rightarrow A \rightarrow \mathit{String}$$

$\mathit{SimpleDT}$ and $\mathit{deriveShow}$ do not require compiler support beyond our (general) meta-programming primitives, although the value of type $\mathit{SimpleDT}\ \ A$ could be provided by the compiler for additional convenience. The type of $\mathit{deriveShow}$ guarantees its correct termination and well-typedness of generated programs (modulo the primitives' soundness). To the best of our knowledge, this is the first demonstration of strongly typed, general datatype-generic meta-programs, with support for syntactic analysis of terms and types and using the language's standard computational model.

The second application domain is proof tactics. A tactic is a meta-program that analyses the type of a proof obligation and produces a proof term (possibly including remaining proof obligations) using general or domain-specific reasoning. Several proof assistants provide special-purpose languages for writing custom tactics [20, 50, 51]. These are often imperative and only guarantee weak type-safety (generated code is checked after execution of meta-program) or partial strong type-safety (generated code is guaranteed type-correct but meta-programs may not terminate). Gonthier et al. argue that tactics without strong type-safety can be hard to maintain and compose [26]. Chlipala discusses a performance advantage of precisely-typed and terminating meta-programs since generated proofs do not need to be calculated if they are known to exist [14]. To demonstrate that we can do better, we present an account of Coq's $\mathit{assumption}$ tactic with a very precise type, guaranteeing that it will always terminate and produce a guaranteed type-correct term under a precise condition. The tactic uses a functional computational model and dependent pattern matching for syntactic analysis of terms, types and typing contexts.

We have implemented our primitives in Agda and our example meta-programs are accepted by Agda's type-checker.[1] Unfortunately, this does not mean our work is readily usable. The practicality of our implementation is currently hampered by long compilation times. However, we will argue that this problem is not intrinsic, but caused by the inefficient evaluation strategy of Agda's compile-time evaluator. The soundness of our approach depends on the soundness of our primitives, which we can currently not provide guarantees about. We believe that our work gives a strong motivation to investigate both of these aspects further, since we provide strong evidence for the additional power that the system offers for meta-programming in general and the hard problems of well-typed tactics and datatype-generic programming in particular.

1.1 Contributions

Our first contribution in this work is the definition of novel meta-programming primitives in a dependently-typed language, starting from a partial formalisation of the language's meta-theory. We also contribute the (to our knowledge first) demonstration of using such a formalisation for meta-programming, with compelling examples in two important application domains: datatype-generic programming and proof tactics. Our meta-programming model works with the language's standard functional computational model, and meta-programs are written in the same way as normal programs. Modulo the soundness of our primitives, meta-programs can be given strong and precise guarantees of termination and correctness of the generated code. Finally, our proof-of-concept applications in these two application domains are interesting in their own right. For both

[1] Code available on `http://people.cs.kuleuven.be/dominique.devriese/permanent/tsmp.zip`.

$$
\begin{array}{l}
\textbf{data}\ \mathit{Constant} : (\mathit{arity} : \mathbb{N}) \to \mathit{Set}\ \textbf{where}\\
\quad \text{(empty for now)}\\
\textbf{data}\ \mathit{Binder} : \mathit{Set}\ \textbf{where}\ \Pi\ \Lambda : \mathit{Binder}\\
\textbf{data}\ \mathit{Expr}\ (n : \mathbb{N}) : \mathit{Set}\ \textbf{where}\\
\quad \mathit{set} \quad : \mathit{Expr}\ n\\
\quad \mathit{var} \quad : \mathit{Fin}\ n \to \mathit{Expr}\ n\\
\quad \mathit{appl} \quad : \mathit{Expr}\ n \to \mathit{Expr}\ n \to \mathit{Expr}\ n\\
\quad \mathit{constant} : \{\mathit{arity} : \mathbb{N}\} \to \mathit{Constant}\ \mathit{arity} \to\\
\qquad\qquad \mathit{Vec}\ (\mathit{Expr}\ n)\ \mathit{arity} \to \mathit{Expr}\ n\\
\quad \mathit{bind} \quad : \mathit{Binder} \to \mathit{Expr}\ n \to \mathit{Expr}\ (\mathit{suc}\ n) \to \mathit{Expr}\ n\\
\mathit{pi} \quad : \{n : \mathbb{N}\} \to \mathit{Expr}\ n \to \mathit{Expr}\ (\mathit{suc}\ n) \to \mathit{Expr}\ n\\
\mathit{pi} \quad = \mathit{bind}\ \Pi\\
\mathit{lambda} : \{n : \mathbb{N}\} \to \mathit{Expr}\ n \to \mathit{Expr}\ (\mathit{suc}\ n) \to \mathit{Expr}\ n\\
\mathit{lambda} = \mathit{bind}\ \Lambda
\end{array}
$$

Figure 1. The representation of terms.

$$
\begin{array}{l}
\mathit{Sub} \quad : \mathbb{N} \to \mathbb{N} \to \mathit{Set}\\
\_/\_ \quad : \{m\ n : \mathbb{N}\} \to \mathit{Expr}\ m \to \mathit{Sub}\ m\ n \to \mathit{Expr}\ n\\
\mathit{weaken} : \{n : \mathbb{N}\} \to \mathit{Expr}\ n \to \mathit{Expr}\ (\mathit{suc}\ n)\\
\_[\_] \quad : \{n : \mathbb{N}\} \to \mathit{Expr}\ (\mathit{suc}\ n) \to \mathit{Expr}\ n \to \mathit{Expr}\ n
\end{array}
$$

Figure 2. Substitutions (implementations omitted).

$$
\begin{array}{l}
\textbf{data}\ \_\leadsto_0\_\ \{n\} : \mathit{Expr}\ n \to \mathit{Expr}\ n \to \mathit{Set}\ \textbf{where}\\
\quad \mathit{reduceApplication} : \forall\ \{s\}\ b\ \mathit{val} \to\\
\qquad \mathit{appl}\ (\mathit{lambda}\ s\ b)\ \mathit{val} \leadsto_0 b\ [\mathit{val}]\\
\textbf{data}\ \_\leadsto\_\ \{n\} : \mathit{Expr}\ n \to \mathit{Expr}\ n \to \mathit{Set}\ \textbf{where}\\
\quad \cdots\ \text{(congruence closure of } \_\leadsto_0\_)\\
\_\leadsto_*\_ : \{n : \mathbb{N}\} \to \mathit{Expr}\ n \to \mathit{Expr}\ n \to \mathit{Set}\\
\_\leadsto_*\_ = \cdots\ \text{(transitive-reflexive closure of } \_\leadsto\_)\\
\_\approx\_ : \{n : \mathbb{N}\} \to \mathit{Expr}\ n \to \mathit{Expr}\ n \to \mathit{Set}\\
x \approx y = \exists\,(\lambda\ n \to x \leadsto_* n \times y \leadsto_* n)
\end{array}
$$

Figure 3. Full β-reduction and β-equivalence for untyped terms.

datatype-generic programming and proof tactics, the prospect of writing general meta-programs with strong and precise guarantees about termination, correctness and completeness and using the language's standard computational model is compelling and novel.

1.2 Outlook

We present the representation of our object language in Section 2. In Section 3, we show how the represented terms and types are brought to life in the meta-language using our meta-programming primitives. In Section 4, we present applications to the fields of datatype-generic programming and proof tactics. We discuss issues like soundness and performance in Section 5, related work in Section 6 and we conclude in Section 7.

2. Self-representation

As discussed, we start from a representation of Agda terms in Agda using a notion of lambda expressions representing terms as well as their types and a typing judgement linking the two together.

Terms Figure 1 shows the definition of Expr, our representation of Agda terms and types as lambda terms, using de Bruijn indices. We represent de Bruijn indices as integers between 0 and $n-1$ using the Agda standard library type $\mathit{Fin}\ n$ [17]. The type Expr is parameterised by the number of free variables in scope. It is defined as a standard inductive data type [21], with an enumeration of its constructors and their types. The set constructor represents the type of types in the object language and free variables are embedded through var. There is a standard function application constructor appl and constants applied to a fixed number of arguments (as determined by the constant's arity) through term constructor $\mathit{constant}$. $\mathit{Vec}\ A\ n$ is another Agda standard library type representing a vector of precisely n values of type A. In what follows, we use $[]$ for the empty vector and for example $[x, y]$ for the vector with elements x and y. Similarly, we write literal Fins as numbers.

The final Expr constructor in Figure 1, bind, is a common representation of two separate binding constructs: lambda expressions $\lambda(x : T) \to b$[2] and dependent function types $(x : T) \to T'$, constructed as $\mathit{bind}\ \Lambda$ and $\mathit{bind}\ \Pi$ respectively. They take two arguments: the type T of the bound variable and the body of the construct (b or T' respectively) with the bound variable additionally in scope in the body. Note by the way that a standard non-dependent function type $s \to t$ can be represented as dependent function $(\_ : s) \to t$. Finally, note in the type of $\mathit{constant}$, pi and lambda that we bind some arguments using curly brackets, indicating that they can be omitted in calls. Agda will then infer their value from the types of the remaining arguments.

Substitutions We use a library of substitutions that is part of the Agda standard library [17], based on a technique by McBride [37]. Figure 2 shows a type of substitutions $\mathit{Sub}\ m\ n$ that will substitute terms with n free variables for all m free variables of other terms. More concretely, the function $\_/\_$ applies a substitution ϕ of type $\mathit{Sub}\ m\ n$ to a term t typed $\mathit{Expr}\ m$ to obtain term $t\ /\ \phi$, typed $\mathit{Expr}\ n$. Note that for example $\_/\_$ is Agda notation for a *mixfix* operator that is applied to two arguments t and ϕ in the form t/ϕ [18]. The function weaken uses the substitutions infrastructure to increase free de Bruijn indices by one and $\_\ [\_]$ substitutes term v for de Bruijn variable 0 in term t, to obtain term $t\ [v]$, shifting other free de Bruijn indices downward in the process.

Convertibility The next thing we define is an untyped notion of strong β-reduction and β-equivalence of terms in Figure 3. It is technically convenient to define primitive reductions in judgement $\_\leadsto_0\_$, a congruence closure of it in $\_\leadsto\_$ and a transitive-reflexive closure of that in $\_\leadsto_*\_$. The $\mathit{reduceApplication}$ rule uses the substitution function $\_\ [\_]$ we saw before. In the type of $\mathit{reduceApplication}$ we use Agda's $\forall$ shorthand notation, which desugars to a normal dependent type. For example $\forall\ \{n\} \to \cdots$ or $\forall\ n \to \cdots$ is short for $\{n : \_\} \to \cdots$ and $(n : \_) \to \cdots$ respectively, i.e. an implicit or normal argument n whose type is inferred by Agda. One $\forall$ symbol can apply to more than one argument. In $\_\approx\_$, we use the $\exists$ and $\times$ types: for a type A and predicate P typed $A \to \mathit{Set}$, $\exists P$ represents a dependent sum type containing tuples (v, pv) with v of type A and pv of type $P\ v$. For types A and B, $A \times B$ represents the cartesian product type of A and B (containing (a, b) with a of type A and b of type B). Two terms t and t' are defined to be convertible ($t \approx t'$) iff there exists a third term n that both t and t' reduce to.

Typing Contexts Figure 4 contains the definition of typing contexts and the more general notion of telescopes. A telescope is a sequence of expressions, each representing the type of a bound variable. The entries may refer to a number of free variables, assumed to be bound outside the telescope. The first index i of the $\mathit{Telescope}$ type indicates how many such *initial* variables are as-

[2] We use Agda notation for lambdas, not the more standard $\lambda x : T.b$.

```
data Telescope (i : ℕ) : ℕ → Set where
  ε     : Telescope i i
  _◁_ : {n : ℕ} → Expr n →
     Telescope i n → Telescope i (suc n)

Context : (n : ℕ) → Set
Context = Telescope 0

lookup : ∀ {n} → Fin n → Context n → Expr n
lookup zero      (t ◁ _) = weaken t
lookup (suc n) (_ ◁ Γ) = weaken (lookup n Γ)
```

Figure 4. Telescopes and Contexts

```
data _⊢_:_ {n} (Γ : Context n) :
        Expr n → Expr n → Set where
  typeSet : Γ ⊢ set : set
  typeVar : ∀ {i} →   Γ ⊢ var i : lookup i Γ
  typePi : ∀ {s t} →   Γ ⊢ s : set   →
    (s ◁ Γ) ⊢ t : set   →   Γ ⊢ pi s t : set
  typeLam : ∀ {s b t} →   Γ ⊢ s : set   →
    (s ◁ Γ) ⊢ b : t   →   Γ ⊢ lambda s b : pi s t
  typeAppl : ∀ {s f t val} →   (s ◁ Γ) ⊢ t : set   →
    Γ ⊢ f : pi s t   →   Γ ⊢ val : s   →
    Γ ⊢ appl f val : appl (lambda s t) val
  typeConv : ∀ {e t t′} →   t ≈ t′   →
    Γ ⊢ e : t′   →   Γ ⊢ t : set   →   Γ ⊢ e : t
```

Figure 5. Typing Judgements.

sumed. Telescopes are dependent: subsequent types can mention variables bound earlier in the telescope. This allows us to represent e.g. the telescope $(n : \mathbb{N})\ (t : \mathit{Expr}\ n)$, where the type of t depends on the value of n. As a consequence of this dependence, each additional entry in a telescope has an additional variable in scope. The second index n of the *Telescope* type is the number of *final* variables: if i variables are initially bound, and we add the bindings of a *Telescope* i n, then in total n variables will be bound, so the telescope contains precisely $n - i$ entries. A typing context *Context* n is a telescope with zero initial and n final bound variables. The *lookup* function looks up the type of a variable in a context. *lookup*'s dependent type ensures that only de Bruijn variables lower than the length of the context can be looked up.

Typing Judgements In Figure 5, we show the typing judgement $\Gamma \vdash v : t$ stating that term v has type t in typing context Γ. The typing judgement models a fairly standard dependent type system, except for the first rule *typeSet*. This rule expresses that *set* has type *set* in any context, a rule which is known as type-in-type and a known source of paradox in dependent type theories [28]. However, we use this rule only for ease of presentation. Our full code avoids type-in-type using a predicative hierarchy of universes similar to Agda's [39]. It uses a level-indexed set_l, the typing rule that $set_l : set_{suc\ l}$ for all l, and a level-indexed typing judgement $\Gamma \vdash_l v : t$ with l such that $\Gamma \vdash_{suc\ l} t : set\ l$ must hold.

In the remaining typing rules in Figure 5 we have *typeVar*, stating that the type of a variable is given by the corresponding entry in the typing context and *typePi*, stating that $(x : S) \to T$ is a type if S and T are types, with $x : S$ added to the context for T. For lambda expressions, *typeLam* says that $\lambda\ (x : S) \to b$ is typed $(x : S) \to T$ if b has type T in a context extended with

```
data ⊢_ : ∀ {n} → Context n → Set where
  ty_ε : ⊢ ε
  ty_◁ : ∀ {n e} {Γ : Context n} →
      ⊢ Γ   →   Γ ⊢ e : set   → ⊢(e ◁ Γ)
data _⊢_:_{n} (Γ : Context n) :
   {m : ℕ} (ρ : Sub m n) (tel : Context m) → Set where
  ··· (omitted)
```

Figure 6. Well-typed Contexts

```
weaken−inj−≈ : ∀ {n} {x y : Expr n} →
     weaken x ≈ weaken y   →   x ≈ y
≈−trans : ∀ {n} {x y z : Expr n} →
     x ≈ y   →   y ≈ z   →   x ≈ z
≈−/ : ∀ {n} {x y} {m} (ρ : Sub Expr n m) →
     x ≈ y → x / ρ ≈ y / ρ
weakenJudgementTop : ∀ {n} {Γ : Context n} {v t t′} →
     Γ ⊢ v : t′   →   t ◁ Γ ⊢ weaken v : weaken t′
substJudgementTop : ∀ {n} {Γ : Context n} {t′ e t v} →
     t′ ◁ Γ ⊢ e : t   →   Γ ⊢ v : t′   →   Γ ⊢ e [v] : t [v]
substContext : ∀ {n} {Γ : Context n} {e t} {t′ t″} →
     t′ ≈ t″   →   Γ ⊢ t′ : set   →   t′ ◁ Γ ⊢ e : t   →
     t″ ◁ Γ ⊢ e : t
⊢−/ : ∀ {m n} {e t} Γ1 Γ2 →   (ϕ : Sub m n)   →
     Γ2 ⊢ ϕ : Γ1   →   Γ1 ⊢ e : t   →   Γ2 ⊢ e / ϕ : t / ϕ
⊢−var : ∀ {n} → {Γ : Context n} → ⊢Γ   →
     (i : Fin n)   →   Γ ⊢ lookup i Γ : set
typesAreSets : ∀ {n} {Γ : Context n} {e t} {l} →
     ⊢ Γ   →   Γ ⊢ e : t   →   Γ ⊢ t : set
substJudgementType : ∀ {n} {Γ : Context n} {e t t′} →
     t ≡ t′   →   Γ ⊢ e : t   →   Γ ⊢ e : t′
```

Figure 7. Meta-theoretic properties of our typing judgements.

$x : S$. According to *typeAppl*, a function application f val has type $((\lambda\ (x : S) \to T)\ val)$ if f has type $(x : S) \to T$ and val has type S. Note that we could equivalently have given such an application the type $T\ [val]$. Finally, the rule *typeConv* states that a type t can be substituted for a convertible type t' in any typing judgement.

In the full version of our code, we extend the calculus with built-in dependent sum types (like the $\exists$ type we have already seen), identity types $x \equiv y : A$ (which contain proofs that x and y of type A are definitionally equal) and the empty type $\bot$ (which does not contain any value). These are modelled by adding suitable constructors for the types, their constructors and eliminators to the *Constant* data type, together with appropriate typing and reduction rules.

More typing judgements In addition to the typing judgement for terms above, we also define typing judgements for contexts and for substitutions. Figure 6 shows the judgement $\vdash\ \Gamma$ expressing that context Γ is well-typed, i.e. that all context entries are sets. Its rule ty_ϵ states that the empty context is always well-typed and $ty_\triangleleft$ says that subsequent entries should be types in their preceding context. We omit the definition of judgement $\Gamma \vdash \phi : tel$[3], which expresses that the terms substituted by substitution ϕ satisfy the type requirements of telescope tel in context Γ.

[3] For ease of presentation, we overload the notation $\_\vdash\_:\_$ in this text.

Meta-theory and helper functions We have proved quite some meta-theory about the reduction, convertibility and typing judgements. For full detail we refer to the full version of our code, but to give you an idea of what is there, Figure 7 shows the types of the most important results. $weaken-inj-\approx$ shows that weakening is injective with respect to convertibility. $\approx$*-trans* shows that convertibility is transitive. $\approx-trans$ is a consequence of the Church-Rosser-property for our reduction rules, which we have proved using a technique for untyped lambda calculi by Tait, described by Martin-Löf [36]. Theorem $\approx$*-/* states that convertibility is invariant under substitutions. Theorems $weakenJudgementTop$, $substJudgementTop$, $substContext$ and $\vdash-/$ state roughly that typings are preserved under weakening, instantiating a variable in the context, replacing a type in the context by a convertible one and applying a substitution to term and type. $\vdash$*-var* is a simple proof that entries in a well-typed context must be sets. By theorem $typesAreSets$, the type of a judgement in a well-typed context must in fact be a type. Finally, $substJudgementType$ is not a theorem but a simple helper function that replaces a judgement's type by a provably equal type (it is a special case of $subst$, the standard eliminator of Agda's singleton type $t \equiv t'$).

Some example terms Let us consider the encoding of a simple example term: the following polymorphic identity function:

$$
\begin{aligned}
&id\ :\ \forall\ (A : Set) \rightarrow A \rightarrow A\\
&id = \lambda\ (A : Set) \rightarrow \lambda\ (v : A) \rightarrow v
\end{aligned}
$$

The type and definition of this function are given by closed expressions $idTyTm$ and $idTm$.

$$
\begin{aligned}
&idTm \quad\ :\ Expr\ 0\\
&idTm \quad\ = lambda\ set\ (lambda\ (var\ 0)\ (var\ 0))\\
&idTyTm\ :\ Expr\ 0\\
&idTyTm = pi\ set\ (fun\ (var\ 0)\ (var\ 0))
\end{aligned}
$$

We can prove that the term $idTm$ satisfies type $idTyTm$ using the typing rules from Figure 5.

$$
\begin{aligned}
&ty_{idTm}\ :\ \varepsilon \vdash idTm : idTyTm\\
&ty_{idTm} = typeLam\ typeSet\ (typeLam\ typeVar\ typeVar)
\end{aligned}
$$

By the $typesAreSets$ theorem, it follows that $idTyTm$ is a type.

$$
\begin{aligned}
&ty_{idTyTm}\ :\ \varepsilon \vdash idTyTm : set\\
&ty_{idTyTm} = typesAreSets\ ty_{\epsilon}\ ty_{idTm}
\end{aligned}
$$

3. Bringing Terms to Life

With this infrastructure in place, we can define our meta-programming primitive $interp$ together with auxiliary primitives $interpCtx$ and $interpSet$. Their types are:

$$
\begin{aligned}
&interpCtx : \{n : \mathbb{N}\}\ \{\Gamma : Context\ n\} \rightarrow\ \vdash\Gamma\ \ \rightarrow\ \ Set\\
&interpSet : \{n : \mathbb{N}\}\ \{\Gamma : Context\ n\}\ \{A : Expr\ n\} \rightarrow\\
&\quad \Gamma \vdash A : set\ \rightarrow\ (ty_{\Gamma} : \vdash\Gamma)\ \rightarrow\ interpCtx\ ty_{\Gamma}\ \rightarrow Set\\
&interp : \{n : \mathbb{N}\}\ \{\Gamma : Context\ n\}\ \{v\ t : Expr\ n\} \rightarrow\\
&\quad (ty_v : \Gamma \vdash v : t)\ \rightarrow\ (ty_{\Gamma} : \vdash\Gamma)\ \rightarrow\\
&\quad (asmpts : interpCtx\ ty_{\Gamma})\ \rightarrow\\
&\quad interpSet\ (typesAreSets\ ty_{\Gamma}\ ty_v)\ ty_{\Gamma}\ asmpts
\end{aligned}
$$

$interpCtx$ turns the types in a well-typed context into a dependent sum type of the context entries' interpretations. It is used by the two other judgements to require values for all of a context's assumptions. $interpSet$ interprets an encoded type, yielding a Set, and $interp$ interprets a term v typed t. In the result type of $interp$ for a proof ty_v of judgement $\Gamma \vdash v : t$, we use the previously mentioned theorem $typesAreSets$ to calculate $typesAreSets\ ty_{\Gamma}\ ty_v$, a proof that $\Gamma \vdash t : set$. The result of $interp$ is then of type t, interpreted using $interpSet$ and this derived judgement.

Interpreting examples Before we go into more details, consider again the previously encoded polymorphic identity function. Remember that the closed terms $idTm$ and $idTyTm$ encode the function and its type and the proofs ty_{idTm} and ty_{idTyTm} witness the typing judgements $\varepsilon \vdash idTm : idTyTm$ and $\varepsilon \vdash idTyTm : set$. Both proofs assume only an empty context, which is always well typed according to the rule ty_{ϵ} in Figure 6. We will discuss the reduction behaviour of our primitives further, but $interpCtx\ ty_{\epsilon}$ (the assumptions in the empty context) reduces to unit type $\top$ (with canonical inhabitant tt). With all of this, we can interpret the encoded type $idTyTm$ to obtain the type $intrp_{idTyTm}$:

$$
intrp_{idTyTm} = interpSet\ ty_{idTyTm}\ ty_{\epsilon}\ tt
$$

More details follow, but $intrp_{idTyTm}$ reduces to $(x{:}Set)\ (x_1{:}x) \rightarrow x$, alpha-equal to the intended type $(A : Set) \rightarrow A \rightarrow A$. Similarly, we can interpret term $idTm$ and its typing proof ty_{idTm} to obtain $intrp_{idTm}$ of type $intrp_{idTyTm}$.

$$
intrp_{idTm} = interp\ ty_{idTm}\ ty_{\epsilon}\ tt
$$

As we intended, $intrp_{idTm}$ reduces to $\lambda\ (x : Set) \rightarrow (x_1 : x) \rightarrow x_1$, alpha-convertible to our intended $\lambda\ (A : Set) \rightarrow \lambda\ (x : A) \rightarrow x$.

Interfacing with the real world In real examples, generated code needs to interface with existing types and values. In staging meta-programming systems, this is supported with a built-in *quoting* primitive, but we use an alternative approach. Suppose for example that we want a meta-program to construct the term $suc\ 2$ from the pre-existing value 2 and function suc. To do this, the meta-program clearly needs to refer to the type $\mathbb{N}$, the function suc and the value 2 in the generated object code, but our term encoding does not provide a way to refer to such outside definitions. One solution would be to build natural numbers into our calculus as primitives, but this is not a scalable approach, since we cannot expect to do this for all types we will ever need, let alone a user's custom types.

A better solution lets the meta-program construct the object term in a suitable context, postulating values of the correct types. Real values can then be provided in the interpretation of this context. For our example, we need the context Γ_{ex}:

$$
\Gamma_{ex} = (pi\ (var\ 1)\ (var\ 2)) \lhd\ (var\ 0) \lhd\ set \lhd\ \varepsilon
$$

This definition should be read right-to-left: $\lhd$ is right-associative and the left-most context entries are added last and may refer to the values of entries to their right. It starts with the empty context ε and lists the types for which we want to postulate values. In order, these are a type (of type set), a value of this type (of type $var\ 0$) and a function from this type to itself (of type $pi\ (var\ 1)\ (var\ 2)$). The context is intended to be instantiated to values $\mathbb{N}$, 2 and suc respectively. Note that the de Bruijn variables $var\ 0$, $var\ 1$ and $var\ 2$ in the context all refer to the value of the rightmost context entry of type set; subsequent context entries have an additional variable in scope and the body of a pi as well. Proof $ty\Gamma ex$ of judgement $\vdash\Gamma_{ex}$ shows that context Γ_{ex} is well-typed, i.e. all entries are in fact sets:

$$
\begin{aligned}
ty_{\Gamma ex} = ty_{\lhd}\ (&ty_{\lhd}\ (ty_{\lhd}\ ty_{\epsilon}\ typeSet)\ typeVar)\\
&(typePi\ typeVar\ typeVar)
\end{aligned}
$$

We will fill in the appropriate values for this context's assumptions with the value $asmpts_{\Gamma ex}$ of type $interpCtx\ ty_{\Gamma ex}$:

$$
asmpts_{\Gamma ex} = ((tt, \mathbb{N}), 1), suc
$$

In context Γ_{ex}, we can now construct the value $suc\ 2$ as a term ex. It is an $Expr\ 3$, since it may refer to Γ_{ex}'s three assumptions, and applies the postulated suc function to the postulated value 2.

$$
ex = appl\ (var\ 0)\ (var\ 1)
$$

We construct a proof ty_{ex} of judgement $\Gamma_{ex} \vdash ex : var\ 2$, i.e. that the constructed term ex has the first postulated value ($\mathbb{N}$) as its type, in three steps. First typing rules *typeAppl* and *typeVar* give us proof ty'_{ex}, showing that ex has a more complicated type. We then prove this type convertible to $var\ 2$ in (partly omitted) proof $conv_{ex}$. ty_{ex} then uses typing rule *typeConv* to replace the convertible type.

$$\begin{aligned}
ty'_{ex} &: \Gamma_{ex} \vdash ex : appl\ (lambda\ (var\ 2)\ (var\ 3))\ (var\ 1) \\
ty'_{ex} &= typeAppl\ typeVar\ typeVar\ typeVar \\
conv_{ex} &: appl\ (lambda\ (var\ 2)\ (var\ 3))\ (var\ 1) \approx var\ 2 \\
conv_{ex} &= \cdots (reduceApplication\ (var\ 3)\ (var\ 1)) \\
ty_{ex} &: \Gamma_{ex} \vdash ex : var\ 2 \\
ty_{ex} &= typeConv\ conv_{ex}\ ty'_{ex}\ typeVar
\end{aligned}$$

We can then interpret object program ex to obtain a value of type $interpSet\ (typesAreSets\ ty_{\Gamma ex}\ ty_{ex})\ ty_{\Gamma ex}\ asmpts_{\Gamma ex}$:

$$exInt = interp\ ty_{ex}\ ty_{\Gamma ex}\ asmpts_{\Gamma ex}$$

The reduction behaviour of our primitives that we will talk about next ensures that *exInt*'s type and *exInt* itself reduce to $\mathbb{N}$ and $suc\ 2$ respectively, precisely as we intended.

Sometimes, a meta-program does not just need to refer to an external function *f* in generated code, but also depends on information about such a function's reduction behaviour to prove well-typedness of the generated code. Without going into much detail, the ideas of this section can support this if we add singleton types to the object calculus. Concretely, a context could postulate the external function *f* together with proofs of its reduction behaviour. Such proofs could then be used in the typing of generated programs and the invocation of the interpretation primitive would require actual proofs of the reduction behaviour in the context interpretation.

Reduction behaviour The reduction behaviour of our primitives is an important part of their definition and crucial for the functioning of the previous examples. We present the reduction rules in Figure 8. In general, these rules interpret encoded types, terms and contexts, but only when the well-typedness of the result can be guaranteed. To achieve the latter, we need to ascertain that the provided well-typedness proofs are valid and do not rely on assumptions that might not hold. This is non-trivial because a language like Agda applies strong reductions during type-checking, i.e. reductions can be applied to open terms as well as closed. Non-closed proofs are not necessarily valid, since they may rely on invalid assumptions. We will provide more insight further on and discuss our solution based on the *value patterns* in Figure 8. These are the patterns written in `typewriter` font in the left-hand sides of some reduction rules. Such a value pattern indicates that the rule must only be applied if the corresponding argument is a *value*. The types of these arguments are conversion or typing judgements and their values are finite trees of constructor applications (see Figures 3 and 5). As such, the property of value-ness can easily be checked in the primitives' implementation. But before we discuss the role of the value patterns further, let us take a better look at the reduction rules.

Recall the type of our most important primitive *interp*.

$$\begin{aligned}
&interp : \{n : \mathbb{N}\}\ \{\Gamma : Context\ n\}\ \{v\ t : Expr\ n\} \to \\
&\quad (ty_v : \Gamma \vdash v : t) \to (ty_\Gamma : \vdash \Gamma) \to \\
&\quad (asmpts : interpCtx\ ty_\Gamma) \to \\
&\quad interpSet\ (typesAreSets\ ty_\Gamma\ ty_v)\ ty_\Gamma\ asmpts
\end{aligned}$$

The primitive takes a context Γ, a term v and a type t as hidden arguments, followed by proofs ty_v, ty_Γ of typing judgements $\Gamma \vdash v : t$ and $\vdash \Gamma$ and a value *asmpts* of the context's interpretation type $interpCtx\ ty_\Gamma$. The reduction rules in Figure 8 specify that for certain forms of the judgement ty_v, the primitive application reduces to appropriate right-hand sides. For $ty_v = typeSet$, which implies[4] $v = set$ and $t = set$, the first rule returns interpretation Set. For $ty_v = typeVar$, an interpretation of the ith context assumption is given by primitive *interpVar*, discussed below.

The rules for $ty_v = typePi\ ty_s\ ty_t$ and $typeLam\ ty_s\ ty_b$ interpret terms $pi\ s\ t$ and $lambda\ s\ b$ as respectively the corresponding Agda Π-type and lambda term, recursively constructed from interpretations of s and t resp. b. The bound variable x is made available for the interpretation of t resp. b by placing it in the interpretation of the extended context $s \lhd \Gamma$. For an application of a function to a value, we apply the interpretation of the function to the interpretation of the value. Note the value patterns on the left-hand side that we will come back to further on. Finally, the interpretation of a *typeConv* is simply the interpretation of the judgement whose type it substitutes, on the condition that the arguments are values.

Recall also the type of primitive *interpCtx*:

$$interpCtx : \{n : \mathbb{N}\}\ \{\Gamma : Context\ n\} \to \vdash \Gamma \to Set$$

The primitive takes a context Γ as a hidden argument and a well-typedness proof for it and returns its interpretation, i.e. a type that contains all the context's assumptions. We saw in *interp*'s reduction rules for *typeLam* and *typePi*, how an extended context $s \lhd \Gamma$ is interpreted by a tuple of the s value and the interpretation of Γ. This corresponds to *interpCtx*'s reduction behaviour, that we look at now. The first reduction rule interprets an empty context by the unit type $\top$. More interestingly, a context Γ extended with a type t is interpreted by an interpretation *asmpts* of Γ, and an interpretation of the type t. We use a dependent sum $\exists$ to specify the interpretation of t with respect to the interpretation *asmpts* of the rest of the context.

Now that we know how to interpret a context, we can define reduction rules for *interpVar*, to project out a context's ith entry. Its reduction rules are not surprising, projecting out the top assumption for variable *zero* and recursing for $suc\ i$. The primitive *interpSet* is a version of *interp* that works on types only. Its role is to break the circularity in the types of the primitives. It is implemented in terms of helper primitives $interpSet'$ and *interpVarSet*. We do not discuss their reduction behaviour as it is similar to *interp* and *interpVar* except that we require proof that the judgement's type is convertible to *set* and that this proof is a value in some cases.

Soundness in the presence of open terms To understand the value patterns in five of the reduction rules in Figure 8, we have to explain the powerful form of type-level computation that a dependently typed language like Agda uses. It uses a *strong* form of reductions: reductions can be applied even inside the body of lambda or pi terms. The term $\lambda\ x \to 0 + x$, for example, is considered equal to $\lambda\ x \to x$, because $0 + x$ is reduced to x despite the open variable x. However, such strong reductions can be dangerous because, in the presence of open variables, we may be reasoning under absurd assumptions. Consider the following function:

$$absurdTerm = \lambda\ (prf : Int \equiv Bool) \to cast\ prf\ 3 \lor false$$

The function *absurdTerm* takes a proof *prf* that $Int \equiv Bool$, modelling an equality proof of types *Int* and *Bool*. This proof type is of course empty, but the type-checker is not aware of that. With *prf* and an appropriate *cast* function, we can use a value 3 as a *Bool*. However, this is not problematic, because a correct definition of the *cast* function will never reduce $cast\ prf\ 3$ to 3. Instead, it will block on the open variable *prf* until a value (i.e. *refl*) is somehow substituted for it. This mechanism effectively protects values like 3 from being used at wrong types like *Bool*.

For our primitives, similar issues arise. We can for example assume a proof *tyAbsurd* of judgement $\varepsilon \vdash set : pi\ set\ set$ even

[4] Note: pattern matches that imply equalities about other arguments are standard for dependent pattern matching [25].

$$
\begin{array}{llll}
\mathit{interp}\ \mathit{typeSet} & \mathit{ty}_\Gamma\ \mathit{asmpts} & = & \mathit{Set} \\
\mathit{interp}\ (\mathit{typeVar}\ \{i = i\}) & \mathit{ty}_\Gamma\ \mathit{asmpts} & = & \mathit{interpVar}\ i\ \mathit{ty}_\Gamma\ \mathit{asmpts} \\
\mathit{interp}\ (\mathit{typePi}\ \mathit{ty}_s\ \mathit{ty}_t) & \mathit{ty}_\Gamma\ \mathit{asmpts} & = & (x : \mathit{interpSet}\ \mathit{ty}_s\ \mathit{ty}_\Gamma\ \mathit{asmpts}) \to \mathit{interpSet}\ \mathit{ty}_t\ (\mathit{ty}_\triangleleft\ \mathit{ty}_\Gamma\ \mathit{ty}_s)\ (\mathit{asmpts}, x) \\
\mathit{interp}\ (\mathit{typeLam}\ \mathit{ty}_s\ \mathit{ty}_b) & \mathit{ty}_\Gamma\ \mathit{asmpts} & = & \lambda\ (x : \mathit{interpSet}\ \mathit{ty}_s\ \mathit{ty}_\Gamma\ \mathit{asmpts}) \to \mathit{interp}\ (\mathit{ty}_\triangleleft\ \mathit{ty}_\Gamma\ \mathit{ty}_s)\ \mathit{ty}_b\ (\mathit{asmpts}, x) \\
\mathit{interp}\ (\mathit{typeAppl}\ \mathtt{ty_t}\ \mathtt{ty_f}\ \mathtt{ty_{val}}) & \mathit{ty}_\Gamma\ \mathit{asmpts} & = & \mathit{interp}\ \mathit{ty}_\Gamma\ \mathit{ty}_f\ \mathit{asmpts}\ (\mathit{interp}\ \mathit{ty}_\Gamma\ \mathit{ty}_{val}\ \mathit{asmpts}) \\
\mathit{interp}\ (\mathit{typeConv}\ \mathtt{t{\sim}t'}\ \mathtt{ty_e}\ \mathtt{ty_t}) & \mathit{ty}_\Gamma\ \mathit{asmpts} & = & \mathit{interp}\ \mathit{ty}_\Gamma\ \mathit{ty}_e\ \mathit{asmpts}
\end{array}
$$

$$
\begin{array}{lll}
\mathit{interpCtx}\ \ \mathit{ty}_\epsilon & = & \top \\
\mathit{interpCtx}\ \ (\mathit{ty}_\triangleleft\ \mathit{ty}_\Gamma\ \mathit{ty}_t) & = & \exists\ \lambda\ (\mathit{asmpts} : \mathit{interpCtx}\ \mathit{ty}_\Gamma) \to \mathit{interpSet}\ \mathit{ty}_t\ \mathit{ty}_\Gamma\ \mathit{asmpts}
\end{array}
$$

$$\mathit{interpVar} : \forall\ \{n\}\ \{\Gamma : \mathit{Context}\ n\}\ i \to (\mathit{ty}_\Gamma : \vdash \Gamma) \to (\mathit{asmpts} : \mathit{interpCtx}\ \mathit{ty}_\Gamma) \to \mathit{interpSet}\ ({\vdash}{-}\mathit{var}\ \mathit{ty}_\Gamma\ i)\ \mathit{ty}_\Gamma\ \mathit{asmpts}$$

$$
\begin{array}{llll}
\mathit{interpVar}\ \ \mathit{zero} & (\mathit{ty}_\triangleleft\ \mathit{ty}_\Gamma\ \mathtt{ty_t}) & (\_, \mathit{asmpt}) & = \mathit{asmpt} \\
\mathit{interpVar}\ \ (\mathit{suc}\ i) & (\mathit{ty}_\triangleleft\ \mathit{ty}_\Gamma\ \mathit{ty}_t) & (\mathit{asmpts}, \_) & = \mathit{interpVar}\ \mathit{ty}_\Gamma\ i\ \mathit{asmpts}
\end{array}
$$

$$\mathit{interpSet}\ \mathit{ty}_t\ \mathit{ty}_\Gamma\ \mathit{asmpts} = \mathit{interpSet}'\ \mathit{ty}_t\ {\approx}{-}\mathit{refl}\ \mathit{ty}_\Gamma\ \mathit{asmpts}$$

$$\mathit{interpSet}' : \forall\ \{n\}\ \{\Gamma : \mathit{Context}\ n\}\ \{A\ t\} \to \Gamma \vdash A : t \to t \approx \mathit{set} \to (\mathit{ty}_\Gamma : \vdash \Gamma) \to \mathit{interpCtx}\ \mathit{ty}_\Gamma \to \mathit{Set}$$

$$
\begin{array}{lllll}
\mathit{interpSet}'\ \ \mathit{typeSet} & \mathit{eq} & \mathit{ty}_\Gamma\ \mathit{asmpts} & = & \mathit{Set} \\
\mathit{interpSet}'\ \ (\mathit{typeVar}\ \{i = i\}) & \mathit{eq} & \mathit{ty}_\Gamma\ \mathit{asmpts} & = & \mathit{interpVarSet}\ i\ \mathit{eq}\ \mathit{ty}_\Gamma\ \mathit{asmpts} \\
\mathit{interpSet}'\ \ (\mathit{typePi}\ \mathit{ty}_s\ \mathit{ty}_t) & \mathit{eq} & \mathit{ty}_\Gamma\ \mathit{asmpts} & = & \\
\multicolumn{5}{l}{\quad (x : \mathit{interpSet}\ \mathit{ty}_s\ \mathit{ty}_\Gamma\ \mathit{asmpts}) \to \mathit{interpSet}\ \mathit{ty}_t\ (\mathit{ty}_\triangleleft\ \mathit{ty}_\Gamma\ \mathit{ty}_s)\ (\mathit{asmpts}, x)} \\
\mathit{interpSet}'\ \ (\mathit{typeAppl}\ \mathtt{ty_t}\ \mathtt{ty_f}\ \mathit{ty}_{val}) & \mathtt{eq} & \mathit{ty}_\Gamma\ \mathit{asmpts} & = & \mathit{interp}\ \mathit{ty}_f\ \mathit{ty}_\Gamma\ \mathit{asmpts}\ (\mathit{interp}\ \mathit{ty}_{val}\ \mathit{ty}_\Gamma\ \mathit{asmpts}) \\
\mathit{interpSet}'\ \ (\mathit{typeConv}\ t{\sim}t'\ \mathit{ty}'_A\ \mathit{ty}_t) & \mathit{eq} & \mathit{ty}_\Gamma\ \mathit{asmpts} & = & \mathit{interpSet}'\ \mathit{ty}'_A\ ({\approx}{-}\mathit{trans}\ ({\approx}{-}\mathit{sym}\ t{\sim}t')\ \mathit{eq})\ \mathit{ty}_\Gamma\ \mathit{asmpt}
\end{array}
$$

$$\mathit{interpVarSet} : \forall\ \{n\}\ \{\Gamma : \mathit{Context}\ n\}\ \{l\}\ i \to \mathit{lookup}\ i\ \Gamma \approx \mathit{set} \to (\mathit{ty}_\Gamma : \vdash \Gamma) \to \mathit{interpCtx}\ \mathit{ty}_\Gamma \to \mathit{Set}$$

$$
\begin{array}{lllll}
\mathit{interpVarSet}\ \ \mathit{zero} & \mathtt{eq} & (\mathit{ty}_\triangleleft\ \mathit{ty}_\Gamma\ \mathtt{ty_t}) & (\_\ \mathit{asmpt}) & = \mathit{asmpt} \\
\mathit{interpVarSet}\ \ (\mathit{suc}\ i) & \mathit{eq} & (\mathit{ty}_\triangleleft\ \mathit{ty}_\Gamma\ \mathit{ty}_t) & (\mathit{asmpts}, \_) & = \mathit{interpVarSet}\ i\ (\mathit{weaken}{-}\mathit{inj}{-}{\approx}\ (\mathit{lookup}\ i\ \Gamma)\ \mathit{set}\ \mathit{eq})\ \mathit{ty}_\Gamma\ \mathit{asmpts}
\end{array}
$$

Figure 8. Reduction behaviour of our primitives. Patterns in `typewriter` font are required to be values.

though this type of proofs is empty. Clearly, $\mathit{interp}\ \mathit{tySet}\ \mathit{ty}_\epsilon\ \mathit{tt}$ should then not reduce to Set at type $\mathit{Set} \to \mathit{Set}$, but instead block on the open variable tySet. Similarly, if we assume a proof prf of judgement $\mathit{pi}\ \mathit{set}\ \mathit{set} \approx \mathit{set}$, and use it with $\mathit{typeConv}$ to construct a proof $\mathit{tyAbsurd}'$ of judgement $\varepsilon \vdash \mathit{set} : \mathit{pi}\ \mathit{set}\ \mathit{set}$, then our primitives should block on open variable prf.

By the value patterns in Figure 8, some rules require that certain arguments are values. We have checked for each rule that the right-hand side's type was equal to the declared type, assuming just the information from the left-hand side patterns, similar to how dependent pattern matching can be type-checked [25]. For the five rules with value patterns, this was not the case. In for example the rule for $\mathit{interp}\ (\mathit{typeConv}\ \mathtt{t{\sim}t'}\ \mathtt{ty_e}\ \mathtt{ty_t})\ \mathit{ty}_\Gamma\ \mathit{asmpts}$, the right-hand-side is of type

$$\mathit{interpSet}\ (\mathit{typesAreSets}\ \mathit{ty}_\Gamma\ \mathit{ty}_e)\ \mathit{ty}_\Gamma\ \mathit{asmpts}$$

i.e. the interpretation of t', not t and the convertibility assumption $t \sim t'$ is essential for returning a value of type t' as one of type t. We believe that the value patterns in Figure 8 solve this problem, making our reduction rules valid for open terms, even though the general question of soundness remains open.

The primitives' properties In addition to the reduction behaviour of our primitives, some of our meta-programs require additional properties about them listed in Figure 9. Property $\mathit{castInterp}{-}{\approx}'$ states that for convertible types A and A', the interpretations under $\mathit{interpSet}$ must be the same. The next two properties are related to the interpretation of a type after a well-typed substitution $\Gamma_2 \vdash \phi : \Gamma_1$ between well-typed contexts Γ_1 and Γ_2. $\mathit{interpCompSubCtx}$ says that an interpretation of Γ_1 can be constructed from one of Γ_1 and $\mathit{interpCompSubSet}'$ says that the interpretation of a type t in Γ_2 is the same as that of $t\ /\ \phi$ in Γ_1 using the interpretation of Γ_1 constructed by $\mathit{interpCompSubCtx}$.

We are currently using stub proofs of these properties, based on an Agda primitive called $\mathit{primTrustMe}$. $\mathit{primTrustMe}$ is an unsafe primitive that proves equalities $a \equiv b$ for any set A and values a, b of type A. However, during type-checking, $\mathit{primTrustMe}$ only reduces to refl when a and b are definitionally equal. It is future work to ascertain that these properties follow from the reduction rules of Figure 8 and the proofs of theorems like $\vdash{-}/$.

4. Applications

Our approach allows definitions of powerful meta-programs, manipulating both code and types, in a functional style and with very precise types. In this section, we demonstrate this for two important applications: datatype-generic programming and tactics.

4.1 Datatype-Generic Programming

The field of datatype-generic programming studies the definition of algorithms that work for a wide variety of data types. An example is Haskell's **deriving** *Show* mechanism [35, §4.3.3, §11], which allows a data type A to be annotated with the directive **deriving** *Show* to make the compiler derive an instance of the *Show* type class. Such an instance consists essentially of a function $\mathit{show} :: A \to \mathit{String}$, derived syntactically by the compiler from the data type's constructors and their types. The goal of datatype-generic programming is to allow functions like *show* to be defined in a generic way, i.e. such that they can be defined once but used with a wide variety of data types.

Representing data types To apply our techniques to the field of datatype-generic programming, we start from a syntactic representation of an inductive data type:

$$
\begin{array}{l}
\mathbf{record}\ \mathit{SimpleDT}\ (A : \mathit{Set}) : \mathit{Set}\ \mathbf{where} \\
\quad \mathbf{constructor}\ \mathit{simpleDT} \\
\quad \mathbf{field}\ \mathit{constructors}\ \ : \mathit{List}\ (\mathit{Constructor}\ A) \\
\qquad\qquad \mathit{folder}\qquad\quad\ : \mathit{folderType}\ A\ \mathit{constructors}
\end{array}
$$

$$castInterp{-}\approx' : \forall\ \{n\}\ \{\Gamma : Context\ n\}\ \{A\ A'\} \rightarrow (ty_A : \Gamma \vdash A : set) \ \rightarrow\ (ty'_A : \Gamma \vdash A' : set)\ \rightarrow\ A \approx A'\ \rightarrow$$
$$(ty_\Gamma : \vdash \Gamma)\ \rightarrow\ (asmpts : interpCtx\ ty_\Gamma)\ \rightarrow\ interpSet\ ty_A\ ty_\Gamma\ asmpts \equiv interpSet\ ty'_A\ ty_\Gamma\ asmpts$$
$$interpCompSubCtx : \forall\ \{m\ n\}\ \{\Gamma_1\ \Gamma_2\}\ \{\phi : Sub\ Expr\ m\ n\} \rightarrow$$
$$\Gamma_2 \vdash \phi : \Gamma_1\ \rightarrow\ (ty\Gamma_1 : \vdash \Gamma_1)\ \rightarrow\ (ty\Gamma_2 : \vdash \Gamma_2)\ \rightarrow interpCtx\ ty\Gamma_2\ \rightarrow\ interpCtx\ ty\Gamma_1$$
$$interpCompSubSet' : \forall\ \{m\ n\ t\}\ \{\Gamma_1\ \Gamma_2\}\ \{\phi : Sub\ Expr\ m\ n\} \rightarrow$$
$$(comp : \Gamma_2 \vdash \phi : \Gamma_1)\ \rightarrow\ (ty\Gamma_1 : \vdash \Gamma_1)\ \rightarrow\ (ty_t : \Gamma_1 \vdash t : set)\ \rightarrow\ (ty\Gamma_2 : \vdash \Gamma_2)\ \rightarrow\ (asmpts_2 : interpCtx\ ty\Gamma_2)\ \rightarrow$$
$$interpSet\ (\vdash{-}/comp\ ty_t)\ ty\Gamma_2\ asmpts_2 \equiv interpSet\ ty_t\ ty\Gamma_1\ (interpCompSubCtx\ comp\ ty\Gamma_1\ ty\Gamma_2\ asmpts_2)$$

Figure 9. Primitive properties

According to this definition, a data type A is syntactically described by a list of its constructors and a *folder* or *induction principle* ($List$ is a standard type of finite lists). To keep things simple, we omit well-formedness requirements (like positivity of the definition) and proofs about the reduction behaviour of the folder function, which are required to completely describe a data type, but not needed for our example application. $Constructor$ is the syntactic representation of a single constructor:

$$
\begin{array}{l}
\textbf{data}\ Constructor\ (A : Set) : Set\ \textbf{where} \\
\quad mkConstructor : String \rightarrow (n : \mathbb{N}) \rightarrow \\
\quad\quad (tel : Telescope\ 1\ (n+1))\ \rightarrow\ (ty_{tel} : \Gamma set \vdash tel) \rightarrow \\
\quad\quad \textbf{let}\ ctorT = funCtx\ n\ tel\ (var\ 0) \\
\quad\quad\quad ty_{ctorT}\ :\ \Gamma set \vdash ctorT : set \\
\quad\quad\quad ty_{ctorT} = typeFunCtx\ n\ ty_{tel}\ typeVar \\
\quad\quad \textbf{in}\ interpSet\ ty_{\Gamma_{set}}\ ty_{ctorT}\ (tt, A)\ \rightarrow\ Constructor\ A
\end{array}
$$

We describe a constructor by its name as a $String$, its arity n and a telescope tel containing the types of its arguments. The telescope has one initial variable in scope: the data type A itself, so that it can be referenced in the types of constructor arguments. The telescope tel must be well-typed in the context $\Gamma set = set \triangleleft \varepsilon$, i.e. with the premise that A is a set. From tel, we can calculate the full type $ctorT$ of the constructor as the function that takes the arguments given by tel and produces a value of type A (using omitted helper function $funCtx$). We prove that $ctorT$ is a set (using omitted lemma $typeFunCtx$), interpret it and require a value of it, i.e. the actual constructor. Note how our meta-programming primitives provide the crucial link between the syntactically represented types and the normal type of the actual constructor.

In addition to the list of $Constructor$s, $SimpleDT$ contains an eliminator or *folder* for the data type. Every inductive data type comes with such an induction principle, which models a general way of perform structural induction over the data type. The function $folderType$ syntactically derives the type of this induction principle from the types of the constructors and their interpretations.

$$
\begin{array}{l}
folderType : (A : Set) \rightarrow List\ (Constructor\ A) \rightarrow Set \\
folderType\ A\ constructors = (P : A \rightarrow Set) \rightarrow \\
\quad underFolderAsmpts\ A\ P\ constructors\ ((x : A) \rightarrow P\ x)
\end{array}
$$

Given a set A and a list of A's constructors, $folderType$ returns the type for a corresponding induction principle: it takes a predicate $P : A \rightarrow Set$ (the *motive* [25], describing what the induction principle should produce) and returns a function of type $(x : A) \rightarrow P\ x$ under a number of assumptions. For every constructor, the function $underFolderAsmpts$ syntactically derives the type of an assumption from the constructor's type. This is fairly involved, but presents no fundamental difficulties and we omit it for space reasons.

Let us immediately show some data types and their representations. The simplest example is the empty type, which has zero constructors. Its definition and induction principle look as follows:

$$
\begin{array}{l}
\textbf{data}\ \bot : Set\ \textbf{where} \\
foldBot : (P : \bot \rightarrow Set) \rightarrow (t : \bot) \rightarrow P\ t \\
foldBot\ P\ ()
\end{array}
$$

Note the use of an absurd pattern () in the definition of $foldBot$. This pattern communicates to Agda that no value can ever be given for the argument of type $\bot$, so that a right-hand-side is not needed. It is easy to provide a value of $SimpleDT$ for $\bot$:

$$
\begin{array}{l}
botDT\ :\ SimpleDT\ \bot \\
botDT = simpleDT\ [\,]\ foldBot
\end{array}
$$

$botDT$ specifies that $\bot$ has no constructors and $foldBot$ is its induction principle. Agda successfully type-checks $foldBot$ against the folder type calculated for the empty list of constructors.

For a more complex example, consider the standard definition of natural numbers and its induction principle:

$$
\begin{array}{l}
\textbf{data}\ \mathbb{N} : Set\ \textbf{where}\ zero\ : \mathbb{N} \\
\qquad\qquad\qquad\qquad\quad suc\ \ : \mathbb{N} \rightarrow \mathbb{N} \\
fold\mathbb{N} : (P : \mathbb{N} \rightarrow Set) \rightarrow\ \ P\ zero\ \rightarrow \\
\quad (\forall\, n \rightarrow P\ n \rightarrow P\ (suc\ n))\ \rightarrow\ (n : \mathbb{N}) \rightarrow P\ n \\
fold\mathbb{N}\ P\ Pz\ Ps\ zero \quad\ = Pz \\
fold\mathbb{N}\ P\ Pz\ Ps\ (suc\ n) = Ps\ n\ (fold\mathbb{N}\ P\ Pz\ Ps\ n)
\end{array}
$$

The constructors $zero$ and suc of data type $\mathbb{N}$ are described by $zeroConstr$ and $sucConstr$ of type $Constructor\ \mathbb{N}$:

$$
\begin{array}{l}
zeroConstr = mkConstructor\ \texttt{"zero"}\ 0\ \varepsilon\ ty_\epsilon\ zero \\
sucConstr\ \ = mkConstructor\ \texttt{"suc"}\ 1\ (var\ 0 \triangleleft \varepsilon) \\
\qquad\qquad (ty_\triangleleft\ ty_\epsilon\ typeVar)\ suc
\end{array}
$$

The constructor $zero$ is of arity 0, with the empty telescope describing its arguments. The actual constructor $zero$ is then provided and Agda checks its type against the one calculated from the syntactic description. Constructor suc is of arity 1, taking one value of type $\mathbb{N}$ as its argument (recall that $var\ 0$ in the constructor telescope refers to the data type itself). The constructor telescope is well-typed under Γset's assumption that $var\ 0$ is a set. Again, the actual constructor is given and checked against the type calculated from the description. We can now describe $\mathbb{N}$ with $natDT : SimpleDT\ \mathbb{N}$.

$$natDT = simpleDT\ [zeroConstr, sucConstr]\ fold\mathbb{N}$$

$natDT$ lists $\mathbb{N}$'s constructors and provides induction principle $fold\mathbb{N}$, checked against the type calculated from the constructors.

Derive Show The type $SimpleDT$ is a general syntactic description of inductive data types that permits a general form of datatype-generic meta-program. As a proof-of-concept, we show the function $deriveShow$ that derives a $show$ function for a data type A.

$$
\begin{array}{l}
deriveShow : \forall\ \{A\} \rightarrow SimpleDT\ A \rightarrow A \rightarrow String \\
deriveShow\ (simpleDT\ constructors\ folder) = \text{omitted}
\end{array}
$$

We omit the algorithm's implementation, which takes the description of data type A and exploits the induction principle with motive $P = \lambda\ \_ \rightarrow String$. It syntactically derives arguments for the folder, specifying how values constructed using the different constructors are to be serialised. The hardest part of the code is to convince the type-checker that the folder arguments we construct for the concrete motive $\lambda\ \_ \rightarrow String$ correspond to their expected types for a general predicate P when P is instantiated to $\lambda\ \_ \rightarrow String$ through the context interpretation. This essentially uses the *interpCompSubCtx* and *interpCompSubSet* primitive properties shown in Figure 9.

For our example data types, *deriveShow* derives an (admittedly not very useful) *show* function for $\bot$:

$$\begin{aligned} showBot &: \bot \rightarrow String \\ showBot &= deriveShow\ botDT \end{aligned}$$

showBot's definition reduces to *foldBot* $(\lambda\ \_ \rightarrow String)$, the code that *deriveShow* syntactically generates. From *natDT*, we can derive the function *showNat* of type $\mathbb{N} \rightarrow String$.

$$showNat = deriveShow\ natDT$$

Like for *showBot*, *showNat*'s definition reduces to the generated function $showNat' = fold\mathbb{N}\ (\lambda\ \_ \rightarrow String)$ `"zero"` (...) (final argument omitted). We can apply it to numbers with for example *showNat* 2 producing the string `"(suc (suc zero))"`.

Discussion This account of datatype-generic programming is rudimentary, lacking support for indices and parameters and non-recursive and more general recursive constructor arguments [21]. It does not exclude non-strictly-positive data types and does not contain proofs about the induction principle's reduction behaviour (required to construct proofs about inductive functions). However, we do not see fundamental obstacles for adding any of this.

From a methodological point of view, our account of datatype-generic programming is compelling: meta-programs are written in the language itself, using the language's standard functional computational model. The syntactic description of a data type in *SimpleDT* is general and could be automatically generated by the compiler. Modulo correctness of our primitives, the meta-programs come with strong guarantees about termination, well-typedness of the generated programs and completeness.

SimpleDT and *deriveShow* are implemented in ±1200 lines of code and can be studied in the full version of our code (see the footnote on page 2). This is still much more than what we would like, and in Section 5 we discuss how this could be improved.

4.2 Tactics

Tactics are a form of meta-programs that solve or refine proof obligations in proof assistants. In proof assistants based on dependent type theory, solving a proof obligation is equivalent to producing a program of a specified type in a specified context. Several proof assistants provide support for writing tactics, often in the form of a special-purpose sub-language. Such tactics are generally untyped and provide little upfront guarantees about their correct operation. Even though the correctness of the generated proofs can be checked after generation, Gonthier et al. argue that untyped tactics can be hard to maintain and compose and giving them more precise types is a good approach to solve this issue [26]. There are also performance advantages to tactics that can be guaranteed to terminate correctly without running them, as argued by Chlipala [14].

Our meta-programming primitives show promise for this field, and they lend themselves to a typed form of tactics written in a standard functional style. The input for a tactic is just a syntactic representation of the proof obligation, i.e. a certain type in a certain context. By additionally requiring a typing judgement for the type and interpretations for the context's values, we can use *interpSet* to specify the expected result type of the tactic.

Consider the following analogue of Coq's *assumption* tactic, a simple tactic that solves proof obligations which appear literally in the context. Our account of it enjoys a very precise type:

$$\begin{aligned} &assumptionTactic : \forall\ \{n\ T\}\ \{\Gamma : Context\ n\} \rightarrow \\ &\quad (ty_t : \Gamma \vdash T : set) \rightarrow \\ &\quad (ty_\Gamma : \vdash \Gamma) \rightarrow (asmpts : interpCtx\ ty_\Gamma) \rightarrow \\ &\quad ifYes\ (inContext?\ \Gamma\ T)\ (interpSet\ ty_t\ ty_\Gamma\ asmpts) \end{aligned}$$

The tactic takes a type T, a well-typed context Γ and values for its assumptions. The return type will be explained further, but it specifies exactly what the tactic will return in all cases: either a value of type T if T is present in the context or a value of the unit type otherwise. Let us explain this in more detail.

We use the Agda standard library's *Dec* P type. It models a decision of proposition P, i.e. either a proof of P or a proof of $\neg P$:

$$\begin{aligned} \textbf{data}\ Dec\ (P : Set) : Set\ \textbf{where}\ yes &: P \rightarrow Dec\ P \\ no &: \neg\ P \rightarrow Dec\ P \end{aligned}$$

Based on a decision of some property, the *ifYes* function returns either an argument type or unit type $\top$:

$$\begin{aligned} &ifYes : \{P : Set\} \rightarrow Dec\ P \rightarrow Set \rightarrow Set \\ &ifYes\ (yes\ \_)\ P' = P' \\ &ifYes\ (no\ \_)\ \_ = \top \end{aligned}$$

The *inContext?* algorithm decides whether or not a certain type t is present in context Γ, i.e. if the ith entry in the context is equal to t for some i. It uses a general purpose decision procedure *any?*, which simply tries all i of the bounded type *Fin* n. For a given variable i, we use a general equality decision procedure for terms $\_\stackrel{?}{=}\_$ to check whether the ith context entry is equal to t.

$$\begin{aligned} &InContext : \{n : \mathbb{N}\}\ (\Gamma : Context\ n)\ (t : Expr\ n) \rightarrow Set \\ &InContext\ \Gamma\ t = \exists \lambda\ i \rightarrow lookup\ i\ \Gamma \equiv t \\ &inContext? : \{n : \mathbb{N}\}\ (\Gamma : Context\ n)\ (t : Expr\ n) \rightarrow \\ &\qquad Dec\ (InContext\ \Gamma\ t) \\ &inContext?\ \Gamma\ t = any?\ (\lambda\ i \rightarrow lookup\ i\ \Gamma \stackrel{?}{=} t) \end{aligned}$$

In our *assumptionTactic*, we use a **with** pattern match to make a case distinction based on the decision from *inContext?*. If the type t is not found, we can simply return $\top$ value *tt*. If it is found at position i, we essentially want to return the ith entry in the context but we need to convince Agda that it has the desired type.

$$\begin{aligned} &assumptionTactic\ ty_\Gamma\ ty_t\ asmpts\ \textbf{with}\ inContext?\ \Gamma\ t \\ &assumptionTactic\ \{n\}\ \{t\}\ \{\Gamma\}\ ty_\Gamma\ ty_t\ asmpts \\ &\quad \mid yes\ (i, eq_{\Gamma id}) = \\ &\quad \textbf{let}\ ty_{var\,i} : \Gamma \vdash var\ i : t \\ &\qquad\quad ty_{var\,i} = substJudgementType\ eq_{\Gamma id}\ typeVar \\ &\quad \textbf{in}\ castInterp\ (typesAreSets\ ty_\Gamma\ ty_{var\,i})\ ty_t \\ &\qquad\quad ty_\Gamma\ asmpts\ (interp\ ty_{var\,i}\ ty_\Gamma\ asmpts) \\ &assumptionTactic\ ty_\Gamma\ ty_t\ asmpts \mid no\ \_ = tt \end{aligned}$$

The first step is to use the proof $eq_{\Gamma id}$ that $lookup\ i\ \Gamma \equiv t$ from *inContext?* and the *typeVar* typing rule to produce a proof $ty_{var\,i}$ of judgement $\Gamma \vdash var\ i : t$. We can then obtain the interpretation of the ith variable through the value $interp\ ty_{var\,i}\ ty_\Gamma\ asmpts$. Unfortunately, that value's type is

$$interpSet\ (typesAreSets\ ty_\Gamma\ ty_{var\,i})\ ty_\Gamma\ asmpts$$

What we need is a value of type $interpSet\ ty_t\ ty_\Gamma\ asmpts$, i.e. an interpretation of the same type t, but for a different proof that t is a set. *castInterp*, an omitted special case of property *castInterp*–≈ from Figure 9, is precisely what we need to cast one to the other.

Tactic usage Currently, our tactics can be manually invoked with a context and goal type and well-formedness proofs. The tactic invocation appears as an expression in the code where the goal is needed. In future systems, compiler support can increase convenience by automatically providing the goal type, context and their typing proofs. This could e.g. extend Agda's experimental and underdocumented **quoteGoal** construct. This construct allows the invocation of a reflective solver with the compiler providing a syntactic representation of the goal type. It does not however provide a syntactic representation of the context or a guarantee about well-formedness of the provided type. Also, a more developed tactic API could support returning unsolved sub-goals and tactic combinators like Coq's ";".

5. Discussion

There are some more aspects of our approach that we believe deserve further discussion: the representation of the object language, the performance of our meta-programs, the overhead for writing meta-programs in our system and the soundness of our primitives.

Types and Guarantees Considering our example meta-programs $deriveShow$ and $assumptionTactic$, an important feature of our meta-programming approach is the strong guarantees that the meta-programs' types provide, modulo the soundness of our primitives. First, meta-programs are strongly type-safe: any object code they generate must be well-typed, since they are required to provide a proof of well-typedness to the interpretation primitive. Second, our meta-language Agda checks termination and completeness of pattern matches for all function definitions to guarantee that all functions are total. This guarantee also applies to our meta-programs, so that additionally we automatically get a totality guarantee for our meta-programs. However, this does not completely exclude the use of general recursion in tactics, techniques like Danielsson's partiality monad [16] can be used to model such algorithms.

The representation Meta-programming implies the syntactic analysis and construction of source code and/or types, and we have chosen a fairly well-understood representation to support this: a lambda calculus with de Bruijn indices and a standard separate encoding of typing judgements. However, many different encodings are equally possible, like those based on more advanced representations of binders [12]. It is future work to investigate the advantages that these alternatives might offer for our purposes. We also want to investigate merging $interpSet$ and $interp$, but we cannot currently try this for technical reasons. Finally, we currently represent typing judgements externally, i.e. as a property that can be true or not for an untyped lambda term. This corresponds to standard presentations of type theory, but it may be interesting to explore the benefits of an internal encoding like Danielsson, Chapman or McBride's [9, 15, 38] in our setting.

Performance We do not currently consider our implementation practical, because of performance reasons. For example, type-checking just the $deriveShow$ example for the type of natural numbers currently takes about 2 minutes and 3GB of memory on our system. Such performance likely prohibits all practical applications. However, we do not think this bad performance is inherent to our approach, but rather a consequence of the inefficient call-by-name execution strategy that Agda uses during type-checking. Remember how we previously defined $showNat$ using our $deriveShow$ function. As we mentioned, $showNat$ is definitionally equal to the generated program $showNat' = fold\mathbb{N}\ (\lambda\ \_ \rightarrow String)$ `"zero"` (...). Nevertheless, applying $showNat$ to the numbers 0 and 1 under Agda's evaluator (which is also used during type-checking) takes 2.5 resp. 11 minutes while for $showNat'$, it is instantaneous for numbers up to at least 100. For larger numbers, $showNat$ quickly runs out of memory.

This behaviour is a consequence of Agda's call-by-name evaluation strategy, which repeats the normalisation of $showNat$ for every reduction of $fold\mathbb{N}$. If Agda were to use a more efficient strategy like call-by-need, then the normalisation of $showNat$ to $showNat'$ would occur only once. Very likely, there is a lot more work being duplicated inside the normalisation of $showNat$ and we believe the call-by-name evaluation strategy is responsible for the long execution and type-checking times there as well.

Overhead Writing meta-programs in our approach entails a certain amount of programming overhead. The full code of our datatype-generic meta-programming application $deriveShow$ is ± 1200 lines of code (including the $SimpleDT$ encoding and some reusable parts). This is a lot more than what it would take to write a corresponding untyped meta-program. A significant part is the correctness proof of the meta-program (i.e. the proof that it generates correct code for all inputs).

However, a big part of our $deriveShow$ implementation consists of a rather tedious proof specific to our meta-programming primitives. It concerns the correspondence of a type in a context with a general predicate P of type $A \rightarrow String$, with the value $\lambda\ \_ \rightarrow String$ provided through the interpretation of this context and the same type with an encoding of $\lambda\ \_ \rightarrow String$ already filled in. We expect quite some work can be saved in this proof, but long compilation times have prevented further investigation. On the bright side, our assumption tactic is only about 50 lines in total, for a big part because it reuses general functions like the decision procedure for syntactic term equality. It is likely that additional reusable functions can reduce the meta-programming effort further. For example, a verified type-inference algorithm can be combined with our primitives to obviate the need for manual typing proofs in many cases.

Finally, we also expect that more experience with the definition of interpretation primitives could provide further opportunities to reduce meta-programming effort. For example, it would likely simplify some things to merge $interp$ and $interpSet$, but we currently cannot do so for technical reasons. Additionally, the *irrelevant arguments* [1] that Agda support offer the potential to make Agda understand that the type correctness proofs that our primitives require are only required to exist but do not influence their result value. We expect this could make a big difference for shortening tedious proofs like the one in our definition of $deriveShow$.

Soundness The soundness of our primitives remains an open question, at least if we consider the full version that does not have the unsound $\Gamma \vdash set : set$ rule that we discussed in Section 2. However, we do think there is a relation to the field of foundational logic that we will try to informally explain here. What we are essentially doing is reasoning about Agda terms within Agda itself. In foundational mathematical logic, Gödel's second incompleteness theorem has something to say about a similar situation for first-order logic [24]. An informal statement of the theorem (found on Wikipedia [54]) reads

Theorem 1 (Gödel's Second Incompleteness Theorem). *For any formal effectively generated theory T including basic arithmetical truths and also certain truths about formal provability, if T includes a statement of its own consistency then T is inconsistent.*

A standard proof of this theorem constructs a proposition T in the object theory such that T asserts the unprovability of its own Gödel-encoding. In vague terms, it can be proven that such a term exists as soon as the object language is powerful enough to reason about natural numbers. Such a term leads to a contradiction in combination with the self-consistency proof of the theory.

It is fair to assume the theorem can be generalised to type theory, and applied to our object theory, perhaps after adding singleton types, an empty type and a type of natural numbers. Consistency of a dependent type theory is equivalent with the existence of a closed term of type $\bot$. Using our primitives, it is not hard to construct a function of type $\forall\ \{t\} \rightarrow \varepsilon \vdash t : constant\ bot\ [\,] \rightarrow \bot$, which means that our meta-level primitives imply the consistency of our object theory. This begs the question whether Agda extended with our primitive must therefore necessarily be inconsistent, by the second incompleteness theorem, since it implies its own consistency. We conjecture that this implication is not there, for the reason that our object calculus does not contain the primitive itself, making it a fundamentally weaker theory. What we do is reminiscent of extending a first-order logical theory T with an axiom asserting T's consistency, to obtain a new theory T'. Such an extended theory T' does not in fact prove its own consistency, just that of T, so that the second incompleteness theorem does not apply. Another question that Gödel's result suggests is whether primitives like ours could in principle be implemented as normal functions within the bounds of a meta-language. Even with sufficient additional features like induction-recursion [22], this might not be possible as it would prove the language's own consistency within itself.

For these reasons, we expect that our primitives are not implementable in pure Agda but do not compromise consistency. Because of Gödel incompleteness, we think there are only two options to gain more confidence in them: either prove consistency of the extended calculus in a strictly stronger logical system such as Zermelo-Fraenkel set theory or implement our primitives in pure Agda, relying on axioms that are easier to trust than our primitives. A non-computational axiom asserting strong normalisation of the calculus (as used by Barras [4]) is a good candidate, but it isn't practical in our current implementation because Agda lacks a Prop universe like Coq's.

We think these logical aspects of our work deserve further attention. Nevertheless, even if our primitives were to be proven unsound, we do not think our work would be useless. Our application of interpretation primitives to meta-programming remains relevant as long as the primitives can be restricted to regain soundness. Also, in some applications of a dependently-typed language for programming (rather than proof checking), full certainty about soundness can be less important than powerful meta-programming support.

Staging As discussed in the introduction, our meta-programming primitives do not use the concept of staging like some other solutions [6, 11, 48, 52]. Nevertheless, our $interp$ primitive performs the same function as an unquote primitive in such systems, allowing object programs to invoke a meta-program and use generated code as if it were normal code. The quote primitive in a staging meta-programming system allows to include references to object-level terms in generated code, something which we support in a different way, as discussed in Section 3. Finally, while in these systems, code at all staging levels runs at either compile-time or run-time, but not both. In our system, the question of when to execute meta-programs is an orthogonal matter, not different from the *partial evaluation* of normal functions. Conveniently, partial evaluation is relatively cheap in total dependently-typed languages and for example well supported in the language Idris [7].

We see the orthogonality of our meta-programming primitives w.r.t. staging considerations as an advantage. If desired, it is technically possible to require at compile-time that all invocations of the primitives be unfoldable (producing errors if arguments are not statically known). However, like for partial evaluation, executing a meta-program upfront is not *always* a good idea, especially if we are already sure that the generated code will be well-typed (see e.g. Chlipala's arguments about the performance advantages of reflective meta-programs [14]). It seems that annotations for partial evaluation like in Idris would combine well with our primitives to conveniently let the programmer control when meta-programs are executed. For example, a version of $deriveShow$ with the $SimpleDT\ A$ argument annotated as $[static]$ would generate $show$ functions at compile time instead of run-time.

6. Related Work

In the literature, we find different forms of programming language support for meta-programming. We discuss them according to the guarantees that are provided about object programs.

Many approaches represent code in an untyped way, i.e. without guarantees that the represented source code is well-typed. These techniques have no way of providing strong type-safety of meta-programs, i.e. a guarantee that all the code a meta-program will ever produce is well-typed. In this category, we include approaches that represent code textually, like parser generators [29, 41], C macro's, eval primitives like JavaScript's [45], Java's pluggable annotation processors [19] (at least on the output side). Some approaches generate untyped bytecode [8]. Also in this category are macro approaches which receive and produce an untyped data structure representation of programs and types, like Template Haskell [48], Ltac proof tactics in Coq [20] and macro systems in Lisp-related languages (e.g. Racket [53]). Some provide specific language features for working with such representations. These systems provide the power of meta-programming at a comparatively low cost, but they make it hard to provide upfront guarantees of (strong) type-safety.

Not all meta-programming approaches are based on an explicit syntactic representation of terms or types. Some exploit type system features like Haskell type classes [33], Coq canonical structures [26] or C++ templates [2] to analyse types and produce code as part of the type inference process. These features provide (intentionally or not) a form of type-level computation with at least a notion of type analysis and structural recursion. Gonthier et al. even exploit canonical structures (non-trivially) to obtain a form of syntactic pattern matching and non-determinism with backtracking [26]. Meta-programming systems based on such primitives only support analysing types (but dependent types in Coq may contain terms). The computational model of these primitives is quite different from the underlying language's (unification-based vs. functional), so that meta-programming requires special expertise and techniques. For canonical structures, the computational model is not so well understood [27] and the resulting meta-programs are tightly coupled to the precise behaviour of the inferencer. An advantage of using primitives exposed by the type inferencer is that strong type-safety can be guaranteed comparatively easily [26, 33]. The type class instance search always terminates (with common extensions), but not so for C++ templates and Coq canonical structures. Completeness of pattern matching is not statically checked in any system. More or less in this category, we also have Chlipala's language Ur, which provides value-level folder functions for record types to support a practical form of meta-programming [13] with a form of syntactic analysis of record types, no explicit representation of object code and a functional computational model. Syntactic analysis of terms or general types is not supported.

Other approaches to meta-programming with strong type safety are based on explicit typed representations of code. This requires a powerful meta-language type system, as determined by the complexity of the object language and whether terms, types and typing contexts can all be syntactically constructed and analysed or only some of those. We discuss the related work according to the type system feature used in this representation.

Rudolph and Thiemann represent typed JVM bytecode generators in the Scala Mnemonics library [47], exploiting various features of Scala's type system. Taha and Sheard [52], Chen and Xi [11], Pašalić and Linger [42] and Sheard and Pašalić [49]'s systems are based on GADTs or explicit type equality proofs. Terms of a non-dependently-typed object language are syntactically represented as values of a data type indexed with the meta-level type of the term they represent. Without analysis of types, these techniques appear unsuitable for applications like proof tactics.

In VeriML, Stampoulis and Shao [50, 51] use a contextual type system, inspired by Beluga [43] and Delphin [44], in the meta-language to model a dependently-typed object language. They provide a syntactic model of terms and types, with a certain level of support for parameterising over and pattern matching on typing contexts. Nevertheless, contexts do not seem first class in VeriML's type system. For example, tactics cannot have contexts as their return type, so meta-programs cannot construct them, only start from the ones they receive and extend them locally. Stampoulis and Shao use an imperative meta-language with general recursion because certain tactics use algorithms that are inherently imperative. We agree that such tactics exist, but we do not see why they cannot be modelled in a pure and/or total functional setting like ours, using models like those found in the literature [16, 30, 32]. VeriML tactics are partial: they can fail or loop forever. This has modularity disadvantages: if a tactic t_1 invokes another tactic t_2, then t_1's author cannot be sure that t_2 will actually succeed when it is invoked at t_1's run-time. Stampoulis and Shao partially solve this with a `letstatic` staging construct that forces tactic t_2 to be evaluated at t_1's compile time instead. This works under certain restrictions on t_2's arguments. Because our tactics' types imply termination guarantees by default, we do not need such a system, while potential non-termination can still be modelled, e.g. using the non-termination monad [16]. Stampoulis and Shao link a proof assistant's type checker with custom tactics to obtain the effect of a sound user-extensible conversion rule in the logic [51], allowing a term t of type A to be used at type A' if the equality decision procedure (potentially a custom tactic) can find a proof that $A = A'$. This form of automatic triggering of tactics for solving constraints is interesting and could perhaps be combined with our work as well.

In a dependently-typed meta-language, it is possible to model non-dependent object languages with standard inductively-defined universes using the technique of reflection [5, 14]. Altenkirch and McBride [3] and Chapman et al. [10] provide syntactic models of data types, together with interpretation functions. Chapman et al.'s universe even describes itself as a data type. These authors do not consider syntactic models of terms or types that are not data types. Brady and Hammond [6] provide a universe that models a non-dependent object language. Terms, types as well as contexts are modelled and can be syntactically constructed and analysed.

This universe-based approach can be extended to dependently-typed object languages using the advanced type-theoretic concept of inductive-recursive definitions [22]. This has been studied by Danielsson [15], Chapman [9] and McBride [38]. These authors provide typed syntactic models of dependently-typed calculi in dependently-typed calculi, with different objectives than ours. Where we focus on the applicability of such a model in meta-programming primitives, they aim to prove properties of the modelled language in the meta-language. They use models based on advanced type-theory features like induction-recursion and mutual induction. All three authors use a model of the object calculus with terms indexed by encodings of their types, instead of an external typing judgement like ours. The models that they use are specifically tailored to enable proofs of deep properties like normalisation, and it is unclear if their models also fit our more practical objectives. Finally, these approaches generally try to stay within the limits of the features of an existing dependently typed language (albeit one with powerful features like inductive-recursive definitions). They try hard to fit their models and interpretation functions (more or less equivalent to the normalisation proof of the object language) in a known inductive-recursive schema, not fully successfully [9, 15]. McBride's encoding is accepted by Agda but he has to significantly limit the dependent nature of his object language [38]. As discussed in the introduction, our use of interpretation *primitives* allows us to side-step the interesting but hard problems that these authors tackle, leaving us free to study the application of related techniques to concrete meta-programming applications. It also allows us to use a more conventional encoding of the object language based on external typing judgements.

7. Conclusion

Our primitives present a novel meta-programming model with several desirable characteristics. Our meta-programs use the same functional style and well-understood computational model as normal programs. They can be given precise types that guarantee termination and strong type-safety. Finally, they can construct and analyse terms, types and typing contexts in a type-safe way. Our proof-of-concept applications in the two important application domains of datatype-generic programming and tactics, demonstrate the generality of our approach. Still, we feel this work is only a first exploration of a new approach to meta-programming. Quite some interesting questions remain to be answered in future work.

Acknowledgments

This research is partially funded by the Research Foundation - Flanders (FWO), and by the Research Fund KU Leuven. Dominique Devriese holds a Ph.D. fellowship of the Research Foundation - Flanders (FWO).

References

[1] A. Abel. Irrelevance in type theory with a heterogeneous equality judgement. In *Foundations of Software Science and Computational Structures*, volume 6604 of *Lecture Notes in Computer Science*, pages 57–71. Springer, 2011.

[2] D. Abrahams and A. Gurtovoy. *C++ template metaprogramming: Concepts, tools, and techniques from Boost and beyond*. Addison-Wesley, 2004.

[3] T. Altenkirch and C. McBride. Generic programming within dependently typed programming. In *IFIP TC2 Working Conference on Generic Programming, Schloss Dagstuhl*, pages 1–20. Kluwer, 2003.

[4] B. Barras and G. Huet. *Auto-validation d'un système de preuves avec familles inductives*. PhD thesis, Université de Paris 07, 1999.

[5] S. Boutin. Using reflection to build efficient and certified decision procedures. In *Theoretical Aspects of Computer Software*, volume 1281 of *Lecture Notes in Computer Science*, pages 515–529. Springer, 1997.

[6] E. Brady and K. Hammond. A verified staged interpreter is a verified compiler. In *Generative Programming and Component Engineering*, pages 111–120. ACM, 2006.

[7] E. C. Brady and K. Hammond. Scrapping your inefficient engine: using partial evaluation to improve domain-specific language implementation. In *International Conference on Functional Programming*, pages 297–308. ACM, 2010.

[8] E. Bruneton, R. Lenglet, and T. Coupaye. ASM: a code manipulation tool to implement adaptable systems. *Adaptable and extensible component systems*, 2002.

[9] J. Chapman. Type theory should eat itself. In *International Workshop on Logical Frameworks and Metalanguages: Theory and Practice*, volume 228 of *Electronic Notes in Theoretical Computer Science*, pages 21–36. Elsevier, 2009.

[10] J. Chapman, P.-E. Dagand, C. McBride, and P. Morris. The gentle art of levitation. In *International Conference on Functional Programming*, pages 3–14. ACM, 2010.

[11] C. Chen and H. Xi. Meta-programming through typeful code representation. In *International Conference on Functional Programming*, pages 275–286. ACM, 2003.

[12] A. Chlipala. Parametric higher-order abstract syntax for mechanized semantics. In *International Conference on Functional Programming*, pages 143–156. ACM, 2008.

[13] A. Chlipala. Ur: statically-typed metaprogramming with type-level record computation. In *Programming Languages Design and Implementation*, pages 122–133. ACM, 2010.

[14] A. Chlipala. Certified programming with dependent types. online 2012. URL `http://adam.chlipala.net/cpdt/`.

[15] N. A. Danielsson. A formalisation of a dependently typed language as an inductive-recursive family. In *Types for Proofs and Programs*, volume 4502 of *Lecture Notes in Computer Science*, pages 93–109. Springer, 2007.

[16] N. A. Danielsson. Operational semantics using the partiality monad. In *International Conference on Functional Programming*, pages 127–138. ACM, 2012.

[17] N. A. Danielsson and many others. The Agda standard library, 2009.

[18] N. A. Danielsson and U. Norell. Parsing mixfix operators. In *Implementation and Application of Functional Languages*, volume 5836 of *Lecture Notes in Computer Science*, pages 80–99. Springer, 2008.

[19] J. Darcy. JSR 269: Pluggable annotation processing API, 2011. URL `http://jcp.org/en/jsr/detail?id=269`.

[20] D. Delahaye. A tactic language for the system Coq. In *Logic Programming and Automated Reasoning*, volume 1955 of *Lecture Notes in Artificial Intelligence*, pages 85–95. Springer, 2000.

[21] P. Dybjer. Inductive families. *Formal Aspects of Computing*, 6(4) 440–465, 1994.

[22] P. Dybjer and A. Setzer. A finite axiomatization of inductive-recursive definitions. In *Typed Lambda Calculi and Applications*, volume 1581 of *Lecture Notes in Computer Science*, pages 129–146. Springer, 1999.

[23] S. Fogarty, E. Pasalic, J. Siek, and W. Taha. Concoqtion: indexed types now! In *Symposium on Partial Evaluation and Semantics-Based Program Manipulation*, pages 112–121. ACM, 2007.

[24] K. Gödel. Über formal unentscheidbare sätze der principia mathematica und verwandter systeme i. *Monatshefte für Mathematik*, 38(1) 173–198, 1931.

[25] H. Goguen, C. McBride, and J. McKinna. Eliminating dependent pattern matching. In *Algebra, Meaning, and Computation*, volume 4060 of *Lecture Notes in Computer Science*, pages 521–540. Springer, 2006.

[26] G. Gonthier, B. Ziliani, A. Nanevski, and D. Dreyer. How to make ad hoc proof automation less ad hoc. In *International Conference on Functional Programming*, pages 163–175. ACM, 2011.

[27] G. Gonthier, B. Ziliani, A. Nanevski, and D. Dreyer. How to make ad hoc proof automation less ad hoc. technical appendix, 2011. URL `http://www.mpi-sws.org/~beta/lessadhoc/appendix.pdf`.

[28] A. J. C. Hurkens. A simplification of Girard's paradox. In *Typed Lambda Calculi and Applications*, volume 902 of *Lecture Notes in Computer Science*, pages 266–278. Springer, 1995.

[29] S. C. Johnson. YACC. *UNIX Programmer's Manual*, 2b, 1979.

[30] O. Kiselyov, C.-c. Shan, D. P. Friedman, and A. Sabry. Backtracking, interleaving, and terminating monad transformers: (functional pearl). In *International Conference on Functional Programming*, pages 192–203. ACM, 2005.

[31] R. Lämmel and S. Peyton-Jones. Scrap your boilerplate: a practical design pattern for generic programming. In *Types in Languages Design and Implementation*, pages 26–37. ACM, 2003.

[32] J. Launchbury and S. Peyton Jones. Lazy functional state threads. In *Programming Languages Design and Implementation*, page 35. ACM, 1994.

[33] J. P. Magalhães, A. Dijkstra, J. Jeuring, and A. Löh. A generic deriving mechanism for Haskell. In *Haskell Symposium*, pages 37–48. ACM, 2010.

[34] G. Mainland and G. Morrisett. Nikola: embedding compiled GPU functions in Haskell. In *Haskell Symposium*, pages 67–78. ACM, 2010.

[35] S. Marlow. Haskell 2010 language report. online, 2010. URL `http://www.haskell.org/onlinereport/haskell2010/`.

[36] P. Martin-Löf. An intuitionistic theory of types. draft, 1972. URL `http://cs.ioc.ee/~james/ITT9200/martinlof72.ps`.

[37] C. McBride. Type-preserving renaming and substitution. draft, 2005. URL `http://strictlypositive.org/ren-sub.pdf`.

[38] C. McBride. Outrageous but meaningful coincidences: dependent type-safe syntax and evaluation. In *Workshop on Generic Programming*, pages 1–12. ACM, 2010.

[39] U. Norell. *Towards a practical programming language based on dependent type theory*. PhD thesis, Chalmers, 2007.

[40] Oracle. Java core reflection. online, 1996. URL `http://docs.oracle.com/javase/1.5.0/docs/guide/reflection/spec/java-reflectionTOC.doc.html`.

[41] T. Parr and R. Quong. ANTLR: A predicated-LL(k) parser generator. *Software: Practice and Experience*, 25(7):789–810, 1995.

[42] E. Pašalić and N. Linger. Meta-programming with typed object-language representations. In *Generative Programming and Component Engineering*, volume 3286 of *Lecture Notes in Computer Science*, pages 136–167. Springer, 2004.

[43] B. Pientka and J. Dunfield. Programming with proofs and explicit contexts. In *Principles and Practice of Declarative Programming*, pages 163–173. ACM, 2008.

[44] A. Poswolsky and C. Schürmann. Practical programming with higher-order encodings and dependent types. In *Programming Languages and Systems*, volume 4960 of *Lecture Notes in Computer Science*, pages 93–107. Springer, 2008.

[45] G. Richards, C. Hammer, B. Burg, and J. Vitek. The eval that men do. In *European Conference on Object-Oriented Programming*, volume 6813 of *Lecture Notes in Computer Science*, pages 52–78. Springer, 2011.

[46] A. Rodriguez, S. Holdermans, A. Löh, and J. Jeuring. Generic programming with fixed points for mutually recursive datatypes. In *International Conference on Functional Programming*, 2009.

[47] J. Rudolph and P. Thiemann. Mnemonics: type-safe bytecode generation at run time. *Higher-Order and Symbolic Computation*, 23(3): 371–407, 2010.

[48] T. Sheard and S. P. Jones. Template meta-programming for Haskell. In *Workshop on Haskell*, pages 1–16. ACM, 2002.

[49] T. Sheard and E. Pasalic. Meta-programming with built-in type equality. In *International Workshop on Logical Frameworks and Meta-Languages*, 2004.

[50] A. Stampoulis and Z. Shao. VeriML: typed computation of logical terms inside a language with effects. In *International Conference on Functional Programming*, pages 333–344. ACM, 2010.

[51] A. Stampoulis and Z. Shao. Static and user-extensible proof checking. In *Principles of Programming Languages*, pages 273–284. ACM, 2012.

[52] W. Taha and T. Sheard. MetaML and multi-stage programming with explicit annotations. *Theoretical Computer Science*, 248(1-2):211–242, 2000.

[53] S. Tobin-Hochstadt, V. St-Amour, R. Culpepper, M. Flatt, and M. Felleisen. Languages as libraries. In *Programming Languages Design and Implementation*, pages 132–141. ACM, 2011.

[54] Wikipedia. Gödel's incompleteness theorems, November 2012. URL `http://en.wikipedia.org/wiki/Goedels_incompleteness_theorems`.

Mtac: A Monad for Typed Tactic Programming in Coq

Beta Ziliani
MPI-SWS
beta@mpi-sws.org

Derek Dreyer
MPI-SWS
dreyer@mpi-sws.org

Neelakantan R. Krishnaswami
MPI-SWS
neelk@mpi-sws.org

Aleksandar Nanevski
IMDEA Software Institute
aleks.nanevski@imdea.org

Viktor Vafeiadis
MPI-SWS
viktor@mpi-sws.org

Abstract

Effective support for custom proof automation is essential for large-scale interactive proof development. However, existing languages for automation via *tactics* either (a) provide no way to specify the behavior of tactics within the base logic of the accompanying theorem prover, or (b) rely on advanced type-theoretic machinery that is not easily integrated into established theorem provers.

We present Mtac, a lightweight but powerful extension to Coq that supports dependently-typed tactic programming. Mtac tactics have access to all the features of ordinary Coq programming, as well as a new set of typed tactical primitives. We avoid the need to touch the trusted kernel typechecker of Coq by encapsulating uses of these new tactical primitives in a *monad*, and instrumenting Coq so that it executes monadic tactics during type inference.

Categories and Subject Descriptors D.3.3 [*Programming Languages*]: Language Constructs and Features—Data types and structures; F.3.1 [*Logics and Meanings of Programs*]: Specifying and Verifying and Reasoning about Programs—Mechanical verification

Keywords Interactive theorem proving; custom proof automation; Coq; monads; typed meta-programming; tactics.

1. Introduction

The past decade has seen a dramatic rise in both the popularity and sophistication of interactive theorem proving technology. Proof assistants like Coq and Isabelle are now eminently effective for formalizing "research-grade" mathematics [8, 9], verifying serious software systems [15, 16, 32, 6], and, more broadly, enabling researchers to mechanize and breed confidence in their results. Nevertheless, due to the challenging nature of the verification problems to which these tools are applied, as well as the rich higher-order logics they employ, the mechanization of substantial proofs typically requires a significant amount of manual effort.

To alleviate this burden, theorem provers provide facilities for *custom proof automation*, enabling users to instruct the system how to carry out "obvious" or oft-repeated proof steps automatically. In some systems like Coq, the base logic of the theorem prover is powerful enough that one can use "proof by reflection" to implement automation routines within the base logic itself (*e.g.*, [3]). However, this approach is applicable only to pure decision procedures, and requires them to be programmed in a restricted style (so that their totality is self-evident). In general, one may wish to write automation routines that engage in activities that even a rich type system like Coq's does not sanction—routines, for instance, that do not (provably) terminate on all inputs, that inspect the intensional syntactic structure of terms, or that employ computational effects.

Toward this end, theorem provers typically provide an additional language for *tactic* programming. Tactics support general-purpose scripting of automation routines, as well as fine control over the state of an interactive proof. However, for most existing tactic languages (*e.g.*, ML, Ltac), the price to pay for this freedom is that the behavior of a tactic lacks any static specification within the base logic of the theorem prover (such as, in Coq, a type). As a result of being untyped, tactics are known to be difficult to compose, debug, and maintain.

A number of researchers have therefore explored ways of supporting *typed* tactic programming. One approach, exemplified by Delphin [23], Beluga [21], and most recently VeriML [29], is to keep a strict separation between the "computational" tactic language and the base logic of the theorem prover, thus maintaining flexibility in what tactics can do, but in addition employing rich type systems to encode strong static guarantees about tactic behavior. The main downside of these systems is a pragmatic one: they are not programmable or usable interactively, and due to the advanced type-theoretic machinery they rely on—*e.g.*, for Beluga and VeriML, *contextual modal type theory* [20]—it is not clear how to incorporate them into established interactive theorem provers.

A rather different approach, proposed by Gonthier *et al.* [11] specifically in the context of Coq, is to encapsulate automation routines as *overloaded lemmas*. Like an ordinary lemma, an overloaded lemma has a precise formal specification in the form of a (dependent) Coq type. The key difference is that an overloaded lemma—much like an overloaded function in Haskell—is not proven (*i.e.*, implemented) once and for all up front; instead, every time the lemma is applied to a particular goal, the system will run a user-specified automation routine in order to construct a proof on the fly for that particular instance of the lemma. To program the automation routine, one uses Coq's "canonical structure" mechanism to declare a set of proof-building rules—implemented as Coq terms—that will be fired in a predictable order by the Coq unification algorithm (but may or may not succeed). In effect, one encodes one's automation routine as a *dependently-typed logic program* to be executed by Coq's type inference engine.

The major benefit of this approach is its integration into Coq: it enables users to program tactics in Coq directly, rather than in a

ICFP '13, September 25–27, 2013, Boston, MA, USA.
Copyright is held by the owner/author(s). Publication rights licensed to ACM.
ACM 978-1-4503-2326-0/13/09... $15.00.
http://dx.doi.org/10.1145/2500365.2500579

separate language, while at the same time offering significant additional expressive power beyond what is available in the base logic of Coq. The downside, however, is that the logic-programming style of canonical structures is in most cases not as natural a fit for tactics as a *functional-programming* style would be.[1] Moreover, canonical structures provide a relatively low-level language for writing tactics. The control flow of sophisticated canonical structure programs depends closely on how Coq type inference is implemented, and thus writing even simple tactics requires one to think at the level of the Coq unification algorithm, sometimes embracing its limitations and sometimes working around them. To make up for this, Gonthier *et al.* [11] describe a series of "design patterns" for programming canonical structures effectively. While these design patterns are clearly useful, the desire for them nonetheless suggests that there is a *high-level language* waiting to be born.

1.1 Mtac: A Monad for Typed Tactic Programming in Coq

In this paper, we present a new language—**Mtac**—for typed tactic programming in Coq. Like Beluga and VeriML, Mtac supports general-purpose tactic programming in a direct functional style. Unlike those languages, however, Mtac is not a separate language, but rather a simple extension to Coq. As a result, Mtac tactics (or as we call them, **Mtactics**) have access to all the features of ordinary Coq programming *in addition to* a new set of tactical primitives. Furthermore, like overloaded lemmas, their (partial) correctness is specified statically within the Coq type system itself, and they are fully integrated into Coq, so they can be programmed and used interactively. Mtac is thus, to our knowledge, the first language to support interactive, dependently-typed tactic programming.

The key idea behind Mtac is dead simple. We encapsulate tactics in a *monad*, thus avoiding the need to change the base logic and trusted kernel typechecker of Coq *at all*. Then, we modify the Coq infrastructure so that it executes these monadic tactics, when requested to do so, *during* type inference (*i.e.*, during interactive proof development or when executing a proof script).

More concretely, Mtac extends Coq with:

1. An inductive type family $\bigcirc A$ (read as "maybe A") classifying Mtactics that—if they terminate successfully—will produce Coq terms of type A. The constructors of this type family essentially give the syntax for a monadically-typed tactic language: they include the usual monadic return and bind, as well as a suite of combinators for tactic programming with fixed points, exception handling, pattern matching, and more. (Note: the definition of the type family $\bigcirc A$ does not *per se* require any extension to Coq—it is just an ordinary inductive type family.)
2. A primitive *tactic execution* construct, **run** t, which has type A assuming its argument t is a tactic of type $\bigcirc A$. When (our instrumentation of) the Coq type inference engine encounters **run** t, it executes the tactic t. If that execution terminates, it will either produce a term u of type A (in which case Coq will rewrite **run** t to u) or else an uncaught exception (which Coq will report to the user). If a proof passes entirely through type inference without incurring any uncaught exceptions, that means that all instances of **run** in the proof must have been replaced with standard Coq terms. Hence, there is no need to extend the trusted kernel typechecker of Coq to handle **run**.

Example: Searching in a List. To get a quick sense of what Mtac programming is like, consider the example in Figure 1. Here, search is a tactical term of type $\forall x : A.\ \forall s :$ list $A.\ \bigcirc(x \in s)$. When executed, search x s will search for an element x (of type A) in a list s (of type list A), and if it finds x in s, it will return a proof that $x \in s$. Note, however, that search x s itself is just a Coq term of monadic type $\bigcirc(x \in s)$, and that the execution of the tactic will only occur when this term is **run**.

```
01 Definition search (x : A) :=
02   mfix f [s : list A] :=
03   mmatch s as s' return ○(x ∈ s') with
04   | [l r] l ++ r ⇒
05     mtry
06       il ← f l;
07       ret (in_or_app l r x (or_introl il))
08     with _ ⇒
09       ir ← f r;
10       ret (in_or_app l r x (or_intror ir))
11     end
12   | [s'] (x :: s') ⇒ ret (in_eq _ _)
13   | [y s'] (y :: s') ⇒
14     r ← f s';
15     ret (in_cons y r)
16   | _ ⇒ raise NotFound
17   end.
```

Figure 1. Mtactic for searching in a list.

The implementation of search relies on four new features of Mtac that go beyond what is possible in ordinary Coq programming: it iterates using a potentially unbounded fixed point **mfix** (line 2), it case-analyzes the input list s using a new **mmatch** constructor (line 3), it **raise**-s an exception NotFound if the element x was not found (line 16), and this exception is caught and handled (for backtracking purposes) using **mtry** (line 5). These new features, which we will present in detail in §2, are all constructors of the inductive type family $\bigcirc A$. Regarding **mmatch**, the reason it is different from ordinary Coq **match** is that it supports pattern-matching not only against primitive datatype constructors (*e.g.*, nil and ::) but also against arbitrary terms (*e.g.*, applications of the ++ function for concatenating two lists). For example, search starts out (line 4) by checking whether s is an application of ++ to two subterms l and r. If so, it searches for x first in l and then in r. In this way, **mmatch** supports case analysis of the intensional syntactic structure of open terms, in the manner of VeriML's **holcase** [29] and Beluga's **case** [21].

By **run**-ning search, we can now, for example, very easily prove the following lemma establishing that z is in the list $[x; y; z]$:

Lemma z_in_xyz $(x\ y\ z : A) : z \in [x; y; z]$:= **run** (search _ _)

Note here that we did not even need to supply the inputs to search explicitly: they were picked up from context, namely the goal of the lemma ($z \in [x; y; z]$), which Coq type inference proceeds to unify with the output type of the Mtactic search.

1.2 Contributions and Overview

In the remainder of this paper, we will:

- Describe the design of Mtac in detail (§2).
- Give a number of examples to concretely illustrate the benefits of Mtac programming (§3).
- Present the formalization of Mtac, along with meta-theoretic results such as type safety (§4).
- Explore some technical issues regarding the integration of Mtac into Coq (§5).
- Compare with related work and discuss future work (§6).

The Coq patch and the examples can be downloaded from:

`http://plv.mpi-sws.org/mtac`

[1] In terms of expressivity, there are tradeoffs between the two styles—for further discussion, see §6.

$\bigcirc$	: Type $\to$ Prop
ret	: $\forall A.\ A \to \bigcirc A$
bind	: $\forall A\ B.\ \bigcirc A \to (A \to \bigcirc B) \to \bigcirc B$
raise	: $\forall A.$ Exception $\to \bigcirc A$
mtry	: $\forall A.\ \bigcirc A \to$ (Exception $\to \bigcirc A) \to \bigcirc A$
mfix	: $\forall A\ B.\ ((\forall x : A.\ \bigcirc(B\ x)) \to (\forall x : A.\ \bigcirc(B\ x))) \to \forall x : A.\ \bigcirc(B\ x)$
mmatch	: $\forall A\ B\ (t : A).$ list (Patt $A\ B) \to \bigcirc(B\ t)$
print	: $\forall s :$ string. $\bigcirc$unit
nu	: $\forall A\ B.\ (A \to \bigcirc B) \to \bigcirc B$
abs	: $\forall A\ P\ x.\ P\ x \to \bigcirc(\forall y : A.\ P\ y)$
is_var	: $\forall A.\ A \to \bigcirc$bool
evar	: $\forall A.\ \bigcirc A$
is_evar	: $\forall A.\ A \to \bigcirc$bool
Patt	: $\forall A\ (B : A \to$ Type). Type
Pbase	: $\forall A\ B\ (p : A)\ (b : \bigcirc(B\ p)).$ Patt $A\ B$
Ptele	: $\forall A\ B\ C.\ (\forall x : C.$ Patt $A\ B) \to$ Patt $A\ B$

Figure 2. The $\bigcirc$ and Patt inductive types.

2. Mtac: A Language for Proof Automation

In this section, we describe the syntax and typing of Mtac, our language for typed proof automation.

Syntax of Mtac. Mtac extends CIC, the Calculus of (co-)Inductive Constructions (see *e.g.*, [2]), with a monadic type constructor $\bigcirc A$, representing tactic computations returning results of type A, along with suitable introduction and elimination forms for such computations. We define $\bigcirc$: Type $\to$ Prop as a normal CIC inductive predicate with constructors reflecting our syntax for tactic programming, which are shown in Fig. 2. (We prefer to define $\bigcirc$ inductively instead of axiomatizing it in order to cheaply ensure that we do not affect the logical consistency of CIC.) The $\bigcirc$ constructors include standard monadic return and bind (**ret**, **bind**), primitives for throwing and handling exceptions (**raise**, **mtry**), a fixed point combinator (**mfix**), a pattern matching construct (**mmatch**), and a printing primitive useful for debugging Mtactics (**print**). Mtac also provides more specialized operations for handling parameters and unification variables (**nu**, **abs**, **is_var**, **evar**, **is_evar**), but we defer explanation of those features until §3.2.

First, let us clear up a somewhat technical point. The reason we define $\bigcirc$ as an inductive *predicate* (*i.e.*, whose return sort is Prop rather than Type) has to do with the handling of **mfix**. Specifically, in order to satisfy Coq's syntactic positivity condition on inductive definitions, we cannot declare **mfix** directly with the type given in Figure 2, since that type mentions the monadic type constructor $\bigcirc$ in a negative position. To work around this, in the inductive definition of $\bigcirc A$, we replace the **mfix** constructor with a variant, **mfix**$'$, in "Mendler style" [17, 14], *i.e.*, in which references to $\bigcirc$ are substituted with references to a *parameter* $\odot$:

$$\textbf{mfix}' : \forall A\ B\ \odot.\ (\forall x : A.\ \odot(B\ x) \to \bigcirc(B\ x)) \to ((\forall x{:}A.\ \odot(B\ x)) \to (\forall x{:}A.\ \odot(B\ x))) \to \forall x{:}A.\ \bigcirc(B\ x)$$

The **mfix** from Figure 2 is then recovered simply by instantiating the $\odot$ parameter of **mfix**$'$ with $\bigcirc$, and instantiating its first value parameter with the identity function. However, due to the inherent "circularity" of this trick, it only works if the type $\bigcirc A$ belongs to an impredicative sort like Prop. (In particular, if $\bigcirc A$ were defined in Type, then while **mfix**$'$ would be well-formed, applying **mfix**$'$ to the identity function in order to get an **mfix** would cause a universe inconsistency.) Fortunately, defining $\bigcirc A$ in Prop has no practical impact on Mtac programming. Note that, in CIC, Prop : Type; so it is possible to construct nested types such as $\bigcirc(\bigcirc A)$.

Now, onto the features of Mtac. The typing of monadic **ret** and **bind** is self-explanatory. The exception constructs **raise** and **mtry** are also straightforward: their types assume the existence of an exception type Exception. It is easy to define such a type, as well as a way of declaring new exceptions of that type, in existing Coq (see §5 for details). The print statement **print** takes the string to print onto the standard output and returns the trivial element.

Pattern matching, **mmatch**, expects a term of type A and a sequence of pattern matching clauses of type Patt $A\ B$, which match objects x of type A and return results of type $B\ x$. Binding in the pattern matching clauses is represented as a *telescope*: Pbase p b describes a ground clause that matches the constant p and has body b, and Ptele($\lambda x.\ pc$) adds the binder x to the pattern matching clause pc. So, for example, Ptele($\lambda x.$ Ptele($\lambda y.$ Pbase $(x + y)\ b$) represents the clause that matches an addition expression, binds the left subexpression to x and the right one to y, and then returns some expression b which can mention both x and y. Another example is the clause, Ptele($\lambda x.$ Pbase $x\ b$) which matches any term and returns b.

Note that it is also fine for a pattern to mention free variables bound in the ambient environment (*i.e.*, not bound by the telescope pattern). Such patterns enable one to check that (some component of) the term being pattern-matched is syntactically unifiable with a specific term of interest. We will see examples of this in the search2 and lookup Mtactics in §3.

In our examples and in our Coq development, we often omit inferrable type annotations and use the following notation to improve readability of Mtactics:

$x \leftarrow t; t'$	denotes	**bind** $t\ (\lambda x.\ t')$
mfix $f\ [x : A] := t$	denotes	**mfix** $(\lambda f.\ \lambda x.\ t)$
$\nu x : A.\ t$	denotes	**nu** $(\lambda x : A.\ t)$
mmatch t **as** x **return** $\bigcirc T$ **with** $\mid [\overline{x_1}]\ p_1 \Rightarrow b_1$ ... $\mid [\overline{x_m}]\ p_m \Rightarrow b_m$ **end**	denotes	**mmatch** $(\lambda x.\ T)\ t$ [Ptele $\overline{x_1}$ (Pbase $p_1\ b_1$), ... Ptele $\overline{x_m}$ (Pbase $p_m\ b_m$)]
mtry t **with** ps **end**	denotes	**mtry** $t\ (\lambda e.$ **mmatch** e **with** ps **end**)

where Ptele $x_1 \cdots x_n\ p$ means Ptele($\lambda x_1 \ldots$ Ptele($\lambda x_n.\ p) \cdots$). The type annotation **as** x **return** $\bigcirc T$ in the **mmatch** notation is optional and can be omitted, in which case the returning type is left to the type inference algorithm to infer.

Running Mtactics. Defining $\bigcirc$ as an inductive predicate means that terms of type $\bigcirc A$ can be destructed by case analysis and induction. Unlike other inductive types, $\bigcirc$ supports an additional destructor: *tactic execution*. Formally, we extend Coq with a new construct, **run** t, that takes an Mtactic t of type $\bigcirc A$ (for some A), and runs it *at type-inference time* to return a term t' of type A.

$$\frac{\Gamma \vdash t : \bigcirc A \qquad \Gamma \vdash t \leadsto^* \textbf{ret}\ t'}{\Gamma \vdash \textbf{run}\ t : A}$$

We postpone the definition of the tactic evaluation relation, $\leadsto$, as well as a precise formulation of the rule, to §4, but note that since tactic evaluation is type-preserving, t' has type A, and thus A is inhabited.

3. Mtac by Example

In this section, we offer a gentle introduction to the various features of Mtac by working through a sequence of proof automation examples.

3.1 noalias: Non-Aliasing of Disjointly Allocated Pointers

Our first example, noalias, is taken from Gonthier *et al.* [11]. The goal is to prove that two pointers are distinct, given the assumption that they appear in the domains of disjoint subheaps of a well-defined memory.

In [11], the noalias example was used to illustrate a rather subtle and sophisticated design pattern for composition of overloaded lemmas. Here, it will help illustrate the main characteristics of Mtac, while at the same time emphasizing the relative simplicity and readability of Mtactics compared to previous approaches.

Preliminaries. We will work here with heaps (of type heap), which are finite maps from pointers (of type ptr) to values. We write $h_1 \bullet h_2$ for the disjoint union of h_1 and h_2, and $x \mapsto v$ for the singleton heap containing only the pointer x, storing the value v. The disjoint union may be undefined if h_1 and h_2 overlap, so we employ a predicate def h, which declares that h is in fact defined.

Motivating Example. With these definitions in hand, let us state a goal we would like to solve automatically:

$$\frac{D\ :\ \mathsf{def}\ (h_1 \bullet (x_1 \mapsto v_1 \bullet x_2 \mapsto v_2) \bullet (h_2 \bullet x_3 \mapsto v_3))}{x_1\ \mathtt{!=}\ x_2 \wedge x_2\ \mathtt{!=}\ x_3}$$

Above the line is a hypothesis concerning the well-definedness of a heap mentioning x_1, x_2, and x_3, and below the line is the goal, which is to show that x_1 is distinct from x_2, and x_2 from x_3.

Intuitively, the truth of the goal follows obviously from the fact that x_1, x_2, and x_3 appear in disjoint subheaps of a well-defined heap. This intuition is made formal with the following lemma (in plain Coq):

$$\mathsf{noalias\_manual} : \forall (h{:}\mathsf{heap})\ (y_1\ y_2{:}\mathsf{ptr})\ (w_1{:}A_1)\ (w_2{:}A_2).\\ \mathsf{def}\ (y_1 \mapsto w_1 \bullet y_2 \mapsto w_2 \bullet h) \rightarrow y_1\ \mathtt{!=}\ y_2$$

Unfortunately, we cannot apply this lemma using hypothesis D as it stands, since the heap that D proves to be well-defined is not of the form required by the premise of the lemma—that is, with the pointers in question (x_1 and x_2, or x_2 and x_3) at the very *front* of the heap expression. It is of course possible to solve the goal by: (a) repeatedly applying rules of associativity and commutativity for heap expressions in order to rearrange the heap in the type of D so that the relevant pointers are at the front of the heap expression; (b) applying the noalias_manual lemma to solve the first inequality; and then repeating (a) and (b) to solve the second inequality.

But we would like to do better. What we really want is an Mtactic that will solve these kinds of goals automatically, no matter where the pointers we care about are located inside the heap. One option is to write an Mtactic to perform all the rearrangements necessary to put the two pointers at the front, and then apply the lemma above. The main inconvenience with this approach is that each inequality in the goal requires a new rearrangement of the heap, where each pointer has to be found and then "bubbled up" to the front of the heap. Computationally, this takes twice the size of the heap for each pointer.

Instead, we pursue a solution analogous to the one in [11], breaking the problem into two smaller Mtactics scan and search2, combined in a third Mtactic, noalias.

***The Mtactic* scan.** Figure 3 presents the Mtactic scan. It scans its input heap h to produce a list of the pointers x appearing in singleton heaps $x \mapsto v$ in h. More specifically, it returns a dependent record containing a list of pointers (seq_of, of type list ptr), together with a proof that, if h is well-defined, then (1) the list seq_of is "unique" (denoted uniq seq_of), meaning that all elements in it are distinct from one another, and (2) its elements all belong to the domain of the heap.

To do this, scan inspects the heap and considers three different cases. If the heap is a singleton heap $x \mapsto v$, then it returns a

```
Record form h := Form {
        seq_of :> list ptr;
        axiom_of : def h → uniq seq_of
                         ∧ ∀ x. x ∈ seq_of → x ∈ dom h }.

Definition scan :=
  mfix f [h : heap] : ○(form h) :=
    mmatch h with
    | [x A (v:A)] x ↦ v ⇒ ret (Form [x] ...)
    | [l r] l • r ⇒
        rl ← f l;
        rr ← f r;
        ret (Form (seq_of rl ++ seq_of rr) ...)
    | [h'] h' ⇒ ret (scan_h [] ...)
    end.
```

Figure 3. Mtactic for scanning a heap to obtain a list of pointers.

```
Definition search2 x y :=
  mfix f [s] : ○(uniq s → x != y) :=
    mmatch s with
    | [s'] x :: s' ⇒ r ← search y s'; ret (foundx_pf x r)
    | [s'] y :: s' ⇒ r ← search x s'; ret (foundy_pf y r)
    | [z s'] z :: s' ⇒ r ← f s'; ret (foundz_pf z r)
    | _ ⇒ raise NotFound
    end.
```

Figure 4. Mtactic for searching for two pointers in a list.

singleton list containing x. If the heap is the disjoint union of heaps l and r, it proceeds recursively on each subheap and returns the concatenation of the lists obtained in the recursive calls. Finally, if the heap doesn't match any of the previous cases, then it returns an empty list. Note that this case analysis is not possible using Coq's standard **match** mechanism, because **match** only pattern-matches against primitive datatype constructors. In the case of heaps, which are really finite maps from pointers to values, $x \mapsto v$ and $l \bullet r$ are applications not of primitive datatype constructors but of defined functions ($\mapsto$ and $\bullet$). Thus, in order to perform our desired case analysis, we require the ability of Mtac's **mmatch** mechanism to pattern-match against the *syntax* of heap expressions.

In each case, scan also returns a proof that the output list obeys the aforementioned properties (1) and (2). For presentation purposes, we omit these proofs (denoted with ... in the figures), but they are proven as standard Coq lemmas. (We will continue to omit proofs in this way throughout the paper when they present no interesting challenges. The reader can find them in the source files.)

***The Mtactic* search2.** Figure 4 presents the Mtactic search2. It takes two elements x and y and a list s as input, and searches for x and y in s. If successful, search2 returns a proof that, if s is unique, then x is distinct from y. Similarly to scan, this involves a syntactic inspection and case analysis of the input list s.

When s contains x at the head (*i.e.*, s is of the form $x :: s'$), search2 searches for y in the tail s', using the Mtactic search from §1.1. If this search is successful, producing a proof $r : y \in s'$, then search2 concludes by composing this proof together with the assumption that s is unique, using the easy lemma foundx_pf:

$$\mathsf{foundx\_pf} : \forall x\ y : \mathsf{ptr}.\ \forall s : \mathsf{list\ ptr}.\\ y \in s \rightarrow \mathsf{uniq}\ (x :: s)\ \rightarrow x\ \mathtt{!=}\ y$$

(In the code, the reader will notice that foundx_pf is not passed the arguments y and s explicitly. That is because they are inferrable from the type of r, and thus are treated as implicit arguments.)

```
Definition noalias h (D : def h) : ○(∀ x y. ○(x != y)) :=
  sc ← scan h;
  ret (λ x y ⇒
    s2 ← search2 x y (seq_of sc);
    ret (combine s2 D)).
```

Figure 5. Mtactic for proving that two pointers do not alias.

If s contains y at the head, search2 proceeds analogously. If the head element is different from both x and y, then it calls itself recursively with the tail. In any other case, it throws an exception.

Note that, in order to test whether the head of s is x or y, we rely crucially on the ability of patterns to mention free variables from the context. In particular, the difference between the first two cases of search2's **mmatch** and the last one is that the first two do *not* bind x and y in their telescope patterns (thus requiring the head of the list in those cases to be syntactically unifiable with x or y, respectively), while the third *does* bind z in its telescope pattern (thus enabling z to match anything).

***The Mtactic* noalias.** Figure 5 shows the very short code for the Mtactic noalias, which stitches scan and search2 together. The type of noalias is as follows:

$$\forall h : \mathsf{heap}.\ \mathsf{def}\ h \rightarrow \bigcirc(\forall x\ y.\ \bigcirc(x\ \mathtt{!=}\ y))$$

As the two occurrences of $\bigcirc$ indicate, this Mtactic is *staged*: it takes as input a proof that h is defined and first runs the scan Mtactic on h, producing a list of pointers sc, but then it immediately returns *another* Mtactic. This latter Mtactic in turn takes as input x and y and searches for them in sc. The reason for this staging is that we may wish to prove non-aliasing facts about different pairs of pointers in the same heap. Thanks to staging, we can apply noalias to some D just once and then reuse the Mtactic it returns on many different pairs of pointers, thus avoiding the need to rescan h redundantly.

At the end, the proofs returned by the calls to scan and search2 are composed using a combine lemma with the following type:

```
Lemma combine h x y (sc : form h) :
  (uniq (seq_of sc) → x != y) → def h → x != y.
```

This lemma is trivial to prove by an application of the cut rule.

***Applying the Mtactic* noalias.** The following script shows how noalias can be invoked in order to solve the motivating example from the beginning of this section:

```
pose F := run (noalias D)
by split; apply: run (F _ _)
```

When Coq performs type inference on the **run** in the first line, that forces the execution of (the first scan-ning phase of) the Mtactic noalias on the input hypothesis D, and the standard pose mechanism then binds the result to F. This F has the type

$$\forall x\ y : \mathsf{ptr}.\ \bigcirc(x\ \mathtt{!=}\ y)$$

In the case of our motivating example, F will be an Mtactic that, when passed inputs x and y, will search for those pointers in the list $[x_1; x_2; x_3]$ output by the scan phase.

The script continues with Coq's standard split tactic, which generates two subgoals, one for each proposition in the conjunction. For our motivating example, it generates subgoals x_1 != x_2 and x_2 != x_3. We then solve both goals by executing the Mtactic F. When F is **run** to solve the first subgoal, it will search for x_1 and x_2 in $[x_1; x_2; x_3]$ and succeed; when F is **run** to solve the second subgoal, it will search for x_2 and x_3 in $[x_1; x_2; x_3]$ and succeed. QED. Note that we provide the arguments to F *implicitly* (as _). As in the proof of the z_in_xyz lemma from §1.1, these arguments are

```
Program Definition interactive_search2 x y :=
  mfix f [s] : ○(uniq s → x != y) :=
    mmatch s with
    | [s'] x :: s' ⇒ r ← search y s'; ret _
    | [s'] y :: s' ⇒ r ← search x s'; ret _
    | [z s'] z :: s' ⇒ r ← f s'; ret _
    | _ ⇒ raise NotFound
    end.
Next Obligation. ... Qed.
Next Obligation. ... Qed.
Next Obligation. ... Qed.
```

Figure 6. Interactive construction of search2 using **Program**.

inferred from the respective goals being solved. (We will explain how this inference works in more detail in §5.)

Developing Mtactics Interactively. One key advantage of Mtac is that it works very well with the rest of Coq, allowing us among other things to develop Mtactics interactively.

For instance, consider the code shown in Figure 6. This is an interactive development of the search2 Mtactic, where the developer knows the overall search structure in advance, but not the exact proof terms to be returned, as this can be difficult in general. Here, we have prefixed the definition with the keyword **Program** [27], which allows us to omit certain parts of the definition by writing underscores. **Program** instructs the type inference mechanism to treat these underscores as unification variables, which—unless instantiated during type inference—are exposed as proof obligations. In our case, none of these underscores is resolved, and so we are left with three proof obligations. Each of these obligations can then be solved interactively within a **Next Obligation** ... **Qed** block.

Finally, it is worth pointing out that within such blocks, as well as within the actual definitions of Mtactics, we could be running other more primitive Mtactics.

3.2 tauto: A Simple First-Order Tautology Prover

With this next example, we show how Mtac provides a simple but useful way to write tactics that manipulate contexts and binders. Specifically, we will write an Mtactic implementing a rudimentary tautology prover, modeled after those found in the work on VeriML [29] and Chlipala's CPDT textbook [5]. Compared to VeriML, our approach has the benefit that it does not require any special type-theoretic treatment of contexts: for us, a context is nothing more than a Coq list. Compared to Chlipala's Ltac version, our version is typed, offering a clear static specification of what the tautology prover produces, if it succeeds.

To ease the presentation, we break the problem in two. First, we show a simple propositional prover that uses the language constructs we have presented so far. Second, we extend this prover to handle first-order logic, and we use this extension to motivate some additional features of Mtac.

Warming up the Engine: A Simple Propositional Prover. Figure 7 displays the Mtactic for a simple propositional prover, taking as input a proposition p and, if successful, returning a proof of p:

$$\mathsf{prop\text{-}tauto} : \forall p : \mathsf{Prop}.\ \bigcirc p$$

The Mtactic only considers three cases:

- p is True. In this case, it returns the trivial proof I.
- p is a conjunction of p_1 and p_2. In this case, it proves both propositions and returns the introduction form of the conjunction (conj r_1 r_2).
- p is a disjunction of p_1 and p_2. In this case, it tries to prove the proposition p_1, and if that fails, it tries instead to prove

```
Definition prop-tauto :=
  mfix f [p : Prop] : ○p :=
    mmatch p as p' return ○p' with
    | True ⇒ ret I
    | [p1 p2] p1 ∧ p2 ⇒
          r1 ← f p1;
          r2 ← f p2;
          ret (conj r1 r2)
    | [p1 p2] p1 ∨ p2 ⇒
          mtry
            r1 ← f p1; ret (or_introl r1)
          with _ ⇒
            r2 ← f p2; ret (or_intror r2)
          end
    | _ ⇒ raise NotFound
    end.
```

Figure 7. Mtactic for a simple propositional tautology prover.

```
01  Definition tauto' :=
02    mfix f [c : list dyn; p : Prop] : ○p :=
03      mmatch p as p' return ○p' with
04      | True ⇒ ret I
05      | [p1 p2] p1 ∧ p2 ⇒
06            r1 ← f c p1 ;
07            r2 ← f c p2 ;
08            ret (conj r1 r2)
09      | [p1 p2] p1 ∨ p2 ⇒
10            mtry
11              r1 ← f c p1 ; ret (or_introl r1)
12            with _ ⇒
13              r2 ← f c p2 ; ret (or_intror r2)
14            end
15      | [p1 p2 : Prop] p1 → p2 ⇒
16            ν (y:p1).
17              r ← f (Dyn p1 y :: c) p2;
18              abs y r
19      | [A (q:A → Prop)] (∀ x:A. q x) ⇒
20            ν (y:A).
21              r ← f c (q y);
22              abs y r
23      | [A (q:A → Prop)] (∃ x:A. q x) ⇒
24            X ← evar A;
25            r ← f c (q X);
26            b ← is_evar X;
27            if b then raise ProofNotFound
28            else ret (ex_intro q X r)
29      | [p':Prop] p' ⇒ lookup p' c
30      end.
```

Figure 8. Mtactic for a simple first-order tautology prover.

the proposition p_2. The corresponding introduction form of the disjunction is returned (or_introl r_1 or or_intror r_2).

- Otherwise, it raises an exception, since no proof could be found.

Extending to First-Order Logic. We now extend the previous prover to support first-order logic. This extension requires the tactic to keep track of a context for hypotheses, which we model as a list of (dependent) pairs pairing hypotheses with their proofs. More concretely, each element in the hypothesis context has the type dyn $= \Sigma p$: Prop. p. (In Coq, this is encoded as an inductive type with constructor Dyn $p\ x$, for any $x : p$.)

```
Definition lookup (p : Prop) :=
  mfix f [s : list dyn] : ○p :=
    mmatch s return ○p with
    | [x s'] (Dyn p x) :: s' ⇒ ret x
    | [d s'] d :: s' ⇒ f s'
    | _ ⇒ raise ProofNotFound
    end.
```

Figure 9. Mtactic to look up a proof of a proposition in a context.

Figure 8 shows the first-order logic tautology prover tauto. The fixed point takes the proposition p and is additionally parameterized over a context (c : list dyn). The first three cases of the **mmatch** are similar to the ones in Figure 7, with the addition that the context is passed around in recursive calls.

Before explaining the cases for $\rightarrow$, $\forall$ and $\exists$, let us start with the last one (line 29), since it is the easiest. In this last case, we attempt to prove the proposition in question by simply searching for it in the hypothesis context. The search for the hypothesis p' in the context c is achieved using the Mtactic lookup shown in Figure 9. lookup takes a proposition p and a context, and traverses the context linearly in the hope of finding a dependent pair with p as the first component. If it finds such a pair, it returns the second component. Like the Mtactic search2 from §3.1, this simple lookup routine depends crucially on the ability to match the propositions in the context *syntactically* against the p for which we are searching.

Returning to the tautology prover, lines 15–18 concern the case where $p = p_1 \rightarrow p_2$. Intuitively, in order to prove $p_1 \rightarrow p_2$, one would (1) introduce a *parameter* y witnessing the proof of p_1 into the context, (2) proceed to prove p_2 having $y : p_1$ as an assumption, and (3) abstract any usage of y in the resulting proof. The rationale behind this last step is that if we succeed proving p_2, then the result is *parametric* over the proof of p_1, in the sense that any proof of p_1 will suffice to prove p_2. Steps (1) and (3) are performed by two of the operators we haven't yet described: **nu** and **abs** (the former is denoted by the νx binder). In more detail, the three steps are:

Line 16: It creates a parameter $y : p_1$ using the constructor **nu**. This constructor has type

$$\textbf{nu} : \forall (A\ B : \mathsf{Type}).\ (A \rightarrow \bigcirc B) \rightarrow \bigcirc B$$

(where A and B are left implicit). It is similar to the operator with the same name in [19] and [26]. Operationally, $\nu x : A.\ f$ (which is notation for **nu** $(\lambda x : A.\ f)$), creates a parameter y with type A, pushes it into the local context, and executes $f\{y/x\}$ (where $\cdot\{\cdot/\cdot\}$ is the standard substitution) in the hope of getting a value of type B. If the value returned by f refers to y, then it causes the tactic execution to fail: such a result would lead to an ill-formed term because y is not bound in the ambient context. This line constitutes the first step of our intuitive reasoning: we introduce the parameter y witnessing the proof of p_1 into the context.

Line 17: It calls tauto$'$ recursively, with context c extended with the parameter y, and with the goal of proving p_2. The result is bound to r. This line constitutes the second step.

Line 18: The result r created in the previous step has type p_2. In order to return an element of the type $p_1 \rightarrow p_2$, we abstract y from r, using the constructor

$$\textbf{abs} : \forall (A : \mathsf{Type})\ (P : A \rightarrow \mathsf{Type})\ (y : A).\ P\ y \rightarrow \bigcirc(\forall x : A.\ P\ x)$$

(with A, P implicit). Operationally, **abs** $y\ r$ checks that the first parameter y is indeed a variable, and returns the function

$$\lambda x : A.\ r\{x/y\}$$

In this case, the resulting element has type $\forall x : p_1 .\ p_2$, which, since p_2 does not refer to x, is equivalent to $p_1 \rightarrow p_2$. This constitutes the last step: by abstracting over y in the result, we ensure that the resulting proof term no longer mentions the ν-bound variable (as required by the use of **nu** in line 16).

Lines 19–22 consider the case that the proposition is an abstraction $\forall x : A.\ q\ x$. Here, q is the body of the abstraction, represented as a function from A to Prop. We rely on Coq's use of higher-order pattern unification [18] to instantiate q with a faithful representation of the body. The following lines mirrors the body of the previous case, except for the recursive call. In this case we don't extend the context with the parameter y, since it is not a proposition. Instead, we try to recursively prove the body q replacing x with y (that is, applying q to y).

If the proposition is an existential $\exists x : A.\ q\ x$ (line 23), then the prover performs the following steps:

Line 24: It uses Mtac's **evar** constructor to create a fresh unification variable called X.

Line 25: It calls tauto′ recursively, replacing x for X in the body of the existential.

Lines 26–28: It uses Mtac's **is_evar** mechanism to check whether X is still an uninstantiated unification variable. If it is, then it raises an exception, since no proof could be found. If it is not—that is, if X was successfully instantiated in the recursive call—then it returns the introduction form of the existential, with X as its witness.

Now we are ready to prove an example, where P : nat $\rightarrow$ Prop:

```
Definition exmpl : ∀P x. P x → ∃y. P y := run (tauto [] _).
```

The proof term generated by **run** is

$$\text{exmpl} = \lambda P\ x\ (H : P\ x).\ \text{ex\_intro}\ P\ x\ H$$

3.3 Inlined Proof Automation

Due to the tight integration between Mtac and Coq, Mtactics can be usefully employed in definitions, notations and other Coq terms, in addition to interactive proving. In this respect, Mtac differs from the related systems such as VeriML [29] and Beluga [21], where, to the best of our knowledge, such expressiveness is not currently available due to the strict separation between the object logic and the automation language.

In this section, we illustrate how Mtactics can be invoked from Coq proper. To set the stage, consider the scenario of developing a library for n-dimensional integer vector spaces, with the main type vector n defined as a record containing a list of nats and a proof that the list has size n:

```
Record vector (n : nat) := Vector {
  seq_of : list nat;
  _ : size seq_of = n}.
```

One of the important methods of the library is the accessor function ith, which returns the i-th element of the vector, for $i < n$. One implementation possibility is for ith to check at run time if $i < n$, and return an option value to signal when i is out of bounds. The downside of this approach is that the clients of ith have to explicitly discriminate against the option value. An alternative is for ith to explicitly request a proof that $i < n$ as one of its arguments, as in the following type ascription:

$$\text{ith} : \forall n{:}\text{nat}.\text{vector}\ n \rightarrow \forall i{:}\text{nat}.i < n \rightarrow \text{nat}$$

Then the clients have to construct a proof of $i < n$ before invoking ith, but we show that in some common situations, the proof can be constructed automatically by Mtac, and then passed to ith.

```
Program Definition compare (n1 n2 : nat) : ○(n1 ≤ n2) :=
  r1 ← to_ast nil n1;
  r2 ← to_ast (ctx_of r1) n2;
  match cancel (ctx_of r2) (term_of r1) (term_of r2)
      return ○(n1 ≤ n2) with
  | true ⇒ ret (@sound n1 n2 r1 r2 _)
  | _ ⇒ raise NotLeqException
  end.
Next Obligation. ... Qed.
```

Figure 10. Mtactic for proving inequalities between nat's.

Specifically, we describe an Mtactic compare, which automatically searches for a proof that two natural numbers n_1 and n_2 satisfy $n_1 \leq n_2$. compare is incomplete, and if it fails to find a proof, because the inequality doesn't hold, or because the proof is too complex, it raises an exception.

Once compare is implemented, it can be composed with ith as follows. Given a vector v whose size we denote as vsize v, and an integer i, we introduce the following notation, which invokes compare to automatically construct a proof that $i + 1 \leq$ vsize v (equivalent to $i <$ vsize v).

```
Notation "[ 'ith' v i ]" :=
  (@ith _ v i (run (compare (i+1) (vsize v))))
```

The notation can be used in definitions. For example, given vectors v_1, v_2 of fixed size 2, we could define the inner product of v_1 and v_2 as follows, letting Coq figure out automatically that the indices 0, 1 are within bounds.

```
Definition inner_prod (v1 v2 : vector 2) :=
        [ith v1 0] × [ith v2 0] + [ith v1 1] × [ith v2 1].
```

If we tried to add the summand [ith v_1 2] $\times$ [ith v_2 2], where the index 2 is out of bounds, then compare raises an exception, making the whole definition ill-typed. Similarly, if instead of vector 2, we used the type vector n, where n is a variable, the definition will be ill-typed, because there is no guarantee that n is larger than 1. On the other hand, the following is a well-typed definition, as the indices k and n are clearly within the bound $n + k + 1$.

```
Definition indexing n k (v : vector (n + k + 1)) :=
  [ith v k] + [ith v n].
```

We proceed to describe the implementation of compare, presented in Figure 10. compare is implemented using two main helper functions. The first is the Mtactic to_ast which *reflects* the numbers n_1 and n_2. More concretely, to_ast takes an integer expression, and considers it as a syntactic summation of a number of components. It *parses* this syntactic summation into an explicit list of summands, each of which can be either a constant or a free variable (subexpressions containing operations other than + are treated as free variables).

The second helper is a CIC function cancel which cancels the common terms from the syntax lists obtained by reflecting n_1 and n_2. If all the summands in the syntax list of n_1 are found in the syntax list of n_2, then it must be that $n_1 \leq n_2$ and cancel returns the boolean true. Otherwise, cancel doesn't search for other ways of proving $n_1 \leq n_2$ and simply returns false to signal the failure to find a proof. This failure ultimately results in compare raising an exception. Notice that cancel can't directly work on n_1 and n_2, but has to receive their syntactic representation from to_ast (in the code of compare these are named term_of r_1 and term_of r_2, respectively). The reason is that cancel has to compare names of variables appearing in n_1 and n_2, and has to match against the occurrences of the (non-constructor) function +, and such comparisons and matchings are not possible in CIC.

Alternatively, we could use **mmatch** to implement cancel in Mtac, but there are good reasons to prefer a purely functional Coq implementation when one is possible, as is the case here. With a pure cancel, compare can return a very short proof term as a result (*e.g.*, (sound n_1 n_2 r_1 r_2 _) in the code of compare). An Mtac implementation would have to expose the reasoning behind the soundness of the Mtactic at a much finer granularity, resulting in a larger proof.

We next describe the implementations of the two helpers.

Data Structures for Reflection. There are two main data structures used for reflecting integer expressions. As each expression is built out of variables, constants and +, we syntactically represent the sum as term containing a list of syntactic representations of variables appearing in the expression, followed by a nat constant that sums up all the constants from the expression. We also need a type of variable contexts ctx, in order to determine the syntactic representation of variables. In our case, a variable context is simply a list of nat expression, each element standing for a different variable, and the position of the variable in the context serves as the variable's syntactic representative.

```
Definition ctx := list nat
Record var := Var of nat
Definition term := (list var) × nat
```

Example 1. The expression $n = (1+x)+(y+3)$ may be reflected using a variable context $c = [x, y]$, and a term ([Var 0, Var 1], 4). Var 0 and Var 1 correspond to the two variables in c (x and y, respectively). 4 is the sum of the constants appearing in n.

Example 2. The syntactic representations of 0, successor constructor S, addition and an individual variable, may be given as following term constructors. We use _.1 and _.2 to denote projections out of a pair.

```
Definition syn_zero : term := (nil, 0).
Definition syn_succ (t : term) := (t.1, t.2 + 1).
Definition syn_add (t1 t2 : term) :=
  (t1.1 ++ t2.1, t1.2 + t2.2).
Definition syn_var (i : nat) := ([Var i], 0).
```

In prose, 0 is reflected by an empty list of variable indexes, and 0 as a constant term; if t is a term reflecting n, then the successor S n is reflected by incrementing the constant component of t, etc.

We further need a function interp that takes a variable context G and a term t, and *interprets* t into a nat, as follows.

```
interp_vars (G : ctx) (t : list var) :=
  if t is j :: t' then
    if (vlook G j, interp G t') is (Some v, Some e)
      then Some (v + e) else None
  else Some 0.

interp (G : ctx) (t : term) :=
  if interp_vars G t.1 is Some e
  then Some (e + t.2) else None.
```

First, interp_vars traverses the list of variable indices of t, turning each index into a natural number by looking it up into the context G, and summing the results. The lookup function vlook G j is omitted here, but it either returns Some j-th element of the context G, or None if G has less than j elements. Then, interp simply adds the result of interp_vars to the constant part of the term. For example, if the context $c = [x, y]$ and term $t =$ ([Var 0, Var 1], 4), then interp c t equals Some $(x + y + 4)$.

Reflection by **to_ast.** The to_ast Mtactic is applied twice in compare: once to reflect n_1, and again to reflect n_2. Each time, to_ast is passed as input a variable context, and extends this context with new variables encountered during reflection. To reflect n_1 in compare, to_ast starts with the empty context nil, and to reflect n_2, it starts with the context obtained after the reflection of n_1. This ensures that if the reflections of n_1 and n_2 encounter the same variables, they will use the same syntactic representations for them.

```
Record ast (G : ctx) (n : nat) :=
  Ast {term_of : term;
       ctx_of : ctx;
       _ : interp ctx_of term_of = Some n ∧ prefix G ctx_of}

Definition to_ast : ∀ G n. ○(ast G n) :=
  mfix f [G ; n] :=
    mmatch n with
    | 0 ⇒ ret (Ast G 0 syn_zero G ...)
    | [n'] S n' ⇒
      r ← f G n';
      ret (Ast G (S n') (syn_succ (term_of r))
                (ctx_of r) ...)
    | [n1 n2] n1 + n2 ⇒
      r1 ← f G n1; r2 ← f (ctx_of r1) n2;
      ret (Ast G (n1 + n2)
        (syn_add (term_of r1) (term_of r2)) (ctx_of r2) ...)
    | _ ⇒
      ctx_index ← find n G;
      ret (Ast G n (syn_var ctx_index.2) ctx_index.1 ...)
    end.
```

Figure 11. Mtactic for reflecting nat expressions.

```
Fixpoint cancel_vars (G : ctx) (s1 s2 : list var) : bool :=
  if s1 is v :: s1' then v ∈ s2 &&
    cancel_vars G s1' (remove_var v s2)
  else true.

Definition cancel (G : ctx) (t1 t2 : term) : bool :=
  cancel_vars G t1.1 t2.1 && t1.2 ≤ t2.2.
```

Figure 12. Algorithm for canceling common variables from terms.

The invariants associated with to_ast are encoded in the data structure ast (Figure 11). ast is indexed by the input context G and the number n to be reflected. Upon successful termination of to_ast, the term_of field contains the term reflecting n, and the ctx_of field contains the new variable context, potentially extending G. The third field of ast is a proof formalizing the described properties of term_of and ctx_of.

Referring to Figure 11, the Mtactic to_ast takes the input variable context G and the number n to be reflected, and traverses n trying to syntactically match the head construct of n with 0, S or +, respectively. In each case it returns an ast structure containing the syntactic representation of n, e.g.: syn_zero, syn_succ or syn_add, respectively. In the $n_1 + n_2$ case, to_ast recurses into n_2 by using the variable context returned from reflection of n_1 as an input, similar as in compare. In each case, the Ast constructor is supplied a proof that we omit but can be found in the sources. In the default case, when no constructor matches, n is treated as a variable. The Mtactic find n G (omitted here), searches for n in G, and returns a ctx × nat pair. If n is found, the pair consists of the old context G, and the position of n in G. If n is not found, the pair consists of a new context in which n is cons-ed to G, and the index k, where k is the index of n in the new context. to_ast then repackages the context and the index into an ast structure.

Canceling Common Variables. The cancel function is presented in Figure 12. It takes a variable context G, and terms t_1 and t_2 and tries to determine if t_1 and t_2 syntactically represent two ≤-related

$$\frac{\Gamma;\Sigma \vdash t \overset{\mathsf{whd}}{\rightsquigarrow} t'}{\Gamma \vdash (\Sigma; t) \rightsquigarrow (\Sigma; t')} \qquad \frac{}{\textbf{mfix}\ f\ t \rightsquigarrow f\ (\textbf{mfix}\ f)\ t}$$

$$\frac{t \rightsquigarrow t'}{\textbf{bind}\ t\ f \rightsquigarrow \textbf{bind}\ t'\ f} \qquad \frac{t \rightsquigarrow t'}{\textbf{mtry}\ t\ f \rightsquigarrow \textbf{mtry}\ t'\ f}$$

$$\frac{}{\textbf{bind}\ (\textbf{ret}\ t)\ f \rightsquigarrow f\ t} \qquad \frac{}{\textbf{bind}\ (\textbf{raise}\ t)\ f \rightsquigarrow \textbf{raise}\ t}$$

$$\frac{}{\textbf{mtry}\ (\textbf{ret}\ t)\ f \rightsquigarrow \textbf{ret}\ t} \qquad \frac{}{\textbf{mtry}\ (\textbf{raise}\ t)\ f \rightsquigarrow f\ t}$$

$$\frac{\begin{array}{c} ps_i \overset{\mathsf{whd}*}{\rightsquigarrow} \mathsf{Ptele}\ \overline{x}\ (\mathsf{Pbase}\ p\ b) \\ \Sigma, \overline{?y} \vdash p\{\overline{?y/x}\} \approx t \rhd \Sigma', \overline{?y := t'} \\ \forall j < i.\ ps_j \text{ does not unify with } t \end{array}}{\Gamma \vdash (\Sigma; \textbf{mmatch}\ t\ ps) \rightsquigarrow (\Sigma'; b\{\overline{t'/x}\})}$$

$$\frac{?x \notin \mathsf{dom}(\Sigma)}{(\Sigma; \textbf{evar}_A) \rightsquigarrow (\Sigma, ?x : A; \textbf{ret}\ ?x)}$$

$$\frac{e \overset{\mathsf{whd}*}{\rightsquigarrow} ?x \quad (?x := \_) \notin \Sigma}{(\Sigma; \textbf{is\_evar}\ e) \rightsquigarrow (\Sigma; \textbf{ret}\ \mathsf{true})} \qquad \frac{e \overset{\mathsf{whd}*}{\rightsquigarrow} t \quad t \text{ not unif. variable}}{(\Sigma; \textbf{is\_evar}\ e) \rightsquigarrow (\Sigma; \textbf{ret}\ \mathsf{false})}$$

$$\frac{\Gamma, x : A \vdash (\Sigma; t) \rightsquigarrow (\Sigma'; t')}{\Gamma \vdash (\Sigma; \nu x : A.\ t) \rightsquigarrow (\Sigma'; \nu x : A.\ t')} \qquad \frac{x \notin \mathsf{FV}(v)}{(\nu x.\ v) \rightsquigarrow v}$$

$$\frac{e \overset{\mathsf{whd}*}{\rightsquigarrow} x \quad (x : A) \in \Gamma}{\Gamma \vdash \textbf{abs}\ e\ t \rightsquigarrow \textbf{ret}\ (\lambda y.\ t\{y/x\})} \qquad \frac{(*\ \textit{print } s \textit{ to stdout } *)}{\textbf{print}\ s \rightsquigarrow \textbf{ret}\ \langle\rangle}$$

Figure 13. Operational small-step semantics.

expressions by cancelling common terms, as we described previously. First, the helper cancel_vars iterates over the list of variable representations of t_1, trying to match each one with a variable representation in t_2 (in the process, removing the matched variables by using yet another helper function remove_vars, omitted here). If the matching is successful and all variables of t_1 are included in t_2, then cancel merely needs to check if the constant of t_1 is smaller than the constant of t_2.

We conclude the example with the statement of the correctness lemma of cancel, which is the key component of the soundness proof for compare. We omit the proof here, but it can be found in our Coq files.

```
Lemma sound n1 n2 (a1 : ast [] n1) (a2 : ast (ctx_of a1) n2) :
    cancel (ctx_of a2) (term_of a1) (term_of a2) →
    n1 ≤ n2.
```

In prose, let a_1 and a_2 be reflections of n_1 and n_2 respectively, where the reflection of a_1 starts in the empty context, and the reflection of a_2 starts in the variable context returned by a_1. Then running cancel in the final context of a_2 over the reflected terms of a_1 and a_2 returns true only when it is correct to do so; that is, only when $n_1 \leq n_2$.

4. Operational Semantics

In this section, we let e, e' range over CIC terms and t, t' over Mtactics, *i.e.*, CIC terms of type $\bigcirc A$ for some type A. The operational semantics of Mtac defines the judgment form

$$\Gamma \vdash (\Sigma; t) \rightsquigarrow (\Sigma'; t')$$

where Γ is the typing context containing parameters and (let-bound) local definitions, while Σ and Σ' are contexts for unification variables $?x$. Both kinds of contexts contain both variable declarations (standing for parameters and uninstantiated unification variables, respectively) and definitions (let-bound variables and instantiated unification variables, respectively).

$$\Gamma ::= \cdot \mid \Gamma, x : A \mid \Gamma, x : A := e$$
$$\Sigma ::= \cdot \mid \Sigma, ?x : A \mid \Sigma, ?x : A := e$$

These contexts are needed for weak head reduction of CIC terms ($\Gamma; \Sigma \vdash e \overset{\mathsf{whd}}{\rightsquigarrow} e'$), but also for some of Mtac constructs. Except where noted, every rule just passes around the contexts, so to avoid clutter we omit them. We also omit the types, although we assume that the terms are well-typed in their given contexts and we ensure that this invariant is maintained throughout execution.

Tactic computation may either (a) terminate successfully returning a term, **ret** e, (b) terminate by throwing an exception, **raise** e, (c) diverge, or (d) get blocked. (We explain the possible reasons for getting blocked below.) Hence we have the following tactic values:

Definition 1 (Values). $v \in \text{Values} ::= \textbf{ret}\ e \mid \textbf{raise}\ e$.

Figure 13 shows our operational semantics. The first rule performs a CIC weak head reduction step. Weak head reduction requires both contexts because, among other things, it will unfold definitions of variables and unification variables in head position. For a precise description of Coq's standard reduction rules, see §4.3 of Coq's Reference Manual [31].

Next, we have the standard unfolding of Mtac fixpoints. The next six rules are quite standard and concern the semantics of **bind** and **mtry**: note the symmetry between **bind/ret** and **mtry/raise**.

The most complex rule is the next one concerning pattern matching. It matches the term t with some pattern described in the list ps. Each element ps_i of ps is a pair containing a pattern p and a body b, abstracted over a list of (dependent) variables $\overline{x : A}$. Since patterns are first class citizens in CIC, ps_i is first reduced to weak head normal form in order to expose the pattern and the body. The normalization relation is written $\overset{\mathsf{whd}*}{\rightsquigarrow}$ and, as with the weak head reduction relation, it requires the two contexts that we omit for clarity. Then, we replace each variable x with a corresponding unification variable $?y$ in p, and proceed to unify the result with term t. For this, the context Σ is extended with the freshly created unification variables $\overline{?y}$. After unification is performed, a new unification variable context is returned that might not only instantiate the freshly generated unification variables $\overline{?y}$, but may also instantiate previously defined unification variables. (Instantiating such unification variables is important, for instance, to instantiate the existentials in the tautology prover example of §3.2). We actually require that unification unifies all the freshly generated variables, so that we can safely remove them after substituting them in the body, thereby avoiding context pollution. Finally, we require that patterns are tried in sequence, *i.e.*, that the scrutinee, t, should not be unifiable with any previous pattern ps_j. In case no patterns match the scrutinee, the **mmatch** is blocked.

The semantics for pattern matching is parametric with respect to the unification judgment and thus does not rely on any particular unification algorithm. (Our implementation uses Coq's standard unification algorithm.) We observe that our examples, however, implicitly depend on *higher-order pattern unification* [18]. Higher-order unification is in general undecidable, but Miller identified a decidable subset of problems, the *pattern* fragment, where unification variables appear only in equations of the form $?f\ x_1\ \ldots\ x_n \approx t$, with $x_1, \ldots, x_n$ distinct variables. The $\forall$ and $\exists$ cases of the tautology prover (§3.2) fall into this pattern fragment, and their proper handling depends on higher-order pattern unification.

Another notable aspect of Coq's unification algorithm is that it equates terms up to definitional equality. In particular, if a pattern match at first does not succeed, Coq will take a step of reduction on the scrutinee, try again, and repeat. Thus, the ordering of two patterns in a **mmatch** matters, even if it seems the patterns are syntactically non-overlapping. Take for instance the search example in §1.1. If the pattern for concatenation of lists were moved *after* the patterns for consing, then the consing patterns would actually match against (many) concatenations as well, since the concatenation of two lists is often reducible to a term of the form h :: t.

Related to this, the last aspect of Coq's unification algorithm that we depend on is its *first-order approximation*. That is, in the presence of an equation of the form $c\ t_1\ \ldots\ t_n \approx c\ t'_1\ \ldots\ t'_n$, where c is a constant, the unification algorithm tries to equate each $t_i \approx t'_i$. While this may cause Coq to miss out on some solutions, it has the benefit of being simple and predictable. For instance, consider the equation

$$?l{+}{+}?r \approx [\,]{+}{+}(h :: t)$$

that might result from matching the list $[\,]{+}{+}(h :: t)$ with the pattern for concatenation of lists in the search example from §1.1, with $?l$ and $?r$ fresh unification variables. Here, although there exist many solutions, the algorithm assigns $?l := [\,]$ and $?r := (h :: t)$, an assignment that is intuitively easy to explain.

Coming back to the rules, next is the rule for $\textbf{evar}_A$, which simply extends Σ with a fresh uninstantiated unification variable of the appropriate type. The two following rules govern **is_evar** e and check whether an expression (after reduction to weak head normal form) is an uninstantiated unification variable.

The next two rules define the semantics of the νx binder: the parameter x is pushed into the context and the execution proceeds until a value is reached. The computed value is simply returned if it does not contain the parameter, x; otherwise, $\nu x.\ v$ is blocked. The latter rule is for abstracting over parameters. If the first argument of **abs** weak-head reduces to a parameter, then we abstract it from the second argument of **abs**, thereby returning a function.

The astute reader may wonder why we decided to have νx and **abs** instead of one single constructor combining the semantics of both. Such a combined constructor would always abstract the parameter x from the result, therefore avoiding the final check that the parameter is not free in the result. The reason we decided to keep **nu** and **abs** separate is simple: it is not always desirable to abstract the parameters in the same order as they were introduced. This is the case, for instance, in the Mtactic skolemize for skolemizing a formula (provided in the Mtac distribution). Moreover, sometimes the parameter is not abstracted at all, for instance in the Mtactic fv for computing the list of free variables of a term (also provided in the Mtac distribution).

Coming back to the rules, finally, the last rule replaces a printing command with the trivial value $\langle\rangle$. Informally, we also print out the string s to the standard output, although standard I/O is not formally modeled here.

Assuming that unification is sound, we can show that Mtac reduction is type-preserving.

Theorem 1 (Type preservation)**.** If $\Gamma \vdash (\Sigma; t) \rightsquigarrow (\Sigma'; t')$ and $\Gamma; \Sigma \vdash t : \bigcirc A$, then $\Gamma; \Sigma' \vdash t' : \bigcirc A$.

As mentioned earlier, Mtactic execution can block. Here, we define exactly the cases when execution of a term is blocked.

Definition 2 (Blocked terms)**.** A term t is *blocked* if and only if the subterm in reduction position satisfies one of the following cases:

- It is not an application of one of the $\bigcirc$ constructors and it is not reducible using the standard CIC reduction rules ($\overset{\mathsf{whd}}{\rightsquigarrow}$).
- It is $\nu x.\ v$ and $x \in \mathsf{FV}(v)$.
- It is **abs** $e\ t$ and $e \overset{\mathsf{whd}}{\rightsquigarrow}{}^{*}\ e'$ and $(e' : \_) \notin \Gamma$.
- It is **mmatch** $t\ ps$ and no pattern in ps unifies with t.

With this definition, we can then also establish a standard type safety theorem for Mtac.

Theorem 2 (Type safety)**.** Whenever $\Gamma; \Sigma \vdash t : \bigcirc A$, then either t is a value, or t is blocked, or there exist t' and Σ' such that $\Gamma \vdash (\Sigma; t) \rightsquigarrow (\Sigma'; t')$ and $\Gamma; \Sigma' \vdash t' : \bigcirc A$.

Example: We show the trace of a simple example to get a grasp of the operational semantics. In this example, $\Gamma = \{h : \mathsf{nat}\}$.

$$\textbf{let}\ s := (h :: [\,]){+}{+}[\,]\ \textbf{in}\ \mathsf{search}\ h\ s$$

We want to show that the final term produced by running this Mtactic expresses the fact that h was found at the head of the list on the left of the concatenation, that is,

$$\mathsf{in\_or\_app}\ (h :: [\,])\ [\,]\ (\mathsf{or\_introl}\ (\mathsf{in\_eq}\ h\ [\,]))$$

First, the **let** is expanded, obtaining

$$\mathsf{search}\ h\ ((h :: [\,]){+}{+}[\,])$$

Then, after expanding the definition of search and β-reducing the term, we are left with the fixpoint being applied to the list:

$$(\textbf{mfix}\ f\ [s : \mathsf{list}\ A] := \ldots)\ ((h :: [\,]){+}{+}[\,])$$

At this point the rule for **mfix** triggers, exposing the **mmatch**:

$$\textbf{mmatch}\ ((h :: [\,]){+}{+}[\,])\ \textbf{with} \ldots \textbf{end}$$

Thanks to first-order approximation, the case for append is unified, and its body is executed:

$$\textbf{mtry}\ il \leftarrow f\ (h :: [\,]);\ \textbf{ret}\ \ldots\ \textbf{with}\ \_ \Rightarrow \ldots\ \textbf{end} \qquad (1)$$

where f stands for the fixpoint. The rule for **mtry** executes the code for searching for the element in the sublist $(h :: [\,])$:

$$il \leftarrow f\ (h :: [\,]);\ \textbf{ret}\ (\mathsf{in\_or\_app}\ (h :: [\,])\ [\,]\ h\ (\mathsf{or\_introl}\ il)) \quad (2)$$

The bind rule triggers, after which the fixpoint is expanded and a new **mmatch** exposed:

$$\textbf{mmatch}\ (h :: [\,])\ \textbf{with}\ \ldots\ \textbf{end}$$

This time, the rule for append fails to unify, but the second case succeeds, returning the result in_eq h []. Coming back to (2), il is replaced with this result, getting the expected final result that is in turn returned by the **mtry** of (1).

As a last remark, notice how at each step the selected rule is the only applicable one: the semantics of Mtac is deterministic.

5. Implementation

This section presents a high-level overview of the architecture of our Mtac extension to Coq, explaining our approach for guaranteeing soundness even in the possible presence of bugs in our Mtac implementation.

The main idea we leverage in integrating Mtac into Coq is that Coq distinguishes between fully and partially type-annotated proof terms: Coq's type inference (or *elaboration*) algorithm transforms partially annotated terms into fully annotated ones, which are then fed to Coq's kernel type checker. In this respect Coq follows the typical architecture of interactive theorem provers, ensuring that all proofs are ultimately certified by a small trusted kernel. Assuming that the kernel is correct, no code outside this kernel may generate incorrect proofs. Thus, our Mtac implementation modifies only the elaborator lying outside of Coq's kernel, and leaves the kernel type checker untouched.

Extending Elaboration. The typing judgment used by Coq's elaboration algorithm [24, 25] takes a partially type-annotated term e, a local context Γ, an unification variable context Σ, and an optional expected type B, and returns its type A, and produces a fully annotated term e', and updated unification variable context Σ'.

$$\Gamma; \Sigma \vdash_B e \hookrightarrow e' : A \triangleright \Sigma'$$

If an expected type B, is provided, then the returned type A will be convertible to it, possibly instantiating any unification variables appearing in both A and B. The elaboration judgment serves three main purposes that the kernel typing judgment does not support:

1. To resolve implicit arguments. We have already seen several cases where this is useful (*e.g.*, in §1.1), allowing us to write underscores and let Coq's unification mechanism replace them with the appropriate terms.
2. To insert appropriate coercions. For example, Ssreflect [10] defines the coercion is_true : bool $\rightarrow$ Prop := $(\lambda b.\ b = \mathsf{true})$. So whenever a term of type Prop is expected and a term b of type bool is encountered, elaboration will insert the coercion, thereby returning the term is_true b having type Prop.
3. To perform canonical structure and type class resolution. Ample examples of canonical structures can be found in Gonthier *et al.* [11]. A type class example will be shown towards the end of this section.

We simply extend the elaboration mechanism to perform a fourth task, namely to run Mtactics. We achieve this by adding the following rule for handling **run** t terms:

$$\frac{\Gamma;\Sigma \vdash_{\bigcirc B} t \hookrightarrow t' : \bigcirc A \rhd \Sigma' \qquad \Gamma \vdash (\Sigma';t') \leadsto^{*} (\Sigma''; \mathbf{ret}\ e)}{\Gamma;\Sigma \vdash_{B} \mathbf{run}\ t \hookrightarrow e : A \rhd \Sigma''}$$

This rule first recursively type-checks the tactic body, while also unifying the return type A of the tactic with the expected goal B (if present). This results in the refinement of t to a new term t', which is then executed. If execution terminates successfully returning a value e (which from Theorem 2 will have type A), then that value is returned. Therefore, as a result of elaboration, all **run** t terms are replaced by the terms produced when running them, and thus the kernel type checker does not need to be modified in any way.

Elaboration and the* apply *Tactic. We have just seen *how* the elaborator coerces the return type A of an Mtactic to be equivalent to the goal B, but we did not stipulate in what situations the knowledge of B is available. Our examples so far assumed B was given, and this was indeed the case thanks to the specific ways we invoked Mtac. For instance, at the end of §1.1 we proved a lemma by *direct definition—i.e.*, providing the proof term directly—and in §3.1 we proved the goal by calling the Ssreflect tactic apply: (note the colon!). In both these situations, we were conveniently relying on the fact that Coq passed the knowledge of the goal being proven into the elaboration of **run**.

Unfortunately, not every tactic does this. In particular, the standard Coq tactic apply (without colon) does not provide the elaborator with the goal as expected type, so if we had written apply (**run** $(F\ \_\ \_)$), the Mtactic F would have been executed on unknown parameters, resulting in a different behavior from what we expect. (Specifically, it would have unified the implicits with the first two pointers appearing in the heap, succeeding only if, luckily, these are the pointers in the goal.)

To ensure that information about the goal is available when running Mtactics, we recommend installing Ssreflect [10]. However, we note that using the standard Coq tactic refine instead of apply also works.

One last point about tactics: Mtac is intended as a typed alternative to Ltac for developing custom automation routines, and it is neither intended to replace the built-in tactics (like apply) nor to subsume all uses of existing Coq tactics. For example, the OCaml tactic vm_compute enables dramatic efficiency gains for reflection-based proofs [12], but its performance depends critically on being *compiled*. Mtac is interpreted, and it is not clear how it could be compiled, given the interaction between Mtac and Coq unification.

```
Class runner A (f : ○A) := { eval : A }.

Hint Extern 20 (runner ?f) ⇒
     (exact (Build_runner f (run f)))
     : typeclass_instances.
```

Figure 14. Type class for delayed execution of Mtactics.

Delaying Execution of Mtactics for Rewriting. Consider the goal from §3.1, after doing pose F := **run** (noalias D), unfolding the implicit is_true coercions for clarity:

$$\frac{\begin{array}{l} D\ :\ \mathsf{def}\ (h_1 \bullet (x_1 \mapsto v_1 \bullet x_2 \mapsto v_2) \bullet (h_2 \bullet x_3 \mapsto v_3)) \\ F\ :\ \forall x\ y.\ \bigcirc((x\ \texttt{!=}\ y) = \mathsf{true}) \end{array}}{(x_1\ \texttt{!=}\ x_2) = \mathsf{true} \wedge (x_2\ \texttt{!=}\ x_3) = \mathsf{true}}$$

Previously we solved this goal by applying the Mtactic F twice to the two subgoals x_1 != x_2 and x_2 != x_3. An alternative way in which a Coq programmer would hope to solve this goal is by using Coq's built-in rewrite tactic. rewrite enables one to apply a lemma one or more times to reduce various *subterms* of the current goal. In particular, we intuitively ought to be able to solve the goal in this case by invoking rewrite !(**run** $(F\ \_\ \_)$), where the ! means that the Mtactic F should be applied repeatedly to solve any and all pointer inequalities in the goal. Unfortunately, however, this does not work, because—like Coq's apply tactic—rewrite typechecks its argument without knowledge of the expected type from the goal, and only later unifies the result with the subterms in the goal. Consequently, just as with apply, F gets run prematurely.

Fortunately, we can circumvent this problem, using a cute trick based on Coq's type class resolution mechanism.

Type classes are an advanced Coq feature similar to canonical structures, with the crucial difference that their resolution is triggered by proof search *after* elaboration [28]. We exploit this functionality in Figure 14, by defining the class runner, which is parameterized over an Mtactic f with return type A and provides a value, eval, of the same type. We then declare a **Hint** instructing the type class resolution mechanism how to build an instance of the runner class, which is precisely by running f.

The details of this implementation are a bit of black magic, and beyond the scope of this paper to explain fully. But intuitively, all that is going on is that eval is *delaying* the execution of its Mtactic argument until type class resolution time, at which point information about the goal to be proven is available.

Returning to our example, we can now use the following script:

rewrite !(eval $(F\ \_\ \_)$) .

This will convert the goal to is_true true $\wedge$ is_true true, which is trivially solvable.

In fact, with eval we can even employ the standard apply tactic, with the caveat that eval creates slightly bigger proof terms, as the final proof term will also contain the unevaluated Mtactic inside it.

A Word about Exceptions In ML, exceptions have type exn and their constructors are created via the keyword **exception**, as in

exception MyException **of** string

Porting this model into Coq is difficult as it is not possible to define a type without simultaneously defining its constructors. Instead, we opted for a simple yet flexible approach. We define the type Exception as isomorphic to the unit type, and to distinguish each exception we create them as *opaque*, that is, irreducible. Figure 15 shows how to create two exceptions, the first one parameterized over a string. What is crucial is the sealing of the definition with **Qed**, signaling to Coq that this definition is opaque. The example test_ex illustrates the catching of different exceptions.

```
Definition MyException (s : string) : Exception.
  exact exception.
Qed.

Definition AnotherException : Exception.
  exact exception.
Qed.

Definition test_ex e :=
  mtry (raise e) with
    | AnotherException ⇒ ret ""
    | MyException "hello" ⇒ ret "world"
    | [s] MyException s ⇒ ret s
  end.
```

Figure 15. Exceptions in Mtac.

6. Related Work

Languages for Typechecked Tactics. In the last five years there has been increasing interest in languages that support safe tactics to manipulate proof terms of dependently typed logics. Delphin [23], Beluga [21, 22, 4], and VeriML [29, 30] are languages that, like Mtac, fall into this category. By "safe" we mean that, if the execution of a tactic terminates, then the resulting proof term has the type specified by the tactic.

But, unlike Mtac, these prior systems employ a strict separation of languages: the computational language (the language used to write tactics) is completely different from the logical language (the language of proofs), making the meta-theory heavier than in Mtac. Indeed, our proof of type safety is completely straightforward, as it inherits from CIC all the relevant properties such as type preservation under substitution. Having a simple meta-theory is particularly important to avoid precluding future language extensions—indeed, extensions of the previous systems have often required a reworking of their meta-theory [30, 4].

Another difference between these languages and Mtac is the logical language they support. For Delphin and Beluga it is LF [13], for VeriML it is λHOL [1], and for Mtac it is CIC [2]. CIC is the only one among these that provides support for computation at the term and type level, thereby enabling proofs by reflection (*e.g.*, see §3.3). Instead, in previous systems term reduction must be witnessed explicitly in proofs. To work around this, VeriML's computational language includes a construct letstatic that allows one to stage the execution of tactics, so as to enable equational reasoning at typechecking time. Then, proofs of (in-)equalities obtained from tactics can be directly injected in proof terms generated by tactics. This is similar to our use of **run** in the example from §3.3, with the caveat that letstatic cannot be used within definitions, as we did in the inner_prod example, but rather only inside tactics.

In Beluga and VeriML the representation of objects of the logic in the computational language is based on Contextual Modal Type Theory [20]. Therefore, every object is annotated with the context in which it is immersed. For instance, a term t depending only in the variable x is written in Beluga as $[x.\ t]$, and the typechecker enforces that t has only x free. In Mtac, it is only possible to perform this check dynamically, writing an Mtactic to inspect a term and rule out free variables not appearing in the set of allowed variables (the interested reader may find an example of this Mtactic in the Mtac distribution). On the other hand, the syntax of the language and the meta-theory required to account for contextual objects are significantly heavier than those of Mtac.

Delphin shares with Mtac the $\nu x : A$ binder from [26, 19]. In Delphin, the variable x introduced by this binder is distinguished with the type $A^{\#}$, in order to statically rule out offending terms like $\nu x : A.$ **ret** x. In Mtac, instead, this check gets performed dynamically. Yet again, we see a tension between the simplicity of the meta-theory and the static guarantees provided by the system. In Mtac we favor the former.

```
01 Structure tagged_heap := Tag {untag :> heap}.
02 Definition default_tag := Tag.
03 Definition ptr_tag := default_tag.
04 Canonical Structure union_tag h := ptr_tag h.
05
06 Structure form (s : list ptr) := Form {
07   heap_of :> tagged_heap;
08   _ : def heap_of → uniq s ∧
09       ∀ x. x ∈ s → x ∈ dom heap_of}.
10
11 Canonical Structure union_form s1 s2 h1 h2 :=
12   Form (s1 ++ s2) (union_tag (h1 • h2)) ...
13
14 Canonical Structure ptr_form A x (v : A) :=
15   Form [:: x] (ptr_tag (x ↦ v)) ...
16
17 Canonical Structure default_form h :=
18   Form [::] (default_tag h) ...
```

Figure 16. Scan tactic in lemma overloading style.

From all these systems, VeriML is the only system that provides ML-style references at the computational level. References are useful for writing efficient tactics. For instance, Stampoulis and Shao [29] first present a tautology prover similar to the one in §3.2, with a linear list lookup function. Then, they replace the list of hypotheses with a hash table to efficiently store and lookup hypotheses. In our implementation of Mtac, we have begun to look into this, and the interested reader can find in the Mtac distribution a similar optimized version of the tautology prover, but we have yet to work out its meta-theory.

Finally, a key difference between Mtac and all the aforementioned systems is the ability to program Mtactics interactively, as shown at the end of §3.1. None of the prior systems supports this.

Proof Automation Through Lemma Overloading. At heart, one of the key ideas of Mtac is to get tactic execution to be performed by Coq's type inference engine. In that sense, Mtac is closely related to (and indeed was inspired by) Gonthier *et al.*'s work on lemma overloading using canonical structures [11].

However, as explained in the introduction, whereas Mtac supports a functional style of programming, the style of programming imposed by lemma overloading is that of (dependently-typed) logic programming. For instance, Figure 16 shows the scan algorithm from §3.1 rewritten using canonical structures. Without going into detail, the structure (*a.k.a.* record) form in line 9 is the backbone of the tactic. The (tagged) heap heap_of is the input to the algorithm, and the list of pointers s and the (unnamed) axiom are the output of the algorithm. The "tagging" of the heap (lines 1 to 4) is required in order to specify an order in which the canonical instance declarations in lines 13 to 20 (much like type class instances in Haskell) should be considered during canonical instance resolution.

The reason for using a parameter of the structure (s) to represent one of the outputs of the algorithm is tricky to explain. More generally, knowing where to place the inputs and outputs of overloaded lemmas, and how to compose them together effectively, requires deep knowledge of the unification algorithm of Coq. In fact, the major technical contribution of Gonthier *et al.*'s paper [11] is the development of a set of common "design patterns" to help in dealing with these issues. For instance, in order to encode the noalias tactic as a composition of several overloaded lemmas, Gonthier *et al.* employ a rather sophisticated "parametrized tagging" pattern for reordering of unification subproblems.

In contrast, the Mtac encoding of noalias is entirely straightforward functional programming. Admittedly, the operational semantics of Mtac's **mmatch** construct is also tied to the unification algorithm of Coq, and the lack of a clear specification of this algorithm is an issue we hope to tackle in the near future. But, crucially, the high-level control flow of Mtactics is easy to understand *without* a detailed knowledge of Coq unification.

That said, there are some idioms that canonical structures support but Mtactics do not. In particular, their logic programming style makes them openly extensible (as with Haskell type classes, new instances can be added at any time), whereas Mtactics are closed to extension. It also enables them to be applied in both *backward* and *forward* reasoning, whereas Mtactics are unidirectional.

Simulable Monads. Claret *et al.* [7] present *Cybele*, a framework for building more flexible proofs by reflection in Coq. Like Mtac, it provides a monad to build effectful computations, although these effects are compiled and executed in OCaml. Upon success, the OCaml code creates a *prophecy* that is injected back into Coq to simulate the effects in pure CIC. On the one hand, since the effects Cybele supports must be replayable inside CIC, it does not provide meta-programming features like Mtac's **mmatch**, **nu**, **abs**, and **evar**, which we use heavily in our examples. On the other hand, for the kinds of effectful computations Cybele supports, the proof terms it generates ought to be smaller than those Mtac generates, since Cybele enforces the use of proof by reflection. The two systems thus offer complementary benefits, and can in principle be used in tandem.

Acknowledgments

We are deeply grateful to Chung-Kil Hur for suggesting the Mendler-style encoding of **mfix**, to Arnaud Spiwack for suggesting the use of telescopes for representing patterns, and to Georges Gonthier for the neat type class trick for delaying execution of Mtactics. We would also like to thank Jesper Bengtson and Jonas Jensen, who tested an earlier version of Mtac and gave useful feedback that helped us in polishing the implementation, as well as Nils Anders Danielsson and the anonymous reviewers for their very helpful comments. This research was partially supported by the Spanish MINECO projects TIN2010-20639 Paran10 and TIN2012-39391-C04-01 Strongsoft, AMAROUT grant PCOFUND-GA-2008-229599, and Ramon y Cajal grant RYC-2010-0743.

References

[1] H. Barendregt and H. Geuvers. Proof-assistants using dependent type systems. In A. Robinson and A. Voronkov, editors, *Handbook of automated reasoning*. Elsevier, 2001.

[2] Y. Bertot, P. Castéran, G. Huet, and C. Paulin-Mohring. *Interactive theorem proving and program development : Coq'Art : the calculus of inductive constructions*. Texts in theoretical computer science. Springer, 2004.

[3] S. Boutin. Using reflection to build efficient and certified decision procedures. In *TACS*, volume 1281 of *LNCS*. Springer, 1997.

[4] A. Cave and B. Pientka. Programming with binders and indexed data-types. In *POPL 2012*. ACM, 2012.

[5] A. Chlipala. Certified programming with dependent types. `http://adam.chlipala.net/cpdt`, 2008.

[6] A. Chlipala. Mostly-automated verification of low-level programs in computational separation logic. In *PLDI 2011*. ACM, 2011.

[7] G. Claret, L. del Carmen González Huesca, Y. Régis-Gianas, and B. Ziliani. Lightweight proof by reflection using a posteriori simulation of effectful computation. In *ITP 2013*, volume 7998 of *LNCS*. Springer, 2013.

[8] G. Gonthier. Formal proof — the four-color theorem. *Notices of the AMS*, 55(11):1382–93, 2008.

[9] G. Gonthier, A. Asperti, J. Avigad, Y. Bertot, C. Cohen, F. Garillot, S. Le Roux, A. Mahboubi, R. O'Connor, S. Ould Biha, I. Pasca, L. Rideau, A. Solovyev, E. Tassi, and L. Théry. A machine-checked proof of the odd order theorem. In *ITP 2013*, volume 7998 of *LNCS*. Springer, 2013.

[10] G. Gonthier, A. Mahboubi, and E. Tassi. A small scale reflection extension for the Coq system. Technical report, INRIA, 2008.

[11] G. Gonthier, B. Ziliani, A. Nanevski, and D. Dreyer. How to make ad hoc proof automation less ad hoc. In *ICFP*, 2011.

[12] B. Grégoire and X. Leroy. A compiled implementation of strong reduction. In *ICFP*, 2002.

[13] R. Harper, F. Honsell, and G. Plotkin. A framework for defining logics. *J. ACM*, 40(1):143–184, Jan. 1993.

[14] C.-K. Hur, G. Neis, D. Dreyer, and V. Vafeiadis. The power of parameterization in coinductive proof. In *POPL 2013*. ACM, 2013.

[15] G. Klein, J. Andronick, K. Elphinstone, G. Heiser, D. Cock, P. Derrin, D. Elkaduwe, K. Engelhardt, R. Kolanski, M. Norrish, T. Sewell, H. Tuch, and S. Winwood. seL4: Formal verification of an operating-system kernel. *CACM*, 53(6):107–115, 2010.

[16] X. Leroy. Formal verification of a realistic compiler. *CACM*, 52(7):107–115, 2009.

[17] N. P. Mendler. Inductive types and type constraints in the second-order lambda calculus. *Annals of Pure and Applied Logic*, 51(1–2):159–172, 1991.

[18] D. Miller. Unification of simply typed lamda-terms as logic programming. In *ICLP 1991*. MIT Press, 1991.

[19] A. Nanevski. Meta-programming with names and necessity. In *ICFP 2002*. ACM, 2002.

[20] A. Nanevski, F. Pfenning, and B. Pientka. Contextual modal type theory. *ACM Trans. Comput. Logic*, 9(3), June 2008.

[21] B. Pientka. A type-theoretic foundation for programming with higher-order abstract syntax and first-class substitutions. In *POPL 2008*. ACM, 2008.

[22] B. Pientka and J. Dunfield. Programming with proofs and explicit contexts. In *PPDP 2008*. ACM, 2008.

[23] A. Poswolsky and C. Schürmann. System description: Delphin – a functional programming language for deductive systems. *ENTCS*, 228:113–120, 2009.

[24] C. Sacerdoti Coen. *Mathematical Knowledge Management and Interactive Theorem Proving*. PhD thesis, University of Bologna, 2004.

[25] A. Saïbi. Typing algorithm in type theory with inheritance. In *POPL 1997*. ACM, 1997.

[26] C. Schürmann, A. Poswolsky, and J. Sarnat. The ∇-calculus. Functional programming with higher-order encodings. In *TLCA 2005*, volume 3461 of *LNCS*. Springer, 2005.

[27] M. Sozeau. Subset coercions in Coq. In *TYPES 2006*, volume 4502 of *LNCS*. Springer, 2007.

[28] M. Sozeau and N. Oury. First-class type classes. In *TPHOLs 2008*, volume 5170 of *LNCS*. Springer, 2008.

[29] A. Stampoulis and Z. Shao. VeriML: Typed computation of logical terms inside a language with effects. In *ICFP 2010*. ACM, 2010.

[30] A. Stampoulis and Z. Shao. Static and user-extensible proof checking. In *POPL 2012*. ACM, 2012.

[31] The Coq Development Team. *The Coq Proof Assistant Reference Manual – Version V8.4*, 2012.

[32] J. Ševčík, V. Vafeiadis, F. Zappa Nardelli, S. Jagannathan, and P. Sewell. CompCertTSO: A verified compiler for relaxed-memory concurrency. *J. ACM*, 60(3):22:1–22:50, June 2013.

Fun with Semirings

A functional pearl on the abuse of linear algebra

Stephen Dolan
Computer Laboratory, University of Cambridge
stephen.dolan@cl.cam.ac.uk

Abstract

Describing a problem using classical linear algebra is a very well-known problem-solving technique. If your question can be formulated as a question about real or complex matrices, then the answer can often be found by standard techniques.

It's less well-known that very similar techniques still apply where instead of real or complex numbers we have a *closed semiring*, which is a structure with some analogue of addition and multiplication that need not support subtraction or division.

We define a typeclass in Haskell for describing closed semirings, and implement a few functions for manipulating matrices and polynomials over them. We then show how these functions can be used to calculate transitive closures, find shortest or longest or widest paths in a graph, analyse the data flow of imperative programs, optimally pack knapsacks, and perform discrete event simulations, all by just providing an appropriate underlying closed semiring.

Categories and Subject Descriptors D.1.1 [*Programming Techniques*]: Applicative (Functional) Programming; G.2.2 [*Discrete Mathematics*]: Graph Theory—graph algorithms

Keywords closed semirings; transitive closure; linear systems; shortest paths

1. Introduction

Linear algebra provides an incredibly powerful problem-solving toolbox. A great many problems in computer graphics and vision, machine learning, signal processing and many other areas can be solved by simply expressing the problem as a system of linear equations and solving using standard techniques.

Linear algebra is defined abstractly in terms of fields, of which the real and complex numbers are the most familiar examples. Fields are sets equipped with some notion of addition and multiplication as well as negation and reciprocals.

Many discrete mathematical structures commonly encountered in computer science do not have sensible notions of negation. Booleans, sets, graphs, regular expressions, imperative programs, datatypes and various other structures can all be given natural notions of product (interpreted variously as intersection, sequencing or conjunction) and sum (union, choice or disjunction), but generally lack negation or reciprocals.

Such structures, having addition and multiplication (which distribute in the usual way) but not in general negation or reciprocals, are called semirings. Many structures specifying sequential actions can be thought of as semirings, with multiplication as sequencing and addition as choice. The distributive law then states, intuitively, a followed by a choice between b and c is the same as a choice between a followed by b and a followed by c.

Plain semirings are a very weak structure. We can find many examples of them in the wild, but unlike fields which provide the toolbox of linear algebra, there isn't much we can do with something knowing only that it is a semiring.

However, we can build some useful tools by introducing the *closed semiring*, which is a semiring equipped with an extra operation called *closure*. With the intuition of multiplication as sequencing and addition as choice, closure can be interpreted as iteration. As we see in the following sections, it is possible to use something akin to Gaussian elimination on an arbitrary closed semiring, giving us a means of solving certain "linear" equations over any structure with suitable notions of sequencing, choice and iteration. First, though, we need to define the notion of semiring more precisely.

2. Semirings

We define a semiring formally as consisting of a set R, two distinguished elements of R named 0 and 1, and two binary operations $+$ and $\cdot$, satisfying the following relations for any $a, b, c \in R$:

$$\begin{aligned} a + b &= b + a \\ a + (b + c) &= (a + b) + c \\ a + 0 &= a \\ a \cdot (b \cdot c) &= (a \cdot b) \cdot c \\ a \cdot 0 &= 0 \cdot a = 0 \\ a \cdot 1 &= 1 \cdot a = a \\ a \cdot (b + c) &= a \cdot b + a \cdot c \\ (a + b) \cdot c &= a \cdot c + b \cdot c \end{aligned}$$

We often write $a \cdot b$ as ab, and $a \cdot a \cdot a$ as a^3.

Our focus will be on *closed semirings* [12], which are semirings with an additional operation called *closure* (denoted *) which satisfies the axiom:

$$a^* = 1 + a \cdot a^* = 1 + a^* \cdot a$$

If we have an *affine map* $x \mapsto ax + b$ in some closed semiring, then $x = a^*b$ is a fixpoint, since $a^*b = (aa^* + 1)b = a(a^*b) + b$. So, a closed semiring can also be thought of as a semiring where affine maps have fixpoints.

The definition of a semiring translates neatly to Haskell:

ICFP '13, September 25–27, 2013, Boston, MA, USA.

ACM 978-1-4503-2326-0/13/09... $15.00.
http://dx.doi.org/10.1145/2500365.2500613

```
infixl 9 @.
infixl 8 @+
class Semiring r where
  zero, one :: r
  closure :: r -> r
  (@+), (@.) :: r -> r -> r
```

There are many useful examples of closed semirings, the simplest of which is the Boolean datatype:

```
instance Semiring Bool where
  zero = False
  one = True
  closure x = True
  (@+) = (||)
  (@.) = (&&)
```

It is straightforward to show that the semiring axioms are satisfied by this definition.

In semirings where summing an infinite series makes sense, we can define a^* as:

$$1 + a + a^2 + a^3 + \ldots$$

since this series satisfies the axiom $a^* = 1 + a \cdot a^*$. In other semirings where subtraction and reciprocals make sense we can define a^* as $(1 - a)^{-1}$. Both of these viewpoints will be useful to describe certain semirings.

The real numbers form a semiring with the usual addition and multiplication, where $a^* = (1 - a)^{-1}$. Under this definition, 1^* is undefined, an annoyance which can be remedied by adding an extra element ∞ to the semiring, and setting $1^* = \infty$.

The regular languages form a closed semiring where $\cdot$ is concatenation, $+$ is union, and * is the Kleene star. Here the infinite geometric series interpretation of * is the most natural: a^* is the union of a^n for all n.

3. Matrices and reachability

Given a directed graph G of n nodes, we can construct its adjacency matrix M, which is an $n \times n$ matrix of Booleans where M_{ij} is true if there is an edge from i to j.

We can add such matrices. Using the Boolean semiring's definition of addition (i.e. disjunction), the effect of this is to take the union of two sets of edges.

Similarly, we define matrix multiplication in the usual way, where $(AB)_{ij} = \sum_k A_{ik} \cdot B_{kj}$. The product of two Boolean matrices A, B is thus true at indices ij if there exists any index k such that A_{ik} and B_{kj} are both true. In particular, $(M^2)_{ij}$ is true if there is a path with two edges in G from node i to node j.

In general, M^k represents the paths of k edges in the graph G. A node j is reachable from a node i if there is a path with any number of edges (including 0) from i to j. This reachability relation can therefore be described by the following, where I is the identity matrix:

$$I + M + M^2 + M^3 + \ldots$$

This looks like the infinite series definition of closure from above. Indeed, suppose we could calculate the closure of M, that is, a matrix M^* such that:

$$M^* = I + M \cdot M^*$$

M^* would include the paths of length 0 (the I term), and would be transitively closed (the $M \cdot M^*$ term). So, if we can show that $n \times n$ matrices of Booleans form a closed semiring, then we can use the closure operation to calculate reachability in a graph, or equivalently the reflexive transitive closure of a graph.

Remarkably, for any closed semiring R, the $n \times n$ matrices of elements of R form a closed semiring. This is a surprisingly powerful result: as we see in the following sections, the closure operation can be used to solve several different problems with a suitable choice of the semiring R.

We define addition and multiplication of $n \times n$ matrices in the usual way, where:

$$(A + B)_{ij} = A_{ij} + B_{ij}$$

$$(A \cdot B)_{ij} = \sum_{k=1}^{n} A_{ik} \cdot B_{kj}$$

The matrix $\mathbf{0}$ is the $n \times n$ matrix where every element is the underlying semiring's 0, and the matrix $\mathbf{1}$ has the underlying semiring's 1 along the main diagonal (so $\mathbf{1}_{ii} = 1$) and 0 elsewhere.

In Haskell, we use the type `Matrix`, which represents a matrix as a list of rows, each a list of elements, with a special case for the representation of scalar matrices (matrices which are zero everywhere but the main diagonal, and equal at all points along the diagonal). This special case allows us to define matrices `zero` and `one` without knowing the size of the matrix.

```
data Matrix a = Scalar a
              | Matrix [[a]]
```

To add a scalar to a matrix, we need to be able to move along the main diagonal of the matrix. To make this easier, we introduce some helper functions for dealing with block matrices.

A block matrix is a matrix that has been partitioned into several smaller matrices. We define a type for matrices that have been partitioned into four blocks:

```
type BlockMatrix a = (Matrix a, Matrix a,
                      Matrix a, Matrix a)
```

If `a`, `b`, `c` and `d` represent the $n \times n$ matrices A, B, C, D, then `BlockMatrix (a,b,c,d)` represents the $2n \times 2n$ block matrix:

$$\begin{pmatrix} A & B \\ C & D \end{pmatrix}$$

Joining the components of a block matrix into a single matrix is straightforward:

```
mjoin :: BlockMatrix a -> Matrix a
mjoin (Matrix a, Matrix b,
       Matrix c, Matrix d) =
      Matrix ((a `hcat` b) ++ (c `hcat` d))
  where hcat = zipWith (++)
```

For any $n \times m$ matrix where $n, m \geq 2$, we can split the matrix into a block matrix by peeling off the first row and column:

```
msplit :: Matrix a -> BlockMatrix a
msplit (Matrix (row:rows)) =
    (Matrix [[first]], Matrix [top],
     Matrix left,      Matrix rest)
  where
    (first:top) = row
    (left, rest) = unzip (map (\(x:xs) -> ([x],xs))
                          rows)
```

Armed with these, we can start implementing a `Semiring` instance for `Matrix`.

```
instance Semiring a => Semiring (Matrix a) where
  zero = Scalar zero
  one = Scalar one

  Scalar a @+ Scalar b = Scalar (a @+ b)

  Matrix a @+ Matrix b =
    Matrix (zipWith (zipWith (@+)) a b)

  Scalar s @+ m = m @+ Scalar s
  Matrix [[a]] @+ Scalar b = Matrix [[a @+ b]]
```

```
m @+ s = mjoin (first @+ s, top,
                left,       rest @+ s)
  where (first, top,
         left,  rest) = msplit m

Scalar a @. Scalar b = Scalar (a @. b)
Scalar a @. Matrix b = Matrix (map (map (a @.)) b)
Matrix a @. Scalar b = Matrix (map (map (@. b)) a)
Matrix a @. Matrix b =
  Matrix [[foldl1 (@+) (zipWith (@.) row col)
           | col <- cols] | row <- a]
  where cols = transpose b
```

Defining `closure` for matrices is trickier. Lehmann [12] gave a definition of M^* for an arbitrary matrix M which satisfies the axioms of a closed semiring, and two algorithms for calculating it. The first of these generalises the Floyd-Warshall algorithm for all-pairs shortest paths [6], while the second is a semiring-flavoured form of Gaussian elimination.

Both are specified imperatively, via indexing and mutation of matrices represented as arrays. However, an elegant functional implementation can be derived almost directly from a lemma used to prove the correctness of the imperative algorithms. Given a block matrix

$$M = \begin{pmatrix} A & B \\ C & D \end{pmatrix}$$

Lehmann shows that its closure M^* will satisfy

$$M^* = \begin{pmatrix} A^* + B'\Delta^*C' & B'\Delta^* \\ \Delta^*C' & \Delta^* \end{pmatrix}$$

where $B' = A^*B$, $C' = CA^*$ and $\Delta = D + CA^*B$. The closure of a 1×1 matrix is easily calculated since $(a)^* = (a^*)$, so this leads directly to an implementation of `closure` for matrices:

```
closure (Matrix [[x]]) = Matrix [[closure x]]
closure m = mjoin
  (first' @+ top' @. rest' @. left', top' @. rest',
   rest' @. left',                   rest')
  where
    (first, top, left, rest) = msplit m
    first' = closure first
    top' = first' @. top
    left' = left @. first'
    rest' = closure (rest @+ left' @. top)
```

Multiplying a $p \times q$ matrix by a $q \times r$ matrix takes $O(pqr)$ operations from the underlying semiring. The `closure` function, when given a $n \times n$ matrix, does $O(n^2)$ semiring operations via matrix multiplication (by multiplying $1 \times n$ and $n \times n$ matrices, or $n \times 1$ and $1 \times n$), plus $O(n^2)$ semiring operations via matrix addition and `msplit`, plus one recursive call.

The recursive call to `closure` is passed a $(n-1) \times (n-1)$ matrix, and so the total number of semiring operations done by `closure` for an $n \times n$ matrix is $O(n^3)$. Thus, `closure` has the same complexity as calculating transitive closure using the Floyd-Warshall algorithm.

However, since it processes the entire graph and always produces an answer for all pairs of nodes, it is slower than standard algorithms for checking reachability between a single pair of nodes.

4. Graphs and paths

We've already seen that the reflexive transitive closure of a graph can be found using the above `closure` function, but it seems like a lot of work just to define reachability! However, choosing a richer underlying semiring allows us to calculate more interesting properties of the graph, all with the same `closure` algorithm.

The tropical semiring (more sensibly known as the min-plus semiring) has as its underlying set the nonnegative integers augmented with an extra element ∞, and defines its $+$ and $\cdot$ operators as min and addition respectively. This semiring describes the length of the shortest path in a graph: ab is interpreted as a path through a and then b (so we sum the distances), and $a + b$ is a choice between a path through a and a path through b (so we pick the shorter one). We express this in Haskell as follows, using the value `Unreachable` to represent ∞:

```
data ShortestDistance = Distance Int | Unreachable
instance Semiring ShortestDistance where
  zero = Unreachable
  one = Distance 0
  closure x = one

  x @+ Unreachable = x
  Unreachable @+ x = x
  Distance a @+ Distance b = Distance (min a b)

  x @. Unreachable = Unreachable
  Unreachable @. x = Unreachable
  Distance a @. Distance b = Distance (a + b)
```

For a directed graph with edge lengths, we make a matrix M such that M_{ij} is the length of the edge from i to j, or `Unreachable` if there is none. M is represented in Haskell with the type `Matrix ShortestDistance`, and calling `closure` calculates the length of the shortest path between any two nodes.

To see this, we can appeal again to the infinite series view of closure: $(M^k)_{ij}$ is the length of the shortest path with k edges from node i to node j, and M^* is the sum (which in this semiring means "minimum") of M^k for any k. Thus, $(M^*)_{ij}$ is the length of the shortest path with any number of edges from node i to node j.

Often we're interested in finding the actual shortest path, not just its length. We can define another semiring that keeps track of this data, where paths are represented as lists of edges, each represented as a pair of nodes.

There may not be a unique shortest path. If we are faced with a choice between two equally short paths, we must either have some means of disambiguating them or be prepared to return multiple results. In the following implementation, we choose the former: we assume nodes are ordered and choose the lexicographically least of multiple equally short paths.

```
data ShortestPath n = Path Int [(n,n)] | NoPath
instance Ord n => Semiring (ShortestPath n) where
  zero = NoPath
  one = Path 0 []
  closure x = one

  x @+ NoPath = x
  NoPath @+ x = x
  Path a p @+ Path a' p'
    | a < a'             = Path a p
    | a == a' && p < p'  = Path a p
    | otherwise          = Path a' p'

  x @. NoPath = NoPath
  NoPath @. x = NoPath
  Path a p @. Path a' p' = Path (a + a') (p ++ p')
```

The `@.` operator given here isn't especially fast since `++` takes time linear in the length of its left argument, but this can be avoided by using an alternative data structure with constant-time appends such as difference lists.

We construct the matrix M, where M_{ij} is `Path d [(i,j)]` if there's an edge of length `d` between nodes i and j or `NoPath` if there's none. Calculating M^* in this semiring will calculate not only the length of the shortest path between all pairs of nodes, but give the actual route.

To calculate longest paths we can use a similar construction. We have to be slightly more careful here, because a graph with cycles contains arbitrarily long paths.

As well as nonnegative integer distances, we have two other possible values: `LUnreachable`, indicating that there is no path between two nodes, and `LInfinite`, indicating that there's an infinitely long path due to a cycle of positive length. This forms a semiring as shown:

```
data LongestDistance = LDistance Int
                     | LUnreachable
                     | LInfinite
instance Semiring LongestDistance where
  zero = LUnreachable
  one = LDistance 0

  closure LUnreachable = LDistance 0
  closure (LDistance 0) = LDistance 0
  closure _ = LInfinite

  x @+ LUnreachable = x
  LUnreachable @+ x = x
  LInfinite @+ _ = LInfinite
  _ @+ LInfinite = LInfinite
  LDistance x @+ LDistance y = LDistance (max x y)

  x @. LUnreachable = LUnreachable
  LUnreachable @. x = LUnreachable
  LInfinite @. _ = LInfinite
  _ @. LInfinite = LInfinite
  LDistance x @. LDistance y = LDistance (x + y)
```

We can find the widest path (also known as the highest-capacity path) by using min instead of addition as semiring multiplication (to pick the narrowest of successive edges in a path). By working with real numbers as edge weights, interpreted as the probability of failure of a given edge, we can calculate the most reliable path.

There is an intuition for closure for an arbitrary graph and an arbitrary semiring. Each edge of the graph is assigned an element of the semiring, which make up the elements of the matrix M. Any path (sequence of edges) is assigned the product of the elements on each edge, and M^*_{ij} is the sum of the products assigned to every path from i to j. The fact that product distributes over sum means we can calculate this, using the above `closure` algorithm, in polynomial time.

We can use this intuition to construct powerful graph analyses, simply by making an appropriate semiring and calculating the closure of a graph's adjacency matrix. For instance, we can make a semiring of subsets of nodes of a graph, where $+$ is intersection and $\cdot$ is union. We set $M_{ij} = \{i, j\}$, and calculate M^*. Each path is assigned the set of nodes visited along that path, and taking the "sum over all paths" calculates the intersection of those sets, or the nodes visited along all paths. Thus, M^*_{ij} gives the set of nodes that are visited along all paths from i to j, or in other words, the graph dominators of j with start node i.

5. "Linear" equations and regular languages

One of the sharpest tools in the toolbox of linear algebra is the use of matrix techniques to solve systems of linear equations.

Since we get to specify the semiring, we define what "linear" means. Many problems can then be described as systems of "linear" equations, even though they're far from linear in the classical sense.

Suppose we have a system of equations in some semiring on a set of variables $x_1, \ldots, x_n$, where each x_i is defined by a linear combination of the variables and a constant term. That is, each

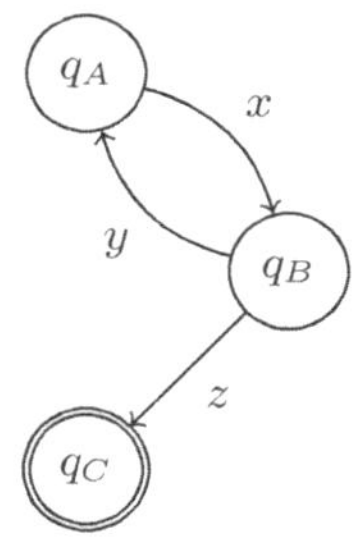

$$\begin{pmatrix} A \\ B \\ C \end{pmatrix} = \begin{pmatrix} 0 & x & 0 \\ y & 0 & z \\ 0 & 0 & 0 \end{pmatrix} \begin{pmatrix} A \\ B \\ C \end{pmatrix} + \begin{pmatrix} 0 \\ 0 \\ 1 \end{pmatrix}$$

Figure 1. A finite state machine and its matrix representation

equation is of the following form, where a_{ij} and b_i are givens:

$$x_i = a_{i1}x_1 + a_{i2}x_2 + \cdots + b_i$$

We arrange the unknowns x_i into a column vector X, the coefficients A into a square matrix A and the constants b into a column vector B. The system of equations now becomes:

$$X = AX + B$$

This equation defines X as the fixpoint of an affine map. As we saw in section 2, it therefore has a solution $X = A^*B$, which can be calculated with our definition of `closure` for matrices.

The above was a little cavalier with matrix dimensions. Technically, our machinery for solving such equations is only defined for $n \times n$ matrices, not column vectors. However, we can extend the column vectors X and B to $n \times n$ matrices by making a matrix all of whose columns are equal. Solving the equation with such matrices comes to the same answer as using column vectors directly, so we keep working with column vectors. Happily, our Haskell code for manipulating matrices accepts column and row vectors without problems, as long as we don't try to calculate the closure of anything but a square matrix.

If we have some system that maps input to output, where the mapping can be described as a linear map $X \mapsto AX + B$, then the fixpoint $X = A^*B$ gives a "stable state" of the system.

As we see below, Kleene's proof that all finite state machines accept a regular language and the McNaughton-Yamada algorithm [15] for constructing a regular expression to describe a state machine can also be described as such "linear" systems.

Given a description of a finite state machine, we can write down a regular grammar describing the language it accepts. For every transition $q_A \xrightarrow{x} q_B$, we have a grammar production $A \to xB$, and for every accepting state q_A we have a production $A \to \varepsilon$.

We can group these productions by their left-hand sides to give a system of equations. For instance, in the machine of Figure 1 there is a state q_B with transitions $q_B \xrightarrow{y} q_A$ and $q_B \xrightarrow{z} q_C$, so we get the equation:

$$B = yA + zC$$

In the semiring of regular languages (where addition is union, multiplication is concatenation, and closure is the Kleene star), these are all linear equations. For an n-state machine, we define the $n \times n$ matrix $\mathbf{M}$ where $\mathbf{M}_{ij}$ is the symbol on the transition from the ith state to the jth, or 0 (the empty language) if there is no such transition. The vector $\mathbf{A}$ is constructed by setting $\mathbf{A}_i$ to 1 (the language containing only ε) when the ith state is accepting, and 0 otherwise. The languages are represented by the vector of unknowns L, where L_i is the language accepted starting in the ith state. For our example machine, $\mathbf{M}$ and $\mathbf{A}$ are shown at the right of Figure 1.

Then, the regular grammar is described by:

$$\mathbf{L} = \mathbf{M} \cdot \mathbf{L} + \mathbf{A}$$

This equation has a solution given by $\mathbf{L} = \mathbf{M}^* \cdot \mathbf{A}$. We can use our existing `closure` function to solve these equations and build a regular expression that describes the language accepted by the finite state machine.

In Haskell, we define a "free" semiring which simply records the syntax tree of semiring expressions. To qualify as a semiring we must have `a @+ b == b @+ a`, `a @. one == a`, and so on. We sidestep this by cheating: we don't define an `Eq` instance for `FreeSemiring`, and consider two `FreeSemiring` values equal if they are equal according to the semiring laws. However, to make our `FreeSemiring` values more compact, we do implement certain simplifications like $0x = 0$.

```
data FreeSemiring gen =
    Zero
  | One
  | Gen gen
  | Closure (FreeSemiring gen)
  | (FreeSemiring gen) :@+ (FreeSemiring gen)
  | (FreeSemiring gen) :@. (FreeSemiring gen)

instance Semiring (FreeSemiring gen) where
  zero = Zero
  one = One

  Zero @+ x = x
  x @+ Zero = x
  x @+ y = x :@+ y

  Zero @. x = Zero
  x @. Zero = Zero
  One @. x = x
  x @. One = x
  x @. y = x :@. y

  closure Zero = One
  closure x = Closure x
```

If we construct $\mathbf{M}$ as a `Matrix (FreeSemiring Char)`, then calculating $\mathbf{M}^* \cdot \mathbf{A}$ will give us a vector of `FreeSemiring Char`, each element of which can be interpreted as a regular expression describing the language accepted from a particular state.

For the example of Figure 1, `closure` then tells us that the language accepted with state A as the starting state is $x(yx)^*z$. This algorithm produces a regular expression that accurately describes the language accepted by a given state machine, but it is not in general the shortest such expression.

6. Dataflow analysis

Many program analyses and optimisations can be computed by *dataflow analysis*. As an example, we consider the classical liveness analysis, which computes which assignments in an imperative program assign values which will never be read ("dead"), and which ones may be used again ("live").

We construct the program's control flow graph by dividing it into control-free basic blocks and with edges indicating where there are jumps between blocks. For a given basic block b, the set of variables live at the start of the block (IN_b) are those used by the basic block itself (USE_b) before their first definition, and those which are live at the end of the block (OUT_b) but not assigned a new value during the block (DEF_b). The variables live at the end of a basic block are those live at the start of any successor.

This gives a system of equations:

$$\mathrm{IN}_b = (\mathrm{OUT}_b \cap \overline{\mathrm{DEF}_b}) \cup \mathrm{USE}_b$$
$$\mathrm{OUT}_b = \bigcup_{b' \in \mathrm{succ}(b)} \mathrm{IN}_{b'}$$

```
x := 1
z := 0

while x < y:

    x := x * 2
    z := z - 1

return x
```

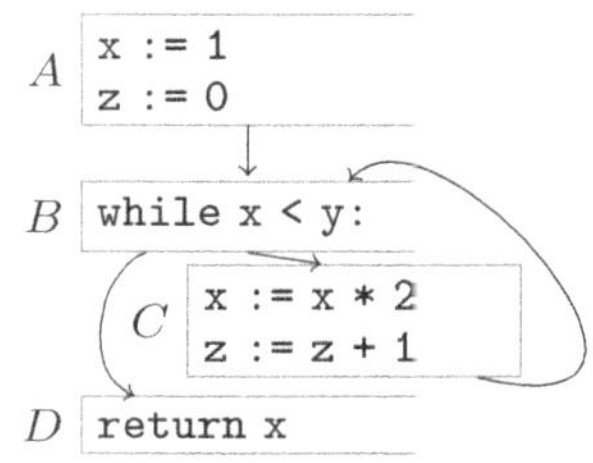

Figure 2. A simple imperative program to calculate the smallest power of two greater than the input `y`, and its control flow graph. The variable `z` does not affect the output.

An example program is given in Figure 2, where DEF and USE are as follows:

$$\mathrm{DEF}_A = \{\mathtt{x}, \mathtt{z}\} \qquad \mathrm{USE}_A = \emptyset$$
$$\mathrm{DEF}_B = \emptyset \qquad \mathrm{USE}_B = \{\mathtt{x}, \mathtt{y}\}$$
$$\mathrm{DEF}_C = \{\mathtt{x}, \mathtt{z}\} \qquad \mathrm{USE}_C = \{\mathtt{x}, \mathtt{z}\}$$
$$\mathrm{DEF}_D = \emptyset \qquad \mathrm{USE}_D = \{\mathtt{x}\}$$

If we solve for IN_b and OUT_b, we find that `z` is not live upon entry to D (that is, $\mathtt{z} \notin \mathrm{IN}_D$). However, `z` is considered live on entry to C, even though it is never affects the output of the program. We see how to remedy this using *faint variables analysis* below, but first we show how the classical live variables analysis can be calculated using our semiring machinery.

We define a semiring of sets of variables, where 0 is the empty set, 1 is the set of all variables in the program, $+$ is union, $\cdot$ is intersection, and $x^* = 1$ for all sets x. Our system of equations can be represented as follows in this semiring:

$$\begin{aligned}\mathrm{OUT}_b &= \sum_{b' \in \mathrm{succ}(b)} \mathrm{IN}_{b'} \\ &= \sum_{b' \in \mathrm{succ}(b)} \overline{\mathrm{DEF}_{b'}} \cdot \mathrm{OUT}_{b'} + \mathrm{USE}_{b'} \\ &= \left(\sum_{b' \in \mathrm{succ}(b)} \overline{\mathrm{DEF}_{b'}} \cdot \mathrm{OUT}_{b'} \right) + \left(\sum_{b' \in \mathrm{succ}(b)} \mathrm{USE}_{b'} \right)\end{aligned}$$

This is a system of affine equations over the variables OUT_b, with coefficients $\overline{\mathrm{DEF}_{b'}}$ and constant terms $\sum_{b' \in \mathrm{succ}(b)} \mathrm{USE}_{b'}$. As before, we can solve it by building a matrix M containing the coefficients and a column vector A containing the constant terms. The solution vector OUT_b is given by $M^* \cdot A$ using the same `closure` algorithm.

Dataflow analyses can be treated more generally by studying the *transfer functions* of each basic block. We consider backwards analyses (like liveness analysis), where the transfer functions specify IN_b given OUT_b (the discussion applies equally well to forwards analyses, with suitable relabelling).

The equations have the following form:

$$\mathrm{IN}_b = f_b(\mathrm{OUT}_b)$$
$$\mathrm{OUT}_b = \operatorname*{join}_{b' \in \mathrm{succ}(b)} \mathrm{IN}_{b'}$$

or, more compactly,

$$\mathrm{OUT}_b = \operatorname*{join}_{b' \in \mathrm{succ}(b)} f(\mathrm{OUT}_{b'})$$

For many standard analyses, we can define a semiring where f_b is linear, and join is summation. This semiring is often the semiring of sets of variables (as above) or expressions, or its dual where $+$

is intersection, $\cdot$ is union, 0 is the entire set of variables and 1 is the empty set.

Such analyses are often referred to as bit-vector problems [11], as the sets can be represented efficiently using bitwise operations.

The available expressions analysis can be expressed as a linear system using this latter semiring, where the set of available expressions at the start of a block is the intersection of the sets of available expressions at the end of each predecessor.

Other analyses don't have such a simple structure. The *faint variables analysis* is an extension of live variables analysis which can detect that certain assignments are useless even though they are considered "live" by the standard analysis. For instance, in Figure 2, the variable `z` was considered live at the start of block C, even though all statements involving `z` can be deleted without affecting the meaning of the program. Live variable analysis will consider `x` "live" since it may be used on the next iteration. Faint variable analysis finds the *strongly live* variables: those used to compute a value which is not dead.

We can write transfer functions for faint variables analysis, which when given OUT_b compute IN_b. For instance, in our example $\mathtt{x} \in \mathrm{IN}_C$ if $\mathtt{x} \in \mathrm{OUT}_C$ (since `x` is used to compute the new value of `x`), and similarly $\mathtt{z} \in \mathrm{IN}_C$ if $\mathtt{z} \in \mathrm{OUT}_C$.

These transfer functions don't fall into the class of bitvector problems, and so our previous tactic won't work directly. However, they are in the more general class of *distributive dataflow* problems [10]: they have the property that $f_b(A \cup B) = f_b(A) \cup f_b(B)$. Happily, such transfer functions form a semiring.

We define a datatype to describe such functions which distribute over set union. For more generality, we consider an arbitrary commutative monoid instead of limiting ourselves to set union. Haskell has a standard definition of monoids, but they are not generally required to be commutative. We define the typeclass Commutative-Monoid for those monoids which are commutative. It has no methods and instances are trivial; it serves only as a marker by which the programmer can certify his monoid does commute.

```
class Monoid m => CommutativeMonoid m
instance Ord a => CommutativeMonoid (Set a)
```

With that done, we can define the semiring of transfer functions:

```
newtype Transfer m = Transfer (m -> m)
instance (Eq m, CommutativeMonoid m) =>
          Semiring (Transfer m) where
  zero = Transfer (const mempty)
  one = Transfer id
  Transfer f @+ Transfer g =
     Transfer (\x -> f x `mappend` g x)
  Transfer f @. Transfer g = Transfer (f . g)
```

Multiplication in this semiring is composition and addition is pointwise `mappend`, which is union in the case of sets. The distributive law is satisfied assuming all of the transfer functions themselves distribute over `mappend`.

The closure of a transfer function is a function f^* such that $f^* = 1 + f \cdot f^*$. When applied to an argument, we expect that $f^*(x) = x + f(f^*(x))$. The closure can be defined as a fixpoint iteration, which will give a suitable answer if it converges:

```
  closure (Transfer f) =
    Transfer (\x -> fixpoint (\y -> x `mappend` f y) x)
    where fixpoint f init =
            if init == next
              then init
              else fixpoint f next
          where next = f init
```

Convergence of this fixpoint iteration is not automatically guaranteed. However, it always converges when the transfer functions and the monoid operation are monotonic increasing in an order of finite height (such as the set of variables in a program), so this gives us a valid definition of `closure` for our transfer functions.

We can then calculate M^*, where M is the matrix of basic block transfer functions. M^* gives us their "transitive closure", which are the transfer functions of the program as a whole. Calling these functions with a trivial input (say, the empty set of variables in the case of faint variable analysis) allows us to generate the solution to the dataflow equations.

7. Polynomials, power series and knapsacks

Given any semiring R, we can define the semiring of polynomials in one variable x whose coefficients are drawn from R, which is written $R[x]$. We represent polynomials as a list of coefficients, where the ith element of the list represents the coefficient of x^i. Thus, $3 + 4x^2$ is represented as the list $[3, 0, 4]$.

We can start defining an instance of `Semiring` for such lists. The zero and unit polynomials are given by (where the `one` on the right-hand-side refers to `r`'s `one`):

```
instance Semiring r => Semiring [r] where
  zero = []
  one = [one]
```

Addition is fairly straightforward: we add corresponding coefficients. If one list is shorter than the other, it's considered to be padding with zeros to the correct length (since $1 + 2x = 1 + 2x + 0x^2 + 0x^3 + \ldots$).

```
  [] @+ y = y
  x @+ [] = x
  (x:xs) @+ (y:ys) = (x @+ y):(xs @+ ys)
```

The head of the list representation of a polynomial is the constant term, and the tail is the sum of all terms divisible by x. So, the Haskell value `a:p` corresponds to the polynomial $a + px$, where p is itself a polynomial. Multiplying two of these gives us:

$$(a + px)(b + qx) = ab + (aq + pb + pqx)x$$

This directly translates into an implementation of polynomial multiplication:

```
  [] @. _ = []
  _ @. [] = []
  (a:p) @. (b:q) = (a @. b):(map (a @.) q @+
                              map (@. b) p @+
                              (zero:(p @. q)))
```

If we multiply a polynomial with coefficients a_i (that is, the polynomial $\sum_i a_i x^i$) by one with coefficients b_i resulting in the polynomial with coefficients c_i, then the coefficients are related by:

$$c_n = \sum_{i=0}^{n} a_i b_{n-i}$$

This is the discrete convolution of two sequences. Our definition of `@.` is in fact a pleasantly index-free definition of convolution.

In order to give a valid definition of `Semiring`, we must define the operation s^* such that $s^* = 1 + s \cdot s^*$. This seems impossible: for instance, there is no polynomial p such that $p = 1 + xp$, since the degrees of both sides don't match.

To form a closed semiring, we need to generalise somewhat and consider not just polynomials, but arbitrary *formal power series*, which are polynomials which may be infinite, giving us the semiring $R[[x]]$.

Our power series are purely formal, representing sequences of elements from a closed semiring. We have no notion of "evaluating" such a series by specifying x. We think of the formal power series $1 + x + x^2 + x^3 \ldots$ as the sequence $1, 1, 1, \ldots$, and require no infinite sums, limits or convergence. As such, "multiplication by x" simply means "shifting the series by one place", and we can write $pxq = pqx$ (but not $pqx = qpx$) even when the underlying semiring does not have commutative multiplication.

Since Haskell's lists are lazily defined and may be infinite, our existing definitions for addition and multiplication work for such power series, as demonstrated by McIlroy in his functional pearl [14].

Given a power series $s = a + px$, we seek its closure $s^* = b + qx$, such that $s^* = 1 + s \cdot s^*$:

$$\begin{aligned} b + qx &= 1 + (a + px)(b + qx) \\ &= 1 + ab + aqx + p(b + qx)x \end{aligned}$$

The constant terms must satisfy $b = 1 + ab$, so a solution is given by $b = a^*$. The other terms must satisfy $q = aq + ps^*$. This states that q is the fixpoint of an affine map, so a solution is given by $q = a^*ps^*$ and thus $s^* = a^*(1 + ps^*)$. This translates neatly into lazy Haskell as follows:

```
closure [] = one
closure (a:p) = r
  where r = [closure a] @. (one:(p @. r))
```

This allows us to solve affine equations of the form $x = bx + c$, where the unknown x and the parameters b and c are all power series over an arbitrary semiring. This form of problem arises naturally in some dynamic programming problems. As an example, we consider the unbounded integer knapsack problem.

We are given n types of item, with nonnegative integer weights $w_1, \ldots, w_n$ and nonnegative integer values $v_1, \ldots, v_n$. Our knapsack can only hold a weight W, and we want to find out the maximal value that we can fit in the knapsack by choosing some number of each item, while remaining below or equal to the weight limit W. This problem is NP-hard, but admits an algorithm with complexity polynomial in W (this is referred to as a *pseudo-polynomial time algorithm* since in general W can be exponentially larger than the description of the problem).

The algorithm calculates a table t, where $t(w)$ is the maximum value possible within a weight limit w. We set $t(0)$ to 0, and for all other w:

$$t(w) = \max_{0 \le w_i \le w} (v_i + t(w - w_i))$$

This expresses that the optimal packing of the knapsack to weight w can be found by looking at all of the elements which could be inserted and choosing the one that gives the highest value.

The algebraic structure of this algorithm becomes more clear when we rewrite it using the max-plus semiring that we earlier used to calculate longest paths, which we implemented in Haskell as `LongestDistance`. Confusingly, in this semiring the unit element is the number 0, since that is the identity of the semiring's multiplication, which is addition of path lengths. The zero element of this semiring is ∞, which is the identity of max.

We take v_i and $t(w)$ to be elements of this semiring. Then, in this semiring's notation,

$$t(0) = 1$$

$$t(w) = \sum_{i=0}^{w} v_i \cdot t(w - w_i)$$

We can combine the two parameters v_i and w_i into a single polynomial $V = \sum_i v_i x^{w_i}$. For example, suppose we fill our knapsack with four types of coin, of values 1, 5, 7 and 10 and weights 3, 6, 8 and 6 respectively. The polynomial V is given by:

$$V = x^3 + 5x^6 + 7x^8 + 10x^6$$

Since we are using the max-plus semiring, this is equivalent to:

$$V = x^3 + 10x^6 + 7x^8$$

Represented as a list, the wth element of V is the value of the most valuable item with weight w (which is zero if there are no items of weight w). Similarly, we represent $t(w)$ as the power series $T = \sum_i t(i)x^i$. The list representation of T has as its wth element the maximal value possible within a weight limit w.

We can now see that the definition of $t(w)$ above is in fact the convolution of T and V. Together with the base case, that $t(0)$ is the semiring's unit, this gives us a simpler definition of $t(w)$:

$$T = 1 + V \cdot T$$

The above can equally be written as $T = V^*$, and so we get the following elegant solution to the unbounded integer knapsack problem (where `!!` is Haskell's list indexing operator):

```
knapsack values maxweight = closure values !! maxweight
```

Note that our previous intuition of x^* being the infinite sum $1 + x + x^2 + \ldots$ applies nicely here: the solution to the integer knapsack problem is the maximum value attainable by choosing no items, or one item, or two items, and so on for any number of items.

Instead of using the `LongestDistance` semiring, we can define `LongestPath` in the same way that we defined `ShortestPath` above, with max in place of min. Using this semiring, our above definition of `knapsack` still works and gives the set of elements chosen for the knapsack, rather than just their total value.

8. Linear recurrences and Petri nets

The power series semiring has another general application: it can express linear recurrences between variables. Since the definition of "linear" can be drawn from an arbitrary semiring, this is quite an expressive notion.

As we are discussing functional programming, we are obliged by tradition to calculate the Fibonacci sequence.

The nth term of the Fibonacci sequence is given by the sum of the previous two terms. We construct the formal power series F whose nth coefficient is the nth Fibonacci number. Multiplying this sequence by x^k shifts along by k places, so we can rewrite the recurrence relation as:

$$1 + xF + x^2F = F$$

This defines $F = 1 + (x + x^2)F$, and so $F = (x + x^2)^*$. So, we can calculate the Fibonacci sequence as `closure [0,1,1]`.

There are of course much more interesting things that can be described as linear recurrences and thus as formal power series. Cohen et al. [4] showed that a class of Petri nets known as *timed event graphs* can be described by linear recurrences in the max-plus semiring (the one we previously used for longest paths and knapsacks).

A timed event graph consists of a set of *places* and a set of *transitions*, and a collection of directed edges between places and transitions. Atomic, indistinguishable *tokens* are consumed and produced by transitions and held in places.

In a timed event graph, unlike a general Petri net, each place has exactly one input transition and exactly one output transition, as well as a nonnegative integer delay, which represents the processing time at that place. When a token enters a place, it is not eligible to leave until the delay has elapsed.

When all of the input places of a transition have at least one token ready to leave, the transition "fires". One token is removed from each input place, and one token is added to each output place of the transition. For simplicity, we assume that transitions are instant, and that a token arrives at all of the output places of a transition as soon as one is ready to leave each of the input places. If desired, transition processing times can be simulated by adding extra places.

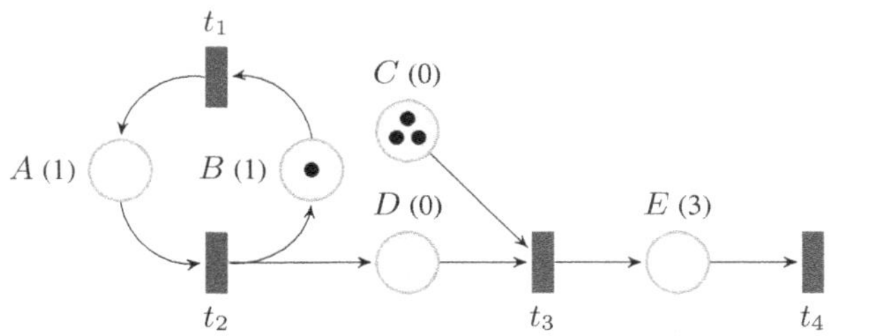

Figure 3. A timed event graph with four transitions t_1, t_2, t_3, t_4 and five places A, B, C, D, E with delays in parentheses, where all but two of the places are initially empty.

In Figure 3, the only transition which is ready to fire at time 0 is t_1. When it fires, it removes a token from B and adds one to A. This makes transition t_2 fire at time 1, which adds a token to B causing t_1 to fire at time 2, then t_2 to fire at time 3 and so on.

When t_2 fires at times $1, 3, 5, \ldots$, a token is added to place D. The first three times this happens, t_3 fires, but after that the supply of tokens from C is depleted. t_4 fires after the tokens have waited in E for a delay of three steps, so t_4 fires at times 4, 6 and 8.

Simulating such a timed event graph requires calculating the times at which tokens arrive and leave each place. For each place p, we define the sequences $\mathrm{IN}(p)$ and $\mathrm{OUT}(p)$. The ith element of $\mathrm{IN}(p)$ is the time at which a token arrives into p for the ith time. The ith element of $\mathrm{OUT}(p)$ is the time at which a token becomes available from p for the ith time, which may be some time before it actually leaves p.

In the example of Figure 3, we have:

$$
\begin{aligned}
\mathrm{IN}(A) &= 0, 2, 4, 6 \ldots & \mathrm{OUT}(A) &= 1, 3, 5, 7 \ldots \\
\mathrm{IN}(B) &= 1, 3, 5, 7 \ldots & \mathrm{OUT}(B) &= 0, 2, 4, 6 \ldots \\
\mathrm{IN}(C) &= \text{—} & \mathrm{OUT}(C) &= 0, 0, 0 \\
\mathrm{IN}(D) &= 1, 3, 5, 7 \ldots & \mathrm{OUT}(D) &= 1, 3, 5, 7 \ldots \\
\mathrm{IN}(E) &= 1, 3, 5 & \mathrm{OUT}(E) &= 4, 6, 8
\end{aligned}
$$

We say that a place p' is a predecessor of p (and write $p' \in \mathrm{pred}(p)$) if the output transition of p' is the input transition of p. Since transitions fire instantly, a place receives a token as soon as all of its predecessors are ready to produce one.

$$\mathrm{IN}(p)_i = \max_{p' \in \mathrm{pred}(p)} \mathrm{OUT}(p')_i$$

Exactly when the ith token becomes available from a place p depends on the amount of time tokens spend processing at p, which we write as $\mathrm{delay}(p)$, and on the number of tokens initially in p, which we write as $\mathrm{nstart}(p)$. The times at which the first $\mathrm{nstart}(p)$ tokens become ready to leave p are given by the sequence $\mathrm{START}(p)$, which is nondecreasing and each element of which is less than $\mathrm{delay}(p)$. In the example we assume the initial tokens of B and C are immediately available, so we have $\mathrm{START}(B) = 0$ and $\mathrm{START}(C) = 0, 0, 0$.

Thus, the time that the ith token becomes available from p is given by:

$$\mathrm{OUT}(p)_i = \begin{cases} \mathrm{START(p)}_i & i < \mathrm{nstart}(p) \\ \mathrm{IN}(p)_{i-\mathrm{nstart}(p)} + \mathrm{delay}(p) & i \geq \mathrm{nstart}(p) \end{cases}$$

By adopting the convention that $\mathrm{IN}(p)_i$ is $-\infty$ when $i < 0$ and that $\mathrm{START}(p)_i$ is $-\infty$ when $i < 0$ or $i \geq \mathrm{nstart}(p)$, we can write the above more succinctly as:

$$\mathrm{OUT}(p)_i = \max(\mathrm{START(p)}_i, \mathrm{IN}(p)_{i-\mathrm{nstart}(p)} + \mathrm{delay}(p))$$

This gives a set of recurrences between the sequences: the value of $\mathrm{OUT}(p)$ depends on the previous values of $\mathrm{IN}(p)$.

We now shift notation to make the semiring structure of this problem apparent. We return to the max-plus algebra, previously used for longest distances and knapsacks, where we write max as $+$, and addition as $\cdot$. Instead of sequences, let's talk about formal power series, where the ith element of the sequence is now the coefficient of x^i. With our semiring goggles on, the above equations now say:

$$
\begin{aligned}
\mathrm{IN}(p) &= \sum_{p' \in \mathrm{pred}(p)} \mathrm{OUT}(p') \\
\mathrm{OUT}(p) &= \mathrm{delay}(p) \cdot x^{\mathrm{nstart(p)}} \cdot \mathrm{IN}(p) + \mathrm{START}(p)
\end{aligned}
$$

We can eliminate $\mathrm{IN}(p)$ by substituting its definition into the second equation:

$$\mathrm{OUT}(p) = \sum_{p' \in \mathrm{pred}(p)} \mathrm{delay}(p) \cdot x^{\mathrm{nstart(p)}} \cdot \mathrm{OUT}(p') + \mathrm{START}(p)$$

What we're left with is a system of affine equations, where the unknowns, the coefficients and the constants are all formal power series over the max-plus semiring.

We can solve these exactly as before. We build the matrix $\mathbf{M}$ containing all of the $\mathrm{delay}(p) \cdot x^{\mathrm{nstart}(p)}$ coefficients, and the column vector $\mathbf{S}$ containing all of the $\mathrm{START}(p)$ sequences, and then calculate $\mathbf{M}^* \cdot \mathbf{S}$ (which, as before, can be done with a single call to `closure` and a multiplication by $\mathbf{S}$). The components of the resulting vector are power series; their coefficients give $\mathbf{OUT}(p)$ for each place p.

Thus, we can simulate a timed event graph by representing it as a linear system and using our previously-defined semiring machinery.

9. Discussion

It turns out that very many problems can be solved with linear algebra, for a definition of "linear" suited to the problem at hand. There are surprisingly many questions that can be answered with a call to `closure` with the right `Semiring` instance. Even still, this paper barely scratches the surface of this rich theory. Much more can be found in books by Gondran and Minoux [9], Golan [7, 8] and others.

The connections between regular languages, path problems in graphs, and matrix inversion have been known for some time. The relationship between regular languages and semirings is described in Conway's book [5]. Backhouse and Carré [3] used regular algebra to solve path problems (noting connections to classical linear algebra), and Tarjan [17] gave an algorithm for solving path problems by a form of Gaussian elimination.

A version of closed semiring was given by Aho, Hopcroft and Ullman [2], along with transitive closure and shortest path algorithms. The form of closed semiring that this paper discusses was given by Lehmann [12], with two algorithms for calculating the closure of a matrix: an algorithm generalising the Floyd-Warshall all-pairs shortest-paths algorithm [6], and another generalising Gaussian elimination, demonstrating the equivalence of these two in their general form. More recently, Abdali and Saunders [1] reformulate the notion of closure of a matrix in terms of "eliminants", which formalise the intermediate steps of Gaussian elimination.

The use of semirings to describe path problems in graphs is widespread [9, 16]. Often, the structures studied include the extra axiom that $a + a = a$, giving rise to *idempotent semirings* or *dioids*. Such structures can be partially ordered, and it becomes possible to talk about least fixed points of affine maps. These have proven strong enough structures to build a variant of classical real analysis [13].

Cohen et al. [4], as well as providing the linear description of Petri nets we saw in section 8, go on to develop an analogue of classical linear systems theory in a semiring. In this theory, they explore semiring versions of many classical concepts, such as stability of a linear system and describing a system's steady-state as an eigenvalue of a transfer matrix.

Acknowledgments

The author is grateful to Alan Mycroft for suffering through early drafts of this work and offering helpful advice, and to Raphael Proust, Stephen Roantree and the anonymous reviewers for their useful comments, and finally to Trinity College, Cambridge for financial support.

References

[1] S. Abdali and B. Saunders. Transitive closure and related semiring properties via eliminants. *Theoretical Computer Science*, 40:257–274, 1985.

[2] A. V. Aho, J. E. Hopcroft, and J. D. Ullman. *The Design and Analysis of Computer Algorithms*. Addison-Wesley, 1974.

[3] R. Backhouse and B. Carré. Regular algebra applied to path-finding problems. *IMA Journal of Applied Mathematics*, 2(15):161–186, 1975.

[4] G. Cohen and P. Moller. Linear system theory for discrete event systems. In *23rd IEEE Conference on Decision and Control*, pages 539–544, 1984.

[5] J. Conway. *Regular algebra and finite machines*. Chapman and Hall (London), 1971.

[6] R. Floyd. Algorithm 97: shortest path. *Communications of the ACM*, 5(6):345, 1962.

[7] J. S. Golan. *Semirings and their applications*. Springer, 1999.

[8] J. S. Golan. *Semirings and affine equations over them*. Kluwer Academic Publishers, 2003.

[9] M. Gondran and M. Minoux. *Graphs, dioids and semirings*. Springer, 2008.

[10] J. Kam and J. Ullman. Global data flow analysis and iterative algorithms. *Journal of the ACM (JACM)*, 23(1):158–171, 1976.

[11] U. Khedker and D. Dhamdhere. A generalized theory of bit vector data flow analysis. *ACM Transactions on Programming Languages and Systems (TOPLAS)*, 16(5):1472–1511, 1994.

[12] D. Lehmann. Algebraic structures for transitive closure. *Theoretical Computer Science*, 4(1):59–76, 1977.

[13] V. P. Maslov. *Idempotent analysis*. American Mathematical Society, 1992.

[14] M. D. McIlroy. Power series, power serious. *Journal of Functional Programming*, 9(3):325–337, 1999.

[15] R. McNaughton and H. Yamada. Regular expressions and state graphs for automata. *IRE Transactions on Electronic Computers*, 9(1):39–47, 1960.

[16] M. Mohri. Semiring frameworks and algorithms for shortest-distance problems. *Journal of Automata, Languages and Combinatorics*, 7(3): 321–350, 2002.

[17] R. Tarjan. Solving path problems on directed graphs. Technical report, Stanford University, 1975.

Efficient Divide-and-Conquer Parsing of Practical Context-Free Languages

Jean-Philippe Bernardy Koen Claessen
Chalmers University of Technology and University of Gothenburg
{bernardy,koen}@chalmers.se

Abstract

We present a divide-and-conquer algorithm for parsing context-free languages efficiently. Our algorithm is an instance of Valiant's (1975), who reduced the problem of parsing to matrix multiplications. We show that, while the conquer step of Valiant's is $O(n^3)$ in the worst case, it improves to $O(\log^3 n)$, under certain conditions satisfied by many useful inputs. These conditions occur for example in program texts written by humans. The improvement happens because the multiplications involve an overwhelming majority of empty matrices. This result is relevant to modern computing: divide-and-conquer algorithms can be parallelized relatively easily.

Categories and Subject Descriptors F.4.2 [*Grammars and Other Rewriting Systems*]: Parsing

Keywords Divide-and-Conquer, Parsing, Complexity, Context-Free Languages, Iteration

1. Introduction

Recent years have seen the rise of parallel computer architectures for the masses. Multicore CPUs and GPUs are legion. One would expect functional programs to be a perfect match for these architectures. Indeed, thanks to the absence of side-effects, functional programs are conceptually easy to parallelise. However, functional programmers have traditionally relied heavily on lists as the data-structure of choice. This tradition hinders the adaptation of functional programs to the age of parallelism. Indeed, the very linear structure of lists imposes a sequential treatment of them. In an eloquent 2009 ICFP invited talk, Guy Steele harangued the functional programming crowds to stop using lists and use sequences, represented as balanced trees. If a computation over them follows the divide-and-conquer skeleton, and uses an associative operator to cheaply combine intermediate results at each node, their fractal structure allows to take advantage of many processors in parallel; in fact as many as there are leaves in the tree.

An additional benefit of the structure its ability to support incremental computation. That is, if one remembers the intermediate results of the computation for each node, then after changing a single leaf in the tree, it suffices to recompute the results for the nodes which are on the path from the root to the given leaf. If the tree is balanced, this means that one only has to run the association operator only a few times to update the result after a single incremental change.

Some problems are naturally solved by divide-and-conquer algorithms. This is the case for example of vector operations, which treat each element independently of the others. However, many problems require creativity to discover efficient divide-and-conquer solutions. This is the case of the problem of parsing context free languages.

Valiant (1975) discovered a divide-and-conquer algorithm for context-free recognition. However, given Valiant's assumptions, the cost of the conquer step is cubic. This means that the conquer step dominates the cost of the algorithm: what we gain by running sub-problems in parallel is dwarfed by the cost of what we must run sequentially. Therefore the divide-and-conquer structure does not yield a significant performance benefit. In this paper, we show that on most inputs, one can carefully implement Valiant's algorithm to get a polylogarithmic conquer step, yielding good overall performance.

We make the following contributions:

- We give a new correctness proof of the Valiant algorithm. We re-construct Valiant algorithm by calculating it from its specification, in a style reminiscent of Bird and de Moor (1997) (Sec. 2.4).
- We characterize a new subclass of context-free languages, corresponding to strings parsed in a hierarchical manner (Def. 8, Sec. 3.1).
- We show that, for languages of the new subclass, the time complexity of the conquer step is $O(\log^3 n)$ (Sec. 3.2).
- We propose a refinement of context-free grammars (and the corresponding modifications of Valiant's parser) which allows to parse iterative structures hierarchically instead of linearly (Sec. 4).
- We conjecture that any given context-free programming language, understood as the set of strings actually written in it (not the language prescribed by its grammar) belong to the subclass that we propose if iteration is represented hierarchically as we prescribe.
- We have implemented the parsing technique described above, and have integrated it in the BNFC parser generator (Forsberg and Ranta 2012).

ICFP '13, September 25–27, 2013, Boston, MA, USA.

ACM 978-1-4503-2326-0/13/09... $15.00.
http://dx.doi.org/10.1145/2500365.2500576

2. Context Free Parsing

In this section we review the basics of context free (CF) parsing, introduce our notation, and review CYK and Valiant algorithms.

2.1 Conventions and Notations

We assume a CF grammar $\mathcal{G}$, given by a quadruple (Σ, N, P, S), where Σ is a finite set of terminals, N is a finite set of non-terminals of which S is the starting symbol, and P a finite set of productions.

We furthermore assume an input $w \in \Sigma^*$ — a sequence of terminal symbols of length $|w|$. The input symbol at position i is denoted $w[i]$. A sub-string of w starting at position i (included) and ending at position j (excluded), is denoted $w[i..j]$. Metasyntactic variables standing for arbitrary strings of terminals will have the form $w_1, w_2, \ldots$. The letters $A, B, C, \ldots$, stand for arbitrary non-terminals, while $\alpha, \beta, \ldots$ stand for arbitrary strings (elements of $(\Sigma \cup N)^*$) and t stands for a terminal symbol. Each production rule associates a non-terminal with a string it can generate.

Definition 1. $\alpha A \beta \longrightarrow \alpha\gamma\beta$ *iff.* $(A ::= \gamma) \in P$

Definition 2. $\overset{*}{\longrightarrow}$ *stands for the reflexive transitive closure of* $\longrightarrow$.

The input string w belongs to the language $\mathcal{L}$ generated by $\mathcal{G}$ iff. $S \overset{*}{\longrightarrow} w$.

Any CF grammar $\mathcal{G}$ defining a language $\mathcal{L}$ can be converted to a grammar $\mathcal{G}'$ in Chomsky Normal Form (CNF) defining the same language $\mathcal{L}$, with $|\mathcal{G}'| \leq |\mathcal{G}|^2$ (Chomsky 1959). Hence we will assume without loss of generality a grammar in CNF. In CNF, the rules are restricted to the following forms

$$
\begin{aligned}
S &::= \epsilon && \text{(nullary)}\\
A &::= t && \text{(unary)}\\
A_0 &::= A_1 A_2 && \text{(binary)}
\end{aligned}
$$

but it is easy to handle the empty string specially, so we conventionally exclude it from the input language and thus exclude the nullary rule. In sum, we assume that P contains only unary and binary rules. The reader avid of details is directed to Lange and Leiß (2009) for a pedagogical account of reduction to CNF.

Given a grammar specified as above, the problem of parsing is reduced to finding a binary tree such that each leaf corresponds to a symbol of the input and a suitable unary rule; and each branch corresponds to a suitable binary rule. Essentially, parsing is equivalent to consider all possible bracketings of the input, and verify that they form a valid parse.

2.2 Charts as Matrices, Parsing as Closure

In this section we show how to specify parsing as an equation on matrices. We start by abstracting away from the grammar, via a ring-like structure. We define the operations $0, +, \cdot$ and σ as follows.

Definition 3 ($0, +, \cdot$ on $\mathcal{P}(N)$)**.**

$$
\begin{aligned}
0 &= \varnothing\\
x + y &= x \cup y\\
x \cdot y &= \{A \mid A_0 \in x, A_1 \in y, A ::= A_0 A_1 \in P\}\\
\sigma_i &= \{A \mid A ::= w[i] \in P\}
\end{aligned}
$$

The $(\cdot)$ operation fully characterizes the binary production rules of the grammar, while σ captures the unary ones. We have the following properties: $(0,+)$ forms a commutative monoid (the usual monoid of sets with union); 0 is absorbing for $(\cdot)$; and $(\cdot)$ distributes over $(+)$. However, and crucially, $(\cdot)$ is *not* associative.

$$
\begin{aligned}
x + 0 &= x\\
0 + x &= x\\
(x + y) + z &= x + (y + z)\\
x \cdot (y + z) &= x \cdot y + x \cdot z\\
x \cdot 0 &= 0\\
0 \cdot x &= 0
\end{aligned}
$$

We will then use matrices of sets of non-terminals to record which non-terminals can generate a given substring. The intention is that $A \in C_{ij}$ iff. $A \overset{*}{\longrightarrow} w[i..j]$. See Fig. 1 for an illustration. In parsing terminology, a structure containing intermediate parse results is called a chart. We call the set of charts $\mathcal{C}$.

Definition 4. $\mathcal{C} = \mathcal{P}(N)^{\mathbb{N}\times\mathbb{N}}$

We lift the operations $0, +, \cdot$ from sets of non-terminals to matrices of sets of nonterminals, in the usual manner.

Definition 5 ($0, +, \cdot$ on $\mathcal{C}$)**.**

$$
\begin{aligned}
0_{ij} &= 0\\
(A + B)_{ij} &= A_{ij} + B_{ij}\\
(A \cdot B)_{ij} &= \sum_k A_{ik} \cdot B_{kj}
\end{aligned}
$$

The properties are lifted accordingly. The operation σ is used to compute an upper diagonal matrix corresponding to the input w, as follows.

Definition 6 (Initial matrix)**.** *The initial matrix, written $I(w)$, is a square matrix of dimension $|w| + 1$ such that*

$$
\begin{aligned}
I(w)_{i,i+1} &= \sigma_i\\
I(w)_{i,j} &= 0 && \textit{if } j \neq i + 1
\end{aligned}
$$

Let $W^{(1)} = I(w)$. Note that $W^{(1)}_{i,i+1} = \sigma_i$ contains all the non-terminals which can generate the substring $w[i..i+1]$. Let $W^{(2)} = W^{(1)}W^{(1)} + I(w)$. It is easy to see that $W^{(2)}_{i,i+2} = \sigma_i \cdot \sigma_{i+1}$, hence it contains all the non-terminals which can generate the substring $w[i..i+2]$. Consider now $W^{(3)} = W^{(2)} \cdot W^{(2)} + I(w)$. We have

$$
\begin{aligned}
W^{(3)}_{i,i+3} &= W^{(2)}_{i,i+2} \cdot W^{(2)}_{i+2,i+3} + W^{(2)}_{i,i+1} \cdot W^{(2)}_{i+1,i+3}\\
&= (\sigma_i \cdot \sigma_{i+1}) \cdot \sigma_{i+2} + \sigma_i \cdot (\sigma_{i+1} \cdot \sigma_{i+2})
\end{aligned}
$$

and

$$
\begin{aligned}
W^{(3)}_{i,i+4} &= W^{(2)}_{i,i+2} \cdot W^{(2)}_{i+2,i+4}\\
&= (\sigma_i \cdot \sigma_{i+1}) \cdot (\sigma_{i+2} \cdot \sigma_{i+3})
\end{aligned}
$$

Hence $W^{(3)}$ contains all possible parsing of 3 symbols, and all *balanced* parsings of 4 symbols. By iterating n times, one obtains all the parsings of n symbols. (However, as a hint to our method for efficient parsing, it suffices to repeat the process $\log n + 1$ times to obtain all balanced parsings of n symbols).

Definition 7 (Transitive closure)**.** *If it exists, the transitive closure of a matrix W, written W^+, is the matrix C such that*

$$C = C \cdot C + W$$

A consequence of the above is $C \supseteq C \cdot C + I(w)$. It is clear by now that, consequently, every possible bracketing of the products $I(w) \cdot \cdots \cdot I(w)$ is contained in C, and thus all possible parsings of $w[i..j]$ are found in C_{ij}. Conversely, because $C \subseteq C{\cdot}C{+}W$, if C_{ij} contains a non-terminal then it must generate $w[i..j]$. Algorithms which parse by computing a chart are known as chart parsers.

The above procedure specifies a recognizer: by constructing $I(w)^+$ one finds if w is parsable, but not the corresponding parse.

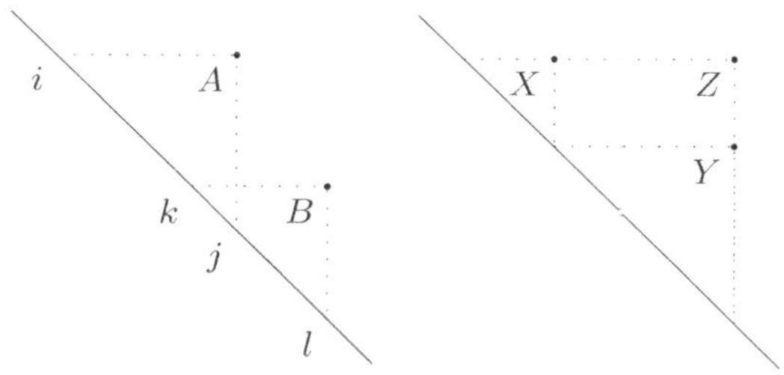

Figure 1. Example charts. In each chart a point at position (x, y) corresponds to a substring starting at x and ending at y. The first parameter x grows downwards and the second y one rightwards. The input string w is represented by the diagonal line. Dots in the upper-right part represent nonterminals. The first chart witnesses $A \xrightarrow{*} w[i..j]$ and $B \xrightarrow{*} w[k..l]$. An instance of the rule $Z ::= XY$ is exemplified on the second chart.

Even though we focus on the recognition problem in this paper, it is straightforward to specify parsers by using matrices of parse trees instead of non-terminals, and adapting the operations accordingly, as we have done in our BNFC implementation.

Following the divide-and-conquer strategy, our parser is based on a function bin combining two charts $I(w_1)^-$, $I(w_2)^+$ and a terminal t into a chart $I(w_1 t w_2)^+$.

2.3 Cocke–Younger–Kasami

A straightforward manner to turn the above specification into an algorithm is as follows.

Let us first remark that the product of two upper triangular matrices is upper triangular. Hence the closure of an upper triangular matrix must also be upper triangular. Hence, in every chart ever considered, every element at the diagonal and below it equals zero. Expanding index-wise the equation $C = C \cdot C + I(w)$ yields:

$$C_{ij} = I(w)_{ij} + \sum_{k=0}^{n} C_{ik} \cdot C_{kj}$$

Because C is upper triangular, $C_{ik} = 0$ if $k \leq i$ and $C_{kj} = 0$ if $k > j$. Hence the sum can be limited to the interval $[i + 1..j]$

$$C_{ij} = I(w)_{ij} + \sum_{k=i+1}^{j} C_{ik} \cdot C_{kj}$$

Observing that the summand equals 0 on the upper diagonal and $I(w)_{ij} = 0$ otherwise, we distinguish on that condition and obtain the two equations:

$$C_{i,i+1} = \sigma_i \tag{1}$$

$$C_{ij} = \sum_{k=i+1}^{j} C_{ik} \cdot C_{kj} \qquad \text{if } j > i + 1 \tag{2}$$

These equations give a method to compute C_{ij} by induction on $j - i$. The equations can be re-interpreted in term of parses and non-terminals as follows. Either

- we parse a single token w_i, and the nonterminals generating it are given directly from unary rules, or
- we parse a longer string. In this case we split it at any intermediate position k, and combine the intermediate results (found in C_{ik} and C_{kj}) in every possible way according to binary rules.

By applying the above rules naively, computation time is exponential in the length of the input; however by memoizing each intermediate result (for example by using lazy dynamic programming (Allison 1992)) the complexity is merely cubic. The resulting dynamic programming algorithm is known as CYK, owing to its independent discoverers: Cocke (1969), Kasami (1965) and Younger (1967).

In the CYK algorithm, any element of the chart is computed only on the basis of elements strictly closer to the diagonal. Hence it can be used to program the combination step of a divide-and-conquer algorithm. The combination of two charts and a terminal $C = bin(A, w[i], B)$, is defined as follows. Elements of C in the upper left corner are copied from A; elements of the bottom right corner are copied from B; and elements from the top right corner are computed using σ_i and the CYK formula (Eq (2)).

Are we done? Unfortunately, no. The above operator has to compute a matrix of size $n \times m$, and computing each element takes time linear in $n + m$. The complexity of bin is therefore cubic; and dwarfs the time spent on computing the sub-charts A and B. For the divide-and-conquer strategy to be efficient, we need the running time of the combination operator to be less than the running time of the recursive calls.

2.4 Valiant

A more subtle way to turn the transitive closure specification into an algorithm is the following. Our task is to find a function $\cdot^+$ which maps a matrix W to its transitive closure $C = W^+$. As above, we do so by refinement of the definition of transitive closure, but we adopt a divide and conquer approach rather than a direct one.

If W is a 1 by 1 matrix, $C = W = 0$. Otherwise, let us divide W and C in blocks as follows (for efficiency the blocks should be roughly of the same size; but the reasoning holds for any sizes):

$$W = \begin{bmatrix} A & X \\ 0 & B \end{bmatrix} \qquad C = \begin{bmatrix} A' & X' \\ 0 & B' \end{bmatrix}$$

Then the condition that C is the transitive closure of W becomes

$$\begin{bmatrix} A' & X' \\ 0 & B' \end{bmatrix} = \begin{bmatrix} A' & X' \\ 0 & B' \end{bmatrix} \cdot \begin{bmatrix} A' & X' \\ 0 & B' \end{bmatrix} + \begin{bmatrix} A & X \\ 0 & B \end{bmatrix}$$

Applying matrix multiplication and sum block-wise:

$$A' = A'A' + A$$
$$X' = A'X' + X'B' + X$$
$$B' = B'B' + B$$

Because A and B are smaller than W (and still upper triangular), we know how to compute A' and B' recursively ($A' = A^+$, $B' = B^+$). There remains to find an algorithm to compute the top-right corner X' of the matrix. That is (renaming variables for convenience) the problem is reduced to finding a recursive function V which maps A, B and X to $Y = V(A, X, B)$, such that $Y = AY + YB + X$. In terms of parsing, the function V combines the chart A of the first part of the input with the chart B of the second part of the input, via a *partial* chart X concerned only with strings starting in A and ending in B, and produces a full chart Y. Let us divide each matrix in blocks again:

$$Y = \begin{bmatrix} Y_{11} & Y_{12} \\ Y_{21} & Y_{22} \end{bmatrix} \qquad X = \begin{bmatrix} X_{11} & X_{12} \\ X_{21} & X_{22} \end{bmatrix}$$

$$A = \begin{bmatrix} A_{11} & A_{12} \\ 0 & A_{22} \end{bmatrix} \qquad B = \begin{bmatrix} B_{11} & B_{12} \\ 0 & B_{22} \end{bmatrix}$$

(Again we assume that splitting can be done; the base cases can be obtained by dropping the first rows and/or the second columns in

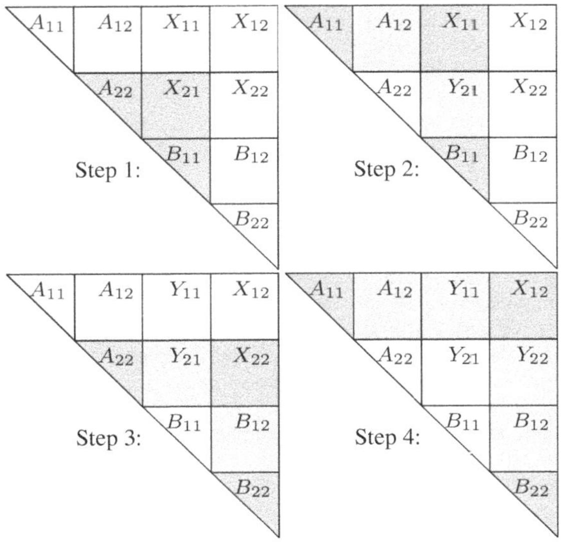

Figure 2. The recursive step of function V. The charts A and B are already complete. To complete the matrix X, that is, compute $Y = V(A, X, B)$, one splits the matrices and performs 4 recursive calls. Each recursive call is depicted graphically. In each figure, to complete the dark-gray square, multiply the light-gray rectangles and add them to the dark-gray square, then do a recursive call on triangular matrix composed of the completed dark-gray square and the triangles.

the above splits.) The condition on Y then becomes

$$\begin{bmatrix} Y_{11} & Y_{12} \\ Y_{21} & Y_{22} \end{bmatrix} = \begin{bmatrix} A_{11} & A_{12} \\ 0 & A_{22} \end{bmatrix} \cdot \begin{bmatrix} Y_{11} & Y_{12} \\ Y_{21} & Y_{22} \end{bmatrix} + \begin{bmatrix} Y_{11} & Y_{12} \\ Y_{21} & Y_{22} \end{bmatrix} \cdot \begin{bmatrix} B_{11} & B_{12} \\ 0 & B_{22} \end{bmatrix} + \begin{bmatrix} X_{11} & X_{12} \\ X_{21} & X_{22} \end{bmatrix}$$

By applying matrix multiplication and sum block-wise:

$$\begin{aligned} Y_{11} &= A_{11}Y_{11} + A_{12}Y_{21} + Y_{11}B_{11} + 0 + X_{11} \\ Y_{12} &= A_{11}Y_{12} + A_{12}Y_{22} + Y_{11}B_{12} + Y_{12}B_{22} + X_{12} \\ Y_{21} &= 0 + A_{22}Y_{21} + Y_{21}B_{11} + 0 + X_{21} \\ Y_{22} &= 0 + A_{22}Y_{22} + Y_{21}B_{12} + Y_{22}B_{22} + X_{22} \end{aligned}$$

By commutativity of $(+)$ and 0 being its unit:

$$\begin{aligned} Y_{11} &= A_{11}Y_{11} + X_{11} + A_{12}Y_{21} + Y_{11}B_{11} \\ Y_{12} &= A_{11}Y_{12} + X_{12} + A_{12}Y_{22} + Y_{11}B_{12} + Y_{12}B_{22} \\ Y_{21} &= A_{22}Y_{21} + X_{21} + 0 + Y_{21}B_{11} \\ Y_{22} &= A_{22}Y_{22} + X_{22} + Y_{21}B_{12} + Y_{22}B_{22} \end{aligned}$$

Because each of the sub-matrices is smaller and because of the absence of circular dependencies, Y can be computed recursively:

$$\begin{aligned} Y_{21} &= V(A_{22}, X_{21}, B_{11}) \\ Y_{11} &= V(A_{11}, X_{11} + A_{12}Y_{21}, B_{11}) \\ Y_{22} &= V(A_{22}, X_{22} + Y_{21}B_{12}, B_{22}) \\ Y_{12} &= V(A_{11}, X_{12} + A_{12}Y_{22} + Y_{11}B_{12}, B_{22}) \end{aligned}$$

We have ignored the base cases so far because they are straightforward, except for the following point. When computing $V(A, X, B)$ on matrices of dimension 1×1, it is guaranteed that A and B are equal to 0. Indeed, in that case X is just above the diagonal. Therefore A and B are on it and must then be 0. The result matrix is therefore equal to X.

In sum, with the above definitions, we have the following expression for V in the recursive case

$$V\left(\begin{bmatrix} A_{11} & A_{12} \\ 0 & A_{22} \end{bmatrix}, \begin{bmatrix} X_{11} & X_{12} \\ X_{21} & X_{22} \end{bmatrix}, \begin{bmatrix} B_{11} & B_{12} \\ 0 & B_{22} \end{bmatrix}\right) = \begin{bmatrix} Y_{11} & Y_{12} \\ Y_{21} & Y_{22} \end{bmatrix}.$$

In the base cases, some or all of the top and/or right sub-matrices are empty and the corresponding recursive calls are omitted. In terms of parsing, initially the partial chart X contains at the bottom-left position a single non-zero element corresponding to the symbol at the interface of A and B. Recursive calls progressively fill this chart, quadrant by quadrant. The above algorithm was first described by Valiant (1975). A graphical summary is shown in Fig. 2.

From Valiant's function V, one can construct the bin operator as follows:

$$bin(A, t, B) = \begin{bmatrix} A & V(A, X, B) \\ 0 & B \end{bmatrix}$$

$$\text{where } X = \begin{bmatrix} 0 & \cdots & \cdots & 0 \\ \vdots & & \iddots & \vdots \\ 0 & 0 & & \vdots \\ \sigma_i & 0 & \cdots & 0 \end{bmatrix}$$

An advantage of Valiant's algorithm over CYK is that it treats whole subcharts at once, via matrix-level multiplication and addition, while CYK explicitly refers to each element of C individually. In particular, when using a sparse-matrix representation, the multiplication of an empty chart with any other chart is instantaneous. The ability to handle this case efficiently is key: we observe that in many cases, charts are sparse, and composition of charts is efficient.

When using a straighforward representation of sparse matrices, the implementation of Valiant's algorithm is an elegant functional program, as can be seen in Fig. 3.

3. Sparse Matrix Assumption and Complexity Analysis

3.1 Model of the Input

In practice, matrices representing charts are expected to be sparse for large inputs, that is, a given substring is unlikely to be generated by a given non-terminal. Indeed, in most cases, the substring starts in the middle of a construction and ends in the middle of some other, usually unrelated other construction. This effect is illustrated in Fig. 4. In the remainder of the paper, we assume that inputs conform to this assumption. Before explaining where it is coming from, we give its formal definition.

Definition 8 (Assumption)**.** *There exists a constant α such that, for any input, the distribution of non-zero elements in the chart C corresponding to it is bounded as follows. For any square subchart A of C above the diagonal,*

$$\#A \leq \left\lceil \alpha \sum_{(i,j)\in \mathrm{dom}(A)} \frac{1}{(j-i)^2} \right\rceil$$

where $\#A$ is the number of non-zero elements in matrix A.

We stress that the assumption involves not a grammar *per se*, but the language itself (i.e. the set of possible input strings we consider), when seen as strings generated by a given grammar in CNF. So, for any given α, every non-trivial grammar will admit strings that break the assumption, but usually the set of strings we consider behaves well in practice.

The above formula merits justification. Before using it to evaluate the complexity of the parsing algorithm, we will build a more

```
import Prelude (Eq (..))
class RingLike a where
  zero :: a
  (+) :: a → a → a
  (·) :: a → a → a
data M a = Q (M a) (M a) (M a) (M a) | Z | One a
q Z Z Z Z = Z
q a b c d = Q a b c d
one x = if x ≡ zero then Z else One x
instance (Eq a, RingLike a) ⇒ RingLike (M a) where
  zero = Z
  Z + x = x
  x + Z = x
  One x + One y = one (x + y)
  Q a11 a12 a21 a22 + Q b11 b12 b21 b22
    = q (a11 + b11) (a12 + b12)
        (a21 + b21) (a22 + b22)
  Z · x = Z
  x · Z = Z
  One x · One y = one (x · y)
  Q a11 a12 a21 a22 · Q b11 b12 b21 b22
    = q (a11 · b11 + a12 · b21) (a11 · b12 + a12 · b22)
        (a21 · b11 + a22 · b21) (a21 · b21 + a22 · b22)
v :: (Eq a, RingLike a) ⇒ M a → M a → M a → M a
v a                 Z                   b = Z
v Z                 (One x)             Z = One x
v (Q a11 a12 Z a22) (Q x11 x12 x21 x22) (Q b11 b12 Z b22)
  = q y11 y12 y21 y22
  where y21 = v a22 x21                               b11
        y11 = v a11 (x11 + a12 · y21              ) b11
        y22 = v a22 (x22 +               y21 · b12) b22
        y12 = v a11 (x12 + a12 · y22 + y11 · b12) b22
```

Figure 3. Data structure for charts as sparse matrices (M), and implementation of the function V. The tricky parts compared to the mathematical development of Sec. 2.4 is the handling of empty matrices. Care must be taken to create empty matrices (Z) whenever they contain only zero elements. This is done by using the smart constructors q and *one* in matrix multiplication. The input matrices a and b are empty iff. the matrix x has dimension one. For concision, this implementation supports only matrices of size 2^n for some n. It can be extended to matrices of arbitrary dimension in a straightforward manner by adding constructors for row and column matrices, to be used as leaves. An implementation supporting arbitrary matrix dimensions, as well as the optimization explained in Sec. 6.2 can be found in the BNFC repository: `https://github.com/BNFC/bnfc/blob/master/source/runtime/Data/Matrix/Quad.hs`

precise intuition for it by examining its consequences and its possible causes.

By symbolically evaluating the sum , we can deduce what the above assumption implies for each of the following shapes for A:

- if A is a square of size n touching the diagonal, then $\#A \leq \lceil \alpha \log n \rceil$
- if A is a square of size n at distance kn to the diagonal with $k \geq 1$, then $\#A \leq \lceil \alpha(2\log(k+1) - \log(k+2) - \log(k)) \rceil$. Hence, remarkably, the upper bound of non-zero elemens in a square chart of dimension n which is at least n elements away from the diagonal is independent from n.

A stochastic way to formulate the idea behind our assumption is the following. When considering k random substrings of size n in a corpus of strings representative of the language, one finds on average that $\frac{\alpha k}{n^2}$ of them correspond to a single nonterminal. That is, by doubling the size of the substring considered, it will be four times less likely to be parsable. This condition agrees with experience.

In order for the assumption to be satisfied, it is also sufficient to assume that the parse trees corresponding to the inputs are balanced. That is, if every node in the chart corresponding to a substring of size n is combinable with exactly one other symbol of size n (precluding ambiguity), then the assumption is verified. In fact the assumption can be relaxed as follows. Consider the triangle-shaped subchart T^n which touches the diagonal and a non-terminal A at distance k from it. We assume all symbols in the triangle but closer to the diagonal combine to form A. If the symbol A can be combined with exactly one other symbol of size βk with $0 < \beta \leq 1$, it will yield exactly one symbol at distance $(1+\beta)k$. Inductively we compute that is of the order of $\frac{\log(n)}{\log(1+\beta)}$ nodes in the triangle, which is compatible with our condition, with $\alpha = 1/\log_2(1-\beta)$.

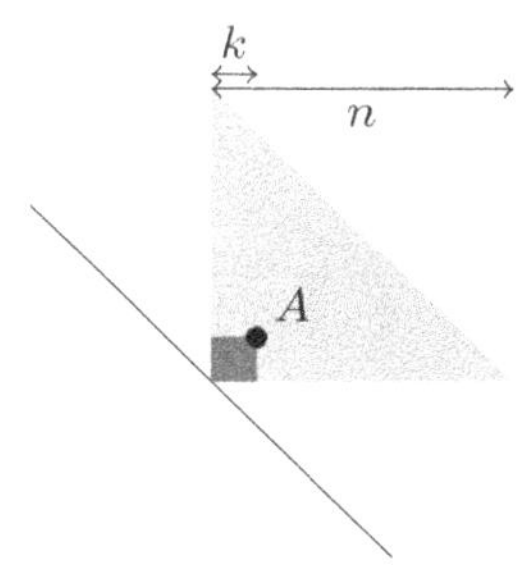

Experiments The assumption we make is not strictly speaking verifiable experimentally, since for any chart there exists an α such that the assumption is verified. However, one can gain confidence in the assumption by plotting the probability of a string to be parsable against its size. One should observe that this probability decreases with the square of the size. In practical terms, given a chart corresponding to a large input, if one observes a drastic cut-off in the density of non-zero elements when departing from a certain distance from the diagonal, then the input is compatible with our assumption. In Fig. 4, we show a chart corresponding to a fragment of C code, obtained using our algorithm. This chart, along with all other inputs for which we have run this experiment, exhibits the expected features. The assumption is also confirmed, albeit indirectly, by observing that the cost analysis which depends on it holds in practice.

Non-suitable inputs Any input which uses nesting in linear proportion to the size of its input will violate our assumption. For example, the lisp program composed of n successive applications of

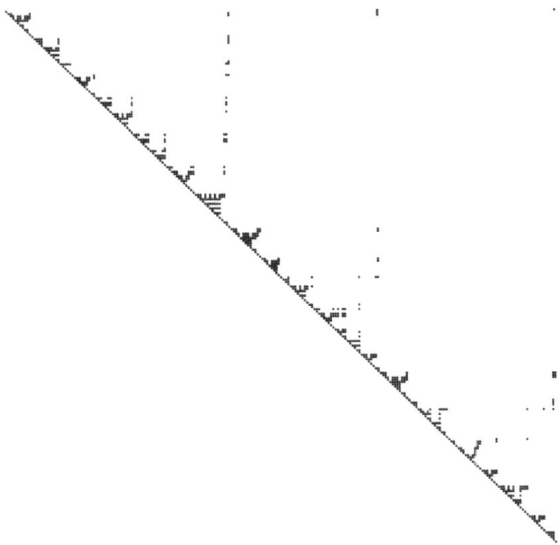

Figure 4. The chart corresponding to a fragment of a C program. The input program can be found in appendix. Two remarkable features merit commentary. First, the staircase shapes, which are explained in Sec. 4.4. Second, some small sub-matrices near the diagonal appear to be dense. These regions correspond to argument lists in the C program, and this iteration structure is implemented by linear recursion rather than our special encoding of Sec. 4.

cons does not satisfy our assumption.

$$(\mathsf{cons}\ x\ (\mathsf{cons}\ x\ (\ldots(\mathsf{cons}\ x\ \mathsf{nil})\ldots)))$$

It appears however that few programs are written in this style, except perhaps for machine-generated ones. Linear constructions are often present, but they are then supported by special syntax. Indeed the above lisp program is invariably written as:

$$(\mathsf{list}\ x\ x \ldots x)$$

Hence we provide special treatment for such special iteration syntaxes. We show in Sec. 4 how to deal with them, while respecting our assumption.

3.2 Cost Estimation

For simplicity we consider only inputs of sizes which are powers of 2. This implies that we only need to consider square matrices in our analysis. We will estimate the cost as the number of elementary multiplications (multiplications on sets of non-terminals) to be performed.

We first remark that because charts are always divided in the middle, a subchart X considered by the algorithm is always square, and at a distance kn to the diagonal, where k is some natural number and n is the dimension of X. When $k = 0$ we say that X touches the diagonal and when $k > 0$ we say that X is far from the diagonal. This distinction is crucial, because matrices touching the diagonal have $O(\log n)$ elements in them, whereas matrix far away have a constant number of elements in them.

3.2.1 Cost of Matrix Multiplications

We start by estimating the cost of the multiplication of two matrices A and B of size n, $M_n(A, B)$. Assuming that $p = \#A$ and $q = \#B$, then matrix multiplication needs to perform $O(pq)$ elementary multiplications. Indeed, each non-zero element in A needs to be multiplied at most with every non-zero element in B. We now assume that A and B are also a subcharts, and distinguish the following cases.

1. Both A and B touch the diagonal. We have $p = O(\log n)$ and $q = O(\log n)$ and thus $M_n(A, B) = O(\log^2 n)$.
2. Either A or B is at least n away from the diagonal. In this case there either p or q is bounded by a constant and thus $M_n(A, B) = O(\log n)$.
3. Both A and B are at least n away from the diagonal. In this case there both p and q are bounded by a constant and thus $M_n(A, B) = O(1)$.

Before proceeding we recall a standard result:

Theorem 1 (Master Theorem, Cormen et al.). *Assume a function T_n constrained by the recurrence*

$$T_n = aT_{\frac{n}{b}} + f(n)$$

(Such an equation will typically come from a divide-and-conquer algorithm, where a is the number of sub-problems at each recursive step, n/b is the size of each sub-problem, and $f(n)$ is the running time of dividing up the problem space into a parts, and combining the sub-results together.)

If we let $e = \log_b a$ and $f(n) = O(n^c \log^d n)$, then

$$\begin{aligned} T_n &= O(n^e) && \text{if } c < e \\ T_n &= O(n^c \log^{d+1} n) && \text{if } c = e \\ T_n &= O(n^c \log^d n) && \text{if } c > e \end{aligned}$$

3.2.2 Cost of the Conquer Step

We proceed to estimate the running cost V_n of the valiant function V on a matrix of size n. We do so assuming that we know the resulting chart $Y = V(A, X, B)$. That is, V_n maps Y to the cost of running $V(A, X, B)$. We have the following recurrence:

$$\begin{aligned} V_n(0) &= 0 \\ V_n \begin{bmatrix} Y_{11} & Y_{12} \\ Y_{21} & Y_{22} \end{bmatrix} &= V_{\frac{n}{2}}(Y_{21}) + V_{\frac{n}{2}}(Y_{11}) + V_{\frac{n}{2}}(Y_{22}) + V_{\frac{n}{2}}(Y_{12}) \\ &\quad + M_{\frac{n}{2}}(A_{12}, Y_{21}) + M_{\frac{n}{2}}(Y_{21}, B_{12}) \\ &\quad + M_{\frac{n}{2}}(A_{12}, Y_{22}) + M_{\frac{n}{2}}(Y_{11}, B_{12}) \end{aligned}$$

Because A and B are upper-triangular matrices, the subcharts A_{12} and B_{12} touch the diagonal. We distinguish two cases: either Y touches the diagonal or it is at least at a distance n from it.

Y ***is far away*** In the latter case we pose $F_n = V_n$ (F for far), and all sub-matrices of Y are far from the diagonal. Hence all matrix multiplications involve at most one matrix touching the diagonal, and the total combined cost of multiplications is $O(\log n)$. The recurrence specializes then to:

$$\begin{aligned} F_n(0) &= 0 \\ F_1(Y) &= 1 \\ F_n \begin{bmatrix} Y_{11} & Y_{12} \\ Y_{21} & Y_{22} \end{bmatrix} &= F_{\frac{n}{2}}(Y_{11}) + F_{\frac{n}{2}}(Y_{12}) + F_{\frac{n}{2}}(Y_{21}) + F_{\frac{n}{2}}(Y_{22}) \\ &\quad + O(\log n) \end{aligned}$$

Because Y has a constant number of non-zero elements, most recursive calls will return immediately, and on average only one recursive call need to be counted. Hence we use the Master Theorem with $a = 1, b = 2$ and $f(n) = O(\log n)$. We are therefore in the case $c = e$, and obtain $F_n = O(\log^2 n)$.

Y ***touches the diagonal*** In the former case, let $V_n = C_n$ (C for close), and Y_{21} touches the diagonal. Hence two of the matrix multiplications involve pairs of matrices at the diagonal, and the combined cost of multiplications is $O(\log^2 n)$. Only the recursive call involving Y_{12} touches the diagonal, and the three others involve

matrices far from it. Therefore the recurrence specializes to:

$$\begin{aligned} C_1 &= 1 \\ C_n &= C_{\frac{n}{2}} + 3F_{\frac{n}{2}} + O(\log^2 n) \\ &= C_{\frac{n}{2}} + O(\log^2 n) \end{aligned}$$

We use the Master Theorem with $a = 1$, $b = 2$ and $f(n) = O(\log^2 n)$. We are therefore in the case $c = e$, and obtain $C_n = O(\log^3 n)$.

3.2.3 Total Cost

We can proceed to compute the total cost of our algorithm on an input string of size $n = |w|$, again using the Master Theorem. We always divide the input into two parts, so $b = 2$. We assume that the input is provided as a balanced tree representing the matrix $I(w)$, and so the cost of the divide step is zero. Therefore $f(n)$ is the cost of the conquer step only. This step involves a matrix close to the diagonal, so $f(n) = C_n = O(\log^3 n)$, and in turn $c = 0$ and $d = 3$.

- If we assume a sequential execution of sub-problems then $a = 2$. In turn, $e = 1$ and $T(n) = O(n)$.
- If we assume perfect parallelisation of sub-problems, or an incremental situation, where one of the sub-solution can be reused, then $a = 1$. In turn, $e = 0$ and $T(n) = O(\log^4 n)$.

Valiant's evaluation for V_n is $O(n^\gamma)$, for some γ between 2 and 3 (the exact value depends on the matrix multiplication algorithm used). In his case $c = \gamma$ and $d = 0$, yielding $T(n) = O(n^\gamma)$ in all cases: according to Valiant's original analysis, making an incremental or parallel version of his algorithm would lead no benefit, while our analysis reveals that a big payoff is at hand.

3.2.4 Experiments

We have conducted two sets of experiments on the running time of the algorithm. All timings were obtained using the CRITERION library (O'Sullivan 2013), on an Intel Core 2 at 2.13GHz. All programs were compiled with GHC 7.6.1. In the first set, we have measured the performance on a practical language on practical inputs, to confirm that the function is fast enough to use as an incremental parser in an interactive setting. To do so, we have run our BNFC implementation on a C grammar to produce the σ and $(\cdot)$ functions, and tested the running time of the V function on a large C program, extracted from the Linux kernel scheduler (`https://github.com/torvalds/linux/blob/master/kernel/sched/core.c` — preprocessor directives as well as `typedefs` found in it were expanded by hand.) The input was divided into a left part and a right part of equal sizes, and a middle symbol. The complete charts for the left and the right part were computed, then we measured the time of the V function on the charts and the singleton chart containing the middle symbol. After collecting 100 samples, CRITERION reported a mean runtime of 320.1469 μs, with a standard deviation of 23.06691 μs. This is well within acceptable limits for interactive use: most people cannot perceive a delay less than a millisecond.

In the second set of experiments, we tested the V function on generated inputs of various sizes, to confirm our calculation of the worst case running time. The grammar is that corresponding to the encoding of t^* (the nonterminal t repeated an arbitrary number of times) using the technique described in Sec. 4 (which ensures that our assumption is verified with α close to 1). The inputs were a repetition of that terminal symbol. The results are shown in Fig. 5. We observe that the measurements, when drawn on a semi-logarithmic scale, fit a quadratic curve.

The observed running therefore appears better than the theoretical cost estimation, which predicts a cubic curve. The best explanation we have for this discrepancy is that we made a pessimistic assumption in our analysis: we have estimated the cost of the matrix product to be at worst $O(\log^2 n)$ if each argument matrix has $O(\log n)$ elements. However, this occurs only if the elements are lined up so that every pair needs to be considered. This case may occur in practice, but we conjecture that it happens so infrequently that it does not contribute significantly to the total running time. This experiment thus suggests that a more precise analysis of the algorithm can be done, which we leave for future work.

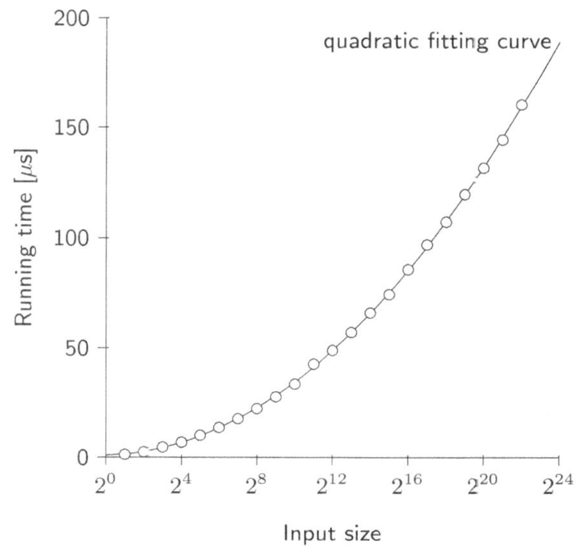

Figure 5. Running time of the V function in function of the size of the input, using semi-logarithmic scale. The grammar is that corresponding to the encoding of t^* using the technique described in Sec. 4. The next data point (input size 2^{23}) could not be obtained due to running out of memory. The curve is the graph of a quadratic function which fits the measurements.

4. Iteration in Context-Free Grammars

4.1 The Problem With Iteration

While we have worked hard to ensure the efficient handling of the non-associative aspect of CF parsing, we have neglected so far that most CF languages feature regular iteration; that is, associative concatenation rules. Without special treatment, such associative rules cause severe inefficiencies in the algorithm as presented so far.

Iteration is technically known as Kleene star, and is written here as a postfix *. In context-free grammars, it can be (and usually is) encoded as either as left or right recursion. For example a rule $A ::= Y^*$ is typically encoded as follows.

$$\begin{aligned} A &::= \epsilon \\ A &::= AY \end{aligned}$$

The problem with this encoding is two-fold. First, inputs consisting mostly of a sequence of Y necessarily violate our assumption on inputs: the depth of the parse tree grows linearly with the size of the input.

Second, the generated AST will necessarily be linear. Consequently, as we have seen in the introduction, this linear shape would preclude efficient parallel or incremental processing of the AST by computations consuming it.

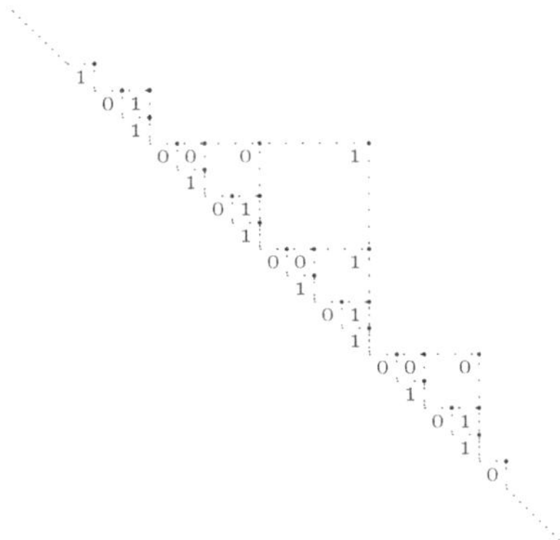

Figure 6. Matching a list using the oracle-sensitive algorithm. We assume that only one non-terminal Y is involved and thus show only the bit-tags. Considering only the non-terminals which cannot be combined using the rule $Y ::= Y^0Y^1$, the charts features a sequence of Y^1 (of increasing size), followed by a sequence of Y^0 (of decreasing size).

One could possibly imagine working around the first problem with creative algorithmic devices. However it is clear that the second problem is intrinsic to the encoding of iteration as linear recursion. Hence we take the stance that special support for iteration is necessary in any parallel or incremental parser.

4.2 Towards an Efficient Encoding

Instead of a linear, unary encoding of iterations, one can attempt a binary tree encoding. One might propose the following encoding:

$$A ::= AA$$
$$A ::= Y$$

However this encoding accepts all possible associations of sequences of Ys, in particular also linear ones. One might attempt to mend the rules by using a more clever encoding, say:

$$A_{k+1} ::= A_k A_k$$

Ignoring that it codes only lists of size 2^n for some n, our second condition on inputs is still be violated. Indeed, in a sequence of Y, any subsequence of length 2^n for some n will be recognized. This means that there will be a lot of overlap between possible parse trees.

In the remainder of the section we describe a way to keep the rule $A ::= AA$, but tweak the parsing algorithm so that for any sequence of Ys only a single association is considered.

4.3 Oracle-Sensitive Parsing

Overview Each nonterminal will come with a bit indicating whether it should be used either as a left or right-child in the parse tree. The bit will be chosen by an oracle upon production of the nonterminal, so that the tree will be balanced. We write Y^b for the non-terminal Y annotated with bit b. The main rule constructing trees is then written:

$$Y ::= Y^0Y^1$$

This restricts which trees are explored. After parsing with this rule, we obtain a sequence of Y^1 (unmatched right children) of growing size followed by a sequence of Y_0 (unmatched left children), as depicted in Fig. 6. These nodes will then be collected using special rules. Assuming that C_0 and D_0 delimit the list of non-terminals Y^*, the collecting rules would be written:

$$C ::= C_0 \qquad D ::= D_0$$
$$::= CY^1 \qquad ::= Y^0D$$

And the final list can be produced by the rule $L ::= CD$.

The delimiters C_0 and D_0 are necessary so that only one collection of Y^1 and only one collection of Y^0 are needed; thereby ensuring a good performance. Without delimiters, every combination of sequences of Y^1 and Y^0 would need to be considered. An intermediate situation is where only one delimiter is present, say the opening one. In that case, only one list of Y^1 is considered, but many sequences of Y^0 would be considered.

Oracle-Sensitive Grammar Formalism In general, we extend productions so that non-terminals on a right-hand-side are tagged with a bit. Formally, we extend the syntax of the productions as follows, where $b_1, b_2, \ldots$ range over bits:

- $A ::= B^{b_1}C^{b_2}$
- $A ::= t$, for $t \in \Sigma$

We allow, as a shorthand, to write non-annotated non-terminal in a production right-hand-side. The production then stands for a pair of rules with either annotation. That is $A ::= \alpha_0 B \alpha_1$ is a shorthand for the pair of rules $A ::= \alpha_0 B^0 \alpha_1$ and $A ::= \alpha_0 B^1 \alpha_1$.

Algorithm An implementation will take a grammar written using a special construction for iteration and translate it to the above formalism appropriately. The parsing algorithm *per se* remains the same as previously, except for the operator combining non-terminals, which is changed as follows.

Definition 9.

$$x \cdot y = \{A^b \mid B^{b_1} \in x, C^{b_2} \in y, A ::= B^{b_1}C^{b_2} \in P\}$$

where the output bit b comes from the oracle.

The transitive closure function modified to use the above version of the $(\cdot)$ operator is called T in the remainder.

Formalization and proof We proceed to prove that the above implementation indeed recognizes the intended language. Firstly, we must define the meaning of our extended grammar formalism and show that it corresponds to our needs.

The main issue is that the algorithm behaves non-deterministically, in the sense that the grammar-writer does not have access to the bits generated by the oracle. The rest of the section is structured as follows:

1. we define a generation relation restricted to a given source bits ρ;
2. we show that the algorithm decides the relation for a specific (but intangible) ρ;
3. we narrow the acceptable grammars to those which are oblivious to ρ (describe languages independent of ρ);
4. we provide a toolkit which enables to identify and construct oblivious grammars;
5. and finally we show that our encoding of iteration preserves obliviousness.

Oracle We define a new generation relation $\overset{\rho}{\longmapsto}$, indexed by a stream of bits ρ. This stream of bits wholly models the oracle.

The meaning of production rules annotated with bits can then be given. We first define a 1-step generation relation indexed by a single bit.

Definition 10 (bit-indexed generation)**.**

- *if* $(A ::= B^{b_1}C^{b_2}) \in P$*, then* $w_0 A^b \alpha \overset{b}{\longmapsto} w_0 B^{b_1} C^{b_2} \alpha$

- *if* $(A ::= x) \in P$, *then* $w_0 A^b \alpha \overset{\rho,\rho}{\longmapsto} w_0 x \alpha$

Crucially, the rules require the relation to act on the first non-terminal in a string. This forces the bit-stream ρ to be used in a deterministic way. Otherwise, the relation could use each bit of ρ in a arbitrary place, essentially bypassing the instructions of the oracle, transmitted via the bitstream ρ.

Definition 11 (stream-indexed generation). *The relation* $\alpha \overset{\rho}{\longmapsto} w$ *is inductively defined as follows.*

- $w \overset{\rho}{\longmapsto} w$
- *If* $\alpha \overset{b}{\longmapsto} \gamma$ *and* $\gamma \overset{\rho}{\longmapsto} w$ *then* $\alpha \overset{b,\rho}{\longmapsto} w$

Algorithm The algorithm decides the $\overset{\rho}{\longmapsto}$ relation, but only for one particular bit-stream ρ (which the grammar-writer has no control over).

Theorem 2.

1. *if* $A^b \in T(I(w))_{ij}$ *then* $\exists \rho. A^b \overset{\rho}{\longmapsto} w_{ij}$
2. *if* $A^b \notin T(I(w))_{ij}$ *then* $\exists \rho. A^b \overset{\rho}{\not\longmapsto} w_{ij}$

Proof. By induction on the decomposition structure of the matrix (done by T). □

Obliviousness Ultimately, we do not want the language defined using our formalism to depend on the actual stream ρ of bits generated by the oracle, since this is out of the control of the grammar writer. That is, if a string is recognized using some ρ, it should be recognized with every ρ.

We first remark that the set of strings generated by any given tagged non-terminal will always depend on ρ. Hence instead we have to consider the strings generated by sets of non-terminals (and in general sets of strings).

We thus define the following relations, using Γ, Δ and Ξ to range over sets of strings.

Definition 12.

- $\Gamma \overset{\exists}{\longmapsto} w$ *iff.* $\exists \rho. \exists \alpha \in \Gamma.\ \alpha \overset{\rho}{\longmapsto} w$
- $\Gamma \overset{\forall}{\longmapsto} w$ *iff.* $\forall \rho. \exists \alpha \in \Gamma.\ \alpha \overset{\rho}{\longmapsto} w$

Definition 13. *A set of strings* Γ *is called* oracle-oblivious *if the set of strings of terminals generated by it is insensitive to non-determinism; that is, for any* w_0, *if* $\Gamma \overset{\exists}{\longmapsto} w_0$ *then* $\Gamma \overset{\forall}{\longmapsto} w_0$.

Definition 14. *We note* $\tilde{A}$ *the set* $\{A^0, A^1\}$.

Definition 15 (well-formed grammar). *A oracle-sensitive grammar is well-formed if* $\tilde{S}$ *is oracle-oblivious.*

We can then show that obliviousness fulfills its purpose: the sensitivity to ρ introduced in the algorithm is indeed hidden by obliviousness.

Theorem 3. *If* $\tilde{A}$ *is oracle-oblivious then*

$$\tilde{A} \overset{\forall}{\longmapsto} w_{ij} \quad \text{iff} \quad A^b \in T(I(w))_{ij}, \text{for some bit } b$$

Proof. The left-to-right direction is the contrapositive of Th. 2.2. The right-to-left direction is obtained by composing Th. 2.1 with the definition of obliviousness for $\tilde{A}$. □

A kit for well-formed grammars Given a grammar definition using bit-annotations arbitrarily, it is hard to decide whether it is well-formed. Hence we define the following relation, which enables us to reason about obliviousness compositionally.

Definition 16. $\Gamma \overset{*}{\Longrightarrow} \Delta$ *iff for every* w_0,

- *if* $\Gamma \overset{\exists}{\longmapsto} w_0$ *then* $\Delta \overset{\exists}{\longmapsto} w_0$.
- *if* $\Delta \overset{\forall}{\longmapsto} w_0$ *then* $\Gamma \overset{\forall}{\longmapsto} w_0$.

The above relation is constructed to transport obliviousness:

Lemma 1. *If* $\Gamma \overset{*}{\Longrightarrow} \Delta$ *and* Δ *is oracle oblivious, then so is* Γ.

Proof. Direct consequence of the definition. □

Lemma 2.

1. $\overset{*}{\Longrightarrow}$ *is reflexive and transitive*
2. *If* $\Gamma \overset{*}{\Longrightarrow} \Delta$ *then* $\Gamma\Xi \overset{*}{\Longrightarrow} \Delta\Xi$ *and* $\Xi\Gamma \overset{*}{\Longrightarrow} \Xi\Delta$
3. *Assume a non-terminal* A *and* Γ *its set of productions. Then* $\tilde{A} \overset{*}{\Longrightarrow} \Gamma$.

Proof. 1. and 3. are a direct consequences of the definitions. The proof of 2. is tedious but straightforward, and similar in style to the proof of Lem. 3 and thus omitted. □

The above lemma means that, if productions are written without bit annotations (they generate all possible annotations), then they preserve obliviousness. Hence, a grammar written without annotations is necessarily well formed. Because our encoding of iteration also preserves obliviousness, this in turn means that, if one uses annotations only to encode iteration in the pattern we prescribe, the grammar will be well-formed.

Encoding iteration As a reminder, we encode $L ::= C_0 Y_0 * D_0$, as

$$\begin{aligned} Y &::= Y_0 \\ &::= Y^0 Y^1 \\ C &::= C_0 \\ &::= C Y^1 \\ D &::= D_0 \\ &::= Y^0 D \\ L &::= C D \end{aligned}$$

Theorem 4. $\tilde{L} \overset{*}{\Longrightarrow} \tilde{C}_0 \tilde{Y}_0^* \tilde{D}_0$

Proof. We construct the relation in the following stages.

1. $\tilde{L}$
2. $\tilde{C}_0 \{Y^1\}^* \{Y^0\}^* \tilde{D}_0$
3. $\tilde{C}_0 \tilde{Y}^* \tilde{D}_0$
4. $\tilde{C}_0 \tilde{Y}_0^* \tilde{D}_0$

Most of the steps are consequences of Lem. 2. Only the step between stages 2. and 3. requires special treatment: it depends on the relation

$$\{Y^1\}^* \{Y^0\}^* \overset{*}{\Longrightarrow} \tilde{Y}^*$$

Proving it requires to preservation lemmas for every w_0:

- if $\{Y^1\}^* \{Y^0\}^* \overset{\exists}{\longmapsto} w_0$ then $\tilde{Y}^* \overset{\exists}{\longmapsto} w_0$.
- if $\tilde{Y}^* \overset{\forall}{\longmapsto} w_0$ then $\{Y^1\}^* \{Y^0\}^* \overset{\forall}{\longmapsto} w_0$.

The first one is an easy consequence of the ability to chose any possible ρ in the $\overset{\exists}{\longmapsto}$ relation. The second one is the angular stone of our method, and is proved in the following lemma. □

Lemma 3. *Let* $w \in \Sigma^*$ *and* $\alpha \in \tilde{Y}^*$. *If* $\alpha \overset{\forall}{\longmapsto} w$ *then there exists* $\beta \in \{Y^1\}^*$ *and* $\gamma \in \{Y^0\}^*$ *such that* $\beta\gamma \overset{\forall}{\longmapsto} w$.

Proof. By induction on the length of α. If α is in the required form, we have the result. If not, then the subsequence Y^0Y^1 can be found at least once in α:

$$\alpha = \alpha_0 Y^0 Y^1 \alpha_1$$

We can decompose w into two parts w_0 and w_1 such that

$$\alpha_0 \overset{\forall}{\longmapsto} w_0$$
$$Y^0Y^1\alpha_1 \overset{\forall}{\longmapsto} w_1$$

But, for any b, we have $Y^b\alpha_1 \overset{b}{\longmapsto} Y^0Y^1\alpha_1$. Therefore, $Y^b\alpha_1 \overset{\forall}{\longmapsto} w_1$ and in turn $\alpha_0 Y^b \alpha_1 \overset{\forall}{\longmapsto} w$.

We can then use the induction hypothesis on $\alpha_0 Y^b \alpha_1$ to obtain β and γ satisfying the conditions of the theorem. □

4.4 Performance

The above encoding yields good performance in practice, even with a straightforward implementation of the oracle providing the stream of bits ρ. Indeed, Fig. 6 shows the chart generated from a sample C program. It exhibits the drastic cut-off in non-zero node density formalized in Def. 8, except for a few linear shapes, as one can observe. These are caused by our implementation of the oracle, which is naive. In our implementation, the bit which is generated is a parameter of the function V, and it is flipped (deterministically) for some recursive calls. This means that, inside a given subchart, all instances of associative rules either right-associate or left-associate, yielding a linear arrangement of results in the chart. Yet, this strategy for bit generation is the best we have found with respect to observed performance. The reason might be that more even distributions of results in the chart worsens the locality of non-zero data, yielding smaller zero subcharts.

5. Related Work

5.1 Our Own Previous Work

Claessen (2004) wrote a paper titled "parallel parsing processes", but which has only tenuous connections with the present work. The paper of 2004 presents a parsing technique based on usual sequential parsers, but where disjunction is represented by processes running concurrently. An advantage of that technique is that the parser processes the input string in chunks that can be discarded as soon as the parser has analyzed them.

Bernardy (2009) has shown how to combine the above idea with the online parsers of Hughes and Swierstra (2003). This makes the resulting parsing algorithm suitable for incremental parsing in an editing environment such as Yi (Bernardy 2008). However the method is brittle, because grammars need to be expressed in a special-purpose formalism, and error-correction must be "bake-in" the grammar. In contrast, the method presented here accepts grammar in Backus-Naur Form (see Sec. 6.6); only iterative structures need to be changed to use the special construction of Sec. 4. One does not have to worry about error recovery since all substrings are parsed.

5.2 Special Support for Iteration

The assumption we make on inputs, which is tied to the balancing of the parse trees is partially inspired by work by Wagner and Graham (1998). They show that linear parse trees cannot be handled efficiently, since updating a structure requires time proportional to its depth. Wagner and Graham then deduce that efficient incremental parsing requires a special purpose support for iteration, as we have done in Sec. 4.

5.3 General CF Parsing

Perhaps the most well known method for parsing general CF languages is that of Tomita (1986). This method has in common with ours that it achieves linear performance on well-behaved inputs, while degrading gracefully to the best possible performance (cubic) in the worst case.

The main difference between the methods is that Tomita's algorithm processes the input sequentially, while we can process it any bottom-up order. This means that the condition for well-behaved inputs is different for either methods. In Tomita's case, the condition is that, at any point during the parsing, the amount of ambiguity is small (bound by a constant), implying that the next action of the parser is most of the time determined by the next symbol in the input. In our case, it is captured by Def. 8, which essentially means that the input should be hierarchical. Tomita's condition does not imply ours: linearly arranged inputs can be deterministic. Checking the other implication is left for future work. It is not easy to conclude: our condition imposes non-local conditions which may or may not restrict non-determinism in a linear processing of the input.

The chief advantage of our method is its divide-and-conquer structure, which means that is can be used in a standard parallel or incremental framework. Tomita inherits essential use of the sequential processing of the input from LR parsing, making his technique not amenable to parallelization.

5.4 Parallel Parsing

There is a wealth of previous work devoted to efficient recognition and parsing of context-free languages on abstract parallel machines, so much that a comprehensive survey of the field does not fit in this paper. The situation can however be summarized as follows: to the best of our knowledge, before this work, algorithms proposed for parallel parsing either need an unrealistic number of processors, or they target a language class which is too restrictive to be of practical interest.

Too many processors Sikkel and Nijholt (1997) describe a parallel algorithm (in section 6.3) which can recognize a string of length n in $O(\log n)$ time, but it requires $O(n^6)$ processors in the worst case.

A line of work involving Rytter gives a dozen of complexity results for various sub-classes of CF and various abstract machines. The most closely related results are perhaps the following.

Chytil et al. (1991) present a simple parallel algorithm recognizing unambiguous context-free languages on a CREW PRAM in time $\log^2 n$ with only n^3 processors. The similarity with our work is that the authors restrict the languages they accept to a well-behaved subset of CF to obtain sensible running time. In our opinion the present work captures better the actual sets of inputs found in the actual practice of CF parsing.

Too restrictive grammars Rytter and Giancarlo (1987) analyze an algorithm which can parse a bracket grammar in $O(\log n)$ time and $O(n/\log n)$ processors. This is fast and does not use too many processors, but is restricted to languages where the grouping of non-terminals is completely explicit in the input: each production rule starts with an opening bracket and ends with a closing bracket.

6. Discussion

6.1 Destructive Updates

We were tempted to solve the problem of iteration by using destructive updates. That is, to have associative rules such as $Y ::= YY$ consume their arguments. That is, when a Y non-terminal is added to the chart using the above rule, the two Y non-terminals that compose it would be removed. We have attempted this solution, but faced a couple of issues, which will not surprise an audience of functional programmers.

- On the theoretical side, reasoning about parsing with destructive updates of the chart has proven too complicated to fit in this paper. The generation relation describing which strings are recognized by a parser is hard to define, let alone reason about. A major difficulty is to combine destructive updates with a notion of non-determinism similar to that described in Sec. 4. Indeed, the user has no control on which particular consuming rule will fire first, since this depends on the particular of the implementation of Valiant's algorithm (the order in which matrix multiplications are run, etc.) and the exact positioning of the substrings.
- On the practical side, the presence of updates makes for a more complicated implementation. It would also mean to abandon (so far unexploited) parallel opportunities in the matrix multiplication and the V function.

6.2 Optimization

In many grammars, a fair proportion of non-terminals occur only either on the left, or on the right of binary productions. Assume for example that A only ever occurs on the left. It is wasteful in this case to consider A for right-combinations, as does the algorithm we have presented so far.

This optimization is available to many CF parsing algorithms, but it is especially useful to us, because it acts in synergy with the detection of empty matrices. Indeed, by having separate matrices of left-combinable and right-combinable non-terminals, each matrix will be sparser. This means some combinations can be discarded *in blocks*, that is, at the level of matrices instead at the level of individual non-terminals.

An additional benefit of this optimization is that it pays for the cost of tagging non-terminals with an extra bit, as we suggest in Sec. 4. Indeed, 0-tagged non-terminals occur only on the left of binary productions, and 1-tagged non-terminals occur only on the right in our encoding of iteration. Therefore this optimization eliminates all the cost of tagging: instead of tagging a non-terminal with a bit, it suffice to insert it only in the relevant matrix.

6.3 Implementation

An implementation of the parsing method presented here, including special support for iteration as presented in Sec. 4 and the optimization presented above, is implemented as a new back-end for the BNFC tool, (Forsberg and Ranta 2012) available in version 2.6. The tool takes a grammar in BNF with annotations for efficient repetition. When running the tool with the option `-cnf`, it produces a Haskell implementation of CNF tables and an instance of the Valiant's algorithm using it. As other BNFC back-ends, our implementation produces full parsers, not mere recognizers.

6.4 Unexploited Parallelism

The parallelisation that we suggest can take advantage of at most a number of processors proportional to the length of the input. When parsing using Valiant's algorithm, there is more parallelism to take advantage of (for example two of the recursive calls in the V function are independent from each other). However, running in parallel all recursive calls to V would require asymptotically more processors than the length of the input. We do believe that this is *not* a reasonable assumption to make when parsing a whole input. However, in the case of incremental parsing, where only a tiny fraction of the input will be re-parsed, one might want to take advantage of such extra parallelism opportunities.

6.5 Unexploited Incrementality

We have suggested that the incremental version of the parser should run the V function $O(\log n)$ times when changing one symbol in the input. In fact, it might be possible to use a better implementation of the chart data structure, which would support an incremental update with a single run of the V function. Indeed, when changing a single symbol of the input, only the part of the chart which depends on that symbol (the square whose bottom-left corner is the symbol in question) needs to be recomputed. This improved re-use of results is left for future work.

6.6 Chomsky Normal-Form

Even though we assume that we transform the grammar to CNF for ease of presentation, this is not actually the best form to use in an implementation. In fact, it is better to convert the grammar to 2NF (where productions have at most 2 symbols) and derive the operations $(\cdot)$ and σ using a slightly modified algorithm, using the method described by Lange and Leiß (2009), as we have done in our implementation.

The conversion from Backus-Naur Form (BNF) to CNF (or 2NF) involves a division of long productions into binary ones. This is usually done by chaining the binary rules linearly. If the productions of the input grammar are long, this impacts negatively the performance of our algorithm, which performs best on balanced inputs. Fortunately it is not difficult to divide long productions into a balanced tree of binary rules.

The CNF grammar is suitable not only for recognition of languages, but also for parsing: the parse trees obtained by the converted grammar are essentially a binarization of the trees obtained by the grammar in BNF. The aspect which cannot be preserved by the conversion is the presence of cycles of unit rules. However, the elimination of such cycles can only be seen as a benefit: they introduce an unbounded amount of ambiguity in the grammar, and are a symptom of a mistake in the grammar specification.

6.7 A New Class of Languages

The assumption we make on the input (depending on a constant α), defines implicitly a new class of languages. The class lies between regular and context-free languages. We call the class α-balanced context-free languages, or BCF(α). The use of the parameter α contrasts with that of the parameter k in classes such as LL(k) or LR(k). While LL(k) or LR(k) restricts the form that a CF grammar can take, BCF(α) does not. Instead, it restricts the form that the strings of the language can take as a whole.

We have found that for a given grammar, programs are written with a shallow nesting structure, instead of a deep one (with the exception of regular iteration) and hence we have anecdotal evidence that any given programming languages is a member of BCF(α). Together with observation that the parsing problem for BCF(α) is simpler than that of general-context free languages, this makes BCF(α) worthy of study.

In fact, because the assumption we make is not one which is enforced by usual CF grammars, but we still observe it to hold in practice, it must mean that the assumption is self-imposed by the writers of these inputs, namely programmers. This is not too surprising, as our assumption can be violated only by programs which exhibit an amount of nesting comparable to the total length of the input. As folklore goes, programmers are adverse to deeply-nested constructions. Indeed, understanding a program with n levels of nesting requires to remember n levels of context. The link between the ability for a computer to efficiently parse an input in parallel and incrementally and for a human to do so is intriguing, and we hope that the present paper sheds an interesting light on it.

6.8 Generalization

The body of the paper does not depend on the particulars of CF recognition: we abstract over it via an arbitrary association operator. This means that other applications can be devised. A natural extension is to support CF *parsing*, as we have done in our implementation. More exotic extensions are also possible. A first example would be to support symbol tables, which are necessary for proper parsing of C. In this extension, non-terminals would be associated with two symbol sets, one that they assume comes from the environment and one which they provide to the environment. The combination operator would reconcile these two sets. A second example is probabilistic parsing. Here, a probability would be associated with each non-terminal and production rule, and the association operator would simply multiply the probabilities.

In fact, our method can be seen as a general way to turn a non-associative operator into an associative one by computing all possible associations. The efficiency is recovered by the ability to filter out most of the results; either because the original operator discards them, or because there is (possibly hidden) associativity which can be taken advantage of.

6.9 The Old as New

It strikes us that a parsing algorithm published in 1975 finds an application in the area of parallelisation for computer architectures of the 2010 decade. Further, Valiant gives no indication that the algorithm described should find any practical parsing application. As it seems, he aims only to tie the complexity of context-free recognition to that of matrix multiplication (via the transitive closure operation).

Indeed, in the case of parsing (in contrast to mere recognition), subtraction of matrices is not defined. Hence one cannot use the efficient Strassen algorithm (Strassen 1969) for multiplication, and in turn the complexity of general context-free parsing using Valiant's method is cubic, and fails to beat the simpler CYK algorithm.

Our contribution is to recognize that Valiant's algorithm performs well for parsing practical inputs, given a special handling of iteration and a sparse matrix representation (even when using the naive matrix multiplication algorithm). If we also account for the ease of making parallel and incremental implementations of the algorithm thanks to its divide and conquer structure, we must classify Valiant's algorithm as a practical method of parsing.

In fact, Valiant's algorithm offers such a combination of simplicity and performance that we believe it deserves a prominent place in textbooks, on par with LALR algorithms.

7. Conclusions

At the start of this work, we set out to find an associative operator with sub-linear complexity that could be used to implement a divide-and-conquer algorithm for parsing. The goal was to obtain a parallelizable parsing algorithm that would double as an incremental parsing algorithm. We managed to find such an operator, but the desired complexity only holds under certain assumptions that luckily do seem to hold in practice. The conditions hold when the recursive nesting depth of a program text only grows, say logarithmically in terms of the total length of the program. An unanticipated result of our work is thus the definition of a new class of languages. We were also forced to come up with a special way of dealing with iteration (frequently occurring in grammars) so it would not break this practical assumption.

Acknowledgments

The proof-method used in the presentation of Valiant's algorithm was suggested by Patrik Jansson. Engaging discussions about the complexity of Valiant algorithm were conducted with Devdatt Dubhashi. Peter Ljunglöf pointed us to some most relevant related work. Thomas Bååth Sjöblom, Darius Blasband, Peter Ljunglöf, as well as anonymous reviewers, gave useful feedback on drafts of the paper. This work has been partially funded by the Swedish Foundation for Strategic Research, under grant RAWFP.

References

L. Allison. Lazy Dynamic-Programming can be eager. *Information Processing Letters*, 43(4):207–212, 1992.

J.-P. Bernardy. Yi: an editor in Haskell for Haskell. In *Proc. of the first ACM SIGPLAN symposium on Haskell*, pages 61–62. ACM, 2008.

J.-P. Bernardy. Lazy functional incremental parsing. In *Proc. of the 2nd ACM SIGPLAN symposium on Haskell*, pages 49–60. ACM, 2009.

R. Bird and O. de Moor. *Algebra of programming*. Prentice-Hall, Inc., 1997.

N. Chomsky. On certain formal properties of grammars. *Information and control*, 2(2):137–167, 1959.

M. Chytil, M. Crochemore, B. Monien, and W. Rytter. On the parallel recognition of unambiguous context-free languages. *Theor. Comp. Sci.*, 81(2):311–316, 1991.

K. Claessen. Parallel parsing processes. *J. Funct. Program.*, 14(6):741–757, 2004.

J. Cocke. *Programming languages and their compilers: Preliminary notes*. Courant Institute of Mathematical Sci.s, New York University, 1969.

T. H. Cormen, C. E. Leiserson, R. L. Rivest, and C. Stein. *Introduction to algorithms, second ed.* MIT press, 2001.

M. Forsberg and A. Ranta. *BNFC Quick reference*, chapter Appendix A, pages 175–192. College Publications, 2012.

R. J. M. Hughes and S. D. Swierstra. Polish parsers, step by step. In *Proc. of ICFP 2003*, pages 239–248. ACM, 2003.

T. Kasami. An efficient recognition and syntax analysis algorithm for context-free languages. Technical report, DTIC Document, 1965.

M. Lange and H. Leiß. To CNF or not to CNF? an efficient yet presentable version of the CYK algorithm. *Informatica Didactica (8)(2008–2010)*, 2009.

B. O'Sullivan. The Criterion benchmarking library, 2013.

W. Rytter and R. Giancarlo. Optimal parallel parsing of bracket languages. *Theor. computer science*, 53(2):295–306, 1987.

K. Sikkel and A. Nijholt. *Parsing of context-free languages*, pages 61–100. Springer-Verlag, 1997.

V. Strassen. Gaussian elimination is not optimal. *Numerische Mathematik*, 13:354–356, 1969. 10.1007/BF02165411.

M. Tomita. *Efficient Parsing for Natural Language*. Kluwer Adademic Publishers, 1986.

L. Valiant. General context-free recognition in less than cubic time. *J. of computer and system sciences*, 10(2):308–314, 1975.

T. A. Wagner and S. L. Graham. Efficient and flexible incremental parsing. *ACM Transactions on Programming Languages and Systems*, 20(5): 980–1013, 1998.

D. Younger. Recognition and parsing of context-free languages in time n^3. *Information and control*, 10(2):189–208, 1967.

Functional Geometry and the *Traité de Lutherie*

[Functional Pearl]

Harry Mairson

Brandeis University

mairson@brandeis.edu

Abstract

We describe a functional programming approach to the design of outlines of eighteenth-century string instruments. The approach is based on the research described in François Denis's book, *Traité de lutherie*. The programming vernacular for Denis's instructions, which we call *functional geometry*, is meant to reiterate the historically justified language and techniques of this musical instrument design. The programming metaphor is entirely Euclidean, involving straightedge and compass constructions, with few (if any) numbers, and no Cartesian equations or grid. As such, it is also an interesting approach to teaching programming and mathematics without numerical calculation or equational reasoning.

The advantage of this language-based, functional approach to *lutherie* is founded in the abstract characterization of common patterns in instrument design. These patterns include not only the abstraction of common straightedge and compass constructions, but of higher-order conceptualization of the instrument design process. We also discuss the role of arithmetic, geometric, harmonic, and subharmonic proportions, and the use of their rational approximants.

Categories and Subject Descriptors D.3.3 [*Programming Languages*]: Language Constructs and Features—Control structures

General Terms Languages

Keywords Euclidean geometry, ruler and compass constructions, *vesica piscis*, proportion and measurement, Pythagorean approximation, chisels, hand planes, animal glue, maple, spruce, ebony, varnish.

1. Introduction

Programming languages don't exist simply to tell machines what to do. Well recognized as the engineering vernacular of software, they are more importantly the collective mother tongue of algorithmic ideas.

This point of view is a virtual credo among computer scientists. That credo has only recently been reiterated in public emphases on "computational thinking" as a way of understanding complex, constructional processes. In other words, programming languages provide a way for us to describe to each other what we know how to do.

We immediately assume, quite naturally, that modern technologies are the ones where this computational thinking is most appropriate and relevant. But people have been building things for a long time. In what way can computational thinking be an intellectual organizing principle for understanding and describing the past, and making sense of the kinds of expertise that flourished and came to maturity?

To that end, we've designed a programming language ("language" may be overblown—in any case, a set of graphics primitives, and more significant, a programming idiom) for realizing outlines of string instruments. The goal of this approach is to mimic accurately the accepted historical traditions for this design, while automating and facilitating the design and the construction process.

1.1 Historical background

Modern *luthiers* (string instrument makers) inherit a tradition embodied in the famous instruments of even more famous historical colleagues: renowned makers include, among others, Andrea Amati—recognized as the father of the violin—and distinguished members of his family, Andrea Guarneri and his family (especially son Giuseppe, and Giuseppe "del Gesù"), Matteo Gofriller, Dominico Montagnana, and the ubiquitous *primus inter pares*, Antonio Stradivari. It is typical for modern makers to copy and modify the canonical designs of these makers. But where did their designs come from? Surely not from an infinite chain of copyists—a non-well founded induction that violates the well-ordering principle. What are the underlying geometric, computational ideas from which these designs originate?

It is misleading to think that these instruments evolved simply from an amorphous, creative, artistic sense. The crude design of string instruments is a fairly inevitable consequence of ergonomics: a resonating box, with rounded corners to avoid bumping and blocking, and a concave middle 'waist' to allow bow access to the strings. But the further refinement of this basic form came from an interaction both musicians and their performance needs, and with the scientific perspective that was emerging simultaneously. Changing peformance requirements (for example, the evolution of the violoncello from a continuo to a virtuoso, solo instrument) caused changes in design. In addition, these string instruments took form during an age of scientific revolution—the era of Copernicus, Kepler, Galileo, Newton—where the experimental mindset, with its associated scientific insights, likely had an impact on instrument designers and makers (Schleske 2004).

In 2006, a French luthier named François Denis published *Traité de lutherie* (Denis 2006), a comprehensive and seminal treatise which attempted to lay out the manner in which string instrument outlines were constructed. There are few, if any, written works on construction technique written at the time these instruments

ICFP '13, September 25–27, 2013, Boston, MA, USA.

http://dx.doi.org/10.1145/2500365.2500617

emerged on the historical, musical scene: Denis' contribution was a historically inspired and *a priori* reconstruction of what some of those techniques likely were. The most striking thing about Denis's book is that the construction methods are entirely Euclidean, when we are used to thinking in a Cartesian way about most everything. The designs are realized without graph paper, without Vernier calipers, protractors, or just about anything having to do with measurement.[1] Instead, virtually everything is done with an (unmarked) ruler, and a compass, save one fixed dimension. That dimension determines, via entirely proportional constructions, all the other ones.

It's worth saying, without reverting to a commutative diagram, that a great majority of our reasoning about a great deal of subjects is Cartesian. We typically learn Euclidean geometry to introduce the notion of *proof*, but by the time we want to *calculate* anything, we've usually moved on to Cartesian, analytic geometry. In other words, a circle isn't a curve: it's an equation. And the same goes for physics, for economics. Even philosophy—think of the "word problems" solved by translation into propositional logic—the utterly Cartesian construction of *analytic* philosophy, which gave rise as well to computer science.

The big Cartesian idea is this: to solve your problem, turn it into equations. Then solve your equations instead (whence the commutative diagram?), and when you're done, translate your solution back to your problem domain. Instead, the Euclidean solution—and that of Denis for instrument design—is this: it's a geometric problem. So you solve it in the geometric world with geometric constructs.

It deserves mentioning that all string instruments are not alike. Of course, there are tonal variations, as a consequence of wood quality, workmanship, and aspects of design. But it should be emphasized that every maker had a signature—not the label inside the instrument as much as the shape of scrolls, pegboxes, necks, corners, purfling, ff-holes—and instrument outline. Professional appraisers can identify the makers of famous instruments by these virtual fingerprints, just as program committees of programming language conferences could identify the authors of conference submissions even under double-blind conditions.

Almost everything we know about how to do this—still considered as a refined, even mysterious, knowledge—was understood virtually a half-millenium ago.[2] But how, and in what way?

1.2 Some comments on Denis's *Traité*

Learning how to carry out Denis's constructions with pencil and paper leads to two immediate conclusions. One is that the descriptions of the constructions are, in effect, a kind of do-this-then-do-that informal straight-line code. They would benefit by a restatement as a functional program, where notions of hierarchy and abstraction have the potential to make greater sense out of many details. A well-structured description can illuminate the big picture of the forest, and the detail of the trees, with no loss of implementation focus at either end.

A second conclusion is that the learning process itself is facilitated by such a development. Not only does this process require the understanding of the big picture and the little details, the inevitable errors encountered in learning how to do this can be made faster, and can be recovered from faster and easier. A mechanical graphics engine attached to this functional description ensures accuracy, rectilinearity, without the accumulated error of physical drafting methods (though similar issues of numerical analysis may arise and need careful treatment).[3] That speed and accuracy is of no small consequence if the analytic methods are to be used also as an experimental, investigative mechanism.

Briefly, a programming characterization of these outlines would serve the following additional goals. First, we can focus on the putative *design process* (program) itself, in an appropriate vernacular, rather than its output. Second, designs of famous instruments could be made public, where they could be downloaded and modified by modern makers. (Their modifications, of proprietary interest, would most likely not be public.) Third, the ease of producing instrument outlines could be a construction prosthetic, aiding the building of molds, around which rib assemblies are constructed. Finally and most interestingly, these programs might be the foundation of a kind of computational art history, where evolution of instruments could be studied more carefully by the more informed evolution of designs. If nothing else, a result would be an effectively automated version of Denis's book.

We are no longer building catapults or pillars or even film cameras. But we are still making violins—a Renaissance technology that was worked out a half-millenium ago. Making them is surely an art, but in every artistic practice, there is method. Scrolls and archings and outlines and all the details of lutherie are not simply a consequence of artistic temperament. There is a method for everything.

The point of this undertaking is to make some of that method explicit in a contemporary vernacular, while showing the greatest respect for the underlying method itself. In other words, don't change the method as much as find a better way of describing it. In preserving this Euclidean perspective, the goal is to take all of the Cartesian, equational calculation—inevitable in programming—and push it all to the effectively invisible back end, so that the interface used is just the Euclidean part. Building a WYSIWYG graphics engine is a canonical entry point to learning about graphics programming, but our real interest here is as much the *language* as the output. All of a sudden, the seemingly static things you learned in high-school geometry become a dynamic programming language.

A virtue of the language is its record of the construction—the opaqueness of WYSIWYG, resolved by a markup language, is that the latter allows you to *see what you did* to get what you got. The challenge is to find appropriate abstraction primitives. Recursion is noticably absent—it doesn't seem particularly relevant. But that doesn't mean that programming is pointless. Recall the principle underlined in (Abelson and Sussman 1996) that to understand a programming language is to identify its primitive operations, means of combination, and means of abstraction. They are all apparent here.

2. Geometric prelude: point, line, circle, and the pentagon

Rather than describe all the bits and pieces of our primitive graphics language, which is just some fairly straightforward graphics prim-

[1] This should be contrasted with the exegesis in Edward Heron-Allen's famous *Violin Making, as it was and is* (Heron-Allen 1885), which was for many years virtually the only go-to book on instrument making, where the design methods are founded on a rectilinearly-based treatise of Antonio Bagatella, *Regole per la costruzione de violini, viole, violoncelli e violoni* (Bagatella 1782).

[2] Simone Sacconi titled his famous monograph *The 'Secrets' of Stradivari* to emphasize that there were no secrets, but rather refined technique (Sacconi 1979). But the cause and effect reflected in that technique is not really analytically understood—instead, luthiers work within a highly functional and successful "envelope" and venture out, experimentally, in search of further optimization.

[3] "Most of all I would like to advise the maker that the greatest care be taken in using the compass to adapt and calculate the measurements because the slightest movement of the position of the hand is capable of causing an error." (Antonio Bagatella, *Regole per la costruzione dei violini-viole, violoncelli e violoni*, Padova, 1782.)

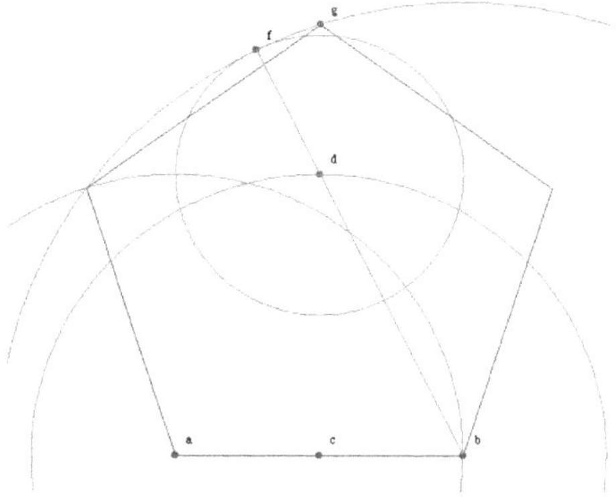

Figure 1. *Constructing a pentagon*

itives on top of Scheme[4], we'll just get on with it. Our demonstration toy problem is how to draw a pentagon with a straightedge and compass.

```
(define (pentagon a s)
  (let ((b (label "b" (xshift a s))))
    (let ((c (label "c"
               (intersect
                 (apply line
                        (intersect (circle a s)
                                   (circle b s)))
                        (line a b)))))
      (let ((d (label "d"
                 (top (intersect
                        (vertical c)
                        (circle c s))))))
        (let ((f (label "f" (top
                   (intersect (line b d)
                              (circle d (distance a c)))))))
          (let ((g (label "g"
                     (top (intersect
                            (vertical c)
                            (circle b (distance b f)))))))
            (let ((p (left (intersect (circle g s)
                                      (circle a s))))
                  (q (right (intersect (circle g s)
                                       (circle b s)))))
              (list (label "a" a) b c d f g p q
                    (makeseg b f)
                    (circle a s) (circle c s)
                    (circle d (distance d f))
                    (circle b (distance b f))
                    (segments (list g p a b q g)) ))))))))
```

Some brief comments on the construction:

(pentagon a s**)** Pentagon at point a with base length s.

(xshift p d**)** Point p shifted d in the x-direction.

(line a b**)** Line through points a, b.

(horizontal p**), (vertical** p**)** Horizontal, vertical lines through point p.

(circle p r**)** Circle with center at p and radius r.

(intersect o_1 o_2**)** Intersection of circles, lines, with possible multiple solutions.[5]

(top S**), (bottom** S**), (left** S**), (right** S**)** Choosing among multiple solutions to an intersection.

(north C**), (south** C**), etc.** Quadrants of a circle.

(label ℓ p**)** Mark point p on the plane with the label ℓ, returning value p.

The overall idea is to specify, then draw. Recall that given a unit length, with a straightedge and compass, the constructable point-to-point distances are those points closed over the unit length and $+, -, \times, \div, \sqrt{}$—i.e., "over radicals".[6] (As a consequence, a straightedge and compass serve as a primitive analog computer.) A pentagon is constructible because with a unit edge, its diameter (distance b-f in Figure 1) is the golden mean $\phi = \frac{1}{2}(1 + \sqrt{5})$.

With this example in mind, there's an overwhelming temptation to start programming up every geometric construction you can find—and there are lots of them, of considerable subtlety (Sutton 2009). We mention, for example, Malfatti's problem (Martin 1998): given a triangle, inscribe three circles that are tangent to each other and to the sides of the circle. This problem wasn't solved until the late nineteenth century (see Steiner's synthetic, geometric construction (Steiner)), though draftsman may well have known the solution long before (Denis, personal communication).

3. Musical prelude: the lute of Arnault of Zwolle

Roughly comparable in detail of the pentagon is the lute design of Henri Arnault of Zwolle, from a manuscript dating from 1440 (Harwood 1960; Zwolle 1440). Arnault was a cleric in the court of French king Louis IX, a polymath prototype of Leonardo da Vinci, only who designed musical instruments instead of instruments of war. His manuscript of 1440 describes the construction of a lute. This lute is the "toy problem" of string instrument metrology: what goes for the lute, goes for the violin and violoncello, only more so.

```
(define (lute rad)
  (let ((c (circle origin rad))
        (d (* 2 rad)))
    (let ((p (label "p" (west c)))
          (q (label "q" (north c)))
          (qprime (label "q'" (south c))))
      (let ((r (label "r"
                 (left (intersect (circle (mirror p) d)
                                  (line (mirror p) q))))))
        (let ((s (label "s" (yshift q (distance q r)))))
          (let ((rose (circle (point 0 (/ rad 2))
                              (* (/ 3 10) rad))))
       (list
         (map (lambda (t)
                (list (label "" (pointfrom origin q t))
                      (label "" (pointfrom origin
                                           (transpose q) t))))
              (list 0 .2 .4 .6 .8 1.0))
         (circle origin rad) (circle q (distance q r))
         ;draw the rose:
         (makearc (center rose) (north rose) (west rose))
         (makearc (center rose) (west rose) (south rose))
         (makearc origin p qprime)
         (makearc (mirror p) p r)
         (makearc q r s))))))))
```

Note that (**mirror** p) produces a point reflected around the y-axis, so arc drawing is only (explicitly) on the left-hand side of the

[4] This situation is deliberately meant to evoke memory of Peter Henderson's *functional geometry* from the 1980s (Abelson and Sussman 1996; Henderson 2002).

[5] To underline the Cartesian and its departure from the Euclidean: reflect on the intersection of two circles, both with equations having x^2 and y^2 terms with coefficient 1. When you subtract one equation from the other, you're left with a linear term—of what? The line that is the bisector of the *vesica piscis*, the "fish bladder" marking their intersection—see, e.g (Wikipedia).

[6] See (Stewart 1973), pp. 57-67.

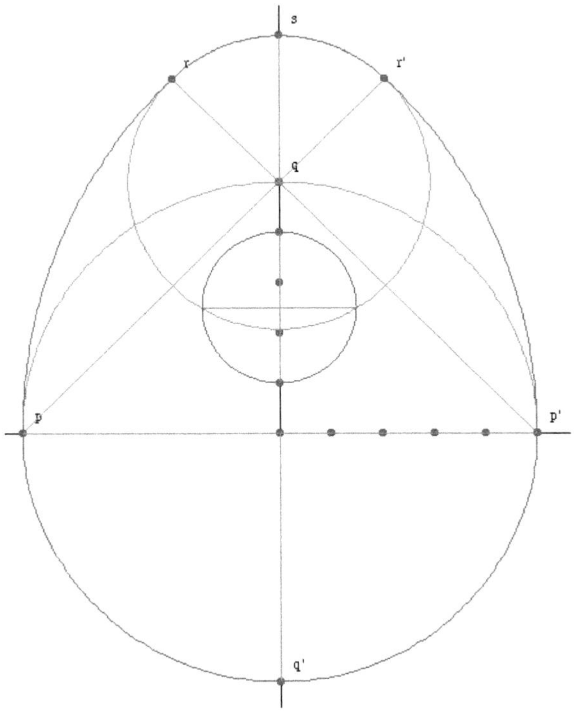

Figure 2. *Lute by Arnault of Zwolle (from a manuscript from 1440), with an approximate soundhole placement*

plane, and mirrored on the right. It's an obvious symmetry that we should take advantage of.

4. Rational approximations

We can make a virtually indistinguishable pentagon by dispensing with the compass almost entirely (or at least, use a "rusty compass" that cannot change dimension), as long as we can draw perpindicular lines. Then, common carpenter's tricks let us code the pentagon with rational, Pythagorean approximants. We use $\frac{14}{9}$ to approximate the height $\sqrt{\phi^2 - \frac{1}{4}}$, $\frac{3}{10}$ for the additional width (beyond the base) $\frac{\phi-1}{2}$, and $\frac{20}{21}$ for the height $\sqrt{1-\left(\frac{\phi-1}{2}\right)^2}$ of the leftmost and rightmost corners:

```
(define (approximate-pentagon a s)
  (let ((b (label "b" (xshift a s))))
    (let ((t (yshift (midpoint a b) (* s (/ 14 9)))))
      (let ((d (yshift (xshift b (* s (/ 3 10)))
                       (* s (/ 20 21))))
            (c (yshift (xshift a (* s (/ -3 10)))
                       (* s (/ 20 21)))))
        (segments (list a b d t c a))))))
```

What works for pentagons works, by extension, for Arnault's lute construction, and describes in greater detail the underlying geometric symmetries of its design. Figure 4 shows a refined analysis of Arnault's lute construction, which is (as Denis points out) not so much the definition of a real lute as much as it is a prototype, an examplar, of a generic recipe for synthesizing lute designs.

This construction method makes the length of the instrument—a critical dimension for tuning and structural stability—a consequence of the design process, rather than a parameter of it. To design the instrument *ab initio* from its length, we need to think a bit

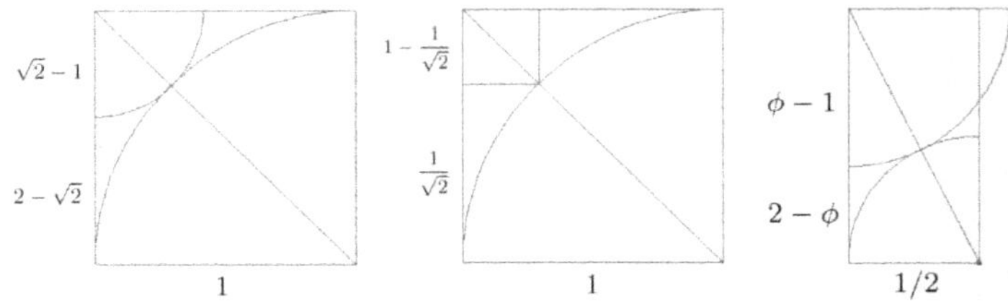

Figure 3. *Harmonic, subharmonic, and geometric sections*

more carefully about the geometry of the underlying construction, in particular its use of harmonic and subharmonic sections.

Notice that the length of the lute is $3m+2s$, where m and s are the radii of circles derived from carefully constructed *geometric sections*. The geometric constructions of these sections are shown in Figures 3 and 4. The highlighted box to the left of the vertical axis of the lute contains a *harmonic section*, and that to the right, a *subharmonic section*. Notice the geometric demonstration that the larger part of a harmonic section equals the smaller part of a subharmonic section that is twice as big.

Now consider the rational approximation of the subharmonic section. Let $s+m=1$ where s and m are an approximation of this section: then a better approximation is $s'=m$ and $m'=s+2m$. Solving $\frac{s}{m}=\frac{s'}{m'}$ gives $s=1-\frac{1}{\sqrt{2}}$, the smaller part of the section. Beginning with $s=m=1$, we get the series of approximants $\frac{1}{3}, \frac{3}{7}, \frac{7}{17}$; luthiers would use initial terms from this series (and those like it) as approximations of its limit. Such constants are mentioned in Arnault's manuscript.[7]

```
(define (approximate-lute s m L)
  (let ((N (+ (* 2 s) (* 3 m))))
    (let ((r (* L (/ (+ m s) N))))
      (let ((q (label "q" (yshift origin (minus r)))))
        (let ((p (label "p" (yshift q L))))
          (let ((cmain (circle (yshift q r) r)))
            (let ((ctop
                    (circle (north cmain)
                            (distance (north cmain) p)))
                  (cright (circle (east cmain) (* r 2))))
 (list
   (apply makeseg    ; bridge
     (intersect cmain
                (horizontal (yshift q (* L (/ s N))))))
   ; sound hole
   (let ((s (yshift p (* (minus L) (/ (+ s (* 3 m)) (* 2 N))))))
     (let ((rs (/ (distance s
                    (left (intersect (horizontal s) cright)))
                  3)))
       (let ((sh (circle s rs)))
         (list sh
               (make-curve q p
                 (list cmain cright ctop)) ))))))))))))
```

(Note that `make-curve` above specifies a curve from `q` to `p`, following the arcs given by circles `cmain`, `cright`, and `ctop`.)

We redraw the lute using this revised code, above, with parameters $s=3$ and $m=4$—note $3/7=.4285\ldots$ is a respectable approximation of $\sqrt{2}-1=.4142\ldots$. The length of the lute is now divided into $3m+2s=18$ parts, and Arnault's written direc-

[7] Recurrences, familiar to students of discrete mathematics, provide the foundation of these proportional sections. Recall $f(x)=\frac{x+1}{x}$ as defining the geometric section (with initial value $x_0=\frac{1}{1}$), $g(x)=\frac{x+2}{x+1}$ as defining the harmonic section (also with initial value x_0), etc.

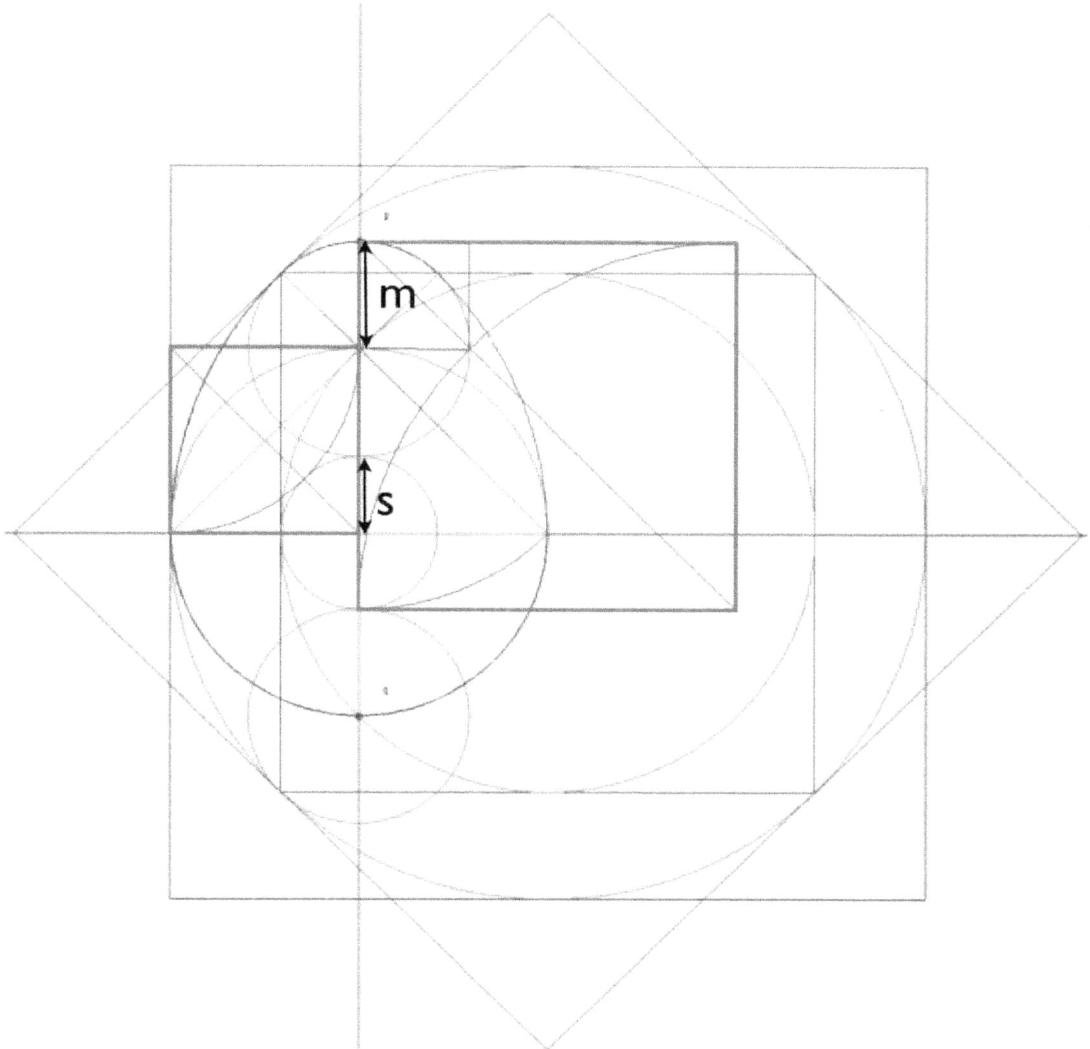

Figure 4. *Geometry of Arnault's lute. The subharmonic section is highlighted on the right, the harmonic section on the left.*

tions that the bridge placement is one-sixth of the instrument length makes rational sense.

Even without this rational approximation, note with $s = \sqrt{2} - 1$ and $m = 2 - \sqrt{2}$, we have $\frac{s}{2m+3s} = \frac{1}{14}(3\sqrt{2} - 2) \approx 0.1602$, realizing Arnault's one-sixth measurement.

Further, the location and size of the soundhole is rationalized through the following argument, a rather striking prestidigitation (see Denis, p. 54 ff.). Its location is said in the manuscript to be halfway from the bridge to the top of the instrument. The length of $3m + 2s$ can be rearranged as $S = m + s$ and $M = 2m + s$. Given the ratio $\frac{s}{m} = \frac{\sqrt{2}-1}{2-\sqrt{2}}$ from the *harmonic* section, we have $\frac{M-S}{S} \approx .5858$ and $\frac{S}{M} \approx .6306$, while the ratio of the *geometric* section is $\frac{2-\phi}{\phi-1} = \phi - 1 \approx .6180$, right between the two.

As a consequence, we can consider the length of the instrument, to sufficient accuracy, as a geometric sequence of overall length $s' + m'$, where the ratio s'/m' can be approximated by Fibonacci numbers of moderate size. Take $s' = 5, m' = 8$ ($m'/s' = 1.625 \approx \phi$). If the bridge is distance s from the bottom of the instrument, then the center of the soundhole is distance $\frac{1}{2}(3m + s)$ from the top of the lute. An exact calculation, following Arnault's specification that the soundhole diameter be one-third of the width, gives a diameter of $(\sqrt{15} - 2)/3 \approx .6243$. Using the approximate geometric section (m', s') above gives $s'/m' = .625$. The point of this rational reconstruction is that layout with carefully chosen approximations comes remarkably close to the analytic calculations.

5. Anatomy of an outline: the Amati violin. Geometric problems and their solutions.

With the preamble of the Arnault lute in mind we can go on to look at the first outline of a violin in the book by Denis: a canonical violin by Andrea Amati. The outline has four essential parts: the framework, which blocks out the regions, and the upper, lower, and middle *bouts*. A key feature of the outline is that it is parameterized by only one fixed dimension: the distance XQ from the top of the outline to the top of the lower bout. All the other dimensions are proportional. The code appears in the Appendix. It needs emphasis that the code is almost a verbatim translation of Denis's construction description.

The do-this-then-do-that of straight line code is not very interesting. But a significant number of low-level details can be abstracted. The curves of all the outlines are made by following sequentially a series of arcs defined by circles, with endpoints, via `(make-curve` p q `(list` C_1 C_2 $\cdots C_k$`))`. There are distances that are partitioned by a series of straightedge and compass sections constructing, for example, a geometric section (geometric-section p q).

Then there are more interesting constructions associated with curious geometric puzzles. For example, given two circles C_1 and C_2 on the plane, and a radius r, find the circle C of radius r that is tangent to both C_1 and C_2. An example of this construction is in the lower bouts of the Amati violin, where the curve is made up of three principal arcs: the middle one is from a circle tangent to others as described here. Solving the equations is a middle-school headache, but the geometric construction is fun.

Similarly, there is a geometric problem in computing reverse curves at the corners of the upper and lower bouts. Given a large circle C that defines the curve at the upper bout, a radius r, and a point p, where is the circle of radius r located that is tangent to the outer side of C, and also tangent to p? Luthiers solved these kinds of problems by construction and without math. With appropriate software, we do the same thing.

```
(define (reverse-curve inner-circle outer pt)
  (let ((outer-radius (- outer (radius inner-circle))))
    (let ((pts (intersect (circle pt (abs outer-radius))
                          (circle (center inner-circle)
                                  (+ outer-radius
                                     (radius inner-circle))))))
      (map (lambda (p) (circle p (abs outer-radius))) pts))))
```

```
(define (inscribe c1 c2 r)
  ; circles tangent to insides of c1, c2 of radius r
  (let ((c1p (circle (center c1) (- (radius c1) r)))
        (c2p (circle (center c2) (- (radius c2) r))))
    (map (lambda (pt) (circle pt r)) (intersect c1p c2p))))
```

Another example comes from the design of a Montagnana violoncello, where a signature characteristic of that maker is found: the principal curve of the upper bout and the reverse curve are not tangent, or mediated by another curve, but instead connected by a straight line. This construction is easy enough by eye, but what is the exact construction? Again, these straightedge and compass constructions have detail, but we can abstract away from them with no loss of detail.

```
(define (tangent small big)
; finds the two lines tangent to (nonintersecting) small,
; big, where the lines are intersecting between them
  (let ((d (line (center small) (center big))))
    (let ((p1 (perpendicular d (center small)))
          (p2 (perpendicular d (center big))))
      (let ((a (top (intersect small p1)))
            (b (bottom (intersect big p2))))
        (let ((i (intersect d (line a b))))
          (let ((j (midpoint i (center big))))
            (let ((pts
                   (intersect big
                              (circle j (distance i j)))))
              (map (lambda (pt) (line i pt)) pts))))))))
```

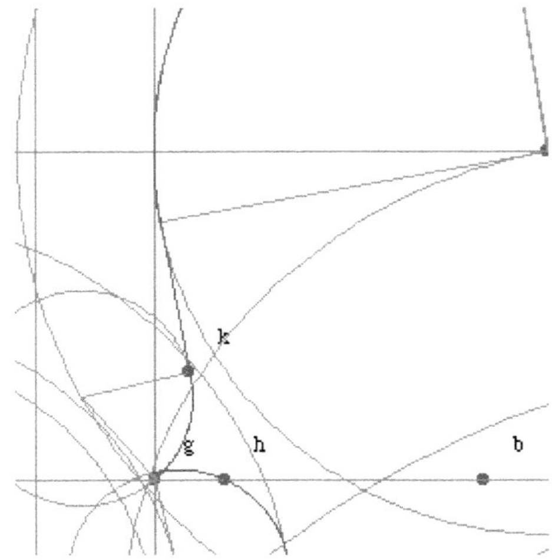

Figure 5. *Detail of Montagnana violoncello, giving upper bout construction using a tangent line between two circles*

6. Abstraction of construction, and of design. Towards a computational art history.

One of the most important tasks which the new science of art could set for itself would be a through analysis of the history of art; to determine the elements, construction and composition in various periods... [the analysis] borders on the problems of the "positive" sciences, the second part... touches the problems of philosophy.
Wassily Kandinsky, **Point and Line to Plane** (Kandinsky 1926)[8]

The code for the Amati violin describes various computational dependencies. Changing some of the integer ratios in the code changes the design, while maintaining the coherence of the form. At some point, the implied constraints may become unsatisfiable (say, a line that must be to the left and to the right of some critical point, causing an intersection that no longer has a solution), and then the implementation cannot draw the outline. For the most part, this breakdown should be regarded as a feature, not a bug—it's an error message in itself. That the instrument is defined as a set of proportional relations, as opposed to curves that must be set to some fixed set of points, lends a certain plasticity to the specification that probably facilitates the satisfaction of these constraints.

A bit more subtle than strictly computational constraints are design constraints. These don't come from the mechanics of layout, but from dimensions that must be satisfied in a final product. For example, the *body stop* of a violincello, measured from the top of the front plate abutting the neck, to the inner nick at the middle of the ff-hole, is typically 400mm. Few modern instruments diverge widely from that dimension, while some old instruments do. It's not clear to me in what way these kinds of constraints should be built into the automated design process.

A clear advantage of this automated drafting is that we can make hypotheses and check them out faster, make mistakes and recover from them faster, than what might be possible with pencil and paper. One question I am looking at is Denis's thesis that Stradivari marks a turning point where the proportional approach is no longer fully explanatory, and that use of metric measurement is necessary. In order to test this assertion, I've been trying to reverse engineer the outline of the 1707 "Countess of Stanlein" Stradivarius violoncello (see (Reuning 2012)), in order to determine whether it could have an effectively proportional description. I've got a first cut at this outline done, and I expect to give more details on this in the full paper.

Abstraction mechanisms give a higher-order representation to the low-level business of straightedge and compass construction. We've given some examples of this abstraction at the more mechanical level, but I would like to be able to raise this abstraction to a more conceptual level, if we could characterize the kind of computing with shapes that is inherent in instrument design. The

[8] It's worth noting that this book was written in 1928, clearly affected by the logical positivists of the Vienna circle and the analytic philosophy movement before it (see, for example, (Galison 1990) for the working out of this striking but somewhat obvious connection). Analytic philosophy is also a significant intellectual precursor of the development of programming languages.

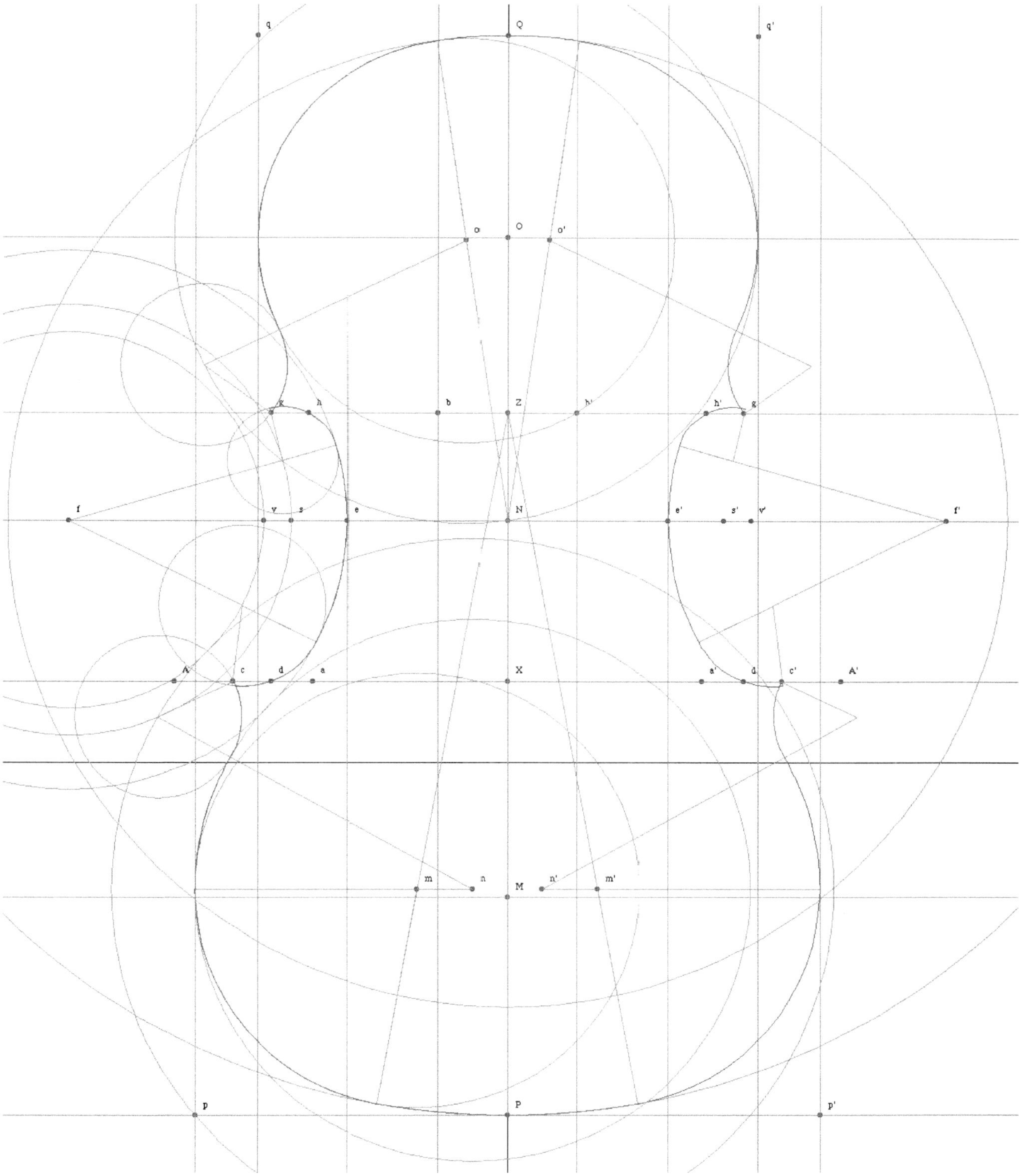

Figure 6. *Violin by Andrea Amati*

Arnault lute gives some hints in this direction, as its outline is a consequence of quadrature, rotation, proportion, and approximation. Bluntly put, if a martini is six parts gin to one part vermouth, what is a Gofriller violoncello? By a familiar analogy: we're used to programming language constructions (say, continuation-passing style) as a basic form, with particular variants (Gödel, Kuroda, Kolmogorov, etc.) derivative from double-negation embeddings; why can't instrument forms be computational variants on a basic theme? What's needed is a kind of grammar of relevant shape and how to compute with it. The thematic homilies of Kandinsky (Kandinsky 1926) given much greater detail in a recent book by George Stiny (Stiny 2008), provide some suggestions of how this work could evolve. In particular, Stiny describes grammars for the evolution of shapes—"how I stopped counting," he says, "and started to see." Good artists know how to see. In this particular example, can their insight, and how it changed, be characterized formally?

7. Historical evidence and the *a priori*

How did luthiers draw outlines? Like many historical and scientific questions, this one has empirical answers, and *a priori* answers. We can look for evidence, as well as analyze from first principles. In his 2010 book on Stradivari, Stewart Pollens writes that he "does not appear to have employed a rigid system of geometry and proportion in designing his violins" and takes a questionable view of such explanations since (and including) the 1782 manuscript of Bagatella (Pollens 2010). The solution of Denis is, on the contrary, heavily *a priori*, with evidence supplied by the 15th-century Arnault manuscript, but not by historical evidence from 18th-century luthiers.

To think that each generation of luthiers has simply copied what came before, perhaps with small modifications, strikes me as the historical equivalent of a non well-founded induction. There has to be a base case. Amati is generally regarded as the first mover in the design of string instruments, as we know them. The solution of Denis is from first principles, effectively contemporaneous with Amati, but also in the spirit of ideas of proportion and symmetry that date from the era of Vitruvius[9], and went on to animate the work of architects, artists, furniture makers, and—as Denis persuasively argues—instrument makers. Nonetheless, it is natural to seek the assurance of empirical confirmation as well. (Such a dissent from Pollens's critique is expressed by Andrew Dipper, the translator of an 18th c. luthier's construction notebook (Dipper 2013), and a cataloguer of items from the Museo Stradivariano in Cremona.)

The situation is analogous to an irreverent remark about the difference between geology and geophysics: geology is the observation of physical phenomena that can't be explained, but geophysics is the explanation of physical phenomena that can't be observed.

8. Conclusions and perspective

A natural and obvious criticism of what I've described here is this: it just using a computer to draw pretty pictures. The pictures are beautiful and of historical and cultural interest, but the programs are not. In response to this point of view, I think that the way we represent what we know is important, and a program clarifies meaning, more than any natural language directions. Moreover, there are inevitably levels of such informal description, from detailed ("do this, then do that") to high-level (literally, "big picture"), and higher-order procedures, well-written, can explain both with no loss of accuracy.

There may be "better" ways of drawing things (for example, with splines), but that doesn't interest me here. What matters is the representation of knowledge that was already known. If research is, literally, the re-searching for things that were already found, then a good justification for it is that in rediscovery, we say it better, or in ways that are more compelling to us. It is a natural progression not only in our understanding of this particular subject, but, more generally, how we represent what we know.

Acknowledgements: In the past half-dozen years, I've become very interested in building string instruments, and in particular, violincellos. I am grateful to Olin Shivers, whose enthusiasm for this project has been a big motivation to me. François Denis has been generous with his time and his advice. Curtis Bryant, a Boston luthier and restorer, has given me a great amount of guidance over several years. Marilyn Wallin taught me a lot about instrument making, varnishing, and setup. George Stiny has been a very helpful guide to relevant literature relating theories of proportion and classical architecture. Thanks also to an inspired reviewer who made many helpful comments. The mistakes I've made and misunderstandings I've had in construction, design, or explanation, are my responsibility and not theirs. Finally, David Van Horn, the POPL workshops co-chair, persuaded me to make a submission to the OBT ("Off the beaten track—New directions in programming language research") workshop; the encouragement I received from him and from workshop participants have motivated this paper.

References

Harold Abelson and Gerald J. Sussman. *Structure and Interpretation of Computer Programs*. MIT Press, Cambridge, Massachusetts, USA, 1996.

Antonio Bagatella. *Regole per la costruzione de violini viole violoncelli e violoni*. Turris, Cremona, 1782.

François Denis. *Traité de lutherie: The violin and the art of measurement*. ALADFI: Association des Luthiers et Archetiers pour le Développement de la Facture Instrumentale, Nice, France, 2006.

Andrew Dipper. *Librem Segreti de Buttegha: The violin and its fabrication, 'a book of workshop secrets'*. Dipper Publications, 2013.

Peter Galison. Aufbau/Bauhaus: Logical positivism and architectural modernism. *Critical Inquiry*, 16(4):709–752, 1990.

Thomas Gordon Smith. *Vitruvius on Architecture*. Monacelli Press, 2003.

Ian Harwood. A fifteenth-century lute design. *Lute Society Journal*, 2, 1960.

Peter Henderson. Functional geometry. *Higher Order Symbol. Comput.*, 15(4):349–365, December 2002. ISSN 1388-3690. . URL `http://dx.doi.org/10.1023/A:1022986521797`.

Edward Heron-Allen. *The Violin, as it was and is*. Ward-Lock, 1885.

Wassily Kandinsky. *Point and Line to Plane*. Dover, New York, 1926.

George Martin. *Geometric Constructions*. Springer, 1998.

Stewart Pollens. *Stradivari*. Cambridge University Press, 2010.

Christopher Reuning. *The "Paganini, Countess of Stanlein" Stradivari Violoncello of 1707*. 2012.

Simone Sacconi. *The 'Secrets' of Stradivari*. Eric Blot (Cremona), 1979.

Martin Schleske. Zeitgeist and violinmaking: Milestones of art and science, a brief journey through time. 2004.

Jakob Steiner. Synthetic solution to a problem of Malfatti. URL `http://en.wikipedia.org/wiki/Malfatti_circles`.

Ian Stewart. *Galois Theory*. Chapman and Hall, 1973.

George Stiny. *Shape: Talking about Seeing and Doing*. MIT Press, 2008.

Andrew Sutton. *Ruler and Compass: practical geometric constructions*. Wooden Books, 2009.

Wikipedia. Vesica Piscis. URL `http://en.wikipedia.org/wiki/Vesica_piscis`.

Henri Arnault of Zwolle. Treatise. *Bibliothèque Nationale, Paris*, ms Lat. 7295, 1440.

[9] See (Gordon Smith 2003), especially Book III.

Appendix: Violin by Andrea Amati

```
(define Amati
  (let ((xq 400)) ;; should be 208mm in the Amati---this is just a screen fit...

; LAYOUT OF THE AREA on which the curves are drawn...
(let ((X (label "X" (point 0 000)))) ; this could be anywhere---just to center it on the output screen
  (let ((A (label "A" (xshift X (- (/ xq 2)))))
        (Q (label "Q" (yshift X xq))))
    (let ((N (label "N" (pointfrom X Q (/ 1 4)))))
      (let ((q (label "q" (xshift (intersect (horizontal Q) (vertical A))
                                  (/ (distance X N) 2))))
            (vv (xshift A (/ (distance X N) 8)))
            (O (label "O" (yshift Q (- (* (distance X N) (/ 5 4))))))
            (Z (label "Z" (yshift N (* (distance X N) (/ 2 3)))))
            (P (label "P" (yshift X (- (* (distance X N) (/ 8 3)))))))
        (let ((p (label "p" (intersect (horizontal P) (vertical vv))))
              (M (label "M" (pointfrom X P (/ 1 2))))
              (a (label "a" (xshift A (/ (distance X Z) 2)))))
          (let ((b (label "b" (xshift Z (- (/ (distance A a) 2))))))
           (let ((ee (label "e" (xshift (intersect (vertical b) (horizontal N)) (- (* (xdistance b p) (/ 3 8)))))))
             (let ((c (label "c" (xshift (intersect (vertical p) (horizontal X)) (/ (xdistance ee p) 4))))
                   (d (label "d" (xshift (intersect (vertical p) (horizontal X)) (/ (xdistance ee p) 2))))
                   (h (label "h" (xshift (intersect (vertical ee) (horizontal Z)) (- (/ (xdistance ee p) 4)))))
                   (g (label "g" (xshift (intersect (vertical ee) (horizontal Z)) (- (/ (xdistance ee p) 2))))))
                (list X A Q N q O Z P p M a b ee c d h g
                      (horizontal N) (horizontal O) (horizontal Z) (horizontal P) (horizontal X) (horizontal M)
                      (vertical p) (vertical q) (vertical b) (vertical ee)

; THE LOWER BOUTS...
(let ((ZMcircle (circle Z (distance Z M)))
      (ZPcircle (circle Z (distance Z P))))
  (let ((m (label "m" (bottom (intersect ZMcircle
                                         (make-line 1 p) ; line w/slope 1 through p
                                         )))))
    (let ((mcircle (circle m (distance M P))))
      (let ((n (label "n" (xshift m (- (distance X Z) (distance M P))))))
        (let ((ncircle (circle n (+ (distance M P) (distance X Z) (- (distance M P)))))
              (reverse-lower-left
                (lower-circle (reverse-curve (circle n (distance X Z)) (+ (distance X Z) (/ (distance X N) 2)) c))))
                   (list m n (circle n (distance n (center reverse-lower-left)))
                         ZPcircle mcircle ncircle reverse-lower-left
                         (make-curve P c (list ZPcircle mcircle ncircle reverse-lower-left)) ))))))

; THE UPPER BOUTS...
(let ((Ncircle (circle N (distance N Q)))
      (o (label "o" (top (intersect
                          (circle N (distance N O))
                          (make-line -1 q) ; line w/slope -1 through q
                          )))))
  (let ((ocircle (circle o (distance O Q))))
    (let ((reverse-upper-left
           (upper-circle (reverse-curve ocircle
                                        (distance N O)
                                        g))))
              (list o (circle o (distance o (center reverse-upper-left)))
                    Ncircle ocircle reverse-upper-left
                    (make-curve Q g (list Ncircle ocircle reverse-upper-left)) ))))

; THE MIDDLE BOUTS...
(let ((f (label "f" (xshift ee (- (distance X Z)))))
      (v (label "v" (xshift ee (- (/ (distance X N) 2)))))
      (s (label "s" (xshift ee (- (/ (distance N Z) 2))))))
  (let ((ecircle (circle f (distance f ee)))
        (vcircle (circle f (distance f v)))
        (scircle (circle f (distance f s))))
    (let ((reverse-lower-middle
            (upper-circle (reverse-curve ecircle (distance f v) d)))
          (reverse-upper-middle
            (lower-circle (reverse-curve ecircle (distance f s) h))))
              (list f v s (circle f (distance f ee)) reverse-upper-middle reverse-lower-middle
                (make-curve g c (list reverse-upper-middle (circle f (distance f ee)) reverse-lower-middle)) ))))))))))))))
```

Programming and Reasoning with Algebraic Effects and Dependent Types

Edwin Brady

School of Computer Science, University of St Andrews, St Andrews, Scotland.
Email: ecb10@st-andrews.ac.uk

Abstract

One often cited benefit of pure functional programming is that pure code is easier to test and reason about, both formally and informally. However, real programs have side-effects including state management, exceptions and interactions with the outside world. Haskell solves this problem using *monads* to capture details of possibly side-effecting computations — it provides monads for capturing state, I/O, exceptions, non-determinism, libraries for practical purposes such as CGI and parsing, and many others, as well as *monad transformers* for combining multiple effects.

Unfortunately, useful as monads are, they do not compose very well. Monad transformers can quickly become unwieldy when there are lots of effects to manage, leading to a temptation in larger programs to combine everything into one coarse-grained state and exception monad. In this paper I describe an alternative approach based on handling *algebraic effects*, implemented in the IDRIS programming language. I show how to describe side effecting computations, how to write programs which compose multiple fine-grained effects, and how, using dependent types, we can use this approach to reason about states in effectful programs.

Categories and Subject Descriptors D.3.2 [*Programming Languages*]: Language Classifications—Applicative (functional) Languages

General Terms Languages, Verification

Keywords Dependent Types, Algebraic Effects

1. Introduction

Pure functions do not have side effects, but real applications do: they may have state, communicate across a network, read and write files, or interact with users, among many other things. Furthermore, real systems may fail due to corrupted or untrusted data. Pure functional programming languages such as Haskell [26] manage such problems using *monads* [31], and allow multiple effects to be combined using a stack of *monad transformers* [17].

Monad transformers are an effective tool for structuring larger Haskell applications. An application using a Read-Execute-Print loop, for example, may have some global state and perform console I/O, and hence be built with an `IO` monad transformed into a state monad using the `StateT` transformer. However, this can create difficulties: the order in which transformers are applied matters (that is, transformers do not commute easily); and it is difficult to invoke a function which uses a subset of the transformers in the stack. To illustrate these problems, consider an evaluator, in Haskell, for a simple expression language:

```
data Expr = Val Int | Add Expr Expr

eval : Expr -> Int
eval (Val i) = i
eval (Add x y) = eval x + eval y
```

If we extend this language with variables, we need to extend the evaluator with an environment, and deal with possible failure if a variable is undefined (we omit the `Val` and `Add` cases):

```
data Expr = Val Int | Add Expr Expr | Var String

type Env = [(String, Int)]

eval :: Expr -> ReaderT Env Maybe Int
eval (Var x) = do env <- ask
                  lift (lookup x env)
```

Here, the `Maybe` monad captures possible failure, and is transformed into a reader monad using the `ReaderT` transformer to store the environment, which is retrieved using `ask`. The `lift` operation allows functions in the inner `Maybe` monad to be called. We can extend the language further, with random number generation:

```
data Expr = Val Int | Add Expr Expr | Var String
          | Random Int

eval :: Expr -> RandT (ReaderT Env Maybe) Int
eval (Var x) = do env <- lift ask
                  lift (lift (lookup x env))
eval (Random x) = getRandomR (0, x)
```

We have added another transformer to the stack, `RandT`, and added `lift` where necessary to access the appropriate monads in the stack. We have built this interpreter from reusable components, the `Maybe` monad and `ReaderT` and `RandT` transformers, which is clearly a good thing. A problem, however, is that the use of `lift` is a little noisy, and will only get worse if we add more monads to the stack, such as `IO`. Bigger problems occur if we need to permute the order of the transformers, or invoke a function which uses a subset:

```
permute :: ReaderT Env (RandT Maybe) a ->
           RandT (ReaderT Env Maybe) a
dropReader :: RandT Maybe a ->
              RandT (ReaderT Env Maybe) a
```

These problems mean that, in general, there is little motivation for separating effects, and a temptation to build an application around

ICFP '13, September 25–27, 2013, Boston, MA, USA.

ACM 978-1-4503-2326-0/13/09... $15.00.
http://dx.doi.org/10.1145/2500365.2500581

one general purpose monad capturing all of an application's state and exception handling needs. This is undesirable, as it limits reuse and hinders modular design. It would be desirable instead to be able to separate effects into specific modular components such as console I/O, file and network handling and operating system interaction, for the same reason that it is desirable to separate the pure fragments of a program from the impure fragments using the `IO` monad. That is, the program's type would give more precise information about its behaviour, making the program easier to reason about and reducing the possibility of errors.

In this paper, I present an alternative approach to combining effects in a pure functional programming language, based on handlers of *algebraic effects* [3], and implemented directly as a domain specific language embedded in a dependently typed host, IDRIS [4, 5].

1.1 Contributions

This paper takes as its hypothesis that algebraic effects provide a cleaner, more composable and more flexible notation for programming with side effects than monad transformers. Although they are not equivalent in power (for example, unlike algebraic effects, monads can express continuations) many common side-effects are captured. The main contribution of this paper is a notation for describing and combining side effects using IDRIS. More specifically:

- An Embedded Domain Specific Language (DSL), `Effects`, for capturing *algebraic effects*, in such a way that they are easily composable, and translatable to a variety of underlying contexts using *effect handlers*.
- A collection of example effects (State, Exceptions, File and Console I/O, random number generation and non-determinism) and their handlers. I show how alternative handlers can be used to evaluate effects in different contexts, for example using an alternative handler to run interactive programs in a pure context.
- I give example programs which combine effects, including an interpreter for an imperative language with mutable variables, to illustrate how effectful applications may be structured.

The `Effects` DSL makes essential use of *dependent types*, firstly to verify that a specific effect is available to an effectful program using simple automated theorem proving, and secondly to track the state of a resource by updating its type during program execution. In this way, we can use the `Effects` DSL to verify implementations of resource usage protocols.

I describe how to *use* `Effects` in Section 2, how it is implemented in Section 3, and give a larger example in Section 4. It is distributed with IDRIS[1]. All of the examples in this paper are available online at `http://idris-lang.org/effects`.

2. `Effects`: an Embedded DSL for Effects Management

In this section, I introduce `Effects`, an embedded domain specific language for managing computational effects in IDRIS. I will introduce specific features of IDRIS as required. In particular, we will use implicit conversions and default implicit arguments in the implementation of `Effects`. A full tutorial is available elsewhere [5]. First, I describe how to use effects which are already defined in the language in order to implement the evaluator described in the introduction. Then, I show how new effects may be implemented.

The framework consists of a DSL representation `Eff` for combining effects, `EffM` for combining mutable effects, and implementations of several predefined effects. We refer to the whole framework with the name `Effects`.

[1] `http://idris-lang.org/`

2.1 Programming with `Effects`

Programs in the `Effects` language are described using the following data type, in the simplest case (I will defer introducing the constructors until later):

```
Eff : (m  : Type -> Type) ->
      (es : List EFFECT) -> (a  : Type) -> Type
```

Note that function types in IDRIS take the form `(x : a) -> b`, with an optional name `x` on the domain of the function. This is primarily to allow the name `x` to be used in the codomain, although it is also useful for documenting the purpose of an argument.

`Eff` is parameterised over a *computation context*, `m`, which describes the context in which the effectful program will be run, a list of side effects `es` that the program is permitted to use, and the program's return type `a`. The name `m` for the computation context is suggestive of a monad, but there is no requirement for it to be so.

Side effects are described using the `EFFECT` type; we will refer to these as *concrete* effects. For example:

```
STATE     : Type -> EFFECT
EXCEPTION : Type -> EFFECT
FILEIO    : Type -> EFFECT
STDIO     : EFFECT
RND       : EFFECT
```

States are parameterised by the type of the state being carried, and exceptions are parameterised by a type representing errors. File I/O allows a single file to be processed, with the type giving the current state of the file (i.e. closed, open for reading, or open for writing). Finally, `STDIO` and `RND` permit console I/O and random number generation respectively. For example, a program with some integer state, which performs console I/O and which could throw an exception of type `Error` might have the following type:

```
example : Eff IO [EXCEPTION Error, STDIO, STATE Int] ()
```

More generally, a program might modify the set of effects available, for example when adding a new effect or updating a dependently typed state. In this case, we describe programs using `EffM`:

```
EffM : (m   : Type -> Type) ->
       (es  : List EFFECT) ->
       (es' : List EFFECT) ->
       (a   : Type) -> Type
```

`EffM` is parameterised over the context and type as before, but separates input effects (`es`) from output effects (`es'`). In fact, `Eff` is defined in terms of `EffM`, with equal input/output effects.

We adopt the convention that the names `es` and `fs` refer to a list of input effects, and `es'` and `fs'` refer to a list of output effects.

2.1.1 First example: State

In general, an effectful program implemented in the `EffM` structure has the look and feel of a monadic program in Haskell, since `EffM` supports do-notation. To illustrate basic usage, let us implement a stateful function, which tags each node in a binary tree with a unique integer, depth first, left to right. We declare trees as follows:

```
data Tree a = Leaf
            | Node (Tree a) a (Tree a)
```

To tag each node in the tree, we write an effectful program which, for each node, tags the left subtree, reads and updates the state, tags the right subtree, then returns a new node with its value tagged. The type expresses that the program requires an integer state:

```
tag : Tree a -> Eff m [STATE Int] (Tree (Int, a))
```

The implementation traverses the tree, using `get` and `put` to manipulate state:

```
tag Leaf = return Leaf
tag (Node l x r)
     = do l' <- tag l
          lbl <- get; put (lbl + 1)
          r' <- tag r
          return (Node l' (lbl, x) r')
```

The `Effects` system ensures, statically, that any effectful functions which are called (`get` and `put` here) require no more effects than are available. The types of these functions are:

```
get : Eff m [STATE x] x
put : x -> Eff m [STATE x] ()
```

Each effect is associated with a *resource*. For example, the resource associated with `STATE Int` is the integer state itself. To *run* an effectful program, we must create a list of resources corresponding to the list of supported effects, and instantiate `m`. Here we instantiate `m` with `id`, resulting in a pure function.

```
tagFrom : Int -> Tree a -> Tree (Int, a)
tagFrom x t = runPure [x] (tag t)
```

In general, to run an effectful program, we use one of the functions `run`, `runWith` or `runPure`, instantiating an environment with resources corresponding to each effect:

```
run     : Applicative m =>
          Env m es -> EffM m es es' a -> m a
runWith : (a -> m a) ->
          Env m es -> EffM m es es' a -> m a
runPure : Env id es -> EffM id es es' a -> a
```

Corresponding functions `runEnv`, `runWithEnv` and `runPureEnv` also return the final resources. The reason `run` needs `m` to be an applicative functor is that it uses `pure` to inject a pure value into `m`. If this is inconvenient, `runWith` can be used. Note that there is no requirement that `m` is a monad; any type transformer is fine. In particular, `id` can be used to translate an effectful program into a pure function. As we will see, the particular choice of `m` can be important. Programs with exceptions, for example, can be run in the context of `IO`, `Maybe` or `Either`. We will return to the definition of `Env` in Section 3.2. For now, it suffices to know that it is a heterogeneous list of values for the initial resources `es`.

2.1.2 Labelled Effects

When we invoke an effect, `Effects` internally searches the list of available effects to check it is supported, and invokes the effect using the corresponding resource. This leads to an important question: what if we have more than one effect which supports the function? A particular situation where this arises is when we have more than one integer state. For example, to count the number of `Leaf` nodes in a tree while tagging nodes, we will need two integer states:

```
tagCount : Tree a ->
     Eff m [STATE Int, STATE Int] (Tree (Int, a))
```

What should be the effect of `get` and `put` in this program? Which effect do they act on? In practice, the earlier effect is chosen. While clearly defined, this is unlikely to be the desired behaviour, so to avoid this problem, effects may also be *labelled* using the `:::` operator. A label can be of any type, and an effect can be converted into a labelled effect using the `:-` operator:

```
(:::) : lbl -> EFFECT -> EFFECT
(:-)  : (l : lbl) -> EffM m [x] [y] t ->
                     EffM m [l ::: x] [l ::: y] t
```

In order to implement `tagCount` now, first we define a type for the labels. We have one state variable representing the leaf count, and one representing the current tag:

```
data Vars = Count | Tag
```

Then, we use these labels to disambiguate the states. To increment the count at each leaf, we use `update`, which combines a `get` and a `put` by applying a function to the state:

```
tagCount : Tree a -> Eff m [Tag   ::: STATE Int,
                            Count ::: STATE Int]
                              (Tree (Int, a))
tagCount Leaf
     = do Count :- update (+1)
          return Leaf
tagCount (Node l x r)
     = do l' <- tagCount l
          lbl <- Tag :- get
          Tag :- put (lbl + 1)
          r' <- tagCount r
          return (Node l' (lbl, x) r')
```

In order to retrieve the count afterwards, we will need access to the environment *after* running `tagCount`. We use `runPureEnv`, which returns the final resource states as well as the result:

```
runPureEnv : Env id xs ->
             EffM id xs xs' a -> (Env id xs', a)
```

To initialise the environment, we give the label name along with the initial value of the resource (where `:=` initialises a label). The order is important here, since resources are initialised in the order given by the list of supported effects.

```
runPureEnv [Tag := 0, Count := 0] (tagCount t)
```

And finally, to implement a pure wrapper function which returns a pair of the count of leaves and a labelled tree, we call `runPureEnv` with the initial resources, and match on the returned resources to retrieve the leaf count:

```
tagCountFrom : Int -> Tree a -> (Int, Tree (Int, a))
tagCountFrom x t
     = let ([_, Count := leaves], tree) =
         runPureEnv [Tag := 0, Count := 0] (tagCount t)
          in (leaves, tree)
```

2.1.3 An Effectful Evaluator revisited

To implement the effectful evaluator from the introduction in `Effects`, we support exceptions, random numbers and an environment mapping from `String` to `Int`:

```
Vars : Type
Vars = List (String, Int)
```

The evaluator invokes supported effects where needed. We use the following effectful functions:

```
get    : Eff m [STATE x] x
raise  : a -> Eff m [EXCEPTION a] b
rndInt : Int -> Int -> Eff m [RND] Int
```

The evaluator itself is written as an instance of `Eff`:

```
eval : Expr ->
       Eff m [EXCEPTION String, RND, STATE Vars] t
```

The implementation simply invokes the required effects with `Effects` checking that they are available:

```
eval (Val x) = return x
eval (Var x) = do vs <- get
                  case lookup x vs of
                    Nothing => raise ("Error " ++ x)
                    Just val => return val
eval (Add l r) = [| eval l + eval r |]
eval (Random upper) = rndInt 0 upper
```

Remark: We have used idiom brackets [20] in this implementation, to give a more concise notation for applicative programming with effects. An application inside idiom brackets, `[| f a b c d |]` translates directly to:

```
pure f <$> a <$> b <$> c <$> d
```

In order to run this evaluator, we must provide initial values for the resources associated with each effect. Exceptions require the unit resource, random number generation requires an initial seed, and the state requires an initial environment. We instantiate `m` with `Maybe` to be able to handle exceptions:

```
runEval : List (String, Int) -> Expr -> Maybe Int
runEval env expr = run [(), 123456, env] (eval expr)
```

Extending the evaluator with a new effect, such as `STDIO` is a matter of extending the list of available effects in its type. We could use this, for example, to print out the generated random numbers:

```
eval : Expr ->
       Eff m [EXCEPTION String, STDIO,
              RND, STATE Vars] t
...
eval (Random upper) = do num <- rndInt 0 upper
                         putStrLn (show num)
                         return num
```

We can insert the `STDIO` effect anywhere in the list without difficulty. The only requirements are that its initial resource is in the corresponding position in the call to `run`, and that `run` instantiates a context which supports `STDIO`, such as `IO`:

```
runEval : List (String, Int) -> Expr -> IO Int
runEval env expr
    = run [(), (), 123456, env] (eval expr)
```

2.2 Implementing effects

In order to implement a new effect, we define a new type (of kind `Effect`) and explain how that effect is interpreted in some underlying context `m`. An `Effect` describes an effectful computation, parameterised by an input resource `res`, an output resource `res'`, and the type of the computation `t`.

```
Effect : Type
Effect = (res : Type) -> (res' : Type) ->
         (t : Type) -> Type
```

We describe effects as algebraic data types. To *run* an effect, we require an interpretation in a computation context `m`. To achieve this, we make effects and contexts instances of a type class, `Handler`, which has a method `handle` explaining this interpretation:

```
class Handler (e : Effect) (m : Type -> Type) where
      handle : res -> (eff : e res res' t) ->
                 (res' -> t -> m a) -> m a
```

Type classes in IDRIS may be parameterised by anything. This means not only types, but also values, and even other type classes. Thus, if a parameter is anything other than a `Type`, it must be given a type label explicitly, like `e` and `m` here.

Handlers are parameterised by the effect they handle, and the context in which they handle the effect. This allows several different context-dependent handlers to be written, e.g. exceptions could be handled differently in an `IO` setting than in a `Maybe` setting. When effects are combined, as in the evaluator example, all effects must be handled in the context in which the program is run.

An effect `e res res' t` updates a resource type `res` to a resource type `res'`, returning a value `t`. The handler, therefore, implements this update in a context `m` which may support side effects. The handler is written in continuation passing style. This is for two reasons: firstly, it returns two values, a new resource and the result of the computation, which is more cleanly managed in a continuation than by returning a tuple; secondly, and more importantly, it gives the handler the flexibility to invoke the continuation any number of times (zero or more).

An `Effect`, which is the internal algebraic description of an effect, is promoted into a concrete `EFFECT`, which is expected by the `EffM` structure, with the `MkEff` constructor:

```
data EFFECT : Type where
     MkEff : Type -> Effect -> EFFECT
```

`MkEff` additionally records the resource state of an effect. In the remainder of this section, we describe how several effects can be implemented in this way: mutable state; console I/O; exceptions; files; random numbers, and non-determinism.

2.2.1 State

In general, effects are described algebraically in terms of the operations they support. In the case of `State`, the supported effects are reading the state (`Get`) and writing the state (`Put`).

```
data State : Effect where
     Get :      State a a a
     Put : b -> State a b ()
```

The resource associated with a state corresponds to the state itself. So, the `Get` operation leaves this state intact (with a resource type `a` on entry and exit) but the `Put` operation may update this state (with a resource type `a` on entry and `b` on exit). That is, a `Put` may update the type of the stored value. We can implement a handler for this effect, for all contexts `m`, as follows:

```
instance Handler State m where
     handle st Get     k = k st st
     handle st (Put n) k = k n ()
```

When running `Get`, the handler passes the current state to the continuation as both the new resource value (the first argument of the continuation `k`) as well as the return value of the computation (the second argument of the continuation). When running `Put`, the new state is passed to the continuation as the new resource value.

We then convert the algebraic effect `State` to a concrete effect usable in an `Effects` program using the `STATE` function, to which we provide the initial state type as follows:

```
STATE : Type -> EFFECT
STATE t = MkEff t State
```

We adopt the convention that algebraic effects, of type `Effect`, have an initial upper case letter. Concrete effects, of type `EFFECT`, are correspondingly in all upper case.

Algebraic effects are promoted to `Effects` programs with concrete effects by using the `mkEffect` function. We will postpone giving the type of `mkEffect` until Section 3.1.2. For now, it suffices to know that it converts an `Effect` to an effectful program. To create the `get` and `put` functions, for example:

```
get : Eff m [STATE x] x
get = mkEffect Get

put : x -> Eff m [STATE x] ()
put val = mkEffect (Put val)
```

We may also find it useful to mutate the *type* of a state, considering that states may themselves have dependent types (we may, for example, add an element to a vector in a state). The `Put` constructor supports this, so we can implement `putM` to update the state's type:

```
putM : y -> EffM m [STATE x] [STATE y] ()
putM val = mkEffect (Put val)
```

Finally, it may be useful to combine **get** and **put** in a single update:

```
update : (x -> x) -> Eff m [STATE x] ()
update f = do val <- get; put (f val)
```

2.2.2 Console I/O

Consider a simplified version of console I/O which supports reading and writing strings. There is no associated resource, although in an alternative implementation we may associate it with an abstract world state, or a pair of handles for **stdin/stdout**. Algebraically:

```
data StdIO : Effect where
     PutStr : String -> StdIO () () ()
     GetStr : StdIO () () String

STDIO : EFFECT
STDIO = MkEff () StdIO
```

The obvious way to handle **StdIO** is via the **IO** monad:

```
instance Handler StdIO IO where
    handle () (PutStr s) k = do putStr s; k () ()
    handle () GetStr     k = do x <- getLine; k () x
```

Unlike the **State** effect, for which the handler worked in *all* contexts, this handler only applies to effectful programs run in an **IO** context. We can implement alternative handlers, and indeed there is no reason that effectful programs in **StdIO** must be evaluated in a monadic context. For example, we can define I/O stream functions:

```
data IOStream a
   = MkStream (List String -> (a, List String))

instance Handler StdIO IOStream where
    ...
```

A handler for **StdIO** in **IOStream** context generates a function from a list of strings (the input text) to a value and the output text. We can build a pure function which simulates real console I/O:

```
mkStrFn : Env IOStream xs -> Eff IOStream xs a ->
          List String -> (a, List String)
mkStrFn {a} env p input = case mkStrFn' of
                               MkStream f => f input
  where injStream : a -> IOStream a
        injStream v = MkStream (\x => (v, []))
        mkStrFn' : IOStream a
        mkStrFn' = runWith injStream env p
```

To illustrate this, we write a simple console I/O program which runs in any context which has a handler for **StdIO**:

```
name : Handler StdIO e => Eff e [STDIO] ()
name = do putStr "Name? "
          n <- getStr
          putStrLn ("Hello " ++ show n)
```

Using **mkStrFn**, we can run this as a pure function which uses a list of strings as its input, and gives a list of strings as its output. We can evaluate this at the IDRIS prompt:

```
*name> show $ mkStrFn [()] name ["Edwin"]
((), ["Name?" , "Hello Edwin\n"])
```

This suggests that alternative, pure, handlers for console I/O, or any I/O effect, can be used for unit testing and reasoning about I/O programs without executing any real I/O.

2.2.3 Exceptions

The exception effect supports only one operation, **Raise**. Exceptions are parameterised over an error type **e**, so **Raise** takes a single argument to represent the error. The associated resource is of unit type, and since raising an exception causes computation to abort, raising an exception can return a value of any type.

```
data Exception : Type -> Effect where
     Raise : e -> Exception e () () b

EXCEPTION : Type -> EFFECT
EXCEPTION e = MkEff () (Exception e)
```

The semantics of **Raise** is to abort computation, therefore handlers of exception effects do not call the continuation **k**. In any case, this should be impossible since passing the result to the continuation would require the ability to invent a value in any arbitrary type **b**! The simplest handler runs in a **Maybe** context:

```
instance Handler (Exception a) Maybe where
     handle _ (Raise err) k = Nothing
```

Exceptions can be handled in any context which supports some representation of failed computations. In an **Either e** context, for example, we can use **Left** to represent the error case:

```
instance Handler (Exception e) (Either e) where
     handle _ (Raise err) k = Left err
```

Given that we can raise exceptions in an **Effects** program, it is also useful to be able to catch them. The **catch** operation runs a possibly failing computation **comp** in some context **m**:

```
catch : Catchable m err =>
         (comp : EffM m xs xs' a) ->
         (handler : err -> EffM m xs xs' a) ->
         EffM m xs xs' a
```

Using **catch** requires that the computation context **m** supports throwing and catching of errors, using the **Catchable** class implemented as part of the IDRIS library:

```
class Catchable (m : Type -> Type) t where
    throw : t -> m a
    catch : m a -> (t -> m a) -> m a
```

This is implemented directly as part of the **Effects** DSL. There is a simple instance for **Maybe**, limited to the unit error:

```
instance Catchable Maybe () where
    throw () = Nothing
    catch Nothing  h = h ()
    catch (Just x) h = Just x
```

The **Either e** instance allows that any type be thrown as an error:

```
instance Catchable (Either e) e where
    throw x = Left x
    catch (Left err) h = h err
    catch (Right x)  h = (Right x)
```

2.2.4 Random numbers

Random number generation can be implemented as an effect, with the resource tracking the *seed* from which the next number will be generated. The **Random** effect supports one operation, **getRandom**, which requires an **Int** resource and returns the next number:

```
data Random : Type -> Type -> Type -> Type where
     GetRandom : Random Int Int Int

RND : EFFECT
RND = MkEff Int Random
```

Handling random number generation shows that it is a state effect in disguise, where the effect updates the seed. This is a simple linear congruential pseudo-random number generator:

```
instance Handler Random m where
    handle seed GetRandom k
         = let seed' = 1664525 * seed + 1013904223 in
               k seed' seed'
```

Alternative handlers could use a different, possibly more secure approach. In any case, we can implement a function which returns a random number between a lower and upper bound as follows:

```
rndInt : Int -> Int -> Eff m [RND] Int
rndInt lower upper
    = do v <- mkEffect GetRandom
         return (v 'mod' (upper - lower) + lower)
```

2.2.5 Resource management: Files

Instead of implementing all I/O operations as a single effect, as with the IO monad, we can separate operations into more fine-grained effects. Another I/O related effect which we can handle separately is file management. Here, we can take advantage of the *resource* associated with an effect, and the fact that resource types are *mutable*, by associating the effect with a file handle parameterised by its current state (i.e. closed, open for reading, or open for writing). File handles are represented as follows, where `File` is a primitive file handle provided by the IDRIS library:

```
data Mode = Read | Write

data OpenFile : Mode -> Type where
     FH : File -> OpenFile m
```

When we declare `FileIO`, we express in the resource transitions how each effect changes the state of the resource:

```
data FileIO : Effect where
     Open  : FilePath -> (m : Mode) ->
             FileIO () (OpenFile m) ()
     Close : FileIO (OpenFile m) () ()
     ReadLine  : FileIO (OpenFile Read)
                        (OpenFile Read) String
     WriteLine : String ->
                 FileIO (OpenFile Write)
                        (OpenFile Write) ()
     EOF       : FileIO (OpenFile Read)
                        (OpenFile Read) Bool
```

We can see from this declaration that opening a file moves from an empty resource to a file open for a specific purpose and that closing a file removes the file resource. Only files which are open for reading may be read, or tested for end of file, and only files open for writing may be written to. Any violation of this resource access protocol will result in a type error. In general, we can use the effect signature of a function to manage resources safely, subsuming the resource management DSL we have previously implemented [9].

The `FILE_IO` effect is parameterised over the current state of a file resource with which it is associated:

```
FILE_IO : Type -> EFFECT
```

The type of `open` expresses that the resource changes from a unit to an open file:

```
open : FilePath -> (m : Mode) ->
       EffM IO [FILE_IO ()] [FILE_IO (OpenFile m)] ()
```

Note that opening a file may fail. We will deal with such exceptional behaviour shortly. Using `EffM`, we have expressed that opening a file causes a change in the resource state. It is then only possible to close a file if there is an open file available:

```
close : EffM IO [FILE_IO (OpenFile m)] [FILE_IO ()] ()
```

Reading is only possible from a file opened for reading:

```
readLine : Eff IO [FILE_IO (OpenFile Read)] String
```

As with `STATE`, we can use labelled resources if we require more than one file handle at a time. We have handlers for `FileIO` for the `IO` context, which does not handle exceptions (in which case failing to open a file is a fatal run-time error), and an `IOExcept e` context which is `IO` augmented with exceptions of type `e` and an instance of the `Catchable` class:

```
data IOExcept err a
ioe_lift : IO a -> IOExcept err a

instance Catchable IOExcept err
```

Assuming we are in a state where we have a file handle available and open for reading, we can read the contents of a file into a list of strings:

```
readLines : Eff (IOExcept String)
                [FILE_IO (OpenFile Read)] (List String)
readLines = readAcc [] where
  readAcc : List String ->
            Eff (IOExcept String)
                [FILE_IO (OpenFile Read)] (List String)
  readAcc acc = do e <- eof
                   if (not e)
                      then do str <- readLine
                              readAcc (str :: acc)
                      else return (reverse acc)
```

To read a file, given a file path, into a list of strings, reporting an error where necessary, we can write the following `readFile` function. We add `STDIO` to the list of effects so that we can report an error to the console if opening the file fails:

```
readFile : FilePath -> Eff (IOExcept String)
                [FILE_IO (), STDIO] (List String)
readFile path = catch (do open path Read
                          lines <- readLines
                          close
                          return lines)
        (\err => do putStrLn ("Failed " ++ err)
                    return [])
```

The effect type of `readFile` means that we must begin *and* end with no open file. This means that omitting the `close` would result in a compile time type error. It would also be a type error to try to invoke `readLines` before the file was open, or if the file was opened for writing instead.

2.2.6 Non-determinism

Following [3], non-determinism can be implemented as an effect `Selection`, in which a `Select` operation chooses one value non-deterministically from a list of possible values:

```
data Selection : Effect where
     Select : List a -> Selection () () a
```

We can handle this effect in a `Maybe` context, trying every choice in a list given to `Select` until the computation succeeds:

```
instance Handler Selection Maybe where
     handle _ (Select xs) k = tryAll xs where
         tryAll [] = Nothing
         tryAll (x :: xs) = case k () x of
                                 Nothing => tryAll xs
                                 Just v => Just v
```

The handler for `Maybe` produces at most one result, effectively performing a depth first search of the values passed to `Select`. The handler runs the continuation for every element of the list until the result of running the continuation succeeds.

Alternatively, we can find *every* possible result by handling selection in a `List` context:

```
instance Handler Selection List where
     handle r (Select xs) k = concatMap (k r) xs
```

We can use the `Selection` effect to implement search problems by non-deterministically choosing from a list of candidate solutions.

For example, a solution to the n-Queens problem can be implemented as follows. First, we write a function which checks whether a point on a chess board attacks another if occupied by a Queen:

```
no_attack : (Int, Int) -> (Int, Int) -> Bool
no_attack (x, y) (x', y')
  = x /= x' && y /= y' && abs (x - x') /= abs (y - y')
```

Then, given a column and a list of Queen positions, we find the rows on which a Queen may safely be placed in that column:

```
rowsIn : Int -> List (Int, Int) -> List Int
rowsIn col qs
   = [ x | x <- [1..8], all (no_attack (x, col)) qs ]
```

Finally, we compute a solution by accumulating a set of Queen positions, column by column, non-deterministically choosing a position for a Queen in each column.

```
addQueens : Int -> List (Int, Int) ->
            Eff m [SELECT] (List (Int, Int))
addQueens 0   qs = return qs
addQueens col qs
   = do row <- select (rowsIn col qs)
        addQueens (col - 1) ((row, col) :: qs)
```

We can run this in `Maybe` context, to retrieve one solution, or in `List` context, to retrieve all solutions. In a `Maybe` context, for example, we can define:

```
getQueens : Maybe (List (Int, Int))
getQueens = run [()] (addQueens 8 [])
```

Then to find the first solution, we run `getQueens` at the REPL:

```
*Queens> show getQueens
"Just [(4, 1), (2, 2), (7, 3), (3, 4),
       (6, 5), (8, 6), (5, 7), (1, 8)]" : String
```

Remark: It is important to note that when combining `SELECT` with other effects, the values of other resources are reset at the beginning of each `select` branch. This means, at least in the current implementation, that state cannot be shared between branches. While perhaps not so important for selection, this may be a problem for other control effects such as co-operative multithreading, for which we may need a more flexible handler if we wish to deal with shared state. We will deal with this issue in future work.

2.3 Effect Polymorphism

Since `Effects` is implemented as an embedding in a host language, we can exploit features of the host language. The means that we can write higher order functions, and functions which are polymorphic in their effects. For example, a `mapEff` function can be implemented corresponding to `fmap` for functors:

```
mapEff : Applicative m =>
         (a -> Eff m xs b) -> List a -> Eff m xs (List b)
mapEff f []        = pure []
mapEff f (x :: xs) = [| f x :: mapEff f xs |]
```

This applies an effectful function across a list, provided that we are in an applicative context, and that the effectful function supports the correct set of effects.

3. The `Effects` DSL implementation

The implementation of `Effects` follows a common pattern in dependently typed DSL implementation, that of the well-typed interpreter [2, 6, 25]. We describe the DSL as a data type, `EffM`, which expresses the properties a program must satisfy in its type, with a corresponding interpreter. The type system guarantees that only programs which satisfy these properties can be interpreted.

3.1 Language representation

The `EffM` data type represents the `Effects` language constructs. It is parameterised over its computation context `m`, and indexed by the list of effects on input and the list of effects on output, as well as the return type of the computation:

```
data EffM : (m   : Type -> Type) ->
            (es  : List EFFECT) ->
            (es' : List EFFECT) -> (a : Type) -> Type
```

For the common case of programs in which the input effects are the same as the output effects, we define `Eff`:

```
Eff : (m : Type -> Type) ->
      (es : List EFFECT) -> (a : Type) -> Type
Eff m es t = EffM m es es t
```

The complete syntax is given in Figure 1 for reference. In this section, we describe the constructs in detail.

Remark: One way of looking at `EffM` is as a flexible monad transformer, augmenting an underlying monad with additional features. In this way we can combine algebraic effects with concepts more difficult to capture, such as partiality and continuations.

3.1.1 Basic constructs

In the simplest case, we would like to inject pure values into the `EffM` representation:

```
return : a -> EffM m es es a
```

Additionally, we have `(>>=)` to support `do` notation:

```
(>>=) : EffM m es es' a ->
        (a -> EffM m es' es'' b) -> EffM m es es'' b
```

The type of `(>>=)` expresses that available effects may change, transitively, across a program. The output of the first action, `es'` becomes the input to the second.

Remark: IDRIS allows ad-hoc name overloading, as well as overloading via type classes. Since it does not support type inference at the top level, as full type inference is undecidable for dependently typed languages, such overloading can be resolved in a type directed way. It is important here, since we cannot make `EffM` an instance of `Monad`, but we would like to use `do`-notation as a natural way of implementing imperative code.

3.1.2 Invoking effects

Recall that an algebraic effect is promoted to an `Effects` program with the `mkEffect` function, the type of which has so far been postponed. We can invoke effects using a helper, `mkEffectP`, which requires a *proof*, `prf`, that the effect is available:

```
mkEffectP : (prf : EffElem e a es) ->
            (eff : e a b t) ->
            EffM m es (updateResTy es prf eff) t
```

If we are invoking an effect `eff`, provided by the algebraic effect `e`, with an input resource type `a`, this is valid only if we can provide a proof that the algebraic effect is present in the input set of resources `es`. This concept is captured in the `EffElem` predicate:

```
data EffElem : (Type -> Type -> Type -> Type) ->
               Type -> List EFFECT -> Type where
     Here : EffElem x a (MkEff a x :: es)
     There : EffElem x a es -> EffElem x a (y :: es)
```

This proof serves two purposes: it provides a guarantee that the effect is available with the correct resource type; and, as we shall see shortly, it serves as an index into the resource set when we *evaluate* programs. After the effect has been handled, its resource type may have been updated. We must therefore update the output

```
data EffM : (m : Type -> Type) -> List EFFECT -> List EFFECT -> Type -> Type where
     return    : a -> EffM m es es a
     (>>=)     : EffM m es es' a -> (a -> EffM m es' es'' b) -> EffM m es es'' b
     mkEffectP : (prf : EffElem e a es) -> (eff : e a b t) -> EffM m es (updateResTy es prf eff) t
     liftP     : (prf : SubList fs es) -> EffM m fs fs' t -> EffM m es (updateWith fs' es prf) t
     (:-)      : (l : ty) -> EffM m [x] [y] t -> EffM m [l ::: x] [l ::: y] t
     new       : Handler e m => res -> EffM m (MkEff res e :: es) (MkEff res' e :: es') a -> EffM m es es' a
     catch     : Catchable m err => EffM m es es' a -> (err -> EffM m es es' a) -> EffM m es es' a
```

Figure 1. The `Effects` DSL data type

resource state in the type. Again, we use the structure of the proof, to update the resource type from `a` to `b`.

```
updateResTy : (es : List EFFECT) ->
              EffElem e a es -> e a b t -> List EFFECT
updateResTy {b} (MkEff a e :: es) Here n
    = (MkEff b e) :: es
updateResTy (x :: es) (There p) n
    = x :: updateResTy es p n
```

The problem with `mkEffectP` is that we must provide an explicit proof that the effect is available. Since the effect list is statically known, IDRIS ought to be able to find such a proof automatically.

IDRIS currently has limited proof search, based on reflection and reification of programs, but it is sufficient for constructing the required proofs. The reflection mechanism itself is beyond the scope of this paper. Briefly, we have the following function, which constructs a tactic for searching for proofs of `EffElem`:

```
findEffElem : Tactic
```

Then, we have a notation for giving *default* implicit arguments to functions. The `mkEffect` function is a wrapper for `mkEffectP` with a default argument which invokes the `findEffElem` tactic. If the proof search fails, this causes a compile time error, reporting that the effect is not available.

```
mkEffect : {default tactics { reflect findEffElem; }
              prf : EffElem e a es} ->
           (eff : e a b t) ->
           EffM m es (updateResTy es prf eff) t
mkEffect {prf} e = mkEffectP prf e
```

Fortunately, there is no need for a user of the library to know anything about this proof search mechanism. Tactic construction for automated proof search is related to the `Ltac` [11] system in Coq, the intention being to make simple proofs automatable.

3.1.3 Effectful sub-programs

As well as invoking algebraic effects directly, we would like to be able to invoke sub-programs, which may use all of the effects available, or a subset. To achieve this, we use the `liftP` construct:

```
liftP : (prf : SubList fs es) ->
        (prog : EffM m fs fs' t) ->
        EffM m es (updateWith fs' es prf) t
```

This requires a proof that the effects available to the sub-program `prog` are a subset (strictly, a sub-list) of the effects available to the outer program, expressed using the following predicate:

```
data SubList : List a -> List a -> Type where
     SubNil : SubList [] []
     Keep   : SubList es fs ->
              SubList (x :: es) (x :: fs)
     Drop   : SubList es fs ->
              SubList es (x :: fs)
```

This predicate describes a sublist in terms of a larger list by saying, for each element of the larger list, whether it is kept or dropped. An alternative base case could state that `[]` is a sub-list of any list, assuming that remaining items are dropped.

The sub-program may itself update the effects it uses, so again the proof serves two purposes: Firstly, to ensure the effects are indeed available; and secondly, to be able to update the effects in the outer program once the sub-program is complete, as follows:

```
updateWith : (fs' : List a) -> (es : List a) ->
             SubList fs es -> List a
updateWith (y :: fs) (x :: es) (Keep rest)
           = y :: updateWith fs es rest
updateWith fs        (x :: es) (Drop rest)
           = x :: updateWith fs es rest
updateWith []        []        SubNil      = []
```

Again, we can construct the necessary proofs of `SubList` automatically, if the sub-program uses a valid set of effects, because all effects are statically known, using a reflected tactic `findSubList`. We implement a wrapper `lift` which builds this proof implicitly:

```
implicit
lift : {default tactics { reflect findSubList; }
           prf : SubList fs es} ->
       (prog : EffM m fs fs' t) ->
       EffM m es (updateWith fs' fs prf) t
lift {prf} e = lift prf e
```

The `implicit` modifier before `lift` states that this function can be used as an *implicit conversion*. Implicit conversions are inspired by a similar feature in Scala [24]. The effect of the `implicit` modifier is, intuitively, that `lift` will be applied to a program in `EffM` if it is required for type correctness. Since type checking is type directed it always has access to the required type of an expression, and the implicit coercions which produce that type, so applying conversions is simple.

Such conversions are, deliberately, limited. They cannot be chained, unlike implicit coercions in Coq, to avoid coherence problems. Furthermore, to avoid ambiguity problems, if there is more than one implicit conversion available then *neither* will be applied. In the `Effects` library, only `lift` is implicit.

Remark: Using `SubList` as it is, rather than some notion of subset, means that in sub-programs the effects must appear in the same order as they appear in the caller's effect list. This is not an inherent limitation; with improved proof search, we should also be able to support effect sets which are *permutations* of another. For the moment, to handle the (uncommon) case where permutations are needed, we provide a `permute` operation, where `Perm es fs` is a proof that `es` is a permutation of `fs`, though we omit further details from the present paper.

```
permute : Perm es fs -> Eff m fs t -> Eff m es t
```

3.1.4 Labelling effects

If we have an effectful program `p` with a single effect, we can *label* that effect using the `(:-)` operator:

```
(:-)  : (l : ty) ->
        EffM m [x] [y] t ->
        EffM m [l ::: x] [l ::: y] t
```

It is sufficient to handle single effects here, because labels can only apply to one effect at a time, and such effectful sub-programs can easily be invoked using an implicit `lift` as described above. Labelling effects does nothing more than adding a label to the effect and its corresponding resource.

3.1.5 Introducing effects

We can introduce a new effect in the course of an effectful program, provided that the effect can be handled in the current computation context `m`:

```
new : Handler e m =>
      res -> EffM m (MkEff res e :: es)
                    (MkEff res' e :: es') a ->
      EffM m es es' a
```

This extends the list of effects, initialised with a resource of type `res`. Once the sub-program is complete, the resource for the new effect is discarded, as is clear from the type of `new`. The effect itself, `e`, is never given explicitly here, which means that it must be clear from the sub-program what the effect is. Typically, this means that the sub-program will be a function with an explicit type.

3.1.6 Handling failure

Finally, if the computation context `m` supports failure handling, we can use the `catch` construct to handle errors:

```
catch : Catchable m err =>
        (prog : EffM m es es' a) ->
        (handler : err -> EffM m es es' a) ->
        EffM m es es' a
```

If the sub-program `prog` fails with an error, of type `err`, then the handler is called wth the error. Note that both `prog` and `handler` transform the effect list from `es` to `es'`. If `prog` fails, then the resources are reset to their starting state. This requires some care, if the effect refers to external resources such as file handles.

3.2 The `Effects` interpreter

Running an effectful program, of type `EffM m es es' t`, should yield a computation of type `m t`, that is, the program returns a value of type `t` in some computation context `m`. We can interpret programs through a traversal of the `EffM` syntax, subject to:

- Keeping track of *resources* corresponding to each effect.
- Invoking the appropriate handlers where necessary.
- Returning two values as part of the computation: the result `t` and an updated collection resources.

To keep track of resources, we build an environment as a heterogeneous list to store the resource corresponding to each effect:

```
data Env  : (m : Type -> Type) ->
            List EFFECT -> Type where
     Nil  : Env m Nil
     (::) : Handler eff m =>
            a -> Env m es -> Env m (MkEff a eff :: es)
```

Using the (overloaded) `Nil` and `(::)` gives us access to list syntax for environments. They are parameterised over a computation context `m`, which allows an effect handler instance to be associated with each entry. As a result `EffM` programs can be independent of context, thus interpretable in several contexts, and effects and hence their handlers can change during execution.

Since we need to return two values, a result and an updated resource collection, we implement the evaluator in continuation passing style, with the two values passed to the continuation. This also helps when invoking handlers, which also require a continuation. The interpreter has the following type:

```
effInt : Env m es -> EffM m es es' a ->
         (Env m es' -> a -> m b) -> m b
```

Effectful programs are invoked using a function of the following form, calling `effInt` with a continuation which simply discards the environment when evaluation is complete.

```
run : Applicative m =>
      Env m es -> EffM m es es' a -> m a
run env prog = effInt env prog (\env, r => pure r)

runPure : Env id es -> EffM id es es' a -> a
runPure env prog = effInt env prog (\env, r => r)
```

The full implementation of `effInt` is given for reference in Figure 2. The interpreter uses a number of helpers in order to manage effects. Firstly, to invoke a handler given a proof that an effect is available, we use `execEff`, defined as follows:

```
execEff : Env m es -> (p : EffElem e res es) ->
          (eff : e res b a) ->
          (Env m (updateResTy es p eff) -> a -> m t) ->
          m t
execEff (val :: env) Here eff' k
    = handle val eff' (\res, v => k (res :: env) v)
execEff (val :: env) (There p) eff k
    = execEff env p eff (\env', v => k (val :: env') v)
```

The proof locates the effect and handler in the environment. Following the interpreter and the handlers, `execEff` is written in continuation passing style, and is used directly to execute effects:

```
effInt env (mkEffectP prf effP) k
                   = execEff env prf effP k
```

Invoking a sub-program with a smaller collection of effects involves dropping the unnecessary resources from the environment, invoking the sub-program, then rebuilding the environment reinstating the resources which were not used. We drop resources from an environment according to the `SubList` proof with `dropEnv`:

```
dropEnv : Env m fs -> SubList es fs -> Env m es
dropEnv [] SubNil = []
dropEnv (v :: vs) (Keep rest) = v :: dropEnv vs rest
dropEnv (v :: vs) (Drop rest) = dropEnv vs rest
```

Correspondingly, `rebuildEnv` rebuilds the outer environment, updating the resources which were updated by the sub-programs:

```
rebuildEnv : Env m fs' -> (prf : SubList fs es) ->
             Env m es -> Env m (updateWith fs' es prf)
rebuildEnv []          SubNil      env = env
rebuildEnv (f :: fs) (Keep rest) (e :: env)
      = f :: rebuildEnv fs rest env
rebuildEnv fs          (Drop rest) (e :: env)
      = e :: rebuildEnv es rest env
```

We can use `dropEnv` and `rebuildEnv` to interpret the execution of sub-programs, dropping resources before invoking, then rebuilding the environment before invoking the continuation:

```
effInt env (liftP prf effP) k
   = let env' = dropEnv env prf in
         effInt env' effP (\envk, p' =>
               k (rebuildEnv envk prf env) p')
```

To introduce a new effect using `new`, we simply extend the environment with the new resources before invoking the sub-program, and drop the extra resource before invoking the continuation:

```
effInt env (new r prog) k
     = let env' = r :: env in
           effInt env' prog
               (\ (v :: envk), p' => k envk p')
```

```
effInt : Env m es -> EffM m es es' a -> (Env m es' -> a -> m b) -> m b
effInt env (return x) k = k env x
effInt env (prog >>= c) k = effInt env prog (\env', p' => effInt env' (c p') k)
effInt env (mkEffectP prf effP) k = execEff env prf effP k
effInt env (liftP prf effP) k = let env' = dropEnv env prf in
                                effInt env' effP (\envk, p' => k (rebuildEnv envk prf env) p')
effInt env (new r prog) k = let env' = r :: env in
                            effInt env' prog (\ (v :: envk), p' => k envk p')
effInt env (catch prog handler) k = catch (effInt env prog k)
                                          (\e => effInt env (handler e) k)
effInt env (l :- prog) k = let env' = unlabel env in
                           effInt env' prog (\envk, p' => k (relabel l envk) p')
```

Figure 2. The `Effects` DSL interpreter

Interpreting a `catch` involves using the `catch` method of the `Catchable` class. We rely on type directed overloading here to disambiguate the `catch`:

```
effInt env (catch prog handler) k
     = catch (effInt env prog k)
             (\e => effInt env (handler e) k)
```

Finally, to interpret a labelled effect, we remove the label, interpret the resulting effect as normal, then replace the label (`unlabel` and `label` have the obvious definitions, with `unlabel` removing a label from a singleton environment, and `relabel` replacing it):

```
effInt env (l :- prog) k
   = let env' = unlabel env in
         effInt env' prog (\envk, p' =>
                              k (relabel l envk) p')
```

4. Example: An Imperative Language Interpreter

As a larger example, I present an interpreter for a small imperative language, `Imp`, which supports variables (requiring an updatable environment), and printing (requiring console I/O). We follow the well-typed interpreter pattern, using a context membership proof to guarantee that local variables are well-scoped. We separate expressions (`Expr`) from statements in the imperative language (`Imp`). First, we define the types, supporting integers, booleans and unit, and a function `interpTy` to convert these to IDRIS types:

```
data Ty = TyInt | TyBool | TyUnit
interpTy : Ty -> Type
```

Expressions include values, variables, random numbers and binary operators derived from IDRIS functions, and are indexed by a context `G` (of type `Vect Ty n`), and the type of the expression:

```
data Expr : Vect Ty n -> Ty -> Type where
     Val : interpTy a -> Expr G a
     Var : HasType i G t -> Expr G t
     Rnd : Int -> Expr G TyInt
     Op  : (interpTy a -> interpTy b -> interpTy c) ->
           Expr G a -> Expr G b -> Expr G c
```

For brevity, we omit the definition of `HasType`. It is sufficient to know that `HasType i G t` states that variable `i` (a de Bruijn index) in context `G` has type `t`. Values of variables are stored in a heterogeneous list corresponding to a vector of their types, with a `lookup` function to retrieve these values:

```
data Vars : Vect Ty n -> Type where
     Nil  : Vars Nil
     (::) : interpTy a -> Vars G -> Vars (a :: G)
lookup : HasType i G t -> Vars G -> interpTy t
```

We can write an evaluator for this simple expression language in `Effects`, using the random number effect, and an environment corresponding to the context `G`:

```
eval : Expr G t ->
       Eff m [RND, STATE (Vars G)] (interpTy t)
eval (Val x) = return x
eval (Var i) = do vars <- get
                  return (lookup i vars)
eval (Rnd upper) = rndInt 0 upper
eval (Op op x y) = [| op (eval x) (eval y) |]
```

Using dependent types, we have expressed a correspondence between the context `G` under which the expression *and* the variables are defined. The imperative fragment is also indexed over a context `G` and the type of a program. We use the unit type for statements (specifically `Print`) which do not have a value:

```
data Imp    : Vect Ty n -> Ty -> Type where
     Let    : Expr G t -> Imp (t :: G) u -> Imp G u
     (:=)   : HasType i G t -> Expr G t -> Imp G t
     Print  : Expr G TyInt -> Imp G TyUnit
     (>>=)  : Imp G a ->
              (interpTy a -> Imp G b) -> Imp G b
     return : Expr G t -> Imp G t
```

Interpreting the imperative fragment requires the local variables to be stored as part of the state, as well as console I/O, for interpreting `Print`. We express this with the following type:

```
interp : Imp G t ->
     Eff IO [STDIO, RND, STATE (Vars G)] (interpTy t)
```

In order to interpret `Let`, which introduces a new variable with a given expression as its initial value, we must update the environment. Before evaluating the scope of the `Let` binding, the environment must be extended with an additional value, otherwise the recursive call will be ill-typed because the state effect must be carrying an environment of the correct length and types. Therefore, we evaluate the expression with `eval`, extend the environment with the result, evaluate the scope, then drop the value.

```
interp (Let e sc)
    = do e' <- eval e
         vars <- get; putM (e' :: vars);
         res <- interp sc
         (_ :: vars') <- get; putM vars'
         return res
```

Calling `eval` is fine here, because it uses a smaller set of effects than `interp`. Also, note that if we forget to drop the value before returning, this definition will be ill-typed because the type of `interp` requires that the environment is unchanged on exit.

Interpreting an assignment simply involves evaluating the expression to be stored in the variable, then updating the state, where `updateVar v vars val'` updates the variable at position v in the environment `vars` with the new value `val'`:

```
interp (v := val)
     = do val' <- eval val
          update (\vars => updateVar v vars val')
          return val'
```

For Print, we simply evaluate the expression and display it, relying on the STDIO effect:

```
interp (Print x) = do e <- eval x
                      putStrLn (show e)
```

Given some program, prog : Imp [] TyUnit a main program would need to set up the initial resources, then call the interpreter:

```
main : IO ()
main = run [(), 123456, []] (interp prog)
```

Though small, this example illustrates the design of a complete application with Effects: a main program sets up the required set of resources and invokes the top level effectful program. This, in turn, invokes effectful programs as necessary, which may use at most the resources available at the point where they are invoked.

5. Related Work

The work presented in this paper arose from dissatisfaction with the lack of composability of monad transformers, and a belief that a dependently typed language ought to handle side-effects more flexibly, in such a way that it would be possible to reason about side-effecting programs. The inspiration for using an *algebraic* representation was Bauer and Pretnar's *Eff* [3], a language based around handlers of algebraic effects. In our Effects system, we have found type classes to be a natural way of implementing handlers, in that they allow different effect handlers to be run in different contexts. Other languages aim to bring effects into their type system, such as Disciple [18], Frank[2] and Koka[3]. These languages are built on well-studied theoretical foundations [13, 16, 27, 28], which we have also applied in this paper. Algebraic effects have also been applied in Haskell, in order to combine I/O effects [30], and more recently [15] with an effect handler library.

In our approach, we have seen that the IDRIS type system can express effects by embedding, without any need to extend the language or type system. We make no attempt to *infer* effect types, however, since our intention is to *specify* effects and *check* that they are used correctly.

While our original motivation was to avoid the need for monad transformers [17] in order to compose effects, there is a clear relationship. Indeed, EffM is in a sense a monad transformer itself, in that it may augment an underlying monad with additional effects. Therefore, we can expect it to be possible to combine effects and monad transformers, where necessary. The problem with modularity of monad transformers is well-known, and addressed to some extent [14], though this still does not allow easy reordering of transformers, or reducing the transformer stack. The Effects approach encourages a more fine-grained separation of effects, by making it easy to call functions which use a smaller set of effects.

Our approach, associating resources with each effect, leads to a natural way of expressing and verifying resource usage protocols, by updating the resource type. This is a problem previously tackled by others, using special purpose type systems [32] or Haskell extensions [19], and in my own previous work [7, 9] by creating a DSL for resource management, but these are less flexible than the present approach in that combining resources is difficult. A related concept is Typestate [1, 29], which allows states to be tracked in types, though again, we are able to implement this directly rather than by extending the language. Implementing and reasoning about state-dependent interactive programs has also been studied using type theory [12, 21].

To some extent, we can now support imperative programming with dependent types, such as supported by Xanadu [33] and Ynot [23]. Ynot in particular is an axiomatic extension to Coq which allows reasoning about imperative programs using Hoare Type Theory [22]. Preconditions and postconditions on operations can be expressed in Effects with input and output resource types. The difficulty in imperative programming with dependent types is that updating one value may affect the type of another, though in our interpreter example in Section 4 we have safely used a dependent type in a mutable state.

6. Conclusions

IDRIS is a new language, with a full dependent type system. This gives us an ideal opportunity to revisit old problems about how to handle effects in a pure functional language. While the conventional approach, based on monads and transformers, has proved successful in Haskell, in this paper we have investigated an alternative approach and found it to be a natural method for defining and using effects. By linking each effect with a *resource* we can even track the state of resources through program execution, and reason about resource usage protocols such as file management.

The Effects approach has a number of strengths, and some weaknesses which we hope to address in future work. The main strength is that many common effects such as state, I/O and exceptions can be combined without the need for monad transformers. Effects can be implemented independently, and combined without further effort. Lifting is automatic; sub-programs using a smaller set of effects can be called without any explicit lifting operation, so as well as being easy to combine effects, programs remain readable. We have described a number of effects which are representable in this setting, and there are several others we have not described which are easy to define, such as parsing, logging, and bounded mutable arrays. Arrays, statically bounded with a dependent type, could even lead to optimisations since the effect system can guarantee that only one copy is needed, therefore the array could have a compact representation with no run-time bounds checking.

Another advantage is that it will be possible to have fine-grained separation of systems effects. We can be precise about needing network support, CGI, graphics, the operating system's environment, etc, rather than including all of these effects in one IO monad.

While using Effects, we are still able to use monads. Effects work *with* monads rather than against them, and indeed effectful programs are generally translated to monadic programs. As a result, concepts which need to be monadic (for example, continuations) can remain so, and still work with Effects.

Further Work

The Effects system is promising as a general approach to effectful programming, but we have only just begun. At present, we are developing more libraries using Effects to assess how well it works in practice as a programming tool, as well as how efficient it is for realistic programs. The most obvious weakness of Effects, is that algebraic effects cannot capture all monads. This does not appear to be a serious problem, however, given that Effects is designed to interact with monads, rather than to replace them. More seriously, but less obviously, there is a small interpreter overhead since EffM is represented as an algebraic data type, with an associated interpreter. We have not yet investigated in depth how to deal with this overhead, or indeed if it is a serious problem in practice, but we expect that partial evaluation [8] or a finally tagless approach [10] would be sufficient.

[2] https://personal.cis.strath.ac.uk/conor.mcbride/pub/Frank/

[3] http://research.microsoft.com/en-us/projects/koka/

Another weakness which we hope to address is that mixing control and resource effects is a challenge. For example, we cannot currently thread state through all branches of a non-deterministic search. If we can address this, it may be possible to represent more sophisticated effects such as co-operative multithreading, or even partiality. One way to tackle this problem could be to introduce a new method of the `Handler` class which manages resources more precisely, with a default implementation calling `handle`.

An implementation detail which could be improved without affecting usage of the library is that effectful sub-programs require ordering of effects to be preserved. We address this with a `permute` operator, requiring a proof that the new effect list is a permutation of the old, but ideally generating these proofs will be automatic.

The `Effects` implementation is entirely within the IDRIS language, with no extensions needed. It takes advantage of dependent types and theorem proving in several small but important ways: heterogeneous lists of resources, proofs of list membership and sublist predicates, and parameterisation of resources. Since modern Haskell supports many of these features, this leads to an obvious question: what would it take to implement `Effects` as an embedded library in Haskell? An interesting topic for further study would be whether this approach to combining effects would be feasible in a more mainstream functional language.

Monad transformers have served us well, and are a good fit for the Haskell type system. However, type systems are moving on. Perhaps now is the time to look for something more effective.

Acknowledgments

This work was supported by the Scottish Informatics and Computer Science Alliance (SICSA). My thanks to the inhabitants of the `#idris` IRC channel on `irc.freenode.net` for their feedback, and to the anonymous referees for their helpful comments.

References

[1] J. Aldrich, J. Sunshine, D. Saini, and Z. Sparks. Typestate-oriented programming. In *Proceedings of the 24th conference on Object Oriented Programming Systems Languages and Applications*, pages 1015–1012, 2009.

[2] L. Augustsson and M. Carlsson. An exercise in dependent types: A well-typed interpreter, 1999. In Workshop on Dependent Types in Programming, Gothenburg.

[3] A. Bauer and M. Pretnar. Programming with Algebraic Effects and Handlers, 2012. Available from `http://arxiv.org/abs/1203.1539`.

[4] E. Brady. Idris, a General Purpose Programming Language: Design and Implementation, 2013. Draft.

[5] E. Brady. Programming in Idris: a Tutorial, 2013. Available from `http://idris-lang.org/tutorial`.

[6] E. Brady and K. Hammond. A verified staged interpreter is a verified compiler. In *Generative Programming and Component Engineering (GPCE 2006)*. ACM, 2006.

[7] E. Brady and K. Hammond. Correct-by-construction concurrency: Using dependent types to verify implementations of effectful resource usage protocols. *Fundamenta Informaticae*, 102:145–176, 2010.

[8] E. Brady and K. Hammond. Scrapping your inefficient engine: Using partial evaluation to improve domain-specific language implementation. In *Proceedings of the 15th International Conference on Functional Programming (ICFP '10)*, pages 297–308. ACM, 2010.

[9] E. Brady and K. Hammond. Resource-safe Systems Programming with Embedded Domain Specific Languages. In *Practical Applications of Declarative Languages*, pages 242–257, 2012.

[10] J. Carette, O. Kiselyov, and C.-C. Shan. Finally tagless, partially evaluated: Tagless staged interpreters for simpler typed languages. *Journal of Functional Programming*, 19(05):509–543.

[11] D. Delahaye. A tactic language for the system Coq. In *Logic for Programming and Automated Reasoning (LPAR)*, volume 1955 of *LNAI*, pages 85–95. Springer, 2000.

[12] P. Hancock and A. Setzer. Interactive Programs in Dependent Type Theory. In *Proceedings of the 14th Annual Conference of the EACSL on Computer Science Logic*, pages 317–331, Aug. 2000.

[13] M. Hyland, G. Plotkin, and J. Power. Combining effects: Sum and tensor. *Theoretical Computer Science*, 357:70–99, 2006.

[14] M. Jaskelioff. Modular monad transformers. In *ESOP 09: Proceedings of the 18th European Symposium on Programming Languages and Systems*, LNCS, pages 64–79. Springer, 2009.

[15] O. Kammar, S. Lindley, and N. Oury. Handlers in action. In *Proceedings of the 18th International Conference on Functional Programming (ICFP '13)*. ACM, 2013.

[16] P. B. Levy. *Call-By-Push-Value*. PhD thesis, Queen Mary and Westfield College, University of London, 2001.

[17] S. Liang, P. Hudak, and M. Jones. Monad transformers and modular interpreters. In *Proceedings of the 22nd ACM SIGPLAN-SIGACT symposium on Principles of Programming Languages*, pages 333–343, New York, New York, USA, Jan. 1995. ACM Press.

[18] B. Lippmeier. Witnessing Purity, Constancy and Mutability. In *7th Asian Symposium on Programming Languages and Systems (APLAS 2009)*, volume 5904 of *LNCS*, pages 95–110. Springer, 2009.

[19] C. McBride. Kleisli arrows of outrageous fortune, 2011. Draft.

[20] C. McBride and R. Paterson. Applicative programming with effects. *Journal of functional programming*, 18(1):1–13, 2008.

[21] M. Michelbrink and A. Setzer. State dependent IO-monads in type theory. *Electronic Notes in Theoretical Computer Science*, 122:127–146, 2005.

[22] A. Nanevski, G. Morrisett, and L. Birkedal. Hoare type theory, polymorphism and separation. *Journal of Functional Programming*, 18(5-6):865–911, Sept. 2008.

[23] A. Nanevski, G. Morrisett, A. Shinnar, P. Govereau, and L. Birkedal. Ynot: Dependent types for imperative programs. In *Proceedings of the 13th International Conference on Functional Programming (ICFP '08)*, pages 229–240. ACM, 2008.

[24] M. Odersky, P. Altherr, V. Cremet, B. Emir, S. Maneth, S. Micheloud, N. Mihaylov, M. Schinz, E. Stenman, and M. Zenger. An overview of the Scala programming language. Technical report, 2004.

[25] E. Pašalic, W. Taha, and T. Sheard. Tagless staged interpreters for typed languages. In *Proceedings of the 7th International Conference on Functional Programming (ICFP '02)*, volume 37, pages 218–229. ACM, Sept. 2002.

[26] S. Peyton Jones. Haskell 98 Language and Libraries: The Revised Report. Technical report, 2002.

[27] G. Plotkin and M. Pretnar. Handlers of Algebraic Effects. In *ESOP 09: Proceedings of the 18th European Symposium on Programming Languages and Systems*, pages 80–94, 2009.

[28] M. Pretnar. *The Logic and Handling of Algebraic Effects*. PhD thesis, University of Edinburgh, 2010.

[29] R. Strom and S. Yemini. Typestate: A programming language concept for enhancing software reliability. *IEEE Transactions on Software Engineering*, SE-12(1):157–171, 1986.

[30] W. Swierstra. Data types à la carte. *Journal of functional programming*, 18(4):423–436, 2008.

[31] P. Wadler. Monads for functional programming. In J. Jeuring and E. Meijer, editors, *Advanced Functional Programming*, volume 925 of *LNCS*, pages 24–52. Springer, 1995.

[32] D. Walker. A Type System for Expressive Security Policies. In *Proceedings of the 27th ACM SIGPLAN-SIGACT Symposium on Principles of Programming Languages*, POPL '00, pages 254–267. ACM, 2000.

[33] H. Xi. Imperative Programming with Dependent Types. In *15th Annual IEEE Symposium on Logic in Computer Science*, pages 375–387, 2000.

Handlers in Action

Ohad Kammar
University of Cambridge
ohad.kammar@cl.cam.ac.uk

Sam Lindley
University of Strathclyde
Sam.Lindley@ed.ac.uk

Nicolas Oury
nicolas.oury@gmail.com

Abstract

Plotkin and Pretnar's handlers for algebraic effects occupy a sweet spot in the design space of abstractions for effectful computation. By separating effect signatures from their implementation, algebraic effects provide a high degree of modularity, allowing programmers to express effectful programs independently of the concrete interpretation of their effects. A handler is an interpretation of the effects of an algebraic computation. The handler abstraction adapts well to multiple settings: pure or impure, strict or lazy, static types or dynamic types.

This is a position paper whose main aim is to popularise the handler abstraction. We give a gentle introduction to its use, a collection of illustrative examples, and a straightforward operational semantics. We describe our Haskell implementation of handlers in detail, outline the ideas behind our OCaml, SML, and Racket implementations, and present experimental results comparing handlers with existing code.

Categories and Subject Descriptors D.1.1 [*Applicative (Functional) Programming*]; D.3.1 [*Formal Definitions and Theory*]; D.3.2 [*Language Classifications*]: Applicative (functional) languages; D.3.3 [*Language Constructs and Features*]; F.3.2 [*Semantics of Programming Languages*]: Operational semantics

Keywords algebraic effects; effect handlers; effect typing; monads; continuations; Haskell; modularity

1. Introduction

Monads have proven remarkably successful as a tool for abstraction over effectful computations [4, 30, 46]. However, monads as a programming language primitive violate the fundamental encapsulation principle: program to an *interface*, not to an *implementation*.

Modular programs are constructed using abstract interfaces as building blocks. This is *modular abstraction*. To give meaning to an *abstract* interface, we instantiate it with a *concrete* implementation. Given a composite interface, each sub-interface can be independently instantiated with different concrete implementations. This is *modular instantiation*.

The monadic approach to functional programming takes a *concrete* implementation rather than an *abstract* interface as primitive. For instance, in Haskell we might define a state monad:

$$
\begin{array}{l}
\mathbf{newtype}\ State\ s\ a = State\ \{runState :: s \to (a, s)\} \\
\mathbf{instance}\ Monad\ (State\ s)\ \mathbf{where} \\
\quad return\ x = State\ (\lambda s \to (x, s)) \\
\quad m \gg\!= f\ \ = State\ (\lambda s \to \mathbf{let}\ (x, s') = runState\ m\ s\ \mathbf{in} \\
\qquad\qquad\qquad\qquad\qquad\qquad runState\ (f\ x)\ s')
\end{array}
$$

This definition says nothing about the intended use of $State\ s\ a$ as the type of computations that read and write state. Worse, it breaks abstraction as consumers of state are exposed to its concrete implementation as a function of type $s \to (a, s)$. We can of course define the natural get and put operations on state, but their implementations are fixed.

Jones [18] advocates modular abstraction for monads in Haskell using type classes. For instance, we can define the following interface to abstract state computation[1]:

$$
\begin{array}{l}
\mathbf{class}\ Monad\ m \Rightarrow MonadState\ s\ m \mid m \to s\ \mathbf{where} \\
\quad get :: \qquad m\ s \\
\quad put :: s \to m\ ()
\end{array}
$$

The $MonadState$ interface can be smoothly combined with other interfaces, taking advantage of Haskell's type class mechanism to represent type-level sets of effects.

Monad transformers [25] provide a form of modular instantiation for abstract monadic computations. For instance, state can be handled in the presence of other effects by incorporating a state monad transformer within a monad transformer stack.

A fundamental problem with monad transformer stacks is that once a particular abstract effect is instantiated, the order of effects in the stack becomes concrete, and it becomes necessary to explicitly lift operations through the stack. Taming the monad transformer stack is an active research area [16, 17, 38, 42].

Instead of the top-down monad transformer approach, we take a bottom-up approach, simply adding the required features as language primitives. We want modular abstraction, so we add abstract effect interfaces, in fact *abstract operations*, as a language primitive. Abstract operations compose, yielding modular abstraction. We also want modular instantiation, so we add *effect handlers* as a language primitive for instantiating an abstract operation with a concrete implementation. A handler operates on a specified subset of the abstract operations performed by an abstract computation, leaving the remainder abstract, and yielding modular instantiation.

By directly adding the features we require, we obtain modular abstraction and modular instantiation while avoiding many of the pitfalls of monad transformers.

Our first inspiration is the *algebraic theory of computational effects*. Introduced by Plotkin and Power [33–35], it complements Moggi's monadic account of effects by incorporating abstract effect interfaces as primitive. Our second inspiration is the elimination construct for algebraic effects, *effect handlers* [36]. In Plotkin and Power's setting, one defines algebraic effects with respect to an equational theory. As with other handler implementations [2, 6, 29],

[1] From the Monad Transformer Library [12].

ICFP '13, September 25–27, 2013, Boston, MA, USA.

ACM 978-1-4503-2326-0/13/09... $15.00.
http://dx.doi.org/10.1145/2500365.2500590

in this paper we always take the equational theory to be the free theory, in which there are no equations.

We argue that algebraic effects and effect handlers provide a compelling alternative to monads as a basis for effectful programming across a variety of functional programming languages (pure or impure, strict or lazy, statically typed or dynamically typed). Our position is supported by a range of handler libraries we have implemented for Haskell, OCaml, SML, and Racket, backed up by a core calculus of effect handlers with a straightforward operational semantics. This paper focuses on the Haskell library.

Our key contributions are the following:

- A collection of novel features for practical programming with handlers in the presence of effect typing, illustrated through a series of examples.
- A small-step operational semantics for effect handlers.
- A type and effect system for effect handlers.
- Effect handler libraries for Haskell, OCaml, SML, and Racket.
- A performance comparison between our Haskell library and equivalent non-handler code.

The rest of the paper is structured as follows. Section 2 presents handlers in action through a series of small examples. Section 3 introduces our core calculus of effect handlers, λ_{eff}, its effect type system, and small-step operational semantics. Section 4 presents in detail the Haskell effect handlers library, and sketches the design of our libraries for OCaml, SML, and Racket. Section 5 reports on the baseline performance of handlers in comparison with existing (less abstract) code. Section 6 discusses related work, and Section 7 concludes.

2. Handlers in Action

We present our examples in a monadic style, using an extension to Haskell syntax implemented using the Template Haskell [40] and quasiquote [28] features of GHC. Haskell's features allow for a relatively simple, user-friendly and efficient implementation of effects handlers with effect typing in an existing language. (None of our other libraries support effect typing.)

However, all of the examples could in fact be implemented with the same level of expressivity and flexibility in a direct-style, without any monadic boilerplate. Indeed, handlers can be direct-style with or without effect typing, and provide a natural abstraction for adding more controlled effectful computations to the ML family of languages or even to the Lisp family of languages as witnessed by the libraries we have implemented in OCaml, SML, and Racket. In Section 4.3 we outline a practical method to prototype an implementation of handlers for a large set of such languages.

A key reason for focusing on our Haskell library in this paper is that it is the only one that supports effect typing. Effect typing is crucial to the termination of our core calculus (Section 3). More importantly, it it is crucial for our notion of soundness, as it statically ensures that operations do not accidentally go unhandled. Anecdotally, we have observed that such static guarantees are important in practice: when we added effect typing to an early version of our Haskell library, it revealed a number of bugs in our test examples.

The code for our effect handler libraries, examples, and benchmarks is available in the GitHub repository at:

```
http://github.com/slindley/effect-handlers/
```

This repository also includes many other other examples. For instance, we have reimplemented Kiselyov and Shan's HANSEI DSL for probabilistic computation [22], Kiselyov's iteratees [21], and Gonzalez's Pipes library [14], all using handlers.

Template Haskell and Quasiquotes Template Haskell [40] is a facility for compile-time meta programming in Haskell. It provides a data type for manipulating Haskell code as an abstract syntax tree. It also provides constructs for splicing chunks of Haskell together.

Quasiquotes [28] extend Template Haskell splicing functionality with user-defined syntax. Each syntax extension (also known as *quasiquoter*) is associated with a name. To define syntax extension, **ext**, a library writer supplies a parser for **ext** expressions as a function that takes a string and returns a Haskell abstract syntax tree. To invoke the syntax extension, a programmer writes an expression e in quasiquote brackets $[\mathbf{ext} \mid e \,|]$, a *quasiquote*. At compile-time, GHC runs the parser on e and splices in the resulting abstract syntax tree in place of the quasiquote brackets.

2.1 State and Handlers

We introduce the primitives for abstract operations and handlers in our Haskell library through the example of global state.

We define abstract operations for state with the following **operation** quasiquotes

$$
\begin{array}{l}
[\mathbf{operation} \mid \mathit{Get}\ s :: \qquad s\ |] \\
[\mathbf{operation} \mid \mathit{Put}\ s :: s \to ()\ |]
\end{array}
$$

which declare a $\mathit{Get}\ \ s$ operation that takes no parameters and returns values of type s, and a $\mathit{Put}\ \ s$ operation that takes a single parameter of type s and returns values of type $()$. In general an abstract operation declaration has the form

$$[\mathbf{operation} \mid \forall u_1 \ldots u_l . \mathit{Op}\ e_1 \ldots e_m :: A_1 \to \ldots \to A_n \to A\ |]$$

where Op is the name of the operation, $u_1, \ldots, u_l$ are *universal* type variables, $e_1, \ldots, e_m$ are *existential* type variables, $A_1, \ldots, A_n$ are parameter types, and A is the return type. (We will discuss the role of universal and existential type variables in Section 2.2.)

The declarations above automatically derive wrappers get and put for actually invoking the operations. Ideally, we would like their types to be

$$
\begin{array}{l}
\mathit{get} :: \qquad \mathit{Comp}'\ \{\mathit{Get}\ s\}\ s \\
\mathit{put} :: s \to \mathit{Comp}'\ \{\mathit{Put}\ s\}\ ()
\end{array}
$$

where $\mathit{Comp}'\ \ \varepsilon\ \ a$ is the type of abstract computations that can perform abstract operations in the set ε and return a value of type a. But GHC does not have a built-in effect type-system, so we simulate one, encoding sets of operations as type class constraints. Thus, get and put actually have slightly more complicated types:

$$
\begin{array}{l}
\mathit{get} :: [\mathbf{handles} \mid h\ \{\mathit{Get}\ s\}\ |] \Rightarrow \qquad \mathit{Comp}\ h\ s \\
\mathit{put} :: [\mathbf{handles} \mid h\ \{\mathit{Put}\ s\}\ |] \Rightarrow s \to \mathit{Comp}\ h\ ()
\end{array}
$$

We can think of the type variable h as standing for a set of operations, an *effect set* ε. Membership of operation Op in ε is denoted by the quasiquotation $[|\ \mathbf{handles} \mid h\ \{\mathit{Op}\}\ |]$ (which is desugared into a corresponding type class constraint). The reason we write **handles** instead of **contains**, and h instead of ε, is that h is more than just an effect set; it actually ranges over *handlers* for ε. Thus $\mathit{Comp}\ h$ represents computations interpreted by handlers of type h, and the constraint $[|\ \mathbf{handles} \mid h\ \{\mathit{Op}\}\ |]$ really means: handler h handles operation Op. (We will introduce the syntax for handlers shortly.)

We define the type of abstract state computations as follows[2]:

$$
\begin{array}{l}
\mathbf{type}\ \mathit{SComp}\ s\ a = \\
\quad \forall h.([\mathbf{handles} \mid h\ \{\mathit{Get}\ s\}\ |], \\
\qquad [\mathbf{handles} \mid h\ \{\mathit{Put}\ s\}\ |]) \Rightarrow \mathit{Comp}\ h\ a
\end{array}
$$

For example:

[2] We would ideally like to write $[\mathbf{handles} \mid h\ \{\mathit{Get}\ s, \mathit{Put}\ s\}\ |]$ as a single constraint, but Template Haskell currently only allows us to generate one type class constraint per quasiquote.

```
comp :: SComp Int Int
comp = do {x ← get; put (x + 1);
           y ← get; put (y + y); get}
```

Because Haskell is lazy we still require notation for explicitly sequencing computations. We take advantage of the existing **do** notation, and *Comp h* is implemented as a certain kind of universal monad (see Section 4).

We can provide many concrete interpretations of stateful computation, which is where handlers come in. First, we interpret state in the standard monadic way:

```
1 [handler |
2   RunState s a :: s → (a, s)
3     handles {Get s, Put s} where
4       Return x   s → (x, s)
5       Get        k s → k s s
6       Put        s k _ → k () s |]
```

We describe the syntax line by line.

Line 1 begins a **handler** quasiquote.

Line 2 specifies the name, type parameters, and type signature of the handler. Notice that the type signature $s \to (a, s)$ is that of the state monad. The type signature indicates that this handler takes one parameter of type s, which is threaded through the handler, and returns a result of type (a, s).

Line 3 specifies the set of operations handled by the handler.

Line 4 is a *return clause*. It expresses how to return a final value from a computation. In general, a return clause takes the form $Return\ x\ y_1\ \ldots\ y_n \to e$, where x binds the value returned by the computation and $y_1, \ldots, y_n$ bind the handler parameters. Here, the final value is paired up with the single state parameter.

Lines 5 and 6 are *operation clauses*. They express how to handle each operation. In general, an operation clause takes the form $Op\ x_1\ \ldots\ x_m\ k\ y_1\ \ldots\ y_n \to e$, where $x_1, \ldots, x_m$ bind the operation parameters, k binds the continuation of the computation, and $y_1, \ldots, y_n$ bind the handler parameters, here the single state parameter. The continuation k is a curried function which takes a return value followed by a sequence of handler parameters, and yields the interpretation of the rest of the computation. For Get, the return value is the current state, which is threaded through the rest of the computation. For $Put\ s$, the existing state is ignored, the return value is $()$, and the state parameter is updated to s.

Analogously to abstract operation declarations, a handler declaration generates a convenient wrapper, whose name is derived from that of the handler by replacing the first letter with its lower case counterpart.

```
runState :: s → SComp s a → (a, s)
*Main> runState 1 comp
(4, 4)
```

If we do not need to read the final contents of the state, then we can give a simpler interpretation to state [36], using the type that a Haskell programmer might normally associate with a read-only state monad:

```
[handler |
  EvalState s a :: s → a handles {Get s, Put s} where
    Return x   s → x
    Get        k s → k s s
    Put        s k _ → k () s |]

*Main> evalState 1 comp
4
```

More interestingly, we can give other interpretations:

```
[handler |
  LogState s a :: s → (a, [s])
    handles {Get s, Put s} where
      Return x   s → (x, [])
      Get        k s → k s s
      Put        s k _ → let (x, ss) = k () s in (x, s : ss) |]
```

This handler logs the history of all writes to the state. For instance,

```
*Main> logState 1 comp
(4, [2, 4])
```

2.2 State and Open Handlers

The three handlers of Section 2.1 are *closed*. They each handle Get and Put, but cannot interpret computations that might perform other operations. Thus they do not support modular instantiation.

Open handlers extend closed handlers by automatically forwarding all operations that are not explicitly handled. For instance, the following defines a handler that forwards all operations other than Get and Put:

```
[handler |
  forward h.
    OpenState s a :: s → a handles {Get s, Put s} where
      Return x   s → return x
      Get        k s → k s s
      Put        s k _ → k () s |]
```

The type variable h is an artefact of the Haskell implementation. It represents an abstract *parent handler* that will ultimately handle operations forwarded by $OpenState$. It is implicitly added as the first type argument to $OpenState$ (yielding $OpenState\ \ h\ \ s\ \ a$) and $Comp\ \ h$ is implicitly applied to the return type (yielding $Comp\ \ h\ \ a$). Any operations other than Get or Put will be automatically forwarded to h.

To illustrate the composability of open handlers, we return to the logging example. In Section 2.1, we demonstrated how to log Put operations using a special handler. We now factor the logging in such a way that we can *refine* any abstract stateful computation into an equivalent abstract computation that also performs logging, such that both logging and state can be subsequently interpreted in arbitrary ways using suitable handlers.

First we define a new operation for logging each Put:

```
[operation | LogPut s :: s → () |]
```

Now we can define an open handler that inserts a $LogPut$ operation before every Put operation in the original computation, but otherwise leaves it unchanged:

```
[handler |
  forward h handles {Put s, LogPut s}.
    PutLogger s a :: a handles {Put s} where
      Return x   → return x
      Put        s k → do {logPut s; put s; k ()} |]
```

For instance, the computation $putLogger\ \ comp$ is equivalent to:

```
do {x ← get; logPut (x + 1); put (x + 1);
    y ← get; logPut (y + y); put (y + y); get}
```

The constraint (h **handles** $\{Put\ \ s, LogPut\ \ s\}$) asserts that the parent handler h must also handle the $Put\ \ s$ and $LogPut\ \ s$ operations[3].

To obtain the original behaviour of $LogState$, we can define the following open handler:

```
[handler |
  forward h.
    LogPutReturner s a :: (a, [s])
      handles {LogPut s} where
        Return x   → return (x, [])
        LogPut s k → do (x, ss) ← k (); return (x, s : ss) |]
```

[3] Under the hood this aids GHC type inference.

and compose several handlers together:

```
stateWithLog :: s → SComp s a → (a, [s])
stateWithLog s comp = (handlePure ∘ logPutReturner ∘
                        openState s ∘ putLogger) comp
```

where *HandlePure* is a canonical top-level closed handler:

```
[handler |
  HandlePure a :: a handles { } where Return x → x |]
```

which interprets a pure computation as a value of type a.

An alternative interpretation of logging is to output logging messages as they arrive:

```
[handler |
  forward h handles {Io}.(Show s) ⇒
    LogPutPrinter s a :: a handles {LogPut s} where
      Return x    → return x
      LogPut s k →
        do io (putStrLn ("Put: " ++ show s)); k () |]
```

Now we can plug everything together:

```
statePrintLog :: Show s ⇒ s → SComp s a → IO a
statePrintLog s comp = (handleIO   ∘ logPutPrinter ∘
                         openState s ∘ putLogger) comp
```

where *HandleIO* is another top-level closed handler for performing arbitrary operations in the *IO* monad with the *Io* operation:

```
[operation | ∀a.Io :: IO a → a |]
[handler |
  HandleIO a :: IO a handles {Io} where
    Return x    → return x
    Io m      k → do {x ← m; k x} |]
```

The *universal* quantifier in the *Io* operation declaration indicates that it must be handled polymorphically in a. This is in contrast to the declaration of *Get*, for instance:

```
[operation | Get s :: s |]
```

where the type parameter s is *existential*, in the sense that for any handler that handles *Get*, there must exist a fixed type for s. Correspondingly, in any given abstract computation, *Io* can be used at arbitrary types a whereas *Get* must be used at a fixed type s.

Comparing the outputs on our sample computation we obtain:

```
*Main> stateWithLog 1 comp
(4, [2, 4])
*Main> statePrintLog 1 comp
Put: 2
Put: 4
4
```

The pattern of precomposing one closed top-level handler with a sequence of open handlers is common when using our library. The order in which open handlers are composed may or may not change the semantics. For instance, if we were to swap the order of *openState s* and *putLogger* in *statePrintLog* then all of the *Put* operations would be handled before any *PutLog* operations could be generated, so no logging information would ever be output. On the other hand, if we were to swap the order of *logPutPrinter* and *openState s* then the semantics would be unchanged as their actions are orthogonal.

Open handlers allow us to handle a subset of the effects in an abstract computation, thus supporting modular instantiation.

The next three subsections present more involved examples, demonstrating the interaction of user-defined effects with various Haskell features.

2.3 Choice and Failure

Consider abstract operations *Choose* and *Failure*:

```
[operation | ∀a.Choose :: a → a → a |]
[operation | ∀a.Failure ::          a |]
```

The idea is that *Choose* should select one of its two arguments of type a, and *Failure* just aborts. Abstract choice computations are interesting because they admit a range of useful interpretations. Archetypal handlers which we consider include those that enumerate all choices (*AllResults* below) and random sampling (*RandomResult* below). The former is notable as it takes full advantage of the ability for an operation clause to invoke the continuation more than once.

The type of abstract computations over *Choose* and *Failure* is:

```
type CF a = ∀h.([handles | h {Choose} |],
                [handles | h {Failure} |]) ⇒ Comp h a
```

As a simple example, consider the following program:

```
data Toss = Heads | Tails deriving Show
drunkToss :: CF Toss
drunkToss = do {caught ← choose True False;
                if caught then choose Heads Tails
                else failure}
drunkTosses :: Int → CF [Toss]
drunkTosses n = replicateM n drunkToss
```

The abstract computation *drunkToss* simulates a drunk performing one coin toss. If the drunk catches the coin then the result of tossing the coin (*Heads* or *Tails*) is returned. If the coin falls into the gutter then no result is returned. The *drunkTosses* function repeats the process the specified number of times.

We can write a handler that returns all possible results of a *CF* computation as a list, providing a model of non-determinism.

```
[handler |
  AllResults a :: [a] handles {Choose, Failure} where
    Return x     → [x]
    Choose x y k → k x ++ k y
    Failure    k → [] |]
```

This is the first handler we have seen that uses the continuation non-linearly. The *Choose* operation is handled by concatenating the results of invoking the continuation with each alternative. The *Failure* operation is handled by returning the empty list and ignoring the continuation. For example:

```
*Main> allResults (drunkCoins 2)
[[Heads, Heads], [Heads, Tails], [Tails, Heads], [Tails, Tails]]
```

Rather than returning all of the results of a *CF* computation, we might wish to sample a single result at random. In order to keep the implementation of randomness abstract, let us declare a new operation for generating random numbers.

```
[operation | Rand :: Double |]
```

We first give a handler for *Choose* alone.

```
[handler |
  forward h handles {Rand}.
    RandomResult a :: a handles {Choose} where
      Return x     → return x
      Choose x y k → do {r ← rand;
                         k (if r < 0.5 then x else y)} |]
```

Unlike in the *AllResults* handler, the *Choose* operation is handled by supplying one of the arguments to the continuation at random. We can implement randomness using the *IO* monad.

```
[handler |
  HandleRandom a :: IO a
    handles {Rand} where
      Return x   → return x
      Rand     k → do {r ← getStdRandom random; k r} |]
```

Let us now define another open handler for handling *Failure*, interpreting the result of a possibly failing computation with a *Maybe* type.

```
[handler |
  forward h.
    MaybeResult a :: Maybe a handles {Failure} where
      Return x → return (Just x)
      Failure k → return Nothing |]
```

As the body of the handler is pure, there is no need to constrain h with a **handles** clause. We now compose the above three handlers:

```
sampleMaybe :: CF a → IO (Maybe a)
sampleMaybe comp =
  (handleRandom ∘ maybeResult ∘ randomResult) comp
```

The *sampleMaybe* function[4] first uses *randomResult* to handle *Choose* using *Rand*, forwarding *Failure*. Then it uses *maybeResult* to handle *Failure*, forwarding *Rand*. Finally, at the top-level, it uses *handleRandom* to handle *Rand* in the *IO* monad. Here are some example runs:

```
*Main> sampleMaybe (drunkTosses 2)
Nothing
*Main> sampleMaybe (drunkTosses 2)
Just [Heads, Heads]
```

We might decide that rather than stopping on failure, we would like to persevere by trying again:

```
[handler |
  forward h.
    Persevere a :: Comp (Persevere h a) a → a
      handles {Failure} where
        Return x    _ → return x
        Failure   k c → persevere c c |]
```

The parameter to the *Persevere* handler is a computation that must be handled recursively by the handler itself. The *Failure* operation is handled by reinvoking the handler.

We can now persevere until we obtain a sample.

```
sample :: CF a → IO a
sample comp = handleRandom (persevere comp' comp')
  where comp' = randomResult comp
```

For instance:

```
*Main> sample (drunkTosses 5)
[Heads, Tails, Heads, Tails, Heads]
```

In practice, one might use a more sophisticated sampling approach to improve performance by avoiding failures [22].

2.4 Word Count

The *wc* program counts the number of lines, words and characters in an input stream. We first present the abstract operations required to implement this functionality:

```
[operation | ReadChar :: Maybe Char |]
[operation | Finished :: Bool       |]
```

The *ReadChar* operation reads a character if available. The *Finished* operation checks whether the input is finished. Given these operations, we can implement a function that reads a line:

```
readLine :: [handles | h {ReadChar} |] ⇒ Comp h String
readLine =
  do mc ← readChar
     case mc of
       Nothing  → return []
       Just '\n' → return []
       Just c    → do cs ← readLine; return (c : cs)
```

Of course, this implementation does not specify where the input is to be read from. We define a handler that reads from a string:

```
[handler |
  forward h.
    StringReader a :: String → a
      handles {ReadChar, Finished} where
        Return x    _        → return x
        ReadChar k []        → k Nothing []
        ReadChar k (c : cs)  → k (Just c) cs
        Finished  k []       → k True []
        Finished  k cs       → k False cs |]
```

and another that reads from standard input:

```
[handler |
  forward h handles {Io}.
    StdinReader a :: a
      handles {ReadChar, Finished} where
        Return x    → return x
        ReadChar k →
          do b ← io (hIsEOF stdin)
             if b then k Nothing
                  else do c ← io getChar; k (Just c)
        Finished  k → do b ← io (hIsEOF stdin); k b |]
```

With the *readLine* function, we can count the number of lines in an input stream, but *wc* additionally provides facilities to count characters and words. For doing so, we give two handlers, each of which instruments the *readChar* operation in a different way. The first handler counts the number of characters read by enumerating each call to *readChar*:

```
[handler |
  forward h handles {ReadChar}.
    CountChar0 a :: Int → (a, Int)
      handles {ReadChar} where
        Return x    i → return (x, i)
        ReadChar k i → do mc ← readChar
                          case mc of
                            Nothing → k mc i
                            Just _  → k mc $! i + 1 |]
countChar = countChar0 0
```

The second handler counts the number of words read by tracking space characters:

```
[handler |
  forward h handles {ReadChar}.
    CountWord0 a :: Int → Bool → (a, Int)
      handles {ReadChar} where
        Return x    i _ → return (x, i)
        ReadChar k i b → do
          mc ← readChar
          case mc of
            Nothing   →
              (k mc $! (if b then i + 1 else i)) $ False
            Just c    →
              if ( c ≡ ' '  ∨ c ≡ '\t'
                 ∨ c ≡ '\n' ∨ c ≡ '\r') then
                (k mc $! (if b then i + 1 else i)) $ False
              else k mc i True |]
countWord = countWord0 0 False
```

Combining these two handlers, we write a general *wc* function:

```
wc ::
  ([handles | h {ReadChar} |], [handles | h {Finished} |])
    ⇒ Comp h (Int, Int, Int)
wc =
  do ((l, w), c) ← countChar (countWord (loop 0))
     return (c, w, l)
  where loop i = do b ← finished
                    if b then return i
                    else do _ ← readLine; loop $! (i + 1)
```

Here is a version of *wc* that takes a string as input:

[4] We cannot η-reduce *sampleMaybe* as doing so upsets the GHC type checker.

$$
\begin{array}{l}
wcString :: String \to IO\ () \\
wcString\ s = \\
\quad \mathbf{let}\ (c, w, l) = handlePure\ (stringReader\ s\ wc)\ \mathbf{in} \\
\quad putStrLn\ \$\ (show\ l) +\!\!+ \texttt{"\ "} +\!\!+ (show\ w) +\!\!+ \texttt{"\ "} +\!\!+ (show\ c)
\end{array}
$$

Here is a version of wc that uses standard input:

$$
\begin{array}{l}
wcStdin :: IO\ () \\
wcStdin = \mathbf{do} \\
\quad (c, w, l) \leftarrow handleIO\ (stdinReader\ wc) \\
\quad putStrLn\ \$\ (show\ l) +\!\!+ \texttt{"\ "} +\!\!+ (show\ w) +\!\!+ \texttt{"\ "} +\!\!+ (show\ c)
\end{array}
$$

In practice, one might define other handlers in order to support file input, network input, or different forms of buffering.

2.5 Tail

The $tail$ program takes an argument n and prints the last n lines of a text file. In order to implement the functionality of $tail$, we make use of $readLine$ as well as two additional abstract operations: the first to record a line, and the second to print all recorded lines.

$$
\begin{array}{l}
[\mathbf{operation} \mid SaveLine :: String \to ()\ |] \\
[\mathbf{operation} \mid PrintAll :: \qquad\qquad ()\ |]
\end{array}
$$

With these two operations, implementing an abstract tail computation $tailComp$ is straightforward.

$$
\begin{array}{l}
tailComp :: \\
\quad ([\mathbf{handles} \mid h\ \{ReadChar\}\ |], [\mathbf{handles} \mid h\ \{Finished\}\ |], \\
\quad\ [\mathbf{handles} \mid h\ \{SaveLine\}\ |], [\mathbf{handles} \mid h\ \{PrintAll\}\ |]) \\
\qquad \Rightarrow Comp\ h\ () \\
tailComp = \\
\quad \mathbf{do}\ s \leftarrow readLine; saveLine\ s \\
\qquad b \leftarrow finished; \mathbf{if}\ b\ \mathbf{then}\ printAll\ \mathbf{else}\ tailComp
\end{array}
$$

We now just need to handle the $SaveLine$ and $ReadLine$ operations. A naive handler might store all saved lines in memory, and print the last n as required. In practice, a more efficient implementation might store only the last n lines, using a circular array, say.

2.6 Pipes and Shallow Handlers

The behaviour of handlers we have described thus far is such that the continuation of an operation is handled with the current handler (though the parameters passed to the continuation may differ from the current parameters).

Another possible behaviour is for the continuation to return an unhandled computation, which must then be handled explicitly. We call such handlers *shallow handlers* because each handler only handles one step of a computation, in contrast to Plotkin and Pretnar's *deep handlers*. Shallow handlers are to deep handlers as case analysis is to a fold on an algebraic data type.

Shallow handlers sometimes lead to slightly longer code. For example, the $EvalState$ handler from Section 2.1 becomes:

$$
\begin{array}{l}
[\mathbf{shallowHandler} \mid \\
\quad EvalStateShallow\ s\ a :: s \to a \\
\qquad \mathbf{handles}\ \{Get\ s, Put\ s\}\ \mathbf{where} \\
\qquad\quad Return\ x \quad s \to x \\
\qquad\quad Get \qquad k\ s \to evalStateShallow\ (k\ s)\ s \\
\qquad\quad Put \qquad s\ k\ \_ \to evalStateShallow\ (k\ ())\ s\ |]
\end{array}
$$

The need to call the handler recursively in most clauses is characteristic of the style of program one writes with shallow handlers.

In some situations, it is helpful to have access to the unhandled result of the continuation. Consider *pipes* as exemplified by Gonzalez's `pipes` library [14]. A *pipe* is a data structure used to represent composable producers and consumers of data. A consumer can $await$ data and a producer can $yield$ data. A pipe is both a consumer and a producer. It is straightforward to provide such an abstraction with the following operations[5]:

$$
\begin{array}{l}
[\mathbf{operation} \mid Await\ s :: \qquad\quad s\ |] \\
[\mathbf{operation} \mid Yield\ \ s :: s \to ()\ |]
\end{array}
$$

To define a plumbing operator that combines a compatible consumer and producer we write two handlers: one handles the downstream consumer and keeps a suspended producer to resume when needed, the other handles the upstream producer and keeps a suspended consumer. These two handlers are straightforward to write using shallow handlers:

$$
\begin{array}{l}
[\mathbf{shallowHandler} \mid \\
\quad \mathbf{forward}\ h.Down\ s\ a :: Comp\ (Up\ h\ a)\ a \to a \\
\qquad \mathbf{handles}\ \{Await\ s\}\ \mathbf{where} \\
\qquad\quad Return\ x \qquad \_ \quad \to return\ x \\
\qquad\quad Await \qquad k\ prod \to up\ k\ prod\ |]
\end{array}
$$

$$
\begin{array}{l}
[\mathbf{shallowHandler} \mid \\
\quad \mathbf{forward}\ h.Up\ s\ a :: (s \to Comp\ (Down\ h\ a)\ a) \to a \\
\qquad \mathbf{handles}\ \{Yield\ s\}\ \mathbf{where} \\
\qquad\quad Return\ x \quad \_ \qquad \to return\ x \\
\qquad\quad Yield\ s \quad k\ cons \to down\ (k\ ())\ (cons\ s)\ |]
\end{array}
$$

However, transforming these handlers into deep handlers requires some ingenuity. Indeed, we need to work with continuations that are fully handled and we cannot keep the simple mutually recursive structure of the two handlers. Instead, we introduce two mutually recursive type definitions

$$
\begin{array}{l}
\mathbf{data}\ Prod\ \ s\ r = Prod\ (() \to Cons\ s\ r \to r) \\
\mathbf{data}\ Cons\ s\ r = Cons\ (s \to Prod\ s\ r \to r)
\end{array}
$$

which we use to encode the suspended partner of each computation

$$
\begin{array}{l}
[\mathbf{handler} \mid \\
\quad \mathbf{forward}\ h.Down\ s\ a :: Prod\ s\ (Comp\ h\ a) \to a \\
\qquad \mathbf{handles}\ \{Await\ s\}\ \mathbf{where} \\
\qquad\quad Return\ x \quad \_ \qquad\qquad\quad \to return\ x \\
\qquad\quad Await \qquad k\ (Prod\ prod) \to prod\ ()\ (Cons\ k)\ |] \\
[\mathbf{handler} \mid \\
\quad \mathbf{forward}\ h.Up\ s\ a :: Cons\ s\ (Comp\ h\ a) \to a \\
\qquad \mathbf{handles}\ \{Yield\ s\}\ \mathbf{where} \\
\qquad\quad Return\ x \quad \_ \qquad\qquad\quad \to return\ x \\
\qquad\quad Yield\ s \quad k\ (Cons\ cons) \to cons\ s\ (Prod\ k)\ |]
\end{array}
$$

resulting in a more complex program. We believe both deep and shallow handlers are useful. For clarity of presentation, we focus on deep handlers in the rest of this paper. In Section 3.4 and Section 4.2 we outline how shallow handlers differ from the main presentation.

2.7 Other Perspectives

In this paper we primarily treat handlers as a flexible tool for interpreting abstract effectful computations. Before we proceed with the rest of the paper we highlight some alternative perspectives on what handlers are.

Generalised exception handlers. Benton and Kennedy [3] introduced the idea of adding a return continuation to exception handlers. Their return continuation corresponds exactly to the return clause of an effect handler. Effect handler operation clauses generalise exception handler clauses by adding a continuation argument, providing support for arbitrary effects. An operation clause that ignores its continuation argument behaves like a standard exception handler clause.

Taming delimited continuations. A handler invocation delimits the start of a continuation. Each operation clause captures the continuation of the computation currently being handled, that is, the continuation up to the invocation point of the handler. Effect handlers modularise delimited continuations by capturing particular patterns of use. As Andrej Bauer, the co-creator of the Eff [2] lan-

[5] These operations have exactly the same signatures as Get and Put, but their intended interpretation is different. For instance, $yield\ x; yield\ y$ is in no way equivalent to $yield\ y$.

(values)	A, B	$::= 1 \mid A_1 \times A_2 \mid 0 \mid A_1 + A_2 \mid U_E C$
(computations)	C	$::= FA \mid A \to C \mid \top \mid C_1 \,\&\, C_2$
(effect signatures)	E	$::= \{\mathsf{op} : A \to B\} \uplus E \mid \emptyset$
(handlers)	R	$::= A\ {}^{E}\!\!\Rightarrow^{E'}\ C$
(environments)	Γ	$::= x_1 : A_1, \ldots, x_n : A_n$

Figure 1. Types and Effects of λ_{eff}

$$
\begin{array}{lrl}
\text{(values)} & V, W & ::= x \mid () \mid (V_1, V_2) \mid \mathbf{inj}_i\, V \mid \{M\} \\
\text{(computations)} & & \\
& M, N & ::= \mathbf{split}(V, x_1.x_2.M) \mid \mathbf{case_0}(V) \\
& & \mid\ \mathbf{case}(V, x_1.M_1, x_2.M_2) \mid V! \\
& & \mid\ \mathbf{return}\ V \mid \mathbf{let}\ x \leftarrow M\ \mathbf{in}\ N \\
& & \mid\ \lambda x.M \mid M\ V \\
& & \mid\ \langle M_1, M_2 \rangle \mid \mathbf{prj}_i\ M \\
& & \mid\ \mathsf{op}\ V(\lambda x.M) \mid \mathbf{handle}\ M\ \mathbf{with}\ H \\
\text{(handlers)} & H & ::= \{\mathbf{return}\ x \mapsto M\} \mid H \uplus \{\mathsf{op}\ p\ k \mapsto N\}
\end{array}
$$

Figure 2. Syntax of λ_{eff} Terms

guage puts it (personal communication, 2012):

"effects + handlers" : "delimited continuations"
=
"while" : "goto"

Folds over free monads. As we shall see in Section 4, we can define an algebraic data type for a collection of operations, and a handler is exactly a fold (otherwise known as *catamorphism*) over that data type.

3. The λ_{eff}-calculus

In this section, we present a small-step operational semantics and a sound type and effect system for λ_{eff}, a higher-order calculus of effect handlers. Following related work on effect operations [19], effect handlers [36], and monadic reflection [11], which takes Levy's call-by-push-value [24] as the underlying paradigm, we extend Levy's calculus with effect operations and effect handlers. For our purposes, the important features of call-by-push-value are that it makes an explicit distinction between values and computations, and that thunks are first-class objects distinct from functions.

3.1 Syntax and Static Semantics

The types and effects of λ_{eff} are given in Figure 1, the terms are given in Figure 2, and the typing rules are given in Figure 3. In all figures, the interesting parts are highlighted in grey. The unhighlighted parts are standard.

Call-by-push-value makes a syntactic distinction between values and computations. Only value terms may be passed to functions, and only computation terms may compute.

Value types (Figure 1) comprise the value unit type (1), value products ($A_1 \times A_2$), the empty type (0), sums ($A_1 + A_2$), and thunks ($U_E C$). The latter is the type of suspended computations. The effect signature E describes the effects that such computations are allowed to cause.

Computation types comprise value-returning computations (FA), functions ($A \to C$), the computation unit type ($\top$), and computation product types ($C_1 \,\&\, C_2$). Call-by-push-value includes two kinds of products: computation products, which are eliminated by projection, and value products, which are eliminated by binding.

An effect signature is a mapping from operations to pairs of value types, written as a set of type assignments. Each type assignment $\mathsf{op} : A \to B$, specifies the parameter type A and return type B of operation op.

A handler type $A\ {}^{E}\!\!\Rightarrow^{E'}\ C$ has a input value type A, output computation type C, input effect signature E, and output effect signature E'. A handler of this type handles value-returning computations of type FA that can only perform operations in E. The body of the handler itself may only perform operations in E', and its computation type is C. Type environments are standard.

Value terms (Figure 2) include variables and value introduction forms. We write $\{M\}$ for the thunk that represents the suspended computation M as a value. All elimination occurs in computation terms, as is standard for call-by-push-value. We write $\mathbf{split}(V, x_1.x_2.M)$ for the elimination form for value products, which binds the components of the product value V to the variables x_1 and x_2 in the computation M. We write $\langle M_1, M_2\rangle$ for a computation pair and $\mathbf{prj}_i\ M$ for the i-th projection of M. We write $V!$ for the computation that *forces* the thunk V, that is, runs the computation suspended in V. A lambda-abstraction $\lambda x.M$ is *not* a value, so must be suspended to be passed as an argument. Function application, products, and projections are standard.

In λ_{eff} operation applications are in continuation-passing-style. An operation application $\mathsf{op}\ V(\lambda x.M)$ takes a parameter V and a continuation $\lambda x.M$. The intuition is that the operation op is applied to the parameter V, returning a value that is bound to x in the continuation computation M. We restrict the continuation to be a lambda abstraction in order to simplify the operational semantics.

While programming with effects, it is more convenient to work with direct-style operation application. Direct-style application can be defined in terms of continuation-passing-style application: $\widehat{\mathsf{op}}\ V = \mathsf{op}\ V(\lambda x.\mathbf{return}\ x)$, and vice versa: $\mathsf{op}\ V(\lambda x.M) = \mathbf{let}\ x \leftarrow \widehat{\mathsf{op}}\ V\ \mathbf{in}\ M$. Plotkin and Power call the function $\lambda x.\widehat{\mathsf{op}}\ x$ underlying a direct-style application the *generic effect* of op [35].

A handled computation $\mathbf{handle}\ M\ \mathbf{with}\ H$ runs the computation M with the handler H. A handler H consists of a return clause $\mathbf{return}\ x \mapsto M$, and a set of operation clauses of the form $\mathsf{op}\ p\ k \mapsto N$. The return clause $\mathbf{return}\ x \mapsto M$ specifies how to handle a return value. The returned value is bound to x in M. Each operation clause $\mathsf{op}\ p\ k \mapsto N$ specifies how to handle applications of the distinct operation name op. The parameter is bound to p and the continuation is bound to k in N. The body of the continuation continues to be handled by the same handler.

The typing rules are given in Figure 3. The computation typing judgement $\Gamma \vdash_E M : C$ states that in type environment Γ the computation M has type C and effect signature E. Only operations in the current effect signature can be applied. Handling a computation changes the current effect signature to the output effect signature of the handler. The effect signature and type of the handled computation must match up exactly with the input type and effect signature of the handler.

In the handler typing judgement $\Gamma \vdash H : R$, all clauses must have the same output type and effect signature. The input type is determined by the return clause. The effect annotation on the thunked continuation parameter k in an operation clause $\mathsf{op}\ p\ k \mapsto N$ is annotated with the output effect rather than the input effect. The reason for this is that when handling an operation, the handler is automatically wrapped around the continuation.

Syntactic Sugar For convenience, we define syntactic sugar for projecting out the return clause and operation clauses of a handler. For any handler

$$\{\mathbf{return}\ x \mapsto M\} \uplus \{\mathsf{op}_i\ p\ k \mapsto N_i\}_i$$

we write

$$H^{\mathbf{return}} \equiv \lambda x.M \qquad H^{\mathsf{op}_i} \equiv \lambda p_i\ k_i.N_i$$

Value typing $\boxed{\Gamma \vdash V : A}$

$$\frac{(x : A) \in \Gamma}{\Gamma \vdash x : A} \qquad \frac{}{\Gamma \vdash () : 1} \qquad \frac{\Gamma \vdash V_1 : A_1 \quad \Gamma \vdash V_2 : A_2}{\Gamma \vdash (V_1, V_2) : A_1 \times A_2}$$

$$\frac{\Gamma \vdash V : A_i}{\Gamma \vdash \mathbf{inj}_i\, V : A_1 + A_2} \qquad \frac{\Gamma \vdash_E M : C}{\Gamma \vdash \{M\} : U_E C}$$

Computation typing $\boxed{\Gamma \vdash_E M : C}$

$$\frac{\Gamma \vdash V : A_1 \times A_2 \quad \Gamma, x_1 : A_1, x_2 : A_2 \vdash_E M : C}{\Gamma \vdash_E \mathbf{split}(V, x_1.x_2.M) : C}$$

$$\frac{\Gamma \vdash V : 0}{\Gamma \vdash_E \mathbf{case_0}(V) : C}$$

$$\frac{\Gamma \vdash V : A_1 + A_2 \quad \Gamma, x_1 : A_1 \vdash_E M_1 : C \quad \Gamma, x_2 : A_2 \vdash_E M_2 : C}{\Gamma \vdash_E \mathbf{case}(V, x_1.M_1, x_2.M_2) : C}$$

$$\frac{\Gamma \vdash V : U_E C}{\Gamma \vdash_E V! : C} \qquad \frac{\Gamma \vdash V : A}{\Gamma \vdash_E \mathbf{return}\, V : FA}$$

$$\frac{\Gamma \vdash_E M : FA \quad \Gamma, x : A \vdash_E N : C}{\Gamma \vdash_E \mathbf{let}\, x \leftarrow M\, \mathbf{in}\, N : C}$$

$$\frac{\Gamma, x : A \vdash_E M : C}{\Gamma \vdash_E \lambda x.M : A \to C} \qquad \frac{\Gamma \vdash_E M : A \to C \quad \Gamma \vdash V : A}{\Gamma \vdash_E M\, V : C}$$

$$\frac{}{\Gamma \vdash_E \langle\rangle : \top} \qquad \frac{\Gamma \vdash_E M_1 : C_1 \quad \Gamma \vdash_E M_2 : C_2}{\Gamma \vdash_E \langle M_1, M_2\rangle : C_1 \,\&\, C_2}$$

$$\frac{\Gamma \vdash_E M : C_1 \,\&\, C_2}{\Gamma \vdash_E \mathbf{prj}_i\, M : C_i}$$

$$\frac{(\mathrm{op} : A \to B) \in E \quad \Gamma \vdash V : A \quad \Gamma, x : B \vdash_E M : C}{\Gamma \vdash_E \mathrm{op}\, V(\lambda x.M) : C}$$

$$\frac{\Gamma \vdash_E M : FA \quad \Gamma \vdash H : A \,{}^{E}\!\!\Rightarrow^{E'} C}{\Gamma \vdash_{E'} \mathbf{handle}\, M\, \mathbf{with}\, H : C}$$

Handler typing $\boxed{\Gamma \vdash H : A \,{}^{E}\!\!\Rightarrow^{E'} C}$

$$\frac{\begin{array}{c} E = \{\mathrm{op}_i : A_i \to B_i\}_i \\ H = \{\mathbf{return}\, x \mapsto M\} \uplus \{\mathrm{op}_i\, p\, k \mapsto N_i\}_i \\ [\Gamma, p : A_i, k : U_{E'}(B_i \to C) \vdash_{E'} N_i : C]_i \\ \Gamma, x : A \vdash_{E'} M : C \end{array}}{\Gamma \vdash H : A \,{}^{E}\!\!\Rightarrow^{E'} C}$$

Figure 3. Typing Rules for λ_{eff}

3.2 Operational Semantics

The reduction relation ($\longrightarrow$) for λ_{eff} is defined in Figure 4. We use *reduction frames* as an auxiliary notion to simplify our presentation. The β-rules are standard: each β-redex arises as an introduction followed by an elimination. The first three β-rules eliminate value terms; the last three eliminate computation terms.

The *hoist*.op-rule hoists operation applications through hoisting frames. Its purpose is to forward operation applications up to the nearest enclosing handler, so that they can be handled by the *handle*.op-rule.

The *handle*.F-rule returns a value from a handled computation. It substitutes the returned value into the return clause of a handler

Reduction frames

(hoisting frames) $\quad \mathcal{H} ::= \mathbf{let}\, x \leftarrow [\,]\, \mathbf{in}\, N \mid [\,]\, V \mid \mathbf{prj}_i\, [\,]$
(computation frames) $\quad \mathcal{C} ::= \mathcal{H} \mid \mathbf{handle}\, [\,]\, \mathbf{with}\, H$

Reduction $\boxed{M \longrightarrow M'}$

$$\begin{array}{lrcl}
(\beta.\times) & \mathbf{split}((V_1, V_2), x_1.x_2.M_1) & \longrightarrow & M[V_1/x_1, V_2/x_2] \\
(\beta.+) & \mathbf{case}(\mathbf{inj}_i\, V, x_1.M_1, x_2.M_2) & \longrightarrow & M_i[V/x_i] \\
(\beta.U) & \{M\}! & \longrightarrow & M \\
(\beta.F) & \mathbf{let}\, x \leftarrow \mathbf{return}\, V\, \mathbf{in}\, M & \longrightarrow & M[V/x] \\
(\beta.\to) & (\lambda x.M)\, V & \longrightarrow & M[V/x] \\
(\beta.\&) & \mathbf{prj}_i\, \langle M_1, M_2\rangle & \longrightarrow & M_i
\end{array}$$

(*hoist*.op)
$$\frac{x \notin FV(\mathcal{H})}{\mathcal{H}[\mathrm{op}\, V(\lambda x.M)] \longrightarrow \mathrm{op}\, V(\lambda x.\mathcal{H}[M])}$$

(*handle*.F)
$$\frac{H^{\mathrm{return}} = \lambda x.M}{\mathbf{handle}\, (\mathbf{return}\, V)\, \mathbf{with}\, H \longrightarrow M[V/x]}$$

(*handle*.op)
$$\frac{H^{\mathrm{op}} = \lambda p\, k.N \quad x \notin FV(H)}{\begin{array}{l}\mathbf{handle}\, \mathrm{op}\, V(\lambda x.M)\, \mathbf{with}\, H \\ \quad \longrightarrow N[V/p, \{\lambda x.\mathbf{handle}\, M\, \mathbf{with}\, H\}/k]\end{array}}$$

(*frame*)
$$\frac{M \longrightarrow M'}{\mathcal{C}[M] \longrightarrow \mathcal{C}[M']}$$

Figure 4. Operational Semantics for λ_{eff}

in exactly the same way that $\beta.F$-reduction substitutes a returned value into the body of a let binding.

The *handle*.op-rule is the most involved of the reduction rules. A handled operation application $\mathbf{handle}\ \mathrm{op}\ V(\lambda x.M)\ \mathbf{with}\ H$ reduces to the body of the operation clause $H^{\mathrm{op}} = \lambda p\, k.N$ with the parameter V substituted for p and the continuation $\lambda x.M$ substituted for k. Any further operation applications should be handled by the same handler H. Thus, we wrap H around M.

The *frame*-rule allows reduction to take place within any stack of computation frames, that is, inside any *evaluation context*.

The semantics is deterministic, as any term has at most one redex. Furthermore, reduction on well-typed terms always terminates.

Theorem 1 (Termination). *If $\Gamma \vdash_E M : C$ then reduction on M terminates.*

Proof sketch: The proof is by a relatively straightforward adaptation of Lindley's proof of strong normalisation for sums [26]. The interesting rule is *handle*.op, which reinvokes the handler, possibly many times, but always on a subterm of the original computation. As with Ariola et al.'s normalisation result for delimited continuations [1], termination depends crucially on the effect type system. □

Theorem 2 (Type soundness). *If $\vdash_{\{\}} M : FA$ then M reduces to a returned value* **return** *V of type A.*

Proof sketch: Define a *canonical* term to be any computation term of the form: $\mathbf{return}\ V$, $\lambda x.N$, $\langle\rangle$, $\langle V, W\rangle$, or $\mathrm{op}\ V(\lambda x.M)$. Induction on typing derivations shows progress: if $\vdash_E M : C$ then, either there exists M' such that $M \longrightarrow M'$, or M is canonical. By appeal to a substitution lemma, induction on typing derivations shows preservation: if $\Gamma \vdash_E M : C$ and $M \longrightarrow M'$ then $\Gamma \vdash_E M' : C$. □

3.3 Open Handlers

Our presentation of λ_{eff} gives an operational account of closed handlers. We can adapt λ_{eff} to support open handlers by making two small changes. The typing rule for handlers becomes:

$$\frac{\begin{array}{c} E = E' \oplus \{\mathrm{op}_i : A_i \to B_i\}_i \\ H = \{\mathbf{return}\ x \mapsto M\} \uplus \{\mathrm{op}_i\ p\ k \mapsto N_i\}_i \\ [\Gamma, p : A_i, k : U_{E'}(B_i \to C) \vdash_{E'} N_i : C]_i \\ \Gamma, x : A \vdash_{E'} M : C \end{array}}{\Gamma \vdash H : A\ {}^E\!\!\Rightarrow^{E'}\ C}$$

The only change to the original rule is that the input effects are now $E' \oplus E$ instead of just E, where $E' \oplus E$ is the extension of E' by E (where any clashes are resolved in favour of E).

The *handle*.op-rule is refined by extending the meaning of H^{op}, such that it is defined as before for operations that are explicitly handled by H, but is also defined as $\lambda p\,k.\mathrm{op}\ p(\lambda x.k\ x)$ for any other operation op. This means that any operation that is not explicitly handled gets forwarded.

In our simply-typed formalism, it is straightforward to translate any program that uses open handlers into an equivalent program that uses closed handlers. As any open handler handles a bounded number of operations, we can simply write down all of the implicit forwarding clauses explicitly. In practice, it seems desirable to offer both open and closed handlers, as in our Haskell library.

To take full advantage of open handlers in a typed language, one inevitably wants to add some kind of effect polymorphism. Indeed, our Haskell implementation provides effect polymorphism, encoded using type classes. We believe that effect polymorphism can be supported more smoothly using row polymorphism.

We briefly outline one path to supporting row polymorphism. The open handler rule from above can be rewritten as follows:

$$\frac{\begin{array}{c} E = \{\mathrm{op}_i : A_i \to B_i\}_i \uplus E_f \\ E' = E'' \uplus E_f \\ H = \{\mathbf{return}\ x \mapsto M\} \uplus \{\mathrm{op}_i\ p\ k \mapsto N_i\}_i \\ [\Gamma, p : A_i, k : U_{E'}(B_i \to C) \vdash_{E'} N_i : C]_i \\ \Gamma, x : A \vdash_{E'} M : C \end{array}}{\Gamma \vdash H : A\ {}^E\!\!\Rightarrow^{E'}\ C}$$

The key difference is that this version of the rule uses disjoint union $\uplus$ in place of extension $\oplus$, explicitly naming the collection of forwarded effects. One can now instantiate the meta variable E_f with a row variable. We would likely also wish to support polymorphism over E''. This is not difficult to achieve using a Remy-style [37] account of row typing if we insist that E'' only include operations in $\{\mathrm{op}_i\}_i$. We leave a full investigation of effect polymorphism for handlers to future work.

3.4 Shallow Handlers

Our presentation of λ_{eff} gives an operational account of deep handlers. In order to model shallow handlers we can make two small changes. The typing rule for handlers becomes:

$$\frac{\begin{array}{c} E = \{\mathrm{op}_i : A_i \to B_i\}_i \\ H = \{\mathbf{return}\ x \mapsto M\} \uplus \{\mathrm{op}_i\ p\ k \mapsto N_i\}_i \\ [\Gamma, p : A_i, k : U_E(B_i \to FA) \vdash_{E'} N_i : C]_i \\ \Gamma, x : A \vdash_{E'} M : C \end{array}}{\Gamma \vdash H : A\ {}^E\!\!\Rightarrow^{E'}\ C}$$

The only changes with respect to the original rule are to the types of the continuations, which now yield FA computations under the input effect signature E, rather than C computations under the output effect signature E'. The *handle*.op-rule is replaced by the *shallow-handle*.op-rule:

$$(\textit{shallow-handle}.\mathrm{op})\quad \frac{H^{\mathrm{op}} = \lambda p\,k.N \qquad x \notin FV(H)}{\mathbf{handle}\ \mathrm{op}\ V(\lambda x.M)\ \mathbf{with}\ H \longrightarrow N[V/p, \{\lambda x.M\}/k]}$$

which does not wrap the handler around the continuation. Of course, without recursion shallow handlers are rather weak.

4. Implementation

Any signature of operations can be viewed as a free algebra and represented as a functor. Every such functor gives rise to a free monad (Swierstra [43] gives a clear account of free monads for functional programmers). This yields a systematic way of building a monad to represent computations over a signature of operations.

We use our standard state example to illustrate. Concretely we can define the free monad over state as follows:

```
data FreeState s a =
    Ret a
  | Get () (s → FreeState s a)
  | Put s (() → FreeState s a)
instance Monad (FreeState s) where
  return       = Ret
  Ret v    >>= f = f v
  Get () k >>= f = Get () (λx → k x >>= f)
  Put s  k >>= f = Put s  (λx → k x >>= f)
```

The type *FreeState s a* is a particular instance of a free monad. It can be viewed as a computation tree. The leaves are labelled with *Ret v* and the nodes are labelled with *Get* () and *Put s*. There is one edge for each possible return value supplied to the continuation of *Get* and *Put* — a possibly infinite number for *Get* depending on the type of the state, and just one for *Put*. The bind operation performs a kind of substitution. To compute $c \gg\!= f$, the tree $f\ v$ is grafted onto each leaf *Ret v* of c.

The generic free monad construction can be defined as follows:

```
data Free f a = Ret a | Do (f (Free f a))
instance Functor f ⇒ Monad (Free f) where
  return     = Ret
  Ret v >>= f = f v
  Do op >>= f = Do (fmap (>>=f) op)
```

and we can instantiate it with state as follows:

```
data StateFunctor s a = GetF () (s → a) | PutF s (() → a)
  deriving Functor
```

where *FreeState s* is isomorphic to *Free* (*StateFunctor s*).

A handler for state is now simply a unary function whose argument has type *Free* (*StateFunctor s*). For instance:

```
stateH :: Free (StateFunctor s) a → (s → a)
stateH (Ret x)             = λs → x
stateH (Do (GetF () k))    = λs → stateH (k s) s
stateH (Do (PutF s k))     = λ_ → stateH (k ()) s
```

interprets a stateful computation as a function of type $s \to a$.

A limitation of the above free monad construction is that it is *closed* in that it can only handle operations in the signature. A key feature of our library is support for *open handlers* that handle a fixed set of operations in a specified way, and forward any other operations to be handled by an outer handler. To encode openness in GHC we take advantage of type classes and type families.

The code for open free monads is given in Figure 5. We split the type of each operation into two parts: a type declaration that defines the parameters to the operation, and a type family instance that defines the return type of the operation. For instance:

```
[operation | Put s :: s → () |]
```

generates:

```
data Put (e :: ⋆) (u :: ⋆) where
  Put :: s → Put s ()
type instance Return (Put s ()) = ()
```

The first type argument e encodes the *existential* type arguments of an operation, while the second type argument u encodes the *universal* type arguments of an operation. In the case of *Put* there is a single existential type argument s and no universal arguments. Using GADTs we can encode multiple arguments as tuples. Handler types are generated similarly.

Lines 1–2 of Figure 5 declare type families for operation return types and handler result types.

Lines 3–6 define a ternary type class $(h\,\text{`}\mathit{Handles}\text{`}\;op)\;e$. Each instance of this class defines the clause of handler h that handles operation op with existential type arguments bound to e. Of course, we do not supply the universal arguments, as the clause should be polymorphic in them. The functional dependency $h\;op \rightarrow a$ asserts that type a must be uniquely determined by types h and op. This is crucial for correctly implementing open handlers as we discuss further in Section 4.1. The **handles** quasiquoter generates type class constraints on the *Handles* type class.

Lines 7–14 define the monad *Comp h*, which is simply a free monad over the functor defined by those operations op that are handled by h (i.e. such that $(h\,\text{`}\mathit{Handles}\text{`}\;op)\;e$ is defined for some type e).

Lines 15–17 define the auxiliary *doOp* function, which realises an operation as an abstract computation of the appropriate type. The **operation** quasiquoter uses *doOp* to automatically generate a function for each operation. For instance, the above declarations for *Get* and *Put* generate the following functions:

```
get :: (h 'Handles' Get) s ⇒ Comp h s
get = doOp Get
put :: (h 'Handles' Put) s ⇒ s → Comp h ()
put s = doOp (Put s)
```

Finally, Lines 18–21 define the one remaining ingredient for the core library, the *handle* function, which takes a computation, a return clause, and a handler, and returns the result of handling the computation. We supply the return clause independently from the type class mechanism in order to simplify the implementation. The handler is automatically applied to the result of the continuation as specified in the operational semantics. This behaviour contrasts with the closed free monad code presented at the beginning of this subsection, which instead uses explicit recursion as with the shallow handlers for state and pipes.

We are making essential use of the type class mechanism. It is instructive to read the type of *handle* as taking a return clause, a list of operation clauses, one for each op such that $(h\,\text{`}\mathit{Handles}\text{`}\;op)\;e$ for some e, and returning a result. Thus the second argument of type h, as well as providing parameters to the handler, also, albeit indirectly, encodes the list of operation clauses.

The **handler** quasiquoter automatically generates a convenient wrapper meaning that programmers need never directly manipulate the constructor for a handler type — just as automatically generated operation wrappers mean that they need never directly manipulate the constructor for an operation type.

Limitations Our Haskell implementation of handlers has several limitations. First, because handlers are encoded as type classes and type classes are not first-class, neither are handlers. Second, because we abstract over handlers in order to simulate effect typing the types of the operation wrappers are more complex than necessary. Third, because we explicitly mention a parent handler in the type of open handlers, the order in which open handlers are composed can leak into types (this is not as bad as with monad transformers, as lifting is never required, but it is still undesirable).

All of these limitations arise from attempting to encode handlers in Haskell. None is inherent to handlers. We believe that a row-based effect type system along the lines of Leroy and Pesaux [23], Blume et al [5], or Lindley and Cheney [27] would provide a cleaner design.

```
1  type family Return (opApp :: ⋆) :: ⋆
2  type family Result (h :: ⋆) :: ⋆
3  class ((h :: ⋆) 'Handles' (op :: j → k → ⋆)) (e :: j) | h op → e
4    where
5      clause :: op e u →
6        (Return (op e u) → h → Result h) → h → Result h
7  data Comp h a where
8    Ret :: a → Comp h a
9    Do :: (h 'Handles' op) e ⇒
10     op e u → (Return (op e u) → Comp h a) → Comp h a
11 instance Monad (Comp h) where
12   return        = Ret
13   Ret v   >>= f = f v
14   Do op k >>= f = Do op (λx → k x >>= f)
15 doOp :: (h 'Handles' op) e ⇒
16          op e u → Comp h (Return (op e u))
17 doOp op = Do op return
18 handle :: Comp h a → (a → h → Result h) → h → Result h
19 handle (Ret v)     r h = r v h
20 handle (Do op k) r h =
21   clause op (λv h′ → handle (k v) r h′) h
```

Figure 5. Free Monad Implementation

```
1  type family Return (opApp :: ⋆) :: ⋆
2  type family Result (h :: ⋆) :: ⋆
3  class ((h :: ⋆) 'Handles' (op :: j → k → ⋆)) (e :: j) | h op → e
4    where
5      clause :: op e u → (Return (op e u) → h → Result h) →
6                                             h → Result h
7  newtype Comp h a =
8    Comp {handle :: (a → h → Result h) → h → Result h}
9  instance Monad (Comp h) where
10   return v = Comp (λk → k v)
11   Comp c >>= f = Comp (λk → c (λx → handle (f x) k))
12 doOp :: (h 'Handles' op) e ⇒
13          op e u → Comp h (Return (op e u))
14 doOp op = Comp (λk h → clause op k h)
```

Figure 6. Continuation Monad Implementation

The Codensity Monad It is well known that free monad computations can be optimised by composing with the *codensity monad*, which is essentially the continuation monad over a polymorphic return type [45].

The Continuation Monad We can in fact do even better by using the continuation monad directly, meaning that the *Ret* and *Do* constructors disappear completely. The continuation monad code is given in Figure 6. The difference from the free monad code begins on Line 7. The type constructor *Comp h* is exactly that of the continuation monad with return type $h \rightarrow \mathit{Result}\;h$. We choose not to factor through the continuation monad defined in the standard library as doing so hurts performance. The *handle* function is now exactly the deconstructor for *Comp*, while the *doOp* function is just $\mathit{Comp} \circ \mathit{clause}$. We explicitly η-expand *doOp* because GHC is unable to optimise the pointless version.

4.1 Open Handlers and Forwarding

The key trick for implementing forwarding is to parameterise a handler H by its parent handler h. Without this parameter we would have no way of describing the operations that are handled by both H and h. Now we can define the following type class instance:

$$\textbf{instance}\ (h\ \text{`}Handles\text{`}\ op)\ e \Rightarrow (H\ h\ \text{`}Handles\text{`}\ op)\ e\ \textbf{where}$$
$$clause\ op\ k\ h = doOp\ op \ggg= (\lambda x \rightarrow k\ x\ h)$$

The **handler** quasiquoter generates this boilerplate automatically for open handlers.

The functional dependency $(H\ \ h)\ op \rightarrow e$ is crucial here. Without it GHC would be unable to resolve the *clause* function. For instance, consider the *OpenState* handler. This must select from the following instances for *Get*:

$$\textbf{instance}\ (OpenState\ h\ s\ a\ \text{`}Handles\text{`}\ Get)\ s\ \textbf{where}$$
$$clause\ Get\ k\ (OpenState\ s) = k\ s\ (OpenState\ s)$$

$$\textbf{instance}\ (h\ \text{`}Handles\text{`}\ op)\ t \Rightarrow$$
$$(OpenState\ h\ s\ a\ \text{`}Handles\text{`}\ op)\ t\ \textbf{where}$$
$$clause\ op\ k\ h = doOp\ op \ggg= (\lambda x \rightarrow k\ x\ h)$$

Without the functional dependency the latter is chosen. This is because GHC tries to ensure that the same version of *clause* is used for *Get* t for any t, and the former is only valid if s is equal to t. The functional dependency asserts that t must be equal to s.

Because the type variable t does not appear in either of the types $OpenState\ \ h\ \ s\ \ a$ or op, and there is a functional dependency which states that $OpenState\ \ h\ \ s\ \ a$ and op uniquely determine e, GHC's default type inference gives up. Enabling the `UndecidableInstances` language option fixes this. We believe that our basic use of `UndecidableInstances` is well-founded (and decidable!), because of the type class constraint $(h\ \text{`}Handles\text{`}\ op)\ t$ which implies that h and op already uniquely determine t.

4.2 Shallow Handlers

It is relatively straightforward to adapt our free monad implementation to implement shallow handlers. The key change is to the type of the continuation argument of the *clause* function which must return a computation. It seems less clear how to adapt the continuation monad implementation.

4.3 Delimited Continuations

We now sketch an implementation of (open) effect handlers in terms of *delimited continuations* [8, 9]. These ideas underlie our OCaml, SML, and Racket implementations.

A variety of different delimited continuation operators are covered in the literature. Shan has recently shown that the four basic choices are straightforwardly inter-definable [39][6]. We choose to describe our implementation in terms of a minor variant of Danvy and Filinski's **shift** and **reset** operators [8] called **shift0** and **reset0**. The behaviour of **shift0** and **reset0** can be concisely summarised through the following reduction rule:

$$\textbf{reset0}\,(\mathcal{E}[\textbf{shift0}\,(\lambda k.M)]) \longrightarrow M[(\lambda x.\textbf{reset0}\,(\mathcal{E}[x]))/k]$$

where $\mathcal{E}$ ranges over call-by-value evaluation contexts.

The **reset0** operator delimits the start of a continuation, and the **shift0** operator captures the continuation up to the nearest enclosing **reset0**. Crucially, the captured continuation is wrapped in a further **reset0**. It is instructive to compare the above rule with the *handle*.op-rule, where **handle** – **with** H plays a similar role to **reset0**.

The implementations rely on the following key ingredients:

- A global (or thread-local) variable keeps a stack of handlers in the current dynamic scope.
- Each handler includes a map from the handled operations to the corresponding operation clause.

[6] These encodings do not preserve memory behaviour, so can sometimes introduce memory leaks.

To handle an effectful computation **handle** M **with** H:

- The handler H is added to the top of the stack.
- We invoke $\textbf{reset0}\,(H^{\textbf{return}}\ M)$.

To apply an operation (in direct style) $\widehat{\text{op}}\ p$:

1. We invoke **shift0** to capture the continuation k up to (but excluding) the next operation handler.
2. The top-most handler H is popped from the stack.
3. We let $k' = \lambda x.push\ H;\ \textbf{reset0}\,(k\ x)$, where $push\ H$ pushes H back onto the stack.
4. The clause corresponding to the operation, that is H^{op}, is applied to the parameter p and the continuation k'.
5. If there is no clause corresponding to this operation, it will be forwarded by the handler. If no other handlers enclose the operation, an exception is raised.

To support shallow handlers, one replaces **shift0** and **reset0** with **control0** and **prompt0**, which behave like **shift0** and **reset0**, except no **prompt0** is wrapped around the continuation:

$$\textbf{prompt0}\,(\mathcal{E}[\textbf{control0}\,(\lambda k.M)]) \longrightarrow M[(\lambda x.\mathcal{E}[x])/k]$$

4.4 Dynamic and Static Operations

Our Haskell implementation uses one static type per operation. A program execution cannot dynamically create a new operation. Because they do not provide effect typing, our other implementations do support dynamic operations, which can be created, closed upon and garbage collected. This makes some programs easier to write. For example, references can be represented as pairs of dynamically generated *Put* and *Get* operations. With only static operations, one has to parameterise *Put* and *Get* by some representation of a reference, and explicitly manage all of the state in a single handler.

Static effect typing for dynamic operations presents challenges:

- Writing an effect type system for dynamic operations involves some form of dependent types, as operations are now first-class objects of the language.
- Dynamic operations are difficult to implement as efficiently as static operations. In particular, it is not clear how to use the type system to pass only the relevant effects to each scope.

5. Performance Evaluation

To evaluate the performance of our Haskell library, we implemented a number of micro-benchmarks, comparing handler code against monadic code that makes use of existing libraries. The code for the micro-benchmarks can be found in the GitHub repository at:

`http://github.com/slindley/effect-handlers/Benchmarks`

Detailed performance results can be found in Appendix A.

Our primary goal was to check that the handler abstraction does not cripple performance. We rely on GHC to optimise away many of the abstractions we introduce. In the future we envisage building handlers into the core of a programming language. We might reasonably hope to do significantly better than in the library-based approach by tailoring optimisations to be aware of handlers.

The results confirm that the Haskell library performs adequately. The performance of the continuation monad implementation of handlers is typically no worse than around two thirds that of baseline code. In some cases the continuation monad implementation actually outperforms existing implementations. The continuation monad implementation always outperforms the codensity monad implementation (sometimes by more than an order of magnitude), which always outperforms the free monad implementation. Usually standard handlers outperform shallow handlers, pipes being an exception, where for large numbers of nested sub-pipes shallow handlers outperform even the continuation monad implementation of standard handlers.

6. Related Work

Algebraic Effects and Effect Handlers Effect operations were pioneered by Plotkin and Power [35], leading to an algebraic account of computational effects [34] and their combination [15]. Effect handlers were added to the theory in order to support exception handling [36]. Recent work incorporates additional computational effects within the algebraic framework, for example, local state [41], and applies the algebraic theory of effects to new problem domains, such as effect-dependent program transformations [19], and logical-relations arguments [20].

While mostly denotational in nature, operational accounts of algebraic effects (without handlers) do exist. Plotkin and Power [33] gave operational semantics to algebraic effects in a call-by-value setting, and Johann et al. [32] gave operational semantics to algebraic effects in a call-by-name setting.

Effect Handler Implementations Bauer and Pretnar's effectful strict statically-typed language *Eff* [2] has built-in support for algebraic effects and effect handlers. Like our ML implementations, it lacks an effect type system. Eff implements dynamic generation of new operations and effects, which we only consider statically. Visscher has implemented the `effects` library [44] for Haskell inspired by Eff. The core idea is to layer continuation monads in the style of Filinski [10], using Haskell type classes to automatically infer lifting between layers. McBride's language *Frank* [29] is similar to Eff, but with an effect system along the lines of ours. It supports only shallow handlers and employs a novel form of effect polymorphism which elides effect variables entirely. Brady [6] has implemented an effect handlers library for the dependently-typed language Idris. It takes advantage of dependent types for resource tracking. The current design has some limitations compared with the other handler implementations. In particular, the composition of other effects with non-determinism is not well-behaved.

Monadic Reflection and Layered Monads Filinski's work on monadic reflection and layered monads is closely related to effect handlers [11]. Monadic reflection supports a similar style of composing effects. The key difference is that monadic reflection interprets monadic computations in terms of other monadic computations, rather than abstracting over and interpreting operations. Filinski's system is nominal (an effect is the name of a monad), whereas ours is structural (an effect is a collections of operations).

Monad Transformers and Inferred Lifting Jaskelioff and Moggi [17] develop the theory of monad transformers and lifting of effect operations. Jaskelioff's Monatron [16] is a monad transformer library based on this development.

Schrijvers and Oliveira [38] infer lifting in Haskell using a zipper structure at the level of type classes to traverse the monad transformer stack. Swamy et al. [42] add support for monads in ML, inferring not only where and how to lift operations, but also where to insert return and bind statements. In both approaches, once the required monad transformers have been defined, the desired lifting is inferred automatically.

7. Conclusion

Algebraic effects and handlers provide a promising approach for supporting effectful computations in functional languages. By offering a new form of modularity, they create possibilities for library design and reusability that are just beginning to emerge. This paper shows that implementing these constructs is within the reach of current compiler technology.

Acknowledgments

The λ_{eff} calculus stemmed from discussions of the first author with Andrej Bauer and Matija Pretnar in Ljubljana and Swansea.

The authors would like to thank Stevan Andjelkovic, Danel Ahman, Bob Atkey, Andrej Bauer, Brian Campbell, James Cheney, Derek Dreyer, Andrzej Filinski, Ben Kavanagh, Neel Krishnaswami, Conor McBride, James McKinna, Gordon Plotkin, Matija Pretnar, Alex Simpson, Sam Staton, Phil Wadler, and the POPL 2013, PLDI 2013, and ICFP 2013 referees, for useful conversations, comments and suggestions. We are grateful to Gabriel Gonzalez for pointing out a flaw in the pipes benchmarks in an earlier draft of this paper. The type system originated from a visit by the first author to Andrej Bauer and Matija Pretnar in Ljubljana, supported by the Laboratory for Foundations of Computer Science. This work was supported by a Google Research Award, EPSRC grants EP/J014591/1 and EP/H005633/1, a SICSA studentship, an Edinburgh University Informatics School studentship, and an Isaac Newton Trust starter grant.

References

[1] Z. M. Ariola, H. Herbelin, and A. Sabry. A type-theoretic foundation of delimited continuations. *Higher-Order and Symbolic Computation*, 22(3):233–273, 2009.

[2] A. Bauer and M. Pretnar. Programming with algebraic effects and handlers. *CoRR*, abs/1203.1539, 2012.

[3] N. Benton and A. Kennedy. Exceptional syntax. *J. Funct. Program.*, 11(4):395–410, 2001.

[4] N. Benton, J. Hughes, and E. Moggi. Monads and effects. In *APPSEM 2000*. Springer-Verlag, 2002.

[5] M. Blume, U. A. Acar, and W. Chae. Exception handlers as extensible cases. In *APLAS*. Springer-Verlag, 2008.

[6] E. Brady. Programming and reasoning with algebraic effects and dependent types. In *ICFP*. ACM, 2013.

[7] B. C. d. S. Oliveira, T. Schrijvers, and W. R. Cook. MRI: Modular reasoning about interference in incremental programming. *J. Funct. Program.*, 22(6):797–852, 2012.

[8] O. Danvy and A. Filinski. Abstracting control. In *LFP*. ACM, 1990.

[9] M. Felleisen. The theory and practice of first-class prompts. In *POPL*. ACM, 1988.

[10] A. Filinski. Representing layered monads. In *POPL*. ACM, 1999.

[11] A. Filinski. Monads in action. In *POPL*. ACM, 2010.

[12] A. Gill. The mtl package (2.1.2), 2012. `http://hackage.haskell.org/package/mtl`.

[13] G. Gonzalez. pipes-2.5: Faster and slimmer, 2012. `http://www.haskellforall.com/2012/10/pipes-25-faster-and-slimmer.html`.

[14] G. Gonzalez. The pipes package (3.2.0), 2013. `http://hackage.haskell.org/package/pipes`.

[15] M. Hyland, G. D. Plotkin, and J. Power. Combining effects: Sum and tensor. *Theoret. Comput. Sci.*, pages 70–99, 2006.

[16] M. Jaskelioff. Monatron: An extensible monad transformer library. In *IFL*. Springer-Verlag, 2008.

[17] M. Jaskelioff and E. Moggi. Monad transformers as monoid transformers. *Theoret. Comput. Sci.*, 411(51–52), 2010.

[18] M. P. Jones. Functional programming with overloading and higher-order polymorphism. In *Advanced Functional Programming*, 1995.

[19] O. Kammar and G. D. Plotkin. Algebraic foundations for effect-dependent optimisations. In *POPL*. ACM, 2012.

[20] S. Katsumata. Relating computational effects by $\top\top$-lifting. *Inf. Comput.*, 222, 2013.

[21] O. Kiselyov. Iteratees. In *FLOPS*. Springer-Verlag, 2012.

[22] O. Kiselyov and C.-c. Shan. Embedded probabilistic programming. In *DSL*. Springer-Verlag, 2009.

[23] X. Leroy and F. Pessaux. Type-based analysis of uncaught exceptions. *ACM Trans. Program. Lang. Syst.*, pages 340–377, 2000.

[24] P. B. Levy. *Call-By-Push-Value: A Functional/Imperative Synthesis*, volume 2 of *Semantics Structures in Computation*. Springer, 2004.

[25] S. Liang, P. Hudak, and M. P. Jones. Monad transformers and modular interpreters. In *POPL*. ACM, 1995.

[26] S. Lindley. Extensional rewriting with sums. In *TLCA*. Springer-Verlag, 2007.

[27] S. Lindley and J. Cheney. Row-based effect types for database integration. In *TLDI*. ACM, 2012.

[28] G. Mainland. Why it's nice to be quoted: quasiquoting for Haskell. In *Haskell*. ACM, 2007.

[29] C. McBride. Frank (0.3), 2012. `http://hackage.haskell.org/package/Frank`.

[30] E. Moggi. Computational lambda-calculus and monads. In *LICS*. IEEE Computer Society, 1989.

[31] B. O'Sullivan. The criterion package (0.8.0.0), 2013. `http://hackage.haskell.org/package/criterion`.

[32] A. S. Patricia Johann and J. Voigtländer. A generic operational metatheory for algebraic effects. In *LICS*. IEEE Computer Society, 2010.

[33] G. D. Plotkin and J. Power. Adequacy for algebraic effects. In *FoSSaCS*. Springer-Verlag, 2001.

[34] G. D. Plotkin and J. Power. Notions of computation determine monads. In *FoSSaCS*. Springer-Verlag, 2002.

[35] G. D. Plotkin and J. Power. Algebraic operations and generic effects. *Appl. Categ. Structures*, 11(1):69–94, 2003.

[36] G. D. Plotkin and M. Pretnar. Handlers of algebraic effects. In *ESOP*. Springer-Verlag, 2009.

[37] D. Rémy. Type inference for records in a natural extension of ML. In C. A. Gunter and J. C. Mitchell, editors, *Theoretical Aspects Of Object-Oriented Programming. Types, Semantics and Language Design*. MIT Press, 1993.

[38] T. Schrijvers and B. C. d. S. Oliveira. Monads, zippers and views: virtualizing the monad stack. In *ICFP*. ACM, 2011.

[39] C.-c. Shan. A static simulation of dynamic delimited control. *Higher-Order and Symbolic Computation*, 20(4):371–401, 2007.

[40] T. Sheard and S. L. P. Jones. Template meta-programming for Haskell. *SIGPLAN Notices*, 37(12):60–75, 2002.

[41] S. Staton. Two cotensors in one: Presentations of algebraic theories for local state and fresh names. *Electr. Notes Theor. Comput. Sci.*, 249:471–490, 2009.

[42] N. Swamy, N. Guts, D. Leijen, and M. Hicks. Lightweight monadic programming in ML. In *ICFP*. ACM, 2011.

[43] W. Swierstra. Data types à la carte. *J. Funct. Program.*, 18(4):423–436, 2008.

[44] S. Visscher. The effects package (0.2.2), 2012. `http://hackage.haskell.org/package/effects`.

[45] J. Voigtländer. Asymptotic improvement of computations over free monads. In *MPC*. Springer-Verlag, 2008.

[46] P. Wadler. Monads for functional programming. In *Advanced Functional Programming*. Springer-Verlag, 1995.

A. Performance Results

All performance testing was conducted with the `-O2` compiler flag enabled using a PC with a quad-core Intel i7-3770K CPU running at 3.50GHz CPU and 32GB of RAM, running GHC 7.6.1 on Ubuntu Linux 12.10. We used O'Sullivan's `criterion` library [31] to sample each micro-benchmark ten times.

The code for the micro-benchmarks can be found in the GitHub repository at:

`http://github.com/slindley/effect-handlers/Benchmarks`

A.1 State

As a basic sanity check we tested the following function on state:

$$\begin{array}{l} count :: SComp\ Int\ Int \\ count = \\ \quad \mathbf{do}\ i \leftarrow get; \\ \quad\quad \mathbf{if}\ i \equiv 0\ \mathbf{then}\ return\ i \\ \quad\quad \mathbf{else\ do}\ put\ (i-1); count \end{array}$$

We used 10^8 as the initial value for the state. We tested implementations using: the state monad, three different versions of standard deep handlers, and one implementation of shallow handlers. As a control, we also tested a pure version of *count*. In each case we used open handlers for interpreting state.

Implementation	Time (ms)	Relative Speed
pure	51	1.00
state monad	51	1.00
handlers (continuations)	77	0.67
handlers (free monad)	5083	0.01
handlers (codensity)	2550	0.02
shallow handlers	5530	0.01

Table 1. State

The results are shown in Table 1. GHC is optimised for monadic programming, so there is no cost to using a state monad over a pure program. The continuation monad implementation runs at two thirds of the speed of the baseline. The free monad implementation is a hundred times slower than the baseline. Using a codensity monad gives a two times speed-up to the free monad implementation. Shallow handlers are implemented using a free monad and are slowest of all.

A.2 Flat Pipes

We tested our pipes implementation using a flat pipeline previously used by the author of the `pipes` library for comparing performance between the `pipes` library and other libraries [13]. The pipeline consists of a producer that yields in turn the integers in the sequence $[1 \mathinner{..} n]$, for some n, connected to a consumer that ignores all inputs and loops forever. The `pipes` library optionally takes advantage of GHC rewrite rules to define special code optimisations for `pipes` code. We tested against `pipes` with and without the rewrite rules enabled. The results are shown in Table 2 for $n = 10^8$. The continuation monad implementation is nearly twice as fast as the `pipes` library without rewrite rules enabled. Enabling the rewrite rules makes a significant difference. In this case the `pipes` library is faster than the continuation monad implementation. The free monad and codensity implementations are slower than the `pipes` library, but the differential is much smaller than in the case of the *count* micro-benchmark. Interestingly, shallow handlers outperform the free monad implementation of standard handlers.

Implementation	Time (ms)	Relative Speed
`pipes` library	3398	1.00
`pipes` library + rewrites	1304	2.61
handlers (continuations)	1820	1.87
handlers (free monad)	6736	0.50
handlers (codensity)	3918	0.87
shallow handlers	5239	0.65

Table 2. Flat Pipes

A.3 Nested Pipes

To test the scalability of handlers we implemented a deeply-nested pipes computation constructed from 2^n sub-pipes, for a range of values of n. The results are shown in Table 5. They are intriguing as the relative performance varies according to the number of sub-pipes. The relative performance is shown graphically in Figure 7. The `pipes` library always out-performs all of our libraries, even with GHC rewrite rules disabled. The continuation monad implementation is relatively constant at around two thirds the speed of the `pipes` library. What is particularly notable is that as the level of nesting increases, the performance of shallow handlers eventually overtakes that of the continuation monad implementation.

One possible reason for the `pipes` library outperforming our continuation monad implementation on nested pipes is that it is in fact based on a free monad, and the implementation takes advantage of the reified representation of computations to optimise the case where an input is forwarded through several pipes.

We are not sure why shallow pipes perform so well on deeply-nested pipes, but suspect it may be due to the simpler definition of pipes for shallow handlers, as compared with that for standard handlers, opening up optimisation opportunities along the lines of those explicitly encoded in the `pipes` library.

We conjecture that the anomalous dip at 2^{11} sub-pipes for the bottom three lines in Figure 7 is due to cache effects.

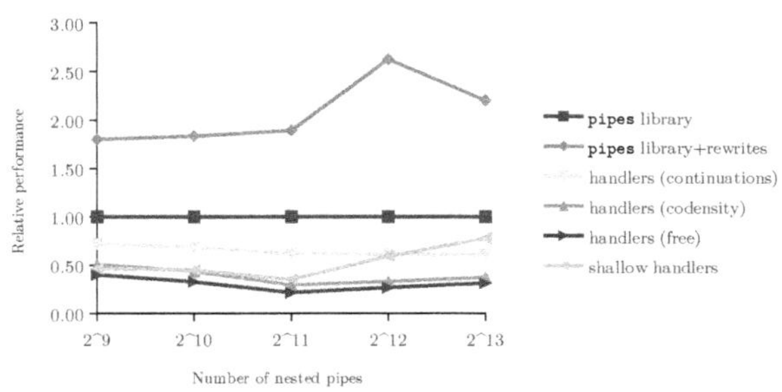

Figure 7. Relative Performance of Nested Pipes

A.4 The n-Queens Problem

To test the performance of handlers that invoke the continuation zero or many times, we implemented the classic n-queens problem in terms of an n-ary *Choose* operation:

$$[\textbf{operation} \mid \forall a. \mathit{Choose} :: [a] \rightarrow a \mid]$$

We wrote a handler that returns the first correct solution for the n-queens problem, and tested against a hand-coded n-queens solver. We tested both algorithms with $n = 20$.

Implementation	Time (ms)	Relative Speed
hand-coded	160	1.00
handlers	237	0.67

Table 3. n-Queens

The results are shown in Table 3. The handler version is about two thirds the speed of the hand-coded version.

A.5 Aspect-Oriented Programming

Effect handlers can be used to implement a form of aspect-oriented programming. We tested an expression evaluator taken from Oliveira et al.'s work on monadic mixins [7]. The expression evaluator is extended to output logging information whenever entering or exiting a recursive call, and to output the environment whenever entering a recursive call. We compared a hand-coded evaluator with Oliveira et al.'s mixin-based evaluator and an evaluator implemented using our continuation monad implementation of standard handlers. We tested each evaluator on the same randomly generated expression containing 2^{12} leaf nodes.

Implementation	Time (ms)
hand-coded	6516
mixins	6465
handlers (continuations)	6526

Table 4. Aspect-Oriented Programming

The results are shown in Table 4. The performance is almost identical for each of the three implementations, indicating no abstraction overhead.

2^9 sub-pipes

Implementation	Time (ms)	Relative Speed
`pipes` library	41	1.00
`pipes` library + rewrites	23	1.80
handlers (continuations)	57	0.72
handlers (free monad)	103	0.40
handlers (codensity)	81	0.51
shallow handlers	88	0.47

2^{10} sub-pipes

Implementation	Time (ms)	Relative Speed
`pipes` library	90	1.00
`pipes` library + rewrites	49	1.84
handlers (continuations)	131	0.69
handlers (free monad)	275	0.33
handlers (codensity)	206	0.44
shallow handlers	198	0.45

2^{11} sub-pipes

Implementation	Time (ms)	Relative Speed
`pipes` library	209	1.00
`pipes` library + rewrites	111	1.89
handlers (continuations)	336	0.62
handlers (free monad)	990	0.21
handlers (codensity)	716	0.29
shallow handlers	595	0.35

2^{12} sub-pipes

Implementation	Time (ms)	Relative Speed
`pipes` library	721	1.00
`pipes` library + rewrites	274	2.63
handlers (continuations)	1181	0.61
handlers (free monad)	2701	0.27
handlers (codensity)	2178	0.33
shallow handlers	1216	0.59

2^{13} sub-pipes

Implementation	Time (ms)	Relative Speed
`pipes` library	1931	1.00
`pipes` library + rewrites	877	2.20
handlers (continuations)	3147	0.61
handlers (free monad)	6172	0.31
handlers (codensity)	5188	0.37
shallow handlers	2470	0.78

Table 5. Nested Pipes

Computer Science as a School Subject

Simon Peyton Jones
Microsoft Research Cambridge
simonpj@microsoft.com

Abstract

Computer science is one of the richest, most exciting disciplines on the planet, yet any teenager will tell you that ICT (as it is called in UK schools — "information and communication technology") is focused almost entirely on the use and application of computers, and in practice covers nothing about how computers work, nor programming, nor anything of the discipline of computer science as we understand it. Over the last two decades, computing at school has drifted from writing adventure games on the BBC Micro to writing business plans in Excel.

This is bad for our young people's education, and it is bad for our economy. Nor is this phenomenon restricted to the UK: many countries are struggling with the same issues. Our young people should be educated not only in the application and use of digital technology, but also in how it works, and its foundational principles. Lacking such knowledge renders them powerless in the face of complex and opaque technology, disenfranchises them from making informed decisions about the digital society, and deprives our nations of a well-qualified stream of students enthusiastic and able to envision and design new digital systems.

Can anything be done, given the enormous inertia of our various countries' educational systems? Sometimes, yes. After a decade of stasis, change has come to the UK. Over the last 18 months, there has been a wholesale reform of the English school computing curriculum, and substantial movement in Scotland and Wales. It now seems likely that computer science will, for the first time, become part of every child's education. This change has been driven not by institutions or by the government, but by a grass-roots movement of parents, teachers, university academics, software developers, and others. A key agent in this grass-roots movement—although not the only one—is the Computing At School Working Group (CAS).

In this talk I will describe how CAS was born and developed, and the radical changes that have taken place since in the UK. I hope that this may be encouraging for those pushing water uphill in other parts of the world, and I will also try to draw out some lessons from our experience that may be useful to others.

Categories and Subject Descriptors K.3.2 [*Computers and Education*]: Computer and Information Science Education

Keywords Computing; School curricula

Further reading:

- Computing at School Working Group: `http://computingatschool.org.uk/`
- *Shut down or restart: the way forward for computing in UK schools*, Royal Society, January 2012: `http://royalsociety.org/education/policy/computing-in-schools/report/`
- Papers on the issues in the UK: `http://research.microsoft.com/~simonpj/papers/cas/`
- Broader papers on the issues: `http://community.computingatschool.org.uk/resources/46`

ICFP '13, September 25–27, 2013, Boston, MA, USA.
ACM 978-1-4503-2326-0/13/09.
http://dx.doi.org/10.1145/2500365.2500609

Correctness of an STM Haskell Implementation

Manfred Schmidt-Schauß David Sabel
Goethe-University Frankfurt, Germany
{schauss,sabel}@ki.cs.uni-frankfurt.de

Abstract

A concurrent implementation of software transactional memory in Concurrent Haskell using a call-by-need functional language with processes and futures is given. The description of the small-step operational semantics is precise and explicit, and employs an early abort of conflicting transactions. A proof of correctness of the implementation is given for a contextual semantics with may- and should-convergence. This implies that our implementation is a correct evaluator for an abstract specification equipped with a big-step semantics.

Categories and Subject Descriptors D.3.1 [*Programming Languages*]: Formal Definitions and Theory—Semantics; D.3.2 [*Programming Languages*]: Language Classifications—Applicative (functional) languages; D.3.3 [*Programming Languages*]: Language Constructs and Features—Concurrent programming structures; F.3.2 [*Logics and Meanings of Programs*]: Semantics of Programming Languages—Operational semantics; F.1.2 [*Computation by Abstract Devices*]: Modes of Computation—Parallelism and concurrency

General Terms Languages, Theory, Verification

Keywords Functional Programming, Concurrent Programming, Semantics, Software Transactional Memory, Haskell

1. Introduction

Due to the recent development in hardware and software, concurrent and parallel programming is getting more and more important, and thus there is a need for semantical investigations in concurrent programming. In this paper we investigate programming models of concurrent processes (threads) where several processes may access shared memory. Concurrent access and independency of processes lead to the well-known problems of conflicting memory use and thus requires protection of critical sections to ensure mutual exclusion. Over the years several programming primitives like locks, semaphores, monitors, etc. have been introduced and used to ensure this atomicity of memory operations in a concurrent setting. However, the explicit use of locking mechanisms is error-prone – the programmer may omit to set or release a lock resulting in deadlocks or race conditions – and it is also often inefficient, since setting too many locks may sequentialize program execution and prohibit concurrent evaluation. Another obstacle of lock-based concurrency is that composing larger programs from smaller ones is usually impossible [6].

A recent approach to overcome these difficulties is software transactional memory (STM) [6, 7, 16, 17] where operations on the shared memory are viewed as *transactions* on the memory, i.e. several small operations (like read and write of memory locations) are compound to a transaction and then the system (the transaction manager) ensures that the transaction is performed in an atomic, isolated, and consistent manner. I.e., the programmer can assume that all the transactions are performed sequentially and isolated, while the runtime system may perform them concurrently and interleaved and may even try sequences of actions several times (invisible to the programmer). This removes the burden from the programmer to set locks and to keep track of them. Composability of transactions is another very helpful feature of STM. We focus on the Haskell-based approach in [6, 7], which provides even more advantages like separation of different kinds of side effects (`IO` and `STM`) by monadic programming and the type system of Haskell. Memory-transactions are indicated in the program by marking a sequence of actions as atomic.

Though STM is easy to use for the programmer, implementing a *correct* transaction manager is considerably harder. Hurdles are an exact specification of the correctness properties, of course to provide an implementation, and to prove its correctness and the validity of the properties. In this paper we will address and solve these problems for a functional, concurrent language which models Concurrent Haskell extended by memory transactions. As a specification calculus, we start with *SHF* (STM-Haskell with futures) that is rather close to STM-Haskell [6, 7] and shares some ideas with the concurrent call-by-need process calculus investigated in [12]. In contrast to STM-Haskell threads are modelled by futures (which are however implementable in Concurrent Haskell using `unsafeInterleaveIO` in a safe manner [13]), *SHF* has no explicit exceptions, it uses call-by-need evaluation and bindings in the environment for sharing, and – for simplicity – it is equipped with a monomorphic type system. We keep the monadic modelling for the separation of `IO` and `STM` and the composability, in particular the selection composability by `orElse`. A big-step operational semantics is given for *SHF*, which is obviously correct, since transactions are executed in isolation, and their effects on the shared memory are only observable after a successful execution. However, this semantics is *not implementable*, due to undecidable execution conditions in the big-step semantics. Thus the purpose of defining *SHF* standard reduction is not the implementation but the *specification* of a correct interpreter for *SHF*.

Secondly, we define a concurrent implementation of *SHF* by introducing the concurrent calculus *CSHF*. *CSHF* is close to a real implementation, since its operational semantics is formulated as a detailed, precise and complete small-step reduction semantics where all precautions and retries of the transactions are explic-

ICFP '13, September 25–27, 2013, Boston, MA, USA.

http://dx.doi.org/10.1145/10.1145/2500365.2500585

itly represented. I.e., the small-step reductions are defined with an appropriate granularity to make them implementable. Features of *CSHF* are registration of threads at transactional variables (TVars) and forced aborts of transactions in case of conflicts. All applicability conditions for the reductions are decidable. *CSHF* is designed to enable concurrent (i.e. interleaved) execution of threads as much as possible, i.e. there are only very short phases where internal locking mechanisms are used to prevent race conditions.

We also implemented *CSHF* as a prototypical library in Haskell[1], which provides the same core interface as Haskell's STM implementation[2], and is (in contrast to *CSHF*) polymorphically typed. Internally it performs the steps as they are defined by the small-step semantics of *CSHF*. Our implementation behaves as expected and thus gives evidence of the correct design of *CSHF*.

The main goal of our investigation is to show that the concurrent implementation fulfills the specification. Here we use the strong criterion of contextual equivalence w.r.t. may- as well as should-convergence in both calculi, where may-convergence means that a process has the ability to evaluate to a successful process, and should-convergence means that the ability to become successful is never lost on every reduction path. Observing also should-convergence for contextual equivalence ensures that it is not permitted to transform a program P that cannot reach an error-state (i.e. a state that is not may-convergent) into a program that can reach an error-state. Compared with must-convergence, which requires termination on every computation path, should-convergence in combination with may-convergence judges busy-wait as non-erroneous behavior, and also contextual equivalence is invariant under restricting reductions to fair ones (see e.g. [10, 12]). Compared with definitions of contextual equivalences that include evaluation traces, using may- and should-convergence provides a coarser definition of equivalence.

In Main Theorem 4.3 we obtain the important result that the implementation mapping ψ is *observationally correct* [15], i.e. for every context D and process P in *SHF* it holds: $D[P]$ may-converges (or should-converges, resp.), if, and only if $\psi(D)[\psi(P)]$ is may-convergent (should-convergent) in *CSHF*. Observational correctness thus shows that may- and should-convergence is preserved and reflected by the implementation ψ (i.e. ψ is convergence equivalent) and the tests used for contextual equivalence are translated in a compositional way. A direct consequence is also that ψ is *adequate*, i.e. the implementation preserves all contextual inequalities and thus does not introduce new equalities (which would introduce confusion in the implementation). Note that even the proof of convergence equivalence of ψ is a strong result, since it implies that *CSHF* is a correct evaluator for *SHF*.

Our notion of correctness is rather strong, since it implies the properties of the concurrent program that are aimed at in other papers like atomicity, opacity, asf. A surprising insight is that early abortion of conflicting transactions is *necessary* to make the implementation correct, where "early" means that a committing transaction must abort other conflicting transactions. This equivalence of *SHF* and *CSHF* has the following consequences: There is a guarantee that error-free *SHF*-programs are mapped to error-free *CSHF*-ones; error-freeness of a concurrent program means that no execution possibility leads to a state which is a dead end insofar as success can not be reached from this state. In particular if the *SHF*-program is free of deadlocks, then the translated CSHF-program is also free of deadlocks. The implementation CSHF will also guarantee a form of global progress or liveness, if threads are fairly executed: If several transactions in CSHF are active, and at least one transaction could potentially reach its commit-phase if running alone, then either the whole process terminates successfully (for other reasons), or at least one of the transactions will reach its commit-phase also under concurrent execution.

Comparing our results with the implementation of STM-Haskell in [7], our work is a justification for the correctness of most of the design decisions of their implementation. However, the implementations behave slightly different which will be discussed in Section 5. The reason for not using the STM-Haskell implementation in [7] is that "formalizing" this implementation as a calculus is not easily possible, since e.g. it requires a test for pointer equality, which is cumbersome in a call-by-need calculus with indirections (represented by binding chains).

Outline. In Section 2 we define the (specification) calculus *SHF*, by explaining its syntax and operational semantics. The concurrent implementation in form of the calculus *CSHF* is introduced in Section 3. In Section 4 we provide the translation ψ : *SHF* $\rightarrow$ *CSHF* and prove that ψ is observationally correct which shows correctness of the implementation. We discuss related work in Section 5 and finally conclude in Section 6. Due to space reasons not all proofs are included in the paper but can be found in the technical report [14].

2. The SHF-Calculus

The syntax of *SHF* and its *processes Proc* is in Fig. 1(a). We assume a countable infinite set of variables (denoted by $x, y, z, \ldots$) and a countable infinite set of *identifiers* (denoted by u, u') to identify threads.

In a *parallel composition* $P_1 \mid P_2$ the processes P_1 and P_2 run concurrently, and the *name restriction* $\nu x.P$ restricts the scope of x to process P. A *concurrent thread* $\langle u \wr x \rangle \Leftarrow e$ has *identifier* u and evaluates the expression e binding the result to the variable x (called the *future* x). A process has usually one distinguished thread, the *main thread*, denoted by $\langle u \wr x \rangle \stackrel{\text{main}}{\Longleftarrow} e$. Evaluation of the main thread is enforced, which does not hold for other threads. *TVars* $x\,\mathbf{t}\,e$ are the transactional (mutable) variables with name x and content e. They can only be accessed inside STM-transactions. *Bindings* $x = e$ model globally shared expressions, where we call x a *binding variable*. Futures and names of TVars are called *component-names*.

We assume a partitioned set of *data constructors*, where each family represents a type constructor T. The T-data constructors are ordered (denoted with $c_1, \ldots, c_{|T|}$). Each type constructor T and each data constructor c has an arity $\text{ar}(T) \geq 0$ ($\text{ar}(c) \geq 0$, resp.). The functional language has variables, *abstractions* $\lambda x.e$, and *applications* $(e_1\ e_2)$, *constructor applications* $(c\ e_1 \ldots e_{\text{ar}(c)})$, `case`-*expressions* where for every type constructor T there is one $\texttt{case}_T$-construct. For $\texttt{case}_T$ there is exactly one `case`-*alternative* $(c_{T,i}\ x_1 \ldots x_{\text{ar}(c_{T,i})} \rightarrow e_i)$ for every constructor $c_{T,i}$ of type constructor T where the variables x_i become bound with scope e_i. In a *pattern* $c_{T,i}\ x_1 \ldots x_{\text{ar}(c_{T,i})}$ the variables x_i must be pairwise distinct. We sometimes abbreviate the `case`-alternatives with $alts$. Further constructs are `seq`-*expressions* $(\texttt{seq}\ e_1\ e_2)$ for strict evaluation, and `letrec`-*expressions* to implement local sharing and recursive bindings. In $\texttt{letrec}\ x_1 = e_1, \ldots, x_n = e_n\ \texttt{in}\ e$ the variables x_i must be pairwise distinct and the bindings $x_i = e_i$ are recursive, i.e. the scope of x_i is $e_1, \ldots, e_n$ and e.

Monadic expressions comprise variants for the IO- and the STM-monad of the "bind" operator `>>=` for sequential composition of actions, and the `return`-operator. For the STM-monad `newTVar`, `readTVar`, and `writeTVar` are available to create and access TVars, the primitive `retry` to abort and restart the STM-transaction, and `orElse` $e_1\ e_2$ to compose an STM-transaction from e_1, e_2: `orElse` returns if e_1 is successful and if it catches a `retry`

[1] The documented source code and some instructions are available from http://www.ki.cs.uni-frankfurt.de/research/stm

[2] http://hackage.haskell.org/package/stm

$$P, P_i \in \mathit{Proc} ::= P_1 \mid P_2 \mid \nu x.P \mid \langle u \wr x\rangle \Leftarrow e \mid x = e \mid x\,\mathbf{t}\,e$$

$$\begin{aligned}e, e_i \in \mathit{Expr} ::=\ & x \mid m \mid \lambda x.e \mid (e_1\ e_2) \mid (c\ e_1 \ldots e_{\mathrm{ar}(c)})\\ & \mid \mathtt{seq}\ e_1\ e_2 \mid \mathtt{letrec}\ x_1 = e_1, \ldots, x_n = e_n\ \mathtt{in}\ e\\ & \mid \mathtt{case}_T\ e\ \mathtt{of}\ alt_{T,1} \ldots alt_{T,|T|}\\ & \quad \text{where } alt_{T,i} = (c_{T,i}\ x_1 \ldots x_{\mathrm{ar}(c_{T,i})} \to e_i)\end{aligned}$$

$$\begin{aligned}m \in \mathit{MExpr} ::=\ & \mathtt{return}_{\mathtt{IO}}\ e \mid e_1 \gg\!=_{\mathtt{IO}} e_2 \mid \mathtt{future}\ e\\ & \mid \mathtt{atomically}\ e \mid \mathtt{return}_{\mathtt{STM}}\ e \mid e_1 \gg\!=_{\mathtt{STM}} e_2 \mid \mathtt{retry}\\ & \mid \mathtt{orElse}\ e_1\ e_2 \mid \mathtt{newTVar}\ e \mid \mathtt{readTVar}\ e \mid \mathtt{writeTVar}\ e\end{aligned}$$

$$\tau, \tau_i \in \mathit{Typ} ::= \mathtt{IO}\ \tau \mid \mathtt{STM}\ \tau \mid \mathtt{TVar}\ \tau \mid (T\ \tau_1\ \ldots\ \tau_n) \mid \tau_1 \to \tau_2$$

(a) Syntax of Processes, Expressions, Monadic Expressions and Types

Functional values:	abstractions $\lambda x.e$ and constructor applications $(c\,e_1\ \ldots\ e_n)$
Monadic values:	all monadic expressions $m \in \mathit{MExpr}$
Values:	functional values and monadic values
cx-values:	$(c\,x_1 \ldots x_n)$ and monadic values where all arguments are variables

(b) Functional values, monadic values, cx-values, and values

$$\begin{aligned}(P_1 \mid P_2) \mid P_3 &\equiv P_1 \mid (P_2 \mid P_3) & P_1 \mid P_2 &\equiv P_2 \mid P_1\\ \nu x_1.\nu x_2.P &\equiv \nu x_2.\nu x_1.P & P_1 &\equiv P_2 \text{ if } P_1 =_\alpha P_2\\ (\nu x.P_1) \mid P_2 &\equiv \nu x.(P_1 \mid P_2) \text{ if } x \notin FV(P_2)\end{aligned}$$

(c) Structural Congruence

$$\begin{aligned}\mathbb{D} \in PC &::= [\cdot] \mid \mathbb{D} \mid P \mid P \mid \mathbb{D} \mid \nu x.\mathbb{D}\\ \mathbb{E} \in EC &::= [\cdot] \mid (\mathbb{E}\ e) \mid (\mathtt{case}\ \mathbb{E}\ \mathtt{of}\ alts) \mid (\mathtt{seq}\ \mathbb{E}\ e)\\ \mathbb{M}_{\mathtt{STM}} \in MC_{\mathtt{STM}} &::= \mathbb{M}_{\mathtt{IO}}[\mathtt{atomically}\ \widehat{\mathbb{M}}_{\mathtt{STM}}]\\ \mathbb{F} \in FC &::= \mathbb{E} \mid (\mathtt{readTVar}\ \mathbb{E}) \mid (\mathtt{writeTVar}\ \mathbb{E}\ e)\\ \mathbb{M}_{\mathtt{IO}} \in MC_{\mathtt{IO}} &::= [\cdot] \mid \mathbb{M}_{\mathtt{IO}} \gg\!=_{\mathtt{IO}} e\\ \widehat{\mathbb{M}}_{\mathtt{STM}} \in \widehat{MC}_{\mathtt{STM}} &::= [\cdot] \mid \widehat{\mathbb{M}}_{\mathtt{STM}} \gg\!=_{\mathtt{STM}} e \mid \mathtt{orElse}\ \widehat{\mathbb{M}}_{\mathtt{STM}}\ e\\ \mathbb{L}_Q \in LC_Q &::= \langle u \wr x\rangle \Leftarrow \mathbb{M}_Q[\mathbb{F}] \mid \langle u \wr x\rangle \Leftarrow \mathbb{M}_Q[\mathbb{F}[x_n]] \mid x_n = \mathbb{E}_n[x_{n-1}] \mid \ldots \mid x_2 = \mathbb{E}_2[x_1] \mid x_1 = \mathbb{E}_1\\ & \quad \text{where } Q \in \{\mathtt{IO}, \mathtt{STM}\} \text{ and } \mathbb{E}_1 \neq [\cdot]\end{aligned}$$

(d) Process-, Monadic-, Evaluation-, and Forcing-Contexts

$$\begin{aligned}\mathtt{future} &:: (\mathtt{IO}\ \alpha) \to \mathtt{IO}\ \alpha & \mathtt{readTVar} &:: (\mathtt{TVar}\ \alpha) \to \mathtt{STM}\ \alpha & (\gg\!=_{\mathtt{IO}}) &:: (\mathtt{IO}\ \alpha_1) \to (\alpha_1 \to \mathtt{IO}\ \alpha_2) \to \mathtt{IO}\ \alpha_2\\ \mathtt{atomically} &:: (\mathtt{STM}\ \alpha) \to \mathtt{IO}\ \alpha & \mathtt{writeTVar} &:: (\mathtt{TVar}\ \alpha) \to \alpha \to \mathtt{STM}\ () & (\gg\!=_{\mathtt{STM}}) &:: (\mathtt{STM}\ \alpha_1) \to (\alpha_1 \to \mathtt{STM}\ \alpha_2) \to \mathtt{STM}\ \alpha_2\\ \mathtt{return}_{\mathtt{STM}} &:: \alpha \to \mathtt{STM}\ \alpha & \mathtt{newTVar} &:: \alpha \to \mathtt{STM}(\mathtt{TVar}\ \alpha) & \mathtt{orElse} &:: (\mathtt{STM}\ \alpha) \to (\mathtt{STM}\ \alpha) \to (\mathtt{STM}\ \alpha)\\ \mathtt{return}_{\mathtt{IO}} &:: \alpha \to \mathtt{IO}\ \alpha & \mathtt{retry} &:: (\mathtt{STM}\ \alpha)\end{aligned}$$

(e) Polymorphic types of operators

$$\frac{\Gamma(x) = \tau,\quad \Gamma \vdash e :: \mathtt{IO}\ \tau}{\Gamma \vdash \langle u \wr x\rangle \Leftarrow e :: \mathtt{wt}} \qquad \frac{\Gamma(x) = \tau,\quad \Gamma \vdash e :: \tau}{\Gamma \vdash x = e :: \mathtt{wt}} \qquad \frac{\Gamma \vdash P_1 :: \mathtt{wt},\quad \Gamma \vdash P_2 :: \mathtt{wt}}{\Gamma \vdash P_1 \mid P_2 :: \mathtt{wt}} \qquad \frac{\Gamma(x) = \mathtt{TVar}\ \tau,\quad \Gamma \vdash e :: \tau}{\Gamma \vdash x\,\mathbf{t}\,e :: \mathtt{wt}} \qquad \frac{\Gamma \vdash P :: \mathtt{wt}}{\Gamma \vdash \nu x.P :: \mathtt{wt}}$$

$$\frac{\Gamma(x) = \tau}{\Gamma \vdash x :: \tau} \qquad \frac{\Gamma(x) = \tau_1,\quad \Gamma \vdash e :: \tau_2}{\Gamma \vdash (\lambda x.e) :: \tau_1 \to \tau_2} \qquad \frac{\Gamma \vdash e_1 :: \tau_1 \to \tau_2,\quad \Gamma \vdash e_2 :: \tau_1}{\Gamma \vdash (e_1\ e_2) :: \tau_2} \qquad \frac{\Gamma \vdash e_i :: \tau_i, i = 1,2 \quad \tau_1 = \tau_3 \to \tau_4 \text{ or } \tau_1 = (T \ldots)}{\Gamma \vdash (\mathtt{seq}\ e_1\ e_2) :: \tau_2}$$

$$\frac{\forall i : \Gamma(x_i) = \tau_i,\quad \forall i : \Gamma \vdash e_i :: \tau_i,\quad \Gamma \vdash e :: \tau}{\Gamma \vdash (\mathtt{letrec}\ x_1 = e_1, \ldots, x_n = e_n\ \mathtt{in}\ e) :: \tau} \qquad \frac{\Gamma \vdash e :: \tau_1 \text{ and } \tau_1 = (T \ldots),\quad \forall i : \Gamma \vdash (c_i\ x_{1,i} \ldots x_{n_i,i}) :: \tau_1,\quad \forall i : \Gamma \vdash e_i :: \tau_2}{\Gamma \vdash (\mathtt{case}_T\ e\ \mathtt{of}\ (c_1\ x_{1,1} \ldots x_{n_1,1} \to e_1) \ldots (c_m\ x_{1,m} \ldots x_{n_m,m} \to e_m)) :: \tau_2}$$

$$\frac{\forall i : \Gamma \vdash e_i :: \tau_i,\quad \tau_1 \to \ldots \to \tau_n \to \tau_{n+1} \in \mathtt{types(c)}}{\Gamma \vdash (c\,e_1\ \ldots\ e_{\mathrm{ar}(c)}) :: \tau_{n+1}}$$

where c is a constructor, or a monadic operator and $\mathtt{types}(c)$ is the set of monomorphic types of a constructor or a monadic operator c

(f) Typing rules

Figure 1. The calculus *SHF*, syntax and contexts

in e_1 then it proceeds with e_2. For the IO-monad the `future`-operator creates threads, and `atomically` lifts an STM-transaction into the IO-monad by executing the transaction.

Variable binders are introduced by abstractions, `letrec`, `case`-alternatives, and $\nu x.P$. This induces a notion of free and bound variables and α-renaming and α-equivalence (denoted by $=_\alpha$). Let $FV(P)$ ($FV(e)$, resp) be the free variables of process P (expression e, resp.). We assume the *distinct variable convention* to hold, that α-renaming is implicitly performed, if necessary.

A *context* is a process or an expression with a hole (denoted by $[\cdot]$). We write $C[e]$ ($C[P]$, resp.) for filling the hole of context C by expression e (process P, resp.). For processes we use a *structural congruence* $\equiv$ to equate obviously equal processes, which is the least congruence satisfying the equations of Fig. 1(c).

SHF is equipped with a monomorphic type system. The syntax of monomorphic types *Typ* is given in Fig. 1(a), where $(\mathtt{IO}\ \tau)$ means a monadic IO-action with return type τ, $(\mathtt{STM}\ \tau)$ means an STM-transaction action, $(\mathtt{TVar}\ \tau)$ stands for a `TVar`-reference with content type τ, $(T\ \tau_1\ \ldots\ \tau_n)$ is a type for an n-ary type constructor T, and $\tau_1 \to \tau_2$ is a function type. Although the type system is monomorphic, we "overload" the constructors and the monadic operators by assuming that they have a polymorphic type according to the usual conventions, however, in the language they are used as monomorphic. The polymorphic types of the monadic operators are shown in Fig. 1(e) where α, α_i are type variables.

To fix the types during reduction and for transformations, we assume that every variable x is explicitly typed and thus has a built-in type $\Gamma(x)$. For contexts, we assume that the hole $[\cdot]$ is typed and carries a type label. The notation $\Gamma \vdash e :: \tau$ ($\Gamma \vdash P :: \mathtt{wt}$, resp.) means that expression e (process P, resp.) can be typed with type τ (can be typed, resp.) using Γ. The typing rules are given in Fig. 1(f). Note that $\langle u \wr x\rangle \Leftarrow e$ is well-typed if x is of type τ and e is of type $\mathtt{IO}\ \tau$, and that an `STM`- or an `IO`-type for the first argument of `seq` is forbidden, to enable that the monad laws hold (see [13]).

Definition 2.1. A variable x is an *introduced variable* if it is a binding variable or a component-name. A process is *well-formed*, if all introduced variables and identifiers are pairwise distinct, and it has at most one main thread. A process P is *well-typed* iff P is well-formed and $\Gamma \vdash P :: \mathtt{wt}$ holds. An expression e is *well-typed with type* τ iff $\Gamma \vdash e :: \tau$ holds.

Monadic STM Computations:

(lunit$_{\text{STM}}$) $\langle u \wr y\rangle \Leftarrow \mathbb{M}_{\text{STM}}[\texttt{return}_{\text{STM}}\ e_1 \gg\!=_{\text{STM}}\ e_2] \xrightarrow{SHFA} \langle u \wr y\rangle \Leftarrow \mathbb{M}_{\text{STM}}[e_2\ e_1]$

(read) $\langle u \wr y\rangle \Leftarrow \mathbb{M}_{\text{STM}}[\texttt{readTVar}\ x] \mid x\,\mathbf{t}\,e \xrightarrow{SHFA} \nu z.(\langle u \wr y\rangle \Leftarrow \mathbb{M}_{\text{STM}}[\texttt{return}_{\text{STM}}\ z] \mid z = e \mid x\,\mathbf{t}\,z)$ where z is fresh

(write) $\langle u \wr y\rangle \Leftarrow \mathbb{M}_{\text{STM}}[\texttt{writeTVar}\ x\ e_2] \mid x\,\mathbf{t}\,e_1 \xrightarrow{SHFA} \langle u \wr y\rangle \Leftarrow \mathbb{M}_{\text{STM}}[\texttt{return}_{\text{STM}}\ ()] \mid x\,\mathbf{t}\,e_2$

(nvar) $\langle u \wr y\rangle \Leftarrow \mathbb{M}_{\text{STM}}[\texttt{newTVar}\ e] \xrightarrow{SHFA} \nu x.(\langle u \wr y\rangle \Leftarrow \mathbb{M}_{\text{STM}}[\texttt{return}_{\text{STM}}\ x] \mid x\,\mathbf{t}\,e)$ where x is fresh

(ortry) $$\frac{\nu X.\mathbb{D}[\langle u \wr y\rangle \Leftarrow \mathbb{M}_{\text{STM}}[\texttt{orElse}\ e_1\ e_2]] \xrightarrow{SHFA,*} \nu X.\mathbb{D}'[\langle u \wr y\rangle \Leftarrow \mathbb{M}_{\text{STM}}[\texttt{orElse}\ \texttt{retry}\ e_2]]}{\nu X.\mathbb{D}[\langle u \wr y\rangle \Leftarrow \mathbb{M}_{\text{STM}}[\texttt{orElse}\ e_1\ e_2]] \xrightarrow{SHFA} \nu X.\mathbb{D}[\langle u \wr y\rangle \Leftarrow \mathbb{M}_{\text{STM}}[e_2]]}$$ where the context $\mathbb{M}_{\text{STM}}$ is maximal, i.e. $e_1 \neq \widehat{\mathbb{M}_{\text{STM}}}[\texttt{orElse}\ e'\ e'']$

(orret) $\langle u \wr y\rangle \Leftarrow \mathbb{M}_{\text{STM}}[\texttt{orElse}\ (\texttt{return}_{\text{STM}}\ e_1)\ e_2] \xrightarrow{SHFA} \langle u \wr y\rangle \Leftarrow \mathbb{M}_{\text{STM}}[\texttt{return}_{\text{STM}}\ e_1]$

(retryup) $\langle u \wr y\rangle \Leftarrow \mathbb{M}_{\text{STM}}[\texttt{retry} \gg\!=_{\text{STM}}\ e_1] \xrightarrow{SHFA} \langle u \wr y\rangle \Leftarrow \mathbb{M}_{\text{STM}}[\texttt{retry}]$

Monadic IO Computations:

(lunit$_{\text{IO}}$) $\langle u \wr y\rangle \Leftarrow \mathbb{M}_{\text{IO}}[\texttt{return}_{\text{IO}}\ e_1 \gg\!=_{\text{IO}}\ e_2] \xrightarrow{SHF} \langle u \wr y\rangle \Leftarrow \mathbb{M}_{\text{IO}}[e_2\ e_1]$

(fork) $\langle u \wr y\rangle \Leftarrow \mathbb{M}_{\text{IO}}[\texttt{future}\ e] \xrightarrow{SHF} \nu z, u'.(\langle u \wr y\rangle \Leftarrow \mathbb{M}_{\text{IO}}[\texttt{return}\ z] \mid \langle u' \wr z\rangle \Leftarrow e)$
where z, u' are fresh and the created thread is not the main thread

(unIO) $\langle u \wr y\rangle \Leftarrow \texttt{return}\ e \xrightarrow{SHF} y = e$ if the thread is not the main-thread

(atomic) $$\frac{\nu X.\mathbb{D}_1[\langle u \wr y\rangle \Leftarrow \mathbb{M}_{\text{IO}}[\texttt{atomically}\ e]] \xrightarrow{SHFA,*} \nu X.\mathbb{D}_1'[\langle u \wr y\rangle \Leftarrow \mathbb{M}_{\text{IO}}[\texttt{atomically}\ (\texttt{return}_{\text{STM}}\ e')]]}{\mathbb{D}[\langle u \wr y\rangle \Leftarrow \mathbb{M}_{\text{IO}}[\texttt{atomically}\ e]] \xrightarrow{SHF} \mathbb{D}'[\langle u \wr y\rangle \Leftarrow \mathbb{M}_{\text{IO}}[\texttt{return}_{\text{IO}}\ e']]}$$
where $\mathbb{D} = \nu X.(\mathbb{D}_1 \mid \mathbb{D}_2)$ and $\mathbb{D}_1$ contains all bindings and TVars of $\mathbb{D}$, $\mathbb{D}_2$ contains all futures of $\mathbb{D}$, and $\mathbb{D}' = \nu X.(\mathbb{D}_1' \mid \mathbb{D}_2)$

Functional Evaluation:

(feval$_{\text{IO}}$) $P \xrightarrow{SHF} P'$, if $P \xrightarrow{a} P'$ for $a \in \{\text{cp}_{\text{IO}}, \text{abs}_{\text{IO}}, \text{mkb}_{\text{IO}}, \text{lbeta}_{\text{IO}}, \text{case}_{\text{IO}}, \text{seq}_{\text{IO}}\}$

(feval$_{\text{STM}}$) $P \xrightarrow{SHFA} P'$, if $P \xrightarrow{a} P$ for $a \in \{\text{cp}_{\text{STM}}, \text{abs}_{\text{STM}}, \text{mkb}_{\text{STM}}, \text{lbeta}_{\text{STM}}, \text{case}_{\text{STM}}, \text{seq}_{\text{STM}}\}$

The reductions with parameter $Q \in \{\texttt{STM}, \texttt{IO}\}$ are defined as follows:

(cp$_Q$) $\mathbb{L}_Q[x_1] \mid x_1 = x_2 \mid \ldots \mid x_{n-1} = x_n \mid x_n = v \rightarrow \mathbb{L}_Q[v] \mid x_1 = x_2 \mid \ldots \mid x_{n-1} = x_n \mid x_n = v$,
if v is an abstraction, a cx-value or a component-name

(abs$_Q$) $\mathbb{L}_Q[x_1] \mid x_1 = x_2 \mid \ldots \mid x_{m-1} = x_m \mid x_m = c\,e_1 \ldots e_n$
$\rightarrow \nu y_1, \ldots y_n.(\mathbb{L}_Q[c\,y_1\ \ldots\ y_n] \mid x_1 = x_2 \mid \ldots \mid x_{m-1} = x_m \mid x_m = c\,y_1\ \ldots\ y_n \mid y_1 = e_1 \mid \ldots \mid y_n = e_n)$
if c is a constructor, or $\texttt{return}_{\text{STM}}$, $\texttt{return}_{\text{IO}}$, $\gg\!=_{\text{STM}}$, $\gg\!=_{\text{IO}}$, `orElse`, `atomically`, `readTVar`, `writeTVar`, `newTVar`, or `future` and $n \geq 1$, and some e_i is not a variable, and where $y_1, \ldots, y_n$ are fresh.

(mkb$_Q$) $\mathbb{L}_Q[\texttt{letrec}\ x_1 = e_1, \ldots, x_n = e_n\ \texttt{in}\ e] \rightarrow \nu x_1, \ldots, x_n.(\mathbb{L}_Q[e] \mid x_1 = e_1 \mid \ldots \mid x_n = e_n)$, where $x_1, \ldots, x_n$ are fresh

(lbeta$_Q$) $\mathbb{L}_Q[((\lambda x.e_1)\ e_2)] \rightarrow \nu x.(\mathbb{L}_Q[e_1] \mid x = e_2)$

(case$_Q$) $\mathbb{L}_Q[\texttt{case}_T\ (c\,e_1\ \ldots\ e_n)\ \texttt{of}\ \ldots((c\,y_1\ \ldots\ y_n) \rightarrow e)\ldots] \rightarrow \nu y_1, \ldots, y_n.(\mathbb{L}_Q[e] \mid y_1 = e_1 \mid \ldots \mid y_n = e_n])$, if $n > 0$

(case$_Q$) $\mathbb{L}_Q[\texttt{case}_T\ c\ \texttt{of}\ \ldots(c \rightarrow e)\ldots] \rightarrow \mathbb{L}_Q[e]$

(seq$_Q$) $\mathbb{L}_Q[(\texttt{seq}\ v\ e)] \rightarrow \mathbb{L}_Q[e]$, if v is a functional value

Closure: $$\frac{P_i \equiv \mathbb{D}[P_i'], P_1' \xrightarrow{SHF} P_2'}{P_1 \xrightarrow{SHF} P_2} \qquad \frac{P_i \equiv \mathbb{D}[P_i'], P_1' \xrightarrow{SHFA} P_2'}{P_1 \xrightarrow{SHFA} P_2}$$

Figure 2. The calculus SHF, reductions

We define a reduction relation $\xrightarrow{SHF}$ (called *standard reduction*) for SHF. This reduction relation is on the one hand a small-step reduction, since several $\xrightarrow{SHF}$-steps are performed sequentially before evaluation stops. However, it uses as a condition the success of the intermediate reduction relation $\xrightarrow{SHFA}$ in a big-step manner for the atomic execution of an STM-transaction (i.e. the evaluation of e in `atomically` e and of `orElse` $e\ e'$).

Definition 2.2. A well-formed process P is *successful*, if P has a main thread of the form $\langle u \wr x\rangle \overset{\text{main}}{\Longleftarrow} \texttt{return}\,e$, i.e. $P \equiv \nu x_1 \ldots \nu x_n.(\langle u \wr x\rangle \overset{\text{main}}{\Longleftarrow} \texttt{return}\ e \mid P')$.

Definition 2.3. The *standard reduction rules* are given in Fig. 2 where the used contexts are defined in Fig. 1(d). Standard reductions are permitted only for well-formed, non-successful processes.

In the following we will denote the transitive closure of a relation $\xrightarrow{R}$ by $\xrightarrow{R,+}$ and the reflexive-transitive closure by $\xrightarrow{R,*}$. We will also use the notation $\xrightarrow{SHF,a}$ where a is the name of a reduction rule to make explicit which reduction is used by a $\xrightarrow{SHF}$-step.

We define the $\xrightarrow{SHF}$*-redex*: For (lunit), (fork), it is the expression in the context $\mathbb{M}$, for (unIO), it is $\langle u \wr y\rangle \Leftarrow \texttt{return}\ e$, for (mkb), (lbeta), (case), (seq), (cp), (abs) it is the expression (or variable) in the context $\mathbb{L}$. We define the $\xrightarrow{SHFA}$*-redex*: For (lunit$_{\text{STM}}$), (read), (write), (nvar), (ortry), (orret) it is the expression in the context $\mathbb{M}_{\text{STM}}$, for (mkb$_{\text{STM}}$), (lbeta$_{\text{STM}}$), (case$_{\text{STM}}$), (seq$_{\text{STM}}$), (cp$_{\text{STM}}$), (abs$_{\text{STM}}$) it is the expression (or variable) in the context $\mathbb{L}_{\text{STM}}$.

We explain the standard reduction rules of Fig. 2. The standard (big-step) reduction is $\xrightarrow{SHF}$, whereas $\xrightarrow{SHFA,*}$ defines the evaluation of STM-transactions. The $\xrightarrow{SHFA,*}$-reduction sequences will only be performed, if they terminate successfully, see rule (atomic).

The rules are divided into three classes: Rules for monadic computations in the STM-monad, rules for monadic computations in the IO-monad, and rules for functional evaluation.

We start with explaining the most interesting rules – the rules for the STM-monad: The rule (lunit) implements the semantics of the monadic sequencing operator `>>=`. The rules (read), (write), and (nvar) access and create TVars. The rule (ortry) is a big-step rule: if a $\xrightarrow{SHFA,*}$-reduction sequence starting with `orElse` e_1 e_2 ends in `orElse retry` e_2, then the effects are ignored, and `orElse` e_1 e_2 is replaced by e_2. If the reduction of e_1 ends with `return` e, then rule (orret) is used to keep the result as the result of `orElse` e_1 e_2.

For the IO-monad there is also a rule (lunit) for the bind-operator. The rule (atomic) executes an STM-action in the IO-monad. It is also a big-step rule. If for a single thread the $\xrightarrow{SHFA,*}$-reduction successfully produces a return, then the transaction is performed in one step of the $\xrightarrow{SHF}$-reduction. If the $\xrightarrow{SHFA,*}$-reduction ends in a `retry`, in a stuck expressions or does not terminate, then there is no $\xrightarrow{SHF}$-reduction, and hence it is omitted from the operational semantics.

The rule (fork) spawns a new concurrent thread and returns the newly created future as the result. The rule (unIO) binds the result of a monadic computation to a functional binding, i.e. the value of a concurrent future becomes accessible.

The rules for functional evaluation implement call-by-need reduction. The rules (cp) and (abs) inline a needed binding $x = e$ where e must be an abstraction, a cx-value, or a component name. To implement call-by-need evaluation the arguments of constructor applications and monadic expressions are shared by new bindings, similar to lazy copying [18]. Since the variable (binding-) chains are transparent, there is no need to copy binding-variables to other places in the expressions. The rule (mkb) moves `letrec`-bindings into the global bindings. The rule (lbeta) is the sharing variant of β-reduction. The (case)-reduction reduces a `case`-expression, where perhaps bindings are created to implement sharing. The (seq)-rule evaluates a `seq`-expression.

Since the reduction rules only introduce variables which are fresh and never introduce a main thread, $\xrightarrow{SHF}$ preserves well-formedness. Also type preservation holds, since every reduction keeps the type of subexpressions. Contextual equivalence equates processes P_1, P_2 if their observable behavior is indistinguishable if P_1 and P_2 are plugged into any process context. For concurrent calculi observing may-convergence, i.e. whether a process can be reduced to a successful process, is *not* sufficient and thus we will also observe should-convergence (see [10, 11]).

Definition 2.4. A process P *may-converges* (written as $P\downarrow$), iff it is well-formed and reduces to a successful process, (see Definition 2.2), i.e. $P\downarrow$ iff P is well-formed and $\exists P' : P \xrightarrow{SHF,*} P' \wedge P'$ successful. If $P\downarrow$ does not hold, then P *must-diverges* written as $P\Uparrow$. A process P *should-converges* (written as $P\Downarrow$), iff it is well-formed and remains may-convergent under reduction, i.e. $P\Downarrow$ iff P is well-formed and $\forall P' : P \xrightarrow{SHF,*} P' \implies P'\downarrow$. If P is not should-convergent then we say P *may-diverges* written as $P\uparrow$, which is also equivalent to $\exists P' : P \xrightarrow{SHF,*} P' \wedge P'\Uparrow$.

Contextual approximation $\leq_c$ and *contextual equivalence* $\sim_c$ on processes are defined as $\leq_c := \leq_\downarrow \cap \leq_\Downarrow$ and $\sim_c := \leq_c \cap \geq_c$ where for $\zeta \in \{\downarrow, \Downarrow\}$: $P_1 \leq_\zeta P_2$ iff $\forall \mathbb{D} \in PC : \mathbb{D}[P_1]\zeta \implies \mathbb{D}[P_2]\zeta$.

The definition of $\xrightarrow{SHF}$ implies that non-wellformed processes are always must-divergent. Also, the process construction by $\mathbb{D}[P]$ is always well-typed if P is well-typed, since we assume that variables have a built-in type.

Clearly, SHF implements memory transactions in a correct way: Every single transaction is executed atomically and isolated from any other transaction. So SHF is a correct specification of STM. However, the semantics has two drawbacks:

- It is impossible to implement the standard reduction: The rules (atomic) and (ortry) have undecidable preconditions, since they include checking whether a $\xrightarrow{SHFA}$-reduction halts successfully.
- Since the transactions are executed sequentially, there is only poor concurrency.

In the next section we will give an implementation using SHF as specification, which overcomes those drawbacks.

3. A Concurrent Implementation of STM Evaluation

We introduce a concurrent (small-step) evaluation enabling much more concurrency which is closer to an abstract machine than the big-step semantics. The executability of every single step is decidable, and every state has a finite set of potential successors. The undecidable conditions in the rules (atomic) and (ortry) of SHF are now implemented by tentatively executing the transaction, under concurrency, thus allowing other threads to execute. Transaction execution should guarantee an equivalent linearized execution of transactions. Our ultimate goal is to show that the concurrent execution is *correct*, i.e. to show that it is semantically equivalent to the big-step reduction defined for SHF. However, our approach uses minimal locking times and thus has a potential danger of conflicts and retries. Instead of using an optimistic read/write approach which performs a rollback in case of a conflict [8], we will follow a similar, but slightly more pessimistic read and write: there are no locks at the start of a transaction, initial reads copy contents to the local store, other reads and writes are local; only at the end of a successful transaction there is a commit phase with global writes such that updates become visible to other transactions where a real, but internal, locking is used for a short time. To have a correct overall execution, conflicting transactions will be stopped by sending them a retry-notification (so-called early conflict detection), where the knowledge of the potential conflicts is memorized at the TVars.

We view a transaction as a function $V_1 \to V_2$ from a set of (read) input TVars V_1 to a set of modified TVars V_2 where V_1, V_2 may have common elements. The guarantee must be that at the end of transaction execution, the complete transaction could be atomically and instantaneously executed on the TVars V_1, V_2. During this commit phase other running transactions that have read any variable of V_2, need to be aborted (restarted) due to a conflict.

More concretely, the ideas of CSHF are as follows:

- For every transaction there is a *local copy* for every TVar it accesses. All reads and writes are performed in the local copies invisible to other concurrently executed threads.
- For later conflict detection every global TVar is equipped with a set of registered threads. Before obtaining a local copy the thread identifier is added to this set.
- For book-keeping of the accessed TVars every thread has a transaction log, where read, written, and created TVars are remembered.
- If an executing transaction (thread) results in `retry`, its local copies of the TVars are removed, its registrations on TVars are removed and the transaction starts over again. If `retry` occurs inside an `orElse` then the treatment is different (see next item).

- To implement the nesting of `orElse`, the local copies of the TVars are stacks, where the stack depth matches the depth of the `orElse`-nesting. In case that a transaction stops with `retry` inside the left argument of `orElse`, all these stacks are popped and the right argument of `orElse` is executed. However, read TVars must remain in the transaction log, since their values may have an influence on the control. For the same reason, also the registration at the global TVars must not be changed.
- If a transaction executed all its actions, then it starts its *commit phase*. To ensure consistency, first all read and all to-be-written TVars are locked by the thread identifier of the committing transaction. This locking is done in one atomic step. After the locks are set, no other thread is able to access the locked TVars. Then there are several steps performed which may be interleaved by other transactions (accessing other TVars):
  - The committing thread removes its registration from all TVars it has accessed.
  - The committing thread reads the registration sets to obtain the thread identifiers of all the conflicting transactions which have to be aborted. The corresponding threads are *notified* by the committing transaction to abort and restart their transaction. This can be seen as throwing an exception from the committing thread to all other threads which have become inconsistent now. This is indeed implemented in this way in our prototype. In the operational semantics below, simply the current code of the other transactions is replaced by `retry` and thus notified threads perform as if they got a (transaction) `retry`: first they unregister their thread identifier and then restart.
  - The committing thread updates the global content of the TVars and then removes the locks.
  - The final steps of the committing thread are to add newly created TVars as global TVars and then to remove all the local copies.

Another design decision in the calculus description below is that sharing by bindings is carefully maximized, including transparent variable-variable-binding chains. One reason is that this leads to manageable correctness proofs. Another design principle is to avoid negative conditions: There must not be any conditions that rely on a test whether there are no occurrences of TVars or threads satisfying certain conditions.

Now we detail on this idea and introduce the calculus *CSHF* which has a concurrent evaluation of transactions and a modified *SHF*-syntax: there is an addition of labels, of memory-cells at threads and a stack for the `orElse`s. First we describe the syntax changes of the language, and then exactly describe the rules, which are close to a concurrent abstract machine for SHF.

Definition 3.1 (Syntax of *CSHF*). The syntax of *CSHF*-processes is almost the same as for *SHF*-processes where, however, there are some extensions and changes. Instead of TVars $x\,\mathbf{t}\,e$ there are two constructs:

1. *Global* TVars are represented by $x\,\mathbf{tg}\,e\,u\,g$, where the additional third argument u is a locking label and may be empty (written as $-$) or a thread identifier u that locks the TVar, and g is a list of thread identifiers for those threads that want to be notified for a retry, when x is updated.
2. A *stack of thread-local* TVars is represented by $u\,\mathbf{tls}\,s$, where u is a thread identifier and s is a stack of sets with *local* TVars $x\,\mathbf{tl}\,e$ as elements, where x is a name of a TVar and e is an expression.

A thread may have a *transaction log*, which is only available if a thread is within a transaction. It is written over the thread-arrow as $\langle u\wr y\rangle \overset{T,L;K}{\Longleftarrow} e$ where T is a set of TVars (i.e. the names of the TVars) that are read during the transaction; L is a stack of triples (L_a, L_n, L_w) where L_a is a set of the names of all TVars which are accessed during the transaction, L_n a set of names of newly generated TVars, L_w a set of locally updated (or written) TVars, and the stack reflects the depth of the `orElse`-execution; K is a set of TVar-names that is locked by a thread in the commit-phase.

Additional (labeled) variants of the operators `orElse` and `atomically` are required: The operator `orElse!` indicates that `orElse` is active, and the operator `atomically!` indicates that a transaction is active, where `atomically!` has as a second argument an expression that is a saved copy of the start expression and that will again be activated after rollback and restart. I.e., the sets of monadic expressions and $MC_{\mathtt{STM}}$-contexts are adapted as:

$$\begin{array}{rl} m \in \mathit{MExpr} & ::= \mathtt{return_{IO}}\,e \mid e_1 \mathbin{>\!\!>\!\!=_{\mathtt{IO}}} e_2 \mid \mathtt{future}\,e \\ & \mid \mathtt{return_{STM}}\,e \mid e_1 \mathbin{>\!\!>\!\!=_{\mathtt{STM}}} e_2 \mid \mathtt{atomically}\,e \\ & \mid \mathtt{atomically!}\,e\,e' \mid \mathtt{retry} \mid \mathtt{orElse}\,e_1\,e_2 \mid \mathtt{orElse!}\,e_1\,e_2 \\ & \mid \mathtt{newTVar}\,e \mid \mathtt{readTVar}\,e \mid \mathtt{writeTVar}\,e \end{array}$$

$$\mathbb{M}_{\mathtt{STM}} \in \mathit{MC}_{\mathtt{STM}} ::= \mathbb{M}_{\mathtt{IO}}[\mathtt{atomically!}\,\widehat{\mathbb{M}}_{\mathtt{STM}}\,e]$$
$$\widehat{\mathbb{M}}_{\mathtt{STM}} \in \widehat{\mathit{MC}_{\mathtt{STM}}} ::= [\cdot] \mid \widehat{\mathbb{M}}_{\mathtt{STM}} \mathbin{>\!\!>\!\!=_{\mathtt{STM}}} e \mid \mathtt{orElse!}\,\widehat{\mathbb{M}}_{\mathtt{STM}}\,e$$

A thread that has a transaction log is called *transactional*, otherwise it is called non-transactional. A *CSHF*-process that only has non-transactional threads and no $u\,\mathbf{tls}\,s$-components is called *non-transactional*; otherwise, it is called *transactional*.

We say a thread is currently *performing a transaction*, if the current evaluation focusses on the arguments of `atomically!` (see the reduction $\xrightarrow{CSHF}$ below).

Definition 3.2. A *CSHF*-process P is *well-formed* iff the following holds: Variable names of TVars, threads, and binders are introduced at most once; i.e. threads, bindings, and global TVars are unique per variable. For every component $x\,\mathbf{tl}\,e$ in a stack-entry of $u\,\mathbf{tls}\,s$, either there is also a global TVar $x\,\mathbf{tg}\,e\,o\,g$, or the TVar is in the L_n-component of the thread-memory (the locally generated TVars). Moreover, for every thread identifier u, there is at most one process component $u\,\mathbf{tls}\,s$. In every stack entry, names of TVars occur at most once. For every thread identifier u in $u\,\mathbf{tls}\,s$ there exists a thread with this identifier.

Though the syntax of *CSHF* is slightly different from *SHF*, we use the same names for the context classes *PC*, *EC*, $MC_{\mathtt{STM}}$, *MC*, *FC*, $MC_{\mathtt{IO}}$, and LC_Q. If necessary, then we distinguish the context classes using an index C (for concurrent). For the *PC*-contexts we assume that also transactional threads are permitted.

Definition 3.3 (Operational Semantics of *CSHF*). A well-formed *CSHF*-process P reduces to another *CSHF*-process P' (denoted by $P \xrightarrow{CSHF} P'$) iff $P \equiv D[P_1]$ and $P' \equiv D[P_1']$ and $P_1 \rightarrow P_1'$ by a reduction rule in Fig. 3, 4, and 5.

We explain the execution of a transaction and the use of the transaction log, where we also point to the reduction rules.

Start of a transaction (atomic): When the execution is started a new empty transaction log is created.

Read-operations: (readl) and (readg): A read first looks into the local store. If no local TVar exists, then the global value is copied into the local store and the own thread identifier is added to the notify-list of the global TVar.

Write-operations (writel) and (writeg): A write command always writes into the local store, perhaps preceded by a copy from the global into the local store .

Monadic IO Computations:

(lunit$_{\text{IO}}$) $\langle u \wr y \rangle \Leftarrow \mathbb{M}_{\text{IO}}[\texttt{return}_{\text{IO}}\ e_1 \gg\!=_{\text{IO}}\ e_2] \xrightarrow{CSHF} \langle u \wr y \rangle \Leftarrow \mathbb{M}_{\text{IO}}[e_2\ e_1]$

(fork) $\langle u \wr y \rangle \Leftarrow \mathbb{M}_{\text{IO}}[\texttt{future}\ e] \xrightarrow{CSHF} \nu z, u'.(\langle u \wr y \rangle \Leftarrow \mathbb{M}_{\text{IO}}[\texttt{return}\ z] \mid \langle u' \wr z \rangle \Leftarrow e)$
where z, u' are fresh and the created thread is not the main thread

(unIO) $\langle u \wr y \rangle \Leftarrow \texttt{return}\ e \xrightarrow{SHF} y = e$ if the thread is not the main-thread

Monadic STM Computations:

(atomic) $\langle u \wr y \rangle \Leftarrow \mathbb{M}_{\text{IO}}[\texttt{atomically}\ e] \xrightarrow{CSHF} \nu z.\langle u \wr y \rangle \stackrel{\emptyset,[\emptyset]}{\Longleftarrow} \mathbb{M}_{\text{IO}}[\texttt{atomically!}\ z\ z] \mid u\ \mathbf{tls}\ [\emptyset] \mid z = e$

(lunit$_{\text{STM}}$) $\langle u \wr y \rangle \stackrel{T,L}{\Longleftarrow} \mathbb{M}_{\text{STM}}[\texttt{return}_{\text{STM}}\ e_1 \gg\!=_{\text{STM}}\ e_2] \xrightarrow{CSHF} \langle u \wr y \rangle \stackrel{T,L}{\Longleftarrow} \mathbb{M}_{\text{STM}}[e_2\ e_1]$

(readl) $\langle u \wr y \rangle \stackrel{T,L}{\Longleftarrow} \mathbb{M}_{\text{STM}}[\texttt{readTVar}\ x] \mid u\ \mathbf{tls}\ (\{x\ \mathbf{tl}\ e_1\} \dot\cup r) : s$
$\xrightarrow{CSHF} \nu z.(\langle u \wr y \rangle \stackrel{T,L}{\Longleftarrow} \mathbb{M}_{\text{STM}}[\texttt{return}_{\text{STM}}\ z] \mid z = e_1 \mid u\ \mathbf{tls}\ (\{x\ \mathbf{tl}\ z\} \dot\cup r) : s$

(readg) $\langle u \wr y \rangle \stackrel{T,L}{\Longleftarrow} \mathbb{M}_{\text{STM}}[\texttt{readTVar}\ x] \mid x\ \mathbf{tg}\ e_1 - g \mid u\ \mathbf{tls}\ r : s$
$\xrightarrow{CSHF} \nu z.(\langle u \wr y \rangle \stackrel{T',L'}{\Longleftarrow} \mathbb{M}_{\text{STM}}[\texttt{return}_{\text{STM}}\ z] \mid z = e_1 \quad u\ \mathbf{tls}\ (\{x\ \mathbf{tl}\ z\} \dot\cup r) \quad s \mid x\ \mathbf{tg}\ z - g')$
if $x \notin L_a$ where $L = (L_a, L_n, L_w) : L_r$, $L' = (L_a \cup \{x\}, L_n, L_w) : L_r$, $T' = T \cup \{x\}$ and $g' = (\{u\} \cup g)$

(writel) $\langle u \wr y \rangle \stackrel{T,L}{\Longleftarrow} \mathbb{M}_{\text{STM}}[\texttt{writeTVar}\ x\ e_1] \mid u\ \mathbf{tls}\ (\{x\ \mathbf{tl}\ e_2\} \dot\cup r : s) \xrightarrow{CSHF} \langle u \wr y \rangle \stackrel{T,L'}{\Longleftarrow} \mathbb{M}_{\text{STM}}[\texttt{return}_{\text{STM}}\ ()] \mid u\ \mathbf{tls}\ (\{x\ \mathbf{tl}\ e_1\} \dot\cup r : s)$
where $L = (L_a, L_n, L_w) : L_r$, $L' = (L_a, L_n, L_w \cup \{x\}) : L_r$

(writeg) $\langle u \wr y \rangle \stackrel{T,L}{\Longleftarrow} \mathbb{M}_{\text{STM}}[\texttt{writeTVar}\ x\ e_1] \mid x\ \mathbf{tg}\ e_2 - g \mid u\ \mathbf{tls}\ (r : s)$
$\xrightarrow{CSHF} \langle u \wr y \rangle \stackrel{T,L'}{\Longleftarrow} \mathbb{M}_{\text{STM}}[\texttt{return}_{\text{STM}}\ ()] \mid x\ \mathbf{tg}\ e_2 - g \mid u\ \mathbf{tls}\ (\{x\ \mathbf{tl}\ e_1\} \dot\cup r : s)$
if $x \notin L_a$, where $L = (L_a, L_n, L_w) : L_r$, $L' = (L_a \cup \{x\}, L_n, L_w \cup \{x\}) : L_r$

(nvar) $\langle u \wr y \rangle \stackrel{T,L}{\Longleftarrow} \mathbb{M}_{\text{STM}}[\texttt{newTVar}\ e] \mid u\ \mathbf{tls}\ (r : s) \xrightarrow{CSHF} \nu x.(\langle u \wr y \rangle \stackrel{T,L'}{\Longleftarrow} \mathbb{M}_{\text{STM}}[\texttt{return}_{\text{STM}}\ x] \mid u\ \mathbf{tls}\ (\{x\ \mathbf{tl}\ e)\} \dot\cup r : s)$
where $L = (L_a, L_n, L_w)$ and $L' = (\{x\} \cup L_a, \{x\} \cup L_n, L_w)$

(retryup) $\langle u \wr y \rangle \stackrel{T,L}{\Longleftarrow} \mathbb{M}_{\text{STM}}[\texttt{retry} \gg\!=_{\text{STM}}\ e_1] \xrightarrow{CSHF} \langle u \wr y \rangle \stackrel{T,L}{\Longleftarrow} \mathbb{M}_{\text{STM}}[\texttt{retry}]$

(orElse) $\langle u \wr y \rangle \stackrel{T,L}{\Longleftarrow} \mathbb{M}_{\text{STM}}[\texttt{orElse}\ e_1\ e_2] \mid (u\ \mathbf{tls}\ (\{x_1\ \mathbf{tl}\ e_{1,1}, \ldots, x_n\ \mathbf{tl}\ e_{1,n}\} : s)$
$\xrightarrow{CSHF} \nu z_1, \ldots z_n.(\langle u \wr y \rangle \stackrel{T,L'}{\Longleftarrow} \mathbb{M}_{\text{STM}}[\texttt{orElse!}\ e_1\ e_2] \mid u\ \mathbf{tls}\ ((\{x_1\ \mathbf{tl}\ z_1, \ldots, x_n\ \mathbf{tl}\ z_n\} : (\{x_1\ \mathbf{tl}\ z_1, \ldots, x_n\ \mathbf{tl}\ z_n\}) : s)$
$\mid z_1 = e_{1,1} \mid \ldots \mid z_n = e_{1,n})$
where $L = (L_a, L_n, L_w) : L_r$, $L' = (L_a, L_n, L_w) : ((L_a, L_n, L_w) : L_r)$

(orRetry) $\langle u \wr y \rangle \stackrel{T,L}{\Longleftarrow} \mathbb{M}_{\text{STM}}[\texttt{orElse!}\ \texttt{retry}\ e_2] \mid u\ \mathbf{tls}\ (r : s) \xrightarrow{CSHF} \langle u \wr y \rangle \stackrel{T,L'}{\Longleftarrow} \mathbb{M}_{\text{STM}}[e_2] \mid u\ \mathbf{tls}\ s$ where $L = L_e : L'$

(orReturn) $\langle u \wr y \rangle \stackrel{T,L}{\Longleftarrow} \mathbb{M}_{\text{STM}}[\texttt{orElse!}\ (\texttt{return}_{\text{STM}}\ e_1)\ e_2] \mid u\ \mathbf{tls}\ (r : s) \xrightarrow{CSHF} \langle u \wr y \rangle \stackrel{T,L}{\Longleftarrow} \mathbb{M}_{\text{STM}}[\texttt{return}_{\text{STM}}\ e_1] \mid u\ \mathbf{tls}\ (r : s)$

(retryCGlob) $\langle u \wr y \rangle \stackrel{T,L}{\Longleftarrow} \mathbb{M}_{\text{IO}}[\texttt{atomically!}\ \texttt{retry}\ e] \mid x\ \mathbf{tg}\ e_1 - g \xrightarrow{CSHF} \langle u \wr y \rangle \stackrel{T',L}{\Longleftarrow} \mathbb{M}_{\text{IO}}[\texttt{atomically!}\ \texttt{retry}\ e] \mid x\ \mathbf{tg}\ e_1 - g'$
if $x \in T$, where $T' = T \setminus \{x\}$, $g' = g \setminus \{u\}$

(retryEnd) $\langle u \wr y \rangle \stackrel{\emptyset,L}{\Longleftarrow} \mathbb{M}_{\text{IO}}[\texttt{atomically!}\ \texttt{retry}\ e] \mid u\ \mathbf{tls}\ (r : s) \xrightarrow{CSHF} \langle u \wr y \rangle \Leftarrow \mathbb{M}_{\text{IO}}[\texttt{atomically}\ e]$

Figure 3. Concurrent Implementation of SHF, transaction reductions

OrElse-Evaluation: If evaluation descends into the left expression of `orElse`, then the stacks of TVar-names and of local TVars are extended by duplicating their top element in rule (orElse). For the final write in the commit phase only the top of the stack is relevant. If evaluation of the left expression is successful, the stack remains as it is (by rule (orReturn)). In case of a retry, the top element is popped (by rule (orRetry)) and the execution of the second expression then uses the stack before executing the `orElse`. Note that the information on the read TVars is kept in the set T, since the values may have an influence on the outcome of the `orElse`-tree execution. This is necessary, since the big-step semantics of SHF enforces a left-to-right evaluation of the `orElse`-tree, where the leftmost successful try will be kept. Note that this is semantically different from making a non-deterministic choice of one of the successful possibilities in the `orElse`-tree.

Commit-Phase: At the end of a transaction, there is a lock-protected sequence of updates: A thread that is in its commit-phase first locks all its globally read and to-be-updated TVars (rule (writeStart)). Locked variables cannot be accessed by other threads for reading, or modifying the notify-list. Then all own notification-entries are removed (rule (writeClear)). All the threads, which are unequal to the running thread, and that are in the notify-list of the updated TVars, will be stopped by replacing the current transaction expression by `retry` (rule (sendRetry)). This mechanism is like raising (synchronous) exceptions to influence other threads. The to-be-updated TVars are written into the global store (rule (writeTV)), then the locks are released (rule (unlockTV)) and fresh TVars are also moved to the global store (rule (writeTVn)). Finally, the transaction log is removed (rule (writeEnd)).

Rollback and Restart: A transaction is rolled back and restarted by the `retry`-command (if it is not inside an `orElse`-command). This can occur by a user programmed `retry`, or if the transaction gets stopped by a conflicting transaction which is committing. The thread removes the notification entries (rule (retryCGlob)) and then the transaction code is replaced by the original expression (rule (retryEnd)).

Also, it is easy to extend the monomorphic type system to $CSHF$ and to see that reduction keeps well-typedness.

The commit-phase uses thread-local memory K, written over the thread-arrow after a semicolon.
The third memory-component is the set of locked TVars.

(writeStart) start of commit: locking the read and to-be-written TVars

$\langle u \wr y \rangle \stackrel{T,L}{\Longleftarrow} \mathbb{M}_{\mathtt{IO}}[\mathtt{atomically!}\ (\mathtt{return_{STM}}\ e_1)\ e] \mid x_1\ \mathbf{tg}\ e'_1 - g_1 \mid \ldots \mid x_n\ \mathbf{tg}\ e'_n - g_n$
$\xrightarrow{CSHF} \langle u \wr y \rangle \stackrel{T,L;K}{\Longleftarrow} \mathbb{M}_{\mathtt{IO}}[\mathtt{atomically!}\ (\mathtt{return_{STM}}\ e_1)\ e] \mid x_1\ \mathbf{tg}\ e'_1\ u\ g_1 \mid \ldots \mid x_n\ \mathbf{tg}\ e'_n\ u\ g_n$
where $K := \{x_1, \ldots, x_n\} = T \cup (L_a \setminus L_n)$ and $L = (L_a, L_n, L_w) : L_r$

(writeClear) removing the notify-entries of u:

$\langle u \wr y \rangle \stackrel{T,L;K}{\Longleftarrow} \mathbb{M}_{\mathtt{IO}}[\mathtt{atomically!}\ (\mathtt{return_{STM}}\ e_1)\ e] \mid x\ \mathbf{tg}\ e_2\ u\ g \xrightarrow{CSHF} \langle u \wr y \rangle \stackrel{T',L;K}{\Longleftarrow} \mathbb{M}_{\mathtt{IO}}[\mathtt{atomically!}\ (\mathtt{return_{STM}}\ e_1)\ e] \mid x\ \mathbf{tg}\ e_2\ u\ g'$
if $x \in T$ where $g' = g \setminus \{u\}$ and $T' = T \setminus \{x\}$

(sendRetry) Sending other threads (that are in transactions) a retry:

$\langle u \wr y \rangle \stackrel{\emptyset,L;K}{\Longleftarrow} \mathbb{M}_{\mathtt{IO}}[\mathtt{atomically!}\ (\mathtt{return_{STM}}\ e_1)\ e] \mid x\ \mathbf{tg}\ e_2\ u\ g \mid \langle u' \wr z \rangle \stackrel{T',L'}{\Longleftarrow} \mathbb{M}'_{\mathtt{IO}}[\mathtt{atomically!}\ e_3\ e_4]$
$\xrightarrow{CSHF} \langle u \wr y \rangle \stackrel{\emptyset,L;K}{\Longleftarrow} \mathbb{M}_{\mathtt{IO}}[\mathtt{atomically!}\ (\mathtt{return_{STM}}\ e_1)\ e] \mid x\ \mathbf{tg}\ e_2\ u\ g' \mid \langle u' \wr z \rangle \stackrel{T',L'}{\Longleftarrow} \mathbb{M}'_{\mathtt{IO}}[\mathtt{atomically!}\ \mathtt{retry}\ e_4]$
if $x \in L_w$, $g \neq \emptyset$, $u' \in g$, where $L = (L_a, L_n, L_w) : L_r$, and $g = g' \dot\cup \{u'\}$

(writeTV) Overwriting the global TVars with the local TVars of u:

$\langle u \wr y \rangle \stackrel{\emptyset,L;K}{\Longleftarrow} \mathbb{M}_{\mathtt{IO}}[\mathtt{atomically!}\ (\mathtt{return_{STM}}\ e_1)\ e] \mid x\ \mathbf{tg}\ e_2\ u\ [] \mid u\ \mathbf{tls}\ (\{x\ \mathbf{tl}\ e_3\} \dot\cup r : s)$
$\xrightarrow{CSHF} \langle u \wr y \rangle \stackrel{\emptyset,L';K}{\Longleftarrow} \mathbb{M}_{\mathtt{IO}}[\mathtt{atomically!}\ (\mathtt{return_{STM}}\ e_1)\ e] \mid x\ \mathbf{tg}\ e_3\ u\ [] \mid u\ \mathbf{tls}\ (r : s)$
if for all $z \in L_w \setminus L_n$ the g is empty in the component $z\ \mathbf{tg}\ e_2\ u\ g$, and if $L_w \setminus L_n \neq \emptyset$
where $L = (L_a, L_n, L_w) : L_r$, $x \in L_w \setminus L_n$, $L' = (L_a, L_n, L_w \setminus \{x\}) : L_r$.

(unlockTV) Unlocking the locked TVars:

$\langle u \wr y \rangle \stackrel{\emptyset,L;K}{\Longleftarrow} \mathbb{M}_{\mathtt{IO}}[\mathtt{atomically!}\ (\mathtt{return_{STM}}\ e_1)\ e] \mid x\ \mathbf{tg}\ e_2\ u\ [] \xrightarrow{CSHF} \langle u \wr y \rangle \stackrel{\emptyset,L;K'}{\Longleftarrow} \mathbb{M}_{\mathtt{IO}}[\mathtt{atomically!}\ (\mathtt{return_{STM}}\ e_1)\ e] \mid x\ \mathbf{tg}\ e_3 - []$
if $L_w \setminus L_n = \emptyset$, and $K \neq \emptyset$ where $L = (L_a, L_n, L_w) : L_r$, and $K' = K \setminus \{x\}$

(writeTVn) Moving the freshly generated TVars of u into global store:

$\langle u \wr y \rangle \stackrel{\emptyset,L;\emptyset}{\Longleftarrow} \mathbb{M}_{\mathtt{IO}}[\mathtt{atomically!}\ (\mathtt{return_{STM}}\ e_1)\ e] \mid u\ \mathbf{tls}\ (\{x\ \mathbf{tl}\ e_3\} \dot\cup r : s)$
$\xrightarrow{CSHF} \langle u \wr y \rangle \stackrel{\emptyset,L;\emptyset}{\Longleftarrow} \mathbb{M}_{\mathtt{IO}}[\mathtt{atomically!}\ (\mathtt{return_{STM}}\ e_1)\ e] \mid x\ \mathbf{tg}\ e_3 - []$
if $x \in L_n$, where $L = (L_a, L_n, L_w) : L_r$ and $L' = (L_a, L_n \setminus \{x\}, \emptyset) : L_r$

(writeEnd) Removing local store and end of commit of transaction:

$\langle u \wr y \rangle \stackrel{\emptyset,L;\emptyset}{\Longleftarrow} \mathbb{M}_{\mathtt{IO}}[\mathtt{atomically!}\ (\mathtt{return_{STM}}\ e_1)\ e] \mid u\ \mathbf{tls}\ (r : s) \xrightarrow{CSHF} \langle u \wr y \rangle \Leftarrow \mathbb{M}_{\mathtt{IO}}[\mathtt{return_{IO}}\ e_1]$
if no other rules of the commit-phase for u are applicable, i.e., if $L_n = L_w = \emptyset$, where $L = (L_a, L_n, L_w) : L_r$.

Figure 4. Concurrent Implementation of SHF, commit phase of transaction

Definition 3.4. A $CSHF$-process P is *successful*, iff it is well-formed and the main thread is of the form $\langle u \wr y \rangle \stackrel{\text{main}}{\Longleftarrow} \mathtt{return}\ e$. *May- and should-convergence* in $CSHF$ are defined by: $P{\downarrow}_{CSHF}$ iff P is well-formed and $\exists P' : P \xrightarrow{CSHF,*} P' \wedge P'$ successful. $P{\Downarrow}_{CSHF}$, iff P is well-formed and $\forall P' : P \xrightarrow{CSHF,*} P' \implies P'{\downarrow}_{CSHF}$. *Must- and may-divergence* of process P are the negations of may- and should-convergence and are denoted by $P{\Uparrow}_{CSHF}$, and $P{\uparrow}_{CSHF}$, resp., where $P{\uparrow}_{CSHF}$ is also equivalent to $P \xrightarrow{CSHF,*} P'$ such that $P'{\Uparrow}_{CSHF}$.

Contextual approximation $\leq_{CSHF}$ and *equivalence* $\sim_{CSHF}$ in $CSHF$ are defined as $\leq_{CSHF} := \leq_{\downarrow_{CSHF}} \cap \leq_{\Downarrow_{CSHF}}$ and $\sim_{CSHF} := \leq_{CSHF} \cap \geq_{CSHF}$ where for $\zeta \in \{\downarrow_{CSHF}, \Downarrow_{CSHF}\}$: $P_1 \leq_\zeta P_2$ iff $\forall \mathbb{D} \in PC_C : \mathbb{D}[P_1]\zeta \implies \mathbb{D}[P_2]\zeta$.

4. Correctness of the Concurrent Implementation

In this section we show that $CSHF$ can be used as a correct evaluator for SHF and its semantics. Hence, we provide a translation from SHF into $CSHF$:

Definition 4.1. The translation ψ of an SHF-process into a $CSHF$-process is defined homomorphically on the structure of processes: Usually it is the identity on the constructs; the only exception is $\psi(x\ \mathbf{t}\ e) := x\ \mathbf{tg}\ e - []$, i.e. initially, the list of threads to be notified is empty and the TVar is not locked. $CSHF$-processes $\psi(P)$ where P is an SHF-process are the *initial* $CSHF$-processes.

We are mainly interested in $CSHF$-reductions that start with initial $CSHF$-processes. Since only transactions can introduce local TVars which are removed at the end of a transaction, the following lemma holds:

Lemma 4.2. *Every initial CSHF-process is well-formed provided the corresponding SHF-process is well-formed. Also, every reduction descendant of an initial CSHF-process is well-formed.*

The correctness theorem we want to prove is the following:

Main Theorem 4.3. *The translation $\psi : SHF \to CSHF$ is observational correct, i.e. for all process contexts D and SHF-processes P the equivalences $D[P]{\downarrow} \iff \psi(D)(\psi(P)){\downarrow}_{CSHF}$ and $D[P]{\Downarrow} \iff \psi(D)(\psi(P)){\Downarrow}_{CSHF}$ hold. This also implies that ψ is adequate, i.e. $\psi(P_1) \sim_{CSHF} \psi(P_2) \implies P_1 \sim_c P_2$.*

Adequacy is a direct consequence of observational correctness (see [15]). Since the translation ψ is compositional, i.e. $\psi(D)(\psi(P)) = \psi(D[P])$ for any processes context D and pro-

Functional Evaluation

(feval$_{\text{IO}}$) $P \xrightarrow{CSHF} P'$, if $P \xrightarrow{a} P'$ for $a \in \{\text{cp}_{\text{IO}}, \text{abs}_{\text{IO}}, \text{mkb}_{\text{IO}}, \text{lbeta}_{\text{IO}}, \text{case}_{\text{IO}}, \text{seq}_{\text{IO}}\}$

(feval$_{\text{STM}}$) $P \xrightarrow{CSHF} P'$, if $P \xrightarrow{a} P'$ for $a \in \{\text{cp}_{\text{STM}}, \text{abs}_{\text{STM}}, \text{mkb}_{\text{STM}}, \text{lbeta}_{\text{STM}}, \text{case}_{\text{STM}}, \text{seq}_{\text{STM}}\}$

The reductions with parameter $Q \in \{\texttt{STM}, \texttt{IO}\}$ are defined as follows

(cp$_Q$) $\mathbb{L}_Q[x_1] \mid x_1 = x_2 \mid \ldots \mid x_{n-1} = x_n \mid x_n = v \to \mathbb{L}_Q[v] \mid x_1 = x_2 \mid \ldots \mid x_{n-1} = x_n \mid x_n = v$,
if v is an abstraction, a cx-value, or a component name

(abs$_Q$) $\mathbb{L}_Q[x_1] \mid x_1 = x_2 \mid \ldots \mid x_{m-1} = x_m \mid x_m = c\, e_1 \ldots e_n$
$\to \nu y_1, \ldots y_n.(\mathbb{L}_Q[c\, y_1 \ldots y_n] \mid x_1 = x_2 \mid \ldots \mid x_{m-1} = x_m \mid x_m = c\, y_1 \ldots y_n \mid y_1 = e_1 \mid \ldots \mid y_n = e_n)$
if c is a constructor, or $\texttt{return}_{\text{STM}}$, $\texttt{return}_{\text{IO}}$, $\texttt{>>=}_{\text{STM}}$, $\texttt{>>=}_{\text{IO}}$, `orElse`, `atomically`, `readTVar`, `writeTVar`, `newTVar`, or `future`, and $n \geq 1$, and some e_i is not a variable.

(mkb$_Q$) $\mathbb{L}_Q[\texttt{letrec}\ x_1 = e_1, \ldots, x_n = e_n\ \texttt{in}\ e] \to \nu x_1, \ldots, x_n.(\mathbb{L}_Q[e] \mid x_1 = e_1 \mid \ldots \mid x_n = e_n)$

(lbeta$_Q$) $\mathbb{L}_Q[((\lambda x.e_1)\ e_2)] \to \nu x.(\mathbb{L}_Q[e_1] \mid x = e_2)$

(case$_Q$) $\mathbb{L}_Q[\texttt{case}_T\ (c\, e_1 \ldots e_n)\ \texttt{of}\ \ldots((c\, y_1 \ldots y_n) \to e)\ldots] \to \nu y_1, \ldots, y_n.(\mathbb{L}_Q[e] \mid y_1 = e_1 \mid \ldots \mid y_n = e_n])$ if $n > 0$

(case$_Q$) $\mathbb{L}_Q[\texttt{case}_T\ c\ \texttt{of}\ \ldots(c \to e)\ldots] \to \mathbb{L}_Q[e]$

(seq$_Q$) $\mathbb{L}_Q[(\texttt{seq}\ v\ e)] \to \mathbb{L}_Q[e]$, if v is a functional value

Figure 5. Concurrent implementation of *SHF*, functional reductions

cess P, for the proof of observational correctness it is sufficient to show that ψ preserves and reflects may- and should convergence:

Theorem 4.4. *The translation $\psi : SHF \to CSHF$ is convergence equivalent, i.e. for all SHF-processes P the equivalences $P{\downarrow} \iff \psi(P){\downarrow}_{CSHF}$ and $P{\Downarrow} \iff \psi(P){\Downarrow}_{CSHF}$ hold.*

In the remainder of this section we will prove this theorem to complete the proof of Main Theorem 4.3. Thus we have to show that may- and should-convergence are the same for the big-step semantics and the concurrent implementation.

In order to be on solid ground, we first analyze the invariants during transactions and properties of the valid configurations.

Lemma 4.5. *The following properties hold during a CSHF-reduction on a well-formed CSHF-process that is reachable from a non-transactional CSHF-process.*

1. *For every component x **tl** e, either $x \in L_n$ of the top entry in L, or there is a global TVar x. For every pair of thread identifier u, and TVar-name x, every stack element of the TVar-stack for u contains at most one entry x **tl** e.*
2. *If u is in a notify-list of a global TVar, then thread u is transactional.*
3. *Every transaction that starts the commit-phase for thread u by performing the rule (writeStart) is able to perform all other rules until (writeEnd) is performed, without retry, nontermination or getting stuck.*

For proving convergence equivalence of ψ (Theorem 4.4) we have to show four parts: preservation of may-convergence ($P{\downarrow} \Rightarrow \psi(P){\downarrow}_{CSHF}$), reflection of may-convergence ($\psi(P){\downarrow}_{CSHF} \Rightarrow P{\downarrow}$), preservation of should-convergence ($P{\Downarrow} \Rightarrow \psi(P){\Downarrow}_{CSHF}$), and reflection of should-convergence ($\psi(P){\Downarrow}_{CSHF} \Rightarrow P{\Downarrow}$).

4.1 Preservation of May-Convergence

We have to show that $P{\downarrow}$ implies $\psi(P){\downarrow}_{CSHF}$, which is not completely straightforward, since the big-step reduction $\xrightarrow{SHFA,*}$ can be tried for free, and only in the case of success, i.e., a $\texttt{return}_{\text{STM}}$ is obtained by an atomic transaction, the changes of the $\xrightarrow{SHFA,*}$-reduction sequence are kept. Also, if an `orElse`-expression is reduced, the big-step reduction is permitted to evaluate the second expression, if it is known that the first one would end in a retry. This is different in *CSHF*, since the execution has to first evaluate the left expression of an `orElse`-expression, and only in case it "retries", the second expression will be evaluated where the changes of the TVars are not kept, but changes belonging to functional evaluation in the bindings are kept. Analyzing the behavior exhibits that these changes of the process can be proved as convergence equivalent transformations.

As a base case, the following lemma holds:

Lemma 4.6. *If P is successful, then $\psi(P)$ is successful.*

An easy case are non-(atomic)-standard reductions:

Lemma 4.7. *If $P_1 \xrightarrow{SHF,a} P_2$ where $a \neq$ (atomic), then $\psi(P_1) \xrightarrow{CSHF} \psi(P_2)$.*

The more complex cases arise for the transactions in the big-step reduction. In this case the state of the concurrent implementation consists of stacks, global TVars and stacks of local TVars. We consider several program transformations related to reduction rules, which are chosen such that it is sufficient to simulate the modifications in the bindings of the retried *CSHF*-standard reductions and then to rearrange reduction sequences of the concurrent implementation.

Definition 4.8 (*CSHF* special transformations). The *special transformations* are defined in Fig. 6 where we assume that they are closed w.r.t. $\mathbb{D}$-contexts and structural congruence, i.e. for any transformation $\xrightarrow{a}$ with $a \in \{\text{(cpBE)}, \text{(absB)}, \text{(funrB)}, \text{(absG)}, \text{(absAt)}, \text{(gc)}\}$ we extend its definition as follows: If $P \equiv \mathbb{D}[P']$, $Q \equiv \mathbb{D}[Q']$, and $P' \xrightarrow{a} Q'$, then also $P \xrightarrow{a} Q$.

We require the notion of convergence equivalence for program transformations, which is analogously defined to convergence equivalence of translations:

Definition 4.9. If $P_1{\downarrow}_{CSHF} \iff P_2{\downarrow}_{CSHF}$ and $P_1{\Downarrow}_{CSHF} \iff P_2{\Downarrow}_{CSHF}$ then we write $P_1 \sim_{ce} P_2$. A program transformation ξ (i.e. a binary relation over *CSHF*-processes) is *convergence equivalent* iff $P_1\ \xi\ P_2$ always implies $P_1 \sim_{ce} P_2$.

In the technical report [14] we prove:

Lemma 4.10. *The rules in Fig. 6 are convergence equivalent.*

First we observe the effects of global retries:

Lemma 4.11. *If there is a CSHF-reduction sequence $P_1 \xrightarrow{CSHF,*} P_2$, where an STM-transaction is started in the first reduction for thread u, and the last reduction is a global retry, i.e. (retryEnd) for thread u, of the transaction, then $P_1\ (\xrightarrow{CSHF} \cup \xrightarrow{spt})^*\ P_2$ where $\xrightarrow{spt}$ is the union of the CSHF-special-transformations*

(cpBE)	$x = \mathbb{E}[x_1] \mid x_1 = x_2 \mid \ldots \mid x_{m-1} = x_m \mid x_m = v \longrightarrow x = \mathbb{E}[v] \mid x_1 = x_2 \mid \ldots \mid x_{m-1} = x_m \mid x_m = v$, if v is an abstraction, a cx-value or a component-name, and $\mathbb{E} \neq [\cdot]$.
(absB)	$x = c\, e_1 \ldots e_n \longrightarrow \nu x_1, \ldots x_n . x = c\, x_1 \ldots x_n \mid x_1 = e_1 \mid \ldots \mid x_n = e_n$.
(funrB)	Every functional rule (without the surrounding $\mathbb{L}$-context) in a context $x = \mathbb{E}[\cdot]$, but not (cp) and not (abs).
(absG)	$x\, \mathbf{tg}\, e\, o\, g \longrightarrow \nu z . x\, \mathbf{tg}\, z\, o\, g \mid z = e$ where $o \in \{-, u\}$
(absAt)	$\langle x \wr u \rangle \Leftarrow \mathbb{M}_{\mathtt{IO}}[(\mathtt{atomically}\ e)] \longrightarrow \langle x \wr u \rangle \Leftarrow \mathbb{M}_{\mathtt{IO}}[(\mathtt{atomically}\ z)] \mid z = e$.
(gc)	$\nu x_1, \ldots, x_n . P \mid x_1 = e_1 \mid \ldots \mid x_n = e_n \longrightarrow \nu x_1, \ldots x_n . P$ if for all $i = 1, \ldots, n$: x_i does not occur free in P.
(cpxgc)	$\nu x . C[x, \ldots, x] \mid x = y \longrightarrow C[y, \ldots, y]$ where C is a multi-context, where all holes are in an $\mathbb{A}$-context, and all occurrences of x are indicated in the notation, i.e., there are no other occurrences. $\mathbb{A}$ is the class of expression contexts where the hole is not within an abstraction nor in a letrec-expression, nor in an alternative of a case and not in an argument of a constructor.

Figure 6. Special Transformations for *CSHF*

(cpBE), (absB), (funrB), (absG), and inverse (gc)-transformations from Definition 4.8.

Proof. A global retry removes all generated local TVars for this thread. There may remain changes in the global TVars and in the bindings: Transformations (absG) may be necessary for global TVars. Functional transformations in the sharing part are still there, but may be turned into non-standard reductions, if these were triggered only by the thread u. Since (cp)-effects in the thread expression are eliminated after a retry in an `orElse`: These may be (cpBE), (absB), (funrB). Various reductions generate bindings which are no longer used after removal of the first expression in an `orElse`, which can be simulated by a reverse (gc). These special reductions replace the transaction reductions for thread u, but the others remain, hence the lemma holds. □

Lemma 4.12. *If* $P_1 \xrightarrow{SHF,atomic} P_2$*, then* $\psi(P_1) \xrightarrow{CSHF,*} P_2'$*, and* $P_2' \xrightarrow{sptx,*} \psi(P_2)$*, where* $\xrightarrow{sptx}$ *consists of special transformations in Fig. 6 and their inverses.*

Proof. The correspondence between the contents of the global TVar x in *CSHF* for a single thread u is the local TVar x on the top of the stack, or the global TVar if there is no local TVar for x. The rules that change the bindings permanently in the atomic-transaction reduction are: (atomic), (readl), (readg), (orElse), which can be simulated by sequences of (absG) and reverse (gc). The effects of the functional rules ((cp$_Q$), (abs$_Q$), (mkb$_Q$), (lbeta$_Q$), (case$_Q$)) that survive a retry are either simulated by (mkb$_Q$), (lbeta$_Q$), (case$_Q$) in a binding, or by (cpBE), (absB), or inverse (gc). An (ortry)-reduction in *SHF* can be simulated in *CSHF* by a sequence of reductions starting with (orElse) and ending with (orRetry). However, since (ortry) undoes all changes, in *CSHF* it is necessary to undo the changes in bindings by the special transformations.

In [14] we show that the claimed rearrangement is possible. □

Theorem 4.13. *For all SHF-processes P, we have* $P\downarrow \implies \psi(P)\downarrow_{CSHF}$.

Proof. This follows by an induction on the length of the given reduction sequence for P. The base case is covered in Lemma 4.6. Lemmas 4.7, 4.12, and 4.10 show that if $P_1 \xrightarrow{SHF} P_2$, then there is some *CSHF*-process P_2' such that $\psi(P_1) \xrightarrow{CSHF,*} P_2'$ with $P_2' \sim_{ce} \psi(P_2)$. This is sufficient for the induction step. □

4.2 Reflection of May-Convergence

In this section we distinguish the different reduction steps within a *CSHF*-reduction sequence $\psi(P_1) \xrightarrow{*} P_2$ for the different threads u. A (sendRetry)-reduction belongs to the sending thread. A subsequence of the reduction sequence starting with (atomic) and ending with (writeEnd), which includes exactly the u-reduction steps in between, and where no other (atomic) or (writeEnd)-reductions are contained is called a *transaction*. A prefix of a transaction is also called a *partial transaction*. The subsequence of an u-transaction for thread u starting with (writeStart) and ending with (writeEnd) is called the *commit-phase* of the transaction. If the subsequence for thread u starts with (atomic) and ends with (retryEnd), without intermediate (atomic) or (retryEnd), then it is an *aborted transaction*. The subsequence from the first (retryCGlob) until (retryEnd) is the *abort-phase* of the aborted transaction. A prefix of an aborted transaction is also called a *partial aborted transaction*.

Theorem 4.14. *For all SHF-processes P, we have* $\psi(P)\downarrow_{CSHF} \implies P\downarrow$.

Proof. Let $\psi(P_1) \xrightarrow{CSHF,*} P_2$ where P_2 is successful. Since the transactions in the reduction sequence may be interleaved with other transactions and reduction steps, we have to rearrange the reduction sequence in order to be able to retranslate it into *SHF*.
Partial Transactions that do not contain a (writeStart) within the reduction sequence can be eliminated and thereby replaced by interspersed special transformations using Lemma 4.11, which again can be eliminated from the successful reduction sequence by Lemma 4.10. If the partial transaction contains a (writeStart), then the missing reduction steps can be added within the reduction sequence before a successful process is reached, since the commit-phase does not change the successful-property of processes.
Aborted Transactions can be omitted since they are replaceable by special transformations, which again can be removed.
Grouping Transactions: We can now assume that within the reduction sequence $\psi(P_1) \xrightarrow{CSHF,*} P_2$ where P_2 is successful, all transactions are completed, and that there are no aborted ones. Now we rearrange the reduction sequence: The (writeEnd)-reduction step is assumed to be the point of attraction for every transaction. Moving single reduction steps starts from the rightmost non-grouped transaction. For this u-transaction, we move the reduction steps that belong to it in the direction of its (writeEnd), i.e., to the right. The reduction steps that belong to the same transaction and are between (writeStart) and (writeEnd) can be moved to the right squeezing out the non-u-reduction steps, which is possible, since the locking prevents other transaction reduction steps of other threads to be in between, and since there are no functional reduction steps in between.

Now we speak of the u-*block* of reduction steps, if every reduction step in it belongs to the same transaction and ends with (writeStart). The block is complete, if the first (leftmost) reduction step is (atomic). The interesting part of the reduction sequence is like $\xrightarrow{a}; S; B^u$, where B^u is the u-block; S is a reduction sequence of non-u-reduction steps and $\xrightarrow{a}$ is the reduction step that we want to move to the right, before B^u. For the reduction steps for u that are before (writeStart), we distinguish functional and non-functional reductions. Every standard functional reduction is triggered (or requested) by one or more threads. This must be taken into account when reasoning about shifting functional transactional reduction steps within reduction sequences. Another issue is which reductions are in S. Since we started with the rightmost transaction, the steps in S are either non-transactional ones, or if they are transactional ones, then these are for another thread. It is obvious that S does not contain a commit-phase of a transaction that aborts u. Thus $\xrightarrow{a}$ cannot be a u-read of a TVar that is committed in S; it can be a u-write of a TVar, even if writing this TVar is committed in S, since there is no registration of threads at written TVars, and so the rules can be interchanged. Hence, if $\xrightarrow{a}$ is a non-functional transaction step, then it can be moved to the u-block. If $\xrightarrow{a}$ is a functional transaction that is only requested by u, then it will also be moved to the u-block. Now assume that $\xrightarrow{a}$ is a functional transaction that is also requested by another transaction of thread u'. If all such threads are either u or their blocks are to the right of the u-block, then we move the reduction in front of the u-block. Otherwise, i.e, if at least one requesting transaction is in S, then $\xrightarrow{a}$ is now a part of S.

Thus the general situation is: the u-block is the current focus of shifting and there may be more blocks to the right of this block; S consists of functional reductions requested by threads in S, and of other reduction steps. Also in this general case the following holds: functional reductions $\xrightarrow{a}$ that are only requested by u, can be moved to the u-block. Finally, there will be an (atomic)-reduction, and after the move, we have a complete u-block that corresponds to a complete transaction. If the moving is done exhaustively, then the reduction sequence is almost in a form that can be backtranslated into SHF. Every reduction steps that are not within transactions for a thread can be backtranslated as a SHF-reduction.

The last issue in the backtranslation are the local retries in `orElse`-expressions in $CSHF$, which do not have an effect on the TVars, but may apply functional reductions to the bindings, however, in SHF the `orElse`-retries are without any effect.

We use Lemma 4.10 to correctly backtranslate transactions, in particular (orElse)-reductions, including the retries in the transaction. The backtranslation is done from left to right. The plan is to show that the `orElse`-computation tree that is done sequentially in $CSHF$, will also be performed in the same sequence in SHF. A difference are that $\xrightarrow{SHFA,*}$-reductions are part of the reductions in $CSHF$. Therefore, consider the case that evaluation of the left expression e_1 in a `orElse` ends in a retry. In $CSHF$, all the functional reductions in the reduction sequence corresponding to e_1 can be shifted in the reduction sequence to the right end of the complete reduction sequence, which can then be ignored leaving the sequence successful. Using induction on the depth of the `orElse`-expressions, we can show that there is a backtranslation of the transaction for thread u as an atomic reduction in SHF.

From a bird eyes point of view, a successful $CSHF$-reduction of a process P is first rearranged into another a successful $CSHF$-reduction, and then an interleaved rearrangement and backtranslation leads to a converging SHF-reduction sequence for P as a SHF-process. □

Corollary 4.15. *Let P be an SHF-process. Then $P\Uparrow \iff \psi(P)\Uparrow_{CSHF}$.*

4.3 Reflection of Should-Convergence

Instead of proving reflection of should-convergence directly, we equivalently show preservation of may-divergence. The proof is analogous to the preservation of may-convergence in Theorem 4.13, where now, however, the reduction sequence ends in a must-divergent process. Using Corollary 4.15 as a base case shows that may-divergence is preserved:

Theorem 4.16. *For all SHF-processes P, we have $P\uparrow \implies \psi(P)\uparrow_{CSHF}$.*

4.4 Preservation of Should-Convergence

This is the last part of the analysis. A needed lemma is the following (proved in [14]), which shows that partial transactions can be eliminated:

Lemma 4.17. *Let P_0 be a nontransactional process, $P_0 \xrightarrow{CSHF,*} P_1$ with $P_1\Uparrow_{CSHF}$, such that $P \xrightarrow{Q} P_1$ is a suffix of the reduction and $P \xrightarrow{Q} P_1$ is a partial transaction for a thread u starting with (atomic) but the commit-phase and the retry-phase is missing, i.e. there is no reduction (writeStart) nor a (retryCGlob) for thread u. Then $P\Uparrow_{CSHF}$.*

Now we show reflection of of may-divergence, which is equivalent to preservation of should-convergence.

Theorem 4.18. *For all SHF-processes P, we have $\psi(P)\uparrow_{CSHF} \implies P\uparrow$.*

Proof. Assume given a non-transactional $CSHF$-process $\psi(P)$ with $\psi(P) \xrightarrow{CSHF,*} P_1$ and $P_1\Uparrow_{CSHF}$. The reasoning is as in Theorem 4.14 with some differences, since we have to ensure the condition $P_1\Uparrow_{CSHF}$, which is more complex than the "successful"-condition. *Partial transactions:* If it includes a (writeStart) or a (retryCGlob), then the transaction can be completed by $P_1 \xrightarrow{CSHF,*} P_1'$ where $P_1'\Uparrow_{CSHF}$, and so we can assume that these do not exist. If the partial transaction does neither include a (writeStart) nor a (retryCGlob), then using the same arguments as in Theorem 4.14, we see that we can assume that the partial transaction is grouped before P_1, i.e. the transaction ends with the partial transaction $P_1'' \xrightarrow{CSHF,*} P_1$. Lemma 4.17 shows that $P_1''\uparrow_{CSHF}$, which permits to assume that the partial transaction can be omitted. *Aborted transactions:* can be omitted since they are replaceable by special transformations, which again can be removed due to Lemma 4.10. *Grouping transaction:* same arguments as in the proof of Theorem 4.14. *Final retranslation:* similar to the proof of Theorem 4.14. □

4.5 Summary

We have proved in Theorems 4.13, 4.14, 4.16, and 4.18 that the translation ψ mapping SHF-processes into $CSHF$-processes is convergence equivalent. Thus we have proved Theorem 4.4 and thus also Main Theorem 4.3 (observational correctness and adequacy of ψ), since ψ is compositional. This shows that $CSHF$ is a correct evaluator for SHF-processes w.r.t. the big-step semantics.

Instead of permitting to retry a transaction too often, the strategy from [7] can be applied: activate retried transactions only if some of the read TVars is modified. Our proofs can be used to show that this restriction of reductions is equivalent to the $CSHF$-semantics.

Note that omitting the send retry for abortion would make the implementation incorrect (non-adequate): a thread that runs into a loop if TVar x contains a 1 and returns otherwise, may block this thread indefinitely, which is not the case in the specification SHF.

5. Related Work

General remarks on STM are in [4, 8]. [4] argue that more research is needed to reduce the runtime overhead of STM. We believe that ease of maintenance of programs and the increased concurrency provided by STM may become more important in the future.

The paper which strongly influenced our work is [7]. *SHF* borrows from the operational semantics of STM Haskell, where differences are that our calculus is extended by futures, models also the call-by-need evaluation, but does not include exceptions and is restricted to monomorphic typing. However, since futures can be safely implemented in Concurrent Haskell by using `unsafeInterleaveIO` [13], this difference is rather small. Moreover, our correctness proofs do not rely on having futures in the language and thus would also hold, if threads only have a thread identifier but not a resulting value.

Harris et al. [7] describe the current implementation of STM Haskell in the Glasgow Haskell Compiler (GHC), however no formal treatment of this implementation is given. The approach taken in the GHC implementation is close to ours with the difference that instead of aborting transactions by the committing transaction (i.e. sending retries in *CSHF*), transactions abort and restart themselves by temporarily checking their local transaction log against the status of the global memory, and thus detecting conflicts. This is comparable to our approach, and we are convinced that the implementations are closely related. However, modelling their approach in a formal semantics would require more effort: For instance, in the GHC implementation comparing the local content (stored in the transaction log) and the global content of a TVar is done by pointer equality. Including this equality either has to be defined as a side condition of a reduction rule or has to be built in as a language construct. One also has to make design decisions like the following: Should indirections (i.e. bindings like $x = y$) be respected, by the pointer equality test? For example, if the local content of a TVar is x and the global content is y where the bindings are $x = z \mid z = s \mid y = w \mid w = z$, are x and y equal? Semantically, this is correct (but hard to express in a small-step semantics). Testing such cases in GHC's STM implementation shows that indirections are not respected in the current implementation.

In contrast the semantics of *CSHF* does not need to compare pointers, since it uses the registration mechanism. A difference between our semantics and STM-Haskell is that in *CSHF* reading the content of a TVar and thereafter writing the same content is always a modification which may result in aborting other transactions, while in STM-Haskell perhaps the pointer remains the same and thus no conflict modification is detected. Thus our approach may have slightly more restarts than the STM-Haskell implementation. A potential semantical problem in [7] is that exceptions may make local values of TVars visible outside the transaction.

A semantical investigation of STM is in [2], where a call-by-name functional core language with concurrent processes is defined, and a contextual equivalence is used as equality. Also strong results are obtained by proving correctness of the monad laws and other program equivalences w.r.t. their semantics. However, [2] only considers may-convergence in the contextual equivalence, which is too weak for reasoning about non-deterministic (and concurrent) calculi. Also, `seq` is missing in [2] which is used in Haskell and known to change the semantics, such that validity of the monad laws only holds under further typing restrictions (see [12]). A further difference to our work is that [2] use pointer equality. [5] propose opacity (transactions can only see a committed state of all TVars), which is satisfied by CSHF; the complexity bounds from [5] are not applicable to CSHF, since we use visible reads.

[9] propose to investigate correctness of an implementation, but stick to testing. [1] consider correctness of implementing STM in a small calculus with call-by-value reduction and a monadic extension similar to the STM/IO-extension in [7]. The main reasoning tool is looking for traces of effects, and arguing about commuting and shifting the effects within traces, where several important properties are proved. It is hard to compare the results with ours, however, from an abstract level, their proof method appears to ignore the should-convergence restriction: There is no argument on forced aborts of transactions.

[3] investigate liveness properties and show that certain combinations of good properties are impossible in a model using infinite traces, random aborts and without fairness conditions.

6. Conclusion

We have presented a big-step semantics for STM-Haskell as a specification, and a small-step concurrent implementation. Using formal reasoning and the strong notion of contextual equivalence with may- and should-convergence we prove correctness of the implementation.

Further research directions are to consider smarter strategies for earlier aborts and retries of conflicting transactions, extending the language, e.g. by exceptions, and a polymorphic type system.

References

[1] A. Bieniusa and P. Thiemann. Proving isolation properties for software transactional memory. In *Proc. ESOP'11, LNCS* 6602, pp. 38–56, Springer 2011.

[2] J. Borgström, K. Bhargavan, and A. D. Gordon. A compositional theory for STM Haskell. In *Proc. Haskell '09*, pp. 69–80. ACM, 2009.

[3] V. Bushkov, R. Guerraoui, and M. Kapalka. On the liveness of transactional memory. In *Proc. PODC'12*, pp. 9–18. ACM, 2012.

[4] C. Cascaval, C. Blundell, M. M. Michael, H. W. Cain, P. Wu, S. Chiras, and S. Chatterjee. Software transactional memory: why is it only a research toy? *Commun. ACM*, 51(11):40–46, 2008.

[5] R. Guerraoui and M. Kapalka. On the correctness of transactional memory. In *Proc. PPoPP'08*, pp. 175–184. ACM, 2008.

[6] T. Harris, S. Marlow, S. Peyton Jones, and M. Herlihy. Composable memory transactions. In *Proc. PPoPP'05*, pp. 48–60. ACM, 2005.

[7] T. Harris, S. Marlow, S. L. Peyton Jones, and M. Herlihy. Composable memory transactions. *Commun. ACM*, 51(8):91–100, 2008.

[8] T. Harris, J. R. Larus, and R. Rajwar. *Transactional Memory, 2nd edition*. Synthesis Lectures on Computer Architecture. Morgan & Claypool Publishers, 2010.

[9] L. Hu and G. Hutton. Towards a verified implementation of software transactional memory. In *Proc. TFP'08*, vol. 9, pp. 129–144. Intellect, 2009.

[10] A. Rensink and W. Vogler. Fair testing. *Inform. and Comput.*, 205(2): 125–198, 2007.

[11] D. Sabel and M. Schmidt-Schauß. A call-by-need lambda-calculus with locally bottom-avoiding choice: Context lemma and correctness of transformations. *Math. Structures Comput. Sci.*, 18(03):501–553, 2008.

[12] D. Sabel and M. Schmidt-Schauß. A contextual semantics for Concurrent Haskell with futures. In *Proc. PPDP'11*, pp. 101–112. ACM, 2011.

[13] D. Sabel and M. Schmidt-Schauß. Conservative concurrency in Haskell. In *Proc. LICS'12*, pp. 561–570. IEEE, 2012.

[14] M. Schmidt-Schauß and D. Sabel. Correctness of an STM Haskell implementation. Frank report 50, Institut f. Informatik. Goethe-University Frankfurt, 2013. available at `http://www.ki.informatik.uni-frankfurt.de/papers/frank/`.

[15] M. Schmidt-Schauß, J. Niehren, J. Schwinghammer, and D. Sabel. Adequacy of compositional translations for observational semantics. In *Proc. IFIP TCS'08, IFIP* 273, pp. 521–535. Springer, 2008.

[16] N. Shavit and D. Touitou. Software transactional memory. In *Proc. PODC'95*, pp. 204–213. ACM, 1995.

[17] N. Shavit and D. Touitou. Software transactional memory. *Distributed Computing, Special Issue*, 10:99–116, 1997.

[18] M. C. J. D. van Eekelen, M. J. Plasmeijer, and J. E. W. Smetsers. Parallel graph rewriting on loosely coupled machine architectures. In *Proc. CTRS'90, LNCS* 516, pp. 354–369. Springer, 1990.

Programming with Permissions in *Mezzo*

François Pottier
INRIA
francois.pottier@inria.fr

Jonathan Protzenko
INRIA
jonathan.protzenko@ens-lyon.org

Abstract

We present *Mezzo*, a typed programming language of ML lineage. *Mezzo* is equipped with a novel static discipline of duplicable and affine permissions, which controls aliasing and ownership. This rules out certain mistakes, including representation exposure and data races, and enables new idioms, such as gradual initialization, memory re-use, and (type)state changes. Although the core static discipline disallows sharing a mutable data structure, *Mezzo* offers several ways of working around this restriction, including a novel dynamic ownership control mechanism which we dub "adoption and abandon".

Categories and Subject Descriptors D.3.2 [*Programming Languages*]: Language Classifications—Multiparadigm languages

Keywords static type systems; side effects; aliasing; ownership

1. Introduction

Programming with mutable, heap-allocated data structures is hard. In many typed imperative programming languages, including Java, C#, and ML, the type system keeps track of the structure of objects, but not of how they are aliased. As a result, a programming mistake can cause undesired sharing, which in turn leads to breaches of abstraction, invariant violations, race conditions, and so on. Furthermore, the fact that sharing is uncontrolled implies that the type of an object must never change. This forbids certain idioms, such as delayed initialization, and prevents the type system from keeping track of the manner in which objects change state through method calls. In order to work around this limitation, programmers typically use C# and Java's null pointer, or ML's option type. This implies that a failure to follow an intended protocol is not detected at compile time, but leads to a runtime error. In short, there is a price to pay for the simplicity of traditional type systems: the bugs caused by undesired sharing, or by the failure to follow an object protocol, are not statically detected.

This paper presents the design of a new programming language, *Mezzo*, which attempts to address these issues. One motivating principle behind the design of *Mezzo* is that one should be able to express precise assertions about the current *state* of an object or data structure. The type system should keep track of *state changes* and forbid using an object in a manner that is inconsistent with its current state. An example is a socket that moves from state "ready", to "connected", then to "closed". The "close" function, for instance, should be invoked only if the socket is currently in the state "connected", and changes its state to "closed". Another example is a collection, which must not be accessed while an iterator exists, but can be used again once iteration is over.

Although state and state change play an important role in many programs, no mainstream programming language builds these notions into its static discipline. External tools must be used, such as typestate checking tools [13, 5, 6] or tools for constructing proofs of programs, based for instance on separation logic [4, 20] or on the Spec# methodology [3]. Instead, we explore the possibility of reasoning about state within the type system. This has well-known potential benefits. A property that is expressed as a type is checked early, often, and at little cost. Furthermore, we believe that, in the future, such a type system can serve as a strong foundation for performing proofs of programs.

Obviously, if two "principals" separately think that "the socket s is currently connected", and if one of them decides to close this socket, then the other will be left with an incorrect belief about s. Thus, precise reasoning about state and state changes requires that information about a mutable object (or data structure) be recorded in at most "one place" in the type system. In *Mezzo*, this place is a *permission*. Permissions keep track not only of the structure of data, as does a traditional type system, but also of must-alias and must-not-alias (i.e. equality and disjointness) information. Like a separation logic assertion [29], a permission has an ownership reading: to have access to a description of a part of the heap is to own this part of the heap. Because "to describe is to own", we need not explicitly annotate types with owners, as done in Ownership Types [10] or Universe Types [14].

We do not think of the "type" of an object and of its "state" as two distinct notions: a permission describes both at once. Whereas previous work on permissions [5] distinguishes between a fixed type structure and "permissions" that evolve with time, in *Mezzo*, both "type" and "state" can change over time. This yields greater expressiveness: for instance, gradual initialization and memory re-use become possible. This also yields greater simplicity and conciseness: for instance, when we write polymorphic code that manipulates a list, a single type variable a denotes not only "what" the list elements are (e.g., sockets) but also in what "state" they are and to what extent we "own" them.

The choices described above form our basic design premises. *Mezzo* can be viewed as an experiment, whose aim is to determine to what extent these choices are viable. Beyond these decisions, we strive to make the language as simple as possible. *Mezzo* is a high-level programming language: we equip it with first-class functions, algebraic data types, and require a garbage collector. We could have chosen classes and objects instead of (or in addition to) algebraic data types; this could be a topic for future research. We equip *Mezzo* with a simple distinction between duplicable permissions (for immutable data) and exclusive permissions (for

ICFP '13, September 25–27, 2013, Boston, MA, USA.

ACM 978-1-4503-2326-0/13/09... $15.00.
http://dx.doi.org/10.1145/2500365.2500598

mutable data). Although more advanced varieties of permissions exist in the literature, including read-only views of mutable data and fractional permissions [7], we wish to evaluate how far one can go without these advanced notions; if desired, they could in principle be added to *Mezzo*.

By default, *Mezzo*'s permission discipline imposes a restrictive aliasing regime: the mutable part of the heap must form a forest. *Mezzo* offers several mechanisms for evading this restriction. One, adoption and abandon, is new. It allows arbitrary aliasing patterns within a region of the heap and achieves soundness via dynamic checks. We describe it in detail in §7. The second mechanism is Boyland's nesting [7]. It can be viewed as a form of adoption and abandon that requires no runtime checks but is (for many purposes) less powerful. The last mechanism is locks in the style of concurrent separation logic [25, 18, 19, 8].

Mezzo's static discipline has been formally defined and mechanically proved sound[1]. The formalization, which is available online [26], includes adoption and abandon, but does not (at present) cover nesting, locks, or concurrency. The statement of soundness guarantees that "well-typed programs do not go wrong", except possibly when the dynamic check performed at "abandon" fails. In a concurrent extension of *Mezzo*, it would in addition guarantee that "well-typed programs are data-race-free". The proof is syntactic. We extend the typing judgement to a pair of a program under execution and its heap, and establish the standard subject reduction and progress lemmas.

A prototype type-checker has been implemented and is publicly available [27]. Several small libraries, totaling a few thousand lines of code, have been written, and are also available online [27]. They include immutable data structures (lists), mutable data structures (lists, doubly-linked lists, binary search trees, hash tables, resizable arrays, and FIFO queues, see §7), persistent data structures implemented via imperative means (suspensions, persistent arrays), and a few algorithms (memoization; graph search). At the time of this writing, an interpreter is available, and a simple compiler (which translates *Mezzo* down to untyped OCaml) is being developed.

The paper begins with a motivating example (§2), which cannot be type-checked in ML, and which serves to informally illustrate *Mezzo*'s permission discipline. Then, we define the syntax of types, permissions, and expressions (§3) and informally explain the ownership reading of permissions for immutable and mutable data (§4). We present the typing rules (§5) and introduce a few syntactic conventions that make the surface language more palatable (§6). We explain adoption and abandon, illustrate them with a second example (§7), and discuss nesting and locks more briefly (§8). Finally, we explain where *Mezzo* lies in the design space and compare it with some of the previous approaches found in the literature (§9).

2. *Mezzo* by example

Figure 1 presents code for the concatenation of two immutable lists. This example showcases several of *Mezzo*'s features, and allows us to explain the use of permissions. We review the code first (§2.1), then briefly explain how it is type-checked (§2.2 and §2.3).

2.1 Code

Our purpose is to write code that concatenates two *immutable* lists `xs` and `ys` to produce a new *immutable* list. The traditional, purely functional implementations of concatenation have linear space overhead, as they implicitly or explicitly allocate a reversed copy of `xs`. Our implementation, on the other hand, is written in *destination-passing style*, and has constant space overhead. Roughly speaking, the list `xs` is traversed and copied on the fly. When the end of `xs` is reached, the last cell of the copy is made to point to `ys`.

```
1  data list a =
2    Nil | Cons { head: a; tail: list a }
3
4  data mutable mlist a =
5    MNil | MCons { head: a; tail: list a }
6
7  val rec appendAux [a] (
8      consumes dst: MCons { head: a; tail: () },
9      consumes xs: list a,
10     consumes ys: list a) : (| dst @ list a) =
11   match xs with
12   | Nil ->
13       dst.tail <- ys;
14       tag of dst <- Cons
15   | Cons ->
16       let dst' = MCons { head = xs.head;
17                          tail = () } in
18       dst.tail <- dst';
19       tag of dst <- Cons;
20       appendAux (dst', xs.tail, ys)
21   end
22
23 val append [a] (
24     consumes xs: list a,
25     consumes ys: list a) : list a =
26   match xs with
27   | Nil ->
28       ys
29   | Cons ->
30       let dst = MCons { head = xs.head;
31                         tail = () } in
32       appendAux (dst, xs.tail, ys);
33       dst
34   end
```

Figure 1. Tail-recursive concatenation of immutable lists

The `append` function (Figure 1, line 23) is where concatenation begins. If `xs` is empty, then the concatenation of `xs` and `ys` is `ys` (line 27). Otherwise (line 29), `append` allocates an *unfinished, mutable* cell `dst` (line 30). This cell contains the first element of the final list, namely `xs.head`. It is in an intermediate state: it cannot be considered a valid list, since its `tail` field contains the unit value `()`. It is now up to `appendAux` to finish the work by constructing the concatenation of `xs.tail` and `ys` and writing the address of that list into `dst.tail`. Once `appendAux` returns, `dst` *has become* a well-formed list (this is indicated by the postcondition "`dst @ list a`" on line 10) and is returned by `append`.

The function `appendAux` expects an unfinished, mutable cell `dst` and two lists `xs` and `ys`. Its purpose is to write the concatenation of `xs` and `ys` into `dst.tail`, at which point `dst` can be considered a well-formed list. If `xs` is `Nil` (line 12), the `tail` field of `dst` is made to point to `ys`. Then, `dst`, a mutable `MCons` cell, is "frozen" by a tag update instruction and becomes an immutable `Cons` cell. (This instruction compiles to a no-op.) If `xs` is a `Cons` cell (line 15), we allocate a new destination cell `dst'`, let `dst.tail` point to it, freeze `dst`, and repeat the process via a tail-recursive call.

This example illustrates several important aspects of *Mezzo*.

Expressiveness In a traditional typed programming language, such as Java or OCaml, list concatenation in destination-passing style is possible, but its result must be a mutable list, because an *immutable* list cell cannot be gradually initialized.

[1] The formalization concerns a slightly lower-level language, Core Mezzo. In Core Mezzo, fields are numbered, whereas in *Mezzo* they are named and field names can be overloaded. At present, Core Mezzo is missing some of the features of *Mezzo*, including parameterized algebraic data types and mode constraints. We hope to add them in the future.

State change The call `appendAux(dst, xs, ys)` changes the "type" of `dst` from "unfinished, mutable list cell' to "well-formed, immutable list". This type-changing update is sound because one must be the "unique owner" of the mutable cell `dst` for this call to be permitted.

Ownership transfer In fact, the call `appendAux(dst, xs, ys)` also changes the "type" of `xs` and `ys` from "immutable list" to "unknown". Indeed, the postcondition of `appendAux` guarantees nothing about `xs` and `ys`. In other words, the caller gives up the permission to use `xs` and `ys` as lists, and in return gains the permission to use `dst` as a list. In other words, the ownership of the list elements is transferred from `xs` and `ys` to `dst`. This is required for soundness. We do not know what the list elements are (they have abstract type `a`). They could be mutable objects, whose "unique ownership" property must not be violated[2].

2.2 Permissions

Permissions do not exist at runtime: they are purely an artefact of the type system. An atomic permission $x\,@\,t$ represents the right to use the program variable x at type t. Two permissions P_1 and P_2 can be combined to form a composite permission $P_1 * P_2$. The conjunction $*$ is separating [29] at mutable memory locations and requires agreement at immutable locations (§4.1). The empty permission, a unit for conjunction, is written empty.

When execution begins, a program conceptually possesses an empty permission. As execution progresses through the code, permissions come and go. At any program point, there is a certain *current permission*. Most of the time, the manner in which permissions evolve and flow is implicit. It must be made explicit in a few places: in particular, every function type must include explicit pre- and postconditions.

Let us continue our discussion of the concatenation example (Figure 1). We explain in an informal manner how the function `append` is type-checked. This allows us to illustrate how permissions are used and how they evolve.

The typing rules appear in Figure 4; a subset of the permission subsumption rules appear in Figure 6. In the following, we refer to some of these rules, but defer their detailed explanation to §5.

The `append` function is defined at line 23. At the beginning of the function's body, by the typing rule FUNCTION, permissions for the formal arguments are available. Thus, the current permission is:

$$xs\,@\,\mathsf{list}\ a * ys\,@\,\mathsf{list}\ a$$

This permission represents the right to use `xs` and `ys` as lists of elements of type a.

This permission soon evolves, thanks to the `match` construct, which examines the tag carried by `xs`. By the typing rule MATCH, as we learn that `xs` is a `Nil` cell, we replace our permission about `xs` with a more precise one, which incorporates the knowledge that the tag of `xs` is `Nil`. At line 27, the current permission becomes:

$$xs\,@\,\mathsf{Nil} * ys\,@\,\mathsf{list}\ a$$

$xs\,@\,\mathsf{Nil}$ is a *structural permission*: it asserts that `xs` points to a memory block whose tag is Nil (and which has zero fields). Similarly, at line 29, the current permission becomes:

$$xs\,@\,\mathsf{Cons}\,\{\mathsf{head} : a; \mathsf{tail} : \mathsf{list}\ a\} * ys\,@\,\mathsf{list}\ a$$

The structural permission for `xs` asserts that `xs` points to a memory block that carries the tag Cons and has a `head` field of type a and a `tail` field of type $\mathsf{list}\ a$.

[2] We later note (§4.1) that if at a call site the variable `a` is instantiated with a duplicable type, say `int`, then the permissions `xs @ list int` and `ys @ list int` are considered duplicable, so they can in fact be duplicated prior to the call `appendAux(dst, xs, ys)`, hence are not lost.

At this stage, the type-checker performs an implicit operation. It applies the permission subsumption rule DECOMPOSEBLOCK. This causes fresh names hd and tl to be introduced for the `head` and `tail` fields of this structural permission. This yields the following conjunction:

$$\begin{array}{l} xs\,@\,\mathsf{Cons}\,\{\mathsf{head} : (=hd); \mathsf{tail} : (=tl)\} * \\ hd\,@\,a * tl\,@\,\mathsf{list}\ a * \\ ys\,@\,\mathsf{list}\ a \end{array}$$

This is our first encounter of a singleton type, which we write $=hd$. A permission of the form $x\,@\,{=y}$ asserts that the variables x and y denote the same value. In particular, if they denote memory locations, this means that x and y point to the same object: this is a *must-alias* constraint. We write $x = y$ for $x\,@\,{=y}$. Similarly, in the structural permission above, the fact that the head field has type $=hd$ means that the value of this field is hd. We write $\mathsf{head} = hd$ for $\mathsf{head} : (=hd)$.

By the typing rules NEW and LET, when the cell `dst` is allocated (line 30), a permission for `dst` appears, namely:

$$dst\,@\,\mathsf{MCons}\,\{\mathsf{head} = hd; \mathsf{tail} : ()\}$$

We now see how singleton types help reason about sharing. At this point, we have three permissions that mention hd. We know that hd is stored in the head field of xs; we know that hd is stored in the head field of dst; and we have a permission to use hd at type a. We do not need a borrowing convention [24] in order to fix which of xs or dst owns hd. Instead, the system knows that the object hd is accessible via two paths, namely $xs.\mathsf{head}$ and $dst.\mathsf{head}$, and can be used under either name. This use of singleton types is taken from Alias Types [30].

By the typing rules READ and APPLICATION, in order to call `appendAux(dst, xs.tail, ys)` (line 32), we need the following conjunction of permissions. It is the precondition of `appendAux`, suitably instantiated:

$$dst\,@\,\mathsf{MCons}\,\{\mathsf{head} : a; \mathsf{tail} : ()\} * tl\,@\,\mathsf{list}\ a * ys\,@\,\mathsf{list}\ a$$

Are we able to satisfy this requirement? The answer is positive. The subsumption rules EXISTSINTRO and DECOMPOSEBLOCK allow combining the permissions $\mathsf{MCons}\,\{\mathsf{head} = hd; \mathsf{tail} : ()\}$ and $hd\,@\,a$ (both of which are present) to obtain the first conjunct above. The second and third conjuncts above are present already.

By APPLICATION, the precondition of `appendAux` is consumed (taken away from the caller). After the call, the postcondition of `appendAux` is added to the current permission, which is then:

$$xs\,@\,\mathsf{Cons}\,\{\mathsf{head} = hd; \mathsf{tail} = tl\} * dst\,@\,\mathsf{list}\ a$$

The conjunct that concerns xs is of no use, and is in fact silently discarded when we reach the end of the Cons branch within `append`. The conjunct that concerns dst is used to check that this branch satisfies `append`'s advertised return type, namely $\mathsf{list}\ a$. Similarly, in the Nil branch, the permission $ys\,@\,\mathsf{list}\ a$ shows that a value of appropriate type is returned. In conclusion, `append` is well-typed.

2.3 To loop or to tail call?

In-place concatenation (that is, melding) of mutable lists can also be implemented by a tail-recursive function. The pattern is analogous to that of Figure 1, but the code is simpler, because the first list is not copied, and "freezing" is not required.

These algorithms are traditionally viewed as iterative and implemented using a `while` loop. Berdine *et al.*'s iterative formulation of mutable list melding [4], which is proved correct in separation logic, has a complex loop invariant, involving two "list segments", and requires an inductive proof that the concatenation of two list segments is a list segment. In contrast, in the tail-recursive approach, the "loop invariant" is the type of the recursive function (e.g., `appendAux` in Figure 1). This type is reasonably natural and does not involve list segments.

How do we get away without list segments and without inductive reasoning? The trick is that, even though `appendAux` is tail-recursive, which means that no code is executed after the call by `appendAux` to itself, a *reasoning step* still takes place after the call. Immediately before the call, the current permission can be written as follows:

$$\begin{array}{r}xs \mathbin{@} \mathsf{Cons}\,\{\mathsf{head} = hd; \mathsf{tail} = tl\} \ast \\ dst \mathbin{@} \mathsf{Cons}\,\{\mathsf{head} : a; \mathsf{tail} = dst'\} \ast \\ dst' \mathbin{@} \mathsf{MCons}\,\{\mathsf{head} : a; \mathsf{tail} : ()\} \ast \\ tl \mathbin{@} \mathsf{list}\ a \ast ys \mathbin{@} \mathsf{list}\ a\end{array}$$

The call "`appendAux (dst', xs.tail, ys)`" consumes the last three permissions and produces instead $dst' \mathbin{@} \mathsf{list}\ a$. The first two permissions are "framed out", i.e., implicitly preserved. After the call, we have:

$$\begin{array}{r}xs \mathbin{@} \mathsf{Cons}\,\{\mathsf{head} = hd; \mathsf{tail} = tl\} \ast \\ dst \mathbin{@} \mathsf{Cons}\,\{\mathsf{head} : a; \mathsf{tail} = dst'\} \ast \\ dst' \mathbin{@} \mathsf{list}\ a\end{array}$$

Dropping the first permission and combining the last two yields:

$$dst \mathbin{@} \mathsf{Cons}\,\{\mathsf{head} : a; \mathsf{tail} : \mathsf{list}\ a\}$$

which can be folded back to $dst \mathbin{@} \mathsf{list}\ a$, so `appendAux` satisfies its postcondition. In short, the code is tail-recursive, but the manner in which one reasons about it is recursive.

Minamide [22] proposes a notion of "data structure with a hole", or in other words, a segment, and applies it to the problem of concatenating immutable lists. Walker and Morrisett [35] offer a tail-recursive version of mutable list concatenation in a low-level typed intermediate language, as opposed to a surface language. The manner in which they avoid reasoning about list segments is analogous to ours. There, because the code is formulated in continuation-passing style, the reasoning step that takes place "after the recursive call" amounts to composing the current continuation with a coercion. Maeda *et al.* [21] study a slightly different approach, also in the setting of a typed intermediate language, where separating implication offers a way of defining list segments. Our approach could be adapted to an iterative setting by adopting a new proof rule for `while` loops. This is noted independently by Charguéraud [9, §3.3.2] and by Tuerk [34].

3. Syntax

3.1 Types

We work with the "internal syntax" of types. The surface syntax adds a few syntactic conventions, which we explain later on (§6). For the moment, the reader may ignore the two underlined constructs in Figure 2.

Types have kinds. The base kinds are type, term, and perm. The standard types, such as function types, tuple types, etc. have kind type. The types of kind term are program variables. If a variable x is bound (by let, fun, or match) in the code, then x may appear not only in the code, but also in a type: it is a type of kind term. The types of kind perm are permissions. First-order arrow kinds are used to classify parameterized algebraic data types.

In Figure 2, we use the meta-variables T and X to stand for types and variables of arbitrary kind; we use t and P to suggest that a type has kind type and perm, respectively; we use a and x to suggest that a variable has kind type and term, respectively. We omit the definition of the kinding judgment; it appears in the extended version of this paper [28].

The *structural type* $\mathsf{A}\,\{\vec{f} : \vec{t}\}$ describes a block in the heap whose tag is currently A and whose fields $\vec{f}$ currently have the types $\vec{t}$. An example, taken from §2, is $\mathsf{MCons}\,\{\mathsf{head} : a; \mathsf{tail} : ()\}$.

$\kappa ::=$	$\mathsf{type} \mid \mathsf{term} \mid \mathsf{perm} \mid \kappa \to \kappa$	kind
$T, t, P ::=$		type or permission
	X	variable $(a, x, \ldots)$
	$t \to t$	function type
	$(\vec{t})$	tuple type
	$\mathsf{A}\,\{\vec{f} : \vec{t}\}\ \mathsf{adopts}\, t$	structural type
	$T\,\vec{T}$	n-ary type application
	$\forall (X : \kappa)\, T$	universal quantification
	$\exists (X : \kappa)\, T$	existential quantification
	$=x$	singleton type
	$(t \mid P)$	type/permission conjunction
	dynamic	(see §7)
	$x \mathbin{@} t$	atomic permission
	empty	empty permission
	$P \ast P$	permission conjunction
	$x : t$	name introduction (see §6)
	consumes T	consumes annotation (see §6)
$d ::=$		algebraic data type definition
	mutable? data $d\ (\vec{X} : \vec{\kappa}) = \vec{b}$ adopts t	
$b ::=$	$\mathsf{A}\,\{\vec{f} : \vec{t}\}$	algebraic data type branch

Figure 2. Syntax of types and permissions

$e ::=$		expression
	x	variable
	let $p = e$ in e	local definition
	fun $[\vec{X} : \vec{\kappa}]\ (x : t) : t = e$	anonymous function
	$e\,[t : \kappa]$	type instantiation
	$e\ e$	function application
	$(\vec{e})$	tuple
	$\mathsf{A}\,\{\vec{f} = \vec{e}\}$	data constructor application
	$e.f$	field access
	$e.f \leftarrow e$	field update
	match e with $\vec{p} \to \vec{e}$	case analysis
	tag of $e \leftarrow A$	tag update
	give e to e	adoption
	take e from e	abandon
	fail	dynamic failure
$p ::=$		pattern
	x	variable
	$(\vec{p})$	tuple pattern
	$\mathsf{A}\,\{\vec{f} = \vec{p}\}$	data constructor pattern

Figure 3. Syntax of expressions

The data constructor A must refer to a previously defined algebraic data type, and the fields $\vec{f}$ must match the definition of A. The types $\vec{t}$, however, need not match the types that appear in the definition of A. For instance, in the definition of MCons, the type of the tail field is mlist a, not (). This implies that the above structural type cannot be folded to mlist a; the tail field must be updated first. A structural type may include a clause of the form adopts t, whose meaning is explained later on (§7). If omitted, adopts $\bot$ is the default.

An example of a type application $T\,\vec{T}$ is list int. We sometimes refer to this as a *nominal type*, as opposed to a structural type.

The universal and existential types are in the style of System F. A (base) kind annotation is mandatory; if omitted, type is the default. The bottom type $\perp$ and the top type unknown can be defined as $\forall a.a$ and $\exists a.a$, respectively.

The conjunction of a type and a permission is written $(t \mid P)$. Because permissions do not exist at runtime, a value of this type is represented at runtime as a value of type t. Such a conjunction is typically used to express function pre- and postconditions. The type $(() \mid P)$ is abbreviated as $(\mid P)$.

Algebraic data type definitions are prefixed with the keyword data. They are anologous to Haskell's and OCaml's. Each branch is explicitly named by a data constructor and carries a number of named fields. If a definition begins with the keyword mutable, then the tag and all fields are considered mutable, and can be modified via tag update and field update instructions; otherwise, they are considered immutable. Examples appear at the top of Figure 1. Like a structural type, an algebraic data type definition may include an adopts clause; if omitted, adopts $\perp$ is the default.

3.2 Expressions

Expressions (Figure 3) form a fairly standard λ-calculus with tuples and algebraic data structures. A function definition must be explicitly annotated with the function's type parameters, argument type, and return type. One reason for this is that the argument and return type serve as pre- and postconditions and in general cannot be inferred. Furthermore, we have System F-style polymorphism. Explicit type abstractions are built into function definitions. Type applications must in principle be explicit as well. The prototype type-checker allows omitting them and performs a limited form of type inference, which is outside the scope of this paper.

4. Ownership, modes, and extent

We wrote earlier (§1) that "to have a permission for x" can be understood informally as "to own x". Roughly speaking, this is true, but we must be more precise, for two reasons. First, we wish to distinguish between mutable data, on which we impose a "unique owner" policy, and immutable data, for which there is no such restriction. For this reason, types and permissions come in several flavors, which we refer to as *modes* (§4.1). Second, in a permission of the form $x @ t$, the type t describes the *extent* to which we own x. If xs is a list cell, do we own just this cell? the entire spine? the spine and the elements? The answer is given by the type t. For instance (§4.2), $xs @ \text{Cons}\{\text{head} = hd; \text{tail} = tl\}$ represents the ownership of just the cell xs, because the singleton types $=hd$ and $=tl$ denote the ownership of an empty heap fragment. On the other hand, $xs @ \text{Cons}\{\text{head} : a; \text{tail} : \text{list } a\}$ gives access to the entire list spine. (Because list is an immutable algebraic data type, this is read-only, shared access.) It further gives access to all of the list elements, insofar as the type a allows this access. In this example, a is a variable: one must wait until a is instantiated to determine what the elements are and to what extent we own them.

4.1 Modes

A subset of the permissions are considered *duplicable*, which means that they can be implicitly copied (DUPLICATE, Figure 6). Copying a permission for an object x means that x may be shared: it may be used via different pointers, or by different threads simultaneously. Thus, a duplicable permission does not represent unique ownership; instead, it denotes *shared knowledge*. Because the system does not control with whom this knowledge is shared, this knowledge must never be invalidated, lest some principals be left with an outdated version of the permission. Therefore, a duplicable permission denotes *shared, permanent knowledge*. The permissions that describe read-only, immutable data are duplicable: for instance, $xs @ \text{Cons}\{\text{head} = hd; \text{tail} = tl\}$ and $xs @ \text{list int}$ are duplicable.

A subset of the permissions are considered *exclusive*. An exclusive permission for an object x represents the "unique ownership" of x. In other words, such a permission grants *read-write access* to the memory block at address x and guarantees that no-one else has access to this block. The permissions that describe mutable memory blocks are exclusive: for instance, $xs @ \text{MCons}\{\text{head} = hd; \text{tail} = tl\}$ is exclusive. An exclusive permission is analogous to a "unique" permission in other systems [5] and to a separation logic assertion [29].

By lack of space, we must unfortunately omit the definition of the predicates "t is duplicable" and "t is exclusive", which are used in the typing rules (Figure 4). They can be found in the extended version of this paper.

No permission is duplicable and exclusive. Some permissions are neither duplicable nor exclusive. "$xs @ \text{list (ref int)}$", which describes an immutable list of references to integers, illustrates this. It must not be duplicated: this would violate the "unique owner" property of the list elements. It is not exclusive: the list cell at `xs` is an immutable object, and this permission does not guarantee exclusive access to this cell. Another example is "`x @ a`". Because `a` is a type variable, one cannot assume that this permission is duplicable (or exclusive)[3].

Every permission is affine. One can implicitly drop a permission that one does not need.

The language is designed so that the type-checker (and the programmer!) can always tell what *mode* a permission P satisfies: duplicable, exclusive, or neither (hence, affine). Modes form an upper semi-lattice, whose top element is "affine", and where "duplicable" and "exclusive" are incomparable. Because algebraic data types are recursively defined, their mode analysis requires a fixed point computation, whose details we omit.

If t and u are exclusive types, then the conjunction $x @ t * y @ u$ implies that x and y are *distinct* addresses. In other words, *conjunction of exclusive permissions is separating*. On the other hand, if t and/or u are duplicable, x and y may be aliases. Conjunction is not in general separating. *Conjunction of duplicable permissions* requires agreement between the two conjuncts. The reader is referred to the draft paper that accompanies the type soundness proof [26] for a formal definition of the semantics of conjunction.

4.2 Extent

Every type t has an ownership reading: that is, the permission $x @ t$ represents certain access rights about x. However, the extent of these rights (or, in separation logic terminology, their footprint) depends on the type t.

A singleton type $=y$, for instance, has empty extent. Indeed, the permission $x @ =y$, which we usually write $x = y$, asserts that x and y are equal, but does not allow assuming that x is a pointer, let alone dereferencing it.

A structural type such as $\text{Cons}\{\text{head} = hd; \text{tail} = tl\}$ has an extent of one memory block. The permission $xs @ \text{Cons}\{\text{head} = hd; \text{tail} = tl\}$ gives us (read-only, shared) access to the block at address xs, and guarantees that its head and tail fields contain the values hd and tl, respectively, but (as per the semantics of singleton types) guarantees nothing about hd and tl.

What is the extent of a "deep" composite type, such as the structural type $\text{Cons}\{\text{head} : a; \text{tail} : \text{list } a\}$ or the nominal type list a? What does it mean to own a list? In order to answer these questions, one must understand how a composite permission is decomposed into a conjunction of more elementary permissions.

[3] *Mezzo* allows the programmer to explicitly assume that a type variable `a` is duplicable, or exclusive. This mechanism is not treated in this paper.

A structural permission, such as xs @ Cons {head : a; tail : list a}, can be decomposed by introducing a fresh name for each of the values stored in the fields. (See DECOMPOSEBLOCK in Figure 6.) The result is a more verbose, but logically equivalent, permission:

$$\exists hd, tl.(xs \mathbin{@} \mathsf{Cons}\,\{\mathsf{head} = hd; \mathsf{tail} = tl\} * hd \mathbin{@} a * tl \mathbin{@} \mathsf{list}\ a)$$

The meaning and extent of the original structural permission is now clearer: it grants access to the cell at xs *and* to the first list element (to the extent dictated by the type a) *and* to the rest of the list.

The meaning of a nominal permission, such as xs @ list a, is just the disjunction of the meanings of its unfoldings, namely xs @ Nil and xs @ Cons {head : a; tail : list a}.

If a is (instantiated with) an exclusive type, then we find that xs @ list a implies that the list elements are *pairwise distinct*, and grants read-only access to the list spine and exclusive access to the list elements.

5. Type assignment

5.1 The typing judgment

The typing judgment takes the form $K; P \vdash e : t$. It is inductively defined in Figures 4 and 5. The kind environment K maps variables to kinds. This judgment means that, by consuming the permission P, the expression e produces a value of type t. It is analogous to a Hoare logic or separation logic triple, where P is the precondition and t is the postcondition.

The typing judgement relies on a well-kindedness judgement of the form $K \vdash t : \kappa$. It ensures that types are well-kinded and that the syntactic facilities of the surface syntax (§6) are used properly. For conciseness, in the typing rules, we omit all freshness and well-kindedness side conditions.

The typing rules require many sub-expressions to be variables. For instance, the rule READ cannot handle a field access expression of the form $e.f$: instead, it requires $x.f$. This requirement is met by first performing a monadic transformation, which introduces extra let constructs. Furthermore, the pattern matching rules (Figure 5) cannot handle deep patterns: they require shallow patterns. Again, this requirement is met by introducing extra let constructs. We omit the details of these transformations.

VAR is the axiom rule. It is worth noting that, in conjunction with the subsumption rule EQUALITYREFLEXIVE (Figure 6), it allows proving that x has type $=x$, even in the absence of any hypothesis about x.

LET corresponds to the sequence rule of separation logic.

FUNCTION states that a *duplicable* permission P that exists at the function definition site is also available within the function body. Requiring P to be duplicable allows us to consider every function type duplicable. Thus, a function can be shared without restriction and can be invoked as many times as desired, provided of course that one is able to satisfy its precondition. If one wishes to write a function that captures a non-duplicable permission P, and can be invoked at most once, this is still possible. Indeed, a type $t_1 \multimap t_2$ of "one-shot" functions can be defined as:

$$\exists (p : \mathsf{perm})\ (((t_1 \mid p) \rightarrow t_2) \mid p)$$

This is a conjunction of a function whose precondition is p and of one copy of p. Because p is abstract, it is considered affine. Hence, at most one call is possible, after which p is consumed and the function becomes unusable.

APPLICATION corresponds to the rule for procedure calls in separation logic. The caller gives up the permission x_2 @ t_2, which is consumed, and in return gains a permission for the result of the function call, at type t_1. In other words, because types have an ownership reading, a function type $t_1 \rightarrow t_2$ describes not only the shape of the function's arguments and results, but also the side effects that the function may perform, as well as the transfers of ownership that occur from the caller to the callee and back.

NEW uses a structural type to describe the newly-allocated memory block in an exact manner. TUPLE is analogous.

READ requires a structural permission x @ A $\{F[f : t]\}$, which guarantees that x points to a memory block that contains a field named f, and allows us to dereference $x.f$[4]. READ concludes that the field access expression $x.f$ has type t, and that the structural permission x @ A $\{F[f : t]\}$ is preserved. There is a catch: because the type t occurs twice in this postcondition, we must require t to be duplicable, or the rule would be unsound. Fortunately, this is not a problem: by using DECOMPOSEBLOCK (Figure 6; also explained earlier, see §2.2 and §4.2), it is possible to arrange for t to be a singleton type, which is duplicable.

Like READ, WRITE requires a structural permission, of the form x_1 @ A $\{F[f : t_1]\}$. It checks that this permission is exclusive, i.e., the data constructor A is associated with a mutable algebraic data type. This ensures that we have write access. In fact, since we have exclusive access to x_1, a strong (type-changing) update is sound. The permission is changed to x_1 @ A $\{F[f : t_2]\}$, where t_2 is the type of x_2. Without loss of generality, one may let t_2 be the singleton type $=x_2$. This allows the type-checker to record that $x_1.f$ and x_2 are now aliases. If desired, the permissions x_1 @ A $\{F[f = x_2]\}$ and x_2 @ t_2 can later be combined by DECOMPOSEBLOCK to yield x_1 @ A $\{F[f : t_2]\}$. Because DECOMPOSEBLOCK, read from right to left, involves a loss of information, it is typically applied by the type-checker only "on demand", i.e., to satisfy a function postcondition or a type annotation.

MATCH is used to type-check a case analysis construct. Each branch is type-checked independently. We currently do not check that the case analysis is exhaustive, but plan to add this feature in the future. The premise relies on a judgment of the form $K; P \vdash$ let $p = x$ in $e : t$. This is not a new judgment; it is an ordinary typing judgement, but, for clarity, the typing rules that have a conclusion of this form are isolated in Figure 5. Although these rules may appear somewhat daunting, they are in fact quite straightforward. LETTUPLE checks that x is a tuple, i.e., we have a permission of the form x @ $(t_1, \ldots, t_n)$. If that is the case, then matching x against the tuple pattern $(x_1, \ldots, x_n)$ is permitted, and gives rise to a conjunction of permissions of the form x_i @ t_i. Because the permission for x is not lost, the types t_i are duplicated, so they are required to be duplicable. Again, this requirement causes no loss of generality, since one can arrange to introduce singleton types ahead of time. LETDATAMATCH is analogous to LETTUPLE, but concerns a (mutable or immutable) memory block. LETDATAMISMATCH concerns the situation where the pattern, which mentions the data constructor B, will clearly not match x, which is statically known to have the tag A. In that case, the branch is dead code, and is considered well-typed. LETDATAUNFOLD *refines* a nominal permission, such as x @ list a, by replacing it with a structural one, such as x @ Cons {head : a; tail : list a}, obtained by unfolding the algebraic data type and specializing it with respect to the data constructor that appears in the pattern. We omit the exact definition of unfolding.

WRITETAG type-checks a *tag update* instruction, which modifies the tag carried by a memory block. Like WRITE, it requires an exclusive permission for this block. It further requires the new tag B to carry the same number of fields as the previous tag A. (Thus, the block does not have to be enlarged or shrunk.) The structural permission is updated in a straightforward way. The

[4] We write $F[f : t]$ for a sequence of field/type pairs in which the pair $f : t$ occurs. The adopts clause, if present, is irrelevant. We overload field names: there could exist multiple data constructors with a field named f. There can be at most one permission of the form x @ A $\{F[f : t]\}$, though, which allows disambiguation to take place.

Var
$$K; x \,@\, t \vdash x : t$$

Let
$$\frac{K; P \vdash e_1 : t_1 \qquad K, x : \mathsf{term}; x \,@\, t_1 \vdash e_2 : t_2}{K; P \vdash \mathsf{let}\ x = e_1\ \mathsf{in}\ e_2 : t_2}$$

Function
$$\frac{K, \vec{X} : \vec{\kappa}, x : \mathsf{term}; P * x \,@\, t_1 \vdash e : t_2 \qquad P \text{ is duplicable}}{K; P \vdash \mathsf{fun}\ [\vec{X} : \vec{\kappa}]\ (x : t_1) : t_2 = e : \forall(\vec{X} : \vec{\kappa})\ t_1 \rightarrow t_2}$$

Instantiation
$$\frac{K; P \vdash e : \forall(X : \kappa)\ t_1}{K; P \vdash e : [T_2/X]t_1}$$

Application
$$K; x_1 \,@\, t_2 \rightarrow t_1 * x_2 \,@\, t_2 \vdash x_1\ x_2 : t_1$$

Tuple
$$K; \vec{x} \,@\, \vec{t} \vdash (\vec{x}) : (\vec{t}\,)$$

New
$$\frac{\mathsf{A}\,\{\vec{f}\} \text{ is defined}}{K; \vec{x} \,@\, \vec{t} \vdash \mathsf{A}\,\{\vec{f} = \vec{x}\} : \mathsf{A}\,\{\vec{f} : \vec{t}\}}$$

Read
$$\frac{t \text{ is duplicable} \qquad P \text{ is } x \,@\, \mathsf{A}\,\{F[f : t]\}\ \mathsf{adopts}\ u}{K; P \vdash x.f : (t \mid P)}$$

Write
$$\frac{\mathsf{A}\,\{\ldots\} \text{ is exclusive}}{K; x_1 \,@\, \mathsf{A}\,\{F[f : t_1]\}\ \mathsf{adopts}\ u * x_2 \,@\, t_2 \vdash x_1.f \leftarrow x_2 : (\,| \ x_1 \,@\, \mathsf{A}\,\{F[f : t_2]\}\ \mathsf{adopts}\ u)}$$

Match
$$\frac{\text{for every } i, \quad K; P \vdash \mathsf{let}\ p_i = x\ \mathsf{in}\ e_i : t}{K; P \vdash \mathsf{match}\ x\ \mathsf{with}\ \vec{p} \rightarrow \vec{e} : t}$$

WriteTag
$$\frac{\mathsf{A}\,\{\ldots\} \text{ is exclusive} \qquad \mathsf{B}\,\{\vec{f}'\} \text{ is defined} \qquad \#\vec{f} = \#\vec{f}'}{K; x \,@\, \mathsf{A}\,\{\vec{f} : \vec{t}\}\ \mathsf{adopts}\ u \vdash \mathsf{tag\ of}\ x \leftarrow B : (\,| \ x \,@\, \mathsf{B}\,\{\vec{f}' : \vec{t}\}\ \mathsf{adopts}\ u)}$$

Give
$$\frac{t_2 \text{ adopts } t_1}{K; x_1 \,@\, t_1 * x_2 \,@\, t_2 \vdash \mathsf{give}\ x_1\ \mathsf{to}\ x_2 : (\,| \ x_2 \,@\, t_2)}$$

Take
$$\frac{t_2 \text{ adopts } t_1}{K; x_1 \,@\, \mathsf{dynamic} * x_2 \,@\, t_2 \vdash \mathsf{take}\ x_1\ \mathsf{from}\ x_2 : (\,| \ x_1 \,@\, t_1 * x_2 \,@\, t_2)}$$

Fail
$$K; P \vdash \mathsf{fail} : t$$

Sub
$$\frac{K; P_2 \vdash e : t_1 \qquad P_1 \leq P_2 \qquad t_1 \leq t_2}{K; P_1 \vdash e : t_2}$$

Frame
$$\frac{K; P_1 \vdash e : t}{K; P_1 * P_2 \vdash e : (t \mid P_2)}$$

ExistsElim
$$\frac{K, X : \kappa; P \vdash e : t}{K; \exists(X : \kappa)\ P \vdash e : t}$$

Figure 4. Typing rules

LetTuple
$$\frac{(\vec{t}\,) \text{ is duplicable} \qquad K, \vec{x} : \mathsf{term}; P * x \,@\, (\vec{t}\,) * \vec{x} \,@\, \vec{t} \vdash e : t}{K; P * x \,@\, (\vec{t}\,) \vdash \mathsf{let}\ (\vec{x}) = x\ \mathsf{in}\ e : t}$$

LetDataMatch
$$\frac{(\vec{t}\,) \text{ is duplicable} \qquad K, \vec{x} : \mathsf{term}; P * x \,@\, \mathsf{A}\,\{\vec{f} : \vec{t}\}\ \mathsf{adopts}\ u * \vec{x} \,@\, \vec{t} \vdash e : t}{K; P * x \,@\, \mathsf{A}\,\{\vec{f} : \vec{t}\}\ \mathsf{adopts}\ u \vdash \mathsf{let}\ \mathsf{A}\,\{\vec{f} = \vec{x}\} = x\ \mathsf{in}\ e : t}$$

LetDataMismatch
$$\frac{\mathsf{A} \text{ and } \mathsf{B} \text{ belong to a common algebraic data type}}{K; P * x \,@\, \mathsf{A}\,\{\vec{f} : \vec{t}\}\ \mathsf{adopts}\ u \vdash \mathsf{let}\ \mathsf{B}\,\{\vec{f}' = \vec{x}\} = x\ \mathsf{in}\ e : t}$$

LetDataUnfold
$$\frac{x \,@\, \mathsf{A}\,\{\vec{f} : \vec{t}\}\ \mathsf{adopts}\ u \text{ is an unfolding of } T\ \vec{T} \qquad K; P * x \,@\, \mathsf{A}\,\{\vec{f} : \vec{t}\}\ \mathsf{adopts}\ u \vdash \mathsf{let}\ \mathsf{A}\,\{\vec{f} = \vec{x}\} = x\ \mathsf{in}\ e : t}{K; P * x \,@\, T\ \vec{T} \vdash \mathsf{let}\ \mathsf{A}\,\{\vec{f} = \vec{x}\} = x\ \mathsf{in}\ e : t}$$

Figure 5. Auxiliary typing rules for pattern matching

EqualityReflexive
$$\mathsf{empty} \leq (x = x)$$

EqualsForEquals
$$(y_1 = y_2) * [y_1/x]P \equiv (y_1 = y_2) * [y_2/x]P$$

Duplicate
$$\frac{P \text{ is duplicable}}{P \leq P * P}$$

MixStar
$$x \,@\, t * P \equiv x \,@\, (t \mid P)$$

Weaken
$$P_1 * P_2 \leq P_2$$

ExistsIntro
$$[T/X]P \leq \exists(X : \kappa)\ P$$

ExistsAtomic
$$x \,@\, \exists(X : \kappa)\ t \equiv \exists(X : \kappa)\ (x \,@\, t)$$

DecomposeBlock
$$y \,@\, \mathsf{A}\,\{F[f : t]\}\ \mathsf{adopts}\ u \equiv \exists(x : \mathsf{term})\ (y \,@\, \mathsf{A}\,\{F[f = x]\}\ \mathsf{adopts}\ u * x \,@\, t)$$

Fold
$$\frac{\mathsf{A}\,\{\vec{f} : \vec{t}\}\ \mathsf{adopts}\ u \text{ is an unfolding of } T\ \vec{T}}{x \,@\, \mathsf{A}\,\{\vec{f} : \vec{t}\}\ \mathsf{adopts}\ u \leq x \,@\, T\ \vec{T}}$$

Unfold
$$\frac{\mathsf{A}\,\{\vec{f} : \vec{t}\}\ \mathsf{adopts}\ u \text{ is an unfolding of } T\ \vec{T} \qquad T\ \vec{T} \text{ has only one branch}}{x \,@\, T\ \vec{T} \leq x \,@\, \mathsf{A}\,\{\vec{f} : \vec{t}\}\ \mathsf{adopts}\ u}$$

DynamicAppears
$$\frac{t \text{ is exclusive}}{x \,@\, t \leq x \,@\, t * x \,@\, \mathsf{dynamic}}$$

Figure 6. Permission subsumption (not all rules shown)

types $\vec{t}$ of the fields do not change. The names of the fields change from $\vec{f}$ to $\vec{f}'$, where the sequences of fields are ordered in the same way as in the (user-provided) definitions of A and B. It is worth noting that A and B need not belong to the same algebraic data type: thus, a memory block can be re-used for a completely new purpose. Furthermore, the tag B may be associated with an immutable algebraic data type: in that case, the block is *frozen*, that is, becomes forever immutable. This feature is exploited in the concatenation of immutable lists (Figure 1, line 19).

GIVE and TAKE are explained later on (§7).

SUB is analogous to Hoare's rule of consequence. It relies on permission subsumption, $P_1 \leq P_2$, defined in Figure 6 and discussed further on (§5.2), and on subtyping, $t_1 \leq t_2$, defined as $x @ t_1 \leq x @ t_2$ for a fresh x.

FRAME is analogous to the frame rule of separation logic.

5.2 The permission subsumption judgment

A subset[5] of the subsumption rules appears in Figure 6. Since $x = y$ is sugar for $x @ =y$, the rule EQUALITYREFLEXIVE can be understood as a claim that x inhabits the singleton type $=x$. EQUALSFOREQUALS shows how equations are exploited: if y_1 and y_2 are known to be equal, then they are interchangeable. (We write $\equiv$ for subsumption in both directions.) DUPLICATE states that a permission that is syntactically considered duplicable can in fact be duplicated. MIXSTAR introduces and eliminates $(t \mid P)$. WEAKEN states that every permission is affine. EXISTSINTRO introduces an existential permission; EXISTSATOMIC converts between an existential permission and an existential type. When read from left to right, DECOMPOSEBLOCK, which was discussed earlier (§2.2, §4.2), introduces a fresh name x for the value stored in $y.f$. When read from right to left, it forgets such a name. (In that case, it is typically used in conjunction with EXISTSINTRO.) This rule is related to Sing#'s explicit "expose" [15]. FOLD folds an algebraic data type definition, turning a structural type into a nominal type. Unfolding is normally performed by case analysis (see LETDATAUNFOLD in Figure 5), but in the special case where an algebraic data type has only one branch (i.e., it is a record type), it can be implicitly unfolded by UNFOLD. DYNAMICAPPEARS is explained later on (§7).

5.3 The *Mezzo* type-checker

Implementing a checker for a highly non-deterministic system such as *Mezzo* poses technical challenges. Our type-checker greedily introduces fresh auxiliary names so as to "normalize" the types and permissions at hand. A persistent union-find data structure keeps track of the permissions of the form "$x = y$". The use of flexible variables enables a limited form of type inference. At present, the implemented type-checker is not complete with respect to the type assignment rules. This is only a brief overview: a follow-up paper devoted to the implementation of *Mezzo* is in the works.

6. Surface syntax

The internal syntax, which we have been using so far, can be fairly verbose. To remedy this, we introduce two syntactic conventions, which rely on the *name introduction* construct and on the consumes keyword (Figure 2). Two transformations eliminate these constructs, so as to obtain a type expressed in the internal syntax. They are formalized in the extended version of the present paper [28]. Here, we give only an intuition.

[5] The reader is referred to the extended version of this paper [28] for the full set of rules. The omitted rules include: conjunction is commutative, associative, and has unit empty; covariance and contravariance of the type constructors; and a few more.

6.1 The name introduction form

The construct $x : t$ allows introducing a name x for a component of type t. This allows writing "dependent function types", such as $(x_1 : t_1) \rightarrow (x_2 : t_2)$, where by convention x_1 is bound within t_1 and t_2, while x_2 is bound within t_2. This is desugared by quantifiying x_1 universally *above* the arrow and quantifying x_2 existentially in the right-hand side of the arrow.

As an example, consider the type of `:=`, the function that writes a reference. This function expects a pair of a reference x whose content has type a and of a value of type b, which it stores into x. At the end, x has become a reference whose content has type b. The variable x must be mentioned in the pre- and postcondition. In the internal syntax, the type of `:=` is:

$$\forall a, b. \forall (x : \mathsf{term})\ ((=x \mid x @ \mathsf{ref}\ a), b) \rightarrow (\mid x @ \mathsf{ref}\ b)$$

Thanks to the name introduction form, instead of planning ahead and quantifying x in front of the function type, one names the first argument "x" on the fly. Thus, in the surface syntax, one writes:

$$\forall a, b. (\mathsf{consumes}\ x : \mathsf{ref}\ a, \mathsf{consumes}\ b) \rightarrow (\mid x @ \mathsf{ref}\ b)$$

This is not significantly shorter, because of the consumes keyword, which must be used in the surface syntax, as explained below. In actual use, though, the comfort afforded by this feature is critical.

6.2 The consumes annotation

Often, a permission is required *and returned* by a function, in which case it is unpleasant to have to write this permission twice, in the precondition and postcondition. Drawing inspiration from Sing# [15], we adopt the convention that, in the surface syntax, *by default, the permission for the argument is required and returned*, i.e., it is *not* consumed.

For instance, the type of the list `length` function, which in the internal syntax is:

$$\forall a. \forall (x : \mathsf{term})(=x \mid x @ \mathsf{list}\ a) \rightarrow (\mathsf{int} \mid x @ \mathsf{list}\ a)$$

can in the surface syntax be written in a much more pleasant form:

$$\forall a. \mathsf{list}\ a \rightarrow \mathsf{int}$$

The type list a is mentioned once, instead of twice, and as a side effect, the need to name the argument x vanishes.

When a permission *is* consumed, though, we need a way of indicating this. This is the purpose of the `consumes` keyword. When a component is marked with this keyword, the permission for this component is required and not returned. This keyword makes sense only in the left-hand side of an arrow.

Since internal syntax and surface syntax interpret the function type differently, a translation is required, regardless of whether `consumes` is used. Consider a function type of the form $t \rightarrow u$, where t does not contain any name introduction forms. Let t_1 stand for $[\tau/\mathsf{consumes}\ \tau]t$, i.e., a copy of t where the consumes keyword is erased. Let t_2 stand for $[\top/\mathsf{consumes}\ \tau]t$, i.e., a copy of t where every component marked with this keyword is replaced with $\top$[6]. Then, the translation of this function type is $(x : t_1) \rightarrow (u \mid x @ t_2)$. The parts of the argument that are *not* marked as consumed are returned to the caller.

The type of the function `insert`, which appears in Figure 7 and is discussed in §7.1, states that the first argument is consumed, while the second argument is not. Its translation into the internal syntax is as follows:

$$\forall (a : \mathsf{type})\ \forall (x : \mathsf{term})$$
$$(=x \mid x @ (a, \mathsf{bag}\ a)) \rightarrow (\mid x @ (\mathsf{unknown}, \mathsf{bag}\ a))$$

[6] Here, we write $\top$ for unknown or empty, depending on whether the `consumes` keyword is applied to a type or a permission.

```
abstract bag a
val create: [a] () -> bag a
val insert: [a] (consumes a, bag a) -> ()
val retrieve: [a] bag a -> option a
```

Figure 7. An interface for bags

```
data mutable cell a =
  Cell { elem: a; next: dynamic }

data mutable bag a =
     Empty { head, tail: () }
  | NonEmpty { head, tail: dynamic }
adopts cell a

val create [a] () : bag a =
  Empty { head = (); tail = () }

val insert [a] (consumes x: a, b: bag a) : () =
  let c = Cell { elem = x; next = () } in
  c.next <- c;
  give c to b;
  match b with
  | Empty ->
      tag of b <- NonEmpty;
      b.head <- c;
      b.tail <- c
  | NonEmpty ->
      take b.tail from b;
      b.tail.next <- c;
      give b.tail to b;
      b.tail <- c
  end

val retrieve [a] (b: bag a) : option a =
  match b with
  | Empty ->
      None
  | NonEmpty ->
      take b.head from b;
      let x = b.head.elem in
      if b.head == b.tail then begin
        tag of b <- Empty;
        b.head <- ();
        b.tail <- ()
      end else begin
        b.head <- b.head.next
      end;
      Some { value = x }
  end
```

Figure 8. A FIFO implementation of bags

6.3 Function definitions

In the internal syntax, functions take the form fun $(x : t_1) : t_2 = e$, where one variable, namely x, is bound in e. In the surface syntax, instead, functions take the form fun $t_1 : t_2 = e$ The argument type t_1 is interpreted as a pattern, and the names that it introduces are considered bound in e. An example is fun $(x : \mathsf{int}, y : \mathsf{int}) : \mathsf{int} = x + y$, where $(x : \mathsf{int}, y : \mathsf{int})$ is the type of the argument, int is the type of the result, and x and y are bound in the function body, which is $x + y$.

7. Adoption and abandon

The permission discipline that we have presented so far has limited expressive power. It can describe immutable data structures with arbitrary sharing and tree-shaped mutable data structures. However, because mutable memory blocks are controlled by exclusive permissions, it cannot describe mutable data structures with sharing.

7.1 Overview

In order to illustrate this problem, let us imagine how one could implement a "bag" abstraction. A bag is a mutable container, which supports two operations: inserting a new element and retrieving an arbitrary element.

We would like our implementation to offer the interface in Figure 7. There, `bag` is presented as an abstract type. Because it is not explicitly declared duplicable, it is regarded as affine. Hence, a bag "has a unique owner", i.e., is governed by a non-duplicable permission. The function `create` creates a new bag, whose ownership is transferred to the caller. The type of `insert` indicates that `insert(x, b)` requires the permissions "`x @ t`" and "`b @ bag t`", for some type `t`, and returns only the latter. Thus, the caller gives up the ownership of `x`, which is "transferred to the bag". Conversely, the call "`let o = retrieve b in ...`" produces the permission "`o @ option a`", which means that the ownership of the retrieved element (if there is one) is "transferred from the bag to the caller".

To implement bags, we choose a simple data structure, namely a mutable singly-linked list. One inserts elements at the tail and extracts elements at the head, so this is a FIFO implementation. One distinguished object `b`, "the bag", has pointers to the head and tail of the list, so as to allow constant-time insertion and extraction. (We use "object" as a synonym for "memory block".)

This data structure is not tree-shaped: the last cell in the list is accessible via two distinct paths. In order to type-check this code, we must allow the ownership hierarchy and the structure of the heap to differ. More specifically, we would like to view the list cells as collectively owned by the bag `b`. That is, we wish to keep track of just one exclusive permission for the *group* formed by the list cells, as opposed to one permission per cell.

We use the name `b` as a name for this group. When a cell `c` joins the group, we say that `b` *adopts* `c`, and when `c` leaves the group, we say that `b` *abandons* `c`. In other words, the bag `b` is an *adopter*, and the list cells `c` are its *adoptees*. In terms of ownership, adopter and adoptees form a unit: the exclusive permission that controls `b` also represents the ownership of the group, and is required by the adoption and abandon operations.

Adoption requires and consumes an exclusive permission for the cell `c` that is about to be adopted: the ownership of `c` is transferred to the group. Conversely, abandon produces an exclusive permission for the cell `c` that is abandoned: the group relinquishes the ownership of `c`.

Abandon must be carefully controlled. If a cell could be abandoned twice, two permissions for it would appear, which would be unsound. Due to aliasing, though, it is difficult to statically prevent this problem. Instead, we decide to record *at runtime* which object is a member of which group, and to verify *at runtime* that abandon is used in a safe way.

7.2 Details

Let us now explain in detail the dynamic semantics of adoption and abandon (what these operations do) as well as their static semantics (what the type-checker requires).

Adopter fields We maintain a pointer from every adoptee to its adopter. Within every object, there is a hidden "`adopter`" field, which contains a pointer to the object's current adopter, if it has one, and `null` otherwise. This information is updated when an object is adopted or abandoned. In terms of space, the cost of this design decision is one field per object.

The type dynamic The permission "`c @ dynamic`" guarantees that `c` is a pointer to a memory block and grants read access to the field `c.adopter`. This can be used to verify the identity of `c`'s adopter. In other words, "`c @ dynamic`" can be viewed as a permission to perform a *dynamic group membership test*. It is a duplicable permission. It appears spontaneously when `c` is known to be a (mutable) object: this is stated by the rule DYNAMICAPPEARS in Figure 6.

In the bag implementation, shown in Figure 8, the `head` and `tail` fields of a non-empty `bag` object, as well as the `next` field of every `cell` object, have type `dynamic` (lines 2 and 6). Because `dynamic` is duplicable, sharing is permitted: for instance, the pointers `b.head` and `b.tail` might happen to be equal.

Adopts clauses When a cell `c` is adopted, the exclusive permission that describes it, namely "`c @ cell a`", disappears. Only "`c @ dynamic`" remains. As a result, the information that `c` is a cell is lost: the type-checker can no longer tell how many fields exist in the object `c` and what they contain. When the bag `b` later abandons `c`, we would like the permission "`c @ cell a`" to re-appear. How can the type-checker recover this information?

Fortunately, when `b` abandons `c`, the type-checker has access to the type of `b`. Thus, provided the type of the adopter determines the type of its adoptees, this problem is solved.

For an object `b` of type `t` to serve as an adopter, where `t` is an algebraic data type, we require that the definition of `t` contain the clause "`adopts u`" and that `t` and `u` be exclusive types. This is illustrated in Figure 8, where the definition of "`bag a`" says "`adopts cell a`" (line 7).

Because the type of the adoptees must not be forgotten when an algebraic data type is unfolded, structural permissions also carry an `adopts` clause. In the case of bags, for instance, the permission "`b @ bag a`" is refined by the `match` constructs of lines 16 and 29 into either "`b @ Empty { head, tail: () } adopts cell a`" or "`b @ NonEmpty { head, tail: dynamic } adopts cell a`", and, conversely, either of these permissions can be folded back to "`b @ bag a`".

We write that "`t` adopts `u`" if either `t` is an algebraic data type whose definition contains the clause "`adopts u`" or `t` is a structural type that contains the clause "`adopts u`".

Adoption The syntax of adoption is "`give c to b`". This instruction requires two permissions "`c @ u`" and "`b @ t`", where `t` adopts `u` (GIVE, Figure 4). At the program point that follows this instruction, the permission "`b @ t`" remains available, but "`c @ u`" has been consumed. Fortunately, not everything about `c` is forgotten. The permission "`c @ dynamic`", which is present before the adoption instruction because "`c @ u`" spontaneously gives rise to "`c @ dynamic`", remains present after adoption.

The runtime effect of this operation is to write the address `b` to the field `c.adopter`. The exclusive permission "`c @ u`" guarantees that this field exists and that its value, prior to adoption, is `null`.

In the bag implementation (Figure 8), adoption is used at the beginning of `insert` (line 15), after a fresh cell `c` has been allocated and initialized. This allows us to maintain the (unstated) invariant that every cell that is reachable from `b` is adopted by `b`.

Abandon The syntax of abandon is "`take c from b`". This instruction requires "`b @ t`" and "`c @ dynamic`", where `t` adopts "`u`", for some type `u` (TAKE, Figure 4). After this instruction, "`b @ t`" remains available. Furthermore, the permission "`c @ u`" appears.

The runtime effect of this operation is to check that the field `c.adopter` contains the address `b` and to write `null` into this field, so as to reflect the fact that `b` abandons `c`. If this check fails, the execution of the program is aborted.

In the bag implementation (Figure 8), abandon is used near the beginning of `retrieve`, at line 33. There, the first cell in the queue, `b.head`, is abandoned by `b`. This yields a permission at type "`cell a`" for this cell. This permission lets us read `b.head.elem` and `b.head.next` and allows us to produce the permission "`x @ a`", where `x` is the value found in `b.head.elem`.

Abandon and adoption are also used inside `insert`, at lines 22 and 24. There, the bag `b` is non-empty, and the cell `b.tail` must be updated in order to reflect the fact that it is no longer the last cell in the queue. However, we cannot just go ahead and access this cell, because the only permission that we have at this point for this cell is at type "`dynamic`". Instead, we must take the cell out of the group, update it, and put it back. We allow writing "`taking b.tail from b begin ... end`" as sugar for such a well-parenthesized use of `take` and `give`.

7.3 Discussion

To the best of our knowledge, adoption and abandon are new. Naturally, the concept of group, or region, has received sustained interest in the literature [11, 12, 16, 32]. Regions are usually viewed either as a dynamic memory management mechanism or as a purely static concept. Adoption and abandon, on the other hand, offer a dynamic ownership control mechanism, which complements our static permission discipline.

Adoption and abandon are a very flexible mechanism, but also a dangerous one. Because abandon involves a dynamic check, it can cause the program to encounter a fatal failure at runtime. In principle, if the programmer knows what she is doing, this should never occur. There is some danger, but that is the price to pay for a simpler static discipline. After all, the danger is effectively less than in ML or Java, where a programming error that creates an undesired alias goes completely undetected—until the program misbehaves in one way or another.

One might wonder why the type dynamic is so uninformative: it gives no clue as to the type of the adoptee or the identity of the adopter. Would it be possible to parameterize it so as to carry either information? The short answer is negative. The type dynamic is duplicable, so the information that it conveys should be stable (i.e., forever valid). However, the type of the adoptee, or the identity of the adopter, may change with time, through a combination of strong updates and `give` and `take` instructions. Thus, it would not make sense for dynamic to carry more information.

That said, we believe that adoption and abandon will often be used according to certain restricted protocols, for which more information is stable, hence can be reflected at the type level. For instance, in the bag implementation, a cell only ever has one adopter, namely a specific bag b. In that case, one could hope to work with a parameterized type dynamic$'$ b, whose meaning would be "either this object is currently not adopted, or it is adopted by b". Ideally, dynamic$'$ would be defined on top of dynamic in a library module, and its use would lessen the risk of confusion.

8. Other means of permitting sharing

Adoption and abandon is not the only way of sharing mutable data. We now describe two other mechanisms, namely nesting and locks.

8.1 Nesting

Nesting [7] is a mechanism by which an object x adopts (so to speak) a permission P. It is a purely static mechanism. The act of nesting P in x has no runtime effect, but consumes P and produces a witness, a permission which Boyland writes $P \prec x$. Because nesting is irreversible, such a witness is duplicable.

Once P has been nested in x, whoever has exclusive ownership of x may decide to temporarily recover P. This is done via two symmetric operations, say "focus" and "defocus", which in the presence of $P \prec x$ convert between $x @ t$ and $P * (P \multimap x @ t)$

(where the type t is arbitrary, but must be exclusive). The permission $P \multimap x @ t$ means that P has been "carved out" of x. While this is the case, $x @ t$ is temporarily lost: in order to recover it, one must give up P. Thus, it is impossible to simultaneously carve *two* permissions out of x.

Nesting subsumes Fähndrich and DeLine's adoption and focus [16]. We view it as a purely static cousin of adoption and abandon. Adoption is more flexible in several important ways: it allows accessing two adoptees at the same time, and allows abandoning an object forever. Nesting has advantages over adoption and abandon: it cannot fail at runtime; it has no time or space overhead; one may nest a permission, whereas one adopts an object; and nesting is heterogeneous, i.e., an object x can nest multiple distinct permissions, whereas, in the case of adoption and abandon, all adoptees of x must have the same type.

Nesting can be axiomatized in *Mezzo* as a trusted library, whose interface appears in the extended version of this paper [28]. In principle, this requires extending the proof of type soundness; we have not done so. When applicable, nesting seems preferable to adoption; however, adoption is more widely applicable.

8.2 Locks

Dynamically-allocated locks in the style of concurrent separation logic [25, 18, 19, 8] are another dynamic mechanism for mediating access to a permission. A new lock, of type lock P, where P is an arbitrary permission, is created via a function `new`. The functions `acquire` and `release` both take the lock as an argument; `acquire` produces the permission P, which `release` consumes. The type lock P is duplicable, so an arbitrary number of threads can share the lock and simultaneously attempt to acquire it. Within a critical section, delimited by `acquire` and `release`, the "lock invariant" P is available, whereas, outside of it, it is not. The "invariant" P can in fact be broken within the critical section, provided it is restored when one reaches the end of the section.

Locks introduce a form of *hidden state* into the language. Because the permission $l @$ lock P is duplicable, it can be captured by a closure. As a result, it becomes possible for a function to perform a side effect, even though its type does not reveal this fact (the pre- and postcondition are empty). *Mezzo*'s modest library for memoization exploits this feature.

Locks can be used to encode "weak" (duplicable) references in the style of ML and duplicable references with affine content in the style of Alms [33], both of which support arbitrary sharing.

Locks can be axiomatized in *Mezzo* as a library, whose interface appears in the extended version of this paper [28]. Again, the proof of type soundness must be extended; we have begun this work. We view locks as complementary to adoption and abandon and nesting. In a typical usage scenario, a lock protects an adopter, which in turn controls a group of adoptees (or of nested permissions). This allows a group of objects to be collectively protected by a single lock. It should be noted that (we believe) adoption and abandon are sound in a concurrent setting.

9. Related work

The literature offers a wealth of type systems and program logics that are intended to help write correct programs in the presence of mutable, heap-allocated state. We review a few of them and contrast them with *Mezzo*.

Ownership Types [10] and its descendants restrict aliasing. Every object is owned by at most one other object, and an "owner-as-dominator" principle is enforced: every path from a root to an object x must go through x's owner. Universe Types [14] impose a slightly different principle, "owner-as-modifier". Arbitrary paths are allowed to exist in the heap, but only those that go through x's owner can be used to modify x. This approach is meant to support program verification, as it allows the owner to impose an object invariant. Permission systems [5, 7, 17] annotate pointers not with owners, but with permissions. The permission carried by a pointer tells how this pointer may be used (e.g. for reading and writing, only for reading, or not at all) and how other pointers to the same object (if they exist) might be used by others.

The systems mentioned so far are refinements (restrictions) of a traditional type discipline. Separation logic [29] departs from this approach and obeys a principle that we dub "owner-as-asserter". (In O'Hearn's words, "ownership is in the eye of the asserter" [25].) Objects are described by logical assertions. To assert is to own: if one knows that "x is a linked list", then one may read and write the cells that form this list, and nobody else may. Whereas the previously mentioned systems combine structural descriptions (i.e., types) with owner or permission annotations, separation logic assertions are at once structural descriptions and claims of ownership.

Mezzo follows the "owner-as-asserter" principle. In the future, this should allow us to annotate permissions with logical assertions and use that as a basis for the specification and proof of *Mezzo* programs. A tempting research direction is to translate *Mezzo* into F* [31]. This purely functional programming language is equipped with affine values, with powerful facilities for expressing program specifications and proofs, and with a notion of proof erasure.

Although our permission discipline is partly inspired by separation logic [29], it is original in several ways. It presents itself as a type system, as opposed to a program logic. This makes it less expressive than a program logic, but more pervasive, in the sense that it can (and must) be used at every stage of a program's development, without proof obligations. It distinguishes between immutable and mutable data, supports first-class functions, and takes advantage of algebraic data types in novel ways.

As far as we know, Ownership or Universe Types cannot express uniqueness or ownership transfer. Müller and Rudich [23] extend Universe Types with these notions. They rely on the fact that each object maintains, at runtime, a pointer to its owner. The potential analogy with our `adopter` fields deserves further study.

The use of singleton types to keep track of equations, and the idea that pointers can be copied, whereas permissions are affine, are inspired by Alias Types [30]. Linear [1] and affine [33] type systems support strong updates and often view permissions (or "capabilities") as ordinary values, which hopefully the compiler can erase. By offering an explicit distinction between permissions and values, we guarantee that permissions are erased, and we are able to make the flow of permissions mostly implicit. Through algebraic data types and through the type constructor $(t \mid P)$, we retain the ability to tie a permission to a value, if desired.

Regions [30, 16, 1] have been widely used as a technical device that allows a type to indirectly refer to a value or set of values. In *Mezzo*, types refer to values directly. This simplifies the metatheory and the programmer's view.

Gordon *et al.* [17] ensure data-race freedom in an extension of C#. They qualify types with permissions in the set immutable, isolated, writable, or readable. The first two roughly correspond to our immutable and mutable modes, whereas the last two have no *Mezzo* analogue. Shared (writable) references allow legacy sequential code to be considered well-typed. A salient feature is the absence of an alias analysis, which simplifies the system considerably. This comes at a cost in expressiveness: mutable global variables, as well as shared objects protected by locks, are disallowed.

Plaid [2] and *Mezzo* exhibit several common traits. A Plaid object does not belong to a fixed class, but can move from one "state" to another: this is related to *Mezzo*'s tag update. Methods carry state pre- and postconditions, which are enforced via permissions [5]. Plaid is more ambitious in that states are organized in an extensible hierarchy, whereas algebraic data types are flat and closed.

10. Conclusion and future work

Mezzo is a high-level functional and imperative programming language where the traditional concept of "type" is replaced with a more powerful concept of "permission". Distinguishing duplicable, exclusive, and affine permissions allows reasoning about state changes. We strive to achieve a balance between simplicity and expressiveness by marrying a static discipline of permissions and a novel dynamic form of adoption and abandon. By adding other mechanisms for controlling sharing, such as nesting and locks, we augment the expressiveness of the language and emphasize that the permission discipline is sufficiently powerful to express these notions. *Mezzo* is type-safe: well-typed programs cannot go wrong (but an abandon operation can fail). We have carried out a machine-checked proof of type safety [26]. In the future, we would like to extend *Mezzo* with support for shared-memory concurrency. We believe that, beyond locks (§8.2), many abstractions (threads, channels, tasks, etc.) can be axiomatized so as to guarantee that well-typed code is data-race-free.

References

[1] Amal Ahmed, Matthew Fluet, and Greg Morrisett. L^3: A linear language with locations. *Fundamenta Informaticæ*, 77(4):397–449, 2007.

[2] Jonathan Aldrich, Joshua Sunshine, Darpan Saini, and Zachary Sparks. Typestate-oriented programming. In *Companion to Object-Oriented Programming, Systems, Languages, and Applications (OOPSLA)*, pages 1015–1022, 2009.

[3] Mike Barnett, K. Rustan M. Leino, and Wolfram Schulte. The Spec# programming system: An overview. In *Construction and Analysis of Safe, Secure and Interoperable Smart devices (CASSIS)*, volume 3362 of *Lecture Notes in Computer Science*, pages 49–69. Springer, 2004.

[4] Josh Berdine, Cristiano Calcagno, and Peter W. O'Hearn. Smallfoot: Modular automatic assertion checking with separation logic. In *Formal Methods for Components and Objects*, volume 4111 of *Lecture Notes in Computer Science*, pages 115–137. Springer, 2005.

[5] Kevin Bierhoff and Jonathan Aldrich. Modular typestate checking of aliased objects. In *Object-Oriented Programming, Systems, Languages, and Applications (OOPSLA)*, pages 301–320, 2007.

[6] Kevin Bierhoff, Nels E. Beckman, and Jonathan Aldrich. Practical API protocol checking with access permissions. In *European Conference on Object-Oriented Programming (ECOOP)*, volume 5653 of *Lecture Notes in Computer Science*, pages 195–219. Springer, 2009.

[7] John Tang Boyland. Semantics of fractional permissions with nesting. *ACM Transactions on Programming Languages and Systems*, 32(6), 2010.

[8] Alexandre Buisse, Lars Birkedal, and Kristian Støvring. A step-indexed Kripke model of separation logic for storable locks. *Electronic Notes in Theoretical Computer Science*, 276:121–143, 2011.

[9] Arthur Charguéraud. *Characteristic Formulae for Mechanized Program Verification*. PhD thesis, Université Paris 7, 2010.

[10] David G. Clarke, John M. Potter, and James Noble. Ownership types for flexible alias protection. In *Object-Oriented Programming, Systems, Languages, and Applications (OOPSLA)*, pages 48–64, 1998.

[11] Karl Crary, David Walker, and Greg Morrisett. Typed memory management in a calculus of capabilities. In *Principles of Programming Languages (POPL)*, pages 262–275, 1999.

[12] Robert DeLine and Manuel Fähndrich. Enforcing high-level protocols in low-level software. In *Programming Language Design and Implementation (PLDI)*, pages 59–69, 2001.

[13] Robert DeLine and Manuel Fähndrich. Typestates for objects. In *European Conference on Object-Oriented Programming (ECOOP)*, volume 3086 of *Lecture Notes in Computer Science*, pages 465–490. Springer, 2004.

[14] Werner Dietl and Müller Peter. Universes: Lightweight ownership for JML. *Journal of Object Technology*, 4(8):5–32, 2005.

[15] Manuel Fähndrich, Mark Aiken, Chris Hawblitzel, Orion Hodson, Galen Hunt, James R. Larus, and Steven Levi. Language support for fast and reliable message-based communication in Singularity OS. In *EuroSys*, pages 177–190, 2006.

[16] Manuel Fähndrich and Robert DeLine. Adoption and focus: practical linear types for imperative programming. In *Programming Language Design and Implementation (PLDI)*, pages 13–24, 2002.

[17] Colin S. Gordon, Matthew J. Parkinson, Jared Parsons, Aleks Bromfield, and Joe Duffy. Uniqueness and reference immutability for safe parallelism. In *Object-Oriented Programming, Systems, Languages, and Applications (OOPSLA)*, pages 21–40, 2012.

[18] Alexey Gotsman, Josh Berdine, Byron Cook, Noam Rinetzky, and Mooly Sagiv. Local reasoning for storable locks and threads. Technical Report MSR-TR-2007-39, Microsoft Research, 2007.

[19] Aquinas Hobor, Andrew W. Appel, and Francesco Zappa Nardelli. Oracle semantics for concurrent separation logic. In *European Symposium on Programming (ESOP)*, volume 4960 of *Lecture Notes in Computer Science*, pages 353–367. Springer, 2008.

[20] Bart Jacobs and Frank Piessens. The VeriFast program verifier. Technical Report CW-520, Department of Computer Science, Katholieke Universiteit Leuven, 2008.

[21] Toshiyuki Maeda, Haruki Sato, and Akinori Yonezawa. Extended alias type system using separating implication. In *Types in Language Design and Implementation (TLDI)*, 2011.

[22] Yasuhiko Minamide. A functional representation of data structures with a hole. In *Principles of Programming Languages (POPL)*, pages 75–84, 1998.

[23] Peter Müller and Arsenii Rudich. Ownership transfer in universe types. In *Object-Oriented Programming, Systems, Languages, and Applications (OOPSLA)*, pages 461–478, 2007.

[24] Karl Naden, Robert Bocchino, Jonathan Aldrich, and Kevin Bierhoff. A type system for borrowing permissions. In *Principles of Programming Languages (POPL)*, pages 557–570, 2012.

[25] Peter W. O'Hearn. Resources, concurrency and local reasoning. *Theoretical Computer Science*, 375(1–3):271–307, 2007.

[26] François Pottier. Type soundness for Core Mezzo. Unpublished, January 2013.

[27] François Pottier and Jonathan Protzenko. *Mezzo*. `http://gallium.inria.fr/~protzenk/mezzo-lang/`, July 2013.

[28] François Pottier and Jonathan Protzenko. Programming with permissions in *Mezzo* (long version). Unpublished, July 2013.

[29] John C. Reynolds. Separation logic: A logic for shared mutable data structures. In *Logic in Computer Science (LICS)*, pages 55–74, 2002.

[30] Frederick Smith, David Walker, and Greg Morrisett. Alias types. In *European Symposium on Programming (ESOP)*, volume 1782 of *Lecture Notes in Computer Science*, pages 366–381. Springer, 2000.

[31] Nikhil Swamy, Juan Chen, Cédric Fournet, Pierre-Yves Strub, Karthik Bhargavan, and Jean Yang. Secure distributed programming with value-dependent types. In *International Conference on Functional Programming (ICFP)*, pages 266–278, 2011.

[32] Nikhil Swamy, Michael Hicks, Greg Morrisett, Dan Grossman, and Trevor Jim. Safe manual memory management in Cyclone. *Science of Computer Programming*, 62(2):122–144, 2006.

[33] Jesse A. Tov and Riccardo Pucella. Practical affine types. In *Principles of Programming Languages (POPL)*, pages 447–458, 2011.

[34] Thomas Tuerk. Local reasoning about while-loops. Unpublished, 2010.

[35] David Walker and Greg Morrisett. Alias types for recursive data structures. In *Types in Compilation (TIC)*, volume 2071 of *Lecture Notes in Computer Science*, pages 177–206. Springer, 2000.

Wellfounded Recursion with Copatterns

A Unified Approach to Termination and Productivity

Andreas Abel
Department of Computer Science,
Ludwig-Maximilians-University Munich, Germany
andreas.abel@ifi.lmu.de

Brigitte Pientka
School of Computer Science,
McGill University, Montreal, Canada
bpientka@cs.mcgill.ca

Abstract

In this paper, we study strong normalization of a core language based on System F_ω which supports programming with finite and infinite structures. Building on our prior work, finite data such as finite lists and trees are defined via constructors and manipulated via pattern matching, while infinite data such as streams and infinite trees is defined by observations and synthesized via copattern matching. In this work, we take a type-based approach to strong normalization by tracking size information about finite and infinite data in the type. This guarantees compositionality. More importantly, the duality of pattern and copatterns provide a unifying semantic concept which allows us for the first time to elegantly and uniformly support both well-founded induction and coinduction by mere rewriting. The strong normalization proof is structured around Girard's reducibility candidates. As such our system allows for non-determinism and does not rely on coverage. Since System F_ω is general enough that it can be the target of compilation for the Calculus of Constructions, this work is a significant step towards representing observation-centric infinite data in proof assistants such as Coq and Agda.

Categories and Subject Descriptors D.3.3 [*Programming Languages*]: Language Constructs and Features—Data types and structures, Patterns, Recursion; F.3.3 [*Logics and Meanings of Programs*]: Studies of Program Constructs—Program and recursion schemes, Type structure; F.4.1 [*Mathematical Logic and Formal Languages*]: Mathematical Logic—Lambda calculus

General Terms Languages, Theory

Keywords Recursion, Coinduction, Pattern matching, Productivity, Strong normalization, Type-based termination

1. Introduction

Integrating infinite data and coinduction with dependent types is tricky. For example, in the Calculus of (Co)Inductive Constructions, the core theory underlying Coq (INRIA 2012), coinduction is broken, since computation does not preserve types (Giménez 1996). In Agda (Norell 2007), a dependently typed proof and programming environment based on Martin-Löf Type Theory, inductive and coinductive types cannot be mixed in a compositional way (Altenkirch and Danielsson 2010). In previous work (Abel et al. 2013) we have introduced *copatterns* as a novel perspective on defining infinite structures that might serve as a new foundation for coinduction in dependently-typed languages, overcoming the problems in the present solutions.

In the copattern approach, finite data such as finite lists and trees are defined as usual via constructors and manipulated via pattern matching, while infinite data such as streams and infinite trees are defined by observations and synthesized via copattern matching. For example, instead of conceiving streams as built by the constructor cons, we consider the observations head and tail about streams as primitive. Programs about streams are defined in terms of the observations head and tail.

Our previous work left the question of termination of recursive function and the productivity of infinite objects open. Both issues are crucial since we want to program inductive proofs as recursive functions and coinductive proofs as infinite objects or corecursive functions producing infinite objects. In this article, we adapt type-based termination (Hughes et al. 1996; Amadio and Coupet-Grimal 1998; Barthe et al. 2004; Blanqui 2004; Abel 2008b; Sacchini 2013) to definitions by copatterns.

A syntactic termination check would ensure that recursive calls occur only with arguments smaller than the ones of the original call. In type-based termination, inductive types are tagged with a size expression that denotes the (ordinal) maximal height of the trees inhabiting it, i. e., an upper bound on the number of constructors in the longest path of the tree. To prove termination of a recursive function means to show that it can safely handle arguments of arbitrary size. This can be established by well-founded induction: to show that a function can handle arguments up to a fixed size a, we may assume it already safely processes arguments of any smaller size $b < a$. This induction principle can be turned into a typing rule for recursive functions, using sized types and size quantification. How can this be dualized to coinduction? A stream is *productive* if we can make arbitrarily deep observations, i. e., if we can take its tail arbitrarily many times. To show that a stream definition is productive, we also proceed by well-founded induction. To show that it can safely handle a observations, we may assume that b observations are fine for any $b < a$. The number of observations we can safely make is called the *depth* of the stream, or more general, of the coinductive structure. One should not be mislead and think of the depth as "size"; streams do not have a size since they are not tree-structures in memory—they only exist as processes that continuously yield elements on demand. But it is fruitful to transfer the

ICFP '13, September 25–27, 2013, Boston, MA, USA.

ACM 978-1-4503-2326-0/13/09... $15.00.
http://dx.doi.org/10.1145/2500365.2500591

concept of *depth* to (co)recursive functions. The depth of a function is the maximal size of arguments it can safely handle. As we are only interested in streams of infinite depth in the end, we care only about functions of infinite depth. Yet to establish productivity and termination, we need to induct on depth.

The type-based termination approach is in contrast to common approaches taken in systems such as Coq (INRIA 2012) and Agda (Norell 2007) which employ a syntactic guardedness check to ensure corecursive programs are productive: all corecursive calls must occur under a constructor. This ensures that the next unit of information can be computed in a finite amount of time (Sijtsma 1989). However, this approach has also known limitations: it is difficult to handle higher-order programs such as $g\,f\ =\ \mathsf{cons}\,0\,(f\,(g\,f))$ where the productivity of g depends on the behavior of the function f. It is also not compositional, i. e., we cannot easily abstract over a constructor cons in a productive program and replace it with a function f. Both limitations are due to the lack of information we have about f in the syntactic guardedness check. Types on the other hand already track information about each argument to a definition and its output. Type-based termination piggy-backs on the typing analysis and avoids a separate formal system to traverse the definitions. By indexing types with sizes, we are able to carry more precise information about input and output arguments and their relation which is then verified simultaneously while type checking the definitions.

The contributions of our work are:

- We present $\mathsf{F}_\omega^{\mathsf{cop}}$, an extension of System F_ω by inductive and coinductive types, sizes and bounded size quantification, pattern and copattern matching and lexicographic termination measures.
- In contrast to previous approaches on type-based termination, we use well-founded induction on ordinals instead of conventional induction that distinguishes between zero, successor and limit ordinals. Disposing of this case distinction, we operate within constructive foundations of mathematics (Taylor 1996).
- Well-founded induction leads to a construction of inductive types by inflationary iteration, which has been utilized to justify cyclic proofs in the sequent calculus (Sprenger and Dam 2003). We are the first to utilize inflationary iteration in a type system.
- Well-founded induction alleviates the need for a semi-continuity check for sized types of recursive functions (Hughes et al. 1996; Abel 2008b) which sometimes disguises itself as a monotonicity check (Barthe et al. 2004; Blanqui 2004; Barthe et al. 2008; Sacchini 2013). Thus, we put type-based termination on leaner and better understandable foundations.
- Since we construct infinite objects by copattern matching, standard rewriting becomes strongly normalizing even for corecursive definitions, and productivity becomes an instance of termination. Thus, we achieve a unified treatment of recursion and corecursion that is central to type-based termination.
- Our typing rules are formulated as a bidirectional type-checking algorithm that can be implemented as such. See, e. g., MiniAgda (Abel 2012).
- We prove soundness of $\mathsf{F}_\omega^{\mathsf{cop}}$ by an untyped term model based on Girard's reducibility candidates. The proof exhibits semantic counterparts of pattern and copattern typing and accounts for incomplete and overlapping rewrite rules.

Due to lack of space, we leave out $\mathsf{F}_\omega^{\mathsf{cop}}$'s inference rules concerning the kind and type level, the description of program typing, and most details of the soundness proof. The full development can be found in the extended version (Abel and Pientka 2013).

2. Copatterns and Termination

Let us illustrate how to program with copatterns using a simple example of generating a stream of zeros. A streams s over an element type A is given by the two *observations* head and tail: We can inspect the head of s by applying the projection s .head and obtain an element of A. To obtain the tail of s, we use the projection s .tail. We can then define the stream of zeros recursively by the following two clauses:

$$\begin{aligned}\mathsf{zeros}\ .\mathsf{head} &= 0\\ \mathsf{zeros}\ .\mathsf{tail} &= \mathsf{zeros}\end{aligned}$$

More generally, zeros can be coded as repeat 0 with

$$\begin{aligned}\mathsf{repeat}\ a\ .\mathsf{head} &= a\\ \mathsf{repeat}\ a\ .\mathsf{tail} &= \mathsf{repeat}\ a\end{aligned}$$

The left hand side of each clause is considering the definiendum, here repeat, in a *copattern*, here $\cdot\ a$ .head and $\cdot\ a$ .tail, resp. A copattern consists of a hole, $\cdot$, applied to a sequence of patterns and/or projections. The hole is filled, e. g., by the definiendum. In this case, we have first a variable pattern, a, and then a projection head/tail.

The definition of repeat is *complete* because the given copatterns are covering all possible cases (Abel et al. 2013). Rewriting with the equations for repeat terminates in all situations, since one projection is consumed in each rewriting step. For example, projecting the $(n+1)$st element (counting from 0) of repeat a, i. e., repeat a .tail^{n+1} .head reduces in one step to repeat a .tail^{n} .head and after n more steps to repeat a .head.

2.1 Example: Fibonacci

Let us look at programming with copatterns and type-based termination for a more interesting example, the stream of Fibonacci numbers. It can be elegantly implemented in terms of zipWith $f\ s\ t$ which pointwise applies the binary function f to the elements of streams s and t.

$$\begin{aligned}\mathsf{zipWith}\ f\ s\ t\ .\mathsf{head} &= f\ (s\ .\mathsf{head})\ (t\ .\mathsf{head})\\ \mathsf{zipWith}\ f\ s\ t\ .\mathsf{tail} &= \mathsf{zipWith}\ f\ (s\ .\mathsf{tail})\ (t\ .\mathsf{tail})\end{aligned}$$

$$\begin{aligned}\mathsf{fib}\ .\mathsf{head} &= 0\\ \mathsf{fib}\ .\mathsf{tail}\ .\mathsf{head} &= 1\\ \mathsf{fib}\ .\mathsf{tail}\ .\mathsf{tail} &= \mathsf{zipWith}\ (+)\ \mathsf{fib}\ (\mathsf{fib}\ .\mathsf{tail})\end{aligned}$$

The last equation states in terms of streams that the $(n+2)$nd element of the Fibonacci stream is the sum of the nth and the $(n+1)$st. It looks like fib is a terminating definition since fib .tail .tail only refers to fib and fib .tail, thus, one projection is removed in each recursive call. However, termination of fib is also dependent on good properties of zipWith. For instance, the following faulty clause for zipWith would make fib .tail .tail .head loop:

$$\mathsf{zipWith}\ f\ s\ t\ .\mathsf{head} = f\ (s\ .\mathsf{tail}\ .\mathsf{head})\ (t\ .\mathsf{tail}\ .\mathsf{head})$$

$$\begin{aligned}&\mathsf{fib}\ .\mathsf{tail}\ .\mathsf{tail}\ .\mathsf{head}\\ &\ = \mathsf{zipWith}\ (+)\ \mathsf{fib}\ (\mathsf{fib}\ .\mathsf{tail})\ .\mathsf{head}\\ &\ = (\mathsf{fib}\ .\mathsf{tail}\ .\mathsf{head}) + (\mathsf{fib}\ .\mathsf{tail}\ .\mathsf{tail}\ .\mathsf{head})\\ &\ = (\mathsf{fib}\ .\mathsf{tail}\ .\mathsf{head}) + (\mathsf{fib}\ .\mathsf{tail}\ .\mathsf{head}) + (\mathsf{fib}\ .\mathsf{tail}\ .\mathsf{tail}\ .\mathsf{head})\\ &\ = \ldots\end{aligned}$$

The problem is that the faulty zipWith adds again one tail projection that has been removed in going from the original call fib .tail .tail to the recursive call fib .tail, thus, we are left with the same number of projections, leading to an infinite call cycle.

What we learn from this counterexample is that in order to reason about termination of stream expressions, we need to trade the naive image of streams as infinite sequences for a notion of streams that can safely be subjected to α many projections, where

$\alpha \leq \omega$ can be a natural number or (the smallest) infinity ω. We refer to such streams as *sized streams*, or streams having *depth* α. Clearly, if a stream of depth α is required, we can safely supply a stream of depth $\beta \geq \alpha$, thus, sized streams are subject to contravariant subtyping.

The original zipWith delivers, if called with input streams of depth α, an output stream of the same depth. This allows us to reason about the termination of fib as follows. We show that fib is a stream of arbitrary depth α by induction on $\alpha \leq \omega$. Cases $\alpha < 2$ are easy. The interesting case is $\alpha = n + 2$ when we take two tail projections and then another n projections, thus, $n + 2$ projections in total. Then we may assume (by induction hypothesis) that on the rhs taking up to $n + 1$ projections of fib is fine, thus, fib and fib .tail behave well under another n projections—they both can be assigned depth n using subtyping. Passing them to zipWith (+) returns in turn a stream of the same depth n, hence the lhs fib .tail .tail can be assigned depth n and, consequently, fib depth $n + 2$, which was our goal.

The faulty zipWith, however, needs streams of depth $n + 1$ to deliver a stream of depth n. Since fib .tail can only safely be assumed to have depth n, not depth $n + 1$, the termination proof attempt fails, and rightfully so.

In this model proof we assumed that taking a projection will decrease the depth by exactly one. In the following, we will loosen this assumption and let projections take us to any strictly smaller depth.

2.2 Type-based termination for copatterns

In this section, we present the key ideas behind $\mathsf{F}^{\mathsf{cop}}_{\omega}$, our polymorphic core language for type-based termination checking of recursive definitions involving inductive and coinductive types. We illustrate how the integration of size expressions into the type system captures and mechanizes the informal reasoning about termination employed in the previous section.

Size quantification for inductive and coinductive types. Besides quantification over types $\forall A{:}{*}.\,B$ we have quantification over sizes $\forall i{<}a.\,B$. To unify these two forms of quantification we add to the base kind $*$ of types the base kinds $<a$ denoting sets of ordinals below a and conceive $\forall i{<}a.\,B$ as shorthand for $\forall i{:}({<}a).\,B$. Thus, size expressions fall in the same syntactic class as type expressions. We introduce a special ordinal ∞, the closure ordinal for all (co)inductive types we consider. As far as streams are concerned, ∞ can be thought of as ω. In general, valid size expressions are of the form $a ::= i + n \mid \infty + n$ where i is a size variable and n a concrete number (we drop $+0$).

The type of streams of depth a over element type A will be denoted by $\mathsf{Stream}^a A$, and we consider the following typing rules for the projections:

$$\frac{s : \mathsf{Stream}^a A}{s\ .\mathsf{head} : \forall i{<}a^{\uparrow}.\,A} \qquad \frac{s : \mathsf{Stream}^a A}{s\ .\mathsf{tail} : \forall i{<}a^{\uparrow}.\,\mathsf{Stream}^i A} \tag{1}$$

These rules state that if you want to project a stream of depth a, you will need to provide a *witness* that you are able to do so, i. e., an ordinal $i < a^{\uparrow}$. In case of tail, this witness serves also as the depth of the projected stream. For instance, if $s : \mathsf{Stream}^{i+2} A$, then $s\ .\mathsf{tail}\ (i+1)\ .\mathsf{head}\ i : A$. *Bound normalization* $a^{\uparrow}$, defined by $(i+n)^{\uparrow} = i + n$ and $(\infty + n)^{\uparrow} = \infty + 1$, allows us to turn bounds $a \geq \infty$ into $\infty + 1$ and project from the fixpoint $\mathsf{Stream}^{\infty} A$ without information loss. For $s : \mathsf{Stream}^{\infty} A$ we have $s\ .\mathsf{tail}\ \infty : \mathsf{Stream}^{\infty} A$ since $\infty < \infty^{\uparrow} = \infty + 1$, reflecting that the tail of a fully defined stream has infinite depth as well.

In practice, we often use the following derived rule which eliminates the universal quantifier and directly compares sizes.

$$\frac{s : \mathsf{Stream}^a A}{s\ .\mathsf{head}\ b : A}\ b < a^{\uparrow} \qquad \frac{s : \mathsf{Stream}^a A}{s\ .\mathsf{tail}\ b : \mathsf{Stream}^b A}\ b < a^{\uparrow}$$

More generally, following previous work (Abel et al. 2013), we represent coinductive types as recursive records νR, with $R = \{d_1 : F_1; \ldots d_n : F_n\}$ giving (sized) types to the projections $d_{1..n}$ as follows:

$$\frac{r : \nu^a R}{r\ .d_k : \forall i{<}a^{\uparrow}.\,F_k(\nu^i R)}$$

For instance, with $\mathsf{Stream}^i A = \nu^i\{\mathsf{head} : \lambda X.\,A; \mathsf{tail} : \lambda X.\,X\}$ we obtain the typing of head and tail presented above (1). Considering R as a finite map from projections to type constructors, we write R_{d_k} for F_k.

Dually, inductive types are recursive variants μS with $S = \langle c_1 : F_1; \ldots; c_n : F_n\rangle$ and constructor typing

$$\frac{t : \exists i{<}a^{\uparrow}.\,F_k(\mu^i S)}{c_k\ t : \mu^a S}.$$

For instance, finite lists can be defined as follows: $\mathsf{List}^i A = \mu^i\langle \mathsf{nil} : \lambda X.\,1;\ \mathsf{cons} : \lambda X.\,A \times X\rangle$. Integrating the quantifier rules, we derive the following inferences for constructors and destructors:

$$\frac{s : S_c(\mu^b S)}{c^b s : \mu^a S}\ b < a^{\uparrow} \qquad \frac{r : \nu^a R}{r\ .d\,b : R_d(\nu^b R)}\ b < a^{\uparrow}.$$

Specifying termination measures. The polymorphically typed version of zipWith officially looks as follows, where we write $\forall i{\leq}a$ as abbreviation for $\forall i{<}(a+1)$:

$$\begin{array}{l} \mathsf{zipWith} : \forall i{\leq}\infty.\,|i| \Rightarrow \forall A{:}{*}.\,\forall B{:}{*}.\,\forall C{:}{*}. \\ \qquad (A \to B \to C) \to \\ \qquad \mathsf{Stream}^i A \to \mathsf{Stream}^i B \to \mathsf{Stream}^i C \end{array}$$

$$\begin{array}{l} \mathsf{zipWith}\ i\ A\ B\ C\ f\ s\ t\ .\mathsf{head}\ j = f\ (s\ .\mathsf{head}\ j)\ (t\ .\mathsf{head}\ j) \\ \mathsf{zipWith}\ i\ A\ B\ C\ f\ s\ t\ .\mathsf{tail}\ j\ \ = \mathsf{zipWith}\ j\ A\ B\ C\ f \\ \qquad\qquad\qquad\qquad\qquad (s\ .\mathsf{tail}\ j)\ (t\ .\mathsf{tail}\ j) \end{array}$$

The first equation has type C and the second one type $\mathsf{Stream}^j C$. The kind of j is $<i$ due to the typing of head and tail, thus, zipWith is well-defined (and terminating) by induction on its first argument, the size argument. The associated termination measure is located after the size variable(s) and, in general, a tuple $|a, b, c|$ of size expressions under the lexicographic order.[1] In this case, it is just the unary tuple $|i|$, meaning that the termination measure is just the value of size variable i. The measure is not officially part of the type; it is rather an annotation that allows us to termination check the clauses without having to infer a termination order.

High-level idea of size-based termination checking. When we check a corecursive definition such as the second clause of zipWith we start with traversing the left hand side (lhs). We first introduce assumption $i{\leq}\infty$ into the context and now hit the measure annotation $|i|$ in the type. At this point we introduce the assumption $\mathsf{zipWith} : \forall j{\leq}\infty.\,|j|{<}|i| \Rightarrow \forall A{:}{*}.\,\forall B{:}{*}.\,\forall C{:}{*}.\,(A \to B \to C) \to \mathsf{Stream}^j A \to \mathsf{Stream}^j B \to \mathsf{Stream}^j C$ which will be used to check the recursive call on the right hand side (rhs). It has a constraint $|j| < |i|$, a lexicographic comparison of size expression tuples (which here just means $j < i$), that is checked before applying zipWith j to A. Continued checking of the lhs introduces further assumptions $A, B, C : *$, $f : A \to B \to C$, $s : \mathsf{Stream}^i A$, $t : \mathsf{Stream}^i B$, and $j < i$. Checking the rhs succeeds since the

[1] The notation for termination measures is taken from Xi (2002)

constraint $|j| < |i|$ is satisfied and s .tail j : $\mathsf{Stream}^j A$ and t .tail j : $\mathsf{Stream}^j B$.

In the following, we abbreviate $\forall A{:}*$ to just $\forall A$ and $\forall i{\le}\infty$ to just $\forall i$. With all size and type-arguments, the definition of the Fibonacci stream becomes:

$$\begin{array}{ll}
\mathsf{fib} : \forall i.\, |i| \Rightarrow \mathsf{Stream}^i\mathbb{N} & \\
\mathsf{fib}\, i\ .\mathsf{head}\ j & = 0 \\
\mathsf{fib}\, i\ .\mathsf{tail}\ j\ .\mathsf{head}\ k & = 1 \\
\mathsf{fib}\, i\ .\mathsf{tail}\ j\ .\mathsf{tail}\ k & = \mathsf{zipWith}\ k\ \mathbb{N}\ \mathbb{N}\ \mathbb{N}\ (+)\ (\mathsf{fib}\, k) \\
 & \quad (\mathsf{fib}\, j\ .\mathsf{tail}\ k)
\end{array}$$

In the last line, the lhs introduces size variables i and $j < i$ and $k < j$ and an assumption $\mathsf{fib} : \forall i'.\, |i'| < |i| \Rightarrow \mathsf{Stream}^{i'}\mathbb{N}$ and expects a rhs of type $\mathsf{Stream}^k\mathbb{N}$. Since $k < j < i$, both recursive calls are valid, and the expressions $\mathsf{fib}\, k$ and $\mathsf{fib}\, j$ .tail k both have type $\mathsf{Stream}^k\mathbb{N}$. With $\mathsf{zipWith}\ k\,\mathbb{N}\,\mathbb{N}\,\mathbb{N} : \mathsf{Stream}^k\mathbb{N} \to \mathsf{Stream}^k\mathbb{N} \to \mathsf{Stream}^k\mathbb{N}$, the rhs is well-typed, and fib is terminating.

2.3 Example: Stream processor

Ghani et al. (2009) describe programs for continuous stream functions $\mathsf{Stream}\,A \to \mathsf{Stream}\,B$ in terms of a mixed coinductive-inductive data type SP with two constructors $\mathsf{get} : (A \to \mathsf{SP}) \to \mathsf{SP}$ and $\mathsf{put} : (B \times \mathsf{SP}) \to \mathsf{SP}$. We use this example to illustrate how our foundation supports size-based reasoning on such mixed datatypes and lexicographic termination measures for mutually recursive functions. A stream processor can either get an element $v : A$ from the input stream and enter a new state, depending on the read value, or it can put an element $w : B$ on the output stream and enter a new state. To be productive, it can only read finitely many values from the input stream before writing a value on the output stream, thus, SP is actually a nesting of a least fixed-point into a greatest one: $\mathsf{SP} = \nu X.\, \mu Y.\, (A \to Y) + (B \times X)$. We express this nesting by the definition of two data types, an inductive variant SP_μ and a coinductive record type SP_ν.

$$\begin{array}{lcl}
\mathsf{SP}^i_\mu\, X & = & \mu^i\langle \mathsf{get} : \lambda Y.\, A \to Y;\ \mathsf{put} : \lambda Y.\, B \times X\rangle \\
\mathsf{SP}^i_\nu & = & \nu^i\{\mathsf{out} : \lambda X.\, \mathsf{SP}^\infty_\mu X\}
\end{array}$$

Inside the coinductive type, we use the inductive type SP_μ at size ∞ since we want to allow an arbitrary (finite) number of gets between two puts. We get the following derived rules for typing constructors and destructors:

$$\frac{f : A \to \mathsf{SP}^b_\mu X}{\mathsf{get}^b f : \mathsf{SP}^a_\mu X}\ b < a^\uparrow \qquad \frac{w : B \qquad sp : X}{\mathsf{put}^b(w, sp) : \mathsf{SP}^a_\mu X}\ b < a^\uparrow$$

$$\frac{sp : \mathsf{SP}^a_\nu}{sp\ .\mathsf{out}\, b : \mathsf{SP}^\infty_\mu\, \mathsf{SP}^b_\nu}\ b < a^\uparrow$$

In the context of stream processors it is convenient to consider streams as given by a single destructor force which returns head and tail in a pair, thus, $\mathsf{Str}^i A = \nu^i\{\mathsf{force} : \lambda X.\, A \times X\}$. Dedicated projections hd and tl can be defined by

$$\begin{array}{lcl}
\mathsf{hd} & : & \forall i.\, \mathsf{Str}^{i+1} A \to A \\
\mathsf{hd}\, i\, s & = & \mathsf{fst}\,(s\ .\mathsf{force}\, i) \\[4pt]
\mathsf{tl} & : & \forall i.\, \mathsf{Str}^{i+1} A \to \mathsf{Str}^i A \\
\mathsf{tl}\, i\, s & = & \mathsf{snd}\,(s\ .\mathsf{force}\, i)
\end{array}$$

with fst and snd the obvious first and second projections from pairs. Via bound normalization, facilitating $\mathsf{Str}^\infty = \mathsf{Str}^{\infty+1}$, we obtain instances $\mathsf{hd}\,\infty : \mathsf{Str}^\infty A \to A$ and $\mathsf{tl}\,\infty : \mathsf{Str}^\infty A \to \mathsf{Str}^\infty A$.

Running a stream processor on an input stream produces an output stream as follows (informally coded in a Haskell-like language):

$$\begin{array}{lcl}
\mathsf{run}\,(\mathsf{get}\, f)\,(v, vs) & = & \mathsf{run}\,(f\, v)\, vs \\
\mathsf{run}\,(\mathsf{put}(w, sp))\, vs & = & (w,\ \mathsf{run}\ sp\ vs)
\end{array}$$

We represent this function via two mutually recursive functions, one handling SP_μ and one SP_ν:

$$\begin{array}{ll}
\mathsf{run}_\mu : \forall i \forall j.\, |i, j{+}1| \Rightarrow \mathsf{SP}^j_\mu(\mathsf{SP}^i_\nu) \to \mathsf{Str}^\infty A \to B \times \mathsf{Str}^i B & \\
\mathsf{run}_\mu\, i\, j\,(\mathsf{get}^{j'} f) \qquad\quad vs = \mathsf{run}_\mu\, i\, j'\,(f\,(\mathsf{hd}\,\infty\, vs))\,(\mathsf{tl}\,\infty\, vs) & \\
\mathsf{run}_\mu\, i\, j\,(\mathsf{put}^{j'}(w, sp))\ vs = (w,\ \mathsf{run}_\nu\, i\, sp\, vs) & \\[4pt]
\mathsf{run}_\nu : \forall i.\, |i, 0| \Rightarrow \mathsf{SP}^i_\nu \to \mathsf{Str}^\infty A \to \mathsf{Str}^i B & \\
\mathsf{run}_\nu\, i\, sp\, vs\ .\mathsf{force}\, i' \qquad = \mathsf{run}_\mu\, i'\,\infty\,(sp\ .\mathsf{out}\, i')\, vs &
\end{array}$$

The recursive run_μ handles a sequence of gets terminated by put and emits the head of a forced stream $B \times \mathsf{Str}^i B$. The tail is produced by the corecursive run_ν which, upon forcing, calls run_μ again. The termination is guaranteed by the lexicographic measures, which decrease in each recursive call:

$$\begin{array}{llll}
\mathsf{run}_\mu \to \mathsf{run}_\mu : & |i, j+1| > |i, j'+1| & & \text{since } j > j' \\
\mathsf{run}_\mu \to \mathsf{run}_\nu : & |i, j+1| > |i, 0| & & \\
\mathsf{run}_\nu \to \mathsf{run}_\mu : & |i, 0| \quad\ > |i', \infty+1| & & \text{since } i > i'
\end{array}$$

Note that since we are not doing induction on SP^i_ν, but coinduction into Str^i, we could use SP^∞_ν instead of SP^i_ν in the types of run_μ and run_ν. However, the given types are more precise: instead of a stream processor of infinite depth, they only require a stream processor of depth i to produce a stream of depth i.

3. Syntax

In this section, we formally define $\mathsf{F}^{\mathsf{cop}}_\omega$, our higher-order polymorphic lambda-calculus with sized inductive and coinductive types, polarized higher-order subtyping, and definitions by pattern and copattern matching. As in previous work (Abel 2008b) we choose System F_ω rather than System F as basis since the notion of a *type constructor* is required (at least, semantically) if one wants to talk its fixed-points, i. e., about (co)inductive types.

$$\begin{array}{llll}
\mathsf{SizeVar} & \ni i, j & & \\
\mathsf{SizeExp} & \ni a, b & ::= i + n \mid \infty + n & (n \ge 0) \\
\mathsf{SizeExp}^+ & \ni a^+, b^+ & ::= a \mid n & \\
\mathsf{Measure} & \ni \mathfrak{m} & ::= \cdot \mid a^+, \mathfrak{m} & \\[4pt]
\mathsf{Pol} & \ni \pi & ::= \circ \mid + \mid - \mid \top & \\
\mathsf{SizeCxt} & \ni \Psi & ::= \cdot \mid \Psi, i{:}\pi({<}a) &
\end{array}$$

Figure 1. Sizes and measures.

3.1 Sizes

Fig. 1 gives a grammar for sizes, measures, and size contexts. A *size expression* a consists of a base, which is either a size variable i or ∞, and an offset, a natural number n.

$$a ::= i + n \mid \infty + n$$

We omit the offset when 0. Each size variable i comes with a bound $i < a$, which is recorded in a *size context*

$$\Psi ::= \cdot \mid \Psi, i{:}\pi({<}a).$$

A size context is considered as finite map from size variables i to their *polarity* π (see below) and their *kind* $<a$. We write $\le a$ for $<(a+1)$ and size for $\le\infty$. *Extended size expressions* a^+ allow as a third base, n, i.e. just a natural number. *Measures* $\mathfrak{m}$ are tuples of extended size expressions. There are a number of trivial judgements concerning well-formedness and partial ordering of (extended) size expressions and measures (see Table 1). These judgements may use the bounds stored in size context Ψ and are all defined as expected; their inference rules can be found in the extended version.

$\Psi \vdash a$	size a is well-formed
$\Psi \vdash a < b$	strict size comparison
$\Psi \vdash a \leq b$	size comparison
$\Psi \vdash a^+$	extended size a^+ is well-formed
$\Psi \vdash a^+ < b^+$	strict comparison
$\Psi \vdash a^+ \leq b^+$	comparison
$\Psi \vdash_n \mathfrak{m}$	measure $\mathfrak{m}$ is a well-formed n-tuple
$\Psi \vdash \mathfrak{m} < \mathfrak{m}'$	strict lexicographic measure comparison
$\Psi \vdash \mathfrak{m} \leq \mathfrak{m}'$	lexicographic measure comparison
$\Psi \vdash \exists\Psi'$	Ψ' is consistent for each valuation of Ψ

Table 1. Size-related judgements.

In constraint-based systems, strong normalization is usually lost in inconsistent contexts.[2] While our size contexts Ψ are always consistent, i. e., enjoy a valuation[3] η of the declared size variables (by natural numbers even), we need sometimes a stronger property that a size context extension Ψ' is consistent with a fixed valuation η of Ψ, i. e., Ψ' must be consistent even when we apply η to its declared bounds. For instance, $i{\leq}\infty\ j{<}i$ is consistent, but $j{<}i$ is not a consistent extension of $i{\leq}\infty$ under valuation $\eta(i) = 0$, since there is no solution for j. We write $\boxed{\Psi \vdash \exists\Psi'}$ if Ψ' consistently extends Ψ in this sense. This judgement is inspired by Blanqui and Riba (2006).

$$
\begin{array}{llll}
\mathsf{SKind} & \ni \iota & ::= & * \mid o \mid \iota \to \iota' \\
\mathsf{Kind} & \ni \kappa & ::= & * \mid {<}a \mid \pi\kappa \to \kappa' \\
\mathsf{TyCxt} & \ni \Delta & ::= & \cdot \mid \Delta, X{:}\pi\kappa \\
\mathsf{Cxt} & \ni \Gamma & ::= & \cdot \mid \Gamma, x : {}'A \mid \Gamma, x : {}^?A \\
\\
\mathsf{TyVar} & \ni X, Y, Z, i, j & & \\
\mathsf{TyAtom} & \ni K & ::= & a \mid X \mid 1 \mid \times \quad \to \mid \forall_\kappa \mid \exists_\kappa \\
\mathsf{Type} & \ni F, G, A, B, C & ::= & K \mid \lambda X{:}\iota.\, F \mid F\,G \\
 & & & \mid \mu^a S \mid \nu^a R \\
\\
\mathsf{Var} & \ni x, y, z & & \\
\mathsf{Cons} & \ni c & & \\
\mathsf{Proj} & \ni d & & \\
\mathsf{Variant} & \ni S & ::= & \langle c_1{:}F_1; \ldots; c_n{:}F_n\rangle \quad n \geq 0 \\
\mathsf{Record} & \ni R & ::= & \{d_1{:}F_1; \ldots; d_n{:}F_n\} \quad n \geq 0 \\
\\
\mathsf{MType} & \ni {}'A, {}'B & ::= & \forall\Psi.\, \mathfrak{m} \Rightarrow A \\
\mathsf{CType} & \ni {}^?A, {}^?B & ::= & \forall\Psi.\, \mathfrak{c} \Rightarrow A \\
\mathsf{Cond} & \ni \mathfrak{c} & ::= & \mathfrak{m} {<} \mathfrak{m}'
\end{array}
$$

Figure 2. Kinds and type constructors.

3.2 Kinds and type constructors

The type constructors of F_ω are assigned kinds $\iota ::= * \mid \iota \to \iota'$, with base kind $*$ classifying all proper types and function kinds $\iota \to \iota'$ the (higher-order) type operators. We add a second base kind $\iota ::= \cdots \mid o$ that classifies size expressions, which we locate at the type level, since they are computationally irrelevant and can be erased during compilation, just as the types are.

[2] For instance, in extensional type theory, X : Type, $p : X = (X \to X) \vdash (\lambda x{:}X.\, x\, x)(\lambda x{:}X.\, x\, x) : X$. The blame is on the false equality assumption $X = X \to X$ which is used for type conversion.

[3] A valuation η of size context Ψ is a map from size variables i to sizes $\eta(i)$ that fulfills the constraints for the size variables given by Ψ. Formally, $\eta(i) < [\![a]\!]_\eta$ must hold in case $i{:}\pi({<}a) \in \Psi$, where $[\![a]\!]_\eta$ is the value of size expression a in environment η.

These *simple kinds* ι form with the type constructor a simply-"typed" type-level lambda calculus. We *refine* these kinds into $\mathsf{F}_\omega^{\mathsf{cop}}$-kinds

$$\kappa ::= * \mid {<}a \mid \kappa \xrightarrow{\pi} \kappa'$$

where ${<}a$ refines o into the kind of size expressions $b < a$. The *polarized function kind* $\kappa \xrightarrow{\pi} \kappa'$, also written $\pi\kappa \to \kappa'$, allows us to express that the classified type constructor is co-variant ($\pi = +$), contravariant ($\pi = -$), constant ($\pi = \top$) or mixed-variant or of unknown variance ($\pi = \circ$). The polarities π are partially ordered $\circ \leq +, - \leq \top$ according to their information content. This and the order on size expressions induce a subkinding relation $\Psi \vdash \kappa \leq \kappa'$ on kinds of the same structure, i. e., the same underlying simple kind $|\kappa| = |\kappa'|$. Here, when comparing two o-kinds $({<}a) \leq ({<}b)$, we resort to size comparison $a \leq b$. The default variance is $\circ$ (no information) and we may omit it, writing simply $\kappa \to \kappa'$ or $\Psi, i{:}({<}a)$, which is further abbreviated by $\Psi, i{<}a$.

Kinding or *type variable contexts* $\Delta ::= \cdot \mid \Delta, X{:}\pi\kappa$, which provide scoping and kinding information for type constructors, generalize size contexts from bounds $({<}a)$ to arbitrary kinds κ. We may use a Δ where a Ψ is formally required, silently erasing all non-size variables from Δ. More generally, context *restriction* $\Delta \restriction \vec{X}$ of context Δ to a set of variables $\vec{X}$ deletes the bindings for all $Y \notin \vec{X}$ from Δ.

$\Psi \vdash \kappa$	kind κ is well-formed in Ψ
$\Psi \vdash \kappa \leq \kappa'$	κ is a subkind of κ'
$\Delta \vdash \Delta'$	kinding context Δ' is well-formed in Δ
$\Delta \vdash \exists\Delta'$	Δ' is consistent for each valuation of Δ

Table 2. Kind-related judgements.

The judgement $\Delta \vdash \exists\Delta'$ (see Table 2) states that Δ' is consistent for each valuation of Δ. Only the size declarations matter here, so it is a straightforward extension of $\Psi \vdash \exists\Psi'$.

Figure 2 contains a grammar for the type constructors of $\mathsf{F}_\omega^{\mathsf{cop}}$. Its core is a simply-kinded lambda-calculus $X \mid \lambda X{:}\iota.\, F \mid F\,G$ with constants $1, \times, \to, \forall_\kappa$, and $\exists_\kappa$ to form unit, product, function, universal, and existential types. Size expressions a are considered type constructors so that sizes can be abstracted over and applied. We use the following short-hands:

$\lambda X F$	for	$\lambda X{:}\iota.\, F$	if ι inferable
$A \times B$	for	$(\times)\, A\, B$	product type
$A \to B$	for	$(\to)\, A\, B$	function type
$\forall X{:}\kappa.\, A$	for	$\forall_\kappa(\lambda X{:}\lvert\kappa\rvert.\, A)$	universal type
$\exists X{:}\kappa.\, A$	for	$\exists_\kappa(\lambda X{:}\lvert\kappa\rvert.\, A)$	existential type
$\forall i{<}a.\, A$	for	$\forall_{<a}\,(\lambda i{:}o.\, A)$	bounded universal
$\exists i{<}a.\, A$	for	$\exists_{<a}\,(\lambda i{:}o.\, A)$	bounded existential
$\forall i.\, A$	for	$\forall i{:}\mathsf{size}.\, A$	"unbounded" universal
$\exists i.\, A$	for	$\forall i{:}\mathsf{size}.\, A$	"unbounded" existential.

We also write $\forall\Delta.\, A$ for the universal abstraction of all type variables of Δ in type A.

The simple kind annotation ι in $\lambda X{:}\iota.\, F$ allows us to infer a unique simple kind for closed type constructors. The simple kind of an open type constructor depends only on the simple kinds of its free type variables. This property simplifies the interpretation $[\![F]\!]$ of type constructors as set-theoretic functions on semantic types we will give later.

For the purpose of type checking, we are only interested in β-normal type constructors. We write $F \mathbin{@^\iota} G$ for the normalizing application of F to an argument G of simple kind ι. We may write $@^\kappa$ instead of $@^{|\kappa|}$, or even just $@$.

Sized inductive $\mu^a S$ and coinductive types $\nu^a R$ are given in terms of *variant rows* S and *record rows* R. A variant row $S =$

$\langle c_1{:}F_1; \ldots; c_n{:}F_n\rangle$ is a finite map from variant labels c_i, called *constructors*, to type constructors $S_{c_i} = F_i$. Dually, a record row R maps record labels d, called *destructors* or *projections*, to type constructors R_d. Instead of presenting, for instance, streams as $\nu^a X. \{\mathsf{head} : A;\ \mathsf{tail} : X\}$, we move the abstraction over X into the record row as $\nu^a\{\mathsf{head} : \lambda X.A;\ \mathsf{tail} : \lambda X.X\}$, in order to formulate the typing rules more conveniently.

Finally, we have *constrained types* $\forall\Psi.\ \mathfrak{m}{<}\mathfrak{m}' \Rightarrow A$ that allow its inhabitants to be used only if the condition $\mathfrak{m} < \mathfrak{m}'$ is fulfilled. We use them to restrict recursive calls to situations where the termination measure has decreased. Recursive function definitions come with *measured types* $'A ::= \forall\Delta.\ \mathfrak{m} \Rightarrow A$. These are not proper types but rather blueprints for constrained types. The idea is that kinding context Δ declares some size variables that are used in measure $\mathfrak{m}$ (and type A). When we analyze the body of a recursive function of measure type $'A$ and the variables of Δ are in scope (thus, the measure $\mathfrak{m}$ is well-formed), we make a copy $'B = \forall\Delta'.\mathfrak{m}' \Rightarrow A'$ of $'A$ by renaming the variables of Δ to Δ'. Then, by *measure replacement* $'B^{<\mathfrak{m}}$ we create the constrained type $\forall\Delta'.\ \mathfrak{m}'{<}\mathfrak{m} \Rightarrow A'$ which is used to type the recursive occurrences of the function in its body.

$\Delta \vdash A$	type A is well-formed
$\Delta \vdash F \rightrightarrows \kappa$	F has kind κ (inference)
$\Delta \vdash F \leftleftarrows \kappa$	F has kind κ (checking)
$\Delta \vdash \Gamma$	typing context Γ is well-formed
$\Delta \vdash A \le A'$	A is subtype of A'
$\Delta \vdash F \le^\pi F' \rightrightarrows \kappa$	F is hi.-ord. subtype of F' (κ inferred)
$\Delta \vdash F \le^\pi F' \leftleftarrows \kappa$	F is hi.-ord. subtype of F' (κ given)

Table 3. Type-related judgements.

Table 3 lists judgements for well-kindedness and partial ordering of types and type constructors. The judgements for types A only invoke the judgments for type constructors F in checking mode at base kind ($\leftleftarrows *$). The judgements for constructors are *bidirectional* with inference mode that computes the kind κ and checking mode that starts with a given κ. Bidirectional checking is complete since we are only interested in normal type constructors.

The rules for these judgements are given in an extended version of this article. A thorough discussion of polarized higher-order subtyping, i. e., subtyping for type constructors that take variance into account, is available in Abel (2008a) and Steffen (1998), we just recapitulate the basic principle here: A constructor F with $X_1{:}\pi_1\kappa_1, \ldots, X_n{:}\pi_n\kappa_n \vdash F \leftleftarrows \kappa$ is interpreted as an operator

$$\lambda X_1 \ldots \lambda X_n.F\ :\ \kappa_1 \stackrel{\pi_1}{\to} \ldots \kappa_n \stackrel{\pi_n}{\to} \kappa$$

with variance given as noted in its kinding context. This induces the kinding rules, for instance $X{:}-*, Y{:}+* \vdash X \to Y : *$ is valid since function space is contravariant in its domain and covariant in its codomain. In particular, the hypothesis rule $X{:}\pi\kappa \vdash X : \kappa$ is only valid if $\pi \le +$, i. e., $\pi = \circ$ which just states that $\lambda X.X : \kappa \to \kappa$ is a well-formed operator, or $\pi = +$ which additionally states that $\lambda X.X$ is monotone. Using the hypothesis rule on $\pi = -$ or $\pi = \top$ is invalid since $\lambda X.X$ is neither an antitone nor a constant operator.

Given a partial order $G \le G'$, its π-parameterized version $G \le^\pi G'$ can be defined as follows:

$$\begin{array}{lcl} G \le^+ G' &=& G \le G' \\ G \le^- G' &=& G' \le G \\ G \le^\circ G' &=& G \le G' \text{ and } G' \le G \\ G \le^\top G' &=& \text{true} \end{array}$$

π-variance of a constructor $F \rightrightarrows \pi\kappa \to \kappa'$ means that $F\,G \le F\,G' \rightrightarrows \kappa$ whenever $G \le^\pi G' \leftleftarrows \kappa$. (The reader is advised to play through the four cases for π in his mind.) Theoretically, the π-parameterized versions $\Delta \vdash F \le^\pi F' \ldots$ of higher-order subtyping could be defined from a non-parameterized version $\Delta \vdash F \le F' \ldots$, but to avoid the potential exponential blowup due to duplication of work in case of $\le^\circ$, the π-parameterized versions are taken as primitive.

Exp	$\ni r, s, t$	$::= u \mid v \mid \lambda\vec{D}$	term
Intro	$\ni v$	$::= () \mid (t_1, t_2) \mid c\,t \mid {}^G t$	introduction
App	$\ni u$	$::= x \mid f \mid r\,e$	applicative
Fun	$\ni f, g$		function name
Elim	$\ni e$	$::= t \mid G \mid .d$	elimination
Pat	$\ni p$	$::= x \mid () \mid (p_1, p_2) \mid c\,p \mid {}^X p$	pattern
Copat	$\ni q$	$::= p \mid X \mid .d$	copattern
PatSp	$\ni \mathbf{q}$	$::= \vec{q}$	pattern spine
DCl	$\ni D$	$::= \{\mathbf{q} \to t\}$	def. clause
Def	$\ni \vec{D}$	$::= \{D_1; \ldots; D_n\}$	def. clauses

Figure 3. Terms, (co)patterns, and clauses.

3.3 Terms and (co)patterns

Figure 3 presents the abstract syntax of $\mathsf{F}_\omega^{\mathsf{cop}}$ *terms* t, which are categorized into *introductions* v, *applicative terms* u, and *anonymous objects* $\lambda\vec{D}$. Introductions $()$, (t_1, t_2), $c\,t$ and ${}^G t$ construct tuples and inductive and existential types. Applicative terms x, f, and $r\,e$ are identifiers and generalized applications of a term r to an *elimination* e, which can be a term s for function elimination, a type G for instantiation of a polymorphic function, or a destructor $.d$ for projection from a coinductive type.

For each introduction form v we have the corresponding form of pattern p, and for each elimination form e there is a copattern q. Application copatterns are just patterns p to match the argument, type application copatterns Q are either type variables X or the special size pattern ∞, which matches anything, and projection copatterns are simply destructors d that match the same destructor in an elimination. A sequence of $\vec{q}$ of copatterns is called a pattern spine $\mathbf{q}$, in correspondence to an *elimination spine* $\vec{e}$.

Generalized lambda abstraction $\lambda\vec{D}$ introduces an object whose behavior is given by the clauses $\vec{D}$, each of which consists of a lhs, a (possibly empty) copattern sequence $\vec{q}$, and a rhs, a term t. Objects subsume both record and λ expressions of traditional functional languages. Here are a few simple examples:

$\lambda\{x \to t\}$	ordinary λ-abstraction $\lambda x t$
$\lambda\{X \to t\}$	type abstraction $\Lambda X t$
$\lambda\{(x, y) \to x\}$	first projection from pair
$\lambda\{{}^X x\, y \to y\, X\, x\}$	elimination of existential
$\lambda\{A\, x\, y\, .\mathsf{head}\ \infty \to x$	
$;\ A\, x\, y\, .\mathsf{tail}\ \ \infty \to y\}$	cons for $\mathsf{Stream}^\infty A$
$\lambda\{\cdot \to s;\ \cdot \to t\}$	non-deterministic choice $s \oplus t$

The meaning, given by the operational semantics, is that whenever $\lambda\vec{D}$ is applied to a sequence of eliminations $\vec{e}$ that match the copatterns $\vec{q}$ of a clause with rhs t under a substitution σ and a type substitution τ, then $(\lambda\vec{D})\,\vec{e}$ reduces to $t\sigma\tau$, the rhs instantiated by the substitutions computed from pattern matching. Using $\boxed{\vec{e}\,/\,\vec{q} \searrow \sigma; \tau}$ for *pattern matching*, the basic rule for *contraction* $\boxed{r \mapsto r'}$ becomes:

$$\frac{\vec{e}\,/\,\mathbf{q}_k \searrow \sigma; \tau}{\lambda\{\overrightarrow{\mathbf{q} \to t}\}\ \vec{e}\,\vec{e}\,' \mapsto t_k\sigma\tau\,\vec{e}\,'}$$

As usual, r is called a *redex* and r' its *reduct* if $r \mapsto r'$. We allow overlapping lhss, a spine $\vec{e}$ may match different pattern spines $\mathbf{q}$, resulting in different contractions of the same redex. Also, if no lhs in the clauses $\vec{D}$ matches $\vec{e}$, the expression $\lambda\vec{D}\ \vec{e}$ is *stuck*. While a coverage checker as described in previous work (Abel et al. 2013) could exclude overlapping and incomplete clauses in well-typed programs, we do not require coverage in this paper and confine ourselves to show *strong normalization*, i. e., the absence of infinite reduction sequences.

Not all stuck terms are pathological; since we are matching the whole pattern spine in one go, partially applied functions such as $\lambda\{xy \to t\}s$ are stuck, but can become unstuck if more arguments are supplied. The existence of partially applied functions will require careful treatment in the normalization proof, because non-contractibility of a non-introduction term is not preserved under application (as would be in the case of λ-calculus).

Decl	$\ni \delta ::= f : A = \vec{D}$	declaration
MDecl	$\ni {}'\delta ::= f : {}'A = \vec{D}$	declaration with measure
Block	$\ni \beta ::= \mathsf{mutual}_m\ {}'\vec{\delta}$	mutual block
Prg	$\ni P ::= \vec{\beta}; u$	program
Sig	$\ni \Sigma ::= \vec{\delta}$	signature

Figure 4. Declarations, blocks, and programs.

3.4 Declarations and programs

An $\mathsf{F}_\omega^{\mathsf{cop}}$ program consists of a sequence $\vec{\beta}$ of mutual blocks and an applicative term u, the *entry point* (this could be the name of the main function or a call to the main function with some initial arguments). Each *mutual block* $\mathsf{mutual}_m {}'\vec{\delta}$ is a sequence ${}'\vec{\delta}$ of mutually recursive declarations with a lexicographic termination measure of length m. Each *declaration* $f : {}'A = \vec{D}$ assigns to a function symbol f its measured type ${}'A$ and its clauses $\vec{D}$. Measures serve their purpose during checking of the mutual block and are discarded afterwards. Erasure of measure $(\!|{}'\delta|\!)$ yields a (unmeasured) declaration $f : A = \vec{D}$; after checking a mutual block and erasing the measures, the individual declarations of the block become part of the signature Σ which is used for type-checking and evaluation of the remainder of the program. An applied function $f\,\vec{e}$ reduces if one of its clauses does:

$$\frac{(\lambda\vec{D})\,\vec{e} \mapsto t}{f\,\vec{e} \mapsto t}(f : A = \vec{D}) \in \Sigma$$

The one-step reduction relation $\boxed{t \longrightarrow t'}$ is the compatible closure of the contraction relation $t \mapsto t'$, i. e., $t \longrightarrow t'$ if t' is the result of contracting exactly one redex in (an arbitrary subterm of) t. Strong normalization of reduction will be shown to hold for well-typed programs.

$\Delta;\Gamma \vdash r \rightrightarrows C$	Infer type C for term r
$\Delta;\Gamma \vdash t \leftleftarrows C$	Term t checks against type C
$\Delta;\Gamma \vdash \{\mathbf{q} \to t\} \leftleftarrows A$	Clause $\mathbf{q} \to t$ checks against type A
$\Delta;\Gamma \vdash \vec{D} \leftleftarrows A$	Clauses D check against type A
$\Delta;\Gamma \vdash_{\Delta_0} p \leftleftarrows A$	Pattern p checks against type A
$\Delta;\Gamma \mid A \vdash_{\Delta_0} \mathbf{q} \rightrightarrows C$	Pattern spine $\mathbf{q}$ eliminates A into C

Table 4. Type checking.

3.5 Type checking

Table 4 lists the judgements involved in type checking $\mathsf{F}_\omega^{\mathsf{cop}}$ programs. Type-checking terms is bidirectional and a straightforward adaption of Abel et al. (2013) to polymorphism, bounded quantification, and constraints. The rules are given in figures 5 and 6, and we briefly explain them.

Inference $\boxed{\Delta;\Gamma \vdash r \rightrightarrows C}$. A function symbol f's type $\Sigma(f)$ is looked up in the signature, and a variable x's type $\Gamma(x)$ in the typing context. If $\Gamma(x)$ is a constrained type $\forall\Psi.\ \mathfrak{c} \Rightarrow A$, the variable x must be immediately applied to size arguments $\vec{a}$ satisfying both Ψ and the condition $\mathfrak{c}$; after all, a constrained type is, for consistency reasons, not a proper type for an expression. An application $r\,s$ of a function r of inferred type $A \to B$ has type B if the argument s checks against type A. Instantiation $r\,G$ of a polymorphic term r of inferred type $\forall_\kappa F$ has type $F\ @^\kappa\ G$ if G has kind κ. In particular, r could be of type $\forall i{<}a.\ A$, then G must be a size expression $< a$ to succeed. If r is of coinductive type $\nu^a R$, then $r\,.d$ has type $\forall j{<}a^\uparrow.R_d\,(\nu^j R)$, see Section 2.3.

There are two rules to switch direction. Checking r against type C succeeds if r's type is inferred as A and A is a subtype of C. Also, we can add *type ascription* $(t : A)$ to the term language; then inference of $(t : A)$ succeeds and yields A if A is a well-formed type and t checks against A. While type ascription is needed to bidirectionally type check redexes or stuck terms, it is dispensable if one confines to checking normal terms (in the sense that no elimination is applied to a λ in the source program). We will consider type ascriptions be removed before execution of the program, so they do not pop up in the operational and denotational semantics.

Checking $\boxed{\Delta;\Gamma \vdash t \leftleftarrows C}$. Introductions and λs are checked against a given type. Checking a pair ${}^G t$ of a type expression G and a term t against an existential type $\exists_k F$ succeeds if G has kind κ and t is of the correct instance $F\ @^\kappa\ G$. Checking a constructor term $c\,t$ against an inductive type $\mu^a S$ succeeds if t checks against $\exists j < a^\uparrow.\ S_c\,(\mu^j S)$. This means that t should be essentially a pair ${}^b t'$ of a size $b < a^\uparrow$ and t' be a correct argument to constructor c, i. e., having variant S_c instantiated to $\mu^j S$. If $a \geq \infty$, by bound normalization $b = \infty$ is a valid size index, which implies that in a value v in the fixpoint $\mu^\infty S$ all size witnesses can uniformly be ∞. To check $\lambda\vec{D}$ we check all clauses D_k.

Clause checking $\boxed{\Delta;\Gamma \vdash \{\mathbf{q} \to t\} \leftleftarrows A}$. We first check that pattern spine $\mathbf{q}$ eliminates indeed type A. As a result, we obtain a kinding context Δ' which binds the type variables X contained in $\mathbf{q}$ and a typing context Γ' which binds the pattern variables x contained in $\mathbf{q}$'s patterns, and a remaining type C of lhs and rhs. We now need to make sure that $\Delta \vdash \exists\Delta'$ such that any valuation of Δ can be extended to a valuation of Δ'. Complementing the original contexts $\Delta;\Gamma$ by the pattern contexts $\Delta';\Gamma'$ we check the rhs t against C.

Pattern spine checking $\boxed{\Delta;\Gamma \mid A \vdash_{\Delta_0} \mathbf{q} \rightrightarrows C}$. We eliminate type A which is well-formed in Δ_0. If there are no copatterns in $\mathbf{q}$, thus, the clause has an empty lhs, we simply return A which must be the type of the rhs. If we encounter an application pattern p, the eliminated type must be a function type $A \to B$. We check p against A and obtain pattern contexts $\Delta_1;\Gamma_1$. We continue to check the remaining copatterns, obtaining more pattern contexts $\Delta_2;\Gamma_2$ and a result type C, which we return together with the concatenated pattern contexts. Concatenation, and thus, pattern spine checking fails if the contexts do not have disjoint domains. A common variable would mean a non-linear lhs, which we exclude.

If we encounter a projection pattern $.d$, the eliminated type must be a coinductive type $\nu^a R$. Taking projection $.d$ yields type $\forall j{<}a^\uparrow.\ R_d(\nu^j R)$, thus, we continue to eliminate this type by ap-

$\boxed{\Delta; \Gamma \vdash r \rightrightarrows C}$ Expression typing (inference mode). In: Δ, Γ, r with $\Delta \vdash \Gamma$. Out: C with $\Delta \vdash C$

$$\frac{}{\Delta; \Gamma \vdash f \rightrightarrows \Sigma(f)} \qquad \frac{(x{:}A) \in \Gamma}{\Delta; \Gamma \vdash x \rightrightarrows A} \qquad \frac{(x : \forall \Psi.\, \mathfrak{c} \Rightarrow A) \in \Gamma \quad \Delta \vdash \vec{a} \leftleftarrows \Psi \quad \tau = \vec{a}/\hat{\Psi} \quad \Delta \vdash \mathfrak{c}\tau}{\Delta; \Gamma \vdash x\, \vec{a} \rightrightarrows A\tau}$$

$$\frac{\Delta; \Gamma \vdash r \rightrightarrows A \to B \quad \Delta; \Gamma \vdash s \leftleftarrows A}{\Delta; \Gamma \vdash r\, s \rightrightarrows B} \qquad \frac{\Delta; \Gamma \vdash r \rightrightarrows \nu^a R}{\Delta; \Gamma \vdash r.d \rightrightarrows \forall j{<}a^{\uparrow}.\, R_d\,(\nu^j R)} \qquad \frac{\Delta; \Gamma \vdash r \rightrightarrows \forall_\kappa F \quad \Delta \vdash G \leftleftarrows \kappa}{\Delta; \Gamma \vdash r\, G \rightrightarrows F\ @^\kappa\ G}$$

Switching.

$$\frac{\Delta \vdash A \quad \Delta; \Gamma \vdash t \leftleftarrows A}{\Delta; \Gamma \vdash (t : A) \rightrightarrows A} \qquad \frac{\Delta; \Gamma \vdash r \rightrightarrows A \quad \Delta \vdash A \leq C}{\Delta; \Gamma \vdash r \leftleftarrows C}$$

$\boxed{\Delta; \Gamma \vdash t \leftleftarrows C}$ Expression typing (checking mode). In: $\Delta; \Gamma, t, C$ with $\Delta \vdash \Gamma$ and $\Delta \vdash C$. Out: success/failure.

$$\frac{}{\Delta; \Gamma \vdash () \leftleftarrows 1} \qquad \frac{\Delta; \Gamma \vdash t_1 \leftleftarrows A_1 \quad \Delta; \Gamma \vdash t_2 \leftleftarrows A_2}{\Delta; \Gamma \vdash (t_1, t_2) \leftleftarrows A_1 \times A_2} \qquad \frac{\Delta; \Gamma \vdash t \leftleftarrows \exists j{<}a^{\uparrow}.\, S_c\,(\mu^j S)}{\Delta; \Gamma \vdash c\, t \leftleftarrows \mu^a S}$$

$$\frac{\Delta \vdash G \leftleftarrows \kappa \quad \Delta; \Gamma \vdash t \leftleftarrows F\ @^\kappa\ G}{\Delta; \Gamma \vdash {}^{G}t \leftleftarrows \exists_\kappa F} \qquad \frac{\Delta; \Gamma \vdash \vec{D} \leftleftarrows A}{\Delta; \Gamma \vdash \lambda \vec{D} \leftleftarrows A}$$

$\boxed{\Delta; \Gamma \vdash D \leftleftarrows A}$ and $\boxed{\Delta; \Gamma \vdash \vec{D} \leftleftarrows A}$ definition typing. In: Δ, Γ, A, D or $\vec{D}$ with $\Delta \vdash \Gamma$ and $\Gamma \vdash A$. Out: success/failure.

$$\frac{\Delta'; \Gamma' \mid A \vdash_\Delta \vec{q} \rightrightarrows C \quad \Delta \vdash \exists \Delta' \quad \Delta, \Delta'; \Gamma, \Gamma' \vdash t \leftleftarrows C}{\Delta; \Gamma \vdash \{\vec{q} \to t\} \leftleftarrows A} \qquad \frac{\Delta; \Gamma \vdash D_k \leftleftarrows A \text{ for all } k}{\Delta; \Gamma \vdash \vec{D} \leftleftarrows A}$$

Figure 5. Type checking rules.

$\boxed{\Delta; \Gamma \vdash_{\Delta_0} p \leftleftarrows A}$ Pattern typing (linear). In: Δ_0, p, A with $\Delta_0 \vdash A$. Out: Δ, Γ with $\Delta_0, \Delta; \Gamma \vdash p \leftleftarrows A$.

$$\frac{}{\cdot; x{:}A \vdash_{\Delta_0} x \leftleftarrows A} \qquad \frac{}{\cdot; \cdot \vdash_{\Delta_0} () \leftleftarrows 1} \qquad \frac{\Delta_1; \Gamma_1 \vdash_{\Delta_0} p_1 \leftleftarrows A_1 \quad \Delta_2; \Gamma_2 \vdash_{\Delta_0} p_2 \leftleftarrows A_2}{\Delta_1, \Delta_2; \Gamma_1, \Gamma_2 \vdash_{\Delta_0} (p_1, p_2) \leftleftarrows A_1 \times A_2}$$

$$\frac{\Delta; \Gamma \vdash_{\Delta_0} p \leftleftarrows \exists j{<}a^{\uparrow}.\, S_c\,(\mu^j S)}{\Delta; \Gamma \vdash_{\Delta_0} c\, p \leftleftarrows \mu^a S} \qquad \frac{\Delta; \Gamma \vdash_{\Delta_0, X:\kappa} p \leftleftarrows F\ @^\kappa\ X}{X{:}\kappa, \Delta; \Gamma \vdash_{\Delta_0} {}^{X}p \leftleftarrows \exists_\kappa F}$$

$\boxed{\Delta; \Gamma \mid A \vdash_{\Delta_0} \vec{q} \rightrightarrows C}$ Pattern spine typing. In: $\Delta_0, A, \vec{q}$ with $\Delta_0 \vdash A$. Out: Δ, Γ, C with $\Delta_0, \Delta; \Gamma \vdash C$ and $\Delta_0, \Delta; \Gamma, z{:}A \vdash z\, \vec{q} \rightrightarrows C$.

$$\frac{}{\cdot; \cdot \mid A \vdash_{\Delta_0} \cdot \rightrightarrows A} \qquad \frac{\Delta_1; \Gamma_1 \vdash_{\Delta_0} p \leftleftarrows A \quad \Delta_2; \Gamma_2 \mid B \vdash_{\Delta_0} \vec{q} \rightrightarrows C}{\Delta_1, \Delta_2; \Gamma_1, \Gamma_2 \mid A \to B \vdash_{\Delta_0} p\, \vec{q} \rightrightarrows C}$$

$$\frac{\Delta; \Gamma \mid \forall j{<}a^{\uparrow}.\, R_d\,(\nu^j R) \vdash_{\Delta_0} \vec{q} \rightrightarrows C}{\Delta; \Gamma \mid \nu^a R \vdash_{\Delta_0} .d\, \vec{q} \rightrightarrows C} \qquad \frac{\Delta; \Gamma \mid F\ @^\kappa\ X \vdash_{\Delta_0, X:\kappa} \vec{q} \rightrightarrows C}{X{:}\kappa, \Delta; \Gamma \mid \forall_\kappa F \vdash_{\Delta_0} X\, \vec{q} \rightrightarrows C}$$

Figure 6. Pattern Typing.

plying it to a fresh size variable. The general form of a universal type $\forall_\kappa F$ is eliminated by a type variable pattern X; we record $X{:}\kappa$ in the type variable pattern context and continue eliminating $F\ @^\kappa\ X$.

Pattern typing $\boxed{\Delta; \Gamma \vdash_{\Delta_0} p \leftleftarrows A}$. This judgement checks pattern p against type A which is valid in kinding context Δ_0, and returns pattern contexts $\Delta; \Gamma$. Pattern x succeeds against any type, returning singleton context $x{:}A$. The empty tuple $()$ succeeds against the unit type 1, binding no variables. The pair pattern (p_1, p_2) succeeds against the product type $A_1 \times A_2$ if each component p_i checks against its type A_i. The resulting pattern contexts are concatenated, checking for disjointness. A constructor pattern $c\,p$ checks against an inductive type $\mu^a S$ if p checks against $\exists j < a^{\uparrow}.\, S_c\,(\mu^j S)$. The latter succeeds if $p = {}^{j}p'$, then we add size variable $j{<}a$ to the pattern context and continue checking p' against $S_c\,(\mu^j S)$. This is an instance of checking against the general existential type $\exists_\kappa F$.

In the next section, we will validate all the typing rules by exhibiting a semantics of strongly normalizing terms based on Girard's reducibility candidates (Girard et al. 1989).

4. Semantics

In this section we show strong normalization of $\mathsf{F}_\omega^{\mathsf{cop}}$ by a term model. Types are interpreted as reducibility candidates à la Girard adapted to our needs. Our semantic constructions rely only on the terms and the operational semantics of $\mathsf{F}_\omega^{\mathsf{cop}}$, not to the types, kinds, or inference rules. Based on the operational semantics, semantic types and kinds are constructed that interpret the syntactic types, yet syntactic types are never used for semantic constructions.[4] We consider this conceptual hygiene important from a philosophic perspective: we use types just as a vehicle to assign properties to our programs; clearly, they have no run-time significance. While in the end we managed to keep syntactic types out of the semantic constructions, it was hard to get the semantic counterpart (Lemma 9) of pattern spine typing (Figure 6) right.

One clarification: Since $\mathsf{F}_\omega^{\mathsf{cop}}$ has Church-style polymorphism with explicit type abstraction and application, we can of course not talk about terms and operational semantics without mentioning syntactic types. However, we never refer to the structure of syntactic types, they remain abstract, and we could remove everything but type variables from our type language without altering the construction of semantic types and semantic typing "judgements". In particular, in the construction of the semantic universal type $\forall_{\mathcal{K}}\mathcal{F} = \{r \in \mathsf{SN} \mid r\,G \in \mathcal{F}(\mathcal{G}) \text{ for all } G \in \mathsf{Type}, \mathcal{G} \in \mathcal{K}\}$ there is no connection between the syntactic type constructor G and the semantic type constructor $\mathcal{G}$ (of semantic kind $\mathcal{K}$). Type applications serve only to make type-checking decidable, they do not play any role in evaluation.

Preliminaries. We use partially applied relations to denote sets. For instance, we write $(t \longrightarrow \_)$ or simply $t\longrightarrow$ for the set $\{t' \mid t \longrightarrow t'\}$ of reducts of t. Similarly, $<\alpha = \{\beta \mid \beta < \alpha\}$. The identity substitution is denoted by σ_{id}.

Strong normalization. Classically, a term t is strongly normalizing if it admits no infinite reduction sequences $t \longrightarrow t_1 \longrightarrow t_2$ starting with t. Inductively, we define $t \in \mathsf{SN}$ if all of its reducts are already in SN:

$$\frac{(t \longrightarrow \_) \subseteq \mathsf{SN}}{t \in \mathsf{SN}}$$

Naturally, if $t \in \mathsf{SN}$ then all its reducts and subterms are also strongly normalizing.

We extend the notion SN to other syntactic categories: An elimination e is strongly normalizing, $e \in \mathsf{SN}$, if it either is not a term (but a type G or a projection $.d$), or if it is a strongly normalizing term. A definition clause $D = \{\vec{q} \to t\}$ is strongly normalizing if $t \in \mathsf{SN}$.

Simulation. Our typing rules (see Figure 5) state that a definition $\lambda\vec{D} : A$ or $(f : A = \vec{D})$ is well-typed if each of the clauses D_k is of type A, individually. In the absence of a coverage check, there is no concept of "the clauses make sense *together*". We would like to see this independence of clauses reflected in our semantics. In particular, we would like to have *compositionality*, i. e., if each clause of a definition is semantically meaningful (in particular, does not lead to non-termination), then the clauses are meaningful together. For functions, our type-checker works exactly like that: each clause is checked individually, using the termination measure; an interaction between clauses need not be taken into account.

One idea is to say that a defined function $f : A = \vec{D}$ reduces non-deterministically to one of its clauses D_k, however, this immediately destroys strong normalization, because D_k might mention f. We need to defer unfolding of f until the pattern of one of its clauses matches. Thus, instead we say that $f\,\vec{e}$ reduces if $(\lambda\vec{D})\vec{e}$ reduces; f is simulated by its clauses $\vec{D}$. In general, a term r is *simulated* by terms $\vec{r}$, written $\boxed{r \rhd \vec{r}}$, iff each of its contractions under some eliminations is accounted for by one of the terms $\vec{r}$, formally $\forall\vec{e}, t.\ r\,\vec{e} \mapsto t \implies \exists k.\ r_k\,\vec{e} \mapsto t$. Closing reducibility candidates by simulation is one of the new ideas of our proof.

Lemma 1 (Simulation)**.**

1. *$\lambda\{D_1; \dots; D_n\} \rhd \lambda D_1, \dots, \lambda D_n$.*
2. *If $(f : A = \vec{D}) \in \Sigma$ then $f \rhd \lambda\vec{D}$.*
3. *If $r \rhd r_1, \dots, r_n$ then $r\,e \rhd r_1\,e, \dots, r_n\,e$.*

[4] Humbly following the masters (Vouillon and Melliès 2004).

4.1 Semantic Types

In order to show strong normalization we model types as sets of strongly normalizing terms, more precisely, as reducibility candidates à la Girard. We choose reducibility candidates over Tait's saturated sets, since they allow us to show strong normalization in the absence of standardization and confluence. As a consequence, we can model definitions with incomplete and overlapping patterns.

A set of terms $\mathcal{A}$ is a *reducibility candidate* (Girard et al. 1989), written $\mathcal{A} \in \mathsf{CR}$, if the following conditions hold.

CR1 $\mathcal{A} \subseteq \mathsf{SN}$: "each term in $\mathcal{A}$ is strongly normalizing".

CR2 if $t \in \mathcal{A}$ then $(t \longrightarrow \_) \subseteq \mathcal{A}$: "$\mathcal{A}$ is closed under reduction".

CR3 if $t \in \mathsf{Ne}$ and $(t \longrightarrow \_) \subseteq \mathcal{A}$ then $t \in \mathcal{A}$: "$\mathcal{A}$ contains a neutral already if all its redexes are in $\mathcal{A}$".

CR4 if $t \notin \mathsf{Intro}$ and $(t \longrightarrow \_) \subseteq \mathcal{A}$ and $t \rhd \vec{t} \in \mathcal{A}$ then $t \in \mathcal{A}$: "$\mathcal{A}$ is closed under simulation".

Condition **CR4**, is new; it introduces multi-clause objects $\lambda\vec{D}$ and function symbols f into a semantic type (candidate).

Lemma 2 (Multi-clause objects)**.**

1. *If $\lambda D_1, \dots, \lambda D_n \in \mathcal{A}$ then $\lambda\vec{D} \in \mathcal{A}$.*
2. *If $(f : A = \vec{D}) \in \Sigma$ and $\lambda\vec{D} \in \mathcal{A}$, then $f \in \mathcal{A}$.*

In **CR3**, Ne is a suitable set of so-called *neutral* terms. These are "good", i. e., inhabit a candidate, as soon as all their reducts are good. For Girard's technique to work, neutral terms need to include redexes such as $(\lambda x.t)\,s\,\vec{e}$ and variables x, and need to be closed under application, i. e., r neutral implies $r\,s$ neutral. In case of pure lambda calculus, any term which is not a lambda-abstraction can be considered neutral.

In our setting of matching the whole pattern spine $\vec{q}$ against the eliminations $\vec{e}$, things are more subtle. For instance, the partial application $\lambda\{x\,y \to x\,x\}\,\delta$ with $\delta = \lambda\{x \to x\,x\}$ is stuck (and even in normal form). However, it cannot be neutral and inhabit every candidate (following **CR3**), in particular semantic function types, since it reduces to the diverging term $\delta\,\delta$ if applied to one more argument. Thus, we can only accept stuck terms as neutral which cannot become unstuck by extra eliminations. This leads to the following definition:

Definition 3 (Neutral term, terminally stuck)**.** *A applicative term $u \in \mathsf{App}$ is* terminally stuck *if $u\,\vec{e}$ is not a redex for all eliminations $\vec{e}$. A term r is* neutral, *written $r \in \mathsf{Ne}$, if it is a redex or terminally stuck.*

As Girard's, our refined notion of neutrality includes redexes, variables, and is closed under eliminations. Further, if $r \in \mathsf{Ne}$ then any reduction in $r\,e$ is either a reduction in r or in e. A reducibility candidate $\mathcal{A}$ is never empty since $\mathsf{Var} \subseteq \mathcal{A}$ by virtue of **CR3**.

Closure. For a set $\mathcal{A} \subseteq \mathsf{SN}$ which is closed under reduction let $\overline{\mathcal{A}}$ be the least reducibility candidate $\supseteq \mathcal{A}$. Inductively, $\overline{\mathcal{A}}$ is defined as the closure under neutrals and simulation:

$$\frac{t \in \mathcal{A}}{t \in \overline{\mathcal{A}}} \qquad \frac{t \in \mathsf{Ne} \qquad (t \longrightarrow \_) \subseteq \overline{\mathcal{A}}}{t \in \overline{\mathcal{A}}}$$

$$\frac{t \notin \mathsf{Intro} \qquad (t \longrightarrow \_) \subseteq \overline{\mathcal{A}} \qquad t \rhd \vec{t} \in \overline{\mathcal{A}}}{t \in \overline{\mathcal{A}}}$$

$\mathcal{A} \mapsto \overline{\mathcal{A}}$ is a *closure operation*, i. e., it is *monotone* ($\mathcal{A} \subseteq \mathcal{B}$ implies $\overline{\mathcal{A}} \subseteq \overline{\mathcal{B}}$), *extensive* ($\mathcal{A} \subseteq \overline{\mathcal{A}}$), and *idempotent* ($\overline{\overline{\mathcal{A}}} \subseteq \overline{\mathcal{A}}$). Note that the closure operator never adds introduction terms such as $\overline{()}$, $\overline{(t_1, t_2)}$, $\overline{c\,t}$, or $\overline{{}^G t}$ to a term set $\mathcal{A}$. Thus, for introductions $v \in \overline{\mathcal{A}}$ we have $v \in \mathcal{A}$ already.

CR is closed under arbitrary intersections and forms, under the inclusion $\subseteq$ order, a complete lattice with greatest element SN and least element $\overline{\emptyset}$.

Semantic types. In the following, let $\mathcal{A}, \mathcal{B} \in \mathsf{CR}$ be candidates, P a proposition, $\mathcal{K}$ some index set and $\mathcal{F} \in \mathcal{K} \to \mathsf{CR}$ a family of reducibility candidates. The following operations, except the conditional $P \Rightarrow \mathcal{A}$, construct new candidates from existing ones.

$$
\begin{array}{lcl}
\mathcal{A} \twoheadrightarrow \mathcal{B} & = & \{r \in \mathsf{SN} \mid \forall s \in \mathcal{A}.\, r\, s \in \mathcal{B}\} \\
\forall_{\mathcal{K}} \mathcal{F} & = & \{r \in \mathsf{SN} \mid \forall G \in \mathsf{Type}, \mathcal{G} \in \mathcal{K}.\, r\, G \in \mathcal{F}(\mathcal{G})\} \\
P \Rightarrow \mathcal{A} & = & \{r \in \mathsf{Exp} \mid r \in \mathcal{A} \text{ if } P\} \\
\mathbf{1} & = & \overline{\{()\}} \\
\mathcal{A}_1 \times \mathcal{A}_2 & = & \overline{\{(t_1, t_2) \mid t_1 \in \mathcal{A}_1 \text{ and } t_2 \in \mathcal{A}_2\}} \\
\exists_{\mathcal{K}} \mathcal{F} & = & \overline{\{{}^G t \mid G \in \mathsf{Type}, \exists \mathcal{G} \in \mathcal{K}, t \in \mathcal{F}(\mathcal{G})\}}
\end{array}
$$

Note that the condition $r \in \mathsf{SN}$ in the definition of $\mathcal{A} \twoheadrightarrow \mathcal{B}$ is redundant, since $x \in \mathcal{A}$ by **CR3** and $r\, x \in \mathsf{SN}$ implies $r \in \mathsf{SN}$. However, in the definition of $\forall_{\mathcal{K}} \mathcal{F}$ it is important since $\mathcal{K}$ could be empty, e. g., $\mathcal{K} = <0$. Conditional types are not first-class; $P \Rightarrow \mathcal{A}$ only forms a candidate if P is true, otherwise, it is just a set of expressions.

Lemma 4 (Semantic typing rules)**.** *The following inferences are trivial consequences of the construction of semantic types:*

$$
\frac{r \in \mathcal{A} \twoheadrightarrow \mathcal{B} \qquad s \in \mathcal{A}}{r\, s \in \mathcal{B}} \qquad \frac{r \in \forall_{\mathcal{K}} \mathcal{F} \qquad \mathcal{G} \in \mathcal{K}}{r\, G \in \mathcal{F}(\mathcal{G})}
$$

$$
\frac{}{() \in \mathbf{1}} \qquad \frac{t_1 \in \mathcal{A}_1 \qquad t_2 \in \mathcal{A}_2}{(t_1, t_2) \in \mathcal{A}_1 \times \mathcal{A}_2} \qquad \frac{\mathcal{G} \in \mathcal{K} \qquad t \in \mathcal{F}(\mathcal{G})}{{}^G t \in \exists_{\mathcal{K}} \mathcal{F}}
$$

Besides definitions (which we will treat in Section 4.5), rules for constructors and destructors are missing. We will describe semantic (co)inductive types in the next section.

4.2 Ordinals and Fixed-Points

Previous approaches to type-based termination (Hughes et al. 1996; Amadio and Coupet-Grimal 1998; Barthe et al. 2004; Blanqui 2004; Sacchini 2013) have defined approximants of least $\boldsymbol{\mu}^\alpha \mathcal{F}$ and greatest fixed-points $\boldsymbol{\nu}^\alpha \mathcal{F}$ of monotone type constructors $\mathcal{F} \in \mathsf{CR} \xrightarrow{+} \mathsf{CR}$ by conventional induction on ordinal α, distinguishing zero (0), successor ($\alpha + 1$), and limit ordinals (λ).

$$
\begin{array}{lcl@{\qquad}lcl}
\boldsymbol{\mu}^0 \ \mathcal{F} & = & \overline{\emptyset} & \boldsymbol{\nu}^0 \ \mathcal{F} & = & \mathsf{SN} \\
\boldsymbol{\mu}^{\alpha+1} \mathcal{F} & = & \mathcal{F}(\boldsymbol{\mu}^\alpha \mathcal{F}) & \boldsymbol{\nu}^{\alpha+1} \mathcal{F} & = & \mathcal{F}(\boldsymbol{\nu}^\alpha \mathcal{F}) \\
\boldsymbol{\mu}^\lambda \ \mathcal{F} & = & \overline{\bigcup_{\alpha<\lambda} \boldsymbol{\mu}^\alpha \mathcal{F}} & \boldsymbol{\nu}^\lambda \ \mathcal{F} & = & \bigcap_{\alpha<\lambda} \boldsymbol{\nu}^\alpha \mathcal{F}
\end{array}
$$

In this work, we adopt the approach of Sprenger and Dam (2003) for approximations in μ-calculus and use *well-founded induction* instead, which amounts to construct $\boldsymbol{\mu}^\alpha \mathcal{F}$ by *inflationary iteration* and $\boldsymbol{\nu}^\alpha \mathcal{F}$ by *deflationary iteration*.

$$
\boldsymbol{\mu}^\alpha \mathcal{F} = \overline{\bigcup_{\beta<\alpha} \mathcal{F}(\boldsymbol{\mu}^\beta \mathcal{F})} \qquad \boldsymbol{\nu}^\alpha \mathcal{F} = \bigcap_{\beta<\alpha} \mathcal{F}(\boldsymbol{\nu}^\beta \mathcal{F})
$$

In this definition, $\mathcal{F}$ does not have to be monotone to obtain an ascending chain of approximants in case of $\boldsymbol{\mu}$ and a descending chain for $\boldsymbol{\nu}$. However, if $\mathcal{F}$ is monotone, one can derive above equations as special cases for α being zero, successor, or limit ordinal, *if such a distinction on ordinals exists*. Intuitionistically, this distinction is not valid (Taylor 1996); by building on well-founded induction, we remain within constructive foundations.

Let α, β, γ range over ordinals. We write $\forall_{\beta<\alpha} \mathcal{F}(\beta)$ for $\forall_{<\alpha} \mathcal{F}$ and analogously for $\exists$. Let $\mathcal{S} \in \mathsf{Cons} \rightharpoonup \mathsf{CR} \to \mathsf{CR}$ and $\mathcal{R} \in \mathsf{Proj} \rightharpoonup \mathsf{CR} \to \mathsf{CR}$ where we write the first argument, the constructor c, or the destructor d, resp., as index, thus, $\mathcal{S}_c$ and $\mathcal{R}_d$ resp. We define the αth approximants $\boldsymbol{\mu}^\alpha \mathcal{S}, \boldsymbol{\nu}^\alpha \mathcal{R} \in \mathsf{CR}$ of recursive variant and record type as follows.

$$
\begin{array}{lcl}
\boldsymbol{\mu}^\alpha \mathcal{S} & = & \overline{\{c\, t \mid c \in \mathsf{dom}(\mathcal{S}) \text{ and } t \in \exists_{\beta<\alpha} \mathcal{S}_c(\boldsymbol{\mu}^\beta \mathcal{S})\}} \\
\boldsymbol{\nu}^\alpha \mathcal{R} & = & \{r \in \mathsf{SN} \mid \forall d \in \mathsf{dom}(\mathcal{R}).\, r.d \in \forall_{\beta<\alpha} \mathcal{R}_d(\boldsymbol{\nu}^\beta \mathcal{R})\}
\end{array}
$$

Since $\exists_{<\alpha} \mathcal{F}$ is monotonic in α for any $\mathcal{F}$, so is $\boldsymbol{\mu}^\alpha \mathcal{S}$. Dually $\forall_{<\alpha} \mathcal{F}$ and $\boldsymbol{\nu}^\alpha \mathcal{R}$ are antitonic in α. We obtain chains:

$$
\begin{array}{l}
\overline{\emptyset} \ = \boldsymbol{\mu}^0 \mathcal{S} \subseteq \boldsymbol{\mu}^1 \mathcal{S} \subseteq \ldots \subseteq \boldsymbol{\mu}^\gamma \mathcal{S} \subseteq \boldsymbol{\mu}^{\gamma+1} \mathcal{S} \subseteq \ldots \\
\mathsf{SN} = \boldsymbol{\nu}^0 \mathcal{R} \supseteq \boldsymbol{\nu}^1 \mathcal{R} \supseteq \ldots \supseteq \boldsymbol{\nu}^\gamma \mathcal{R} \supseteq \boldsymbol{\nu}^{\gamma+1} \mathcal{R} \supseteq \ldots
\end{array}
$$

If $\boldsymbol{\mu}^\alpha \mathcal{S} = \boldsymbol{\mu}^\gamma \mathcal{S}$ for some $\alpha > \gamma$ then $\boldsymbol{\mu}^\beta \mathcal{S} = \boldsymbol{\mu}^\gamma \mathcal{S}$ for all $\beta > \gamma$ and we say that the chain has become *stationary* at γ. Since the set Exp of expressions is countable and all elements of these chains are subsets of Exp, the chains must become stationary latest at the first uncountable ordinal Ω. We call the ordinal at which all such chains of our language are stationary the *closure ordinal* and denote it by ∞.

Since it does not make sense to inspect chains beyond the closure ordinal, we introduce *bound normalization*

$$
\alpha^\uparrow = \begin{cases} \infty + 1 & \text{if } \alpha \geq \infty, \\ \alpha & \text{otherwise.} \end{cases}
$$

Note that $\boldsymbol{\mu}^\alpha \mathcal{S} = \boldsymbol{\mu}^{\alpha^\uparrow} \mathcal{S}$ and $\boldsymbol{\nu}^\alpha \mathcal{R} = \boldsymbol{\nu}^{\alpha^\uparrow} \mathcal{R}$. In the following we will talk about ordinals that are as big as $\infty + n$ for finite n, but not bigger ones, so all ordinals will be in $\mathsf{O} = \{\alpha \mid \alpha < \infty + \omega\}$, a set closed under successor. As size index to a least or greatest fixed point, only the ordinals in $\mathsf{Size} = \{\alpha \mid \alpha \leq \infty\}$ are interesting. Thus, if no bound for an ordinal β is given, we assume $\beta \in \mathsf{Size}$, for instance, we write $\exists_\beta \mathcal{F}(\beta)$ instead of $\exists_{\beta \in \mathsf{Size}} \mathcal{F}(\beta)$ or $\exists_{\mathsf{Size}} \mathcal{F}$.

The stationary point $\boldsymbol{\mu}^\infty \mathcal{S}$ is a pre-fixed point in the sense that $t \in \mathcal{S}_c(\boldsymbol{\mu}^\infty \mathcal{S})$ implies $c^\infty t \in \boldsymbol{\mu}^{\infty+1} \mathcal{S} = \boldsymbol{\mu}^\infty \mathcal{S}$. Dually, $\boldsymbol{\nu}^\infty \mathcal{R}$ is a post-fixed point as $r \in \boldsymbol{\nu}^\infty \mathcal{R} = \boldsymbol{\nu}^{\infty+1} \mathcal{R}$ implies $r.d\,\infty \in \mathcal{R}_d(\boldsymbol{\nu}^\infty \mathcal{R})$. Note that we do not require $\mathcal{R}$ or $\mathcal{S}$ to be monotone for the implications to hold in these directions. Yet we do if we want $\boldsymbol{\mu}^\infty \mathcal{S}$ and $\boldsymbol{\nu}^\infty \mathcal{R}$ to be fixed-points.

Lemma 5 (Fixed-points)**.** *If $\mathcal{S}_c, \mathcal{R}_d$ be monotone for all $c \in \mathsf{dom}(\mathcal{S})$ and $d \in \mathsf{dom}(\mathcal{R})$, then*

1. $\boldsymbol{\mu}^\infty \mathcal{S} = \overline{\{c^b t \mid c \in \mathsf{dom}(\mathcal{S}), b \in \mathsf{Type}, t \in \mathcal{S}_c(\boldsymbol{\mu}^\infty \mathcal{S})\}}$, *and*
2. $\boldsymbol{\nu}^\infty \mathcal{R} = \{r \mid \forall d \in \mathsf{dom}(\mathcal{R}), b \in \mathsf{Type}.\ r.d\ b \in \mathcal{R}_d(\boldsymbol{\nu}^\infty \mathcal{R})\}$.

Proof. For 1, it is sufficient to show $\subseteq$, meaning that $\boldsymbol{\mu}^\infty \mathcal{S}$ is a post-fixed point. Note that by definition

$$
\boldsymbol{\mu}^\infty \mathcal{S} = \overline{\bigcup_{\beta<\infty} \{c^b t \mid c \in \mathsf{dom}(\mathcal{S}), b \in \mathsf{Type}, t \in \mathcal{S}_c(\boldsymbol{\mu}^\beta \mathcal{S})\}},
$$

so we conclude by monotonicity of $\mathcal{S}_c$ and the closure operator, using $\boldsymbol{\mu}^\beta \mathcal{S} \subseteq \boldsymbol{\mu}^\infty \mathcal{S}$. For 2, it is sufficient to show that $\boldsymbol{\nu}^\infty \mathcal{R}$ is a pre-fixed point. So, if $r.d\ b \in \mathcal{R}_d(\boldsymbol{\nu}^\infty \mathcal{R})$ for all $d \in \mathsf{dom}(\mathcal{R})$ and $b \in \mathsf{Type}$, then $r \in \boldsymbol{\nu}^\infty \mathcal{R}$. It is sufficient to show $r.d\ b \in \mathcal{R}_d(\boldsymbol{\nu}^\beta \mathcal{R})$ for all $\beta < \infty$, and this follows from $\boldsymbol{\nu}^\infty \mathcal{R} \subseteq \boldsymbol{\nu}^\beta \mathcal{R}$ by monotonicity of $\mathcal{R}_d$. □

4.3 Kinds

Higher kinds are interpreted as π-variant set-theoretical function spaces $\mathcal{K}_1 \xrightarrow{\pi} \mathcal{K}_2$ over the base kinds CR and $<\alpha$. For ρ a *size valuation* mapping size variables to ordinals, *kind interpretation* $[\![\kappa]\!]_\rho$ is defined in the obvious way.

A *semantic kinding context* $\mathcal{D}$ maps type variables X to semantic kinds $\mathcal{K}$. Semantic kinding contexts classify *type environments* ρ mapping type variables to semantic types or type constructors; we have $\rho \in \mathcal{D}$ if $\rho(X) \in \mathcal{D}(X)$ for all $X \in \mathsf{dom}(\mathcal{D})$. Since kinds in $\mathcal{D}$ can depend on size variables declared earlier in $\mathcal{D}$, semantic kinding contexts are dependent. Given $\mathcal{D}$ and a family $\mathcal{D}'(\rho \in \mathcal{D})$, the dependent concatenation of $\mathcal{D}$ and $\mathcal{D}'$ is written $\Sigma_{\mathcal{D}}\mathcal{D}'$.

4.4 Type constructors

Type constructors of higher kind are interpreted as operators on semantic types. For ρ a *type environment* mapping type variables to semantic types or type constructors, *type interpretation* $[\![F]\!]_\rho$ maps the syntactic type constructors to the corresponding semantic ones.

Kind and type interpretation model the kind- and type-level judgements in the usual way. For lack of space, we cannot provide more detail here, see the extended version of this paper instead.

4.5 Patterns, copatterns, λ-abstractions

In this section, we explain patterns and copatterns by developing semantic notions of pattern and pattern spine typing. These provide us with semantic conditions when a definition $\lambda\vec{D}$ inhabits a semantic type $\mathcal{A}$. As a consequence, we can prove soundness of syntactic pattern, pattern spine, and expression typing.

Semantic typing contexts and semantic pattern typing. A semantic typing context $\mathcal{E} \in \mathsf{CXT}(\cdot)$ ($\mathcal{E}$ for typing *environment*) is a finite map from term variables to semantic types, so $\mathcal{E} \in \mathsf{Var} \rightharpoonup \mathsf{CR}$. We write $\cdot$ for the empty semantic typing context, $x{:}\mathcal{A}$ for the singleton and $\mathcal{E}, \mathcal{E}'$ for the disjoint union. *Semantic substitution typing* $\sigma \in \mathcal{E}$ is defined as $\sigma(x) \in \mathcal{E}(x)$ for all $x \in \mathsf{dom}(\mathcal{E})$.

A parameterized semantic typing context $\mathcal{E} \in \mathsf{CXT}(\mathcal{D})$ is a family $\mathcal{E}(\rho)$ of semantic typing contexts indexed by semantic type substitutions ρ that belong to a semantic kinding context $\mathcal{D}$. Each instance $\mathcal{E}(\rho)$ is a partial function from variables to semantic types. We overload the notation for non-parameterized semantic typing contexts by setting $\cdot(\rho) = \cdot$ and $(x{:}\mathcal{A})(\rho) = x{:}\mathcal{A}(\rho)$ and $(\mathcal{E}, \mathcal{E}')(\rho) = \mathcal{E}(\rho), \mathcal{E}'(\rho)$ with $\mathsf{dom}(\mathcal{E}(\rho)) \cap \mathsf{dom}(\mathcal{E}'(\rho)) = \emptyset$.

For two differently parameterized semantic typing contexts $\mathcal{E}_1 \in \mathsf{CXT}(\mathcal{D}_1)$ and $\mathcal{E}_2 \in \mathsf{CXT}(\mathcal{D}_2)$ we let their disjoint union $\mathcal{E}_1 * \mathcal{E}_2 \in \mathsf{CXT}(\mathcal{D}_1, \mathcal{D}_2)$ be defined by $(\mathcal{E}_1 * \mathcal{E}_2)(\rho_1 \in \mathcal{D}_1, \rho_2 \in \mathcal{D}_2) = (\mathcal{E}_1(\rho_1), \mathcal{E}_2(\rho_2))$. Further, if $\mathcal{E} \in \mathsf{CXT}(\Sigma_{\mathcal{D}}\mathcal{D}')$ and $\rho \in \mathcal{D}$ we let the partial application $\mathcal{E}(\rho, \_) \in \mathsf{CXT}(\mathcal{D}'(\rho))$ be defined by $\mathcal{E}(\rho, \_)(\rho') = \mathcal{E}(\rho, \rho')$.

If $\mathcal{C}(\mathcal{G})(\rho)$ is a type parameterized by another type $\mathcal{G}$ and a type substitution ρ, we let $\mathcal{C}X$ be defined by $(\mathcal{C}X)(\rho) = \mathcal{C}(\rho(X))(\rho \setminus X)$. In particular, $(\mathcal{C}X)(\mathcal{G}/X, \rho) = \mathcal{C}(\mathcal{G})(\rho)$. The notations $\mathcal{D}X$ and $\mathcal{E}X$ are defined analogously.

A pattern p is semantically of type $\mathcal{A}$ in context $\mathcal{E}$ if it acts as a bidirectional (invertible) map from $\mathcal{E}$ to $\mathcal{A}$, i. e., $p\sigma \in \mathcal{A}$ for all $\sigma \in \mathcal{E}$, and, for any substitution σ with $p\sigma \in \mathcal{A}$ we have $\sigma \in \mathcal{E}$. Extending this to type substitutions we define *semantic pattern typing* by

$$\boxed{\mathcal{A} \,/\, p \searrow \mathcal{D}; \mathcal{E}} \;:\!\iff\; \forall \tau, \sigma.\ (\exists \rho \in \mathcal{D}.\ \sigma \in \mathcal{E}(\rho)) \iff p\tau\sigma \in \mathcal{A}.$$

Here, and in the following, τ denotes a syntactic type substitution. Note that it is unconstrained, it needs not bear a relationship with the semantic type substitution ρ.

One could have expected that semantic pattern typing implies that p matches any introduction term $v \in \mathcal{A}$. But since we are not interested in pattern coverage, but merely strong normalization, we do not require this strong guarantee.[5]

Lemma 6 (Semantic pattern typing). *The following implications, written as rules, hold.*

$$\frac{}{\mathcal{A} \,/\, x \searrow \cdot; (x{:}\mathcal{A})} \qquad \frac{}{\mathbf{1} \,/\, () \searrow \cdot; \cdot}$$

$$\frac{\mathcal{A}_1 \,/\, p_1 \searrow \mathcal{D}_1; \mathcal{E}_1 \qquad \mathcal{A}_2 \,/\, p_2 \searrow \mathcal{D}_2; \mathcal{E}_2}{\mathcal{A}_1 \times \mathcal{A}_2 \,/\, (p_1, p_2) \searrow \mathcal{D}_1, \mathcal{D}_2; \mathcal{E}_1 * \mathcal{E}_2}$$

$$\frac{\exists_{\beta<\alpha^\uparrow} \mathcal{S}_c(\boldsymbol{\mu}^\beta \mathcal{S}) \,/\, p \searrow \mathcal{D}; \mathcal{E}}{\boldsymbol{\mu}^\alpha \mathcal{S} \,/\, c\,p \searrow \mathcal{D}; \mathcal{E}}$$

$$\frac{\mathcal{F}(\mathcal{G}) \,/\, p \searrow \mathcal{D}(\mathcal{G}); \mathcal{E}(\mathcal{G}) \textit{ for all } \mathcal{G} \in \mathcal{K}}{\exists_{\mathcal{K}} \mathcal{F} \,/\, {}^X p \searrow \Sigma_{X:\mathcal{K}}\mathcal{D}; \mathcal{E}X}$$

Theorem 7 (Soundness of pattern typing). *Let* $\vdash \Delta_0, \Delta$ *and* $\Delta_0, \Delta \vdash \Gamma$. *If* $\Delta; \Gamma \vdash_{\Delta_0} p \Leftarrow A$ *and* $\rho_0 \in [\![\Delta_0]\!]$ *then* $[\![A]\!]_{\rho_0} \,/\, p \searrow [\![\Delta]\!]_{\rho_0}; [\![\Gamma]\!]_{(\rho_0, \_)}$.

Proof. By induction on $\Delta; \Gamma \vdash_{\Delta_0} p \Leftarrow A$ using the inferences of Lemma 6. □

Semantic typing in context. Given a parameterized semantic type $\mathcal{C} \in \mathcal{D}' \to \mathsf{CR}$ we define weakening $\mathsf{W}_{\mathcal{D}}\mathcal{C} \in (\mathcal{D}, \mathcal{D}') \to \mathsf{CR}$ of $\mathcal{C}$ by semantic kinding context $\mathcal{D}$ as $(\mathsf{W}_{\mathcal{D}}\mathcal{C})(\rho \in \mathcal{D}, \rho') = C(\rho')$. Given a semantic type family $\mathcal{C} \in (\mathcal{D}, \mathcal{D}') \to \mathsf{CR}$ and a semantic type substitution $\rho \in \mathcal{D}$, we let the partial application $\mathcal{C}(\rho, \_) \in \mathcal{D}' \to \mathsf{CR}$ be defined by $\mathcal{C}(\rho, \_)(\rho') = \mathcal{C}(\rho, \rho')$. Semantic typing under a context is defined by

$$\boxed{\mathcal{D}; \mathcal{E} \vdash t \in \mathcal{C}} \;:\!\iff\; \forall \rho \in \mathcal{D}, \sigma \in \mathcal{E}(\rho), \tau.\ t\tau\sigma \in \mathcal{C}(\rho)$$

Let P be a proposition depending on the pattern variables and pattern type variables of a copattern spine $\vec{q}$. We define the following shorthand for the replacement of the pattern variables by expressions obtained from matching $\vec{q}$ against an elimination list $\vec{e}$:

$$\boxed{P[\vec{e}/\vec{q}]} \;:\!\iff\; \exists \tau, \sigma.\ \vec{e} \,/\, \vec{q} \searrow \tau; \sigma \,\wedge\, P\tau\sigma$$

Semantic pattern spines. A pattern spine $\vec{q}$ has to be understood by its purpose, to serve as the lhs of a definition. Semantically, q eliminates type $\mathcal{A}$ into $\mathcal{C}$ at contexts $\mathcal{D}; \mathcal{E}$ if any definition $\lambda\{\vec{q} \to t\}$ that can be formed with $\vec{q}$ is in $\mathcal{A}$ as long as the rhs t is in $\mathcal{C}$ under contexts $\mathcal{D}; \mathcal{E}$. We further generalize this to partially applied definitions $\lambda\{\vec{q}'\,\vec{q} \to t\}\vec{e}$ where $\vec{e}$ matches $\vec{q}'$. We let

$$\boxed{\mathcal{A} \mid \vec{q} \searrow \mathcal{D}; \mathcal{E}; \mathcal{C}} \;:\!\iff\; \forall t, \vec{e} \in \mathsf{SN}.\forall \vec{q}'.$$
$$\mathcal{D}; \mathcal{E} \vdash t[\vec{e}/\vec{q}'] \in \mathcal{C} \implies \lambda\{\vec{q}'\vec{q} \to t\}\vec{e} \in \mathcal{A}.$$

Lemma 8 (Semantic clause typing). *The following implication holds:*

$$\frac{\mathcal{A} \mid \vec{q} \searrow \mathcal{D}; \mathcal{E}; \mathcal{C} \qquad \mathcal{D}; \mathcal{E} \vdash t \in \mathcal{C} \qquad \rho \in \mathcal{D}}{\lambda\{\vec{q} \to t\} \in \mathcal{A}}$$

Proof. With $\sigma_{\mathsf{id}} \in \mathcal{E}(\rho)$ we have $t = t\sigma_{\mathsf{id}} \in \mathcal{C}(\rho) \subseteq \mathsf{SN}$. The rest follows by definition of semantic pattern spine typing with empty $\vec{e}$ and empty $\vec{q}'$. Note that we cannot proceed if $\mathcal{D}$ is inconsistent. □

Lemma 9 (Semantic pattern spine typing). *The following implications hold.*

$$\frac{}{\mathcal{A} \mid \cdot \searrow \cdot; \cdot; \mathcal{A}} \qquad \frac{\mathcal{A}_1 \,/\, p \searrow \mathcal{D}_1; \mathcal{E}_1 \qquad \mathcal{A}_2 \mid \vec{q} \searrow \mathcal{D}_2; \mathcal{E}_2; \mathcal{C}}{\mathcal{A}_1 \to \mathcal{A}_2 \mid p\,\vec{q} \searrow \mathcal{D}_1, \mathcal{D}_2; \mathcal{E}_1 * \mathcal{E}_2; \mathsf{W}_{\mathcal{D}_1}\mathcal{C}}$$

[5] On the contrary, we can live with junk introductions in our semantic types. For instance, it would not endanger normalization to throw the empty tuple into each semantic type.

$$\frac{\forall_{\beta<\alpha^\uparrow} \mathcal{R}_d\,(\boldsymbol{\nu}^\beta \mathcal{R}) \mid \vec{q} \searrow \mathcal{D}; \mathcal{E}; \mathcal{C}}{\boldsymbol{\nu}^\alpha \mathcal{R} \mid .d\,\vec{q} \searrow \mathcal{D}; \mathcal{E}; \mathcal{C}}$$

$$\frac{\forall \mathcal{G} \in \mathcal{K}.\ \mathcal{F}(\mathcal{G}) \mid \vec{q} \searrow \mathcal{D}(\mathcal{G}); \mathcal{E}(\mathcal{G}); \mathcal{C}(\mathcal{G})}{\boldsymbol{\forall}_{\mathcal{K}} \mathcal{F} \mid X\,\vec{q} \searrow \Sigma_{X:\mathcal{K}} \mathcal{D}; \mathcal{E}X; \mathcal{C}X}$$

Theorem 10 (Soundness of pattern spine typing). *Let* $\vdash \Delta_0, \Delta$ *and* $\Delta_0, \Delta \vdash \Gamma$. *If* $\Delta; \Gamma \mid A \vdash_{\Delta_0} \vec{q} \rightrightarrows C$ *and* $\rho_0 \in [\![\Delta_0]\!]$ *then* $[\![A]\!]_{\rho_0} \mid \vec{q} \searrow [\![\Delta]\!]_{\rho_0}; [\![\Gamma]\!]_{(\rho_0,-)}; [\![C]\!]_{(\rho_0,-)}$.

Proof. By induction on $\Delta; \Gamma \mid A \vdash_{\Delta_0} \vec{q} \rightrightarrows C$ using Lem. 9. □

Semantic declaration and signature well-formedness. Having understood definitons by clauses $\lambda\vec{D}$ we can now show that any well-typed term inhabits its corresponding semantic type. For function symbols f, we simply assume it, by postulating a sematically well-formed signature Σ. We define $\boxed{\models \delta}$ and $\boxed{\models \Sigma}$ by

$$\begin{array}{lll} \models (f : A = \vec{D}) & :\Longleftrightarrow & f \in [\![A]\!] \\ \models \Sigma & :\Longleftrightarrow & \forall \delta \in \Sigma.\ \models \delta. \end{array}$$

Theorem 11 (Soundness of expression typing). *Assume* $\models \Sigma$. *Let* $\vdash \Delta$ *and* $\Delta \vdash \Gamma$ *and* $\Delta \vdash C$ *and* $\mathcal{D} = [\![\Delta]\!]$ *and* $\mathcal{E}(\rho) = [\![\Gamma]\!]_\rho$ *and* $\mathcal{C}(\rho) = [\![C]\!]_\rho$.

1. *If* $\Delta; \Gamma \vdash r \rightrightarrows C$ *in* Σ *then* $\mathcal{D}; \mathcal{E} \vdash r \in \mathcal{C}$.
2. *If* $\Delta; \Gamma \vdash t \leftleftarrows C$ *in* Σ *then* $\mathcal{D}; \mathcal{E} \vdash t \in \mathcal{C}$.
3. *If* $\Delta; \Gamma \vdash \vec{D} \leftleftarrows C$ *in* Σ *then* $\mathcal{D}; \mathcal{E} \vdash \lambda\vec{D} \in \mathcal{C}$.

What remains to be proven is that well-typed programs yield, after measure erasure, semantically well-formed signatures. This is shown mutual block by mutual block using a lexicographic induction on ordinals as given by the termination measure assigned to each block. A formal description of program typing and its soundness proof has to be delegated to the long version of this paper due to lack of space.

5. Conclusion

Our work provides a uniform type-based approach to proving termination of (co)inductive definitions. It is centered around patterns and copatterns which allow us to reason about both finite and infinite data by well-founded induction. Proving strong normalization for this language is a significant step towards understanding well-founded corecursion in terms of the depth of observation we can safely make.

As a next step, we plan to extend our work to full dependently typed systems to allow coinductive definitions to be defined and reasoned with by observations. This will put coinduction in these systems on a robust foundation. We have already implemented size-based type checking for patterns and copatterns in MiniAgda (Abel 2012) which gives us confidence in the approach.

References

A. Abel. Polarized subtyping for sized types. *Math. Struct. in Comput. Sci.*, 18:797–822, 2008a. Special issue on subtyping, edited by Healfdene Goguen and Adriana Compagnoni.

A. Abel. Semi-continuous sized types and termination. *Logical Meth. in Comput. Sci.*, 4(2:3):1–33, 2008b. CSL'06 special issue.

A. Abel. Type-based termination, inflationary fixed-points, and mixed inductive-coinductive types. *Electr. Proc. in Theor. Comp. Sci.*, 77:1–11, 2012. Proceedings of FICS 2012.

A. Abel and B. Pientka. Wellfounded recursion with copatterns: A unified approach to termination and productivity. URL `http://www.tcs.ifi.lmu.de/~abel/icfp13-long.pdf`. Extended version, 2013.

A. Abel, B. Pientka, D. Thibodeau, and A. Setzer. Copatterns: Programming infinite structures by observations. In *Proc. of the 40th ACM Symp. on Principles of Programming Languages, POPL 2013*, pages 27–38. ACM Press, 2013.

T. Altenkirch and N. A. Danielsson. Termination checking in the presence of nested inductive and coinductive types. Short note supporting a talk given at PAR 2010, Workshop on Partiality and Recursion in Interactive Theorem Provers, FLoC 2010, 2010.

R. M. Amadio and S. Coupet-Grimal. Analysis of a guard condition in type theory (extended abstract). In *Proc. of the 1st Int. Conf. on Foundations of Software Science and Computation Structure, FoSSaCS'98*, volume 1378 of *Lect. Notes in Comput. Sci.*, pages 48–62. Springer, 1998.

G. Barthe, M. J. Frade, E. Giménez, L. Pinto, and T. Uustalu. Type-based termination of recursive definitions. *Math. Struct. in Comput. Sci.*, 14 (1):97–141, 2004.

G. Barthe, B. Grégoire, and C. Riba. Type-based termination with sized products. In *Computer Science Logic, 22nd Int. Wksh., CSL 2008, 17th Annual Conf. of the EACSL*, volume 5213 of *Lect. Notes in Comput. Sci.*, pages 493–507. Springer, 2008.

F. Blanqui. A type-based termination criterion for dependently-typed higher-order rewrite systems. In *Rewriting Techniques and Applications (RTA 2004), Aachen, Germany*, volume 3091 of *Lect. Notes in Comput. Sci.*, pages 24–39. Springer, 2004.

F. Blanqui and C. Riba. Combining typing and size constraints for checking the termination of higher-order conditional rewrite systems. In *Proc. of the 13th Int. Conf. on Logic for Programming, Artificial Intelligence, and Reasoning, LPAR 2006*, volume 4246 of *Lect. Notes in Comput. Sci.*, pages 105–119. Springer, 2006.

N. Ghani, P. Hancock, and D. Pattinson. Representations of stream processors using nested fixed points. *Logical Meth. in Comput. Sci.*, 5(3), 2009.

E. Giménez. *Un Calcul de Constructions Infinies et son application a la vérification de systèmes communicants*. PhD thesis, Ecole Normale Supérieure de Lyon, 1996. Thèse d'université.

J.-Y. Girard, Y. Lafont, and P. Taylor. *Proofs and Types*, volume 7 of *Cambridge Tracts in Theoret. Comput. Sci.* Cambridge University Press, 1989.

J. Hughes, L. Pareto, and A. Sabry. Proving the correctness of reactive systems using sized types. In *Proc. of the 23rd ACM Symp. on Principles of Programming Languages, POPL'96*, pages 410–423, 1996.

INRIA. *The Coq Proof Assistant Reference Manual*. INRIA, version 8.4 edition, 2012. URL `http://coq.inria.fr/`.

U. Norell. *Towards a Practical Programming Language Based on Dependent Type Theory*. PhD thesis, Dept of Comput. Sci. and Engrg., Chalmers, Göteborg, Sweden, 2007.

J. L. Sacchini. Type-based productivity of stream definitions in the calculus of constructions. In *Logics in Computer Science (LICS 2013), June 25-28, 2013, New Orleans*, 2013.

B. A. Sijtsma. On the productivity of recursive list definitions. *ACM Trans. Prog. Lang. Syst.*, 11(4):633–649, 1989.

C. Sprenger and M. Dam. On the structure of inductive reasoning: Circular and tree-shaped proofs in the μ-calculus. In *Proc. of the 6th Int. Conf. on Foundations of Software Science and Computational Structures, FoSSaCS 2003*, volume 2620 of *Lect. Notes in Comput. Sci.*, pages 425–440. Springer, 2003.

M. Steffen. *Polarized Higher-Order Subtyping*. PhD thesis, Technische Fakultät, Universität Erlangen, 1998.

P. Taylor. Intuitionistic sets and ordinals. *J. Symb. Logic*, 61(3):705–744, 1996.

J. Vouillon and P.-A. Melliès. Semantic types: A fresh look at the ideal model for types. In *Proc. of the 31st ACM Symp. on Principles of Programming Languages, POPL 2004*, pages 52–63. ACM Press, 2004.

H. Xi. Dependent types for program termination verification. *J. Higher-Order and Symb. Comput.*, 15(1):91–131, 2002.

Productive Coprogramming with Guarded Recursion

Robert Atkey
bob.atkey@gmail.com

Conor McBride
University of Strathclyde
Conor.McBride@strath.ac.uk

Abstract

Total functional programming offers the beguiling vision that, just by virtue of the compiler accepting a program, we are guaranteed that it will always terminate. In the case of programs that are not intended to terminate, e.g., servers, we are guaranteed that programs will always be *productive*. Productivity means that, even if a program generates an infinite amount of data, each piece will be generated in finite time. The theoretical underpinning for productive programming with infinite output is provided by the category theoretic notion of final coalgebras. Hence, we speak of *co*programming with non-well-founded *co*data, as a dual to programming with well-founded data like finite lists and trees.

Systems that offer facilities for productive coprogramming, such as the proof assistants Coq and Agda, currently do so through syntactic guardedness checkers, which ensure that all self-recursive calls are guarded by a use of a constructor. Such a check ensures productivity. Unfortunately, these syntactic checks are not compositional, and severely complicate coprogramming.

Guarded recursion, originally due to Nakano, is tantalising as a basis for a flexible and compositional type-based approach to coprogramming. However, as we show, guarded recursion by itself is not suitable for coprogramming due to the fact that there is no way to make finite observations on pieces of infinite data. In this paper, we introduce the concept of *clock variables* that index Nakano's guarded recursion. Clock variables allow us to "close over" the generation of infinite codata, and to make finite observations, something that is not possible with guarded recursion alone.

Categories and Subject Descriptors D.1.1 [*Programming techniques*]: Applicative (functional) programming; D.2.4 [*Software Engineering*]: Software/Program Verification; D.3.3 [*Programming Languages*]: Language Constructs and Features—Data types and structures

General Terms Languages, Theory, Types, Recursion

Keywords coalgebras, corecursion, guarded recursion, total functional programming

1. Introduction

Coprogramming refers to the practice of explicitly manipulating codata, the non-well-founded dual of well-founded data like finite lists and trees. Codata are useful for representing the output of an infinite process as a never ending stream, or for representing potentially infinite search trees of possibilities. The natural way to express codata is as a recursively defined coprogram. However, for recursively defined coprograms to be safely used in a total setting, the system must ensure that all recursive definitions are productive. The state of the art for productivity checking is currently either awkward syntactic guardedness checkers, or more flexible sized type systems that explicitly label everything with size information.

In this paper, we investigate the use of *guarded recursion* (due to Hiroshi Nakano [20]) as a lightweight typing discipline for enabling productive coprogramming. As we show in this introduction, guarded recursion by itself is not suitable for coprogramming, due to the strict segmentation of time inherent in putting guardedness information in types. We therefore introduce the concept of *clock variables* to take us from the finite-time-sliced world of guarded recursion to the infinite world of codata.

The contributions we make in this paper are the following:

1. We define a core type system for comfortable productive coprogramming, combining three key features: initial algebras, Nakano's guarded recursion and our main conceptual contribution: quantification over clock variables. We show that by combining the three key features of our system, we obtain a system for programming with *final coalgebras*, the category theoretic description of codata. The combination of guarded recursion and clock quantification allows us to dispense with the clunky syntactic guardedness checks, and move to a flexible, compositional and local type-based system for ensuring guardedness.
2. We define a domain-theoretic denotational model that effectively interprets our system in the untyped lazy λ-calculus. We use a multiply-step-indexed model of types to prove that all well-typed programs are either terminating or productive and to show the correctness of our reconstruction of final coalgebras.
3. A side benefit of the combination of guarded recursion and clock quantification is that, due to the careful tracking of what data is available when through guarded types, we are able to accurately type, and show safe, strange circular functional programs like Bird's replaceMin example.

Despite the large amount of recent work on guarded recursion (we provide references throughout this introduction), this is the first paper that formally links guarded recursion to productive coprogramming. As recently noted by Birkedal and Møgelberg [4], "guarded recursive types can be used to [sic] as a crutch for higher-order programming with coinductive types". In this paper, we show that this is indeed possible.

1.1 Guardedness checkers and guarded recursion

Several systems with support for corecursion, such as Coq (as described by Giménez [12]) and Agda (as described by Danielsson and Altenkirch [9]), make use of syntactic guardedness checks to

ICFP '13, September 25–27, 2013, Boston, MA, USA.

ACM 978-1-4503-2326-0/13/09... $15.00.
http://dx.doi.org/10.1145/2500365.2500597

ensure productivity of programs defined using corecursion. Without these checks, the soundness of these systems cannot be guaranteed. An unfortunate aspect of these guardedness checks is their non-compositionality. We demonstrate the problem with an example, and see how Nakano's guarded recursion can be used to provide a compositional type-based guardedness check.

We will use Haskell notation for each of our informal examples, since it serves to illustrate the issues concisely. Consider the following Haskell declaration of a type of infinite streams of integers:

$$\textbf{data}\ \text{Stream} = \mathsf{StreamCons}\ \text{Integer Stream}$$

An example of a Stream is the infinite stream of 1s:

$$\begin{array}{l} \mathit{ones} :: \text{Stream} \\ \mathit{ones} = \mathsf{StreamCons}\ 1\ \mathit{ones} \end{array}$$

It is easy to see that this recursive definition is *guarded*; *ones* is only invoked recursively within an application of the stream constructor StreamCons. This definition of *ones* defines an infinite data structure, but each piece of the data structure is delivered to us in finite time. Hence, *ones* is productive.

An example of a non-guarded definition is the filter function, extended from finite lists to infinite streams:

$$\begin{array}{l} \mathit{filter} :: (\text{Integer} \to \text{Bool}) \to \text{Stream} \to \text{Stream} \\ \mathit{filter}\ f\ (\mathsf{StreamCons}\ z\ s) = \\ \quad \textbf{if}\ f\ z\ \textbf{then}\ \mathsf{StreamCons}\ z\ (\mathit{filter}\ f\ s)\ \textbf{else}\ \mathit{filter}\ f\ s \end{array}$$

This definition is not guarded: in the **then**-case of the conditional, the recursive call to *filter* is not within an application of the stream constructor StreamCons. A syntactic guardedness checker is right to reject this definition: consider the case when all of the elements of the stream are filtered out; *filter* will never return anything, and so will be non-productive.

Syntactic guardedness checkers are not always so helpful. The following higher-order function defines a general merge function on pairs of streams:

$$\begin{array}{l} \mathit{mergef} :: (\text{Integer} \to \text{Integer} \to \text{Stream} \to \text{Stream}) \to \\ \qquad\qquad \text{Stream} \to \text{Stream} \to \text{Stream} \\ \mathit{mergef}\ f\ (\mathsf{StreamCons}\ x\ xs)\ (\mathsf{StreamCons}\ y\ ys) = \\ \quad f\ x\ y\ (\mathit{mergef}\ f\ xs\ ys) \end{array}$$

Any syntactic checker looking for constructors to guard recursive calls will reject this function: there are no constructors anywhere in the definition! This rejection is with good reason: there are functions that we could pass to *mergef* that would render it unproductive. For example, this function will cause *mergef* to hang on all pairs of streams:

$$\begin{array}{l} \mathit{badf} :: \text{Integer} \to \text{Integer} \to \text{Stream} \to \text{Stream} \\ \mathit{badf}\ x\ y\ s = s \end{array}$$

On the other hand, there are plenty of good functions *f* that we could use with *mergef* to obtain productive functions, but a syntactic guardedness checker does not allow us to express this fact.

A possible way out of this problem is to retain the syntactic guardedness check, and work around it by changing the type of *f*. For instance, we could change the required type of *f* to:

$$f :: \text{Integer} \to \text{Integer} \to \text{Integer}$$

to allow for merging functions that operate element-wise. Or we could change the type to

$$f :: \text{Integer} \to \text{Integer} \to (\text{Integer}, [\text{Integer}])$$

which would allow for the functional argument to replace each pair of elements from the input streams with a non-empty list of values. The general trick is to make f return "instructions" on how to transform the stream back to *mergef*, which then executes them in a way that the syntactic guardedness checker can see is guarded. This technique has been elaborated in detail by Danielsson [8]. However, it is difficult to see whether we could capture all the possibilities for good *f*s in a single type. We could give yet another type which would accommodate the behaviour of the following possible value of *f*:

$$f\ x\ y\ s = \mathsf{StreamCons}\ x\ (\mathit{map}\ (+y)\ s)$$

Incorporating the forms of all the possible productive definitions into a single type seems impractical. Moreover, we complicate the definition of *mergef*, which is now forced to become essentially an implementation of a virtual machine for running little stream transformer programs returned by its functional argument, rather than the simple one line definition we gave above.

A more promising type-based solution is provided by Nakano [20]. Nakano introduces a guardedness type constructor that represents values that may only be used in a guarded way. Thus Nakano transports the guardedness checks from the syntactic level into the type system. We write this constructor, applied to a type A, as $\triangleright A$ (Nakano uses the notation $\bullet A$, but the $\triangleright A$ notation has become more common, and conveys an intuitive idea of displacement in time). A useful way to think of $\triangleright A$ is as a value of A that is only available "tomorrow", and the temporal gap between today and tomorrow can only be bridged by the application of a constructor such as StreamCons. The reading of $\triangleright A$ as a value of A tomorrow is explicitly supported in the step-indexed semantics we present in Section 3 by means of a clock counting down to zero.

We now alter the type of *f* to be:

$$f :: \text{Integer} \to \text{Integer} \to \triangleright\text{Stream} \to \text{Stream}$$

This type captures the intuition that the stream argument to *f* must only be used in a guarded way. To introduce guarded types into the system, we must make some changes to the types of our primitives. We alter the type of the constructor StreamCons as follows, and also introduce a stream deconstructor that we previously implicitly used via pattern matching:

$$\begin{array}{l} \mathsf{StreamCons} :: \text{Integer} \to \triangleright\text{Stream} \to \text{Stream} \\ \mathsf{deStreamCons} :: \text{Stream} \to (\text{Integer}, \triangleright\text{Stream}) \end{array}$$

The type of StreamCons shows that it takes a guarded stream "tomorrow", and produces a non-guarded stream "today". This is in line with the temporal intuition we have of the type $\triangleright$Stream. The inverse operation deStreamCons takes a full stream and returns the integer and the *guarded* remainder of the stream.

To give the guardedness type constructor force, Nakano proposes the following alternative type of the fixpoint operator for defining recursive values:

$$\textbf{fix} :: (\triangleright A \to A) \to A$$

(The standard typing of the **fix** operator is $(A \to A) \to A$.) Nakano's alternative typing ensures that recursive definitions must be guarded by only allowing access to recursively generated values "tomorrow".

To actually program with the guardedness constructor, we equip it with the structure of an applicative functor [18]:

$$\begin{array}{l} \textbf{pure} :: A \to \triangleright A \\ (\circledast) :: \triangleright(A \to B) \to \triangleright A \to \triangleright B \end{array}$$

Note that $\triangleright$ is not a monad: a join operation of type $\triangleright(\triangleright A) \to \triangleright A$ would allow us to collapse multiple guardedness obligations.

This method for integrating Nakano's guardedness type constructor into a typed λ-calculus is not the only one. Nakano uses a system of subtyping with respect to the guardedness type constructor that has a similar effect to assuming that $\triangleright$ is an applicative functor. We propose to treat $\triangleright$ as an applicative functor here, due to the greater ease with which it can be incorporated into a standard functional programming language like Haskell. Krishnaswami and

Benton [14, 15] have presented an alternative method that annotates members of the typing context with the level of guardedness that applies to them. Severi and de Vries [22] have generalised Krishnaswami and Benton's approach for any typed λ-calculus derived from a Pure Type System (PTS), including dependently typed systems. These calculi have nice proof theoretic properties, such as being able to state productivity in terms of infinitary strong normalisation.

With the guardedness type constructor, and its applicative functor structure, we can rewrite the *mergef* function to allow the alternative typing which only allows functional arguments that will lead to productive definitions.

$$\begin{aligned}
&\mathit{mergef} :: (\text{Integer} \to \text{Integer} \to \triangleright\text{Stream} \to \text{Stream}) \to \\
&\qquad \text{Stream} \to \text{Stream} \to \text{Stream} \\
&\mathit{mergef}\, f = \mathbf{fix}\ (\lambda g\ xs\ ys. \\
&\qquad\qquad \mathbf{let}\ (x, xs') = \mathsf{deStreamCons}\ xs \\
&\qquad\qquad\quad (y, ys') = \mathsf{deStreamCons}\ ys \\
&\qquad\qquad \mathbf{in}\, f\ x\ y\ (g \circledast xs' \circledast ys'))
\end{aligned}$$

Aside from the explicit uses of **fix** and deStreamCons, which were hidden by syntactic sugar in our previous definition, the only substantial changes to the definition are the uses of applicative functor apply ($\circledast$). These uses indicate operations that are occurring under a guardedness type constructor.

1.2 From the infinite to the finite

The type system for guarded recursion that we described above allowed us to remove the syntactic guardedness check and replace it with a compositional type-based one. However, aside from proposing applicative functor structure as a convenient way to incorporate the guardedness type constructor into a functional language, we have not gone much beyond Nakano's original system. We now describe a problem with guarded recursion when attempting to combine infinite and finite data. We propose a solution to this problem in the next subsection.

Consider the *take* function that reads a finite prefix of an infinite stream into a list. This function will have the following type:

$$\mathit{take} :: \text{Natural} \to \text{Stream} \to [\text{Integer}]$$

where we wish to regard the type [Integer] as the type of *finite* lists of integers. The explicit segregation of well-founded and non-well-founded types is important for our intended applications of total functional programming and theorem proving.

We also assume that the type Natural of natural numbers is well-founded, so we may attempt to write *take* by structural recursion on its first argument. However, we run into a difficulty, which we have highlighted.

$$\begin{aligned}
&\mathit{take} :: \text{Natural} \to \text{Stream} \to [\text{Integer}] \\
&\mathit{take}\ 0\ s = [] \\
&\mathit{take}\ (n+1)\ s = x : \mathit{take}\ n\ s' \\
&\quad \mathbf{where}\ (x, s') = \mathsf{deStreamCons}\ s
\end{aligned}$$

The problem is that the variable s', which we have obtained from deStreamCons, has type $\triangleright$Stream. However, to invoke the *take* function structurally recursively, we need something of type Stream, without the guardedness restriction.

We analyse this problem in terms of our intuitive reading of $\triangleright$Stream as a stream that is available "tomorrow". Nakano's typing discipline slices the construction of infinite data like Stream into discrete steps. In contrast, a well-founded data type like [Integer] lives entirely in the moment. While a stream is being constructed, this slicing is required so that we do not get ahead of ourselves and attempt to build things today from things that will only be available tomorrow. But once a stream has been fully constructed, we ought to be able to blur the distinctions between the days of its construction. We accomplish this in our type system by means of *clock variables*, and quantification over them.

1.3 Clock variables

We extend the type system with *clock variables* κ. A clock variable κ represents an individual time sequence that can be used for safe construction of infinite data like streams. In our model, clock variables are interpreted as counters running down to zero in the style of step-indexed models. By quantifying over all counters we are able to accommodate all possible finite observations on an infinite data structure.

We annotate the guardedness type constructor with a clock variable to indicate which time stream we are considering: $\triangleright^\kappa A$. Infinite data types such as streams are now annotated by their clock variable, indicating the time stream that they are being constructed on. We have the following new types for the constructor and deconstructor:

$$\begin{aligned}
&\mathsf{StreamCons}^\kappa :: \text{Integer} \to \triangleright^\kappa\text{Stream}^\kappa \to \text{Stream}^\kappa \\
&\mathsf{deStreamCons}^\kappa :: \text{Stream}^\kappa \to (\text{Integer}, \triangleright^\kappa\text{Stream}^\kappa)
\end{aligned}$$

We now regard the type Stream^κ as the type of infinite streams in the process of construction. A finished infinite stream is represented by *quantifying* over the relevant clock variable: $\forall\kappa.\text{Stream}^\kappa$. If we think of each possible downward counting counter that κ could represent, then this universally quantified type allows for any counter large enough to allow us any finite extraction of data from the stream. We use the notation $\Lambda\kappa.e$ and $e[\kappa]$ to indicate clock abstraction and application respectively, in the style of explicitly typed System F type abstraction and application.

The fixpoint operator is parameterised by the clock variable:

$$\mathbf{fix} :: \forall\kappa.(\triangleright^\kappa A \to A) \to A$$

as is the applicative functor structure carried by $\triangleright^\kappa$:

$$\begin{aligned}
&\mathbf{pure} :: \forall\kappa.A \to \triangleright^\kappa A \\
&(\circledast) :: \forall\kappa.\triangleright^\kappa(A \to B) \to \triangleright^\kappa A \to \triangleright^\kappa B
\end{aligned}$$

We also add an additional piece of structure to eliminate guarded types that have been universally quantified:

$$\mathbf{force} :: (\forall\kappa.\ \triangleright^\kappa A) \to (\forall\kappa.\ A)$$

Intuitively, if we have a value that, for any time stream, is one time step away, we simply instantiate it with a time stream that has at least one step left to run and extract the value. Note that the universal quantification is required on the right hand side since κ may appear free in the type A. The **force** operator has a similar flavour to the **runST** :: $(\forall s.\text{ST}\ s\ a) \to a$ for the ST monad [16, 19]. In both cases, rank-2 quantification is used to prevent values from "leaking" out from the context in which it is safe to use them.

Using **force** we may write a deconstructor for completed streams of type $\forall\kappa.\text{Stream}^\kappa$.

$$\begin{aligned}
&\mathsf{deStreamCons} :: (\forall\kappa.\text{Stream}^\kappa) \to (\text{Integer}, \forall\kappa.\text{Stream}^\kappa) \\
&\mathsf{deStreamCons}\ x = \\
&\qquad (\Lambda\kappa.\mathbf{fst}\ (\mathsf{deStreamCons}^\kappa\ (x[\kappa])), \\
&\qquad\ \mathbf{force}\ (\Lambda\kappa.\mathbf{snd}\ (\mathsf{deStreamCons}^\kappa\ (x[\kappa]))))
\end{aligned}$$

In this definition we have made use of a feature of our type system that states that the type equality $\forall\kappa.A \equiv A$ holds whenever κ is not free in A. Our system also includes other type equalities that demonstrate how clock quantification interacts with other type formers. These are presented in Section 2.2.

In the presence of clock variables, our definition of *take* is well-typed and we get the function we desire: taking a finite observation of a piece of infinite data:

$$\begin{array}{l} \mathit{take} :: \text{Natural} \to (\forall\kappa.\text{Stream}^\kappa) \to [\text{Integer}] \\ \mathit{take}\ 0\ s = [] \\ \mathit{take}\ (n+1)\ s = x : \mathit{take}\ n\ s' \\ \quad \textbf{where}\ (x, s') = \mathsf{deStreamCons}\ s \end{array}$$

Clock variables also allow us to make clear in the types fine distinctions between functions that are extensionally equal, but differ in their productivity. In plain Haskell, the following two stream mapping functions have the same behaviour on any *completely constructed* stream. The first *map* processes each element one at a time

$$\begin{array}{l} \mathit{map}\ f\ s = \mathsf{StreamCons}\ (f\ x)\ (\mathit{map}\ f\ s') \\ \quad \textbf{where}\ (x, s') = \mathsf{deStreamCons}\ s \end{array}$$

while *maap* processes elements two at a time by pattern matching:

$$\begin{array}{l} \mathit{maap}\ f\ (\mathsf{StreamCons}\ x\ (\mathsf{StreamCons}\ y\ s'')) \\ \quad = \mathsf{StreamCons}\ (f\ x)\ (\mathsf{StreamCons}\ (f\ y)\ (\mathit{maap}\ f\ s'')) \end{array}$$

If all the elements of the input are available at once, then *map* and *maap* have the same behaviour. However, if these functions are passed streams that are still being constructed, then their behaviour can differ significantly. Consider these two definitions of a stream of natural numbers, using *map* and *maap*:

$$\begin{array}{l} \mathit{nats} = \mathsf{StreamCons}\ 0\ (\mathit{map}\ (\lambda x.\ x+1)\ \mathit{nats}) \\ \mathit{badnats} = \mathsf{StreamCons}\ 0\ (\mathit{maap}\ (\lambda x.\ x+1)\ \mathit{badnats}) \end{array}$$

Running *nats* produces the infinite stream of natural numbers, as expected, but running *badnats* produces nothing. The function *maap* expects two elements to be available on its input stream, while *badnats* has only provided one.

Even though *map* and *maap* are extensionally equal, they have different behaviour on partially constructed streams. We can state this different behaviour using the following types in our system:

$$\begin{array}{l} \mathit{map} :: \forall\kappa.(\text{Integer} \to \text{Integer}) \to \text{Stream}^\kappa \to \text{Stream}^\kappa \\ \mathit{maap} :: (\text{Integer} \to \text{Integer}) \to (\forall\kappa.\text{Stream}^\kappa) \to (\forall\kappa.\text{Stream}^\kappa) \end{array}$$

Thus, *map*'s type states that the input stream and output stream run on the same clock κ, so each element of the output will only require one element of the input. This is exactly what *nats* requires, and our type system will accept the definition of *nats*. In contrast, *maap*'s type states that it requires a fully constructed stream as input. The definition of *badnats* does not provide this, and so our type system will reject it.

By using clock quantification to "close over" the guardedness, our approach thus *localises* the discipline which makes the productivity of definitions plain, without affecting the types at which the defined objects are used. Abel's *sized types* impose a similar discipline, but globally [1].

1.4 Final coalgebras from initial algebras, guards and clocks

In the previous subsection, we informally stated that the type Stream $=$ $\forall\kappa.$Stream$^\kappa$ represents exactly the type of infinite streams of integers. We make this informal claim precise by using the category theoretic notion of final coalgebra. A key feature of our approach is that we decompose the notion of final coalgebra into three parts: initial algebras, Nakano-style guarded types, and clock quantification.

Initial algebras In Section 2 we present a type system that includes a notion of strictly positive type operator. We include a least fixpoint operator $\mu X.F[X]$. For normal strictly positive type operators F (i.e. ones that do not involve the $\rhd^\kappa$ operator), $\mu X.F[X]$ is exactly the normal least fixpoint of F. Thus we can define the normal well-founded types of natural numbers, lists, trees and so on. Our calculus contains constructors $\mathsf{Cons}_F :: F[\mu X.F] \to \mu X.F$ for building values of these types, and recursion combinators for eliminating values:

$$\mathsf{primRec}_{F,A} :: (F[(\mu X.F) \times A] \to A) \to \mu X.F[X] \to A$$

We opt to use primitive recursion instead of a fold operator (i.e. $\mathit{fold} :: (F[A] \to A) \to \mu X.F[X] \to A$) because it allows for constant time access to the top-level of an inductive data structure.

We show in the proof of Theorem 2 that $\mu X.F$ is the carrier of the initial F-algebra in our model. Therefore, we may use standard reasoning techniques about initial algebras to reason about programs written using the $\mathsf{primRec}$ combinator.

Guarded final coalgebras When we consider strictly positive type operators of the form $F[\rhd^\kappa X]$, where κ does not appear in F then, in addition to $\mu X.F[\rhd^\kappa X]$ being the least fixpoint of the operator $F[\rhd^\kappa -]$, it is also the *greatest* fixpoint. This initial-final coincidence is familiar from domain theoretic models of recursive types (see, e.g., Smyth and Plotkin [23]), and has previously been observed as a feature of guarded recursive types by Birkedal *et al.* [6].

The *unfold* combinator that witnesses $\mu X.F[\rhd^\kappa X]$ as final can be implemented in terms of the **fix** operator, and Cons:

$$\begin{array}{l} \mathit{unfold}_F :: \forall\kappa.(A \to F[\rhd^\kappa A]) \to A \to \mu X.F[\rhd^\kappa X] \\ \mathit{unfold}_F = \Lambda\kappa.\lambda f.\textbf{fix}\ (\lambda g\ a.\mathsf{Cons}\ (\mathit{fmap}_F\ (\lambda x.g \circledast x)\ (f\,a))) \end{array}$$

where $\mathit{fmap}_F :: (A \to B) \to (F[A] \to F[B])$ is the functorial mapping combinator associated with the strictly positive type operator F. Note that without the additional $\rhd^\kappa$ in $F[\rhd^\kappa -]$, there would be no way to define *unfold*, due to the typing of **fix**.

To make observations on elements, we define a deCons_F combinator for every F, using the primitive recursion

$$\begin{array}{l} \mathit{deCons}_F :: \forall\kappa.(\mu X.F[\rhd^\kappa X]) \to F[\rhd^\kappa \mu X.F[\rhd^\kappa X]] \\ \mathit{deCons}_F = \Lambda\kappa.\mathsf{primRec}\ (\lambda x.\ \mathit{fmap}_{F[\rhd^\kappa -]}\ (\lambda y.\textbf{fst}\ y)\ x) \end{array}$$

The proof of Theorem 3 shows that these definitions of unfold_F and deCons_F exhibit $\mu X.F[\rhd^\kappa X]$ as the final $F[\rhd^\kappa -]$-coalgebra, using deCons_F as the structure map. This means that $\mathit{unfold}_F[\kappa]f$ is the unique $F[\rhd^\kappa -]$-coalgebra homomorphism from A to $\mu X.F[\rhd^\kappa -]$.

Final coalgebras Theorem 3 only gives us final coalgebras in the case when the recursion in the type is guarded by the type constructor $\rhd^\kappa -$. So we do not yet have a dual to the least fixpoint type constructor $\mu X.F$. However, as we hinted above in the case of streams, we can use clock quantification to construct a final F-coalgebra, where F need not contain an occurrence of $\rhd^\kappa -$.

For the type $\forall\kappa.\mu X.F[\rhd^\kappa -]$ we define an unfold^ν_F operator, in a similar style to the unfold_F operator above. However, this operator takes an argument of type $(A \to F[A])$, with no mention of guardedness.

$$\begin{array}{l} \mathit{unfold}^\nu_F :: (A \to F[A]) \to A \to \forall\kappa.\mu X.F[\rhd^\kappa X] \\ \mathit{unfold}^\nu_F = \lambda f\,a.\Lambda\kappa. \\ \qquad \textbf{fix}\ (\lambda g\ a.\mathsf{Cons}_F\ (\mathit{fmap}_F(\lambda x.g \circledast \textbf{pure}\ x)\ (f\,a)))\ a \end{array}$$

We can also define the corresponding deconstructor, building on the definition of deCons_F above, but also using the **force** construct in conjunction with clock quantification. This is a generalisation of the definition of $\mathsf{deStreamCons}$ above.

$$\begin{array}{l} \mathit{deCons}^\nu_F :: (\forall\kappa.\mu X.F[\rhd^\kappa X]) \to F[\forall\kappa.\mu X.F[\rhd^\kappa X]] \\ \mathit{deCons}^\nu_F = \lambda x.\ \mathit{fmap}_F\ (\lambda x.\textbf{force}\ x)\ (\Lambda\kappa.\ \mathit{deCons}_F[\kappa]\ (x[\kappa])) \end{array}$$

In the application of fmap_F, we make use of the type equalities in our calculus, which allow us to treat the types $\forall\kappa.F[X]$ and $F[\forall\kappa.X]$ as equivalent, when κ does not appear in F. We present the type equalities in Section 2.2, and prove them sound in Section 3.4.

Our last main technical result, Theorem 4, states that, in the semantics we define Section 3, $\forall\kappa.\mu X.F[\rhd^\kappa -]$ actually is the final F-coalgebra. The use of clock quantification has allowed us to remove mention of the guardedness type constructor, and given us a way to safely program and reason about F-coalgebras.

1.5 Circular traversals of trees

We now present a perhaps unexpected application of the use of clock quantification that does not relate to ensuring productivity of recursive programs generating infinite data. An interesting use of laziness in functional programming languages is to perform single-pass transformations of data structures that would appear to require at least two passes. A classic example, due to Bird [3], is the *replaceMin* function that replaces each value in a binary tree with the minimum of all the values in the tree, in a single pass. In normal Haskell, this function is written as follows:

```
replaceMin :: Tree → Tree
replaceMin t = let (t', m) = replaceMinBody t m in t'
    where
      replaceMinBody (Leaf x) m = (Leaf m, x)
      replaceMinBody (Br l r) m =
              let (l', m_l) = replaceMinBody l m
                  (r', m_r) = replaceMinBody r m
              in (Br l' r', min m_l m_r)
```

The interesting part of this function is the first **let** expression. This takes the minimum value m computed by the traversal of the tree and passes it into the *same* traversal to build the new tree. This function is a marvel of declarative programming: we have declared that we wish the tree t' to be labelled with the minimum value in the tree t just by stating that they be the same, without explaining at all why this definition makes any sense. Intuitively, the reason that this works is that the overall minimum value is never used in the computation of the minimum, only the construction of the new tree. The computation of the minimum and the construction of the new tree conceptually exist at different moments in time, and it is only safe to treat them the same after both have finished.

Using explicit clock variables we can give a version of the *replaceMin* definition that demonstrates that we have actually defined a total function from trees to trees. The use of clock variables allows us to be explicit about the time when various operations are taking place.

Out first step is to replace the circular use of **let** with a *feedback* combinator defined in terms of the **fix** operator:

$$\mathit{feedback} : \forall\kappa.\ (\rhd^{\kappa} U \to (B[\kappa], U)) \to B[\kappa]$$
$$\mathit{feedback} = \Lambda\kappa.\lambda f.\mathbf{fst}\ (\mathbf{fix}\ (\lambda x.\ f\ (\mathbf{pure}\ (\lambda x.\mathbf{snd}\ x) \circledast x)))$$

In the application of the **fix** operator, $x : \rhd^{\kappa}(B \times U)$. The notation $B[\kappa]$ indicates that κ may appear free in the type B.

We now rewrite the *replaceMinBody* function so that we can apply *feedback* to it. We have highlighted the changes from the previous definition.

```
replaceMinBody :: Tree → ∀κ. ▷κ Integer → (▷κ Tree, Integer)
replaceMinBody (Leaf x) m = (pure Leaf ⊛ m, x)
replaceMinBody (Br l r) m =
          let (l', m_l) = replaceMinBody l m
              (r', m_r) = replaceMinBody r m
          in (pure Br ⊛ l' ⊛ r', min m_l m_r)
```

The changes required are minor: we must change the type, and use the applicative functor structure of $\rhd^{\kappa}$ to indicate when computations are taking place "tomorrow".

Applying *feedback* to *replaceMinBody*, and using **force** to remove the now redundant occurrence of $\rhd^{\kappa}$, we can define the full *replaceMin* function in our system:

```
replaceMin :: Tree → Tree
replaceMin t = force (Λκ.feedback[κ] (replaceMinBody[κ]) t)
```

$$\frac{X \in \Theta}{\Delta;\Theta \vdash X : \mathtt{type}} \qquad \frac{}{\Delta;\Theta \vdash 1 : \mathtt{type}}$$

$$\frac{\Delta;\Theta \vdash A : \mathtt{type} \qquad \Delta;\Theta \vdash B : \mathtt{type}}{\Delta;\Theta \vdash A \times B : \mathtt{type}}$$

$$\frac{\Delta;\Theta \vdash A : \mathtt{type} \qquad \Delta;\Theta \vdash B : \mathtt{type}}{\Delta;\Theta \vdash A + B : \mathtt{type}}$$

$$\frac{\Delta;- \vdash A : \mathtt{type} \qquad \Delta;\Theta \vdash B : \mathtt{type}}{\Delta;\Theta \vdash A \to B : \mathtt{type}}$$

$$\frac{\Delta;\Theta, X \vdash A : \mathtt{type}}{\Delta;\Theta \vdash \mu X.A : \mathtt{type}} \qquad \frac{\Delta,\kappa;\Theta \vdash A : \mathtt{type}}{\Delta;\Theta \vdash \forall\kappa.A : \mathtt{type}}$$

$$\frac{\Delta;\Theta \vdash A : \mathtt{type} \qquad \kappa \in \Delta}{\Delta;\Theta \vdash \rhd^{\kappa} A : \mathtt{type}}$$

Figure 1. Well-formed types and type operators

By the soundness property of our system that we prove in Section 3, we are assured that we have defined a total function from trees to trees. The standard Haskell type system does not provide this guarantee.

1.6 Models of guarded recursion

To substantiate the claims we have made in this introduction, in Section 3 we construct a multiply-step-indexed model of the type system we present in the next section. The multiple step-indexes are required for the multiple clock variables in our system, each representing separate time streams. Step-indexed models were introduced by Appel and McAllester [2] to prove properties of recursive types. The use of step-indexing serves to break the circularity inherent in recursive types. Dreyer *et al.* [10] exposed the connection between Nakano's guarded recursion and step indexed models. More recently, Birkedal *et al.* [4, 6] have elaborated this connection, particularly in the direction of dependent types.

Alternative semantics for guarded recursion have involved ultrametric spaces, for example Birkedal *et al.* [5] and Krishnaswami and Benton [15]. Hutton and Jaskelioff [13] have also used an approach based on metric spaces for identifying productive stream generating functions.

Finally, we mention the syntactic approach of Severi and de Vries [22], who define the notion of infinitary strong normalisation to prove productivity of dependent type systems with guarded recursion.

2. A type system with clocks and guards

In the introduction, we presented our motivating examples in terms of a Haskell-like language informally extended with a Nakano-style guard modality and clock quantification. To formally state the properties of our combination of clock quantification, clock-indexed guard modalities and inductive types, in this section we define an extension of the simply-typed λ-calculus with these features. In the next section, we define a semantics for our system in which we can formally state the results that we claimed in the introduction.

2.1 Well-formed types with clock variables

The types of our system include two kinds of variable that may occur free and bound: clock variables in the clock quantifier and the clock-indexed guard modality, as well as type variables occurring in strictly positive positions for the inductive types. We therefore formally define when a type is well-formed with respect to contexts of clock and type variables, using the rules displayed in Figure 1.

The well-formedness judgement for types ($\Delta; \Theta \vdash A : \mathtt{type}$) is defined with respect to a *clock context* Δ and a *type variable context* Θ. Clock contexts are lists of clock variables, $\Delta = \kappa_1, ..., \kappa_n$, and type variable contexts are lists of type variable names, $\Theta = X_1, ..., X_n$. Type variables are only used to manage the scope of the nested least fixpoint type operator μ; there is no type polymorphism in the type system we present here. We generally use Roman letters A, B, C to stand for types, but we also occasionally use F and G when we wish to emphasise that types with free type variables are strictly positive type operators. For any type A, we define $fc(A)$ to be the set of free clock variables that appear in A.

Most of the type well-formedness rules are standard: we have a rule for forming a type from a type variable that is in scope and rules for forming the unit type 1, product types $A \times B$, sum types $A + B$, function types $A \to B$ and least fixpoint types $\mu X.A$. We enforce the restriction to strictly positive type operators by disallowing occurrences of free type variables in the domain component of function types. In Section 2.3, we will see that each of the standard type constructors will have the usual corresponding term-level constructs; our system subsumes the simply typed λ-calculus with products, sums and least fixpoint types.

The remaining two rules are for forming clock quantification $\forall\kappa.A$ types and the clock-indexed Nakano-style guard modality $\rhd^{\kappa} A$. The type formation rule for clock quantification is very similar to universal type quantification from standard polymorphic type theories like System F.

As we described in the introduction in Section 1.3, we have augmented the Nakano-style delay modality with a clock variable. This allows us to distinguish between guardedness with respect to multiple clocks, and hence to be able to close over all the steps guarded by a particular clock.

2.2 Type Equality

The examples we presented in the introduction made use of several type equalities allowing us to move clock quantification through types. For instance, in the definition of the deStreamCons stream deconstructor in Section 1.3, we made use of a type equality to treat a value of type $\forall\kappa.$Integer as having the type Integer. Intuitively, this is valid because a value of type Integer exists independently of any clock, therefore we can remove the clock quantification. In general, clock quantification commutes with almost all strictly positive type formers, except for guards indexed by the same clock variable. For those, we must use **force**.

The following rules are intended to be read as defining a judgement $\Delta; \Theta \vdash A \equiv B : \mathtt{type}$, indicating that the well-formed types $\Delta; \Theta \vdash A : \mathtt{type}$ and $\Delta; \Theta \vdash B : \mathtt{type}$ are to be considered equal. In addition to these rules, the relation $\Delta \vdash A \equiv B : \mathtt{type}$ is reflexive, symmetric, transitive and a congruence.

$$
\begin{array}{rll}
\forall\kappa.A & \equiv A & (\kappa \notin fc(A)) \\
\forall\kappa.A + B & \equiv (\forall\kappa.A) + (\forall\kappa.B) & \\
\forall\kappa.A \times B & \equiv (\forall\kappa.A) \times (\forall\kappa.B) & \\
\forall\kappa.A \to B & \equiv A \to \forall\kappa.B & (\kappa \notin fc(A)) \\
\forall\kappa.\forall\kappa'.A & \equiv \forall\kappa'.\forall\kappa.A & (\kappa \neq \kappa') \\
\forall\kappa.\rhd^{\kappa'} A & \equiv \rhd^{\kappa'}\forall\kappa.A & (\kappa \neq \kappa') \\
\forall\kappa.\mu X.F[A, X] & \equiv \mu X.F[\forall\kappa.A, X] & (fc(F) = \emptyset)
\end{array}
$$

In the last rule, F must be strictly positive in A as well as X.

After we define the terms of our system in the next sub-section, it will become apparent that several of the type equality rules could be removed, and their use replaced by terms witnessing the conversions back and forth. In the case of product types, we could define the following pair of terms (using the syntax and typing rules we define below):

$$
\begin{array}{l}
\lambda x.(\Lambda\kappa.\mathbf{fst}\ (x[\kappa]), \Lambda\kappa.\mathbf{snd}\ (x[\kappa])) \\
\qquad\qquad : (\forall\kappa.A \times B) \to (\forall\kappa.A) \times (\forall\kappa.B)
\end{array}
$$

and

$$
\begin{array}{l}
\lambda x.\Lambda\kappa.(\mathbf{fst}\ x\ [\kappa], \mathbf{snd}\ x\ [\kappa]) \\
\qquad\qquad : (\forall\kappa.A) \times (\forall\kappa.B) \to \forall\kappa.A \times B
\end{array}
$$

Indeed, the denotational semantics we present in Section 3 will interpret both of these functions as the identity. However, not all the type equality rules are expressible in terms of clock abstraction and application, for instance, the $\forall\kappa.A \equiv A$ rule and the rule for sum types. Moreover, our definition of deCons in Section 1.4 is greatly simplified by having clock quantification commute with all type formers uniformly (recall that we made crucial use of the equality $\forall\kappa.F[-] \equiv F[\forall\kappa.-]$). Therefore, we elect to include type equalities for commuting clock quantification with all type formers uniformly.

2.3 Well-typed Terms

The terms of our system are defined by the following grammar:

$$
\begin{array}{rl}
e, f, g ::= & x \mid * \mid \lambda x.\ e \mid f e \mid (e_1, e_2) \mid \mathbf{fst}\ e \mid \mathbf{snd}\ e \\
& \mid \mathbf{inl}\ e \mid \mathbf{inr}\ e \mid \mathbf{case}\ e\ \mathbf{of}\ \mathbf{inl}\ x.f; \mathbf{inr}\ y.g \\
& \mid \mathsf{Cons}_F\ e \mid \mathsf{primRec}_F\ e \mid \Lambda\kappa.e \mid e[\kappa'] \\
& \mid \mathbf{pure}\ x \mid f \circledast e \mid \mathbf{fix}\ f \mid \mathbf{force}\ e
\end{array}
$$

The *well-typed* terms of our system are defined by the typing judgement $\Delta; \Gamma \vdash e : A$, given by the rules presented in Figure 2. Terms are judged to be well-typed with respect to a clock variable context Δ, and a typing context Γ consisting of a list of variable : type pairs: $x_1 : A_1, ..., x_n : A_n$. We only consider typing contexts where each type is well-formed with respect to the clock variable context Δ, and the *empty* type variable context. The result type A in the typing judgement must also be well-formed with respect to Δ and the empty type variable context.

We have split the typing rules in Figure 2 into five groups. The first group includes the standard typing rules for the simply-typed λ-calculus with unit, product and sum types. Apart from the additional clock variable contexts Δ, these rules are entirely standard. The second group contains the rules for the inductive types $\mu X.F$. Again, apart from the appearance of clock variable contexts, these rules are the standard constructor and primitive recursion constructs for inductive types.

The third group of rules cover clock abstraction and application, and the integration of the type equality rules we defined in the previous section. In the κ-App rule, we have used the notation $A[\kappa \mapsto \kappa']$ to indicate the substitution of the clock variable κ' for κ. These rules are as one might expect for System F-style quantification with non-trivial type equality, albeit that in the κ-App rule the κ' clock variable cannot already appear in the type. This disallows us from using the same clock variable twice, preventing multiple "time-streams" becoming conflated.

The fourth group of rules state that the clock-indexed guard modality supports the **pure** and apply ($\circledast$) operations of an applicative functor. When we define a denotational semantics of our calculus in the next section, these operations will be interpreted simply as the identity function and normal function application respectively, meaning that the applicative functor laws hold trivially.

Finally, the fifth group of rules presents the typing for Nakano's guarded **fix** combinator, now indexed by a clock variable, and our **force** combinator for removing the guard modality when it is protected by a clock quantification.

2.4 Type operators are functorial

In Section 1.4 we used a functorial mapping function $fmap_F : (A \to B) \to F[A] \to F[B]$, which we claimed was defined

1. Simply-typed λ-calculus with products and sums

$$\frac{x : A \in \Gamma}{\Delta;\Gamma \vdash x : A}\ (\textsc{Var}) \qquad \frac{}{\Delta;\Gamma \vdash * : 1}\ (\textsc{Unit}) \qquad \frac{\Delta;\Gamma, x : A \vdash e : B}{\Delta;\Gamma \vdash \lambda x.\, e : A \to B}\ (\textsc{Abs}) \qquad \frac{\Delta;\Gamma \vdash f : A \to B \quad \Delta;\Gamma \vdash e : A}{\Delta;\Gamma \vdash fe : B}\ (\textsc{App})$$

$$\frac{\Delta;\Gamma \vdash e_1 : A \quad \Delta;\Gamma \vdash e_2 : B}{\Delta;\Gamma \vdash (e_1, e_2) : A \times B}\ (\textsc{Pair}) \qquad \frac{\Delta;\Gamma \vdash e : A \times B}{\Delta;\Gamma \vdash \mathbf{fst}\ e : A}\ (\textsc{Fst}) \qquad \frac{\Delta;\Gamma \vdash e : A \times B}{\Delta;\Gamma \vdash \mathbf{snd}\ e : B}\ (\textsc{Snd}) \qquad \frac{\Delta;\Gamma \vdash e : A}{\Delta;\Gamma \vdash \mathbf{inl}\ e : A + B}\ (\textsc{Inl})$$

$$\frac{\Delta;\Gamma \vdash e : B}{\Delta;\Gamma \vdash \mathbf{inr}\ e : A + B}\ (\textsc{Inr}) \qquad \frac{\Delta;\Gamma \vdash e : A - B \quad \Delta;\Gamma, x : A \vdash f : C \quad \Delta;\Gamma, y : B \vdash g : C}{\Delta;\Gamma \vdash \mathbf{case}\ e\ \mathbf{of}\ \mathbf{inl}\ x.f; \mathbf{inr}\ y.g : C}\ (\textsc{Case})$$

2. Least Fixpoint Types

$$\frac{\Delta;\Gamma \vdash e : F[\mu X.F[X]]}{\Delta;\Gamma \vdash \mathsf{Cons}_F\ e : \mu X.F[X]}\ (\textsc{Cons}) \qquad \frac{\Delta;\Gamma \vdash e : F[(\mu X.F[X]) \times A] \to A}{\Delta;\Gamma \vdash \mathsf{primRec}_F\ e : \mu X.F[X] \to A}\ (\textsc{PrimRec})$$

3. Clock Abstraction and Application, and Type Equality

$$\frac{\Delta, \kappa;\Gamma \vdash e : A \quad \kappa \notin fc(\Gamma)}{\Delta;\Gamma \vdash \Lambda\kappa.e : \forall\kappa.A}\ (\kappa\text{-}\textsc{Abs}) \qquad \frac{\Delta;\Gamma \vdash e : \forall\kappa.A \quad \kappa' \in \Delta \quad \kappa' \notin fc(A)}{\Delta;\Gamma \vdash e[\kappa'] : A[\kappa \mapsto \kappa']}\ (\kappa\text{-}\textsc{App})$$

$$\frac{\Delta;\Gamma \vdash e : A \quad \Delta \vdash A \equiv B}{\Delta;\Gamma \vdash e : B}\ (\textsc{TyEq})$$

4. Applicative Functor Structure for $\rhd^\kappa -$

$$\frac{\Delta;\Gamma \vdash e : A \quad \kappa \in \Delta}{\Delta;\Gamma \vdash \mathbf{pure}\ e : \rhd^\kappa A}\ (\textsc{DePure}) \qquad \frac{\Delta;\Gamma \vdash f : \rhd^\kappa(A \to B) \quad \Delta;\Gamma \vdash e : \rhd^\kappa A}{\Delta;\Gamma \vdash f \circledast e : \rhd^\kappa B}\ (\textsc{DeApp})$$

5. Fix and Force

$$\frac{\Delta;\Gamma \vdash f : \rhd^\kappa A \to A}{\Delta;\Gamma \vdash \mathbf{fix}\ f : A}\ (\textsc{Fix}) \qquad \frac{\Delta;\Gamma \vdash e : \forall\kappa.\rhd^\kappa A}{\Delta;\Gamma \vdash \mathbf{force}\ e : \forall\kappa.A}\ (\textsc{Force})$$

Figure 2. Well-typed terms

$$\begin{aligned}
&\mathit{fmap}_F : \overrightarrow{(A \to B)} \to F[\vec{A}] \to F[\vec{B}]\\
&\mathit{fmap}_{X_i}\ \vec{f}x = f_i\, x\\
&\mathit{fmap}_1\ \vec{f}x = *\\
&\mathit{fmap}_{F\times G}\ \vec{f}x = (\mathit{fmap}_F\ \vec{f}\ (\mathbf{fst}\ x), \mathit{fmap}_G\ \vec{f}\ (\mathbf{snd}\ x))\\
&\mathit{fmap}_{F+G}\ \vec{f}x = \mathbf{case}\ x\ \mathbf{of}\ \mathbf{inl}\ y.\mathbf{inl}\ (\mathit{fmap}_F\ \vec{f}\ y)\\
&\qquad\qquad\qquad \mathbf{inr}\ z.\mathbf{inr}\ (\mathit{fmap}_G\ \vec{f}\ z)\\
&\mathit{fmap}_{A\to F}\vec{f}x = \lambda a.\mathit{fmap}_F\ \vec{f}\ (x\ a)\\
&\mathit{fmap}_{\rhd^\kappa F}\ \vec{f}x = \mathbf{pure}\ (\mathit{fmap}_F\ \vec{f}) \circledast x\\
&\mathit{fmap}_{\forall\kappa.F}\ \vec{f}x = \Lambda\kappa.\mathit{fmap}_F\ \vec{f}\ (x[\kappa])\\
&\mathit{fmap}_{\mu X.F}\vec{f}x = \mathsf{primRec}\ (\lambda x.\mathsf{Cons}(\mathit{fmap}_F\ \vec{f}\ (\lambda x.\ \mathbf{snd}\ x)\ x))\ x
\end{aligned}$$

Figure 3. fmap_F for all type operators F

for each strictly positive type operator F. We define this operator by structural recursion on the derivation of F, using the clauses in Figure 3. Due to the presence of nested least fixpoint types in our calculus, we handle n-ary strictly positive type operators.

2.5 Programming with guarded types and clocks

Lists and Trees, Finite and Infinite Using the least fixpoint type operator $\mu X.F$, we can reconstruct many of the usual inductive data types used in functional programming. For example, the OCaml declaration:

$$\mathbf{type}\ \text{list} = \mathsf{NilList} \mid \mathsf{ConsList}\ \mathbf{of}\ A \times \text{list}$$

of finite lists of values of type A, can be expressed as the type $\mu X.1 + A \times X$ in our system, where we have replaced the two constructors $\mathsf{NilList}$ and $\mathsf{ConsList}$ with a use of the sum type former. Likewise, the type of binary trees labelled with As that we used in Section 1.5 can be written as $\mu X.A + X \times X$.

A similar data type declaration in Haskell has a different interpretation. If we make the following declaration in Haskell:

$$\mathbf{data}\ \text{List} = \mathsf{NilList} \mid \mathsf{ConsList}\ A\ \text{List}$$

then the type List includes both finite lists of As, and infinite lists of As (a similar effect can be achieved in OCaml by use of the **lazy** type constructor). Haskell's type system is too weak to distinguish the definitely finite from the possibly infinite case, and it is often left to the documentation to warn the programmer that some functions will be non-productive on infinite lists (for example, the *reverse* function).

Making use of Nakano's guard modality $\rhd^\kappa -$, we are able to express Haskell-style possibly infinite lists as the guarded inductive type $\mu X.1 + A \times \rhd^\kappa A$. As we saw in the introduction, infinite lists can be constructed using the guarded **fix** operator. For example, the infinite repetition of a fixed value can be written in our system as:

$$\lambda a.\mathbf{fix}\ (\lambda l.\mathsf{Cons}\ (\mathbf{inr}\ (a, l)))$$

If we restrict ourselves to only one clock variable, and always use guarded recursive types, then we obtain a programming language similar to a monomorphic Haskell, except with a guarantee that all functions are productive.

Co-inductive Streams As we saw in Section 1.2, programming with guarded types is productive, but they are fundamentally incompatible with normal inductive types. Recall that if we define infinite streams of As as $\text{Stream}^\kappa\ A = \mu X.A \times \triangleright^\kappa X$, then there is no way of defining a function *tail* : $\text{Stream}^\kappa\ A \to \text{Stream}^\kappa\ A$; the best we can do is *tail* : $\text{Stream}^\kappa\ A \to \triangleright^\kappa \text{Stream}^\kappa\ A$. The rest of the stream only exists "tomorrow".

Clock quantification fixes this problem. We define:

$$\text{Stream}\ A = \forall\kappa.\mu X.A \times \triangleright^\kappa A$$

Now we can define the two deconstructors for making observations on streams, with the right types:

$$\begin{aligned}
&\mathit{head}\ :\ \text{Stream}\ A \to A\\
&\mathit{head} = \lambda s.\Lambda\kappa.\mathsf{primRec}\ (\lambda x.\mathbf{fst}\ x)\ (s[\kappa])
\end{aligned}$$

$$\begin{aligned}
&\mathit{tail}\ :\ \text{Stream}\ A \to \text{Stream}\ A\\
&\mathit{tail} = \lambda s.(\mathbf{force}\ (\Lambda\kappa.\mathsf{primRec}\ (\lambda x.\mathbf{pure}(\lambda x.\mathbf{fst}\ x) \circledast (\mathbf{snd}\ x))\\
&\qquad\qquad (s[\kappa])))
\end{aligned}$$

In the definition of *head* we use the fact that κ cannot appear in A to apply the first type equality rule from Section 2.2.

Stream Processing Ghani, Hancock and Pattinson [11] define a type of representations of continuous functions on streams using a least fixpoint type nested within a greatest fixpoint. A continuous function on streams is a function that only requires a finite amount of input for each element of the output. Ghani *et al.*'s type is expressed in our system as follows:

$$\text{SP}\ I\ O = \forall\kappa.\mu X.\mu Y.(I \to Y) + (O \times \triangleright^\kappa X)$$

where SP stands for "Stream Processor" and I and O stand for input and output respectively. In this type, the outer fixpoint permits the production of infinitely many Os, due to the guarded occurrence of X, while the inner fixpoint only permits a finite amount of Is to be read from the input stream. This kind of nested fixpoint is not expressible within Coq, but is possible with Agda's support for coinductive types [9].

Defining the application of an SP I O to a stream of Is serves as an interesting example of programming with guards and clocks. We make use of a helper function for unfolding values of type SP I O that have already been instantiated with some clock:

$$\mathit{step} : \mathit{SP}^\kappa\ I\ O \to \mu Y.(I \to Y) \times (O \times \triangleright^\kappa(\mathit{SP}^\kappa\ I\ O))$$

where $\mathit{SP}^\kappa\ I\ O$ is $\mathit{SP}\ I\ O$ instantiated with the clock κ.

The definition of stream processor application goes as follows, where we permit ourselves a little pattern matching syntactic sugar for pairs:

$$\begin{aligned}
&\mathit{apply} : \text{SP}\ I\ O \to \text{Stream}\ I \to \text{Stream}\ O\\
&\mathit{apply} =\\
&\lambda sp\ s.\Lambda\kappa.\mathbf{fix}(\lambda rec\ sp\ s.\\
&\qquad \mathsf{primRec}\ (\lambda x\ s.\mathbf{case}\ x\ \mathbf{of}\\
&\qquad\qquad \mathbf{inl}\ f.f\ (\mathit{head}\ s)(\mathit{tail}\ s)\\
&\qquad\qquad \mathbf{inr}\ (o, sp').\\
&\qquad\qquad\quad \mathsf{Cons}(o, rec \circledast sp' \circledast \mathbf{pure}\ s))\\
&\qquad (\mathit{step}\ sp))\\
&\quad (sp\ [\kappa])\ s
\end{aligned}$$

This function consists of two nested loops. The outer loop, expressed using **fix**, generates the output stream. This loop is running on the clock κ, introduced by the $\Lambda\kappa$. We have instantiated the stream processor with the same clock; this causes the steps of the output stream to be in lockstep with the output steps of the stream processor, exactly as we might expect. The inner loop, expressed using primRec, recurses over the finite list of input instructions from the stream processor, pulling items from the input stream as needed. The input stream is *not* instantiated with the same clock as the stream processor and the output stream: we need to access an arbitrary number of elements from the input stream for each step of the stream processor, so their clocks cannot run in lockstep.

The Partiality Monad The partiality monad is a well-known coinductively defined monad that allows the definition of functions via general recursion, even in a total language. The partiality monad is defined as $\text{Partial}\ A = \nu X.A + X$. Hence, a value of type Partial A consists of a stream of **inr**s, either continuing forever, or terminating in an **inl** with a value of type A. Using the partiality monad, possibly non-terminating computations can be represented, with non-termination represented by an infinite stream that never returns a value. Capretta [7] gives a detailed description.

To express the partiality monad in our system, we decompose it into a guarded least fixpoint and clock quantification, just as we did for streams and stream processors above:

$$\begin{aligned}
\text{Partial}^\kappa\ A &= \mu X.A + \triangleright^\kappa X\\
\text{Partial}\ A &= \forall\kappa.\text{Partial}^\kappa\ A
\end{aligned}$$

For convenience, we define two constructors for $\text{Partial}^\kappa\ A$, corresponding to the two components of the sum type:

$$\begin{aligned}
&\mathit{now}^\kappa\ : A \to \text{Partial}^\kappa\ A\\
&\mathit{now}^\kappa\ = \lambda a.\ \mathsf{Cons}\ (\mathbf{inl}\ a)
\end{aligned}$$

$$\begin{aligned}
&\mathit{later}^\kappa\ : \triangleright^\kappa(\text{Partial}^\kappa\ A) \to \text{Partial}^\kappa\ A\\
&\mathit{later}^\kappa\ = \lambda p.\ \mathsf{Cons}\ (\mathbf{inr}\ p)
\end{aligned}$$

It is straightforward to use guarded recursion and clock quantification to define the *return* and bind functions that demonstrate that Partial is indeed a monad. For an example of a possibly non-terminating function that can be expressed using the partiality monad, we define the following function *collatz*. For each natural number n, this function only terminates if the Collatz sequence starting from n reaches 1. Whether or not this sequence reaches 1 for all n is a famous unsolved question in number theory.

$$\begin{aligned}
&\mathit{collatz} : \text{Natural} \to \text{Partial}\ 1\\
&\mathit{collatz} = \lambda n.\Lambda\kappa.\mathbf{fix}\ (\lambda rec\ n.\mathbf{if}\ n = 1\ \mathbf{then}\ \mathit{now}^\kappa\ (*)\\
&\qquad\qquad \mathbf{else\ if}\ n\ \mathit{mod}\ 2 = 0\ \mathbf{then}\\
&\qquad\qquad\quad \mathit{later}^\kappa\ (rec \circledast (\mathbf{pure}\ (n/2)))\\
&\qquad\qquad \mathbf{else}\\
&\qquad\qquad\quad \mathit{later}^\kappa\ (rec \circledast (\mathbf{pure}\ (3 * n + 1))))\ n
\end{aligned}$$

The partiality monad is not a drop-in replacement for general recursion. The type Partial A reveals information about the number of steps that it takes to compute a value of type A. Therefore, it is possible to write a timeout function that runs a partial computation for a fixed number of steps before giving up:

$$\mathit{timeout} : \text{Natural} \to \text{Partial}\ A \to A + 1$$

The partiality monad allows us to write possibly non-terminating functions, but also allows us to make more observations on them.

3. A denotational semantics for clocks and guards

We have claimed that the typing discipline from the previous section guarantees that programs will be productive. We now substantiate this claim by defining a domain-theoretic model of our system, and showing that the denotation of a well-typed closed term is never $\bot$. We accomplish this by using a multiply-step-indexed interpretation of types, where the multiple step indexes correspond to the multiple clock variables that may be in scope.

$$
\begin{aligned}
[\![x]\!]\eta &= \eta(x) \\
[\![*]\!]\eta &= \mathsf{Unit} \\
[\![\lambda x.\, e]\!]\eta &= \mathsf{Lam}\ (\lambda v.\ [\![e]\!](\eta[x \mapsto v])) \\
[\![f e]\!]\eta &= \begin{cases} d_f\ ([\![e]\!]\eta) & \text{if } [\![f]\!]\eta = \mathsf{Lam}\ d_f \\ \bot & \text{otherwise} \end{cases} \\
[\![(e_1, e_2)]\!]\eta &= \mathsf{Pair}\ ([\![e_1]\!]\eta, [\![e_2]\!]\eta) \\
[\![\textbf{fst}\ e]\!]\eta &= \begin{cases} d_1 & \text{if } [\![e]\!]\eta = \mathsf{Pair}\ (d_1, d_2) \\ \bot & \text{otherwise} \end{cases} \\
[\![\textbf{snd}\ e]\!]\eta &= \begin{cases} d_2 & \text{if } [\![e]\!]\eta = \mathsf{Pair}\ (d_1, d_2) \\ \bot & \text{otherwise} \end{cases} \\
[\![\textbf{inl}\ e]\!]\eta &= \mathsf{Inl}\ ([\![e]\!]\eta) \\
[\![\textbf{inr}\ e]\!]\eta &= \mathsf{Inr}\ ([\![e]\!]\eta) \\
\left[\!\!\left[\begin{array}{l} \textbf{case}\ e\ \textbf{of} \\ \quad \textbf{inl}\ x.f \\ \quad \textbf{inr}\ y.g \end{array} \right]\!\!\right]\eta &= \begin{cases} [\![f]\!](\eta[x \mapsto d]) & \text{if } [\![e]\!]\eta = \mathsf{Inl}\ d \\ [\![g]\!](\eta[y \mapsto d]) & \text{if } [\![e]\!]\eta = \mathsf{Inr}\ d \\ \bot & \text{otherwise} \end{cases}
\end{aligned}
$$

Figure 4. Semantics for the simply-typed portion of our system

3.1 Semantics of terms

We interpret terms in (a mild extension of) the standard domain theoretic model of the untyped lazy λ-calculus, described by Pitts [21]. A feature of this semantics is the erasure of anything to do with the guardedness type constructor $\triangleright^{\kappa}$ – and the clock quantification. The **fix** operator is interpreted as the domain-theoretic fixpoint, i.e., exactly the usual interpretation of general recursion.

We assume a directed complete partial order with bottom ($\mathrm{DCPO}_\bot$), D, satisfying the following recursive domain equation:

$$D \cong (D \to D)_\bot \oplus (D \times D)_\bot \oplus D_\bot \oplus D_\bot \oplus 1_\bot$$

where $\oplus$ represents the coalesced sum that identifies the $\bot$ element of all the components. We are guaranteed to be able to obtain such a D by standard results about the category $\mathrm{DCPO}_\bot$ (see, e.g., Smyth and Plotkin [23]). The five components of the right hand side of this equation will be used to carry functions, products, the left and right injections for sum types and the unit value respectively. We use the following symbols to represent the corresponding continuous injective maps into D:

$$
\begin{array}{ll}
\mathsf{Lam} : (D \to D) \to D & \mathsf{Pair} : D \times D \to D \\
\mathsf{Inl} : D \to D & \mathsf{Inr} : D \to D \\
\mathsf{Unit} : 1 \to D &
\end{array}
$$

We will write Unit instead of Unit $*$.

Let V be the set of all possible term-level variable names. Environments η are modelled as maps from V to elements of D. Terms are interpreted as continuous maps from environments to elements of D. The clauses for defining the interpretation of parts of our system that are just the simply-typed λ-calculus are standard, and displayed in Figure 4. It can be easily checked that this collection of equations defines a continuous function $[\![-]\!] : (V \to D) \to D$, since everything is built from standard parts.

The applicative functor structure for the guard modality is interpreted just as the identity function and normal application, as we promised in Section 2.3:

$$
\begin{aligned}
[\![\textbf{pure}\ e]\!]\eta &= [\![e]\!]\eta \\
[\![f \circledast e]\!]\eta &= \begin{cases} d_f\ ([\![e]\!]\eta) & \text{if } [\![f]\!]\eta = \mathsf{Lam}\ d_f \\ \bot & \text{otherwise} \end{cases}
\end{aligned}
$$

Our interpretation simply translates the **fix** operator as the usual fixpoint operator $\mathrm{fix}\ f = \bigsqcup_n f^n(\bot)$ in $\mathrm{DCPO}_\bot$. The **force** operator

$$
\begin{aligned}
\mathrm{fmap}_{\mathrm{X}}\ \vec{f}\ x &= d_f(x) \quad (f_X = \mathsf{Lam}\ d_f) \\
\mathrm{fmap}_{1}\ \vec{f}\ x &= \mathsf{Unit} \\
\mathrm{fmap}_{\mathrm{F}\times\mathrm{G}}\ \vec{f}\ (\mathsf{Pair}\ (x, y)) &= \mathsf{Pair}\ (\mathrm{fmap}_{\mathrm{F}}\ \vec{f}\ x, \mathrm{fmap}_{\mathrm{G}}\ \vec{f}\ y) \\
\mathrm{fmap}_{\mathrm{F}+\mathrm{G}}\ \vec{f}\ (\mathsf{Inl}\ x) &= \mathsf{Inl}\ (\mathrm{fmap}_{\mathrm{F}}\ \vec{f}\ x) \\
\mathrm{fmap}_{\mathrm{F}+\mathrm{G}}\ \vec{f}\ (\mathsf{Inr}\ x) &= \mathsf{Inr}\ (\mathrm{fmap}_{\mathrm{G}}\ \vec{f}\ x) \\
\mathrm{fmap}_{\mathrm{A}\to\mathrm{F}}\ \vec{f}\ (\mathsf{Lam}\ g) &= \mathsf{Lam}\ (\lambda v.\mathrm{fmap}_{\mathrm{F}}\ \vec{f}\ (g\ v)) \\
\mathrm{fmap}_{\triangleright^{\kappa}\mathrm{F}}\ \vec{f}\ x &= \mathrm{fmap}_{\mathrm{F}}\ \vec{f}\ x \\
\mathrm{fmap}_{\forall\kappa.\mathrm{F}}\ \vec{f}\ x &= \mathrm{fmap}_{\mathrm{F}}\ \vec{f}\ x \\
\mathrm{fmap}_{\mu\mathrm{X}.\mathrm{F}}\ \vec{f}\ x &= \mathrm{primrec}\ (\mathrm{fmap}_{\mathrm{F}}\ \vec{f}) \\
&\qquad (\mathrm{fmap}_{\mathrm{F}}\ \vec{f}\ \mathrm{snd})\ x
\end{aligned}
$$

where

$$\mathrm{snd}\ (\mathsf{Pair}\ (x, y)) = y$$

All unhandled cases are defined to be equal to $\bot$.

Figure 5. Semantic $\mathrm{fmap}_{\mathrm{F}}$ for $\Delta; \Theta \vdash F : \mathtt{type}$

is interpreted as a no-operation.

$$
\begin{aligned}
[\![\textbf{fix}\ f]\!]\eta &= \begin{cases} \mathrm{fix}\ d_f & \text{if } [\![f]\!]\eta = \mathsf{Lam}\ d_f \\ \bot & \text{otherwise} \end{cases} \\
[\![\textbf{force}\ e]\!]\eta &= [\![e]\!]\eta
\end{aligned}
$$

Finally, we interpret the constructor Cons_F and primitive recursion eliminator $\mathsf{primRec}_F$ for least fixpoint types. The interpretation of construction is straightforward: the constructor itself disappears at runtime, so the interpretation simply ignores it:

$$[\![\mathsf{Cons}_F\ e]\!]\eta = [\![e]\!]\eta$$

To define the semantic counterpart of the $\mathsf{primRec}_F$ operator, we first define a higher-order continuous function $\mathrm{primrec} : (D \to D \to D) \to (D \to D) \to D$ in the model. This is very similar to how one would define a generic $\mathsf{primRec}_F$ in Haskell using general recursion, albeit here in an untyped fashion.

$$
\begin{aligned}
&\mathrm{primrec}\ \mathit{fmap}\ f = \\
&\quad \mathsf{Lam}\ (\mathrm{fix}\ (\lambda g x.\ f\ (\mathit{fmap}\ (\mathsf{Lam}\ (\lambda x.\mathsf{Pair}\ (x, g\ x))))\ x))
\end{aligned}
$$

The first argument to primrec is intended to specify a functorial mapping function. For each of the syntactic types $\Delta; \Theta \vdash F : \mathtt{type}$ defined in Figure 1, we define a suitable $\mathrm{fmap}_{\mathrm{F}} : D^{|\Theta|} \to D \to D$, where $|\Theta|$ is the number of type variables in Θ. This definition is presented in Figure 5.

With these definitions we can define the interpretation of the syntactic $\mathsf{primRec}_F$ operator. Note that the syntactic type constructor F here always has exactly one free type variable, so $\mathrm{fmap}_{\mathrm{F}}$ has type $D \to D \to D$, as required by primrec.

$$
\begin{aligned}
&[\![\mathsf{primRec}_F\ f]\!]\eta = \\
&\quad \begin{cases} \mathrm{primrec}\ \mathrm{fmap}_{\mathrm{F}}\ d_f & \text{if } [\![f]\!]\eta = \mathsf{Lam}\ d_f \\ \bot & \text{otherwise} \end{cases}
\end{aligned}
$$

This completes the interpretation of the terms of our programming language in our untyped model. We now turn to the semantic meaning of types, with the aim of showing, in Section 3.5, that each well-typed term's interpretation is semantically well-typed.

3.2 Interpretation of clock variables

For a clock context Δ, we define $[\![\Delta]\!]$ to be the set of clock environments: mappings from the clock variables in Δ to the natural numbers. We use δ, δ' etc. to range over clock environments. For δ and δ' in $[\![\Delta]\!]$, we say that $\delta \sqsubseteq \delta'$ (in $[\![\Delta]\!]$) if for all $\kappa \in \Delta$,

$\delta(\kappa) \leq \delta'(\kappa)$. The intended interpretation of some $\delta \in [\![\Delta]\!]$ is that δ maps each clock κ in Δ to a natural number stating how much time that clock has left to run. The ordering $\delta \sqsubseteq \delta'$ indicates that the clocks in δ have at most as much time left as the clocks in δ'. We use the notation $\delta[\kappa \mapsto n]$ to denote the clock environment mapping κ to n and κ' to $\delta(\kappa')$ when $\kappa \neq \kappa'$.

3.3 Semantic types

We interpret types as $[\![\Delta]\!]$-indexed families of partial equivalence relations (PERs) over the semantic domain D. Recall that a PER on D is a binary relation on D that is symmetric and transitive, but not necessarily reflexive. Since PERs are binary relations, we will treat them as special subsets of the cartesian product $D \times D$. We write $\mathrm{PER}(D)$ for the set of all partial equivalence relations on D, and $\top_D$ for the PER $D \times D$. We require that our $[\![\Delta]\!]$-indexed families of PERs contravariantly respect the partial ordering on elements of $[\![\Delta]\!]$. This ensures that, as the time left to run on clocks increases, the semantic type becomes ever more precise. When we interpret clock quantification as intersection over all approximations, we capture the common core of all the approximations.

Formally, a semantic type for a clock context Δ is a function $A : [\![\Delta]\!] \to \mathrm{PER}(D)$, satisfying contravariant Kripke monotonicity: for all $\delta' \sqsubseteq \delta$, $A\delta \subseteq A\delta'$. We write $\mathrm{ClkPER}(\Delta)$ for the collection of all semantic types for the clock context Δ. In Section 4, we will formally consider morphisms between semantic types, and so turn each $\mathrm{ClkPER}(\Delta)$ into a category. Note that we do *not* require that any of our PERs are admissible. Admissible PERs always include the pair $(\bot, \bot)$, precisely the values we wish to exclude.

We now define semantic counterparts for each of the syntactic type constructors we presented in Section 2.1.

Unit, Product, Coproduct and Function Types The constructions for unit, product and coproduct types are straightforward. The unit type will be interpreted by a constant family of PERs:

$$1\delta = \{(\mathsf{Unit}, \mathsf{Unit})\}$$

This trivially satisfies Kripke monotonicity.

Given semantic types A and B, their product is defined to be

$$(A \times B)\delta = \left\{ \begin{array}{l} (\mathsf{Pair}(x, y), \mathsf{Pair}(x', y')) \\ \quad \mid (x, x') \in [\![A]\!]\delta \wedge (y, y') \in [\![B]\!]\delta \end{array} \right\}$$

and their coproduct is

$$(A + B)\delta = \begin{array}{c} \{(\mathsf{Inl}(x), \mathsf{Inl}(x')) \mid (x, x') \in [\![A]\!]\delta\} \\ \cup \\ \{(\mathsf{Inr}(y), \mathsf{Inr}(y')) \mid (y, y') \in [\![B]\!]\delta\} \end{array}$$

Since A and B are assumed to be semantic types, it immediately follows that $A \times B$ and $A + B$ are semantic types.

To interpret function types, we use the usual definition for Kripke-indexed logical relations, by quantifying over all smaller clock environments. Given semantic types A and B, we define:

$$(A \to B)\delta = \left\{ \begin{array}{l} (\mathsf{Lam}(f), \mathsf{Lam}(f')) \\ \quad \mid \forall \delta' \sqsubseteq \delta, (x, x') \in A\delta'. \, (fx, f'x') \in B\delta' \end{array} \right\}$$

It follows by the standard argument for Kripke logical relations that this family of PERs is contravariant in clock environments.

Guarded Modality Given a semantic type A, we define the semantic guard modality $\rhd^\kappa$ as follows, where κ is a member of the clock context Δ:

$$(\rhd^\kappa A)\delta = \begin{cases} \top_D & \text{if } \delta(\kappa) = 0 \\ A(\delta[\kappa \mapsto n]) & \text{if } \delta(\kappa) = n + 1 \end{cases}$$

The semantic type operator $\rhd^\kappa$ acts differently depending on the time remaining on the clock κ in the current clock environment δ. When the clock has run to zero, $\rhd^\kappa A$ becomes completely uninformative, equating all pairs of elements in the semantic domain D. If there is time remaining, then $\rhd^\kappa A$ equates a pair iff A would with one fewer steps remaining. For Kripke monotonicity, we want to prove that $(d, d') \in (\rhd^\kappa A)\delta$ implies $(d, d') \in (\rhd^\kappa A)\delta'$ when $\delta' \sqsubseteq \delta$. If $\delta'(\kappa) = 0$ then $(\rhd^\kappa A)\delta' = D \times D \ni (d, d')$. If $\delta'(\kappa) = n' + 1$ then $\delta(\kappa) = n + 1$ with $n' \leq n$. So $(d, d') \in A(\delta[\kappa \mapsto n])$, and so by A's Kripke monotonicity, $(d, d') \in A(\delta'[\kappa \mapsto n']) = (\rhd^\kappa A)\delta'$.

Clock Quantification The semantic counterpart of clock quantification takes us from semantic types in $\mathrm{ClkPER}(\Delta, \kappa)$ to semantic types in $\mathrm{ClkPER}(\Delta)$. Given a semantic type A in $\mathrm{ClkPER}(\Delta, \kappa)$, we define

$$\forall_\kappa A = \bigcap_{n \in \mathbb{N}} A(\delta[\kappa \mapsto n])$$

For Kripke monotonicity, if $(d, d') \in (\forall \kappa. A)\delta$ then $\forall n. \, (d, d') \in A(\delta[\kappa \mapsto n])$. Since A is a semantic type, $\forall n. \, (d, d') \in A(\delta'[\kappa \mapsto n])$, hence $(d, d') \in (\forall \kappa. A)\delta'$.

Complete Lattice Structure In order to define the semantic counterpart of the least fixpoint type operator, we make use of the lattice structure of $\mathrm{ClkPER}(\Delta)$. Given $A, B \in \mathrm{ClkPER}(\Delta)$, we define a partial order: $A \subseteq B$ if $\forall \delta. A\delta \subseteq B\delta$. It is easy to see that $\mathrm{ClkPER}(\Delta)$ is closed under arbitrary intersections, and so is a complete lattice.

Each of the semantic type constructors above is monotonic with respect to the partial order on $\mathrm{ClkPER}(\Delta)$ (with the obvious proviso that $A \to B$ is only monotonic in its second argument).

Least Fixpoint Types We make use of the Knaster-Tarski theorem [24] to produce the least fixpoint of a monotone function on $\mathrm{ClkPER}(\Delta)$. See Loader [17] for an similar usage in a setting without guarded recursion. Given a monotone function $F : \mathrm{ClkPER}(\Delta) \to \mathrm{ClkPER}(\Delta)$, we define:

$$(\mu F) = \bigcap \{A \in \mathrm{ClkPER}(\Delta) \mid FA \subseteq A\}$$

For any monotone F, μF is immediately a semantic type by construction, since semantic types are closed under intersection. As an initial step towards semantic type soundness for our calculus, we demonstrate a semantic well-typedness result for the primrec function we defined in Section 3.1.

Lemma 1. *Let $F : \mathrm{ClkPER}(\Delta) \to \mathrm{ClkPER}(\Delta)$ be a monotone function. Let* $\mathrm{fmap} : D \to D \to D$ *be such that for all $\delta \in [\![\Delta]\!]$, for all $A, B \in \mathrm{ClkPER}(\Delta)$, and for all $(g, g') \in (A \to B)\delta$ and $(x, x') \in FA\delta$, we have $(\mathrm{fmap}\ g\ x, \mathrm{fmap}\ g'\ x') \in FB\delta$. Then, for all $\delta \in [\![\Delta]\!]$ and for all $(f, f') \in (F(\mu F \times C) \to C)\delta$, where C is a semantic type, we have*

$$(\mathrm{primrec\ fmap}\ f, \mathrm{primrec\ fmap}\ f') \in (\mu F \to C)\delta$$

Proof. (Sketch) By induction on the least fixpoint $F(\mu F) = \mu F$, using the Knaster-Tarski theorem. □

This lemma only states that our semantic primrec recursion operator is semantically well-typed. We will show in Theorem 2 that primrec also witnesses μF as the carrier of the initial F-algebra, as we claimed in Section 1.4.

3.4 Interpretation of syntactic types

A well-formed type $\Delta; \Theta \vdash A : \texttt{type}$ is interpreted as monotonic function $[\![A]\!] : \mathrm{ClkPER}(\Delta)^{|\Theta|} \to \mathrm{ClkPER}(\Delta)$, where $|\Theta|$ denotes the number of type variables in Θ. The interpretation is defined in the clauses in Figure 6. These clauses make use of the constructions of semantic types defined in the previous subsection. In the clause for $\forall\kappa$, we make use of the "clock weakening" operator $-\!\uparrow_\kappa$ which takes a collection of semantic types in $\mathrm{ClkPER}(\Delta)^{|\Theta|}$ to semantic types in $\mathrm{ClkPER}(\Delta, \kappa)^{|\Theta|}$ by pointwise restriction of clock environments in $[\![\Delta, \kappa]\!]$ to clock environments in $[\![\Delta]\!]$.

$$
\begin{aligned}
[\![1]\!]\theta &= 1\\
[\![X]\!]\theta &= \theta(X)\\
[\![A\times B]\!]\theta &= [\![A]\!]\theta \times [\![B]\!]\theta\\
[\![A+B]\!]\theta &= [\![A]\!]\theta + [\![B]\!]\theta\\
[\![A\to B]\!]\theta &= [\![A]\!]\emptyset \to [\![B]\!]\theta\\
[\![\rhd^{\kappa} A]\!]\theta &= \rhd^{\kappa}([\![A]\!]\theta)\\
[\![\forall\kappa.A]\!]\theta &= \forall_{\kappa}([\![A]\!](\theta{\uparrow_{\kappa}}))\\
[\![\mu X.F]\!]\theta &= \mu(\lambda X.[\![F]\!](\theta, X))
\end{aligned}
$$

Figure 6. Interpretation of well-formed types

The next lemma states that syntactic substitution and semantic substitution commute. The proof is a straightforward induction on the well-formed type A. Note the side condition that $\kappa \notin fc(A)$, matching the side condition on the κ-APP typing rule.

Lemma 2. *Assume that $\Delta;\Theta \vdash A$: $\mathtt{type}$, $\kappa, \kappa' \in \Delta$ and $\kappa' \notin fc(A)$. Then for all $\delta \in [\![\Delta[\kappa \mapsto \kappa']]\!]$ and $\theta \in \mathrm{ClkPER}(\Delta)^{|\Theta|}$,*

$$[\![A]\!]\theta(\delta[\kappa \mapsto \delta(\kappa')]) = [\![A[\kappa \mapsto \kappa']]\!](\theta[\kappa \mapsto \kappa'])\delta.$$

The syntactic type equality judgement $\Delta;\Theta \vdash A \equiv B : \mathtt{type}$ that we defined in Section 2.2 is interpreted as equality of semantic types. The following lemma states that this interpretation is sound.

Lemma 3. *If $\Delta;\Theta \vdash A \equiv B : \mathtt{type}$ then for all $\theta \in \mathrm{ClkPER}(\Delta)^{|\Theta|}$, $[\![A]\!]\theta = [\![B]\!]\theta$.*

The next lemma states that we may use the semantic fmap_F functions defined in Figure 5 with the primrec operator, by showing that fmap_F always satisfies the hypotheses of Lemma 1.

Lemma 4. *For all $\Delta;\Theta \vdash F : \mathtt{type}$, the fmap_F defined in Figure 5 are all semantically well-typed: For all $\delta \in [\![\Delta]\!]$, for all $\overrightarrow{A, B} \in \mathrm{ClkPER}(\Delta)$, and for all $(g, g') \in \overrightarrow{(A \to B)\delta}$ and $(x, x') \in FA\delta$, we have $(\mathrm{fmap}_F\ \vec{g}\ x, \mathrm{fmap}_F\ \vec{g'}\ x') \in FB\delta$.*

It may seem that we could prove this lemma by using the syntactic definition of *fmap* from Figure 3 and then applying Theorem 1. However, the semantic well-typedness of our interpretation of primRec depends on the semantic well-typedness of fmap, so we must prove this lemma directly in the model to break the circularity.

3.5 Semantic type soundness

We now state our first main result: the semantic type soundness property of our system. To state this result, we define the semantic interpretation of contexts as a clock-environment indexed collection of PERs over environments:

$$[\![\Gamma]\!]\delta = \{(\eta, \eta') \mid \forall (x : A) \in \Gamma.\ (\eta(x), \eta'(x)) \in [\![A]\!]\delta\}$$

Theorem 1. *If $\Delta;\Gamma \vdash e : A$, then for all $\delta \in [\![\Delta]\!]$ and $(\eta, \eta') \in [\![\Gamma]\!]\delta$, $([\![e]\!]\eta, [\![e]\!]\eta') \in [\![A]\!]\delta$.*

Proof. (Sketch) By induction on the derivation of $\Delta;\Gamma \vdash e : A$. The most interesting cases are for **fix** and primRec. In essence, the case for **fix** goes through by induction on the value of the counter assigned to the clock variable κ in the current clock environment. The case for primRec is given by Lemma 1 and Lemma 4. □

Corollary 1. *If $-;- \vdash e : A$ then for all η, $[\![e]\!]\eta \neq \bot$.*

By this corollary, the denotation of a closed program is never $\bot$, so well-typed programs always yield a proper value. When the result type A is the stream type $\forall\kappa.\mu X.B \times \rhd^{\kappa} X$, we can deduce that the denotation of e will always be infinite streams of elements of B. We further elaborate this point in the next section, showing that this type is the carrier of the final $(B \times -)$-coalgebra.

4. Properties of fixpoint types

Using the denotational model of the previous section, we are now in a position to formally state and sketch the proofs of the properties of fixpoint types that we claimed in Section 1.4. Our claimed results are statements in category theoretic language about the initiality and finality of various (co)algebras. Therefore, we first construct suitable categories to work in.

Definition 1. *For each clock variable context Δ, the category $\mathrm{ClkPER}(\Delta)$ has as objects semantic types over Δ. Morphisms $f : A \to B$ are continuous functions $f : D \to D$ such that for all $\delta \in [\![\Delta]\!]$ and $(a, a') \in A\delta$, $(fa, fa') \in B\delta$ Two morphisms f, f' are considered equivalent if for all $\delta \in [\![\Delta]\!]$ and $(a, a') \in A\delta$, $(fa, f'a') \in B\delta$.*

Each well-typed term $\Delta; x : A \vdash e : B$ defines a morphism $[\![e]\!] : [\![A]\!] \to [\![B]\!]$ in $\mathrm{ClkPER}(\Delta)$. We can define equality between terms in our syntactic type system in terms of the equality on morphisms in this definition. Moreover, each well-formed type operator $\Delta; X \vdash F[X] : \mathtt{type}$ defines a (strong) realisable endofunctor on $\mathrm{ClkPER}(\Delta)$ that is monotonic on objects, using the semantic fmap_F defined in Figure 5 to define the action on morphisms. We have already checked (Lemma 4) that this is well-defined, and it is straightforward to check that the usual functor laws hold. In what follows, whenever we refer to an endofunctor on $\mathrm{ClkPER}(\Delta)$, we mean a realisable functor that is monotonic on objects, and we will use fmap_F to refer to the action of a functor F on morphisms.

Initial Algebras Recall that, for any functor F, an F-algebra is a pair of an object A and a morphism $k : FA \to A$. A homomorphism h between (A, k_A) and (B, k_B) is a morphism $h : A \to B$ such that $h \circ k_A = k_B \circ \mathit{fmap}_F\ h$. An *initial* F-algebra is an F-algebra (A, k_A) such that for any other F-algebra (B, k_B), there is a unique homomorphism $h : (A, k_A) \to (B, k_B)$.

Theorem 2. *If F is an endofunctor on $\mathrm{ClkPER}(\Delta)$, then μF is the carrier of an initial F-algebra.*

Proof. (Sketch) Since μF is a fixpoint of F, the morphism $F(\mu F) \to \mu F$ is simply realised by the identity map. Given any other F-algebra (B, k_B), define a morphism $\mu F \to B$ using the primrec operator from Lemma 1. Checking that this gives an F-algebra homomorphism is straightforward, proving uniqueness uses induction on elements of μF, by the Knaster-Tarski theorem. □

Guarded Final Co-Algebras Theorem 2 applies to all functors F, and in particular functors of the form $F(\rhd^{\kappa} -)$ on the category $\mathrm{ClkPER}(\Delta, \kappa)$. As well as $\mu(F(\rhd^{\kappa} -))$ being the carrier of an initial algebra, it is also the carrier of a final $F(\rhd^{\kappa} -)$-coalgebra.

Coalgebras are the formal dual of algebras: for an endofunctor F, an F-coalgebra is a pair of an object A and a morphism $k_A : A \to FA$. A homomorphism $h : (A, k_A) \to (B, k_B)$ of coalgebras is a morphism $h : A \to B$ such that $\mathit{fmap}_F\ h \circ k_A = k_B \circ h$. A *final* F-coalgebra is an F-coalgebra (B, k_B) such that for any other F-coalgebra (A, k_A), there is a unique F-coalgebra homomorphism unfold $k_A : (A, k_A) \to (B, k_B)$.

Theorem 3. *If F is an endofunctor on $\mathrm{ClkPER}(\Delta)$, then $\mu(F(\rhd^{\kappa} -))$ is the carrier of a final $F(\rhd^{\kappa} -)$-coalgebra in $\mathrm{ClkPER}(\Delta, \kappa)$.*

Proof. (Sketch) As for Theorem 2, since $\mu(F(\rhd^{\kappa} -))$ is a fixpoint of $F(\rhd^{\kappa} -)$, the morphism $\mu(F(\rhd^{\kappa} -)) \to F(\rhd^{\kappa}(\mu(F(\rhd^{\kappa} -))))$ is simply realised by the identity map. Given any other F-coalgebra (A, k_A), define a morphism unfold $k_A : A \to \mu(F(\rhd^{\kappa} -))$ as $\mathrm{fix}\ (\lambda g\ a.\ \mathrm{fmap}_F\ g\ (k_A\ a))$. It is straightforward to prove that this is an F-coalgebra homomorphism. Uniqueness is proved for each possible clock environment δ by induction on $\delta(\kappa)$. □

The syntactic counterpart of the construction we used in this proof is exactly the term we used in Section 1.4 for the definition of *unfold*. It is also easy to check that the term *deCons* we defined there is semantically equivalent to the identity. Therefore, Theorem 3 substantiates the claim we made in Section 1.4 that $\mu X.F[\triangleright^{\kappa} -]$ is the syntactic description of the carrier of a final $F[\triangleright^{\kappa} -]$-coalgebra.

Final Co-Algebras Theorem 3 gives final coalgebras in the categories $\text{ClkPER}(\Delta, \kappa)$, where we have a spare clock variable. By using clock quantification, we can close over this clock variable, and get the final F-coalgebra, not just the final $F(\triangleright^{\kappa} -)$-coalgebra.

Theorem 4. *For an endofunctor F on $\text{ClkPER}(\Delta)$, $\forall_{\kappa}.\mu(F(\triangleright^{\kappa} -))$ is the carrier of a final F-coalgebra in $\text{ClkPER}(\Delta)$.*

Proof. (Sketch) Almost identical to the proof for Theorem 3. □

This final theorem, along with the examples we presented in Section 2.5, substantiates our claim that the combination of clocks and guards that we have presented in this paper is a viable and comfortable setting in which to productively coprogram.

5. Conclusions and Further Work

We have presented a semantics for a small total calculus with primitive recursion for inductive data and a compositional treatment of corecursion, ensuring causality via the applicative structure of a *local* notion of time. In effect, we use time-based typing to grow a given total language, where all computation terminates within one 'day', into a larger total language, where additional recursion is justified clearly by the advancing clock. Functions from clocked inputs to clocked outputs enforce precise producer-consumer contracts—today's output must be computed only from today's input—documenting their utility as components of productive processes. Quantifying clock variables localises the time stream to a particular construction whose clients can then use it 'in the moment'. The method, made local, can be iterated, with inner clocks justifying the totality of computations within one 'day' of an outer clock.

At present, however, we have used local time only to justify productive corecursion, with only primitive recursion for inductive types. It seems pressing to ask whether local time might similarly liberalise termination checking, with a local clock measuring time into the past and ensuring that recursive calls receive old enough inputs that their outputs are ready when we need them. We are actively seeking a semantics for such a system, but it currently seems more difficult to pin down.

In due course, we should like to grow this experimental calculus to a full blown dependent type theory where (co)recursive constructions are checked to be total within nested local time streams, then exported to their clients without clocking. At least we have now established what local time streams are and how to extract productive processes from them.

Acknowledgements We would like to thank Lars Birkedal, Rasmus Møgelberg, and Paula Severi for extremely useful comments and discussions.

References

[1] A. Abel. Termination checking with types. *ITA*, 38(4):277–319, 2004.

[2] A. W. Appel and D. A. McAllester. An indexed model of recursive types for foundational proof-carrying code. *ACM Trans. Program. Lang. Syst.*, 23(5):657–683, 2001.

[3] R. S. Bird. Using Circular Programs to Eliminate Multiple Traversals of Data. *Acta Informatica*, 21:239–250, 1984.

[4] L. Birkedal and R. E. Møgelberg. Intensional type theory with guarded recursive types qua fixed points on universes. In *ACM/IEEE Symposium on Logic in Computer Science (LICS 2013)*, 2013.

[5] L. Birkedal, J. Schwinghammer, and K. Støvring. A metric model of guarded recursion. In *Presented at FICS 2010*, 2010.

[6] L. Birkedal, R. E. Møgelberg, J. Schwinghammer, and K. Støvring. First steps in synthetic guarded domain theory: step-indexing in the topos of trees. *Log. Meth. in Computer Science*, 8(4), 2012.

[7] V. Capretta. General recursion via coinductive types. *Log. Meth. in Computer Science*, 1(2), 2005.

[8] N. A. Danielsson. Beating the productivity checker using embedded languages. In *Workshop on Partiality and Recursion in Interactive Theorem Provers (PAR 2010)*, volume 43 of *EPTCS*, pages 29–48, 2010.

[9] N. A. Danielsson and T. Altenkirch. Mixing induction and coinduction. Draft, 2009.

[10] D. Dreyer, A. Ahmed, and L. Birkedal. Logical step-indexed logical relations. *Log. Meth. in Computer Science*, 7(2), 2011.

[11] N. Ghani, P. Hancock, and D. Pattinson. Representations of stream processors using nested fixed points. *Log. Meth. in Computer Science*, 5(3), 2009.

[12] E. Giménez. Codifying guarded definitions with recursive schemes. In *Types for Proofs and Programs, International Workshop TYPES'94*, volume 996 of *Lecture Notes in Computer Science*, pages 39–59, 1994.

[13] G. Hutton and M. Jaskelioff. Representing contractive functions on streams. Submitted, 2011.

[14] N. R. Krishnaswami and N. Benton. A semantic model for graphical user interfaces. In *ACM SIGPLAN international conference on Functional Programming, ICFP 2011*, pages 45–57, 2011.

[15] N. R. Krishnaswami and N. Benton. Ultrametric semantics of reactive programs. In *IEEE Symposium on Logic in Computer Science, LICS 2011*, pages 257–266, 2011.

[16] J. Launchbury and S. L. Peyton Jones. Lazy functional state threads. In *Proceedings of the ACM SIGPLAN'94 Conference on Programming Language Design and Implementation (PLDI)*, pages 24–35, 1994.

[17] R. Loader. Equational Theories for Inductive Types. *Annals of Pure and Applied Logic*, 84(2):175–217, 1997.

[18] C. McBride and R. Paterson. Applicative programming with effects. *J. Funct. Prog.*, 18(1):1–13, 2008.

[19] E. Moggi and A. Sabry. Monadic encapsulation of effects: a revised approach (extended version). *J. Funct. Prog.*, 11(6):591–627, 2001.

[20] H. Nakano. A modality for recursion. In *IEEE Symposium on Logic in Computer Science (LICS 2000)*, pages 255–266, 2000.

[21] A. M. Pitts. Computational adequacy via 'mixed' inductive definitions. In *Mathematical Foundations of Programming Semantics, Proc. 9th Int. Conf.*, volume 802 of *Lecture Notes in Computer Science*, pages 72–82. Springer-Verlag, Berlin, 1994.

[22] P. Severi and F.-J. de Vries. Pure type systems with corecursion on streams: from finite to infinitary normalisation. In *ACM SIGPLAN International Conference on Functional Programming, ICFP'12*, 2012.

[23] M. B. Smyth and G. D. Plotkin. The category-theoretic solution of recursive domain equations. *SIAM J. Comput.*, 11(4):761–783, 1982.

[24] A. Tarski. A lattice-theoretical fixpoint theorem and its applications. *Pacific Journal of Mathematics*, 5(2):285–309, 1955.

Unifying Structured Recursion Schemes

Ralf Hinze Nicolas Wu Jeremy Gibbons

Department of Computer Science, University of Oxford, Wolfson Building, Parks Road, Oxford, OX1 3QD, England

{ralf.hinze,nicolas.wu,jeremy.gibbons}@cs.ox.ac.uk

Abstract

Folds over inductive datatypes are well understood and widely used. In their plain form, they are quite restricted; but many disparate generalisations have been proposed that enjoy similar calculational benefits. There have also been attempts to unify the various generalisations: two prominent such unifications are the 'recursion schemes from comonads' of Uustalu, Vene and Pardo, and our own 'adjoint folds'. Until now, these two unified schemes have appeared incompatible. We show that this appearance is illusory: in fact, adjoint folds subsume recursion schemes from comonads. The proof of this claim involves standard constructions in category theory that are nevertheless not well known in functional programming: Eilenberg-Moore categories and bialgebras.

Categories and Subject Descriptors D.1.1 [*Programming Techniques*]: Applicative (Functional) Programming; D.3.2 [*Programming Languages*]: Language Classifications—applicative (functional) languages; F.3.2 [*Logics and Meanings of Programs*]: Semantics of Programming Languages—algebraic approaches to semantics

General Terms Languages; Theory; Verification

Keywords recursion schemes; adjunctions; comonads; bialgebras; distributive laws

1. Introduction

It has long been understood that explicit recursion is the 'goto' of pure functional programming [22], and should be considered harmful to program comprehension and analysis. Instead, structured recursion operators such as catamorphisms (folds) [10, 19] ought to be used wherever possible: they make termination manifest, and enjoy many useful calculational properties which would otherwise have to be established afresh for each new application.

However, catamorphisms are relatively restricted. There are many other structured patterns of recursion, equally harmless and worth capturing, that do not quite fit the scheme. Variations that have been proposed in the past include folds with parameters and accumulating folds [25], which may depend on constant or varying additional arguments; mutumorphisms [8], which are pairs of mutually recursive functions; zygomorphisms [18], which consist of a main recursive function and an auxiliary one on which it depends; paramorphisms [21], in which the body of structural recursion has access to immediate subterms as well as to their images under the recursion; histomorphisms [26], in which the body has access to the recursive images of all subterms, not just the immediate ones; and so-called generalised folds [4], which use polymorphic recursion to handle nested datatypes.

The many divergent generalisations of catamorphisms can be bewildering to the uninitiated, and there have been attempts to unify them. One approach is the identification of recursion schemes from comonads [30] (which we call 'rsfcs' for short). Comonads capture the general idea of 'evaluation in context' [27], and rsfcs make contextual information available to the body of the recursion. This pattern subsumes zygomorphisms and histomorphisms.

A more recent attempt [11] uses adjunctions as the common thread. Adjoint folds arise by inserting a left adjoint functor into the recursive characterisation, thereby adapting the form of the recursion; they subsume accumulating folds, mutumorphisms (and hence zygomorphisms), and generalised folds.

Given that adjoint folds and rsfcs cover some of the same examples, it seems reasonable to suspect a deeper relationship between them. That suspicion is strengthened by the observation that every adjunction induces a comonad, and every comonad can be factored into adjoint functors. And indeed, the suspicion turns out to be well founded. In this paper, we show that rsfcs are subsumed by adjoint folds. Moreover, although the converse does not hold, we identify those adjoint folds that correspond to rsfcs.

Technically speaking, our contributions are as follows:

- We provide a fresh account of adjoint folds, making essential use of liftings and conjugates. Very briefly, adjoint folds are parametrised by an adjunction $\mathsf{L} \dashv \mathsf{R}$ and a distributive law $\sigma : \mathsf{L} \circ \mathsf{D} \dot{\to} \mathsf{C} \circ \mathsf{L}$ that connects data structure to control structure.
- We show that that rsfcs [30] are subsumed by adjoint folds.
- We state precisely the relationship to the (type) fusion rule of categorical fixed-point calculus [1]. In essence, type fusion allows us to fuse an application of a left adjoint with an initial algebra to form another initial algebra, $\mathsf{L}\,(\mu\mathsf{C}) \cong \mu\mathsf{D}$, under the stronger assumption that σ is an isomorphism.
- We prove that adjoint folds can be framed as rsfcs, if a distributive isomorphism σ exists.

We dissect most of the proofs into two parts: first, we establish a bijection between certain arrows and homomorphisms; second, we instantiate the bijections to initial or free algebras.

The unified approach to recursion schemes is based on adjoint folds and unfolds, so no new theory is needed. This is good news indeed! The message of this paper is that the existing theory is more general than we anticipated. The unification is more than merely an intellectual curiosity: it promises concrete returns, too—for example, through general techniques for combining different recursion schemes (most functions actually use a combination of recursion schemes).

ICFP '13, September 25–27, 2013, Boston, MA, USA.

ACM 978-1-4503-2326-0/13/09...$15.00.
http://dx.doi.org/10.1145/2500365.2500578

Because of space limitations, we focus on algebras and inductive types; but everything dualises elegantly to a theory of adjoint unfolds [11] that subsumes patterns such as apomorphisms [31] and futumorphisms [26]; we return to this point in Section 9.

The paper is organised as follows: Section 2 presents a smörgåsbord of Haskell examples, which are picked up later; Section 3 summarises some of the theoretical background; Section 4 walks through a basic example of our unifying theory of adjoint folds, which is set out in Section 5; Section 6 shows that all rsfcs are adjoint folds, and Section 7 identifies those adjoint folds that are rsfcs; and finally, Section 8 discusses related work, and Section 9 concludes and points out directions for future work.

2. A Zoo of Morphisms

In this section we exhibit a number of specimens from the zoo of morphisms, which will serve to illustrate the theory that follows. We use Haskell as a lingua franca for codifying our categorical constructions as programs. However, throughout the paper we are careful to distinguish between inductive and coinductive types, which Haskell conflates.

Catamorphism The most basic recursion scheme is the *catamorphism*, known more colloquially as *fold*. A catamorphism decomposes an inductively defined structure, replacing each of the constructors with a provided argument. An example of this pattern is to compute the depth of a binary tree.

$$\begin{aligned}
&\mathbf{data}\ \mathit{Tree} = \mathit{Empty} \mid \mathit{Node}\ \mathit{Tree}\ \mathbb{N}\ \mathit{Tree}\\
&\mathit{depth} :: \mathit{Tree} \to \mathbb{N}\\
&\mathit{depth}\ (\mathit{Empty}) \quad = 0\\
&\mathit{depth}\ (\mathit{Node}\ l\ a\ r) = 1 + (\mathit{depth}\ l\ \text{`}\mathit{max}\text{`}\ \mathit{depth}\ r)
\end{aligned}$$

Folds with parameters Folds with constant parameters take an additional argument, on which results may depend. List concatenation is a canonical example:

$$\begin{aligned}
&\mathit{cat} :: ([a],[a]) \to [a]\\
&\mathit{cat}\ ([\,], \quad \mathit{ys}) = \mathit{ys}\\
&\mathit{cat}\ (x : \mathit{xs}, \mathit{ys}) = x : \mathit{cat}\ (\mathit{xs}, \mathit{ys}) \quad .
\end{aligned}$$

Here, the second component of the pair is the parameter; *cat* is not just a fold because the pair argument is not of an an inductive type.

In folds with accumulating parameters, the additional argument may vary in recursive calls. Haskell's *foldl* is an example. More interesting examples are provided by downwards accumulations on trees [9]; for example, replacing every element with its depth (if the accumulator is initialised to 0):

$$\begin{aligned}
&\mathit{depths} :: (\mathit{Tree}, \mathbb{N}) \to \mathit{Tree}\\
&\mathit{depths}\ (\mathit{Empty}, \quad n) = \mathit{Empty}\\
&\mathit{depths}\ (\mathit{Node}\ l\ a\ r, n) = \mathit{Node}\ (\mathit{depths}\ (l, n{+}1))\ n\ (\mathit{depths}\ (r, n{+}1)) \quad .
\end{aligned}$$

This is a rather simple example; in general, the accumulating parameter will vary in different ways in different branches.

Paramorphism The *paramorphism* models primitive recursion: the body has access not only to the results of recursive calls, but also to the substructures on which these calls are made. An example of a paramorphism is counting the words in a string:

$$\begin{aligned}
&\mathit{wc} :: [\mathit{Char}] \to \mathit{Int}\\
&\mathit{wc}\ [\,] = 0\\
&\mathit{wc}\ (c : \mathit{cs})\\
&\quad \mid \neg\,(\mathit{isSpace}\ c) \wedge (\mathit{null}\ \mathit{cs} \vee \mathit{isSpace}\ (\mathit{head}\ \mathit{cs})) = \mathit{wc}\ \mathit{cs} + 1\\
&\quad \mid \mathit{otherwise} \qquad\qquad\qquad\qquad\qquad\quad = \mathit{wc}\ \mathit{cs} \quad .
\end{aligned}$$

Note that in the clause for non-empty lists, the result depends not only on a recursive call *wc cs* on the substructure, but also on the substructure *cs* itself.

Zygomorphism A variation is the *zygomorphism*, where the recursion is aided by an auxiliary function:

$$\begin{aligned}
&\mathit{perfect} :: \mathit{Tree} \to \mathbb{B}\\
&\mathit{perfect}\ \mathit{Empty} \qquad = \mathit{True}\\
&\mathit{perfect}\ (\mathit{Node}\ l\ a\ r) = \mathit{perfect}\ l \wedge \mathit{perfect}\ r \wedge (\mathit{depth}\ l == \mathit{depth}\ r) \quad .
\end{aligned}$$

The function *perfect* is not a simple fold, since it relies on an auxiliary traversal of the tree structure using *depth*.

Mutumorphism A *mutumorphism* generalises the idea of a zygomorphism, allowing the recursive functions to rely mutually on one another. For example, consider the *odd* and *even* functions:

$$\begin{aligned}
&\mathit{odd} :: \mathbb{N} \to \mathbb{B} &&\mathit{even} :: \mathbb{N} \to \mathbb{B}\\
&\mathit{odd}\ 0 \qquad = \mathit{False} &&\mathit{even}\ 0 \qquad = \mathit{True}\\
&\mathit{odd}\ (n+1) = \mathit{even}\ n &&\mathit{even}\ (n+1) = \mathit{odd}\ n \quad .
\end{aligned}$$

Here, the functions work as a pair in tandem as they recurse through the structure of natural numbers.

Nested datatypes Functions over nested datatypes such as perfect trees or random-access lists have to deal with the polymorphic recursion. For example, consider summing a perfect tree of numbers:

$$\begin{aligned}
&\mathbf{data}\ \mathit{Perfect}\ a = \mathit{Zero}\ a \mid \mathit{Succ}\ (\mathit{Perfect}\ (a,a))\\
&\mathbf{instance}\ \mathit{Functor}\ \mathit{Perfect}\ \mathbf{where}\\
&\quad \mathit{fmap}\ f\ (\mathit{Zero}\ a) = \mathit{Zero}\ (f\ a)\\
&\quad \mathit{fmap}\ f\ (\mathit{Succ}\ p) = \mathit{Succ}\ (\mathit{fmap}\ (\lambda\,(x,y) \to (f\,x, f\,y))\ p)\\
&\mathit{total} :: \mathit{Perfect}\ \mathbb{N} \to \mathbb{N}\\
&\mathit{total}\ (\mathit{Zero}\ n) = \quad n\\
&\mathit{total}\ (\mathit{Succ}\ p) = \quad \mathit{total}\ (\mathit{fmap}\ (\lambda\,(a,b) \to a+b)\ p) \quad .
\end{aligned}$$

This is not a straightforward fold, because the recursive call of *total* is not applied directly to a subterm—indeed, it cannot be so applied, because the subterm p of *Succ p* has type *Perfect* $(\mathbb{N},\mathbb{N})$ rather than *Perfect* $\mathbb{N}$.

Histomorphism Histomorphisms capture tabulation, as used in dynamic programming. For example, consider the unbounded knapsack problem: given an integer capacity c, and as many copies as needed of each of a collection of items (w_i, v_i) with *positive* integer weight w_i and value v_i, compute the maximum value that will fit in the knapsack. Thus, given capacity 15 and items $[(12,4),(1,2),(2,2),(1,1),(4,10)]$, the maximum value possible is 36, using three copies each of the second and fifth items.

The naive recursive solution takes exponential time (we suppose here that the maximum value of the empty list of candidate solutions is zero):

$$\begin{aligned}
&\mathit{knapsack} :: [(\mathbb{N},\mathbb{R})] \to \mathbb{N} \to \mathbb{R}\\
&\mathit{knapsack}\ \mathit{wvs}\ c\\
&\quad = \mathit{maximum}\ [v + \mathit{knapsack}\ \mathit{wvs}\ (c{-}w) \mid (w,v) \leftarrow \mathit{wvs}, w \leqslant c] \quad .
\end{aligned}$$

However, by tabulating the results for each capacity in $0\,..\,c$, one can compute the answer in pseudo-polynomial time:

$$\begin{aligned}
&\mathit{knapsack}\ \mathit{wvs}\ c = \mathit{table}\ !!\ c\ \mathbf{where}\\
&\quad \mathit{table} = [\mathit{ks}\ i \mid i \leftarrow [0\,..\,c]]\\
&\quad \mathit{ks}\ i \quad = \mathit{maximum}\ [v + \mathit{table}\ !!\ (i{-}w) \mid (w,v) \leftarrow \mathit{wvs}, w \leqslant i] \quad .
\end{aligned}$$

Lazy evaluation works out the data dependencies automatically; but each element of the table depends only on elements with lower indices, so even without lazy evaluation it suffices to fill the table in index order.

Now, the general question is whether the recursion equations above have unique solutions? The answer is yes for all of them. However, up to now the proofs involved two seemingly incompatible techniques: most of the examples can be identified as adjoint folds; some of them (in particular *knapsack*) are subsumed by recursion schemes from comonads. Before we show how to unify the two approaches, we first need to introduce a bit of theory.

3. Background

This paper assumes a basic knowledge of category theory, in that the reader should be familiar with the notions of functors, natural transformations, and product and functor categories. In this section we fix the notation and establish categorical concepts that will be used in the remainder of the paper. For the most part this material is standard and can safely be glossed over on an initial reading. An exception is perhaps the material on functor squares and conjugates, which will need particular attention.

3.1 Functor Squares

A *functor square* consists of four functors and a natural transformation between them (to read off the type of λ, it might help to tilt your head 45° to the left when looking at this diagram):

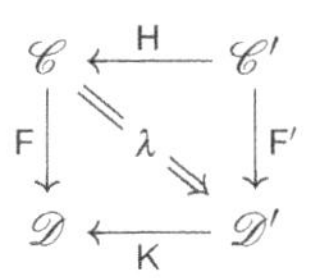

$$\lambda : \mathsf{F} \circ \mathsf{H} \dot{\to} \mathsf{K} \circ \mathsf{F}' \ .$$

For brevity, we call λ a *distributive law*, even though the name is traditionally used for the special case in which opposite functors are comonads or monads. Functor squares can be horizontally (and also vertically, not shown below) composed:

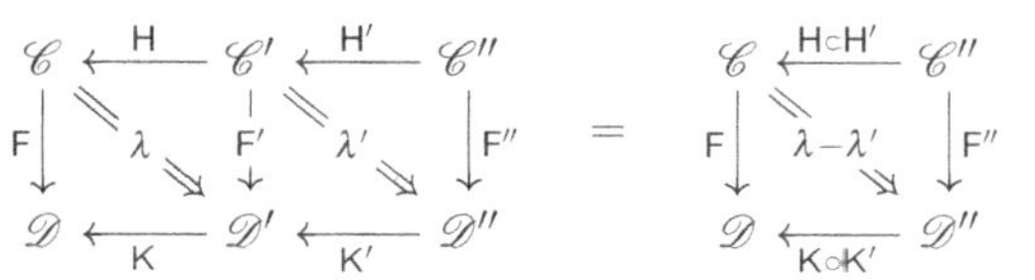

where the horizontal composition $\lambda - \lambda'$ of the distributive laws λ and λ' is given by a combination of horizontal ($\circ$) and vertical ($\cdot$) composition of natural transformations ($\circ$ binds tighter than $\cdot$):

$$\lambda - \lambda' = \mathsf{K} \circ \lambda' \cdot \lambda \circ \mathsf{H}' \ .$$

This composition is associative, with $id_{\mathsf{F}} : \mathsf{F} \circ \mathsf{Id} \dot{\to} \mathsf{Id} \circ \mathsf{F}$ as its neutral element.

3.2 Algebras and Coalgebras

Algebras and coalgebras form the basis for the categorical description of structured recursion schemes.

Given an endofunctor $\mathsf{F} : \mathscr{C} \to \mathscr{C}$, an F-algebra is a pair (a, A), where $a : \mathsf{F}\, A \to A$ is an arrow and $A : \mathscr{C}$ is an object, which are known as the *action* and *carrier* of the algebra. (We deviate a little from the standard notation (A, a), in order to have a syntax that distinguishes algebras from coalgebras.) Since the action determines its carrier, it is often used by itself to refer to the F-algebra. An F-homomorphism between algebras (a, A) and (b, B) is an arrow $h : A \to B : \mathscr{C}$ such that $h \cdot a = b \cdot \mathsf{F}\, h$.

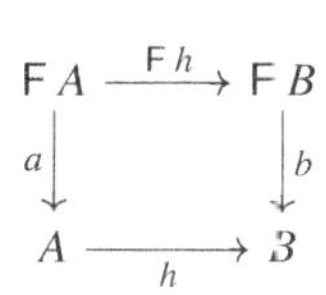

Clearly, F-homomorphisms compose and have an identity, so it follows that F-algebras and F-homomorphisms form a category, which we call F-$\mathbf{Alg}(\mathscr{C})$. The initial object of this category, if it exists, is given by $(in, \mu\mathsf{F})$ and called the *initial* F*-algebra*. The initiality implies that to each F-algebra, (a, A), there exists a unique F-homomorphism, $(\!|a|\!) : (in, \mu\mathsf{F}) \to (a, A)$, called a *fold*. The algebra *in* is, in fact, an isomorphism, so $\mu\mathsf{F}$ is a fixed-point of F (the least fixed-point), a fact known as Lambek's lemma.

Example 3.1. The semantics of the inductive datatype *Tree* is given by the initial algebra $\mu\mathsf{Tree}$, where the so-called *base functor*

$$\textbf{data}\ \mathsf{Tree}\ \mathit{tree} = \mathsf{Empty} \mid \mathsf{Node}\ \mathit{tree}\ \mathbb{N}\ \mathit{tree}$$

abstracts away from the recursive occurrences of *Tree*. The Haskell rendering of the isomorphism *in*, the action of the initial algebra,

$$\begin{aligned} & in :: \mathsf{Tree}\ \mathit{Tree} \to \mathit{Tree} \\ & in\ (\mathsf{Empty}) \quad\ \ = \mathit{Empty} \\ & in\ (\mathsf{Node}\ l\ a\ r) = \mathit{Node}\ l\ a\ r \end{aligned}$$

amounts to a simple renaming of constructors. □

Dually, given an endofunctor $\mathsf{G} : \mathscr{C} \to \mathscr{C}$, a G-coalgebra is a pair (C, c), where $C : \mathscr{C}$ is the carrier and $c : C \to \mathsf{G}\, C$ is the action of the coalgebra. A G-homomorphism between coalgebras (C, c) and (D, d) is an arrow $h : C \to D : \mathscr{C}$ that satisfies $\mathsf{G}\, h \cdot c = d \cdot h$. Just as before, a category G-$\mathbf{Coalg}(\mathscr{C})$ can be formed from G-coalgebras and G-homomorphisms. The final object of this category, if it exists, is given by $(\nu\mathsf{G}, out)$ and called the *final* G*-coalgebra*.

The category F-$\mathbf{Alg}(\mathscr{C})$ has more structure than $\mathscr{C}$. The forgetful or underlying functor $\mathsf{U}^{\mathsf{F}} : \mathsf{F}\text{-}\mathbf{Alg}(\mathscr{C}) \to \mathscr{C}$ forgets about the additional structure: $\mathsf{U}^{\mathsf{F}}\ (a, A) = A$ and $\mathsf{U}^{\mathsf{F}}\ h = h$. An analogous functor can be defined for coalgebras: $\mathsf{U}_{\mathsf{G}} : \mathsf{G}\text{-}\mathbf{Coalg}(\mathscr{C}) \to \mathscr{C}$.

Liftings and coliftings A functor $\bar{\mathsf{H}} : \mathsf{F}\text{-}\mathbf{Alg}(\mathscr{C}) \to \mathsf{G}\text{-}\mathbf{Alg}(\mathscr{D})$ is called a *lifting* of $\mathsf{H} : \mathscr{C} \to \mathscr{D}$ iff $\mathsf{H} \circ \mathsf{U}^{\mathsf{F}} = \mathsf{U}^{\mathsf{G}} \circ \bar{\mathsf{H}}$. Given a distributive law $\lambda : \mathsf{H} \circ \mathsf{F} \dot{\leftarrow} \mathsf{G} \circ \mathsf{H}$, we can define a lifting as follows:

$$\mathsf{H}^{\lambda}\ (a, A) = (\mathsf{H}\, a \cdot \lambda\, A, \mathsf{H}\, A) \ , \tag{3.1a}$$

$$\mathsf{H}^{\lambda}\ h = \mathsf{H}\, h \ . \tag{3.1b}$$

For liftings, the action on the carrier and on homomorphisms is fixed; the action on the algebra is determined by the distributive law. Liftings of the identity functor, that is, $\mathsf{H} = \mathsf{Id}$ and $\lambda = \alpha : \mathsf{F} \dot{\leftarrow} \mathsf{G}$, are often written as α-$\mathbf{Alg}(\mathscr{C}) : \mathsf{F}\text{-}\mathbf{Alg}(\mathscr{C}) \to \mathsf{G}\text{-}\mathbf{Alg}(\mathscr{C})$. Liftings compose in an attractive way: $\mathsf{H}^{\lambda} \circ \mathsf{H}'^{\lambda'} = (\mathsf{H} \circ \mathsf{H}')^{\lambda - \lambda'}$.

Since we use the action of an algebra to refer to the algebra itself, we often abbreviate $\mathsf{H}\, a \cdot \lambda\, A$ by $\mathsf{H}^{\lambda}\ a$.

Dually, $\underline{\mathsf{H}} : \mathsf{F}\text{-}\mathbf{Coalg}(\mathscr{C}) \to \mathsf{G}\text{-}\mathbf{Coalg}(\mathscr{D})$ is a colifting of $\mathsf{H} : \mathscr{C} \to \mathscr{D}$ iff $\mathsf{U}_{\mathsf{G}} \circ \underline{\mathsf{H}} = \mathsf{H} \circ \mathsf{U}_{\mathsf{F}}$. Given $\lambda : \mathsf{H} \circ \mathsf{F} \dot{\to} \mathsf{G} \circ \mathsf{H}$ we can define a colifting as follows:

$$\mathsf{H}_{\lambda}\ (C, c) = (\mathsf{H}\, C, \lambda\, C \cdot \mathsf{H}\, c) \ , \tag{3.2a}$$

$$\mathsf{H}_{\lambda}\ h = \mathsf{H}\, h \ . \tag{3.2b}$$

3.3 Adjunctions

Adjunctions were introduced by Kan [14] and are so pervasive in the study of category theory that Mac Lane [17, p.vii] noted "Adjoint functors arise everywhere." Our work supports this view: adjunctions provide a unified framework for program transformation.

Given categories $\mathscr{C}, \mathscr{D}$, we say that functors $\mathsf{L} : \mathscr{C} \leftarrow \mathscr{D}$ and $\mathsf{R} : \mathscr{C} \to \mathscr{D}$ form an adjunction, written $\mathsf{L} \dashv \mathsf{R} : \mathscr{C} \rightharpoonup \mathscr{D}$ or

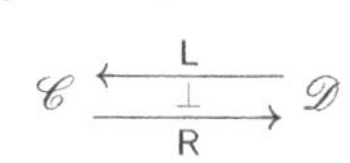

iff there is a bijection between the sets of arrows

$$\lfloor - \rfloor : \mathscr{C}(\mathsf{L}\, A, B) \cong \mathscr{D}(A, \mathsf{R}\, B) : \lceil - \rceil$$

that is natural both in A and B. We say that L is a *left adjoint* for R, and R a *right adjoint* for L; the isomorphism $\lfloor - \rfloor$ is called the *left adjunct*, and its inverse $\lceil - \rceil$ the *right adjunct*. The arrows $\lfloor f \rfloor$ and $\lceil g \rceil$ are also called the *transposes* of f and g.

That the adjuncts $\lfloor - \rfloor$ and $\lceil - \rceil$ are mutually inverse can be captured using an equivalence:

$$f = \lceil g \rceil \iff \lfloor f \rfloor = g \ , \tag{3.3}$$

for all $f : \mathsf{L}\,A \to B : \mathscr{C}$ and $g : A \to \mathsf{R}\,B : \mathscr{D}$. The naturality properties of the adjuncts can be expressed as fusion laws.

$$\mathsf{R}\,k \cdot \lfloor f \rfloor \cdot h = \lfloor k \cdot f \cdot \mathsf{L}\,h \rfloor \qquad (3.4a)$$

$$k \cdot \lceil g \rceil \cdot \mathsf{L}\,h = \lceil \mathsf{R}\,k \cdot g \cdot h \rceil \qquad (3.4b)$$

These equations imply that the adjuncts are uniquely defined by their actions on the identity: $\mathsf{R}\,k \cdot \lfloor id \rfloor = \lfloor k \rfloor$ and $\lceil id \rceil \cdot \mathsf{L}\,h = \lceil h \rceil$. An alternative definition of adjunctions is based on the two natural transformations $\epsilon = \lceil id \rceil$ and $\eta = \lfloor id \rfloor$, which are called the *counit* $\epsilon : \mathsf{L} \circ \mathsf{R} \dot{\to} \mathsf{Id}$ and the *unit* $\eta : \mathsf{Id} \dot{\to} \mathsf{R} \circ \mathsf{L}$ of the adjunction. The equivalence (3.3) can also be framed in terms of the units:

$$f = \epsilon\,B \cdot \mathsf{L}\,g \iff \mathsf{R}\,f \cdot \eta\,A = g \ . \qquad (3.5)$$

Adjunctions satisfy a wealth of properties. An important property is that adjoint functors are uniquely defined up to isomorphism: if $\mathsf{L}_1 \dashv \mathsf{R}_1$ and $\mathsf{L}_2 \dashv \mathsf{R}_2$, then

$$\mathsf{L}_2 \cong \mathsf{L}_1 \iff \mathsf{R}_1 \cong \mathsf{R}_2 \ . \qquad (3.6)$$

This equivalence can be used as a reasoning principle: often one isomorphism is trivial and can be used to establish the other.

Left adjoints preserve initial objects, $\mathsf{L}\,0 \cong 0$. Dually, right adjoints preserve final objects, $\mathsf{R}\,1 \cong 1$. In general, left adjoints preserve colimits (LAPC) and right adjoints preserve limits (RAPL).

Example 3.2. Coproducts and products arise as left and right adjoints $(+) \dashv \Delta \dashv (\times)$ of the diagonal functor $\Delta : \mathscr{C} \to \mathscr{C} \times \mathscr{C}$ defined by $\Delta\,A = (A, A)$ and $\Delta f = (f, f)$.

The bijections express that pairs of arrows with the same source (respectively, target) are in one-to-one correspondence with arrows to a product (respectively, from a coproduct). In the case of products, the left adjunct $\lfloor (f_1, f_2) \rfloor = f_1 \vartriangle f_2$ is known as the 'split' combinator, and the counit $\epsilon = (outl, outr)$ arises from the projections. □

Example 3.3. Perhaps the best-known example of an adjunction is currying: a function of two arguments can be treated as a function of the first argument whose values are functions of the second.

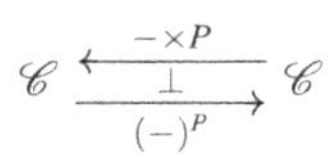

The right adjoint of pairing with P is the exponential from P. □

Example 3.4. For a signature expressed as a functor F, the terms involving variables of type A constitute the free algebra $\mathsf{Free}^{\mathsf{F}}\,A$ on A. The functor $\mathsf{Free}^{\mathsf{F}} : \mathscr{C} \to \mathsf{F}\text{-}\mathbf{Alg}(\mathscr{C})$ arises as the left adjoint of the forgetful functor U^{F}. Dually, cofree G-coalgebras arise as the right adjoint of U_{G}.

The first bijection expresses that the compositional evaluation of a term is uniquely determined by the action on variables. Initial algebras and final coalgebras arise as special cases (LAPC and RAPL): $(in, \mu\mathsf{F}) \cong \mathsf{Free}^{\mathsf{F}}\,0$ (closed terms as open terms where the variables are drawn from 0) and $(\nu\mathsf{G}, out) \cong \mathsf{Cofree}_{\mathsf{G}}\,1$. □

Adjunctions can be lifted to functor categories: $\mathsf{L} \dashv \mathsf{R}$ implies both $\mathsf{L} \circ - \dashv \mathsf{R} \circ -$ and $- \circ \mathsf{R} \dashv - \circ \mathsf{L}$. The latter adjunctions capture the following bijections between natural transformations:

$$\mathscr{C}^{\mathscr{X}}(\mathsf{L} \circ \mathsf{F}, \mathsf{G}) \cong \mathscr{D}^{\mathscr{X}}(\mathsf{F}, \mathsf{R} \circ \mathsf{G}) \ , \qquad (3.7a)$$

$$\mathscr{X}^{\mathscr{C}}(\mathsf{F} \circ \mathsf{R}, \mathsf{G}) \cong \mathscr{X}^{\mathscr{D}}(\mathsf{F}, \mathsf{G} \circ \mathsf{L}) \ . \qquad (3.7b)$$

Conjugates Next we introduce a concept that will be at the heart of our framework. Just as natural transformations relate functors, conjugates relate adjoint pairs of functors. Given the adjunctions $\mathsf{L} \dashv \mathsf{R} : \mathscr{C} \rightharpoonup \mathscr{D}$ and $\mathsf{L}' \dashv \mathsf{R}' : \mathscr{C}' \rightharpoonup \mathscr{D}'$, and functors $\mathsf{H} : \mathscr{C} \to \mathscr{C}'$ and $\mathsf{K} : \mathscr{D} \to \mathscr{D}'$, the distributive laws $\sigma : \mathsf{L}' \circ \mathsf{K} \dot{\to} \mathsf{H} \circ \mathsf{L}$ and $\tau : \mathsf{K} \circ \mathsf{R} \dot{\to} \mathsf{R}' \circ \mathsf{H}$ are *conjugates*, written $\sigma \dashv \tau$, if one of the following conditions holds

$$\lfloor \mathsf{H}\,f \cdot \sigma\,A \rfloor' = \tau\,B \cdot \mathsf{K}\,\lfloor f \rfloor \ , \qquad (3.8a)$$

$$\mathsf{H}\,\lceil g \rceil \cdot \sigma\,A = \lceil \tau\,B \cdot \mathsf{K}\,g \rceil' \ , \qquad (3.8b)$$

for all $f : \mathsf{L}\,A \to B : \mathscr{C}$ and $g : A \to \mathsf{R}\,B : \mathscr{D}$. The equivalence of the two conditions is a consequence of (3.7). In fact, each natural transformation uniquely determines the other:

$$\sigma\,A = \lceil \tau\,(\mathsf{L}\,A) \cdot \mathsf{K}\,(\eta\,A) \rceil' \ , \qquad (3.9a)$$

$$\tau\,B = \lfloor \mathsf{H}\,(\epsilon\,B) \cdot \sigma\,(\mathsf{R}\,B) \rfloor' \ . \qquad (3.9b)$$

We obtain two distributive laws for the price of one; this fact will be used a lot. The following diagrams record the types.

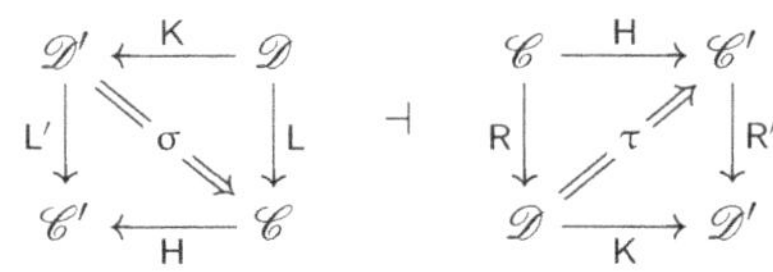

(As an aside, the data—the functors H and K and the laws σ and τ—are also called an *adjoint square*, a pair of functor squares, from $\mathsf{L} \dashv \mathsf{R}$ to $\mathsf{L}' \dashv \mathsf{R}'$. Above, we have taken the first steps towards defining the *double* category of adjoint squares [24].)

Example 3.5. A lifting $\bar{\mathsf{H}}$ provides an important example of a conjugate between categories of algebras where the second transformation $\tau : \mathsf{H} \circ \mathsf{U}^{\mathsf{F}} = \mathsf{U}^{\mathsf{G}} \circ \bar{\mathsf{H}}$ is manifestly the identity. □

4. Warm-up: An Easy Instance of Adjoint Folds

Before we introduce the unified framework, it is instructive to walk through a specific instance. In Section 2 we have discussed that functions defined by mutual recursion, *mutumorphisms*, are not simple folds. They are, however, in one-to-one correspondence with folds. Mutumorphisms are captured by the following scheme:

$$x_1 \cdot in = b_1 \cdot \mathsf{D}\,(x_1 \vartriangle x_2) \quad \text{and} \quad x_2 \cdot in = b_2 \cdot \mathsf{D}\,(x_1 \vartriangle x_2) \ .$$

The split combinator makes the results of both recursive calls available to the 'algebras' $b_i : \mathsf{D}\,(B_1 \times B_2) \to B_i$. Think of $x_i : \mu\mathsf{D} \to B_i$ as unknowns; we aim to show that they are uniquely determined by the two equations. We proceed in two steps:

First, we abstract away from the initial algebra $(in, \mu\mathsf{D})$, generalising to an arbitrary D-algebra (a, A), and turn the two equations into a form we can work with. Product categories provide a natural setting, simply because we have two equations. (Recall that split $\vartriangle$ is the left adjunct of $\Delta \dashv (\times)$, see Example 3.2.)

$$
\begin{aligned}
& x_1 \cdot a = b_1 \cdot \mathsf{D}\,(x_1 \vartriangle x_2) \quad \text{and} \quad x_2 \cdot a = b_2 \cdot \mathsf{D}\,(x_1 \vartriangle x_2) \\
\iff & \quad \{ \text{ product category } \mathscr{C} \times \mathscr{C} \ \} \\
& (x_1, x_2) \cdot (a, a) = (b_1, b_2) \cdot (\mathsf{D}\,(x_1 \vartriangle x_2), \mathsf{D}\,(x_1 \vartriangle x_2)) \\
\iff & \quad \{ \text{ definition of } \Delta \text{ and definition of } \lfloor - \rfloor \ \} \\
& (x_1, x_2) \cdot \Delta\,a = (b_1, b_2) \cdot \Delta\,(\mathsf{D}\,\lfloor (x_1, x_2) \rfloor) \\
\iff & \quad \{ \text{ set } x := (x_1, x_2) \text{ and } b := (b_1, b_2) \ \} \\
& x \cdot \Delta\,a = b \cdot \Delta\,(\mathsf{D}\,\lfloor x \rfloor)
\end{aligned}
$$

We obtain a single equation, where the algebra a is wrapped in a left adjoint. From here, a short calculation demonstrates that the transpose of x is a homomorphism:

$$\begin{array}{ll} & x \cdot \Delta a = b \cdot \Delta\,(\mathsf{D}\,\lfloor x \rfloor) \ : \ \Delta\,(\mathsf{D}\,A) \to B \\ \iff & \{\ \lfloor - \rfloor \text{ and } \lceil - \rceil \text{ are isomorphisms (3.3)}\ \} \\ & \lfloor x \cdot \Delta a \rfloor = \lfloor b \cdot \Delta\,(\mathsf{D}\,\lfloor x \rfloor)\rfloor \\ \iff & \{\ \lfloor - \rfloor \text{ is natural (3.4a)}\ \} \\ & \lfloor x \rfloor \cdot a = \lfloor b \rfloor \cdot \mathsf{D}\,\lfloor x \rfloor \ : \ \mathsf{D}\,A \to (\times)\,B\ . \end{array}$$

Thus, $\lfloor x \rfloor$ is a D-homomorphism, and so x is the transpose of a D-homomorphism. Furthermore, b is the transpose of a D-algebra—this is an important observation. Let us record the correspondence (note that B is an object of $\mathscr{C} \times \mathscr{C}$, that is, a pair of objects in $\mathscr{C}$, and recall that $\lfloor x \rfloor = x_1 \vartriangle x_2$).

$$\begin{array}{ccc} \Delta\,(\mathsf{D}\,A) & \xrightarrow{\Delta\,(\mathsf{D}\,\lfloor x \rfloor)} & \Delta\,(\mathsf{D}\,((\times)\,B)) \\ \Delta a \downarrow & & \downarrow b \\ \Delta A & \xrightarrow[x]{} & B \end{array} \quad \iff \quad \begin{array}{ccc} \mathsf{D}\,A & \xrightarrow{\mathsf{D}\,\lfloor x \rfloor} & \mathsf{D}\,((\times)\,B) \\ a \downarrow & & \downarrow \lfloor b \rfloor \\ A & \xrightarrow[\lfloor x \rfloor]{} & (\times)\,B \end{array}$$

Second, we instantiate (a, A) to the initial algebra $(in, \mu\mathsf{D})$. The solution of the original pair of equations is then given by

$$x_1 \vartriangle x_2 = (\!|b_1 \vartriangle b_2|\!)\ ,$$

which is Fokkinga's mutu-CHARN law [7].

Several special cases are worth singling out. If x_2 does not depend on x_1, we obtain *zygomorphisms* (ie $b_2 := b \cdot \mathsf{D}\ outr$ and consequently $x_2 := (\!|b|\!)$). Further, when b_2 is the identity, the zygomorphism specialises to a paramorphism (ie $b_2 := in \cdot \mathsf{D}\ outr$ and consequently $x_2 := (\!|in|\!) = id$). Pushing this to the extreme, if we have two independent homomorphisms (ie $b_1 := b_1 \cdot \mathsf{D}\ outl$ and $b_2 := b_2 \cdot \mathsf{D}\ outr$ and consequently $x_1 = (\!|b_1|\!)$ and $x_2 = (\!|b_2|\!)$), we derive the *banana-split law* [3], an important program optimisation that replaces a double tree traversal by a single one.

$$(\!|b_1|\!) \vartriangle (\!|b_2|\!) = (\!|b_1 \cdot \mathsf{D}\ outl \vartriangle b_2 \cdot \mathsf{D}\ outr|\!) \qquad (4.1)$$

The law can also be justified in a different way: $(\!|b_1|\!) \vartriangle (\!|b_2|\!)$ is the unique homomorphism *to a product algebra*:

$$(b_1, B_1) \times (b_2, B_2) = (b_1 \cdot \mathsf{D}\ outl \vartriangle b_2 \cdot \mathsf{D}\ outr, B_1 \times B_2)\ .$$

We shall see later that this is not just a lucky coincidence.

5. A Unified Framework for Recursion Schemes

This section introduces the promised unifying theory for recursion schemes. As noted in the introduction, the unifying concept, called *generalised iteration* in [20] and *adjoint fold* in [11], is not new. (So no new theory is needed, which is good.) What is novel is the presentation, which makes essential use of conjugate pairs of distributive laws and liftings, rendering the proofs concise and elegant. However, since the concepts from category theory are perhaps somewhat remote from the daily practice of the programmer in the cubicle, we first take a short detour, which hopefully helps to connect the abstract concepts to concrete programs.

5.1 Detour: Mendler-style Folds

Mendler-style folds [23, 28] arise from taking a logical (specifically, second-order simply-typed lambda calculus) rather than an algebraic approach to inductive datatypes. As such, they provide a smooth transition path from explicit recursion to the use of recursion schemes. To illustrate, the semantics of *depth* is roughly the fixed-point of the so-called *base function* depth

$$\begin{array}{ll} \mathsf{depth}\ depth\ (\mathsf{Empty}) & = 0 \\ \mathsf{depth}\ depth\ (\mathsf{Node}\ l\ a\ r) & = 1 + (depth\ l\ \text{`}max\text{`}\ depth\ r)\ , \end{array}$$

which abstracts away from the recursive calls. There is an additional twist: we have replaced the *Tree* constructors by the corresponding Tree constructors, which results in a rank-1 type:

$$\mathsf{depth} :: \forall tree\ .\ (tree \to \mathbb{N}) \to (\mathsf{Tree}\ tree \to \mathbb{N})\ .$$

The polymorphic type guarantees that the original recursion equation, $depth \cdot in = \mathsf{depth}\ depth$ has a *unique* solution. (Because of the occurrence of *in*, we said 'roughly the fixed-point'.)

Translated into category theory, *Mendler-style folds* are solutions in an unknown $x : \mu\mathsf{D} \to B$ to recursion equations of the form

$$x \cdot in = \Psi\,(\mu\mathsf{D})\,x\ ,$$

where the base function Ψ is a natural transformation of type $\mathscr{C}(-, B) \dot{\to} \mathscr{C}(\mathsf{D}\,-, B)$. Very briefly, the Yoneda lemma [17] shows that the space of base functions such as Ψ is isomorphic to the space of D-algebras. Thus, Mendler-style folds are in one-to-one correspondence with standard folds of the form

$$x \cdot in = b \cdot \mathsf{D}\,x\ .$$

Conversely, a standard fold is a Mendler-style fold, as the right-hand side as a function in x satisfies the naturality requirement.

5.2 Detour: Mendler-style Adjoint Folds

We have noted in Section 2 that many functions do not quite fit the pattern of simple folds: *depths*, for instance, uses an accumulating parameter. However, to provide a precise semantics we can take a similar approach as in the previous section. We define a base function that additionally replaces the *Tree* constructors on the left-hand side (and only those) by the corresponding Tree constructors.

$$\begin{array}{l} \mathsf{depths} :: \forall tree\ .\ ((tree, \mathbb{N}) \to Tree) \to ((\mathsf{Tree}\ tree, \mathbb{N}) \to Tree) \\ \mathsf{depths}\ depths\ (\mathsf{Empty}, \quad n) = Empty \\ \mathsf{depths}\ depths\ (\mathsf{Node}\ l\ a\ r, n) \\ \quad = Node\ (depths\ (l, n+1))\ n\ (depths\ (r, n+1)) \end{array}$$

The type of the base function is similar to what we had before, except that *tree* and Tree *tree* are wrapped in a left adjoint: $(-, \mathbb{N})$ or, categorically speaking, $- \times \mathbb{N}$. Nonetheless, one can show that $\mathsf{depths} \cdot (in \times \mathbb{N}) = \mathsf{depths}\ depths$ has a *unique* solution.

This motivates the following generalisation of Mendler-style folds. Given an adjunction $\mathsf{L} \dashv \mathsf{R}$, an *Mendler-style adjoint fold* $x : \mathsf{L}\,(\mu\mathsf{D}) \to B$ is the unique solution to the recursion equation

$$x \cdot \mathsf{L}\,in = \Psi\,(\mu\mathsf{D})\,x\ , \qquad (5.1)$$

where the base function Ψ is now a natural transformation of type $\mathscr{C}(\mathsf{L}\,-, B) \dot{\to} \mathscr{C}(\mathsf{L}\,(\mathsf{D}\,-), B)$.

The main difficulty in translating the examples of Section 2 into adjoint folds is to identify the left adjoint. For some examples this is obvious, eg for *depths* we use the curry adjunction $- \times \mathbb{N} \dashv (-)^{\mathbb{N}}$; for others it is less obvious, eg for *total* the left adjoint is type application (applying a functor to a constant object), which has a right adjoint under some mild conditions [11].

5.3 Adjoint Folds

Standard folds are restricted to the case that the control structure of a function ever follows the structure of its input data. Mendler-style adjoint folds loosen this tight coupling. The control structure is given implicitly through the adjunction, but it can also be made explicit by introducing a 'control functor'.

Definition 5.1 (Adjoint recursion equation). Given an adjunction $\mathsf{L} \dashv \mathsf{R} : \mathscr{C} \rightharpoonup \mathscr{D}$, functors $\mathsf{C} : \mathscr{C} \to \mathscr{C}$ and $\mathsf{D} : \mathscr{D} \to \mathscr{D}$, and a distributive law $\sigma : \mathsf{L} \circ \mathsf{D} \dot{\to} \mathsf{C} \circ \mathsf{L}$, an adjoint recursion equation in the unknown $x : \mathsf{L}\,(\mu\mathsf{D}) \to B$ has the form

$$x \cdot \mathsf{L}\,in = b \cdot \mathsf{C}\,x \cdot \sigma\,(\mu\mathsf{D})\ , \qquad (5.2)$$

where $b : \mathsf{C}\,B \to B$.

The functor C is called control functor because it governs the recursive call structure. The diagram below displays the functors involved (D as in data functor, C as in control functor).

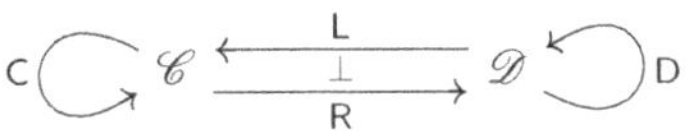

(5.3)

The distributive law $\sigma : \mathsf{L} \circ \mathsf{D} \dot{\to} \mathsf{C} \circ \mathsf{L}$ serves as an impedance matcher relating data and control functors.

Adjoint folds arise as unique solutions of adjoint recursion equations—we postpone the proof of uniqueness until Section 5.4. As in the vanilla case, Mendler-style adjoint folds (5.1) and adjoint folds (5.2) are interchangeable. Every adjoint fold is a Mendler-style one, as the right-hand side of (5.2) as a function in x satisfies the naturality requirement. The other direction is more interesting: Given a base function $\Psi : \mathscr{C}(\mathsf{L}\,-, B) \dot{\to} \mathscr{C}(\mathsf{L}\,(\mathsf{D}\,-), B)$, we have to construct a control functor C, a distributive law $\sigma : \mathsf{L} \circ \mathsf{D} \dot{\to} \mathsf{C} \circ \mathsf{L}$ and a C-algebra $b : \mathsf{C}\,B \to B$. The first two pieces of data are induced by the adjunction: a canonical choice for the control structure is $\mathsf{C} = \mathsf{L} \circ \mathsf{D} \circ \mathsf{R}$—we simply go round in a loop (5.3). Using this definition, the type of σ expands to $\mathsf{L} \circ \mathsf{D} \dot{\to} \mathsf{L} \circ \mathsf{D} \circ \mathsf{R} \circ \mathsf{L}$, which suggests defining $\sigma = \mathsf{L} \circ \mathsf{D} \circ \eta$. Finally, the C-algebra is derived from the base function: $b = \Psi\,(\mathsf{R}\,B)\,(\epsilon\,B) : \mathsf{L}\,(\mathsf{D}\,(\mathsf{R}\,B)) \to B$. For the proof of $\Psi\,X\,x = b \cdot \mathsf{C}\,x \cdot \sigma\,X$ we refer to the original paper [11].

Recursive Haskell programs are easily framed as Mendler-style adjoint folds (5.1). Adjoint folds (5.2) are, however, preferable for the theoretical development as they avoid sophistications such as natural transformations between hom-functors.

5.4 Transposed Homomorphisms

To show that (5.2) has a unique solution, we proceed in two steps, following the pattern set out in Section 4.

First, we abstract away from the initial algebra $(in, \mu\mathsf{D})$, generalising to an arbitrary D-algebra (a, A), and establish a bijection between arrows $x : \mathsf{L}\,A \to B$ satisfying

$$x \cdot \mathsf{L}\,a = b \cdot \mathsf{C}\,x \cdot \sigma\,A \ , \tag{5.4}$$

and D-algebra homomorphisms. The central step in the calculation below is the penultimate one, which replaces the distributive law $\sigma : \mathsf{L} \circ \mathsf{D} \dot{\to} \mathsf{C} \circ \mathsf{L}$ by its conjugate $\tau : \mathsf{D} \circ \mathsf{R} \dot{\to} \mathsf{R} \circ \mathsf{C}$, effectively shifting the recursive call to the right.

$$\begin{array}{ll} & x \cdot \mathsf{L}\,a = b \cdot \mathsf{C}\,x \cdot \sigma\,A \ : \ \mathsf{L}\,(\mathsf{D}\,A) \to B \\ \iff & \{ \lfloor - \rfloor \text{ and } \lceil - \rceil \text{ are isomorphisms (3.3)} \} \\ & \lfloor x \cdot \mathsf{L}\,a \rfloor = \lfloor b \cdot \mathsf{C}\,x \cdot \sigma\,A \rfloor \\ \iff & \{ \lfloor - \rfloor \text{ is natural (3.4a)} \} \\ & \lfloor x \rfloor \cdot a = \mathsf{R}\,b \cdot \lfloor \mathsf{C}\,x \cdot \sigma\,A \rfloor \\ \iff & \{ \sigma \dashv \tau \text{ conjugates (3.8a)} \} \\ & \lfloor x \rfloor \cdot a = \mathsf{R}\,b \cdot \tau\,B \cdot \mathsf{D}\,\lfloor x \rfloor \\ \iff & \{ \text{definition of lifting (3.1a)} \} \\ & \lfloor x \rfloor \cdot a = \mathsf{R}^{\tau}\,b \cdot \mathsf{D}\,\lfloor x \rfloor \ : \ \mathsf{D}\,A \to \mathsf{R}\,B \end{array}$$

Voilà: the transpose $\lfloor x \rfloor : (a, A) \to \mathsf{R}^{\tau}\,(b, B)$ is a D-homomorphism between a and a lifting of b. To fix some terminology, we call x a *transposed homomorphism*, or *traho* for short.

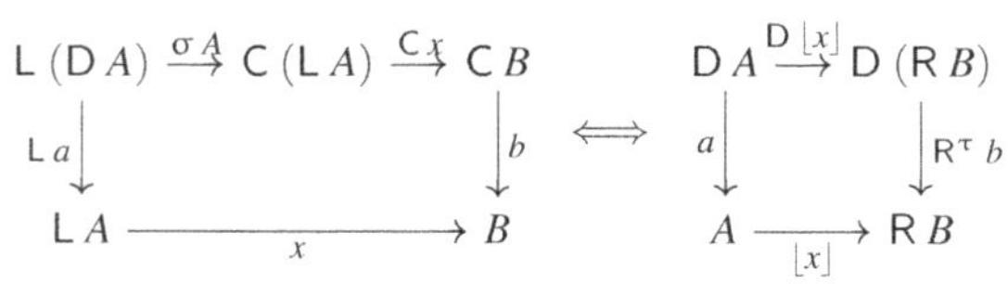

(5.5)

Second, if we instantiate (a, A) to the initial algebra $(in, \mu\mathsf{D})$, we obtain the following

Theorem 5.2 (Adjoint folds). *The adjoint recursion equation* (5.2) *has the unique solution* $x = \lceil (\!| \mathsf{R}^{\tau}\,b |\!) \rceil$, *where* $\tau : \mathsf{D} \circ \mathsf{R} \dot{\to} \mathsf{R} \circ \mathsf{C}$ *is the conjugate of* σ. *The arrow* x *is called an* adjoint fold.

Proof. This is an immediate consequence of initiality.

$$\begin{array}{ll} & x \cdot \mathsf{L}\,in = b \cdot \mathsf{C}\,x \cdot \sigma\,(\mu\mathsf{D}) \\ \iff & \{ \text{see above} \} \\ & \lfloor x \rfloor \cdot in = \mathsf{R}^{\tau}\,b \cdot \mathsf{D}\,\lfloor x \rfloor \\ \iff & \{ (in, \mu\mathsf{D}) \text{ initial} \} \\ & \lfloor x \rfloor = (\!| \mathsf{R}^{\tau}\,b |\!) \\ \iff & \{ \lfloor - \rfloor \text{ and } \lceil - \rceil \text{ are isomorphisms (3.3)} \} \\ & x = \lceil (\!| \mathsf{R}^{\tau}\,b |\!) \rceil \end{array}$$

□

So an adjoint fold is a traho from the initial algebra. Using the bijection (5.5) we can easily generalise from initial to free algebras. Then $\lfloor x \rfloor$ can be seen as evaluating a first-order term, and is uniquely determined by an evaluation function for variables.

There is an interesting observation to be made. Adjoint folds arise out of a situation that is not symmetric. The distributive law τ allows us to lift the right adjoint R to categories of algebras:

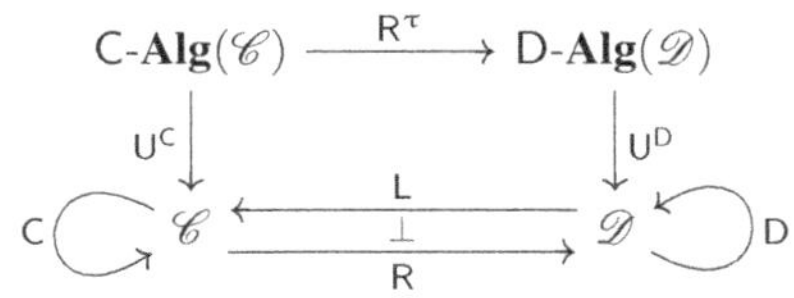

(5.6)

$$\sigma : \mathsf{L} \circ \mathsf{D} \dot{\to} \mathsf{C} \circ \mathsf{L} \ \dashv \ \tau : \mathsf{D} \circ \mathsf{R} \dot{\to} \mathsf{R} \circ \mathsf{C} \ .$$

Alas, we cannot lift the left adjoint L with the data at hand: a lifting of L requires a distributive law of type $\mathsf{C} \circ \mathsf{L} \dot{\to} \mathsf{L} \circ \mathsf{D}$. The asymmetry can be traced back to the definition of algebras. Consider the type of an action, $a : \mathsf{D}\,A \to A$; the base functor D only appears to the left of the arrow, in a contravariant position. Symmetry can be restored if σ is an isomorphism, an important special case, which we explore in the Section 5.5. But first, let us look at an example.

Example 5.3. Mutumorphisms are an instance of adjoint folds where the control functor is the canonical one and $\sigma = \Delta \circ \mathsf{D} \circ \eta$.

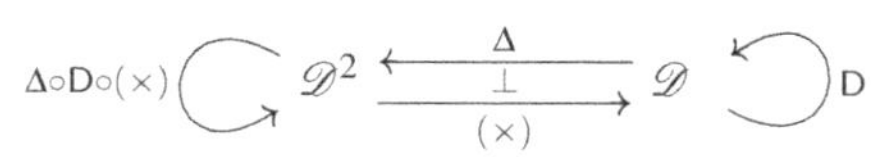

The conjugate of σ is $\tau = \eta \circ \mathsf{D} \circ (\times)$ (3.9b) and thus

$$(\times)^{\tau}\,(b_1, b_2) = b_1 \vartriangle b_2 \ .$$

Note that the lifted product functor is just the left adjunct. □

When we discussed adjoint folds (Section 5.3), we introduced the canonical control functor $\mathsf{C} = \mathsf{L} \circ \mathsf{D} \circ \mathsf{R}$. For this case the development above can be simplified. The functor C comes equipped with a canonical pair of distributive laws:

$$\sigma = \mathsf{L} \circ \mathsf{D} \circ \eta : \mathsf{L} \circ \mathsf{D} \dot{\to} \mathsf{C} \circ \mathsf{L} \ \dashv \ \tau = \eta \circ \mathsf{D} \circ \mathsf{R} : \mathsf{D} \circ \mathsf{R} \dot{\to} \mathsf{R} \circ \mathsf{C} \ .$$

The proof of uniqueness then boils down to a two-stepper (this is the proof of Section 4, more abstractly):

$$\begin{array}{ll} & x \cdot \mathsf{L}\,a = b \cdot \mathsf{L}\,(\mathsf{D}\,\lfloor x \rfloor) \ : \ \mathsf{L}\,(\mathsf{D}\,A) \to B \\ \iff & \{ \lfloor - \rfloor \text{ and } \lceil - \rceil \text{ are isomorphisms (3.3)} \} \\ & \lfloor x \cdot \mathsf{L}\,a \rfloor = \lfloor b \cdot \mathsf{L}\,(\mathsf{D}\,\lfloor x \rfloor) \rfloor \\ \iff & \{ \lfloor - \rfloor \text{ is natural (3.4a)} \} \\ & \lfloor x \rfloor \cdot a = \lfloor b \rfloor \cdot \mathsf{D}\,\lfloor x \rfloor \ : \ \mathsf{D}\,A \to \mathsf{R}\,B \ . \end{array}$$

This is indeed an instance of the previous development: some easy calculations show that $\mathsf{R}^{\tau}\, b = \lfloor b \rfloor$ and $\mathsf{L}\,(\mathsf{D}\,\lfloor x \rfloor) = \mathsf{C}\,x \cdot \sigma\,A$.

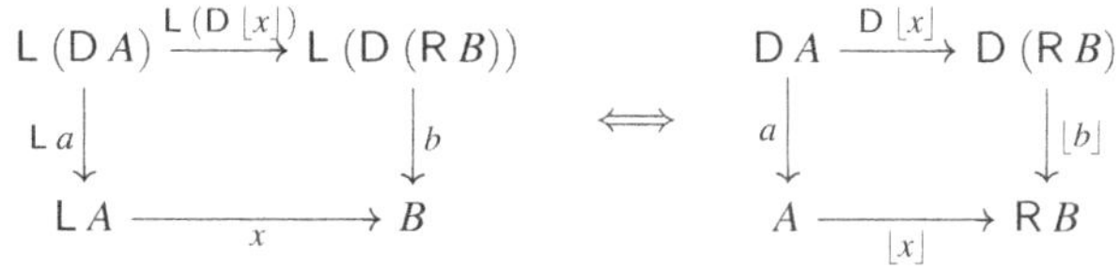

(5.7)

Now, if (a, A) is initial, then $x = \lceil (\!| \lfloor b \rfloor |\!) \rceil$. We further explore the canonical control functor in Section 5.6.

5.5 Type Fusion

Let us now assume that the distributive law σ is an isomorphism. Then we can continue the first calculation of Section 5.4 'in the opposite direction'. We start with (5.4) and reason

$$\begin{aligned} & x \cdot \mathsf{L}\,a = b \cdot \mathsf{C}\,x \cdot \sigma\,A \;:\; \mathsf{L}\,(\mathsf{D}\,A) \to B \\ \iff & \{\ \sigma \text{ is an isomorphism }\} \\ & x \cdot \mathsf{L}\,a \cdot \sigma^{\circ}\,A = b \cdot \mathsf{C}\,x \\ \iff & \{\ \text{definition of lifting (3.1a)}\ \} \\ & x \cdot \mathsf{L}^{\sigma^{\circ}}\,a = b \cdot \mathsf{C}\,x \;:\; \mathsf{C}\,(\mathsf{L}\,A) \to B\ . \end{aligned}$$

Overall, we have established the following one-to-one correspondence between algebra homomorphisms.

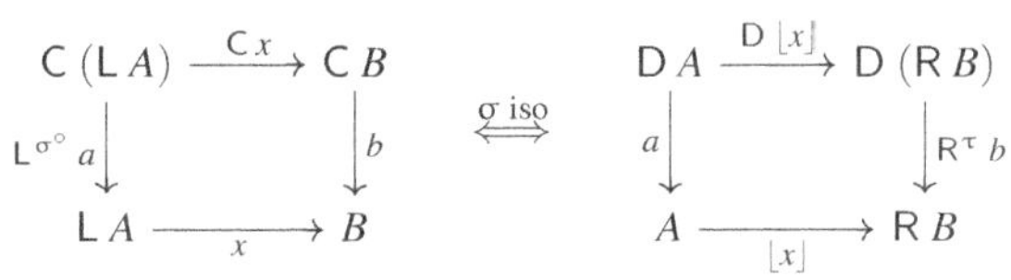

In other words, jointly with L we have lifted the entire adjunction $\mathsf{L} \dashv \mathsf{R}$ to an adjunction $\mathsf{L}^{\sigma^{\circ}} \dashv \mathsf{R}^{\tau}$ between categories of algebras.

$$\mathsf{C}\text{-}\mathbf{Alg}(\mathscr{C})(\mathsf{L}^{\sigma^{\circ}}\,(a, A), (b, B)) \cong \mathsf{D}\text{-}\mathbf{Alg}(\mathscr{D})((a, A), \mathsf{R}^{\tau}\,(b, B))$$

We arrive at a situation that is perfectly symmetric. Trahos appear at some intermediate stage, at the point where we apply the assumption that the distributive law σ is an isomorphism.

We can now complete (5.6) with the missing left adjoints.

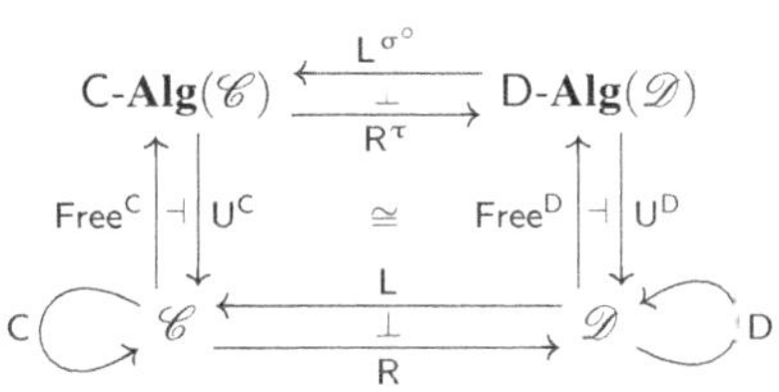

(5.8)

$$\sigma : \mathsf{L} \circ \mathsf{D} \cong \mathsf{C} \circ \mathsf{L} \;\dashv\; \tau : \mathsf{D} \circ \mathsf{R} \dot{\to} \mathsf{R} \circ \mathsf{C}$$

Overall, we have four (!) adjunctions, which form a commuting square of adjunctions. The proof of this fact makes use of the hgih-level reasoning principle (3.6). If we instantiate (3.6) to the compositions of left and right adjoints (note that left adjoints are composed in the opposite order) we obtain:

$$\mathsf{Free}^{\mathsf{C}} \circ \mathsf{L} \cong \mathsf{L}^{\sigma^{\circ}} \circ \mathsf{Free}^{\mathsf{D}} \iff \mathsf{U}^{\mathsf{D}} \circ \mathsf{R}^{\tau} \cong \mathsf{R} \circ \mathsf{U}^{\mathsf{C}}\ .$$

Since R^{τ} is a lifting, the isomorphism on the right is valid—indeed, it is even an equality. Consequently, the compositions of left adjoints are isomorphic, as well. We record the following

Theorem 5.4. *Let $\mathsf{L} \dashv \mathsf{R} : \mathscr{C} \rightharpoonup \mathscr{D}$ be an adjunction, and let $\mathsf{C} : \mathscr{C} \to \mathscr{C}$ and $\mathsf{D} : \mathscr{D} \to \mathscr{D}$ be functors.*

$$\mathsf{L} \circ \mathsf{D} \cong \mathsf{C} \circ \mathsf{L} \implies \mathsf{L} \circ \mathsf{D}^{*} \cong \mathsf{C}^{*} \circ \mathsf{L}$$

Proof. Plugging in the definitions, $\mathsf{F}^{*} = \mathsf{U}^{\mathsf{F}} \circ \mathsf{Free}^{\mathsf{F}}$, we conclude

$$\mathsf{L} \circ \mathsf{U}^{\mathsf{D}} \circ \mathsf{Free}^{\mathsf{D}} = \mathsf{U}^{\mathsf{C}} \circ \mathsf{L}^{\sigma^{\circ}} \circ \mathsf{Free}^{\mathsf{D}} \cong \mathsf{U}^{\mathsf{C}} \circ \mathsf{Free}^{\mathsf{C}} \circ \mathsf{L}\ . \qquad \square$$

As a corollary (using $\mu\mathsf{F} \cong \mathsf{F}^{*}\,0$ and $\mathsf{L}\,0 \cong 0$) we obtain the fusion rule of Backhouse et al. [1]'s categorical fixed-point calculus.

Corollary 5.5 (Type fusion).

$$\mathsf{L} \circ \mathsf{D} \cong \mathsf{C} \circ \mathsf{L} \implies \mathsf{L}\,(\mu\mathsf{D}) \cong \mu\mathsf{C}$$

Example 5.6. The diagonal functor Δ satisfies a simple property: $\Delta \circ \mathsf{D} = \mathsf{D}^2 \circ \Delta$. Since Δ is a left adjoint, Corollary 5.5 implies

$$\Delta\,(\mu\mathsf{D}) \cong \mu\mathsf{D}^2\ .$$

The initial algebra of D^2, a functor over a product category, consists of two copies of $\mu\mathsf{D}$—we will later need this simple fact. The conjugate of the distributive law $id : \Delta \circ \mathsf{D} = \mathsf{D}^2 \circ \Delta$ is $\tau = \mathsf{D}\,outl \vartriangle \mathsf{D}\,outr$ (3.9b) and thus

$$(\times)^{\tau}\,(b_1, b_2) = b_1 \cdot \mathsf{D}\,outl \vartriangle b_2 \cdot \mathsf{D}\,outr\ .$$

Instantiating Diagram (5.8) we can see the global picture.

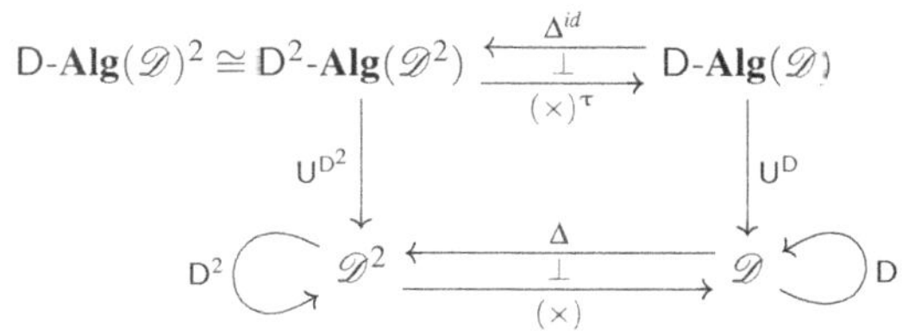

Since $\mathsf{D}^2\text{-}\mathbf{Alg}(\mathscr{D}^2) \cong \mathsf{D}\text{-}\mathbf{Alg}(\mathscr{D})^2$, we obtain that $(\times)^{\tau}$ modulo the isomorphism is the product functor for $\mathsf{D}\text{-}\mathbf{Alg}(\mathscr{D})$, which gives us the entire infrastructure for products: *outl*, *outr* and $\vartriangle$. (This also provides us with another proof of the banana-split law (4.1)) $\square$

We have now encountered two control functors associated with the adjunction $\Delta \dashv (\times)$: the canonical one $\Delta \circ \mathsf{D} \circ (\times)$ and the 'perfect' control functor D^2. The next section relates the two.

5.6 Comparing Control Functors

Adjoint folds involve several pieces of data: an adjunction, an algebra, and a control functor equipped with a conjugate pair of distributive laws. The latter is perhaps the most mysterious, especially if we try to link the Haskell programs in Section 2 *directly* to the recursion scheme of adjoint folds (5.2). Mendler-style folds provide a stepping stone, suggesting that there is a canonical choice for the control functor: $\mathsf{C} = \mathsf{L} \circ \mathsf{D} \circ \mathsf{R}$ with

$$\sigma = \mathsf{L} \circ \mathsf{D} \circ \eta : \mathsf{L} \circ \mathsf{D} \dot{\to} \mathsf{C} \circ \mathsf{L} \;\dashv\; \tau = \eta \circ \mathsf{D} \circ \mathsf{R} : \mathsf{D} \circ \mathsf{R} \dot{\to} \mathsf{R} \circ \mathsf{C}\ .$$

We now justify the adjective 'canonical' for this choice: we show that every other control functor can be reduced to the canonical one. Assume that we have another control functor C' with

$$\sigma' : \mathsf{L} \circ \mathsf{D} \dot{\to} \mathsf{C}' \circ \mathsf{L} \;\dashv\; \tau' : \mathsf{D} \circ \mathsf{R} \dot{\to} \mathsf{R} \circ \mathsf{C}'\ .$$

Using bijection (3.7b), the distributive law σ' gives rise to a natural transformation $\gamma : \mathsf{L} \circ \mathsf{D} \circ \mathsf{R} \dot{\to} \mathsf{C}' = \mathsf{C} \dot{\to} \mathsf{C}'$, namely $\gamma = \mathsf{C} \circ \epsilon \cdot \sigma' \circ \mathsf{R}$. This natural transformation in turn induces the lifting γ-$\mathbf{Alg}(\mathscr{C})$, which maps C'-algebras to C-algebras. Since it is a lifting of the identity functor, γ-$\mathbf{Alg}(\mathscr{C})$ is faithful. Moreover, we have the following commutative diagrams of functors.

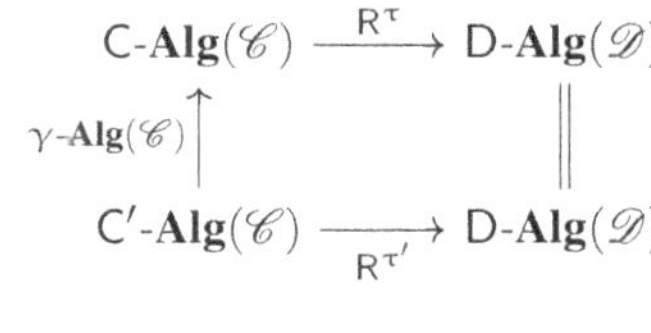

(5.9)

We first note that γ relates $\sigma \dashv \tau$ and $\sigma' \dashv \tau'$ in the following way (the proofs are routine but uninstructive).

$$\sigma' = \gamma \circ \mathsf{L} \cdot \sigma \qquad (5.10a)$$

$$\tau' = \mathsf{R} \circ \gamma \cdot \tau \qquad (5.10b)$$

For the proof of (5.9) it suffices to concentrate on the algebras:

$$\mathsf{R}^{\tau}\ (\gamma\text{-}\mathbf{Alg}(\mathscr{C})\ a) = \mathsf{R}\ (a \cdot \gamma\, A) \cdot \tau\, A = \mathsf{R}\, a \cdot \tau'\, A = \mathsf{R}^{\tau'}\ a\ .$$

Furthermore, every traho can be translated into a traho that uses the canonical control functor:

$$\begin{aligned} & x \cdot \mathsf{L}\, a = b \cdot \mathsf{C}'\, x \cdot \sigma'\, A \\ \iff & \{\ (5.10a)\ \} \\ & x \cdot \mathsf{L}\, a = b \cdot \mathsf{C}'\, x \cdot \gamma\ (\mathsf{L}\, A) \cdot \sigma\, A \\ \iff & \{\ \gamma \text{ is natural and } x : \mathsf{L}\, A \to B\ \} \\ & x \cdot \mathsf{L}\, a = b \cdot \gamma\, B \cdot \mathsf{C}\, x \cdot \sigma\, A \\ \iff & \{\ \text{definition of lifting (3.1b)}\ \} \\ & x \cdot \mathsf{L}\, a = \gamma\text{-}\mathbf{Alg}(\mathscr{C})\ b \cdot \mathsf{C}\, x \cdot \sigma\, A\ . \end{aligned}$$

Example 5.7. In Section 4 we noted that the banana-split law (4.1) arises as an extreme case of mutumorphisms. Mutumorphisms are based on the canonical control functor $\mathsf{C} = \Delta \circ \mathsf{D} \circ (\times)$; banana-split employs the control functor D^2. The lifting $\gamma\text{-}\mathbf{Alg}(\mathscr{C}^2) : \mathsf{D}^2\text{-}\mathbf{Alg}(\mathscr{C}^2) \to \mathsf{C}\text{-}\mathbf{Alg}(\mathscr{C}^2)$ induced by $\gamma = (\mathsf{D}\ outl, \mathsf{D}\ outr) : \mathsf{C} \to \mathsf{D}^2$ serves as the adaptor, translating D^2- into C-algebras. □

6. Recursion Schemes from Comonads

Recursion schemes from comonads [30], rsfcs for short, form a general recursion principle that makes use of a comonad N to provide 'contextual information' to the algebra. Like adjoint folds, it is 'doubly generic': it is parametric in the datatype $\mu\mathsf{F}$, and in the comonad N. As a particularly nice example, histomorphisms, the Squiggol rendering of course-of-values recursion, employ the cofree comonad, which makes available the results of recursive calls on *all* subterms. (An even better choice is the cofree *recursive* comonad [29].) To this end it makes use of a coalgebra $fan : \mu\mathsf{F} \to \mathsf{N}\ (\mu\mathsf{F})$ that embeds a subterm in a context. For the cofree comonad, *fan* maps a term to the cotree of all subterms. The coalgebra can be defined generically in terms of a distributive law $\lambda : \mathsf{F} \circ \mathsf{N} \dot{\to} \mathsf{N} \circ \mathsf{F}$, which is subject to certain conditions (6.6), detailed below.

Definition 6.1 (Comonadic recursion equation)**.** Given a functor F, a comonad $(\mathsf{N}, \epsilon, \delta)$, and a distributive law $\lambda : \mathsf{F} \circ \mathsf{N} \dot{\to} \mathsf{N} \circ \mathsf{F}$, a comonadic recursion equation in the unknown $f : \mu\mathsf{F} \to B$ has the form

$$f \cdot in = b \cdot \mathsf{F}\ (\mathsf{N} f \cdot fan)\ , \qquad (6.1)$$

where $fan = (\!(\mathsf{N}\ in \cdot \lambda\ (\mu\mathsf{F}))\!) : \mu\mathsf{F} \to \mathsf{N}\ (\mu\mathsf{F})$ and $b : \mathsf{F}\ (\mathsf{N}\ B) \to B$.

The composition $\mathsf{N} f \cdot fan$ creates a context that makes the results of 'recursive calls' available to the algebra b, which is a context-sensitive algebra—an $(\mathsf{F} \circ \mathsf{N})$-algebra, rather than merely an F-algebra. Uustalu et al. [30] showed the following

Theorem 6.2 (Rsfcs)**.** *The comonadic recursion equation* (6.1) *has the unique solution* $f = \epsilon\ B \cdot (\!(\mathsf{N}\, b \cdot \lambda\ (\mathsf{N}\ B) \cdot \mathsf{F}\ (\delta\ B))\!)$.

A couple of remarks are in order. The recursion scheme involves both algebras and coalgebras, and combines them in an interesting way. We noted above that *fan* is a coalgebra, but it is actually a bit more: it is a coalgebra *for the comonad* N. Furthermore, the algebra *in* and the coalgebra *fan* go hand-in-hand. They are related by the distributive law λ and form what is known as a λ-bialgebra, a combination of an algebra and a coalgebra with a common carrier.

We postpone our proof of Theorem 6.2 to Section 6.3, after we have provided the necessary background in the following sections, which can be skipped by those already familiar with the material.

6.1 Background: Eilenberg-Moore Categories

Comonads and monads Functional programmers have embraced monads, and to a lesser extent, comonads, to capture effectful and context-sensitive computations. A comonad is a functor $\mathsf{N} : \mathscr{C} \to \mathscr{C}$ equipped with natural transformations $\epsilon : \mathsf{N} \dot{\to} \mathsf{Id}$ (counit), that extracts a value from a context, and $\delta : \mathsf{N} \dot{\to} \mathsf{N} \circ \mathsf{N}$ (comultiplication), that duplicates a context, such that the following laws hold:

$$\epsilon \circ \mathsf{N} \cdot \delta = \mathsf{N}\ , \qquad (6.2a)$$

$$\mathsf{N} \circ \epsilon \cdot \delta = \mathsf{N}\ , \qquad (6.2b)$$

$$\delta \circ \mathsf{N} \cdot \delta = \mathsf{N} \circ \delta \cdot \delta\ . \qquad (6.2c)$$

The first two properties, the counit laws, state that duplicating a context and then discarding a duplicate is the same as doing nothing. The third property, the coassociative law, equates the two ways of duplicating a context twice. Monads (M, η, μ) are dual to comonads, with transformations $\eta : \mathsf{Id} \dot{\to} \mathsf{M}$ (unit) and $\mu : \mathsf{M} \circ \mathsf{M} \dot{\to} \mathsf{M}$ (multiplication) that obey dual properties.

Huber [13] discovered that an adjunction $(\epsilon, \mathsf{L} \dashv \mathsf{R}, \eta)$ induces a comonad $(\mathsf{L} \circ \mathsf{R}, \epsilon, \mathsf{L} \circ \eta \circ \mathsf{R})$ and a monad $(\mathsf{R} \circ \mathsf{L}, \eta, \mathsf{R} \circ \epsilon \circ \mathsf{L})$. For example, the adjunction $\mathsf{Free}^{\mathsf{F}} \dashv \mathsf{U}^{\mathsf{F}}$ induces the so-called *free monad* $\mathsf{F}^* = \mathsf{U}^{\mathsf{F}} \circ \mathsf{Free}^{\mathsf{F}}$, the carrier of the free F-algebra, representing first-order terms with variables. (The comonad that arises is less interesting.) Dually, the adjunction $\mathsf{U}_{\mathsf{G}} \dashv \mathsf{Cofree}_{\mathsf{G}}$ induces the *cofree comonad* $\mathsf{G}_\infty = \mathsf{U}_{\mathsf{G}} \circ \mathsf{Cofree}_{\mathsf{G}}$. This can be seen as the type of generalised streams of observations—'generalised' because the 'tail' is a G-structure of 'streams' rather than just a single one; we obtain streams for $\mathsf{G} = \mathsf{Id}$. (Now the monad is less interesting.)

Coalgebras for a comonad A coalgebra for a comonad N is an N-coalgebra (C, c) that respects ϵ and δ:

$$\epsilon\ C \cdot c = id_C\ , \qquad (6.3a)$$

$$\delta\ C \cdot c = \mathsf{N}\ c \cdot c\ . \qquad (6.3b)$$

If we first create a context and then focus, we obtain the original value. Creating a nested context is the same as first creating a context and then duplicating it. For example, the so-called cofree coalgebra $(\mathsf{N}\ C, \delta\ C)$ is respectful, which follows directly from (6.2b) and (6.2c). The second law (6.3b) also enjoys an alternative reading: c is a homomorphism of type $(C, c) \to (\mathsf{N}\ C, \delta\ C)$. This observation is at the heart of the Eilenberg-Moore construction, which we discuss below. Coalgebras that respect ϵ and δ, and coalgebra homomorphisms between them, form a category, known as the *(co)-Eilenberg-Moore category* and denoted $\mathscr{C}_{\mathsf{N}}$. Eilenberg-Moore categories generalise categories of coalgebras: $\mathsf{G}\text{-}\mathbf{Coalg}(\mathscr{C}) \cong \mathscr{C}_{\mathsf{N}}$ where $\mathsf{N} = \mathsf{G}_\infty$ is the cofree comonad.

Eilenberg-Moore construction As noted above, every adjunction generates a comonad. The converse is also true: every comonad N induces an adjunction that generates N—in fact, in two canonical ways. One construction was discovered by Kleisli [15], the other by Eilenberg and Moore [6]. We shall need the latter, which constructs a right adjoint to the forgetful functor $\mathsf{U}_{\mathsf{N}} : \mathscr{C}_{\mathsf{N}} \to \mathscr{C}$.

$$\mathscr{C} \underset{\mathsf{Cofree}_{\mathsf{N}}}{\overset{\mathsf{U}_{\mathsf{N}}}{\underset{\bot}{\rightleftarrows}}} \mathscr{C}_{\mathsf{N}}$$

The functor $\mathsf{Cofree}_{\mathsf{N}}$ maps an object to the cofree coalgebra for N:

$$\mathsf{Cofree}_{\mathsf{N}}\ B = (\mathsf{N}\ B, \delta\ B)\ , \qquad (6.4a)$$

$$\mathsf{Cofree}_{\mathsf{N}}\ f = \mathsf{N} f\ . \qquad (6.4b)$$

The counit $\epsilon : \mathsf{U}_{\mathsf{N}} \circ \mathsf{Cofree}_{\mathsf{N}} \dot{\to} \mathsf{Id}$ of the adjunction $\mathsf{U}_{\mathsf{N}} \dashv \mathsf{Cofree}_{\mathsf{N}}$ is the counit of N; the unit $\eta : \mathsf{Id} \dot{\to} \mathsf{Cofree}_{\mathsf{N}} \circ \mathsf{U}_{\mathsf{N}}$ defined $\eta\ (C, c) = c$ extracts the action of a coalgebra, which is an N-coalgebra homomorphism of type $(C, c) \to (\mathsf{N}\ C, \delta\ C)$ (6.3b). The bijection framed in terms of the units reads:

$$f = \epsilon\, B \cdot \mathsf{U_N}\, h \iff \mathsf{Cofree_N}\, f \cdot \eta\,(C,c) = h \ ,$$

for all $f : \mathsf{U_N}\,(C,c) \to B$ and $h : (C,c) \to \mathsf{Cofree_N}\, B$. The adjunction $\mathsf{U_N} \dashv \mathsf{Cofree_N}$ indeed generates the comonad N: we have $\mathsf{U_N} \circ \mathsf{Cofree_N} = \mathsf{N}$ and $\delta = \mathsf{U_N} \circ \eta \circ \mathsf{Cofree_N}$. Since $\mathsf{U_N}$ is faithful, we can simplify the bijection slightly:

$$f = \epsilon\, B \cdot h \iff \mathsf{N}\, f \cdot c = h \ , \qquad (6.5)$$

for all $f : C \to B$ and homomorphisms $h : (C,c) \to (\mathsf{N}\, B, \delta\, B)$. Have we seen an arrow of the form $\mathsf{N}\, f \cdot c$ before?

6.2 Background: Bialgebras

A bialgebra combines an algebra and a coalgebra with a common carrier. Bialgebras come in many flavours; we need the variant that combines F-algebras and coalgebras for a comonad N. The two functors have to interact coherently, described by a distributive law.

Distributive laws A distributive law $\lambda : \mathsf{F} \circ \mathsf{N} \dot{\to} \mathsf{N} \circ \mathsf{F}$ of an endofunctor F over a comonad N is a natural transformation satisfying the two coherence conditions:

$$\epsilon \circ \mathsf{F} \cdot \lambda = \mathsf{F} \circ \epsilon \ , \qquad (6.6a)$$

$$\delta \circ \mathsf{F} \cdot \lambda = \mathsf{N} \circ \lambda \cdot \lambda \circ \mathsf{N} \cdot \mathsf{F} \circ \delta \ . \qquad (6.6b)$$

We can use λ to colift F to the category $\mathscr{C}_\mathsf{N}$. The coherence conditions guarantee that $\mathsf{F}_\lambda : \mathscr{C}_\mathsf{N} \to \mathscr{C}_\mathsf{N}$ preserves respect for ϵ and δ. Dually, λ induces the lifting $\mathsf{N}^\lambda : \mathsf{F}\text{-}\mathbf{Alg}(\mathscr{C}) \to \mathsf{F}\text{-}\mathbf{Alg}(\mathscr{C})$. Now, the coherence conditions ensure that N^λ is a comonad with $\bar{\epsilon}\,(a,A) = \epsilon\, A$ and $\bar{\delta}\,(a,A) = \delta\, A$. In particular, the lifted transformations $\bar{\epsilon} : \mathsf{N}^\lambda \dot{\to} \mathsf{Id}$ and $\bar{\delta} : \mathsf{N}^\lambda \dot{\to} \mathsf{N}^\lambda \circ \mathsf{N}^\lambda$ are F-algebra homomorphisms.

Bialgebras Let $\lambda : \mathsf{F} \circ \mathsf{N} \dot{\to} \mathsf{N} \circ \mathsf{F}$ be a distributive law for the endofunctor F over the comonad N. A *λ-bialgebra* (a,X,c) consists of an F-algebra (a,X) and a coalgebra (X,c) for the comonad N such that the *pentagonal law* holds:

$$c \cdot a = \mathsf{N}\, a \cdot \lambda\, X \cdot \mathsf{F}\, c \ . \qquad (6.7)$$

Loosely speaking, the law allows us to swap the algebra a and the coalgebra c. A λ-bialgebra homomorphism is both an F-algebra and an N-coalgebra homomorphism. λ-bialgebras and their homomorphisms form a category, denoted λ-$\mathbf{Bialg}(\mathscr{C})$.

The pentagonal law (6.7) also has two asymmetric renderings, which relate it to liftings and coliftings.

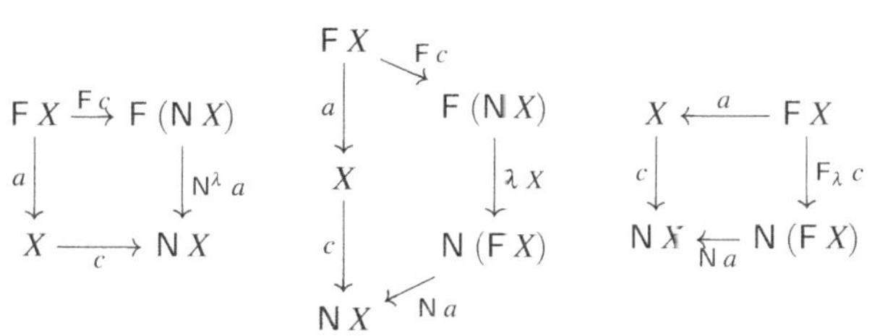

(6.8)

The diagram on the left shows that $c : (a,X) \to \mathsf{N}^\lambda\,(a,X)$ is an F-algebra homomorphism. Dually, the diagram on the right identifies $a : \mathsf{F}_\lambda\,(X,c) \to (X,c)$ as an N-coalgebra homomorphism. Thus, we can interpret the bialgebra (a,X,c) both as an algebra over a coalgebra $(a,(X,c))$, or as a coalgebra over an algebra $((a,X),c)$. Formally, we have the following isomorphisms of categories:

$$\mathsf{F}_\lambda\text{-}\mathbf{Alg}(\mathscr{C}_\mathsf{N}) \cong \lambda\text{-}\mathbf{Bialg}(\mathscr{C}) \cong (\mathsf{F}\text{-}\mathbf{Alg}(\mathscr{C}))_{\mathsf{N}^\lambda} \ . \qquad (6.9)$$

The alternative interpretations are useful to determine initial and final objects in λ-$\mathbf{Bialg}(\mathscr{C})$. To determine the initial object, we use the 'coalgebra over algebra' view, as categories of G-coalgebras have a trivial initial object: $(0, 0 \dashrightarrow \mathsf{G}\, 0)$, where 0 is the initial object in the underlying category and $0 \dashrightarrow \mathsf{G}\, 0$ the unique arrow from it. Consequently, $(in, \mu\mathsf{F}, fan)$ with $fan = (\!|\mathsf{N}^\lambda\ in|\!)$ is indeed initial.

6.3 Recursion Schemes from Comonads are Adjoint Folds

We now return to the proof of Theorem 6.2 using our new vocabulary to derive the unique solution. Somewhat surprisingly, as an immediate consequence of this proof, it turns out that rsfcs are an instance of adjoint folds, when previously, the two frameworks were thought of as being orthogonal [11]. Of course, the derivation is not strictly necessary, but it helps to relate the present development to prior work [30], and it hopefully helps to understand why rsfcs are an instance of adjoint folds. The development will follow the pattern we have already established.

First, we abstract away from the initial object $(in, \mu\mathsf{F}, fan)$, generalising to an arbitrary λ-bialgebra (a,A,c). The goal is to establish a bijection between arrows $f : A \to B$ satisfying $f \cdot a = b \cdot \mathsf{F}\,(\mathsf{N}\, f \cdot c)$ and λ-bialgebra homomorphisms $h : (a,A,c) \to (b_\sharp, \mathsf{N}\, B, \delta\, B)$, where $b_\sharp$ is a to-be-determined F-algebra. Now, we already know that arrows of type $f : A \to B$ and N-coalgebra homomorphisms $h : (A,c) \to (\mathsf{N}\, B, \delta\, B)$ are in one-to-one correspondence (6.5). So we identify $\mathsf{N}\, f \cdot c$ as the transpose of f and simplify f's equation to $f \cdot a = b \cdot \mathsf{F}\, h$. It remains to show that h is an F-algebra homomorphism of type $(a,A) \to (b_\sharp, \mathsf{N}\, B)$.

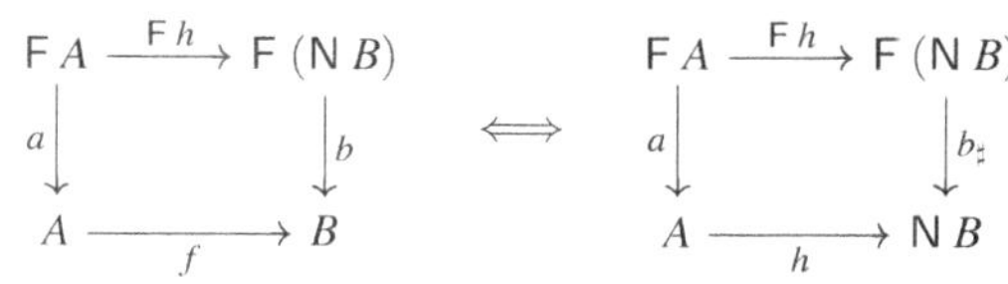

(6.10)

The strategy for the proof is clear: we have to transmogrify f into $\mathsf{N}\, f \cdot c$. Thus, we apply N to both sides of $f \cdot a = b \cdot \mathsf{F}\, h$ and then 'swap' a and c using the pentagonal law (6.7).

$$\begin{array}{ll} & f \cdot a = b \cdot \mathsf{F}\, h \\ \Longrightarrow & \{\ \mathsf{N}\ \text{functor}\ \} \\ & \mathsf{N}\, f \cdot \mathsf{N}\, a = \mathsf{N}\, b \cdot \mathsf{N}\,(\mathsf{F}\, h) \\ \Longrightarrow & \{\ \text{Leibniz}\ \} \\ & \mathsf{N}\, f \cdot \mathsf{N}\, a \cdot \mathsf{F}_\lambda\, c = \mathsf{N}\, b \cdot \mathsf{N}\,(\mathsf{F}\, h) \cdot \mathsf{F}_\lambda\, c \\ \iff & \{\ a : \mathsf{F}_\lambda\,(A,c) \to (A,c)\ (6.7)\ \} \\ & \mathsf{N}\, f \cdot c \cdot a = \mathsf{N}\, b \cdot \mathsf{N}\,(\mathsf{F}\, h) \cdot \mathsf{F}_\lambda\, c \\ \iff & \{\ \mathsf{F}_\lambda\, h : \mathsf{F}_\lambda\,(A,c) \to \mathsf{F}_\lambda\,(\mathsf{N}\, B, \delta\, B)\ \text{and}\ \mathsf{F}_\lambda\, h = \mathsf{F}\, h\ \} \\ & h \cdot a = \mathsf{N}\, b \cdot \mathsf{F}_\lambda\,(\delta\, B) \cdot \mathsf{F}\, h \end{array}$$

The proof makes essential use of the fact that a and h are N-coalgebra homomorphisms, and that F_λ preserves coalgebra homomorphisms. Along the way, we have derived a formula for $b_\sharp$:

$$b_\sharp = \mathsf{N}\, b \cdot \mathsf{F}_\lambda\,(\delta\, B) = \mathsf{N}\, b \cdot \lambda\,(\mathsf{N}\, B) \cdot \mathsf{F}\,(\delta\, B) \ . \qquad (6.11)$$

We have to show that $(b_\sharp, \mathsf{N}\, B, \delta\, B)$ is a λ-bialgebra. Since $\mathsf{F}_\lambda\,(\mathsf{N}\, B, \delta\, B)$ is a coalgebra for the comonad N, we can conclude using (6.5) that $b_\sharp$ is a coalgebra homomorphism of type $\mathsf{F}_\lambda\,(\mathsf{N}\, B, \delta\, B) \to (\mathsf{N}\, B, \delta\, B)$, which establishes the desired result. Furthermore $b = \epsilon\, B \cdot b_\sharp$, which allows us to complete the proof.

$$\begin{array}{ll} & h \cdot a = b_\sharp \cdot \mathsf{F}\, h \\ \Longrightarrow & \{\ \text{Leibniz}\ \} \\ & \epsilon\, B \cdot h \cdot a = \epsilon\, B \cdot b_\sharp \cdot \mathsf{F}\, h \\ \iff & \{\ f = \epsilon\, B \cdot h\ \text{and}\ b = \epsilon\, B \cdot b_\sharp\ \} \\ & f \cdot a = b \cdot \mathsf{F}\, h \end{array}$$

We have discovered an important fact: b and $b_\sharp$ are also related by the Eilenberg-Moore adjunction $\mathsf{U_N} \dashv \mathsf{Cofree_N}$! Using the notation for adjuncts, the right-hand side of (6.10) reads $\lfloor f \rfloor \cdot a = \lfloor b \rfloor \cdot \mathsf{F}\, \lfloor f \rfloor$. This looks suspiciously like the right-hand side of (5.7), which relates trahos (adjoint folds) and homomorphisms. However, the original equation for f does not seem to fit into the picture. This is because it omits the forgetful functor $\mathsf{U_N}$. If we make it explicit, we obtain the the following bijection, which is indeed an instance of (5.7).

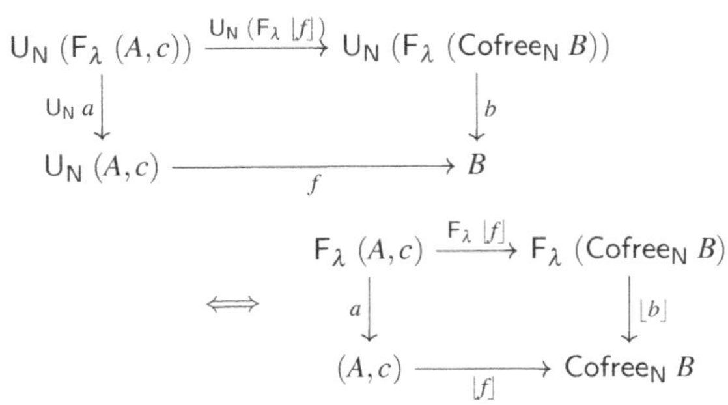

If we simplify the composition of functors using $\mathsf{U_N} \circ \mathsf{F}_\lambda = \mathsf{F} \circ \mathsf{U_N}$ and $\mathsf{U_N} \circ \mathsf{F}_\lambda \circ \mathsf{Cofree_N} = \mathsf{F} \circ \mathsf{U_N} \circ \mathsf{Cofree_N} = \mathsf{F} \circ \mathsf{N}$, we obtain the original equivalence (6.10). The somewhat pedantic diagrams above explicate all the information implicit in (6.10). For example, we can read off that a is an N-coalgebra homomorphism.

The *second* step should be routine by now. If we instantiate (a, A, c) to the initial λ-bialgebra $(in, \mu\mathsf{F}, fan)$, we obtain that the unique solution of the original equation (6.1) is $f = \lceil (\!| \lfloor b \rfloor |\!) \rceil$ or, expressed using the vocabulary of [30], $f = \epsilon\, B \cdot (\!| b_{\ddagger} |\!)$. We record

Theorem 6.3. *A recursion scheme from the comonad* N *and the distributive law* $\lambda : \mathsf{F} \circ \mathsf{N} \dot{\to} \mathsf{N} \circ \mathsf{F}$ *can be framed as an adjoint fold based on the Eilenberg-Moore adjunction* $\mathsf{U_N} \dashv \mathsf{Cofree_N}$, *using the canonical control functor* $\mathsf{U_N} \circ \mathsf{F}_\lambda \circ \mathsf{Cofree_N} = \mathsf{F} \circ \mathsf{N}$.

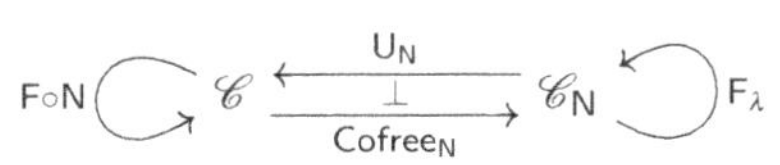

Let us conclude the section by investigating an alternative control functor: since $\mathsf{U_N} \circ \mathsf{F}_\lambda = \mathsf{F} \circ \mathsf{U_N}$, the functor F itself can be used as the control! For this case the distributive law σ is an isomorphism, even an identity, so we can invoke the machinery of Section 5.5 and lift the adjunction $\mathsf{U_N} \dashv \mathsf{Cofree_N}$ to an adjunction between categories of algebras. The conjugate of $\sigma = id$ is just λ, we have $\mathsf{U_N} \circ \tau = \lambda$. (The coherence condition (6.6b) shows that λ is an N-coalgebra homomorphism of type $\mathsf{F}_\lambda \circ \mathsf{Cofree_N} \dot{\to} \mathsf{Cofree_N} \circ \mathsf{F}$.)

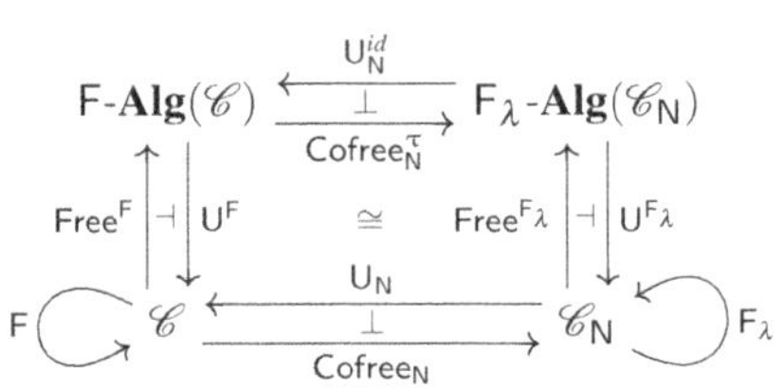

In the upper right corner we find the category of λ-bialgebras (6.9). This shows that the underlying functor $\lambda\text{-}\mathbf{Bialg}(\mathscr{C}) \to \mathsf{F}\text{-}\mathbf{Alg}(\mathscr{C})$, which forgets about the algebra part, has a right adjoint. Since right adjoints preserve final objects, we immediately obtain that $\mathsf{Cofree}^{\tau}_{\mathsf{N}}\ (\mathsf{F}\ 1 \dashrightarrow 1, 1)$ is the final bialgebra.

7. When is an Adjoint Fold an Rsfc?

We have seen that all rsfcs are adjoint folds; and indeed, previous work has shown that the two share some connection—zygomorphisms have been modelled both by using rsfcs [30] and as adjoint folds [11]. But what about the reverse direction: when is an adjoint fold also modelled by using an rsfc? In this section we show that an adjoint fold based on the canonical control functor can be captured as an rsfc, if additionally a distributive isomorphism exists.

An adjoint fold is based on an adjunction $\mathsf{L} \dashv \mathsf{R}$, and an rsfc on a comonad. Thus, using Huber's result, an obvious choice for the comonad is $\mathsf{N} = \mathsf{L} \circ \mathsf{R}$. However, we also need to manufacture a distributive law $\lambda : \mathsf{F} \circ \mathsf{N} \dot{\to} \mathsf{N} \circ \mathsf{F}$. Now, one can show that a conjugate pair $\sigma \dashv \tau$ of distributive laws, *where* σ *is an isomorphism*, induces a distributive law for an endofunctor over comonad [32]. Consequently, we assume the following data (we rename F to C to bring the subsequent development in line with Section 5.5):

$$\sigma : \mathsf{L} \circ \mathsf{D} \cong \mathsf{C} \circ \mathsf{L} \quad \dashv \quad \tau : \mathsf{D} \circ \mathsf{R} \dot{\to} \mathsf{R} \circ \mathsf{C} \ .$$

These are the same assumptions as for the type fusion rule, Corollary 5.5. We shall see shortly that this is not a mere coincidence.

Under these assumptions we aim to show that the following two diagrams are equivalent. On the left we have the diagram for adjoint folds based on the canonical control functor (5.7); on the right we have the diagram for recursion schemes from comonads (6.1).

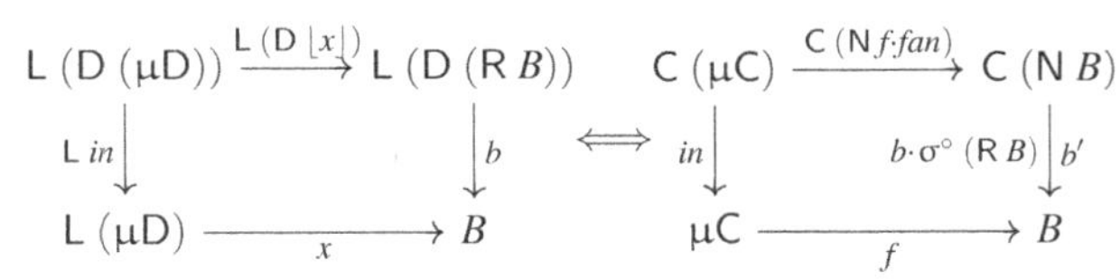

The functions x and f are related by the isomorphism $\mathsf{L}\ (\mu\mathsf{D}) \cong \mu\mathsf{C}$, provided by Corollary 5.5. The main task is to relate the upper arrows. To this end we derive a simple formula for fan, which uses the assumption that $\mathsf{N} = \mathsf{L} \circ \mathsf{R}$ is a composition of adjoint functors.

But first, we have to set up the infrastructure. From the data above we can generate two distributive laws [32]:

$$\alpha = \tau - \sigma^{\circ} = \mathsf{R} \circ \sigma^{\circ} \cdot \tau \circ \mathsf{L} : \mathsf{D} \circ \mathsf{M} \dot{\to} \mathsf{M} \circ \mathsf{D} \ , \quad (7.1a)$$

$$\gamma = \sigma^{\circ} - \tau = \mathsf{L} \circ \tau \cdot \sigma^{\circ} \circ \mathsf{R} : \mathsf{C} \circ \mathsf{N} \dot{\to} \mathsf{N} \circ \mathsf{C} \ . \quad (7.1b)$$

The distributive law γ satisfies the two requirements for λ (6.6) (note that $\mathsf{N}^{\gamma} = \mathsf{L}^{\sigma^{\circ}} \circ \mathsf{R}^{\tau}$); the distributive law α of an endofunctor over a monad enjoys analogous conditions:

$$\alpha \cdot \mathsf{D} \circ \eta = \eta \circ \mathsf{D} \ , \quad (7.2a)$$

$$\alpha \cdot \mathsf{D} \circ \mu = \mu \circ \mathsf{D} \cdot \mathsf{M} \circ \alpha \cdot \alpha \circ \mathsf{M} \ . \quad (7.2b)$$

Next we construct an initial γ-bialgebra. Since $\mathsf{L}\ (\mu\mathsf{D}) \cong \mu\mathsf{C}$, we know that $(\mathsf{L}^{\sigma^{\circ}}\ in, \mathsf{L}\ (\mu\mathsf{D}))$ is initial in $\mathsf{C}\text{-}\mathbf{Alg}(\mathscr{C})$. To determine a formula for *fan*, the corresponding coalgebra part, we have to delve a bit deeper into the theory. The Eilenberg-Moore adjunction $\mathsf{U_N} \dashv \mathsf{Cofree_N}$ has an important property: it is the largest adjunction that generates N, in the sense that for every adjunction $\mathsf{L} \dashv \mathsf{R}$ there is a unique adjoint square from $\mathsf{L} \dashv \mathsf{R}$ to $\mathsf{U_N} \dashv \mathsf{Cofree_N}$, see the diagram on the left below. (Since the distributive laws of the adjoint square are identities, it is actually a so-called *map of adjunctions*.)

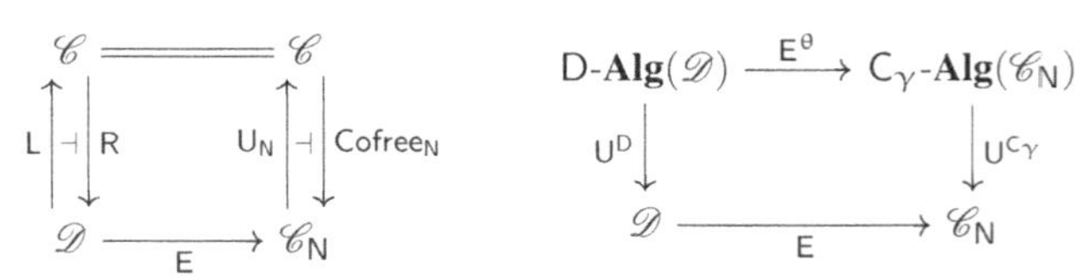

The so-called *comparison functor* $\mathsf{E} : \mathscr{D} \to \mathscr{C}_{\mathsf{N}}$ is defined

$$\mathsf{E}\, A = (\mathsf{L}\, A, \mathsf{L}\ (\eta\, A)) \ , \quad (7.3a)$$

$$\mathsf{E} f = \mathsf{L} f \ . \quad (7.3b)$$

Since the distributive laws of the adjoint square are identities, we have $\mathsf{U_N} \circ \mathsf{E} = \mathsf{Id} \circ \mathsf{L}$ and $\mathsf{E} \circ \mathsf{R} = \mathsf{Cofree_N} \circ \mathsf{Id}$.

Note that the carrier of $\mathsf{E}\, A$ is $\mathsf{L}\, A$, which suggests that the coalgebra part of the initial γ-bialgebra is perhaps just $\mathsf{L}\ (\eta\ (\mu\mathsf{D}))$.

Then it remains to verify that $\mathsf{L}^{\sigma^\circ}\ in$ and $\mathsf{L}\ (\eta\ (\mu\mathsf{D}))$ satisfy the pentagonal law. We prove, in fact, a slightly more general result: we show that $(\mathsf{L}^{\sigma^\circ}\ a, \mathsf{L}\ A, \mathsf{L}\ (\eta\ A))$ is a γ-bialgebra, by lifting the comparison functor E to categories of algebras, see diagram on the right above. To this end, we need a distributive law $\theta : \mathsf{E} \circ \mathsf{D} \dot{\leftarrow} \mathsf{C}_\gamma \circ \mathsf{E}$. We claim that σ° itself fits the bill: $\mathsf{U}_\mathsf{N} \circ \theta = \sigma^\circ$. (Note that $\mathsf{U}_\mathsf{N} \circ \mathsf{E} \circ \mathsf{D} \dot{\leftarrow} \mathsf{U}_\mathsf{N} \circ \mathsf{C}_\gamma \circ \mathsf{E} = \mathsf{L} \circ \mathsf{D} \dot{\leftarrow} \mathsf{C} \circ \mathsf{L}$). In other words, we have to show that σ° is a natural N-coalgebra homomorphism of type $\mathsf{E} \circ \mathsf{D} \dot{\leftarrow} \mathsf{C}_\gamma \circ \mathsf{E}$. Plugging in the definitions, we reason

$$
\begin{array}{ll}
 & \mathsf{L} \circ \eta \circ \mathsf{D} \cdot \sigma^\circ \\
= & \{\ \alpha \text{ respects } \eta \text{ (7.2a)}\ \} \\
 & \mathsf{L} \circ \alpha \cdot \mathsf{L} \circ \mathsf{D} \circ \eta \cdot \sigma^\circ \\
= & \{\ \sigma^\circ \text{ is natural}\ \} \\
 & \mathsf{L} \circ \alpha \cdot \sigma^\circ \circ \mathsf{M} \cdot \mathsf{C} \circ \mathsf{L} \circ \eta \\
= & \{\ \sigma^\circ - \alpha = \sigma^\circ - \tau - \sigma^\circ = \gamma - \sigma^\circ\ \} \\
 & \mathsf{N} \circ \sigma^\circ \cdot \gamma \circ \mathsf{L} \cdot \mathsf{C} \circ \mathsf{L} \circ \eta\ .
\end{array}
$$

We have derived the following attractive definition of *fan*:

$$
fan = \mathsf{L}\ (\eta\ (\mu\mathsf{D}))\ , \qquad (7.4)
$$

which is in most cases a much more efficient implementation than $(\!|\mathsf{N}\ in \cdot \lambda\ (\mu\mathsf{F})|\!)$.

We are now ready to show that adjoint folds are recursion schemes from comonads, provided that a distributive isomorphism $\sigma : \mathsf{L} \circ \mathsf{D} \cong \mathsf{C} \circ \mathsf{L}$ exists. Here is the diagram for rsfcs with applications of the isomorphism σ made explicit.

$$
\begin{array}{ccccccc}
\mathsf{L}\ (\mathsf{D}\ (\mu\mathsf{D})) & \xrightarrow{\sigma\ (\mu\mathsf{D})} & \mathsf{C}\ (\mathsf{L}\ (\mu\mathsf{D})) & \xrightarrow{\mathsf{C}\ (\mathsf{N}\ x \cdot fan)} & \mathsf{C}\ (\mathsf{N}\ B) & \xrightarrow{\sigma^\circ\ (\mathsf{R}\ B)} & \mathsf{L}\ (\mathsf{D}\ (\mathsf{R}\ B)) \\
\downarrow{\scriptstyle \mathsf{L}\ in} & & \downarrow{\scriptstyle \mathsf{L}^{\sigma^\circ}\ in} & & \downarrow{\scriptstyle b \cdot \sigma^\circ\ (\mathsf{R}\ B)} & & \downarrow{\scriptstyle b} \\
\mathsf{L}\ (\mu\mathsf{D}) & = & \mathsf{L}\ (\mu\mathsf{D}) & \xrightarrow[x]{} & B & = & B
\end{array}
$$

Thus, it remains to show that $\mathsf{L}\ \lfloor x \rfloor = \mathsf{N}\ x \cdot fan$.

$$
\begin{array}{ll}
 & \mathsf{L}\ \lfloor x \rfloor \\
= & \{\ \lfloor - \rfloor \text{ expressed in terms of } \eta\text{; (3.4a) with } k, f, h := x, id, id\ \} \\
 & \mathsf{L}\ (\mathsf{R}\ x \cdot \eta\ (\mu\mathsf{D})) \\
= & \{\ \mathsf{L} \text{ functor and definition of } fan \text{ (7.4)}\ \} \\
 & \mathsf{N}\ x \cdot fan
\end{array}
$$

We record the result in the following

Theorem 7.1. *An adjoint fold based on the adjunction* $\mathsf{L} \dashv \mathsf{R}$ *and the canonical control functor can be framed as a recursion scheme for the comonad* $\mathsf{N} = \mathsf{L} \circ \mathsf{R}$ *if there is a control functor* C *and a conjugate pair of distributive laws with* σ *an isomorphism:*

$$
\sigma : \mathsf{L} \circ \mathsf{D} \cong \mathsf{C} \circ \mathsf{L} \quad \dashv \quad \tau : \mathsf{D} \circ \mathsf{R} \dot{\to} \mathsf{R} \circ \mathsf{C}\ .
$$

The distributive law $\lambda : \mathsf{C} \circ \mathsf{N} \dot{\to} \mathsf{N} \circ \mathsf{C}$ *is given by* $\sigma^\circ - \tau$.

Example 7.2. Mutumorphisms are an instance of rsfcs using $\sigma = id : \Delta \circ \mathsf{D} = \mathsf{D}^2 \circ \Delta$, see Example 5.6. Since the isomorphism is an identity, we can transform the diagram for adjoints folds almost directly into a corresponding diagram for rsfcs ($A := \mu\mathsf{D}$).

$$
\begin{array}{ccc}
\Delta\ (\mathsf{D}\ A) & \xrightarrow{\Delta\ (\mathsf{D}\ \lfloor x \rfloor)} & \Delta\ (\mathsf{D}\ ((\times)\ B)) \\
\downarrow{\scriptstyle \Delta\ in} & & \downarrow{\scriptstyle b} \\
\Delta\ A & \xrightarrow[x]{} & B
\end{array}
\quad \Longleftrightarrow \quad
\begin{array}{ccc}
\mathsf{D}^2\ (\Delta\ A)) & \xrightarrow{\mathsf{D}^2\ (\Delta\ \lfloor x \rfloor)} & \mathsf{D}^2\ (\Delta\ ((\times)\ B)) \\
\downarrow{\scriptstyle \Delta\ in} & & \downarrow{\scriptstyle b} \\
\Delta\ A & \xrightarrow[x]{} & B
\end{array}
$$

In the upper right corner we discover the comonad $\mathsf{N} = \Delta \circ (\times)$, which works over a product category. As $fan = \Delta\ (id \vartriangle id)$, we have $\Delta\ \lfloor x \rfloor = \Delta\ ((\times)\ x \cdot (id \vartriangle id)) = \mathsf{N}\ x \cdot fan$. If we identify $\Delta\ (\mu\mathsf{D})$ and $\mu\mathsf{D}^2$ so that $\Delta\ in = in$, the diagram for rsfcs emerges. □

We have seen in the previous section that an rsfc (based on a comonad N and a distributive law $\lambda : \mathsf{F} \circ \mathsf{N} \dot{\to} \mathsf{N} \circ \mathsf{F}$) can be framed as an adjoint fold, which in turn is based on the Eilenberg-Moore adjunction $\mathsf{U}_\mathsf{N} \dashv \mathsf{Cofree}_\mathsf{N}$. Now, what happens if we go round in a circle, instantiating the development above to $\mathsf{D} = \mathsf{F}_\lambda$, $\mathsf{C} = \mathsf{F}$, and $id : \mathsf{U}_\mathsf{N} \circ \mathsf{F}_\lambda = \mathsf{F} \circ \mathsf{U}_\mathsf{N}$? Recall that $\mathsf{U}_\mathsf{N} \circ \tau = \lambda$; consequently,

$$
\gamma = \sigma^\circ - \tau = \mathsf{U}_\mathsf{N} \circ \tau \cdot id^\circ \circ \mathsf{Cofree}_\mathsf{N} = \lambda\ .
$$

Hence, we obtain back the original rsfc!

We have seen that mutumorphisms based on $\Delta \dashv (\times)$ can be modelled by using an rsfc. Of course, this does not work for every adjunction. As an example, consider the curry adjunction. One would need a control functor C such that:

$$
\sigma : (- \times P) \circ \mathsf{D} \cong \mathsf{C} \circ (- \times P)\ .
$$

Such a control functor is not guaranteed to exist for all datatypes.

8. Related Work

Adjoint folds Mendler-style adjoint folds first appeared in a paper by Bird and Paterson [4], where they were used to show that generalised folds are uniquely defined. (Somewhat ironically, adjoint folds were *only* used in the proofs, not as a general recursion principle.) The algebraic variant of adjoint folds that we have employed throughout was introduced by Matthes and Uustalu [20] under the name *generalised iteration*. The first author of the present paper explored the design space of adjoint folds [11], identifying the adjunctions underlying various recursion schemes. The paper also shows how to combine recursion schemes by combining the underlying adjunctions. Alas, we wrote "However, we cannot reasonably expect that adjoint (un)folds subsume all existing species of morphisms. For instance, a largely orthogonal extension of standard folds are *recursion schemes from comonads*."

Recursion schemes from comonads Recursion schemes from comonads are due to Uustalu et al. [30]. Simultaneously and independently, Bartels [2] introduced the dual construction under name *λ-coiteration*. Technically, his work is closest to ours in the use of λ-bialgebras, although our proofs differ considerably in that we make use of the Eilenberg-Moore construction. Bartels also discussed variations of the scheme that do not rely on a monad structure. These and further variations were used in a recent ICFP paper [12] to prove the unique fixed-point principle correct.

Categorical fixed-point calculus The roots of the initial algebra approach to the semantics of datatypes can be traced back to the work of Lambek [16] on fixed points in categories. Lambek suggests that lattice theory provides a fruitful source of inspiration for results in category theory. These ideas were picked up by Backhouse et al. [1], where a number of lattice-theoretic fixed-point rules were generalised to categories, type fusion being one of them.

Category theory Most of the category theory utilised in this paper is fairly standard—[17] is a good reference—except perhaps the material on distributive laws and conjugates. An extensive account of the relationship between adjunctions and monads is provided by Vidal and Tur [32]. Roughly speaking, they show that the Eilenberg-Moore construction is a right biadjoint to the Huber construction.

9. Conclusion

As one might expect, everything dualises elegantly. There is insufficient space to tell the full story here; but the essential fact is that adjoint unfolds subsume anamorphisms, apomorphisms, generalised unfolds, λ-coiteration, futumorphisms, and other dual patterns that have not yet been formally christened. Table 1 provides an overview of the various morphisms and their duals, and shows how they are captured in the framework of adjoint (un)folds.

(a) catamorphism [10, 19]	$\mathsf{Id} \dashv \mathsf{Id}$	*depth*	(b) anamorphism [10, 19]	$\mathsf{Id} \dashv \mathsf{Id}$
mutumorphism [8]	$\Delta \dashv (\times)$	*even/odd*	(mutumorphism)	$(+) \dashv \Delta$
special case: zygomorphism [18]		*perfect*	—	
special case: paramorphism [21]		*wc*	apomorphism [31]	
fold with a parameter [25]	$- \times P \dashv (-)^P$	*cat, depths*	—	
generalised fold [4]	$(- \circ \mathsf{P}) \dashv \mathsf{Ran}_\mathsf{P}$	*total*	(generalised unfold)	$\mathsf{Lan}_\mathsf{P} \dashv (- \circ \mathsf{P})$
recursion scheme from a comonad [30]	$\mathsf{U}_\mathsf{N} \dashv \mathsf{Cofree}_\mathsf{N}$		λ-coiteration [2]	$\mathsf{Free}^\mathsf{M} \dashv \mathsf{U}^\mathsf{M}$
special case: histomorphism [26]		*knapsack*	*special case:* futumorphism [26]	

Table 1. Adjoint folds (a) and unfolds (b); Lan_P and Ran_P are left and right Kan extensions, $\mathsf{Free}^\mathsf{M} \dashv \mathsf{U}^\mathsf{M}$ is the Eilenberg-Moore adjunction

This paper shows again the importance of adjunctions. They have played a pivotal role in the categorical analysis of logic; we believe that will prove just as important in the theory of programming. The unification of recursion schemes we have presented is mathematically satisfying: in the economy of expression it provides (for example, for reasoning about products in $\mathsf{F}\text{-}\mathbf{Alg}(\mathscr{C})$), and especially in the simple reassurance it provides through things just fitting together in the right way. But it is more than merely an intellectual curiosity: the additional structure we have uncovered promises concrete returns, too—for example, through general techniques for combining different recursion schemes, by composing the corresponding adjunctions. In practice, most functions do indeed use a combination of recursion schemes (in particular, functions over parametric datatypes).

In future work, we intend to explore the calculational properties of adjoint folds; our earlier paper [11] lists several laws, and it would be interesting to know whether the laws for recursion schemes from comonads of Uustalu et al. [30] are instances of these. Another interesting direction is to explore the use of *recursive* coalgebras [5] (or *corecursive* algebras) in λ-bialgebras.

Acknowledgments

This work has been funded by EPSRC grant number EP/J010995/1, on Unifying Theories of Generic Programming. The authors would like to thank the anonymous reviewers and José Pedro Magalhães for their helpful and constructive comments.

References

[1] R. Backhouse, M. Bijsterveld, R. van Geldrop, and J. van der Woude, "Categorical fixed point calculus," in *CTCS*, ser. LNCS, vol. 953. Springer, 1995, pp. 159–179.

[2] F. Bartels, "Generalised coinduction," *Mathematical Structures in Computer Science*, vol. 13, pp. 321–348, 2003.

[3] R. Bird and O. de Moor, *Algebra of Programming*. London: Prentice Hall, 1997.

[4] R. Bird and R. Paterson, "Generalised folds for nested datatypes," *Formal Aspects of Computing*, vol. 11, no. 2, pp. 200–222, 1999.

[5] V. Capretta, T. Uustalu, and V. Vene, "Recursive coalgebras from comonads," *Information and Computation*, vol. 204, no. 4, pp. 437–468, 2006.

[6] S. Eilenberg and J. C. Moore, "Adjoint functors and triples," *Illinois J. Math*, vol. 9, no. 3, pp. 381–398, 1965.

[7] M. M. Fokkinga, "Law and order in algorithmics," Ph.D. dissertation, University of Twente, Feb. 1992.

[8] ——, "Tupling and mutumorphisms," *The Squiggolist*, vol. 1, no. 4, pp. 81–82, Jun. 1990.

[9] J. Gibbons, "Generic downwards accumulations," *Science of Computer Programming*, vol. 37, no. 1-3, pp. 37–65, 2000.

[10] T. Hagino, "Category theoretic approach to data types," Ph.D. dissertation, University of Edinburgh, 1987.

[11] R. Hinze, "Adjoint folds and unfolds—an extended study," *Science of Computer Programming*, Aug. 2012.

[12] R. Hinze and D. W. James, "Proving the unique fixed-point principle correct: an adventure with category theory," in *ICFP*. ACM, 2011, pp. 359–371.

[13] P. J. Huber, "Homotopy theory in general categories," *Math. Ann.*, vol. 144, pp. 361–385, 1961.

[14] D. M. Kan, "Adjoint functors," *Trans. AMS*, vol. 87, no. 2, pp. 294–329, 1958.

[15] H. Kleisli, "Every standard construction is induced by a pair of adjoint functors," *Proc. AMS*, vol. 16, no. 3, pp. 544–546, Jun. 1965.

[16] J. Lambek, "A fixpoint theorem for complete categories," *Math. Zeitschr.*, vol. 103, pp. 151–161, 1968.

[17] S. Mac Lane, *Categories for the Working Mathematician*, 2nd ed., ser. Graduate Texts in Mathematics. Berlin: Springer-Verlag, 1998.

[18] G. Malcolm, "Algebraic data types and program transformation," Ph.D. dissertation, University of Groningen, 1990.

[19] ——, "Data structures and program transformation," *Science of Computer Programming*, vol. 14, no. 2–3, pp. 255–280, 1990.

[20] R. Matthes and T. Uustalu, "Substitution in non-wellfounded syntax with variable binding," *TCS*, vol. 327, no. 1–2, pp. 155–174, 2004.

[21] L. Meertens, "Paramorphisms," *Formal Aspects of Computing*, vol. 4, pp. 413–424, 1992.

[22] E. Meijer, M. Fokkinga, and R. Paterson, "Functional programming with bananas, lenses, envelopes and barbed wire," in *FPLCA*, ser. LNCS, vol. 523. Springer, 1991, pp. 124–144.

[23] N. P. Mendler, "Inductive types and type constraints in the second-order lambda calculus," *Ann. Pure Appl. Logic*, vol. 51, no. 1–2, pp. 159–172, 1991.

[24] P. H. Palmquist, "The double category of adjoint squares," in *Midwest Category Seminar V*, ser. LNM. Springer, 1971, vol. 195, pp. 123–153.

[25] A. Pardo, "Generic accumulations," in *Working Conference on Generic Programming*, vol. 243. Kluwer Academic Publishers, Jul. 2002, pp. 49–78.

[26] T. Uustalu and V. Vene, "Primitive (co)recursion and course-of-value (co)iteration, categorically," *Informatica, Lith. Acad. Sci.*, vol. 10, no. 1, pp. 5–26, 1999.

[27] ——, "Comonadic notions of computation," in *CMCS*, ser. ENTCS, vol. 203(5), 2008, pp. 263–284.

[28] ——, "Mendler-style inductive types, categorically," *Nordic J. Comput.*, vol. 6, pp. 343–361, 1999.

[29] ——, "The recursion scheme from the cofree recursive comonad," *ENTCS*, vol. 229, no. 5, pp. 135–157, 2011, proceedings of the Second Workshop on Mathematically Structured Functional Programming (MSFP 2008).

[30] T. Uustalu, V. Vene, and A. Pardo, "Recursion schemes from comonads," *Nordic J. Comput.*, vol. 8, pp. 366–390, Sep. 2001.

[31] V. Vene and T. Uustalu, "Functional programming with apomorphisms (corecursion)," *Proceedings of the Estonian Academy of Sciences: Physics, Mathematics*, vol. 47, no. 3, pp. 147–161, 1998.

[32] J. C. Vidal and J. S. Tur, "Kleisli and Eilenberg-Moore constructions as parts of biadjoint situations," *Extracta Mathematicae*, vol. 25, no. 1, pp. 1–61, 2010.

Higher-Order Functional Reactive Programming without Spacetime Leaks

Neelakantan R. Krishnaswami
Max Planck Institute for Software Systems (MPI-SWS)
neelk@mpi-sws.org

Abstract

Functional reactive programming (FRP) is an elegant approach to declaratively specify reactive systems. However, the powerful abstractions of FRP have historically made it difficult to predict and control the resource usage of programs written in this style.

In this paper, we give a new language for higher-order reactive programming. Our language generalizes and simplifies prior type systems for reactive programming, by supporting the use of streams of streams, first-class functions, and higher-order operations. We also support many temporal operations beyond streams, such as terminatable streams, events, and even resumptions with first-class schedulers. Furthermore, our language supports an efficient implementation strategy permitting us to eagerly deallocate old values and statically rule out *spacetime leaks*, a notorious source of inefficiency in reactive programs. Furthermore, these memory guarantees are achieved *without* the use of a complex substructural type discipline.

We also show that our implementation strategy of eager deallocation is safe, by showing the soundness of our type system with a novel step-indexed Kripke logical relation.

Categories and Subject Descriptors D.3.2 [*Dataflow Languages*]

Keywords Functional reactive programming; Kripke logical relations; temporal logic; guarded recursion; dataflow; capabilities; comonads

1. Introduction

Interactive programs engage in an ongoing dialogue with the environment. An interactive program receives an input event from the environment, and computes an output event, and then waits for the next input, which may in turn be affected by the earlier outputs the program has made. Examples of such systems range from embedded controllers and sensor networks, up to graphical user interfaces, web applications, and video games.

Programming interactive applications in general purpose programming languages can be very confusing, since the different components of the program do not typically interact via structured control flow (such as loops or direct procedure calls), but instead operate by registering state-manipulating callbacks with one another, which are then implicitly invoked by an event loop. Reasoning about such programs is difficult, since each of these features – higher-order functions, aliased imperative state, and concurrency – is challenging on its own, and their combination takes us to the outer limits of what verification can cope with.

These difficulties, plus the critical nature of many reactive systems, have inspired a great deal of research into languages, libraries and analysis techniques for reactive programming. Two of the main strands of work on this problem are the *synchronous dataflow languages*, and *functional reactive programming*.

Synchronous dataflow languages, such Esterel [5], Lustre [7], and Lucid Synchrone [39], implement a computational model inspired by Kahn networks. Programs are fixed networks of stream-processing nodes that communicate with each other, each node consuming and producing a statically-known number of primitive values at each clock tick. These languages deliver strong guarantees on space and time usage, and so see wide use in applications such as hardware synthesis and embedded control software.

Functional reactive programming, introduced by Elliott and Hudak [15], also works with time-varying values (rather than mutable state) as a primitive abstraction. However, it provides a much richer model than synchronous languages do. Signals are first-class values, and can be used freely, including in higher-order functions and signal-valued signals, which permits writing programs which dynamically grow and alter the dataflow network. FRP has been applied to problem domains such as robotics, games, music, and GUIs, illustrating the power of the FRP model.

However, this power comes at a steep price. Modeling A-valued signals as streams A^ω (in the real-valued case, $A^\mathbb{R}$) and reactive systems as functions $\mathsf{Input}^\omega \to \mathsf{Output}^\omega$ has several problems. First, this model does not enforce causality (that is, output at time n depends only upon inputs at earlier times), nor does it ensure that feedback (used to define signals recursively) is well-founded. Second, since the model of FRP abstracts away from resource usage, it is easy to write programs with significant resource leaks by inadvertently accumulating the entire history of a signal – that is,"space leaks".[1] For example, consider the simple program below:

$$\mathsf{bad\_const} : S\,\mathbb{N} \to S\,(S\,\mathbb{N}) \qquad 1$$
$$\mathsf{bad\_const}\ ns = \mathsf{cons}(ns, \mathsf{bad\_const}\ ns) \qquad 2$$

The bad_const function takes a stream of numbers as an argument, and then returns that stream constantly. So if it receives the stream $(a, b, c, \ldots)$, then it returns a stream of streams with $(a, b, c, \ldots)$ as its first element, with $(a, b, c, \ldots)$ as its second element, and so on

[1] In reactive programming, the phrase "space leak" usually refers only to memory leaks arising from capturing too much history, since they form the species of memory leak that functional programmers are unused to debugging. Relatedly, there are also "time leaks", which occur when a signal is sampled infrequently. Under lazy evaluation, infrequent sampling can lead to the head of a stream growing to become a large computation.

ICFP '13, September 25-27, Boston, MA, USA..

ACM 978-1-4503-2326-0/13/09... $15.00.
http://dx.doi.org/10.1145/2500365.2500588

indefinitely. This is a perfectly natural, even boring, *mathematical* function on streams, but many *implementations* leak memory. Consider the following diagram, illustrating how a stream data structure evolves over time:

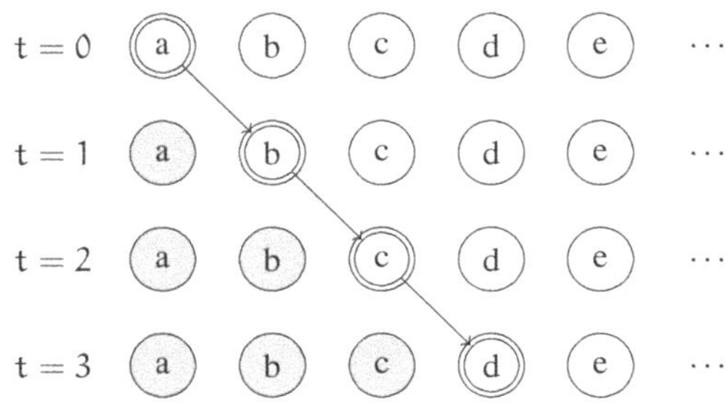

Here, a stream is a computation incrementally producing values. At time 0, the stream yields the value "a", and at time 1, it yields the value "b", and so on. Each value in a double-circle represents the stream's *current value* at time t, and the values in white circles represent the stream's *future values*, and the values in gray circles represent the stream's *past values*. (So there are n gray circles at time n.)

If a pointer to the head of a stream persists, then at time n all of the first $n + 1$ values of the stream will be accessible, and so we will need to store all the values the stream has produced – all of the grey nodes, plus the double-circled node. Thus, at time n, we will have to store n elements of history, which means that the memory usage of the bad_const function will be $O(n)$ at time n. So the accidental use of a function like bad_const in a long-running program will eventually consume all of the memory available.

To avoid this problem, a number of alternative designs, such as such as *event-driven FRP* [43] and *arrowized FRP* [35], have been proposed. The common thread in this work is to give up on treating signals as first-class values, and instead offer a collection of combinators to construct stream transformer functions (that is, functions of type $S\ A \to S\ B$) from smaller ones. Streams of streams (and other time-dependent values) are forbidden, and each of the exported combinators is designed to ensure that only efficient stream transformers can be constructed.

Restricting programmers to indirect access to streams is akin to a first-order programming style, since it makes it difficult to abstract over stream-manipulating operations. This restriction is also quite similar to those synchronous dataflow languages impose, and Liu et al. [30] exploit this resemblance to develop a compilation scheme (reminiscent of the Bohm-Jacopini theorem) to compile arrow programs into efficient single-loop code, much as compilers for Esterel and Lucid do. Sculthorpe and Nilsson [40] extend the arrowized approach further, by using dependent types to enforce causality.

However, dynamic modification of the dataflow graph is very natural for interactive programs. For example, in a graphical program, we may wish to associate dataflow networks with windows, which are created and destroyed as a program executes. To support this, arrowized FRP libraries need to add additional combinators to restore dynamic behavior. These combinators make unwanted memory leaks possible once more (though less easily than in the original FRP). They also have a somewhat *ad-hoc* flavor: since first-class and higher-order stream types are unavailable, somewhat complex and strange types are needed to encode typical usage patterns.

To recover a more natural programming style, Krishnaswami and Benton [27] proposed a lambda-calculus for stream programming based on the guarded recursion calculus of Nakano [34], which ensured by typing that all definitions are causal and well-founded. Jeffrey [19] and Jeltsch [22] further observed that it is possible to use the formulas of linear temporal logic [38] as types for reactive programs. However, while all of these papers offer a coherent account of causality (not using values from the future, and ensuring that all recursive definitions are guarded), none of them have much to say about the memory behavior of their programs.

To resolve this problem, Krishnaswami et al. [28] gave a calculus which retains the causality checking and fully higher order style of [19, 22, 27], but which also uses linear types to control the memory usage of reactive programs. This calculus passes around linearly-typed tokens representing the right to allocate stream values, which ensures that no program can ever allocate a dataflow graph which is larger than the total number of permissions passed in. This solution works, but is *too precise* to be useful in practice. The exact size of the dataflow graph is revealed in a program's type, and so even modest refactorings lead to massive changes in the type signature of program components.

Contributions Our contributions are as follows:

1. We give a new implementation strategy, described using operational semantics, for higher-order reactive programming. Our semantics rules out space and time leaks *by construction*, making it *impossible* to write programs which accidentally retain temporal values over long periods of time.

   To accomplish this, we describe the semantics of reactive programs with two operational semantics. The first semantics explains how to evaluate program terms in the current clock tick, and the second is a "tick relation" for advancing the clock.

   Expressions in a reactive language can be divided into two classes, those which must be evaluated now, and those which must be evaluated later, on future clock ticks. We evaluate current expressions using a call-by-value strategy, and we suspend future expressions by placing them in mutable thunks on the heap, in a style reminiscent of call-by-need. Evaluating current expressions in a call-by-value style prevents time leaks, by making streams head-strict [42].

   Future expressions can only be evaluated in the future, and the tick relation describes how to advance the clock into the future. This semantics works by going through the heap of thunks, and forcing each expression scheduled for execution on the current time step. Furthermore, we achieve our goal of blocking space leaks through the simple but drastic measure of *deleting all old values*, thereby making it operationally impossible to accidentally retain a reference to a value past its lifetime.

2. We give a simple type theory for a higher-order reactive programming language.

   Our type system generalizes earlier work on using temporal logic [19, 22, 27] to type reactive programs. Instead of using formulas of temporal logic as types, we take a standard simply-typed lambda calculus, and introduce a *delay modality* $\bullet A$ of terms of type A that can be evaluated "on the next tick of the clock", and add to that the new notion of a *temporal recursive type* $\hat{\mu}\alpha.\ A$, which allows defining types which are recursive through time.

   This recursive type construct allows *encoding* all of the standard temporal operators as derived constructions within our calculus – streams, events, and even resumptions are all definable within our system, as are higher-order functions to construct and manipulate elements of these types.

   To retain control over space leaks, we simplify the work of Krishnaswami et al. [28] on using linear types to prevent space leaks in reactive systems. We introduce a new kind of *type-based capability* which grants the *right* to allocate memory, without having to enumerate the exact *amount* of memory used. As a result, we do not need the complexities of a substructural type system, and moreover we no longer reflect exact memory usage in types, which improves the modularity of reactive programs.

3. We show that our type discipline is sound by means of a novel step-indexed Kripke logical relation.

   Deleting old values naturally raises the question of what happens if we accidentally reference a deleted value. Our logical relation lets us prove that no well-typed program will ever dereference a deallocated location, and that expressions whose types say they do not allocate memory, do not actually allocate memory. Furthermore, the logical relation shows that the expression relation is total for well-typed terms, despite the presence of a term-level fixed point. This demonstrates that we can only define well-founded and causal loop structures.

Supplementary Material Full proofs of the main results in this paper, and statements and proofs of all the supporting lemmas, can be found in the accompanying technical report.

2. Programming Language

We begin with a description of our language design. We give the syntax of types, terms, and values in Figure 1, the syntax of contexts in Figure 2, and the typing rules in Figures 3, 4, and 5. The operational semantics of expressions is in Figure 6, and the semantics of advancing the clock is in Figure 7.

Overview In a reactive language, an explicit notion of time is exposed to the programmer, and so we will need to extend the operational semantics to account for time, and then give a modified type system which properly reflects the semantics.

Our operational semantics consists of two relations. The expression relation $\langle\sigma; e\rangle \Downarrow \langle\sigma'; v\rangle$ describes how to evaluate an expression within a single timestep. This relation, given in Figure 6, is a standard big-step, call-by-value operational semantics for a functional language with a store. As we will see, the use of a call-by-value semantics rules out time leaks, since they are inherently an artifact of lazy evaluation.

However, the stores are not unrestricted heaps in the style of ML. Since reactive languages allow programmers to schedule *when* different expressions should be executed, there are program expressions which should not be executed right away. We put these expressions into a store, with the idea that the code stored in the heap will be evaluated later. In terms of reactive programming idioms, the store represents *the dataflow graph* of the program, which contains the nodes that will supply values on later ticks of the clock. In terms of functional programming idioms, the store implements *lazy evaluation*, in a variant of call-by-need where thunks are explicitly scheduled for later execution.

To actually advance the clock, we give the *tick relation* $\sigma \Longrightarrow \sigma'$, which describes (Figure 7) how the store σ is transformed into a store σ' when the clock ticks. As expected, our relation evaluates all of the computations scheduled for evaluation on the next tick. The tick semantics also makes space leaks impossible, by construction: brutally but expediently it *deletes all values* that are more than one tick old.

It is now trivially the case that it is impossible to inadvertently store a history too long – but, at what price? Surprisingly, we can show that the price is low. We give a type discipline, which not only ensures that all well-typed programs are *safe* (in that they never try to access a deleted value), but which is also *expressive*, in that natural reactive programs (higher-order or not) are still well-typed.

Since the passage of time is a central feature of our operational semantics, we introduce three *temporal qualifiers*, now, later, and stable, to explain *when* some expression is well-typed, and when a variable may be used. The now qualifier means "in the present time step", the later qualifier means "on the next time step", and the stable qualifier means "at any time step, present or future".

As a result, our typing judgment takes the form $\Gamma \vdash e : A\ q$, where q is a qualifier. So the informal reading of the typing judgment is "under hypotheses Γ, the expression e has type A at time q." Just as expressions have temporal qualifiers, so too do the hypotheses in the context. The context Γ (with a grammar given in Figure 2) consists of a list of hypotheses of the form $x : A\ q$, which gives not just a type A for each variable x, but also gives a qualifier q controlling when we may use the variable x.

Types, Terms, and Expression Evaluation The core of our programming language is essentially the simply-typed lambda calculus. The basic types include product types $A \times B$ with pairs (e, e') and projections $\mathsf{fst}\, e$ and $\mathsf{snd}\, e$, disjoint unions $A + B$ with injections $\mathsf{inl}\, e$ and $\mathsf{inr}\, e$ and a case statement $\mathsf{case}(e, \mathsf{inl}\, x \to e', \mathsf{inr}\, y \to e'')$, and function types $A \to B$ with lambda-abstractions $\lambda x.\, e$ and applications $e\ e'$, as well as a variety of primitive types (such as numbers $\mathbb{N}$ and booleans bool). The typing rules for these constructs are all given in Figure 3, and are all standard. Similarly, the reduction rules for these terms are given in the first half of Figure 6, and are also standard.

To this, we add a number of features to deal with time.

First, we have the next-step operator $\bullet A$. The intuitive reading of this type is that an inhabitant of $\bullet A$ is a term that, when evaluated on the next time step, will yield a value of type A – the type of "A's tomorrow". The introduction form is the delay term $\delta_{e'}(e)$, which says that e is a term to evaluate on the next time step. Consequently, its typing rule $\bullet$I requires e to be typechecked later. The elimination form is a binding-style elimination form, $\mathsf{let}\ \delta(x) = e\ \mathsf{in}\ e'$. The typing rule $\bullet$E asserts that e is of type $\bullet A$, and the variable x is of type A, but with the later qualifier. This ensures that the body e' does not use e's value before it is available.

Operationally, we do not evaluate the body e of a delayed expression $\delta_{e'}(e)$ right away. Instead, we extend the store with a pointer $l : e$ later to a thunk e, which will be evaluated on the next time step. These pointers implement a form of call-by-need, ensuring that even if we use a delayed variable multiple times, the delayed expression will itself only be evaluated once. This can be seen in the reduction rule for $\mathsf{let}\ \delta(x) = e\ \mathsf{in}\ e'$. Here, if e evaluates to the pointer l, the reduction rule substitutes $!l$, a dereferencing of the pointer, for x in e'.

The allocation of a thunk extends the reactive program's dataflow graph, and the growth of the dataflow graph is something we must control. To achieve this, we use the subscripted argument e' in the delay introduction form $\delta_{e'}(e)$. This argument must be of the allocation type alloc, and indicates a permission to allocate heap storage. Since the type alloc represents a pure capability [32], we have no introduction or elimination forms for it; a token (denoted by $\diamond$ in our syntax) representing this capability must be passed in to a closed program by the runtime system of the language. Thus, programmers may control whether or not a function allocates by controlling whether or not they pass it an allocation capability.

Pointer expressions l, dereference expressions $!l$, and resource tokens $\diamond$ are all internal forms of our language, and cannot be written by a programmer. (As a result, there are no typing rules for them.)

Values of $\bullet A$ type are time-dependent, in the sense that their representation changes over time: when the clock ticks, the dataflow graph/store is evaluated, and pointers are updated. This means that they should only be used on particular time steps. Other types, such as natural numbers or booleans, consist of values whose representation does not change over time. These *stable values* may safely be used at many different times. Values of other types, such as functions $A \to B$, are either time-dependent or stable, depending on whether or not they capture any time-dependent values in their environment.

So we also introduce a modal type $\Box A$, which contains only those values of type A which are *stable*. The introduction form $\mathsf{stable}(e)$ ensures that e has the type A under the stable qualifier, and the elimination form $\mathsf{let\ stable}(x) = e \mathsf{\ in\ } e'$ takes a term e of type $\Box A$, and binds x to a stable variable. Since values of certain types (base types, and products and sums of same) are always stable, we also introduce a term $\mathsf{promote}(e)$, which takes a term of an inherently stable type A (as judged by the judgment $A\ \mathsf{stable}$, defined in Figure 5) and returns a value of type $\Box A$.

In order to get interesting temporal data structures, we introduce a *temporal recursive type*, $\hat{\mu}\alpha.\ A$. This type has the expected introduction $\mathsf{into}\ e$ and elimination $\mathsf{out}\ e$ forms, but their types are slightly nonstandard. When constructing a term $\mathsf{into}\ e$ of recursive type $\hat{\mu}\alpha.\ A$, we require e to have the type $[\bullet(\hat{\mu}\alpha.\ A)/\alpha]A$. That is, every occurrence of α in A is substituted with $\bullet(\hat{\mu}\alpha.\ A)$, which is the recursive type *on the next time step*. This lets us use the next-step modality to define data whose structure repeats over time, rather than proceeding only a constant number of steps into the future.

In addition to type-level recursion, we also have a term-level recursion operator $\mathsf{fix}\,x.\ e$. There are no restrictions on the types we may take fixed points at; we only require that if $\mathsf{fix}\,x.\ e$ is of type A, then we assume x is a later variable. This ensures that we can never construct an unguarded loop.

We also include a stream type $\mathsf{S}\,A$, with an introduction form $\mathsf{cons}(e, e')$ and an elimination form $\mathsf{let\ cons}(x, xs) = e \mathsf{\ in\ } e'$. The stream type can be encoded using the other constructs of the language (see Section 3.2), but we include it in order to give a more readable syntax to our examples. However, the $\mathsf{cons}(e, e')$ form does help illustrate why we chose a call-by-value evaluation strategy. Under call-by-value, the head of the stream e is always evaluated to a value. As a result, "time leaks" are impossible, since the head gets reduced to a value on every tick, and so it doesn't matter how frequently a stream is sampled.

Finally, the variable rule HYP says that we can only use a variable now, if it is either stable, or if it is available now. Then, there are the TSTABLE and TLATER rules, which show how to derive terms with the stable and later qualifiers, in terms of the now qualifier. The key to this are the context-clearing operations defined in Figure 2. The $\Gamma^{\Box}$ context operation deletes every now and later hypothesis, ensuring that stable terms may only depend on stable variables. The $\Gamma^{\bullet}$ operation takes a context, and deletes every hypothesis marked now, and changes every later hypothesis to now, ensuring that terms which are typechecked later (1) view the later variables as if they were available in the present, and (2) do not access any variables containing possibly out-of-date values.

Dataflow Graphs The store σ is used to represent the dataflow graph of the program, and contains a collection of pointers, which can be viewed as the nodes in a dataflow graph. Each node is either a suspended expression $l : e\ \mathsf{later}$ to be evaluated on the next tick of the clock, or points to a presently available value $l : v\ \mathsf{now}$, or is undefined $l : \mathsf{null}$ and points to nothing.

Advancing Time We give the tick relation $\sigma \Longrightarrow \sigma'$ in Figure 7, which explains how to advance time for a dataflow graph.

If the dataflow graph σ is empty, then of course the updated store is also empty. In order to evaluate a store $\sigma, l : e\ \mathsf{later}$, we first update the rest of the dataflow graph σ to σ', and then evaluate e in the result store σ' to a value v, updating the pointer to $l : v\ \mathsf{now}$. However, when we see a store $\sigma, l : v\ \mathsf{now}$ containing a value, we evaluate the store, but null out the pointer, setting it to $l : \mathsf{null}$. Finally, once nulled out, null pointers stay nulled out.

This feature of the operational semantics suffices to ensure that FRP-specific space leaks are *impossible* – because our dataflow graph never stores values for more than a single tick, it follows that values can never accumulate and build up into a memory leak. As a result, values in dataflow nodes can never persist in memory unless the programmer explicitly writes code to retain them. (Of course, all the memory leaks traditional to functional programming are still possible – we have simply ensured that reactivity has not added any *new* sources of leaks.)

It is worth reiterating that it is the operational semantics, and not the type system, which ensures the absence of space leaks: because we *delete* everything old, it is simply impossible to remember the past unless the programmer explicitly writes the code to do so. The type system merely acts as a set of guard rails, ensuring that we do not accidentally follow any invalid pointers.

Making dataflow nodes transient is a significant departure from existing imperative implementation strategies for FRP libraries, such as Scala.React [31] or Racket's FrTime [9, 10]. In these libraries, dataflow nodes are persistent, and last across many time steps, and clever heuristics are used to order updates.

Abandoning this strategy pays many dividends. We have already observed that accidental space leaks are no longer possible, but there are also further practical benefits. A real implementation needs to garbage collect null nodes. Fortunately, the structure of our typing rules ensures that well-typed program terms never contain locations that outlive their tick, and as a result, the usual reachability heuristic of standard garbage collectors will work unchanged.

In contrast, persistent dataflow nodes need to manage dependencies explicitly, and as a result, each dataflow cell knows both which cells it reads, and which cells read it. This bidirectional linkage means that if one cell is reachable, all cells are reachable, defeating garbage collection unless special (and often expensive) measures such as weak references are used.

Complete Programs Finally, we need to say a word about what complete programs in our language are. Since we use an object-capability style to control the growth of the dataflow graph, a user program must be a function type, so that it can receive a capability as an argument. Furthermore, since alloc is not a stable type, we will need to supply a fresh capability on each tick.

For this reason, we take user programs to be closed terms of type $\mathsf{S\,alloc} \to A$. If e is such a term, then we will begin evaluation of the program with the call $e\ (\mathsf{fix}\,xs.\ \mathsf{cons}(\diamond, \delta_{\diamond}(xs)))$. The term $\mathsf{fix}\,xs.\ \mathsf{cons}(\diamond, \delta_{\diamond}(xs))$ computes into a term which produces a stream yielding an allocation token $\diamond$ at each tick, but this term cannot itself be typed under our type system, Modeling the fact that the runtime system of the language possesses certain capabilities that user programs do not.

As a result, our metatheory needs to be done in a "semantic" style, using a step-indexed Kripke logical relation, rather than showing soundness through the usual syntactic progress and preservation lemmas.

3. Examples

3.1 Stream Functions

Basic Examples We begin with the constant function on streams. It takes a natural number as an input, and returns a constant stream of that number.

```
1  const : S alloc → ℕ → S ℕ
2  const us n =
3    let cons(u, δ(us')) = us in
4    let stable(x) = promote(n) in
5    cons(x, δ_u(const us' x))
```

In this example, we have a function const which receives a stream of permissions us to allocate, and a number n on line 2. On line 3, we take the head and tail of the permission stream, with a pattern-matching-style nested delay elimination to bind us' to

$$
\begin{array}{llll}
\text{Types} & A & ::= & b \mid A \times B \mid A + B \mid A \to B \\
& & \mid & \bullet A \mid \Box A \mid \hat{\mu}\alpha.\ A \mid S\,A \mid \mathsf{alloc} \\
\text{Terms} & e & ::= & \mathsf{fst}\ e \mid \mathsf{snd}\ e \mid (e, e') \\
& & \mid & \mathsf{inl}\ e \mid \mathsf{inr}\ e \mid \mathsf{case}(e, \mathsf{inl}\ x \to e', \mathsf{inr}\ y \to e'') \\
& & \mid & \lambda x.\ e \mid e\ e' \\
& & \mid & \delta_{e'}(e) \mid \mathsf{let}\ \delta(x) = e\ \mathsf{in}\ e' \\
& & \mid & \mathsf{stable}(e) \mid \mathsf{let}\ \mathsf{stable}(x) = e\ \mathsf{in}\ e' \\
& & \mid & \mathsf{into}\ e \mid \mathsf{out}\ e \\
& & \mid & \mathsf{cons}(e, e') \mid \mathsf{let}\ \mathsf{cons}(x, xs) = e\ \mathsf{in}\ e' \\
& & \mid & \mathsf{fix}\ x.\ e \mid x \mid \mathsf{promote}(e) \\
& & \mid & l \mid !l \mid \diamond \\
\text{Values} & v & ::= & (v, v') \mid \mathsf{inl}\ v \mid \mathsf{inr}\ v' \mid \lambda x.\ e \\
& & \mid & l \mid \diamond \mid \mathsf{stable}(v) \mid \mathsf{into}\ v \mid \mathsf{cons}(v, v') \\
\text{Stores} & \sigma & ::= & \cdot \mid \sigma, l : v\ \mathsf{now} \mid \sigma, l : e\ \mathsf{later} \mid \sigma, l : \mathsf{null}
\end{array}
$$

Figure 1. Syntax

$$
\begin{array}{llll}
\text{Qualifiers} & q & ::= & \mathsf{now} \mid \mathsf{stable} \mid \mathsf{later} \\
\text{Contexts} & \Gamma & ::= & \cdot \mid \Gamma, x : A\ q
\end{array}
$$

$$
\begin{array}{lcl}
(\cdot)^\bullet & = & \cdot \\
(\Gamma, x : A\ \mathsf{later})^\bullet & = & \Gamma^\bullet, x : A\ \mathsf{now} \\
(\Gamma, x : A\ \mathsf{stable})^\bullet & = & \Gamma^\bullet, x : A\ \mathsf{stable} \\
(\Gamma, x : A\ \mathsf{now})^\bullet & = & \Gamma^\bullet \\
\\
(\cdot)^\Box & = & \cdot \\
(\Gamma, x : A\ \mathsf{stable})^\Box & = & \Gamma^\Box, x : A\ \mathsf{stable} \\
(\Gamma, x : A\ \mathsf{later})^\Box & = & \Gamma^\Box \\
(\Gamma, x : A\ \mathsf{now})^\Box & = & \Gamma^\Box
\end{array}
$$

Figure 2. Hypotheses, Contexts and Operations on Them

$$\boxed{\Gamma \vdash e : A\ q}$$

$$\frac{\Gamma \vdash e : A\ \mathsf{now} \qquad \Gamma \vdash e' : B\ \mathsf{now}}{\Gamma \vdash (e, e') : A \times B\ \mathsf{now}}\ \times\mathrm{I}$$

$$\frac{\Gamma \vdash e : A \times B\ \mathsf{now}}{\Gamma \vdash \mathsf{fst}\ e : A\ \mathsf{now}}\ \times\mathrm{LE} \qquad \frac{\Gamma \vdash e : A \times B\ \mathsf{now}}{\Gamma \vdash \mathsf{snd}\ e : B\ \mathsf{now}}\ \times\mathrm{RE}$$

$$\frac{\Gamma \vdash e : A\ \mathsf{now}}{\Gamma \vdash \mathsf{inl}\ e : A + B\ \mathsf{now}}\ +\mathrm{LI} \qquad \frac{\Gamma \vdash e : B\ \mathsf{now}}{\Gamma \vdash \mathsf{inr}\ e : A + B\ \mathsf{now}}\ +\mathrm{RI}$$

$$\frac{\begin{array}{c}\Gamma \vdash e : A + B\ \mathsf{now} \\ \Gamma, x : A\ \mathsf{now} \vdash e' : C\ \mathsf{now} \qquad \Gamma, y : B\ \mathsf{now} \vdash e'' : C\ \mathsf{now}\end{array}}{\Gamma \vdash \mathsf{case}(e, \mathsf{inl}\ x \to e', \mathsf{inr}\ y \to e'') : C\ \mathsf{now}}\ +\mathrm{E}$$

$$\frac{\Gamma, x : A\ \mathsf{now} \vdash e : B\ \mathsf{now}}{\Gamma \vdash \lambda x.\ e : A \to B\ \mathsf{now}}\ \to\mathrm{I}$$

$$\frac{\Gamma \vdash e : A \to B\ \mathsf{now} \qquad \Gamma \vdash e' : A\ \mathsf{now}}{\Gamma \vdash e\ e' : B\ \mathsf{now}}\ \to\mathrm{E}$$

Figure 3. Standard Typing Rules

$$\boxed{\Gamma \vdash e : A\ q\ \text{continued}}$$

$$\frac{\Gamma \vdash e : A\ \mathsf{later} \qquad \Gamma \vdash e' : \mathsf{alloc}\ \mathsf{now}}{\Gamma \vdash \delta_{e'}(e) : \bullet A\ \mathsf{now}}\ \bullet\mathrm{I}$$

$$\frac{\Gamma \vdash e : \bullet A\ \mathsf{now} \qquad \Gamma, x : A\ \mathsf{later} \vdash e' : C\ \mathsf{now}}{\Gamma \vdash \mathsf{let}\ \delta(x) = e\ \mathsf{in}\ e' : C\ \mathsf{now}}\ \bullet\mathrm{E}$$

$$\frac{\Gamma \vdash e : [\bullet(\hat{\mu}\alpha.\ A)/\alpha]A\ \mathsf{now}}{\Gamma \vdash \mathsf{into}\ e : \hat{\mu}\alpha.\ A\ \mathsf{now}}\ \mu\mathrm{I}$$

$$\frac{\Gamma \vdash e : \hat{\mu}\alpha.\ A\ \mathsf{now}}{\Gamma \vdash \mathsf{out}\ e : [\bullet(\hat{\mu}\alpha.\ A)/\alpha]A\ \mathsf{now}}\ \mu\mathrm{E}$$

$$\frac{\Gamma \vdash e : A\ \mathsf{stable}}{\Gamma \vdash \mathsf{stable}(e) : \Box A\ \mathsf{now}}\ \Box\mathrm{I}$$

$$\frac{\Gamma \vdash e : \Box A\ \mathsf{now} \qquad \Gamma, x : A\ \mathsf{stable} \vdash e' : C\ \mathsf{now}}{\Gamma \vdash \mathsf{let}\ \mathsf{stable}(x) = e\ \mathsf{in}\ e' : C\ \mathsf{now}}\ \Box\mathrm{E}$$

$$\frac{\Gamma \vdash e : A\ \mathsf{now} \qquad A\ \mathsf{stable}}{\Gamma \vdash \mathsf{promote}(e) : \Box A\ \mathsf{now}}\ \textsc{Promote}$$

$$\frac{\Gamma \vdash e : A\ \mathsf{now} \qquad \Gamma \vdash e' : \bullet(S\,A)\ \mathsf{now}}{\Gamma \vdash \mathsf{cons}(e, e') : S\,A\ \mathsf{now}}\ \mathrm{SI}$$

$$\frac{\begin{array}{c}\Gamma \vdash e : S\,A\ \mathsf{now} \\ \Gamma, x : A\ \mathsf{now}, xs : \bullet(S\,A)\ \mathsf{now} \vdash e' : C\ \mathsf{now}\end{array}}{\Gamma \vdash \mathsf{let}\ \mathsf{cons}(x, xs) = e\ \mathsf{in}\ e' : C\ \mathsf{now}}\ \mathrm{SE}$$

$$\frac{\Gamma^\Box, x : A\ \mathsf{later} \vdash e : A\ \mathsf{now}}{\Gamma \vdash \mathsf{fix}\ x.\ e : A\ \mathsf{now}}\ \textsc{Fix}$$

$$\frac{x : A\ q \qquad q \in \{\mathsf{now}, \mathsf{stable}\}}{\Gamma \vdash x : A\ \mathsf{now}}\ \textsc{Hyp}$$

$$\frac{\Gamma^\Box \vdash e : A\ \mathsf{now}}{\Gamma \vdash e : A\ \mathsf{stable}}\ \mathrm{T}\textsc{Stable} \qquad \frac{\Gamma^\bullet \vdash e : A\ \mathsf{now}}{\Gamma \vdash e : A\ \mathsf{later}}\ \mathrm{T}\textsc{Later}$$

Figure 4. Typing

$$\boxed{A\ \mathsf{stable}}$$

$$\frac{A\ \mathsf{stable} \qquad B\ \mathsf{stable}}{A \times B\ \mathsf{stable}} \qquad \frac{A\ \mathsf{stable} \qquad B\ \mathsf{stable}}{A + B\ \mathsf{stable}}$$

$$\frac{}{b\ \mathsf{stable}} \qquad \frac{}{\Box A\ \mathsf{stable}}$$

Figure 5. Stability of Types

$$\boxed{\langle \sigma; e\rangle \Downarrow \langle \sigma'; v\rangle}$$

$$\frac{}{\langle \sigma; v\rangle \Downarrow \langle \sigma; v\rangle}$$

$$\frac{\langle \sigma; e_1\rangle \Downarrow \langle \sigma'; v_1\rangle \qquad \langle \sigma'; e_2\rangle \Downarrow \langle \sigma''; v_2\rangle}{\langle \sigma; (e_1, e_2)\rangle \Downarrow \langle \sigma''; (v_1, v_2)\rangle}$$

$$\frac{\langle \sigma; e\rangle \Downarrow \langle \sigma'; (v_1, v_2)\rangle}{\langle \sigma; \mathsf{fst}\ e\rangle \Downarrow \langle \sigma'; v_1\rangle} \qquad \frac{\langle \sigma; e\rangle \Downarrow \langle \sigma'; (v_1, v_2)\rangle}{\langle \sigma; \mathsf{snd}\ e\rangle \Downarrow \langle \sigma'; v_2\rangle}$$

$$\frac{\langle \sigma; e\rangle \Downarrow \langle \sigma'; v\rangle}{\langle \sigma; \mathsf{inl}\ e\rangle \Downarrow \langle \sigma'; \mathsf{inl}\ v\rangle} \qquad \frac{\langle \sigma; e\rangle \Downarrow \langle \sigma'; v\rangle}{\langle \sigma; \mathsf{inr}\ e\rangle \Downarrow \langle \sigma'; \mathsf{inr}\ v\rangle}$$

$$\frac{\langle \sigma; e\rangle \Downarrow \langle \sigma'; \mathsf{inl}\ v\rangle \qquad \langle \sigma'; [v/x]e'\rangle \Downarrow \langle \sigma''; v''\rangle}{\langle \sigma; \mathsf{case}(e, \mathsf{inl}\ x \to e', \mathsf{inr}\ y \to e'')\rangle \Downarrow \langle \sigma''; v''\rangle}$$

$$\frac{\langle \sigma; e\rangle \Downarrow \langle \sigma'; \mathsf{inr}\ v\rangle \qquad \langle \sigma'; [v/y]e''\rangle \Downarrow \langle \sigma''; v''\rangle}{\langle \sigma; \mathsf{case}(e, \mathsf{inl}\ x \to e', \mathsf{inr}\ y \to e'')\rangle \Downarrow \langle \sigma''; v''\rangle}$$

$$\frac{\begin{array}{c}\langle \sigma; e_1\rangle \Downarrow \langle \sigma'; \lambda x.\ e_1'\rangle \\ \langle \sigma'; e_2\rangle \Downarrow \langle \sigma''; v_2\rangle \qquad \langle \sigma''; [v_2/x]e_1'\rangle \Downarrow \langle \sigma'''; v\rangle\end{array}}{\langle \sigma; e_1\ e_2\rangle \Downarrow \langle \sigma'''; v\rangle}$$

$$\frac{\langle \sigma; e'\rangle \Downarrow \langle \sigma'; \diamond\rangle \qquad l \notin \mathrm{dom}(\sigma')}{\langle \sigma; \delta_{e'}(e)\rangle \Downarrow \langle (\sigma', l : e\ \mathsf{later}); l\rangle}$$

$$\frac{\langle \sigma; e\rangle \Downarrow \langle \sigma'; l\rangle \qquad \langle \sigma'; [!l/x]e'\rangle \Downarrow \langle \sigma''; v\rangle}{\langle \sigma; \mathsf{let}\ \delta(x) = e\ \mathsf{in}\ e'\rangle \Downarrow \langle \sigma''; v\rangle} \qquad \frac{l : v\ \mathsf{now} \in \sigma}{\langle \sigma; !l\rangle \Downarrow \langle \sigma; v\rangle}$$

$$\frac{\langle \sigma; e\rangle \Downarrow \langle \sigma'; v\rangle}{\langle \sigma; \mathsf{into}\ e\rangle \Downarrow \langle \sigma'; \mathsf{into}\ v\rangle} \qquad \frac{\langle \sigma; e\rangle \Downarrow \langle \sigma'; \mathsf{into}\ v\rangle}{\langle \sigma; \mathsf{out}\ e\rangle \Downarrow \langle \sigma'; v\rangle}$$

$$\frac{\langle \sigma; e\rangle \Downarrow \langle \sigma'; v\rangle}{\langle \sigma; \mathsf{stable}(e)\rangle \Downarrow \langle \sigma'; \mathsf{stable}(v)\rangle}$$

$$\frac{\langle \sigma; e\rangle \Downarrow \langle \sigma'; v\rangle}{\langle \sigma; \mathsf{promote}(e)\rangle \Downarrow \langle \sigma'; \mathsf{stable}(v)\rangle}$$

$$\frac{\langle \sigma; e\rangle \Downarrow \langle \sigma'; \mathsf{stable}(v)\rangle \qquad \langle \sigma'; [v/x]e'\rangle \Downarrow \langle \sigma''; v''\rangle}{\langle \sigma; \mathsf{let}\ \mathsf{stable}(x) = e\ \mathsf{in}\ e'\rangle \Downarrow \langle \sigma''; v''\rangle}$$

$$\frac{\langle \sigma; e\rangle \Downarrow \langle \sigma'; v\rangle \qquad \langle \sigma'; e'\rangle \Downarrow \langle \sigma''; v'\rangle}{\langle \sigma; \mathsf{cons}(e, e')\rangle \Downarrow \langle \sigma''; \mathsf{cons}(v, v')\rangle}$$

$$\frac{\langle \sigma; e\rangle \Downarrow \langle \sigma'; \mathsf{cons}(v, l)\rangle \qquad \langle \sigma'; [v/x, l/xs]e'\rangle \Downarrow \langle \sigma''; v''\rangle}{\langle \sigma; \mathsf{let}\ \mathsf{cons}(x, xs) = e\ \mathsf{in}\ e'\rangle \Downarrow \langle \sigma''; v''\rangle}$$

$$\frac{\langle \sigma; [\mathsf{fix}\ x.\ e/x]e\rangle \Downarrow \langle \sigma'; v\rangle}{\langle \sigma; \mathsf{fix}\ x.\ e\rangle \Downarrow \langle \sigma'; v\rangle}$$

Figure 6. Expression Semantics

$$\boxed{\sigma \Longrightarrow \sigma'}$$

$$\frac{}{\cdot \Longrightarrow \cdot} \qquad \frac{\sigma \Longrightarrow \sigma' \qquad \langle \sigma'; e\rangle \Downarrow \langle \sigma''; v\rangle \qquad l \notin \mathrm{dom}(\sigma'')}{\sigma, l : e\ \mathsf{later} \Longrightarrow \sigma'', l : v\ \mathsf{now}}$$

$$\frac{\sigma \Longrightarrow \sigma' \qquad l \notin \mathrm{dom}(\sigma')}{\sigma, l : v\ \mathsf{now} \Longrightarrow \sigma', l : \mathsf{null}} \qquad \frac{\sigma \Longrightarrow \sigma' \qquad l \notin \mathrm{dom}(\sigma')}{\sigma, l : \mathsf{null} \Longrightarrow \sigma', l : \mathsf{null}}$$

Figure 7. Tick Semantics

a later variable. On line 4, we make use of the fact that natural numbers are *stable* in order to rebind n to the stable variable x. This lets us refer to x in both the head and tail of the cons-cell on line 5. The head of the cons cell is just x itself, and the tail is a delayed stream, which we may allocate since we have a permission u.

Below, we give a summation function, which takes a stream of numbers and returns a stream containing the cumulative sum of the stream. To implement this, we introduce an auxiliary function sum_acc which stores the sum in an accumulator variable, and then call it with an initial sum of 0.

```
sum_acc : S alloc → S ℕ → ℕ → S ℕ
sum_acc us ns acc =
  let cons(u, δ(us')) = us in
  let cons(n, δ(ns')) = ns in
  let stable(x) = promote(n + acc) in
  cons(x, δ_u(sum_acc us' ns' x))

sum : S alloc → S ℕ → S ℕ
sum us ns = sum_acc us ns 0
```

Higher-Order Stream Operations Our language permits the free use of streams of streams, as well as higher-order functions on streams. We illustrate this with a simple function which takes a stream, and returns the stream of successive tails of that stream.

```
tails : S alloc → S A → S (S A)
tails us xs =
  let cons(u, δ(us')) = us in
  let cons(x, δ(xs')) = xs in
  cons(xs, δ_u(tails us' xs'))
```

The higher-order map functional is definable as follows:

```
map : S alloc → □(A → B) → S A → S B
map us h xs =
  let cons(u, δ(us')) = us in
  let cons(x, δ(xs')) = xs in
  let stable(f) = h in
  cons(f x, δ_u(map us' stable(f) xs'))
```

Note that the map functional calls its argument function on every element of the input stream. As a result, we need to use the function at many different time steps, and so we need to give the functional argument the stable type $\square(A \to B)$ to ensure that we can safely use it both now and later.

The fact that all computable streams are definable in our language is witnessed by giving the unfold operation, which shows that the universal property of streams is definable within the language.

```
unfold : S alloc → □(X → A × •X) → X → S A
unfold us h x =
  let cons(u, δ(us')) = us in
  let stable(f) = h in
  let (a, δ(x')) = f x in
  cons(a, δ_u(unfold us' stable(f) x'))
```

Dynamic Changes of Streams Switching behavior is directly programmable in our language. The swap function below takes a number n, and two streams xs and ys. It yields the same values as xs on the first n time steps, and afterward the same values as ys.

```
swap : S alloc → ℕ → S A → S A → S A
swap us n xs ys =
  if n = 0 then
    ys
  else
    let cons(u, δ(us')) = us in
    let cons(x, δ(xs')) = xs in
    let cons(y, δ(ys')) = ys in
    let stable(m) = promote(n) in
    cons(x, δ_u(swap us' (m − 1) xs' ys'))
```

What is interesting about this example is that there is nothing surprising about it: it is basically an ordinary functional program. Unlike many other approaches to reactive programming, we program conditional behavior with ordinary conditional control flow.

3.2 Type Encodings

Streams In order to make the examples more readable, we included streams as a primitive type in our language, but that is actually unnecessary, since they are encodable using recursive types:

$$\mathsf{S}\,A \triangleq \hat{\mu}\alpha.\ A \times \alpha$$

This encoding looks completely conventional, but because unfolding a recursive type requires guarding the recursive type with a delay modality before substituting, this type is isomorphic to:

$$\mathsf{S}\,A \simeq A \times \bullet(A \times \bullet(A \times \ldots))$$

From a logical perspective, the stream type $\mathsf{S}\,A$ corresponds to the "always" operator of temporal logic, which asserts that at every time step, we always have a witness to the proposition A.

Events In reactive programs, there are often operations which take a length of time observable to the user. For example, downloading a file is an operation which can take many ticks to happen, and the file value is not available for use until the operation is complete.

Such operations, which we call "events", are surprisingly difficult to model in a stream-based paradigm, since nothing happens until the completion of the process, and once the final event happens, no more events occur. Stream-based languages have used a number of tricks to encode behaviours like this, but when we have a temporal recursive type, it is straightforward to define a type of events:

$$\mathsf{E}\,A \triangleq \hat{\mu}\alpha.\ A + \alpha$$

Here, we simply replace the product with a sum, which means that an element of type A is either immediately available, or we have to wait until the next tick to try again. (That is, $\mathsf{E}\,A \simeq A + \bullet(\mathsf{E}\,A)$.)Events make implementing dynamic switching behavior very natural.

```
switch : S alloc → S A → E (S A) → S A
switch us xs e =
  let cons(u, δ(us')) = us in
  let cons(x, δ(xs')) = xs in
  case(out e,
       inl ys → ys,
       inr t → let δ(e') = t in
               cons(x, δ_u(switch us' xs' e')))
```

In this example, the call switch us xs e behaves like xs until the event e returns a stream ys, and then it behaves like ys.

Events correspond to the "eventually" operator of temporal logic. Since the eventually operator forms a closure operator on the Kripke structure of times, the event type constructor correspondingly forms a monad, whose monadic operations may be defined as follows:

```
return : A → E A
return x = into (inl x)

bind : S alloc → □(A → E B) → E A → E B
bind us h e =
  let cons(u, δ(us')) = us in
  let stable(f) = h in
  case(out e,
       inl a → f a,
       inr t → let δ(e') = t in
               into (inr (δ_u(bind us' stable(f) e'))))
```

Here, we perform sequencing by taking a function that maps elements of A to B events, and waiting until an A-event yields an A to apply the function. Because we do not know when we will need to invoke the function, bind requires it to be stable.

Events are closely related to promises and futures [4, 16], in that they are proxies for computations which have not yet completed constructing a value. However, unlike most implementations of futures, our type $\mathsf{E}\,A$ permits clients to test whether or not the computation has finished. Because we embed our events into a synchronous programming language, this choice does not introduce nondeterminism into our programming language.

Until Just as the always and eventually operators in temporal logic can be merged into the "until" operator, we can also give a combined operation for processes that produce values of type A until they terminate, producing a value of type B.

$$A\,\mathcal{U}\,B \triangleq \hat{\mu}\alpha.\ B + (A \times \alpha)$$

Note that streams correspond to producing elements of A until the empty type, $\mathsf{S}\,A \simeq A\,\mathcal{U}\,0$, and events correspond to yielding units until B, $\mathsf{E}\,B \simeq 1\,\mathcal{U}\,B$.

Resumptions The fact that we have function spaces and arbitrary recursive types enables us to go well beyond the expressive power of temporal logic. In this example, we will illustrate this by showing how resumptions [37], a simple interleaving model of concurrency, may be encoded in our type system.

$$\mathsf{R}_{I,O}\,A \triangleq \hat{\mu}\alpha.\ \alpha \times (A + (I \to O \times \alpha))$$

Elements of the type $\mathsf{R}_{I,O}\,A$ can be thought of as representations of thread values, in an interleaving model of concurrency. The left-hand-side of the pair $\alpha \times (A + (I \to O \times \alpha))$ can be seen as what to do when the thread is not executed on this tick, and the right-hand-side says that either the thread finishes execution with a value of A, or it takes an input message of type I and yields an output message of type O, and continues computing.

Given two threads, we can implement a scheduler which takes two threads and interleaves their execution until one of them finishes.

```
1  par : S alloc → R_{I,O} A × R_{I,O} A → R_{I,O} A
2  par us (p1, p2) =
3    let cons(u, δ(us')) = us in
4    case((snd (out p1),
5         inl a → p1,
6         inr f → let δ(p1') = fst (out p1) in
7                 let δ(p2') = fst (out p2) in
8                 let p' = δ_u(par us' p1' p2') in
9                 let f' = λi. let (o, δ(p1'')) = f i in
10                             into (o, δ_u(par us' p2' p1'')) in
11                into (p', inr f'))
```

One line 5, we see that if the first process p_1 completes on this tick, then the parallel composition completes on this tick. If p_1 does not complete, then we need to return (1) how to defer the parallel composition, and (2) the I/O behavior of the parallel composition. We construct the deferred computation for the parallel composition by taking (on lines 6-8) the deferred computations for each process individually, and then resuming their parallel composition on the next tick. On line 9-10, we define the function f', which produces the same I/O as p_1 on this tick, defers p_2 to the next tick, and then on the next tick schedules p_2 for execution and defers p_1's next action.

Definability of Fixed Points Our calculus has a term-level fixed point operator $\mathsf{fix}\, x.\ e$. However, fixed points are *definable*, illustrating the high expressiveness that guarded recursive types permit. We will show the inhabitation of the type $\Box(\bullet A \to A) \to \mathsf{S\,Alloc} \to A$, in three steps. First, we define the recursive type $X \triangleq \hat{\mu}\alpha.\ \Box(\mathsf{S\,alloc} \to \alpha \to A)$. We use this type to define the operation selfapp, which takes an element of type X and applies it to itself, wrapped around a call to a function $f : \bullet A \to A$:

```
selfapp : (•A → A) → S alloc → X → A
selfapp f us v =
  let cons(u, δ(us')) = us in
  let stable(w) = out v in
  f (δ_u(w us' (into (stable w))))
```

Next, we can use this self-application function to implement a fixed-point combinator.

```
fixedpoint : □(•A → A) → S alloc → A
fixedpoint h us =
  let stable(f) = h in
  selfapp f us (into (stable(selfapp f)))
```

This fixed point operator is essentially a variant of Curry's fixed point combinator [11] $Y \triangleq \lambda f.\ (\lambda x.\ f\ (x\ x))\ (\lambda x.\ f\ (x\ x))$, with extra noise to deal with the modal operators and iso-recursive types. The most significant difference is that we need to additionally pass in a stream of allocation tokens to ensure that we can construct the necessary delay thunks.

3.3 Blocking Space Leaks Without Ruling Out Buffering

Our operational semantics makes it impossible to implicitly retain values across multiple time ticks, and our type systems statically rejects programs which try. For example, if we try to program a function which takes a stream and returns that stream constantly, then it fails to typecheck, as we desire:

```
scary_const : S alloc → S ℕ → S (S ℕ)
scary_const us ns =
  let cons(u, δ(us')) = us in
  let stable(xs) = promote(ns) in  — TYPE ERROR
  cons(xs, δ_u(scary_const us' xs))
```

The reason for this error is that we need to use the argument stream at multiple times, and since streams are not a stable type, we cannot promote them into a stable variable, which we need in order to use the stream value at multiple times. So we get a compile-time error.

We blocked this function definition because implementing it would require potentially unbounded buffering, and we do not want to do that implicitly, since that would mean that variable references could create unexpected memory leaks.

However, there are many legitimate programs which need to retain data across multiple time steps: for example, we may wish to retain data to compute a moving average. Our language does not *prohibit* these kinds of programs; instead, it demands that programmers *explicitly* write all the buffering code.

As an extreme (and somewhat ridiculous) example, we will write the function scary_const, which takes a stream argument and repeats it constantly.

```
buffer : S alloc → ℕ → S ℕ → S ℕ
buffer us n xs =
  let cons(u, δ(us')) = us in
  let cons(x, δ(xs')) = xs in
  let stable(x') = promote(x) in
  cons(n, δ_u(buffer us' x' xs'))

forward : S alloc → S ℕ → •(S ℕ)
forward us xs =
  let cons(u, δ(us')) = us in
  let cons(x, δ(xs')) = xs in
  let stable(x') = promote(x) in
  δ_u(buffer us' x' xs')

scary_const : S alloc → S ℕ → S (S ℕ)
scary_const us xs =
  let cons(u, δ(us')) = us in
  let δ(xs') = forward us xs in
  cons(xs, δ_u(scary_const us' xs'))
```

In this example, we use a function buffer, which appends a natural number to the head of a stream, and then use buffer to define a function forward, which pushes its argument one tick into the future, and then define scary_const, which repeatedly calls forward to keep moving the argument one tick into the future.

This definition makes the memory leak explicit in the source code: our program repeatedly calls forward on the argument stream to scary_const, using more memory each time.

In general, it is possible to define buffering for a recursive type $\hat{\mu}\alpha.\ A$, if the expression A is constructed from the variable α, sums of bufferable types $A + B$, products of bufferable types $A \times B$, any stable type $\Box A$, or delays of bufferable types $\bullet A$. It is not possible to buffer arbitrary members of function types $A \to B$, because the environment of a function closure cannot be examined.

4. Metatheory

Overview Kripke logical relations have a long history in giving semantics to higher-order stateful languages [2, 13, 36]. Since our dynamic dataflow graph can be viewed as a store, they are a natural tool for showing the soundness of our type system.

The basic idea behind the technique of logical relations is to give a family of sets of closed terms $[\![A]\!]$ by induction on the structure of the type A, each of which possesses the soundness property we desire. Then, we prove a theorem (the fundamental property) that shows that every well-typed term $e : A$ lies within the set $[\![A]\!]$, and from that we can conclude that the language is sound.

In a Kripke logical relation, in addition to the type, the relations are also indexed by some contextual information, the *world*, which is used to relativize the interpretation of each type. In our setting, this contextual information will include the store terms are to evaluate under, as well as the permission information telling us whether the term may extend the dataflow graph.

Recursive types make defining relations by induction on the syntax of a type difficult, since semantically we expect a recursive type to be defined in terms of its unfolding, and unfolding a recursive type can make it larger. To resolve this issue, we make use of the idea of *step-indexing*, originally introduced by Appel and McAllester [3], in which we extend the world with a natural number n, and interpret a recursive type only at strictly smaller numbers.

In this section, we give a high-level overview of our definitions, and a brief tour of the soundness proof. We give the full proof in the technical report [25] provided in the supplementary material.

Supportedness and Location Permutations Before we can describe the structure of our logical relation, there is one technical issue we need to discuss. The allocation rule in the expression semantics is non-deterministic – it chooses a location that is not in the current heap. However, the tick semantics $\sigma \Longrightarrow \sigma'$, when given

$$\boxed{e \sqsubseteq \sigma}$$

$$e \sqsubseteq \sigma \triangleq \text{free locations of } e \subseteq \mathrm{dom}(\sigma)$$

$$\boxed{\sigma\ \mathsf{supported}}$$

$$\frac{}{\cdot\ \mathsf{supported}} \qquad \frac{\sigma\ \mathsf{supported} \quad v \sqsubseteq \sigma}{\sigma, l : v\ \mathsf{now\ supported}}$$

$$\frac{\sigma\ \mathsf{supported} \quad e \sqsubseteq \sigma}{\sigma, l : e\ \mathsf{later\ supported}} \qquad \frac{\sigma\ \mathsf{supported}}{\sigma, l : \mathsf{null\ supported}}$$

Figure 8. Definition of Supportedness

a nonempty store, removes the most recently-allocated location l from the store, updates the older heap, and then updates the removed location. The technical question is: what happens if the update of the older heap allocates l itself?

Intuitively, this is not a serious problem, since our allocator could always have chosen a different location to have allocated. To formalize this intuition, we introduce the idea of *supportedness*, described in Figure 8. We write $e \sqsubseteq \sigma$ if all of the free locations in e are in the domain of σ. We write σ $\mathsf{supported}$, when every pointer containing an expression or value is supported by the heap cells allocated earlier (that is, to the left in the list). Then, we can prove the following three lemmas.

Lemma 1 (Permutability). *We have that:*

1. *If* $\pi \in \mathrm{Perm}$ *and* $\langle\sigma; e\rangle \Downarrow \langle\sigma'; v\rangle$ *then* $\langle\pi(\sigma); \pi(e)\rangle \Downarrow \langle\pi(\sigma'); \pi(v)\rangle$.
2. *If* $\pi \in \mathrm{Perm}$ *and* $\sigma \Longrightarrow \sigma'$ *then* $\pi(\sigma) \Longrightarrow \pi(\sigma')$.

Lemma 2 (Supportedness). *We have that:*

1. *If* σ $\mathsf{supported}$ *and* $e \sqsubseteq \sigma$ *and* $\langle\sigma; e\rangle \Downarrow \langle\sigma'; v\rangle$ *then* $v \sqsubseteq \sigma'$ *and* σ' $\mathsf{supported}$.
2. *If* σ $\mathsf{supported}$ *and* $\sigma \Longrightarrow \sigma'$ *then* σ' $\mathsf{supported}$.

Lemma 3 (Quasi-determinacy). *We have that:*

1. *If* $\langle\sigma; e\rangle \Downarrow \langle\sigma'; v'\rangle$ *and* $\langle\sigma; e\rangle \Downarrow \langle\sigma''; v''\rangle$ *and* σ $\mathsf{supported}$ *and* $e \sqsubseteq \sigma$, *then there is a* $\pi \in \mathrm{Perm}$ *such that* $\pi(\sigma') = \sigma''$ *and* $\pi(\sigma) = \sigma$.
2. *If* $\sigma \Longrightarrow \sigma'$ *and* $\sigma \Longrightarrow \sigma''$ *and* σ $\mathsf{supported}$ *then there is a* $\pi \in \mathrm{Perm}$ *such that* $\pi(\sigma') = \sigma''$ *and* $\pi(\sigma) = \sigma$.

Here, Perm is the set of finite permutations on locations, and $\pi(e)$ and $\pi(\sigma)$ lift it to expressions and stores in the obvious way. Together, these lemmas imply that we can rename locations however we like, and that the nondeterminism of the allocator can *only* affect how locations are named.

Kripke Worlds We now describe the structure of the worlds we use in our logical relation, which we lay out in Figure 9.

A world w is a triple (n, σ, a). Here, n is a step index, indicating that an element of this relation must be good for at least n ticks into the future. The term a is a *capability*. The capability $\top$ means that we *do not* have the permission to extend the dataflow graph, and $\bot$ means that we *do* have the permission to extend the graph. Finally, the store σ must be an element of Heap_n, which is the set of supported heaps for which the tick relation is defined for at least n steps. That is, if $\sigma \in \mathrm{Heap}_n$, then there are $\sigma_1, \ldots, \sigma_n$ such that $\sigma \Longrightarrow \sigma_1 \Longrightarrow \cdots \Longrightarrow \sigma_n$. As a notational shorthand, we write $w.n$ for the step index of w, $w.\sigma$ for the store component of w, and $w.a$ for the capability of w. We also write $\pi(w)$ to mean the world $(w.n, \pi(w.\sigma), w.a)$.

In most applications, step-indexing has been used purely as a technical device to force the inductive definition of types to be well-founded. In our setting, in contrast, steps have a concrete operational reading, corresponding directly to the passage of time: a step index of n tells us that the tick relation can definitely tick at least n times.

Each of these components has an associated preorder $\leq$. A step index n' is below an index n, if n' is less than or equal to n. A heap σ' is below a heap σ, $\sigma' \leq \sigma$, if σ' is an extension of σ – that is, if σ' has a larger domain than σ, and agrees with it on the overlap. Finally, a capability a' is below a, if either they are the same, or a' is $\bot$ and a is $\top$.

The intuition behind the order on worlds is that $w' \leq w$ when w' is a possible future state of w. In the future of w, we may have extended the dataflow graph, or we can potentially receive a capability to allocate from our environment.

The Logical Relations In Figure 10, we define three logical relations.

The set $\mathcal{V}[\![A]\!]\,\rho\ w$ defines the *value relation*, the set of closed values semantically inhabiting the type A at the world w, with the parameter ρ giving the type interpretation of each of the free variables in A. The set $\mathcal{E}[\![A]\!]\,\rho\ w$ gives the *expression relation*, the set of expressions semantically inhabiting the type A (that is, they will evaluate to a value of type A if they are run on the current tick). Similarly, we also define $\mathcal{L}[\![A]\!]\,\rho\ w$, the *later expression relation*. These are the expressions that will evaluate to a value of type A if they are run on the *next* time step.

Both the expression relation $\mathcal{E}[\![A]\!]\,\rho\ w$ and the later relation $\mathcal{L}[\![A]\!]\,\rho\ w$ are defined in terms of the value relation. The expression relation consists of closed, supported expressions, which evaluate to values in the value relation. Furthermore, the expression evaluation may extend the heap only if the world contains the capability to allocate. If it does not, then the store will be untouched.

The later relation $\mathcal{L}[\![A]\!]\,\rho\ w$ is defined by cases. If the world's step index is 0, then we place no constraints on it – it is simply the set of closed, supported expressions. If the world's step index is $n + 1$ and the tick relation sends the current world's store to σ', then terms are in $\mathcal{L}[\![A]\!]\,\rho\ w$ if they are in the expression relation of A, at step n and store σ'. That is, it consists of those expressions that will be in the expression relation *on the next tick*.

The value relation is defined by induction on the syntax of the type A. Matters first become interesting in the function case. First, we require that a lambda term $\lambda x.\ e$ inhabiting $\mathcal{V}[\![A \to B]\!]\,\rho\ w$ be *supported* with respect to the heap component of the world. As is usual, we quantify over all future worlds $w' \leq w$, but we also quantify over *location permutations* $\pi \in \mathrm{Perm}$.

Then, we consider all arguments e' coming from the A expression relation at the permuted world $\pi(w')$, and assert that applying the term to the renamed function should also be in the B expression relation at $\pi(w')$. The extra renaming requirement semantically formalizes the idea that we need to ignore the exact choice of names (and indeed is very similar to the definition of the function space in nominal set theory [17]).

The later type $\bullet A$ is interpreted as the set of pointers l, which point to an expression $l : e$ later where e is in the later relation of A. As with functions, we quantify over future worlds and renamings. The interpretation of the stability modality $\mathcal{V}[\![\square A]\!]\,\rho\ w$ contains values $\mathsf{stable}(v)$, where $v \in \mathcal{V}[\![A]\!]\,\rho\ (w.n, \cdot, \top)$. That is, these values v are not allowed to depend upon the store, or to assume that they have the capability to extend the heap.

Recursive types $\hat{\mu}\alpha.\ A$ are interpreted by the interpretation of A, where the environment is extended by the interpretation of $\bullet(\hat{\mu}\alpha.\ A)$. Superficially, this looks like a circular definition, except that the next-step modality is defined in terms of the later relation for $\hat{\mu}\alpha.\ A$,

$$\text{Heap}_0 = \{\sigma \in \text{Store} \mid \sigma \text{ supported}\}$$

$$\text{Heap}_{n+1} = \left\{ \sigma \in \text{Store} \;\middle|\; \begin{array}{l} \sigma \text{ supported} \wedge \\ \exists \sigma'.\ \sigma \Longrightarrow \sigma' \wedge \sigma' \in \text{Heap}_n \end{array} \right\}$$

$$\text{Cap} = \{\top, \bot\}$$

$$\text{World} = \{(n, \sigma, a) \mid n \in \mathbb{N} \wedge \sigma \in \text{Heap}_n \wedge a \in \text{Cap}\}$$

$$\sigma' \leq \sigma \iff \exists \sigma_0.\ \sigma \cdot \sigma_0 = \sigma'$$

$$a' \leq a \iff a = a' \vee (a' = \bot \wedge a = \top)$$

$$(n', \sigma', a') \leq (n, \sigma, a) \iff n' \leq n \wedge \sigma' \leq \sigma \wedge a' \leq a$$

Figure 9. Worlds

which lowers the step index, making the definition well-founded. Finally, the semantic interpretation of alloc is the token $\diamond$, if the world has the capability, and is the empty set otherwise.

Soundness The key property we prove is the following:

Theorem 1 (Fundamental Property). *The following properties hold:*

1. *If* $\cdot \vdash e : A$ later, *then* $e \in \mathcal{L}[\![A]\!] \cdot w$.
2. *If* $\cdot \vdash e : A$ stable, *then* $e \in \mathcal{E}[\![A]\!] \cdot (w.n, \cdot, \top)$.
3. *If* $\cdot \vdash e : A$ now, *then* $e \in \mathcal{E}[\![A]\!] \cdot w$.

The proof of this theorem follows the usual pattern for soundness proofs by logical relations. We extend the definition of the expression relation to define environments binding expressions to variables, and then prove by induction on the syntax of the typing derivation that all substitutions of well-typed terms by well-formed environments are in the logical relation. As usual, a fair number of auxiliary lemmas must be proved (such as the monotonicity of the value relation, and the stability of all relations under renaming of locations), and we refer interested readers to the companion technical report [25] for details. Once we have the fundamental property, we get a soundness property as an almost immediate corollary.

Corollary 1. *(Soundness) If* $\cdot \vdash e : A$, *then* $\langle \cdot; e \rangle \Downarrow \langle \sigma; v \rangle$. *Furthermore, for all* n, $v \in \mathcal{V}[\![A]\!]\, \rho\, (n, \sigma, \bot)$.

Note that expression evaluation always terminates. This shows that our type discipline enforces well-founded use of fixed points $\text{fix}\, x.\ e$. Also, note that $\sigma \in \text{Heap}_n$ for any n, and so we can tick the clock as often as we like. Thus, if we compute a stream value, then each time we tick the clock, the tail pointer will point to a new cons cell, whose head contains the next value of the stream, and whose tail is the pointer to chase on the next tick.

5. Implementation

While the work described here is largely theoretical, that theory arises from an attempt to understand the correctness of a new language, AdjS (the implementation can be downloaded from the author's website), whose type system closely tracks the type system of this paper. (The major extensions are polymorphism and linear types, and a system to infer uses of the promote(e) operation.) The attempt to prove the soundness of the type system was fortuitous: in the course of the formalization we discovered two soundness bugs in our implementation!

The first soundness bug was that the AdjS compiler has both delay types $\bullet A$ and $S\,A$ as primitive, but only required an allocation token to construct a stream. The second soundness bug was that we had originally treated the allocation type alloc as a promotable stable type. Each of these bugs made it possible to build a value of type $\square(\bullet A)$, and use it to access a thunk after its lifetime has ended.

There remain a few features of the implementation which we have not completely formalized. First, the operational semantics in this paper forces every thunk when time elapses. Our actual implementation is lazier about this, only forcing thunks when they are read. It should still be the case that no thunk is forced, except on its scheduled tick, but it is additionally possible for thunks to go unforced. This is not difficult to model, but it seemed to complicate the definition of Kripke extension without sufficient expository advantages to compensate.

More seriously, we have not given a correctness proof of our implementation of linear types. While we do have both denotational and type-theoretic models of linear guarded types [26], we do not yet have a soundness proof of our implementation strategy for it, in the same way that this paper shows the soundness of our implementation strategy of the functional part of the language. This is because the linear types are used to model GUI widgets, and we need a plausible, yet tractable, operational semantics for the GUI widgets. This does not seem impossibly out of reach, though: recently Lerner et al. [29] have given a formal model of the HTML DOM, and we are currently investigating using a simplified version of their event model to build the operational semantics we need.

In order to make the synchrony hypothesis (namely, that all computations finish quickly relative to the size of a tick), our implementation runs at a fixed clock speed of 60 Hz. This does mean that the runtime wakes even when nothing is happening. However, we do not foresee many issues in increasing the clock speed, since Haskell implementations demonstrate that it is possible to sustain very high rates of thunk allocation. In contrast, Elliott [14] gives an implementation of streams using futures. In our terms, his stream type $S\,A$ is $\mu\alpha.\ A \times E\,\alpha$, where the recursive type is guarded by an event constructor instead of a unit delay. This means that each stream can run at a different rate, permitting the system to quiesce until events become available, at the cost of complicating the merging of streams.

6. Related Work

Implementing Reactive Programming DSLs for reactive programming languages tend to fall into one of two camps. The "purist" camp, such as Yampa [35], typically features fairly simple implementation strategies and limited dynamic behaviour, which fairly closely track the semantic model of stream programming. The "pragmatist" camp, such the Froc library for Ocaml [12], FrTime [10], and Scala.React [31], feature more sophisticated implementations based on dataflow engines and change propagation, and better support for dynamic behavior.

Now, it has long been recognized that there are connections between lazy evaluation and the synchronous dataflow paradigm [6], but the precise relationship between the two semantics has been unclear to date. Our semantics clarifies this connection, by decomposing streams into a recursive type over the next-step modality of temporal logic. We then show that thunking and lazy evaluation can be used to give *realizers* for the next-step modality, and that the synchrony assumption (that is, a global notion of time) enables *scheduling* when these thunks are forced. In other words, we show that two standard functional programming evaluation strategies – call-by-value and call-by-need – jointly supply all the computational primitives well-behaved reactive programs need.

We can also clarify what parts of the sophisticated implementations used by the pragmatist languages are necessary, and which parts are optimizations. These languages typically work by building a graph of dataflow nodes (which might be thought of as a kind of generalized spreadsheet), and incrementally recomputing values when node values change. The recomputations are guided by the dependency structure of the dataflow graph, often using quite so-

$$
\begin{array}{lcl}
\mathcal{V}\llbracket \alpha \rrbracket\, \rho\, w & = & \rho(\alpha)\, w \\
\mathcal{V}\llbracket A + B \rrbracket\, \rho\, w & = & \{\mathsf{inl}\, v \mid v \in \mathcal{V}\llbracket A \rrbracket\, \rho\, w\} \cup \{\mathsf{inr}\, v \mid v \in \mathcal{V}\llbracket B \rrbracket\, \rho\, w\} \\
\mathcal{V}\llbracket A \times B \rrbracket\, \rho\, w & = & \{(v_1, v_2) \mid v_1 \in \mathcal{V}\llbracket A \rrbracket\, \rho\, w \wedge v_2 \in \mathcal{V}\llbracket B \rrbracket\, \rho\, w\} \\
\mathcal{V}\llbracket A \to B \rrbracket\, \rho\, w & = & \left\{ \lambda x.\, e \;\middle|\; \begin{array}{l} \lambda x.\, e \sqsubseteq w.\sigma \wedge \\ \forall \pi \in \mathrm{Perm}, w' \leq w, e' \in \mathcal{E}\llbracket A \rrbracket\, \rho\, \pi(w').\ [e'/x]\pi(e) \in \mathcal{E}\llbracket B \rrbracket\, \rho\, \pi(w') \end{array} \right\} \\
\mathcal{V}\llbracket \bullet A \rrbracket\, \rho\, w & = & \{l \mid w.\sigma = (\sigma_0, l : e\ \mathsf{later}, \sigma_1) \wedge \forall \pi \in \mathrm{Perm}, w' \leq (w.n, \sigma_0, w.a).\ \pi(e) \in \mathcal{L}\llbracket A \rrbracket\, \rho\, \pi(w')\} \\
\mathcal{V}\llbracket \Box A \rrbracket\, \rho\, w & = & \{\mathsf{stable}(v) \mid v \in \mathcal{V}\llbracket A \rrbracket\, \rho\, (w.n, \cdot, \top)\} \\
\mathcal{V}\llbracket \hat{\mu}\alpha.\, A \rrbracket\, \rho\, w & = & \{\mathsf{into}\, v \mid v \in \mathcal{V}\llbracket A \rrbracket\, (\rho, \mathcal{V}\llbracket \bullet(\hat{\mu}\alpha.\, A) \rrbracket\, \rho\, w/\alpha)\, w\} \\
\mathcal{V}\llbracket S\, A \rrbracket\, \rho\, w & = & \{\mathsf{cons}(v, v') \mid v \in \mathcal{V}\llbracket A \rrbracket\, \rho\, w \wedge v' \in \mathcal{V}\llbracket \bullet S\, A \rrbracket\, \rho\, w\} \\
\mathcal{V}\llbracket \mathsf{alloc} \rrbracket\, \rho\, w & = & \{\diamond \mid w.a = \bot\} \\
 & & \\
\mathcal{E}\llbracket A \rrbracket\, \rho\, (n, \sigma, a) & = & \left\{ e \;\middle|\; \begin{array}{l} e \sqsubseteq \sigma \wedge \\ \forall \sigma' \leq \sigma.\ \exists \sigma'' \leq \sigma', v \in \mathcal{V}\llbracket A \rrbracket\, \rho\, (n, \sigma'', a). \\ \quad \langle \sigma'; e \rangle \Downarrow \langle \sigma''; v \rangle \wedge (a = \top \implies \sigma'' = \sigma') \end{array} \right\} \\
 & & \\
\mathcal{L}\llbracket A \rrbracket\, \rho\, (0, \sigma, a) & = & \{e \in \mathrm{Expr} \mid e \sqsubseteq \sigma\} \\
\mathcal{L}\llbracket A \rrbracket\, \rho\, (n+1, \sigma, a) & = & \{e \in \mathrm{Expr} \mid e \sqsubseteq \sigma \wedge \sigma \Longrightarrow \sigma' \wedge \forall w' \leq (n, \sigma', a).\ e \in \mathcal{E}\llbracket A \rrbracket\, \rho\, w'\}
\end{array}
$$

Figure 10. The Logical Relation

phisticated techniques: for example, Froc is explicitly based on the implementation strategies in self-adjusting computation [1].

Our decomposition also clarifies the semantics of imperative implementation techniques of FRP, by showing how imperative state supports a purely functional surface language. Again, the decomposition of streams via recursive types and the later modality is crucial. *Imperative state* is essential, since it lets us implement the later modality with memoization, and thereby avoid redundant multiple recomputations when we reference a later variable multiple times. However, *persistent state with identity* is not necessary to implement higher-order FRP, and abandoning it enables significant simplifications over the dataflow graph strategy. In a traditional dataflow graph, streams are primitives, and represented by dataflow nodes with persistent identity. This greatly complicates correctness proofs: in [27], we gave such a representation Modeling pure streams with dataflow nodes, and were forced to give a vastly more complex logical relation to account for the persistence of dataflow nodes.

Logics of Time and Space To our knowledge, Sculthorpe and Nilsson [41] first suggested using temporal logic to verify FRP programs. There, they gave a standard (albeit dependently-typed) arrowized FRP system, and temporal logic was used to describe the behavior of these programs. Jeffrey [19] and Jeltsch [22] were the first to suggest using LTL directly as a type system for FRP.

Jeltsch [21] proposes a design for a Haskell FRP library with some similarities with our approach. As in our approach, streams are viewed as a kind of generator which incrementally produce values. However, instead of using temporal modalities to control when streams are used, the types of streams are indexed with polymorphic type parameters ("era parameters") in the style of Haskell's `runST` operation. Though no correctness proof is given, the use of polymorphism suggests that the techniques of Jeffrey [20] may be applicable.

The Modal μ-calculus Our use of recursive types to model temporal operations naturally invites comparisons to the modal μ-calculus [24]. The μ-calculus takes the propositional calculus, adds a next-step modality, and adds constructors for inductive and coinductive formulas.

The biggest difference is that the μ-calculus restricts recursive variables to occur in strictly positive position, but places no guardedness condition on those variables. In contrast, our notion of recursive type is drawn from Nakano [34], who uses a guardedness condition instead of a positivity condition, allowing variables to occur negatively as long as they occur underneath a delay operator.

Permitting negative occurrences is extremely powerful: as we have seen, term-level fixed points can be defined using recursive types with negative occurrences. The definability of fixed points in turn means that guarded recursive types enjoy a form of limit-colimit coincidence similar to the same property in domain theory. In type-theoretic terms, inductive and coinductive interpretations of a guarded recursive type coincide. This means that it is not possible to distinguish may (coinductive) and must (inductive) properties: for example, our event type constructor says that an event may occur, but does not say it will necessarily occur. (Recently, Jeltsch [23] has investigated potential applications of must-operators to reactive programming.)

Our choice to use guarded recursive types was guided by the nature of interactive programs: if we begin to download a file, there is no way to be *sure* that the download necessarily completes (such as the wifi may go down). As a result, placing must-properties in types is perhaps philosophically arguable. (On a pragmatic note, expressing fixed points with guarded recursion leads to very natural and idiomatic code.)

Our stable type $\Box A$ is not found in the modal μ-calculus, but may be understood as a constructivization of the always modality. When passing from a model-theoretic semantics to a proof theory, it is often the case that a single model-theoretic concept bifurcates into two or more proof-theoretic concepts. The always modality exemplifies this: under a computational interpretation,"always A" can either be interpreted as a single value of type A which is always available (that is, stability $\Box A$), or as a different A on each tick (that is, streams $S\,A$).

Very recently, Cave et al. [8] proposed a type-theoretic constructivization of the modal μ-calculus (without the $\Box A$ modality). In particular, they use inductive and coinductive types instead of a Nakano-style recursive type, and use it to express fairness properties (for example, of schedulers) with types. While it is too early to make a detailed comparison (larger examples are needed), having calculi with both kinds of type recursion available seems like a valuable tool for understanding the design space.

Stability and Permissions Our stability judgment and promotion rule are inspired by the mobility judgment in the distributed language

ML5 [33]. We wanted to identify values we could use at multiple times, and they wanted to identity values they could use at multiple locations. Promotion is actually definable in our calculus, as a kind of eta-expansion. However, operationally these coercions traverse the entire data structure, and so for efficiency's sake we added it as a primitive. Allocation permissions were introduced by Hofmann [18], to control memory allocation in a linearly-typed language. Our observation that in an intuitionistic setting, these tokens correspond to an object capability style [32] seems to be new, and potentially has applications beyond reactive programming. However, we do not yet have a full Curry-Howard explanation of allocation permissions.

Acknowledgments

I would like to thank Derek Dreyer, Bob Harper, and the anonymous referees for helpful discussions and suggestions.

References

[1] U. A. Acar. *Self-Adjusting Computation*. PhD thesis, Carnegie Mellon University, 2005.

[2] A. Ahmed, D. Dreyer, and A. Rossberg. State-dependent representation independence. In *Principles of Programming Languages (POPL)*, pages 340–353, 2009.

[3] A. Appel and D. McAllester. An indexed model of recursive types for foundational proof-carrying code. *ACM Transactions on Programming Languages and Systems (TOPLAS)*, 23(5):657–683, 2001.

[4] H. Baker and C. Hewitt. The incremental garbage collection of processes. In *Symposium on Artificial Intelligence Programming Languages*, August 1977.

[5] G. Berry and L. Cosserat. The ESTEREL synchronous programming language and its mathematical semantics. In *Seminar on Concurrency*, pages 389–448. Springer, 1985.

[6] P. Caspi and M. Pouzet. Synchronous Kahn networks. In *Proceedings of the first ACM SIGPLAN international conference on Functional programming*, ICFP '96, pages 226–238, New York, NY, USA, 1996. ACM. ISBN 0-89791-770-7. .

[7] P. Caspi, D. Pilaud, N. Halbwachs, and J. Plaice. LUSTRE: A declarative language for real-time programming. In *Principles of Programming Languages (POPL)*, 1987.

[8] A. Cave, F. Ferreira, P. Panangaden, and B. Pientka. Fair reactive programming. Technical report, McGill University, 2013.

[9] G. H. Cooper. *Integrating Dataflow Evaluation into a Practical Higher-Order Call-by-Value Language*. PhD thesis, Brown University, 2008.

[10] G. H. Cooper and S. Krishnamurthi. Embedding dynamic dataflow in a call-by-value language. In *European Symposium on Programming (ESOP)*, pages 294–308, 2006.

[11] H. B. Curry. The Paradox of Kleene and Rosser. *Transactions of the American Mathematical Society*, 50(3):454–516, Nov. 1941.

[12] J. Donham. Froc: a library for functional reactive programming in OCaml. `http://jaked.github.com/froc/`, 2010.

[13] D. Dreyer, G. Neis, and L. Birkedal. The impact of higher-order state and control effects on local relational reasoning. In *International Conference on Functional Programming (ICFP)*, pages 143–156, 2010.

[14] C. Elliott. Push-pull functional reactive programming. In *Haskell Symposium*, 2009. URL `http://conal.net/papers/push-pull-frp`.

[15] C. Elliott and P. Hudak. Functional reactive animation. In *International Conference on Functional Programming (ICFP)*, 1997.

[16] D. Friedman and D. Wise. The impact of applicative programming on multiprocessing. In *International Conference on Parallel Processing*, pages 263–272, 1976.

[17] M. J. Gabbay and A. M. Pitts. A new approach to abstract syntax with variable binding. *Formal Aspects of Computing*, 13:341–363, 2001.

[18] M. Hofmann. Linear types and non-size-increasing polynomial time computation. In *Logic in Computer Science (LICS)*, 1999.

[19] A. Jeffrey. LTL types FRP: linear-time temporal logic propositions as types, proofs as functional reactive programs. In *Programming Languages Meets Program Verification (PLPV)*, pages 49–60, 2012.

[20] A. Jeffrey. Causality for free!: parametricity implies causality for functional reactive programs. In *Programming Languages Meets Program Verification (PLPV)*, pages 57–68, 2013.

[21] W. Jeltsch. Signals, not generators! *Trends in Functional Programming*, 10:145–160, 2009.

[22] W. Jeltsch. Towards a common categorical semantics for linear-time temporal logic and functional reactive programming. *Electronic Notes in Theoretical Computer Science*, 286:229–242, Sept. 2012.

[23] W. Jeltsch. Temporal logic with "until", functional reactive programming with processes, and concrete process categories. In *Programming Languages Meets Program Verification (PLPV)*, pages 69–78, 2013.

[24] D. Kozen. Results on the propositional μ-calculus. *Theoretical Computer Science*, 27(3):333 – 354, 1983.

[25] N. R. Krishnaswami. Proofs for higher-order reactive programming without spacetime leaks (supplementary material). Technical report, Max Planck Institute for Software Systems (MPI-SWS), 2013.

[26] N. R. Krishnaswami and N. Benton. A semantic model for graphical user interfaces. In *International Conference on Functional programming (ICFP)*, pages 45–57, 2011.

[27] N. R. Krishnaswami and N. Benton. Ultrametric semantics of reactive programs. In *Logic in Computer Science (LICS)*, pages 257–266, 2011.

[28] N. R. Krishnaswami, N. Benton, and J. Hoffmann. Higher-order functional reactive programming in bounded space. In *Principles of Programming Languages (POPL)*, pages 45–58, 2012.

[29] B. S. Lerner, M. J. Carroll, D. P. Kimmel, H. Q.-D. La Vallee, and S. Krishnamurthi. Modeling and reasoning about DOM events. In *Conference on Web Application Development (WebApps)*, 2012.

[30] H. Liu, E. Cheng, and P. Hudak. Causal commutative arrows and their optimization. In *International Conference on Functional Programming (ICFP)*, 2009.

[31] I. Maier and M. Odersky. Deprecating the Observer Pattern with Scala.React. Technical report, EPFL, 2012.

[32] M. Miller. *Robust composition: Towards a unified approach to access control and concurrency control*. PhD thesis, Johns Hopkins University, 2006.

[33] T. Murphy VII., K. Crary, and R. Harper. Type-safe distributed programming with ML5. In *Conference on Trustworthy Global Computing (TGC)*, pages 108–123, 2008.

[34] H. Nakano. A modality for recursion. In *Logic in Computer Science (LICS)*, pages 255–266, 2000.

[35] H. Nilsson, A. Courtney, and J. Peterson. Functional reactive programming, continued. In *ACM Haskell Workshop*, page 64, 2002.

[36] A. Pitts and I. Stark. Operational reasoning for functions with local state. *Higher Order Operational Techniques in Semantics*, 1998.

[37] G. D. Plotkin. A powerdomain construction. *SIAM Journal of Computation*, 5(3):452–487, 1976.

[38] A. Pnueli. The temporal logic of programs. In *Foundations of Computer Science (FOCS)*, pages 46 –57, 1977.

[39] M. Pouzet. *Lucid Synchrone, version 3. Tutorial and reference manual*. Université Paris-Sud, LRI, 2006.

[40] N. Sculthorpe and H. Nilsson. Safe functional reactive programming through dependent types. In *International Conference on Functional Programming (ICFP)*, 2009.

[41] N. Sculthorpe and H. Nilsson. Keeping calm in the face of change. *Higher Order Symbolic Computation*, 23(2):227–271, June 2010.

[42] P. Wadler, W. Taha, and D. MacQueen. How to add laziness to a strict language, without even being odd. In *Workshop on Standard ML*, 1998.

[43] Z. Wan, W. Taha, and P. Hudak. Event-driven FRP. In *Practical Applications of Declarative Languages (PADL)*, pages 155–172, 2002.

Functional Reactive Programming with Liveness Guarantees

As relations are to set-valued functions, so event sources are to behaviours

Alan Jeffrey
Bell Labs, Alcatel-Lucent
ajeffrey@bell-labs.com

Abstract

Functional Reactive Programming (FRP) is an approach to the development of reactive systems which provides a pure functional interface, but which may be implemented as an abstraction of an imperative event-driven layer. FRP systems typically provide a model of behaviours (total time-indexed values, implemented as pull systems) and event sources (partial time-indexed values, implemented as push systems). In this paper, we investigate a type system for event-driven FRP programs which provide liveness guarantees, that is every input event is guaranteed to generate an output event. We show that FRP can be implemented on top of a model of sets and relations, and that the isomorphism between event sources and behaviours corresponds to the isomorphism between relations and set-valued functions. We then implement sets and relations using a model of continuations using the usual double-negation CPS transform. The implementation of behaviours as pull systems based on futures, and of event sources as push systems based on the observer pattern, thus arises from first principles. We also discuss a Java implementation of the FRP model.

Categories and Subject Descriptors D.1.1 [*Software*]: Programming Techniques—Applicative (Functional) Programming

General Terms Design, Theory

Keywords Functional Reactive Programming, Concurrency, Liveness

1. Introduction

Many classes of programs are *reactive*: they run for a long period of time during which they interact with their environment. Examples of reactive programs include control systems, servers, and any program with a graphical user interface.

Many reactive programs are implemented using an event-driven model, in which stateful components send and receive events which update their state, and may cause side-effects such as network traffic or screen updates. The event-driven model forms the basis of Actors [12], and the Model View Controller architecture of Smalltalk [5].

ICFP '13, September 25–27, 2013, Boston, MA, USA.

http://dx.doi.org/10.1145/2500365.2500584

The event-driven model has a number of challenging features, including:

- *Concurrency*: reactive programs often have concurrent features such as dealing with multiple simultaneous events. This either leads to multithreaded languages such as Java, with complex concurrency models [4, Ch. 17], or single-threaded languages such as ECMAScript which do not naturally support multicore execution, and rely on cooperative multitasking.
- *Imperative programming*: components are stateful, and may respond to events by updating their internal state. These hidden side-effects can result in complex implicit component interdependencies.
- *Referential opacity*: since components support mutable state, component identity is important. The semantics for components is not referentially transparent, since creating a component and copying it is not equivalent to creating multiple components.
- *Callbacks*: the idiom for programming in an event-driven model is registering callbacks rather than blocking function calls. For example, in ECMAScript an HTTP request is not a blocking method call, but instead a non-blocking call which registers a callback to handle the result of the HTTP request. This essentially requires the programmer to convert their program to Continuation Passing Style (CPS) [22]. Manual CPS transformation can be error-prone, for example, calling the wrong continuation, or mistakenly calling a continuation twice. In the absence of call/cc, CPS transformation is a whole-program translation, so can require a large codebase to be rewritten.

Functional Reactive Programming allows reactive programs to be written in a pure functional style. Originally developed by Elliot and Hudak [11] as part of the Fran functional animation system, there are now a number of implementations, including Agda FRP [15], Flapjax [20], Frappé [8], Froc [9], FrTime [7], Grapefruit [16], Reactive [10], Reactive-Banana [2], and Yampa [23].

Comparing FRP with the event-driven model, we have:

- *Pure functional model*: there are no implicit interactions caused by shared mutable state, and a simple concurrency model.
- *Referentially transparent*: signals can be copied without altering their semantics.
- *Direct*: FRP programs are given in direct style rather than CPS.

Comparing FRP with synchronous dataflow languages such as Esterel [3], some key distinctions are:

- *Fine-grained time*: FRP often models time as a continuous domain (such as $\mathbb{R}$) or using a much finer unit of time than the sample frequency of a synchronous language (such as 1ms).

- *Higher-order signals*: FRP allows signals of signals, which model dynamically reconfigurable dataflow networks.
- *Embedded DSL*: FRP is typically implemented as an embedded DSL library in a functional host language (often Haskell, but also Agda [13], ECMAScript [20], Java [8], OCaml [9], or Scheme [7]).

In this paper, we consider the problem of *liveness* of an FRP program.

- We develop a type system and model of FRP which provides liveness guarantees.
- We show how to define guarded fixed points, and provide liveness in the presence of recursion.
- We give an implementation of FRP in terms of programming over sets and relations, which are in turn implemented using callbacks.
- We discuss a multithreaded Java implementation of the model.

This is the first work to provide liveness guarantees for event-based programs in FRP. Moreover, in implementing FRP in terms of a model of sets and relations:

- The isomorphism between event sources and behaviours corresponds to the isomorphism between relations and set-valued functions.
- The implementation of sets and relations using the usual double-negation CPS transform allows the implementation of behaviours as pull systems based on futures, and of event sources as push systems based on the observer pattern, to arise from first principles.
- The implementation of event sources as relations allows naturally for concurrent execution, and in particular for out-of-order arrival of events. Most combinators naturally allow for concurrency, and it is only combinators which rely on ordering (such as an accumulation function) which force an order on events.

This is the first such investigation of the relationship between FRP and a CPS implementation of sets and relations, and the first implementation of concurrent FRP using out-of-order events.

2. History-free programs

In this section, we present our core FRP model, with types, combinators, and their semantics. For readability, we present the model in pseudo-Haskell: the actual implementation is in Java, as discussed in Section 6. We start by presenting the combinators for history-free programs: history-sensitive programs are discussed in the next section.

The semantics of FRP is defined in terms of *behaviours* over a total order Time, whose semantics are given as total functions from time to values:

$$[\![\mathsf{Behaviour}\ A]\!] = \mathsf{Time} \rightarrow [\![A]\!]$$

and *event sources* which are partial functions:

$$[\![\mathsf{Event}\ A]\!] = \mathsf{Time} \rightarrow [\![A]\!]_\bot$$

where:

$$X_\bot = \{\bot\} \cup \{\mathsf{lift}\, x \mid x \in X\}$$

We will sometimes refer to *signals* when we want to talk about both behaviours and events.

The timestamps for events are based on the time an event first enters the FRP system, not the current wall-clock time. For example, a function on event sources which processes a event x with timestamp t to an event $f(x)$ will still emit $f(x)$ with timestamp t, irrespective of the running time of f.

Signal types come with a collection of combinators such as:

$$\begin{aligned} &\mathsf{map} : (A \rightarrow B) \rightarrow \mathsf{Event}\ A \rightarrow \mathsf{Event}\ B \\ &\mathsf{filter} : (A \rightarrow \mathsf{Boolean}) \rightarrow \mathsf{Event}\ A \rightarrow \mathsf{Event}\ A \end{aligned}$$

whose semantics are as one might expect:

$$[\![\mathsf{map}]\!]\ f\ \sigma\ t = \begin{cases} \mathsf{lift}\,(f\ x) & \text{if } \sigma\ t = \mathsf{lift}\, x \\ \bot & \text{otherwise} \end{cases}$$

$$[\![\mathsf{filter}]\!]\ f\ \sigma\ t = \begin{cases} \mathsf{lift}\, x & \text{if } \sigma\ t = \mathsf{lift}\, x \text{ and } f\ x \\ \bot & \text{otherwise} \end{cases}$$

For example, a simple web server, which responds "Hello, World!" to any `GET` request might be written:

```
server : Event HTTPRequest → Event HTTPResponse
server reqs = getResps where
  getReqs = filter isGetRequest reqs
  getResps = map hello getReqs
  hello req = httpResponse 200 "Hello, World!"
```

assuming a library for HTTP messages:

```
isGetRequest : HTTPRequest → Boolean
httpResponse : Integer → String → HTTPResponse
```

Unfortunately, this server has a serious problem: it suffers from a lack of *liveness*, in that a non-`GET` request will result in no response at all. To fix this, we introduce explicit error handling:

```
server : Event HTTPRequest → Event HTTPResponse
server reqs = union getResps otherResps where
  (getReqs, otherReqs) = partition isGetRequest reqs
  getResps = map hello getReqs
  otherResps = map error otherReqs
  hello req = httpResponse 200 "Hello, World!"
  error req = httpResponse 405 "Method not supported."
```

This uses combinators for partitioning and recombining events:

$$\begin{aligned} &\mathsf{partition} : (A \rightarrow \mathsf{Boolean}) \rightarrow \mathsf{Event}\ A \rightarrow (\mathsf{Event}\ A \times \mathsf{Event}\ A) \\ &\mathsf{union} : \mathsf{Event}\ A \rightarrow \mathsf{Event}\ A \rightarrow \mathsf{Event}\ A \end{aligned}$$

The semantics of partitioning is simple:

$$[\![\mathsf{partition}]\!]\ f\ \sigma = ([\![\mathsf{filter}]\!]\ f\ \sigma, [\![\mathsf{filter}]\!]\ (\neg \circ f)\ \sigma)$$

The semantics of recombining is not so simple, since we have to account for the possibility that events will arrive simultaneously from both sources. The easiest thing to do is to prioritize one source over the other, for example to prioritize the first source:

$$[\![\mathsf{union}]\!]\ \sigma\ \tau\ t = \begin{cases} \mathsf{lift}\, x & \text{if } \sigma\ t = \mathsf{lift}\, x \\ \tau\ t & \text{otherwise} \end{cases}$$

Unfortunately, this approach is problematic for three reasons:

- This semantics for union xs ys is not commutative, even though in its idiomatic usage xs and ys have disjoint domains.
- The types for partition and union permit the original buggy server, so do not provide liveness guarantees.
- The implementation of union xs ys is difficult, in that an event from ys at time t cannot be emitted until we know that xs will not generate an event at time t. This may cause events from ys to be unnecessarily buffered, and requires the presence of negative information (xs will not generate an event at time t).

For these reasons, we propose an alternative type system for behaviours and events. Rather than event sources being partial func-

$$[\![\mathsf{Event}\,T\,A]\!] = [\![T]\!] \to [\![A]\!]$$
$$[\![\mathsf{Behaviour}\,T\,A]\!] = [\![T]\!] \to [\![A]\!]$$
$$[\![\mathsf{Minus}\,T\,S]\!] = [\![T]\!] \setminus [\![S]\!]$$

$$\mathsf{event} : \mathsf{Behaviour}\,T\,A \to \mathsf{Event}\,T\,A$$
$$[\![\mathsf{event}]\!]\,\sigma = \sigma$$

$$\mathsf{buffer} : \mathsf{Event}\,T\,A \to \mathsf{Behaviour}\,T\,A$$
$$[\![\mathsf{buffer}]\!]\,\sigma = \sigma$$

$$\mathsf{map} : (A \to B) \to \mathsf{Event}\,T\,A \to \mathsf{Event}\,T\,B$$
$$[\![\mathsf{map}]\!]\,f\,\sigma\,t = f\,(\sigma\,t)$$

$$\mathsf{map} : (A \to B) \to \mathsf{Behaviour}\,T\,A \to \mathsf{Behaviour}\,T\,B$$
$$[\![\mathsf{map}]\!]\,f\,\sigma\,t = f\,(\sigma\,t)$$

$$\mathsf{map2} : (A \to B \to C) \to \mathsf{Behaviour}\,T\,A \to \mathsf{Behaviour}\,T\,B \to \mathsf{Behaviour}\,T\,C$$
$$[\![\mathsf{map2}]\!]\,f\,\sigma\,\tau\,t = f\,(\sigma\,t)\,(\tau\,t)$$

$$\mathsf{map2} : (A \to B \to C) \to \mathsf{Event}\,T\,A \to \mathsf{Behaviour}\,T\,B \to \mathsf{Event}\,T\,C$$
$$[\![\mathsf{map2}]\!]\,f\,\sigma\,\tau\,t = f\,(\sigma\,t)\,(\tau\,t)$$

$$\mathsf{partition} : (A \to \mathsf{Boolean}) \to \mathsf{Event}\,T\,A \to \exists(S \le T)(\mathsf{Event}\,S\,A \times \mathsf{Event}\,(\mathsf{Minus}\,T\,S)\,A)$$
$$[\![\mathsf{partition}]\!]\,f\,\sigma = (X, \tau, \rho) \text{ where } X = \{t \mid f\,(\sigma\,t)\} \text{ and } \tau\,t = \sigma\,t \text{ and } \rho\,t = \sigma\,t$$

$$\mathsf{union} : \mathsf{Event}\,S\,A \to \mathsf{Event}\,(\mathsf{Minus}\,T\,S)\,A \to \mathsf{Event}\,T\,A$$
$$[\![\mathsf{union}]\!]\,\sigma\,\tau = \sigma \cup \tau$$

Figure 1. History-free fragment, where $[\![S]\!] \subseteq [\![T]\!] \subseteq \mathsf{Time}$ is locally finite and well-ordered

tions with domain Time, we propose viewing them as total functions whose domain is a subset of Time, that is:

$$[\![\mathsf{Event}\,T\,A]\!] = [\![T]\!] \to [\![A]\!]$$

Since event sources are total, they guarantee *liveness* in the sense that they will produce a value for any time in $[\![T]\!]$. For symmetry, we parameterize behaviours by the times at which they change:

$$[\![\mathsf{Behaviour}\,T\,A]\!] = [\![T]\!] \to [\![A]\!]$$

To ensure the existence of fixed points, as discussed in Section 3, we require that $[\![T]\!] \subseteq \mathsf{Time}$ is locally finite (that is every interval $[s,t]$ from $[\![T]\!]$ is finite) and well-ordered (every non-empty subset of T has a least element). Note that T is being used as a *phantom type* [19]: it is a fiction of the types for signals, and its implementation is not necessarily as a subset of Time.

Semantically, events and behaviours are equivalent, and indeed they form an isomorphism given by:

$$\mathsf{event} : \mathsf{Behaviour}\,T\,A \to \mathsf{Event}\,T\,A$$
$$\mathsf{buffer} : \mathsf{Event}\,T\,A \to \mathsf{Behaviour}\,T\,A$$

As we shall see, their implementations are quite different (behaviours are implemented as pull systems, and events are implemented as push systems). In particular, the event function introduces no overhead, but the buffer function introduces buffering, and so may have a significant memory overhead.

We are careful about when we use Behaviour types and when we use Event types to ensure that the only source of buffering from the primitives is the buffer function. For example, we provide two functions for mapping a binary function over two signals:

$$\mathsf{map2} : (A \to B \to C) \to \mathsf{Behaviour}\,T\,A \to \mathsf{Behaviour}\,T\,B \to \mathsf{Behaviour}\,T\,C$$
$$\mathsf{map2} : (A \to B \to C) \to \mathsf{Event}\,T\,A \to \mathsf{Behaviour}\,T\,B \to \mathsf{Event}\,T\,C$$

In both cases, one of the signals must be a behaviour, and if we wish to combine two event sources, we must first buffer one of them, for example if $\mathsf{xs}, \mathsf{ys} : \mathsf{Event}\,T\,\mathsf{Integer}$ then:

$$\mathsf{map2}\,(\cdot + \cdot)\,\mathsf{xs}\,(\mathsf{buffer}\,\mathsf{ys}) : \mathsf{Event}\,T\,\mathsf{Integer}$$

We do *not* provide a combinator:

$$\mathsf{map2} : (A \to B \to C) \to \mathsf{Event}\,T\,A \to \mathsf{Event}\,T\,A \to \mathsf{Event}\,T\,A$$

since $\mathsf{map2}\,f\,\mathsf{xs}\,\mathsf{ys}$ cannot be implemented without buffering: an event with timestamp t may arrive from xs at wall-clock time t_1, with the matching event from ys arriving at wall-clock time t_2; events must be buffered to allow for the differences in wall-clock time.

The type for map is unchanged, and its semantics is simplified, since events are now total:

$$\mathsf{map} : (A \to B) \to \mathsf{Event}\,T\,A \to \mathsf{Event}\,T\,B$$
$$[\![\mathsf{map}]\!]\,f\,\sigma\,t = f\,(\sigma\,t)$$

The type for filter must change: if xs has domain T, then filter f xs will not have domain T, but will instead have some subdomain of T. To model this, we use *bounded existential types* [6], with semantics:

$$[\![\exists(A \le B)(F\,A)]\!] = \{(X, [\![F]\!]X) \mid X \subseteq [\![B]\!]\}$$

The type and semantics of filter are then:

$$\mathsf{filter} : (A \to \mathsf{Boolean}) \to \mathsf{Event}\,T\,A \to \exists(S \le T)(\mathsf{Event}\,S\,A)$$
$$[\![\mathsf{filter}]\!]\,f\,\sigma = (X, \tau) \text{ where } X = \{t \mid f\,(\sigma\,t)\} \text{ and } \tau\,t = \sigma\,t$$

For example, if:

$$[\![\mathsf{things}]\!] = \{0 \mapsto \mathsf{apple}, 1 \mapsto \mathsf{cat}, 2 \mapsto \mathsf{banana}\}$$

then:

$$[\![\text{filter isFruit things}]\!] = (\{0,2\}, \{0 \mapsto \text{apple}, 2 \mapsto \text{banana}\})$$

For partitioning, we could just continue to treat a partition as a pair of filters, which would give the type:

$$\begin{aligned}&\text{partition} : (A \to \text{Boolean}) \to \text{Event}\,T\,A \to \\ &\quad (\exists(S \leq T)(\text{Event}\,S\,A) \times \exists(R \leq T)(\text{Event}\,R\,A))\end{aligned}$$

However, with this type, we have lost the information that T has been partitioned into S and R. Instead, we provide a more refined type, in which we set R to be $\text{Minus}\,T\,S$:

$$\begin{aligned}&\text{partition} : (A \to \text{Boolean}) \to \text{Event}\,T\,A \to \\ &\quad \exists(S \leq T)(\text{Event}\,S\,A \times \text{Event}\,(\text{Minus}\,T\,S)\,A)\end{aligned}$$

where $\text{Minus}\,T\,S$ is interpreted as set subtraction (maintaining an invariant that $[\![S]\!] \subseteq [\![T]\!]$):

$$[\![\text{Minus}\,T\,S]\!] = [\![T]\!] \setminus [\![S]\!]$$

The semantics of partition is:

$$\begin{aligned}&[\![\text{partition}]\!]\,f\,\sigma = (X, \tau, \rho) \text{ where} \\ &\quad X = \{t \mid f\,(\sigma\,t)\} \text{ and } \tau\,t = \sigma\,t \text{ and } \rho\,t = \sigma\,t\end{aligned}$$

For example:

$$\begin{aligned}&[\![\text{partition isFruit things}]\!] = \\ &\quad (\{0,2\}, \{0 \mapsto \text{apple}, 2 \mapsto \text{banana}\}, \{1 \mapsto \text{cat}\})\end{aligned}$$

The benefit of this refined type for partition is that it allows for a better treatment of union:

$$\begin{aligned}&\text{union} : \text{Event}\,S\,A \to \text{Event}\,(\text{Minus}\,T\,S)\,A \to \text{Event}\,T\,A \\ &[\![\text{union}]\!]\,\sigma\,\tau = \sigma \cup \tau\end{aligned}$$

For example, if we define:

$$\begin{aligned}&\text{mkDog xs} = \text{union fruit dogs where} \\ &\quad (\text{fruit}, \text{rest}) = \text{partition isFruit xs} \\ &\quad \text{dogs} = \text{map}\,(\lambda x\,.\,\text{dog})\,\text{rest}\end{aligned}$$

then we have:

$$[\![\text{mkDog things}]\!] = \{0 \mapsto \text{apple}, 1 \mapsto \text{dog}, 2 \mapsto \text{banana}\}$$

This addresses the three issues we highlighted earlier:

- The semantics of union is commutative.
- The fixed version of the HTTP server typechecks with type $\text{server} : \text{Event}\,T\,\text{HTTPRequest} \to \text{Event}\,T\,\text{HTTPResponse}$. The buggy server does not typecheck with this type. In general, the semantics of $\text{Event}\,T\,A$ require liveness for all of T.
- The implementation of union xs ys is simple: when an event from either xs or ys is generated, it can immediately be emitted. No negative information is required.

In Figure 1 we summarize the history-free fragment of our model.

3. History-sensitive programs

So far the FRP combinators only allow history-free programs to be defined, in that output behaviour at time t can only depend on input behaviour at time t, not at any time before t. We now present combinators which support history-sensitive programming.

The simplest form of history-sensitivity is the delay function, which takes a behaviour, and delays it by one unit of time:

$$\begin{aligned}&\text{delay} : \text{Behaviour}\,T\,A \to \text{Event}\,(\text{Tail}\,T)\,A \\ &[\![\text{delay}]\!]\,\sigma\,t_{i+1} = \sigma\,t_i\end{aligned}$$

For example:

$$[\![\text{delay things}]\!] = \{1 \mapsto \text{apple}, 2 \mapsto \text{cat}\}$$

Here we are making use of the requirement that T is a locally finite and well-ordered, since this means that:

$$[\![T]\!] = \{t_0 < t_1 < t_2 < \cdots\}$$

In particular we can then define the tail of T to be every element other than the least one:

$$[\![\text{Tail}\,T]\!] = \text{if } [\![T]\!] = \emptyset \text{ then } \emptyset \text{ else } [\![T]\!] \setminus \{t_0\}$$

We can similarly define the tail of a behaviour to be every element but the first:

$$\begin{aligned}&\text{tail} : \text{Behaviour}\,T\,A \to \text{Behaviour}\,(\text{Tail}\,T)\,A \\ &[\![\text{tail}]\!]\,\sigma\,t = \sigma\,t\end{aligned}$$

For example:

$$[\![\text{tail things}]\!] = \{1 \mapsto \text{cat}, 2 \mapsto \text{banana}\}$$

We cannot, however, provide a matching head function with type $\text{Behaviour}\,T\,A \to A$, since t_0 may be in the future (and indeed T may be empty, so no such A may exist). Instead, we allow a peek function, which allows the first element to be inspected as long as an event is being produced:

$$\begin{aligned}&\text{peek} : \text{Behaviour}\,T\,A \to (A \to \text{Event}\,T\,B) \to \text{Event}\,T\,B \\ &[\![\text{peek}]\!]\,\sigma\,f = f\,(\sigma\,t_0)\end{aligned}$$

For example:

$$[\![\text{peek things}\,(\lambda x\,.\,\text{if isFruit x then ys else zs})]\!] = [\![\text{ys}]\!]$$

These functions allow signals to be decomposed, we can also compose them, for example:

$$\begin{aligned}&\text{cons} : A \to \text{Event}\,(\text{Tail}\,T)\,A \to \text{Event}\,T\,A \\ &[\![\text{cons}]\!]\,x\,\sigma\,t = \begin{cases} x & \text{if } t = t_0 \\ \sigma\,t & \text{otherwise}\end{cases}\end{aligned}$$

for example:

$$\begin{aligned}&[\![\text{cons dog (event (tail things))}]\!] \\ &\quad = \{0 \mapsto \text{dog}, 1 \mapsto \text{cat}, 2 \mapsto \text{banana}\}\end{aligned}$$

Finally, we consider recursively defined behaviours. We will only allow the solution to guarded equations, in the sense that behaviour at time t_{i+1} can only depend on recursive behaviour up to time t_i. We ensure this by introducing an explicit delay, that is we are solving:

$$\sigma = f\,([\![\text{delay}]\!]\,\sigma)$$

Since all definable functions on signals are causal (output at time t only depends on input up to time t) we have that σ's value at time t_{i+1} only depends on $f\,([\![\text{delay}]\!]\,\sigma)$'s value at time t_{i+1}, which only depends on $([\![\text{delay}]\!]\,\sigma)$'s value up to time t_{i+1}, which only depends on σ's value up to time t_i. Thus, σ is well-defined. For a more formal treatment of the well-definedness of guarded equations, see Krishnaswami and Benton's ultrametric space semantics [18], or the author's use of parametricity to ensure causality [14].

Unfortunately, the obvious type for fixed points:

$$\text{fix} : (\text{Event}\,(\text{Tail}\,T)\,A \to \text{Behaviour}\,T\,A) \to \text{Behaviour}\,T\,A$$

has a problem. We are maintaining an invariant that all time domains are locally finite and well-ordered, but if we were to allow fix to exist for all T, then we could use it to inhabit $\text{Behaviour}\,\mathbb{R}^+\,A$, for example:

$$\text{fix}(\lambda\text{xs}\,.\,\text{buffer}(\text{cons}(0, \text{xs})))$$

Since $\mathbb{R}^+$ is locally infinite and non-well-ordered, this would be problematic. To avoid this, we introduce a type of *clocks*, which is only inhabited when $T \subseteq \text{Time}$ is locally finite and well-ordered, in which case its semantics is trivial:

$$[\![\text{Clock}\,T]\!] = \{*\}$$

$$[\![\mathsf{Tail}\, T]\!] = \text{if } [\![T]\!] = \emptyset \text{ then } \emptyset \text{ else } [\![T]\!] \setminus \{t_0\}$$
$$[\![\mathsf{Clock}\, T]\!] = \{*\}$$

$$\mathsf{peek} : \mathsf{Behaviour}\, T\, A \to (A \to \mathsf{Event}\, T\, B) \to \mathsf{Event}\, T\, B$$
$$[\![\mathsf{peek}]\!]\, \sigma\, f = f\, (\sigma\, t_0)$$

$$\mathsf{tail} : \mathsf{Behaviour}\, T\, A \to \mathsf{Behaviour}\, (\mathsf{Tail}\, T)\, A$$
$$[\![\mathsf{tail}]\!]\, \sigma\, t = \sigma\, t$$

$$\mathsf{delay} : \mathsf{Behaviour}\, T\, A \to \mathsf{Event}\, (\mathsf{Tail}\, T)\, A$$
$$[\![\mathsf{delay}]\!]\, \sigma\, t_{i+1} = \sigma\, t_i$$

$$\mathsf{cons} : A \to \mathsf{Event}\, (\mathsf{Tail}\, T)\, A \to \mathsf{Event}\, T\, A$$
$$[\![\mathsf{cons}]\!]\, x\, \sigma\, t = \begin{cases} x & \text{if } t = t_0 \\ \sigma\, t & \text{otherwise} \end{cases}$$

$$\mathsf{clock} : \mathsf{Behaviour}\, T\, A \to \mathsf{Clock}\, T$$
$$[\![\mathsf{clock}]\!]\, \sigma = *$$

$$\mathsf{fix} : \mathsf{Clock}\, T \to (\mathsf{Event}\, (\mathsf{Tail}\, T)\, A \to \mathsf{Behaviour}\, T\, A) \to \mathsf{Behaviour}\, T\, A$$
$$[\![\mathsf{fix}]\!]\, c\, f = \sigma \text{ where } \sigma = f\, ([\![\mathsf{delay}]\!]\, \sigma)$$

Figure 2. History-sensitive fragment of our FRP model, where $[\![T]\!] = \{t_0 < t_1 < t_2 < \cdots\}$

The modified type for fix uses a clock element to ensure that it is safe to inhabit Behaviour $T\ A$:

$$\mathsf{fix} : \mathsf{Clock}\, T \to (\mathsf{Event}\, (\mathsf{Tail}\, T)\, A \to \mathsf{Behaviour}\, T\, A) \to \mathsf{Behaviour}\, T\, A$$
$$[\![\mathsf{fix}]\!]\, c\, f = \sigma \text{ where } \sigma = f\, ([\![\mathsf{delay}]\!]\, \sigma)$$

For example, we can use fix to define a constant behaviour:

$$\mathsf{constant} : \mathsf{Clock}\, T \to A \to \mathsf{Behaviour}\, T\, A$$
$$\mathsf{constant}\, \mathsf{c}\, \mathsf{x} = \mathsf{fix}\, \mathsf{c}\, (\lambda \mathsf{xs}\, .\, \mathsf{buffer}(\mathsf{cons}(\mathsf{x}, \mathsf{xs})))$$
$$[\![\mathsf{constant}]\!]\, c\, x\, t = x$$

We can also use fix to define an accumulator function:

$$\mathsf{accum} : (B \to A \to B) \to B \to \mathsf{Behaviour}\, T\, A \to \mathsf{Behaviour}\, T\, B$$
$$\mathsf{accum}\, \mathsf{f}\, \mathsf{y}\, \mathsf{xs} = \mathsf{fix}\, (\mathsf{clock}\, \mathsf{xs})\, (\lambda \mathsf{ys}\, .\, \mathsf{buffer}(\mathsf{map2}\, \mathsf{f}\, \mathsf{cons}(\mathsf{y}, \mathsf{ys})\, \mathsf{xs}))$$

making use of a function to extract a clock from a behaviour:

$$\mathsf{clock} : \mathsf{Behaviour}\, T\, A \to \mathsf{Clock}\, T$$
$$[\![\mathsf{clock}]\!]\, \sigma = *$$

For example if:

$$\sigma = \{t_0 \mapsto x_0, t_1 \mapsto x_1\ t_2 \mapsto x_2, \ldots\}$$

then:

$$[\![\mathsf{accum}]\!]\, (\cdot + \cdot)\, 0\, \sigma = \{t_0 \mapsto x_0, t_1 \mapsto (x_0 + x_1), t_2 \mapsto (x_0 + x_1 + x_2), \ldots\}$$

In Figure 2 we summarize the history-sensitive fragment of our FRP model.

4. Implementation of behaviours and events

The implementation of signals is built on top of a library of sets and relations. In Figure 3 we give the model of sets and relations, we defer discussing its implementation until the next section. It provides two types, for sets and relations:

$$[\![\mathsf{Set}\, A]\!] = \mathcal{P}\, [\![A]\!]$$
$$\mathsf{Relation}\, A\, B = \mathsf{Set}\, (A \times B)$$

together with a collection of combinators for these types. Of particular interest is the isomorphism between relations ($\mathcal{P}\,(X \times Y)$)

$$[\![\mathsf{Set}\, A]\!] = \mathcal{P}\, [\![A]\!]$$
$$\mathsf{Relation}\, A\, B = \mathsf{Set}\, (A \times B)$$

$$\mathsf{buffer} : \mathsf{Relation}\, A\, B \to A \to \mathsf{Set}\, B$$
$$[\![\mathsf{buffer}]\!]\, R\, x = \{y \mid (x, y) \in R\}$$

$$\mathsf{empty} : \mathsf{Set}\, A$$
$$[\![\mathsf{empty}]\!] = \emptyset$$

$$\mathsf{singleton} : A \to \mathsf{Set}\, A$$
$$[\![\mathsf{singleton}]\!]\, x = \{x\}$$

$$\mathsf{union} : \mathsf{Set}\, A \to \mathsf{Set}\, A \to \mathsf{Set}\, A$$
$$[\![\mathsf{union}]\!]\, X\, Y = X \cup Y$$

$$\mathsf{pmap} : (A \to \mathsf{Set}\, B) \to \mathsf{Set}\, A \to \mathsf{Set}\, B$$
$$[\![\mathsf{pmap}]\!]\, f\, X = \{y \mid x \in X, y \in f\, x\}$$

$$\mathsf{fix} : ((A \to \mathsf{Set}\, B) \to (A \to \mathsf{Set}\, B)) \to A \to \mathsf{Set}\, B$$
$$[\![\mathsf{fix}]\!]\, f = \text{the smallest } g \text{ such that } \forall x\, .\, f\, g\, x \subseteq g\, x$$

Figure 3. Model of sets and relations

and set-valued functions ($X \to \mathcal{P}\, Y$) given by the functions:

$$\mathsf{relation} : \mathsf{Set}\, A \to (A \to \mathsf{Set}\, B) \to \mathsf{Relation}\, A\, B$$
$$\mathsf{relation}\, \mathsf{xs}\, \mathsf{f} = \mathsf{pmap}\, (\lambda \mathsf{x}\, .\, \mathsf{map}\, (\mathsf{x}, \cdot)\, (\mathsf{f}\, \mathsf{x}))\, \mathsf{xs}$$
$$[\![\mathsf{relation}]\!]\, X\, f = \{(x, y) \mid x \in X, y \in f\, x\}$$

$$\mathsf{buffer} : \mathsf{Relation}\, A\, B \to A \to \mathsf{Set}\, B$$
$$[\![\mathsf{buffer}]\!]\, R\, x = \{y \mid (x, y) \in R\}$$

Given a relation R whose domain (that is $\{x \mid \exists y\, .\, (x, y) \in R\}$) is X, we have:

$$[\![\mathsf{relation}]\!]\, X\, ([\![\mathsf{buffer}]\!]\, R) = R$$

and given a function f whose domain (that is $\{x \mid \exists y\, .\, y \in f\, x\}$) is X, we have:

$$[\![\mathsf{buffer}]\!]\, ([\![\mathsf{relation}]\!]\, X\, f) = f$$

We shall see later that this isomorphism generates the isomorphism between behaviours and event sources.

The combinators include a fixed point function:

$$\mathsf{fix} : ((A \to \mathsf{Set}\ B) \to (A \to \mathsf{Set}\ B)) \to A \to \mathsf{Set}\ B$$
$$[\![\mathsf{fix}]\!]\ f = \text{the smallest } g \text{ such that } \forall x \,.\, f\ g\ x \subseteq g\ x$$

This function is well-defined because the only implementable functions are monotone with respect to $\subseteq$.

Using the combinators given in Figure 3, we can derive other combinators such as:

$$\mathsf{map} : (A \to B) \to \mathsf{Set}\ A \to \mathsf{Set}\ B$$
$$\mathsf{map\ f} = \mathsf{pmap}\ (\lambda \mathsf{x}\,.\,\mathsf{singleton(f\ x)})$$
$$[\![\mathsf{map}]\!]\ f\ X = \{f\ x \mid x \in X\}$$

$$\mathsf{pmapr} : (B \to \mathsf{Set}\ C) \to \mathsf{Relation}\ A\ B \to \mathsf{Relation}\ A\ C$$
$$\mathsf{pmapr\ f} = \mathsf{pmap}\ (\lambda(\mathsf{x},\mathsf{y})\,.\,\mathsf{map}\ (x,\cdot)\ (\mathsf{f\ y}))$$
$$[\![\mathsf{pmapr}]\!]\ f\ R = \{(x,z) \mid (x,y) \in R, z \in f\ y\}$$

$$\mathsf{filter} : (A \to \mathsf{Boolean}) \to \mathsf{Set}\ A \to \mathsf{Set}\ A$$
$$\mathsf{filter\ f} = \mathsf{pmap}\ (\lambda \mathsf{x}\,.\,\mathsf{if\ f\ x\ then\ singleton\ x\ else\ empty})$$
$$[\![\mathsf{filter}]\!]\ f\ X = \{x \mid x \in X, f\ x\}$$

$$\mathsf{domain} : \mathsf{Relation}\ A\ B \to \mathsf{Set}\ A$$
$$\mathsf{domain} = \mathsf{map}\ (\lambda(\mathsf{x},\_)\,.\,\mathsf{x})$$
$$[\![\mathsf{domain}]\!]\ R = \{x \mid \exists y\,.\,(x,y) \in R\}$$

In particular, we can implement the categorical structure of relations, with identity and composition:

$$\mathsf{diagonal} : \mathsf{Set}\ A \to \mathsf{Relation}\ A\ A$$
$$\mathsf{diagonal} = \mathsf{map}\ (\lambda \mathsf{x}\,.\,(\mathsf{x},\mathsf{x}))$$
$$[\![\mathsf{diagonal}]\!]\ X = \{(x,x) \mid x \in X\}$$

$$\mathsf{comp} : \mathsf{Relation}\ A\ B \to \mathsf{Relation}\ B\ C \to \mathsf{Relation}\ A\ C$$
$$\mathsf{comp\ q\ r} = \mathsf{pmapr}\ (\mathsf{buffer\ r})\ \mathsf{q}$$
$$[\![\mathsf{comp}]\!]\ Q\ R = \{(x,z) \mid (x,y) \in Q, (y,z) \in R\}$$

We shall now consider an implementation of FRP using sets and relations, beginning with the implementation of clocks. A clock is implemented as an abstract datatype whose implementation is:

```
data Clock T = Clock {
  times : Set Time,
  first : Set Time,
  prev : Relation Time Time,
  parent : T
}
```

We maintain the following invariants about $\mathsf{c} : \mathsf{Clock}\ T$, where $[\![T]\!] \subseteq \mathsf{Time}$ is locally finite and well-ordered, and so $[\![T]\!]$ is of the form $\{t_0 < t_1 < t_2 < \cdots\}$:

- $[\![\mathsf{times\ c}]\!] = [\![T]\!]$.
- $[\![\mathsf{first\ c}]\!] = \{t_0\}$ (or $\emptyset$ when $[\![T]\!] = \emptyset$).
- $[\![\mathsf{prev\ c}]\!] = \{(t_{i+1}, t_i) \mid t_{i+1} > t_0\}$.

Note that every element of $\mathsf{Clock}\ T$ is equal (and in fact we use memoization to ensure that every T has at most one $\mathsf{Clock}\ T$). Clocks are needed as a way to access at run time the total order on T. We can implement a function:

```
tail : Clock T → Clock (Tail T)
tail c = Clock {
  times = domain (prev c)
  first = pmap (λt . domain(filter (λ(_, u) . t = u) (prev c))) (first c)
  prev = pmap (λt . filter (λ(_, u) . t < u) (prev c)) (first c)
  parent = c
}
```

The reason for having a parent element is to implement:

$$\mathsf{tail}^{-1} : \mathsf{Clock}\ (\mathsf{Tail}\ T) \to \mathsf{Clock}\ T$$

The concrete implementation of $\mathsf{Tail}\ T$ is:

$$\mathsf{data\ Tail}\ T = \mathsf{Tail}\ \{\mathsf{clock} : \mathsf{Clock}\ T\}$$

so we can define:

$$\mathsf{tail}^{-1}\ \mathsf{c} = \mathsf{clock\ (parent\ c)}$$

The implementation of $\mathsf{Minus}\ T$ and minus^{-1} are similar. We can now turn our attention from clocks to behaviours and event sources. The concrete implementation of a behaviour is a clock together with a function from time to sets of events:

```
data Behaviour T A = Behaviour {
  clock : Clock T,
  function : Time → Set A
}
```

and the concrete implementation of an event source is a clock together with a relation between time and events:

```
data Event T A = Event {
  clock : Clock T,
  relation : Relation Time A
}
```

As we shall see when we look at the implementation of sets and relations, behaviours are implemented as pull systems, and event sources are implemented as push systems. We maintain the following invariants about $\mathsf{xs} : \mathsf{Behaviour}\ T\ A$ and $\mathsf{ys} : \mathsf{Event}\ T\ A$:

- For any $t \in [\![T]\!]$, the set $[\![\mathsf{function\ xs}]\!]\ t$ is a singleton.
- The domain of $[\![\mathsf{relation\ ys}]\!]$ is $[\![T]\!]$.
- For any $(t,x) \in [\![\mathsf{relation\ ys}]\!] \ni (t,y)$, we have $x = y$.

These invariants mean that it is straightforward to translate the concrete semantics of signal to their abstract semantics:

$$[\![\mathsf{xs}]\!]\ t = \text{the unique } x \text{ such that } x \in [\![\mathsf{function\ xs}]\!]\ t$$
$$[\![\mathsf{ys}]\!]\ t = \text{the unique } x \text{ such that } (t,x) \in [\![\mathsf{relation\ ys}]\!]$$

We can then implement the FRP combinators, and verify that they maintain the invariants and have the expected semantics. Most are quite straightforward given the model of sets and relations, for example the isomorphism between behaviours and events is just given by lifting the isomorphism between functions to sets and relations:

```
event : Behaviour T A → Event T A
event (Behaviour c f) = Event c (relation (times c) f)

buffer : Event T A → Behaviour T A
buffer (Event c r) = Behaviour c (buffer r)
```

$[\![\mathsf{Not}\, A]\!] = [\![A]\!] \to 2$

$\mathsf{buffer} : \mathsf{Not}\,(\mathsf{Not}\,(A \times B)) \to A \to \mathsf{Not}\,(\mathsf{Not}\, B)$

$[\![\mathsf{buffer}]\!]\; k\, x\, \ell = k\,(\lambda\,(x', y)\, .\, (x = x') \wedge \ell(y))$

$\mathsf{discard} : \mathsf{Not}\, A$

$[\![\mathsf{discard}]\!]\; x = \mathsf{false}$

$\mathsf{doubleNot} : A \to \mathsf{Not}\,(\mathsf{Not}\, A)$

$[\![\mathsf{doubleNot}]\!]\; x\, k = k\, x$

$\mathsf{andthen} : \mathsf{Not}\, A \to \mathsf{Not}\, A \to \mathsf{Not}\, A$

$[\![\mathsf{andthen}]\!]\; k\, \ell\, x = k\, x \vee \ell\, x$

$\mathsf{copmap} : (B \to \mathsf{Not}\,(\mathsf{Not}\, A)) \to \mathsf{Not}\, A \to \mathsf{Not}\, B$

$[\![\mathsf{copmap}]\!]\; f\, k\, y = f\, y\, k$

$\mathsf{fix} : ((A \to \mathsf{Not}\, B) \to (A \to \mathsf{Not}\, B)) \to A \to \mathsf{Not}\, B$

$[\![\mathsf{fix}]\!]\; f =$ the smallest g such that $\forall x\, .\, \forall y\, .\, f\, g\, x\, y \Rightarrow g\, x\, y$

Figure 4. Model of continuations

The delay function is implemented by mapping the behaviour over the previous time relation:

$$\mathsf{delay} : \mathsf{Behaviour}\; T\; A \to \mathsf{Event}\,(\mathsf{Tail}\; T)\; A$$
$$\mathsf{delay}\,(\mathsf{Behaviour}\; c\; f) = \mathsf{Event}\,(\mathsf{tail}\; c)\,(\mathsf{pmapr}\; f\,(\mathsf{prev}\; c))$$

The cons function is just the union of the head and the tail:

$$\mathsf{cons} : A \to \mathsf{Event}\,(\mathsf{Tail}\; T)\; A \to \mathsf{Event}\; T\; A$$
$$\mathsf{cons}\; x\,(\mathsf{Event}\; c\; r) = \mathsf{Event}\; c'\,(\mathsf{union}\; r\; r')\; \text{where}$$
$$c' = \mathsf{tail}^{-1}\, c$$
$$r' = \mathsf{map}\,(\mathsf{first}\; c')\,(\lambda t\, .\, (t, x))$$

The union function is just union of relations:

$$\mathsf{union} : \mathsf{Event}\; S\; A \to \mathsf{Event}\,(\mathsf{Minus}\; T\; S)\; A \to \mathsf{Event}\; T\; A$$
$$\mathsf{union}\,(\mathsf{Event}\; \_\; q)\,(\mathsf{Event}\; c\; r) = \mathsf{Event}\,(\mathsf{minus}^{-1}\; c)\,(\mathsf{union}\; q\; r)$$

We defer a discussion of the implementation of partition to Section 6. The implementation and verification of the remaining primitives is straightforward.

5. Implementation of sets and relations

The implementation of signals is built on top of a library of continuations. In Figure 4 we give the model of continuations, we defer discussing its implementation until the next section. It provides a type of continuations:

$$[\![\mathsf{Not}\, A]\!] = [\![A]\!] \to 2$$

together with a collection of combinators for these types. These combinators correspond directly to the combinators for sets, since we can define:

$$\mathsf{data\; Set}\; A = \mathsf{Set}\,\{\mathsf{unSet} : \mathsf{Not}\,(\mathsf{Not}\, A)\}$$

and then define:

$$\mathsf{buffer}\,(\mathsf{Set}\; xs) = \mathsf{Set} \cdot (\mathsf{buffer}\; xs)$$
$$\mathsf{empty} = \mathsf{Set\; discard}$$
$$\mathsf{singleton}\; x = \mathsf{Set}\,(\mathsf{doubleNot}\; x)$$
$$\mathsf{union}\,(\mathsf{Set}\; xs)\,(\mathsf{Set}\; ys) = \mathsf{Set}\,(\mathsf{andthen}\; xs\; ys)$$
$$\mathsf{pmap}\; f\,(\mathsf{Set}\; xs) = \mathsf{Set}\,(\mathsf{comap}\,(\mathsf{copmap}\,(\mathsf{unSet} \cdot f)))$$
$$\mathsf{fix}\; f = \mathsf{Set} \cdot \mathsf{fix}\,(\lambda g\, .\, \mathsf{unSet} \cdot f\,(\mathsf{Set} \cdot g))$$

```
public class Events<T,A> {

  public final Clock<T> clock;
  public final Relation<Time,A> relation;

  public<B> Events<T,B>
    map(Function<A,B> f) { ... }
  public Behaviour<T,A>
    buffer() { ... }
  public PartitionedEvents<?,T,A>
    partition(Predicate<A> p) { ... }
  ...

}

public interface PartitionedEvents<S extends T,T,A> {

  public Events<S,A> yes();
  public Events<Minus<T,S>,A> no();
  public<Z> Z
    split(Function2<
      Events<S,A>,
      Events<Minus<T,S>,A>,
      Z> f);

}
```

Figure 5. Event sources in Java

where:

$$\mathsf{comap} : (B \to A) \to \mathsf{Not}\, A \to \mathsf{Not}\, B$$
$$\mathsf{comap}\; f = \mathsf{copmap}\,(\lambda y\, .\, \mathsf{doubleNot}\,(f\; y))$$

We can translate from the concrete semantics of sets to their abstract semantics as:

$$[\![xs]\!] = \{x \mid [\![\mathsf{unSet}\; xs]\!]\,(\lambda x'\, .\, x = x')\}$$

It is straightforward to verify that the combinators on sets have their expected semantics.

We have now shown that a model of FRP can be translated into a model of sets and relations, and from there to continuations. Composing these translations, we get:

$$\mathsf{Behaviour}\; T\; A \subseteq \mathsf{Clock}\; T \times (\mathsf{Time} \to \mathsf{Not}\,(\mathsf{Not}\, A))$$
$$\mathsf{Event}\; T\; A \subseteq \mathsf{Clock}\; T \times \mathsf{Not}\,(\mathsf{Not}\,(\mathsf{Time} \times A))$$

that is:

- Behaviours are implemented as *pull* systems: a user of a behaviour can call it with a time $t \in [\![T]\!]$, and receive back a *future* value, of type $\mathsf{Not}\,(\mathsf{Not}\, A)$. A client can then register callbacks of type $\mathsf{Not}\, A$ with the future, which will be executed when the value is known. Since we maintain an invariant that behaviours return singletons, each callback will be executed precisely once.
- Events are implemented as *push* systems: a user of an event can register a callback of type $\mathsf{Not}(\mathsf{Time} \times A)$ with it, which will be executed with pairs (t, x) whenever an event x arrives at time t. We maintain an invariant that each time t has a unique x, and that all times $t \in [\![T]\!]$ will generate an event.

It is interesting that the implementation of reactive programs as push or pull systems, and the uses of futures and the observer pattern fall out naturally from the translation of signals to sets and relations, and then to continuations. Moreover, the isomorphism between push systems and pull systems is given by the isomorphism between relations and set-valued functions.

```
public<T> Events<T,HttpResponse>
  responses(Events<T,HttpRequest> requests)
{
  return requests.partition(request ->
    request.isGetRequest()
  ).split((getReqs,otherReqs) ->
    getReqs.map(request ->
      new HttpResponse(200,"Hello, World!")
    ).union(otherReqs.map(request ->
      new HttpResponse(405)
    ))
  );
}
```

Figure 6. Example "Hello, World!" server implemented in Java

```
public interface Not<A> {

  public void accept(A x);

  default public<B> Not<B> comap(Function<B,A> f) {
    return y -> { this.accept(f.apply(y)); };
  }
  default public Not<A> andthen(Not<A> other) {
    return x -> { this.accept(x); other.accept(x); };
  }
  ...

}


public interface Not2<A,B> {

  public void accept(A x, B y);
  ...

}
```

Figure 7. Continuation classes in Java

6. Java implementation

The FRP implementation is in Java, and is a direct translation of the model discussed in Sections 2–5. Part of the interface for event sources is given in Figure 5, and is the Java equivalent of the relevant fragment of Figure 1. We make use of Java 8's support for anonymous functions (where $\lambda x \,.\, M$ is written in Java as `x -> M`).

There is a slight difference in the way Java treats bounded existential types, which is by wildcarding (the ? type in the return type of `partition`). Java does not support direct unpacking of existential types, and instead unpacking must be performed by helper functions. For example in Java one cannot write:

```
Events<T,Integer> xs = ...;
PartitionedEvents<S,T,Integer> p =
  xs.partition(x -> 0 <= x);
Events<S,Integer> pos = p.yes();
Events<Minus<T,S>,Integer> neg = p.no();
return pos.union(neg.map(Math.abs));
```

because there is no way to introduce the new bound type variable S. Instead, one writes:

```
Events<T,Integer> xs = ...;
```

```
public class NotImpl<A> implements Not<A> {

  protected List<Not<A>> conts;
  final WeakReference<NotNotImpl<A>> not;

  public NotImpl(NotNotImpl<A> not) {
    this.not = new WeakReference<>(not);
  }

  public void accept(A x) {
    List<Not<A>> ks;
    NotNotImpl<A> not;
    synchronized(this) {
      ks = this.conts;
      not = this.not.get();
      if (not != null) {
        not.values = new List<>(x,not.values);
      }
    }
    while (ks != null) {
      ks.hd.accept(x); ks = ks.tl;
    }
  }

}

public class NotNotImpl<A> implements Not<Not<A>> {

  protected List<A> values;
  final NotImpl<A> not = new NotImpl<>(this);

  public void accept(Not<A> k) {
    List<A> xs;
    synchronized(this.not) {
      xs = this.values;
      this.not.conts = new List<>(k,this.not.conts);
    }
    while (xs != null) {
      k.accept(xs.hd); xs = xs.tl;
    }
  }

}
```

Figure 8. Mutable implementation of continuations

```
return xs.partition(x ->
  0 <= x
).split((pos,neg) ->
  pos.union(neg.map(Math.abs))
)
```

Inside the anonymous helper function, an anonymous type variable S is created, `pos` is given type `Events<S,Integer>` and `neg` is given type `Events<Minus<T,S>,Integer>`.

The example "Hello, World!" web application is shown in Figure 6. An implementation of an asynchronous servlet allows it to execute in any servlet container, resulting in the interactions:

```
$ curl -i localhost:8080/hello
HTTP/1.1 200 OK
Content-Length: 13
Server: Jetty(9.0.0.M5)

Hello, World!
```

```
public class FunctionNotNotRef<A,B>
  implements Function<A,Not<Not<B>>>,
    Not<Function<A,Not<Not<B>>>>
{

  protected Function<A,Not<Not<B>>> delegate;
  protected HashMap<A,NotNotImpl<B>> cache =
    new HashMap<>();

  public Not<Not<B>> apply(A x) {
    Function<A,Not<Not<B>>> f;
    NotNotImpl<B> k = null;
    synchronized (this) {
      f = this.delegate;
      if (f == null) {
        k = this.cache.get(x);
        if (k == null) {
          k = new NotNotImpl<B>();
          this.cache.put(x,k);
        }
      }
    }
    if (f == null) {
      return k;
    } else {
      return f.apply(x);
    }
  }

  public void accept(Function<A,Not<Not<B>>> f) {
    HashMap<A,NotNotImpl<B>> cache;
    synchronized (this) {
      cache = this.cache;
      this.cache = null;
      this.delegate = f;
    }
    for(
      Entry<A,NotNotImpl<B>> e : cache.entrySet()
    ) {
      A x = e.getKey();
      Not<B> k = e.getValue().not;
      f.apply(x).accept(k);
    }
  }

}

public<A,B> Function<A,Not<Not<B>>> fix(
  Function<
    Function<A,Not<Not<B>>>,
    Function<A,Not<Not<B>>>
  > f
) {
  FunctionNotNotRef<A,B> g =
    new FunctionNotNotRef<A,B>();
  Function<A,Not<Not<B>>> h =
    f.apply(g);
  g.accept(h);
  return h;
}
```

Figure 9. Implementation of fix

```
public class FunctionNotNotImpl<A,B>
  implements Function<A,Not<Not<B>>>, Not2<A,B>
{

  final WeakHashMap<A,NotNotImpl<B>> cache =
    new WeakHashMap<>();

  public synchronized NotNotImpl<B> apply(A x) {
    NotNotImpl<B> k = this.cache.get(x);
    if (k == null) {
      k = new NotNotImpl<B>();
      this.cache.put(x,k);
    }
    return k;
  }

  public void accept(A x, B y) {
    this.apply(x).not.accept(y);
  }

}

public<A,B> Function<A,Not<Not<B>>>
  buffer(Not<Not2<A,B>> k)
{
  FunctionNotNotImpl<A,B> f =
    new FunctionNotNotImpl<A,B>();
  k.accept(f);
  return f;
}
```

Figure 10. Implementation of buffer

and:

```
curl -i -d "Stuff" localhost:8080/hello
HTTP/1.1 405 Method Not Allowed
Content-Length: 0
Server: Jetty(9.0.0.M5)
```

Most of the work in the FRP implementation is in implementing the continuation classes `Not<A>` which represents Not A and `Not2<A,B>` which represents Not $(A \times B)$. The implementation of `Not<A>` is as an interface with a single abstract method `void accept(A x)`. This method is allowed to be side-effecting (although care is required from any programmer working at this low level to respect the high-level semantics). Figure 7 shows some of the implementation of the classes.

One implementation of continuations is a pair of mutable containers, given in Figure 8. One is a container of Not A continuations, and implements Not A; the other is a container of A values, and implements Not (Not A). When a new continuation is added (by calling `accept` on the value container), it is applied to all of the existing values. Similarly when a new value is added (by calling `accept` on the continuation container), all the existing continuations are applied to it. Note that there is only a weak reference from the continuation container to the value container, so the value container can be garbage collected without impacting the continuation container.

To ensure thread-safety of the implementation, appropriate locking is used on critical sections. Note that we never call any callbacks while holding a lock, so there is never any attempt to acquire two locks simultaneously. Thus, the code is deadlock-free, and will not introduce issues with liveness.

```
public class ClockImpl<T> extends Clock<T> {

  final Not<Time> ntimes;
  final Not<Time> nfirst;
  final Not2<Time,Time> nprev;
  ...

}

public class EventsImpl<T,A> extends Events<T,A> {

  final public ClockImpl<T> clock;
  final public Not2<Time,A> nrelation;
  ...

}

public class PartitionedEventsImpl<T,A>
  implements PartitionedEvents<T,T,A>
{

  final Predicate<A> pred;
  final EventsImpl<T,A> yes;
  final EventsImpl<Minus<T,T>,A> no;

  final WeakHashMap<Time,Boolean> flags;
  final HashMap<Time,Time> prevUnknown;
  final HashMap<Time,Time> nextUnknown;
  final HashMap<Time,Time> prevSame;
  final HashMap<Time,Time> nextSame;
  Time first = null;

  public PartitionedEventsImpl(
    Predicate<A> pred, Events<T,A> xs
  ) {
    this.pred = pred;
    this.yes = new EventsImpl<>(...);
    this.no = new EventsImpl<>(...);
    xs.relation.pairs.accept(this::acceptEvent);
    ...
  }

  public void emitTime(Time t, Boolean flag) {
    if (flag) { this.yes.clock.ntimes.accept(t); }
    else { this.no.clock.ntimes.accept(t); }
  }

  public void emitEvent(Time t, A x, Boolean flag) {
    if (flag) { this.yes.nrelation.accept(t,x); }
    else { this.no.nrelation.accept(t,x); }
  }

  public void acceptEvent(Time t, A x) {
  Boolean tflag = this.pred.apply(x);
    synchronized (this) { this.flags.put(t,tflag); }
    this.emitEvent(t,x,tflag);
    this.emitTime(t,tflag);
    ...
  }

  ...

}
```

Figure 11. Implementation of partition

The two methods of $\mathsf{Not}\,A$ which require effort are fix (which finds the fixed point of set-valued functions) and buffer (which implements half of the isomorphism between relations and set-valued functions). These two functions are implemented similarly, in that under the hood they are based on mutable continuations, and use a `HashMap` to buffer values. The implementations are given in Figures 9 and 10.

In the case of fix, we make use of a class `FunctionNotNotRef` which implements $A \to \mathsf{Not}\,(\mathsf{Not}\,B)$ by acting as a delegate to another function of the same type. Crucially, the delegate may be set after the reference has been created, so the function has to respond to `apply` in the absence of its delegate. It does so by creating a new mutable $\mathsf{Not}\,(\mathsf{Not}\,A)$, which it stores in a cache before returning. When the delegate is set, it runs through the cache, initializing all of the cached continuations appropriately. Thus, a suitable mix of buffering and mutable state allows cyclic structures to be built which give the appearance of pure functional fixed points.

The implementation of buffer is similar, but there is one crucial difference. In the case of fix, the buffering is only required after the reference has been created, but its delegate is initialized. In most cases, this will be transitory, and the buffer will not be long-lived. In the case of buffer, the buffer will be long-lived, and we need to take care that it does not cause a space leak. For this reason, we use a weak hash map to store the buffer. When a key in the buffer can be garbage collected, it will be, and the corresponding value will be removed.

In its use in the FRP implementation, `FunctionNotNotImpl` is always used to implement a function of type $\mathsf{Time} \to \mathsf{Not}\,(\mathsf{Not}\,A)$, and so every use of buffering will introduce a `WeakHashMap` whose keys are `Time`. This makes `Time` objects quite expensive: even though each `Time` object is small (just containing a `long` timestamp) each live `Time` object is also keeping alive many entries in a buffer. For this reason, the FRP interface does not expose `Time` objects to user code, since it would be very easy to introduce a space leak by holding on to a time object. In our setting, this is the form that *time leaks* take [21], even though Java is a strict language.

There is one method of signals which we implement directly at a low level rather than going through the abstraction of sets and relations. An outline of the implementation of partition is given in Figure 11. It uses implementations of $\mathsf{Clock}\,T$ and $\mathsf{Event}\,T\,A$ which are backed by mutable sets to create two new event sources `yes` and `no`. When an event `x` arrives at time `t`, it calls `pred` on `x` to determine whether to send the event on to `yes` or to `no`. Most of the effort is in implementing `yes.clock` and `no.clock`, and to do this we maintain the following data structures:

- `flags` is a map from `Time` to `Boolean` such that $(t, b) \in [\![\texttt{flags}]\!]$ whenever there is some $(t, x) \in [\![\texttt{xs.relation}]\!]$ and $[\![\texttt{pred}]\!]\, x = b$,
- `prevUnknown` is a map from `Time` to `Time` such that $(t, s) \in [\![\texttt{prevUnknown}]\!]$ whenever $s \to t$ and either s or t is not in the domain of $[\![\texttt{flags}]\!]$,
- `nextUnknown` is the inverse of `prevUnknown`,
- `prevSame` is a map from `Time` to `Time` such that $(t, s) \in [\![\texttt{prevSame}]\!]$ whenever $s \to^{*}_{?/c} t$ and there is no $r \to_{?/c} s$,
- `nextSame` is a map from `Time` to `Time` such that $(s, t) \in [\![\texttt{prevSame}]\!]$ whenever $s \to^{*}_{b/?} t$ and there is no $t \to_{b/?} u$, and
- `first` $\in [\![\texttt{xs.clock.first}]\!]$,

where we write:

- $s \to t$ whenever $(t, s) \in [\![\texttt{xs.clock.prev}]\!]$,

- $s \rightarrow_{b/c} t$ whenever $s \rightarrow t$ and $(s, b) \in [\![\texttt{flags}]\!] \ni (t, c)$,
- $s \rightarrow_{b/?} t$ whenever $s \rightarrow_{b/c} t$ for some c, and
- $s \rightarrow_{?/c} t$ whenever $s \rightarrow_{b/c} t$ for some b.

This data is enough to construct `yes.clock` and `no.clock`, for example $(t, s) \in [\![\texttt{yes.clock.prev}]\!]$ whenever:

$$s \rightarrow_{\mathsf{true/true}} t \quad \text{or} \quad s \rightarrow_{\mathsf{true/false}} \cdot \rightarrow^{*}_{\mathsf{false/false}} \cdot \rightarrow_{\mathsf{false/true}} t$$

One unusual feature of our FRP implementation is that it allows out-of-order arrival of events. Due to multithreading, it is possible that an event (t, x) will arrive before an event (u, y) even when $t > u$. For example FrTime [7] makes use of an ordering scheme similar to that of Acar's [1] self-adjusting computation to ensure in-order arrival of events. In our setting, we are prioritizing liveness over execution order, and so we only introduce time dependencies where they are needed (for example in `accum`) and allow most event sources to proceed at their own pace.

7. Comparison with push/pull FRP

The most closely related work is Elliott's [10] *push-pull FRP*. Elliott reconstructs the behaviour and event source types using futures. Elliott's type Future A can be encoded in our system as:

$$\mathsf{Future}\,A = \mathsf{Not}\,(\mathsf{Not}\,(\mathsf{Time} \times A))$$

so Elliott's type for event sources:

$$\mathsf{Event}\,A = \mathsf{Future}\,(A \times \mathsf{Event}\,A)$$

is the equivalent of:

$$\mathsf{Event}\,A = \mathsf{Not}\,(\mathsf{Not}\,(\mathsf{Time} \times A \times \mathsf{Event}\,A))$$

Comparing this to our type:

$$\mathsf{Event}\,T\,A = \mathsf{Not}\,(\mathsf{Not}\,(\mathsf{Time} \times A))$$

we can see some of the important distinctions between the approaches:

- Push-pull FRP is based on the one-shot Future type, rather than the implementation of Set using callbacks.
- In push-pull FRP, events are guaranteed to arrive in order. If $(s, x, \sigma) \in \rho$ and $(t, y, \tau) \in \sigma$ then $s < t$. In our implementation of FRP, events may arrive out-of-order. In particular, push-pull FRP uses McCarthy amb to implement union. Out-of-order events also occur in Jeltsch's push-based FRP [17, §4.2.6].
- Push-pull FRP does not make use of the isomorphism between relations and set-valued functions.

There are also some differences of focus: we have focused on liveness, which is not an issue in push-pull FRP, and we have not focussed on continuous-time behaviours.

8. Conclusions and future work

We have presented a model of FRP which provides liveness guarantees by static typing. The implementation of FRP is based on a model of sets and relations, which in turn is implemented using continuations. This implementation shows how the pull implementation of behaviours using futures, and the push implementation of event sources using the observer pattern, arise naturally.

There are two areas of future work: on stopping space and time leaks and on distribution.

Currently, there is effort made to ensure that signals do not cause space and time leaks, by appropriate use of weak pointers. However, it is possible for users to cause a leak by keeping a reference to a signal live. We are already tracking time domains, so it should be possible to use them as Jeltsch's [16] era parameters, and ensure that signals do not have to buffer all their events.

The Java implementation of the FRP library is already linked against a servlet class, to allow it to be used as the processing engine in an HTTP server. It would be interesting to see if HTTP could be used as the communication protocol between FRP instances, and so build a distributed FRP implementation.

References

[1] U. A. Acar. *Self-Adjusting Computation*. PhD thesis, Carnegie Mellon Univ., 2005.

[2] H. Apfelmus. `http://www.haskell.org/haskellwiki/Reactive-banana`.

[3] G. Berry and G. Gonthier. The Esterel synchronous programming language: Design, semantics, implementation. *Sci. Computer Programming*, 19(2):87–152, 1992.

[4] G. Bracha, J. Gosling, B. Joy, and G. Steele. *The Java Language Specification*. Sun Microsystems, third edition, 2005.

[5] S. Burbeck. Applications programming in Smalltalk-80: How to use model-view-controller (MVC), 1987.

[6] L. Cardelli and P. Wegner. On understanding types, data abstraction, and polymorphism. *ACM Comput. Surv.*, 28(150), 1985.

[7] G. H. Cooper and S. Krishnamurthi. Embedding dynamic dataflow in a call-by-value language. In *Proc. European Symp. on Programming*, pages 294–308, 2006.

[8] A. Courtney. Frappé: Functional reactive programming in Java. In *Proc. Symp. Pratical Aspects of Declarative Languages*, pages 29–44, 2001.

[9] J. Donham. Functional reactive programming in OCaml. `https://github.com/jaked/froc`.

[10] C. Elliott. Push-pull functional reactive programming. In *Proc. Haskell Symp.*, 2009.

[11] C. Elliott and P. Hudak. Functional reactive animation. In *Proc. Int. Conf. Functional Programming*, pages 263–273, 1997.

[12] C. Hewitt, P. Bishop, and R. Steiger. A universal modular actor formalism for artificial intelligence. *Proc. Int. Joint Conf. Artificial Intelligence*, pages 235–245, 1973.

[13] A. S. A. Jeffrey. `https://github.com/agda/agda-frp-js/`.

[14] A. S. A. Jeffrey. Causality for free!: Parametricity implies causality for functional reactive programs. In *Proc. ACM Workshop Programming Languges meets Program Verification*, pages 57–68, 2013.

[15] A. S. A. Jeffrey. Provably correct web applications: FRP in Agda in HTML5. In *Proc. Int. Symp. Practical Aspects of Declarative Languages*, 2013.

[16] W. Jeltsch. Signals, not generators! In *Proc. Symp. Trends in Functional Programming*, pages 283–297, 2009.

[17] W. Jeltsch. *Strongly Typed and Efficient Functional Reactive Programming*. PhD thesis, BTU Cottbus, 2012.

[18] N. Krishnaswami and N. Benton. Ultrametric semantics of reactive programs. In *Proc. IEEE Logic in Computer Science*, pages 257–266, 2011.

[19] D. Leijen and E. Meijer. Domain specific embedded compilers. In *Proc. Conf. Domain-Specific Languages*, pages 109–122, 1999.

[20] L. A. Meyerovich, A. Guha, J. Baskin, G. H. Cooper, M. Greenberg, A. Bromfield, and S. Krishnamurthi. Flapjax: A programming language for ajax applications. In *Proc, ACM Conf. Object-Oriented Programming Systems, Languages and Applications*, pages 1–20, 2009.

[21] H. Nilsson, A. Courtney, and J. Peterson. Functional reactive programming, continued. In *Proc. ACM Workshop on Haskell*, pages 51–64, 2002.

[22] G. Plotkin. Call-by-name, call-by-value, and the λ-calculus. *Theoretical Computer Science*, 1:125–159, 1975.

[23] Yale Haskell Group. Yampa library for programming hybrid systems. `http://www.haskell.org/haskellwiki/Yampa`.

A Short Cut to Parallelization Theorems

Akimasa Morihata
Tohoku University
morihata@riec.tohoku.ac.jp

Abstract

The third list-homomorphism theorem states that if a function is both *foldr* and *foldl*, it has a divide-and-conquer parallel implementation as well. In this paper, we develop a theory for obtaining such parallelization theorems. The key is a new proof of the third list-homomorphism theorem based on shortcut deforestation. The proof implies that there exists a divide-and-conquer parallel program of the form of $h\ (x\ `merge`\ y) = h_1\ x \odot h_2\ y$, where h is the subject of parallelization, *merge* is the operation of integrating independent substructures, h_1 and h_2 are computations applied to substructures, possibly in parallel, and $\odot$ merges the results calculated for substructures, if (i) h can be specified by two certain forms of iterative programs, and (ii) *merge* can be implemented by a function of a certain polymorphic type. Therefore, when requirement (ii) is fulfilled, h has a divide-and-conquer implementation if h has two certain forms of implementations. We show that our approach is applicable to structure-consuming operations by catamorphisms (folds), structure-generating operations by anamorphisms (unfolds), and their generalizations called hylomorphisms.

Categories and Subject Descriptors D.1. [*Programming Techniques*]: Concurrent Programming—Parallel Programming; D.1.2 [*Programming Techniques*]: Automatic Programming—Program Transformation; D.3.3 [*Programming Languages*]: Language Construct and Features—Polymorphism

Keywords Divide-and-conquer Parallelism; Shortcut Deforestation; Third List-homomorphism Theorem

1. Introduction

Functional programs are suitable for parallel evaluation. Since they are side-effect free, we can simultaneously evaluate independent subexpressions. However, sometimes there are not enough independent tasks. For example, consider the list-summation function.

$$\begin{aligned} sum\ [\,] &= 0 \\ sum\ (a : x) &= a + sum\ x \end{aligned}$$

There are essentially no independent tasks in this case, and therefore, we cannot gain any advantage from parallel computing.

We can improve parallelizablity by transforming it to a different implementation.

$$\begin{aligned} sum\ [\,] &= 0 \\ sum\ [a] &= a \\ sum\ (x +\!\!+\ y) &= sum\ x + sum\ y \end{aligned}$$

Here, the third equation intends to express a divide-and-conquer implementation: the total sum of a longer list $x +\!\!+\ y$ is calculated by summing up the results of shorter sublists x and y. By evaluating $sum\ x$ and $sum\ y$ in parallel, we can achieve a parallel speedup.

It is preferable that such divide-and-conquer implementations be systematically obtained from standard, sequential implementations. The third list-homomorphism theorem (Gibbons 1996a) is useful for this purpose.

Theorem 1 (The third list-homomorphism theorem (Gibbons 1996a)). *For any function $h :: [A] \to B$, suppose that there exist $f_\triangleleft :: A \to B \to B$, $f_\triangleright :: B \to A \to B$, and $e :: B$ such that*

$$h = foldr\ f_\triangleleft\ e = foldl\ f_\triangleright\ e.$$

Then, there exists an operator $(\odot) :: B \to B \to B$ such that

$$h\ (x +\!\!+\ y) = h\ x \odot h\ y$$

for any x and y □

The theorem states that if a function can be written by both *foldr* and *foldl*, it can be evaluated in a divide-and-conquer manner as well. It has been used (Gibbons 1996a,b; Gorlatch 1999; Geser and Gorlatch 1999; Morita et al. 2007; Liu et al. 2011; Chi and Mu 2011) as a basis of deriving divide-and-conquer parallel programs from sequential programs written by *foldr* and/or *foldl*.

One might expect that there are similar parallelization theorems that essentially state "two implementations of certain forms imply a divide-and-conquer implementation". Suppose that a computation on a data structure can be implemented by two different iteration patterns. This fact implies order insensitivity, namely, we can to some extent change the order of operations applied to elements. Order insensitivity is an indication of a potential parallelism. Indeed, several such parallelization theorems are known, including the generalization of the third list-homomorphism to tree operations (Morihata et al. 2009) and their dual (Mu and Morihata 2011). Yet, it was unclear when such parallelization theorems hold.

The aim of this paper is to develop a theory for this kind of parallelization. We consider a general divide-and-conquer pattern expressed in the form,

$$h\ (x\ `merge`\ y) = h_1\ x \odot h_2\ y \tag{2}$$

Here, $h :: S \to B$ is the subject of parallelization and $merge :: S_1 \to S_2 \to S$ is a function of integrating substructures x and y. The equation means that we can calculate h for $x\ `merge`\ y$ by calculating $h_1 :: S_1 \to B_1$ and $h_2 :: S_2 \to B_2$ for substructures x and y, possibly in parallel, and then merging them by using $(\odot) :: B_1 \to B_2 \to B$. We prove Equation (2) holds if:

- h can be written by using h_1 as well as by using h_2, where h_1 and h_2 are certain forms of recursive functions, and

ICFP '13, September 25–27, 2013, Boston, MA, USA.
Copyright © 2013 ACM 978-1-4503-2326-0/13/09... $15.00.
http://dx.doi.org/10.1145/2500365.2500580

- *merge* can be specified by a function of a certain polymorphic type.

Therefore, if *merge* satisfies the latter condition, we have a parallelization theorem stating that h has a divide-and-conquer implementation if it has two implementations of certain forms.

Now let us outline our development.

First, we try to determine when $\odot$ exists for given h, *merge*, h_1, and h_2 in Equation (2). A necessary and sufficient condition for this has been developed by Mu and Morihata (2011). However, it is unsatisfactory. To apply it to the case of the third list-homomorphism theorem, it requires m_2 such that

$$h\ (x +\!\!+\ y) = m_2\ (x, h\ y), \quad (3)$$

instead of h being *foldr*. Equation (3) is apparently less intuitive. Functional programmers routinely write their programs by using *foldr* and/or *foldl*, and one of the most interesting points of the third list-homomorphism theorem is that such routines lead to parallel programs. We would thus like to keep this point.

Our key insight is to view Equation (3) as a *deforestation* problem (Wadler 1988): we would like to develop an implementation, specified by m_2, that avoids generating an intermediate list by $+\!\!+$. We adopt shortcut deforestation (Gill et al. 1993; Gill 1996) for this purpose. When h is *foldr*, shortcut deforestation shows that such an m_2 exists because $+\!\!+$ can be specified by a function of a certain polymorphic type. A similar discussion holds for the case of *foldl*. In summary, shortcut deforestation enables us to prove the third list-homomorphism theorem from the fact that $+\!\!+$ can be implemented with certain polymorphic functions.

The generalizations of shortcut deforestation (Takano and Meijer 1995; Johann 2002) enable us to naturally generalize our approach from *foldr*/*foldl* to a class of data-consuming operations called catamorphisms or folds (Malcolm 1990; Meijer et al. 1991; Bird and de Moor 1997). Moreover, our approach can also deal with their dual, i.e., data-generating operations called anamorphisms or unfolds. Roughly speaking, we consider divide-and-conquer structure generations of the form,

$$h\ (v \odot w) = h_1\ v \text{ `}merge\text{' } h_2\ w, \quad (4)$$

and prove that when *merge* has implementations using functions of certain polymorphic types, $\odot$ in Equation (4) exists if h has two implementations by anamorphisms. Furthermore, we can also deal with hylomorphisms, which subsume both catamorphisms and anamorphisms. These generalizations suggest that our approach is a modest and yet important step towards a new vista of functional parallel programming.

Our major contributions are summarized as follows.

- We provide a new proof to the third list-homomorphism theorem by using shortcut deforestation (Section 3). Shortcut deforestation has been well studied for optimizing functional programs; however, to the best of the author's knowledge, its connection to parallelization has not been noticed.
- We show that the proof can be naturally generalized to catamorphisms (Section 4). It subsumes the study by Morihata et al. (2009).
- We prove that similar theorems hold for anamorphisms, and moreover, the results for catamorphisms and anamorphisms can be further generalized to hylomorphisms (Section 5). The result for anamorphisms is a generalization of the study by Mu and Morihata (2011). To the best of the author's knowledge, generalizations to hylomorphisms have not been studied so far.

2. Preliminary

2.1 Functions and Right Inverses

We will use Haskell notations with some extensions. For defining functions, we may use functions rather than constructors in patterns, such as $sum\ (x +\!\!+\ y) = sum\ x + sum\ y$. The semantics of such equations are their least fixed point. We may sometimes equate the curried variants with the uncurried definitions of binary operators. For example, $(+\!\!+)$ may be regarded as a function of type $([a], [a]) \to [a]$. We write id_A to denote the identity function on type A. Subscripts will be omitted if they are not important or apparent from the context.

We restrict ourselves to using total, terminating, and well-defined functions that deal with finite structures. For simplicity of presentations, we may sometimes use functions that appear to be partial or possibly non-terminating, and in such cases, we will assume that bad behaviors are avoided somehow. For example, in the above *sum*, we do not consider binding empty lists to x nor y, so as to avoid non-termination.

A function g is said to be a right inverse of a function f if $f = f \circ g \circ f$. That is, for any value v in the range of f, $v = f\ (g\ v)$. For example, $wrap\ a = [a]$ is a right inverse of *sum*, *maximum*, etc., and *id* is a right inverse of idempotent functions such as *sort* and *filter p*. Any function has a right inverse if its domain is enumerable or the axiom of choice is assumed under the set-theoretic model of functions. We will assume the existence of right inverses, and use f^{-1} to denote a right inverse of f.

2.2 Categories

In order to formalize datatype-generic theorems, we will follow the preceding studies (Malcolm 1990; Meijer et al. 1991; Bird and de Moor 1997) and borrow some of the notions from category theory.

A category consists of a collection of objects and a collection of arrows between objects. We mainly consider the category $\mathfrak{Set}$, in which objects are sets, arrows are functions, and compositions of arrows are function compositions.

Functors are mappings between categories. They should preserve identity arrows and arrow compositions. Formally, in $\mathfrak{Set}$, F is a functor if $\mathsf{F} id_A = id_{\mathsf{F}A}$ and $\mathsf{F}(f \circ g) = \mathsf{F}f \circ \mathsf{F}g$. An easy way to understand functors is to regard them as type constructors. For example, F_{Int} defined by $\mathsf{F}_{Int} X = (Int, X)$ for a type X and $\mathsf{F}_{Int} f\ (n, x) = (n, f\ x)$ for a function f and an integer n is a functor.

A bifunctor is a binary operator, and it behaves as a functor if one of its operands is fixed. Formally, $\dagger$ is a bifunctor if $id_A \dagger id_B = id_{A \dagger B}$ and $(f \circ f') \dagger (g \circ g') = (f \dagger g) \circ (f' \dagger g')$. A typical bifunctor is the product $\times$ defined by $A \times B = (A, B)$ for types A and B and $(f \times g)\ (a, b) = (f\ a, g\ b)$ for functions f and g.

2.3 Algebras and Catamorphisms

For a functor F, an F-algebra is a pair $(A, \phi :: \mathsf{F}A \to A)$. An algebra morphism between two F-algebras, from (A_1, ϕ_1) to (A_2, ϕ_2), is an arrow $h :: A_1 \to A_2$ such that $h \circ \phi_1 = \phi_2 \circ \mathsf{F}h$. An F-algebra is said to be initial if there exists a unique algebra morphism to each F-algebra. An initial F-algebra is unique up to isomorphisms, and we denote it as $(\mu\mathsf{F}, in_\mathsf{F})$. The unique algebra morphism from the initial F-algebra is called a catamorphism (aka fold). $(\!|\phi|\!)_\mathsf{F}$ denotes a catamorphism to an F-algebra (A, ϕ). Catamorphisms have two important properties:

- $(\!|in_\mathsf{F}|\!)_\mathsf{F} = id_{\mu\mathsf{F}}$.
- $(\!|\phi|\!)_\mathsf{F} \circ in_\mathsf{F} = \phi \circ \mathsf{F}(\!|\phi|\!)_\mathsf{F}$.

Roughly speaking, the initial F-algebra captures a data structure: F determines its shape (its branching structure) and in_F corresponds to constructors. In $\mathfrak{Set}$, $\mu\mathsf{F}$ is the least fixed point of $X = \mathsf{F}X$.

For example, the initial $\mathsf{L_c}$-algebra $(\mu\mathsf{L_c}, in_{\mathsf{L_c}})$, where $\mathsf{L_c}X = \{(1,())\} \cup \{(2,(n,x)) \mid n \in Int \wedge x \in X\}$, $in_{\mathsf{L_c}}\ (1,()) = []$, and $in_{\mathsf{L_c}}\ (2,(n,x)) = n : x$, captures "cons" lists of integers. Catamorphisms for $\mathsf{L_c}$-algebras consists of the following variants of *foldr*.

$$
\begin{array}{lcl}
foldr :: (\mathsf{L_c}A \to A) \to [Int] \to A \\
foldr\ \phi\ [] & = & \phi\ (1,()) \\
foldr\ \phi\ (n : x) & = & \phi\ (2,(n, foldr\ \phi\ x))
\end{array}
$$

According to $in_{\mathsf{L_c}}$, $[]$ and $n : x$ are interpreted as $(1,())$ and $(2,(n,x))$, respectively. They are passed to ϕ after a recursive call.

Similarly, "snoc" lists, in which elements are added to the last, can be captured by the initial $\mathsf{L_s}$-algebra $(\mu\mathsf{L_s}, in_{\mathsf{L_s}})$, where $\mathsf{L_s}X = \{(1,())\} \cup \{(2,(x,n)) \mid x \in X \wedge n \in Int\}$, $in_{\mathsf{L_c}}\ (1,()) = []$, and $in_{\mathsf{L_c}}\ (2,(x,n)) = x +\!\!+ [n]$. Catamorphisms for $\mathsf{L_s}$-algebras are *foldl*.

$$
\begin{array}{lcl}
foldl :: (\mathsf{L_s}A \to A) \to [Int] \to A \\
foldl\ \phi\ [] & = & \phi\ (1,()) \\
foldl\ \phi\ (x +\!\!+ [n]) & = & \phi\ (2,(foldl\ \phi\ x, n))
\end{array}
$$

In order to make their connections to catamorphisms explicit, we will use the above definitions rather than the standard definitions of *foldr* and *foldl*. While they are defined only for lists of integers, we could deal with polymorphic structures as well, by using bifunctors; however, for simplicity of presentations, we will only consider structures that consist of integers.

2.4 Shortcut Deforestation

We will use shortcut deforestation (Gill et al. 1993) and its generalizations. Deforestation (Wadler 1988) is a method of eliminating intermediate data structures passed between two functions, often called a generator and a consumer. We will make use of the following generalization of shortcut deforestation, which is a variant of the cata-augment rule (Gill 1996; Johann 2002).

Theorem 5. *For any initial* F*-algebra* $(\mu\mathsf{F}, in_\mathsf{F})$ *and functors* G *and* H*, we have*

$$\mathsf{H}(\!|\phi|\!)_\mathsf{F} \circ gen\ in_\mathsf{F} = gen\ \phi \circ \mathsf{G}(\!|\phi|\!)_\mathsf{F}$$

if $gen :: \forall\alpha.\ (\mathsf{F}\alpha \to \alpha) \to \mathsf{G}\alpha \to \mathsf{H}\alpha$. □

Suppose that the consumer is a catamorphism, $(\!|\phi|\!)_\mathsf{F}$, and the generator is a function of a certain polymorphic type using the given constructors, $gen\ in_\mathsf{F}$. Then, Theorem 5 enables us to eliminate the intermediate structure by using ϕ instead of in_F and preprocessing the additional input (the α part in $\mathsf{G}\alpha$) by $(\!|\phi|\!)_\mathsf{F}$.

3. Proving the Third List-homomorphism Theorem by Shortcut Deforestation

First, we show that the third list-homomorphism theorem can be proved by using shortcut deforestation with an abstract result (Lemma 6). The proof leads to the generalizations studied in the following sections.

3.1 Necessary and Sufficient Conditions for Simultaneous Computations

Our starting point is the following lemma, which is essentially due to Mu and Morihata (2011).

Lemma 6. *For any bifunctor* $\dagger$ *and functions* $h :: (A \dagger B) \to C$, $h_1 :: A \to A'$*, and* $h_2 :: B \to B'$*, there exist* $m_1 :: (A' \dagger B) \to C$ *and* $m_2 :: (A \dagger B') \to C$ *such that*

$$\hat{h} = m_1 \circ (h_1 \dagger id) = m_2 \circ (id \dagger h_2)$$

if and only if there exists $m :: (A' \dagger B') \to C$ *such that*

$$\hat{h} = m \circ (h_1 \dagger h_2).$$

In fact, $m = \hat{h} \circ (h_1^{-1} \dagger h_2^{-1})$.

Proof. We will later prove its generalization, Lemma 12. □

Our objective is to calculate $\hat{h}$. Since its input consists of subcomponents A and B, we would like to apply h_1 and h_2 to them simultaneously. It follows from Lemma 6 that such a parallel evaluation is possible if $\hat{h}$ can be calculated in the following two ways: we apply h_1 to the A part and then merge the result with B by using m_1; we apply h_2 and then merge it by using m_2. The theorem also states that the function m, which is used for merging the results of the two components, can be derived from the right inverses of h_1 and h_2.

For example, consider $mod_k\ (n_1 + n_2)$ where $mod_k\ n = mod\ n\ k$. Lemma 6 is applicable because $mod_k\ (n_1 + n_2) = mod_k\ (mod_k\ n_1 + n_2) = mod_k\ (n_1 + mod_k\ n_2)$. Now we reason as follows.

$$
\begin{array}{l}
\quad mod_k\ (n_1 + n_2) \\
= \{\ \text{Lemma 6; since } mod_k \text{ is idempotent, } id \text{ is its right inverse}\ \} \\
\quad mod_k\ (id\ (mod_k\ n_1) + id\ (mod_k\ n_2)) \\
= \{\ \text{unfolding } id\ \} \\
\quad mod_k\ (mod_k\ n_1 + mod_k\ n_2)
\end{array}
$$

Therefore, we can calculate $mod_k\ n_1$ and $mod_k\ n_2$ in parallel and get $mod_k\ (n_1 + n_2)$. This would be worthwhile if the cost of mod_k is proportional to the input.

3.2 Shortcut Deforestation for Confirming the Premises

Lemma 6 appears to be so generic that it can subsume the third list-homomorphism theorem. However, this intuition is wrong. In the case of the third list-homomorphism theorem, we would like to find m such that $h\ (x +\!\!+ y) = m\ (h\ x, h\ y)$. Lemma 6 requires the following condition.

$$\exists m_1, m_2.\ h\ (x +\!\!+ y) = m_1\ (h\ x, y) = m_2\ (x, h\ y) \qquad (7)$$

However, this condition is not satisfactory. For instance, in the case of sum, we can fulfill Requirement (7) by $m_1\ (v,y) = v + sum\ y$ and $m_2\ (x,w) = sum\ x + w$, but it appears to be almost equivalent to developing a parallel implementation. It would more easier for functional programmers to confirm that h is both *foldr* and *foldl*.

To resolve this issue, we use shortcut deforestation, in particular Theorem 5. Recall that *foldr* and *foldl* are catamorphisms for two representations of lists. Therefore, Requirement (7) follows from Theorem 5 if $+\!\!+$ can be specified by two polymorphic functions. It is actually possible.

$$
\begin{array}{lcl}
x +\!\!+ y = gen_1\ in_{\mathsf{L_s}}\ (x,y) = gen_2\ in_{\mathsf{L_c}}\ (x,y) \\
gen_1 :: \forall\alpha.\ (\mathsf{L_s}\alpha \to \alpha) \to (\alpha, [Int]) \to \alpha \\
gen_1\ \phi\ (x, []) & = & x \\
gen_1\ \phi\ (x, y +\!\!+ [b]) & = & \phi\ (2, (gen_1\ \phi\ (x,y), b)) \\
gen_2 :: \forall\beta.\ (\mathsf{L_c}\beta \to \beta) \to ([Int], \beta) \to \beta \\
gen_2\ \phi\ ([], y) & = & y \\
gen_2\ \phi\ (a : x, y) & = & \phi\ (2, (a, gen_2\ \phi\ (x,y)))
\end{array}
$$

Now we prove Theorem 1.

Proof of Theorem 1. From Lemma 6, it is sufficient to show that Requirement (7) is met. Since $h = foldl\ \phi_1 = foldr\ \phi_2$, Theorem 5 guarantees that it is satisfied by $m_1 = gen_1\ \phi_1$ and $m_2 = gen_2\ \phi_2$. □

4. Generalizing The Third List-homomorphism Theorem

4.1 Meta-theorems for Parallelizing Catamorphisms

Our approach can be naturally generalized to arbitrary catamorphisms. Let us consider parallelizing $h\ (x\ \text{`}merge\text{`}\ y)$. We assure that there exists m such that $h\ (x\ \text{`}merge\text{`}\ y) = m\ (h_1\ x, h_2\ y)$ by proving that (i) h can be written as two kinds of catamorphisms and (ii) $merge$ can be written as two kinds of polymorphic functions. To be precise, we use two merging functions because two different catamorphisms have different types. The idea is embodied in the following theorem.

Theorem 8. *Let $(\mu\mathsf{F}, in_\mathsf{F})$ and $(\mu\mathsf{G}, in_\mathsf{G})$ be two initial algebras and $\dagger$ be a bifunctor. Assume that $merge_1 :: (\mu\mathsf{F} \dagger \mu\mathsf{G}) \to \mu\mathsf{F}$ and $merge_2 :: (\mu\mathsf{F} \dagger \mu\mathsf{G}) \to \mu\mathsf{G}$ are defined by using polymorphic functions as follows.*

$$\begin{array}{l} merge_1 = gen_1\ in_\mathsf{F} \\ gen_1 :: \forall\alpha.\ (\mathsf{F}\alpha \to \alpha) \to (\alpha \dagger \mu\mathsf{G}) \to \alpha \\ merge_2 = gen_2\ in_\mathsf{G} \\ gen_2 :: \forall\beta.\ (\mathsf{G}\beta \to \beta) \to (\mu\mathsf{F} \dagger \beta) \to \beta \end{array}$$

Then, for any $\hat{h} :: (\mu\mathsf{F} \dagger \mu\mathsf{G}) \to C$ such that

$$\hat{h} = (\!|\phi_1|\!)_\mathsf{F} \circ merge_1 = (\!|\phi_2|\!)_\mathsf{G} \circ merge_2,$$

there exists an m such that

$$\hat{h} = m \circ ((\!|\phi_1|\!)_\mathsf{F} \dagger (\!|\phi_2|\!)_\mathsf{G}).$$

In fact, $m = \hat{h} \circ ((\!|\phi_1|\!)_\mathsf{F}^{-1} \dagger (\!|\phi_2|\!)_\mathsf{G}^{-1})$.

Proof. We will prove a more general theorem, Theorem 9. □

Theorem 8 works as a meta-theorem that derives theorems like the third list-homomorphism theorem. Given a structure $\mu\mathsf{F} \dagger \mu\mathsf{G}$ that contains substructures, $\mu\mathsf{F}$ and $\mu\mathsf{G}$, suppose that there exist two merging functions, $merge_1$ and $merge_2$, defined by using polymorphic functions, gen_1 and gen_2. Then, if $\hat{h}$ can be described by two patterns, each of which is a composition of a catamorphism and a merging function, $\hat{h}$ can be calculated by simultaneously applying $(\!|\phi_1|\!)_\mathsf{F}$ and $(\!|\phi_2|\!)_\mathsf{G}$ to the substructures.

Theorem 8 directly generalizes the third list-homomorphism theorem. In this case, $\mathsf{F} = \mathsf{L_s}$, $\mathsf{G} = \mathsf{L_c}$, $\dagger = \times$, and both $merge_1$ and $merge_2$ are $(+\!\!+)$. Two catamorphisms correspond to $foldl$ and $foldr$. An isomorphism between the snoc lists ($\mu\mathsf{L_s}$) and the cons lists ($\mu\mathsf{L_c}$) is implicitly used.

We can generalize Theorem 8. Note that shortcut deforestation is applicable if there is a composition of a catamorphism and a merging function. This implies that $\hat{h}$ can include other computations.

Theorem 9. *Let $(\mu\mathsf{F}, in_\mathsf{F})$ and $(\mu\mathsf{G}, in_\mathsf{G})$ be two initial algebras, $\dagger$ be a bifunctor, and H_1 and H_2 be functors. Furthermore, suppose that $merge_1 :: (\mu\mathsf{F} \dagger \mu\mathsf{G}) \to \mathsf{H}_1\mu\mathsf{F}$ and $merge_2 :: (\mu\mathsf{F} \dagger \mu\mathsf{G}) \to \mathsf{H}_2\mu\mathsf{G}$ are defined as follows.*

$$\begin{array}{l} merge_1 = gen_1\ in_\mathsf{F} \\ gen_1 :: \forall\alpha.\ (\mathsf{F}\alpha \to \alpha) \to (\alpha \dagger \mu\mathsf{G}) \to \mathsf{H}_1\alpha \\ merge_2 = gen_2\ in_\mathsf{G} \\ gen_2 :: \forall\beta.\ (\mathsf{G}\beta \to \beta) \to (\mu\mathsf{F} \dagger \beta) \to \mathsf{H}_2\beta \end{array}$$

Then, for any $\hat{h} :: (\mu\mathsf{F} \dagger \mu\mathsf{G}) \to C$, $\epsilon_1 :: \mathsf{H}_1 A \to C$, $\epsilon_2 :: \mathsf{H}_2 B \to C$, $\phi_1 :: \mathsf{F}A \to A$, and $\phi_2 :: \mathsf{F}B \to B$ such that

$$\hat{h} = \epsilon_1 \circ \mathsf{H}_1(\!|\phi_1|\!)_\mathsf{F} \circ merge_1 = \epsilon_2 \circ \mathsf{H}_2(\!|\phi_2|\!)_\mathsf{G} \circ merge_2,$$

there exists $m :: A \dagger B \to C$ such that

$$\hat{h} = m \circ ((\!|\phi_1|\!)_\mathsf{F} \dagger (\!|\phi_2|\!)_\mathsf{G}).$$

In fact, $m = \hat{h} \circ ((\!|\phi_1|\!)_\mathsf{F}^{-1} \dagger (\!|\phi_2|\!)_\mathsf{G}^{-1})$.

Proof. From Lemma 6, it is sufficient to show that there exist m_1 and m_2 such that

$$\hat{h} = m_1 \circ ((\!|\phi_1|\!)_\mathsf{F} \dagger id) = m_2 \circ (id \dagger (\!|\phi_2|\!)_\mathsf{G}).$$

Theorem 5 shows $m_1 = \epsilon_1 \circ gen_1\ \phi_1$ and $m_2 = \epsilon_2 \circ gen_2\ \phi_2$. We will prove the former case here; the proof of the other case is similar.

$$\begin{array}{cl} \hat{h} & = \{\ \text{premise, and unfolding } merge_1\ \} \\ & \quad \epsilon_1 \circ \mathsf{H}_1(\!|\phi_1|\!)_\mathsf{F} \circ gen_1\ in_\mathsf{F} \\ & = \{\ \text{Theorem 5}\ \} \\ & \quad \epsilon_1 \circ gen_1\ \phi_1 \circ ((\!|\phi_1|\!)_\mathsf{F} \dagger id) \end{array}$$

□

Theorem 9 states that if each $merge_i$ is implemented by a function of a certain polymorphic type, we obtain a parallelization theorem that parallelize $\hat{h}$ specified by a catamorphism with an additional function, ϵ_i. It is worth noting that the additional function improves expressiveness. For example, Theorem 9 can cope with mutumorphisms (Fokkinga 1989) and adjoint folds (Hinze 2013).

Keen readers might notice that parallelization theorems derived from Theorem 9 are applicable to almost all computations. For instance, since $h = h \circ foldl\ in_{\mathsf{L_s}} = h \circ foldr\ in_{\mathsf{L_c}}$ for any $h :: [Int] \to C$, Theorem 9 is applicable to any list operation. However, in this case, the theorem does not provide any useful insight for obtaining efficient parallel programs: Note that id is the right inverse of both of $foldl\ in_{\mathsf{L_s}}$ and $foldr\ in_{\mathsf{L_c}}$; hence, the theorem yields $h\ (x +\!\!+ y) = h\ (id\ (foldl\ in_{\mathsf{L_s}}\ x) +\!\!+ id\ (foldr\ in_{\mathsf{L_c}}\ y))$, which is trivial because $id \circ foldl\ in_{\mathsf{L_s}} = id \circ foldr\ in_{\mathsf{L_c}} = id$.

As we observed above, the parallel implementations obtained from our theorems might be useless and/or terribly slow. This is a limitation of our approach. We will discussions this issue in Section 6.2.

Another issue is the way of dividing the given structure. In order to use Theorems 8 and 9, we need to provide a division, specified by $\mu\mathsf{F} \dagger \mu\mathsf{G}$, of the input. The division determines efficiency of the obtained parallel programs. For linear structures such as lists, it is reasonable to divide the input at the middle. For more complex structures, it is nontrivial to provide a good division that supports recursive divisions, yields substructures of similar sizes, and is achieved efficiently. However, ways of providing good divisions are beyond the scope of this paper.

4.2 Deriving Divide-and-conquer Tree Operations

Let us demonstrate the use of Theorem 9 by developing a parallelization theorem for the binary trees defined below.

$$\textbf{data}\ Tree = Lf\ Int\ \mid\ Nd\ Tree\ Int\ Tree$$

First, we decide the way of dividing trees. A naive strategy is to isolate siblings and thereby deal with them in parallel. Our theorem proves that a tree operation can be implemented with this strategy if it is both left-to-right, namely iterating the left subtree first, and right-to-left, namely iterating the right subtree first.

Instead, we will employ a different approach because the above strategy is little effective if the input tree is slender and tall, like a list. To exploit more parallelism, we divide up a tree not only at the root but also at an arbitrary internal node. Division at an internal node results in three substructures: two subtrees, and a one-hole context that retains the upper part. Therefore, we need a data structure for representing one-hole contexts. We will use Huet's zipper (Huet 1997).

$$\overset{\text{root}}{\longrightarrow} (n_1, t_1) \overset{\text{left}}{\longrightarrow} (t_2, n_2) \overset{\text{right}}{\longrightarrow} (t_3, n_3) \overset{\text{right}}{\longrightarrow} \sim$$

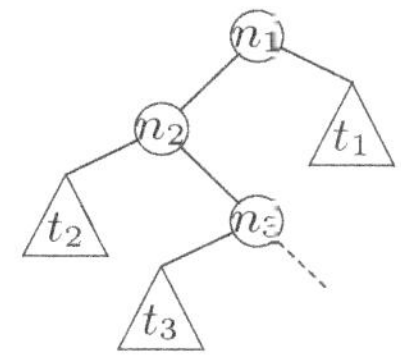

Figure 1. Correspondence between a zipper structure and a one-hole context: the dashed line denotes the hole, and thus, the corresponding subtree is missing.

$$\begin{aligned} \textbf{data}\ \mathit{Zipper} \ =\ & \overset{\text{root}}{\longrightarrow} \mid \mathit{Zipper}\ (\mathit{Int}, \mathit{Tree}) \overset{\text{left}}{\longrightarrow} \\ & \mid \mathit{Zipper}\ (\mathit{Tree}, \mathit{Int}) \overset{\text{right}}{\longrightarrow} \end{aligned}$$

For readability, we will use *postfix* constructors, $\overset{\text{left}}{\longrightarrow}$ and $\overset{\text{right}}{\longrightarrow}$. Figure 1 outlines the correspondence between the zipper structure and the one-hole context. Zippers essentially retain the paths from their root to their hole. $\overset{\text{left}}{\longrightarrow}$ and $\overset{\text{right}}{\longrightarrow}$ correspond to paths to the left and right children, respectively. The following operator, $(\triangleleft) :: \mathit{Zipper} \to \mathit{Tree} \to \mathit{Tree}$, plugs a tree into the hole of a zipper.

$$\begin{aligned} \overset{\text{root}}{\longrightarrow} \triangleleft t \quad &= t \\ (z\ (n, r) \overset{\text{left}}{\longrightarrow}) \triangleleft t \quad &= z \triangleleft \mathit{Nd}\ t\ n\ r \\ (z\ (l, n) \overset{\text{right}}{\longrightarrow}) \triangleleft t \quad &= z \triangleleft \mathit{Nd}\ l\ n\ t \end{aligned}$$

Next, we formalize zippers by using initial algebras. We make isomorphisms $\mathit{Zipper} \sim \mu\mathsf{F}$ and $\mathit{Tree} \sim \mu\mathsf{G}$, as follows.

$$\begin{aligned} \mathsf{F}X \ =\ & \{(1, ())\} \\ & \cup \{(2, (x, n, t)) \mid x \in X \wedge n \in \mathit{Int} \wedge t \in \mathit{Tree}\} \\ & \cup \{(3, (x, t, n)) \mid x \in X \wedge t \in \mathit{Tree} \wedge n \in \mathit{Int}\} \\ \mathit{in}_{\mathsf{F}}\ (1, ()) \quad &= \overset{\text{root}}{\longrightarrow} \\ \mathit{in}_{\mathsf{F}}\ (2, (x, n, t)) \quad &= x\ (n, t) \overset{\text{left}}{\longrightarrow} \\ \mathit{in}_{\mathsf{F}}\ (3, (x, t, n)) \quad &= x\ (t, n) \overset{\text{right}}{\longrightarrow} \end{aligned}$$

$$\begin{aligned} \mathsf{G}X \ =\ & \{(1, n) \mid n \in \mathit{Int}\} \\ & \cup \{(2, (x_1, n, x_2)) \mid x_1, x_2 \in X \wedge n \in \mathit{Int}\} \\ \mathit{in}_{\mathsf{G}}\ (1, n) \quad &= \mathit{Lf}\ n \\ \mathit{in}_{\mathsf{G}}\ (2, (x_1, n, x_2)) \quad &= \mathit{Nd}\ x_1\ n\ x_2 \end{aligned}$$

Next, we prepare two merging functions. It is natural to choose $(\triangleleft)$ as merge_2. We also need merge_1 that merges a tree into a zipper. However, while merging a zipper with a tree results in a tree, a zipper represents not a tree but a one-hole context. Thus, we use $(\blacktriangleleft) :: \mathit{Zipper} \to \mathit{Tree} \to (\mathit{Zipper}, \mathit{Int})$, characterized as follows, as the other merging function. It calculates a zipper as well as an integer, which corresponds to the value of the missing leaf.

$$z \blacktriangleleft t = (z', n) \ \text{ such that } \ z \triangleleft t = z' \triangleleft \mathit{Lf}\ n$$

Finally, let us confirm that they can be implemented by functions of the required polymorphic type.

$$\begin{aligned} & z \blacktriangleleft t = \mathit{gen}_1\ \mathit{in}_{\mathsf{F}}\ (z, t) \\ & \quad \textbf{where}\ \mathit{gen}_1 :: \forall\alpha.\ (\mathsf{F}\alpha \to \alpha) \to (\alpha, \mathit{Tree}) \to (\alpha, \mathit{Int}) \\ & \qquad \mathit{gen}_1\ \phi\ (z, \mathit{Lf}\ n) \quad = (z, n) \\ & \qquad \mathit{gen}_1\ \phi\ (z, \mathit{Nd}\ l\ n\ r) = \mathit{gen}_1\ \phi\ (\phi\ (2, (z, n, r)), l) \end{aligned}$$

$$\begin{aligned} & z \triangleleft t = \mathit{gen}_2\ \mathit{in}_{\mathsf{G}}\ (z, t) \\ & \quad \textbf{where}\ \mathit{gen}_2 :: \forall\beta.\ (\mathsf{G}\beta \to \beta) \to (\mathit{Zipper}, \beta) \to \beta \\ & \qquad \mathit{gen}_2\ \phi\ (\overset{\text{root}}{\longrightarrow}, t) \quad = t \\ & \qquad \mathit{gen}_2\ \phi\ (z\ (n, r) \overset{\text{left}}{\longrightarrow}, t) \ = \mathit{gen}_2\ \phi\ (z, \phi\ (2, (t, n, r))) \\ & \qquad \mathit{gen}_2\ \phi\ (z\ (l, n) \overset{\text{right}}{\longrightarrow}, t) = \mathit{gen}_2\ \phi\ (z, \phi\ (2, (l, n, t))) \end{aligned}$$

Now that all the requirements are fulfilled, the following corollary follows from Theorem 9.

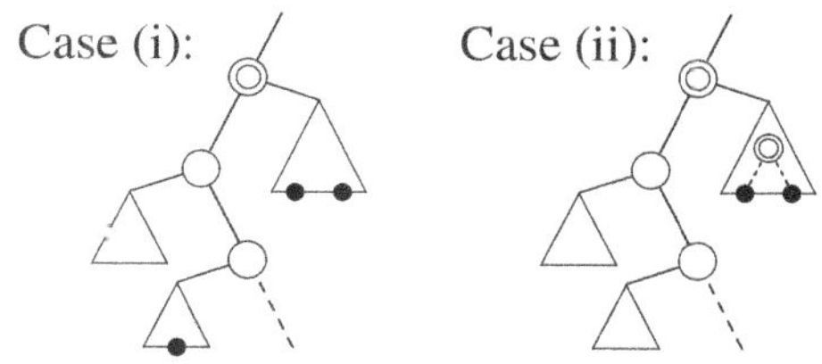

Figure 2. Top-down calculation of the least common ancestor: the black bullets denote null pointers, and the double circles denote candidates of the least common ancestors. The dashed lines denote subtrees that have not been explored yet.

Corollary 10. *For any* $\hat{h} :: (\mathit{Zipper} \times \mathit{Tree}) \to C$, $\phi_1 :: \mathsf{F}A \to A$, $\phi_2 :: \mathsf{G}B \to B$, $\epsilon_1 :: (A \times \mathit{Int}) \to C$, *and* $\epsilon_2 :: B \to C$,

$$\begin{aligned} \hat{h}\ (z, t) \ &=\ \textbf{let}\ (z', n) = z \blacktriangleleft t\ \textbf{in}\ \epsilon_1\ ((\![\phi_1]\!)_{\mathsf{F}}\ z', n) \\ &=\ \epsilon_2\ ((\![\phi_2]\!)_{\mathsf{G}}\ (z \triangleleft t)) \end{aligned}$$

implies that there exists $m :: (A \times B) \to C$ *such that*

$$\hat{h}\ (z, t) = m\ ((\![\phi_1]\!)_{\mathsf{F}}\ z, (\![\phi_2]\!)_{\mathsf{G}}\ t).$$

Actually, $m = \hat{h} \circ ((\![\phi_1]\!)_{\mathsf{F}}^{-1} \times (\![\phi_2]\!)_{\mathsf{G}}^{-1})$. □

While catamorphisms on trees are bottom-up, those on zippers are top-down. Thus, Corollary 10 enables us to derive parallel programs from top-down and bottom-up implementations.

In order to implement the obtained programs, we need an implementation of our division strategy. For this purpose, we can use the m-bridge technique (Reif 1993), which enables us to divide a tree into reasonably-sized segments, each of which is either a subtree or a one-hole context. Its details are beyond the scope of this paper and thus omitted.

Example: Least Common Ancestor

Let us demonstrate the use of Corollary 10 by deriving a parallel program for finding the least common ancestor of null pointers. We assume that the address of each node is stored as its node value; thus, null pointers are 0-valued leaves.

It is easy to implement the task in a bottom-up manner. Let lca be the function,

$$\begin{aligned} & \mathit{lca}\ (\mathit{Lf}\ n) \quad\ = \textbf{if}\ n \equiv 0\ \textbf{then}\ \mathit{Just}\ n\ \textbf{else}\ \mathit{Nothing} \\ & \mathit{lca}\ (\mathit{Nd}\ l\ n\ r) = \mathit{lca}_{aux}\ (\mathit{lca}\ l)\ n\ (\mathit{lca}\ r) \\ & \quad \textbf{where}\ \mathit{lca}_{aux}\ (\mathit{Just}\ \_)\ n\ (\mathit{Just}\ \_) \ = \mathit{Just}\ n \\ & \qquad\quad \mathit{lca}_{aux}\ (\mathit{Just}\ n_1)\ \_\ \mathit{Nothing} \ = \mathit{Just}\ n_1 \\ & \qquad\quad \mathit{lca}_{aux}\ \mathit{Nothing}\ \_\ (\mathit{Just}\ n_2) \ = \mathit{Just}\ n_2 \\ & \qquad\quad \mathit{lca}_{aux}\ \mathit{Nothing}\ \_\ \mathit{Nothing} \ \ = \mathit{Nothing} \end{aligned}$$

lca results in $\mathit{Nothing}$ if the tree contains no null pointer, and $\mathit{Just}\ n$ otherwise, where n is the address of the least common ancestor. lca_{aux} integrates the results of subtrees: if both subtrees contain null pointers, it returns the root; otherwise, it propagates the results of the subtrees.

From this definition, it is easy to see that lca is a catamorphism for Tree (i.e., $\mu\mathsf{G}$): $\mathit{lca} = (\![\phi_2]\!)_{\mathsf{G}}$, where $\phi_2\ (1, n) =$ **if** $n \equiv 0$ **then** $\mathit{Just}\ n$ **else** $\mathit{Nothing}$ and $\phi_2\ (2, (v_1, n, v_2)) = \mathit{lca}_{aux}\ v_1\ n\ v_2$.

To apply Corollary 10, we also need a top-down implementation of lca by using a catamorphism on Zipper (i.e., $\mu\mathsf{F}$). In calculating lca while going down a path, we face possibly three situations: (i) null pointers have been found on two different subtrees along the path, and therefore, the least common ancestor has been already known; (ii) null pointers have been found in exactly one subtree, and thus, the least common ancestor is either one in the subtree or the branching node to the subtree, and (iii) no null pointer has been found. Figure 2 shows cases (i) and (ii). We use the following datatype for expressing these cases.

$$\mathbf{data}\ Result_{lca} = Fixed\ Int \mid Or\ Int\ Int \mid None$$

Fixed n corresponds to the first case, where n is the least common ancestor. *Or* $n_1\ n_2$ retains two possible candidates, and the least common ancestor is n_1 if another null pointer will be found, and n_2 otherwise. *None* means that no null pointer is found.

The following is a zipper version of *lca*.

$$\begin{aligned}
&lca_{Zipper}\ (z, n) = \epsilon_1\ (lca_Z\ z, n)\\
&lca_Z\ (\overset{\text{root}}{\rightarrow}) \quad = None\\
&lca_Z\ (z\ (n, r) \overset{\text{left}}{\rightarrow}) \quad = lca^Z_{aux}\ (lca_Z\ z)\ n\ (lca\ r)\\
&lca_Z\ (z\ (l, n) \overset{\text{right}}{\rightarrow}) \quad = lca^Z_{aux}\ (lca_Z\ z)\ n\ (lca\ l)\\
&\quad \mathbf{where}\ lca^Z_{aux}\ (Fixed\ n)\ _\ _ = Fixed\ n\\
&\qquad lca^Z_{aux}\ (Or\ n_1\ n_2)\ _\ (Just\ _) = Fixed\ n_1\\
&\qquad lca^Z_{aux}\ (Or\ n_1\ n_2)\ _\ Nothing = Or\ n_1\ n_2\\
&\qquad lca^Z_{aux}\ None\ n_1\ (Just\ n_2) = Or\ n_1\ n_2\\
&\qquad lca^Z_{aux}\ None\ _\ Nothing = None\\
&\epsilon_1\ (Fixed\ n', _) = Just\ n'\\
&\epsilon_1\ (Or\ n_1\ n_2, n) = \mathbf{if}\ n \equiv 0\ \mathbf{then}\ Just\ n_1\ \mathbf{else}\ Just\ n_2\\
&\epsilon_1\ (None, n) = \mathbf{if}\ n \equiv 0\ \mathbf{then}\ Just\ n\ \mathbf{else}\ Nothing
\end{aligned}$$

Although the above is rather complicated, it can be implemented by a zipper catamorphism: $lca_Z = (\!|\phi_1|\!)_{\mathsf{F}}$ where $\phi_1\ (1, ()) = None$ and $\phi_1\ (2, (z, n, t)) = \phi_1\ (3, (z, t, n)) = lca^Z_{aux}\ z\ n\ (lca\ t)$.

We have confirmed that Corollary 10 is applicable. Therefore, there is a divide-and-conquer implementation of *lca*. Moreover, the implementation can be derived from the right inverses of *lca* and lca_Z, which are not difficult to find.

$$\begin{aligned}
&lca^{-1}\ (Just\ n) = Nd\ n\ (Lf\ 0)\ (Lf\ 0)\\
&lca^{-1}\ Nothing = Lf\ 1\\
&lca_Z^{-1}\ (Fixed\ n) = \overset{\text{root}}{\rightarrow} (n, Lf\ 0) \overset{\text{left}}{\rightarrow} (1, Lf\ 0) \overset{\text{left}}{\rightarrow}\\
&lca_Z^{-1}\ (Or\ n_1\ n_2) = \overset{\text{root}}{\rightarrow} (n_1, Nd\ n_2\ (Lf\ 0)\ (Lf\ 0)) \overset{\text{left}}{\rightarrow}\\
&lca_Z^{-1}\ None = \overset{\text{root}}{\rightarrow}
\end{aligned}$$

Now let us work out a divide-and-conquer implementation of $lca\ (z \lhd t)$. In the following, we will focus on the case of $lca_Z\ z = Or\ n_1\ n_2$ and $lca\ t = Just\ n$.

$$\begin{aligned}
&\quad lca\ (z \lhd t)\\
&= \{\ \text{Corollary 10}\ \}\\
&\quad lca\ (lca_Z^{-1}\ (lca_Z\ z) \lhd lca^{-1}\ (lca\ t))\\
&= \{\ \text{unfolding } lca_Z^{-1}, lca^{-1}, \text{and } (\lhd)\ \}\\
&\quad lca\ (Nd\ (Nd\ n\ (Lf\ 0)\ (Lf\ 0))\ n_1 (Nd\ n_2\ (Lf\ 0)\ (Lf\ 0)))\\
&= \{\ \text{unfolding } lca\ \}\\
&\quad Just\ n_1
\end{aligned}$$

Similar calculations will yield implementations for the other cases. We will omit them. Consequently, we obtain the following program.

$$\begin{aligned}
&lca\ (z \lhd t) = lca^{DC}_{aux}\ (lca_Z\ z)\ (lca\ t)\\
&\quad \mathbf{where}\ lca^{DC}_{aux}\ (Fixed\ n)\ _ = Just\ n\\
&\qquad lca^{DC}_{aux}\ (Or\ n_1\ n_2)\ (Just\ _) = Just\ n_1\\
&\qquad lca^{DC}_{aux}\ (Or\ n_1\ n_2)\ Nothing = Just\ n_2\\
&\qquad lca^{DC}_{aux}\ None\ (Just\ n) = Just\ n\\
&\qquad lca^{DC}_{aux}\ None\ Nothing = Nothing
\end{aligned}$$

This program implemented by using the m-bridge technique runs in $O(\mathrm{N}/\mathrm{P} + \mathrm{P})$ time for a tree of size N on the PRAM of P processors. Hence, if $\mathrm{N} \gg \mathrm{P}$, it finds the least common ancestor in time $O(\mathrm{N}/\mathrm{P})$ regardless of the height of the tree.

4.3 Deriving Divide-and-conquer Set Operations

As an another application of Theorem 9, let us consider parallelizing set manipulations described by the following $fold_{Set}$. Let $add\ a\ x = \{a\} \cup x$.

$$\begin{aligned}
fold_{Set}\ (\oplus)\ e\ \emptyset &= e\\
fold_{Set}\ (\oplus)\ e\ (add\ a\ x) &= a \oplus fold_{Set}\ (\oplus)\ e\ x
\end{aligned}$$

To make the function well-defined, we need $a \oplus (b \oplus v) = b \oplus (a \oplus v)$ and $a \oplus (a \oplus v) = a \oplus v$ for v in the range of $fold_{Set}\ (\oplus)\ e$. Among the algebras that have these properties, $\emptyset$ and *add* form the initial one and $fold_{Set}$ corresponds to the catamorphisms.

Theorem 9 leads to a parallelization theorem for $fold_{Set}$, which states that any set operation implemented by $fold_{Set}$ is potentially parallelizable.

Corollary 11. *For any* $\hat{h} :: Set\ A \rightarrow C$, $\epsilon :: B \rightarrow C$, $(\oplus) :: (A, B) \rightarrow B$, *and* $e :: B$

$$\hat{h} = \epsilon \circ fold_{Set}\ (\oplus)\ e$$

implies that there exists m *such that*

$$\hat{h}\ (x \cup y) = m\ (fold_{Set}\ (\oplus)\ e\ x, fold_{Set}\ (\oplus)\ e\ y),$$

where $m\ (v, w) = \hat{h}\ ((fold_{Set}\ (\oplus)\ e)^{-1}\ v \cup (fold_{Set}\ (\oplus)\ e)^{-1}\ w)$.

Proof. From Theorem 9 and the commutativity of $(\cup)$, it is sufficient to show that $(\cup)$ can be specified by a certain polymorphic function.

$$\begin{aligned}
&x \cup y = gen\ add\ \emptyset\ (x, y)\\
&\quad \mathbf{where}\ gen :: \forall \beta.\ (A \rightarrow \beta \rightarrow \beta) \rightarrow \beta \rightarrow (Set\ A, \beta) \rightarrow \beta\\
&\qquad gen\ (\oplus)\ e\ (\emptyset, y) = y\\
&\qquad gen\ (\oplus)\ e\ (add\ a\ x, y) = a \oplus gen\ (\oplus)\ e\ (x, y)
\end{aligned}$$ □

Remark To be precise, Corollary 11 is not an instance of Theorem 9: *gen* takes not a function of the type of $\mathsf{P}\beta \rightarrow \beta$, where P is a functor such that $\mu\mathsf{P} \sim Set\ A$, but $(\oplus) :: (A \rightarrow \beta \rightarrow \beta)$ with $e :: \beta$. Especially, *gen* is unaware of the algebraic properties of P, such as the associativity and the commutativity, which make P different from $\mathsf{L_c}$. Hence, the fact that *gen* has that polymorphic type is actually not sufficient to prove the corollary, though the rest of the proof is straightforward and is very similar to that of Theorem 9. We use this formalization because it seems difficult to take the algebraic properties of P into account without spoiling relational parametricity (Reynolds 1983; Wadler 1989), which is the basis of shortcut deforestation.

Example: Finding Celebrities

We apply Corollary 11 to the "finding celebrities" problem studied by Bird and Curtis (2006). In the attendees of a party, we call a person a celebrity if he/she is known by all the attendees but knows only the other celebrities. A set of celebrities is unique, but may be empty. From the perspective of graph theory, it can be viewed as a problem on a directed graph to find a clique that satisfies a kind of isolation property.

Assume that there is a celebrity[1]. Bird and Curtis (2006) showed that the following linear-time program finds the set of celebrities.

$$\begin{aligned}
&celeb = fold_{Set}\ step\ \emptyset\\
&\quad \mathbf{where}\\
&\qquad step\ a\ \emptyset = \{a\}\\
&\qquad step\ a\ (add\ b\ y) = (\mathbf{if}\ b\ \text{`}know\text{`}\ a\ \mathbf{then}\ \{a\}\ \mathbf{else}\ \emptyset)\\
&\qquad\qquad \cup\ (\mathbf{if}\ a\ \text{`}know\text{`}\ b\ \mathbf{then}\ add\ b\ y\ \mathbf{else}\ \emptyset)
\end{aligned}$$

[1] To be precise, so as to let *celeb* be a function, we assume that every subset of the input has a nonempty set of celebrities.

It might be hard to see that this program correctly finds celebrities. Nevertheless, Corollary 11 states that it is parallelizable. Moreover, since *celeb* is idempotent, *id* is its right inverse. Therefore, we can obtain the following divide-and-conquer implementation.

$$
\begin{aligned}
celeb\ (x \cup y) &= \{\text{ Corollary 11 }\} \\
&\quad fold_{Set}\ step\ \emptyset\ (id\ (celeb\ x) \cup id\ (celeb\ y)) \\
&= \{\text{ Unfolding } id \text{, and a simplification }\} \\
&\quad fold_{Set}\ step\ (celeb\ y)\ (celeb\ x)
\end{aligned}
$$

We can improve efficiency as follows. We call two persons friends if they know each other. Observe that a friend of a celebrity is a celebrity, whereas a friend of a non-celebrity is not. In fact, *celeb* maintains a chain of friendship relations. Now, we check whether $a \in celeb\ x$ and $b \in celeb\ y$ know each other.

b **knows** a**:** If a (and thereby any of $celeb\ x$) is not a celebrity, b (as well as $celeb\ y$) is not either. Therefore, if there are celebrities, they should contain $celeb\ x$.

b **does not know** a**:** Apparently a is not a celebrity, and thus, none of $celeb\ x$ is a celebrity.

The same goes for $celeb\ y$. Consequently, we obtain the following program.

$$
\begin{aligned}
&celeb\ (x \cup y) = m\ (celeb\ x, celeb\ y) \\
&\quad \textbf{where}\ m\ (\emptyset, \hat{y}) = \hat{y} \\
&\qquad m\ (\hat{x}, \emptyset) = \hat{x} \\
&\qquad m\ (add\ a\ \hat{x}, add\ b\ \hat{y}) \\
&\qquad\quad = (\textbf{if}\ b\ `know`\ a\ \textbf{then}\ add\ a\ \hat{x}\ \textbf{else}\ \emptyset) \\
&\qquad\quad \cup (\textbf{if}\ a\ `know`\ b\ \textbf{then}\ add\ b\ \hat{y}\ \textbf{else}\ \emptyset)
\end{aligned}
$$

Suppose that sets are implemented by linked lists that support constant-time concatenations. Then, m is a constant-time function, and hence, we can find the celebrities in $O(N/P + \log P)$ time on a PRAM of P processors, where N is the number of attendees.

5. Dualization and Generalization to Hylomorphisms

So far, we have developed a theory for deriving parallel programs from two catamorphisms, i.e., structure-consuming operations. In parallel programs, data distributions, rather than consumptions, often form bottlenecks. Therefore, data generations should be parallelized: each processor receives a seed of the data and generates part of the data independently. We can view the development of such parallel data generations as a parallelization of the dual of catamorphisms, called anamorphisms (Malcolm 1990; Meijer et al. 1991; Bird and de Moor 1997), which generate structures. Here, we provide a theorem for deriving divide-and-conquer implementations for programs specified by anamorphisms.

Moreover, we show that our theory can be further generalized to compositions of catamorphisms and anamorphisms, called hylomorphisms. In hylomorphisms, structures are generated and immediately consumed; thus, they correspond to a kind of "on-the-fly" structure manipulation.

5.1 Brief Introduction to Relations

Following Mu and Morihata (2011), we will use relations rather than functions for formalizing the dualization. Since inputs and outputs are symmetric for relations, properties about relations can be dualized by taking relational converses. We stress that our objective is the development of functions rather than relations. Relations are only used for formalizations and proofs.

In the following, we briefly introduce relations (Details can be found in (Bird and de Moor 1997)). A relation R between two sets A and B is a subset of $B \times A$. We write its type as $R :: A \to B$. A relation $R :: A \to B$ is a function if $\forall (b, a), (b', a) \in R.\ b = b'$ and $\forall a \in A.\ \exists (b, a) \in R$. We may write $b = R\ a$ to mean $(b, a) \in R$ if R is a function, and $b \leftarrow R\ a$ otherwise. The relational composition of $R :: A \to B$ and $S :: B \to C$ is defined by $(c, a) \in (S \circ R) \iff (\exists b.\ (c, b) \in S \land (b, a) \in R)$. Note that it generalizes the function compositions. The relational converse of $R :: A \to B$, denoted by $R^\circ :: B \to A$, is defined by $(a, b) \in R^\circ \iff (b, a) \in R$. Note that $(R \circ S)^\circ = S^\circ \circ R^\circ$.

In order to formalize structure manipulations using relations, we extend our categorical model from $\mathfrak{Set}$ to $\mathfrak{Rel}$, where objects are sets, arrows are relations, and arrow compositions are relational compositions. In $\mathfrak{Rel}$, we require that each functor F preserves converses, i.e., $(\mathsf{F}R)^\circ = \mathsf{F}(R^\circ)$. Such functors are called relators. All of the standard functors are relators, and therefore, we will take functors to mean relators. We also require bifunctors to have similar properties.

Lemma 6 can be generalized to relations.

Lemma 12. *For any bifunctor* $\dagger$*, the relations* $H :: A_1 \dagger A_2 \to B$*,* $H_1 :: A_1 \to B_1$*,* $H_2 :: A_2 \to B_2$*,* $R_1 :: B_1 \to A_1$ *and* $R_2 :: B_2 \to A_2$*, assume* $H_1 \circ R_1 \circ H_1 = H_1$ *and* $H_2 \circ R_2 \circ H_2 = H_2$*. Then, there exist relations* $M_1 :: B_1 \dagger A_2 \to B$ *and* $M_2 :: A_1 \dagger B_2 \to B$ *such that*

$$H = M_1 \circ (H_1 \dagger id) = M_2 \circ (id \dagger H_2)$$

if and only if there exists a relation $M :: (B_1 \dagger B_2) \to B$ *such that*

$$H = M \circ (H_1 \dagger H_2).$$

Proof. The "if" part is easy. $M_1 = M \circ (id \dagger H_2)$ and $M_2 = M \circ (H_1 \dagger id)$ apparently satisfy the requirement.

The "only if" part is a generalization of Mu and Morihata (2011) from the product to arbitrary bifunctors. The proof is almost the same as theirs, and $M = H \circ (R_1 \dagger R_2)$ satisfies the requirement.

$$
\begin{aligned}
H &= \{\text{ premise }\} \\
&\quad M_1 \circ (H_1 \dagger id) \\
&= \{\ H_1 \circ R_1 \circ H_1 = H_1 \text{, and } \dagger \text{ is a bifunctor }\} \\
&\quad M_1 \circ (H_1 \dagger id) \circ (R_1 \dagger id) \circ (H_1 \dagger id) \\
&= \{\text{ premise }\} \\
&\quad M_2 \circ (id \dagger H_2) \circ (R_1 \dagger id) \circ (H_1 \dagger id) \\
&= \{\ H_2 \circ R_2 \circ H_2 = H_2 \text{, and } \dagger \text{ is a bifunctor }\} \\
&\quad M_2 \circ (id \dagger H_2) \circ (R_1 \dagger R_2) \circ (H_1 \dagger H_2) \\
&= \{\text{ premise }\} \\
&\quad H \circ (R_1 \dagger R_2) \circ (H_1 \dagger H_2)
\end{aligned}
$$

□

5.2 Dualization

5.2.1 Anamorphisms

The dual of an F-algebra, called an F-coalgebra, is a pair $(A, \psi :: A \to \mathsf{F}A)$. An F-coalgebra morphism from (A_1, ψ_1) to (A_2, ψ_2) is an arrow $h :: A_1 \to A_2$ such that $\mathsf{F}h \circ \psi_1 = \psi_2 \circ h$. From any F-coalgebra, a final F-coalgebra has a unique coalgebra morphism. A final F-coalgebra is unique up to isomorphisms and is denoted by $(\nu\mathsf{F}, out_\mathsf{F})$. $[\!(\psi)\!]_\mathsf{F}$ denotes the unique coalgebra morphism from the F-coalgebra (A, ψ), and is called an anamorphism or an unfold. Anamorphisms have the following two properties.

- $[\!(out_\mathsf{F})\!]_\mathsf{F} = id_{\nu\mathsf{F}}$.
- $\mathsf{F}[\!(\psi)\!]_\mathsf{F} \circ \psi = out_\mathsf{F} \circ [\!(\psi)\!]_\mathsf{F}$.

Anamorphisms are generalizations of *unfoldr*. More precisely, in $\mathfrak{Set}$, the following *unfoldr* captures the anamorphisms for $(\nu\mathsf{L_c}, out_{\mathsf{L_c}})$.

$$
\begin{aligned}
&unfoldr :: (A \to \mathsf{L_c}A) \to A \to [Int] \\
&unfoldr\ \psi\ a = \textbf{case}\ \psi\ a\ \textbf{of}\ (1, ()) \to [\,] \\
&\qquad\qquad\qquad\qquad\quad (2, (n, a')) \to n : unfoldr\ \psi\ a'
\end{aligned}
$$

Similarly, the following *unfoldl* captures the anamorphisms for snoc lists.

$$\begin{aligned} &\mathit{unfoldl} :: (A \to \mathsf{L_s}A)) \to A \to [\mathit{Int}] \\ &\mathit{unfoldl}\ \psi\ a\ =\ \textbf{case}\ \psi\ a\ \textbf{of}\ (1,()) \to [\,] \\ &\qquad\qquad\qquad\qquad (2,(a',n)) \to \mathit{unfoldl}\ \psi\ a' \mathbin{+\!\!\!+} [n] \end{aligned}$$

They can be defined in $\mathfrak{Rel}$ as well, but we will omit them because we are less interested in relational programs.

In $\mathfrak{Rel}$, the initial F-algebra and the final F-coalgebra have a close connection. For a final F-coalgebra $(\nu\mathsf{F}, \mathit{out}_\mathsf{F})$, there exists unique h such that $\mathsf{F}h \circ \psi = \mathit{out}_\mathsf{F} \circ h$ for any F-coalgebra (A, ψ). This is equivalent to that there exists unique h° such that $\psi^\circ \circ \mathsf{F}h^\circ = h^\circ \circ \mathit{out}_\mathsf{F}^\circ$ for any F-algebra (A, ψ°). Thus, $(\nu\mathsf{F}, \mathit{out}_\mathsf{F})$ is a final F-coalgebra if and only if $(\nu\mathsf{F}, \mathit{out}_\mathsf{F}^\circ)$ is an initial F-algebra. In other words, $\mathit{in}_\mathsf{F} = \mathit{out}_\mathsf{F}^\circ$ and $\mu\mathsf{F} = \nu\mathsf{F}$. Moreover, this discussion also clarifies $(\![\phi]\!)_\mathsf{F}^\circ = [\![\phi^\circ]\!]_\mathsf{F}$ and $(\![\phi^\circ]\!)_\mathsf{F} = [\![\phi]\!]_\mathsf{F}^{\circ}$[2].

5.2.2 Parallelization Theorem for Anamorphisms

Since anamorphisms are converses of catamorphisms in $\mathfrak{Rel}$, one may think that theorems about catamorphisms can be immediately dualized by taking the relational converses. However, there is a technical difficulty. It is known that nondeterminism and partiality complicate relational parametricity (Reynolds 1983; Wadler 1989); therefore, we cannot simply generalize Theorem 5 to relations.

Nevertheless, the following theorem for parallelizing anamorphisms holds.

Theorem 13. *Suppose the same situation as Theorem 9 about the initial algebras* $(\mu\mathsf{F}, \mathit{in}_\mathsf{F})$ *and* $(\mu\mathsf{G}, \mathit{in}_\mathsf{G})$*, functors* H_1 *and* H_2*, bifunctor* $\dagger$*, and functions* $\mathit{merge}_1 :: \mu\mathsf{F} \dagger \mu\mathsf{G} \to \mathsf{H}_1\mu\mathsf{F}$ *and* $\mathit{merge}_2 :: \mu\mathsf{F} \dagger \mu\mathsf{G} \to \mathsf{H}_2\mu\mathsf{G}$*. Then, for any relation* $\hat{h} :: C \to (\mu\mathsf{F} \dagger \mu\mathsf{G})$ *such that*

$$\hat{h} = \mathit{merge}_1^\circ \circ \mathsf{H}_1[\![\psi_1]\!]_\mathsf{F} \circ \tau_1 = \mathit{merge}_2^\circ \circ \mathsf{H}_2[\![\psi_2]\!]_\mathsf{G} \circ \tau_2,$$

where $\psi_1 :: A \to \mathsf{F}A$ *and* $\psi_2 :: B \to \mathsf{G}B$ *are functions (however* $\tau_1 :: C \to \mathsf{H}_1 A$ *and* $\tau_2 :: C \to \mathsf{H}_2 B$ *may be relations), there exists a relation* $s :: C \to (A \dagger B)$ *such that*

$$\hat{h} = ([\![\psi_1]\!]_\mathsf{F} \dagger [\![\psi_2]\!]_\mathsf{G}) \circ s.$$

Actually, $s = ([\![\psi_1]\!]_\mathsf{F}^{-1} \dagger [\![\psi_2]\!]_\mathsf{G}^{-1}) \circ \hat{h}$.

Proof. The key is the following lemma. It can be proved from relational parametricity. Because its proof contains the techniques of relational calculations, we leave it for the Appendix.

Lemma 14. *For any initial algebra* $(\mu\mathsf{F}, \mathit{in}_\mathsf{F})$*, functor* G*, bifunctor* $\dagger$*, functions* $g :: \forall\alpha.\ (\mathsf{F}\alpha \to \alpha) \to (\alpha \dagger B) \to \mathsf{G}\alpha$ *and* $\psi :: A \to \mathsf{F}A$*, there exists a relation* $R :: \mathsf{G}A \to (A \dagger B)$ *such that*

$$(g\ \mathit{in}_\mathsf{F})^\circ \circ \mathsf{G}[\![\psi]\!]_\mathsf{F} = ([\![\psi]\!]_\mathsf{F} \dagger \mathit{id}) \circ R. \qquad \square$$

Now, by taking the converse of Lemma 12, we can see that it is sufficient that there exist s_1 and s_2 such that

$$\hat{h} = ([\![\psi_1]\!]_\mathsf{F} \dagger \mathit{id}) \circ s_1 = (\mathit{id} \dagger [\![\psi_2]\!]_\mathsf{F}) \circ s_2.$$

We prove the case of s_1. The case of s_2 is similar.

$$\begin{aligned} \hat{h}\ =&\ \ \{\text{ premise }\} \\ &\ \ \mathit{merge}_1^\circ \circ \mathsf{H}_1[\![\psi_1]\!]_\mathsf{F} \circ \tau_1 \\ =&\ \ \{\text{ Lemma 14, and let } s_1 = R \circ \tau_1 \ \} \\ &\ \ ([\![\psi]\!]_\mathsf{F} \dagger \mathit{id}) \circ s_1 \end{aligned} \qquad \square$$

[2] This might appear to be strange. Usually $\mu\mathsf{F}$ and $\nu\mathsf{F}$ are respectively interpreted as a set of all finite structures and one of all possibly infinite structures. However, in the presence of relational converses, one can generate infinite structures if and only if one can consume them as well; therefore, $\mu\mathsf{F}$ and $\nu\mathsf{F}$ coincide.

The objective is to generate either $\mu\mathsf{F}$ or $\mu\mathsf{G}$. We use $\hat{h}$ to obtain $\mu\mathsf{F} \dagger \mu\mathsf{G}$, which can be transformed into $\mu\mathsf{F}$ and $\mu\mathsf{G}$ by merge_1 and merge_2, respectively. $\hat{h}$ potentially generates all possible divisions, namely, those from which each merge_i yields the final result. If $\hat{h}$ has two implementations, each of which consists of an anamorphisms after an additional computation, Theorem 13 guarantees that the independent substructures can be generated in parallel. To be precise, there exists a relation s that yields seeds from which all possible divisions can be calculated.

5.2.3 Example: *downfrom*

Here, we illustrate the use of Theorem 13 with a small example, an *downfrom* function defined as follows.

$$\mathit{downfrom}\ n = \textbf{if}\ n \equiv 0\ \textbf{then}\ [\,]\ \textbf{else}\ n : \mathit{downfrom}\ (n-1)$$

We can write *downfrom* by two anamorphisms, *unfoldl* and *unfoldr*.

$$\begin{aligned} &\mathit{downfrom} = \mathit{unfoldl}\ \psi_1 \circ \tau_1 = \mathit{unfoldr}\ \psi_2 \\ &\tau_1\ n = (n, 1) \\ &\psi_1\ (n,m) = \textbf{if}\ n < m\ \textbf{then}\ (1,())\ \textbf{else}\ (2,((n,m+1),m)) \\ &\psi_2\ (n,m) = \textbf{if}\ n \equiv 0\ \textbf{then}\ (1,())\ \textbf{else}\ (2,(n,n-1)) \end{aligned}$$

Now let $\hat{h} = (\mathbin{+\!\!\!+})^\circ \circ \mathit{downfrom}$; namely, $\hat{h}\ n$ generates (x, y) such that $x \mathbin{+\!\!\!+} y = \mathit{downfrom}\ n$. Recall that lists have two appropriate merging functions, both being essentially $(\mathbin{+\!\!\!+})$. Thus, from Theorem 13, we can find s such that $\hat{h} = (\mathit{unfoldl}\ \psi_1 \times \mathit{unfoldr}\ \psi_2) \circ s$, as follows. Note that $(\mathit{unfoldl}\ \psi_1)^{-1}\ [n, n-1, \ldots, m] = (n, m)$ and $(\mathit{unfoldr}\ \psi_2)^{-1}\ [n, n-1, \ldots, 1] = n$.

$$\begin{aligned} &\ \ ((n_1, m), n_2) \leftarrow s\ n \\ \Leftrightarrow&\ \ \{\text{ Theorem 13 }\} \\ &\ \ \exists(x,y) \leftarrow \hat{h}\ n.\ (\mathit{unfoldl}\ \psi_1)^{-1}\ x = (n_1, m)\ \wedge \\ &\qquad\qquad\qquad (\mathit{unfoldr}\ \psi_2)^{-1}\ y = n_2 \\ \Leftrightarrow&\ \ \{\text{ unfolding } \hat{h}\ \} \\ &\ \ \exists x, y.\ x \mathbin{+\!\!\!+} y = [n, n-1, \ldots, 1]\ \wedge \\ &\qquad (\mathit{unfoldl}\ \psi_1)^{-1}\ x = (n_1, m) \wedge (\mathit{unfoldr}\ \psi_2)^{-1}\ y = n_2 \\ \Leftrightarrow&\ \ \{\text{ unfolding } \mathbin{+\!\!\!+}\ \} \\ &\ \ \exists k.\ (\mathit{unfoldl}\ \psi_1)^{-1}\ [n, n-1, \ldots, k+1] = (n_1, m)\ \wedge \\ &\qquad (\mathit{unfoldr}\ \psi_2)^{-1}\ [k, k-1, \ldots, 1] = n_2 \\ \Leftrightarrow&\ \ \{\text{ unfolding } (\mathit{unfoldl}\ \psi_1)^{-1} \text{ and } (\mathit{unfoldr}\ \psi_2)^{-1}\ \} \\ &\ \ \exists k.\ (n, k+1) = (n_1, m) \wedge k = n_2 \end{aligned}$$

Consequently, we have proven that

$$\mathit{downfrom}\ n = \mathit{unfoldl}\ \psi_1\ (n, k+1) \mathbin{+\!\!\!+} \mathit{unfoldr}\ \psi_2\ k$$

for any $n \geq k \geq 0$. This equation expresses a divide-and-conquer implementation of *downfrom*, where the prefix and suffix are generated independently.

5.2.4 Difficulties of Parallelizing Anamorphisms

Theorem 13 is theoretically interesting, and it has a few applications such as those discussed by Mu and Morihata (2011). However, from the author's own experience, Theorem 13 is more difficult to use than Theorem 9.

First of all, Theorem 13 concerns relations. One may want to take a functional approach, namely, develop a function s' such that $\mathit{downfrom} = (\mathbin{+\!\!\!+}) \circ (\mathit{unfoldl}\ \psi_1 \times \mathit{unfoldr}\ \psi_2) \circ s'$. Unfortunately, this is not always satisfactory: $s' n = ((n, n), n-1)$ satisfies the requirement, and it yields $[n]$ and $[n-1, n-2, \ldots, 1]$ after applying $(\mathit{unfoldl}\ \psi_1 \times \mathit{unfoldr}\ \psi_2)$. Since the prefix part is always a singleton, it is like a variant of *unfoldr* rather than divide-and-conquer. Theorem 13 states, by using relations, that we could generate not particular but arbitrary prefix/suffix pairs.

Another problem is that it is usually more difficult to derive right inverses for anamorphisms. On one hand, right inverses of catamorphisms generate structures. This means that we are often able to find a non-recursive right inverse that yields a structure of a constant size, like *wrap*. This fact is also helpful for automatic parallelization (Morita et al. 2007). On the other hand, right inverses of anamorphisms consume structures, and therefore, they are essentially recursive functions. Needless to say, recursive functions are more difficult to reason about.

5.3 Hylomorphisms

Next, we consider hylomorphisms, which are compositions of catamorphisms and anamorphisms. Given an initial algebra $(\mu\mathsf{F}, in_\mathsf{F})$, a hylomorphism $\llbracket \phi, \psi \rrbracket_\mathsf{F}$ is defined by $\llbracket \phi, \psi \rrbracket_\mathsf{F} = (\!|\phi|\!)_\mathsf{F} \circ [\!(\psi)\!]_\mathsf{F}$. The composition makes sense because the initial F-algebra and the final F-coalgebra coincide in our setting.

Hylomorphisms are generalizations of catamorphisms and anamorphisms, $(\!|\phi|\!)_\mathsf{F} = \llbracket \phi, out_\mathsf{F} \rrbracket_\mathsf{F}$ and $[\!(\psi)\!]_\mathsf{F} = \llbracket in_\mathsf{F}, \psi \rrbracket_\mathsf{F}$. Moreover, hylomorphisms include functions that do not explicitly concern structures. Instead, they implicitly construct and consume structures in the form of recursion trees. For example, $prod\ n = \mathbf{if}\ n \equiv 1\ \mathbf{then}\ 1\ \mathbf{else}\ n * prod\ (n-1)$ is a hylomorphism, because $prod = foldr\ (*)\ 1 \circ downfrom$. The intermediate list corresponds to a series of arguments of recursive calls.

5.3.1 Parallelization Theorem for Hylomorphisms

Combining Theorems 9 and 13 yields a parallelization theorem for hylomorphisms.

Theorem 15. *Suppose the same situation as Theorems 9 and 13 about the initial algebras* $(\mu\mathsf{F}, in_\mathsf{F})$ *and* $(\mu\mathsf{G}, in_\mathsf{G})$, *functors* H_1 *and* H_2, *bifunctor* $\dagger$, *and functions* $merge_1 :: (\mu\mathsf{F} \dagger \mu\mathsf{G}) \to \mathsf{H}_1\mu\mathsf{F}$ *and* $merge_2 :: (\mu\mathsf{F} \dagger \mu\mathsf{G}) \to \mathsf{H}_2\mu\mathsf{G}$. *Assume that for* $\hat{h} :: C_1 \to C_2$ *there exist* $\tau_1 :: C_1 \to \mathsf{H}_1 A_1$, $\tau_2 :: C_1 \to \mathsf{H}_2 B_1$, $\psi_1 :: A_1 \to \mathsf{F}A_1$, $\psi_2 :: B_1 \to \mathsf{G}B_1$, $\phi_1 :: \mathsf{F}A_2 \to A_2$, $\phi_2 :: \mathsf{G}B_2 \to B_2$, $\epsilon_1 :: \mathsf{H}_1 A_2 \to C_2$, *and* $\epsilon_2 :: \mathsf{H}_2 B_2 \to C_2$ *such that we have the following conditions.*

- *$merge_1$ and $merge_2$ are surjective*
- $\hat{h} = \epsilon_1 \circ \mathsf{H}_1 \llbracket \phi_1, \psi_1 \rrbracket_\mathsf{F} \circ \tau_1 = \epsilon_2 \circ \mathsf{H}_2 \llbracket \phi_2, \psi_2 \rrbracket_\mathsf{G} \circ \tau_2$
- $merge_1^\circ \circ \mathsf{H}_1 [\!(\psi_1)\!]_\mathsf{F} \circ \tau_1 = merge_2^\circ \circ \mathsf{H}_2 [\!(\psi_2)\!]_\mathsf{G} \circ \tau_2$
- $\epsilon_1 \circ \mathsf{H}_1 (\!|\phi_1|\!)_\mathsf{F} \circ merge_1 = \epsilon_2 \circ \mathsf{H}_2 (\!|\phi_2|\!)_\mathsf{G} \circ merge_2$

Then, there exist $m :: (A_2 \dagger B_2) \to C_2$ *and* $s :: C_1 \to (A_1 \dagger B_1)$ *such that*

$$\hat{h} = m \circ (\llbracket \phi_1, \psi_1 \rrbracket_\mathsf{F} \dagger \llbracket \phi_2, \psi_2 \rrbracket_\mathsf{G}) \circ s.$$

Actually, $m = \epsilon_1 \circ \mathsf{H}_1 (\!|\phi_1|\!)_\mathsf{F} \circ merge_1 \circ ((\!|\phi_1|\!)_\mathsf{F}^{-1} \dagger (\!|\phi_2|\!)_\mathsf{G}^{-1})$ *and* $s = ([\!(\psi_1)\!]_\mathsf{F}^{-1} \dagger [\!(\psi_2)\!]_\mathsf{G}^{-1}) \circ merge_1^\circ \circ \mathsf{H}_1 [\!(\psi_1)\!]_\mathsf{F} \circ \tau_1$.

Proof.

$$\begin{aligned}
& \hat{h} = \epsilon_1 \circ \mathsf{H}_1 \llbracket \phi_1, \psi_1 \rrbracket_\mathsf{F} \circ \tau_1 = \epsilon_2 \circ \mathsf{H}_2 \llbracket \phi_2, \psi_2 \rrbracket_\mathsf{G} \circ \tau_2 \\
\Leftrightarrow\ & \{ \text{hylomorphisms and functors} \} \\
& \hat{h} = \epsilon_1 \circ \mathsf{H}_1 (\!|\phi_1|\!)_\mathsf{F} \circ \mathsf{H}_1 [\!(\psi_1)\!]_\mathsf{F} \circ \tau_1 \\
& \quad = \epsilon_2 \circ \mathsf{H}_2 (\!|\phi_2|\!)_\mathsf{G} \circ \mathsf{H}_2 [\!(\psi_2)\!]_\mathsf{G} \circ \tau_2 \\
\Leftrightarrow\ & \{ \text{for any surjective function } f,\ f \circ f^\circ = id \} \\
& \hat{h} = \epsilon_1 \circ \mathsf{H}_1 (\!|\phi_1|\!)_\mathsf{F} \circ merge_1 \circ merge_1^\circ \circ \mathsf{H}_1 [\!(\psi_1)\!]_\mathsf{F} \circ \tau_1 \\
& \quad = \epsilon_2 \circ \mathsf{H}_2 (\!|\phi_2|\!)_\mathsf{G} \circ merge_2 \circ merge_2^\circ \circ \mathsf{H}_2 [\!(\psi_2)\!]_\mathsf{G} \circ \tau_2 \\
\Rightarrow\ & \{ \text{Theorems 9 and 13} \} \\
& \exists m, s.\ \hat{h} = m \circ ((\!|\phi_1|\!)_\mathsf{F} \dagger (\!|\phi_2|\!)_\mathsf{G}) \circ ([\!(\psi_1)\!]_\mathsf{F} \dagger [\!(\psi_2)\!]_\mathsf{G}) \circ s \\
\Leftrightarrow\ & \{ \text{bifunctor and hylomorphisms} \} \\
& \exists m, s.\ \hat{h} = m \circ (\llbracket \phi_1, \psi_1 \rrbracket_\mathsf{F} \dagger \llbracket \phi_2, \psi_2 \rrbracket_\mathsf{G}) \circ s
\end{aligned}$$

□

In Theorem 15, we essentially parallelize the catamorphism part and anamorphism part independently, by using Theorems 9 and 13, and then reconstruct hylomorphisms. It is worth noting that the derived implementation does not need intermediate data structures between the catamorphisms and anamorphisms.

5.3.2 Example: Calculating Power Series

As an example, let us calculate $a_0 + a_1 x + \cdots a_n x^n$ for a given $[a_1, \ldots, a_n]$ and x.

$$\begin{aligned}
& power_series\ as\ x = ps\ (as, x, 0) \\
& \quad \mathbf{where}\ ps\ ([], _, _) \quad = 0 \\
& \qquad\qquad ps\ (a : as, x, k) = a * x^k + ps\ (as, x, k+1)
\end{aligned}$$

Although *power_series* is not a catamorphism, because of the additional parameters x and k, it is essentially a hylomorphism. Consider $ana = unfoldr\ \psi$ and $cata = foldr\ \phi$ where ψ and ϕ are defined as follows; then, $ps = cata \circ ana$.

$$\begin{aligned}
\psi\ ([], _, _) &= (1, ()) \\
\psi\ (a : as)\ x\ k &= (2, ((a, x, k), (as, x, k+1))) \\
\phi\ (1, ()) &= 0 \\
\phi\ (2, ((a, x, k), r)) &= a * x^k + r
\end{aligned}$$

In order to apply Theorem 15, we would like to implement *ana* and *cata* in terms of *unfoldl* and *foldl*. This is not difficult.

$$\begin{aligned}
& ana\ (as, x, k) = unfoldl\ \psi'\ (as, x, k + length\ as - 1) \\
& \psi'\ ([], _, _) \quad = (1, ()) \\
& \psi'\ (as +\!\!+ [a])\ x\ k = (2, ((as, x, k-1), (a, x, k))) \\
& cata = foldl\ \phi' \\
& \phi'\ (1, ()) \quad = 0 \\
& \phi'\ (2, (r, (a, x, k))) = r + a * x^k
\end{aligned}$$

Therefore, from Theorem 15, there exist m and s such that

$$ps = m \circ (\llbracket \phi', \psi' \rrbracket_{\mathsf{L_s}} \times \llbracket \phi, \psi \rrbracket_{\mathsf{L_c}}) \circ s.$$

In order to derive m and s, we need the right inverses of the catamorphisms and anamorphisms. These are not difficult to construct. Accordingly, s is derived from *ana*:

$$\begin{aligned}
& ((as_1, x_1, k_1), (as_2, x_2, k_2)), \leftarrow s\ ([a_0, \ldots, a_n], x, k) \\
\Leftrightarrow\ & \{ \text{Theorem 15 and the definition of } ana \} \\
& \exists r_1, r_2.\ r_1 +\!\!+ r_2 = [(a_0, x, k), \ldots, (a_n, x, k+n)] \wedge \\
& \qquad (as_1, x_1, k_1) = (unfoldl\ \psi')^{-1}\ r_1 \wedge \\
& \qquad (as_2, x_2, k_2) = (unfoldr\ \psi)^{-1}\ r_2 \\
\Leftrightarrow\ & \{ \text{unfolding } (unfoldl\ \psi')^{-1} \text{ and } (unfoldr\ \psi)^{-1} \} \\
& \exists k'.\ (as_1, x_1, k_1) = ([a_0, \ldots, a_{k'-1}], x, k + k' - 1) \wedge \\
& \qquad (as_2, x_2, k_2) = ([a_{k'}, \ldots, a_n], x, k + k')
\end{aligned}$$

and, m is derived from *cata*:

$$\begin{aligned}
& m\ (v_1, v_2) \\
=\ & \{ \text{Theorem 15} \} \\
& cata\ ((foldl\ \phi')^{-1}\ v_1 +\!\!+ (foldr\ \phi)^{-1}\ v_2) \\
=\ & \{ \text{unfolding } (foldl\ \phi')^{-1} \text{ and } (foldr\ \phi)^{-1} \} \\
& cata\ ([(v_1, _, 0)] +\!\!+ [(v_2, _, 0)]) \\
=\ & \{ \text{unfolding } +\!\!+ \text{ and } cata \} \\
& v_1 + v_2.
\end{aligned}$$

In summary, we have derived the following divide-and-conquer implementation, where k' is any integer of $1 \leq k' \leq n$.

$$\begin{aligned}
& ps\ ([a_0, \ldots, a_n], x, k) = \\
& \quad \llbracket \phi', \psi' \rrbracket_{\mathsf{L_s}}\ ([a_1, \ldots, a_{k'-1}], x, k + k' - 1) \\
& \quad + \llbracket \phi, \psi \rrbracket_{\mathsf{L_c}}\ ([a_{k'}, \ldots, a_n], x, k + k')
\end{aligned}$$

Theorem 15 is especially useful for dealing with functions, like *power_series*, that are not catamorphisms because of their having tiny additional computations such as distributing values. Parallelizing their anamorphism parts is usually not difficult; often they can be reduced to a few well-known patterns. Their parallelization can thus be achieved by parallelizing catamorphisms.

6. Limitations

6.1 Problems Unsuitable for Our Formalism

Although we have generalized the third list-homomorphism theorem, there are still several cases that do not fit our formalism.

For example, consider dividing a list into two sublists, each of which consists of even/odd-numbered elements. A typical application is the fast Fourier transformation. Here, we show a compact program by Misra (1994). We assume that lists x and y are of the same length, n, which is a power of two.

$$
\begin{aligned}
& \mathit{fft}\ (\mathit{interleave}\ x\ y) \\
& \quad = \mathbf{let}\ p = \mathit{fft}\ x \\
& \qquad\quad q = \mathit{fft}\ y \\
& \qquad\quad \omega_n = \exp(-\pi \mathrm{i}/n) \\
& \qquad \mathbf{in}\ \mathit{zipWith}\ (+)\ p\ (\mathit{zipWith}\ (*)\ [\omega_n^0, \omega_n^1, \ldots, \omega_n^{n-1}]\ q) +\!\!\!+ \\
& \qquad\qquad \mathit{zipWith}\ (-)\ p\ (\mathit{zipWith}\ (*)\ [\omega_n^0, \omega_n^1, \ldots, \omega_n^{n-1}]\ q)
\end{aligned}
$$

$$
\begin{aligned}
\mathit{interleave}\ ([\,], [\,]) &= [\,] \\
\mathit{interleave}\ (a : x, b : y) &= a : b : \mathit{interleave}\ (x, y)
\end{aligned}
$$

The problem is that it seems impossible to implement $\mathit{interleave}$ using a function of the required polymorphic type. We require that $\mathit{interleave}$ consumes one of the input and keeps the other as it is, but $\mathit{interleave}$ simultaneously consumes both inputs.

We face a similar problem in manipulating sorted lists. The merging operations for sorted lists are as follows.

$$
\begin{aligned}
\mathit{merge}\ ([\,], y) &= y \\
\mathit{merge}\ (x, [\,]) &= x \\
\mathit{merge}\ (a : x, b : y) &= \mathbf{if}\ a \leq b\ \mathbf{then}\ a : \mathit{merge}\ x\ (b : y) \\
&\qquad\qquad\quad \mathbf{else}\ b : \mathit{merge}\ (a : x)\ y
\end{aligned}
$$

Since merge simultaneously manipulates both lists, it seems impossible for it to have the required polymorphic type.

Another problem is that our theorems are not very useful for deriving specific subclasses of divide-and-conquer implementations. Recall that Theorem 1 derives programs of the form of $h\ (x +\!\!\!+ y) = h\ x \odot h\ y$. For the sake of efficiency, we may want h to have more specific implementations. For example, we may require $(\odot)$ to be $(+\!\!\!+)$, like *map* and *filter*. However, our theorems do not have enough flexibility to take account of such additional requirements.

6.2 Computational Complexities of Derived Implementations

The efficiency of the obtained divide-and-conquer programs is a very important consideration because, without it, there would be no reason to use parallel programs. However, our theorems state nothing about efficiency. Moreover, as mentioned in Section 4.1, they can *deal with* almost every function if we disregard efficiency. This fact may cast doubt on the usefulness of our theorems.

Actually, it is possible to have a discussion about computational costs—not about the time complexity but about the communication complexity. Recall Lemma 6. The lemma suggests that we can evaluate h_1 and h_2 independently, i.e., on different processors, and communicate their results. Therefore, the sizes of the ranges of h_1 and h_2 provide an estimate of how much information the divide-and-conquer implementation needs to communicate. More formally, if either h_1 or h_2 results in an $O(f(\mathrm{N}))$-bit output for any N-bit input, the communication complexity of $\hat{h}$ is $O(f(\mathrm{N}))$. For example, since sum is both *foldr* and *foldl*, there exists m such that $\mathit{sum} \circ (+\!\!\!+) = m \circ (\mathit{sum} \times \mathit{sum})$, and therefore, its communication complexity is $O(1)$ if we regard the sizes of integers as constant.

Low communication cost implementations are often fast. Therefore, the viewpoint of communication complexity would provide a strategy for developing efficient implementations. For example, in the case of Theorem 9, it is reasonable to melt away as much information as possible by using the catamorphism part and to let each ϵ_i be a tiny computation, such as a projection from a tuple.

However, this strategy is not always useful. In particular, it is useless for parallelizing isomorphisms. For example, consider calculating Fibonacci numbers.

$$
\begin{aligned}
& \mathit{fib}\ n = \mathbf{let}\ (a, b) = \mathit{fib}'\ n\ \mathbf{in}\ a \\
& \quad \mathbf{where}\ \mathit{fib}'\ 0 = (1, 0) \\
& \qquad\qquad \mathit{fib}'\ n = \mathbf{let}\ (a, b) = \mathit{fib}'\ (n-1)\ \mathbf{in}\ (a+b, a)
\end{aligned}
$$

fib' is a hylomorphism, and moreover, Theorem 15 is applicable. Hence, $\mathit{fib}'\ (n_1 + n_2) = \mathit{fib}'\ (\mathit{fib}'^{-1}\ (\mathit{fib}'\ n_1) + \mathit{fib}'^{-1}\ (\mathit{fib}'\ n_2))$. However, because fib' is injective[3], this is a kind of tautology and does not improve efficiency at all.

In fact, there is an efficient divide-and-conquer algorithm for calculating Fibonacci numbers. In the following, $(\cdot)$ denotes matrix multiplication.

$$
\begin{aligned}
& \mathit{fib}\ n = \mathbf{let}\ \begin{pmatrix} a & b \\ 0 & c \end{pmatrix} = \mathit{fib}''\ n\ \mathbf{in}\ a \\
& \mathbf{where}\ \mathit{fib}''\ 0 \qquad = \begin{pmatrix} 1 & 0 \\ 0 & 1 \end{pmatrix} \\
& \qquad\quad \mathit{fib}''\ 1 \qquad = \begin{pmatrix} 1 & 1 \\ 0 & 1 \end{pmatrix} \\
& \qquad\quad \mathit{fib}''\ (n_1 + n_2) = \mathit{fib}''\ n_1 \cdot \mathit{fib}''\ n_2
\end{aligned}
$$

The key is to retain rather redundant information, in the form of matrices, for efficiently merging the results of subcomputations. However, our theorems are not helpful for introducing such redundant information.

In summary, it seems reasonable to conclude that our theorems specify necessary, rather than sufficient, conditions for certain kinds of divide-and-conquer parallel evaluations. They are still unique and interesting, because most of the existing parallelization methods discuss only sufficient conditions.

7. Discussion

We have studied a theory for developing parallelization theorems in the form of "two iterative implementations lead to a parallel implementation". The key is a new proof of the third list-homomorphism theorem based on shortcut deforestation. The proof can be easily generalized to catamorphisms. We found that similar results hold for anamorphisms and moreover hylomorphisms. These results may help to usher in a new paradigm for parallel functional programming.

7.1 Generalizations of the Third List-homomorphism Theorem

There have been several studies on generalizing the third list-homomorphism theorem.

Morihata et al. (2009) generalized the third list-homomorphism theorem to deal with manipulations of algebraic data structures. Their idea is to use zipper structures for reducing operations of algebraic data structures to those of lists and thereby to exploit parallelization methods for list operations. Our theorems generalize theirs. We showed that reductions to lists are not essential; moreover, our theorems can deal with other structures besides algebraic data structures.

Mu and Morihata (2011) pointed out that the proof of the third list-homomorphism theorem has an interesting structure that leads to the dualization and generalization of the theorem. The proof structure they focused on is essentially Lemma 12. Our theory is built upon their approach. We have shown that this proof structure

[3] *fib* is not injective because $\mathit{fib}\ 0 = \mathit{fib}\ 1 = 1$.

alone is insufficient for obtaining useful theorems like the third list-homomorphism theorem and demonstrated that shortcut deforestation can be an aid.

Gibbons et al. (2001) showed necessary and sufficient conditions for functions being catamorphisms or anamorphisms. A function h characterized by $h\ (x +\!\!+\ y) = h\ x \odot h\ y$ is a catamorphism on yet another list structure, called *join lists*, in which lists are constructed by $+\!\!+$. Therefore, their theory provides a necessary and sufficient condition for functions being such divide-and-conquer list operations. However, the necessary and sufficient condition is similar to the premise of Lemma 6, and thus, not as useful as the third list-homomorphism theorem. It is also worth noting that our theorems are not restricted to deriving catamorphisms/anamorphisms. For instance, the divide-and-conquer $downfrom$ is not an anamorphism.

7.2 Parallelization of Recursive Functions

The third list-homomorphism theorem have been used as a basis of parallelization (Gibbons 1996a,b; Gorlatch 1999; Geser and Gorlatch 1999; Morita et al. 2007; Liu et al. 2011; Chi and Mu 2011). The study by Morita et al. (2007) is the most related to ours, because like ours, it relies on the derivation of right inverses. They built an automatic parallelization system on a method of automatically finding right inverses. The system could be used to automate parallelizations based on Theorem 9; moreover, it would also be useful when applying Theorem 15 to functions whose anamorphism parts are easy to deal with. However, it cannot derive right inverses that contain recursions, and hence, cannot automate parallelizations based on Theorem 13.

There are other methods of deriving parallel implementations from sequential recursive functions, such as (Hu et al. 1997; Chin et al. 1998; Hu et al. 1998; Keller and Chakravarty 1998; Xu et al. 2004; Matsuzaki et al. 2006; Morihata and Matsuzaki 2010). While they only deal with functions that operate on linear structures (Hu et al. 1997; Chin et al. 1998; Hu et al. 1998; Xu et al. 2004) or trees (Keller and Chakravarty 1998; Matsuzaki et al. 2006; Morihata and Matsuzaki 2010), any initial algebra is in the domain of our theory. Moreover, while most of the existing methods only consider functions that consume structures, ours can deal with anamorphisms and hylomorphisms as well. Thus, one can argue that ours is one of the most generic theories, whereas each of others has its own strong point, such as suitability for automation and efficiency of the resulting parallel programs.

7.3 Connections to Shortcut Deforestation

Our methods rely on shortcut deforestation (Gill et al. 1993; Gill 1996; Takano and Meijer 1995; Johann 2002) and its basis, parametricity (Reynolds 1983; Wadler 1989). We viewed Theorem 5 as follows: the polymorphic type guarantees that the structure α in the argument $\mathsf{G}\alpha$ is to be used as is, according to the parameter passed to gen; therefore, we need to process that part in advance, possibly in parallel with other computations. Similar observations have been appeared in the literature on deforestation of monadic programs (Ghani and Johann 2007) and accumulative programs (Katsumata and Nishimura 2008). This is not surprising. For example, for deforesting accumulative programs, we can consume structures constructed in accumulative parameters before they actually form a part of the output. This means that, like parallelization, deforestation of accumulative programs require the order of computations to be changed. Further studies on connections between deforestation and parallelizations may lead to more interesting insights.

We used parametricity rather than shortcut deforestation to prove the theorem about anamorphisms, namely Theorem 13. One might think that it is more natural to use the dual of the shortcut deforestation, often called the unfoldr-destroy rule (Takano and Meijer 1995; Svenningsson 2002). We did not take this approach for two reasons. First, as mentioned in Section 5.2.4, it is essential to formalize the theorem by using relations, and therefore, function-based approaches are not suitable for our purpose. Secondly, in order to use the unfoldr-destroy rules, we should implement $merge$ by using a function of yet another polymorphic type. This, however, makes the generalization to hylomorphisms (Theorem 15) less elegant.

We required that the merging operations be implemented by functions of certain polymorphic types. There have been a few studies (Launchbury and Sheard 1995; Chitil 1999; Yokoyama et al. 2005) on automatically deriving such polymorphic implementations. They would enable us to automatically obtain parallelization theorems even for user-defined data structures.

Acknowledgments

The author is grateful to Shin-Cheng Mu and Zhenjiang Hu. My discussion with them were helpful in the preliminary developments. The author is also grateful to anonymous reviewers for pointing out a flaw of Corollary 11 and giving comments useful to improve presentations. The author is supported by a JSPS Grant-in-Aid for Young Scientists (B) 24700019.

References

R. S. Bird and S. A. Curtis. Functional pearls: Finding celebrities: A lesson in functional programming. *J. Funct. Program.*, 16(1):13–20, 2006.

R. S. Bird and O. de Moor. *Algebra of Programming*. Prentice Hall, 1997.

Y.-Y. Chi and S.-C. Mu. Constructing list homomorphisms from proofs. In *Programming Languages and Systems - 9th Asian Symposium, APLAS 2011, Proceedings*, volume 7078 of *Lecture Notes in Computer Science*, pages 74–88. Springer, 2011.

W.-N. Chin, A. Takano, and Z. Hu. Parallelization via context preservation. In *Proceedings of the 1998 International Conference on Computer Languages, ICCL '98*, pages 153–162. IEEE, 1998.

O. Chitil. Type inference builds a short cut to deforestation. In *Proceedings of the 4th ACM SIGPLAN International Conference on Functional Programming, ICFP'99*, pages 249–260. ACM, 1999

M. M. Fokkinga. Tupling and mutumorphisms. *Squiggolist*, 1(4), 1989.

A. Geser and S. Gorlatch. Parallelizing functional programs by generalization. *J. Funct. Program.*, 9(6):649–673, 1999.

N. Ghani and P. Johann. Monadic augment and generalised short cut fusion. *J. Funct. Program.*, 17(6):731–776, 2007.

J. Gibbons. The third homomorphism theorem. *J. Funct. Program.*, 6(4): 657–665, 1996.

J. Gibbons, Computing downwards accumulations on trees quickly. *Theor. Comput. Sci.*, 169(1):67–80, 1996.

J. Gibbons, G. Hutton, and T. Altenkirch. When is a function a fold or an unfold? *Electr. Notes Theor. Comput. Sci.*, 44(1):146–160, 2001.

A. Gill. *Cheap Deforestation for Non-strict Functional Languages*. PhD thesis, Department of Computing Science, Glasgow University, 1996.

A. Gill, J. Launchbury, and S. Peyton Jones. A short cut to deforestation. In *FPCA'93 Conference on Functional Programming Languages and Computer Architecture*, pages 223–232. ACM, 1993.

S. Gorlatch. Extracting and implementing list homomorphisms in parallel program development. *Sci. Comput. Program.*, 33(1):1–27, 1999.

R. Hinze. Adjoint folds and unfolds—an extended study. *Sci. Comput. Program.*, 2013. In Press.

Z. Hu, H. Iwasaki, and M. Takechi. Formal derivation of efficient parallel programs by construction of list homomorphisms. ACM Trans. Program. Lang. Syst., 3(19):444–461, 1997.

Z. Hu, M. Takeichi, and W.-N. Chin. Parallelization in calculational forms. In *POPL '98: Proceedings of the 25th ACM SIGPLAN-SIGACT Symposium on Principles of Programming Languages*, pages 316–328. ACM, 1998.

G. P. Huet. The zipper. *J. Funct. Program.*, 7(5):549–554, 1997.

P. Johann. A generalization of short-cut fusion and its correctness proof. *Higher-Order and Symbolic Computation*, 15(4):273–300, 2002.

S. Katsumata and S. Nishimura. Algebraic fusion of functions with an accumulating parameter and its improvement. *J. Funct. Program.*, 18 (5-6):781–819, 2008.

G. Keller and M. M. T. Chakravarty. Flattening trees. *Euro-Par '98 Parallel Processing, 4th International Euro-Par Conference, Proceedings*, volume 1470 of *Lecture Notes in Computer Science*, pages 709–719. Springer, 1998.

J. Launchbury and T. Sheard. Warm fusion: Deriving build-catas from recursive definitions. In *Conference Record of FPCA'95 SIGPLAN-SIGARCH-WG2.8 Conference on Functional Programming Languages and Computer Architecture*, pages 314–323. ACM, 1995.

Y. Liu, Z. Hu, and K. Matsuzaki. Towards systematic parallel programming over MapReduce. In *Parallel Processing - 17th International Conference, Euro-Par 2011, Proceedings, Part II*, volume 6853 of *Lecture Notes in Computer Science*, pages 39–50. Springer, 2011.

G. Malcolm. Data structures and program transformation. *Sci. Comput. Program.*, 14(2-3):255–279, 1990.

K. Matsuzaki, Z. Hu, and M. Takeichi. Towards automatic parallelization of tree reductions in dynamic programming. In *SPAA 2006: Proceedings of the 18th Annual ACM Symposium on Parallel Algorithms and Architectures*, pages 39–48. ACM, 2006.

E. Meijer, M. M. Fokkinga, and R. Paterson. Functional programming with bananas, lenses, envelopes and barbed wire. In *Functional Programming Languages and Computer Architecture, 5th ACM Conference, Proceedings*, volume 523 of *Lecture Notes in Computer Science*, pages 124–144. Springer, 1991.

J. Misra. Powerlist: A structure for parallel recursion. *ACM Trans. Program. Lang. Syst.*, 16(6):1737–1767, 1994.

A. Morihata and K. Matsuzaki. Automatic parallelization of recursive functions using quantifier elimination. In *Functional and Logic Programming, 10th International Symposium, FLOPS 2010, Proceedings*, volume 6009 of *Lecture Notes in Computer Science*, pages 321–336. Springer, 2010.

A. Morihata, K. Matsuzaki, Z. Hu, and M. Takeichi. The third homomorphism theorem on trees: Downward & upward lead to divide-and-conquer. In *Proceedings of the 36th ACM SIGPLAN-SIGACT Symposium on Principles of Programming Languages, POPL 2009*, pages 177–185. ACM, 2009.

K. Morita, A. Morihata, K. Matsuzaki, Z. Hu, and M. Takeichi. Automatic inversion generates divide-and-conquer parallel programs. In *Proceedings of the ACM SIGPLAN 2007 Conference on Programming Language Design and Implementation*, pages 146–155. ACM, 2007.

S.-C. Mu and A. Morihata. Generalising and dualising the third list-homomorphism theorem: functional pearl. In *Proceeding of the 16th ACM SIGPLAN International Conference on Functional Programming, ICFP 2011*, pages 385–391. ACM, 2011.

J. H. Reif, editor. *Synthesis of Parallel Algorithms*. Morgan Kaufmann Publishers, 1993.

J. C. Reynolds. Types, abstraction and parametric polymorphism. *Information Processing*, 83:513–523, 1983.

J. Svenningsson. Shortcut fusion for accumulating parameters & zip-like functions. In *Proceedings of the 7th ACM SIGPLAN International Conference on Functional programming, ICFP'02*, pages 124–132. ACM, 2002.

A. Takano and E. Meijer. Shortcut deforestation in calculational form. In *Conference Record of FPCA'95 SIGPLAN-SIGARCH-WG2.8 Conference on Functional Programming Languages and Computer Architecture*, pages 306–313. ACM, 1995.

P. Wadler. Deforestation: Transforming programs to eliminate trees. In *ESOP'88, 2nd European Symposium on Programming, Proceedings*, volume 300 of *Lecture Notes in Computer Science*, pages 344–358. Springer, 1988.

P. Wadler. Theorems for free! In *FPCA'89 Conference on Functional Programming Languages and Computer Architecture*, pages 347–359. ACM, 1989.

D. N. Xu, S.-C. Khoo, and Z. Hu. PType system: A featherweight parallelizability detector. In *Programming Languages and Systems: Second Asian Symposium, APLAS 2004, Proceedings*, volume 3302 of *Lecture Notes in Computer Science*, pages 197–212. Springer, 2004.

T. Yokoyama, Z. Hu, and M. Takeichi. Calculation rules for warming-up in fusion transformation. In *On-line Pre-Review Processings of the Sixth Symposium on Trends in Functional Programming, TFP 2005*, pages 399–412, 2005.

Appendix: Proof of Lemma 14

We prove the following equation.

$$\mathsf{G}[\!(\psi)\!]_{\mathsf{F}}^{\circ} \circ g\ in_{\mathsf{F}} = \mathsf{G}[\!(\psi)\!]_{\mathsf{F}}^{\circ} \circ g\ in_{\mathsf{F}} \circ ([\!(\psi)\!]_{\mathsf{F}} \dagger id) \circ ([\!(\psi)\!]_{\mathsf{F}}^{\circ} \dagger id) \quad (16)$$

Since $\dagger$ is a bifunctor (i.e., a *birelator*), Lemma 14 follows from its converse, where $R = (\mathsf{G}[\!(\psi)\!]_{\mathsf{F}}^{\circ} \circ g\ in_{\mathsf{F}} \circ ([\!(\psi)\!]_{\mathsf{F}} \dagger id))^{\circ}$.

For the relations R and S, $R \subseteq S$ is defined by set-theoretic inclusion. Note that $R \subseteq S$ implies $P \circ R \circ Q \subseteq P \circ S \circ Q$. We can prove Equation (16) by showing both directions of inclusions. We first prove $\supseteq$ as follows.

$$\begin{array}{cl}
& \mathsf{G}[\!(\psi)\!]_{\mathsf{F}}^{\circ} \circ g\ in_{\mathsf{F}} \circ ([\!(\psi)\!]_{\mathsf{F}} \dagger id) \circ ([\!(\psi)\!]_{\mathsf{F}}^{\circ} \dagger id) \\
= & \{\ \dagger \text{ is a bifunctor }\} \\
& \mathsf{G}[\!(\psi)\!]_{\mathsf{F}}^{\circ} \circ g\ in_{\mathsf{F}} \circ ([\!(\psi)\!]_{\mathsf{F}} \circ [\!(\psi)\!]_{\mathsf{F}}^{\circ} \dagger id) \\
\subseteq & \{\ \text{Since } [\!(\psi)\!]_{\mathsf{F}} \text{ is a function, } [\!(\psi)\!]_{\mathsf{F}} \circ [\!(\psi)\!]_{\mathsf{F}}^{\circ} \subseteq id\ \} \\
& \mathsf{G}[\!(\psi)\!]_{\mathsf{F}}^{\circ} \circ g\ in_{\mathsf{F}} \circ (id \dagger id) \\
= & \{\ \dagger \text{ is a bifunctor }\} \\
& \mathsf{G}[\!(\psi)\!]_{\mathsf{F}}^{\circ} \circ g\ in_{\mathsf{F}}
\end{array}$$

The other direction can be proved by using relational parametricity.

$$\begin{array}{cl}
& \mathsf{G}[\!(\psi)\!]_{\mathsf{F}}^{\circ} \circ g\ in_{\mathsf{F}} \subseteq \mathsf{G}[\!(\psi)\!]_{\mathsf{F}}^{\circ} \circ g\ in_{\mathsf{F}} \circ ([\!(\psi)\!]_{\mathsf{F}} \dagger id) \circ ([\!(\psi)\!]_{\mathsf{F}}^{\circ} \dagger id) \\
\Leftrightarrow & \{\ f \circ R \subseteq S \iff R \subseteq f^{\circ} \circ S \text{ for any function } f\ \} \\
& \mathsf{G}[\!(\psi)\!]_{\mathsf{F}} \circ \mathsf{G}[\!(\psi)\!]_{\mathsf{F}}^{\circ} \circ g\ in_{\mathsf{F}} \subseteq g\ in_{\mathsf{F}} \circ ([\!(\psi)\!]_{\mathsf{F}} \dagger id) \circ ([\!(\psi)\!]_{\mathsf{F}}^{\circ} \dagger id) \\
\Leftrightarrow & \{\ \mathsf{G} \text{ is a functor and } \dagger \text{ is a bifunctor }\} \\
& \mathsf{G}([\!(\psi)\!]_{\mathsf{F}} \circ [\!(\psi)\!]_{\mathsf{F}}^{\circ}) \circ g\ in_{\mathsf{F}} \subseteq g\ in_{\mathsf{F}} \circ ([\!(\psi)\!]_{\mathsf{F}} \circ [\!(\psi)\!]_{\mathsf{F}}^{\circ} \dagger id) \\
\Leftarrow & \{\ \text{relational parametricity; note that } \mathsf{F} \text{ is a functor }\} \\
& [\!(\psi)\!]_{\mathsf{F}} \circ [\!(\psi)\!]_{\mathsf{F}}^{\circ} \circ in_{\mathsf{F}} \subseteq in_{\mathsf{F}} \circ \mathsf{F}[\!(\psi)\!]_{\mathsf{F}} \circ \mathsf{F}[\!(\psi)\!]_{\mathsf{F}}^{\circ} \\
\Leftrightarrow & \{\ in_{\mathsf{F}} \text{ is an isomorphism, and } in_{\mathsf{F}}^{\circ} = out_{\mathsf{F}}\ \} \\
& out_{\mathsf{F}} \circ [\!(\psi)\!]_{\mathsf{F}} \circ [\!(\psi)\!]_{\mathsf{F}}^{\circ} \circ out_{\mathsf{F}}^{\circ} \subseteq \mathsf{F}[\!(\psi)\!]_{\mathsf{F}} \circ \mathsf{F}[\!(\psi)\!]_{\mathsf{F}}^{\circ} \\
\Leftrightarrow & \{\ \text{universal property of anamorphisms }\} \\
& \mathsf{F}[\!(\psi)\!]_{\mathsf{F}} \circ \psi \circ \psi^{\circ} \circ \mathsf{F}[\!(\psi)\!]_{\mathsf{F}}^{\circ} \subseteq \mathsf{F}[\!(\psi)\!]_{\mathsf{F}} \circ \mathsf{F}[\!(\psi)\!]_{\mathsf{F}}^{\circ} \\
\Leftarrow & \{\ \text{since } \psi \text{ is a function, } \psi \circ \psi^{\circ} \subseteq id\ \} \\
& \mathit{True}
\end{array}$$

□

Using Circular Programs for Higher-Order Syntax

Functional pearl

Emil Axelsson Koen Claessen

Chalmers University of Technology

{emax,koen}@chalmers.se

Abstract

This pearl presents a novel technique for constructing a first-order syntax tree directly from a higher-order interface. We exploit circular programming to generate names for new variables, resulting in a simple yet efficient method. Our motivating application is the design of embedded languages supporting variable binding, where it is convenient to use higher-order syntax when constructing programs, but first-order syntax when processing or transforming programs.

Categories and Subject Descriptors D.3.1 [*Formal Definitions and Theory*]: Syntax; D.3.2 [*Language Classifications*]: Applicative (functional) languages

Keywords higher-order syntax; embedded languages; circular programming

1. Introduction

Imagine a simple Haskell data type for expressions of the lambda calculus:

```
data Exp = Var Name       -- Variable
         | Lam Name Exp   -- Abstraction
         | App Exp Exp    -- Application
         deriving (Show)
```

The `Var` and `Lam` constructors use explicit names to refer to variables, where names belong to the abstract type `Name`. When constructing expressions in this representation, we have to keep track of the scope of bound variables. As an example, the term $\lambda x.(\lambda y.y)(\lambda z.z)x$ – a verbose definition of the identity function – can be represented as follows (assuming an integer representation of names):

```
identity_FO :: Exp
identity_FO = Lam 1
  (App (App (Lam 2 (Var 2)) (Lam 3 (Var 3)))
       (Var 1)
  )
```

Because it is so easy to mix up variable names, it is common to instead use *higher-order syntax* (HOS) in embedded languages. A HOS interface for the lambda calculus is given in Fig. 1. HOS allows us to write the above example in a much more convenient form:

```
app :: Exp → Exp → Exp
lam :: (Exp → Exp) → Exp
```

Figure 1: Higher-order interface for the lambda calculus

```
identity :: Exp
identity = lam (λx →
    app (app (lam (λy → y)) (lam (λz → z)))
        x
  )
```

By using binding in the host language to represent binding in the object language, it is impossible to refer to unbound variables. Note that the HOS interface does not include a constructor for variables. Those are implicitly introduced by `lam`.

How can we implement the interface in Fig. 1 without changing the original `Exp` data type? That is the question that this pearl will answer. As we shall see in Sec. 4, this problem is highly relevant to the implementation of embedded languages.

First attempt. The difficulty is in implementing `lam`. A first attempt may lead to the following code:

```
lam f = Lam n (f (Var n))
  where
    n = ???
```

Now, the problem is to choose a name `n` that does not interfere with other names in the expression. The name must be

ICFP '13, September 25–27, 2013, Boston, MA, USA.

ACM 978-1-4503-2326-0/13/09... $15.00.
http://dx.doi.org/10.1145/2500365.2500614

```
bot   :: Name
prime :: Name → Name

-- prime law:
∀ a . prime a > a

-- Maximum:
(⊔) :: Name → Name → Name
m ⊔ n | m ≥ n = m
      | n > m = n
```

Figure 2: Creation and manipulation of names

chosen so that (1) the binding does not accidentally capture free variables in the body, and (2) uses of the new variable are not captured by other bindings in the body.

Abstract representation of names. In order to allow freedom in the representation of names, we will use the operations in Fig. 2 to create, manipulate and reason about names. A name can be any totally ordered type implementing the given interface. The law for `prime` states that this function always increases the order of a name. Since no operation decreases the order of a name, we can argue that `bot` is the smallest name, as long as we only create names using the given interface.

For the examples in this pearl, we will use the following implementation of names:

```
type Name = Integer
bot       = 0
prime     = succ
```

Note also that `(⊔)` is equivalent to the `max` function.

2. Alternatives

This section gives two alternative implementations of the HOS interface. These provide sufficient background to develop our new method in Sec. 3. Some additional alternatives are mentioned in the related work (Sec. 4).

2.1 Threading a name supply

As a reference, let us first consider a non-solution – one that does involve changing the `Exp` type. The idea is to prevent capturing by using a unique name in each binding. This can be done by threading a name supply through the `lam` and `app` functions, which requires us to change `Exp` to a state-passing function:[1]

```
type ExpNS = Name → (Exp, Name)
```

[1] We will use subscripts as a way to distinguish different implementations of similar functions and types throughout the paper.

```
fromExpNS :: ExpNS → Exp
fromExpNS e = fst (e (prime bot))
```

The implementation of application will just thread the state, first through the function and then through the argument. Abstraction is a bit more involved.

```
appNS :: ExpNS → ExpNS → ExpNS
appNS f a = λn →
    let (f',o) = f n
        (a',p) = a o
    in  (App f' a', p)

lamNS :: (ExpNS → ExpNS) → ExpNS
lamNS f = λn →
    let var   = λo → (Var n, o)
        (a,p) = f var (prime n)
    in  (Lam n a, p)
```

The incoming name `n` is used for the new variable. The variable expression `var` just passes its name supply through unchanged. The body `(f var)` is given `(prime n)` as the incoming name, which ensures that all its bindings will use names that are different from `n`.

An example shows how the names are chosen:

```
*Main> fromExpNS identityNS
Lam 1 (App (App (Lam 2 (Var 2)) (Lam 3 (Var 3)))
(Var 1))
```

The expression $\texttt{identity}_{NS}$ is defined as `identity` but with $_{NS}$ subscripts on `app` and `lam`. We will use the same convention for $\texttt{identity}_{SPEC}$ below.

The name supply method does not solve the original problem, as it uses a different representation of expressions. Also, the tedious state threading in $\texttt{app}_{NS}$ and $\texttt{lam}_{NS}$ leaves a bad taste in the mouth. On the more practical side, the fact that $\texttt{Exp}_{NS}$ is a function leads to some additional problems:

- It is not directly possible to pattern match on expressions. Pattern matching is commonly used to define smart constructors that simplify expressions on the fly [6].
- It is not possible to observe any implicit sharing [5, 7] in the expression. After all, a shared sub-expression can appear in many contexts with different name supplies.

For all these reasons, we leave $\texttt{Exp}_{NS}$ behind and look for a better alternative.

2.2 Speculative naming

Recall, the problem is to implement `lam` without changing the `Exp` type, which means that there will not be any name supply available. Let us thus return to our original attempt at defining `lam`:

```
lam f = Lam n (f (Var n)) where n = ???
```

We have no name supply, yet we need to pick a name that does not interfere with the body of the expression. One way to solve this puzzle is to speculatively evaluate the function `f` to find out which names are used in the body, then pick a different name for the variable, and apply `f` again:

```
lamSPEC :: (Exp → Exp) → Exp
lamSPEC f = Lam n' (f (Var n'))
  where
    ph = Var bot      -- Placeholder
    n  = maxV (f ph) -- Speculation
    n' = prime n
```

The placeholder `ph` used in the first application of `f` uses the smallest name `bot`, which is assumed only to be used for speculative evaluation, not for bound variables. The $\mathtt{max_V}$ function simply traverses the body to find the greatest occurring variable name:

```
maxV :: Exp → Name
maxV (Var n)   = n
maxV (App f a) = maxV f ⊔ maxV a
maxV (Lam _ a) = maxV a
```

Selecting `n' = prime n` ensures absence of capturing: there could be other variables of that name in scope, but they are anyway not used in the body.

Since we are now constructing the `Exp` type directly, the $\mathtt{app_{SPEC}}$ constructor is identical to `App`:

```
appSPEC = App
```

Our running example shows how the names are chosen:

```
*Main> identitySPEC
Lam 2 (App (App (Lam 1 (Var 1)) (Lam 1 (Var 1)))
(Var 2))
```

So, the method works, but can you spot the problems with the implementation of $\mathtt{lam_{SPEC}}$?

One problem is that $\mathtt{max_V}$ has to traverse the whole body, leading to quadratic complexity in expressions with nested lambdas. However, there is a much more severe problem: The function `f` is applied twice in each lambda, which means that an expression with n nested lambdas requires 2^n applications!

Deeply nested lambdas are not uncommon in embedded languages where variable binding is used to represent shared sub-expressions (as, for example, in reference [6]). Thus, the exponential complexity renders the above method unusable in practice.

3. Our method: circular speculation

The speculative application in the previous method is used to resolve the circular dependency arising from the fact that we need to examine the body before constructing it. In a classic paper, Richard Bird poses the Repmin problem that has a similar circular dependency [2]. The Repmin problem is to define a function that converts a tree into a tree of identical shape, but where all leaves have been replaced by the minimal leaf in the original tree. A naive solution would traverse the tree twice – once to find the minimal leaf, and once to construct the new tree. Bird's solution uses circular programming to collapse the two traversals into one.

For the Repmin problem, circular programming reduces two traversals into one more complicated traversal, which makes it unclear if the approach saves any computation at all. However, in case of nested traversals, cutting the number of recursive calls in each step can reduce the complexity class!

Can we use circular programming to avoid the exponential blowup in $\mathtt{lam_{SPEC}}$? Let us try:

```
lamCIRC :: (Exp → Exp) → Exp
lamCIRC f = Lam n' body
  where
    body = f (Var n')
    n    = maxV body
    n'   = prime n
```

This version avoids the separate speculation by using the correct name right away. Although this function type checks, unfortunately it does not work.

Why?

The problem is that $\mathtt{max_V}$ can no longer distinguish the new variable from other variables in the body. Thus, $\mathtt{max_V}$ returns a name that is at least as high as `n'`, giving $\mathtt{n} \geq \mathtt{n'}$. At the same time, we have `n' = prime n` which gives us $\mathtt{n'} > \mathtt{n}$. This contradiction manifests itself as an infinite loop in $\mathtt{lam_{CIRC}}$.

3.1 A different perspective

The simple speculative method involved finding a name that is not used in the body of a binding. As previously said, this ensures absence of capturing. However, another way to avoid capturing is to only look at the variables that are bound in the body, and pick a name that is not bound. Then there is still a risk of capturing a free variable, but as long as all bindings and variables are created using the same method, this will never happen (see Sec. 3.2).

The function that finds the greatest bound variable is a slight variation of $\mathtt{max_V}$:

```
maxBV :: Exp → Name
maxBV (Var _)   = bot
maxBV (App f a) = maxBV f ⊔ maxBV a
maxBV (Lam n a) = n ⊔ maxBV a
```

```
app :: Exp → Exp → Exp
app = App

lam :: (Exp → Exp) → Exp
lam f = Lam n body
  where
    body = f (Var n)
    n    = prime (maxBV body)
```

Figure 3: Implementation of the higher order interface using circular programming

Fig. 3 gives a complete definition of the HOS interface using circular programming. The trick is that since $\mathtt{max}_{\mathtt{BV}}$ does not look at `Var` constructors, it can produce a value without forcing evaluation of the new variable. Thus, the infinite loop is broken.

For the `identity` example (but not in general), our method chooses the same names as the simple speculative method:

```
*Main> identity
Lam 2 (App (App (Lam 1 (Var 1)) (Lam 1 (Var 1)))
(Var 2))
```

3.2 The law of the jungle: to capture or to be captured

When choosing a name for a new binding, there are two problems we want to avoid: (1) the binding captures a free variable in the body, and (2) uses of the new variable are captured by other bindings in the body. For closed terms, capturing can only happen when a binder shadows a variable in scope. Thus, to check for absence of capturing, it is enough to check for absence of shadowing:

```
safe :: Exp → Bool
safe (Var _)   = True
safe (App f a) = safe f && safe a
safe (Lam n a) = n > maxBV a && safe a
```

The above function checks that no binding is shadowed by another binding in its body. The requirement that each binding introduces a variable that is greater than all bound variables in the body is overly conservative (it is enough that the new variable is distinct from the bound variables in the body), but suffices for our purposes. Note that by assuming closed terms and only considering shadowing, we can reason about capture-avoidance purely in terms of binders, ignoring any uses of the variables. We trust that our HOS implementation only produces closed expressions.

We will argue for the correctness of our method by showing that any term constructed using the HOS interface – `app` and `lam` – is safe. To simplify reasoning, we only consider Haskell terms t built using direct application of those functions and variables.

Definition 1. A HOS term is defined by the following grammar:

$$t \;::=\; v \;\mid\; \mathtt{app}\ t\ t \;\mid\; \mathtt{lam}\ (\lambda v\ .\ t)$$

Definition 2. We use $c \vdash t \Downarrow e$ to denote evaluation of the term t to value e (of type `Exp`) in context c. A context is a mapping from Haskell variables to expressions of type `Exp`. We omit the definition of evaluation from the paper.

Definition 3. We extend the notion of safety to contexts: $\mathtt{safe}_{\mathtt{CXT}}\ c$ holds if all variables in c map to safe expressions.

Theorem 1. Evaluation of a term t in a safe context c results in a safe expression:

$$\forall\, c\ t\ e\ .\ \ \mathtt{safe}_{\mathtt{CXT}}\ c\ \ \&\ \ c \vdash t \Downarrow e \ \ \Rightarrow\ \ \mathtt{safe}\ e$$

The proof is by induction on terms. The base case, for variables, is proved by noting that looking up a variable in a safe context must result in a safe expression. The case for `app` is shown by a straightforward use of the induction hypothesis. For `lam`, we see in Fig. 3 that it evaluates to `Lam n body`. This expression is safe if `n` is greater than all bound variables in the body and the body is safe. The first requirement is trivially fulfilled by the definition of `lam`. To show that `body` is safe, we expand it to `f (Var n)`, where `f` is equal to $\lambda v\ .\ t$ for some variable v and term t. Thus, the evaluation of the body in context c must be equal to the evaluation of t in context $(v \mapsto \mathtt{Var\ n} : c)$. Assuming that c is safe, this extended context is also safe; hence the induction hypothesis implies that the result of evaluating the body is safe. □

3.3 Achieving linear complexity

So far, we have prevented the exponential complexity in the simple speculative solution by only computing the body once in `lam`. However, since `lam` has to traverse the whole body to find the greatest bound variable, we still have quadratic complexity in the number of nested lambdas. Fortunately, the reasoning in Sec. 3.2 shows us that `lam` actually traverses most of the body in vain!

The `safe` property states that each binding introduces a variable that is greater than all bound variables in the body. This means that we can make an improved version of $\mathtt{max}_{\mathtt{BV}}$ that only looks at the closest binders:

```
maxBV+ :: Exp → Name
maxBV+ (Var _)   = bot
maxBV+ (App f a) = maxBV+ f ⊔ maxBV+ a
maxBV+ (Lam n _) = n
```

Lemma 1. For safe expressions, $\mathtt{max}_{\mathtt{BV}+}$ gives the same result as $\mathtt{max}_{\mathtt{BV}}$:

$$\mathtt{safe}\ e \quad \Rightarrow \quad \mathtt{max}_{\mathtt{BV}+}\ e \ = \ \mathtt{max}_{\mathtt{BV}}\ e$$

Proof by induction on expressions. □

Swapping in $\mathtt{max}_{\mathtt{BV}+}$ in the definition of `lam` gives us a more efficient implementation:

```
lam+ f = Lam n body
  where
    body = f (Var n)
    n    = prime (maxBV+ body)
```

Here, $\mathtt{max}_{\mathtt{BV}+}$ traverses the body down to the closest binders, which in the worst case means traversing most of the expression. However, since the result is a `Lam` expression, the body will never have to be traversed again by uses of $\mathtt{max}_{\mathtt{BV}+}$ from lambdas higher up in the expression. Thus, the total effect of all uses of $\mathtt{max}_{\mathtt{BV}+}$ is *one extra traversal* of the expression. This means that the complexity of building an expression is linear in the size of the expression, giving an amortized complexity of $O(1)$ for each `lam` and `app`.

Theorem 2. Let t_+ range over terms built using `app` and $\mathtt{lam}_+$. Evaluation of a term t_+ in a safe context c results in a safe expression:

$$\forall c\, t_+\, e \,.\ \ \mathtt{safe}_{\mathtt{CXT}}\ c \ \&\ c \vdash t_+ \Downarrow e \quad \Rightarrow \quad \mathtt{safe}\ e$$

Proof using induction on terms t_+ and lemma 1. □

4. Discussion and related work

The problem solved in this pearl is not just a theoretical exercise – it is of great interest to the implementation of embedded domain-specific languages (EDSLs). There are many EDSLs that rely on a higher-order interface towards the user and a first-order representation for analysis and code generation: Lava [3], Pan [6], Nikola [8], Accelerate [10], Obsidian [12] and Feldspar [1], to name some. All of these EDSLs employ some kind of higher-order to first-order conversion.

The simple speculative method in Sec. 2.2 was originally suggested by Lennart Augustsson in a private communication with the authors. One of the anonymous referees also brought to our attention that a similar method is used in reference [4] to construct a first-order term with de Bruijn indexes from a higher-order interface.

A common method for implementing higher-order language constructs is to use *higher-order abstract syntax* (HOAS) [11]. A HOAS version of the lambda calculus would be like our `Exp` but where the `Lam` constructor mimics the type of `lam`:

```
data Exp
  = Var Name
  | App Exp Exp
  | Lam (Exp → Exp)
```

The advantage of this representation is that the constructors have a direct correspondence to the HOS interface in Fig. 1. However, working with this type is not convenient. As soon as we need to look inside a lambda, we need to come up with a variable name to pass to the binding function, which means that the name generation problem we have battled in this paper will reappear in each analysis. Another problem is HOAS to HOAS transformations where the binding functions have to be reconstructed after transforming under a lambda.

Instead, a common approach is to have a separate data type for first-order abstract syntax (FOAS) and a function to convert from HOAS to FOAS. This technique is used, for example, in Accelerate and recent versions of Feldspar. Although the technique is quite useful, it has some practical concerns:

- It requires defining two separate but almost identical data types (or play tricks to merge the two into one).
- Care has to be taken not to destroy implicit sharing during conversion [10].

In a blog post, McBride [9] proposes an implementation of higher-order syntax that, like our solution, does not require a separate HOAS data type. His term representation uses typed de Bruijn indexes and a type class to compute the index of a variable depending on its use site. Since de Bruijn indexes depend on the nesting depth of binders, a value-level implementation would require passing an environment while building expressions (with problems similar to the ones in Sec. 2.1). McBride cleverly avoids the problem by lifting the environment to the type level. Unfortunately, this also leads to more complicated types in the user interface.

It should be noted that our technique using circular speculation assumes that all bindings and variables are created using the `lam` function. This restriction is fine in an embedded language front end where terms are constructed from scratch, but it makes the approach unsuitable for introducing new bindings in existing terms. Consider the following transformation:

```
trans (Lam n a) = Lam n (trans' a)
```

If `trans'` introduces a new binder using `lam`, this introduction will be unaware of the fact that `n` is in scope leading to potential capturing. To avoid capturing, we would have to use `lam` on the right-hand side to introduce a fresh variable `x`, and substitute `x` for `n` in the body (assuming the existence of a suitable substitution function `subst`):

```
trans (Lam n a) = lam (λx → trans' (subst n x a))
```

```
data Exp = Var Name         -- Variable
         | Lam Name Exp    -- Abstraction
         | App Exp Exp     -- Application
         deriving (Show)

app :: Exp → Exp → Exp
app = App

lam :: (Exp → Exp) → Exp
lam f = Lam n body
  where
    body = f (Var n)
    n    = prime (maxBV body)

type Name = Integer

bot   :: Name
prime :: Name → Name
(⊔)   :: Name → Name → Name

bot   = 0
prime = succ
(⊔)   = max

maxBV :: Exp → Name
maxBV (Var _)   = bot
maxBV (App f a) = maxBV f ⊔ maxBV a
maxBV (Lam n _) = n
```

Figure 4: Final solution

Although this version does avoid capturing, the whole approach is a bit fragile, and the need for renaming makes it quite inefficient.

5. Conclusion

We have presented a simple solution to the problem of generating first-order syntax with binders from a higher-order interface. The key is to use circular programming to be able to examine the body of a binding "before" deciding which name to bind. Despite its simplicity, our solution possesses characteristics that makes it quite suitable for practical EDSLs. In particular, our solution

- does not require a separate data type for higher-order abstract syntax,
- is efficient and implementable in plain Haskell 98.

Our technique also serves as a real example where circular programming is used to change the complexity class of an algorithm. Bird's circular solution to the Repmin problem uses one traversal instead of two, possibly leading to a smaller constant factor for the algorithmic complexity. In our case, circular programming allows us to build an expression in linear time instead of exponential.

The complete final solution is given in Fig. 4.

Acknowledgments

This work has been partially funded by the Swedish Foundation for Strategic Research, under grant RAWFP. We would like to thank Anders Persson, Jean-Philippe Bernady, Joel Svensson, Josef Svenningsson, Mary Sheeran and Michał Pałka for useful input on this pearl.

References

[1] E. Axelsson, K. Claessen, M. Sheeran, J. Svenningsson, D. Engdal, and A. Persson. The design and implementation of Feldspar. In *Implementation and Application of Functional Languages*, volume 6647 of *LNCS*, pages 121–136. Springer Berlin Heidelberg, 2011.

[2] R. Bird. Using circular programs to eliminate multiple traversals of data. *Acta Informatica*, 21(3):239–250, 1984.

[3] P. Bjesse, K. Claessen, M. Sheeran, and S. Singh. Lava: hardware design in Haskell. In *Proceedings of the third ACM SIGPLAN international conference on Functional programming*, ICFP '98, pages 174–184. ACM, 1998.

[4] V. Capretta and A. P. Felty. Combining de Bruijn indices and higher-order abstract syntax in Coq. In *Types for Proofs and Programs*, volume 4502 of *Lecture Notes in Computer Science*, pages 63–77. Springer Berlin Heidelberg, 2007.

[5] K. Claessen and D. Sands. Observable sharing for functional circuit description. In *Advances in Computing Science, ASIAN'99*, volume 1742 of *LNCS*, pages 62–73. Springer, 1999.

[6] C. Elliott, S. Finne, and O. De Moor. Compiling embedded languages. *Journal of Functional Programming*, 13(3):455–481, May 2003.

[7] A. Gill. Type-safe observable sharing in Haskell. In *Proceedings of the 2nd ACM SIGPLAN symposium on Haskell*, Haskell '09, pages 117–128. ACM, 2009.

[8] G. Mainland and G. Morrisett. Nikola: embedding compiled GPU functions in Haskell. In *Proceedings of the third ACM Haskell symposium on Haskell*, Haskell '10, pages 67–78. ACM, 2010.

[9] C. McBride. I am not a number, I am a classy hack. 2010. URL http://www.e-pig.org/epilogue/?p=773.

[10] T. L. McDonell, M. M. Chakravarty, G. Keller, and B. Lippmeier. Optimising purely functional GPU programs. Accepted for publication at ICFP 2013.

[11] F. Pfenning and C. Elliot. Higher-order abstract syntax. In *Proceedings of the ACM SIGPLAN 1988 conference on Programming Language design and Implementation*, PLDI '88, pages 199–208. ACM, 1988.

[12] J. Svensson, M. Sheeran, and K. Claessen. Obsidian: A domain specific embedded language for parallel programming of graphics processors. In *Implementation and Application of Functional Languages*, volume 5836 of *LNCS*, pages 156–173. Springer Berlin Heidelberg, 2011.

Weak Optimality, and the Meaning of Sharing

Thibaut Balabonski

INRIA, Gallium team

thibaut.balabonski@inria.fr

Abstract

In this paper we investigate laziness and optimal evaluation strategies for functional programming languages. We consider the weak λ-calculus as a basis of functional programming languages, and we adapt to this setting the concepts of optimal reductions that were defined for the full λ-calculus. We prove that the usual implementation of call-by-need using sharing is optimal, that is, normalizing any λ-term with call-by-need requires exactly the same number of reduction steps as the shortest reduction sequence in the weak λ-calculus without sharing. Furthermore, we prove that optimal reduction sequences without sharing are not computable. Hence sharing is the only computable means to reach weak optimality.

Categories and Subject Descriptors I.1.3 [*Languages and Systems*]: Evaluation strategies

General Terms Theory, Languages

Keywords Strategies, Laziness, Weak reduction, Sharing, Optimality, Computability.

1. Introduction

The computation steps described by a functional program can usually be scheduled in many different ways. However, the schedules do not all have the same efficiency. Consider for instance the following program:

```
let   id  x  =  x
and  cst1 x  =  1
and  diag x  =  (x, x)
in
     diag (cst1 (id 2))
```

Its *reduction space*, that is, the directed graph that sums up all the possible evaluations of the program, is pictured in Fig. 1. Each evaluation strategy choses a path in this graph.

In particular, *call-by-value* reaches the result in three evaluation steps, with one inefficiency: it evaluates the argument `id 2`, which is *not needed*, since its value is going to be discarded by the function `cst1`. *Call-by-name* also reaches the result in three evaluation steps, with another inefficiency: it performs twice the call to the function `cst1` that is *duplicated* by the function `diag`.

ICFP '13, September 25–27, 2013, Boston, MA, USA.

Copyright is held by the owner/author(s). Publication rights licensed to ACM.

ACM 978-1-4503-2326-0/13/09... $15.00.

http://dx.doi.org/10.1145/2500365.2500606

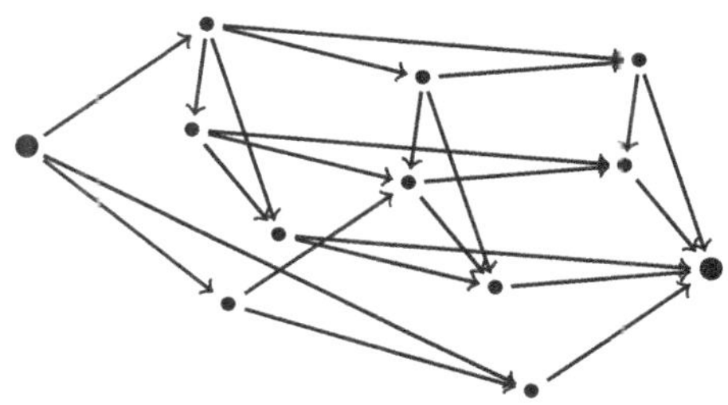

Figure 1. Reduction space

There are two ways of evaluating this program in only two steps. The first one is an hybrid strategy that first performs the call to `cst1` and then the call to `diag`. The second one, *call-by-need*, combines call-by-name with an additional mechanism of *memoization* or *sharing*, which enables a re-use of already-computed results, and which is meant to make up for duplications. This additional mechanism adds shortcuts in the original single-step reduction space.

Since its introduction by Wadsworth's in 1971, call-by-need is considered as a good strategy for avoiding at the same time non-needed and duplicated computation steps. The point of this paper is to turn this folkloric fact into a precise theorem.

In particular we will prove that call-by-need is an *optimal* strategy with respect to some reasonable restriction of the λ-calculus, that is, call-by-need always reaches the result of a computation in the least number of evaluation steps, or, call-by-need always picks the shortest path in some realistic reduction space.

The restriction that we consider comes from the following remark: the λ-calculus is too powerful for most functional programming languages. Indeed, while different languages use different strategies, most of them use only a subset of the reduction space known as *weak evaluation*, in which no anticipated evaluation of a function body is performed before the function is applied to its arguments. With this restriction to weak evaluation we lose some strategies, and the shortest path in the full reduction space of the λ-calculus may not be preserved in the weak reduction space, as shown in the following example.

Example 1.1.

Let a be a fresh variable. Consider the λ-term

$$t \quad = \quad (\lambda x.x(xa))(\lambda y.(\lambda z.z)y)$$

Its normal form is a, and it can be reached in four β-steps by first reducing $\lambda y.(\lambda z.z)y$ to $\lambda y.y$. If we restrict ourselves to weak reduction however, we need five steps to reach the result.

However, we consider weak evaluation as more realistic than the full λ-calculus, since this restriction is crucial for the implementation, and thus in this paper we investigate *weak optimality*, that is, the evaluation strategies that are optimal in the restricted-, weak-reduction space.

The main contributions are the following:

- We adapt Lévy's theory of optimal evaluation to the weak λ-calculus (Section 4), and identify two strategies that reach optimality (Section 6). One of these weakly optimal strategies is the original *call-by-need*, which proves the good behavior of Wadsworth's technique. The second weakly optimal strategy does not use sharing at all, which proves that the new reduction sequences allowed by sharing are not shorter than the shortest single-step reduction sequences.
- We prove that optimal single-step reduction strategies cannot be computable (Section 3). This result completes the previous statement by showing that, while sharing does not enable strictly shorter reduction sequences, call-by-need nevertheless offers a computable way of reaching weak optimality.
- We use a labelling of the weak λ-calculus as a simple way to give a faithful account of all the causal dependencies between computation events (Section 4).
- We show that the weak λ-calculus, while it has the appearance of the λ-calculus, has the properties of a first-order rewriting system (Section 5).

Since it is a better fit for a conference format, we focus here on the case of the weak λ-calculus. However, the results of the paper hold for the more general case of weak reduction in orthogonal higher-order rewriting. The interested reader is referred to the author's doctoral dissertation [Bal12b].

2. The weak λ-calculus

In this section we recall the definitions and the basic properties of the weak λ-calculus. As in the previous paper [Bal12c], the λ-calculus is expressed in the higher-order rewriting framework of *Combinatory Reduction Systems (CRS)*. This may seem artificial at the beginning, but it will allow a clean handling of the labels and of the connection between weak reduction and first-order rewriting.

First, let us introduce the *CRS* in a nutshell. We see here only the basic syntax and mechanisms; a comprehensive presentation can be found in [KvOvR93].

Definition 2.1 (*Combinatory Reduction Systems / CRS*). *The grammar of* **metaterms** *in a* CRS *is:*

$$t \quad ::= \quad x \mid [x]t \mid f(t_1, ..., t_n) \mid Z(t_1, ..., t_n)$$

where x is a **variable**, *$[x]$ denotes the* **binding** *of a variable, f is an n-ary* **function symbol** *taken in a* **signature** *$\mathcal{S}$, and Z is an n-ary* **metavariable**.

A **term** *is a metaterm without metavariable, and an n-ary* **context** *is a term that contains n occurrences of the special nullary symbol $\square$ (the* **hole**). *A* **reduction rule** *is a pair $L \to R$ of closed metaterms satisfying the following conditions:*

- *the metavariables in L appear as $Z(x_1, ..., x_n)$ with $x_1, ..., x_n$ distinct bound variables; and*
- *all the metavariables of R also appear in L.*

A rule matches a term by application of a **valuation** *σ that maps n-ary metavariables to n-ary contexts avoiding variable capture.* **Reduction** *by a rule $L \to R$ with valuation σ in a context c is $c[L^\sigma] \to c[R^\sigma]$.*

Example 2.2.

The λ-calculus can be seen as a CRS *with:*

- *a signature $\mathcal{S}_\lambda = \{\lambda, @\}$ where the symbol λ is unary and the application symbol $@$ is binary;*
- *a unique reduction rule $@(\lambda([x]Z(x)), Z') \to Z(Z')$.*

The λ-term $(\lambda x.x)y$ is encoded in the CRS *term $@(\lambda([x]x), y)$. However, we will still use usual λ-calculus notation wherever this can lighten the presentation.*

Example 2.3.

First order rewriting systems, also called Term Rewriting Systems (TRS) *are also a particular case of* CRS, *where metaterms do not contain any binders.*

The absence of binders has some consequences. In particular, since any metavariable Z appearing in the left member L of a reduction rule $L \to R$ is supposed to appear as $Z(x_1, \ldots, x_n)$ where the x_i's are bound variables, we are restricted to nullary metavariables that appear simply as Z. This restricts a lot the reduction rules that can be defined, and explains the simpler behavior of first-order compared to higher-order rewriting.

In this paper we will consider a signature that strictly contains the one of the λ-calculus.

Definition 2.4 (Terms). *From now on we consider the signature*

$$\mathcal{S} = \{\varepsilon, \lambda, @\} \cup \mathcal{F}$$

where:

- *ε is a unary symbol called* **dummy** *symbol, and*
- *$\mathcal{F} = \bigcup_{n \in \mathbb{N}} \mathcal{F}_n$ where for all n, $\mathcal{F}_n$ is a countable set of n-ary symbols called* **supercombinators**.

From now on, by **term** *we mean a CRS term over the signature $\mathcal{S}$. Write Λ for the set of terms. We use the usual notion of* **position** *in a term. Write $t|_p$ for the* **subterm** *of t rooted at position p, and call two positions p_1 and p_2* **disjoint** *if none is a prefix of the other. We also use the usual notion of* **free variables**. *Write $t^{\{x:=u\}}$ for the* **substitution** *by u of all the free occurrences of the variable x in t. Write $\mathtt{dom}(\sigma)$ for the domain of a n-ary substitution σ. A* **context** *is a term also containing the nullary symbol $\square$, called* **hole**. *Replacement $c[t]$ of a hole in a context c by a term t is as usual.*

The supercombinator symbols in the sets $\mathcal{F}_n$ are used in Section 5 for the reduction of the weak λ-calculus to a first-order rewriting system. Until then they play no role and may be safely ignored.

The dummy symbol ε has no meaning in itself. It is needed for the causal interpretation of labels (Section 4.5), and serves in particular as a container for dynamically created labels. As a consequence, occurrences of ε should not interfere with β-reduction. This leads to the following countable set of rules to simulate β-reduction by allowing any number of ε's between the application and the λ-abstraction.

Definition 2.5 (Beta-reduction). *The rules for β-reduction are as follows:*

$$\begin{array}{lrcl} \beta_0: & @(\lambda x.Z(x), Z') & \to_\beta & \varepsilon(Z(Z')) \\ \beta_1: & @(\varepsilon(\lambda x.Z(x)), Z') & \to_\beta & \varepsilon(Z(Z')) \\ \beta_2: & @(\varepsilon(\varepsilon(\lambda x.Z(x))), Z') & \to_\beta & \varepsilon(Z(Z')) \\ \ldots & & & \end{array}$$

Write $\rho : t \to t'$ a reduction step ρ from a term t to a term t'. Write $\mathtt{src}(\rho) = t$ for the **source** *of ρ, $\mathtt{tgt}(\rho) = t'$ for its* **target**, *and $\mathtt{root}(\rho)$ for the position in $\mathtt{src}(\rho)$ of the redex reduced by ρ. A* **normal form** *is a term that is the source of no reduction step. The usual notions of* **ancestors** *and* **descendants** *[Ter03], which track subterms along reduction in the λ-calculus are straightforwardly adapted*[1]*, as illustrated in Example 2.6. A* **residual** *of a redex r is a*

[1] The book [Ter03] gives several definitions of descendants that differ in particular in how they treat variables. In this paper we only need to consider the descendants of applications, hence the simplest definition is enough.

descendant of r which is still a redex. A redex r in the target $\mathtt{tgt}(\rho)$ of a reduction step ρ is **created** *by ρ if it is not a residual of a redex in the source $\mathtt{src}(\rho)$. A* **development** *of a set of redexes $\mathcal{R}$ in a term t is a reduction sequence $\varrho : t \twoheadrightarrow t'$ where each step reduces a residual of a redex in $\mathcal{R}$. A development ϱ is* **complete** *if there is no remaining residual of any redex in $\mathcal{R}$. A redex r in a term t is* **needed** *if any reduction sequence from t to a normal form reduces at least one residual of r.*

The ε's in the right hand sides of the β-rules are used for the correct labelling of collapsing reductions (Section 4.5). The use of the dummy symbol ε is inspired by the notion of *expansion* in term rewriting systems [Ter03, Chap. 8].

Example 2.6.

The rule β_1 enables a reduction step

$$\rho \quad : \quad @(\varepsilon(\lambda x.@(x,x)),y) \quad \to \quad \varepsilon(@(y,y))$$

The two occurrences of y in the target are the descendants of the y in the source, and the latter is the ancestor of the formers. The ε in the source has no descendant and the ε in the target has no ancestor.

In the usual, non-weak λ-calculus, β-reduction can be applied in any context. In contrast, the weak λ-calculus introduces some restrictions on the contexts in which a reduction rule can be applied. Intuitively, reduction will be forbidden at any position (called *frozen*) that belongs to the "effective scope" of a binder, which we call *skeleton*. This restriction is formally based on the following definitions.

Definition 2.7 (Free expression)**.** *A* **free expression**[2] *of a λ-term $\lambda x.t$ is a subterm s of t such that any free variable occurrence in s is also free in $\lambda x.t$. A free expression is* **maximal** *if it is not a subterm of another free expression.*

Definition 2.8 (Prefix)**.** *A* **n-ary prefix** *of a λ-term t is a n-ary context c such that there are n λ-terms $t_1, \dots, t_n$ satisfying $t = c[t_1,\dots,t_n]$.*

We will be mostly interested in the prefix that is obtained by removing all the maximal free expressions of a λ-abstraction $\lambda x.t$, which represents the parts of the term that are not independent from the binder, and which we call **skeleton** of $\lambda x.t$. Example 2.9 illustrates this notion, and definition 2.10 then gives a direct definition.

Example 2.9.

Suppose w_1 and w_2 are two variables, and consider the λ-term

$$t = \lambda x.(\lambda y.y)(\lambda z.z(w_1w_2)x)$$

Its maximal free expressions are $\lambda y.y$ and w_1w_2, while its skeleton is the binary prefix

$$\lambda x.\Box(\lambda z.z\Box x)$$

The skeleton is marked with bold lines in the following picture.

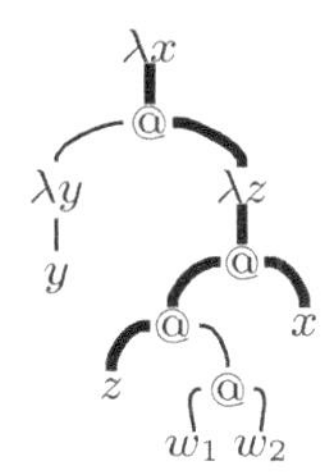

Definition 2.10 (Skeleton)**.** *For any set of variables θ, call* **θ-skeleton** *of a λ-term t and write $\langle\langle t\rangle\rangle^\theta$ for the prefix of t defined as follows:*

$$\langle\langle t\rangle\rangle^\theta \quad = \quad \Box \qquad\qquad \theta\cap\mathtt{fv}(t)=\emptyset$$

Otherwise:

$$\begin{array}{rcll}
\langle\langle x\rangle\rangle^\theta & = & x & x\in\theta \\
\langle\langle \varepsilon(t)\rangle\rangle^\theta & = & \varepsilon(\langle\langle t\rangle\rangle^\theta) & \\
\langle\langle \lambda x.t\rangle\rangle^\theta & = & \lambda x.\langle\langle t\rangle\rangle^{\theta\cup\{x\}} & \\
\langle\langle t_1t_2\rangle\rangle^\theta & = & \langle\langle t_1\rangle\rangle^\theta\langle\langle t_2\rangle\rangle^\theta & \\
\langle\langle f(t_1,\dots,t_n)\rangle\rangle^\theta & = & f(\langle\langle t_1\rangle\rangle^\theta,\dots,\langle\langle t_n\rangle\rangle^\theta) &
\end{array}$$

Call **skeleton** *of a λ-abstraction $\lambda x.t$ its prefix $\lambda x.\langle\langle t\rangle\rangle^{\{x\}}$. Write $\langle\langle\Lambda\rangle\rangle$ for the set of all skeletons.*

Definition 2.11 (Frozen positions)**.** *A position p of a λ-term t is called* **frozen** *if it is contained in the skeleton of a λ-abstraction of t. Call a* **frozen redex** *any β-redex whose main @ symbol (the root of the redex) occurs at a frozen position.*

Definition 2.12 (Weak β-reduction)**. Weak β-reduction** *is defined by the application of the β-reduction rules to any β-redex that is not frozen.*

From now on we call **redex** only a *non-frozen* redex, that is a redex for weak reduction. A **weak normal form** is a term that contains no (non-frozen) redex.

Example 2.13.

Let a be a fresh variable. Consider the λ-term

$$t \quad = \quad \lambda x.@(\lambda y.y, @(x, @(\lambda z.z, a)))$$

Its frozen positions are ϵ, 1, 12, and 121 (corresponding to λx, x, and the two applications in between). Hence the redex $@(\lambda y.y, @(x, @(\lambda z.z, a)))$ is frozen, while the redex $@(\lambda z.z, a)$ is not. The weak normal form of t is $\lambda x.@(\lambda y.y, @(x,a))$.

This notion of weak β-reduction first appeared in works by Howard [How70] and by Çagman and Hindley [cH98], as a mean to describe in the syntax of the λ-calculus the reduction behavior of the combinators S and K of Combinatory Logic. For this reason it has been called *combinatory weak reduction*. In this setting, Çagman and Hindley proved in particular that the weak λ-calculus had the Church-Rosser property.

Proposition 2.14 (Church-Rosser, Çagman and Hindley [cH98])**.** *The weak λ-calculus is confluent.*

3. (Un-)Computability

In this section we prove the Uncomputability Theorem 3.14, which states that any optimal strategy for the weak λ-calculus, that is any reduction strategy that selects a shortest weak reduction sequence for any λ-term, is necessarily uncomputable. A similar result has already been proved by Barendregt et al. for the usual non-weak λ-calculus [BBKV76]. However, a key step of their proof does not hold if we restrict ourselves to weak reduction. In Section 3.1 we review the structure of the proof of Barendregt et al. and show where it gets broken by weak reduction. Then in Section 3.2 we patch their proof thanks to an original use of the λ-lifting transformation.

In this whole section we ignore the dummy symbol ε and the supercombinator symbols in $\mathcal{F}$.

3.1 Barendregt et al.'s proof of uncomputability

The proof by Barendregt et al. proceeds by exhibiting two recursively inseparable sets of λ-terms $\mathcal{A}$ and $\mathcal{B}$[3] and by showing how to separate them using a hypothetical optimal reduction strategy. The set $\mathcal{A}$ (resp. $\mathcal{B}$) is defined as "the set of all λ-terms admitting

[2] Originally called *abstractable expression* by Wadsworth.

[3] $\mathcal{A}$ and $\mathcal{B}$ are **recursively inseparable** if there is no recursive set $\mathcal{C}$ such that $\mathcal{A}\subset\mathcal{C}$ and $\mathcal{B}\cap\mathcal{C}=\emptyset$.

some cleverly-chosen t_a (resp. t_b) as normal form", and these two sets $\mathcal{A}$ and $\mathcal{B}$ are known to be recursively inseparable thanks to a result by Scott [Sco68].

The two sets $\mathcal{A}$ and $\mathcal{B}$ are then separated using a total computable function $\varphi(.)$ on λ-terms such that:

- Each $\varphi(t)$ contains exactly two β-redexes, written r_t^a and r_t^b.
- From $\varphi(t)$, any optimal reduction strategy reduces r_t^a if $t \twoheadrightarrow t_a$, and r_t^b if $t \twoheadrightarrow t_b$ (and nothing is specified if t reduces neither to t_a nor to t_b).

Their first step in defining the λ-term $\varphi(t)$ is to build an *enumerator*, that is a λ-term e in normal form such that, if n_t is a Gödel number for a λ-term t, and if $\ulcorner n_t \urcorner$ is a representation in the λ-calculus of n_t, then $e\ulcorner n_t \urcorner \twoheadrightarrow t$. This enumerator e works by building applicative combinations of the standard S, K, and I combinators. In particular $e\ulcorner n_t \urcorner$ reduces to $(t)_{CL}$, the usual encoding of t in combinatory logics S, K, I. Then, after reverting all the combinators into λ-terms, which gives a λ-term $((t)_{CL})_\lambda$, it is folklore that $((t)_{CL})_\lambda \twoheadrightarrow t$.

However, the latter is not true anymore in the weak λ-calculus, as the following example shows.

Example 3.1.

Consider the λ-term

$$t = \lambda x.xx$$

Then we have

$$\begin{array}{rcl} (t)_{CL} & = & SII \\ ((t)_{CL})_\lambda & = & (\lambda xyz.xz(yz))(\lambda x.x)(\lambda x.x) \end{array}$$

and $((t)_{CL})_\lambda \twoheadrightarrow t$ in the non-weak λ-calculus. However, the weak normal form of $((t)_{CL})_\lambda$ is

$$\lambda z.((\lambda x.x)z)((\lambda x.x)z)$$

Hence we do not have $((t)_{CL})_\lambda \twoheadrightarrow t$ in the weak λ-calculus.

The next section provides a new function $\varphi(.)$ that is suited for use with the weak λ-calculus.

3.2 Uncomputability for the weak λ-calculus

First, let us state that Scott's inseparability result is still valid for the weak λ-calculus.

Proposition 3.2 (Inseparability, Scott [Sco68]). *Let $\mathcal{A}$ and $\mathcal{B}$ be two non-empty sets of λ-terms that are closed under weak β-reduction. Then $\mathcal{A}$ and $\mathcal{B}$ are recursively inseparable.*

Proof. Similar to Barendregt's proof [Bar84, Chap. 6], that does not need non-weak β-reduction. □

The main mechanism of our function $\varphi(.)$ is a decomposition of a λ-term into several components, all of which are in weak normal form. We rely on the fact that any skeleton is a normal form for weak reduction (all the positions of a skeleton are indeed frozen), and we use a technique inspired by λ-lifting to represent a λ-term as an assembly of skeletons.

The first step, corresponding to what Danvy and Schultz call "parameter lifting" [DS00], makes each λ-abstraction closed by extracting its maximal free expressions[4].

[4] Note that ordinary λ-lifting extracts only the free variables; switching to free expressions corresponds to fully lazy λ-lifting [PJ87].

Definition 3.3 (Free Expressions Lifting ($\texttt{fel}$)).

$$\begin{array}{rcl} \texttt{fel}(x) & = & x \\ \texttt{fel}(t_1 t_2) & = & \texttt{fel}(t_1)\texttt{fel}(t_2) \\ \texttt{fel}(\lambda x.t) & = & (\lambda y_1 \ldots y_n x.s[y_1, \ldots, y_n])\texttt{fel}(t_1)\ldots\texttt{fel}(t_n) \\ & & s = \langle\langle t \rangle\rangle^{\{x\}} \\ & & t = s[t_1, \ldots, t_n] \\ & & y_1, \ldots, y_n \textit{ fresh variables} \end{array}$$

Lemma 3.4 (Free expressions lifting). *For any λ-term t we have $\texttt{fel}(t) \twoheadrightarrow t$.*

Proof. By induction on t. □

Example 3.5.

Suppose a, b and c are three free variables and consider the term

$$t = \lambda x_1.((\lambda x_2.x_2 a)b)(x_1 c)$$

Then free expression lifting proceeds as follows:

$$\begin{array}{rcl} \texttt{fel}(t) & = & (\lambda y_1 y_2 x_1.y_1(x_1 y_2))\texttt{fel}((\lambda x_2.x_2 a)b)\texttt{fel}(c) \\ & = & (\lambda y_1 y_2 x_1.y_1(x_1 y_2))(\texttt{fel}(\lambda x_2.x_2 a)\texttt{fel}(b))\texttt{fel}(c) \\ & = & (\lambda y_1 y_2 x_1.y_1(x_1 y_2))((\lambda y_1' x_2.x_2 y_1')\texttt{fel}(a)\texttt{fel}(b))\texttt{fel}(c) \\ & = & (\lambda y_1 y_2 x_1.y_1(x_1 y_2))((\lambda y_1' x_2.x_2 y_1')ab)c \end{array}$$

Moreover, we have $\texttt{fel}(t) \twoheadrightarrow t$ in three weak reduction steps.

The second step, corresponding to what Danvy and Schultz call "block floating", moves each function to toplevel. This is done by replacing each skeleton by a fresh variable and mapping these new variables to the skeletons they denote.

Definition 3.6 (Skeletons Floating ($\texttt{sf}$)).

$$\begin{array}{rcl} \texttt{sf}(x) & = & (x, \emptyset) \\ \texttt{sf}(t_1 t_2) & = & (u_1 u_2, \sigma_1 \uplus \sigma_2) \\ & & \forall i \in \{1,2\}, \texttt{sf}(t_i) = (u_i, \sigma_i) \\ \texttt{sf}(\lambda x.t) & = & (z, \{z := \lambda x.t\}) \qquad z \textit{ fresh} \end{array}$$

where $\uplus$ is the union of two substitutions with disjoint domains.

Lemma 3.7 (Skeletons floating). *Let t be a λ-term and p a position. Write $\texttt{sf}(t) = (u, \sigma)$. Then $u^\sigma = t$.*

Proof. By induction on t. □

Example 3.8.

Consider the term $\texttt{fel}(t)$ obtained at the end of example 3.5. Skeletons floating $\texttt{sf}(\texttt{fel}(t))$ yields the term

$$u = z_1(z_2 ab)c$$

and the substitution

$$\sigma = \{ z_1 := \lambda y_1 y_2 x_1.y_1(x_1 y_2); \; z_2 := \lambda y_1' x_2.x_2 y_1' \}$$

such as $u^\sigma = \texttt{fel}(t)$.

Finally, the result of the two previous steps allows us to decompose a λ-term t as an application $s_0 s_1 \ldots s_n$ with $n \geq 1$ and where each s_i is a weak normal form.

Definition 3.9 (Decomposition). *Let t be a λ-term. Write*

$$\texttt{sf}(\texttt{fel}(t)) = (u, \sigma)$$

- *If $\texttt{dom}(\sigma) = \emptyset$, then define*

$$\texttt{dec}(t) = (\lambda z.u)I$$

- *Otherwise write $\texttt{dom}(\sigma) = \{z_1, \ldots, z_n\}$, and define*

$$\texttt{dec}(t) = (\lambda z_1 \ldots z_n.u)\sigma(z_1)\ldots\sigma(z_n)$$

Lemma 3.10 (Decomposition). *For any λ-term t we have* $\mathtt{dec}(t) \twoheadrightarrow t$.

Proof. By case on whether skeletons floating yields an empty substitution or not. □

Definition 3.11 (Separating function). *The* **separating function** *$\varphi(.)$ is defined as follows: let t be a λ-term; write* $\mathtt{dec}(t) = s_0 s_1 ... s_n$*; then*

$$\varphi(t) = (\lambda x.x s_0 x)(\lambda y.y s_1 \ldots s_n (II))$$

where $I = \lambda z.z$ is the identity.

Example 3.12.

Consider the term t from example 3.5. Its decomposition is

$$\begin{aligned}\mathtt{dec}(t) &= (\lambda z_1 z_2.z_1(z_2 ab)c) \\ &\quad (\lambda y_1 y_2 x_1.y_1(x_1 y_2)) \\ &\quad (\lambda y_1' x_2.x_2 y_1')\end{aligned}$$

where each of the three components is a weak normal form, and where we can check that $\mathtt{dec}(t) \twoheadrightarrow t$ *in five weak reduction steps. Finally we define*

$$\begin{aligned}\varphi(t) &= (\lambda x.x(\lambda z_1 z_2.z_1(z_2 ab)c)x) \\ &\quad (\lambda y.y(\lambda y_1 y_2 x_1.y_1(x_1 y_2))(\lambda y_1' x_2.x_2 y_1')(II))\end{aligned}$$

Lemma 3.13 (Separation). *Consider an optimal strategy $\xrightarrow{\mathtt{opt}}$ for the weak λ-calculus, and let $s_0, s_1, \ldots, s_n$ be λ-terms in weak normal form. Write $u = (\lambda x.x s_0 x)(\lambda y.y s_1 \ldots s_n(II))$, where $I = \lambda z.z$ is the identity. Then the following holds:*

- *If* $s_0 s_1 \ldots s_n \twoheadrightarrow \lambda xyz.z$ *then* $u \xrightarrow{\mathtt{opt}} (\lambda y.y s_1 \ldots s_n(II)) s_0 (\lambda y.y s_1 \ldots s_n(II))$
- *If* $s_0 s_1 \ldots s_n \twoheadrightarrow a$ *then* $u \xrightarrow{\mathtt{opt}} (\lambda x.x s_0 x)(\lambda y.y s_1 \ldots s_n I)$

Proof. Similar to Barendregt's [Bar84, Lemma 13.5.5]. □

Now we are able to prove the Uncomputability Theorem 3.14.

Theorem 3.14 (Uncomputability). *There is no computable optimal reduction strategy for the weak λ-calculus.*

Proof. Define $\mathcal{A} = \{t \in \Lambda \mid t \twoheadrightarrow \lambda xyz.z\}$ and $\mathcal{B} = \{t \in \Lambda \mid t \twoheadrightarrow a\}$. Both sets are closed by weak β-reduction, hence by Scott's Inseparability Proposition 3.2 the sets $\mathcal{A}$ and $\mathcal{B}$ are recursively inseparable.

Now suppose there is a recursive optimal strategy $\xrightarrow{\mathtt{opt}}$ for the weak λ-calculus. Then the set

$$\mathcal{C} = \{t \in \Lambda \mid \varphi(t) \xrightarrow{\mathtt{opt}} t' \text{ at position } \varepsilon\}$$

is computable. And yet, by Separation Lemma 3.13 the set $\mathcal{C}$ separates $\mathcal{A}$ and $\mathcal{B}$. Contradiction. □

Finally, we have proved that optimal reduction strategies for the weak λ-calculus cannot be computable. In the following sections we will investigate other approaches to optimality, in particular by using sharing.

4. Weak optimality

In this section we adapt Vuillemin-Lévy's theory of optimality [Lé80] to the weak λ-calculus, which will give a characterization of optimal reduction in a setting in which some sharing of computation is allowed.

4.1 A short introduction to Vuillemin-Lévy's optimality

This approach is intended to give a lower bound on the number of evaluation steps needed for normalizing a term, by characterizing an ideal case in which there is no unneeded computation step and no duplication at all. Since such an ideal reduction sequence cannot be reached in the pure λ-calculus –it is either non-existing or non-computable– this characterization of optimality proceeds by identifying *families* of computation steps that regroup all the duplicates of a given original redex. Hence, the families describe which redexes should be *shared* in order to achieve a computation without duplication.

The main idea behind families is the following: consider a reduction sequence $\varrho : t_1 \to t_2 \to \ldots \to t_n$ and two redexes r_1 and r_2 in t_n. If there is a redex r_0 in one of the t_i's that is a common ancestor to r_1 and r_2, then r_1 and r_2 are in the same family (they are two duplicate copies of the original r_0). Hence two redexes are in the same family if their duplication could have been avoided by first reducing a common ancestor.

Example 4.1.

In this reduction sequence we follow the underlined expression $\underline{(\lambda z.z)(\lambda w.w)}$.

$$\begin{aligned}&(\lambda x.xx)(\lambda y.(\underline{(\lambda z.z)(\lambda w.w)}y)) \\ \to\ &(\lambda y.(\underline{(\lambda z.z)(\lambda w.w)}y))(\lambda y.(\underline{(\lambda z.z)(\lambda w.w)}y)) \\ \to\ &\underline{(\lambda z.z)(\lambda w.w)}(\lambda y.(\underline{(\lambda z.z)(\lambda w.w)}y))\end{aligned}$$

The two occurrences of $\underline{(\lambda z.z)(\lambda w.w)}$ are residuals of the first occurrences; they are in the same family.

However, this criterion is not enough: two redexes can be in the same family even if their common ancestor is not visible in the sequence ϱ.

Example 4.2.

Now reduce the two underlined occurrences in the last term of example 4.1. We observe two new redexes (underlined below) that have no visible ancestor, and therefore no visible common ancestor.

$$\underline{(\lambda w.w)(\lambda y.\underline{(\lambda w.w)y})}$$

Such a common ancestor exists somewhere though. Consider this other possible evaluation sequence and follow the underlined terms.

$$\begin{aligned}&(\lambda x.xx)(\lambda y.((\lambda z.z)(\underline{\lambda w.w})y)) \\ \to\ &(\lambda x.xx)(\lambda y.(\underline{(\lambda w.w)y})) \\ \to\ &(\lambda y.(\underline{(\lambda w.w)y}))(\lambda y.(\underline{(\lambda w.w)y})) \\ \to\ &\underline{(\lambda w.w)(\lambda y.\underline{(\lambda w.w)y})}\end{aligned}$$

Hence, by permuting the original sequence we have found a common ancestor to the two underlined redexes, which are thus in the same family. Reducing them both finally yields the term

$$\lambda y.y$$

Hence, the definition of families requires to reason globally on the reduction spaces and the permutations of their steps. To circumvent this problem, Lévy also gave a direct characterization of families, through a labelled λ-calculus that is shown to be stable by permutation of reduction steps. With this additional tool, the labels directly tell which redexes should be reduced in a shared way. Unfortunately the definition does not give an implementation. One of the difficulties is that optimal sharing in the λ-calculus requires sharing contexts (as the context $(\lambda w.w)\Box$ in the previous example). The first algorithms realizing optimal sharing in the non-weak λ-calculus were found ten years later [Lam90].

In this section we characterize families and optimality for the weak λ-calculus. We use an abstract characterization of Vuillemin-

Lévy optimality that has been proposed by Glauert and Khasidashvili.

4.2 Glauert & Khasidashvili's Deterministic Family Structures

Glauert and Khasidashvili [GK96] propose an abstract framework for characterizing optimality that is composed by two layers:

1. a well-behaved notion of residual (so-called *Deterministic Residual Structure* or *DRS*); and
2. a notion of family built above the notion of residual and enjoying additional good properties (so-called *Deterministic Family Structure*, or *DFS*).

Deterministic Residual Structures are defined by only two axioms, which are usually satisfied by the natural notions of residual in λ-calculus-based systems.

Definition 4.3 (Deterministic Residual Structure, DRS [GK96]). *A* **Deterministic Residual Structure (DRS)** *is a rewriting system equipped with a residual relation satisfying the following properties:*

- **[FD]** *All developments are terminating; all complete developments of a given set of redexes have the same target; all complete developments of a given set of redexes define the same residuals.*
- **[Acyclicity]** *Let r and r_e be two distinct redexes of a term t such that r erases[5] r_e. Then r_e does not erase r.*

The definition of *Deterministic Family Structures* is more complex. First, since the families of redexes in a term t are linked to the history of t –that is to [the permutations of] a reduction sequence of which t is the target– this definition considers families of *reduction steps with history*.

Definition 4.4 (Reduction step with history). *A* **reduction step with history** *is a pair (ϱ, ρ) where ϱ is a reduction sequence, ρ is a reduction step, and $\texttt{tgt}(\varrho) = \texttt{src}(\rho)$. Two reduction steps with history (ϱ_1, ρ_1) and (ϱ_2, ρ_2) are* **coinitial** *if $\texttt{src}(\varrho_1) = \texttt{src}(\varrho_2)$.*

Second, we need to include the notions of residual and of permutation in the definition of families. For this they define a notion of *copy*, which has to be understood as a residual relation modulo permutation.

Definition 4.5 (Copy). *Let (ϱ_1, ρ_1) and (ϱ_2, ρ_2) be two coinitial reduction steps with history. Suppose ϱ_1 has no residual after ϱ_2[6]. Let ϱ_2/ϱ_1 be a complete development of the residuals of ϱ_2 after ϱ_1. If ρ_2 is a residual of ρ_1 after ϱ_2/ϱ_1, then (ϱ_2, ρ_2) is said to be a* **copy** *of (ϱ_1, ρ_1), written $(\varrho_1, \rho_1) \rhd (\varrho_2, \rho_2)$.*

Definition 4.6 (Deterministic Family Structure [GK96]). *Let R be a DRS. Let $\simeq$ be an equivalence relation over coinitial reduction steps with history, whose equivalence classes are called* **families**. *Write $\texttt{Fam}(\varrho, \rho)$ for the family (ie the equivalence class) of a reduction step with history (ϱ, ρ). Let $\hookrightarrow$ be a binary relation over families, called* **contribution** *relation. The triple $(R, \simeq, \hookrightarrow)$ is a* **Deterministic Family Structure (DFS)** *if the following axioms are satisfied:*

- **[Initial]** *For any coinitial distinct reduction steps ρ_1 and ρ_2 we have $\texttt{Fam}(\emptyset, \rho_1) \neq \texttt{Fam}(\emptyset, \rho_2)$.*
- **[Copy]** $\rhd\ \subseteq \simeq$.
- **[FFD]** *Any reduction sequence that contracts redexes of a finite number of families is finite.*
- **[Creation]** *For any reduction step with history (ϱ, ρ), if ρ creates a reduction step ρ' then $\texttt{Fam}(\varrho, \rho) \hookrightarrow \texttt{Fam}(\varrho\rho, \rho')$.*
- **[Contribution]** *For any two families ϕ_1 and ϕ_2, we have $\phi_1 \hookrightarrow \phi_2$ if and only if for any reduction step with history $(\varrho_2, \rho_2) \in \phi_2$ there is a reduction step with history $(\varrho_1, \rho_1) \in \phi_1$ such that $\varrho_1\rho_1$ is a prefix of ϱ_2.*

Definition 4.7 (Family reduction). *In a DFS, a* **family reduction step** *is a complete development of a set $\mathcal{R}$ of redexes of a term t which all belong to a given family ϕ. It is* **complete** *if $\mathcal{R}$ contains all the redexes of t that belong to the family ϕ. It is* **needed** *if one of the redexes of $\mathcal{R}$ is needed.*

Family reduction gives a new, richer reduction space in which shared evaluation is possible. From now on, we are interested in optimality in this bigger reduction space, that is in optimality with sharing.

Proposition 4.8 (Optimality in DFS [GK96]). *In any DFS, a family reduction sequence that reduces only complete needed families is optimal.*

Our goal for the rest of the section is to build a DFS over the weak λ-calculus, in order to characterize weak optimality. That means we need to give a concrete definition of the abstract concept of family and to prove that all the axioms are satisfied. Here is a summary of the required ingredients:

- we need to exhibit concrete notions of family ($\simeq$) and of contribution ($\hookrightarrow$); following Lévy, we will do this through a labelling of the weak λ-calculus presented in Section 4.4;
- in Section 4.3 we derive a classification of redex creations that both guide the definition of labels and enables the proof of the [Creation] axiom; and
- in Section 4.5 we show that the labels give a faithful account of the causal dependencies between reduction steps, which will be the core of the proof of the [Contribution] axiom.

The proof of the finite development axioms [FD] and [FFD] is postponed to Section 5, where we establish a connection between the weak labelled λ-calculus and a first-order rewriting system, which allows us to re-use finite development results from the first-order rewriting literature.

4.3 Redex creation in the weak λ-calculus

In this subsection we do not use the dummy symbol ε yet.

In the λ-calculus, a redex is a connection between a λ-abstraction and an argument. Hence a redex is created each time a new connection of this kind appears.

Example 4.9.

The three reduction steps below show the three ways of connecting a λ-abstraction $\underline{\lambda x.t}$ to an argument $\underline{u}$ described by Lévy [Lé78].

$$\begin{array}{rcl} ((\lambda y.\underline{\lambda x.t})v)\underline{u} & \rightarrow & (\lambda x.t^{\{y:=v\}})u \\ ((\lambda y.y)\underline{\lambda x.t})\underline{u} & \rightarrow & (\lambda x.t)u \\ (\lambda y.y\underline{u})\underline{\lambda x.t} & \rightarrow & (\lambda x.t)u \end{array}$$

These examples are valid independently of the restriction to weak reduction.

In the weak λ-calculus there is a new creation case, which can be observed when a frozen redex gets unfrozen.

Example 4.10.

In the source of the following reduction step, the expression $(\underline{\lambda x.yx})\underline{u}$ is not a redex because it is frozen by the variable y.

$$(\lambda y.((\underline{\lambda x.yx})\underline{u}))t \quad \rightarrow \quad (\lambda x.tx)u$$

[5] r **erases** r_e means that r_e has no residual after the reduction of r.

[6] This means that any "task" of ϱ_1 is either completed or erased by ϱ_2.

For the rest of this paper, it is enough to classify the redex creations in two categories: either the left part of an application evaluates to a λ-abstraction, or an application subterm is affected by a substitution. This classification is formalized by Redex creation Theorem 4.12. We begin with a lemma that considers the case of a redex creation at the root of a term.

Lemma 4.11 (Root redex creation). *Let $\rho : t = c[r] \to c[r'] = t'$ be a reduction step with $r = (\lambda x.u)v$ and $r' = u^{\{x:=v\}}$. Suppose $c \neq \Box$ and t' is a redex $r_c = (\lambda y.u_c)v_c$ that is created by ρ. Then the following holds:*

(1) $c = \Box v_c$ *and* $r' = \lambda y.u_c$.

Proof. Case analysis on $c \neq \Box$:

- Case $c = \lambda z.c'$, or $c = f(t_1, \ldots, c', \ldots, t_n)$. Then there exists u' such that $t' = \lambda z.u'$ (resp. $t' = f(t_1, \ldots, u', \ldots, t_n)$). Contradiction with the hypothesis that t' is a redex.
- Case $c = (\lambda y.u_c)c'$. Then the ancestor t of r_c is already a redex. Contradiction with the hypothesis that the redex r_c is created by ρ.
- Case $c = c'v_c$. Case analysis on c':
  - Case $c' = \Box$. Then $c = \Box v_c$ and $r' = \lambda y.u_c$. Hence proposition (1) holds.
  - Case $c' = t_1c''$ or $c''t_2$. Then $c = t_1c''v_c$ or $c = c''t_2v_c$, and there exists a pair t'_1, t'_2 such that $t' = t'_1t'_2v_c$. Contradiction with the hypothesis that t' is a redex
  - Case $c' = f(t_1, \ldots, c'', \ldots, t_n)$ is similar.
  - Case $c' = \lambda y.c''$. Then $c = (\lambda y.c'')v_c$, and the ancestor t of r_c is already a redex. Contradiction with the hypothesis that the redex r_c is created by ρ. □

Theorem 4.12 (Redex creation). *Let $\rho : t = c[r] \to c[r'] = t'$ be a reduction step with $r = (\lambda x.u)v$ and $r' = u^{\{x:=v\}}$. Let $r_c = (\lambda y.u_c)v_c$ be a redex in t' that is created by ρ. Write $t' = c_c[r_c]$. Then one of the following holds:*

(1) $c = c_c[\Box v_c]$ *and* $r' = \lambda y.u_c$.
(2) *The position* $\texttt{root}(r_c)$ *is a descendant of a position of the* x*-skeleton of* u.

Proof. Case analysis on the relative positions $\texttt{root}(r')$ and $\texttt{root}(r_c)$.

- If $\texttt{root}(r')$ and $\texttt{root}(r_c)$ are disjoint, then the redex r_c already exists in t. Contradiction with the hypothesis that the redex r_c is created by ρ.
- If $\texttt{root}(r_c)$ is a prefix of $\texttt{root}(r')$, then there is a c' such that $r_c = c'[r']$ and $t' = c_c[c'[r']]$. Since r_c is created by ρ, its ancestor $c'[r]$ is not a redex in $t = c_c[c'[r]]$. Suppose $c'[r]$ is a frozen redex. Then in $c'[r]$ there is a free occurrence of a variable x that is bound in c_c. Case analysis on the position of this variable occurrence:
  - If x appears in r, then r is a frozen redex. Contradiction with the hypothesis that the redex r is reduced
  - If x appears in c', then $r_c = c'[r']$ still contains x and r_c is a frozen redex. Contradiction with the hypothesis that r_c is a redex.

  Hence $c'[r]$ is not a frozen redex, and we can apply Root redex creation Lemma 4.11 to the step $c'[r] \to c'[r']$ to conclude.
- If $\texttt{root}(r')$ is a prefix of $\texttt{root}(r_c)$, then r_c is a subterm of $r' = u^{\{x:=v\}}$, and there are three cases to consider:
  - If r_c is in a substituted occurrence of v, then its ancestor is already a redex. Contradiction with the hypothesis that the redex r_c is created by ρ.
  - If $\texttt{root}(r_c)$ is in the x-skeleton of u but is not the position of an occurrence of x, then proposition (2) holds.
  - If $\texttt{root}(r_c)$ is in u but not in the x-skeleton of u, then the ancestor of r_c is equal to r_c and is already a redex. Contradiction with the hypothesis that the redex r_c is created by ρ. □

4.4 Weak labelled λ-calculus

From now on we use the full signature $\mathcal{S}$.

The classification of redex creations 4.12 will guide the definition of the labels following a simple principle: the labels have to record all possible redex creations. More precisely, each redex r (and by extension each reduction step ρ) is given a *name* that contains all the information relevant to the creation of r. Thus we expect at least two things:

- If a redex r is created by a reduction step ρ, then the name of ρ should influence the name of r in some way.
- Once a redex is created, its name never changes.

These two properties are formalized in Direct contribution Lemma 4.21 and Residuals Lemma 4.22. These properties will allow us to use the labels to define Lévy-style redex families.

A label is either an atomic label (here a position for technical convenience) or a combination $[\Omega, \alpha]$ of a name Ω and a label α. A name is a sequence of labels obtained by collecting the individual labels of the meaningful positions of the corresponding redex. Most of these definitions are taken from the previous paper [Bal12c]; the obtained system is a slight simplification of a labelling presented by Blanc, Lévy and Maranget [BLM07].

Definition 4.13 (Labels). *The set $\mathcal{L}$ of* **labels** *and the set $\mathcal{N}$ of* **redex names** *are defined by the following grammar:*

Labels $\mathcal{L}$	α	$::=$	$p \mid [\Omega, \alpha]$	p *position*
Names $\mathcal{N}$	Ω	$::=$	$\alpha_1 \ldots \alpha_n$	$n \geq 2$

The labelled signature $\mathcal{S}^{\mathcal{L}}$ is defined as

$$\mathcal{S}^{\mathcal{L}} = \{f^{\alpha} \mid f \in \mathcal{S},\ \alpha \in \mathcal{L}\}$$

where arities are preserved. Let $(.)^{\bullet}$ be the forgetful morphism that maps terms over $\mathcal{S}^{\mathcal{L}}$ to terms over $\mathcal{S}$ by removing their labels. For any term t over $\mathcal{S}^{\mathcal{L}}$ and any position $p \in \texttt{pos}(t)$, write $\tau_p(t)$ for the label of t at position p. In this section, call **initial** *a term over $\mathcal{S}^{\mathcal{L}}$ whose labels are all atomic (that is, a position) and different.*

The *contribution* relation is a straightforward containment relation on the labels. The strength of this simple syntactic notion is that it is equivalent to a more semantic notion of causal dependency between reduction steps, which we will prove in Section 4.5.

Definition 4.14 (Contribution). *The* **direct contribution** *relation $\hookrightarrow_{dc}$ is defined on names by the following criterion: $\Omega \hookrightarrow_{dc} \Omega_1[\Omega, \alpha]\Omega_2$ for any name Ω, any possibly empty names Ω_1, Ω_2, and any label α. The* **contribution** *relation $\hookrightarrow_c$ is the transitive closure of $\hookrightarrow_{dc}$.*

Definition 4.15 (Name of a redex). *A* **labelled redex** *is a term over $\mathcal{S}^{\mathcal{L}}$ of the form*

$$r = @^{\omega}(\varepsilon^{\alpha_1}(\ldots\varepsilon^{\alpha_n}(\lambda^{\gamma}x.t)), u)$$

Its **name** *is the sequence*

$$\texttt{name}(r) = \omega\alpha_1 \ldots \alpha_n\gamma$$

Labelled β-reduction introduces the name of the reduced redex at all the places identified by Redex creation Theorem 4.12 as possibly related to a redex creation: the labels of the skeleton are modified, and a new label is created at the root of the reduced redex.

Definition 4.16 (Uniform relabelling). *For any labelled n-ary context c and any label Ω, the* uniform relabelling $[\Omega, c]$ *of c by Ω is* *defined by the following equations:*

$$\begin{aligned}
[\Omega, \Box] &= \Box \\
[\Omega, x] &= x \\
[\Omega, \varepsilon^{\alpha}(c)] &= \varepsilon^{[\Omega,\alpha]}(c) \\
[\Omega, \lambda^{\alpha}x.c] &= \lambda^{[\Omega,\alpha]}x.[\Omega, c] \\
[\Omega, @^{\alpha}(c_1, c_2)] &= @^{[\Omega,\alpha]}([\Omega, c_1], [\Omega, c_2]) \\
[\Omega, f^{\alpha}(c_1, \dots, c_n)] &= f^{[\Omega,\alpha]}([\Omega, c_1], \dots, [\Omega, c_n])
\end{aligned}$$

Definition 4.17 (Labelled β-reduction). **Labelled β-reduction** *is defined by the following rule scheme:*

$$\begin{gathered}
@^{\omega}(\varepsilon^{\alpha_1}(\dots\varepsilon^{\alpha_n}(\lambda^{\gamma}x.s[Z_1, \dots, Z_n])), Z) \\
\to_{\beta} \\
[\omega\alpha_1\dots\alpha_n\gamma, \varepsilon^{\epsilon}(s)]^{\{x:=Z\}}[Z_1, \dots, Z_n]
\end{gathered}$$

where s is a $\{x\}$-skeleton.

Example 4.18.

In this example we work on a labelling of the ordinary λ-term $((\lambda x.xa)(\lambda y.y))b$. Consider the labelled term

$$t \quad = \quad @^{\alpha}(@^{\beta}(\varepsilon^{\gamma}(\lambda^{\delta}x.@^{\eta}(\varepsilon^{\iota}(x), \varepsilon^{\nu}(a))), \lambda^{\mu}y.y), \varepsilon^{\kappa}(b))$$

The term t contains a labelled redex

$$r \quad = \quad @^{\beta}(\varepsilon^{\gamma}(\lambda^{\delta}x.@^{\eta}(\varepsilon^{\iota}(x), \varepsilon^{\nu}(a))), \lambda^{\mu}y.y)$$

with name $\Omega = \beta\gamma\delta$. The skeleton of the λ-abstraction of r is

$$\lambda^{\delta}x.@^{\eta}(\varepsilon^{\iota}(x), \Box)$$

This skeleton is the only part whose labels are modified by labelled β-reduction. Hence

$$t \quad \to \quad @^{\alpha}(\varepsilon^{[\beta\gamma\delta,\epsilon]}(@^{[\beta\gamma\delta,\eta]}(\varepsilon^{[\beta\gamma\delta,\iota]}(\lambda^{\mu}y.y), \varepsilon^{\nu}(a))), \varepsilon^{\kappa}(b))$$

In the target of this reduction step, a labelled redex

$$r_c \quad = \quad @^{[\beta\gamma\delta,\eta]}(\varepsilon^{[\beta\gamma\delta,\iota]}(\lambda^{\mu}y.y), \varepsilon^{\nu}(a))$$

with name $\Omega_c = [\beta\gamma\delta, \eta][\beta\gamma\delta, \iota]\mu$ such that $\Omega \hookrightarrow_{dc} \Omega_c$.

Finally, we define a notion of *parallel labelled reduction* that is meant to represent shared evaluation.

Definition 4.19 (Parallel reduction). *Write $\bar{\rho} : t \Rightarrow t'$ if there exists a name Ω and a complete development $\varrho : t \twoheadrightarrow t'$ of all the labelled β-redexes in t of name Ω.*

4.5 Causality

In this section we show that the labels give a faithful account of causality in our system. Causal soundness Lemma 4.26 and Causal completeness Lemma 4.28 show that the set $\mathcal{N}$ of the names that contribute to a given redex name Ω is exactly the set of the names of the reduction steps that are needed to create a redex of name Ω from an initial term.

We formalize this fact using the following notion of *needed names*, which extends the notion of needed redexes.

Definition 4.20 (Needed name). *A name Ω_1 is said to be* **needed** *for a name Ω_2, written $\Omega_1 \hookrightarrow_n \Omega_2$, if every reduction sequence $\varrho\rho_2$ with $\mathtt{src}(\varrho\rho_2)$ initial and $\mathtt{name}(\rho_2) = \Omega_2$ is such that ϱ contains a reduction step of name Ω_1.*

This subsection is devoted to the proof that the semantic notion of neededness $\hookrightarrow_n$ is equivalent to the syntactic notion of contribution $\hookrightarrow_c$ (Causality Theorem 4.29). We begin with three lemmas that are not new, but that are useful to derive stronger causality properties.

Lemma 4.21 (Direct contribution). *For any reduction step $\rho : t \to t'$ of name Ω, if ρ_c is a reduction step from t' of name Ω_c that is created by ρ, then $\Omega \hookrightarrow_{dc} \Omega_c$.*

Proof. By a case analysis on the creation of ρ_c, guided by Redex creation Theorem 4.12. □

Lemma 4.22 (Residuals). *For any reduction step $\rho : t \to t'$, if ρ_a is a reduction step from t of name Ω, then any descendant in t' of $\mathtt{root}(\rho_a)$ is the root of a redex with same name Ω.*

Proof. Similar to the proof given by Blanc, Lévy, and Maranget [BLM07]. The main point is that a non-frozen redex cannot be relabelled. □

Lemma 4.23 (Finite developments). *Let t be a labelled λ-term and $\mathcal{R}$ a set of reduction steps from t. Then the three following hold:*

- *All the developments of $\mathcal{R}$ are finite.*
- *All the complete developments of $\mathcal{R}$ have the same target.*
- *All the complete developments of $\mathcal{R}$ define the same descendants and residuals.*

Proof. Deduced from finite developments for orthogonal TRS once the results from Section 5 are established. □

Causal soundness is the inclusion of $\hookrightarrow_c$ in $\hookrightarrow_n$. It is proved by tracking the origins of the labels and by checking that the labels do not record spurious contributions.

Lemma 4.24 (Reversed direct contribution). *Let ϱ be a reduction sequence from an initial term. If the target of ϱ contains a label of the form $[\Omega, \alpha]$, then the sequence ϱ contains a reduction step of name Ω.*

Proof. By induction on the length of ϱ, remarking that, at each step, any label $[\Omega, \alpha]$ is created or descends from an identical label. □

Lemma 4.25 (Direct neededness). *Let ϱ be a reduction sequence from an initial term. Let ρ be a reduction step from $t = \mathtt{tgt}(\varrho)$ and name Ω. If Ω' is a name such that $\Omega' \hookrightarrow_{dc} \Omega$, then ϱ contains a reduction step of name Ω'.*

Proof. Write $\Omega = \omega_1 \dots \omega_n$. By definition there exists i such that $\omega_i = [\Omega', \alpha]$. By definition of the name of a redex, there exists a position $p \in \mathtt{pos}(t)$ such that $\tau_p(t) = [\Omega', \alpha]$ for some label α. Then by Lemma 4.24 the reduction sequence ϱ contains a reduction step of name Ω'. □

Lemma 4.26 (Causal soundness). *Let Ω_1 and Ω_2 be two names such that $\Omega_1 \hookrightarrow_c \Omega_2$. Then $\Omega_1 \hookrightarrow_n \Omega_2$.*

Proof. By induction on the length of a shortest sequence $\Omega_1 \hookrightarrow_{dc} \dots \hookrightarrow_{dc} \Omega_2$.

- If $\Omega_1 \hookrightarrow_{dc} \Omega_2$, then by Direct neededness Lemma 4.25 any reduction sequence from an initial term to a term containing of redex of name Ω_2 contains a reduction step of name Ω_1, which means that $\Omega_1 \hookrightarrow_n \Omega_2$.
- If $\Omega_1 \hookrightarrow_{dc} \Omega_3 \hookrightarrow_c \Omega_2$ and $\Omega_3 \hookrightarrow_n \Omega_2$, then similarly $\Omega_1 \hookrightarrow_n \Omega_3$ and by transitivity of neededness $\Omega_1 \hookrightarrow_n \Omega_2$. □

Causal completeness is the inclusion of $\hookrightarrow_n$ in $\hookrightarrow_c$. It is proved by checking that reduction steps whose names are not comparable can be permuted.

Lemma 4.27 (Permutation). *If $t_0 \Rightarrow_{\Omega_0} t_1 \Rightarrow_{\Omega} t_2$ and $\Omega_0 \not\hookrightarrow_c \Omega$, then one of the following holds:*

- *$t_0 \Rightarrow_{\Omega} t_2$.*
- *There is a t_1' such that $t_0 \Rightarrow_{\Omega} t_1' \Rightarrow_{\Omega_0} t_2$.*

Proof. Since $\Omega_0 \not\hookrightarrow_c \Omega$, by contraposition of Direct contribution Lemma 4.21 the redexes of name Ω in t_1 are the residuals of redexes in t_0. In particular $t_0 \Rightarrow_{\Omega_0} t_1 \Rightarrow_{\Omega} t_2$ is a complete development of the set of all redexes in t_0 of name Ω_0 or Ω. By Finite developments Lemma 4.23 the term t_2 is the target of any complete development of these redexes, and in particular of the one first developing all the redexes of name Ω and then developing all the redexes of name Ω_0 if they have not been erased by the first step. □

Lemma 4.28 (Causal completeness)**.** *Let Ω_0 and Ω be two names such that $\Omega_0 \hookrightarrow_n \Omega$. Then $\Omega_0 \hookrightarrow_c \Omega$.*

Proof. Write $\bar{\mathcal{R}}$ for the set of all parallel labelled reduction sequences of minimal length from an initial term to a term containing redexes of name Ω. There is a n such that every sequence $\bar{\varrho} \in \bar{\mathcal{R}}$ has the form $\Rightarrow_{\Omega_1^\varrho} \dots \Rightarrow_{\Omega_n^\varrho}$. Write $\bar{\mathcal{R}}^*$ for the set of all sequences $\bar{\varrho} \in \bar{\mathcal{R}}$ for which there is at least one $i \in \{1, \dots, n\}$ such that $\Omega_i^\varrho \not\hookrightarrow_c \Omega$.

Suppose $\bar{\mathcal{R}}^*$ is not empty and let i be the greatest integer such that there is a sequence $\bar{\varrho} \in \bar{\mathcal{R}}^*$ satisfying $\Omega_i^\varrho \not\hookrightarrow_c \Omega$. Let $\bar{\varrho}$ be such a sequence in $\bar{\mathcal{R}}^*$ satisfying $\Omega_i^\varrho \not\hookrightarrow_c \Omega$. The sequence $\bar{\varrho}$ has the form $\Rightarrow_{\Omega_1^\varrho} \dots \Rightarrow_{\Omega_i^\varrho} \Rightarrow_{\Omega_{i+1}^\varrho} \dots \Rightarrow_{\Omega_n^\varrho}$.

By definition of $\bar{\varrho}$ we have $\Omega_{i+1}^\varrho \hookrightarrow_c \Omega$. Since $\Omega_i^\varrho \not\hookrightarrow_c \Omega$, by transitivity of $\hookrightarrow_c$ we get $\Omega_i^\varrho \not\hookrightarrow_c \Omega_{i+1}^\varrho$. Then by Permutation Lemma 4.27 we can build one of the following sequences:

- A sequence $\Rightarrow_{\Omega_1^\varrho} \dots \Rightarrow_{\Omega_{i-1}^\varrho} \Rightarrow_{\Omega_{i+1}^\varrho} \dots \Rightarrow_{\Omega_n^\varrho}$ strictly shorter than $\bar{\varrho}$, which contradicts the minimality of the length of $\bar{\varrho}$.
- A sequence $\Rightarrow_{\Omega_1^\varrho} \dots \Rightarrow_{\Omega_{i+1}^\varrho} \Rightarrow_{\Omega_i^\varrho} \dots \Rightarrow_{\Omega_n^\varrho}$ with $\Omega_i^\varrho \not\hookrightarrow_c \Omega$, of same length as $\bar{\rho}$ but which contradicts the maximality of i.

Hence the set $\bar{\mathcal{R}}^*$ must be empty, and every name Ω_0 that appears in a reduction sequence in $\bar{\mathcal{R}}$ satisfies $\Omega_0 \hookrightarrow_c \Omega$.

Finally, let Ω_0 be a name such that $\Omega_0 \hookrightarrow_n \Omega$. By definition 4.20, every reduction sequence ϱ from an initial term to a term that contains redexes of name Ω contains a step of name Ω_0. It is in particular the case of any reduction sequence developing a sequence in $\bar{\mathcal{R}}$. Hence $\Omega_0 \hookrightarrow_c \Omega$. □

Finally, Causal soundness Lemma 4.26 and Causal completeness Lemma 4.28 can be combined to prove that the syntactic contribution relation $\hookrightarrow_c$ and the semantic neededness relation $\hookrightarrow_n$ are equal.

Theorem 4.29 (Causality)**.** $\hookrightarrow_c = \hookrightarrow_n$.

4.6 The labelled weak λ-calculus as a DFS

Using the labels of Section 4.4 we get a straightforward definition for families.

Definition 4.30 (Families)**.** *The* **family relation** $\simeq$ *over reduction steps with history is defined by the following condition: $(\varrho_1, \rho_1) \simeq (\varrho_2, \rho_2)$ if and only if the reduction steps ρ_1 and ρ_2 have the same name. Hence families correspond to names, and we extend the* **contribution relation** $\hookrightarrow_c$ *to families.*

Notice that we do not use the histories ϱ_1 and ϱ_2 in the previous definition. Indeed, thanks to the causal labelling, the labels in the target of a reduction sequence ϱ already contains all the relevant pieces of information about ϱ.

Lemma 4.31. *The labelled weak λ-calculus equipped with its family relation is a Deterministic Family Structure.*

Proof. We first check that the labelled weak λ-calculus is a *DRS*:

[FD] Direct application of the Finite developments Lemma 4.23.

[Acyclicity] In the λ-calculus, if a redex r erases a redex r_e, then r_e is a strict subterm of r. The subterm relation being acyclic, there is no possible cross-erasure.

The axioms for DFS are then checked as follows:

[Initial] Let ρ_1 and ρ_2 be two reduction steps from a common initial term t. If ρ_1 and ρ_2 are different, in particular they apply to different positions and have different names.

[Copy] Suppose $(\varrho_1, \rho_1) \rhd (\varrho_2, \rho_2)$, then in particular $\rho_2 \in \rho_1/(\varrho_2/\varrho_1)$. By Residuals Lemma 4.22 the reduction steps ρ_2 and ρ_1 have the same name, hence (ϱ_1, ρ_1) and (ϱ_2, ρ_2) are in the same family.

[FFD] Orthogonal TRS satisfy the Finite Family Developments property [vO97]. Hence the weak λ-calculus does the same by Bisimulation Proposition 5.10.

[Creation] Direct application of Direct contribution Lemma 4.21.

[Contribution] This axiom can be reworded as $\hookrightarrow_c = \hookrightarrow_n$. Conclusion by Causality Theorem 4.29. □

Thus, by Glauert and Khasidashvili's Optimality Proposition 4.8, any complete needed weak family reduction sequence is optimal, which we call *weak optimality*. Such concrete reduction strategies will be detailed in Section 6.

5. Weak reduction and first-order rewriting

In this section we show that the weak λ-calculus behaves as an orthogonal first-order rewriting system[7]. First in Section 5.1 we recall the formalization of λ-lifting as a higher-order rewriting system given in the previous paper [Bal12c], which can be used to prove that the weak λ-calculus is strongly bisimilar to an orthogonal first-order term rewriting system; then in Section 5.2 we show that the transformation moreover preserves concepts and properties such as residuals or neededness.

5.1 Fully lazy λ-lifting

We formalize fully lazy λ-lifting as a higher-order rewriting system that replaces a skeleton by a single supercombinator symbol. The labelling of the transformation presented here is a slight simplification of the one of the previous paper [Bal12c], but it has roughly the same properties.

Definition 5.1 (Expansor)**.** *An* **expansor** *is a bijection $\psi : \mathcal{F} \to \langle\langle \Lambda \rangle\rangle$ that preserves arity. For any $f, g \in \mathcal{F}$ we say that g* **contains** *f and we write $g \supset f$ if f appears in the expansion $\psi(g)$. An expansor ψ is* **well-founded** *if there is no infinite sequence $f_1 \supset f_2 \supset \dots$.*

For the rest of the paper, let ψ be a fixed well-founded expansor. Such a bijection between $\mathcal{F}$ and $\langle\langle \Lambda \rangle\rangle$ exists since for any n the set of n-ary contexts is countable.

For any λ-term t containing $\mathcal{F}$-symbols, the expansor ψ describes a structure that is implicit in t, in some sense hidden in the $\mathcal{F}$-symbols. The notion of *extended position* in a λ-term t gives a partial account of this structure by indicating ordinary positions of t as well as "internal" positions of the $\mathcal{F}$-symbols.

Definition 5.2 (Extended positions)**.** *The set of the* **ψ-extended positions** *of a λ-term, or simply* **ψ-positions** *of t, written $\mathsf{pos}_\psi(t)$, is defined as follows:*

$$\begin{aligned} \mathsf{pos}_\psi(x) &= \{\epsilon\} \\ \mathsf{pos}_\psi(\lambda x.t) &= \{\epsilon\} \cup 1 \cdot \mathsf{pos}_\psi(t) \\ \mathsf{pos}_\psi(t_1 t_2) &= \{\epsilon\} \cup 1 \cdot \mathsf{pos}_\psi(t_1) \cup 2 \cdot \mathsf{pos}_\psi(t_2) \\ \mathsf{pos}_\psi(f(t_1, ..., t_n)) &= \{\epsilon\} \cup (0 \cdot \mathsf{pos}_\psi(\psi(f))) \cup (\textstyle\bigcup_i i \cdot \mathsf{pos}_\psi(t_i)) \end{aligned}$$

[7] A rewriting system is **orthogonal** when its rewriting rules cannot interfere with each other.

This set if finite since ψ is well-founded.

Example 5.3.

Consider the λ-term

$$t \quad = \quad f(@(z_1, z_2), z_3)$$

and suppose the following expansions (with f and g two binary symbols):

$$\begin{array}{rcl} \psi(f) & = & \lambda x.\Box g(\Box, x) \\ \psi(g) & = & \lambda y.y\Box\Box \end{array}$$

The following picture shows t and the expansions of the symbols f and g.

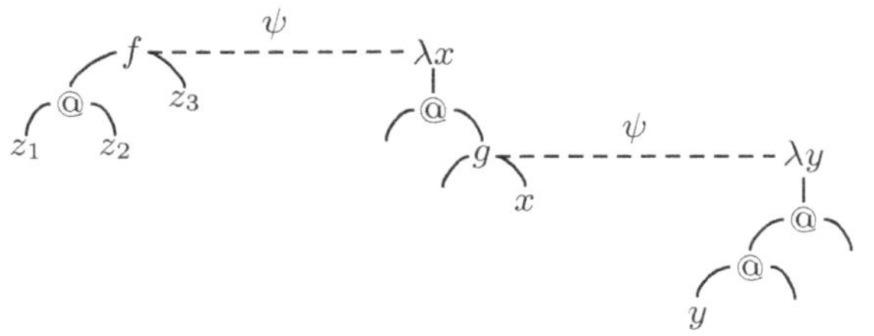

The set of positions of t is $\texttt{pos}(t) \;=\; \{\epsilon, 1, 11, 12, 2\}$. The set of ψ-positions of t is:

$$\texttt{pos}_\psi(t) \quad = \quad \{\epsilon, 1, 11, 12, 2, 0, 01, 012, 0122, 0120, 01201, 012011, 0120111\}$$

The following table gives a correspondence between some ψ-positions of t and symbols from t, $\psi(f)$, or $\psi(g)$.

ϵ	f
0	λx
012	g
0120	λy

With the next two definitions we propose an initial labelling that takes into account the expansions of the term. Intuitively, each node is labelled by the position it would have if the term were fully expansed.

Definition 5.4 (Expansed positions). *Let c be a n-ary context and $p \in \texttt{pos}(c)$ a position of c. The* **expansion** *of p relative to c is the position $(p)^{c,\psi}$ defined by:*

$$\begin{array}{rcll} (\epsilon)^{c,\psi} & = & \epsilon & \\ (1 \cdot p)^{\varepsilon(c),\psi} & = & 1 \cdot (p)^{c,\psi} & \\ (1 \cdot p)^{\lambda x.c,\psi} & = & 1 \cdot (p)^{c,\psi} & \\ (i \cdot p)^{c_1 c_2,\psi} & = & i \cdot (p)^{c_i,\psi} & i \in \{1, 2\} \\ (i \cdot p)^{f(c_1,\ldots,c_n),\psi} & = & (q_i)^{\psi(f),\psi} \cdot (p)^{c_i,\psi} & i \in \{1, \ldots, n\} \\ & & & q_i \text{ position of } i^{th} \text{ hole in } \psi(f) \end{array}$$

Definition 5.5 (Extended initial labelling). *For any position p, the function $i_p(.)$ maps λ-terms to labelled λ-terms through the following rules:*

$$\begin{array}{rcl} i_p(x) & = & x \\ i_p(\varepsilon(t)) & = & \varepsilon^p(i_{p\cdot 1}(t)) \\ i_p(\lambda x.t) & = & \lambda^p x.i_{p\cdot 1}(t) \\ i_p(t_1 t_2) & = & @^p(i_{p\cdot 1}(t_1), i_{p\cdot 2}(t_2)) \\ i_p(f(t_1, \ldots, t_n)) & = & f^p(i_{p\cdot q_1}(t_1), \ldots, i_{p\cdot q_n}(t_n)) \\ & & \forall j.\ q_j = (j)^{f(t_1,\ldots,t_n),\psi} \end{array}$$

Let t be a λ-term. The **initial labelling** *of t is the labelled λ-term $i_\epsilon(t)$, also written $i(t)$.*

Example 5.6.

Consider the λ-term $t = f(@(z_1, z_2), z_3)$ from example 5.3. Then

$$i(t) \quad = \quad f^\epsilon(@^{11}(z_1, z_2), z_3)$$

With this extended initial labelling, we can now define the *target system*, that is the first-order rewriting system to which the weak λ-calculus is bisimilar.

Definition 5.7 (Target redex). *A* **target redex** *is a term over $\mathcal{S}^\mathcal{L}$ of the form*

$$@^\omega(\varepsilon^{\alpha_1}(\ldots \varepsilon^{\alpha_n}(f^\gamma(t_1, \ldots, t_n))), u)$$

Its **name** *is the sequence*

$$\texttt{name}(r) = \omega\alpha_1 \ldots \alpha_n\gamma$$

Definition 5.8 (Source & Target reductions). *The* **source reduction** *is the labelled β-reduction of definition 4.17. The* **target reduction** *is given by the following rule scheme:*

$$\begin{array}{c} @^\omega(\varepsilon^{\alpha_1}(\ldots \varepsilon^{\alpha_n}(f^\gamma(Z_1, \ldots, Z_n))), Z) \\ \to_f \\ [\omega\alpha_1 \ldots \alpha_n\gamma,\ [\Omega_k, \ldots [\Omega_1, \varepsilon^\epsilon(i_p(s))]]\ ]^{\{x := Z\}}[Z_1, \ldots, Z_n] \end{array}$$

where $\gamma = [\Omega_k, \ldots [\Omega_1, p]]$ and $\psi(f) = \lambda x.s$.

Definition 5.9 (Lambda-lifting). *The λ-lifting rewriting system is defined by the following rules applied in any context (no restriction to weak reduction here).*

- *For any label α, variable x, and $\{x\}$-skeleton s, the pair $\lambda^\alpha x.s[Z_1, ..., Z_n] \;\to_c\; (\psi^{-1}(\lambda x.s^\bullet))^\alpha(Z_1, ..., Z_n)$ is a λ-* **lifting rule of rank** *0.*
- *A pair $f(Z_1, \ldots, Z_n) \to f'(Z_1, \ldots, Z_n)$ is called a* **λ-lifting rule of rank** *$n + 1$ if there is a reduction step $\psi(f) \to \psi(f')$ by a λ-lifting rule of rank n.*

Proposition 5.10 (Bisimulation, Balabonski [Bal12c]). *The λ-lifting relation $\twoheadrightarrow_{\texttt{lft}}$ is a strong bisimulation in the global system.*

It is also known that the λ-lifting reduction relation is convergent, and compatible with sharing. In the next section we add new results that ensure that $\twoheadrightarrow_{\texttt{lft}}$ preserves the properties that are useful to the study of optimality.

5.2 Properties preserved by the reduction to first order

For any term t, write $\texttt{lift}(t)$ for the normal form of t by λ-lifting. Similarly, for any position p of a term t, write $\texttt{lift}(p)$ for the set of its descendants along any complete lifting of t, and for any source reduction step ρ from t, write $\texttt{lift}(\rho)$ for the residual of ρ after any complete lifting of t.

In this section we show that $\texttt{lift}(.)$ preserves descendants, residuals, and neededness.

Lemma 5.11 (Labels and descendants). *Let t be a labelled term whose labels are initial and different, and $t \twoheadrightarrow t'$ be a reduction sequence. Then a position $p' \in \texttt{pos}(t')$ is a descendant of a position $p \in \texttt{pos}(t)$ if and only if there are names $\Omega_1, \ldots, \Omega_n$ such that $\tau_{t'}(p') = [\Omega_n, \ldots [\Omega_1, \tau_t(p)]]$.*

Proof. By induction on the length of the sequence, with the following generalized statement:

For any labelled term t, reduction sequence $\varrho : t \to t'$, and position p_0, write

$$\begin{array}{l} P_\alpha = \{p \in \texttt{pos}(t) \mid \exists k,\ \exists \Omega_k \ldots \Omega_1,\ \tau_p(t) = [\Omega_k, \ldots [\Omega_1, p_0]]\} \\ P'_\alpha = \{p' \in \texttt{pos}(t') \mid \exists k',\ \exists \Omega_{k'} \ldots \Omega_1,\ \tau_p(t) = [\Omega_{k'}, \ldots [\Omega_1, p_0]]\} \end{array}$$

for the sets of the positions of t and t' where p_0 appears. Then

$$P'_\alpha = P_\alpha / \varrho \qquad \Box$$

With this characterization of descendants, we can use confluence results on a labelled system to get results about descendants and residuals.

Lemma 5.12 (Preservation of descendants). *Let t be a λ-term, $p \in \texttt{pos}(t)$ a position, and $\rho : t \to t'$ a source reduction step. Then $\texttt{lift}(p/\rho) = \texttt{lift}(p)/\texttt{lift}(\rho)$.*

Proof. By Bisimulation Proposition 5.10 we have the following diagram:

$$\begin{array}{ccc} t & \overset{\varrho_{\mathit{lft}}}{\twoheadrightarrow} & \texttt{lift}(t) \\ \rho \downarrow & & \downarrow \texttt{lift}(\rho) \\ t' & \overset{\varrho'_{\mathit{lft}}}{\twoheadrightarrow} & \texttt{lift}(t') \end{array}$$

By definition of descendants along a reduction sequence we have $\texttt{lift}(p/\rho) = (p/\rho)/\varrho'_{\mathit{lft}} = p/(\rho\varrho'_{\mathit{lft}})$ as well as $p/(\varrho_{\mathit{lft}}\texttt{lift}(\rho)) = (p/\varrho_{\mathit{lft}})/\texttt{lift}(\rho) = \texttt{lift}(p)/\texttt{lift}(\rho)$. Since the sequences $\rho\varrho'_{\mathit{lft}}$ and $\varrho_{\mathit{lft}}\texttt{lift}(\rho)$ have same target, by Labels and descendants Lemma 5.11 we also have $p/(\rho\varrho'_{\mathit{lft}}) = p/(\varrho_{\mathit{lft}}\texttt{lift}(\rho))$. By combining these equations we get $\texttt{lift}(p/\rho) = \texttt{lift}(p)/\texttt{lift}(\rho)$. □

The preservation of residuals is an immediate corollary of the preservation of descendants.

Lemma 5.13 (Preservation of residuals). *Let $\rho : t \to t'$, $\rho_a : t \to u$ and $\rho_r : t' \to u'$ be three source reduction steps. Then ρ_r is a residual of ρ_a after ρ if and only if $\texttt{lift}(\rho_r)$ is a residual of $\texttt{lift}(\rho_a)$ after $\texttt{lift}(\rho)$.*

Finally, we deduce that λ-lifting also preserves the notion of neededness, which will allow us in the next section to transfer a result on needed strategies from first-order rewriting to the weak λ-calculus.

Theorem 5.14 (Preservation of neededness). *Let t be a normalizing term. Then a source reduction step ρ from t is needed if and only if the target reduction step $\texttt{lift}(\rho)$ is needed in the target system.*

Proof. Let ρ be a needed source reduction step from t. Let $\varrho^f = \rho^f_1 \dots \rho^f_n$ be a normalizing target reduction sequence from $\texttt{lift}(t)$. By Bisimulation Proposition 5.10 we have a normalizing source reduction sequence $\varrho = \rho_1 \dots \rho_n$ from t. By hypothesis ρ is needed, hence there exists i such that ρ_i is a residual of ρ. By Preservation of residuals Lemma 5.13, the reduction step ρ^f_i is a residual of $\texttt{lift}(\rho)$. Hence $\texttt{lift}(\rho)$ is needed.

We show similarly that if $\texttt{lift}(\rho)$ is needed, then ρ is also needed. □

The properties stated in this section show that the weak λ-calculus, while it has the appearance of the λ-calculus, has the properties of a first-order rewriting system. This first-order essence of weak reduction will become even more apparent in the next section.

6. Two weakly optimal strategies

We conclude our investigation by identifying two strategies that realize the weak optimality characterized in Section 4. The first strategy (Section 6.1) is *call-by-need*: Wadsworth's well-known technique for efficient evaluation of the λ-calculus [Wad71], which is also the source of mainstream lazy evaluation mechanisms. The second strategy (Section 6.2) is a bit more intriguing, since it reaches optimality without using any sharing (but of course, following Uncomputability Theorem 3.14 the latter cannot be computable).

6.1 Call-by-need

As shown in the previous paper [Bal12c], the labelled weak λ-calculus defined in Section 4 describes a graph-based evaluation mechanism for the λ-calculus, which is exactly the one proposed by Wadsworth [Wad71]. This is done through the technique of sharing-via-labelling [Mar91, Bal12a], that has first been introduced by Maranget.

The main idea is as follows: if two subterms t^δ have the same label δ, then they represent the same node in the corresponding graph (this node is marked with a star in the picture below), and have to be reduced in only one step.

$$\begin{array}{l} @^\alpha(@^\beta(t^\gamma, \underline{t^\delta}), \underline{t^\delta}) \\ \Rightarrow @^\alpha(@^\beta(t^\gamma, t'^\varsigma), t'^\varsigma) \end{array}$$

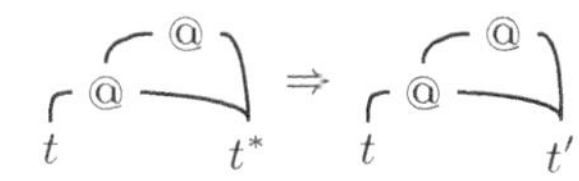

This principle allows us to interpret labelled terms as graphs, provided a consistency property of the labels is satisfied: two subterms that have the same label must be equal.

Finally, the following proposition ensures that parallel reduction preserves the consistency of labels, and thus describes a graph rewriting system. Moreover, this graph rewriting system is known to correspond to Wadsworth's original technique [Bal12c].

Proposition 6.1 (Sharing-via-labelling, Balabonski [Bal12c]). *The following property is preserved by parallel reduction:*

Sharing *If $\tau_{p_1}(t) = \tau_{p_2}(t)$ then $t|_{p_1} = t|_{p_2}$.*

Hence Wadsworth's call-by-need implements complete family reduction. Moreover, call-by-need is known to reduce only needed redexes [BKKS87], and thus Glauert and Khasidashvili's Optimality Proposition 4.8 applies.

Theorem 6.2 (Optimality). *Wadsworth's call-by-need is a weakly optimal reduction strategy.*

Besides marking a well-known reduction strategy as weakly optimal, this optimality theorem reveals a difference between weak and non-weak reduction: while any implementation of non-weak optimality requires a sharing of contexts (see example 4.2), the sharing of subterms expressible by sharing-via-labelling is enough for weak optimality.

6.2 Innermost needed reduction

Now we are going to combine the results of the previous sections to prove that the shortest weak reduction sequences without sharing have the same length as the complete needed family reduction sequences. First we transfer a sufficient condition for a reduction strategy to be optimal from the first-order rewriting literature to our system, then we check that this condition describes a subset of complete needed family reduction.

Proposition 6.3 describes a sufficient condition for a reduction strategy to be optimal in orthogonal term rewriting systems, that has been established by Khasidashvili. Using our formalization of λ-lifting, we transfer this result to the weak λ-calculus.

Proposition 6.3 (Khasidashvili's optimality criterion [Kha93]). *Let t be a term in an orthogonal* TRS, *and ϱ a normalizing reduction sequence of source t in which each step reduces an innermost needed redex. Then no normalizing reduction sequence of source t is shorter than ϱ.*

Theorem 6.4 (Optimality criterion). *Let t be a λ-term, and ϱ a normalizing weak reduction sequence of source t in which each step reduces an innermost needed redex. Then no normalizing weak reduction sequence of source t is shorter than ϱ.*

Proof. Suppose there is a normalizing weak reduction sequence ϱ' of source t that is shorter than ϱ. Let ϱ_f (resp. ϱ'_f) be the image of ϱ (resp. ϱ') in the target system. By Bisimulation Proposition 5.10, ϱ_f and ϱ'_f have the same source, are both normalizing, and ϱ'_f is shorter than ϱ_f. Moreover, by Preservation of neededness Theorem 5.14, each reduction step in the sequence ϱ_f reduces an innermost needed redex. Hence by Khasidashvili's Optimality Proposition 6.3 the reduction sequence ϱ_f is of minimal length, which contradicts the existence of the sequences ϱ'_f and ϱ'. □

This criterion shows once again that weak reduction is closer to first-order rewriting than to the usual non-weak λ-calculus. Indeed, Guerrini proved with a counter-example that innermost needed reduction is not optimal in the non-weak λ-calculus [Gue96].

Lemma 6.5. *An innermost needed reduction step does not duplicate any needed redex.*

Proof. Deduced from Khasidashvili's results [Kha93] using λ-lifting. □

Thus an innermost needed reduction sequence performs only needed reduction steps on redexes that have not been duplicated, and such a sequence is an instance of complete needed family reduction.

Theorem 6.6 (Optimality). *Innermost needed reduction is a weakly optimal reduction strategy.*

This optimality theorem gives away another important difference between weak and non-weak reduction. Indeed, Lamping exhibited an example for which non-weak Lévy-optimality cannot be realized without sharing [Lam90].

7. Conclusion

We characterized optimal evaluation in the weak λ-calculus and identified two interesting weakly optimal strategies: the well-known call-by-need strategy, and innermost needed reduction. The latter illustrates the fact that the weak λ-calculus has the properties of a first-order rewriting system, and also shows that weakly optimal evaluation does not require sharing. However, we also showed that the optimal strategies without sharing cannot be computable. Finally, in the setting of weak reduction the meaning of sharing is not to make the shortest path shorter, but rather to make it effectively reachable.

Acknowledgments

Thanks to Delia Kesner, Olivier Danvy and Vincent van Oostrom, who offered me the tools to explore this topic. Thanks also to François Pottier, Mike Rainey, and the ICFP reviewers for their helpful comments and suggestions.

References

[Bal12a] Thibaut Balabonski. Axiomatic sharing-via-labelling. In Ashish Tiwari, editor, *RTA*, volume 15 of *LIPIcs*, pages 85–100. Schloss Dagstuhl - Leibniz-Zentrum fuer Informatik, 2012.

[Bal12b] Thibaut Balabonski. *La pleine paresse, une certaine optimalité.* Ph.D. thesis, Université Paris 7 – Diderot, 2012.

[Bal12c] Thibaut Balabonski. A unified approach to fully lazy sharing. In John Field and Michael Hicks, editors, *POPL*, pages 469–480. ACM, 2012.

[Bar84] Hendrik Pieter Barendregt. *The Lambda Calculus – Its Syntax and Semantics*, volume 103 of *Studies in Logic and the Foundations of Mathematics*. North-Holland Publishing Company, Amsterdam, revised edition edition, 1984.

[BBKV76] Hendrik Pieter Barendregt, Jan A. Bergstra, Jan Willem Klop, and Henri Volken. Some notes on lambda reduction. Technical Report 22, University of Utrecht, Dpt. of mathematics, 1976.

[BKKS87] Hendrik Pieter Barendregt, Richard Kennaway, Jan Willem Klop, and M. Ronan Sleep. Needed reduction and spine strategies for the lambda calculus. *Information and Computation*, 75(3):191–231, 1987.

[BLM07] Tomasz Blanc, Jean-Jacques Lévy, and Luc Maranget. Sharing in the weak lambda-calculus revisited. In Erik Barendsen, Herman Geuvers, Venanzio Capretta, and Milad Niqui, editors, *Reflections on Type Theory, Lambda Calculus, and the Mind*, pages 41–50. ICIS, Faculty of Science, Radbout University Nijmegen, 2007. Essays Dedicated to Henk Barendregt on the Occasion of his 60th Birthday.

[cH98] Naim Çagman and J. Roger Hindley. Combinatory weak reduction in lambda calculus. *Theoretical Computer Science*, 198(1-2):239–247, 1998.

[DS00] Olivier Danvy and Ulrik Pagh Schultz. Lambda-dropping: transforming recursive equations into programs with block structure. *Theoretical Computer Science*, 248(1-2):243–287, 2000.

[GK96] John R. W. Glauert and Zurab Khasidashvili. Relative normalization in deterministic residual structures. In Hélène Kirchner, editor, *CAAP*, volume 1059 of *Lecture Notes in Computer Science*, pages 180–195. Springer, 1996.

[Gue96] Stefano Guerrini. *Theoretical and Practical Issues of Optimal Implementations of Functional Languages*. Ph.D. thesis, Università di Pisa, 1996.

[How70] William Alvin Howard. Assignment of ordinals to terms for primitive recursive functionals of finite type. In *Intuitionism and Proof Theory*, pages 443–458, 1970.

[Kha93] Zurab Khasidashvili. Optimal normalization in orthogonal term rewriting systems. In Claude Kirchner, editor, *RTA*, volume 690 of *Lecture Notes in Computer Science*, pages 243–258. Springer, 1993.

[KvOvR93] Jan Willem Klop, Vincent van Oostrom, and Femke van Raamsdonk. Combinatory reduction systems: Introduction and survey. *Theoretical Computer Science*, 121(1&2):279–308, 1993.

[Lam90] John Lamping. An algorithm for optimal lambda calculus reduction. In Frances E. Allen, editor, *POPL*, pages 16–30. ACM Press, 1990.

[Lé78] Jean-Jacques Lévy. *Réductions correctes et optimales dans le lambda-calcul*. Ph.D. thesis, Université Paris VII, 1978.

[Lé80] Jean-Jacques Lévy. Optimal reductions in the lambda-calculus. In *To H.B. Curry: Essays on Combinatory Logic, Lambda Calculus and Formalisms*, pages 159–191, 1980.

[Mar91] Luc Maranget. Optimal derivations in weak lambda-calculi and in orthogonal terms rewriting systems. In David S. Wise, editor, *POPL*, pages 255–269. ACM Press, 1991.

[PJ87] Simon L. Peyton-Jones. *The Implementation of Functional Programming Languages*. Prentice-Hall, 1987.

[Sco68] Dana Scott. A system of functional abstraction, 1968. Lectures delivered at University of California, Berkeley, Cal., 1962/63.

[Ter03] Terese. *Term Rewriting Seminar – Terese*. Vol. 55 of Cambridge Tracts in Theoretical Computer Science. Cambridge University Press, 2003.

[vO97] Vincent van Oostrom. Finite family developments. In Hubert Comon, editor, *RTA*, volume 1232 of *Lecture Notes in Computer Science*, pages 308–322. Springer, 1997.

[Wad71] Christopher P. Wadsworth. *Semantics and Pragmatics of the Lambda Calculus*. Ph.D. thesis, Oxford, 1971.

System FC with Explicit Kind Equality

Stephanie Weirich Justin Hsu Richard A. Eisenberg

Department of Computer and Information Science, University of Pennsylvania
Philadelphia, PA, USA
{sweirich,justhsu,eir}@cis.upenn.edu

Abstract

System FC, the core language of the Glasgow Haskell Compiler, is an explicitly-typed variant of System F with first-class type equality proofs called *coercions*. This extensible proof system forms the foundation for type system extensions such as type families (type-level functions) and Generalized Algebraic Datatypes (GADTs). Such features, in conjunction with kind polymorphism and datatype promotion, support expressive compile-time reasoning.

However, the core language lacks explicit *kind* equality proofs. As a result, type-level computation does not have access to kind-level functions or promoted GADTs, the type-level analogues to expression-level features that have been so useful. In this paper, we eliminate such discrepancies by introducing kind equalities to System FC. Our approach is based on dependent type systems with heterogeneous equality and the "Type-in-Type" axiom, yet it preserves the metatheoretic properties of FC. In particular, type checking is simple, decidable and syntax directed. We prove the preservation and progress theorems for the extended language.

Categories and Subject Descriptors F.3.3 [*Studies of Program Constructs*]: Type structure

General Terms Design, Languages

Keywords Haskell, Dependent types, Equality

1. Introduction

Is Haskell a dependently typed programming language? Many would say no, as Haskell fundamentally does not allow expressions to appear in types (a defining characteristic of dependently-typed languages). However, the type system of the Glasgow Haskell Compiler (GHC), Haskell's primary implementation, supports two essential features of dependently typed languages: *flow-sensitive typing* through Generalized Algebraic Datatypes (GADTs) (Peyton Jones et al. 2006; Schrijvers et al. 2009), and rich *type-level computation* through type classes (Jones 2000), type families (Chakravarty et al. 2005), datatype promotion and kind polymorphism (Yorgey et al. 2012). These two features allow clever Haskellers to encode programs that are typically reputed to need dependent types.

ICFP '13, September 25–27, 2013, Boston, MA, USA.

ACM 978-1-4503-2326-0/13/09... $15.00.
http://dx.doi.org/10.1145/2500365.2500599

However, these encodings cannot accommodate all dependently-typed programs. GADTs and type families are supported in FC, GHC's typed intermediate language, through the use of first-class type equalities (Sulzmann et al. 2007). However, FC lacks first-class *kind equalities* limiting its expressiveness. As a result, *GADTs cannot be promoted*, because the type equalities in their definition cannot be lifted to kind equalities. Furthermore, *GADTs cannot be indexed by kinds*, which would require reasoning about kind equality. Finally, although type families permit types to be defined computationally, the lack of kind equalities means there are *no kind families* in GHC. Although these features seem esoteric, they are often necessary for encoding dependently-typed programs in GHC (Eisenberg and Weirich 2012). We give concrete examples that require these features in Section 2.

Our goal in this paper is to eliminate such nonuniformities with a single blow, by unifying types and kinds. In essence, we augment FC's type language with dependent kinds—kinds that can depend on types. This process is not without challenges—this dependency has complex interactions with type equality. However, our ultimate goal is to better support dependently typed programming in GHC, and resolving these issues is an critical step.

Specifically, we make the following technical contributions:

- We describe an explicitly-typed intermediate language with explicit equality proofs for both types *and kinds* (Sections 3 and 4). The language is no toy: it is an extension of the System FC intermediate language used by GHC (Sulzmann et al. 2007; Weirich et al. 2011; Yorgey et al. 2012; Vytiniotis et al. 2012).
- We extend the *type preservation* proof of FC to cover the new features (Section 5). The treatment of datatypes requires an important property: *congruence* for the equational theory. In other words, we can derive a proof of equality for any form of type or kind, given equality proofs of subcomponents. The computational content of this theorem, called *lifting*, generalizes the standard substitution operation. This operation is required in the operational semantics for datatypes.
- We prove the *progress* theorem in the presence of kind coercions and dependent coercion abstraction. The progress theorem holds under consistent sets of equality axioms. Our modifications require new conditions on axioms to ensure consistency, and proving consistency requires significant changes to the proof from prior work. We discuss these changes and their consequences in Section 6.

We have implemented our extensions to FC in a development branch[1] of GHC to demonstrate that our modifications are compatible with the existing system, and do not invalidate existing Haskell

[1] Available online, from
`http://www.cis.upenn.edu/~eir/packages/nokinds/`.

programs. This implementation involves extensions to the core language syntax, type checker and stepper (used in optimizations).

Although our designs are inspired by the rich theory of dependent type systems, applying these ideas in the context of Haskell means that our language differs in many ways from existing work. We detail these comparisons in Section 7.

The scope of this paper only includes the design and implementation of kind equalities in the FC intermediate language; we have not yet modified GHC's source language, so promoted GADTs, kind-indexed GADTs and kind families are not (yet) available to programmers. Although the required syntactic extensions are minor, extending GHC's constraint solver requires careful integration with existing features. Furthermore, the encodings that work around Haskell's restriction that terms cannot appear in types often impose heavy syntactic overheads—improved source-level support for dependently-typed programming should also address this issue. We describe this important future work in Section 8.

For reasons of space, several technical details and the proofs are deferred to the extended version of the paper, available at `http://www.cis.upenn.edu/~sweirich/nokinds-extended.pdf`.

2. Why kind equalities?

Kind equalities enable new, useful features. In this section we use an extended example to demonstrate how *kind-indexed GADTs*, *promoted GADTs*, and *kind families* might be used in practice. Below, code snippets that require kind equalities in their compilation to FC are highlighted in gray—all other code snippets compile.[2]

The running example below defines "shallowly" and "deeply" indexed representations of types, and shows how they may be used for Generic Programming. The former use Haskell's types as indices (Crary et al. 1998; Yang 1998), whereas the latter use an algebraic datatype (also known as a *universe*) (Altenkirch and McBride 2002; Norell 2002). (Magalhães (2012) gives more details describing how extensions to Haskell, including the ones described in this paper, benefit generic programming.)

Shallow indexing Consider a GADT for type representations:

```
data TyRep :: * → * where
 TyInt  :: TyRep Int
 TyBool :: TyRep Bool
```

GADTs differ from ordinary algebraic datatypes in that they allow each data constructor to constrain the type parameters to the datatype. For example, the `TyInt` constructor requires that the single parameter to `TyRep` be `Int`.

We can use type representations for type-indexed programming—a simple example is computing a default element for each type.

```
zero :: ∀ a. TyRep a → a
zero TyInt  = 0           -- 'a' must be Int
zero TyBool = False       -- 'a' must be Bool
```

This code pattern matches the type representation to determine what value to return. Because of the nonuniform type index, pattern matching recovers the identity of the type variable `a`. In the first case, because the data constructor is `TyInt`, this parameter must be `Int`, so `0` can be returned. In the second case the parameter `a` must be equal to `Bool`, so returning `False` is well-typed.

However, the GADT above can only be used to represent types of kind $\star$. To represent type constructors with kind $\star \to \star$, such as `Maybe` or `[]`, we could create a separate datatype, perhaps called `TyRep1`. However, this approach is ugly and inflexible—what about tuples? Do we need a `TyRep2`, `TyRep3`, and more?

[2] with GHC 7.6 and the language extensions `PolyKinds`, `DataKinds`, `GADTs`, `ExplicitForAll` and `TypeFamilies`.

We might hope that kind polymorphism (Yorgey et al. 2012), which allows datatypes to be parameterized by kind variables as well as type variables, could be the solution. For example, the following kind polymorphic type takes two phantom arguments, a kind variable κ and a type variable a of kind κ.

```
data Proxy (a :: k) = P
```

However, kind polymorphism is not enough to unify the representations for `TyRep`—the type representation (shown below) should constrain its *kind* parameter.

```
data TyRep :: ∀ k. k → * where
  TyInt   :: TyRep Int
  TyBool  :: TyRep Bool
  TyMaybe :: TyRep Maybe
  TyApp   :: TyRep a → TyRep b → TyRep (a b)
```

This `TyRep` type takes two parameters, a kind `k` and a type of that kind (not named in the kind annotation). The data constructors constrain `k` to a concrete kind. For the example to be well-formed, `TyInt` must constrain the *kind* parameter to $\star$. Similarly, `TyMaybe` requires the kind parameter to be $\star \to \star$. We call this example a *kind-indexed GADT* because the datatype is indexed by both kind and type information.

Pattern matching with this datatype refines kinds as well as types—determining whether a type is of the form `TyApp` makes new kind and type equalities available. For example, consider the `zero` function extended with a default value of the `Maybe` type.

```
zero :: ∀ (a :: *). TyRep a → a
zero TyInt                = 0
zero TyBool               = False
zero (TyApp TyMaybe _)    = Nothing
```

In the last case, the `TyApp` pattern introduces the kind variable `k`, the type variables `b :: k → *` and `c :: k`, and the type equality `a ∼ b c`. The `TyMaybe` pattern adds the kind equality `k ∼ *` and type equality `b ∼ Maybe`. Combining the equalities, we can show that `Maybe c`, the type of `Nothing`, is well-kinded and equal to `a`.[3]

Deep indexing Kind equalities enable additional features besides kind-indexed GADTs. The previous example used Haskell types directly to index type representations. With datatype promotion, we can instead define a datatype (a *universe*) for type information.

```
data Ty = TInt | TBool
```

We can use this datatype to index the representation type.

```
data TyRep :: Ty → * where
 TyInt  :: TyRep TInt
 TyBool :: TyRep TBool
```

Note that the kind of the parameter to this datatype is `Ty` instead of `*`—datatype promotion allows the type `Ty` to be used as a kind and allows its constructors, `TyInt` and `TyBool`, to appear in types.

To use these type representations, we describe their connection with Haskell types via a *type family* (a function at the type level).

```
type family I (t :: Ty) :: *
type instance I TInt  = Int
type instance I TBool = Bool
```

`I` is a function that maps the (promoted) data constructor `TInt` to the Haskell type `Int`, and similarly `TBool` to `Bool`.

[3] Note that although this definition of `zero` is exhaustive, it is unlikely that an extended version of GHC will be able to determine that fact automatically.

We can use these type representations to define type-indexed operations, like before.

```
zero :: ∀ (a :: Ty). TyRep a → I a
zero TyInt  = 0
zero TyBool = False
```

Pattern matching `TyInt` refines `a` to `TInt`, which then uses the type family definition to show that the result type is equal to `Int`.

Dependently typed languages do not require an argument like `TyRep` to implement operations such as `zero`—they can match directly on the type of kind `Ty`. This is not allowed in Haskell, which maintains a separation between types and expressions. The `TyRep` argument is an example of a *singleton* type, a standard way of encoding dependently typed operations in Haskell.

Note that this representation is no better than the shallow version in one respect—`I` must produce a type of kind $\star$. What if we wanted to encode `TMaybe` with `Ty`?

To get around this issue, we use a GADT to represent different kinds of types. We first need a universe of kinds.

```
data Kind = Star | Arr Kind Kind
```

`Kind` is a normal datatype that, when promoted, can be used to index the `Ty` datatype, making it a (standard) GADT.

```
data Ty :: Kind → * where
  TInt   :: Ty Star
  TBool  :: Ty Star
  TMaybe :: Ty (Arr Star Star)
  TApp   :: Ty (Arr k1 k2) → Ty k1 → Ty k2
```

This indexing means that `Ty` can only represent well-kinded types. For example `TMaybe` has type `Ty (Arr Star Star)` and `TApp TMaybe TBool` has type `Ty Star`, while the value `TApp TInt` would be rejected. Although this GADT can be expressed in GHC, the corresponding `TyRep` type requires two new extensions: *promoted GADTs* and *kind families*.

With the current design of FC, only a subset of Haskell 98 datatypes can be promoted. In particular, GADTs cannot be used to index other GADTs. The extensions proposed in this work allow the GADT `Ty` above to be used as an index to `TyRep` or to be interpreted by the type family `I`, as shown below.

```
data TyRep (k :: Kind) (t :: Ty k) where
  TyInt   :: TyRep Star TInt
  TyBool  :: TyRep Star TBool
  TyMaybe :: TyRep (Arr Star Star) TMaybe
  TyApp   :: TyRep (Arr k1 k2) a → TyRep k1 b
          → TyRep k2 (TApp a b)
```

We now need to adapt the type family `I` to work with the new promoted GADT `Ty`. To do so, we must classify its return kind, and for that, we need a *kind family*—a function that produces a kind by pattern matching a type or kind argument. For example, we can interpret values of the `Kind` datatype as Haskell kinds like so:

```
kind family IK (k :: Kind)
kind instance IK Star = *
kind instance IK (Arr k1 k2) = IK k1 → IK k2
```

This interpretation of kinds is necessary to define the interpretation of types—without it, this definition does not "kind-check":

```
type family I (t :: Ty k) :: IK k
type instance I TInt       = Int
type instance I TBool      = Bool
type instance I TMaybe     = Maybe
type instance I (TApp a b) = (I a) (I b)
```

However, once `I` has been defined, `Ty` and `TyRep` can be used in type-indexed operations as before.

```
zero :: ∀ (a :: Ty Star). TyRep Star a → I a
zero TyInt             = 0
zero TyBool            = False
zero (TyApp TyMaybe _) = Nothing
```

The examples above demonstrate all three features that kind equalities enable: kind-indexed GADTs, kind families, and promoted GADTs. While these examples are all derived from generic programming, we have also been able to use these features to express dependently typed programs from McBride (2012) and Oury and Swierstra (2008). We omit these examples for lack of space.

We note that the Haskell syntax used in the gray boxes above is hypothetical, as we have not extended the surface language. However, an important first step is to enhance the core language, System FC, so that it is expressive enough to support these features. We now turn to this task.

3. System FC

System FC is the typed intermediate language of GHC. GHC's advanced features, such as GADTs and type families, are compiled into FC as type equalities. This section reviews the current status of System FC, describes that compilation, and puts our work in context. FC has evolved over time, from its initial definition (Sulzmann et al. 2007), to extensions FC_2 (Weirich et al. 2011), and $F_C^{\uparrow}$ (Yorgey et al. 2012). In this paper, we use the name FC for the language and all of its variants. Our technical discussion contrasts our new extensions with the most recent prior version, $F_C^{\uparrow}$.

Along with the usual kinds (κ), types (τ) and expressions (e), FC contains coercions (γ) that are proofs of type equality. The judgement

$$\Gamma \vdash_{\mathsf{co}} \gamma : \tau_1 \sim \tau_2$$

checks that the coercion γ proves types τ_1 and τ_2 equal. These proofs are used to change the types of expressions. For example, if γ is a proof of $\tau_1 \sim \tau_2$, and the expression e has type τ_1, then the expression $e \triangleright \gamma$ (pronounced "e casted by γ") has type τ_2.

Making type conversion explicit ensures that the FC typing relation $\Gamma \vdash_{\mathsf{tm}} e : \tau$ is syntax-directed and decidable. This is not the case in the source language; there type checking requires nonlocal reasoning, such as unification and type class resolution. Furthermore, in the presence of certain flags (such as `UndecidableInstances`), it may not terminate.

Straightforward type checking is an important sanity check on the internals of GHC—transformations and optimizations must preserve typability. Therefore, all information necessary for type checking is present in FC expressions. This information includes explicit type abstractions and applications (System FC is an extension of System F_ω (Girard 1972)) as well as explicit proofs of type equality.

For example, type family definitions are compiled to *axioms* about type equality that can be used in FC coercion proofs. A type family declaration and instance in source Haskell

```
type family F a :: *
type instance F Bool = Int
```

generates the following FC axiom declaration:

$$\mathsf{axF} : \mathsf{F\ Bool} \sim \mathsf{Int}$$

When given a source language function of type

```
g :: ∀ a. a → F a → Char
```

the expression `g True 3` translates to the FC expression

$$g\ \mathsf{Bool}\ \mathsf{True}\ (3 \rhd \mathbf{sym}\,\mathsf{axF})$$

that instantiates g at type Bool and coerces 3 to have type F Bool. The coercion $\mathbf{sym}\,\mathsf{axF}$ is a proof that $\mathsf{Int} \sim \mathsf{F\ Bool}$.

GADTs are compiled into FC so that pattern matching on their data constructors introduces *type equality assumptions* into the context. For example, consider the following simple GADT.

```
data T :: * → * where
  TInt :: T Int
```

This declaration could have also been written as a normal datatype where the type parameter is constrained to be equal to `Int`.

```
data T a = (a ~ Int) ⇒ TInt
```

In fact, all GADTs can be rewritten in this form using equality constraints. Pattern matching makes this constraint available to the type checker. For example, the type checker concludes below that 3 has type `a` because the type `Int` is known to be equal to `a`.

```
f :: T a → a
f TInt = 3
```

In the translation to FC, the TInt data constructor takes this equality constraint as an explicit argument.

$$\mathsf{TInt} : \forall\, a{:}\, \star\,.\,(a \sim \mathsf{Int}) \Rightarrow T\ a$$

When pattern matching on values of type $T\ a$, this proof is available for use in a cast.

$$\begin{array}{l} f = \Lambda a{:}\,\star\,.\lambda x{:}\,T\ a.\ \mathbf{case}\ x\ \mathbf{of} \\ \qquad \mathsf{TInt}\ (c{:}\,a \sim \mathsf{Int}) \to (3 \rhd \mathbf{sym}\ c) \end{array}$$

Coercion assumptions and axioms can be composed to form larger proofs. FC includes a number of forms in the coercion language that witness the reflexivity, symmetry and transitivity of type equality. Furthermore, equality is a congruent relation over types. For example, if we have proofs of $\tau_1 \sim \tau_2$ and $\tau_1' \sim \tau_2'$, then we can form a proof of the equality $\tau_1\,\tau_1' \sim \tau_2\,\tau_2'$. Finally, composite coercion proofs can be decomposed. For example, data constructors T are injective, so given a proof of $T\,\tau_1 \sim T\,\tau_2$, a proof of $\tau_1 \sim \tau_2$ can be produced.

Explicit coercion proofs are like explicit type arguments: they are erasable from expressions and do not effect the operational behavior of an expression. (We make this precise in Section 5.3.) To ensure that coercions do not suspend computation, FC includes "push rules". For example, when a coerced value is applied to an argument, the coercion must be "pushed" to the argument and result of the application so that β-reduction can occur.

$$\frac{\Gamma \vdash_{\mathsf{co}} \gamma\ :\ \sigma_1 \to \sigma_2 \sim \tau_1 \to \tau_2}{(v \rhd \gamma)\ e \longrightarrow (v\ (e \rhd \mathbf{sym}\,(\mathbf{nth}^1\ \gamma))) \rhd \mathbf{nth}^2\ \gamma}\ \textsc{S\_Push}$$

In this rule, if the expression $(v \rhd \gamma)\ e$ is well typed, then γ must be a proof of the equality $\sigma_1 \to \sigma_2 \sim \tau_1 \to \tau_2$. The coercions $\mathbf{sym}\,(\mathbf{nth}^1\ \gamma)$ and $\mathbf{nth}^2\ \gamma$ decompose this proof into coercions for the argument $(\tau_1 \sim \sigma_1)$ and result $(\sigma_2 \sim \tau_2)$ of the application.

4. System FC with kind equalities

The main idea of this paper is to augment FC with proofs of equality between kinds and to use these proofs to explicitly coerce the kinds of types. We do so via new type form: if type τ has kind κ_1, and γ is a proof that kind κ_1 equals kind κ_2, then $\tau \rhd \gamma$ is type τ casted to kind κ_2. There are several challenges to this extension, which we address with the following technical solutions.

H	$::=$	Type constants
	$\mid\ (\to)$	Arrow
	$\mid\ \star$	Type/Kind
	$\mid\ T$	Type constructor
	$\mid\ K$	Promoted data constructor
w	$::=$	Type-level names
	$\mid\ a$	Type variables
	$\mid\ F$	Type functions
	$\mid\ H$	Type constants
$\sigma,\ \tau,\ \kappa$	$::=$	Types and Kinds
	$\mid\ w$	Names
	$\mid\ \forall\, a{:}\,\kappa.\,\tau$	Polymorphic types
	$\mid\ \forall\, c{:}\,\phi.\,\tau$	Coercion abstr. type
	$\mid\ \tau_1\,\tau_2$	Type/kind application
	$\mid\ \tau \rhd \gamma$	Casting
	$\mid\ \tau\,\gamma$	Coercion application
ϕ	$::= \sigma \sim \tau$	Propositions (coercion kinds)
$\gamma,\ \eta$	$::=$	Coercions
	$\mid\ c$	Variables
	$\mid\ C\,\overline{\rho}$	Axiom application
	$\mid\ \langle\tau\rangle$	Reflexivity
	$\mid\ \mathbf{sym}\,\gamma$	Symmetry
	$\mid\ \gamma_1 \fatsemi \gamma_2$	Transitivity
	$\mid\ \forall_\eta(a_1, a_2, c).\gamma$	Type/kind abstr. cong.
	$\mid\ \forall_{(\eta_1,\eta_2)}(c_1, c_2).\gamma$	Coercion abstr. cong.
	$\mid\ \gamma_1\,\gamma_2$	Type/kind app. cong.
	$\mid\ \gamma(\gamma_2, \gamma_2')$	Coercion app. cong.
	$\mid\ \gamma \rhd \gamma'$	Coherence
	$\mid\ \gamma@\gamma'$	Type/kind instantiation
	$\mid\ \gamma@(\gamma_1, \gamma_2)$	Coercion instantiation
	$\mid\ \mathbf{nth}^i\ \gamma$	nth argument projection
	$\mid\ \mathbf{kind}\,\gamma$	Kind equality extraction
ρ	$::= \tau \mid \gamma$	Type or coercion
$e,\ u$	$::=$	Expressions
	$\mid\ x$	Variables
	$\mid\ \lambda x{:}\,\tau.\ e$	Abstraction
	$\mid\ e_1\ e_2$	Application
	$\mid\ \Lambda a{:}\,\kappa.\ e$	Type/kind abstraction
	$\mid\ e\,\tau$	Type/kind application
	$\mid\ \lambda c{:}\,\phi.\ e$	Coercion abstraction
	$\mid\ e\,\gamma$	Coercion application
	$\mid\ e \rhd \gamma$	Casting
	$\mid\ K$	Data constructors
	$\mid\ \mathbf{case}\ e\ \mathbf{of}\ \overline{p \to u}$	Case analysis
	$\mid\ \mathbf{contra}\,\gamma\,\tau$	Absurdity
p	$::= K\ \Delta\ \overline{x{:}\tau}$	Patterns
Δ	$::=$	Telescopes
	$\mid\ \varnothing$	Empty
	$\mid\ \Delta,\ a{:}\,\kappa$	Type variable binding
	$\mid\ \Delta,\ c{:}\,\phi$	Coercion variable binding

Figure 1. Basic Grammar

- *Unifying kinds and types.* A language with kind polymorphism, kind equalities, kind coercions, type polymorphism, type equalities and type coercions quickly becomes redundant (and somewhat overwhelming).

  Therefore, we follow pure type systems (Barendregt 1992) and unify the syntax of types and kinds, allowing us to reuse type coercions as kind coercions.[4] Although there is no syntactic distinction between types and kinds, we informally use the word *type* (metavariables τ and σ) for those members that classify runtime expressions, and *kind* (metavariable κ) for those members that classify expressions of the type language.

  As in pure type systems, types and kinds share semantics—there is a common judgement for the validity of both. Furthermore, our rules include the $\star{:}\star$ axiom which means that there is no real distinction between types and kinds. This choice simplifies many aspects of the language design.

  Languages such as Coq and Agda avoid the $\star{:}\star$ axiom because it introduces inconsistency, but that is not an issue here. The FC type language is already inconsistent in the sense that all kinds are inhabited. The type safety property of FC depends on the consistency of its *coercion* language, not its *type* language. See Section 6 and Section 7 for more discussion of this issue.[5]

- *Making type equality "heterogeneous".* As kinds classify types, kind equality has nontrivial interactions with type equality.

  Because kind coercions are explicit, there are equivalent types that do not have syntactically identical kinds Therefore, like McBride's "John Major" equality (2002), our definition of type equality $\tau_1 \sim \tau_2$ is heterogeneous—the types τ_1 and τ_2 could have kinds κ_1 and κ_2 that have no syntactic relation to each other. A proof γ of $\tau_1 \sim \tau_2$ implies not only that τ_1 and τ_2 are equal, but also that their kinds are equal. The new coercion form **kind** γ extracts the proof of $\kappa_1 \sim \kappa_2$ from γ.

  Another difficulty comes from the need to equate polymorphic types that have coercible but not syntactically equal kinds for the bound variable. We discuss the modification to this coercion form in Section 4.3.1.

- *Coercion irrelevance.* Coercions should be irrelevant to both the operational semantics *and* type equivalence. The fact that a coercion is used to change the type of an expression, or the kind of a type, should not influence the evaluation of the expression or the equalities available for the type. For the former, we maintain irrelevance by updating FC's "push rules" to the new semantics (see Section 5 for details). For the latter, we carefully construct our coercion forms to ignore coercions inside types (Section 4.3.2).

- *Dependent coercion abstraction.* As in prior versions of FC, coercions are first class—they can be passed as arguments to functions and stored in data structures (as the arguments to data constructors of GADTs). However, this system differs from earlier versions in that the type form for these objects, written $\forall\, c{:}\, \phi.\, \tau$, *names* the abstracted proof with the variable c and allows the type τ to refer to this coercion.

  This extension is necessary for some kind-indexed GADTs. For example, consider the following datatype, which is polymorphic over a kind and type parameter.

[4] GHC already uses a shared datatype for types and kinds, so this merge brings the formalism closer to the actual implementation.

[5] If a consistent type language were desired for FC for other reasons, we believe that the ideas presented in this paper are adaptable to the stratification of $\star$ into *universe levels* (Luo 1994), as is done in Coq and Agda.

```
data T :: ∀ k. k → * where
  K :: ∀ (b :: *). b → T b
```

The single data constructor K constrains the kind to be $\star$ but does not otherwise constrain the type.

After translation, the data constructor should be given the following FC type, where the abstracted kind coercion c is used to cast the kind of the parameter k.

$$\mathsf{K}{:}\, \forall\, k{:}\, \star,\ b{:}\, k.\, \forall\, c{:}\, (k \sim \star).\, (b \rhd c) \to \mathsf{T}\, k\, b$$

4.1 Type system overview

The next few subsections go into more detail about these technical points. We start with a quick tour of the type system.

The new syntax for FC appears in Figure 1; forms that are new or modified in this paper are highlighted—these modifications are primarily in the type and coercion languages. Also, note that $\star$ is a new type constant and κ is a metavariable for types. The only difference in the grammar for expressions is that type abstractions and kind abstractions have been merged. In general, the type system and operational semantics for the expression language is the same here as in prior versions of FC.

A context Γ is a list of assumptions for term variables (x), type variables/datatypes/data constructors (w), coercion variables (c), and coercion axioms (C).

$$\Gamma ::= \varnothing \mid \Gamma,\ x{:}\,\tau \mid \Gamma,\ w{:}\,\kappa \mid \Gamma,\ c{:}\,\phi \mid \Gamma,\ C{:}\ \forall \Delta.\, \phi$$

The type system includes the following judgements:

$\vdash_{\mathsf{wf}} \Gamma$	Context validity	(Figure 5)
$\Gamma \vdash_{\mathsf{ty}} \tau : \kappa$	Type/kind validity	(Figure 2)
$\Gamma \vdash_{\mathsf{pr}} \phi\ \mathsf{ok}$	Proposition validity	(Figure 3)
$\Gamma \vdash_{\mathsf{tm}} e : \tau$	Expression typing	(extended version)
$\Gamma \vdash_{\mathsf{co}} \gamma : \phi$	Coercion validity	(Figure 4)
$\Gamma \vdash_{\mathsf{tel}} \overline{\rho} \Leftarrow \Delta$	Telescope arg. validity	(extended version)

Each of the judgements is syntax directed: given the information before the colon (if present), a simple algorithm determines if the judgement holds, and recovers the information after the colon.

4.2 Type and kind formation

We next describe our extensions and modifications to the rules classifying FC types into kinds, which appear in Figure 2. Some of these rules are unchanged or only slightly modified from prior versions of FC.

For example, rule K_VAR looks up the kind of a type-level name from the typing context. Unlike previous systems, this rule now covers the kinding of promoted constructors, since w ranges over them. Recall that datatype promotion allows data constructors, such as `TInt`, to appear in types and be the arguments of type functions. Previously, the types of data constructors had to be explicitly promoted to kinds (Yorgey et al. 2012). Now, *any* data constructor may freely be used as a type. When the constructor is used as a type, its kind is the same as the type of the constructor when used as a term.

Rule K_ARROW gives the expected kind for the arrow type constructor. We use the usual syntactic sugar for arrow types, writing $\tau_1 \to \tau_2$ for $(\to)\, \tau_1\, \tau_2$. Note that the kind of the arrow type constructor is itself an arrow type. However, that circularity does not cause difficulty. After that, the rule K_ALLT describes when polymorphic types are well formed.

The next two rules describe when type application is well-formed. Application is overloaded in these rules, but the system is still syntax-directed—the type of the first component determines which rule applies. We do not combine function types $\sigma_1 \to \sigma_2$

$$\boxed{\Gamma \vdash_{\mathsf{ty}} \tau : \kappa}$$

$$\frac{\vdash_{\mathsf{wf}} \Gamma \quad w{:}\kappa \in \Gamma}{\Gamma \vdash_{\mathsf{ty}} w : \kappa} \ \textsc{K\_Var}$$

$$\frac{\vdash_{\mathsf{wf}} \Gamma}{\Gamma \vdash_{\mathsf{ty}} (\to) : \star \to \star \to \star} \ \textsc{K\_Arrow}$$

$$\frac{\Gamma, a{:}\kappa \vdash_{\mathsf{ty}} \tau : \star \quad \Gamma \vdash_{\mathsf{ty}} \kappa : \star}{\Gamma \vdash_{\mathsf{ty}} \forall\, a{:}\kappa.\, \tau : \star} \ \textsc{K\_AllT}$$

$$\frac{\Gamma \vdash_{\mathsf{ty}} \tau_1 : \kappa_1 \to \kappa_2 \quad \Gamma \vdash_{\mathsf{ty}} \tau_2 : \kappa_1}{\Gamma \vdash_{\mathsf{ty}} \tau_1\, \tau_2 : \kappa_2} \ \textsc{K\_App}$$

$$\frac{\Gamma \vdash_{\mathsf{ty}} \tau_1 : \forall\, a{:}\kappa_1.\, \kappa_2 \quad \Gamma \vdash_{\mathsf{ty}} \tau_2 : \kappa_1}{\Gamma \vdash_{\mathsf{ty}} \tau_1\, \tau_2 : \kappa_2[\tau_2/a]} \ \textsc{K\_Inst}$$

$$\frac{\vdash_{\mathsf{wf}} \Gamma}{\Gamma \vdash_{\mathsf{ty}} \star : \star} \ \textsc{K\_StarInStar}$$

$$\frac{\Gamma \vdash_{\mathsf{ty}} \tau_1 : \forall\, c{:}\phi.\, \kappa \quad \Gamma \vdash_{\mathsf{co}} \gamma_1 : \phi}{\Gamma \vdash_{\mathsf{ty}} \tau_1\, \gamma_1 : \kappa[\gamma_1/c]} \ \textsc{K\_CApp}$$

$$\frac{\Gamma, c{:}\phi \vdash_{\mathsf{ty}} \tau : \star \quad \Gamma \vdash_{\mathsf{pr}} \phi\ \mathsf{ok}}{\Gamma \vdash_{\mathsf{ty}} \forall\, c{:}\phi.\, \tau : \star} \ \textsc{K\_AllC}$$

$$\frac{\Gamma \vdash_{\mathsf{ty}} \tau : \kappa_1 \quad \Gamma \vdash_{\mathsf{co}} \eta : \kappa_1 \sim \kappa_2 \quad \Gamma \vdash_{\mathsf{ty}} \kappa_2 : \star}{\Gamma \vdash_{\mathsf{ty}} \tau \rhd \eta : \kappa_2} \ \textsc{K\_Cast}$$

Figure 2. Kind and type formation rules

$$\boxed{\Gamma \vdash_{\mathsf{pr}} \phi\ \mathsf{ok}}$$

$$\frac{\Gamma \vdash_{\mathsf{ty}} \sigma_1 : \kappa_1 \qquad \Gamma \vdash_{\mathsf{ty}} \sigma_2 : \kappa_2}{\Gamma \vdash_{\mathsf{pr}} \sigma_1 \sim \sigma_2\ \mathsf{ok}} \ \textsc{Prop\_Equality}$$

Figure 3. Proposition formation rule

and polymorphic types $\forall\, a{:}\kappa.\, \sigma$ into a single form because of type erasure: term arguments are necessary at runtime, whereas type arguments may be erased. Although this distinction is meaningless at the kind level, it is benign. Identifying these forms at the kind level while retaining the distinction at the term level would needlessly complicate the language.

The rules K_STARINSTAR, K_CAST and K_CAPP and K_ALLC check the new type forms. The first says that $\star$ has kind $\star$.

To preserve the syntax-directed nature of FC, we must make the use of kind equality proofs explicit. We do so via the new form $\tau \rhd \gamma$ of kind casts: when given a type τ of kind κ_1 and a proof γ that kind κ_1 equals kind κ_2, the cast produces a type of kind κ_2. Because equality is heterogeneous, the K_CAST rule requires a third premise to ensure that the new kind has the correct classification, so that inhabited types have kind $\star$.

To promote GADTs we must be able to promote data constructors that take coercions as arguments, requiring the new application form $\tau\,\gamma$. For example, the data constructor TInt (from Section 3) requires a type argument τ and a proof that $\tau \sim \mathsf{Int}$. Note that there is no type-level abstraction over coercion—the form $\tau\,\gamma$ can only appear when the head of τ is a promoted datatype constructor.

4.3 Coercions

Coercions are proof terms witnessing the equality between types (and kinds), and are classified by propositions ϕ. The rules under which the proofs can be derived appear in Figure 4, with the validity

$$\boxed{\Gamma \vdash_{\mathsf{co}} \gamma : \phi}$$

$$\frac{\Gamma \vdash_{\mathsf{ty}} \tau : \kappa}{\Gamma \vdash_{\mathsf{co}} \langle \tau \rangle : \tau \sim \tau} \ \textsc{CT\_Refl}$$

$$\frac{\Gamma \vdash_{\mathsf{co}} \gamma : \tau_1 \sim \tau_2}{\Gamma \vdash_{\mathsf{co}} \mathbf{sym}\,\gamma : \tau_2 \sim \tau_1} \ \textsc{CT\_Sym}$$

$$\frac{\Gamma \vdash_{\mathsf{co}} \gamma_1 : \tau_1 \sim \tau_2 \quad \Gamma \vdash_{\mathsf{co}} \gamma_2 : \tau_2 \sim \tau_3}{\Gamma \vdash_{\mathsf{co}} \gamma_1 \mathbin{⨾} \gamma_2 : \tau_1 \sim \tau_3} \ \textsc{CT\_Trans}$$

$$\frac{\begin{array}{c}\Gamma \vdash_{\mathsf{co}} \gamma_1 : \tau_1' \sim \tau_2' \quad \Gamma \vdash_{\mathsf{co}} \gamma_2 : \tau_1 \sim \tau_2 \\ \Gamma \vdash_{\mathsf{ty}} \tau_1'\,\tau_1 : \kappa_1 \quad \Gamma \vdash_{\mathsf{ty}} \tau_2'\,\tau_2 : \kappa_2\end{array}}{\Gamma \vdash_{\mathsf{co}} \gamma_1\,\gamma_2 : \tau_1'\,\tau_1 \sim \tau_2'\,\tau_2} \ \textsc{CT\_App}$$

$$\frac{\begin{array}{l}\Gamma \vdash_{\mathsf{co}} \gamma_1 : \tau_1 \sim \tau_1' \\ \Gamma \vdash_{\mathsf{ty}} \tau_1\,\gamma_2 : \kappa \quad \Gamma \vdash_{\mathsf{ty}} \tau_1'\,\gamma_2' : \kappa'\end{array}}{\Gamma \vdash_{\mathsf{co}} \gamma_1(\gamma_2, \gamma_2') : \tau_1\,\gamma_2 \sim \tau_1'\,\gamma_2'} \ \textsc{CT\_CApp}$$

$$\frac{\begin{array}{l}\Gamma \vdash_{\mathsf{co}} \eta : \kappa_1 \sim \kappa_2 \\ \Gamma,\ a_1{:}\kappa_1,\ a_2{:}\kappa_2,\ c{:}\ a_1 \sim a_2 \vdash_{\mathsf{co}} \gamma : \tau_1 \sim \tau_2 \\ \Gamma \vdash_{\mathsf{ty}} \forall\, a_1{:}\kappa_1.\, \tau_1 : \star \quad \Gamma \vdash_{\mathsf{ty}} \forall\, a_2{:}\kappa_2.\, \tau_2 : \star\end{array}}{\Gamma \vdash_{\mathsf{co}} \forall_{\eta}(a_1, a_2, c).\gamma : (\forall\, a_1{:}\kappa_1.\, \tau_1) \sim (\forall\, a_2{:}\kappa_2.\, \tau_2)} \ \textsc{CT\_AllT}$$

$$\frac{\begin{array}{l}\Gamma \vdash_{\mathsf{co}} \eta_1 : \sigma_1 \sim \sigma_1' \quad \phi_1 = \sigma_1 \sim \sigma_2 \\ \Gamma \vdash_{\mathsf{co}} \eta_2 : \sigma_2 \sim \sigma_2' \quad \phi_2 = \sigma_1' \sim \sigma_2' \\ c_1 \# |\gamma| \quad c_2 \# |\gamma| \\ \Gamma,\ c_1{:}\phi_1,\ c_2{:}\phi_2 \vdash_{\mathsf{co}} \gamma : \tau_1 \sim \tau_2 \\ \Gamma \vdash_{\mathsf{ty}} \forall\, c_1{:}\phi_1.\, \tau_1 : \star \quad \Gamma \vdash_{\mathsf{ty}} \forall\, c_2{:}\phi_2.\, \tau_2 : \star\end{array}}{\Gamma \vdash_{\mathsf{co}} \forall_{(\eta_1, \eta_2)}(c_1, c_2).\gamma : (\forall\, c_1{:}\phi_1.\, \tau_1) \sim (\forall\, c_2{:}\phi_2.\, \tau_2)} \ \textsc{CT\_AllC}$$

$$\frac{\Gamma \vdash_{\mathsf{co}} \gamma : \tau_1 \sim \tau_2 \quad \Gamma \vdash_{\mathsf{ty}} \tau_1 \rhd \gamma' : \kappa}{\Gamma \vdash_{\mathsf{co}} \gamma \rhd \gamma' : \tau_1 \rhd \gamma' \sim \tau_2} \ \textsc{CT\_Coh}$$

$$\frac{c{:}\phi \in \Gamma \quad \vdash_{\mathsf{wf}} \Gamma}{\Gamma \vdash_{\mathsf{co}} c : \phi} \ \textsc{CT\_Var}$$

$$\frac{C{:}\ \forall\, \Delta.\, (\tau_1 \sim \tau_2) \in \Gamma \quad \Gamma \vdash_{\mathsf{tel}} \overline{\rho} \Leftarrow \Delta}{\Gamma \vdash_{\mathsf{co}} C\,\overline{\rho} : \tau_1[\overline{\rho}/\Delta] \sim \tau_2[\overline{\rho}/\Delta]} \ \textsc{CT\_Axiom}$$

$$\frac{\begin{array}{l}\Gamma \vdash_{\mathsf{co}} \gamma : H\,\overline{\rho} \sim H\,\overline{\rho}' \\ \rho_i = \tau \quad \rho_i' = \tau'\end{array}}{\Gamma \vdash_{\mathsf{co}} \mathbf{nth}^{i}\,\gamma : \tau \sim \tau'} \ \textsc{CT\_Nth}$$

$$\frac{\Gamma \vdash_{\mathsf{co}} \gamma_1 : (\forall\, a_1{:}\kappa_1.\, \tau_1) \sim (\forall\, a_2{:}\kappa_2.\, \tau_2)}{\Gamma \vdash_{\mathsf{co}} \mathbf{nth}^{1}\,\gamma_1 : \kappa_1 \sim \kappa_2} \ \textsc{CT\_Nth1TA}$$

$$\frac{\begin{array}{l}\Gamma \vdash_{\mathsf{co}} \gamma_1 : (\forall\, a_1{:}\kappa_1.\, \tau_1) \sim (\forall\, a_2{:}\kappa_2.\, \tau_2) \\ \Gamma \vdash_{\mathsf{co}} \gamma_2 : \sigma_1 \sim \sigma_2 \\ \Gamma \vdash_{\mathsf{ty}} \sigma_1 : \kappa_1 \quad \Gamma \vdash_{\mathsf{ty}} \sigma_2 : \kappa_2\end{array}}{\Gamma \vdash_{\mathsf{co}} \gamma_1 @ \gamma_2 : \tau_1[\sigma_1/a_1] \sim \tau_2[\sigma_2/a_2]} \ \textsc{CT\_Inst}$$

$$\frac{\Gamma \vdash_{\mathsf{co}} \gamma : (\forall\, c{:}\kappa_1 \sim \kappa_2.\, \tau) \sim (\forall\, c'{:}\kappa_1' \sim \kappa_2'.\, \tau')}{\Gamma \vdash_{\mathsf{co}} \mathbf{nth}^{1}\,\gamma : \kappa_1 \sim \kappa_1'} \ \textsc{CT\_Nth1CA}$$

$$\frac{\Gamma \vdash_{\mathsf{co}} \gamma : (\forall\, c{:}\kappa_1 \sim \kappa_2.\, \tau) \sim (\forall\, c'{:}\kappa_1' \sim \kappa_2'.\, \tau')}{\Gamma \vdash_{\mathsf{co}} \mathbf{nth}^{2}\,\gamma : \kappa_2 \sim \kappa_2'} \ \textsc{CT\_Nth2CA}$$

$$\frac{\begin{array}{l}\Gamma \vdash_{\mathsf{co}} \gamma : (\forall\, c_1{:}\phi_1.\, \tau_1) \sim (\forall\, c_2{:}\phi_2.\, \tau_2) \\ \Gamma \vdash_{\mathsf{co}} \gamma_1 : \phi_1 \quad \Gamma \vdash_{\mathsf{co}} \gamma_2 : \phi_2\end{array}}{\Gamma \vdash_{\mathsf{co}} \gamma@(\gamma_1, \gamma_2) : \tau_1[\gamma_1/c_1] \sim \tau_2[\gamma_2/c_2]} \ \textsc{CT\_InstC}$$

$$\frac{\Gamma \vdash_{\mathsf{co}} \gamma : \tau_1 \sim \tau_2 \quad \Gamma \vdash_{\mathsf{ty}} \tau_1 : \kappa_1 \quad \Gamma \vdash_{\mathsf{ty}} \tau_2 : \kappa_2}{\Gamma \vdash_{\mathsf{co}} \mathbf{kind}\,\gamma : \kappa_1 \sim \kappa_2} \ \textsc{CT\_Ext}$$

Figure 4. Coercion formation rules

rule for ϕ appearing in Figure 3. These rules establish properties of the type equality relation:

- Equality is an *equivalence relation*, as seen in rules CT_REFL, CT_SYM, and CT_TRANS.
- Equality is *congruent*—types with equal subcomponents are equal. Every type formation rule (except for the base cases like variables and constants) has an associated congruence rule. The exception is kind coercion $\tau \triangleright \gamma$, where the congruence rule is derivable (see Section 4.3.2). The congruence rules are mostly straightforward; we discuss the rules for quantified types (rules CT_ALLT and CT_ALLC) in Section 4.3.1.
- Equality can be *assumed*. Coercion variables and axioms add assumptions about equality to the context and appear in proofs (using rules CT_VAR and CT_AXIOM respectively). These axioms for type equality are allowed to be *axiom schemes*—they may be parameterized and must be instantiated when used.

  The general form of the type of an axiom, $C\colon \forall \Delta. \phi$ gathers multiple parameters in a *telescope*, a context denoted with Δ of type and coercion variables, each of which scope over the remainder of the telescope as well as the body of the axiom. We specify the list of instantiations for a telescope with $\overline{\rho}$, a mixed list of types and coercions. When type checking an axiom application, we must type check its list of arguments $\overline{\rho}$ against the given telescope. The judgement form $\Gamma \vdash_{\mathsf{tel}} \overline{\rho} \Leftarrow \Delta$ (presented in the extended version of this paper) checks each argument ρ in turn against the binding in the telescope, scoping variables appropriately.
- Equality can be *decomposed* using the next six rules. For example, because we know that datatypes are injective type functions, we can decompose a proof of the equivalence of two datatypes into equivalence proofs for any pair of corresponding type parameters (CT_NTH). Furthermore, the equivalence of two polymorphic types means that the kinds of the bound variables are equivalent (CT_NTH1TA), and that all instantiations of the bound variables are equivalent (CT_INST). The same is true for coercion abstraction types (rules CT_NTH1CA, CT_NTH2CA, and CT_INSTC).
- Equality is *heterogeneous*. If γ is a proof of the equality $\tau_1 \sim \tau_2$, then $\mathbf{kind}\,\gamma$ extracts a proof of equality between the kinds of τ_1 and τ_2.

4.3.1 Congruence rules for quantified types

In prior versions of FC, the coercion $\forall a\colon \kappa.\gamma$ proved the equality proposition $\forall\, a\colon \kappa.\, \tau_1 \sim \forall\, a\colon \kappa.\, \tau_2$, using the following rule:

$$\frac{\Gamma \vdash_{\mathsf{ty}} \kappa : \star \qquad \Gamma,\, a\colon \kappa \vdash_{\mathsf{co}} \gamma : \tau_1 \sim \tau_2}{\Gamma \vdash_{\mathsf{co}} \forall\, a\colon \kappa.\gamma : (\forall\, a\colon \kappa.\, \tau_1) \sim (\forall\, a\colon \kappa.\, \tau_2)} \quad \text{CT\_ALLTX}$$

This rule sufficed because the only quantified types that could be shown equal had the same syntactic kinds κ for the bound variable. However, we now have a nontrivial equality between kinds. We need to be able to show a more general proposition, $\forall\, a\colon \kappa_1.\, \tau_1 \sim \forall\, a\colon \kappa_2.\, \tau_2$, even when κ_1 is not syntactically equal to κ_2.

Without this generality, the language does not satisfy the preservation theorem, which requires that the equality relation be substitutive—given a valid type σ where a appears free, and a proof $\Gamma \vdash_{\mathsf{co}} \gamma : \tau_1 \sim \tau_2$, we must be able to derive a proof between $\sigma[\tau_1/a]$ and $\sigma[\tau_2/a]$. For this property to hold, if a occurs in the kind of a quantified type (or coercion) variable $\forall\, b\colon a.\, \tau$, then we must be able to derive $\forall\, b\colon \tau_1.\, \tau \sim \forall\, b\colon \tau_2.\, \tau$.

Rule CT_ALLT shows when two polytypes are equal. The first premise requires a proof η that the kinds of the bound variables are equal. But, these two kinds might not be *syntactically* equal, so we must have two type variables, a_1 and a_2, one of each kind. The second premise of the rule adds both bindings $a_1\colon \kappa_1$ and $a_2\colon \kappa_2$ to the context as well as an assertion c that a_1 and a_2 are equal. The polytypes themselves can only refer to their own variables, as verified by the last two premises of the rule.

The other type form that includes binding is the coercion abstractions, $\forall\, c\colon \phi.\, \tau$. The rule CT_ALLC constructs a proof that two such types of this form are equal. We can only construct such proofs when the abstracted propositions relate correspondingly equal types, as witnessed by proofs η_1 and η_2. The proof term introduces two coercion variables into the context, similar to the two type variables above. Due to proof irrelevance, there is no need for a proof of equality between coercions themselves. Note that the kind of c_1 is *not* that of η_1: the kind of c_1 is built from types in both η_1 and η_2.

The rule CT_ALLC also restricts how the variables c_1 and c_2 can be used in γ. The premises $c_1 \# |\gamma|$ and $c_2 \# |\gamma|$ prevent these variables from appearing in the relevant parts of γ. (The freshness operator $\#$ requires its two arguments to have disjoint sets of free variables.) This restriction stems from our proof technique for the consistency of this proof system; we define the erasure operation $|\cdot|$ and discuss this issue in more detail in Section 6.

$\boxed{\vdash_{\mathsf{wf}} \Gamma}$

$$\frac{\Gamma \vdash_{\mathsf{ty}} \forall\, \overline{a\colon \kappa}.\star : \star \qquad T \# \Gamma}{\vdash_{\mathsf{wf}} \Gamma,\, T\colon \forall\, \overline{a\colon \kappa}.\star} \quad \text{GWF\_TYDATA}$$

$$\frac{\Gamma \vdash_{\mathsf{ty}} \forall\, \overline{a\colon \kappa}.\forall\, \Delta.\, (\overline{\sigma} \to T\ \overline{a}) : \star \qquad K \# \Gamma}{\vdash_{\mathsf{wf}} \Gamma,\, K\colon \forall\, \overline{a\colon \kappa}.\forall\, \Delta.\, (\overline{\sigma} \to T\ \overline{a})} \quad \text{GWF\_CON}$$

$$\frac{\Gamma, \Delta \vdash_{\mathsf{pr}} \phi\ \mathsf{ok} \qquad C \# \Gamma}{\vdash_{\mathsf{wf}} \Gamma,\, C\colon \forall\, \Delta.\, \phi} \quad \text{GWF\_AX}$$

Figure 5. Context formation rules (excerpted)

4.3.2 Coercion irrelevance and coherence

Although the type system includes a judgement for type equality, and types may include explicit coercion proofs, the system does not include a judgement that states when two coercions proofs are equal. The reason is that this relation is trivial—all coercions should be considered equivalent. As a result, coercion proofs are irrelevant to type equality.

This "proof irrelevance" is guaranteed by several of the coercion rules. Consider the congruence rule for coercion application, CT_CAPP: there are no restrictions on γ_2 and γ_2' other than well-formedness. Another example is rule CT_INSTC—again, no relation is required between the coercions γ_1 and γ_2.

Not only is the identity of coercion proofs irrelevant, but it is always possible to equate a type with a casted version of itself. The coherence rule, CT_COH, essentially says that the use of kind coercions can be ignored when proving type equalities. Although this rule seems limited, it is sufficient to derive the elimination and congruence rules for coerced types, as seen below.

$$\frac{\Gamma \vdash_{\mathsf{co}} \gamma : \tau_1 \sim \tau_2 \quad \Gamma \vdash_{\mathsf{ty}} \tau_1 \triangleright \eta_1 : \kappa_1 \quad \Gamma \vdash_{\mathsf{ty}} \tau_2 \triangleright \eta_2 : \kappa_2}{\Gamma \vdash_{\mathsf{co}} (\mathbf{sym}\,((\mathbf{sym}\,\gamma) \triangleright \eta_2)) \triangleright \eta_1 : \tau_1 \triangleright \eta_1 \sim \tau_2 \triangleright \eta_2}$$

(Again, note that there is no relation required between η_1 and η_2.) We use the syntactic sugar $\gamma \triangleright \eta_1 \sim \eta_2$ to abbreviate the coercion $(\mathbf{sym}\,((\mathbf{sym}\,\gamma) \triangleright \eta_2)) \triangleright \eta_1$.

4.4 Datatypes

Because we focus on the treatment of equality in the type language, we omit most of the discussion of the expression language and its operational semantics. However, since we have collapsed types and kinds, we must revise the treatment of datatypes, whose constructors can contain types and kinds as arguments. Previously, the arguments to datatype constructors were ordered with all kind arguments occurring before all type arguments (Yorgey et al. 2012). In this language, we cannot divide up the arguments in this way. Therefore, we again use the technique of telescopes to describe the more complex dependency between arguments.

The validity rules for contexts (see Figure 5) restrict datatype constants T to have kind $\forall\, \overline{a{:}\kappa}.\star$. We call the variables $\overline{a}$ the *parameters* of the datatype. For example, the kind of the datatype List is $\forall\, a{:}\star.\star$ and the kind of the datatype TyRep (the first version from Section 2) is $\forall\, k{:}\star,\ t{:}k.\star$. Furthermore, datatypes can only be parameterized by types and kinds, not coercions.

Likewise, the same validity rules force data constructors K to have types/kinds of the form

$$\forall\, \overline{a{:}\kappa}.\forall\,\Delta.(\overline{\sigma} \to T\ \overline{a}).$$

Each data constructor K must produce an element of T applied to all of its parameters $\overline{a{:}\kappa}$. Above, the form $\forall\,\Delta.\tau$ is syntactic sugar for a list of nested quantified types. The scope of the bound variables includes both the remainder of the telescope Δ and the form within the quantification (in this case, $\overline{\sigma} \to T\ \overline{a}$).

The telescope Δ describes the *existential* arguments to the data constructor. These arguments may be either coercions or types, and because of the dependency, must be allowed to freely intermix. For example, the data constructor TyInt from Section 2 (a data constructor belonging to TyRep : $\forall\, k{:}\star,\ t{:}k.\star$) includes two coercions in its telescope, one asserting that the kind parameter k is $\star$, the second asserting that the type parameter t is Int:

$$\mathsf{TyInt} : \forall\, k{:}\star,\ t{:}k.\forall\, c_1{:}k \sim \star,\ c_2{:}t \sim \mathsf{Int}.\,\mathsf{TyRep}\,k\,t$$

Likewise, the data constructor TyApp existentially binds k', a, b, and c—one kind and two type variables followed by a coercion.

$$\begin{array}{c}\mathsf{TyApp} : \forall k{:}\star,\ t{:}k.\forall k'{:}\star,\ a{:}k' \to k,\ b{:}k',\ c{:}t \sim a\ b.\\ \mathsf{TyRep}\,(k' \to k)\ a \to \mathsf{TyRep}\,k'\ b \to \mathsf{TyRep}\,k\ t\end{array}$$

A datatype value is of the form $K\ \overline{\tau}\ \overline{\rho}\ \overline{e}$, where $\overline{\tau}$ denotes the parameters (which cannot include coercions), $\overline{\rho}$ instantiate the existential arguments, and $\overline{e}$ is the list of usual expression arguments to the data constructor.

5. The "push" rules and the preservation theorem

Now that we have defined our extensions, we turn to the metatheory: preservation and progress. While the operational semantics is largely unchanged from prior work, we detail here a few key differences. The most intricate part of the operational semantics of FC are the "push" rules, which ensure that coercions do not interfere with the small step semantics. Coercions are "pushed" into the subcomponents of values whenever a coerced value appears in an elimination context. System FC has four push rules, one for each such context: term application, type application, coercion application, and pattern matching on a datatype. The first three are straightforward and are detailed in previous work (Yorgey et al. 2012). In this section, we focus on pattern matching and the S_KPUSH rule.

5.1 Pushing coercions through constructors

When pattern matching on a coerced datatype value of the form $K\ \overline{\tau}\ \overline{\rho}\ \overline{e} \rhd \gamma$, the coercion must be distributed over all of the arguments of the data constructor, producing a new scrutinee $K\ \overline{\tau'}\ \overline{\rho'}\ \overline{e'}$ as shown in Figure 6. In the rest of this section, we explain the rule by describing the formation of the *lifting context* Ψ and its use in the definition of $\overline{\tau'}$, $\overline{\rho'}$ and $\overline{e'}$.

The S_KPUSH rule uses a *lifting* operation $\Psi(\cdot)$ on expressions which coerces the type of its argument ($\overline{e}$ in Figure 6). For example,

$$\frac{\begin{array}{l}K{:}\forall\,\overline{a{:}\kappa}.\forall\,\Delta.\overline{\sigma} \to (T\ \overline{a}) \in \Gamma\\ \Psi = \mathsf{extend}(\mathsf{context}(\gamma); \overline{\rho}; \Delta)\\ \overline{\tau'} = \Psi_2(\overline{a})\\ \overline{\rho}' = \Psi_2(dom\,\Delta)\\ \text{for each } e_i \in \overline{e},\\ \quad e_i' = e_i \rhd \Psi(\sigma_i)\end{array}}{\begin{array}{l}\mathbf{case}\ ((K\ \overline{\tau}\ \overline{\rho}\ \overline{e}) \rhd \gamma)\ \mathbf{of}\ \overline{p \to u} \longrightarrow\\ \quad \mathbf{case}\ (K\ \overline{\tau'}\ \overline{\rho'}\ \overline{e'})\ \mathbf{of}\ \overline{p \to u}\end{array}}\ \text{S\_KPUSH}$$

Figure 6. The S_KPUSH rule

suppose we have a data constructor K of type $\forall\, a{:}\star.\,F\ a \to T\ a$ for some type function F and some type constructor T. Consider what happens when a case expression scrutinee $(K\ \mathsf{Int}\ e){\rhd}\gamma$, where γ is a coercion of type $T\ \mathsf{Int} \sim T\ \tau'$. The push rule should convert this expression to $K\ \tau'\ (e \rhd \gamma')$ for some new coercion γ' showing $F\ \mathsf{Int} \sim F\ \tau'$. To produce γ', we need to lift the type $F\ a$ to a coercion along the coercion $\mathbf{nth}^1\ \gamma$, which shows $\mathsf{Int} \sim \tau'$.

In previous work, lifting was written $\sigma[a \mapsto \gamma]$, defined by analogy with substitution. Because of the similar syntax of types and coercion proofs, we could think of lifting as replacing a type variable with a coercion to produce a new coercion. That intuition holds true here, but we require more machinery to make this precise.

Lifting contexts We define lifting with respect to a *lifting context* Ψ, which maps type variables to triples (τ_1, τ_2, γ) and coercion variables to pairs (η_1, η_2). The forms τ_1 and η_1 refer to the original, uncoerced parameters to the data constructor (Int in our example). The forms τ_2 and η_2 refer to the new, coerced parameters to the data constructor (like τ' in our example). Finally, the coercion γ witnesses the equality of τ_1 and τ_2. No witness is needed for the equality between η_1 and η_2—equality on proofs is trivial.

The lifting operation is defined by structural recursion on its type argument. This operation is complicated by type forms that bind fresh variables: $\forall\, a{:}\kappa.\tau$ and $\forall\, c{:}\phi.\tau$. Lifting over these types introduces new mappings in the lifting context, marked with $\overset{\bullet}{\mapsto}$.

$$\begin{array}{rlll}\Psi ::= \emptyset & \mid\ \Psi, a{:}\kappa \mapsto (\tau_1, \tau_2, \gamma) & \mid & \Psi, c{:}\phi \mapsto (\gamma_1, \gamma_2)\\ & \mid\ \Psi, a{:}\kappa \overset{\bullet}{\mapsto} (a_1, a_2, c) & \mid & \Psi, c{:}\phi \overset{\bullet}{\mapsto} (c_1, c_2)\end{array}$$

(We use the notation $\overset{?}{\mapsto}$ to refer to a mapping created either with $\mapsto$ or with $\overset{\bullet}{\mapsto}$.) A lifting context Ψ induces two multisubstitutions $\Psi_1(\cdot)$ and $\Psi_2(\cdot)$, as follows:

Definition 5.1 (Lifting context substitution). *$\Psi_1(\cdot)$ and $\Psi_2(\cdot)$ are multisubstitutions, applicable to types, coercions, telescopes, typing contexts, and even other lifting contexts.*

1. *For each $a{:}\kappa \overset{?}{\mapsto} (\tau_1, \tau_2, \gamma)$ in Ψ, $\Psi_1(\cdot)$ maps a to τ_1 and $\Psi_2(\cdot)$ maps a to τ_2.*
2. *For each $c{:}\phi \overset{?}{\mapsto} (\gamma_1, \gamma_2)$ in Ψ, $\Psi_1(\cdot)$ maps c to γ_1 and $\Psi_2(\cdot)$ maps c to γ_2.*

The two substitution operations satisfy straightforward substitution lemmas, defined and proved in the extended version of this paper. The usual substitution lemmas, which substitute a single type or coercion, are a direct corollary of these lemmas.

We can now define *lifting:*[6]

Definition 5.2 (Lifting). *We define the lifting of types to coercions, written $\Psi(\tau)$, by induction on the type structure. The following equations, to be tried in order, define the operation. (Note that the last line uses the syntactic sugar introduced in Section 4.3.2.)*

[6] This definition is not just for the proof—it is implemented in GHC as part of the optimizer to reduce case expressions.

$$
\begin{array}{ll}
\Psi(a) & = \gamma \text{ when } a{:}\,\kappa \overset{?}{\mapsto} (\tau_1, \tau_2, \gamma) \in \Psi \\
\Psi(\tau) & = \langle\tau\rangle \text{ when } \tau \# dom(\Psi) \\
\Psi(\tau_1\,\tau_2) & = \Psi(\tau_1)\,\Psi(\tau_2) \\
\Psi(\tau\,\gamma) & = \Psi(\tau)(\Psi_1(\gamma), \Psi_2(\gamma)) \\
\Psi(\forall\, a{:}\,\kappa.\,\tau) & = \forall_{\Psi(\kappa)}(a_1, a_2, c).\Psi'(\tau) \\
& \quad \text{where } \Psi' = \Psi, a{:}\,\kappa \overset{\bullet}{\mapsto} (a_1, a_2, c) \\
& \quad \text{and } a_1, a_2, c \text{ are fresh} \\
\Psi(\forall\, c{:}\,\sigma_1 \sim \sigma_2.\,\tau) & = \forall_{(\Psi(\sigma_1),\Psi(\sigma_2))}(c_1, c_2).\Psi'(\tau) \\
& \quad \text{where } \Psi' = \Psi, c{:}\,\sigma_1 \sim \sigma_2 \overset{\bullet}{\mapsto} (c_1, c_2) \\
& \quad \text{and } c_1, c_2 \text{ are fresh} \\
\Psi(\tau \rhd \gamma) & = \Psi(\tau) \rhd \Psi_1(\gamma) \sim \Psi_2(\gamma)
\end{array}
$$

The lifting lemma establishes the correctness of the lifting operation and shows that equality is congruent.

Lemma 5.3 (Lifting Lemma). *If Ψ is a valid lifting context for context Γ and the telescope Δ, and $\Gamma, \Delta \vdash_{\mathsf{ty}} \tau : \kappa$, then*

$$\Gamma \vdash_{\mathsf{co}} \Psi(\tau) \;:\; \Psi_1(\tau) \sim \Psi_2(\tau)$$

Lifting context creation In the S_KPUSH rule, the actual context Ψ used for lifting is built in two stages. First, $\mathsf{context}(\gamma)$ defines a lifting context with coercions for the parameters to the datatype.

Definition 5.4 (Lifting context generation). *If $\Gamma \vdash_{\mathsf{co}} \gamma \;:\; T\,\overline{\sigma} \sim T\,\overline{\sigma'}$, and $T{:}\,\forall\,\overline{a{:}\,\kappa}.\,\star \in \Gamma$, where the lists $\overline{\sigma}$, $\overline{\sigma'}$, and $\overline{a{:}\,\kappa}$ are all of length n, then define* $\mathsf{context}(\gamma)$ *as*

$$\mathsf{context}(\gamma) = \overline{a_i{:}\,\kappa_i \mapsto (\sigma_i, \sigma'_i, \mathbf{nth}^i\,\gamma)}^{i \in 1..n}$$

Intuitively, $(\mathsf{context}(\gamma))_1(\tau)$ replaces all parameters a in τ with the corresponding type on the left of $\sim$ in the type of γ. Similarly, $(\mathsf{context}(\gamma))_2(\tau)$ replaces a with the corresponding type on the right of $\sim$.

Next, this initial lifting context is extended with coercions using the operation $\mathsf{extend}(\cdot)$, which adds mappings for the variables in Δ, the existential parameters to the data constructor K. Due to the dependency, we define the operation recursively. The intuition still holds: $(\mathsf{extend}(\Psi; \overline{\rho}; \Delta))_1(\tau)$ replaces free variables in τ with their corresponding "from" types, while $(\mathsf{extend}(\Psi; \overline{\rho}; \Delta))_2(\tau)$ replaces a variables with their corresponding "to" types.

Definition 5.5 (Lifting context extension). *Define the operation of lifting context extension, written* $\mathsf{extend}(\Psi; \overline{\rho}; \Delta)$*, as:*

$$
\begin{array}{l}
\mathsf{extend}(\Psi; \varnothing; \varnothing) \quad = \quad \Psi \\
\mathsf{extend}(\Psi; \overline{\rho}, \tau; \Delta,\ a{:}\,\kappa) \quad = \\
\qquad \Psi', a{:}\,\kappa \mapsto (\tau, \tau \rhd \Psi'(\kappa), \mathbf{sym}\,(\langle\tau\rangle \rhd \Psi'(\kappa))) \\
\qquad \text{where } \Psi' = \mathsf{extend}(\Psi; \overline{\rho}; \Delta) \\
\mathsf{extend}(\Psi; \overline{\rho}, \gamma; \Delta,\ c{:}\,\sigma_1 \sim \sigma_2) \quad = \\
\qquad \Psi', c{:}\,\sigma_1 \sim \sigma_2 \mapsto (\gamma, \mathbf{sym}\,(\Psi'(\sigma_1)) \fatsemi \gamma \fatsemi \Psi'(\sigma_2)) \\
\qquad \text{where } \Psi' = \mathsf{extend}(\Psi; \overline{\rho}; \Delta)
\end{array}
$$

5.2 Type preservation

Now that we have explained the most novel part of the operational semantics, we can state the preservation theorem.

Theorem 5.6 (Preservation). *If $\Gamma \vdash_{\mathsf{tm}} e \;:\; \tau$ and $e \longrightarrow e'$ then $\Gamma \vdash_{\mathsf{tm}} e' \;:\; \tau$.*

The proof of this theorem is by induction on the typing derivation, with a case analysis on the small-step. Most of the rules are straightforward, following directly by induction or by substitution. The "push" rules require reasoning about coercion propagation. We include the details of the rules that differ from previous work (Weirich et al. 2010) in the extended version of this paper.

5.3 Correctness of push rules: The type erasure theorem

We care not only that the push rules preserve types, but that they do "the right thing." Do these rules reduce to no-ops if we erase types and coercions?

To state this formally, we define an erasure operation $|\cdot|$ over expressions. This operation erases types, coercions, and equality propositions to trivial forms $\bullet_{\mathsf{ty}}$, $\bullet_{\mathsf{co}}$ and $\bullet_{\mathsf{prop}}$ and removes all casts. The full definition of this operation appears in the extended version of this paper, and we present only the interesting cases here:

$$|e\,\tau| = |e|\,\bullet_{\mathsf{ty}} \qquad |e\,\gamma| = |e|\,\bullet_{\mathsf{co}} \qquad |e \rhd \gamma| = |e|$$

With this operation, we can state that erasing types, coercions and casts does not change how expressions evaluate e.

Theorem 5.7 (Type erasure). *If $e \longrightarrow e'$, then either $|e| = |e'|$ or $|e| \longrightarrow |e'|$.*

6. Consistency and the progress theorem

The proof for the progress theorem follows the same course as in previous work (Weirich et al. 2010). The progress theorem holds only for *closed, consistent* contexts. A context is *closed* if it does not contain any expression variable bindings—as usual, open expressions could be stuck. We use the metavariable Σ to denote closed contexts.

Theorem 6.1 (Progress). *Assume Σ is a closed, consistent context. If $\Sigma \vdash_{\mathsf{tm}} e_1 \;:\; \tau$ and e_1 is not a value v or a coerced value $v \rhd \gamma$, then there exists an e_2 such that $e_1 \longrightarrow e_2$.*

The definition of consistent contexts is stated using the notions of uncoerced *values* and their types, *value types*. Formally, we define values v and value types ξ, with the following grammars:

$$
\begin{array}{lcl}
v & ::= & \lambda x{:}\,\sigma.\,e \mid \Lambda a{:}\,\kappa.\,e \mid \lambda c{:}\,\phi.\,e \mid K\,\overline{\tau}\,\overline{\rho}\,\overline{e} \\
\xi & ::= & \sigma_1 \to \sigma_2 \mid \forall\, a{:}\,\kappa.\,\sigma \mid \forall\, c{:}\,\phi.\,\sigma \mid T\,\overline{\sigma}
\end{array}
$$

Definition 6.2 (Consistency). *A context Γ is consistent if ξ_1 and ξ_2 have the same head form whenever $\Gamma \vdash_{\mathsf{co}} \gamma \;:\; \xi_1 \sim \xi_2$.*

Although the extensions in this paper have little effect on the structure of this proof compared to prior work, there is still work to do: we need an new notion of acceptable contexts to allow kind equalities, and we must prove that these contexts are consistent.

Our consistency argument proceeds in four steps:

1. Because coercion proofs are irrelevant to type equivalence, we start with an *implicitly coerced* version of the language, where all coercion proofs have been erased. Derivations in the explicit language can be matched up with derivations in the implicit language (Definition 6.3) so showing consistency in the latter implies consistency in the former.
2. We define a *rewrite relation* that reduces types in the implicit system by firing axioms in the context (Figure 7).
3. We specify a sufficient condition, which we write $\mathbf{Good}\,\Gamma$ (Definition 6.5), for a context to be consistent. This condition allows the axioms produced by type and kind family definitions.
4. We show that good contexts are consistent by arguing that the joinability of the rewrite relation is complete with respect to the implicit coercion proof system. Since the rewrite relation and erasure preserve the head form of value types, this gives consistency for both the implicit and explicit systems.

Since we don't want consistency to depend on particular proofs of kind equality, we prove our results with an implicit version of the type language. This implicit language elides coercion proofs and casts from the type language, and has judgements (denoted with a turnstile $\models$) analogous to the explicit language but for a few key

$$\boxed{\Gamma \models \tau \rightsquigarrow \tau'}$$

$$\frac{}{\Gamma \models \tau \rightsquigarrow \tau} \text{ TS\_REFL}$$

$$\frac{\Gamma, \Gamma' \models \kappa \rightsquigarrow \kappa' \quad \Gamma,\ c{:}\, a_1 \sim a_2, \Gamma' \models \sigma \rightsquigarrow \sigma'}{\Gamma, \Gamma' \models \forall\, a_1{:}\, \kappa.\, \sigma \rightsquigarrow \forall\, a_2{:}\, \kappa'.\, \sigma'} \text{ TS\_ALLT}$$

$$\frac{\Gamma \models \tau_1 \rightsquigarrow \tau_1' \quad \Gamma \models \tau_2 \rightsquigarrow \tau_2' \quad \Gamma \models \sigma \rightsquigarrow \sigma'}{\Gamma \models \forall\, c{:}\, \tau_1 \sim \tau_2.\, \sigma \rightsquigarrow \forall\, c{:}\, \tau_1' \sim \tau_2'.\, \sigma'} \text{ TS\_ALLC}$$

$$\frac{\begin{array}{c} C{:}\ \forall\, \Delta.\, (F\, \overline{\tau} \sim \tau') \in \Gamma \\ \sigma_1 = \tau[\overline{\rho}/\Delta] \quad \sigma_1' = \tau'[\overline{\rho}/\Delta] \end{array}}{\Gamma \models F\, \overline{\sigma_1} \rightsquigarrow \sigma_1'} \text{ TS\_RED}$$

$$\frac{c{:}\, a \sim \tau \in \Gamma}{\Gamma \models a \rightsquigarrow \tau} \text{ TS\_VARRED}$$

$$\frac{\Gamma \models \tau \rightsquigarrow \tau' \quad \Gamma \models \sigma \rightsquigarrow \sigma'}{\Gamma \models \tau\, \sigma \rightsquigarrow \tau'\, \sigma'} \text{ TS\_APP}$$

$$\frac{\Gamma \models \tau \rightsquigarrow \tau'}{\Gamma \models \tau\, \bullet_{\mathsf{co}} \rightsquigarrow \tau'\, \bullet_{\mathsf{co}}} \text{ TS\_CAPP}$$

Figure 7. Rewrite relation

differences where coercions are dropped from types. To connect the explicit and implicit systems, we define an erasure operation:

Definition 6.3 (Coercion Erasure). *Given an explicitly typed term τ or coercion γ, we define its* erasure, *denoted $|\tau|$ or $|\gamma|$, by induction on its structure. The interesting cases follow:*

$$\begin{array}{lclclcl} |\tau \rhd \gamma| & = & |\tau| & \quad & |\gamma(\gamma_1, \gamma_2)| & = & |\gamma|(\bullet_{co}, \bullet_{co}) \\ |\tau\, \gamma| & = & |\tau|\, \bullet_{co} & & |\gamma \rhd \gamma'| & = & |\gamma| \\ & & & & |\gamma@(\gamma', \gamma'')| & = & |\gamma|@(\bullet_{co}, \bullet_{co}) \end{array}$$

All other cases follow by simply propagating the $|\cdot|$ operation down the abstract syntax tree. (The full definition of this operation appears in the extended version of this paper.)

We further define the erasure *of a context Γ, denoted $|\Gamma|$, by erasing the types and equality propositions of each binding.*

Lemma 6.4 (Erasure is type preserving). *If a judgement holds in the explicit system, the judgement with coercions erased throughout the context, types and coercions is derivable in the implicit system.*

We define a nondeterministic rewrite relation on open implicit types in Figure 7. We say that σ_1 is *joinable* with σ_2, written $\Gamma \models \sigma_1 \Leftrightarrow \sigma_2$, when both can multi-rewrite to a common reduct.

Consistency does not hold in arbitrary contexts, and it is difficult in general to check whether a context is inconsistent. Therefore, like in previous work (Weirich et al. 2010), we give sufficient conditions written **Good** Γ, for a context to be consistent. Since we are working with the implicit language, these conditions are actually for the *erased* context.

Definition 6.5 (Good contexts). *We have* **Good** Γ *when the following conditions hold:*

1. *All coercion assumptions and axioms in Γ are of the form $C{:}\ \forall\, \Delta.\, (F\, \overline{\tau} \sim \tau')$ or of the form $c{:}\ a_1 \sim a_2$. In the first form, the arguments to the type function must behave like patterns: for all $\overline{\rho}$, every $\tau_i \in \overline{\tau}$ and every τ_i' such that $\Gamma \models \tau_i[\overline{\rho}/\Delta] \rightsquigarrow \tau_i'$, there exists $\overline{\rho}'$ such that $\tau_i' = \tau_i[\overline{\rho'}/\Delta]$ and $\Gamma \models \sigma_m \rightsquigarrow \sigma_m'$ for each $\sigma_m \in \overline{\rho}$ and $\sigma_m' \in \overline{\rho}'$.*
2. *Axioms and coercion assumptions don't overlap. For each $F\, \overline{\tau}$, there exists at most one prefix $\overline{\tau_1}$ of $\overline{\tau}$ such that there exist C and $\overline{\rho}$ where $C{:}\ \forall\, \Delta.\, F\, \overline{\sigma_0} \sim \sigma_1 \in \Gamma$ and $\overline{\tau_1} = \overline{\sigma_0[\overline{\rho}/\Delta]}$. These C and $\overline{\rho}$ are unique for every matching $F\, \overline{\tau_1}$.*
3. *For each a, there is at most one assumption of the form $c{:}\ a \sim a'$ or $c{:}\ a' \sim a$, and $a \neq a'$.*
4. *Axioms equate types of the same kind. For each $C{:}\ \forall\, \Delta.\, (F\, \overline{\tau} \sim \tau')$ in Γ, the kinds of each side must equal: for some κ, $\Gamma, \Delta \models F\, \overline{\tau}\ :\ \kappa$ and $\Gamma, \Delta \models \tau'\ :\ \kappa$ and that kind must not mention bindings in the telescope, $\Gamma \models \kappa\ :\ \star$.*

The main lemma required for consistency is the completeness of joinability. Here, we write $fcv(\gamma) \subseteq dom\, \Gamma'$ to indicate that all coercion variables and axioms used in γ are in the domain of Γ'.

Lemma 6.6 (Completeness). *Suppose that $\Gamma \models \gamma\ :\ \sigma_1 \sim \sigma_2$, and $fcv(\gamma) \subseteq dom\, \Gamma'$ for some subcontext Γ' satisfying* **Good** Γ'. *Then $\Gamma \models \sigma_1 \Leftrightarrow \sigma_2$.*

The proof of this theorem appears in the extended version of this paper. Here, we highlight a technical point about coercions between coercion abstractions. The completeness proof requires that all coercion variables in a coercion γ must satisfy the requirements of Good contexts. As a result, we need to restrict the coercion abstraction equality rule in both the implicit and explicit systems.

$$\frac{\begin{array}{l} \Gamma \models \eta_1\ :\ \sigma_1 \sim \sigma_1' \quad \phi_1 = \sigma_1 \sim \sigma_2 \\ \Gamma \models \eta_2\ :\ \sigma_2 \sim \sigma_2' \quad \phi_2 = \sigma_1' \sim \sigma_2' \\ c_1 \,\#\, \gamma \quad c_2 \,\#\, \gamma \\ \Gamma,\ c_1{:}\phi_1,\ c_2{:}\phi_2 \models \gamma\ :\ \tau_1 \sim \tau_2 \\ \Gamma \models \forall\, c_1{:}\phi_1.\, \tau_1\ :\ \star \quad \Gamma \models \forall\, c_2{:}\phi_2.\, \tau_2\ :\ \star \end{array}}{\Gamma \models \forall_{(\eta_1,\eta_2)}(c_1, c_2).\gamma\ :\ (\forall\, c_1{:}\phi_1.\, \tau_1) \sim (\forall\, c_2{:}\phi_2.\, \tau_2)}$$

In this rule, the variables c_1 and c_2 cannot be used in γ due to the premises $c_1 \,\#\, \gamma$ and $c_2 \,\#\, \gamma$. (The analogous rule in the explicit system includes the premises $c_1 \,\#\, |\gamma|$ and $c_2 \,\#\, |\gamma|$.) This restriction is because c_1 and c_2 may be inconsistent assumptions: perhaps $c_1{:}\ \mathsf{Int} \sim \mathsf{Bool}$. If we were to introduce these into the context, induction would fail.

The consequence of these restrictions is that there are some types that cannot be shown equivalent, even though they are intuitively equivalent. For example, there is no proof of equivalence between the types $\forall\, c_1{:}\ \mathsf{Int} \sim b.\, \mathsf{Int}$ and $\forall\, c_2{:}\ \mathsf{Int} \sim b.\, b$—a coercion between these two types would need to use c_1 or c_2. However, this lack of expressiveness is not significant—in source Haskell, it could only be observed through exotic uses of first-class polymorphism, which are already rare in general. Furthermore, this restriction already exists in GHC[7] and other dependently-typed languages such as Agda and Coq. It is possible that a different consistency proof would validate a rule that does not restrict the use of these variables. However, we leave this possibility to future work.

7. Discussion and related work

Collapsing kinds and types Blurring the distinction between types and kinds is convenient, but is it wise? It is well known that type systems that include the $\Gamma \vdash_{\mathsf{ty}} \star\ :\ \star$ rule are inconsistent logics (Girard 1972). Does that cause trouble? For FC the answer is no—inconsistency here means that all kinds are inhabited, but even without our extensions, all kinds are already inhabited.

The $\Gamma \vdash_{\mathsf{ty}} \star\ :\ \star$ rule often causes type checking to be undecidable in dependently typed languages (Cardelli 1986; Augustsson 1998). This axiom permits the expression of divergent terms—if the type checker tries to reduce them it will loop. However, type checking in FC is decidable—all type equalities are witnessed by finite equality proofs, not potentially infinite reductions.

[7] Currently, coercions between the types $(\mathsf{Int} \sim b) \Rightarrow \mathsf{Int}$ and $(\mathsf{Int} \sim b) \Rightarrow b$ are disallowed

At the source language level, which does reduce type expressions, it is not clear whether adding the $\Gamma \vdash_{\mathsf{ty}} \star : \star$ rule could cause type inference to loop (in the absence of language extensions such as `UndecidableInstances` which already make divergence possible). However, even though this version of FC combines types and kinds, the Haskell source language need not do so (predictable type inference algorithms may require more traditional stratification). This gap would not be new—differing requirements for the core and surface languages have already led FC to be more expressive than source Haskell.

Heterogeneous equality Heterogeneous equality is an essential part of this system. It is primarily motivated by the presence of dependent application (such as rules K_INST and K_CAPP), where the kind of the result depends on the value of the argument. We would like type equivalence to be congruent with respect to application, as is demonstrated by rule CT_APP. However, if all equalities are required to be homogeneous, then not all uses of the rule are valid because the result kinds may differ.

For example, consider the datatype $\mathsf{TyRep} : \forall k{:}\,\star\,.\,\forall b{:}\,k.\,\star$. If we have coercions $\Gamma \vdash_{\mathsf{co}} \gamma_1 : \star \sim \kappa$ and $\Gamma \vdash_{\mathsf{co}} \gamma_2 : \mathsf{Int} \sim \tau$ (with $\Gamma \vdash_{\mathsf{ty}} \tau : \kappa$), then we can construct the proof

$$\Gamma \vdash_{\mathsf{co}} \langle \mathsf{TyRep} \rangle\, \gamma_1\, \gamma_2 \; : \; \mathsf{TyRep}\,\star\,\mathsf{Int} \sim \mathsf{TyRep}\,\kappa\,\tau$$

However, this proof requires heterogeneity because the first part ($\langle \mathsf{TyRep} \rangle\, \gamma_1$) creates an equality between types of different kinds: $\mathsf{TyRep}\,\star$ and $\mathsf{TyRep}\,\kappa$. The first has kind $\star \to \star$, whereas the second has kind $\kappa \to \star$.

The coherence rule (CT_COH) also requires that equality be heterogeneous because it equates types that almost certainly have different kinds. This rule, inspired by Observational Type Theory (Altenkirch et al. 2007), provides a simple way of ensuring that proofs do not interfere with equality. Without it, we would need coercions analogous to the many "push" rules of the operational semantics.

There are several choices in the semantics of heterogeneous equality. We have chosen the most popular, where a proposition $\sigma_1 \sim \sigma_2$ is interpreted as a conjunction: "the types are equal and their kinds are equal". This semantics is similar to Epigram 1 (McBride 2002), the `HeterogeneousEquality` module in the Agda standard library,[8] and the treatment in Coq.[9] Epigram 2 (Altenkirch et al. 2007) uses an alternative semantics, interpreted as "if the kinds are equal then the types are equal". (This relation requires a proof of kind equality before coercing types.) Guru (Stump et al. 2008) and Trellys (Kimmell et al. 2012; Sjöberg et al. 2012) use yet another interpretation which says nothing about the kinds. These differences reflect the design of the type systems—the syntax-directed type system of FC makes the conjunctive interpretation the most reasonable, whereas the bidirectional type system of Epigram 2 makes the implicational version more convenient. As Guru/Trellys demonstrate, it is also reasonable to not require kind equality. We conjecture that without the $\mathbf{kind}\,\gamma$ coercion form, it would be sound to drop the fourth condition from $\mathbf{Good}\,\Gamma$.

Unlike higher-dimensional type theory (Licata and Harper 2012), equality in this language has no computational content. Because of the separation between objects and proofs, FC is resolutely one-dimensional—we do not define what it means for proofs to be equivalent. Instead, we ensure that in any context the identity of equality proofs is unimportant.

The implicit language Our proof technique for consistency, based on erasing explicit type conversions, is inspired by ICC (Miquel 2001). Coercion proofs are irrelevant to the definition of type equality, so to reason about type equality it is convenient to ignore them entirely. Following ICC* (Barras and Bernardo 2008), we could also view the implicit language as the "real" semantics for FC, and consider the language of this paper as an adaptation of that semantics with annotations to make typing decidable. Furthermore, the implicit language is interesting in its own right as it is closer to source Haskell, which also makes implicit use of type equalities.

However, although the implicit language allows type equality assumptions to be used implicitly, it is not extensional type theory (ETT) (Martin-Löf 1984): it separates proofs from programs so that it can weaken the former (ensuring consistency) while enriching the latter (with "type-in-type"). As a result, the proof language of FC is not as expressive as ETT; besides the limitations on equalities between coercion abstractions in Section 6, FC lacks η-equivalence or extensional reasoning for type-level functions.

Explicit equality proofs In concurrent related work, van Doorn, Geuvers and Wiedijk (Geuvers and Wiedijk 2004; van Doorn et al. 2013) develop a variant of pure type systems that replaces implicit conversions with explicit convertibility proofs. There are strong connections to this paper: they too use heterogeneous equality and must significantly generalize the statement of a lifting lemma (which they call "equality of substitutions"). However, there are differences. Their work is based on Pure Type Systems, which generalize over sorts, rules and axioms; we only consider a single instance here. They also show that the system with explicit equalities is equivalent to the system with implicit equalities; we only show one direction. Finally, as their work is based on intensional type theory, it does not address coercion abstraction. Consequently, their analogue to rule CT_ALLT is the following asymmetric rule.

$$\frac{\begin{array}{l}\Gamma \vdash_{\mathsf{co}} \eta : \kappa_1 \sim \kappa_2 \\ \Gamma,\, a_1{:}\,\kappa_1 \vdash_{\mathsf{co}} \gamma : \tau_1 \sim \tau_2[a_1 \rhd \eta / a_2] \\ \Gamma \vdash_{\mathsf{ty}} \forall\, a_1{:}\,\kappa_1.\,\tau_1 : \star \\ \Gamma \vdash_{\mathsf{ty}} \forall\, a_2{:}\,\kappa_2.\,\tau_2 : \star\end{array}}{\Gamma \vdash_{\mathsf{co}} \eta\, a_1{:}\,\kappa_1.\,\gamma : (\forall\, a_1{:}\,\kappa_1.\,\tau_1) \sim (\forall\, a_1{:}\,\kappa_2.\,\tau_2)} \;\textsc{CT\_AllTA}$$

We conjecture that in our system, the above rule is equivalent to CT_ALLT.

8. Conclusions and future work

This work provides the basis for the practical extension of a popular programming language implementation. It does so without sacrificing any important metatheoretic properties. This extension is a necessary step towards making Haskell more dependently typed.

The next step in this research plan is to lift these extensions to the source language, incorporating these features within GHC's constraint solving algorithm. In particular, we plan future language extensions in support of type- and kind-level programming, such as datakinds (datatypes that exist only at the kind-level), kind synonyms and kind families. Although GHC already infers kinds, we will need to extend this mechanism to generate kind coercions and take advantage of these new features.

Going further, we would like to also like to support a true "dependent type" in Haskell, which would allow types to mention expressions directly, instead of requiring singleton encodings. One way to extend Haskell in this way is through elaboration: we believe that the translation between source Haskell and FC could automatically insert the appropriate singleton arguments (Eisenberg and Weirich 2012), perhaps using the class system to determine where they are necessary. This approach would not require further extension to FC. Alternatively, Adam Gundry's forthcoming dissertation[10] includes Π-types in a version of System FC that is

[8] `http://wiki.portal.chalmers.se/agda/agda.php?n=Libraries.StandardLibrary`

[9] `http://coq.inria.fr/stdlib/Coq.Logic.JMeq.html`

[10] Personal communication

strongly influenced by an early draft of this work. If elaboration does not prove to be sufficiently expressive, Gundry's work provides a blueprint for future core language extension.

In either case the interaction between dependent types and type inference brings new research challenges. However, the results in this paper mean that these challenges can be addressed in the context of a firm semantic basis.

Acknowledgments

Thanks to Simon Peyton Jones, Dimitrios Vytiniotis, Iavor Diatchki, José Pedro Magalhães, Adam Gundry and Conor McBride for discussion. This material is based upon work supported by the National Science Foundation under Grant Nos. 0910500 and 1116620.

References

T. Altenkirch and C. McBride. Generic programming within dependently typed programming. In J. Gibbons and J. Jeuring, editors, *Generic Programming*, volume 243 of *IFIP Conference Proceedings*, pages 1–20. Kluwer, 2002.

T. Altenkirch, C. McBride, and W. Swierstra. Observational equality, now! In *Proceedings of the 2007 workshop on Programming Languages meets Program Verification*, PLPV '07, pages 57–68, New York, 2007. ACM.

L. Augustsson. Cayenne—a language with dependent types. In *Proceedings of the third ACM SIGPLAN International Conference on Functional Programming*, ICFP '98, pages 239–250, New York, 1998. ACM. .

H. P. Barendregt. Handbook of logic in computer science (vol. 2). chapter Lambda calculi with types, pages 117–309. Oxford University Press, New York, 1992.

B. Barras and B. Bernardo. The implicit calculus of constructions as a programming language with dependent types. In *Foundations of Software Science and Computational Structures*, volume 4962 of *Lecture Notes in Computer Science*, pages 365–379. Springer, Berlin, Heidelberg, 2008.

L. Cardelli. A polymorphic lambda calculus with type:type. Technical Report 10, Digital Equipment Corporation Systems Research Center, 1986.

M. M. T. Chakravarty, G. Keller, and S. Peyon Jones. Associated type synonyms. In *Proceedings of the tenth ACM SIGPLAN International Conference on Functional Programming*, ICFP '05, pages 241–253, New York, 2005. ACM.

K. Crary, S. Weirich, and G. Morrisett. Intensional polymorphism in type erasure semantics. In *Proceedings of the Third ACM SIGPLAN International Conference on Functional Programming*, ICFP '98, pages 301–313, Baltimore, MD, USA, 1998. ACM.

R. A. Eisenberg and S. Weirich. Dependently typed programming with singletons. In *Proceedings of the 2012 Haskell Symposium*, Haskell '12, pages 117–130, New York, 2012. ACM.

H. Geuvers and F. Wiedijk. A logical framework with explicit conversions. In C. Schuermann, editor, *LFM'04, Proceedings of the Fourth International Workshop on Logical Frameworks and Meta-Languages, Cork, Ireland*, pages 32–45, 2004.

J.-Y. Girard. *Interprétation fonctionnelle et élimination des coupures de l'arithmétique d'ordre supérieu*. PhD thesis, Université de Paris VII, 1972.

M. P. Jones. Type classes with functional dependencies. In *9th European Symposium on Programming, ESOP '00*, volume 1782 of *Lecture Notes in Computer Science*, pages 230–244. Springer, 2000.

G. Kimmell, A. Stump, H. D. Eades III, P. Fu, T. Sheard, S. Weirich, C. Casinghino, V. Sjöberg, N. Collins, and K. Y. Ahn. Equational reasoning about programs with general recursion and call-by-value semantics. In *Sixth ACM SIGPLAN Workshop Programming Languages meets Program Verification (PLPV '12)*, 2012.

D. R. Licata and R. Harper. Canonicity for 2-dimensional type theory. In *Proceedings of the 39th annual ACM SIGPLAN-SIGACT symposium on Principles of programming languages*, POPL '12, pages 337–348, New York, NY, USA, 2012. ACM.

Z. Luo. *Computation and reasoning: a type theory for computer science*. Oxford University Press, Inc., New York, NY, USA, 1994.

J. P. Magalhães. The right kind of generic programming. In *8th ACM SIGPLAN Workshop on Generic Programming, WGP 2012, Copenhagen, Denmark*, New York, NY, USA, 2012. ACM.

P. Martin-Löf. *Intuitionistic Type Theory*. Bibliopolis, 1984.

C. McBride. Elimination with a motive. In *Selected papers from the International Workshop on Types for Proofs and Programs*, TYPES '00, pages 197–216, London, UK, UK, 2002. Springer-Verlag.

C. T. McBride. Agda-curious?: an exploration of programming with dependent types. In P. Thiemann and R. B. Findler, editors, *ICFP*, pages 1–2. ACM, 2012. ISBN 978-1-4503-1054-3.

A. Miquel. The implicit calculus of constructions: extending pure type systems with an intersection type binder and subtyping. In *Proceedings of the 5th international conference on Typed lambda calculi and applications*, TLCA'01, pages 344–359, Berlin, Heidelberg, 2001. Springer-Verlag.

U. Norell. Functional generic programming and type theory, 2002. MSc thesis.

N. Oury and W. Swierstra. The power of Pi. In *Proceedings of the 13th ACM SIGPLAN international conference on Functional programming*, ICFP '08, pages 39–50, New York, NY, USA, 2008. ACM. ISBN 978-1-59593-919-7.

S. Peyton Jones, D. Vytiniotis, S. Weirich, and G. Washburn. Simple unification-based type inference for GADTs. In *Proceedings of the eleventh ACM SIGPLAN International Conference on Functional Programming*, ICFP '06, pages 50–61, New York, NY, USA, 2006. ACM.

T. Schrijvers, S. Peyton Jones, M. Sulzmann, and D. Vytiniotis. Complete and decidable type inference for GADTs. In *Proceedings of the 14th ACM SIGPLAN international conference on Functional programming*, ICFP '09, pages 341–352, New York, NY, USA, 2009. ACM.

V. Sjöberg, C. Casinghino, K. Y. Ahn, N. Collins, H. D. Eades III, P. Fu, G. Kimmell, T. Sheard, A. Stump, and S. Weirich. Irrelevance, heterogenous equality, and call-by-value dependent type systems. In *Fourth workshop on Mathematically Structured Functional Programming (MSFP '12)*, 2012.

A. Stump, M. Deters, A. Petcher, T. Schiller, and T. Simpson. Verified programming in Guru. In *Proceedings of the 3rd workshop on Programming languages meets program verification*, PLPV '09, pages 49–58, New York, NY, USA, 2008. ACM.

M. Sulzmann, M. M. T. Chakravarty, S. P. Jones, and K. Donnelly. System F with type equality coercions. In *Proceedings of the 2007 ACM SIGPLAN international workshop on Types in languages design and implementation*, TLDI '07, pages 53–66, New York, NY, USA, 2007. ACM.

F. van Doorn, H. Geuvers, and F. Wiedijk. Explicit convertibility proofs in pure type systems. Draft paper, in submission, `http://www.cs.ru.nl/~herman/PUBS/ExplicitPTS.pdf`, 2013.

D. Vytiniotis, S. Peyton Jones, and J. P. Magalhães. Equality proofs and deferred type errors: A compiler pearl. In *Proceedings of the 14th ACM SIGPLAN International Conference on Functional Programming, ICFP 2012, Copenhagen, Denmark*, New York, NY, USA, 2012. ACM.

S. Weirich, D. Vytiniotis, S. Peyton Jones, and S. Zdancewic. Generative type abstraction and type-level computation (extended version). Technical report, University of Pennsylvania, Nov. 2010.

S. Weirich, D. Vytiniotis, S. Peyton Jones, and S. Zdancewic. Generative type abstraction and type-level computation. In *Proceedings of the 38th annual ACM SIGPLAN-SIGACT symposium on Principles of programming languages*, POPL '11, pages 227–240, New York, NY, USA, 2011. ACM.

Z. Yang. Encoding types in ML-like languages. In *Proceedings of the Third International Conference on Functional Programming (ICFP)*, pages 289–300, Baltimore, Maryland, USA, 1998. ACM Press.

B. A. Yorgey, S. Weirich, J. Cretin, S. Peyton Jones, D. Vytiniotis, and J. P. Magalhães. Giving Haskell a promotion. In *Proceedings of the 8th ACM SIGPLAN workshop on Types in Language Design and Implementation*, TLDI '12, pages 53–66, New York, NY, USA, 2012. ACM.

The Constrained-Monad Problem

Neil Sculthorpe
ITTC
The University of Kansas
neil@ittc.ku.edu

Jan Bracker
Institut für Informatik
Christian-Albrechts-Universität
jbra@informatik.uni-kiel.de

George Giorgidze
Institut für Informatik
Universität Tübingen
george.giorgidze@uni-tuebingen.de

Andy Gill
EECS / ITTC
The University of Kansas
andygill@ittc.ku.edu

Abstract

In Haskell, there are many data types that would form monads were it not for the presence of type-class constraints on the operations on that data type. This is a frustrating problem in practice, because there is a considerable amount of support and infrastructure for monads that these data types cannot use. Using several examples, we show that a monadic computation can be restructured into a normal form such that the standard monad class *can* be used. The technique is not specific to monads, and we show how it can also be applied to other structures, such as applicative functors. One significant use case for this technique is *domain-specific languages*, where it is often desirable to compile a deep embedding of a computation to some other language, which requires restricting the types that can appear in that computation.

Categories and Subject Descriptors D.3.3 [*Programming Languages*]: Language Constructs and Features—Constraints, Polymorphism, Data types and structures; D.3.2 [*Programming Languages*]: Language Classifications—Applicative (functional) languages

Keywords Class Constraints; Monads; Deep Embeddings; Haskell

1. Motivation

The use of *monads* to structure computation was first suggested by Moggi [27, 28] and Spivey [36], and was then enthusiastically taken up by Wadler [41, 42]. Monads have since proved to be a popular and frequently occurring structure, and are now one of the most prevalent abstractions within the Haskell language.

However, there are many data structures that are monad-like, but cannot be made instances of the Monad type class (Figure 1) because of type-class constraints on their operations. The classic example of this is the Set data type, which imposes an ordering constraint on its operations. This is unfortunate, because the Haskell language and libraries provide a significant amount of infrastructure to support arbitrary monads, including special syntax. We will refer to this situation where type-class constraints prevent a Monad instance from being declared as the "constrained-monad problem". This paper is about investigating solutions to this problem, with an emphasis on the particular solution of normalizing a deep embedding of a monadic computation. We aim to understand the utility of the various solutions, publicize their usefulness, and explain how they relate to each other.

ICFP '13, September 25–27, 2013, Boston, MA, USA.

ACM 978-1-4503-2326-0/13/09... $15.00.
http://dx.doi.org/10.1145/2500365.2500602


```
class Monad (m :: * → *) where
  return :: a → m a
  (>>=)  :: m a → (a → m b) → m b
```

- return a >>= $k \equiv k\ a$ (left identity)
- ma >>= return $\equiv ma$ (right identity)
- $(ma$ >>= $h)$ >>= $k \equiv ma$ >>= $(\lambda a \rightarrow h\ a$ >>= $k)$ (associativity)

Figure 1. Monads and the monad laws.

We begin by giving three concrete examples of the constrained-monad problem: three data types that would be monads were it not for the presence of class constraints on their operations.

1.1 Sets

The `Data.Set` module in the Haskell standard library provides an abstract representation of sets that is implemented using size-balanced binary trees [1] for efficiency. The operations from the module that we will use are as follows:

```
singleton :: a → Set a
toList    :: Set a → [a]
fromList  :: Ord a ⇒ [a] → Set a
unions    :: Ord a ⇒ [Set a] → Set a
```

Notice the Ord class constraint on two of the operations; this is a consequence of the binary-tree implementation.

Ideally we would like to define a Set monad that behaves analogously to the list monad (i.e. modelling non-determinism), except that it should combine duplicate results. For example, we would like to write the following set comprehension,

```
do n ← fromList [3, 2, 1, 2]
   c ← fromList ['a', 'b']
   return (n, c)
```

and be able to evaluate it to the set:

$\{(1, \text{'a'}), (1, \text{'b'}), (2, \text{'a'}), (2, \text{'b'}), (3, \text{'a'}), (3, \text{'b'})\}$

Using the operations provided by `Data.Set`, it appears straightforward to define return and >>= (pronounced "bind") functions that satisfy the monad laws (Figure 1):

```
returnSet :: a → Set a
returnSet = singleton

bindSet :: Ord b ⇒ Set a → (a → Set b) → Set b
bindSet sa k = unions (map k (toList sa))
```

However, the use of unions introduces an Ord constraint in the type of bindSet, which means that a straightforward attempt to define a Monad instance will not type check:

```
instance Monad Set where
  return = returnSet
  (>>=)  = bindSet    -- does not type check
```

The problem is that ≫= must be parametrically polymorphic in its two type parameters, whereas bindSet constrains its second type parameter to ordered types.

1.2 Vectors

In their work on structuring quantum effects, Vizzotto et al. [39] discuss how quantum values can be represented as a vector associating a complex number to each element of a finite set. Furthermore, they observe that such vectors have a structure that is almost a monad, with the application of a linear operator to a vector matching the type of ≫= and obeying the monad laws. Adapting their code slightly, this can be defined as follows[1]:

```
class Finite (a :: *) where
  enumerate :: [a]

type Vec (a :: *) = (a → Complex Double)

returnVec :: Eq a ⇒ a → Vec a
returnVec a = λb → if a ≡ b then 1 else 0

bindVec :: Finite a ⇒ Vec a → (a → Vec b) → Vec b
bindVec va k = λb → sum [va a * (k a) b | a ← enumerate]
```

Notice the presence of class constraints on both returnVec and bindVec; as with the set example, these constraints prevent these functions being used to define a Monad instance. However, the situation is not quite the same as for sets: bindVec has a constraint on its first type parameter, whereas bindSet had a constraint on its second type parameter. Additionally, returnVec is constrained, whereas returnSet was not; and furthermore, the constraint on returnVec differs from the constraint on bindVec.

1.3 Embedding JavaScript

Our Sunroof library [6] provides an Embedded Domain-Specific Language (EDSL) [5, 10] for expressing JavaScript computations in Haskell, and for compiling them to executable JavaScript. Our initial embedding of a JavaScript computation in Haskell used the following Generalized Algebraic Data Type (GADT) [31]:

```
data JS :: * → * where
  Prompt :: JSString                → JS JSString
  Alert  :: JSString                → JS ()
  If     :: JSBool → JS a → JS a → JS a
```

We consider only a small selection of constructors for brevity: Prompt and Alert are deep embeddings of the standard-library functions of the same names; If is a deep embedding of a conditional statement. We have enumerated the functions Prompt and Alert for clarity here, but will later abstract over an arbitrary function (Section 4.3.2).

To allow JS to be compiled, we must constrain any polymorphic types to those that can be successfully translated to JavaScript — a common requirement for this style of EDSL [8, 37]. We represent this constraint with a class called Sunroof, which can generate new variables, print values in their JavaScript form, and, given a right-hand side, generate a JavaScript assignment:

```
type JSCode = String

class Show a ⇒ Sunroof (a :: *) where
  mkVar     :: String → a                  -- New variable of type a
  showJS    :: a → JSCode                  -- Show as JavaScript
  assignVar :: a → JSCode → JSCode         -- Assign to a variable
  assignVar a c = showJS a ++ "=" ++ c ++ ";"
```

The () type is the outlier, so we give its instance here. It is interesting because values of type () are not stored in variables, and expressions of type () are never even computed.

[1] Actually, Vec should be defined as a **newtype** because of limitations on the use of type synonyms in Haskell. However, as this introduces some syntactic clutter, we elide this detail.

```
instance Sunroof () where
  mkVar _        = ()
  showJS ()      = "null"
  assignVar () _ = ""
```

To compile to JavaScript, we use the pattern of compiling JS into a pair consisting of JavaScript code and a JavaScript variable referring to the result of that code. We work inside a state monad [42] called CompM for name supply purposes.

```
compileJS :: Sunroof a ⇒ JS a → CompM (JSCode, a)
compileJS (Prompt s) = do
  (decl, v) ← newVar
  return (concat [decl
                 , assignVar v ("prompt(" ++ showJS s ++ ")")], v)
compileJS (Alert s) =
  return (concat ["alert(", showJS s, ");"], ())
compileJS (If b ja1 ja2) = do
  (decl, v) ← newVar
  (c1, a1)  ← compileJS ja1
  (c2, a2)  ← compileJS ja2
  return (concat [decl
                 , "if(", showJS b, ") {"
                 , c1, assignVar v (showJS a1)
                 , "} else {"
                 , c2, assignVar v (showJS a2)
                 , "}"], v)
```

As JavaScript computations are usually sequences of commands, with some commands returning values that can influence which commands follow, a natural way of expressing these sequences would be to use a monad. In particular, **do**-notation would allow for code that emulates JavaScript closely. For example:

```
js1 :: JS ()
js1 = do reply ← Prompt (string "Name?")
         Alert (string "Hello: " ◇ reply)

string :: String → JSString   -- only signature given
```

For monadic code such as this to be valid, we need to write a Monad instance for JS. Note that we do not want the monadic operations to *interpret* the JavaScript (a shallow embedding); rather we want to construct a representation of the monadic operations (a deep embedding) so that we can later compile them to JavaScript. Thus we add Return and Bind constructors to the JS data type, using the *higher-order abstract syntax* [33] approach of representing a variable binding as a Haskell function:

```
data JS :: * → * where
  ...
  Return :: a                    → JS a
  Bind   :: JS x → (x → JS a) → JS a
```

Note that the semantics of GADTs are such that the x on the Bind constructor is an *existential type* [22]: it is instantiated to a specific type when a Bind is constructed, and then inaccessibly encapsulated by the constructor until the Bind is deconstructed through case analysis.

Using Return and Bind, it is trivial to declare a Monad instance:

```
instance Monad JS where
  return = Return
  (≫=)  = Bind
```

The constrained-monad problem strikes when we try to compile this deep embedding into JavaScript. Initially, compiling the Return and Bind constructors may seem to be straightforward:

```
compileJS (Return a) = return ("", a)
compileJS (Bind jx k) = do
  (c1, x) ← compileJS jx   -- does not type check
  (c2, a) ← compileJS (k x)
  return (c1 ++ c2, a)
```

However, this does not type check. The problem is that the existential type introduced by the Bind constructor is not constrained by the Sunroof type class, and thus we cannot recursively call compileJS on the argument jx. There appears to be a simple solution though — add the Sunroof constraint to the Bind constructor:

$$\mathsf{Bind} :: \mathsf{Sunroof}\ x \Rightarrow \mathsf{JS}\ x \rightarrow (x \rightarrow \mathsf{JS}\ a) \rightarrow \mathsf{JS}\ a$$

However, because the type of Bind is now more constrained than the type of $\gg\!=$, the Monad instance for JS no longer type checks, leaving us in a similar situation to the vector example.

Yet while the same issue has arisen, this example is fundamentally different from the previous two examples. There we wanted to define return and $\gg\!=$ operations that would use their arguments to compute a new set/vector (i.e. a shallow embedding), whereas for Sunroof we are constructing a computation that we can then compile to JavaScript (i.e. a deep embedding).

1.4 Contributions

We have seen three examples of the constrained-monad problem. In each case, the problem was slightly different. The set example only required the second type parameter of $\gg\!=$ to be constrained, the vector example involved two distinct constraints, and in the Sunroof example the objective was to *compile* the computation to JavaScript, rather than to *evaluate* the computation. We will refer to the situation where we want to evaluate a monadic computation to the same type that we are operating on as the *shallow* constrained-monad problem, and to the situation where we want to compile a monadic computation as the *deep* constrained-monad problem (also known as the monad-reification problem).

The problem generalizes beyond monads. There are many other type classes with methods that are parametrically polymorphic in one or more arguments (e.g. Functor). We would like data types with operations that obey the relevant laws to be able to use the existing type-class hierarchy and infrastructure, even if those operations constrain the polymorphic arguments. As the problem is that we have a type class and a data type that are incompatible, a solution must therefore involve either modifying the class, modifying the data type, or both (or modifying the language).

This paper brings together several techniques for working with monads, constraints and deep embeddings, to present a framework for addressing the constrained-monad problem. In the process we demonstrate the compatibility of many of these techniques, and how they can be used to complement each other. The principal solution that we describe involves defining a normal form for a monadic computation, and a GADT to represent a deep embedding of that computation. The GADT explicitly constrains all existential types within the GADT, while still allowing a Monad instance to be declared for that GADT. The deep embedding can then be given multiple interpretations, which can impose different constraints. Finally, we show how the technique can be applied to other control structures, such as applicative functors.

We also survey other solutions to the constrained-monad problem, and related techniques. Some of the techniques we describe are well known, but have not been applied to this problem before. Others are known in functional-programming "folklore" to be able to address either the shallow or deep version of the problem, but have either not been documented, or generalized to the other half of the problem. There is one existing published solution to the deep constrained-monad problem [30], with which we compare in detail.

Our solution is direct, and we show how it can be applied to structures other than monads. Additionally, our solution provides a use case demonstrating the utility of the recent *constraint kinds* [3] GHC extension.

In summary, the contributions of this paper are as follows:

- We describe our solution to the constrained-monad problem. Specifically, we construct a normalized deep embedding of a monadic computation with explicit constraints on the existential types. The normalization eliminates any unconstrained types, allowing a Monad instance to be declared. We demonstrate our solution by applying it to each of the three examples. (Section 2)
- We present a general solution by abstracting from the solutions for each example. (Section 3)
- We survey other solutions to the constrained-monad problem, and compare them to each other and to our solution. (Section 4)
- We apply our solution to several other structures. (Section 5)
- We show how Jones et al. [17]'s technique for specifying constraints at use sites is compatible with our solution, and how it supports multiple interpretations of a computation. (Section 6)

2. Normality can be Constraining

In this section we present our technique for addressing the constrained-monad problem: constraining all existential types by normalizing a deep embedding of the monadic computation. For clarity, we present specialized solutions for each of the three examples.

2.1 Overview of Technique

The main steps of our technique are as follows:

- Separate the monadic structure of the computation from its primitive operations.
- Restructure the computation into a normal form by applying the monad laws.
- Capture that structure in a deep embedding that constrains all existential types.
- Only permit constrained primitive operations to be lifted into the embedding.
- Declare a Monad instance for the embedding.
- Constrain the type parameter of the computation when interpreting the computation.

By *monadic structure* we mean all uses of return and $\gg\!=$. By *primitive operations*, we mean other functions that produce values of type $m\ a$ for the specific monad m with which we are working. The literature refers to primitive operations under a variety of names, including "non-proper morphisms", "effect basis", "instruction sets" and "generic effects". For example, the primitive operations of the Maybe monad are the constructors Just and Nothing, whereas the primitive operations of the state monad [42] are get and put.

The monadic normal form [2] consists of a sequence of right-nested $\gg\!=$s terminating with a return, where the first argument to each $\gg\!=$ is a primitive operation. This can be seen graphically in Figure 2. Any monadic computation constructed from $\gg\!=$, return and primitive operations can be restructured into this normal form by applying the monad laws.

As well as allowing us to overcome the constrained-monad problem, there are two well-known benefits from constructing a normalized deep embedding. First, by applying the monad laws to normalize the structure, the monad laws are enforced *by construction* [24]. Second, by using a deep embedding, the construction of the monadic computation is separated from its interpretation. Consequently, multiple interpretations can be given to a computation [2, 24]. For example, a monadic computation over a probability distribution can be interpreted either non-deterministically by using a state monad where the state is a pseudo-random seed, or by computing the weights of all possible outcomes [2]. Furthermore, of particular relevance to the constrained-monad problem, different interpretations can impose different constraints.

In the remainder of this section, we demonstrate how normalization is the tool we need to constrain all existential types in a monadic computation, by applying it to our three examples.

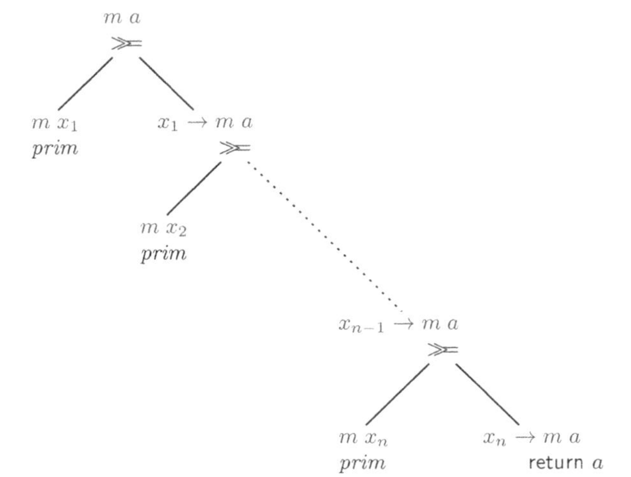

Figure 2. A normal form for monadic computations.

2.2 Sets

We begin by defining a deep embedding of normalized monadic computations over Set as a GADT:

```
data SetM :: * → * where
  Return :: a                           → SetM a
  Bind   :: Set x → (x → SetM a) → SetM a
```

Notice that the first argument to Bind is an actual Set (i.e. the type of primitive operations), not a recursive occurrence of SetM. We recommend that the reader takes a few moments to convince herself that this data type only permits monadic computations in the normal form presented in Figure 2.

We now declare a Monad instance for SetM, using the monad laws to restructure the computation into the normal form:

```
instance Monad SetM where
  return :: a → SetM a
  return = Return

  (≫=) :: SetM a → (a → SetM b) → SetM b
  (Return a)  ≫= k = k a                          -- left identity
  (Bind sx h) ≫= k = Bind sx (λx → h x ≫= k)    -- associativity
```

The use of the monad laws is essential: attempting to define ≫= simply as Bind would not type check, because the first argument to ≫= is a SetM, whereas the first argument to Bind is a Set.

We now need a way to lift a primitive Set into this deep embedding. As there is no constructor for a solitary primitive operation, we use the right-identity law to introduce a Bind and Return:

```
liftSet :: Set a → SetM a
liftSet sa = Bind sa Return   -- right identity
```

If this does not seem obvious, consider that it is similar to creating a singleton list using $(\lambda x \to x : [\,])$.

We can now construct monadic computations over sets by working in the SetM monad. For example, we can express a set comprehension as follows:

```
s1 :: SetM (Int, Char)
s1 = do n ← liftSet (fromList [3, 2, 1, 2])
        c ← liftSet (fromList ['a', 'b'])
        return (n, c)
```

Finally, we need to lower a SetM to a Set. This is a simple matter of folding over the GADT, replacing Return and Bind with returnSet and bindSet (from Section 1.1), respectively:

```
lowerSet :: Ord a ⇒ SetM a → Set a
lowerSet (Return a)  = returnSet a
lowerSet (Bind sx k) = bindSet sx (lowerSet ∘ k)
```

Thus, to express monadic set computations, we can lift primitive Sets into the SetM type, write computations in the SetM monad, and then lower the resulting SetM to a Set. But why does this work? Observe from Figure 2 that, after normalization, the second type parameter of ≫= is the same type (a) throughout the computation, and that this type is the same type as the top-level type parameter. Hence, by constraining the top-level type parameter in the type signature of lowerSet, we constrain the second type parameter of all occurrences of Bind. As the bindSet function only requires its second type parameter to be constrained, we are thus always able to use it in place of Bind. If we had not normalized the computation, then arbitrary existential types could appear as the second type parameter of Bind, and so we could not fold the computation using bindSet.

2.3 Vectors

Having solved the constrained-monad problem for sets, it would seem straightforward to do the same for vectors. And indeed we can define a normalized deep embedding (VecM), declare a monad instance for it, and provide a lifting function, exactly as we did for SetM. However, an attempt to define a similar lowering function fails to type check:

```
-- does not type check
lowerVec :: (Eq a, Finite a) ⇒ VecM a → Vec a
lowerVec (Return a)  = returnVec a
lowerVec (Bind vx k) = bindVec vx (lowerVec ∘ k)
```

The problem is that bindVec constrains its first type parameter (whereas bindSet constrains its second type parameter). That first parameter is not present in the type signature of lowerVec; indeed it is not even a single type: it needs to be instantiated to every existential type within the GADT (types x_1 to x_n in Figure 2). There is no type signature that we can give to lowerVec to express this constraint.

However, we can change the deep embedding such that it constrains the existential types. In this case, we attach the Finite constraint to the Bind constructor:

```
data VecM :: * → * where
  Return :: a                                      → VecM a
  Bind   :: Finite x ⇒ Vec x → (x → VecM a) → VecM a
```

The definition of lowerVec now type checks, because the type of bindVec matches that type of Bind. Indeed, we can even drop the Finite constraint from the type of lowerVec,

```
lowerVec :: Eq a ⇒ VecM a → Vec a
```

as that constraint need only appear on the first type parameter of bindVec. Conversely, the Eq constraint must remain, as that is required by returnVec.

But does adding this constraint interfere with defining a Monad instance for VecM? Perhaps surprisingly, it does not; we can define the monad instance exactly as before:

```
instance Monad VecM where
  return :: a → VecM a
  return = Return

  (≫=) :: VecM a → (a → VecM b) → VecM b
  (Return a)  ≫= k = k a                          -- left identity
  (Bind vx h) ≫= k = Bind vx (λx → h x ≫= k)    -- associativity
```

Initially this may appear magical: a function without class constraints is constructing a GADT containing class constraints. However, observe that (≫=) isn't introducing any new types; it is merely re-associating the existing computation. In the recursive case, it pattern matches on Bind, introducing the Finite constraint, before constructing a new Bind with the same existential type, and thus the necessary constraint is already in scope.

Of course, the Finite constraint has to come from somewhere, and that somewhere is the lifting function, which constructs a Bind without deconstructing an existing Bind:

```
liftVec :: Finite a ⇒ Vec a → VecM a
liftVec va = Bind va Return   -- right identity
```

This addition of a class constraint to the lifting function is key. Consider, the only ways to create a VecM are by using liftVec and Return. As liftVec is constrained, the only way to introduce an unconstrained type is through Return. But by performing normalization, all occurrences of Return except the final occurrence are eliminated. And the type of that final Return can be constrained by the lowering function. Hence, in combination, we can constrain all types within a VecM computation.

2.4 Embedding JavaScript

In the previous two examples we introduced a deep embedding as a means of normalizing a monadic computation, and then defined a lowering function that interpreted the deep embedding as the same type as the underlying primitive operations. The Sunroof example differs in that rather than interpreting the computation as the underlying type, we instead want to compile it to JavaScript.

We begin by splitting a JavaScript computation into two mutually recursive data types[2], one for the primitive operations and one for the (normalized) monadic structure:

```
data JS :: * → * where
  Prompt :: JSString                    → JS JSString
  Alert  :: JSString                    → JS ()
  If     :: JSBool → JSM a → JSM a → JS a

data JSM :: * → * where
  Return :: a                              → JSM a
  Bind   :: Sunroof x ⇒ JS x → (x → JSM a) → JSM a
```

Notice that, as with VecM, we constrain the existential type.

A Monad instance for JSM, and an accompanying lifting function, are defined in exactly the same way as for VecM. We can then successfully complete the compiler for the JS monad:

```
compileJSM :: Sunroof a ⇒ JSM a → CompM (JSCode, a)
compileJSM (Return a)   = return ("", a)
compileJSM (Bind jx k) = do (c1, x) ← compileJS jx
                            (c2, a) ← compileJSM (k x)
                            return (c1 ++ c2, a)
```

We do not repeat the definition of compileJS as it is mostly unchanged from Section 1.3; the only difference is that the recursive calls to compileJS are replaced with calls to compileJSM.

2.5 Discussion

The key to this technique is *normalization*. Once normalized, the only types within a monadic computation are either the type parameters of primitive operations, or the top-level type parameter. Consequently, by constraining the primitives and constraining the top-level type parameter, we can constrain *all* types within the computation. Thus, when interpreting the computation, we can use functions that have class constraints.

As shown by the vector example, the class constraints on the ≫=-like and return-like functions can differ. In general, any constraints on the first type parameter of the ≫=-like function should appear in the context of the Bind constructor, constraining the existential type. Whereas any constraints on either the type parameter of the return-like function, or on the second type parameter of the ≫=-like function, should appear in the context of the interpretation function, constraining the type parameter of the computation.

[2] A non-recursive and more reusable alternative would be to paramaterize JS on a type $m :: * \to *$, and then instantiate that type to JSM. Such an approach is advocated by Lin [24].

Note that while the deep embedding is used to *facilitate* normalization, it is not *necessary*: there are other ways to normalize a monadic computation, as we will discuss in Section 4.4. Furthermore, even using a deep embedding, defining a GADT that *enforces* the normal form is unnecessary. A valid alternative is to define a GADT that allows arbitrary nesting of Binds and occurrences of Returns (such as the JS data type in Section 1.3). We would then normalize that GADT, or normalize during deconstruction of the GADT (as is done by Unimo [24] and RMonad [35]). However, we consider it clearer, and less error-prone, to have the GADT enforce the normal form (as is done by Operational [2]).

3. Generalizing using Constraint Kinds

Each deep embedding in Section 2 was specialized to a particular example. In this section we use the recent *constraint kinds* GHC extension to generalize to a single deep embedding that can be instantiated to any of the examples. This generalized solution is also available in our Constrained-Normal library [34].

3.1 Constraint Kinds

Constraint kinds were implemented by Bolingbroke [3], motivated by a desire to support the constraint synonyms and constraint families proposed by Orchard and Schrijvers [29]. The core idea is to add a new *literal kind* to Haskell called Constraint, which is the kind of a fully applied type class. For example, the Ord and Monad classes would be assigned the following kinds:

```
Ord   :: * → Constraint
Monad :: (* → *) → Constraint
```

The most significant benefit of this extension is the ability to abstract over constraints: data types and type classes can take class constraints as parameters.

The extension also adds syntax for an empty constraint and constraint synonyms; however, as constraint synonyms cannot be partially applied, they are less expressive than defining empty type classes with polymorphic instances. For example, we will later need to instantiate a parameter of kind (* → Constraint) such that it imposes no constraints on the type; so we encode this using the following empty type class:

```
class Unconstrained (a :: *) where
instance Unconstrained a where
```

3.2 Constrained Normal Monads

We now define what we call a *constrained normal monad*: a GADT representing a normalized monadic computation with constrained existential types. This requires parameterizing the GADT on a class constraint c and an underlying type of primitive operations t:

```
data NM :: (* → Constraint) → (* → *) → * → * where
  Return :: a                          → NM c t a
  Bind   :: c x ⇒ t x → (x → NM c t a) → NM c t a
```

This GADT generalizes SetM, VecM and JSM from Section 2, and has a Monad instance defined in the same way.

To accompany NM, we provide a generalized lifting function:

```
liftNM :: c a ⇒ t a → NM c t a
liftNM ta = Bind ta Return
```

Constructing monadic computations is now no harder than when using the specialized solutions in Section 2, for example:

```
s1 :: NM Unconstrained Set (Int, Char)
s1 = do n ← liftNM (fromList [3, 2, 1, 2])
        c ← liftNM (fromList ['a', 'b'])
        return (n, c)
```

A generalized lowering function is slightly more complicated. Recall that lowerSet and lowerVec made use of operations specific to their underlying type, such as returnVec and bindVec. Thus, our generalization has to take those functions as arguments:

```
lowerNM :: ∀ a c t. (a → t a) →
    (∀ x. c x ⇒ t x → (x → t a) → t a) → NM c t a → t a
lowerNM ret bind = lowerNM'
  where lowerNM' :: NM c t a → r
        lowerNM' (Return a)   = ret a
        lowerNM' (Bind tx k)  = bind tx (lowerNM' ∘ k)
```

The type signatures used here require the *scoped type variables* [31] and *rank-2 types* [32] GHC extensions. Notice that the type of *ret* shares its type parameter (a) with the parameter of the NM argument. Thus *ret* need only be applicable at that one specific type, which is sufficient because normalization ensures that there will only be one Return constructor, and it will have that type. The second type parameter of *bind* is that same type a, but its first type parameter can be *any type that type satisfies the constraint* c. This restriction is precisely what allows lowerNM to take constrained functions such as bindVec as arguments. For example:

```
lowerVec :: Eq a ⇒ NM Finite Vec a → Vec a
lowerVec = lowerNM returnVec bindVec

lowerSet :: Ord a ⇒ NM Unconstrained Set a → Set a
lowerSet = lowerNM returnSet bindSet
```

Actually, the inferred type of lowerNM is more general than the type signature we assigned it. Its definition is a fold over the GADT, which could return values of types other than the primitive operation. Renaming lowerNM to foldNM, the inferred type is:

```
foldNM :: ∀ a c r t. (a → r) →
    (∀ x. c x ⇒ t x → (x → r) → r) → NM c t a → r
```

This generalization is useful because it can be used to define interpretations of a monadic computation that differ from the underlying type. For example, we could define compileJSM in terms of foldNM, but not in terms of lowerNM.

A problem arises when we try to use multiple interpretations that impose distinct constraints. Consider the type of the following pretty printer for set computations (its definition is straightforward, but unimportant to the discussion):

```
prettySet :: Show a ⇒ NM Show Set a → String
```

If we try to apply prettySet to s_1 (from Section 3.2), type checking will fail because Show does not match Unconstrained. We can work around this by assigning s_1 a more polymorphic type, thereby allowing it to be interpreted by both lowerSet and prettySet:

```
s1 :: (c Char, c Int) ⇒ NM c Set (Int, Char)
```

However, while this works in this case, there are limitations to this approach. We postpone demonstrating these limitations, and describing an approach to overcoming them, until Section 6.

4. A Survey of Solutions

The constrained-monad problem is well known, and a variety of techniques have been implemented or proposed to address it. In this section we survey the existing solutions, and compare them to each other and the normalized deep-embedding approach.

4.1 Restricted Data Types

An early solution to the constrained-monad problem was Hughes' *restricted data types* [12] proposed language extension. The essence of the idea was to extend Haskell to support data types with attached constraints that scope over the entire type. Hughes's proposed syntax is best seen by example:

```
data Ord a ⇒ RSet a = ...
```

Note however that this is intended to be semantically stronger than the existing meaning of that same syntax in Haskell (which has since been deprecated). Furthermore, the proposal included introducing a keyword **wft** (well-formed type) that would allow the constraints of a data type to be referenced. For example, a context

```
wft (RSet a) ⇒ ...
```

would be semantically equivalent to

```
Ord a ⇒ ...
```

Type classes could then refer to these attached constraints in their methods. For example:

```
class Monad (m :: * → *) where
  return :: wft (m a) ⇒ a → m a
  (>>=)  :: (wft (m a), wft (m b)) ⇒ m a → (a → m b) → m b
```

Instances could then be declared for restricted data types such as RSet, as any attached constraints are brought into scope.

Note that the keyword **wft** is crucial to this approach. Without the keyword, a restricted data type is analogous to a GADT with the constraint on each constructor, except that it is necessary to pattern match on the constructor to bring the constraint into scope. However, this GADT approach is insufficiently constraining: for example, an instance for sets would effectively require return to map *any* type a to a pair of Set a and an Ord a class dictionary, which is impossible to define. The **wft** keyword is needed to allow the Ord constraint to scope over the argument type a.

4.2 Restricted Type Classes

Hughes [12] also suggested an alternative approach: defining *restricted type classes* that take a class constraint as a parameter. For example, a *restricted monad* could be defined as follows:

```
class RMonad (c :: * → Constraint) (m :: * → *) where
  return :: c a ⇒ a → m a
  (>>=)  :: (c a, c b) ⇒ m a → (a → m b) → m b
```

This was prior to the advent of constraint kinds so was not possible at the time, but several simulations of restricted type classes were encoded using various work-arounds [12, 18, 19, 35].

An alternative formulation of restricted type classes uses an associated type function [4] to map the data type to a constraint, rather than taking a constraint as a parameter [3, 29]. Such a function can be given a default definition as Unconstrained, which is convenient when declaring instances for data types that do not require a constraint on their operations. For example:

```
class RMonad (m :: * → *) where
  type Con m :: * → Constraint
  type Con m = Unconstrained

  return :: Con m a ⇒ a → m a
  (>>=)  :: (Con m a, Con m b) ⇒ m a → (a → m b) → m b

instance RMonad Set where
  type Con Set = Ord

  return = returnSet
  (>>=)  = bindSet

instance RMonad [] where
  return a  = [a]
  ma >>= k  = concatMap k ma
```

The restricted-type-class solutions do not require any modification to the data types involved, but they do require either the existing type classes to be modified, or new types classes to be added. In the former case existing code will break, in the latter case the new code will not be compatible with the existing, unrestricted, classes. Thus, for this to be practical, a class author must anticipate the need for constraints when defining the class [12].

4.3 Normalizing using Deep Embeddings

The idea of separating the monadic structure of a computation from its interpretation was pioneered by the Unimo framework [24], and then later used by the MonadPrompt [15] and Operational [2] libraries. The same idea was used by Swierstra [38] to embed IO computations, albeit formulated somewhat differently using free monads (see Section 5.2). Normalization is not an essential part of separating structure from interpretation, but it does have the advantage of enforcing the monad laws: without normalization it is possible to define an interpretation that exhibits different behavior for computations that are equivalent according to the monad laws.

The first use of normalization to overcome the constrained-monad problem of which we are aware was in the RMonad library [35]. The central feature of this library is a restricted-monad class, RMonad. This class is similar to the restricted monads described in Section 4.2, except that it is implemented using a data family [20], with the constructors of the family containing the constraints. We believe this implementation choice was made because constraint kinds were not then available; the implementation could now be simplified using the associated-type-function approach. The RMonad library also provides a (non-normalized) deep embedding over the RMonad class, with an accompanying Monad instance. The library provides a function to interpret that deep embedding, which normalizes the structure and lowers it to the underlying restricted monad. This is essentially the same technique as presented in Section 3, using normalization to ensure that the necessary constraints hold whenever the (restricted) $\gg\!=$ of the restricted monad is applied. The differences are that an RMonad instance is required, and that the only interpretation of the embedding is as that underlying RMonad.

4.3.1 Using the Operational Library

While Unimo, MonadPrompt and Operational do not explicitly handle constraints, it is possible to leverage their deep embedding and normalization functionality when addressing the constrained-monad problem. We will demonstrate this by encoding the technique from Section 3 using Operational, and we note that Unimo and MonadPrompt could use a similar encoding.

The core of Operational is a deep embedding of a normalized monadic computation, which is essentially our NM data type without the constraint parameter[3]:

```
data Program :: (* → *) → * → * where
  Return :: a                             → Program t a
  Bind   :: t x → (x → Program t a) → Program t a
```

For Program to be able to handle constraints, we have to embed the desired constraint into an underlying type. This can be achieved using a GADT:

```
data FinVec :: * → * where
  FV :: Finite a ⇒ Vec a → FinVec a
```

When defining an interpretation, we can pattern match on the GADT to bring the constraint into scope, for example (where lowerProg is defined similarly to lowerNM):

```
lowerVec :: Eq a ⇒ Program FinVec a → Vec a
lowerVec = lowerProg returnVec (λ(FV vx) k → bindVec vx k)
```

This is okay if the user always wants to work with specific pairs of primitive operations and constraints, but does not allow for situations where the user wants to write code that treats one as polymorphic and the other as specialized. However, this can be addressed by abstracting over the constraint and primitive operations:

```
data Box :: (* → Constraint) → (* → *) → * → * where
  Box :: c a ⇒ t a → Box c t a

lowerVec :: Eq a ⇒ Program (Box Finite Vec) a → Vec a
lowerVec = lowerProg returnVec (λ(Box vx) k → bindVec vx k)
```

[3] We simplify slightly, as the Operational implementation uses monad transformers and views, but our encoding is valid using the actual library.

We could now, for example, assign the following polymorphic type to the s_1 computation:

```
s1 :: (c Char, c Int) ⇒ Program (Box c Set) (Int, Char)
```

4.3.2 Constraining the Primitive Operations

If the type of primitive operations is a GADT, then as an alternative to using the Box type from Section 4.3.1, the desired constraint can instead be placed within *each constructor* of the GADT that contains polymorphic types, for example:

```
type JSM (a :: *) = Program JS a

data JS :: * → * where
  If :: Sunroof a ⇒ JSBool → JSM a → JSM a → JS a
  ...
```

Instead of pattern matching on the Box GADT, we can now introduce the constraint by performing a case analysis on the primitive operation. The disadvantages of this approach are that primitive operations must not be an abstract data type, that syntactic clutter is introduced in the form of repeated constraints, and that additional case analyses may sometimes be required. However, a significant advantage is that it becomes possible to constrain existential types that occur within the primitive-operation GADT, or to have different constraints on different constructors. For example, the Prompt and Alert constructors can be generalized to a single Call constructor that is polymorphic in its argument and result type, provided those types have Sunroof instances:

```
data JS :: * → * where
  Call :: (Sunroof a, Sunroof b) ⇒ JSFunction a b → a → JS b
  ...
```

Indeed, this is how Sunroof is actually implemented, using Operational for the monadic deep embedding and normalization [6].

4.4 Normalizing using Continuations

Unimo, Operational, RMonad, and our constrained normal monads are all similar in that they normalize the structure of a monadic computation by capturing that structure as a deep embedding. However, an alternative means of normalizing a monadic computation is to use *continuations*.

Consider the following types:

```
type ContT (r :: *) (t :: * → *) (a :: *) =       (a → t r) → t r
type CodT           (t :: * → *) (a :: *) = ∀ r. (a → t r) → t r
```

These are known as the *continuation monad transformer* [23] and the *codensity monad transformer* [14, 16]. Note however that both ContT r t and CodT t form a monad, regardless of whether the underlying type t is a monad[4]:

```
instance Monad (CodT t) where
  return :: a → CodT t a
  return a = λh → h a

  (>>=) :: CodT t a → (a → CodT t b) → CodT t b
  ca >>= k = λh → ca (λa → (k a) h)
```

A Monad instance for ContT is declared in the same way: ContT is just a special case of CodT that fixes the result type r.

Primitive operations can be lifted into (or lowered from) the codensity monad by providing a $\gg\!=$-like or return-like function, respectively:

```
liftCodT :: (∀ r. t a → (a → t r) → t r) → t a → CodT t a
liftCodT bind ta = bind ta

lowerCodT :: (a → t a) → CodT t a → t a
lowerCodT ret ca = ca ret
```

[4] As with Vec, we elide the detail that ContT and CodT must be **newtypes** for this to be valid Haskell.

A consequence of these definitions is that any monadic computation constructed in the CodT monad will construct a normalized computation with respect to the underlying $\gg\!=$-like and return-like functions. A useful analogy for what happens, suggested by Voigtländer [40], is that it is like using *difference lists* [11] to right-associate nested applications of string concatenation. Alternatively, observe that each primitive operation always appears as the first argument to the underlying $\gg\!=$-like function, as that function is partially applied to the primitive during lifting. And there is always exactly one use of the return-like function, which is when it is used as the final continuation during lowering.

This infrastructure can be used to address the constrained-monad problem, for example:

```
liftVec :: Finite a ⇒ Vec a → CodT Vec a
liftVec = liftCodT bindVec

lowerVec :: Eq a ⇒ CodT Vec a → Vec a
lowerVec = lowerCodT returnVec
```

During lifting the first type parameter of bindVec is exposed, so it can be constrained with Finite. During lowering, the type parameter of returnVec is exposed, so it can be constrained with Eq.

However, what is not exposed is the second type parameter to bindVec, which is the universally quantified r hidden inside CodT. For the vector example that is not a problem, but if we try to lift a Set in a similar manner then the definition will not type check because r is required to satisfy an Ord constraint. Perhaps then we should use ContT instead of CodT, as that exposes a fixed result type that we could constrain? While that would work, it would be unnecessarily restrictive. We don't need r to be a specific type, merely for it to satisfy Ord. Therefore, we define what we shall call the *restricted codensity transformer*:

```
type RCodT (c :: * → Constraint) (t :: * → *) (a :: *)
  = ∀ r. c r ⇒ (a → t r) → t r
```

This type expresses exactly what we need: the result type can be any type that satisfies c. This gives rise to lifting and lowering functions with the following types:

```
liftRCodT  :: (∀ r. c r ⇒ t a → (a → t r) → t r) →
              t a → RCodT c t a
lowerRCodT :: c a ⇒ (a → t a) → RCodT c t a → t a
```

Thus, the shallow constrained-monad problem can be overcome using the restricted codensity transformer with comparable ease to using a normalized deep embedding. However, the two approaches are not equivalent, as becomes evident when we consider interpretations other than lowering to the underlying type. The deep-embedding approach allows multiple interpretations to be given to a monadic computation, whereas the codensity approach only allows a single interpretation. That single interpretation is essentially "hard-wired" into the computation, as the $\gg\!=$-like operation is partially applied to each primitive operation when it is lifted.

There is a work-around though. Rather than using the primitive operations directly, we can first construct a deep embedding of a monadic computation over the primitive-operation type, and then use that deep embedding as the underlying type of the restricted codensity monad. Regardless of how return and $\gg\!=$ are then used, the result after lowering will be a normalized deep embedding. That deep embedding can then be interpreted in whatever way is desired. This is essentially the approach taken by Persson et al. [30] to overcome the monad-reification problem in the Syntactic library, though they build their own specialized type around the continuation monad, rather than defining the general-purpose restricted codensity transformer as we have here.

In our opinion, using the codensity technique for the deep constrained-monad problem in this manner is more complicated than using the normalized-deep-embedding approach, as it requires two levels of structure rather than one: the codensity transformer to perform the normalization, and then the deep embedding to allow multiple interpretations. Whereas a normalized deep embedding provides both with a single structure. Finally, we observe that this two-level approach could be employed with any solution to the constrained-monad problem that only permits one interpretation, such as the RMonad library.

4.5 Normalization and Efficiency

That continuations can be used to overcome the constrained-monad problem has been an obscure piece of functional-programming "folklore" for several years [26], but, to our knowledge, the only published use of the technique was when Persson et al. [30] used it in Syntactic. There have been other uses of continuations to normalize monadic computations, but with the aim of improving efficiency. For example, Voigtländer [40] uses the codensity transformer to improve the efficiency of the tree-substitution monad. This is possible because the monad laws only guarantee the equivalence of the *semantics* of two monadic computations; the laws do not guarantee the equivalence of operational behavior.

However, normalization is not always beneficial to performance. For example, normalizing a set-monad computation defers elimination of duplicate elements until the end, rather than eliminating duplicates in intermediate results [35]. That is, the performance of a normalized set monad will typically be no better than converting to a list, using the list monad, and then converting back to a set again. Note that this change in operational behavior is a consequence of the normalization, and applies regardless of whether a deep embedding or the codensity transformer is used to achieve that normalization. Conversely, using a restricted monad does not cause a change in operational behavior, as no normalization of structure occurs (but nor are the monad laws enforced).

5. The Constrained-Type-Class Problem

The focus of this paper has been monads; a choice we made because of the widespread use of monads in functional programming. However, the essence of the problem — that some data types cannot be made instances of some type classes because of the presence of class constraints on their operations — is not specific to monads, nor are the techniques for overcoming it. In this section we demonstrate that the solutions to the constrained-monad problem are more widely applicable, by applying them to several related type classes: Functor, Applicative and MonadPlus.

5.1 The Constrained-Functor Problem

Consider the Functor type class (Figure 3). As with the Monad class methods, sometimes the only mapping function that exists for a data type imposes constraints on its type parameters, thereby preventing a Functor instance from being declared. For example:

```
mapSet :: Ord b             ⇒ (a → b) → Set a → Set b
mapVec :: (Finite a, Eq b)  ⇒ (a → b) → Vec a → Vec b
```

We have the same options for addressing this problem as we had for monads. Thus, if we are prepared to use a new type class, then we could define a *restricted functor* class:

```
class RFunctor (c :: * → Constraint) (f :: * → *) where
  fmap :: (c a, c b) ⇒ (a → b) → f a → f b
```

We could also use the variant that has an associated type function that maps to a constraint, rather than a constraint parameter.

On the other hand, if we want to use the standard Functor class, then we can take the normalization approach. The normal form for functors is fairly simple: a single fmap applied to a single primitive operation. This ensures that all existential types within the computation appear as parameters on the (single) primitive operation.

```
class Functor (f :: ∗ → ∗) where
  fmap :: (a → b) → f a → f b
```

- fmap id ≡ id (identity)
- fmap g ∘ fmap h ≡ fmap (g ∘ h) (composition)

Figure 3. Functors and the functor laws.

Normalization consists of applying the functor composition law to fuse together all uses of fmap.

Taking the deep-embedding approach to normalization, we can define *constrained normal functors* as follows:

```
data NF :: (∗ → Constraint) → (∗ → ∗) → ∗ → ∗ where
  FMap :: c x ⇒ (x → a) → t x → NF c t a

instance Functor (NF c t) where
  fmap :: (a → b) → NF c t a → NF c t b
  fmap g (FMap h tx) = FMap (g ∘ h) tx   -- composition law

liftNF :: c a ⇒ t a → NF c t a
liftNF ta = FMap id ta   -- identity law

lowerNF :: (∀ x. c x ⇒ (x → a) → t x → t a) → NF c t a → t a
lowerNF fmp (FMap g tx) = fmp g tx
```

Notice the similarities to constrained normal monads (Section 3.2): we define the normal form as a GADT, declare a Functor instance by using laws to convert to that normal form, define a lifting function by using an identity law, and define a lowering function that takes interpretations of the constructors as arguments.

We can also take the codensity approach to normalization, but instead of the codensity transformer, we need to use the related *Yoneda functor transformer* [21], which generates a functor (but not a monad) for any $t :: * \to *$:

```
type Yoneda (t :: ∗ → ∗) (a :: ∗) = ∀ r. (a → r) → t r

instance Functor (Yoneda t) where
  fmap :: (a → b) → Yoneda t a → Yoneda t b
  fmap g ya = λh → ya (h ∘ g)
```

As with codensity, we introduce a restricted version of this transformer by adding a constraint parameter:

```
type RYoneda (c :: ∗ → Constraint) (t :: ∗ → ∗) (a :: ∗)
  = ∀ r. c r ⇒ (a → r) → t r
```

We can then define lifting and lowering functions as follows:

```
liftRYoneda :: (∀ r. c r ⇒ (a → r) → t a → t r) →
                 t a → RYoneda c t a
liftRYoneda fmp ta = λh → fmp h ta

lowerRYoneda :: c a ⇒ RYoneda c t a → t a
lowerRYoneda ya = ya id
```

Notice that liftRYoneda takes an fmap-like function as an argument — this means that the interpretation of fmap is "hard-wired" during construction in a similar manner to the interpretation of ≫= when using the codensity transformer for monads.

5.2 Aside: Free Monads

Every functor induces a monad, known as the *free monad* [38, 40] of that functor:

```
data Free (f :: ∗ → ∗) (a :: ∗) = Pure a | Impure (f (Free f a))

instance Functor f ⇒ Monad (Free f) where
  return :: a → Free f a
  return = Pure

  (≫=) :: Free f a → (a → Free f b) → Free f b
  (Pure a)     ≫= k = k a
  (Impure ffa) ≫= k = Impure (fmap (≫=k) ffa)
```

The data type Free is a deep embedding of a monadic computation, and thus can be given multiple interpretations [38]. Yet this embedding is not as deep as the NM embedding, as it always uses the fmap of the underlying functor, rather than allowing it to be given multiple interpretations. We find it helpful to think of this as constructing a monad from fmap, return and join, where fmap is shallowly embedded and return and join are deeply embedded.

```
class Applicative (f :: ∗ → ∗) where
  pure :: a → f a
  (⊛)  :: f (a → b) → f a → f b
```

- pure id ⊛ fa ≡ fa (identity)
- ((pure (∘) ⊛ fa) ⊛ fb) ⊛ fc ≡ fa ⊛ (fb ⊛ fc) (composition)
- pure g ⊛ pure a ≡ pure (g a) (homomorphism)
- fg ⊛ pure a ≡ pure (λg → g a) ⊛ fg (interchange)

Figure 4. Applicative functors and the applicative-functor laws.

Aside from the lack of constraint parameter, the key distinction between the two embeddings is that, to induce a monad, Free requires the underlying type to be a Functor, whereas NM does not. However, we showed in Section 5.1 that it is possible to generate a functor for any $t :: * \to *$, by using a deep embedding. This provides an alternative way to construct a deep embedding of a monadic computation: take the free monad over the deep embedding of a functor. Doing so results in a type isomorphic to a deep embedding of a normalized monad. This can be seen informally as follows:

```
Free (NF c t) a       ≈ NM c t a
Pure a                ≈ Return a
Impure (FMap k tx)    ≈ Bind tx k
```

5.3 The Constrained-Applicative-Functor Problem

Applicative functors [25] (Figure 4) are a structure that lies between functors and monads, and the usual problem arises if we want to declare an instance for a data type with constrained operations. Defining a class of *restricted applicative functors* is as straightforward as defining restricted monads or restricted functors, so we will just discuss the normalization approach.

The normal form for applicative functors [7] consists of a left-nested sequence of ⊛s (pronounced "apply") terminating in a pure (Figure 5). Our deep embedding of this normal form is as follows:

```
data NAF :: (∗ → Constraint) → (∗ → ∗) → ∗ → ∗ where
  Pure :: a                                → NAF c t a
  Ap   :: c x ⇒ NAF c t (x → a) → t x → NAF c t a
```

Defining an Applicative instance and lifting function require applying the laws of the structure (Figure 4), as usual:

```
instance Applicative (NAF c t) where
  pure :: a → NAF c t a
  pure = Pure

  (⊛) :: NAF c t (a → b) → NAF c t a → NAF c t b
  (Pure g) ⊛ (Pure a) = Pure (g a)                    -- homomorphism
  n1 ⊛ (Pure a)      = Pure (λg → g a) ⊛ n1            -- interchange
  n1 ⊛ (Ap n2 tx) = Ap (Pure (∘) ⊛ n1 ⊛ n2) tx        -- composition

liftNAF :: c a ⇒ t a → NAF c t a
liftNAF ta = Ap (Pure id) ta   -- identity
```

While in many ways similar, there is an important difference between the normal forms for monads and applicative functors. For monads, the top-level type parameter is propagated along the spine of the normal form, giving the same result type at each node (type a in Figure 2). Whereas for applicative functors the type of each node differs, as the function type is progressively saturated with type arguments (see Figure 5). Furthermore, the type of Pure differs from the top-level type parameter. Consequently, an interpretation of applicative functors has to be able to handle these existential types. This is not an obstacle, but does lead to heavy use of rank-2 types when assigning a type to those interpretations. For example:

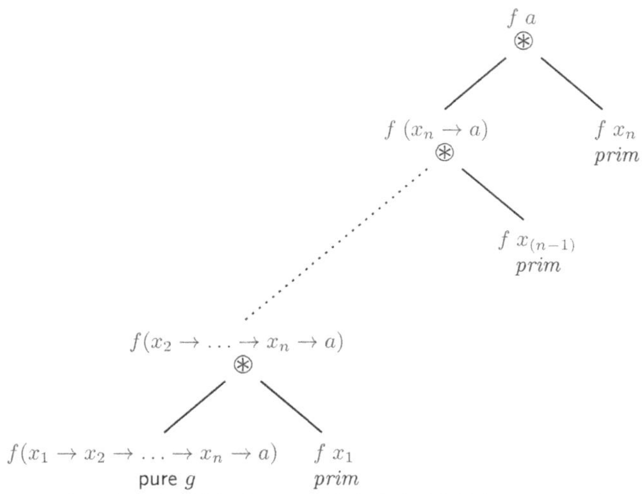

Figure 5. A normal form for applicative computations.

```
foldNAF :: ∀ a c r t. (∀ x. x → r x) →
    (∀ y z. c y ⇒ r (y → z) → t y → r z) → NAF c t a → r a
foldNAF pur app = foldNAF'
  where
    foldNAF' :: ∀ b. NAF c t b → r b
    foldNAF' (Pure b)   = pur b
    foldNAF' (Ap n tx) = app (foldNAF' n) tx
```

The reader may now expect us to define a transformer similar to Codensity and Yoneda, but that generates an applicative functor. However, we were unable to find such a transformer, as we will now explain.

Initially we did not know what type the transformer should have, so we started with the lifting function. We wanted the lifting function to partially apply ⊛, such that the primitive appears as its second argument, which gave us the following type:

```
liftAFT :: (∀ r. t (a → r) → t a → t r) → t a → AFT t a
liftAFT app ta = λtg → app tg ta
```

From this, we inferred a type for the transformer:

```
type AFT t a = ∀ r. t (a → r) → t r
```

It was then straightforward to define a lowering function:

```
lowerAFT :: (∀ x. x → t x) → AFT t a → t a
lowerAFT pur ra = ra (pur id)
```

However, we were unable to define an Applicative instance for AFT t, and have come to the conclusion that it is only possible to define such an instance *if the underlying type t is itself an Applicative*. As the problem we are trying to overcome is that the underlying type is *not* an Applicative, this is no use to us.

We do not claim that there is no transformer type that could solve this problem for applicative functors. Rather, we observe that we found it difficult to apply the Codensity/Yoneda approach to other structures, because it is not obvious what the transformer type should be. Arguably, this problem requires no more inventiveness than deciding on a normal form for the structure (which is needed for the deep-embedding approach). However, our experience has been that it is easier to devise a normal form than to devise a suitable transformer type.

5.4 The Constrained-MonadPlus Problem

Now consider the MonadPlus type class (Figure 6). Defining a restricted version of this type class is straightforward as usual, so we will just discuss the normalization approach. We represent the MonadPlus normal form using two mutually recursive data types:

```
class Monad m ⇒ MonadPlus (m :: * → *) where
  mzero :: m a
  mplus :: m a → m a → m a
```

- mplus mzero $a \equiv a$ (left unit)
- mplus a mzero $\equiv a$ (right unit)
- mplus (mplus a b) $c \equiv$ mplus a (mplus b c) (associativity)
- mzero $\gg\!=$ $k \equiv$ mzero (left zero)
- mplus a $b \gg\!= k \equiv$ mplus ($a \gg\!= k$) ($b \gg\!= k$) (left distribution)

Figure 6. MonadPlus and the MonadPlus laws.

```
type NMP c t a = MZero | MPlus (NMP' c t a) (NMP c t a)
data NMP' :: (* → Constraint) → (* → *) → * → * where
  Return :: a                              → NMP' c t a
  Bind   :: c x ⇒ t x → (x → NMP c t a) → NMP' c t a
```

The first type, NMP, represents a normal form for the monoidal mplus/mzero operations. That normal form is just the free monoid (i.e. a list) over the second type, NMP′. The normal form for NMP′ is the usual monadic normal form, except that the result of the second argument to Bind is the NMP type, rather than NMP′.

Defining a MonadPlus instance for NMP proceeds in a similar manner to the monad and applicative functor cases, so we direct the reader to our Constrained-Normal library [34] for the details. The key step is the application of the left-distribution law (Figure 6) when an MPlus appears as the first argument to ≫=. Likewise, the accompanying lifting function involves applying the right-identity law (and the right-unit law), and the folding function takes interpretations for the four constructors as arguments.

5.5 Discussion

The same idea underlies the normalization technique for all of the structures we have considered, and for each structure we performed the same sequence of steps. First, we identify a normal form that contains no existential types except those that appear on primitive operations. Second, we define a deep embedding of that normal form as a GADT. The GADT takes a class constraint as a parameter, and places that constraint on any existential types within the GADT. Third, we declare the structure's class instance for the GADT; this instance normalizes the computation by applying the algebraic laws of the structure, which typically involves fusing pure computations and thereby eliminating intermediate existential types. Fourth, we define a function to lift a primitive operation into the normal form, which (for the structures we have considered) involved applying one or more identity laws, and required the type parameter of the primitive operation to satisfy the class constraint. Finally, we define a fold for the computation, which takes interpretations for the operations of the structure as arguments.

In sections 4.3.1 and 4.3.2 we discussed variant formulations of a deep embedding for monads that place the class constraint either on the constructors of the primitive operations, or in a Box GADT that can be used as a wrapper around the primitive operations. Both of those techniques generalize to the other structures.

The structures we considered in this section are all specializations or generalizations of monads. That is not a limitation of the technique; these are just well-known structures that we chose as a starting point. We are also investigating the Category and Arrow [13] type classes. Our initial results show that Category is straightforward to normalize, as it has a monoidal structure, but that there may not exist an Arrow normal form that ensures that all existential types appear as type parameters on primitive operations. However, an intermediate structure consisting of a Category with an arr operation (but not a first) does have a suitable normal form: a sequence of alternating pure functions and primitives. We are also interested in investigating recursive structures such as MonadFix and ArrowLoop, but this remains as future work.

Note that for some structures, full normalization is not required to eliminate all unconstrained existential types (and hence to allow the desired class instance). For example, normalizing the *monoidal* structure of the MonadPlus class is unnecessary to infer any constraints, as the mplus and mzero operations do not introduce any existential types; normalizing the *monadic* structure is sufficient. Indeed, the RMonad library [35] takes the approach of only normalizing the monadic structure, not the monoidal structure. However, an advantage of fully normalizing is that the monoid laws are enforced by construction, which is why we chose to do so.

6. Interpretations with Distinct Constraints

In Section 3.2 we demonstrated that it is possible to define multiple interpretations for a constrained normal monad (lowerSet and prettySet), even if those interpretations impose different constraints. However, that approach does not allow both interpretations to be applied to the same computation *if they impose distinct constraints*. Even if the computation is defined to be polymorphic in its constraint parameter, two copies of the computation have to be constructed, one for each interpretation. This is a more general problem that afflicts any data type that has a constraint parameter, but fortunately Jones et al. [17] have recently developed a technique for addressing it. In this section we demonstrate the problem, and then show how Jones et al.'s technique can be applied to overcome it. While we only consider our constrained normal monads, we note that this technique is also compatible with using a Box wrapper and the Operational library (Section 4.3.1), with placing the constraints on the constructors of the primitive operations (Section 4.3.2), and with the other type classes discussed in Section 5.

6.1 Distinct Constraint Parameters are Incompatible

Imagine that we wish to display all elements of all Finite types that appear within a vector computation. We could achieve this by defining a function of the following type:

```
showFin :: NM FiniteShow Vec a → String

class (Finite a, Show a) ⇒ FiniteShow a where
instance (Finite a, Show a) ⇒ FiniteShow a where
```

The definition of showFin is unimportant to the discussion; what matters is that it imposes a Show constraint on the existential types. The need for an auxiliary class representing the intersection of the Finite and Show constraints is irritating, but not a major concern.

Now let us try to both display and evaluate a computation:

```
-- does not type check
showAndLower :: Eq a ⇒ NM FiniteShow Vec a → (String, Vec a)
showAndLower v = (showFin v, lowerVec v)
```

This does not type check because lowerVec requires its argument to have exactly the type NM Finite Vec a, and the constraints Finite and FiniteShow are distinct. To overcome this, we would have to either define a variant of lowerVec that uses FiniteShow instead of Finite, or modify the type of the existing lowerVec function. That is, we must either duplicate or modify existing code, both of which are bad for modularity.

In general, whenever we want to apply two (or more) interpretations that impose distinct constraints to the same computation, we have to duplicate or modify those interpretations to use a new type class representing the intersection of all the required constraints. Note that while in this example one constraint is strictly stronger than the other, in general different interpretations can have disjoint constraints. We want a way to combine existing interpreters that have distinct constraints without modifying those interpreters.

6.2 A List of Existential Types

Jones et al.'s key idea is that, rather than parameterizing a GADT on a constraint, we can parameterize it on *the set of types within that GADT*. We can then constrain those types when we interpret the GADT, rather than during construction. We will demonstrate this technique by applying it to our constrained normal monads. We begin by replacing the constraint parameter with a list of types, making use of the *data kinds* [43] GHC extension:

```
data NM :: [∗] → (∗ → ∗) → ∗ → ∗ where
  Return :: a                                   → NM xs t a
  Bind   :: Elem x xs ⇒ t x → (x → NM xs t a) → NM xs t a
```

Instead of the constraint parameter, the context of the Bind constructor now uses the Elem type class, which represents type-level list membership:

```
class Elem (a :: ∗) (as :: [∗]) where ...
```

The intent is that Elem a as should only be satisfied if the type a is an element of the list of types as, and thus the xs parameter of NM limits the existential types that can appear on Bind constructors.

The definitions of the liftNM and foldNM functions remain unchanged from Section 3.2, but their types are modified to use Elem rather than a constraint parameter:

```
liftNM :: Elem a xs ⇒ t a → NM xs t a
foldNM :: ∀ a r t xs. (a → r) →
  (∀ x. Elem x xs ⇒ t x → (x → r) → r) → NM xs t a → r
```

To use this list of types to constrain the existential types within the GADT, we need another type class:

```
class All (c :: ∗ → Constraint) (as :: [∗]) where ...
```

The intent is that All c as should only be satisfied if c holds for every type in the list as. We can then use All to constrain the existential types when defining an interpretation, for example:

```
lowerVec :: (Eq a, All Finite xs) ⇒ NM xs Vec a → Vec a
showFin  :: (All Finite xs, All Show xs) ⇒ NM xs Vec a → String
```

Our goal, combining multiple interpretations with different constraints, is now straightforward:

```
showAndLower :: (Eq a, All Finite xs, All Show xs) ⇒
                NM xs Vec a → (String, Vec a)
showAndLower v = (showFin v, lowerVec v)
```

An explanation of the methods of the Elem and All classes, and how they are used, is beyond the scope of this paper, so we direct the reader to the original paper by Jones et al. [17].

7. Conclusions

In this paper we surveyed a variety of solutions to the constrained-monad problem, some of which require modifying the data type (normalization, restricted data types), and some of which require modifying the type class (restricted type classes). Some solutions are only proposals, as they require modifications to the Haskell language (restricted data types). Some solutions are better suited to the shallow version of the problem than the deep version (restricted monads, continuations), and some were straightforward to apply to other structures (normalized deep embeddings, restricted type classes). Our solution — using normalized deep embeddings with explicit constraints on the existential types — is pragmatic, simple to understand and implement, and useful in practice.

A valid concern about our technique is whether the benefits of being able to define a monad instance for a data type with constrained operations outweigh the cost of applying the technique. We expect the answer will vary between use cases. However, we observe that if a data type is provided abstractly by a library, then it is possible for all of the work to be done internally by the library implementer. For example, we have constructed an alternative to the `Data.Set` module, and made it available as the Set-Monad library [9]. This library provides an abstract type Set, with the same interface as `Data.Set`. However, it performs normalization internally, and thus is able to provide Monad and other instances for its Set type. That is, the Set type it exposes corresponds to the SetM type described in Section 2.2.

We think that awareness of the ability to reify computations expressed using structures containing existential types will have a significant impact on future EDSL designs. Both Syntactic-based EDSLs [30] and our own Sunroof [6] would be considerably weaker without this ability. Referring to our experience in Sunroof, the ability to perform monadic-bind reification has led to a useful compiler that directly supports multiple threading models and concurrency objects such as mutable variables and channels. We anticipate others using monadic-bind reification to build other effect-based EDSLs.

Acknowledgments

We thank Andrew Farmer and Nicolas Frisby for suggesting the normal form and normalization algorithm for applicative functors. We also thank Heinrich Apfelmus and Ryan Ingram for observing that we could use the Operational and MonadPrompt libraries to perform the monadic normalization, respectively. Finally, we thank Ed Komp, Philip Hölzenspies and the anonymous reviewers for feedback on earlier versions of this paper, and Edward Kmett for his helpful comments on restricted monads. This material is based upon work supported by the National Science Foundation under Grant No. 1117569.

References

[1] S. Adams. Efficient sets — a balancing act. *Journal of Functional Programming*, 3(4):553–561, 1993.

[2] H. Apfelmus. The Operational monad tutorial. *The Monad.Reader*, 15:37–55, 2010.

[3] M. Bolingbroke. Constraint kinds for GHC, 2011. URL `http://blog.omega-prime.co.uk/?p=127`.

[4] M. M. T. Chakravarty, G. Keller, and S. Peyton Jones. Associated type synonyms. In *International Conference on Functional Programming*, pages 241–253. ACM, 2005.

[5] C. Elliott, S. Finne, and O. de Moor. Compiling embedded languages. *Journal of Functional Programming*, 13(3):455–481, 2003.

[6] A. Farmer and A. Gill. Haskell DSLs for interactive web services. In *Cross-model Language Design and Implementation*, 2012.

[7] J. Gibbons and B. C. dos Santos Oliveira. The essence of the iterator pattern. *Journal of Functional Programming*, 19(3–4):377–402, 2009.

[8] A. Gill. Type-safe observable sharing in Haskell. In *Haskell Symposium*, pages 117–128. ACM, 2009.

[9] G. Giorgidze, 2012. URL `http://hackage.haskell.org/package/set-monad`.

[10] P. Hudak. Modular domain specific languages and tools. In *International Conference on Software Reuse*, pages 134–142. IEEE Computer Society, 1998.

[11] J. Hughes. A novel representation of lists and its application to the function "reverse". *Information Processing Letters*, 22(3):141–144, 1986.

[12] J. Hughes. Restricted data types in Haskell. In *Haskell Workshop*, 1999.

[13] J. Hughes. Generalising monads to arrows. *Science of Computer Programming*, 37(1–3):67–111, 2000.

[14] G. Hutton, M. Jaskelioff, and A. Gill. Factorising folds for faster functions. *Journal of Functional Programming*, 20(3&4):353–373, 2010.

[15] R. Ingram and B. Felgenhauer, 2008. URL `http://hackage.haskell.org/package/MonadPrompt`.

[16] M. Jaskelioff. Monatron: An extensible monad transformer library. In *Implementation and Application of Functional Languages 2008*, volume 5836 of *LNCS*, pages 233–248. Springer, 2011.

[17] W. Jones, T. Field, and T. Allwood. Deconstraining DSLs. In *International Conference on Functional Programming*, pages 299–310. ACM, 2012.

[18] E. Kidd. How to make Data.Set a monad, 2007. URL `http://www.randomhacks.net/articles/2007/03/15/data-set-monad-haskell-macros`.

[19] O. Kiselyov. Restricted monads, 2006. URL `http://okmij.org/ftp/Haskell/types.html#restricted-datatypes`.

[20] O. Kiselyov, S. Peyton Jones, and C. Shan. Fun with type functions. In *Reflections on the Work of C.A.R. Hoare*, chapter 14, pages 301–331. Springer, 2010.

[21] E. A. Kmett, 2013. URL `http://hackage.haskell.org/package/kan-extensions`.

[22] K. Läufer and M. Odersky. Polymorphic type inference and abstract data types. *Transactions on Programming Languages and Systems*, 16 (5):1411–1430, 1994.

[23] S. Liang, P. Hudak, and M. Jones. Monad transformers and modular interpreters. In *Principles of Programming Languages*, pages 333–343. ACM, 1995.

[24] C. Lin. Programming monads operationally with Unimo. In *International Conference on Functional Programming*, pages 274–285. ACM, 2006.

[25] C. McBride and R. Paterson. Applicative programming with effects. *Journal of Functional Programming*, 18(1):1–13, 2008.

[26] M. Mitrofanov. A problem defining a monad instance, 2009. URL `http://www.haskell.org/pipermail/haskell-cafe/2009-November/068761.html`.

[27] E. Moggi. Computational lambda-calculus and monads. In *Logic in Computer Science*, pages 14–23. IEEE Press, 1989.

[28] E. Moggi. Notions of computation and monads. *Information and Computation*, 93(1):55–92, 1991.

[29] D. Orchard and T. Schrijvers. Haskell type constraints unleashed. In *International Conference on Functional and Logic Programming*, pages 56–71. Springer, 2010.

[30] A. Persson, E. Axelsson, and J. Svenningsson. Generic monadic constructs for embedded languages. In *Implementation and Application of Functional Languages 2011*, volume 7257 of *LNCS*, pages 85–99. Springer, 2012.

[31] S. Peyton Jones, D. Vytiniotis, S. Weirich, and G. Washburn. Simple unification-based type inference for GADTs. In *International Conference on Functional Programming*, pages 50–61. ACM, 2006.

[32] S. Peyton Jones, D. Vytiniotis, S. Weirich, and M. Shields. Practical type inference for arbitrary-rank types. *Journal of Functional Programming*, 17(1):1–82, 2007.

[33] F. Pfenning and C. Elliott. Higher-order abstract syntax. In *Programming Language Design and Implementation*, pages 199–208. ACM, 1988.

[34] N. Sculthorpe, 2013. URL `http://hackage.haskell.org/package/constrained-normal`.

[35] G. Sittampalam and P. Gavin, 2008. URL `http://hackage.haskell.org/package/rmonad`.

[36] M. Spivey. A functional theory of exceptions. *Science of Computer Programming*, 14(1):25–42, 1990.

[37] J. Svenningsson and E. Axelsson. Combining deep and shallow embedding for EDSL. In *Trends in Functional Programming 2012*, volume 7829 of *LNCS*. Springer.

[38] W. Swierstra. Data types à la carte. *Journal of Functional Programming*, 18(4):423–436, 2008.

[39] J. Vizzotto, T. Altenkirch, and A. Sabry. Structuring quantum effects: Superoperators as arrows. *Mathematical Structures in Computer Science*, 16(3):453–468, 2006.

[40] J. Voigtländer. Asymptotic improvement of computations over free monads. In *Mathematics of Program Construction*, pages 388–403. Springer, 2008.

[41] P. Wadler. Comprehending monads. In *LISP and Functional Programming*, pages 61–78. ACM, 1990.

[42] P. Wadler. The essence of functional programming. In *Principles of Programming Languages*, pages 1–14. ACM, 1992.

[43] B. A. Yorgey, S. Weirich, J. Cretin, S. Peyton Jones, D. Vytiniotis, and J. P. Magalhães. Giving Haskell a promotion. In *Types in Language Design and Implementation*, pages 53–66. ACM, 2012.

Simple and Compositional Reification of Monadic Embedded Languages

Functional Pearl

Josef Svenningsson Bo Joel Svensson

Chalmers University of Technology

{josefs,joels}@chalmers.se

Abstract

When writing embedded domain specific languages in Haskell, it is often convenient to be able to make an instance of the `Monad` class to take advantage of the do-notation and the extensive monad libraries. Commonly it is desirable to compile such languages rather than just interpret them. This introduces the problem of monad *reification*, i.e. observing the structure of the monadic computation. We present a solution to the monad reification problem and illustrate it with a small robot control language. Monad reification is not new but the novelty of our approach is in its directness, simplicity and compositionality.

Categories and Subject Descriptors D.3.2 [*Programming Languages*]: Language Classifications—Applicative (functional) languages; D.3.4 [*Programming Languages*]: Processors—Code generation

Keywords Compiling, embedded language, reification, monads

1. Introduction

Benny is a computer science student working in a project involving programming robots in a low-level imperative language. However, Benny has a budding interest in functional programming using Haskell and has read "The Haskell school of expression" [6]. He gets the idea to implement a language for robot control embedded in Haskell. Benny realises that the capabilities of the robot hardware are very similar to those of the robots that Hudak evaluates graphically in a grid world. There is however a very important difference; the embedded language needs to be compiled into some form that is understood by the robot.

Guided by the capabilities of the target robot, Benny designs an API for robot programming. The robot can perform operations such as *move* that steps the robot forward and *turn* left and right. The robot also has the capability to execute program loops and conditionals and it has a forward facing `sensor` with which it can query the world.

ICFP '13, September 25–27,2013, Boston, MA, USA.

http://dx.doi.org/10.1145/2500365.2500611

The API that Benny designs is simple:

```
move      :: Program ()
turnLeft  :: Program ()
turnRight :: Program ()
sensor    :: Program Bool
cond      :: Program Bool
             -> Program ()
             -> Program ()
             -> Program ()
while     :: Program Bool
             -> Program ()
             -> Program ()
```

Now, Benny wants to express robot programs using the Haskell *do* notation. The motivation behind this is the imperative look and feel of the operations he identified and the potential to use all the control structures in the *Control.Monad* library. For this, a `Monad` instance is needed.

To be able to create a first-order representation of a computation described using monads, Benny needs to solve the problem of *reifying* monads This is the story of how Benny came up with a particularly simple solution to this problem.

1.1 Example programs

Benny is quite happy with his language design and decides to write some programs to try it out.

The first program is called `sMove`, which implements a safe move operation. This operation can be executed by the robot even though it is facing an obstacle, without risk of harming robot or obstacle.

```
sMove :: Program ()
sMove = cond sensor turnRight move
```

The second program moves the robot forward until it stands directly in front of an obstacle such as a wall.

```
moveToWall :: Program ()
moveToWall = while ((liftM not) sensor) move
```

Based on these examples, Benny is quite satisfied with the design of his language and turns to implementing it.

1.2 Implementation and data structures

Enthused by the prospect of compiling these programs to the target language and seeing some robot action, Benny goes to work on the data structures.

Since the language is going to be compiled, Benny realises that the booleans in his language cannot be regular Haskell booleans. The booleans needs to be replaced by boolean typed expressions.

```
type Name = String

data BoolE = Lit Bool
           | Var Name
           | (:||:) BoolE BoolE
           | (:&&:)  BoolE BoolE
           | Not BoolE
```

Following this, the operations that should go into the `Program` data type feel straightforward.

```
data Program a where
  Move      :: Program ()
  TurnLeft  :: Program ()
  TurnRight :: Program ()
  Sensor    :: Program BoolE
  Cond      :: Program BoolE
               -> Program ()
               -> Program ()
  While     :: Program BoolE
               -> Program ()
               -> Program ()
```

Benny continues by naively adding constructors for `Return` and `Bind` to the `Program` data type.

```
data Program a where
  ...
  Return :: a -> Program a
  Bind   :: Program a
            -> (a -> Program b)
            -> Program b
```

Then he writes down the `Monad` instance.

```
instance Monad Program where
  return = Return
  (>>=)  = Bind
```

Proud of his accomplishments, Benny sends his Haskell module in an email to Prof. Björn. Benny knows that Björn is teaching an introductory Haskell course and should be able to provide feedback.

1.3 Problem statement

Meanwhile in Professor Björn's Office

Prof. Björn notices an email from Benny in his inbox and opens it.

> Dear Professor Björn
>
> I am CS student working in a robot control project. Usually, we program our robots in C but I have developed an interest in Haskell programming and thought it'd be natural to try implementing an EDSL. I know you teach an FP course and thought I would ask for your input. Attached to this mail is a file containing an outline of the data types I want to use. Does this look sensible to you?
>
> Thank you
> Benny

Prof. Björn opens the attachment and takes a look at the data type. He particularly notices the constructors `Return` and `Bind` and the `Monad` instance. He shakes his head at Benny's naiveté and writes an email back:

> Hello Benny
>
> I'm afraid your implementation of the monadic primitives can never work. The constructor `Return` can take any arbitrary value that has nothing to do with the language you're designing. These values may be strings, binary trees or higher-order functions from zygomorphisms to histomorphisms. The same problem goes for `Bind`; it has to be able to handle arbitrary values. It cannot possibly work! This is a very difficult problem and such a naive solution is bound to fail.
>
> Prof. Björn
> Dept. of Computer Science and Engineering
> Chalmers University of Technology

While waiting for feedback from Björn, Benny has carried on trying to implement a compiler for his language.

When Björn's email does arrive, Benny is confused. He feels he has already managed to compile the `Program` data type into a representation closer to that which is executed by the robot hardware.

He writes an apprehensive email back to Prof. Björn.

> Hello Prof. Björn
>
> Thanks for your feedback. But I think it does work! Attached to this email you find a file containing my attempt at compiling the `Program` data type into a representation closer to that which is executed by our robots.
>
> I have also attached two example programs that you can compile and then run in the graphical simulator (see figure 1)
>
> Benny

2. Compilation of the monadic robot EDSL

Björn receives Benny's latest email

Björn looks through the `Compiler` module and finds a data type describing a first-order representation of the robot language.

```
data Prg = PMove
         | PTurnRight
         | PTurnLeft
         | PSensor Name
         | PCond BoolE Prg Prg
         | PWhile Name Prg Prg
         | PSeq Prg Prg
         | PSkip
         | PAssign Name BoolE
```

From the `Prg` data type, Björn presumes that the `PSeq` constructor will be the result of compiling `Bind` and that `PSensor` binds a variable which can be used in `PAssign` and `PWhile`. The conclusion is that the representation looks sensible, but he is very interested in seeing the `Program a -> Prg` transformation. The compile function assumes a splittable name supply with the interface described in figure 2.

```
spiralIn :: Int -> Program ()
spiralIn 0 = return ()
spiralIn n = do
  replicateM_ 2 $ do
    replicateM_ n move
    turnLeft
  spiralIn (n-1)
```

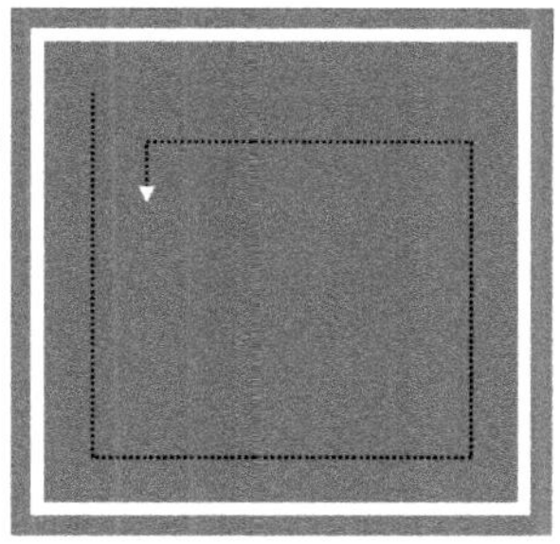

```
followWall :: Program ()
followWall =
  while (return true) $
    cond checkLeft sMove $
            do turnLeft
               move

checkLeft :: Program BoolE
checkLeft = do
  TurnLeft
  s <- Sensor
  TurnRight
  return s
```

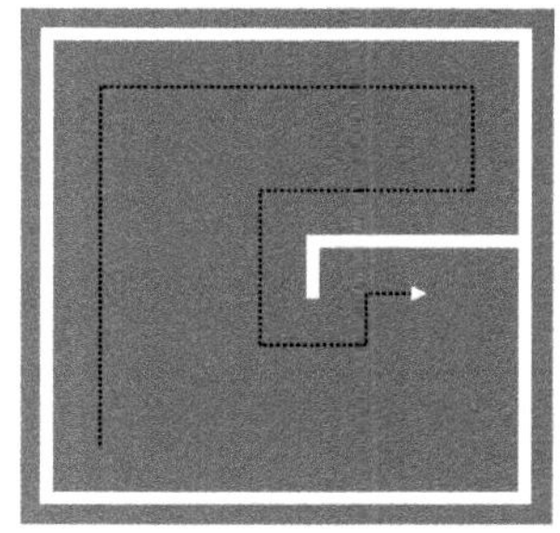

Figure 1. The `spiralIn` and `followWall` programs sent from Benny to Björn in an email

```
newNameSupply :: NameSupply
split2 :: NameSupply ->
          (NameSupply,NameSupply)
split3 :: NameSupply ->
          (NameSupply,NameSupply,NameSupply)
supplyValue :: NameSupply -> Int
```

Figure 2. The interface of the splittable name supply used in the implementation of the compile functions

```
runCompile :: Program a -> Prg
runCompile prg = snd $ compile s prg
  where
    s = newNameSupply

compile :: NameSupply -> Program a -> (a, Prg)
compile s Move = ((),PMove)
compile s TurnRight = ((),PTurnRight)
compile s TurnLeft  = ((),PTurnLeft)
compile s Sensor    = (Var nom,PSensor nom)
  where
    v   = supplyValue s
    nom = "v" ++ show v
compile s (Cond b p1 p2) =
    ((),bp ‘PSeq‘ PCond b’ p1’ p2’)
  where
    (s1,s2,s3) = split3 s
    (b’,bp)    = compile s1 b
    (a1,p1’)   = compile s2 p1
    (a2,p2’)   = compile s3 p2
compile s (While wp prg) = ((),PWhile nom nwp prg’)
  where
    (s1,s2,s3) = split3 s
    (b,wp’)    = compile s1 wp
    (c,prg’)   = compile s2 prg
    nom        = "v" ++ (show $ supplyValue s3)
    nwp        = (wp’ ‘PSeq‘ PAssign nom b)
compile s (Return a) = (a,PSkip)
compile s (Bind pa f) = (b, prg1 ‘PSeq‘ prg2)
  where
    (s1,s2)  = split2 s
    (a,prg1) = compile s1 pa
    (b,prg2) = compile s2 (f a)
```

Björn studies the code in disbelief, saves the module and tries it out on some examples. The code does indeed seem to work and Björn's disbelief is replaced with enthusiasm; this appears to be a simple and convenient way to reify monads.

Björn sends an email to Benny, inviting him to a meeting.

3. Meeting in Björn's office

BJÖRN: Hello, come in.

BENNY: Thanks.

BJÖRN: So, about this robot language! You gave me a bit of a surprise there. I was entirely sure that what you did was impossible.

BENNY: Oh, But I just did the first thing that came to mind. There was no deep thought behind it.

BJÖRN: The problem is [*Björn approaches his whiteboard*] when you try to reify the bind constructor of your representation.

```
Bind :: Program a -> (a -> Program b) -> Program b
```

BJÖRN: You need to come up with an element of type `a` to pass to the function.

BENNY: I didn't realise it was problem.

BJÖRN: But it is! Your solution is that you are careful about the return types of all operations in your language. They are either of unit type or some type which can be guaranteed to be reified. [*Björn scribbles on his whiteboard*]

```
Move :: Program ()
```

```
Sensor :: Program BoolE
```

BJÖRN: This is different from how such constructs are normally implemented. If I had implemented the language I would have given `Sensor` the type `Program Bool` so that I could write an evaluator of type `Program a -> a`, or perhaps `Program a -> M a`. But then adding a monad to the language and reifying it becomes much harder.

BENNY: Yes, now that you mention it, I have seen that style used for defining DSLs.

BJÖRN: Having constructors like `Sensor` return `BoolE` instead of `Bool` is a crucial part of why your method works. It allows the `compile` function to be written in such a way that it can generate the return values statically and pass them as arguments to `Bind`. In a sense you're doing evaluation at the same time as compilation. There's just enough evaluation to remove the monadic constructs. It's a very neat trick!

BENNY: Thank you.

BJÖRN: Another way to think about your trick is that you are using a writer monad to evaluate your language and produce the first-order syntax tree as a side effect. Then you could have used a state monad transformer on top of that for the fresh name supply. But that's a stylistic choice.

BENNY: You seem to be making a big deal out of this. I just did what I thought was the most straightforward thing to do.

3.1 Related work

BJÖRN: Others have solved this problem before but I have never seen a solution as simple as yours and was quite surprised that it works. For example, in this paper [*Björn shows Benny the paper [7]*], the authors use a continuation monad to be able to reify the monadic constructs of their language. If they were to implement your robot language they would use the same `Program` data type as you do. However, they would not expose that to the user of the language. Instead they would create a type like this:

```
data P a =
  P (forall r. ((a -> Program r) -> Program r))
```

BJÖRN: The type `P` is a continuation monad so the monad instance comes naturally. Operations on `P` are defined using `Bind` like this:

```
while :: P BoolE -> P () -> P ()
while c b =
  P (\k -> While (runP c) (runP b) `Bind` k)

cond :: BoolE -> P () -> P () -> P ()
cond b t e =
  P (\k -> Cond b (runP t) (runP e) `Bind` k)

runP :: P a -> Program a
runP (P f) = f (\a -> Return a)
```

BENNY: I see. Continuations are quite magical to me. I could never have come up with that technique. How do they deal with transforming higher-order programs to first-order programs?

BJÖRN: That's a good question. The transformation to first order programs is dealt with by a library called Syntactic. It is described in a separate paper [*Björn pulls out the paper [2] from a pile of papers*]. It's hard to do an apples to apples comparison between Syntactic and your technique. Syntactic solves a much bigger problem than what you're doing so it is naturally more complicated.

BENNY: Ok.

BJÖRN: There are also the papers [5, 8] which solves the problem in a manner that is more similar to yours. They also have explicit constructors `Bind` and `Return` but give them a slightly different type which guarantees that all applications of `Bind` are *normalised*, so that all `Bind`s are right-associated. Unexpectedly, this allows them to make instances of the `Monad` class but at the same time constrain the arguments of `Bind`. Their technique is more complicated than yours, but just as with the case of Syntactic, they solve a more general problem.

However, there is one particular thing I like about your technique.

BENNY: What is that?

BJÖRN: Your technique is compositional.

3.2 Compositionality

BENNY: What does it mean that my technique is compositional?

BJÖRN: The compile function is compositional because there is one case for each constructor and each case deals with exactly one constructor. In particular, the constructors `Return` and `Bind` are handled completely separately from all other language constructs.

BENNY: And that is good ?

BJÖRN: Absolutely! Compositional definitions are nice because they imply that there is no weird semantical interaction between the constructs as they are defined independently. But it also means that it should be possible to factor out the constructors `Return` and `Bind` into a data type of their own. Then, it could be combined with other data types using techniques like Data Types á la Carte [9] or CompData [3]. This way, a language can be designed piece by piece.You can then select the set of pieces required for a particular task or that suits a particular brand of robots.

BENNY: Oh! Interesting.

3.3 The Monad laws

BJÖRN: There is still one problem with your method though.

BENNY: What's that?

BJÖRN: When we make instances of the monad class we expect certain laws to hold. [*Björn writes the laws on his whiteboard*]

```
m >>= return    = m
return a >>= f  = f a
(m >>= f) >>= g = m >>= \a -> f a >>= g
```

BJÖRN: These laws clearly don't hold for your instance. Take the first law for instance. The left hand side will have extra `Bind` and `Return` constructors compared to the right hand side.

BENNY: Hmmm. I hadn't really thought about that. But adding an extra return at the end of a computation shouldn't make a difference in my implementation.

BJÖRN: So, you're saying that your implementation actually obeys the first monad law?

BENNY: Well, at least when I run my programs I will never see any difference between the left hand side and the right hand side.

BJÖRN: Aha, so what you're saying is that if we compare the semantics of programs rather than comparing the programs themselves then we get some useful laws. [*Björn scribbles some new laws on the whiteboard*]

```
eval (m >>= return)     = eval m
eval (return a >>= f)   = eval (f a)
eval ((m >>= f) >>= g)  = eval (m >>= \a -> f a >>= g)
```

BJÖRN: These laws are morally the same as the monad laws, especially if we don't let the user of the robot language ever compare terms in the language.

BENNY: Yes, that captures my intuition very well.

BJÖRN: Ok, good. Can you prove these equations?

BENNY: No, I don't have any experience proving programs correct.

BJÖRN: Well, it shouldn't be that difficult. Let me see what I can come up with.

[*Björn scribbles frenetically on a piece of paper for a couple of minutes.*]

Aha! Your technique is quite general. It can reify monads into any kind of structure which is a monoid. Return translates into the monoid unit and bind translates into the monoid operation.

For example, in your compilation function it is important that the semantics of `PSkip` is the identity of the semantics of `PSeq` and that `PSeq` is associative.

BENNY: Ok, that sounds good. I take that as meaning the method is quite general?

BJÖRN: Yes, requiring a monoid is a very mild restriction.

Look at the time! This was interesting, I got quite carried away. We must round off but please get back to me if you make any more progress on your robot language.

BENNY: Thanks very much for your time. Bye!

BJÖRN: Thank you.

4. Composing reifiable monadic languages

At Benny's computer

Benny was really intrigued by the idea of compositionally building embedded languages and after having read the papers Björn showed him he decides to try his own approach to the problem.

```
data (e1 :+: e2) x a
  = InjL (e1 x a) | InjR (e2 x a)
infixr :+:

class sub :<: sup where
  inj :: sub x a  -> sup x a

instance f :<: f where
  inj = id

instance (f :<: (f :+: g)) where
   inj = InjL

instance (f :<: h) => (f :<: (g :+: h)) where
  inj = InjR . inj
```

Figure 3. Data types from CompData for composing languages.

Inspired by CompData he starts out by adding the code in figure 3 to his file. The data type `:+:` is used for composing languages, and the `:<:` typeclass provides coercions so that the programmer doesn't have to worry about using the right sequence of the `InjL` and `InjR` constructors to inject terms into the composed language.

Benny then starts to add data types for the different language constructs in his robotic language. The different operations for the robot are pleasingly easy to add.

```
data MoveOp x a where
  Move :: MoveOp x ()

data TurnOp x a where
  TurnLeft  :: TurnOp x ()
  TurnRight :: TurnOp x ()

data SensorOp x a where
  Sensor :: SensorOp x BoolE

data CondOp x a where
  Cond :: x BoolE -> x () -> x () -> CondOp x ()

data WhileOp x a where
  While :: x BoolE -> x () -> WhileOp x ()
```

In order to test out these definitions, Benny next turns to implementing a compiler. He realises that the compiler now needs to be implemented as a class with one instance per compilable sub-language.

```
runCompile :: Compile f => f a -> Prg
runCompile prg = snd $ compile s prg
  where s = newNameSupply

class Compile f where
  compile :: NameSupply -> f a -> (a, Prg)

instance Compile (MoveOp x) where
  compile _ Move = ((), PMove)

instance Compile (TurnOp x) where
  compile _ TurnLeft = ((), PTurnLeft)
  compile _ TurnRight = ((), PTurnRight)

instance Compile (SensorOp x) where
  compile s Sensor = (Var nom, PSensor nom)
    where v   = supplyValue s
          nom = "v" ++ show v
```

```
instance Compile x => Compile (CondOp x) where
  compile s (Cond b p1 p2) =
    ((),bp `PSeq` PCond b' p1' p2')
    where (s1,s2,s3) = split3 s
          (b',bp)    = compile s1 b
          (a1,p1')   = compile s2 p1
          (a2,p2')   = compile s3 p2

instance Compile x => Compile (WhileOp x) where
  compile s (While wp p) = ((),PWhile nom nwp p')
    where (s1,s2,s3) = split3 s
          (b,wp')    = compile s1 wp
          (c,p')     = compile s2 p
          nom        = "v" ++ (show $ supplyValue s3)
          nwp        = wp' `PSeq` PAssign nom b

instance (Compile (e1 f), Compile (e2 f))
  => Compile ((e1 :+: e2) f) where
  compile s (InjL a) = compile s a
  compile s (InjR a) = compile s a
```

But when Benny tries to add the monadic operations he finds that they are quite resistant to a compositional treatment. After much struggle he comes up with the following data type definition:

```
data Mops f x a where
  Oper   :: f x a -> Mops f x a
  Return :: a -> Mops f x a
  Bind   :: x a -> (a -> x b) -> Mops f x b
```

The recursion is provided by another data type that Benny calls `MonadExp`.

```
data MonadExp f a = In (Mops f (MonadExp f) a)
```

Benny thinks of the `MonadExp` data type as a representation of a monadic language parameterised over operations `Oper` that are constructed using the constructors of some type `f`. The monad instance for this data type is only slightly more complicated compared to the earlier, non-compositional setting.

```
instance Monad (MonadExp f) where
  return = In . Return
  (>>=) a f = In (Bind a f)
```

Benny can now write the type of his robotic language, built from independent pieces. It is noteworthy that the monadic expressions have to be added on top of all the other language constructs.

```
type Robot = MonadExp (MoveOp :+: TurnOp  :+:
                       CondOp :+: WhileOp :+:
                       SensorOp)
```

Given the definition of his language Benny can now write an injection function which helps writing smart constructors for all the different robot operations.

```
inject :: (sub :<: f)
       => sub (MonadExp f) a
       -> MonadExp f a
inject a = In $ Oper $ inj $ a

move :: (MoveOp :<: f) => MonadExp f ()
move =  inject Move

turnL :: (TurnOp :<: f) => MonadExp f ()
turnL = inject TurnLeft

turnR :: (TurnOp :<: f) => MonadExp f ()
turnR = inject TurnRight

sensor :: (SensorOp :<: f) => MonadExp f BoolE
sensor = inject Sensor
```

```
cond :: (CondOp :<: f)
     => MonadExp f BoolE
     -> MonadExp f () -> MonadExp f () -> MonadExp f ()
cond b p1 p2 = inject $ Cond b p1 p2

while :: (WhileOp :<: f)
      => MonadExp f BoolE
      -> MonadExp f () -> MonadExp f ()
while pb p = inject $ While pb p
```

Things are starting to fall into place. The only remaining bit is to complete the compiler for monadic expressions.

```
instance (Compile x, Compile (f x))
  => Compile (Mops f x) where
  compile s (Oper o) = compile s o
  compile s (Return a) = (a,PSkip)
  compile s (Bind m f) = (b,prg1 `PSeq` prg2)
    where (s1,s2)  = split2 s
          (a,prg1) = compile s1 m
          (b,prg2) = compile s2 (f a)

instance (Compile (f (MonadExp f)))
  => Compile (MonadExp f) where
  compile s (In a) = compile s a
```

Now, Benny has all the functions he needs to compile a simple example program.

```
test1 :: Robot ()
test1 = do
  move
  turnL
  move
  turnL
```

Compiling the program above gives the expected result.

```
PSeq PMove (PSeq PTurnLeft (PSeq PMove PTurnLeft))
```

Benny decides to contact Björn again to show him what he has done.

Dear Prof. Björn

I have attached a file which demonstrates that the monadic constructs can be factored out and compiled separately, just as you suggested.

Thanks
Benny

Benny,

Fascinating! You've managed to factor out the monadic operations so that they can be compiled once and for all. Users of your library don't have to be concerned at all with the semantics of bind and return. Very nice!

I note that the data type for monadic operations cannot be composed as freely as the other operations, but instead has to be applied separately as a final step. Your solution is very similar to how variable binding is handled in the Syntactic library [1].

Prof. Björn
Dept. of Computer Science and Engineering
Chalmers University of Technology

5. Epilogue

This paper shows a simple method of implementing monadic EDSLs. It shows a naïve approach to the monad reification problem which has the additional benefit of being compositional. In section 4, the language is reimplemented in an extensible way and the compile function is shown explicitly to be compositional by treating sub parts of the language separately.

The example language used throughout the story is small and quite limited. But the technique presented in this paper does scale up to larger languages and more complicated language constructs. It is currently used in the implementation of Obsidian, an EDSL for general purpose GPU programming [4]. Obsidian has language constructs which are considerably more advanced than the robot language is this paper. One example is the sequential for-loop which is higher-order (the type parameter `t` is not relevant to the current discussion):

```
SeqFor :: EWord32 -> (EWord32 -> Program t ())
       -> Program t ()
```

There does, however, seem to be restrictions on what kind of language constructs the reification technique presented in this paper can deal with. For instance, the functions from the `MonadPlus` class has resisted our attempts at adding them to an EDSL in the same way as we've added `Return` and `Bind`. The exact limits of the expressiveness of our method is currently unknown to us.

Acknowledgments

We would like to thank Emil Axelsson for very valuable help during the implementation of the methods used in this pearl. We thank Mary Sheeran for suggesting the names Björn & Benny. The ICFP reviewers provided many helpful suggestion which has improved the paper.

This research has been funded by the Swedish Foundation for Strategic Research (which funds the Resource Aware Functional Programming (RAW FP) Project) and by the Swedish Research Council.

References

[1] E. Axelsson. Syntactic. http://hackage.haskell.org/package/syntactic.

[2] E. Axelsson. A generic abstract syntax model for embedded languages. In *Proceedings of the 17th ACM SIGPLAN international conference on Functional programming*, pages 323–334. ACM, 2012.

[3] P. Bahr and T. Hvitved. Parametric compositional data types. In *MSFP*, pages 3–24, 2012.

[4] K. Claessen, M. Sheeran, and B. J. Svensson. Expressive Array Constructs in an Embedded GPU Kernel Programming Language. In *Proceedings of the 7th workshop on Declarative aspects and applications of multicore programming*, DAMP '12, pages 21–30, New York, NY, USA, 2012. ACM. ISBN 978-1-4503-1117-5.

[5] A. Farmer and A. Gill. Haskell DSLs for interactive web services. In *1st International Workshop on Cross-model Language Design and Implementation*, Sep 2012. (published on workshop website, http://workshops.inf.ed.ac.uk/xldi2012/).

[6] P. Hudak. *The Haskell School of Expression: Learning Functional Programming through Multimedia*. Cambridge University Press, New York, NY, USA, 1999. ISBN 0521643384.

[7] A. Persson, E. Axelsson, and J. Svenningsson. Generic monadic constructs for embedded languages. In *Proceedings of the 23rd international conference on Implementation and Application of Functional Languages*, IFL'11, pages 85–99, Berlin, Heidelberg, 2012. Springer-Verlag.

[8] N. Sculthorpe, J. Bracker, G. Giorgidze, and A. Gill. The constrained-monad problem. In *Proceedings of the 18th ACM SIGPLAN international conference on Functional programming*. ACM, 2013.

[9] W. Swierstra. Data types à la carte. *Journal of Functional Programming*, 18(4):423, 2008.

Structural Recursion for Querying Ordered Graphs

Soichiro Hidaka Kazuyuki Asada *
Zhenjiang Hu Hiroyuki Kato
National Institute of Informatics, Japan
{hidaka,asada,hu,kato}@nii.ac.jp

Keisuke Nakano
University of Electro-Communications, Japan
ksk@cs.uec.ac.jp

Abstract

Structural recursion, in the form of, for example, folds on lists and catamorphisms on algebraic data structures including trees, plays an important role in functional programming, by providing a systematic way for constructing and manipulating functional programs. It is, however, a challenge to define structural recursions for graph data structures, the most ubiquitous sort of data in computing. This is because unlike lists and trees, graphs are essentially not inductive and cannot be formalized as an initial algebra in general. In this paper, we borrow from the database community the idea of structural recursion on how to restrict recursions on infinite unordered regular trees so that they preserve the finiteness property and become terminating, which are desirable properties for query languages. We propose a new graph transformation language called λ_{FG} for transforming and querying ordered graphs, based on the well-defined bisimulation relation on ordered graphs with special ε-edges. The language λ_{FG} is a higher order graph transformation language that extends the simply typed lambda calculus with graph constructors and more powerful structural recursions, which is extended for transformations on the sibling dimension. It not only gives a general framework for manipulating graphs and reasoning about them, but also provides a solution to the open problem of how to define a structural recursion on ordered graphs, with the help of the bisimilarity for ordered graphs with ε-edges.

Categories and Subject Descriptors CR-number [*subcategory*]: third-level; D.3.2 [*Programming Languages*]: Language Classifications—Specialized application languages; E.1 [*Data Structures*]: Graphs and networks

Keywords Structural Recursion, Ordered Graphs, Graph Query Language, Bisimulation, Optimization

1. Introduction

Structural recursion, in the form of, for example, folds on lists and catamorphisms (Meijer et al. 1991) on algebraic data structures including trees, plays an important role in functional programming, by providing a systematic way for construction and manipulation of functional programs (Bird and de Moor 1996; Gill et al. 1993; Hu et al. 2006). It is, however, a challenge to define structural recursions for graph data structures, the most ubiquitous sort of data in computing. This is because, unlike lists and trees, graphs are essentially not inductive and cannot be formalized as an initial algebra (Gibbons 1995). Many attempts have been made to resolve this problem by using special trees to represent graphs so that structural recursion on trees can be used to manipulate graphs. This includes the work on representing graphs by trees with specific pointers (Hamana 2009; Dal Zilio et al. 2004; Oliveira and Cook 2012) and by trees with embedded functions (Fegaras and Sheard 1996). However, these attempts have not been so successful, because of the gap between trees (with specific pointers/embedded functions) and graphs, and they require programmers to bridge the gap by explicitly programming these specific pointers and embedded functions.

Would it be possible to define a structural recursion on graphs as if the graphs were trees (special graphs), while using it to manipulate general graphs? Yes, this has been proved to be possible to some extent in the database community, where UnCAL (and its user-level surface syntax UnQL) (Buneman et al. 2000) was introduced to provide a powerful querying method through structural recursion on finite graphs. The graph model of UnCAL is an unordered graph (whose outgoing edges are not ordered), which can be treated as (unordered) *regular trees* (Ginali 1979) given a suitable definition of bisimulation. The benefit of bisimulation is that structural recursion on regular trees can be used for graphs, and moreover, it leads to an interesting and important feature of structural recursion on graphs: *bulk semantics*. With bulk semantics, a structural recursion can be evaluated by first processing all edges of the input graph *in parallel* and then combining the results. Bulk semantics relies on the use of ε-edges (like ε transitions in the labeled transition system) in graphs and provides a smart way of treating shared nodes and cycles in graphs.

Despite usefulness of structural recursion in querying unordered graphs, there are two major limitations with UnCAL. One is that UnCAL can treat only unordered graphs; it cannot treat other graph models, such as the widely used ordered graphs in which the outgoing edges of a node are ordered, e.g., in EMF Ecore, MOF, and KM3 (Jouault and Bézivin 2006). Another limitation is the lack of expressive power of transformations in the sibling dimension. For example, when the edges of input graphs are labeled with natural numbers, we cannot write a transformation in UnCAL that extracts all edges labeled with the average number on the labels of all siblings.

At first sight, it seems that the first limitation could be easily overcome by encoding ordered graphs as unordered ones with suitable edge labels, say by using *hd* and *tl* to represent the first branch and the rest of the branches, respectively. However, there is a fatal problem with this *hd*-*tl* encoding. It is *unsound* in the context of UnCAL where ε-edges must be taken into account for the graph construction and structural recursion. Figure 1 shows

* Current affiliation is The University of Tokyo.

ICFP '13, September 25–27, 2013, Boston, MA, USA.

ACM 978-1-4503-2326-0/13/09.
http://dx.doi.org/10.1145/2500365.2500608

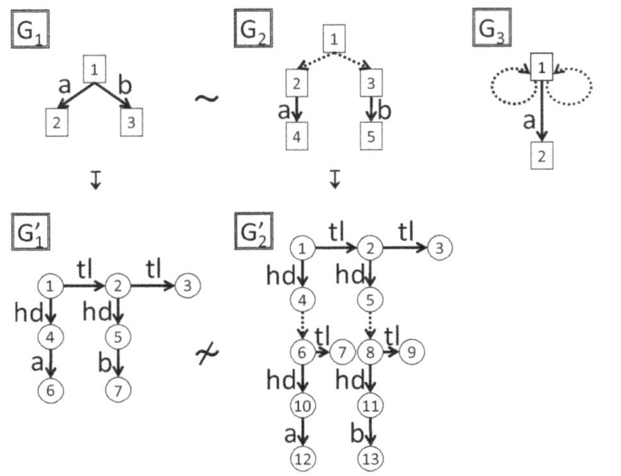

Figure 1. Examples of Head-tail Encoding and Its Unsoundness

an encoding example, where the numbers on the nodes have no particular meaning, since we consider bisimulation. As shown in Figure 1, the ordered graphs G_1 and G_2, where we use dotted arrows to represent ε-edges, are naturally bisimilar (denoted by $\sim$ in the figure), but the corresponding encoded graphs G'_1 and G'_2 ($\mapsto$ in the figure denotes the encoding) are not bisimilar at all.

One might think that we could do the encoding after deleting ε-edges. However, as the graph G_3 in Figure 1 shows, ε-edge elimination of some ordered graphs could produce *infinite width* graphs, and this infinite-width problem is not trivial to solve (see Section 3). Even if we could come up with an encoding, we would still have to show consistency and soundness of the encoding and the corresponding decoding and provide a suitable notion of bisimilarity for ordered graphs having ε-edges, which is very subtle as well (see Section 3). Moreover, we would need an effective way to guarantee that UnCAL transformations map well-encoded graphs to well-encoded graphs that can be successfully decoded later. All these suggest it would be better to design a new language that treats ordered graph directly.

In fact, it has been an *open problem* for more than ten years as to whether the definition of structural recursion in UnCAL can be modified so that it treats ordered graphs rather than unordered ones (the issue was first raised in the conclusion of the paper (Buneman et al. 2000)):

> *... there are some important and interesting areas of research that may well bear fruit. In connection with XML, we have shown how the principles of UnQL will work on an ordered tree. However, it is not clear how they can be extended to an ordered graph model. ... we still lack a complete picture of this topic ...*

In this paper, we provide a solution to this problem; i.e., we define a new structural recursion for ordered graphs. For this, we define the subtle notion of bisimilarity for ordered graphs having ε-edges, and prove *bisimulation genericity* (well-definedness with respect to bisimilarity) of our structural recursion. Note that our (and ref. (Buneman et al. 2000)'s) notion of bisimilarity is different from that of weak bisimilarity used in process algebra. Weak bisimilarity does not fit our purpose, because, for example, the graph union operator (works like the list append in the case of ordered lists) would not be associative.

We propose $\lambda_{\rm FG}$, a powerful higher-order graph transformation language, which is an extension of the simply typed lambda calculus with graph constructors and a more powerful structural recursion for manipulating ordered graphs than what is available in UnCAL. The main contributions of this paper can be summarized as follows.

- We propose a novel definition of bisimilarity between ordered graphs having ε-edges, forming the semantic foundation for $\lambda_{\rm FG}$. Specifically, we show that the branch order is not necessarily finite but of *countable linear order*, even for finite graphs, and clarify that the combination of ε-edges and cycles induces such a countable linear order on the branchings, which would cause issues that do not occur in the unordered case. We show that we can decide whether an ordered graph is empty and whether we can eliminate all ε-edges for a finite ordered graph in such a way that the finite width property of the graph is kept.
- We show that graph constructors and structural recursion on unordered graphs can be adapted to those of ordered ones, forming the core syntax of $\lambda_{\rm FG}$. Specifically, we define a more powerful structural recursion on ordered graphs, which can describe various graph queries including those on the *sibling dimension*. We also prove that (1) any graph query in $\lambda_{\rm FG}$ is *bisimulation generic* in the sense that it returns bisimilar results for bisimilar inputs, and (2) any graph query in $\lambda_{\rm FG}$ *terminates*, transforming *node-finite* graphs to *node-finite* graphs.

  Unlike UnCAL, we also define bisimilarity for higher order functions and prove bisimulation genericity of our structural recursion as a higher order function; this is the key to extending our language to a simply typed lambda calculus, and it makes it clear how we can extend it to rich type systems such as polymorphic/dependent type systems. Moreover, our proof of bisimulation genericity is clearer than the original proof given in (Buneman et al. 2000); this should make further extensions of structural recursion for graphs easier.
- We have implemented an interpreter for $\lambda_{\rm FG}$ that is available at `http://www.biglab.org/src/lambdaFG/`, and we have tested all the examples in this paper. In addition, we demonstrate (but have not implemented) that structural recursions are suitable for query reasoning and query optimization such as fusion and tupling transformations. This shows that our embedding of structural recursions into lambda calculus would be a good foundation to overcome the known impedance mismatch problem that is often raised from a gap between two languages when a query language is used in a general-purpose one for developing a practical application.

Note that in this paper, the "ordered" in "ordered graph" refers to the order on the branchings (rather than, say, the order on the nodes), and "graphs" generally refers to "ordered graphs" that can have ε-edges.

Organization of the Paper We shall start with an overview of $\lambda_{\rm FG}$, a new graph transformation language for querying ordered graphs in Section 2. In Section 3, we discuss the first key technical contribution of this paper, defining ordered graphs, bisimilarity for ordered graphs having ε-edges, and ε-elimination. In Section 4, we give the semantics of our structural recursion and $\lambda_{\rm FG}$ and prove its bisimulation genericity. We demonstrate how to reason about graph transformations and discuss the expressive power of $\lambda_{\rm FG}$ in Section 5. Finally, we discuss related work in Section 6 and conclude the paper in Section 7.

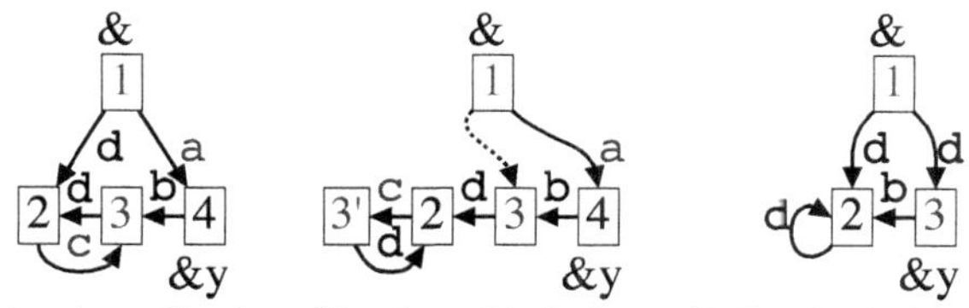

(a) A Simple Graph: G (b) An Equivalent Graph: G' (c) Result of $a2d\_xc$ on (a)

Figure 2. Examples of Graphs

$$
\begin{array}{rcll}
\sigma & ::= & \sigma \to \sigma \mid \sigma + \sigma \mid \sigma \times \sigma & \{\text{ function, coproduct, product types }\} \\
& \mid & \mathbf{List}(\sigma) \mid \mathbf{Bool} & \{\text{ list and boolean types }\} \\
& \mid & \mathbf{Label} \mid \mathbf{G}_Y^X & \{\text{ label and graph types }\} \\
e & ::= & x \mid \lambda x.e \mid e\ e \mid \mathbf{case}\ e\ \mathbf{of}\ \mathbf{in_l}(x) \to e\ \mathbf{or}\ \mathbf{in_r}(y) \to e & \\
& \mid & \mathbf{in_l}\ e \mid \mathbf{in_r}\ e \mid (e, e) \mid \mathbf{pr_l} e \mid \mathbf{pr_r} e & \{\text{ terms of lambda calculus }\} \\
& \mid & \mathbf{nil} \mid \mathbf{cons}(e, e) \mid \mathbf{foldr}(e, e) \mid \ldots & \{\text{ functions for lists }\} \\
& \mid & \mathbf{if}\ e\ \mathbf{then}\ e\ \mathbf{else}\ e & \{\text{ conditional }\} \\
& \mid & a \mid e = e & \{\text{ labels } (a \in \mathcal{L}) \text{ and label equality }\} \\
& \mid & \underline{[]} \mid e \mathbin{\underline{++}} e \mid \underline{[}e : e\underline{]} \mid \underline{[}\&y\underline{]} \mid \&x := e \mid () \mid e \oplus e & \\
& \mid & e \mathbin{@} e \mid \mathbf{cycle}(e) & \{\text{ graph constructors }\} \\
& \mid & \mathbf{isEmpty}(e) & \{\text{ graph emptiness checking }\} \\
& \mid & \mathbf{srec}(e, e) & \{\text{ structural recursion functions }\}
\end{array}
$$

Figure 3. λ_{FG} Language

2. Overview of λ_{FG}

We start with an overview of our transformation language λ_{FG} for transforming (querying) ordered graphs. We introduce our graph model to which closed terms of graph types in λ_{FG} are interpreted. Then we present the syntax and typing rules of λ_{FG} and explain how to represent graphs and write transformations for graphs in λ_{FG}.

2.1 Ordered Graphs

Graphs treated in λ_{FG} are multi-rooted, directed, and edge-labeled. The graph model in λ_{FG} has three prominent features: *ε-edges*, *markers*, and *graph concatenation*. An ε-edge represents a shortcut between the two nodes and behaves like the ε-transition in automata. Nodes may be marked with *input* and *output markers*. These markers are used as an interface to other graphs through ε-edges. Graph concatenation sequentially aligns two graphs in a given order.

Formally, we define an ordered graph as follows. We write $\mathcal{L}$ for a set of *labels* and $\mathcal{L}_\varepsilon$ for $\mathcal{L} \cup \{\varepsilon\}$. Let X and Y be finite sets of input and output markers, respectively; we add the prefix & for markers like $\&x$. Accordingly, an *ordered graph G* (or just *graph*) is defined by a triple (V, B, I), where

- V is a set of *nodes*,
- $B\colon V \to \mathit{List}(\mathcal{L}_\varepsilon \times V + Y)$ is a *branch function* mapping a node to a list of *branches*: a branch in $\mathcal{L}_\varepsilon \times V + Y$ is either a *labeled edge* $\mathsf{Edge}(l, v)$ or an *output marker* $\mathsf{Outm}(\&y)$, and
- $I\colon X \to V$ is a function which determines the *input nodes* (also called *roots*) of the graph.

Note that in the terminology of coalgebra theory, an ordered graph is a coalgebra (V, B) of the endofunctor $\mathit{List}(\mathcal{L}_\varepsilon \times (\text{-}) + Y)$ equipped with a number $|X|$ of initial states I.

Example 1 (Ordered Graph)**.** The ordered graph in Figure 2(a), where the branches are ordered for each node, is represented as (V, B, I), where

$$
\begin{array}{rcl}
V & = & \{1, 2, 3, 4\} \\
B & = & \{1 \mapsto \underline{[}\mathsf{Edge}(\mathsf{d}, 2), \mathsf{Edge}(\mathsf{a}, 4)\underline{]},\ 2 \mapsto \underline{[}\mathsf{Edge}(\mathsf{c}, 3)\underline{]}, \\
& & \ 3 \mapsto \underline{[}\mathsf{Edge}(\mathsf{d}, 2)\underline{]},\ 4 \mapsto \underline{[}\mathsf{Edge}(\mathsf{b}, 3), \mathsf{Outm}(\&y)\underline{]}\} \\
I(\&) & = & 1.
\end{array}
$$
□

In our graph model, every node in the range of function I is called a root. In Example 1, node 1 is the root node. Even though it is called a "root", it may have incoming edges. However, we can convert any graph having such edges incoming to the root into graphs bisimilar to the original one but having no such incoming edges.

We shall write $\mathcal{G}_Y^X$ for the set of ordered graphs with the input marker set X and the output marker set Y. We say that a graph is *finite* if V is a finite set and write $\mathcal{G}\mathrm{f}_Y^X$ for the set of finite ordered graphs. When we say just "finite", it always means finiteness on the set of nodes. We allow a graph to have multiple roots, as a multi-rooted graph is to a forest what a single-rooted graph is to a tree. For single-rooted graphs, we often use the *default marker* & to indicate the root and use $\mathcal{G}_Y$ to denote $\mathcal{G}_Y^{\{\&\}}$.

2.1.1 Graph Equivalence

λ_{FG} uses bisimilarity (also called value-equivalence) as the graph equivalence for ordered graphs. For instance, the graphs G and G' in Figures 2(a) and 2(b) are equivalent. In G', nodes 3 and $3'$ are bisimilar because both nodes only have one outgoing edge labeled d to node 2. Also in G', there is an ε-edge (denoted by the dotted line) from node 1 to node 3, which can be eliminated while maintaining bisimilarity by replacing the ε-edge with an outgoing edge labeled d from node 1 to node 2. The parts that are unreachable from the roots are disregarded. The formal definition of bisimilarity for ordered graphs having ε-edges, which is one of the important results in this paper, is described in Section 3.

Note that the notion of equivalence based on bisimilarity influences the expressiveness of our query language. For example, since we do not distinguish bisimilar graphs like in Figures 2(a) and 2(b) —they have different numbers of nodes—, we cannot count the number of nodes of a graph.

2.2 Syntax of λ_{FG}

The syntax of λ_{FG} is given in Figure 3, and its typing rules are given in Figure 4, though we have omitted some standard typing rules. From here onwards, we will explain the syntax, but will omit the standard explanations for lambda terms and conditionals. We will explain graph constructors and structural recursion in detail in Sections 2.2.1 and 2.2.2 and give their formal semantics in Sections 3.4 and 4. We use the underlined syntax to distinguish certain graph constructors from ordinary list constructors.

$\mathbf{List}(\sigma)$ is the usual list type whose elements belong to σ; **nil**, $\mathbf{cons}(e, e)$, and $\mathbf{foldr}(e, e)$ are standard list functions, and we can add any convenient list functions. These are used for specifying d in $\mathbf{srec}(e, d)$.

Note that we do not include the label ε in the syntax; ε-edges are only used in the semantics. Equality only applies to labels.

We have prepared a set of markers Marker; the metavariables X, Y, and so on denote finite subsets of Marker. Note that we assume type annotations for bound variables, graph constructors, and structural recursions: e.g., $\lambda x^\sigma.e$, $\underline{[]}_Y$, and $\mathbf{srec}_{X,Y,Z}(e, d)$; but we will omit them in this presentation for simplicity. We have a type inference procedure to omit marker set annotations in a way similar to our previous work for UnCAL (Hidaka et al. 2012).

The set of markers α in the type of d is an "abstract" set of markers, which can be viewed as being similar to a type variable in

$$\frac{(a \in \mathcal{L})}{\vdash a\colon \mathbf{Label}} \qquad \frac{\vdash e_1\colon \mathbf{Label} \quad \vdash e_2\colon \mathbf{Label}}{e_1 = e_2 : \mathbf{Bool}}$$

$$\frac{}{\vdash [] : \mathbf{G}_Y} \qquad \frac{\vdash e_1\colon \mathbf{G}_Y^X \quad \vdash e_2\colon \mathbf{G}_Y^X}{\vdash e_1 \mathbin{+\!\!+} e_2\colon \mathbf{G}_Y^X} \qquad \frac{\vdash e_1\colon \mathbf{Label} \quad \vdash e_2\colon \mathbf{G}_Y}{\vdash \lfloor e_1 : e_2 \rfloor : \mathbf{G}_Y}$$

$$\frac{(\&y \in Y)}{\vdash \lfloor \&y \rfloor\colon \mathbf{G}_Y} \qquad \frac{\vdash e\colon \mathbf{G}_Y}{\vdash \&x := e\colon \mathbf{G}_Y^{\{\&x\}}} \qquad \frac{}{\vdash ()\colon \mathbf{G}_Y^{\emptyset}}$$

$$\frac{\vdash e_1\colon \mathbf{G}_Y^{X_1} \quad \vdash e_2\colon \mathbf{G}_Y^{X_2} \quad (X_1 \cap X_2 = \emptyset)}{\vdash e_1 \oplus e_2\colon \mathbf{G}_Y^{X_1 \cup X_2}} \qquad \frac{\vdash e_1\colon \mathbf{G}_Y^X \quad \vdash e_2\colon \mathbf{G}_Z^Y}{\vdash e_1 \mathbin{@} e_2\colon \mathbf{G}_Z^X}$$

$$\frac{\vdash e\colon \mathbf{G}_{X \cup Y}^X \quad (X \cap Y = \emptyset)}{\vdash \mathbf{cycle}(e)\colon \mathbf{G}_Y^X} \qquad \frac{\vdash e\colon \mathbf{G}_Y^X}{\vdash \mathbf{isEmpty}(e)\colon \mathbf{Bool}}$$

$$\frac{\vdash e\colon \mathbf{Label} \times \mathbf{G}_Y \to \mathbf{G}_Z^Z \qquad \vdash d\colon \mathbf{List}(\mathbf{G}_{Z \times \alpha}^Z + \mathbf{G}_{Z \times Y}^Z) \to \mathbf{G}_{Z \times \alpha + Z \times Y}^Z}{\vdash \mathbf{srec}(e, d)\colon \mathbf{G}_Y^X \to \mathbf{G}_{Z \times Y}^{Z \times X}}$$

(Note that we have omitted the typing environments Γ in each rule.)

Figure 4. Typing Rules for Graph-Related Expressions in λ_{FG}

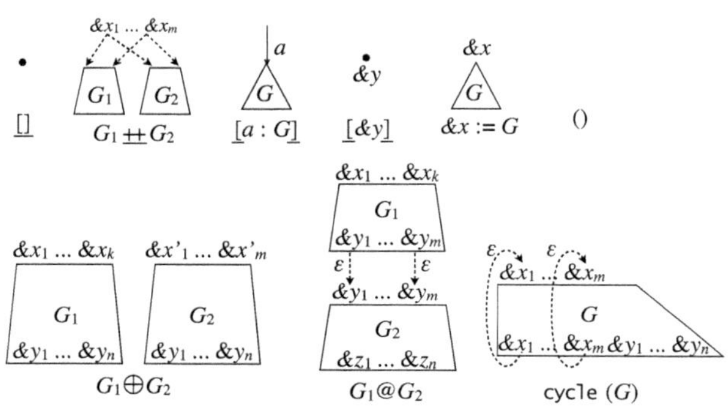

Figure 5. Graph Constructors

polymorphic lambda calculi. This polymorphism in the semantics of our structural recursion is explained in Section 4.

The graph type $\mathbf{G}_Y^X$ is interpreted as a set $\mathcal{G}\mathrm{f}_Y^X$ of *finite* graphs. Similarly to the notation given in Section 2.1 for sets of graphs, we use $\mathbf{G}_Y$ to denote $\mathbf{G}_Y^{\{\&\}}$. The predicate $\mathbf{isEmpty}(e)$ is true if the graph obtained by e has no non-ε-edges in the accessible part.

2.2.1 Graph Construction

λ_{FG} provides useful graph constructors to build arbitrary finite ordered graphs. Figure 5 summarizes the constructors; let us see how type discipline on the input and output markers works for each constructor. First, $\lfloor\rfloor$ constructs a root-only graph with the default input marker and no output markers. For two graphs G_1 and G_2 having identical input markers and output markers, $G_1 \mathbin{+\!\!+} G_2$ *concatenates* them by adding two branching ε-edges from each new root to the corresponding old roots of G_1 and G_2. Next, $\lfloor a : G \rfloor$ extends G with a new fresh root node pointing to the old root of G with an a-labeled edge; the constructor $\lfloor \&y \rfloor$ constructs a graph with a single node marked with an output marker $\&y$ (in (Buneman et al. 2000), $\lfloor a : G \rfloor$ and $\lfloor \&y \rfloor$ are denoted as $\{a : G\}$ and $\&y$, respectively). *Marker renaming* $\&x := G$ associates an input marker $\&x$ with the root node of G (here, G should have only one default input marker $\&$). $()$ constructs a trivial graph that has neither a node nor an edge; and $G_1 \oplus G_2$ constructs a *disjoint union* of G_1 and G_2, i.e., the set of nodes of $G_1 \oplus G_2$ is the disjoint union of those of G_1 and G_2 and branching of nodes (B) is the same as the original. Then, $G_1 \mathbin{@} G_2$ *appends* two graphs by replacing the output markers of G_1 with an ε-edge pointing to the corresponding input nodes of G_2, and $\mathbf{cycle}(G)$ replaces the output marker of G with ε-edges pointing to the corresponding input nodes of G to form cycles.

Note that this set of constructors is powerful enough to describe any finite ordered graphs (although such a description may not be unique). More precisely, for any finite graph, there is a term using graph constructors whose interpretation is bisimilar to the given graph. This can be shown in a quite similar way to that in (Buneman et al. 2000). For instance, the ordered graph in Figure 2(a) can be constructed as follows:

$$\begin{aligned}\&n_1 \mathbin{@} \mathbf{cycle}((&\&n_1 := \lfloor \mathtt{d} : \lfloor \&n_2 \rfloor\rfloor \mathbin{+\!\!+} \lfloor \mathtt{a} : \lfloor \&n_4 \rfloor\rfloor) \oplus \\ &(\&n_2 := \lfloor \mathtt{c} : \lfloor \&n_3 \rfloor\rfloor) \oplus \\ &(\&n_3 := \lfloor \mathtt{d} : \lfloor \&n_2 \rfloor\rfloor) \oplus \\ &(\&n_4 := \lfloor \mathtt{b} : \lfloor \&n_3 \rfloor\rfloor \mathbin{+\!\!+} \lfloor \&y \rfloor)).\end{aligned}$$

2.2.2 Structural Recursion

Structural recursion in λ_{FG} provides a powerful mechanism to describe transformations and queries over ordered graphs that guarantees the termination of the computation and preserves the finiteness of graphs.

In general, the typing rule of $\mathbf{srec}$ is the one given in Figure 4; but here, for ease of explanation, we will use the following simplified variant in which the input graph has no output marker.

$$\frac{\vdash e\colon \mathbf{Label} \times \mathbf{G}_{\emptyset} \to \mathbf{G}_Z^Z \qquad \vdash d\colon \mathbf{List}(\mathbf{G}_{Z \times \alpha}^Z) \to \mathbf{G}_{Z \times \alpha}^Z}{\vdash \mathbf{srec}'(e, d)\colon \mathbf{G}_{\emptyset}^X \to \mathbf{G}_{Z \times \emptyset}^{Z \times X}}$$

This $\mathbf{srec}'$ is obtained as syntax sugar from the original $\mathbf{srec}$:

$$\mathbf{srec}'(e, d) \stackrel{\mathrm{def}}{=} \mathbf{srec}(e, i \circ d \circ p)$$

where $p : \mathbf{List}(\mathbf{G}_{Z \times \alpha}^Z + \mathbf{G}_{Z \times \emptyset}^Z) \to \mathbf{List}(\mathbf{G}_{Z \times \alpha}^Z)$ discards elements in $\mathbf{G}_{Z \times \emptyset}^Z$ in an input list and $i : \mathbf{G}_{Z \times \alpha}^Z \to \mathbf{G}_{Z \times \alpha + Z \times \emptyset}^Z$ is the obvious isomorphism. Throughout this section, we will simply $\mathbf{srec}$ for $\mathbf{srec}'$.

Now let us briefly explain the semantics of $\mathbf{srec}(e, d)$; there are two different styles: *recursive semantics* and *bulk semantics*. Recursive semantics is more concise and useful for reasoning about not only the behavior of a function defined in a recursive way but also program transformation/optimization (This will be considered in Section 5.1). On the other hand, bulk semantics is useful for understanding how a graph is transformed on the whole, for parallel computation, and for proving the termination and finiteness-preserving properties. We will explain recursive semantics in a simple form here and formally describe these two semantics in Section 4.

We introduce a reasonable condition called *production-consumption compatibility (PCC)* on e and d so that we can give a clearer form of recursive semantics. The condition is explained in detail in Section 4.1, and the following examples in this section satisfy it. Furthermore, for simplicity, we consider the following case: $d = \mathbf{foldr}(\odot, \iota_{\odot})$ for some monoid $(\odot, \iota_{\odot})$ on $\mathbf{G}_{Z \times \alpha}^Z$; we consider general d in Section 4.1. The structural recursion function $f \stackrel{\mathrm{def}}{=} \mathbf{srec}(e, d)$ satisfies the following equations (here, equality means the bisimilarity):

$$\begin{array}{lcl} f(\lfloor\rfloor) & = & \iota_{\odot} \\ f(g_1 \mathbin{+\!\!+} g_2) & = & f(g_1) \odot f(g_2) \\ f(\lfloor l : g \rfloor) & = & e(l, g) \mathbin{@} f(g) \\ f(\&x := g) & = & (\oplus_{\&z \in Z}(\&z, \&x) := \lfloor (\&z, \&) \rfloor) \mathbin{@} f(g) \\ f(()) & = & () \\ f(g_1 \oplus g_2) & = & f(g_1) \oplus f(g_2). \end{array} \qquad (1)$$

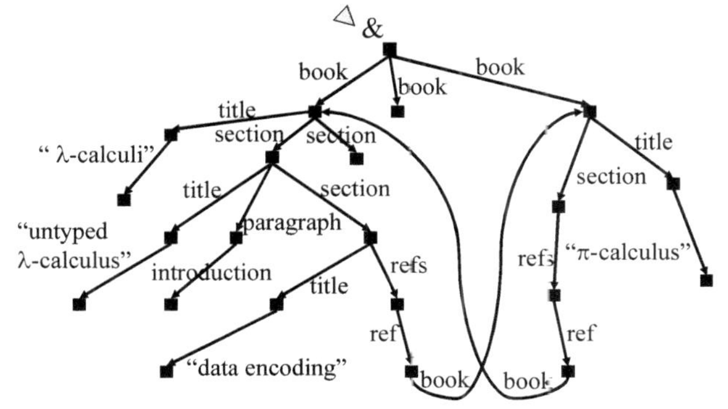

Figure 6. Ordered Graph Representation of Books

Though the above equations do not necessarily determine the functions f uniquely (up to bisimilarity), we can obtain a definition of f by the above equations: graphs can be regarded as infinite trees constructed by the above seven graph constructors (i.e., all the nine graph constructors but @ and **cycle**), and hence the above equations can be taken as a definition by a fixed-point operator.

Thus, f transforms graphs along the structures of graphs; e replaces a label with a new graph, and d (i.e., $\odot$) acts on branches and transforms in sibling directions. The fourth equation is just renaming of input markers and the fifth and sixth equations are cases of multi-rooted graphs; these three equations are straightforward, and so will be omitted in other forms of recursive semantics given later. In the case of the monoid $(\underline{++}, \underline{[]})$—this satisfies PCC with any e—, the above recursive semantics is the same as given in UnCAL (Buneman et al. 2000) except that we treat ordered graphs rather than unordered graphs.

Though the above recursive semantics gives us a definition of the structural recursion, it is not obvious how to make the semantics terminating and that the semantics outputs finite (up to bisimilarity) graphs for given finite input graphs. It is the bulk semantics that shows the termination and finiteness of output graphs; and the bulk semantics satisfies the above equations.

In the following, we give several examples demonstrating the power of our language in transforming ordered graphs. Further examples are given in Sections 4.1 and 5.2.

Example 2. This example shows how we can manipulate edges of the graph and change its shape. The following structural recursion $a2d\_xc$ replaces all labels a with d and contracts c-labeled edges by using the function rc ($r$emove c).

$$\begin{aligned} a2d\_xc &= \mathbf{srec}(rc, \mathbf{foldr}(\underline{++}, \underline{[]})) \\ \mathbf{where}\ rc(l,g) &= \mathbf{if}\ l{=}\mathtt{a}\ \mathbf{then}\ \underline{[}\mathtt{d} : \underline{[\&]}\underline{]} \\ &\qquad \mathbf{else\ if}\ l{=}\mathtt{c}\ \mathbf{then}\ \underline{[\&]}\ \mathbf{else}\ \underline{[}l : \underline{[\&]}\underline{]} \end{aligned}$$

Applying the function $a2d\_xc$ to the graph in Fig. 2(a) yields the graph in Fig. 2(c). Note that $\underline{[\&]}$ can be considered as a hole that will be later filled in with a recursive result. □

Example 3. This example demonstrates that our structural recursion can define transformations in the sibling direction, showing that it is more powerful than the structural recursion in UnCAL. The following function reverses the branches of each node of a graph.

$$\begin{aligned} revBranches &= \mathbf{srec}(idE, \mathbf{foldr}(\underline{\hat{++}}, \underline{[]})) \\ \mathbf{where}\ idE(l,g) &= \underline{[}l : \underline{[\&]}\underline{]} \\ r_1 \underline{\hat{++}} r_2 &= r_2\ \underline{++}\ r_1 \end{aligned}$$ □

Example 4. This example demonstrates the usefulness of nested structural recursion. Figure 6 shows an ordered graph representation of a list of books that contains hierarchical structures with “section”-labeled edges. Since “section”s must be ordered and there would be reference links in books, we can regard books as ordered graphs. The following *nested* structural recursion toc, which is adapted from (Robertson et al. 2009), computes a table-of-contents of books in which sections can be arbitrarily nested:

$$\begin{aligned} toc &= \mathbf{srec}(extractSection, \mathbf{foldr}(\underline{++}, \underline{[]})) \\ \mathbf{where}\ & extractSection(l,g) = \\ &\quad \mathbf{if}\ l{=}\mathtt{section} \\ &\quad \mathbf{then}\ \underline{[}\mathtt{section} : (get\_title(g)\ \underline{++}\ \underline{[\&]})\underline{]} \\ &\quad \mathbf{else}\ \underline{[\&]} \end{aligned}$$

where the function get_title, again defined by a structural recursion, results in the title of the section.

$$\begin{aligned} & get\_title(g) = \mathbf{srec}(extractTitle, \mathbf{foldr}(\underline{++}, \underline{[]})) \\ & \mathbf{where}\ extractTitle(l_1, g_1) = \\ & \quad \mathbf{if}\ l_1{=}\mathtt{title} \\ & \quad \mathbf{then}\ \underline{[}\mathtt{title} : \mathbf{srec}(\lambda(l_2, g_2).\underline{[}l_2 : \underline{[]}\underline{]}, \mathbf{foldr}(\underline{++}, \underline{[]}))\ (g_1)\underline{]} \\ & \quad \mathbf{else}\ \underline{[]} \end{aligned}$$ □

Example 5. We can define complex graph transformations by gluing together smaller ones. Suppose that we want to make a reverse version of the table-of-contents of a book. We can simply define it as

$$tocRev(g) = revBranches\ (toc(g)).$$ □

Before ending the review of λ_{FG}, it is worth remarking that compared with the structural recursion in UnCAL (Buneman et al. 2000), structural recursion in λ_{FG} can deal with ordered graphs and computations on the sibling dimension of graphs; in fact, **srec** in UnCAL does not have the function argument d. As will be seen later, the key to the success of our extension from unordered graphs to ordered ones is a new definition of bisimilarity for ordered graphs having ε-edges, under which (finite) ordered graphs are equivalent to (possibly infinite) regular trees up to bisimilarity.

In the rest of this paper, we will formally define our version of bisimilarity on ordered graphs, give a formal semantics for λ_{FG}, prove the three important properties of λ_{FG}, namely bisimulation genericity, termination, and finiteness-preservation, and demonstrate how to reason about graph transformations.

3. Ordered Graphs and Bisimilarity

As discussed in the introduction, direct manipulation of graphs is difficult. We will tackle this problem by regarding graphs as their equivalent trees so that we can manipulate graphs as if to manipulate trees. To this end, we need to define the semantic equivalence for the graph model of λ_{FG}: bisimilarity between ordered graphs. It should be noticed that ordered graphs have a big problem that does not occur with unordered graphs: i.e., ε-elimination might induce branches with an *infinite* width. In the following, we shall illustrate this problem and show how to define bisimilarity between ordered graphs. We will show an effective procedure to avoid infinite-width graphs.

3.1 Bisimilarity for Ordered Graphs

Let us show some examples of ordered graphs in order to get a feeling for the bisimilarity to be defined. Consider the graphs in Figure 7. Unfolding the graph G_s will yield an infinite tree (the graph in the middle), and performing “ε-elimination” on the infinite tree will give the graph on the right, whose branchings

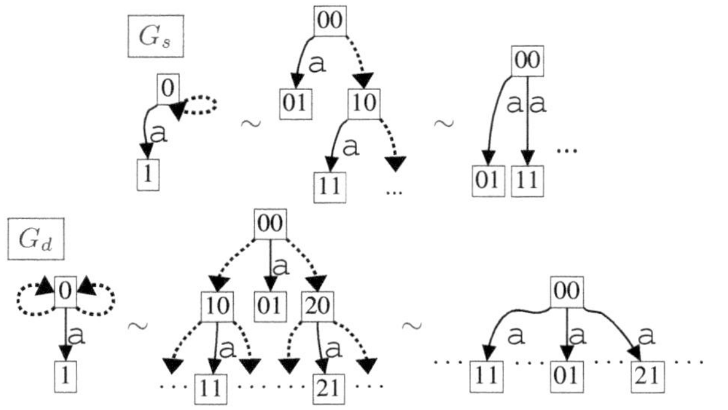

Figure 7. Graphs with Stream Branching and with Dense Branching

look like a stream. However, such infiniteness that occurs in ordered graphs having ε-edges is not just the stream type, as in the next example G_d. Unfolding G_d will yield the tree in the middle, and performing "ε-elimination" will give the graph on the right. This graph has a set of branches behaving like the ordered set $\{n/2^m \in \mathbb{Q} \mid n, m \in \mathbb{N}, 0<n<2^m\}$, which is a dense countable linear ordered set.[1] It is worth noting that, if we were in an unordered setting where the branches are sets (that is, duplications of identical branches are ignored), G_s and G_d after ε-elimination would be bisimilar to the graph with only one branch; consequently, ε-elimination in this case would just delete the ε-loops.

Now let us define bisimilarity between ordered graphs. As can be seen from the above examples, the ε-elimination of an ordered graph might induce a countable width. Therefore, we shall first define a generalized notion of an "ordered graph with a countable width", and then proceed to define bisimilarity for such generalized graphs. To this end, for a set S, we extend the set of lists $List(S)(= \Sigma_{n\in\mathbb{N}} S^n)$ to that of the countable list $CList(S)$ defined as

$$CList(S) \stackrel{\text{def}}{=} \Sigma_{L\in\mathbb{L}} S^L$$

where $\mathbb{N}$ is generalized to $\mathbb{L}$, the set of countable linear ordered sets up to order isomorphism [2]. Replacing $List$ with $CList$, we extend the notion of ordered graph to that of *ordered graph with a countable width*. The set of such extended graphs is denoted by $\mathcal{G}^{\mathrm{c}X}_{Y}$. Certainly, our original ordered graphs $\mathcal{G}^X_Y$ are a subset of $\mathcal{G}^{\mathrm{c}X}_{Y}$.

Once we become aware of the importance of countable linear order, our idea to define bisimilarity between graphs in $\mathcal{G}^{\mathrm{c}X}_{Y}$ is rather simple. Informally, given two graphs, a relation R is a bisimulation relation if for any two R-related nodes v and v', their corresponding *proper branch* sets are related through R. Here a proper branch of a node is defined as a path from v going through zero or more ε-edges and reaching a non-ε-edge.

Now we see the formal definitions. For a branching function $B(v)$, we use $|B(v)|$ to denote the countable linear ordered set L, call $i \in |B(v)|$ *a branch index* of a node v, and write $B(v).i \in \mathcal{L}_\varepsilon \times V + Y$ for the i-th branch.

Definition 6 (Proper Branch). Let $G = (V, B, I) \in \mathcal{G}^{\mathrm{c}X}_{Y}$ and $v \in V$. The path starting from v

$$v\ (= v_0) \stackrel{\varepsilon}{\rightarrow}_{i_0} v_1 \ldots \stackrel{\varepsilon}{\rightarrow}_{i_{n-1}} v_n \rightarrow_{i_n}$$

is called a *proper branch of* v if the i_n-th branch $B(v_n).i_n$ is not an ε-edge; i.e., it is either a non-ε edge or an output marker. The set of all proper branches of v in G is denoted by $\mathrm{Pb}(G, v)$. □

Definition 7 (Order on Proper Branches). Given two proper branches $p = (v \stackrel{\varepsilon}{\rightarrow}_{i_0} v_1 \ldots \stackrel{\varepsilon}{\rightarrow}_{i_{n-1}} v_n \rightarrow_{i_n})$ and $p' = (v \stackrel{\varepsilon}{\rightarrow}_{i'_0} v'_1 \ldots \stackrel{\varepsilon}{\rightarrow}_{i'_{n'-1}} v'_{n'} \rightarrow_{i'_{n'}})$, let their branch index sequences be $\tilde{p} \stackrel{\text{def}}{=} (i_0, \ldots, i_{n-1}, i_n)$ and $\tilde{p'} \stackrel{\text{def}}{=} (i'_0, \ldots, i'_{n'-1}, i'_{n'})$. We define $p \leq_{\mathrm{Pb}} p' \stackrel{\text{def}}{\iff} \tilde{p} \leq_l \tilde{p'}$, where $\leq_l$ is the lexicographical order between branch index sequences. □

Now we are ready to define the bisimilarity.

Definition 8 (Bisimilarity). For two graphs $G = (V, B, I)$ and $G' = (V', B', I')$ in $\mathcal{G}^{\mathrm{c}X}_{Y}$, a relation R between V and V' is called a *bisimulation relation*, if for any vRv', there is an order isomorphism $f\colon (\mathrm{Pb}(G, v), \leq_{\mathrm{Pb}}) \rightarrow (\mathrm{Pb}(G', v'), \leq_{\mathrm{Pb}})$ satisfying the following order-preserving property: For any proper branch $p = (v \stackrel{\varepsilon}{\rightarrow}_{i_0} \ldots v_n \rightarrow_{i_n}) \in \mathrm{Pb}(G, v)$ with $f(p) = (v' \stackrel{\varepsilon}{\rightarrow}_{i'_0} \ldots v'_{n'} \rightarrow_{i'_{n'}}) \in \mathrm{Pb}(G', v')$, we have

- Edge Correspondence: if $B(v_n).i_n = \mathsf{Edge}(l, u)$ for some $l \in \mathcal{L}, u \in V$, then there exists $u' \in V'$ such that $B'(v'_{n'}).i'_{n'} = \mathsf{Edge}(l, u')$ and uRu',
- Marker Correspondence: if $B(v_n).i_n = \mathsf{Outm}(\&y)$ for some $\&y \in Y$, then $B'(v'_{n'}).i'_{n'} = \mathsf{Outm}(\&y)$.

Two graphs G and G' are *bisimilar* (denoted by $G \sim G'$) if there is a bisimulation relation R such that for every input marker $\&x \in X$, $I(\&x)\ R\ I'(\&x)$. □

3.2 Elimination of ε-Edges

The ε-edges are introduced (and necessary) in our internal semantics of graph transformation, but unnecessary ε-edges in the final result should be eliminated. The following definition leads to a procedure to eliminate ε-edges (for example by taking transitive closures) from the graphs and shows that the graph obtained by ε-elimination is bisimilar to the original graph.

Definition 9 (ε-elimination). For a graph $G = (V, B, I) \in \mathcal{G}^{\mathrm{c}X}_{Y}$, the *$\varepsilon$-elimination* ε-elim(G) of G is a graph $(V, B', I) \in \mathcal{G}^{\mathrm{c}X}_{Y}$ where $|B'(v)| \stackrel{\text{def}}{=} \mathrm{Pb}(G, v)$ and $B'(v).p \stackrel{\text{def}}{=} B(v_n).i_n$ for $p = (v \stackrel{\varepsilon}{\rightarrow}_{i_0} \ldots v_n \rightarrow_{i_n})$ in $|B'(v)|$. □

Note that the ε-elimination does not change the sets of nodes.

Proposition 10.

1. For any $G \in \mathcal{G}^{\mathrm{c}X}_{Y}$, ε-elim(G) has no ε-edge, and G and ε-elim(G) are bisimilar.
2. Two graphs $G, G' \in \mathcal{G}^{\mathrm{c}X}_{Y}$ are bisimilar if and only if ε-elim(G) and ε-elim(G') are bisimilar. □

3.3 Decidability of Empty and Finite-Width Graphs

In our graph transformation, i.e., any function from a graph type to a graph type in λ_{FG} like $tocRev$ in Example 5 the input graph is usually an ordered graph that has neither ε-edges nor infinite width, but the result may contain ε-edges in our context. In the following, we show that, given a graph with ε-edges, it is possible to decide whether there is a corresponding bisimilar ordered graph that has neither ε-edges nor infinite width, and there is a procedure to compute out such a bisimilar graph.

Let $\mathrm{FG}_{\not\varepsilon}$ be the set of finite ordered graphs (with finite width and possibly with ε-edges) that are bisimilar to some finite ordered graphs without ε-edge or infinite width. The following procedure

[1] In this paper, the term *countable* includes the finite case.

[2] More precisely, $CList(S)$ is the set of objects of the skeleton of the comma category $(U \downarrow S)$ where $U : \mathbf{CLO} \rightarrow \mathbf{Set}$ is the forgetful functor from the category $\mathbf{CLO}$ of countable linear ordered sets and monotone functions.

answers (decides) whether a finite ordered graph G is in FG$\not\varepsilon$ or not.

1. For each node accessible from a root, check if there is an ε-cycle—a cyclic path consisting only of ε-edges—on the node or not. If there is no ε-cycle, then G is in FG$\not\varepsilon$
2. Otherwise, for every accessible node with an ε-cycle, if there is no proper branch, then graph G is in FG$\not\varepsilon$; otherwise, it is not in FG$\not\varepsilon$.

If G is in FG$\not\varepsilon$, we can effectively eliminate ε-edges; otherwise, it is impossible to eliminate ε-edges and keep the width finite. $\mathbf{isEmpty}(G)$ is true iff G has no non-ε edge in the accessible part, and thus, it is decidable.

Note that this procedure is useful for evaluating $\lambda_{\rm FG}$; though we need ε-edges for the implementation—for structural recursion and for the efficiency of the graph calculation—, practical graphs in the real world have no ε-edges. If a user writes such a practical query, the result should be a graph in FG$\not\varepsilon$; if it is an incorrect query not intended by the user and then if the result has ε-edges, the above procedure can determine this and can warn the user. Note also that, in the FG$\not\varepsilon$ class, since we can eliminate ε-edges, we can use familiar effective procedures for checking bisimilarity and for obtaining the minimum graphs in a similar way to that of unordered graphs.

3.4 Graph Constructors

In Section 2.2.1, we have given an intuitive explanation for our graph constructors; the formal semantics of them should be obvious. As an example, we give the semantic definition of $G_1 \mathbin{\underline{++}} G_2$ (the formal semantics of all graph constructors can be found in Appendix A). For $G_i = (V_i, B_i, I_i) \in \mathcal{G}_Y^X$,

$$G_1 \mathbin{\underline{++}} G_2 \stackrel{\rm def}{=} (V_1 \cup V_2 \cup \{v_1, \ldots, v_m\}, B', I')$$

where

$v_1, \ldots, v_m$ are fresh node identifiers

$\{\&x_1, \ldots, \&x_m\} = Dom(I_1)\ (= Dom(I_2))$

$B' = B_1 \cup B_2 \cup$

$\quad \{v_i \mapsto [\mathsf{Edge}(\varepsilon, I_1(\&x_i)), \mathsf{Edge}(\varepsilon, I_2(\&x_i))] \mid i{=}1, ..., m\}$

$I'(\&x_i) = v_i$.

Above, we assume V_1 and V_2 to be disjoint, which is realized by taking copies of them; recall that node identity is ignored in the context of bisimilarity.

One important property of the graph constructors is that they are bisimulation generic. As an example, consider $G_1 \mathbin{\underline{++}} G_2$; we want to show that $\underline{++}$ is bisimulation generic in the sense that if $G_1 \sim G_1'$ and $G_2 \sim G_2'$, then $G_1 \mathbin{\underline{++}} G_2 \sim G_1' \mathbin{\underline{++}} G_2'$. We say that two graphs are *strongly bisimilar* if they are bisimilar without special treatment of ε-edges (i.e., ε-edges are considered as ordinary edges but labeled ε). It is quite straightforward to see that the graph concatenation constructor $\underline{++}$ is strongly-bisimulation generic. Furthermore, we can see that ε-elim$(G_1 \mathbin{\underline{++}} G_2)$ is bisimilar to ε-elim$(\varepsilon$-elim$(G_1) \mathbin{\underline{++}} \varepsilon$-elim$(G_2))$. This means that strong-bisimulation genericity implies bisimulation genericity for this graph constructor. Similarly we can show other graph constructors are bisimulation generic. This leads to the following proposition.

Proposition 11 (Bisimulation Genericity of Graph Constructors)**.** All the graph constructors are strongly-bisimulation generic and also are bisimulation generic. □

4. Structural Recursion

Here, we give the semantics of our structural recursion; we modify structural recursion for unordered graphs UnCAL (Buneman et al. 2000) to deal with ordered graphs and extend it so that we can transform graphs also in the sibling direction. We start by giving *recursive semantics* of our structural recursion; this enables us to understand the behavior of functions by recursive reasoning. After that, we give the *bulk semantics* of the structural recursion to show the termination and finiteness preserving properties.

Next, we show that our structural recursion and every transformation in $\lambda_{\rm FG}$ are *bisimulation generic*; i.e., they returns bisimilar results for bisimilar inputs. This bisimulation genericity plays an important role in our framework, allowing us to reason about properties of graphs by using (possibly infinite) trees bisimilar to them. To this end, we extend the notion of bisimilarity to higher order functions in Section 4.3 and give the whole semantics of $\lambda_{\rm FG}$.

After that, we will discuss implementation and termination property. Finally, we will summarize relations of conditions and results provided in this section.

Below, we often use the following *marker renaming graphs*: for a "marker renaming" function $f\colon X \to Y$, we define a graph $\lfloor f \rfloor \in \mathcal{G}_Y^X$ as $\lfloor f \rfloor \stackrel{\rm def}{=} \bigoplus_{\&x \in X} \&x := \lfloor f(\&x) \rfloor$. As two use cases, for $G \in \mathcal{G}_Y^X$ with $f: X' \to X$, $\lfloor f \rfloor \mathbin{@} G \in \mathcal{G}_Y^{X'}$ is "input marker renaming" by f: an input marker $f(\&x)$ is replaced with $\&x$ and input markers of G that are not in the image of f are removed. Also, for $G \in \mathcal{G}_Y^X$ with $f: Y \to Y'$, $G \mathbin{@} \lfloor f \rfloor \in \mathcal{G}_{Y'}^X$ is "output marker renaming" by f: an output marker $\&y$ is replaced with $f(\&y)$.

4.1 Recursive Semantics

In Section 2.2.2, we described the recursive semantics of our structural recursion in the simple setting where we ignored output marker cases, assumed production-consumption compatibility (PCC), and restricted d to be the form of $\mathbf{foldr}(\odot, \iota_\odot)$. Here, we will give other forms of recursive semantics, relaxing these restrictions; but we still ignore output marker cases for the sake of simplifying the presentation. (For recursive semantics for the general d without ignoring output markers, see Appendix B.) Hence, in this subsection, the type of d is $\mathbf{List}(\mathbf{G}_{Z\times\alpha}^Z) \to \mathbf{G}_{Z\times\alpha}^Z$. (In bulk semantics, though, we will deal with also output marker cases.)

First, let us explain the polymorphism α in the type of d. This α plays two important roles: It is used to substitute a concrete set for α in order to express recursive semantics and define bulk semantics; it is also used to show bisimulation genericity of the bulk semantics by using relational parametricity. Formally, we should introduce α by formulating $\lambda_{\rm FG}$ as polymorphic typed lambda calculus as well as by introducing sets of markers as types, but to keep the presentation simple, we formulated $\lambda_{\rm FG}$ as a simply typed lambda calculus. In the following explanation of semantics, we will write d_X for the "type application" of d to X on α, and when we interpret $\mathbf{srec}(e, d)$, we introduce the universal quantifier $\forall\alpha.$ for d to bind α. We use the "type application" only in semantics for the above purposes, and do not use syntactically in $\lambda_{\rm FG}$ itself. Thus, $\lambda_{\rm FG}$ is essentially a rank-2 polymorphic lambda calculus; hence, type inference is decidable (Kfoury and Tiuryn 1990).

Now, let us consider recursive semantics of $f = \mathbf{srec}(e, d)$. For general e and d, the straightforward generalization of Equations (1) should be, just in form, as the following:

$$\begin{aligned} & f(\lfloor l_1 : g_1 \rfloor \mathbin{\underline{++}} \cdots \mathbin{\underline{++}} \lfloor l_n : g_n \rfloor) \\ & = d_\emptyset([e(l_1, g_1) \mathbin{@} f(g_1), \ldots, e(l_n, g_n) \mathbin{@} f(g_n)]) . \end{aligned} \tag{2}$$

This equation means that, when we start from the root of a graph, we have the branches $\lfloor l_i : g_i \rfloor$ under the root; then f first computes

$e(l_i, g_i)$ and recursively computes $f(g_i)$; they are connected by @ and finally are transformed in the sibling direction by using d.

However, for general e and d, this recursive semantics is not necessarily correct, i.e., the structural recursion functions defined by bulk semantics given later do not necessarily satisfy this equation. On the other hand, if we evaluate the above recursively, then, since the computation of d depends on $f(g_i)$, and since g_i may include a cyclic path returning to the original root, the evaluation may not terminate. Even if it terminates, the result is not necessarily bisimilar to the result by bulk semantics.

Instead, for general e and d, we have the following recursive semantics.

$$\begin{aligned} & f([l_1 : g_1] +\!\!+ \cdots +\!\!+ [l_n : g_n]) \\ &= d_{\bar{n}}([e(l_1, g_1) @ \lfloor \mathrm{in}_1 \rfloor, \ldots, e(l_n, g_n) @ \lfloor \mathrm{in}_n \rfloor]) \\ &\quad @ \Big((\lfloor \mathrm{iso}_1 \rfloor @ f(g_1)) \oplus \cdots \oplus (\lfloor \mathrm{iso}_n \rfloor @ f(g_n)) \Big) \end{aligned} \tag{3}$$

where $\bar{n} \stackrel{\text{def}}{=} \{1, ..., n\}$, $\mathrm{in}_i : Z \to Z \times \bar{n}$ is defined as $\mathrm{in}_i(\&z) \stackrel{\text{def}}{=} (\&z, i)$, and $\mathrm{iso}_i : Z \times \{i\} \cong Z$ is defined as $\mathrm{iso}_i((\&z, i)) \stackrel{\text{def}}{=} \&z$. This might look a bit complicated, but you can disregard marker-renaming parts $@\lfloor \mathrm{in}_i \rfloor$ and $\lfloor \mathrm{iso}_i \rfloor @$, which are not essential. A noteworthy point in Equation (5) is that d is applied before @ connects $e(l_i, g_i)$ to $f(g_i)$; in Equation (2), the order is reversed.

Now, the PCC condition is naturally introduced as the requirement that the recursive semantics (2) and (3) coincide, i.e., the order of application of d and connecting $e(l_i, g_i)$ with $f(g_i)$ by @ may be interchanged. Formally e: $\mathbf{Label} \times \mathbf{G}_{\emptyset} \to \mathbf{G}_Z^Z$ and d: $\mathbf{List}(\mathbf{G}_{Z \times \alpha}^Z) \to \mathbf{G}_{Z \times \alpha}^Z$ are called *production-consumption compatible (PCC)* if they satisfy the following equation:

$$\begin{aligned} & d_{\emptyset}([e(l_1, g_1) @ g'_1, \ldots, e(l_n, g_n) @ g'_n]) \\ &= d_{\bar{n}}([e(l_1, g_1) @ \lfloor \mathrm{in}_1 \rfloor, \ldots, e(l_n, g_n) @ \lfloor \mathrm{in}_n \rfloor]) \\ &\quad @ \Big((\lfloor \mathrm{iso}_1 \rfloor @ g'_1) \oplus \cdots \oplus (\lfloor \mathrm{iso}_n \rfloor @ g'_n) \Big) \end{aligned}$$

Intuitively, the above condition says that d *consumes* only the information in the graphs *produced* by e and does not traverse beyond the output markers of the graphs produced by e. For example, if we write e such that any $e(l, G)$ has no output markers down to depth three, we can write d that can traverse graphs up to depth three. Note that, if d changes only the positions of graphs in an input list—such positions are regarded as positions of branches—and does not traverse each graph, then d satisfies the PCC condition with any e.

By definition, if e and d satisfy PCC, then $f = \mathbf{srec}(e, d)$ has the recursive semantics (2). Note that, in this paper, we call only the functions defined by the following equivalent semantics *structural recursion functions* (and denoted by $\mathbf{srec}(e, d)$): (i) the bulk semantics (Definition 13), (ii) the recursive semantics (3), and (iii) when PCC holds, the recursive semantics (2) and (1). For example, if e and d do not satisfy PCC, then in this paper we do not call functions defined by the recursive semantics (2) structural recursion functions even if they terminate.

Introducing d is our extension for sibling transformations from the original structural recursion in UnCAL. Note that, no matter whether we use the general recursive semantics (3) or the recursive semantics (2) with PCC, access by d is confined to the graphs produced by e anyway. This is the key restriction on our structural recursion for termination.

Example 12. In this example, d satisfies PCC with any e. To remove the even branches of a graph, we can apply $even\_remove \stackrel{\text{def}}{=} \mathbf{srec}(e, d)$ where $e(l, g) \stackrel{\text{def}}{=} [l : \&]$; and $d([]) \stackrel{\text{def}}{=} []$, $d([g]) \stackrel{\text{def}}{=} g$, and $d(g :: g' :: gs) \stackrel{\text{def}}{=} g +\!\!+ d(gs)$.

In the next example, e and d do not satisfy PCC, but we still can reason that this works as expected from the recursive semantics (3). To contract the even edges of a graph, from (3), it is enough that e is an "identity" and d contracts even labeled edges; i.e., we can apply $even\_contract \stackrel{\text{def}}{=} \mathbf{srec}(e, d)$ where

$$\begin{aligned} & e(l, g) \stackrel{\text{def}}{=} [l : \&], \quad d([]) \stackrel{\text{def}}{=} [], \quad d([g]) \stackrel{\text{def}}{=} g, \\ & d(g :: g' :: gs) \stackrel{\text{def}}{=} g +\!\!+ p(g') +\!\!+ d(gs), \\ & p \stackrel{\text{def}}{=} srec(\lambda(l, g).[\&], \mathbf{foldr}(+\!\!+, [])) \ : \ \mathbf{G}_{\{\&\} \times \alpha}^{\{\&\}} \to \mathbf{G}_{\{\&\} \times \alpha}^{\{\&\}}. \end{aligned}$$

4.2 Bulk Semantics

Here, we give bulk semantics of the structural recursion $\mathbf{srec}(e, d)$ for a general d not assuming PCC nor ignoring output markers.

Before giving the formal definition of the bulk semantics of $\mathbf{srec}(e, d)$, we illustrate the behavior of the semantics in an example $a2d\_xc \stackrel{\text{def}}{=} \mathbf{srec}(rc, \mathbf{foldr}(+\!\!+, []))$ (see Example 2 for rc). Mainly, an evaluation with the bulk semantics consists of three steps; we start with the input graph (a) in Figure 8.

1. *Applying the Map Computation on Edges with e*

   We apply the function rc (which renames a-labeled edges as d-labeled ones and contracts the c-labeled edges) to every l-labeled edge and the graph g following the edge, to yield a graph in $\mathcal{G}_Z^Z$. Let us call the graphs produced by an expression e *e-graphs*. Graph (b) is a graph whose edges are labeled by rc-graphs.

2. *Applying Map Computation on Nodes with d*

   For each edge—from a node v to a node v'—of Graph (b), we replace every output marker $\&z$ of the e-graph with a pair $(\&z, v')$, which will be used in the next "grouping" step. Next, for every node v of Graph (b), we use binary operator $+\!\!+$ to combine all e-graphs which are labels of the branches of v. Let us call the graphs produced using d ($= \mathbf{foldr}(+\!\!+, [])$) *d-graphs*; Graph (c) shows the result. Nodes 1 and 4 have more than one branch which need to be merged using $+\!\!+$. After producing the d-graph for v, we replace each input marker $\&z$ with a pair $(\&z, v)$.

3. *Grouping New Graphs with ε-Edges*

   Now, for each node of Graph (b)—equivalently, for each node of the original graph—, we have a d-graph produced as above. We group all these d-graphs in Graph (c) by connecting every output marker $(\&z, v)$ of every d-graph to the corresponding input node of some d-graph by using an ε-edge. The root of the new graph is that of the d-graph on the original root node. Thereby, we get Graph (d) as an evaluation result of the structural recursion. Graph (e) is the graph obtained by performing ε-elimination on Graph (d). We remark that ε-elimination may increase the number of non-ε edges as this example. (We can further minimize Graph (e) if necessary, resulting the graph in Figure 2(c).)

Before applying a structural recursion function $\mathbf{srec}(e, d)$ to G, we have to perform ε-elimination on G; if ε-$\mathrm{elim}(G)$ has infinite width, we raise an error. Without the ε-elimination, if we extend the bulk semantics to treat input graphs having ε-edges by extending e to $\bar{e}(\varepsilon, g) \stackrel{\text{def}}{=} \lfloor \mathrm{id}_Z \rfloor$, then the $\mathbf{srec}(\bar{e}, d)$ is not necessarily bisimulation generic, as shown by the following counter example. The two graphs on the left are bisimilar, but if we apply the structural recursion function $even\_remove$ in Example 12, the resulting graphs are not bisimilar.

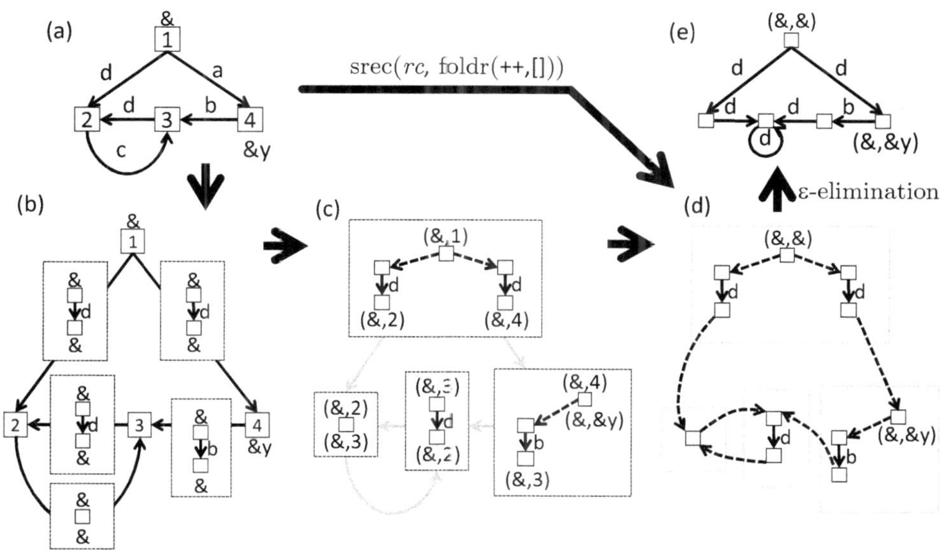

Figure 8. Bulk Semantics of Structural Recursion: An Example of $\mathbf{srec}(rc, \mathbf{foldr}(\underline{+\!\!+}, \underline{[]}))$

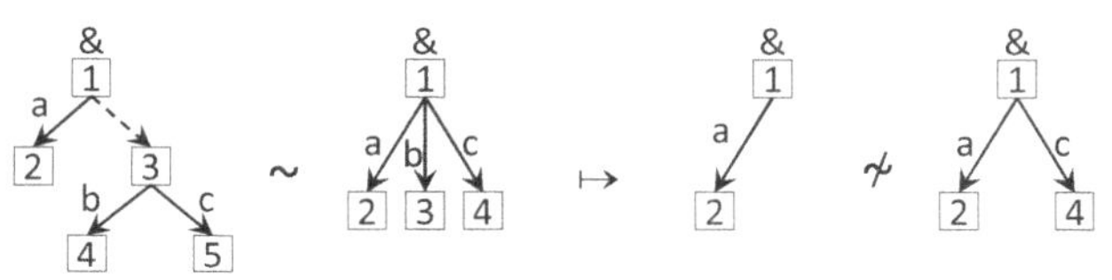

Though, if $d = \mathbf{foldr}(\underline{+\!\!+}, \underline{[]})$ or $d = \mathbf{foldr}(\hat{\underline{+\!\!+}}, \underline{[]})$ (reverse function), then we can show the bisimulation genericity without performing ε-elimination.

Now let us give the formal definition of the bulk semantics of the structural recursion. Note that the following definition is more concise than the one given in (Asada et al. 2012), which mimics the original bulk semantics of UnCAL given in (Buneman et al. 2000); and this simplification makes the proof of bisimulation genericity clearer.

Definition 13 (Bulk Semantics)**.** For functions

$$e\colon \mathcal{L}\times\mathcal{G}_Y \to \mathcal{G}_Z^Z \quad d\colon \forall\alpha.List(\mathcal{G}_{Z\times\alpha}^Z+\mathcal{G}_{Z\times Y}^Z) \to \mathcal{G}_{Z\times\alpha+Z\times Y}^Z,$$

a *structural recursion function* $\mathbf{srec}(e,d)\colon \mathcal{G}_Y^X \to \mathcal{G}_{Z\times Y}^{Z\times X}$ is defined as follows.

Let $G = (V, B, I)$ be a graph in $\mathcal{G}_Y^X$. As explained above, we perform ε-elimination on G in order to ensure bisimulation genericity; hence, we assume G has no ε-edges Let us define $\tilde{e}\colon \mathcal{L}\times V \to \mathcal{G}_Z^Z$ as $e \circ (\mathrm{id}_{\mathcal{L}}\times G|_{(\text{-})})$, where $G|_{(\text{-})}\colon V \to \mathcal{G}_Y$ extracts the subgraph of G whose root is a given node: i.e., $G|_v \stackrel{\text{def}}{=} (V, B, \{\&\mapsto v\})$.

Then, as in the first step explained above, we construct a new branching function $B' \stackrel{\text{def}}{=} \mathbf{map}(\langle\tilde{e},\pi_2\rangle+\mathrm{id}_Y) \circ B$ of type

$$V \xrightarrow{B} List(\mathcal{L}\times V+Y) \xrightarrow{\mathbf{map}(\langle\tilde{e},\pi_2\rangle+\mathrm{id}_Y)} List(\mathcal{G}_Z^Z\times V+Y).$$

This corresponds to a step producing Graph (b) in Figure 8.

As for the second step, first, we construct a function $d'_\alpha \stackrel{\text{def}}{=} d_\alpha \circ \mathbf{map}(p+q)$ of type

$$List(\mathcal{G}_Z^Z\times\alpha+Y) \xrightarrow{\mathbf{map}(p+q)} List(\mathcal{G}_{Z\times\alpha}^Z+\mathcal{G}_{Z\times Y}^Z) \xrightarrow{d_\alpha} \mathcal{G}_{Z\times\alpha+Z\times Y}^Z$$

where $p(G, \&a) \stackrel{\text{def}}{=} G \mathbin{@} \lfloor \&z \mapsto (\&z, \&a)\rfloor$ and $q(\&y) \stackrel{\text{def}}{=} \lfloor \&z \mapsto (\&z, \&y)\rfloor$. Next, by using the following bijective correspondence,

$$oplus : (V\to\mathcal{G}_{Z\times V+Z\times Y}^Z) \xrightarrow{\cong} \mathcal{G}_{Z\times V+Z\times Y}^{Z\times V},$$

$$oplus(f) \stackrel{\text{def}}{=} \bigoplus_{(\&z,v)\in Z\times V}(\&z, v) := (\lfloor\&z\rfloor \mathbin{@} f(v))$$

we obtain a graph $G' \stackrel{\text{def}}{=} oplus(d'_V \circ B') \in \mathcal{G}_{Z\times V+Z\times Y}^{Z\times V}$, which corresponds to (c) in Figure 8; then, in correspondence with (d) in Figure 8, we define

$$\mathbf{srec}(e,d)(G) \stackrel{\text{def}}{=} \lfloor\mathrm{id}_Z\times I\rfloor \mathbin{@} \mathbf{cycle}(G') \quad (\in \mathcal{G}_{Z\times Y}^{Z\times X}).$$

□

It is worth remarking that the above bulk semantics is essentially *root-independent*: the whole part except for the final step—i.e., till constructing $\mathbf{cycle}(G')$—does not use the input function I.

The following is clear from the above bulk semantics.

Proposition 14. *If the functions e and d map finite graphs to finite graphs, so does* $\mathbf{srec}(e,d)$.

From the above bulk semantics, we can show obviously the termination property of λ_{FG}. We can implement the above bulk semantics in an obvious way: We may represent graphs (X, Y, V, B, I) using "set" and "map" (implemented as, e.g., balanced trees); X, Y, and V are as "set"s, and B and I are as "map"s. Then implementation of the bulk semantics is straightforward. It is clear that the computation of the bulk semantics terminates by the above definition and the finiteness on nodes and width of graphs, which is ensured by the above proposition. Our actual implementation in OCaml can be found at `http://www.biglab.org/src/lambdaFG/`; note that d in $\mathbf{srec}$ in the implementation is currently restricted to the form $\mathbf{foldr}(\odot, \iota_\odot)$.

4.3 Semantics of λ_{FG} and Bisimilarity on Functions

Before proving the bisimulation genericity of the structural recursion, we will summarize the whole semantics of λ_{FG}.

A requirement of our semantics is that it should guarantee that any transformation—including the one using higher order functions—in λ_{FG} must be bisimulation generic. To this end, we extend the notion of bisimilarity on graphs to bisimilarity on functions in λ_{FG}. We have defined bisimilarity for graph types $\mathbf{G}_Y^X$, and we can use the equality relations for the other basic types. It is well known that, if we want to lift equivalence relations to function types, we need to switch from the notion of an equivalence relation to that of a *partial equivalence relation*, i.e., equivalence relation on some *subset* of the original set. This is because, in the current case, it is not true that all functions on $\mathcal{G}\mathrm{f}_Y^X$ are bisimulation generic, so we have to focus on its *subset* consisting of bisimulation generic functions.

Formally, for types σ of λ_{FG}, we define binary *logical relations* $\sim_\sigma$ from the above equivalence relations on the base types. Let us recall the logical relation $\sim_\sigma$ only in the essential case, i.e., function types: $\sigma = \sigma_1 \to \sigma_2$ (for other cases, one can consult (Mitchell 1996)). We define a binary relation $\sim_\sigma$ on $[\![\sigma]\!] \overset{\mathrm{def}}{=} [\![\sigma_1]\!] \to [\![\sigma_2]\!]$ as

$$f \sim_\sigma f' \overset{\mathrm{def}}{\iff} \forall x, x' \in [\![\sigma_1]\!].\ (x \sim_{\sigma_1} x' \Rightarrow f(x) \sim_{\sigma_2} f'(x')).$$

For any type σ, $\sim_\sigma$ becomes a partial equivalence relation on $[\![\sigma]\!]$, i.e., an equivalence relation on the subset $|{\sim_\sigma}| \overset{\mathrm{def}}{=} \{x \in [\![\sigma]\!] \mid x \sim_\sigma x\}$. We say a function $f\colon [\![\sigma_1]\!] \to [\![\sigma_2]\!]$ *bisimulation generic* if f is in $|{\sim_{\sigma_1 \to \sigma_2}}|$.

Now from the Basic Lemma of the logical relation (Mitchell 1996), interpretations of all the terms are bisimulation generic if interpretations of all the constants (including constant functions) are bisimulation generic; accordingly, we can form a model (a cartesian closed category) of λ_{FG} such that the interpretations of types are the quotient sets of the partial equivalence relations. We have already shown the bisimulation genericity of graph constructors, and now we will show the same for the structural recursion.

4.4 Bisimulation Genericity of the Structural Recursion

We prove a stronger statement of bisimulation genericity than the original one in (Buneman et al. 2000), which proves only first-order bisimulation genericity, i.e., only bisimulation genericity on graph arguments. In addition, our proof is much clearer than the original naive proof. This simplification should make further extensions of structural recursion easier.

Theorem 15 (Bisimulation Genericity of $\mathbf{srec}$). *The higher order function* $\mathbf{srec}$ *is bisimulation generic; i.e., for* $e_1 \sim e_2$, $d_1 \sim d_2$, *and* $G_1 \sim G_2$, $\mathbf{srec}(e_1, d_1)(G_1) \sim \mathbf{srec}(e_2, d_2)(G_2)$.

We will use the following notions and notations in the proof of the above theorem. We write $R : A_1 \mathrel{-\!\!\!+\!\!\!-} A_2$ for a relation $R \subseteq A_1 \times A_2$; e.g., the diagram on the left below means that if $a_1\, R\, a_2$, then $f_1(a_1)\, S\, f_2(a_2)$.

$$\begin{array}{ccc} A_1 & \xrightarrow{f_1} & B_1 \\ {\scriptstyle R}\,\Big| & & \Big|\,{\scriptstyle S} \\ A_2 & \xrightarrow[f_2]{} & B_2 \end{array} \qquad \begin{array}{ccccc} X_1 & \xrightarrow{I_1} & V_1 & \xrightarrow{B_1} & CList(\mathcal{L}\times V_1 + Y_1) \\ {\scriptstyle S}\,\Big| & & {\scriptstyle R}\,\Big| & & \Big|\,{\scriptstyle CList(\mathcal{L}\times R+T)} \\ X_2 & \xrightarrow[I_2]{} & V_2 & \xrightarrow[B_2]{} & CList(\mathcal{L}\times V_2 + Y_2) \end{array}$$

For $S : X_1 \mathrel{-\!\!\!+\!\!\!-} X_2$ and $T : Y_1 \mathrel{-\!\!\!+\!\!\!-} Y_2$, let us define the relation $\sim_T^S\colon \mathcal{G}_{Y_1}^{X_1} \mathrel{-\!\!\!+\!\!\!-} \mathcal{G}_{Y_2}^{X_2}$: for G_i, let $(V_i, B_i, I_i) = \varepsilon\text{-elim}(G_i)$, then $G_1 \sim_T^S G_2$ if there exists a relation $R : V_1 \mathrel{-\!\!\!+\!\!\!-} V_2$ such that the right diagram above commutes (i.e., each of the two squares is true). We write simply X for the diagonal relation between X and X, then note that $\sim_Y^X\colon \mathcal{G}_Y^X \mathrel{-\!\!\!+\!\!\!-} \mathcal{G}_Y^X$ is the same as $\sim$.

Proof. Let G_i be (V_i, B_i, I_i). From $G_1 \sim G_2$, there exists $R : V_1 \mathrel{-\!\!\!+\!\!\!-} V_2$ such that the following diagram commutes.

$$\begin{array}{ccccc} X & \xrightarrow{I_1} & V_1 & \xrightarrow{B_1} & List(\mathcal{L}\times V_1 + Y) \\ \Big\| & & {\scriptstyle R}\,\Big| & & \Big|\,{\scriptstyle List(\mathcal{L}\times R+Y)} \\ X & \xrightarrow[I_2]{} & V_2 & \xrightarrow[B_2]{} & List(\mathcal{L}\times V_2 + Y) \end{array} \qquad (4)$$

Next, from the assumption that $e_1 \sim e_2$ and $d_1 \sim d_2$, the following diagram commutes.

$$\begin{array}{ccccccc} V_1 & \xrightarrow{B_1} & List(\mathcal{L}\times V_1 + Y) & \xrightarrow{\mathbf{map}(\langle \tilde{e_1}, \pi_2\rangle + \mathrm{id}_Y)} & List(\mathcal{G}_Z^Z \times V_1 + Y) & \xrightarrow{d'_{1\,V_1}} & \mathcal{G}_{Z\times V_1 + Z\times Y}^Z \\ {\scriptstyle R}\,\Big| & & {\scriptstyle List(\mathcal{L}\times R+Y)}\,\Big| & & {\scriptstyle List(\sim_Z^Z \times R+Y)}\,\Big| & & {\scriptstyle \sim_{Z\times R+Z\times Y}^Z}\,\Big| \\ V_2 & \xrightarrow[B_2]{} & List(\mathcal{L}\times V_2 + Y) & \xrightarrow[\mathbf{map}(\langle \tilde{e_2}, \pi_2\rangle + \mathrm{id}_Y)]{} & List(\mathcal{G}_Z^Z \times V_2 + Y) & \xrightarrow[d'_{2\,V_2}]{} & \mathcal{G}_{Z\times V_2 + Z\times Y}^Z \end{array}$$

Note that to show the right square above, we also use the relational parametricity of d_i and hence of d'_i; see Definition 13 for the definition of d'_i. Then, for the above compositions, transposing V_i by using *oplus* as in Definition 13 yields

$$\begin{array}{ccc} 1 & \xrightarrow{G'_1} & \mathcal{G}_{Z\times V_1 + Z\times Y}^{Z\times V_1} \\ \Big\| & & \Big|\,{\scriptstyle \sim_{Z\times R+Z\times Y}^{Z\times R}} \\ 1 & \xrightarrow[G'_2]{} & \mathcal{G}_{Z\times V_2 + Z\times Y}^{Z\times V_2} \end{array} \quad \text{i.e.,}\quad G'_1 \sim_{Z\times R+Z\times Y}^{Z\times R} G'_2. \qquad (5)$$

After that, we can show that

$$\mathbf{cycle}(G'_1) \sim_{Z\times Y}^{Z\times R} \mathbf{cycle}(G'_2), \qquad (6)$$

and from the left square of the diagram (4) we get

$$\lfloor \mathrm{id}_Z \times I_1 \rfloor \ @\ \mathbf{cycle}(G'_1) \sim_{Z\times Y}^{Z\times X} \lfloor \mathrm{id}_Z \times I_2 \rfloor \ @\ \mathbf{cycle}(G'_2)$$

i.e., $\mathbf{srec}(e_1, d_1)(G_1) \sim \mathbf{srec}(e_2, d_2)(G_2)$. □

For readers familiar with category theory, we will elaborate a bit on the general technique behind Equation (6). From the correspondence $Y \mapsto \mathcal{G}_Y$, we can construct a monad on $\mathbf{Set}$; then $\mathbf{cycle}$ becomes an *iteration operator* (dual of fixed point operator) in its Kleisli category. Furthermore, the iteration operator is uniform on values (i.e., functions). The above Equation (6) from Equation (5) is then the uniformity principle on relations (Hasegawa 2002).

4.5 Remark

We conclude this section with a summary of some conditions that we assumed occasionally. (Ignoring output marker cases is just for presentation and not essential.)

We use PCC to obtain more familiar form of recursive semantics (2), and moreover we assumed d to be in the fold form of monoid to obtain simpler recursive semantics (1). The PCC condition and its recursive semantics are also used for optimization given in Section 5.1.

The polymorphism of α of d is used to express recursive semantics and define bulk semantics, and its parametricity is used to prove the bisimulation genericity of the bulk semantics. The preprocessing of ε-elimination for input graphs of structural recursion functions is also used to prove the bisimulation genericity.

Termination and node-finiteness preserving properties of the structural recursion was shown via the bulk semantics, and essentially comes from the suitable restriction of recursion pattern; our structural recursion still has rich expressive power (see Section 5.2) and enables systematic optimization by the recursive semantics (see Section 5.1).

5. Discussion

5.1 Optimization of λ_{FG} Programs

Embedding graph queries into lambda calculus as structural recursions would make query optimization easier and more systematic. This is not only because existing optimization techniques for functional programs can be directly brought in, but also because structural recursion itself has nice algebraic properties for optimization.

Here, we illustrate the usefulness of structural recursion in reasoning and manipulating graph queries with two known transformation techniques, fusion and tupling.

Fusion Transformation Fusion (or called deforestation) (Meijer et al. 1991; Gill et al. 1993; Takano and Meijer 1995) is an important program transformation to turn a composition of two structural recursions into one so that unnecessary intermediate data passed from one structural recursion to another can be removed. The following is our fusion rule showing that a composition of a function f and a structural recursion $\mathbf{srec}(e, d)$ can be merged into one as long as the PCC condition holds for e and d:

$$f \circ \mathbf{srec}(e, d) \;=\; \mathbf{srec}(e' \circ e, d')$$

holds, provided that f is promoted on d and demoted on @; i.e., for some f', we have

$$f \circ d = d' \circ \mathbf{map}\; f' \quad \text{and} \quad f'(g \mathbin{@} r) = e'(g) \mathbin{@} f(r).$$

Tupling Transformation Tupling (Hu et al. 1997) is another important optimization technique. It eliminates multiple traversals of the same data. Our following tupling transformation rule reduces two traversals of G given by two structural recursions into one.

$$\begin{array}{l} (\&x_1 := \mathbf{srec}(e_1, d_1)(G)) \oplus (\&x_2 := \mathbf{srec}(e_2, d_2)(G)) \\ = \mathbf{srec}(e, d)(G) \\ \quad \mathbf{where} \\ \qquad \begin{array}{lcl} e\,(l, g) & = & (\&x_1 := (e_1(l, g) \mathbin{@} \lfloor \&x_1 \rfloor)) \\ & \oplus & (\&x_2 := (e_2(l, g) \mathbin{@} \lfloor \&x_2 \rfloor)) \\ d\; gs & = & (\&x_1 := d_1(\mathbf{map}\;(\lambda g.\lfloor \&x_1 \rfloor \mathbin{@} g)\; gs)) \\ & \oplus & (\&x_2 := d_2(\mathbf{map}\;(\lambda g.\lfloor \&x_2 \rfloor \mathbin{@} g)\; gs)) \end{array} \end{array}$$

The new structural recursion basically computes in parallel two graphs marked by $\&x_1$ and $\&x_2$. Note that the tuple construction and projection that are used in the ordinary tupling technique are encoded here by the disjoint union ($\oplus$) and marker renaming: a pair "(g_1, g_2)" is by $(\&x_1 := (g_1 \mathbin{@} \lfloor \&x_1 \rfloor)) \oplus (\&x_2 := (g_2 \mathbin{@} \lfloor \&x_2 \rfloor))$, and a projection "$\pi_i(g)$" is by $\lfloor \&x_i \rfloor \mathbin{@} g$.

5.2 Expressive Power of λ_{FG}

In the previous sections, we described the definition and properties of λ_{FG}, and showed some interesting query examples. In this section, we discuss the expressive power of λ_{FG} from the user's point of view, to show that λ_{FG} can serve as a basis of query languages on ordered graphs under bisimulation.

As has already been demonstrated by Buneman et al. (2000) in the unordered setting, nesting of $\mathbf{srec}$ can produce a sequence of combinations of label and graph variable bindings $(\lambda(l_1, g_1), \lambda(l_2, g_2), \ldots)$. We can combine this nesting with conditionals on these variables to express variety of join conditions. For example, two nested structural recursions can extract subgraphs following consecutive edges with identical labels. Moreover, regular path expressions of labels can be expressed by $\mathbf{srec}$ with a body e generating multiple roots via tupling (Hu et al. 1997), as shown in Section 5.1. Such an e can be systematically constructed from the regular path expressions of labels via finite state automata, as in Buneman et al. (2000) (while NFA is used in (Buneman et al. 2000), we need DFA to make the result well-defined). These kinds of queries in λ_{FG} can be concisely expressed by using a more user-friendly syntactic sugar like UnQL for UnCAL in (Buneman et al. 2000) (although we do not give any concrete desugaring rules here) so that users do not have to write nested structural recursions with multiple root expressions manually. For example,

$$\mathbf{select}\; e\; \mathbf{where}\; \lfloor path{:}g \rfloor\; \mathbf{in}\; db$$

binds the graph variable g to every subgraph pointed to by a regular path expression $path$ from the root of the graph that db is bound to,

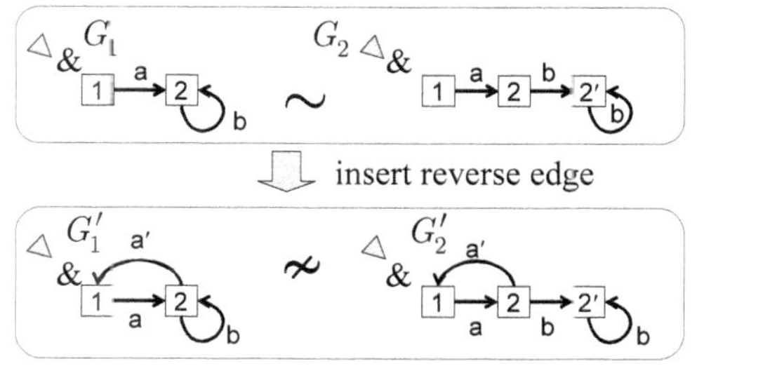

Figure 9. insertion of reverse edge

and will join (++) the graphs generated by the expression e that refers the graph variable g.

It is worth noting that, in case of extracting subgraphs under regular path pattern, we just shortcut the edges with unmatching labels like in the **else** clause of $extractSection$ in Example 4. If there is a cycle of these unmatching labels (labels other than `section` in the example) above the matching subgraph, then the cycle turns into an ε-cycle, meaning that the result of query represents infinite number of that subgraphs. This infinity is no surprising since original input graph essentially includes infinite number of that subgraphs when the cycle is unfolded. The infinity in the result is reported by ε-elimination error in λ_{FG}. Interestingly, this exhibits the expressive power of λ_{FG} to *detect cyclic patterns* specified by the automata mentioned above. For example, $extractSection$ corresponds to automata on the right, which includes a cycle. If this cycle and the ones in the input graph matches, then an ε-cycle is produced.

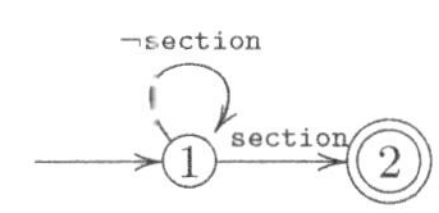

Expressive Power on Sibling Dimension With the parameter d of type $\mathbf{List}(\mathbf{G}^{Z}_{Z\times\alpha} + \mathbf{G}^{Z}_{Z\times Y}) \rightarrow \mathbf{G}^{Z}_{Z\times\alpha+Z\times Y}$ in $\mathbf{srec}$ we can express not only queries such as extracting subgraphs as mentioned above, but also those manipulating siblings of nodes, like reversal (Example 2), removing and contracting even-numbered siblings (Example 12).

Expressiveness under Bisimilarity Equivalence Since our language is bisimulation generic, targeting graphs under bisimilarity equivalence, queries that distinguish bisimilar graphs are not expressible. For example, we cannot count the number of nodes, since two bisimilar graphs may have different numbers of nodes. As another example, we cannot insert a 'reverse' edge. For example, in Figure 9, the graph G_2 is obtained from G_1 by unfolding the cycle formed by the edge labeled `b` at node 2; hence so G_1 and G_2 are bisimilar. The bisimulation relation $S : G_1.\mathrm{V} \times G_2.\mathrm{V}$ is $\{(1, 1), (2, 2), (2, 2')\}$. Now suppose we insert for every `a`-labeled edge a reversed `a'`-labeled edge like in G'_1 and G'_2. Notice the difference between outgoing edges from node 2 and those from node $2'$. In G'_1, there is an outgoing edge `a'` from node 2. However, in G'_2, there is no such edge from node $2'$. So G'_1 and G'_2 are not bisimilar anymore. The essential reason for this bisimulation genericity violation is that the reverse edge on a node is inserted on *incoming* edges while bisimulation is determined by *outgoing* edges. So bisimilar nodes are treated differently.

It would be interesting to combine λ_{FG} with the predicate of bisimilarity on graphs. Since (for ε-eliminable graphs) the bisimilarity is decidable, we can readily introduce such predicate in λ_{FG} and express queries that identify nodes in terms of their bisimilarity.

6. Related Work

Our structural recursion for ordered graphs is very much related to research on algebras of programming (Meijer et al. 1991; Bird and de Moor 1996; Hu et al. 2006), where structural recursions such as folds and catamorphisms are used to structure programs and systematically manipulate programs. In particular, our approach is influenced by the many attempts at defining structural recursions for specific graphs, such as graphs represented by trees with specific pointers (Hamana 2009; Dal Zilio et al. 2004; Oliveira and Cook 2012) and graphs represented by trees with embedded functions (Fegaras and Sheard 1996). However, they do not ensure all of the bisimulation genericity, terminating property, and finiteness preserving property, which are our original goals as explained in the introduction.

In the database community, structural recursion is an important primitive in database queries. Rewriting rules for optimization can be obtained by exploiting axiom of languages based on structural recursion. Although it works for various data models such as relations (Breazu-Tannen et al. 1991), nested collections (Wong 1994), unordered graphs (Buneman et al. 2000), and ordered trees (Robertson et al. 2009), structural recursion for querying ordered graphs has not been established yet.

As described in the introduction, our work was inspired by the structural recursion in UnCAL (Buneman et al. 2000) that is practically used for manipulating unordered graphs. We borrow from database community the idea of how to restrict a structural recursion for infinite regular trees so that a structural recursion for finite graphs preserves finiteness of graphs and becomes terminating, which are desirable properties for query languages. We solve the open problem of dealing with ordered graphs by providing a novel definition of bisimulation relation for ordered graphs. To enhance the expressive power to deal with transformation among children graphs, we extend the original structural recursion from $\mathbf{srec}(e)$ to $\mathbf{srec}(e, d)$ so that d can be used to combine results among children.

A lot of work has been devoted to efficient implementation of graph algorithms in lazy functional languages (Burton and Yang 1990; King and Launchbury 1995; Erwig 1997; Johnsson 1998). The emphasis there is placed on the importance of achieving efficient implementation of general graph algorithms through the monadic model for including actions on the state in the non-strict context. In contrast, we focus on inductive traversals of ordered graphs and aim to provide an efficient way to deal with a specific class of important graph algorithms—graph querying. In addition, unlike the above where graph equivalences are up to isomorphism, our graph equivalences are up to bisimilarity and all our transformations are guaranteed to be bisimulation generic.

Algebraic graph transformations (Ehrig et al. 2006) formalize graph transformations using categories in which objects are graphs and graph patterns to be matched, and matching be graph morphisms. A step of transformations is realized by a pushout complement followed by a pushout in the double-pushout approach. Category theory is elegantly used in the proofs and various constructions like transformation rule compositions. In contrast to our graph model, their graph model is based on graph isomorphism, and order between outgoing edges are not considered.

Picard and Matthes (2012) deal with node-labeled graphs using coinductive data types in Coq proof assistant. Although outgoing edges of their graphs are also ordered and graph equivalence based on bisimulation is considered, ε-edges are not considered.

Our decision procedure on ε-eliminability under finite-width in Section 3.3 is close to the eliminability of ε-transition cycles of weighted automata in Lombardy and Sakarovitch (2012). However, while eliminability of ε-transition cycle in the weighted automata is determined solely by the weight of the ε-edge (whether the weight is starable), we also consider the presence of proper branches. Note also that there is no notion of order between transitions in Lombardy and Sakarovitch (2012), so our ε-elimination cannot be derived from that of weighted automata.

The treatment for ε-edges in the current paper was inspired by (Jacobs 2010). Although there was no consideration of ε-edge itself in that study, the author showed that the trace semantics for some kinds of coalgebra induces iteration operators by forgetting the length of trace paths; the resulting iteration operators can be regarded as ε-elimination. The countable list monad $CList$ is not treated in that paper (or in any literature to the best of our knowledge); it does not satisfy the assumption of the theorem in that paper. Since our definition of bisimilarity agrees with (strong) bisimilarity defined generally by coalgebra theory if graphs contain no ε-edges, Proposition 10 suggests that our bisimilarity for graphs having ε-edges can be equivalently defined by the combination of the usual strong bisimulation and ε-elimination. In this viewpoint, our essential contribution in Sections 3.1 and 3.2 is that we define and exploit $CList$ and define the ε-elimination.

This paper is also related to our another submission (Asada et al. 2013), which also treats an extension of UnCAL. In the current paper, we provide a novel solution to the problem of querying over the ordered graphs, while Asada et al. (2013) shows that the solution can be *partially* generalized with less expressiveness of queries. More specifically, the two papers are technically independent in the following two points. First, though Asada et al. (2013) shows that branch patterns of graphs can be generalized by using monads, the generalization assumes the existence of a monad with an iteration operator. For ordered graph case, the definition of the monad $CList$ with its iteration operator (i.e., the ε-elimination) is the very contribution of the current paper, and Asada et al. (2013) just use the result to include ordered graph case as an example of the generalization. The other point is that the current paper is not an instantiation of Asada et al. (2013); though the current paper extends the structural recursion with d for sibling transformations, it is not achieved in Asada et al. (2013). Also, the decidability of ε-eliminability is not generalized in Asada et al. (2013).

7. Conclusions and Future Work

We presented the first solution to the open problem of how to modify the graph model and structural recursion from unordered graphs to ordered ones and defined a new graph transformation language λ_{FG} for doing so. The key technical contributions are a novel definition of a bisimulation relation on ordered graphs having ε-edges and an extension of structural recursion with an operation for combining sibling results to achieve expressive power on the sibling dimension. We implemented λ_{FG} and showed two important optimization rules.

There are many interesting future paths of study. First, we should analyse structural recursion more thoroughly; for instance, we should examine the circumstances under which structural recursion is productive. A structural recursion is said to be productive, if it produces a finite ordered graph without ε-edges (i.e., $\mathrm{FG}_{\not\varepsilon}$ defined in Section 3.3) for any input ordered graph without ε-edge. Second, following our previous work on bidirectionalizing UnCAL (Hidaka et al. 2010), we are very interested in developing a systematic way to bidirectionalize λ_{FG}.

Acknowledgments

We would like to thank Kazutaka Matsuda for various comments to the current and earlier versions of the paper. We also would like to thank the anonymous reviewers of the present and earlier versions for their thorough comments and constructive suggestions to improve the paper. The research was supported in part by the Grand-Challenging Project on the "Linguistic Foundation for Bidirectional Model Transformation" of the National Institute of Informatics, and a Grant-in-Aid for Scientific Research for Encouragement of Young Scientists (B) No. 20700035, and a Grant-in-Aid for Scientific Research (B) No. 22300012.

References

K. Asada, S. Hidaka, H. Kato, Z. Hu, and K. Nakano. Parameterized graph transformation languages with monads. Technical Report GRACE-TR-2012-07, GRACE Center, National Institute of Informatics, 2012. `http://www.biglab.org/papers.html`.

K. Asada, S. Hidaka, H. Kato, Z. Hu, and K. Nakano. A parameterized graph transformation calculus for finite graphs with monadic branches, 2013. To appear in PPDP'13.

R. Bird and O. de Moor. *Algebras of Programming*. Prentice Hall, 1996.

V. Breazu-Tannen, P. Buneman, and S. Naqvi. Structural recursion as a query language. In *Proc. of the Third International Workshop on Database Programming Languages(DBPL 91)*, pages 9–19, 1991.

P. Buneman, M. F. Fernandez, and D. Suciu. UnQL: a query language and algebra for semistructured data based on structural recursion. *VLDB Journal: Very Large Data Bases*, 9(1):76–110, 2000.

F. W. Burton and H.-K. Yang. Manipulating multilinked data structures in a pure functional language. *Softw. Pract. Exper.*, 20:1167–1185, November 1990.

S. Dal Zilio, D. Lugiez, and C. Meyssonnier. A logic you can count on. POPL'04, pages 135–146, New York, NY, USA, 2004. ACM.

H. Ehrig, K. Ehrig, U. Prange, and G. Taentzer. *Fundamentals of Algebraic Graph Transformation*. Springer-Verlag, 2006.

M. Erwig. Functional programming with graphs. ICFP '97, pages 52–65, New York, NY, USA, 1997. ACM.

L. Fegaras and T. Sheard. Revisiting catamorphisms over datatypes with embedded functions. POPL '96, St. Petersburg Beach, Florida, Jan. 1996.

J. Gibbons. An initial-algebra approach to directed acyclic graphs. In *Mathematics of Program Construction*, MPC '95, pages 282–303, London, UK, 1995. Springer-Verlag.

A. Gill, J. Launchbury, and S. P. Jones. A short cut to deforestation. In *Proc. Conference on Functional Programming Languages and Computer Architecture*, pages 223–232, Copenhagen, June 1993.

S. Ginali. Regular trees and the free iterative theory. *J. Comput. Syst. Sci.*, 18(3):228–242, 1979.

M. Hamana. Initial algebra semantics for cyclic sharing structures. TLCA '09, pages 127–141, Berlin, Heidelberg, 2009. Springer-Verlag.

M. Hasegawa. The uniformity principle on traced monoidal categories. *Electr. Notes Theor. Comput. Sci.*, 69:137–155, 2002.

S. Hidaka, Z. Hu, K. Inaba, H. Kato, K. Matsuda, and K. Nakano. Bidirectionalizing graph transformations. In *ACM SIGPLAN International Conference on Functional Programming*, pages 205–216. ACM, 2010.

S. Hidaka, Z. Hu, H. Kato, K. Matsuda, K. Nakano, and I. Sasano. Marker-directed Optimization of UnCAL Graph Transformations. In *LOPSTR'11*, volume 7225 of *LNCS*, pages 123–138. Springer, 2012.

Z. Hu, H. Iwasaki, M. Takeichi, and A. Takano. Tupling calculation eliminates multiple data traversals. ICFP'97, pages 164–175, Amsterdam, The Netherlands, June 1997. ACM Press.

Z. Hu, T. Yokoyama, and M. Takeichi. Program optimizations and transformations in calculational form. In *Summer School on Generative and Transformational Techniques in Software Engineering*, pages 139–164, Braga, Portugal, 2006. Springer, LNCS 4043.

B. Jacobs. From coalgebraic to monoidal traces. *Electronic Notes in Theoretical Computer Science*, 264(2):125 – 140, 2010. Proceedings of the Tenth Workshop on Coalgebraic Methods in Computer Science (CMCS 2010).

T. Johnsson. Efficient graph algorithms using lazy monolithic arrays. *J. Funct. Program.*, 8:323–333, July 1998.

F. Jouault and J. Bézivin. KM3: A DSL for metamodel specification. In *Formal Methods for Open Object-Based Distributed Systems*, pages 171–185. LNCS 4037, Springer, 2006.

A. J. Kfoury and J. Tiuryn. Type reconstruction in finite-rank fragments of the polymorphic lambda-calculus (extended summary). In *LICS*, pages 2–11, 1990.

D. J. King and J. Launchbury. Structuring depth-first search algorithms in Haskell. POPL '95, pages 344–354, New York, 1995. ACM.

S. Lombardy and J. Sakarovitch. The removal of weighted ε-transitions. CIAA'12, pages 345–352. Springer-Verlag, 2012.

E. Meijer, M. Fokkinga, and R. Paterson. Functional programming with bananas, lenses, envelopes and barbed wire. In *Proc. Conference on Functional Programming Languages and Computer Architecture* (LNCS 523), pages 124–144, Cambridge, Massachuetts, Aug. 1991.

J. C. Mitchell. *Foundations for programming languages*. Foundation of computing series. MIT Press, 1996.

B. C. Oliveira and W. R. Cook. Functional programming with structured graphs. ICFP '12, pages 77–88, New York, 2012. ACM.

C. Picard and R. Matthes. Permutations in Coinductive Graph Representation. In D. Pattinson and L. Schröder, editors, *Coalgebraic Methods in Computer Science*, volume 7399 of *LNCS*, pages 218–237. Springer, 2012.

E. L. Robertson, L. V. Saxton, D. V. Gucht, and S. Vansummeren. Structural recursion as a query language on lists and ordered trees. *Theory of Computing Systems*, 44(4):590–619, 2009.

A. Takano and E. Meijer. Shortcut deforestation in calculational form. FPCA '95, pages 306–313, New York, 1995. ACM.

L. Wong. *Querying Nested Collections*. PhD thesis, Philadelphia, PA, USA, 1994.

A. Semantics of Graph Constructors

Figure 10 summarizes the semantic definitions of all graph constructors in λ_{FG}. In the definitions of $\underline{+\!\!+}$, $\oplus$, and $@$, we assume V_1 and V_2 to be disjoint, which is realized by taking copies of them.

The semantics should be easy to understand with the help of Figure 5 and the intuitive explanations given in Section 2.2.1.

B. Recursive Semantics with Output Markers

In Section 4.1, we gave recursive semantics by omitting output marker case. Throughout here, we consider general case with output markers. Hence, the typing rule is the one in Figure 4.

Now we will give both cases with and without PCC, whose definition will be given at the end. Before that, let us see more simple case, i.e., in addition to PCC, we assume that, for some monoid $(\odot, \iota_\odot)$ on $\mathbf{G}^Z_{Z\times\alpha+Z\times Y}$,

$$d = \mathbf{foldr}(\odot\ \iota_\odot) \circ \mathbf{List}([p,q]) \qquad : \mathbf{List}(\mathbf{G}^Z_{Z\times\alpha}+\mathbf{G}^Z_{Z\times Y}) \rightarrow \mathbf{G}^Z_{Z\times\alpha+Z\times Y}$$

where $p \stackrel{\text{def}}{=} (\text{-})\ @\ \lfloor \mathrm{in_l} \rfloor : \mathbf{G}^Z_{Z\times\alpha} \rightarrow \mathbf{G}^Z_{Z\times\alpha+Z\times Y}$ and $q \stackrel{\text{def}}{=} (\text{-})\ @\ \lfloor \mathrm{in_r} \rfloor : \mathbf{G}^Z_{Z\times Y} \rightarrow \mathbf{G}^Z_{Z\times\alpha+Z\times Y}$. Then, a structural recursion function $f \stackrel{\text{def}}{=} \mathbf{srec}(e,d)$ characterized by the following recursive semantics:

$$\begin{array}{lcl} f(\underline{[]}) & = & \iota_\odot \\ f(g_1 \mathbin{\underline{+\!\!+}} g_2) & = & f(g_1) \odot f(g_2) \\ f(\underline{[}l : g\underline{]}) & = & e(l,g)\ @\ f(g) \\ f(\underline{[}\&y\underline{]}) & = & \lfloor \&z \mapsto (\&z, \&y) \rfloor \\ f(\&x := g) & = & (\oplus_{\&z\in Z}(\&z, \&x) := \underline{[}(\&z, \&)\underline{]})\ @\ f(g) \\ f(()) & = & () \\ f(g_1 \oplus g_2) & = & f(g_1) \oplus f(g_2). \end{array} \tag{7}$$

The fourth equation is the new one for the output marker case. The meaning should be quite easy to understand, and the following more general versions are essentially the same as this.

$$
\begin{array}{lcl}
\underline{[]} & = & (\{root\}, \{root \mapsto []\}, \{\& \mapsto root\}) \textbf{ where } root \text{ is a fresh node} \\
G_1 \mathbin{\underline{++}} G_2 & = & \textbf{let } (V_1, B_1, I_1) = G_1;\ (V_2, B_2, I_2) = G_2 \\
 & & \quad \{\&x_1, \ldots, \&x_m\} = Dom(I_1)\ (= Dom(I_2)) \\
 & & \quad v_1, \ldots, v_m \text{ are fresh node identifiers} \\
 & & \quad B' = B_1 \cup B_2 \cup \\
 & & \qquad \{v_i \mapsto [\mathsf{Edge}(\varepsilon, I_1(\&x_i)), \mathsf{Edge}(\varepsilon, I_2(\&x_i))] \mid i = 1, \ldots, m\} \\
 & & \quad I'(\&x_i) = v_i \\
 & & \textbf{in } (V_1 \cup V_2 \cup \{v_1, \ldots, v_m\}, B', I') \\
\underline{[l : G]} & = & \textbf{let } (V, B, I) = G \\
 & & \quad root \text{ is a fresh node} \\
 & & \textbf{in } (V \cup \{root\}, B \cup \{root \mapsto [\mathsf{Edge}(l, I(\&))]\}, \{\& \mapsto root\}) \\
\underline{[\&y]} & = & (\{v\}, \{v \mapsto [\mathsf{Outm}(\&y)]\}, \{\& \mapsto v\}) \textbf{ where } v \text{ is a fresh node} \\
\&x := G & = & \textbf{let } (V, B, I) = G \textbf{ in } (V, B, \{\&x \mapsto I(\&)\}) \\
G_1 \oplus G_2 & = & \textbf{let } (V_1, B_1, I_1) = G_1;\ (V_2, B_2, I_2) = G_2 \\
 & & \textbf{in } (V_1 \cup V_2, B_1 \cup B_2, I_1 \cup I_2) \\
() & = & (\{\}, \{\}, \{\}) \\
G_1 \mathbin{@} G_2 & = & \textbf{let } (V_1, B_1, I_1) = G_1;\ (V_2, B_2, I_2) = G_2 \\
 & & \quad B'(v_1 (\in V_1)) = [\mathit{fillOutm}\ b \mid b \leftarrow B_1(v_1)] \\
 & & \qquad \textbf{where } \mathit{fillOutm}\ (\mathsf{Edge}(l', v')) = \mathsf{Edge}(l', v') \\
 & & \qquad\qquad \mathit{fillOutm}\ (\mathsf{Outm}(\&y)) = \mathsf{Edge}(\varepsilon, I_2(\&y)) \\
 & & \quad B'(v_2 (\in V_2)) = B_2(v_2) \\
 & & \textbf{in } (V_1 \cup V_2, B', I_1) \\
\textbf{cycle}(G) & = & \textbf{let } (V, B, I) = G \\
 & & \quad B'(v) = [\ \mathit{cyclize}\ b \mid b \leftarrow B(v)] \\
 & & \qquad \textbf{where } \mathit{cyclize}\ (\mathsf{Edge}(l', v')) = \mathsf{Edge}(l', v') \\
 & & \qquad\qquad \mathit{cyclize}\ (\mathsf{Outm}(\&y)) = \textbf{if } \&y \notin Dom(I) \textbf{ then } \mathsf{Outm}(\&y) \\
 & & \qquad\qquad\qquad \textbf{else } \mathsf{Edge}(\varepsilon, I(\&y)) \\
 & & \textbf{in } (V, B', I)
\end{array}
$$

Figure 10. Semantics of Graph Constructors

Now let us see another recursive semantics, with relaxing assumptions. For e and d satisfying PCC, we have the following recursive semantics.

$$
\begin{aligned}
& f(\mathbin{\underline{++}}_{i=1}^{n} \begin{Bmatrix} \underline{[l_i : g_i]} \\ \underline{[\&y_i]} \end{Bmatrix}) \\
&= d_Y ([\begin{Bmatrix} \mathrm{in_l}(e(l_i, g_i) \mathbin{@} f(g_i)) \\ \mathrm{in_r}(\lfloor \&z \mapsto (\&z, \&y_i) \rfloor) \end{Bmatrix}]_{i=1}^{n}) \mathbin{@} \lfloor \nabla_{Z \times Y} \rfloor
\end{aligned} \tag{8}
$$

where $[x_i]_{i=1}^n$ is comprehension representation of a list $[x_1, ..., x_n]$. The above equation is read as follows: for each i on the left hand side, the content of $\{\text{-}\}$ is upper or lower; then on the right hand side, for each i, according to the case on the left hand side, we think the upper or lower.

Compare the above with the following recursive semantics given in Section 4.1, where we omit the case of output markers:

$$
\begin{aligned}
& f(\underline{[l_1 : g_1]} \mathbin{\underline{++}} \ldots \mathbin{\underline{++}} \underline{[l_n : g_n]}) \\
&= d_{\emptyset}([e(l_1, g_1) \mathbin{@} f(g_1), ..., e(l_n, g_n) \mathbin{@} f(g_n)]).
\end{aligned}
$$

In Section 4.1, as well as assuming Y to be $\emptyset$, we simplified the typing of d

$$
\begin{array}{ll}
\text{from} & d : \mathbf{List}(\mathbf{G}^Z_{Z \times \alpha} + \mathbf{G}^Z_{Z \times Y}) \to \mathbf{G}^Z_{Z \times \alpha + Z \times Y} \\
\text{to} & d : \mathbf{List}(\mathbf{G}^Z_{Z \times \alpha}) \to \mathbf{G}^Z_{Z \times \alpha}
\end{array}
$$

hence we did not need to use $\mathrm{in_l}$ and ∇ in Equation (8).

For general d without assuming PCC, we have the following recursive semantics.

$$
\begin{aligned}
& f(\mathbin{\underline{++}}_{i=1}^{n} \begin{Bmatrix} \underline{[l_i : g_i]} \\ \underline{[\&y_i]} \end{Bmatrix}) \\
&= d_n ([\begin{Bmatrix} \mathrm{in_l}(e(l_i, g_i) \mathbin{@} \lfloor \&z \mapsto (\&z, \&i) \rfloor) \\ \mathrm{in_r}(\lfloor \&z \mapsto (\&z, \&y_i) \rfloor) \end{Bmatrix}]_{i=1}^{n}) \\
&\quad \mathbin{@} ((\textstyle\bigoplus_{i=1}^{n} \lfloor \mathrm{iso}_i \rfloor \mathbin{@} \begin{Bmatrix} f(g_i) \\ \underline{[]} \end{Bmatrix}) \oplus \lfloor \mathrm{id}_{Z \times Y} \rfloor)
\end{aligned} \tag{9}
$$

where $\mathrm{iso}_i : Z \times \{i\} \cong Z$.

Production-Consumption Compatibility The PCC condition is defined as follows: e: $\mathbf{Label} \times \mathbf{G}_Y \to \mathbf{G}^Z_Z$ and d: $\mathbf{List}(\mathbf{G}^Z_{Z \times \alpha} + \mathbf{G}^Z_{Z \times Y}) \to \mathbf{G}^Z_{Z \times \alpha + Z \times Y}$ are called *production-consumption compatible (PCC)* if they satisfy the following: For any n, suppose that, for each $i \in n$, $l_i \in \mathcal{L}$, $G_i \in \mathbf{G}_Y$, and $G'_i \in \mathbf{G}^Z_{Z \times Y}$ are given, or $\&y \in Y$ is given. Then the following equation holds

$$
\begin{aligned}
& d_Y ([\begin{Bmatrix} \mathrm{in_l}(e(l_i, G_i) \mathbin{@} G'_i) \\ \mathrm{in_r}(\lfloor \&z \mapsto (\&z, \&y) \rfloor) \end{Bmatrix}]_{i=1}^{n}) \mathbin{@} \lfloor \nabla_{Z \times Y} \rfloor \\
&= d_n ([\begin{Bmatrix} \mathrm{in_l}(e(l_i, G_i) \mathbin{@} \lfloor \&z \mapsto (\&z, i) \rfloor) \\ \mathrm{in_r}(\lfloor \&z \mapsto (\&z, \&y) \rfloor) \end{Bmatrix}]_{i=1}^{n}) \\
&\quad \mathbin{@} ((\textstyle\bigoplus_{i=1}^{n} \lfloor \mathrm{iso}_i \rfloor \mathbin{@} \{ {}^{G'_i}_{\underline{[]}} \}) \oplus \lfloor \mathrm{id}_{Z \times Y} \rfloor)
\end{aligned}
$$

where $\nabla_{Z \times Y} : Z \times Y + Z \times Y \to Z \times Y$ and $\mathrm{iso}_i : Z \times \{i\} \cong Z$.

Modular Monadic Meta-Theory

Benjamin Delaware
University of Texas at Austin
bendy@cs.utexas.edu

Steven Keuchel Tom Schrijvers
Ghent University
{steven.keuchel,tom.schrijvers}@ugent.be

Bruno C. d. S. Oliveira
The University of Hong Kong
bruno@cs.hku.hk

Abstract

This paper presents 3MT, a framework for *modular* mechanized meta-theory of languages with *effects*. Using 3MT, individual language features and their corresponding definitions – *semantic functions*, *theorem statements* and *proofs* – can be built separately and then reused to create different languages with fully mechanized meta-theory. 3MT combines *modular datatypes* and *monads* to define denotational semantics with effects on a per-feature basis, without fixing the particular set of effects or language constructs.

One well-established problem with *type soundness* proofs for denotational semantics is that they are notoriously brittle with respect to the addition of new effects. The statement of type soundness for a language depends intimately on the effects it uses, making it particularly challenging to achieve modularity. 3MT solves this long-standing problem by splitting these theorems into two separate and reusable parts: a *feature theorem* that captures the well-typing of denotations produced by the semantic function of an individual feature with respect to only the effects used, and an *effect theorem* that adapts well-typings of denotations to a fixed superset of effects. The proof of type soundness for a particular language simply combines these theorems for its features and the combination of their effects. To establish both theorems, 3MT uses two key reasoning techniques: *modular induction* and *algebraic laws* about effects. Several effectful language features, including references and errors, illustrate the capabilities of 3MT. A case study reuses these features to build fully mechanized definitions and proofs for 28 languages, including several versions of mini-ML with effects.

Categories and Subject Descriptors D.3.1 [*Programming Languages*]: Formal Definitions and Theory—Semantics

General Terms Languages

Keywords mechanized meta-theory; modularity; monads; side-effects

1. Introduction

Theorem provers are actively used to mechanically verify large-scale formalizations of critical components, including programming language meta-theory [1], compilers [25], large mathematical proofs [15] and operating system kernels [23]. Due to their scale and complexity, these developments can be quite time consuming, often demanding multiple man-years of effort.

It is reasonable to expect that variations can simply extend and reuse the original development in order to leverage the large investment of resources in these formalizations. This is unfortunately often not the case, as even small extensions can require significant additional effort. Adding a new language feature to a programming language formalization or compiler, for example, involves significant redesigns that have a cross-cutting impact on nearly all definitions and proofs in the formalization. This leads to a copy-paste-patch approach to reuse with several modified copies of the original development, making it difficult to compose new features and ultimately leading to a maintenance nightmare. Dissatisfied with this situation, several researchers [1, 15, 43, 44] have called for better ways to modularize mechanical formalizations.

This work extends the current state-of-the-art in modular mechanizations by solving a well-known and long-standing open problem with denotational semantics: type soundness proofs are notoriously brittle with respect to the addition of new effects. This is an important problem because effects are pervasive in programming language formalizations: in addition to extensions to syntax and semantics, new features usually introduce new effects to the denotations. Without a more robust formulation of type soundness, the addition of new effects requires cross-cutting changes to type soundness theorem statements and proofs.

Initially the semantics themselves were also brittle with respect to effects [24, 32], but *monads* [31, 50] have been found to provide the necessary robustness to denotations. Yet as far as we know, the brittleness of (denotational) type soundness proofs has remained an open problem since it was raised by Wright and Felleisen [53] to motivate their own type-soundness approach. The framework we present here, *modular monadic meta-theory* (3MT), is the first in 20 years to provide a substantial solution. Using 3MT, we develop a novel approach to proving type soundness for monadic denotational semantics in a way that is modular in the set of effects used. Proofs for individual features do not depend on effects they do not use and hence are robust to extension.

The solution builds on Meta-Theory à la Carte (MTC) [9], a Coq framework for the mechanization of formal programming language meta-theory that supports modular extension of existing definitions. With MTC it is possible to develop meta-theory which is modular in two dimensions: *language features* on the one hand and *functions* and *proofs* over these features on the other hand. MTC adapts ideas from existing programming language solutions [34, 46] to the *expression problem* [51] for functions and features, and adds *modular induction* for proofs.

3MT adds a third modularity dimension to MTC: modular addition of new *effects*. 3MT enables the separate definition of features with effectful semantic functions and proofs over these functions, and reuse of these features in formalizations of multiple languages.

ICFP '13, September 25–27, 2013, Boston, MA, USA.
Copyright © 2013 ACM 978-1-4503-2326-0/13/09... $15.00.
http://dx.doi.org/10.1145/2500365.2500587

To make denotations robust with respect to effects, 3MT uses the established solution, *monads*. In Coq, *type classes* [52] enable semantic function definitions that are constrained, yet polymorphic in the monad. This allows the inclusion of a feature in any language which supports a superset of its effects. When a language is composed from different effectful features, *monad transformers* [28] are used to instantiate the denotation's monad with all the effects required by the modular components.

To solve the key challenge of modularizing and reusing theorems and proofs of type soundness, we split the classic type soundness theorems into three parts:

1. Reusable *feature theorems* capture the essence of type soundness for an individual feature. They depend only on that feature's syntax, typing relation, semantic function and the effects used therein. At the same time, they abstract over the syntax, semantics and effects of other features. This means that the addition of new features with other types of effects *does not affect* the existing feature theorem proofs.
   To achieve the abstraction over other effects, a feature uses a constrained polymorphic monad. As a consequence, it only establishes the well-typing of the resulting denotations with respect to the effects declared in the constraints.
2. Reusable *effect theorems* fix the monad of denotations and consequently the set of effects. They take well-typing proofs of monadic denotations expressed in terms of a constrained polymorphic monad and which mention only a subset of effects, and turn them into well-typings with respect to a fixed monad and all the effects it provides.
   Effect theorems reason fully at the level of denotations and abstract over the details of language features like syntax and semantic functions.
3. Finally, *language theorems* establish type soundness for a particular language. They require no more effort than to instantiate the set of features and the set of effects (i.e., the monad), thus tying together the respective feature and effect theorems into an overall proof.

To establish the first two theorems, 3MT relies on modular induction and algebraic laws about effects. As far as we know, it applies the most comprehensive set of such laws to date, as each effect utilized by a feature needs to be backed up by laws and interactions between different effects must also be governed by laws. These laws are crucial for modular reasoning in the presence of effects.

In summary, the specific contributions of this work are:

- A reusable framework, 3MT, for mechanized meta-theory of languages with effects. This framework includes a mechanized library for monads, monad transformers and corresponding algebraic laws in Coq. Besides several laws for specific types of effects, the library also includes laws for the interactions between different types of effects.
- A new *modular* proof method for type-soundness proofs of denotational semantics.
- A case study of a family of fully mechanized languages, including a mini-ML variant with errors and references. The case study comprises 28 languages, 8 different effect theorems and 5 features with their feature theorems.

3MT is implemented in the Coq proof assistant and the code is available at `http://www.cs.utexas.edu/~bendy/3MT`.

Code and Notational Conventions While all the code underlying this paper has been developed in Coq, the paper adopts a terser syntax for its many code fragments. For the computational parts, this syntax exactly coincides with Haskell syntax, while it is an extrapolation of Haskell syntax style for propositions and proof concepts. Following MTC, the Coq code requires the impredicative-set option due to the use of Church encodings.

2. Background: Meta-Theory à la Carte

This section summarizes the necessary parts of the *Meta-Theory à la Carte* (MTC) approach to modular datatypes in Coq. For the full details of MTC, we refer the reader to the original paper [9].

2.1 Mendler Church Encodings and Folds for Semantics

MTC encodes data types and folds with a variant of Church encodings [5, 36] based on Mendler folds [47]. The advantage of Mendler folds is that recursive calls are explicit, allowing the user to precisely control the evaluation order. The Mendler-Church encodings represent (least) fixpoints and folds as follows:

$$\mathbf{type}\ Algebra_M\ f\ a = \forall r.(r \rightarrow a) \rightarrow f\ r \rightarrow a$$
$$\mathbf{type}\ Fix_M\ f = \forall a.Algebra_M\ f\ a \rightarrow a$$
$$\begin{aligned}&fold_M :: Algebra_M\ f\ a \rightarrow Fix_M\ f \rightarrow a\\ &fold_M\ alg\ fa = fa\ alg\end{aligned}$$

Mendler algebras ($Algebra_M\ f\ a$) use a function argument of type ($r \rightarrow a$) for their recursive calls. To enforce structurally recursive calls, arguments which appear at recursive positions have a polymorphic type r. Using this polymorphic type prevents case analysis, or any type of inspection, on those arguments. Mendler-Church encodings ($Fix_M\ f$) are functions of type $\forall a.Algebra_M\ f\ a \rightarrow a$. Mendler folds are defined by directly applying a Church encoded value fa to a Mendler algebra alg. All these definitions are non-recursive and can thus be expressed in Coq.

Example As a simple example, consider a language for boolean expressions supporting boolean literals and conditionals:

$$\mathbf{data}\ Logic_F\ e = BLit\ Bool \mid If\ e\ e\ e$$
$$\mathbf{type}\ Value = Bool$$

The evaluation algebra for this language is defined as follows:

$$\begin{aligned}&ifAlg :: Algebra_M\ Logic_F\ Value\\ &ifAlg\ [\![\cdot]\!]\ (BLit\ b) \quad\ \ = b\\ &ifAlg\ [\![\cdot]\!]\ (If\ e_1\ e_2\ e_3) = \mathbf{if}\ [\![e_1]\!]\ \mathbf{then}\ [\![e_2]\!]\ \mathbf{else}\ [\![e_3]\!]\end{aligned}$$

Unlike conventional Church encodings and folds, the recursive calls ($[\![\cdot]\!]$) are explicit and indicate the evaluation order.
The evaluation function simply folds the *ifAlg* algebra:

$$\begin{aligned}&eval :: Fix_M\ Logic_F \rightarrow Value\\ &eval = fold_M\ ifAlg\end{aligned}$$

2.2 Modular Composition of Features

MTC adapts the *Data Types à la Carte* (DTC) [46] approach for composing f-algebras to Mendler algebras.

Modular Functors Because feature syntax is defined by means of functors, such as $Logic_F$, it can easily be composed with functor composition:

$$\mathbf{data}\ (\oplus)\ f\ g\ a = Inl\ (f\ a) \mid Inr\ (g\ a)$$

The syntax of a language of both conditional and simple arithmetic expressions, for example, is $Fix\ (Arith_F \oplus Logic_F)$ where

$$\mathbf{data}\ Arith_F\ e = Lit\ Int \mid Add\ e\ e$$

Feature semantics are expressed as Mendler algebras and can be composed in a similar way.

Type Classes Unlike DTC, MTC defines a number of type classes with laws in order to support proofs. These classes and laws are summarized in the table in Figure 1. The second column notes whether the base instances of a particular class are provided by the user or are automatically inferred with a default instance. Importantly, instances of all these classes for feature compositions (using $\oplus$) are built automatically.

Class Definition	Description
class $Functor\ f$ **where** $fmap :: (a \to b) \to (f\ a \to f\ b)$ $fmap\_id :: fmap\ id \equiv id$ $fmap\_fusion :: \forall g\ h.$ $fmap\ h \circ fmap\ g \equiv fmap\ (h \circ g)$	**Functors** Supplied by the user
class $f \prec: g$ **where** $inj :: f\ a \to g\ a$ $prj :: g\ a \to Maybe\ (f\ a)$ $inj\_prj :: prj\ ga \equiv Just\ fa \to$ $ga \equiv inj\ fa$ $prj\_inj :: prj \circ inj \equiv Just$	Functor Subtyping Inferred
class $(Functor\ f, Functor\ g, f \prec: g) \Rightarrow$ $WF\_Functor\ f\ g$ **where** $wf\_functor :: \forall a\ b\ (h :: a \to b).$ $fmap\ h \circ inj \equiv inj \circ fmap\ h$	Functor Delegation Inferred
class $(Functor\ h, f \prec: h, g \prec: h) \Rightarrow$ $DistinctSubFunctor\ f\ g\ h$ **where** $inj\_discriminate :: \forall a\ (fe :: f\ a)$ $(ge :: g\ a).inj\ fe \not\equiv inj\ ge$	Functor Discrimination Inferred
class $FAlg\ name\ t\ a\ f$ **where** $f\_algebra : Mixin\ t\ f\ a$	**Function Algebras** Supplied by the user
class $(f \prec: g, FAlg\ n\ t\ a\ f, FAlg\ n\ t\ a\ g) \Rightarrow$ $WF\_FAlg\ n\ t\ a\ f\ g$ **where** $wf\_algebra :: \forall rec\ (fa :: f\ t).$ $f\_algebra\ rec\ (inj\ fa) \equiv$ $f\_algebra\ rec\ fa$	Algebra Delegation Inferred
class $(Functor\ f, Functor\ g, f \prec: g) \Rightarrow$ $PAlg\ name\ f\ g\ a$ **where** $p\_algebra :: Algebra\ f\ a$ $proj\_eq :: \forall e.\pi_1\ (p\_algebra\ e) \equiv$ $in_f\ (inj\ (fmap\ \pi_1\ e))$	**Proof Algebras** Supplied by the User

Figure 1. Type classes provided by 3MT

The *Functor* class provides the *fmap* method and is an adaptation of the corresponding type class in Haskell. In contrast with the Haskell version, the two functor laws are part of the definition. The class $\prec:$ represents a subtyping relation between two functors f and g. This class is an adaptation of the corresponding class in DTC and it includes two additional laws which govern the behavior of functor projection and injection (inj_prj and prj_inj). The class $WF\_Functor$ ensures that *fmap* distributes through injection, and the class *DistinctSubFunctor* ensures that injections from two different subfunctors are distinct. Unlike DTC, MTC defines a single generic Coq type class, *FAlg*, for the definition of semantic algebras. *FAlg* is indexed by the name of the semantic function (*name*). Note that the type *Mixin*:

$$\textbf{type}\ Mixin\ t\ f\ a = (t \to a) \to f\ r \to a$$

is a slight generalization of Mendler algebras, which is useful for defining non-inductive language features such as general recursion or higher-order binders. The type class WF_FAlg provides a well-formedness condition for every composite algebra. Finally, the type class *PAlg* provides the definitions for proof algebras.

2.3 Modular Proofs

The main novelty of MTC is its modular approach to inductive proofs. Regular structural induction is not available for Church encodings, so MTC adapts the proof methods used in the *initial algebra semantics of data types* [14, 29] – in particular *universal properties* – to support modular inductive proofs over Church encodings. Proofs are written in the same modular style as functions, using proof algebras (class *PAlg* in Figure 1). These algebras are folded over the terms and can be modularly combined. Unlike function algebras, proof algebras are subject to an additional constraint which ensures the validity of the proofs ($proj\_eq$).

Sublemmas Each feature builds extensible datatypes by abstracting them over a super-functor. Because this super-functor is abstract, the complete set of cases needed by a proof algebra is unknown within a feature. To perform induction, a feature must therefore dispatch proofs to an abstract proof algebra over this super-functor. The components of this proof algebra are built in a distributed fashion among individual features. These components can then be composed to build a complete proof algebra for a concrete composition of functors.

As an example, consider the lemma that the type equality function *eqType* is sound:

$$\forall t_1\ t_2.eqType\ t_1\ t_2 \equiv true \to t_1 \equiv t_2 \qquad (EqP)$$

This property can be captured in a proof algebra:

$$PAlg\ EqF_{name}\ f\ f\ (\exists\ e : EqP\ e)$$

A feature can build a proof of *EqP* for a specific type t by folding this proof algebra over t. Features also provide specific instances of this proof algebra for the types they introduce:

$$PAlg\ EqF_{name}\ TBool_F\ f\ (\exists\ e : EqP\ e)$$

A concrete language with boolean and natural types provides a proof algebra of the lemma by composing the proof algebras for the two separate type functors and instantiating the super-functor f to $TNat_F \oplus TBool_F$. By instantiating f to other functor compositions, the proof algebras of the individual features can easily be reused in other languages.

2.4 No Effect Modularity

Unfortunately, effect modularity is not supported in MTC. Consider two features: mutable references Ref_F and errors Err_F. Both of these introduce an effect to any language, the former state and the latter the possibility of raising an error. These effects show up in the type of their evaluation algebras:

$$eval_{Ref} :: Algebra_M\ Ref_F\ (Env \to (Value, Env))$$
$$eval_{Err} :: Algebra_M\ Err_F\ (Maybe\ Value)$$

MTC supports the composition of two algebras over different functors as long as they have the same carrier. That is not the case here, making the two algebras incompatible. This problem can be solved by anticipating both effects in both algebras:

$$eval_{Ref} :: Algebra_M\ Ref_F\ (Env \to (Maybe\ Value, Env))$$
$$eval_{Err} :: Algebra_M\ Err_F\ (Env \to (Maybe\ Value, Env))$$

This anticipation is problematic for modularity: the algebra for references mentions the effect of errors even though it does not involve them, while a language that includes references does not necessarily feature errors. More importantly, the two algebras cannot be composed with a third feature that introduces yet another effect (e.g., local environments) without further foresight. It is impossible to know in advance all the effects that new features may introduce.

3. The 3MT Monad Library

3MT includes a monad library to support effectful semantic functions using *monads* and *monad transformers*, and provides *algebraic laws* for reasoning. Monads provide a uniform representation for encapsulating computational effects such as mutable state, exception handling, and non-determinism. Monad transformers allow monads supporting the desired set of effects to be built. Algebraic laws are the key to *modular* reasoning about monadic definitions.

3MT implements the necessary definitions of *monads* and *monad transformers* as a Coq library inspired by the Haskell *monad transformer library* (MTL) [28]. Our library refines the MTL in two key ways in order to support modular reasoning using algebraic laws. While algebraic laws can only be documented informally in

```
———— Monad class ————
class Functor m ⇒ Monad m where
  return      :: a → m a
  (>>=)       :: m a → (a → m b) → m b
  return_bind :: return x >>= f ≡ f x
  bind_return :: p >>= return ≡ p
  bind_bind   :: (p >>= f) >>= g ≡
                   p >>= λx → (f x >>= g)
  fmap_bind   :: fmap f t ≡ t >>= (return ∘ f)

———— Failure class ————
class Monad m ⇒ 𝔽_M m where
  fail      :: m a
  bind_fail :: fail >>= f ≡ fail

———— State class ————
class Monad m ⇒ 𝕊_M s m where
  get       :: m s
  put       :: s → m ()
  get_query :: get >> t ≡ t
  put_get   :: put s >> get ≡ put s >> return s
  get_put   :: get >>= put ≡ return ()
  get_get   :: get >>= λs >>= get >>= f s ≡
                 get >>= λs → f s s
  put_put   :: put s1 >> put s2 ≡ put s2

———— Reader class ————
class Monad m ⇒ ℝ_M e m where
  ask          :: m e
  local        :: (e → e) → m a → m a
  ask_query    :: ask >> t ≡ t
  local_return :: local f ∘ return = return
  ask_ask      :: ask >>= λs >>= ask >>= f s ≡
                    ask >>= λs → f s s
  ask_bind     :: t >>= λx → ask >>= λe → f x e ≡
                    ask >>= λe → t >>= λx → f x e
  local_bind   :: local f (t >>= g) ≡
                    local f t >>= local f ∘ g
  local_ask    :: local f ask ≡ ask >>= return ∘ f
  local_local  :: local f ∘ local g ≡ local (g ∘ f)

———— Exception class ————
class Monad m ⇒ 𝔼_M x m where
  throw        :: x → m a
  catch        :: m a → (x → m a) → m a
  bind_throw   :: throw e >>= f ≡ throw e
  catch_throw1 :: catch (throw e) h ≡ h e
  catch_throw2 :: catch t throw ≡ t
  catch_return :: catch (return x) h ≡ return x
  fmap_catch   :: fmap f (catch t h) ≡
                    catch (fmap f t) (fmap f ∘ h)

———— Identity monad ————
newtype 𝕀 a
𝕀     :: a → 𝕀 a
run_𝕀 :: 𝕀 a → a

———— Failure transformer ————
newtype 𝔽_T m a
𝔽_T     :: m (Maybe a) → 𝔽_T m a
run_𝔽_T :: 𝔽_T m a → m (Maybe a)

———— State transformer ————
newtype 𝕊_T s m a
𝕊_T     :: (s → m (a, s)) → 𝕊_T s m a
run_𝕊_T :: 𝕊_T s m a → s → m (a, s)

———— Exception transformer ————
newtype 𝔼_T x m a
𝔼_T     :: m (Either x a) → 𝔼_T x m a
run_𝔼_T :: 𝔼_T x m a → m (Either x a)

———— Reader transformer ————
newtype ℝ_T e m a
ℝ_T     :: (e → m a) → ℝ_T e m a
run_ℝ_T :: ℝ_T e m a → e → m a
```

Figure 2. Key classes, definitions and laws from 3MT's monadic library. The names of algebraic laws are in bold.

Haskell, our library fully integrates them into type class definitions using Coq's expressive type system. Additionally, 3MT systematically includes laws for all monad subclasses, several of which have not been covered in the functional programming literature before.

Library overview Figure 2 summarizes the library's key classes, definitions and laws. The type class *Monad* describes the basic interface of monads. The type $m\ a$ denotes computations of type m which produce values of type a when executed. The function *return* lifts a value of type a into a (pure) computation that simply produces the value. The *bind* function $\gg\!=$ composes a computation $m\ a$ producing values of type a, with a function that accepts a value of type a and returns a computation of type $m\ b$. The function $\gg$ defines a special case of bind that discards the intermediate value:

$$(\gg) :: Monad\ m \Rightarrow m\ a \rightarrow m\ b \rightarrow m\ b$$
$$ma \gg mb = ma \gg\!= \backslash\_ \rightarrow mb$$

The **do** notation is syntactic sugar for the *bind* operator: $\mathbf{do}\ \{x \leftarrow f; g\}$ means $f \gg\!= \lambda x \rightarrow g$.

Particular monads can be built from basic monad types such as the identity monad ($\mathbb{I}$) and monad transformers including the failure ($\mathbb{F}_T$), mutable state ($\mathbb{S}_T$), and exception ($\mathbb{E}_T$) transformers. These transformers are combined into different monad stacks with $\mathbb{I}$ at the bottom. Constructor and extractor functions such as $\mathbb{S}_T$ and $run_{\mathbb{S}_T}$ provide the signatures of the functions for building and running particular monads/transformers.

In order to support extensible effects, a feature needs to abstract over the monad implementation used. Any implementation which includes the required operations is valid. These operations are captured in type classes such as $\mathbb{S}_M$ and $\mathbb{E}_M$, also called *monad subclasses*. The type classes (denoted by subscript M) are used to require a monad stack to support a particular effect without assuming a particular stack configuration.[1] Each class offers a set of primitive operations, such as *get* to access the state for $\mathbb{S}_M$.

Algebraic laws Each monad (sub)class includes a set of algebraic laws that govern its operations. These laws are an integral part of the definition of the monad type classes and constrain the possible implementations to sensible ones. Thus, even without knowing the particular implementation of a type class, we can still modularly reason about its behavior via these laws. This is crucial for supporting modular reasoning [35].

The first three laws for the *Monad* class are standard, while the last law (***fmap_bind***) relates *fmap* and *bind* in the usual way. Each monad subclass also includes its own set of laws. The laws for various subclasses can be found scattered throughout the functional programming literature, such as for failure [13] and state [13, 35]. Yet, as far as we know, 3MT is the first to systematically bring them together. Furthermore, although most laws have been presented in the semantics literature in one form or another, we have not seen some of the laws in the functional programming literature. One such example are the laws for the exception class:

- The ***bind_throw*** law generalizes the ***bind_fail*** law: a sequential computation is aborted by throwing an exception.
- The ***catch_throw***$_1$ law states that the exception handler is invoked when an exception is thrown in a *catch*.
- The ***catch_throw***$_2$ law indicates that an exception handler is redundant if it just re-throws the exception.
- The ***catch_return*** law states that a *catch* around a pure computation is redundant.
- The ***fmap_catch*** law states that pure functions (*fmap f*) distribute on the right with *catch*.

Other definitions Our monad library contains a number of other classes, definitions and laws apart from the definitions discussed here. This includes infrastructure for other types of effects (e.g. writer effects), as well as other infrastructure from the MTL. There are roughly 30 algebraic laws in total.

4. Modular Monadic Semantics

Features can utilize the monad library included with 3MT to construct algebras for semantic functions which are compatible with a range of effects. These modular monadic algebras have the form:

$$eval_{Ref} :: \mathbb{S}_M\ Store\ m \Rightarrow Algebra_M\ Ref_F\ (m\ a)$$
$$eval_{Err} :: \mathbb{E}_M\ ()\ m \Rightarrow Algebra_M\ Err_F\ (m\ a)$$

These algebras use monad subclasses such as $\mathbb{S}_M$ and $\mathbb{E}_M$ to *constrain* the monad required by the feature, allowing the monad to

[1] Supporting two instances of the same effect requires extra machinery [41].

```
— Simplified value interface —
type Value

loc   :: Int → Value
stuck :: Value
unit  :: Value
isLoc :: Value → Maybe Int

— Simplified type interface —
type Type

tRef   :: Type → Type
tUnit  :: Type
isTRef :: Type → Maybe Type

—— Expression functor ——
data Ref_F a = Ref a
  | DeRef a
  | Assign a a

type Store = [Value]
```

```
——— Monadic typing algebra ———
typeof_Ref :: F_M m ⇒
  Algebra_M Ref_F (m Type)
typeof_Ref rec (Ref e) =
  do t ← rec e
     return (tRef t)
typeof_Ref rec (DeRef e) =
  do te ← rec e
     maybe fail return (isTRef te)
typeof_Ref rec (Assign e1 e2) =
  do t1 ← rec e1
     case isTRef t1 of
       Nothing → fail
       Just t → do t2 ← rec e2
                   if (t ≡ t2)
                     then return tUnit
                     else fail
```

```
———————— Monadic evaluation algebra ————————
eval_Ref :: S_M Store m ⇒ Algebra_M Ref_F (m Value)
eval_Ref rec (Ref e) =
  do v   ← rec e
     env ← get
     put (v : env)
     return (loc (length env))
eval_Ref rec (DeRef e) =
  do v   ← rec e
     env ← get
     case isLoc v of
       Nothing → return stuck
       Just n → return (maybe stuck id (fetch n env))
eval_Ref rec (Assign e1 e2) =
  do v   ← rec e1
     env ← get
     case isLoc v of
       Nothing → return stuck
       Just n   → do v2 ← rec e2
                     put (replace n v2 env)
                     return unit
```

Figure 3. Syntax, type, and semantic function definitions for references.

Arithmetic Expressions	$Monad\ m$
Boolean Expressions	$Monad\ m$
Errors	$\mathbb{E}_{\mathrm{M}}\ ()\ m$
References	$\mathbb{S}_{\mathrm{M}}\ Store\ m$
Lambda	$\mathbb{R}_{\mathrm{M}}\ Env\ m, \mathbb{F}_{\mathrm{M}}\ m$

Figure 4. Effects used by the case study's evaluation algebras.

have more effects than those used in the feature. These two algebras can be combined to create a new evaluation algebra with type:

$$(\mathbb{S}_{\mathrm{M}}\ m\ s, \mathbb{E}_{\mathrm{M}}\ m\ x) \Rightarrow Algebra_M\ (Ref_F \oplus Err_F)\ (m\ a)$$

The combination imposes both type class constraints while the monad type remains extensible with new effects. The complete set of effects used by the evaluation functions for the five language features used in our case study of Section 7 are given in Figure 4.

4.1 Example: References

Figure 3 illustrates this approach with definitions for the functor for expressions and the evaluation and typing algebras for the reference feature. Other features have similar definitions.

For the sake of presentation the definitions are slightly simplified from the actual ones in Coq. For instance, we have omitted issues related to the extensibility of the syntax for values (*Value*) and types (*Type*). We refer the interested reader to MTC [9] and the 3MT Coq code for these details. *Value* and *Type* are treated as abstract datatypes with a number of constructor functions: *loc*, *stuck*, *unit*, *tRef* and *tUnit* denote respectively reference locations, stuck values, unit values, reference types and unit types. There are also matching functions *isLoc* and *isTRef* for checking whether a term is a location value or a reference type, respectively.

The type Ref_F is the functor for references. It has constructors for creating references (*Ref*), dereferencing (*DeRef*) and assigning (*Assign*) references. The evaluation algebra $eval_{Ref}$ uses the state monad for its reference environment, which is captured in the type class constraint $\mathbb{S}_{\mathrm{M}}\ Store\ m$. The typing algebra ($typeof_{Ref}$) is also monadic, using the failure monad to denote ill-typing.

4.2 Effect-Dependent Theorems

Monadic semantic function algebras are compatible with new effects and algebraic laws facilitate writing extensible proofs over these monadic algebras. Effects introduce further challenges to proof reuse, however: each combination of effects induces its own type soundness statement. Consider the theorem for a language with references which features a store σ and a store typing Σ that are related through the store typing judgement $\Sigma \vdash \sigma$:

$$\forall e, t, \Sigma, \sigma. \left\{ \begin{array}{c} typeof\ e \equiv return\ t \\ \Sigma \vdash \sigma \end{array} \right\} \rightarrow$$
$$\exists v, \Sigma', \sigma'. \left\{ \begin{array}{c} put\ \sigma \gg [\![e]\!] \equiv put\ \sigma' \gg return\ v \\ \Sigma' \supseteq \Sigma \\ \Sigma' \vdash v : t \\ \Sigma' \vdash \sigma' \end{array} \right\} \qquad (\text{LSOUND}_S)$$

Contrast this with the theorem for a language with errors, which must account for the computation possibly ending in an exception being thrown:

$$\forall e, t. typeof\ e \equiv return\ t \rightarrow$$
$$(\exists v. [\![e]\!] \equiv return\ v \wedge \vdash v : t) \vee (\exists x. [\![e]\!] \equiv throw\ x) \qquad (\text{LSOUND}_E)$$

Clearly, the available effects are essential for the formulation of the theorem. A larger language which involves both exceptions and state requires yet another theorem where the impact of both effects cross-cut one another[2]:

$$\forall e, t, \Sigma, \sigma. \left\{ \begin{array}{c} typeof\ e \equiv return\ t \\ \Sigma \vdash \sigma \end{array} \right\} \rightarrow$$
$$\exists v, \Sigma', \sigma'. \left\{ \begin{array}{c} put\ \sigma \gg [\![e]\!] \equiv put\ \sigma' \gg return\ v \\ \Sigma' \supseteq \Sigma \\ \Sigma' \vdash v : t \\ \Sigma' \vdash \sigma' \end{array} \right\}$$
$$\vee$$
$$\exists x. put\ \sigma \gg [\![e]\!] \equiv throw\ x \qquad (\text{LSOUND}_{ES})$$

Modular formulations of LSOUND_E and LSOUND_S are useless for proving a modular variant of LSOUND_{ES} because their

[2] A similar proliferation of soundness theorems can be found in TAPL [37].

$$\frac{}{\Sigma \vdash_M v_m \ : \ \mathit{fail}} \quad \text{(WFM-ILLTYPED)}$$

$$\frac{\Sigma \vdash v \ : \ t}{\Sigma \vdash_M \mathit{return}\ v \ : \ \mathit{return}\ t} \quad \text{(WFM-RETURN)}$$

Figure 5. Typing rules for pure monadic values.

induction hypotheses have the wrong form. The hypothesis for LSOUND$_E$ requires the result to be of the form $\mathit{return}\ v$, disallowing $\mathit{put}\ \sigma' \gg \mathit{return}\ v$ (the form required by LSOUND$_S$). Similarly, the hypothesis for LSOUND$_S$ does not account for exceptions occurring in subterms. In general, without anticipating additional effects, type soundness theorems with fixed sets of effects cannot be reused modularly.

5. Modular Monadic Type Soundness

In order to preserve a measure of modularity, we do not prove type soundness directly for a given feature, but by means of a more generic theorem. The technique of proving a theorem of interest by means of a more general theorem is well-known. For a conventional monolithic language, for instance, type soundness is often established for any well-formed typing context, even though the main interest lies with the more specific initial, empty context. In that setting, the more general theorem produces a weaker induction hypothesis for the theorem's proof.

Our approach to type soundness follows the core idea of this technique and relies on three theorems:

- FSOUND: a reusable *feature theorem* that is only aware of the effects that a feature uses
- ESOUND: an *effect theorem* for a fixed set of known effects, and
- LSOUND: a *language theorem* which combines the two to prove soundness for a specific language.

In order to maximize compatibility, the statement of the reusable feature theorem cannot hardwire the set of effects. This statement must instead rephrase type soundness in a way that can adapt to any superset of a feature's effects. Our solution is to have the feature theorem establish that the monadic evaluation and typing algebras of a feature satisfy an extensible well-formedness relation, defined in terms of effect-specific typing rules. Thus, a feature's proof of FSOUND uses only the typing rules required for the effects specific to that feature. The final language combines the typing rules of all the language's effects into a closed relation.

Figure 6 illustrates how these reusable pieces fit together to build a proof of soundness. Each feature provides a proof algebra for FSOUND which relies on the typing rules (WFM-X) for the effects it uses. Each unique statement of soundness for a combination of effects requires a new proof of ESOUND. The proof of LSOUND for a particular language is synthesized entirely from a single proof of ESOUND and a combination of proof algebras for FSOUND.

Note that there are several dimensions of modularity here. A feature's proof of FSOUND only depends on the typing rules for the effects that feature uses and can thus be used in any language which includes those typing rules. The typing rules themselves can be reused by any number of different features. ESOUND depends solely on a specific combination of effects and can be reused in any language which supports that unique combination, e.g. both LSOUND$_A$ and LSOUND$_{AR}$ use ESOUND$_{ES}$.

5.1 Soundness for a Pure Feature

The reusable feature theorem FSOUND states that $[\![\cdot]\!]$ and *typeof* are related by the extensible typing relation:

$$\forall e, \Sigma. \quad \Sigma \vdash_M [\![e]\!] : \mathit{typeof}\ e \qquad \text{(FSOUND)}$$

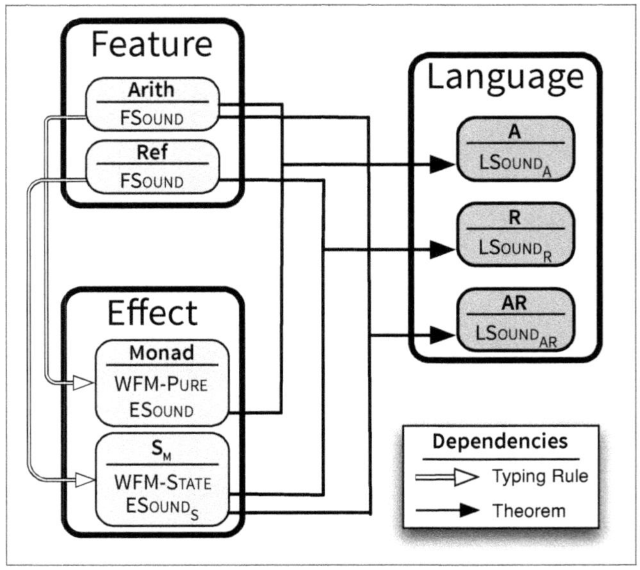

Figure 6. Dependency Graph

Extensible Typing Relation The extensible typing relation has the form:

$$\Sigma \vdash_M v_m : t_m$$

The relation is polymorphic in an environment type *env* and an evaluation monad type m. The parameters Σ, v_m and t_m have types *env*, m *Value* and *Maybe Type* respectively. The modular typing rules for this relation can impose constraints on the environment type *env* and monad type m. A particular language must instantiate *env* and m in a way that satisfies all the constraints imposed by the typing rules used in its features.

Figure 5 lists the two base typing rules of this relation. These do not constrain the evaluation monad and environment types and are the only rules needed for pure features. The (WFM-ILLTYPED) rule denotes that nothing can be said about computations (m_e) which are ill-typed. The (WFM-RETURN) rule ensures that well-typed computations only yield values of the expected type.

To see how the reusable theorem works for a pure feature, consider the proof of soundness for the boolean feature.

Proof Using the above two rules, we can show that FSOUND holds for the boolean feature. The proof has two cases. The boolean literal case is handled by a trivial application of (WFM-RETURN). The second case, for conditionals, is more interesting[3].

$$\begin{array}{l}
(\vdash_M [\![e_c]\!] \ : \ \mathit{typeof}\ e_c) \to \\
\qquad (\vdash_M [\![e_t]\!] \ : \ \mathit{typeof}\ e_t) \to \\
\qquad\qquad (\vdash_M [\![e_e]\!] \ : \ \mathit{typeof}\ e_e) \to \\
\vdash_M \begin{pmatrix}
\textbf{do}\ v \leftarrow [\![e_c]\!] \\
\quad \textbf{case}\ \mathit{isBool}\ v\ \textbf{of} \\
\quad\quad \mathit{Just}\ b \quad \to \\
\quad\quad\quad \textbf{if}\ b\ \textbf{then}\ [\![e_t]\!] \\
\quad\quad\quad\quad \textbf{else}\ [\![e_e]\!] \\
\quad\quad \mathit{Nothing} \to \mathit{stuck}
\end{pmatrix} : \begin{pmatrix}
\textbf{do}\ t_c \leftarrow \mathit{typeof}\ e_c \\
\quad t_t \leftarrow \mathit{typeof}\ e_t \\
\quad t_e \leftarrow \mathit{typeof}\ e_e \\
\quad \mathit{guard}\ (\mathit{isTBool}\ t_c) \\
\quad \mathit{guard}\ (\mathit{eqT}\ t_t\ t_e) \\
\quad \mathit{return}\ t_t
\end{pmatrix}
\end{array} \qquad \text{(WFM-IF-VC)}$$

Because $[\![\cdot]\!]$ and *typeof* are polymorphic in the monad, we cannot directly inspect the values they produce. We can, how-

[3] We omit the environment Σ to avoid clutter.

ever, perform case analysis on the derivations of the proofs produced by the induction hypothesis that the subexpressions are well-formed, $\vdash_M [\![e_c]\!] : \mathit{typeof}\ e_c$, $\vdash_M [\![e_t]\!] : \mathit{typeof}\ e_t$, and $\vdash_M [\![e_e]\!] : \mathit{typeof}\ e_e$. The final rule used in each derivation determines the shape of the monadic value produced by $[\![\cdot]\!]$ and *typeof*. Assuming that only the pure typing rules of Figure 5 are used for the derivations, we can divide the proof into two cases depending on whether e_c, e_t, or e_e was typed with (WFM-ILLTYPED).

- If any of the three derivations uses (WFM-ILLTYPED), the result of *typeof* is *fail*. As *fail* is the zero of the typing monad, (WFM-ILLTYPED) resolves the case.
- Otherwise, each of the subderivations was built with (WFM-RETURN) and the evaluation and typing expressions can be simplified using the ***return_bind*** monad law.

$$\vdash_M \begin{pmatrix} \textbf{case}\ \mathit{isBool}\ v_c\ \textbf{of} \\ \quad \mathit{Just}\ b \quad \rightarrow \\ \quad\quad \textbf{if}\ b\ \textbf{then}\ \mathit{return}\ v_t \\ \quad\quad\quad \textbf{else}\ \mathit{return}\ v_e \\ \quad \mathit{Nothing} \rightarrow \mathit{stuck} \end{pmatrix} : \begin{pmatrix} \textbf{do}\ \mathit{guard}\ (\mathit{isTBool}\ t_c) \\ \quad \mathit{guard}\ (\mathit{eqT}\ t_t\ t_e) \\ \quad \mathit{return}\ t_t \end{pmatrix}$$

After simplification, the typing expression has replaced the bind with explicit values which can be reasoned with. If $\mathit{isTBool}\ t_c$ is *false*, then the typing expression reduces to *fail* and well-formedness again follows from the WFM-ILLTYPED rule. Otherwise $t_c \equiv \mathit{TBool}$, and we can apply the inversion lemma

$$\vdash v : \mathit{TBool} \rightarrow \exists b.\mathit{isBool}\ v \equiv \mathit{Just}\ b$$

to establish that v_c is of the form $\mathit{Just}\ b$, reducing the evaluation to either $\mathit{return}\ v_e$ or $\mathit{return}\ v_t$. A similar case analysis on $\mathit{eqT}\ t_t\ t_e$ will either produce *fail* or $\mathit{return}\ t_t$. The former is trivially true, and both $\vdash_M \mathit{return}\ v_t : \mathit{return}\ t_t$ and $\vdash_M \mathit{return}\ v_e : \mathit{return}\ t_t$ hold in the latter case from the induction hypotheses.

Modular Sublemmas The above proof assumed that only the pure typing rules of Figure 5 were used to type the subexpressions of the **if** expression, which is clearly not the case when the boolean feature is included in an effectful language. Instead, case analyses are performed on the extensible typing relation in order to make the boolean feature theorem compatible with new effects. Case analyses over the extensible $\vdash_M$ relation are accomplished using extensible proof algebras which are folded over the derivations provided by the induction hypothesis, as outlined in Section 2.3.

In order for the boolean feature's proof of FSOUND to be compatible with a new effect, each extensible case analysis requires a proof algebra for the new typing rules the effect introduces to the $\vdash_M$ relation. These proof algebras are examples of *feature interactions* [3] from the setting of modular component-based frameworks. In essence, a feature interaction is functionality (e.g., a function or a proof) that is only necessary when two features are combined. Importantly, these proof algebras do not need to be provided up front when developing the boolean algebra, but can instead be modularly resolved by a separate feature for the interaction of booleans and the new effect.

The formulation of the properties proved by extensible case analysis has an impact on modularity. The conditional case of the previous proof can be dispatched by folding a proof algebra for the property WFM-IF-VC over $\vdash_M [\![v_c]\!] : \mathit{typeof}\ t_c$. Each new effect induces a new case for this proof algebra, however, resulting in an interaction between booleans and every effect. WFM-IF-VC is specific to the proof of FSOUND in the boolean feature; proofs of FSOUND for other features require different properties and thus different proof algebras. Relying on such specific properties can lead to a proliferation of proof obligations for each new effect.

$$\frac{}{\Sigma \vdash_M \mathit{throw}\ x\ :\ t_m} \quad \text{(WFM-THROW)}$$

$$\frac{\Sigma \vdash_M m \gg\!= k\ :\ t_m \qquad \forall\, \Sigma' \supseteq \Sigma\, x\,.\, \Sigma' \vdash_M h\ x \gg\!= k\ :\ t_m}{\Sigma \vdash_M \mathit{catch}\ m\ h \gg\!= k\ :\ t_m} \quad \text{(WFM-CATCH)}$$

Figure 7. Typing rules for exceptional monadic values.

Alternatively, the boolean feature can use a proof algebra for a stronger property that is also applicable in other proofs, cutting down on the number of feature interactions. One such stronger, more general sublemma relates the monadic bind operation to well-typing:

$$\begin{aligned}&(\Sigma \vdash_M v_m : t_m) \rightarrow \\ &(\forall v\, T\, \Sigma' \supseteq \Sigma.\, (\Sigma' \vdash v : T) \rightarrow \Sigma' \vdash_M k_v\, v : k_t\, T) \rightarrow \\ &\qquad \Sigma \vdash_M v_m \gg\!= k_v : t_m \gg\!= k_t \quad \text{(WFM-BIND)}\end{aligned}$$

A proof of WFM-IF-VC follows from two applications of this stronger property. The advantage of WFM-BIND is clear: it can be reused to deal with case analyses in other proofs of FSOUND, while a proof of WFM-IF-VC has only a single use. The disadvantage is that WFM-BIND may not hold for some new effect, while the weaker WFM-IF-VC does, possibly excluding some feature combinations. As WFM-BIND is a desirable property for typing rules, the case study focuses on that approach.

5.2 Type Soundness for a Pure Language

The second phase of showing type soundness is to prove a statement of soundness for a fixed set of effects. For pure effects, the soundness statement is straightforward:

$$\forall v_m\ t.\ \vdash_M v_m : \mathit{return}\ t \Rightarrow \exists v.v_m \equiv \mathit{return}\ v \wedge \vdash v : t \quad \text{(ESOUND}_P\text{)}$$

Each effect theorem is proved by induction over the derivation of $\vdash_M v_m : \mathit{return}\ t$. ESOUND$_P$ fixes the irrelevant environment type to the type () and the evaluation monad to the pure monad $\mathbb{I}$. Since the evaluation monad is fixed, the proof of ESOUND$_P$ only needs to consider the pure typing rules of Figure 5. The proof of the effect theorem is straightforward: WFM-ILLTYPED could not have been used to derive $\vdash_M v_m : \mathit{return}\ t$, and WFM-RETURN provides both a witness for v and a proof that it is of type t.

The statement of soundness for a pure language built from a particular set of features is similar to ESOUND$_P$:

$$\forall e, t.\mathit{typeof}\ e \equiv \mathit{return}\ t \Rightarrow \exists v.[\![e]\!] \equiv \mathit{return}\ v \wedge \vdash v : t \quad \text{(LSOUND)}$$

The proof of LSOUND is an immediate consequence of the reusable proofs of FSOUND and ESOUND$_P$. Folding a proof algebra for FSOUND over e provides a proof of $\vdash_M [\![e]\!] : \mathit{return}\ t$, satisfying the first assumption of ESOUND$_P$. LSOUND follows immediately.

5.3 Errors

The evaluation algebra of the error language feature uses the side effects of the exception monad, requiring new typing rules.

Typing Rules Figure 7 lists the typing rules for monadic computations involving exceptions. WFM-THROW states that $\mathit{throw}\ x$ is typeable with any type. WFM-CATCH states that binding the results of both branches of a *catch* statement will produce a monad with the same type. While it may seem odd that this rule is formulated in terms of a continuation $\gg\!= k$, it is essential for compatibility with the proofs algebras required by other features. As described

$$\frac{\forall \sigma, \Sigma \vdash \sigma \rightarrow \Sigma \vdash_M k\, \sigma : t_m}{\Sigma \vdash_M get \ggg\!\!= k \;:\; t_m} \quad \text{(WFM-GET)}$$

$$\frac{\Sigma' \vdash \sigma \qquad \Sigma' \supseteq \Sigma \qquad \Sigma' \vdash_M k : t_m}{\Sigma \vdash_M put\ \sigma \gg k \;:\; t_m} \quad \text{(WFM-PUT)}$$

Figure 8. Typing rules for stateful monadic values.

in Section 5.1, extensible proof algebras over the typing derivation will now need cases for the two new rules. To illustrate this, consider the proof algebra for the general purpose WFM-BIND property. This algebra requires a proof of:

$$(\Sigma \vdash_M catch\ e\ h \ggg\!\!= k \;:\; t_m) \rightarrow$$
$$(\forall v\, T\, \Sigma' \supseteq \Sigma.\ (\Sigma' \vdash v \;:\; T) \rightarrow \Sigma' \vdash_M \ k_v\ v \;:\; k_t\ T) \rightarrow$$
$$\Sigma \vdash_M (catch\ e\ h \ggg\!\!= k) \ggg\!\!= k_v : t_m \ggg\!\!= k_t$$

With the continuation, we can first apply the associativity law to reorder the binds so that WFM-CATCH can be applied: $(catch\ \ e\ \ h \ggg\!\!= k) \ggg\!\!= k_v = catch\ \ e\ \ h \ggg\!\!= (k \ggg\!\!= k_v)$. The two premises of the rule follow immediately from the inductive hypothesis of the lemma, finishing the proof. Without the continuation, the proof statement only binds $catch\ e\ h$ to v_m, leaving no applicable typing rules.

Effect Theorem The effect theorem, ESOUND$_E$, for a language whose only effect is exceptions reflects that the evaluation function is either a well-typed value or an exception.

$$\forall v_m\ t.\ \vdash_M v_m : return\ t \Rightarrow$$
$$\exists x.v_m \equiv throw\ x \vee \exists v.v_m \equiv return\ v \wedge \vdash v : t \qquad (\text{ESOUND}_E)$$

The proof of ESOUND$_E$ is again by induction on the derivation of $\vdash_M v_m : return\ t$. The irrelevant environment can be fixed to (), while the evaluation monad is the exception monad $\mathbb{E}_\mathrm{T}\ x\ \mathbb{I}$.

The typing derivation is built from four rules: the two pure rules from Figure 5 and the two exception rules from Figure 7. The case for the two pure rules is effectively the same as before, and WFM-THROW is straightforward. In the remaining case, $v_m \equiv catch\ e'\ h$, and we can leverage the fact that the evaluation monad is fixed to conclude that either $\exists v.e' \equiv return\ v$ or $\exists x.e' \equiv throw\ x$. In the former case, $catch\ e'\ h$ can be reduced using ***catch_return***, and the latter case is simplified using ***catch_throw***$_1$. In both cases, the conclusion then follows immediately from the assumptions of WFM-CATCH. The proof of the language theorem LSOUND$_E$ is similar to LSOUND and is easily built from ESOUND$_E$ and FSOUND.

5.4 References

Typing Rules Figure 8 lists the two typing rules for stateful computations. To understand the formulation of these rules, consider LSOUND$_S$, the statement of soundness for a language with a stateful evaluation function. The statement accounts for both the typing environment Σ and evaluation environment σ by imposing the invariant that σ is well-formed with respect to Σ. FSOUND however, has no such conditions (which would be anti-modular in any case). We avoid this problem by accounting for the invariant in the typing rules themselves:

- WFM-GET requires that the continuation k of a get is well-typed under the invariant.
- WFM-PUT requires that any newly installed environment maintains this invariant.

The intuition behind these premises is that effect theorems will maintain these invariants in order to apply the rules.

$$\frac{\forall \gamma.\, \Gamma \vdash \gamma \rightarrow \Gamma \vdash_M k\, \gamma : t_m}{\Gamma \vdash_M ask \ggg\!\!= k \;:\; t_m} \quad \text{(WFM-ASK)}$$

$$\frac{\forall\, \gamma.\, \Gamma \vdash \gamma \rightarrow \Gamma' \vdash f\, \gamma \qquad \Gamma' \vdash_M m \;:\; return\ t'_m \qquad \forall v.\ \vdash v \;:\; t'_m \rightarrow \Gamma \vdash_M (k\ v) : t_m}{\Gamma \vdash_M \ local\, f\ m \ggg\!\!= k\!:\ t_m}$$

(WFM-LOCAL)

$$\frac{}{\Gamma \vdash_M \bot \;:\; t_m} \quad \text{(WFM-BOT)}$$

Figure 9. Typing rules for environment and failure monads.

Effect Theorem The effect theorem for mutable state proceeds again by induction over the typing derivation. The evaluation monad is fixed to $\mathbb{S}_\mathrm{T}\ Sigma\ \mathbb{I}$ and the environment type is fixed to $[\,Type\,]$ with the obvious definitions for $\supseteq$.

- The proof case for the two pure rules is again straightforward.
- For WFM-GET we have that $put\ \sigma \gg [\![e]\!] \equiv put\ \sigma \gg get \ggg\!\!= k$. After reducing this to $k\ \sigma$ with the ***put_get*** law, the result follows immediately from the rule's assumptions.
- Similarly, for WFM-PUT we have that $put\ \ \sigma\ \gg [\![e]\!] \ \equiv put\ \sigma \gg put\ \sigma' \gg k$. After reducing this to $put\ \sigma' \gg k$ with the ***put_put*** law, the result again follows immediately from the rule's assumptions.

5.5 Lambda

The case study represents the binders of the lambda feature using PHOAS [7] to avoid many of the boilerplate definitions and proofs about term well-formedness found in first-order representations.

The Environment Effect Unlike in MTC, 3MT neatly hides the variable environment of the evaluation function with a reader monad $\mathbb{R}_\mathrm{M}$. This new effect introduces the two new typing rules listed in Figure 9. Unsurprisingly, these typing rule are similar to those of Figure 8. The rule for ask is essentially the same as WFM-GET. The typing rule for $local$ differs slightly from WFM-PUT. Its first premise ensures that whenever f is applied to an environment that is well-formed in the original typing environment Γ, the resulting environment is well-formed in some new environment Γ'. The second premise ensures the body of $local$ is well-formed in this environment according to some type T, and the final premise ensures that k is well-formed when applied to any value of type T. The intuition behind binding the $local$ expression in some k is the same as with put.

The Non-Termination Effect The lambda feature also introduces the possibility of non-termination to the evaluation function, which is disallowed by Coq. MTC solves this problem by combining *mixin algebras* with a bounded fixpoint function. This function applies an algebra a bounded number of times, returning a $\bot$ value when the bound is exceeded. Because MTC represented $\bot$ as a value, all evaluation algebras needed to account for it explicitly. In the monadic setting, 3MT elegantly represents $\bot$ with the $fail$ primitive of the failure monad. This allows terminating features to be completely oblivious to whether a bounded or standard fold is used for the evaluation function, resulting in a much cleaner semantics. WFM-BOT allows $\bot$ to have any type.

6. Effect Compositions

As we have seen, laws are essential for proofs of FSOUND. The proofs so far have involved only one effect and the laws regulate the behavior of that effect's primitive operations.

Languages often involve more than one effect, however. Hence, the proofs of effect theorems must reason about the interaction between multiple effects. There is a trade-off between fully instantiating the monad for the language as we have done previously, and continuing to reason about a constrained polymorphic monad. The former is easy for reasoning, while the latter allows the same language proof to be instantiated with different implementations of the monad. In the latter case, additional *effect interaction* laws are required.

6.1 Languages with State and Exceptions

Consider the effect theorem which fixes the evaluation monad to support exceptions and state. The statement of the theorem mentions both kinds of effects by requiring the evaluation function to be run with a well-formed state σ and by concluding that well-typed expressions either throw an exception or return a value. The WFM-CATCH case this theorem has the following goal:

$$(\Sigma \vdash \sigma : \Sigma)$$

$$\rightarrow$$

$$\exists\, \Sigma', \sigma', v. \left\{ \begin{array}{c} put\ \sigma \gg catch\ e\ h \gg= k \equiv put\ \sigma' \gg return\ v \\ \Sigma' \vdash v : t \end{array} \right\}$$

$$\vee$$

$$\exists\, \Sigma', \sigma', x. \left\{ \begin{array}{c} put\ \sigma \gg catch\ e\ h \gg= k \equiv put\ \sigma' \gg throw\ x \\ \Sigma' \vdash \sigma' : \Sigma' \end{array} \right\}$$

In order to apply the induction hypothesis to e and h, we need to precede them by a $put\ \sigma$. Hence, $put\ \sigma$ must be pushed under the $catch$ statement through the use of a law governing the behavior of put and $catch$. There are different choices for this law, depending on the monad that implements both $\mathbb{S}_\mathrm{M}$ and $\mathbb{E}_\mathrm{M}$. We consider two reasonable choices, based on the monad transformer compositions $\mathbb{E}_\mathrm{T}\ x\ (\mathbb{S}_\mathrm{T}\ s\ \mathbb{I})$ and $\mathbb{S}_\mathrm{T}\ s\ (\mathbb{E}_\mathrm{T}\ x\ \mathbb{I})$:

- Either $catch$ passes the current state into the handler:
  $put\ \sigma \gg catch\ e\ h \equiv catch\ (put\ \sigma \gg e)\ h$
- Or $catch$ runs the handler with the initial state:
  $put\ \sigma \gg catch\ e\ h \equiv catch\ (put\ \sigma \gg e)\ (put\ \sigma \gg h)$

The WFM-CATCH case is provable under either choice. As the LSOUND$_{ES}$ proof is written as an extensible theorem, the two cases are written as two separate proof algebras, each with a different assumption about the behavior of the interaction. Since the cases for the other rules are impervious to the choice, they can be reused with either proof of WFM-CATCH.

6.2 Full Combination of Effects

A language with references, errors and lambda abstractions features four effects: state, exceptions, an environment and failure. The language theorem for such a language relies on the effect theorem ESOUND$_{ESRF}$ given in Figure 10. The proof of ESOUND$_{ESRF}$ is similar to the previous effect theorem proofs, and makes use of the full set of interaction laws given in Figure 11. Perhaps the most interesting observation here is that because the environment monad only makes local changes, we can avoid having to choose between laws regarding how it interacts with exceptions. Also note that since we are representing nontermination using a failure monad $\mathbb{F}_\mathrm{M}\ m$, the ***catch_fail*** law conforms to our desired semantics.

7. Case Study

As a demonstration of the 3MT framework, we have built a set of five reusable language features and combined them to build a family of languages which includes a mini-ML [8] variant with references and errors. The study includes pure boolean and arithmetic features as well as effectful features for references, errors and lambda abstractions.

$$\forall \Sigma, \Gamma, \delta, \gamma, \sigma, e_E, e_T. \left\{ \begin{array}{c} \gamma, \delta \vdash e_E \equiv e_T \\ \Sigma \vdash \sigma : \Sigma \\ \Sigma \vdash \gamma : \Gamma \\ typeof\ e_T \equiv return\ t \end{array} \right\} \rightarrow$$

$$\exists\, \Sigma', \sigma', v. \left\{ \begin{array}{c} local\ (\lambda\_.\gamma)\ (put\ \sigma \gg [\![\epsilon]\!]_E) \\ \equiv local\ (\lambda\_.\gamma)\ (put\ \sigma' \gg return\ v) \\ \Sigma' \vdash v : t \end{array} \right\}$$

$$\vee$$

$$\exists\, \Sigma', \sigma', v. \left\{ \begin{array}{c} local\ (\lambda\_.\gamma)\ (put\ \sigma \gg [\![e]\!]_E) \\ \equiv local\ (\lambda\_.\gamma(put\ \sigma' \gg \bot) \\ \Sigma' \vdash \sigma' : \Sigma' \\ \Sigma' \supseteq \Sigma \end{array} \right\}$$

$$\vee$$

$$\exists\, \Sigma', \sigma', v. \left\{ \begin{array}{c} local\ (\lambda\_.\gamma)\ (put\ \sigma \gg [\![e]\!]_E) \\ \equiv local\ (\lambda\_.\Gamma(put\ \sigma' \gg throw\ t) \\ \Sigma' \vdash \sigma' : \Sigma' \\ \Sigma' \supseteq \Sigma \end{array} \right\}$$

(ESOUND$_{ESRF}$)

Figure 10. Effect theorem statement for languages with errors, state, an environment and failure.

The study builds twenty eight different combinations of the features which are all possible combinations with at least one feature providing values.[4] Figure 13 presents the syntax of the expressions, values, and types provided; each line is annotated with the feature that provides that set of definitions.

Four kinds of feature interactions appear in the case study.

- The PHOAS representation of binders requires an auxiliary equivalence relation, the details of which are covered in the MTC paper [9]. The soundness proofs of language theorems

[4] Also available at `http://www.cs.utexas.edu/~bendy/3MT`

——— Exceptional Environment ———

class $(\mathbb{E}_\mathrm{M}\ x\ m, \mathbb{R}_\mathrm{M}\ m) \Rightarrow \mathbb{ER}_\mathrm{M}\ x\ g\ m$ **where**
local_throw $:: local\ f\ (throw\ e) \equiv throw\ e$
local_catch $:: local\ f\ (catch\ e\ h) \equiv$
$catch\ (local\ f\ e)\ (\lambda x.local\ f\ (h\ x))$

——— Exceptional Failure ———

class $(\mathbb{E}_\mathrm{M}\ x\ m, \mathbb{F}_\mathrm{M}\ m) \Rightarrow \mathbb{FS}_\mathrm{M}\ x\ m$ **where**
catch_fail $:: catch\ fail\ h \equiv fail$
fail_neq_throw $:: fail \not\equiv throw\ x$

——— Exceptional State Failure ———

class $(\mathbb{E}_\mathrm{M}\ x\ m, \mathbb{S}_\mathrm{M}\ s\ m, \mathbb{F}_\mathrm{M}\ m) \Rightarrow \mathbb{EFS}_\mathrm{M}\ x\ m$ **where**
put_fail_throw $:: put\ \sigma \gg fail \not\equiv put\ \sigma' \gg throw\ x$

——— Exceptional State ———

class $(\mathbb{E}_\mathrm{M}\ x\ m, \mathbb{F}_\mathrm{M}\ m) \Rightarrow MonadErrorState\ x\ m$ **where**
put_ret_throw $:: put\ \sigma \gg return\ a \not\equiv put\ \sigma' \gg throw\ x$
put_throw $:: \forall A\ B.put\ \sigma \gg throw\_A\ x \equiv put\ \sigma' \gg throw\_A\ x \rightarrow$
$put\ \sigma \gg throw\_B\ x \equiv put\ \sigma' \gg throw\_B\ x$

——— Alternate Exceptional State laws ———

class $(\mathbb{E}_\mathrm{M}\ x\ m, \mathbb{F}_\mathrm{M}\ m) \Rightarrow \mathbb{ES}_{\mathrm{M}_1}\ x\ m$ **where**
put_catch$_1$ $:: put\ \sigma \gg catch\ e\ h \equiv catch\ (put\ \sigma \gg e)\ h$

——— Or ———

class $(\mathbb{E}_\mathrm{M}\ x\ m, \mathbb{F}_\mathrm{M}\ m) \Rightarrow \mathbb{ES}_{\mathrm{M}_2}\ x\ m$ **where**
put_catch$_2$ $:: put\ env \gg catch\ e\ h \equiv$
$catch\ (put\ \sigma \gg e)\ (\lambda x \rightarrow put\ \sigma \gg h\ x)$

Figure 11. Interaction laws

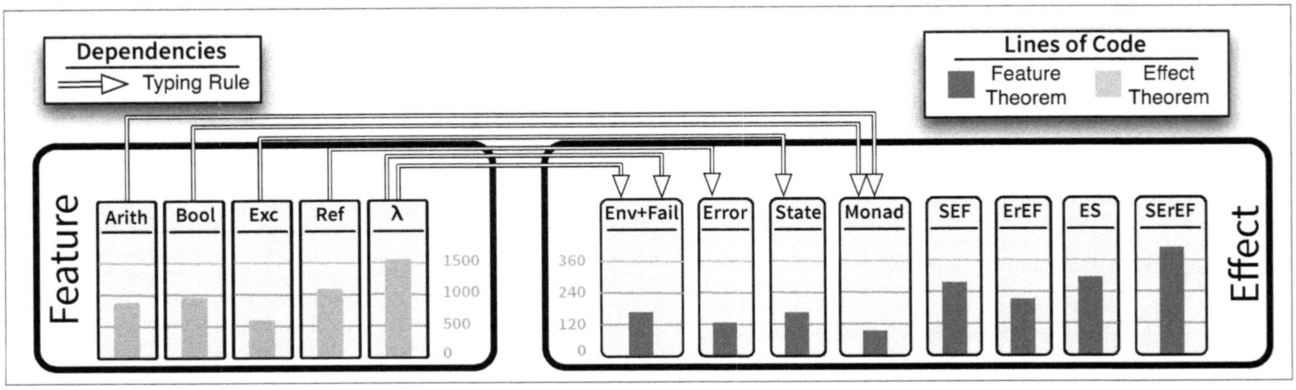

Figure 12. Dependency and size information for the features and effects used in the case study.

e ::= ℕ	e + e	*Arith*
| 𝔹	**if** e **then** e **else** e	*Bool*
| **lam** x : T.e	e e	x	*Lambda*
| **ref** e	!e	e:=e	*References*
| **try** e **with** e	**error**	*Errors*

V ::= ℕ	*Arith*
| 𝔹	*Bool*
| **clos** e $\overline{\text{V}}$	*Lambda*
| **loc** ℕ	*References*

T ::= **Nat**	*Arith*
| **Bool**	*Bool*
| T → T	*Lambda*
| **Ref** T	*References*

Figure 13. mini-ML expressions, values, and types

for languages which include binders proceed by induction over this equivalence relation instead of expressions. The reusable feature theorems of other features need to be lifted to this equivalence relation.

- The effect theorems that feature an environment typing Σ, such as those for state or environment, need a weakening sublemma which states that each well-formed value under Σ is also well-formed under a conservative extension:

$$\Sigma \vdash v : t \rightarrow \Sigma' \supseteq \Sigma \rightarrow \Sigma' \vdash v : t$$

- Inversion lemmas for the well-formed value relation as in the proof of FSOUND for the boolean feature in Section 5.1 are proven by induction over the relation.

The proofs of the first and second kind of feature interactions are straightforward; the inversion lemmas of the third kind can be dispatched by tactics hooked into the type class inference algorithm.

The framework itself consists of about 4,400 LoC of which about 2,000 LoC comprise the implementation of the monad transformers and their algebraic laws. The size in LoC of the implementation of semantic evaluation and typing functions and the reusable feature theorem for each language feature is given in the left box in Figure 12. The right box lists the sizes of the effect theorems. Each language needs on average 110 LoC to assemble its semantic functions and soundness proofs from those of its features and the effect theorem for its set of effects.

8. Related Work

While previous work has explored the basic techniques of modularizing dynamic semantics of languages with effects, our work is the first to show how to also do modular proofs. Adding the ability to do modular proofs required the development of novel techniques for reasoning about modular components with effects.

8.1 Functional Models for Modular Side Effects

Monads and Monad Transformers Since Moggi [31] first proposed monads to model side-effects, and Wadler [50] popularized them in the context of Haskell, various researchers (e.g., [21, 45]) have sought to modularize monads. Monad transformers emerged [6, 28] from this process, and in later years various alternative implementation designs facilitating monad (transformer) implementations, have been developed, including Filinksi's layered monads [10] and Jaskelioff's Monatron [19].

Monads and Subtyping Filinski's MultiMonadic MetaLanguage (M^3L) [11, 12] embraces the monadic approach, but uses subtyping (or subeffecting) to combine the effects of different components. The subtyping relation is fixed at the program or language level, which does not provide the adaptability we achieve with constrained polymorphism.

Algebraic Effects and Effect Handlers In the semantics community the algebraic theory of computational effects [39] has been an active area of research. Many of the laws about effects, which we have not seen before in the context of functional programming, can be found throughout the semantics literature. Our first four laws for exceptions, for example, have been presented by Levy [26].

A more recent model of side effects are effect handlers. They were introduced by Plotkin and Pretnar [38] as a generalization from exception handlers to handlers for a range of computational effects, such as I/O, state, and nondeterminism. Bauer and Pretnar [4] built the language *Eff* around effect handlers and show how to implement a wide range of effects in it. Kammar et al. [22] showed that effect handlers can be implemented in terms of delimited continuations or free monads.

The major advantage of effect handlers over monads is that they are more easily composed, as any composition of effect operations and corresponding handlers is valid. In contrast, not every composition of monads is a monad. In the future, we plan on investigating the use of effect handlers instead of monad transformers, which could potentially reduce the amount of work involved on proofs about interactions of effects.

Other Effect Models Other useful models have been proposed, such as *applicative functors* [30] and *arrows* [17], each with their own axioms and modularity properties.

8.2 Modular Effectful Semantics

There are several works on how to modularize semantics with effects, although none of these works considers reasoning.

Mosses [33] modularizes structural operational semantics by means of a label transition system where extensible labels capture effects like state and abrupt termination. Swierstra [46] presents modular syntax with functor coproducts and modular semantics with algebra compositions. To support effects, he uses modular syntax to define a free monad. The effectful semantics for this free monad is not given in a modular manner, however. Jaskelioff et al. [20] present a modular approach for operational semantics on top of Swierstra's modular syntax, although they do not cover conventional semantics with side-effects. Both Schrijvers and Oliveira [42] and Bahr and Hvitved [2] have shown how to define modular semantics with monads for effects; this is essentially the approach followed in this paper for modular semantics.

8.3 Effects and Reasoning

Non-Modular Monadic Reasoning Although monads are a purely functional way to encapsulate computational-effects, programs using monads are challenging to reason about. The main issue is that monads provide an abstraction over purely functional models of effects, allowing functional programmers to write programs in terms of abstract operations like $\gg=$, $return$, or get and put. One way to reason about monadic programs is to remove the abstraction provided by such operations [18]. However, this approach is fundamentally non-modular.

Modular Monadic Reasoning Several more modular approaches to modular monadic reasoning have been pursued in the past.

One approach to modular monadic reasoning is to exploit *parametricity* [40, 49]. Voigtländer [48] has shown how to derive parametricity theorems for type constructor classes such as $Monad$. Unfortunately, the reasoning power of parametricity is limited, and parametricity is not supported by proof assistants like Coq.

A second technique uses *algebraic laws*. Liang and Hudak [27] present one of the earliest examples of using algebraic laws for reasoning. They use algebraic laws for reader monads to prove correctness properties about a modular compiler. In contrast to our work, their compiler correctness proofs are pen-and-paper and thus more informal than our proofs. Since they are not restricted by a termination checker or the use of positive types only, they exploit features like general recursion in their definitions. Oliveira et al. [35] have also used algebraic laws for the state monad, in combination with parametricity, for modular proofs of non-interference of aspect-oriented advice. Hinze and Gibbons discuss several other algebraic laws for various types of monads [13]. However, as far as we know, we are the first to provide an extensive mechanized library for monads and algebraic laws in Coq.

8.4 Mechanization of Monad Transformers

Huffmann [16] illustrates an approach for mechanizing type constructor classes in Isabelle/HOL with monad transformers. He considers transformer variants of the resumption, error and writer monads, but features only the generic functor, monad and transformer laws. The work tackles many issues that are not relevant for our Coq setting, such as lack of parametric polymorphism and explicit modeling of laziness.

9. Conclusion

In previous work [9] we have shown that it is possible to modularize meta-theory along two dimensions: 1) language constructs and 2) operations and proofs. A significant limitation of that work is that it only considered pure languages.

This work lifts that limitation and shows how to develop modular meta-theory for languages with effects. Our solution uses monads and corresponding algebraic laws for reasoning about different types of effects. The key challenge that we have solved is how to formulate and prove a general type-soundness theorem in a modular way that enables the reuse of feature proofs across multiple languages with different sets of effects. This turned out to be non-trivial because existing formulations of type-soundness are very sensitive to the particular effects used by the language.

As a secondary contribution, our work shows that algebraic laws about effects scale up to realistic verification tasks such as meta-theoretic proofs. As far as we know, it is their largest application to date. In this setting, the proof assistant Coq has been invaluable. While the typically smaller examples in the functional programming community can easily be dealt with by pen-and-paper proofs, that approach would not have been manageable for the large family of type-soundness proofs for mini-ML variants, as keeping track of large goals and hypotheses by hand would be too painful and error-prone.

Acknowledgements We would like to thank the anonymous reviewers for their many comments and suggestions. This work was supported by the National Science Foundation under Grant CCF 0724979.

References

[1] Brian E. Aydemir et al. Mechanized metatheory for the masses: The poplmark challenge. In *Theorem Proving in Higher Order Logics*, volume 3603 of *Lecture Notes in Computer Science*, pages 50–65. Springer, 2005.

[2] Patrick Bahr and Tom Hvitved. Compositional data types. In *Proceedings of the seventh ACM SIGPLAN workshop on Generic programming*, WGP '11, pages 83–94. ACM, 2011.

[3] Don Batory, Jongwook Kim, and Peter Höfner. Feature interactions, products, and composition. In *Proceedings of the 10th ACM international conference on Generative programming and component engineering*, GPCE '11. ACM, 2011.

[4] Andrej Bauer and Matija Pretnar. Programming with algebraic effects and handlers. *CoRR*, abs/1203.1539, 2012.

[5] Corrado Böhm and Alessandro Berarducci. Automatic synthesis of typed -programs on term algebras. *Theoretical Computer Science*, 39(0):135 – 154, 1985.

[6] Pietro Cenciarelli and Eugenio Moggi. A syntactic approach to modularity in denotational semantics. In *In Proceedings of the Conference on Category Theory and Computer Science*, CCTCS '93, 1993.

[7] Adam Chlipala. Parametric higher-order abstract syntax for mechanized semantics. In *Proceedings of the 13th ACM SIGPLAN international conference on Functional programming*, ICFP '08, pages 143–156. ACM, 2008.

[8] Dominique Clément, Thierry Despeyroux, Gilles Kahn, and Joëlle Despeyroux. A simple applicative language: mini-ml. In *Proceedings of the 1986 ACM conference on LISP and functional programming*, LFP '86, pages 13–27. ACM, 1986.

[9] Benjamin Delaware, Bruno C. d. S. Oliveira, and Tom Schrijvers. Meta-theory à la carte. In *Proceedings of the 40th annual ACM SIGPLAN-SIGACT symposium on Principles of programming languages*, POPL '13, pages 207–218. ACM, 2013.

[10] Andrzej Filinski. Representing layered monads. In *Proceedings of the 26th ACM SIGPLAN-SIGACT symposium on Principles of programming languages*, POPL '99, pages 175–188. ACM, 1999.

[11] Andrzej Filinski. On the relations between monadic semantics. *Theor. Comput. Sci.*, 375(1-3):41–75, 2007.

[12] Andrzej Filinski. Monads in action. In *Proceedings of the 37th annual ACM SIGPLAN-SIGACT symposium on Principles of programming languages*, POPL '10, pages 483–494. ACM, 2010.

[13] Jeremy Gibbons and Ralf Hinze. Just do it: simple monadic equational reasoning. In *Proceedings of the 16th ACM SIGPLAN international conference on Functional programming*, ICFP '11, pages 2–14. ACM, 2011.

[14] Joseph A. Goguen, James W. Thatcher, Eric G. Wagner, and Jesse B. Wright. Initial algebra semantics and continuous algebras. *J. ACM*, 24(1), 1977.

[15] Georges Gonthier. Engineering mathematics: the odd order theorem proof. In *Proceedings of the 40th annual ACM SIGPLAN-SIGACT symposium on Principles of programming languages*, POPL '13, pages 1–2. ACM, 2013.

[16] Brian Huffman. Formal verification of monad transformers. In *Proceedings of the 17th ACM SIGPLAN international conference on Functional programming*, ICFP '12, pages 15–16. ACM, 2012.

[17] John Hughes. Generalising monads to arrows. *Sci. Comput. Program.*, 37(1-3):67–111, 2000.

[18] Graham Hutton and Diana Fulger. Reasoning about effects: Seeing the wood through the trees. In *Proceedings of the Ninth Symposium on Trends in Functional Programming*, 2008.

[19] Mauro Jaskelioff. Monatron: An extensible monad transformer library. In *Implementation and Application of Functional Languages*, volume 5836 of *Lecture Notes in Computer Science*, pages 233–248. Springer, 2011.

[20] Mauro Jaskelioff, Neil Ghani, and Graham Hutton. Modularity and implementation of mathematical operational semantics. *Electron. Notes Theor. Comput. Sci.*, 229(5):75–95, 2011.

[21] Mark P. Jones and Luc Duponcheel. Composing monads. Research Report YALEU/DCS/RR-1004, Yale University, 1993.

[22] Ohad Kammar, Sam Lindley, and Nicolas Oury. Handlers in action. In *The 1st ACM SIGPLAN Workshop on Higher-Order Programming with Effects*, HOPE '12, 2012.

[23] Klein et al. sel4: formal verification of an operating-system kernel. *Commun. ACM*, 53(6):107–115, 2010.

[24] Peter Lee. *Realistic Compiler Generation*. MIT Press, Cambridge, MA, 1989.

[25] Xavier Leroy. Formal verification of a realistic compiler. *Commun. ACM*, 52(7):107–115, 2009.

[26] Paul Blain Levy. Monads and adjunctions for global exceptions. *Electron. Notes Theor. Comput. Sci.*, 158:261–287, 2006.

[27] Sheng Liang and Paul Hudak. Modular denotational semantics for compiler construction. In *Proceedings of the 6th European Symposium on Programming Languages and Systems*, ESOP '96, pages 219–234. Springer-Verlag, 1996.

[28] Sheng Liang, Paul Hudak, and Mark Jones. Monad transformers and modular interpreters. In *Proceedings of the 22nd ACM SIGPLAN-SIGACT symposium on Principles of programming languages*, POPL '95, pages 333–343. ACM, 1995.

[29] Grant Malcolm. *Algebraic Data Types and Program Transformation*. PhD thesis, Rijksuniversiteit Groningen, September 1990.

[30] Conor Mcbride and Ross Paterson. Applicative programming with effects. *J. Funct. Program.*, 18(1):1–13, 2008.

[31] Eugenio Moggi. An abstract view of programming languages. Technical Report ECS-LFCS-90-113, Edinburgh University, Department of Computer Science, June 1989.

[32] Peter D. Mosses. A basic abstract semantic algebra. In *Semantics of Data Types*, volume 173 of *Lecture Notes in Computer Science*, pages 87–107. Springer, 1984.

[33] Peter D. Mosses. Modular structural operational semantics. *Journal of Logic and Algebraic Programming*, 6061(0):195 – 228, 2004.

[34] Bruno C. d. S. Oliveira. Modular visitor components. In *Proceedings of the 23rd European Conference on Object-Oriented Programming*, ECOOP 2009, pages 269–293. Springer-Verlag, 2009.

[35] Bruno C. d. S. Oliveira, Tom Schrijvers, and William R. Cook. EffectiveAdvice: disciplined advice with explicit effects. In *Proceedings of the 9th International Conference on Aspect-Oriented Software Development*, AOSD '10, pages 109–120. ACM, 2010.

[36] Frank Pfenning and Christine Paulin-Mohring. Inductively defined types in the calculus of constructions. In *Mathematical Foundations of Programming Semantics*, volume 442 of *Lecture Notes in Computer Science*, pages 209–228. Springer-Verlag, 1990.

[37] Benjamin C. Pierce. *Types and Programming Languages*. MIT Press, 2002.

[38] Gordon Plotkin and Matija Pretnar. Handlers of algebraic effects. In *Programming Languages and Systems: 18th European Symposium on Programming, ESOP 2009*, volume 5502 of *Lecture Notes in Computer Science*, pages 80–94. Springer, 2009.

[39] Gordon D. Plotkin and John Power. Notions of computation determine monads. In *Proceedings of the 5th International Conference on Foundations of Software Science and Computation Structures*, FoSSaCS '02, pages 342–356. Springer-Verlag, 2002.

[40] John C. Reynolds. Types, abstraction and parametric polymorphism. In *IFIP Congress*, pages 513–523, 1983.

[41] Tom Schrijvers and Bruno C. d. S. Oliveira. Monads, zippers and views: virtualizing the monad stack. In *Proceedings of the 16th ACM SIGPLAN international conference on Functional programming*, ICFP '11, pages 32–44. ACM, 2011.

[42] Tom Schrijvers and Bruno C. d. S. Oliveira. The monad zipper. Report CW 595, Dept. of Computer Science, K.U.Leuven, 2010.

[43] Zhong Shao. Certified software. *Commun. ACM*, 53(12):56–66, 2010.

[44] Antonis Stampoulis and Zhong Shao. Veriml: typed computation of logical terms inside a language with effects. In *Proceedings of the 15th ACM SIGPLAN international conference on Functional programming*, ICFP '10, pages 333–344. ACM, 2010.

[45] Guy L. Steele, Jr. Building interpreters by composing monads. In *Proceedings of the 21st ACM SIGPLAN-SIGACT symposium on Principles of programming languages*, POPL '94, pages 472–492. ACM, 1994.

[46] Wouter Swierstra. Data types à la carte. *J. Funct. Program.*, 18(4):423–436, 2008.

[47] Tarmo Uustalu and Varmo Vene. Coding recursion à la Mendler. In *Proceedings 2nd Workshop on Generic Programming, WGP '00*, pages 69–85, 2000.

[48] Janis Voigtländer. Free theorems involving type constructor classes: functional pearl. In *Proceedings of the 14th ACM SIGPLAN international conference on Functional programming*, ICFP '09, pages 173–184. ACM, 2009.

[49] Philip Wadler. Theorems for free! In *Proceedings of the fourth international conference on Functional programming languages and computer architecture*, FPCA '89, pages 347–359. ACM, 1989.

[50] Philip Wadler. Monads for functional programming. In *Proceedings of the Marktoberdorf Summer School on Program Design Calculi*, August 1992.

[51] Philip Wadler. The Expression Problem. Email, November 1998. Discussion on the Java Genericity mailing list.

[52] Philip Wadler and Stephen Blott. How to make ad-hoc polymorphism less ad hoc. In *Proceedings of the 16th ACM SIGPLAN-SIGACT symposium on Principles of programming languages*, POPL '89, pages 60–76. ACM, 1989.

[53] Andrew K. Wright and Matthias Felleisen. A syntactic approach to type soundness. *Information and Computation*, 115(1):38 – 94, 1994.

Modular and Automated Type-Soundness Verification for Language Extensions

Florian Lorenzen
TU Berlin, Germany

Sebastian Erdweg
TU Darmstadt, Germany

Abstract

Language extensions introduce high-level programming constructs that protect programmers from low-level details and repetitive tasks. For such an abstraction barrier to be sustainable, it is important that no errors are reported in terms of generated code. A typical strategy is to check the original user code prior to translation into a low-level encoding, applying the assumption that the translation does not introduce new errors. Unfortunately, such assumption is untenable in general, but in particular in the context of extensible programming languages, such as Racket or SugarJ, that allow regular programmers to define language extensions.

In this paper, we present a formalism for building and automatically verifying the type-soundness of syntactic language extensions. To build a type-sound language extension with our formalism, a developer declares an extended syntax, type rules for the extended syntax, and translation rules into the (possibly further extended) base language. Our formalism then validates that the user-defined type rules are sufficient to guarantee that the code generated by the translation rules cannot contain any type errors. This effectively ensures that an initial type check prior to translation precludes type errors in generated code. We have implemented a core system in PLT Redex and we have developed a syntactically extensible variant of System F_ω that we extend with *let* notation, monadic *do* blocks, and algebraic data types. Our formalism verifies the soundness of each extension automatically.

Categories and Subject Descriptors D.2.4 [*Software/Program Verification*]; I.2.2 [*Automatic Programming*]: Program transformation; D.3.2 [*Language Classifications*]: Extensible languages

General Terms Languages, Verification

Keywords language extensibility, type soundness, automatic verification, metaprogramming, macros, SugarJ

1. Introduction

Whenever code generation is used to abstract from low-level details or to provide high-level interfaces to software developers, type errors in generated code jeopardize the abstraction barrier: First, error messages are in terms of generated code and thus expose programmers to low-level details that should be hidden. Second, manual inspection of generated code may be necessary to identify the cause of the type error. Third, since a type error in generated code may be caused by either a defective generator or by invalid generator input, manual inspection of the generator may be necessary to identify the generator's contract and whether the input adheres to that contract. Type errors in generated code present a serious usability threat for abstractions implemented via code generation.

In this paper, we address above problem in the context of code generators that extend a base language with new language constructs by translation into other constructs of the base language. Such code generators are sometimes referred to as desugarings. Many compilers employ desugarings to transform programs of the input language into a core language, so that subsequent compiler phases can focus on fewer language constructs. Moreover, macro systems empower regular programmers to introduce new language constructs via desugaring transformations. Despite wide-spread application of desugarings, few existing compilers and no existing macro system can *guarantee the absence of type errors in desugared code*.

To this end, we present SoundExt, a formalism for soundly extending a base language with new language constructs. SoundExt statically and modularly validates a language extension and guarantees that desugared code does not contain type errors. More specifically, for each language extension, SoundExt requires the definition of (i) an extended syntax, (ii) type rules for checking programs that use the extended syntax, and (iii) a desugaring transformation that translates a program of the extended syntax into a base-language program. SoundExt then derives proof obligations for each user-defined type rule: For all programs permitted by the type rule, the desugared version of these programs must have the same type. SoundExt synthesizes the corresponding proof for each type rule by instrumenting the inference engine with additional axioms that correspond to the assumptions of the user-supplied type rules. We present the details of our methodology in Section 3, where we also show that the validity of each derived proof obligation entails the following high-level property:

$$\Gamma \vdash_{ext} e : T \;\wedge\; e \rightsquigarrow^* e' \;\wedge\; e' \in Base \quad\Rightarrow\quad \Gamma \vdash_{base} e' : T$$

That is, given a program e that is well-typed in the extended type system, if this program desugars into a base-language program e', then the desugared program is well-typed in the base type system. In other words, type checking the user-supplied program is sufficient to ensure the absence of type errors in desugared code.

To demonstrate the expressiveness of SoundExt, we instantiate the formalism for SugarFomega, a syntactically extensible variant of System F_ω. Besides standard lambda and type abstraction, SugarFomega features variants, records, and higher-order iso-recursive types as well as SugarJ-like macros with flexible syntax [5, 8, 10]. Using this macro system, SugarFomega programmers can introduce new language constructs at the level of expressions, types, and kinds. Accordingly, programmers define additional "type" rules using type and kind judgments. We have implemented language extensions of

ICFP '13, September 25–27, 2013, Boston, MA, USA.

ACM 978-1-4503-2326-0/13/09... $15.00.
http://dx.doi.org/10.1145/10.1145/2500365.2500596

SugarFomega for *let* expressions, monadic *do* blocks (no implicit dictionary passing), and algebraic data types. SoundExt modularly validated each of these extensions and guarantees that they are sound with respect to the type system of System F_ω.

In summary, we make the following contributions:

- We present the design of SoundExt, a formalism for type-sound language extensibility.
- SoundExt automatically verifies the type-soundness of language extensions by deriving type rules for generated programs and proving the admissibility of these type rules.
- To prove admissibility we check derivability by instrumenting the type checker to use a type rule's premises as additional axioms.
- We present a formalization of SoundExt based on PLT Redex and prove that the desugarings of successfully verified language extensions adhere to type preservation and progress.
- We verify that SoundExt extensions compose soundly as long as there is no syntactic overlap.
- We implement the extensible language SugarFomega based on SoundExt and show how SoundExt enables us to soundly extend SugarFomega with *let* expressions, monadic *do* blocks, and algebraic data types.

2. Illustrating example

Figure 1 shows the standard type rules of the simply-typed lambda calculus as they, for example, appear in Pierce's Types and Programming Languages [22]. The soundness of the corresponding type system is an established fact in the programming-language community. However, when extending such a base language, one has to manually reestablish the soundness theorem for the extended language [31]. As we demonstrate with SoundExt in this paper, we can automatically verify the soundness of the extended type system for language extensions that are defined through translation into the base language.

For example, consider the extension of the simply-typed lambda calculus with *let* expressions:

$$e ::= \ldots \mid \text{let}\, x : T = e \,\text{in}\, e$$

We can rewrite *let* expressions to the simply-typed lambda calculus using the following desugaring:

$$\textsf{desugar-let} : (\text{let}\, x : T = e_1 \,\text{in}\, e_2) \dashrightarrow (\lambda x : T.e_2)\; e_1$$

Since we want to detect and report type errors prior to desugaring, we extend the type system of the simply-typed lambda calculus with a type rule for *let* expressions:

$$\text{T-LET}\,\frac{\Gamma \vdash e_1 : T_1 \qquad \Gamma, x : T_1 \vdash e_2 : T_2}{\Gamma \vdash \text{let}\, x : T_1 = e_1 \,\text{in}\, e_2 : T_2}$$

In the hope of preventing type errors in generated code, we use the extended type system to validate a user program prior to any desugaring. This way, the rewrite rule desugar-let will only be applied to a *let* expression that has been checked by T-Let. For example, the expression

$$\text{let}\, n : \text{Nat} = 17 \,\text{in}\, n + n$$

is well-typed since 17 has type Nat and the judgment $n : \text{Nat} \vdash n + n : \text{Nat}$ holds. Therefore, it is safe to apply the rewrite rule, that is, the rewriting generates a well-typed expression:

$$(\lambda n : \text{Nat}.n + n)\; 17$$

Conceptually, there are two sources of possible errors. First, the rewrite rule may be defective and produce ill-typed or wrongly typed code, even though the input *let* expression was well-typed according to T-Let. Second, the type rule may be defective and admit *let* expressions that are not well-typed. For example, a defective rewrite rule $(\text{let}\, x : T = e_1 \,\text{in}\, e_2) \dashrightarrow (e_2\; e_1)$ would translate above

$$\text{T-VAR}\,\frac{x : T \in \Gamma}{\Gamma \vdash x : T} \qquad \text{T-ABS}\,\frac{\Gamma, x : T_1 \vdash e : T_2}{\Gamma \vdash \lambda x : T_1.e : T_1 \to T_2}$$

$$\text{T-APP}\,\frac{\Gamma \vdash e_1 : T_1 \to T_2 \qquad \Gamma \vdash e_2 : T_1}{\Gamma \vdash e_1\; e_2 : T_2}$$

Figure 1. Type rules of the simply-typed lambda calculus.

let expression into the ill-typed expression $(n + n)\; 17$. Conversely, suppose we forgot the first premise in the definition of the type rule T-Let. This defective type rule would admit the expression $(\text{let}\, f : \text{Nat} \to \text{Nat}{=}17 \,\text{in}\, f\, 0)$, which the (correct) rewrite rule desugar-let translates into the ill-typed program $(\lambda f : \text{Nat} \to \text{Nat}.f\, 0)\; 17$. Technically, these two sources of errors are two sides of the same coin: To guarantee the absence of type errors in generated code, we must ensure that *the rewrite rule and the type rule are correct with respect to each other.*

To this end, we can read the type rule T-Let as a contract for the rewrite rule desugar-let: The rewrite rule may assume all input adheres to the type rule T-Let, and the rewrite rule must produce an expression of the type declared in the type rule. In essence, the rewrite rule must be type-preserving with respect to the type rules. If this holds, we can type check the user program once before desugaring and know that the desugared program has the same type.

To verify that user-defined rewrite rules preserve types according to the user-defined type rules, we proceed as follows. We symbolically apply the rewrite rule to the subject of the corresponding type rule. For example, for the *let* extension we obtain the type rule T-Let':

$$\text{T-LET'}\,\frac{\Gamma \vdash e_1 : T_1 \qquad \Gamma, x : T_1 \vdash e_2 : T_2}{\Gamma \vdash (\lambda x : T_1.e_2)\; e_1 : T_2}$$

We could use this type rule to validate the code generated by desugar-let. Instead, we want to show that this type rule is *admissible*, that is, for all expressions typeable through applications of T-Let', there is a derivation in the type system without T-Let' given the same context yielding the same type. Accordingly, we do not need T-Let' to type check the generated code, because the other type rules already are expressive enough.

SoundExt automatically infers proof obligations for the admissibility of derived type rules. But SoundExt also automatically verifies these proof obligations by checking the derivability of type rules, which entails admissibility. We can reuse the type system for checking the derivability of a derived type rule if (i) we interpret all metavariables in the assumptions and conclusion as constants that only unify with themselves and (ii) we temporarily add the assumptions of the derived type rule as axioms to the system. A type rule then is derivable if we can find a derivation of the modified conclusion given the additional axioms.

For example, for T-Let' we try to find a derivation for $\Gamma \vdash (\lambda x : T_1.e_2)\; e_1 : T_2$ given the axioms (Ax1) $\Gamma \vdash e_1 : T_1$ and (Ax2) $\Gamma, x : T_1 \vdash e_2 : T_2$. Indeed, we can infer the following derivation, where the occurring metavariables Γ, x, T_1, T_2, e_1, e_2 are constants.

$$\text{T-APP}\,\frac{\text{T-ABS}\,\dfrac{\text{AX2}\,\dfrac{}{\Gamma, x : T_1 \vdash e_2 : T_2}}{\Gamma \vdash \lambda x : T_1.e_2 : T_1 \to T_2} \qquad \text{AX1}\,\dfrac{}{\Gamma \vdash e_1 : T_1}}{\Gamma \vdash (\lambda x : T_1.e_2)\; e_1 : T_2}$$

This derivation shows that the type rule T-Let' is derivable. As consequence, given an expression that is well-typed according to the user-defined type rule T-Let, we know that the expression generated by desugar-let has the same type as the original *let* expression. Accordingly, no type errors can emerge from the code generated by the desugaring rule.

In the following section we describe the approach followed by SoundExt formally and prove that the derivability of derived type rules indeed entails type preservation of desugarings.

$$
\begin{array}{ll}
t ::= x \mid (c\,\overline{t}) & \textit{Terms} \\
J ::= t \vdash t : t & \textit{Judgments} \\
I ::= \forall \overline{x}.\ \overline{J} \Rightarrow J & \textit{Inference rules} \\
R ::= t \dashrightarrow t & \textit{Rewrite rules} \\
E ::= ext\ \overline{I}\ \overline{R} & \textit{Extensions} \\
B ::= \overline{I} & \textit{Base systems}
\end{array}
$$

Figure 2. Syntax for declaring extensions.

$$
\text{R-MATCH}\ \frac{rewrite\ \overline{R}\ e = e'}{e \rightsquigarrow_{\overline{R}} e'} \qquad \text{R-CON}\ \frac{e_2 \rightsquigarrow_{\overline{R}} e_2' \quad e_1 \not\rightsquigarrow_{\overline{R}} e_1'\ \forall e_1 \in \overline{e_1}}{c\,\overline{e_1}\,e_2\,\overline{e_3} \rightsquigarrow_{\overline{R}} c\,\overline{e_1}\,e_2'\,\overline{e_3}}
$$

Figure 3. Specification of a left-to-right, one-step rewriting.

3. SoundExt

A language extension defines new syntax, type rules for that syntax, and rewritings of that syntax into the base language. SoundExt provides a language for the declaration of such extensions and a verification procedure for checking type soundness of extensions. We verify that our verification procedure is sufficient to guarantee that no type errors are in desugared code.

Our formalization is based on an implementation of SoundExt in PLT Redex [11].[1] However, whereas our PLT Redex implementation contains a concrete rewrite engine and inference engine, we parameterize our formalization over these engines and formulate minimal assumptions. Moreover, like the PLT Redex implementation, our formalization ignores all aspects of concrete syntax and assumes programmers write abstract syntax trees directly; our implementation of SugarFomega (see next section) supports the declaration of concrete syntax for extensions.

3.1 A language for declaring extensions

We define abstract syntax for the declaration of extensions as shown in Figure 2. We use a generic term representation to generalize over the expression, types, and contexts of any particular language. Essentially, a term t is an abstract syntax tree consisting of constructor applications $(c\,\overline{t})$ (overlines denote sequences) and metavariables x. We use these terms for declaration of judgments J. A judgment $t_1 \vdash t_2 : t_3$ relates a subject t_2 to an object t_3 under a context t_1. We conventionally choose metavariable names that resemble type checking as in $\Gamma \vdash e : T$.

Multiple judgments make up an inference rule, where all but the last judgments are premises and free metavariables must be explicitly quantified. For example, we can encode the type rule T-Abs for lambda abstraction in this format:

$$
\begin{aligned}
I_{\text{ABS}} = \forall\, \Gamma\, x\, e\, T_1\, T_2.\ \ & (\texttt{Bind}\ \Gamma\ x\ T_1) \vdash e : T_2 \\
\Rightarrow\ \ & \Gamma \vdash (\texttt{abs}\ x\ T_1\ e) : (\texttt{Fun}\ T_1\ T_2)
\end{aligned}
$$

For axioms, that is, inference rules without premises, we simply write $\forall \overline{x}.\ J$; for inference rules that do not bind any metavariables, we drop the quantifier $\overline{J} \Rightarrow J$.

Similar to inference rules, we can use terms to specify rewritings $e_1 \dashrightarrow e_2$, where e_1 may contain metavariables to pattern match on a term and e_2 is a generation template that can use the metavariables bound during pattern matching. In contrast to inference rules all meta-variables of the left-hand side of a rewrite rule may be instantiated during pattern matching. We therefore omit an explicit quantification. The syntax of rewrite rules is agnostic to the meaning of the terms, it may be an expression or a type, for example. Nevertheless, we restrict ourselves in this section to rewritings of expressions, that is, only terms in the subject position of inference rules. In Section 4 we present a generalized form that also rewrites types.

Based on these definitions, we define an extension as a list of inference rules and rewrite rules.

The base language B only consists of inference rules but no rewrite rules. The dynamic semantics of a base language and its relationship to the static semantics is completely orthogonal to SoundExt since we are only interested in typing statements about base language programs.

[1] Implementation available online: `http://sugarj.org/fomega`

3.2 Assumptions about the rewrite engine

SoundExt is not tied to a specific rewriting algorithm. We assume a function $rewrite\ \overline{R}\ e$ that performs a single rewriting step by one of the rules in $\overline{R}$ or returns $fail$ if no rule is applicable. Since we want to apply the rewrite function to subjects of inference rules that contain metavariables, we must require that rewriting is closed under metavariable substitution:

Assumption 1 (Metavariable substitution-invariance). *If* $rewrite\ \overline{R}\ e[\overline{x}] = e'[\overline{x}]$, *then* $rewrite\ \overline{R}\ e[\overline{t}] = e'\ \overline{t}]$.

We write $e[\overline{x}]$ to denote a term e in which at most the metavariables $\overline{x}$ appear free, and $e[\overline{t}]$ for the substitutions of these metavariables by the terms $\overline{t}$.

This assumption requires that rewriting is independent of metavariable occurrences. For example, consider the following two rewrite rules:

$$
\begin{aligned}
&\textsf{plus1} : (\texttt{Plus}\ (\texttt{Suc}\ m)\ n) \dashrightarrow (\texttt{Suc}\ (\texttt{Plus}\ m\ n)) \\
&\textsf{plus2} : (\texttt{Plus}\ m\ n) \qquad\quad \dashrightarrow n
\end{aligned}
$$

Given the input term $(\texttt{Plus}\ x\ \texttt{Zero})$ with metavariable x, the rewrite function might do pattern matching to apply plus2 and return Zero. However, if we substitue $(\texttt{Suc}\ y)$ for x, rule plus1 becomes applicable and yields $(\texttt{Suc}\ (\texttt{Plus}\ y\ \texttt{Zero}))$. This violates Assumption 1 because applying the same substitution to the old result does not yield the new result. However, it is easy to recover this problem by expanding the pattern matching of plus2:

$$
\textsf{plus2}' : (\texttt{Plus Zero}\ n) \dashrightarrow n
$$

Given this rule, the rewrite function would fail for the input term $(\texttt{Plus}\ x\ \texttt{Zero})$, which is consistent with Assumption 1. In general, a rewrite engine should arrange that if a rewrite rule inspects a subtree, this subtree cannot match a metavariable. In our PLT Redex implementation, we assume that user-defined rewrite rules already adhere to the above properties.

An alternative solution to the problem illustrated by plus1 and plus2 is to require *rewrite* to perform top-to-bottom matching of rules and to reverse the order of the two. In that case, plus2 would be applied for boths inputs. However, this would not relieve us from Assumption 1 and we therefore decided to leave the order of matching unspecified since this poses fewer assumptions on the rewrite engine and has a more declarative feeling.

Based on the function *rewrite*, we define the function $e_1 \rightsquigarrow_{\overline{R}} e_2$ that performs a top-down, left-to-right, one-step rewriting of e_1 using *rewrite* (Figure 3). We write $e \rightsquigarrow^*_{\overline{R}} e'$ for the reflexive, transitive closure of $e \rightsquigarrow_{\overline{R}} e'$.

Finally, we require that *rewrite* does not succeed on terms of the base language. As we will later show, this ensures that the structure of base-language programs is preserved by $\rightsquigarrow_{\overline{R}}$.

Assumption 2 (Rewrite fails on base-language constructors). *For any base-language constructor* c, $rewrite\ \overline{R}\ (c\,\overline{e}) = fail$.

3.3 Assumptions about the inference engine

SoundExt requires developers to declare static analyses for extensions via inference rules. To reason about the user-defined inference rules and to prove their soundness, SoundExt employs an inference engine to compute derivations. As for the rewriting, SoundExt does not require any specific inference engine. Instead, we assume an inference engine that, given inference rules $\overline{I}$ and a judgment J, checks if J can be derived using the rules $\overline{I}$. If successful, the inference engine yields a concrete derivation $\overline{I} \succ J$. Without going into any detail, we require correctness of the inference engine:

Assumption 3 (Correctness)**.** *If the inference engine yields a derivation $\overline{I} \succ J$, then the derivation only consists of valid applications of the rules in $\overline{I}$.*

Since we want to use the inference engine not only for checking concrete programs but also for mechanically proving entailment between judgments, we require proper handling of metavariables by the inference engine. Specifically, like for the rewrite engine, we require that the inference of derivations is closed under metavariable substitution (in the context of logical consequences this property is known as *structurality* [17]):

Assumption 4 (Metavariable substitution-invariance)**.** *If $\overline{I[\overline{x}]} \succ J[\overline{x}]$, then $\overline{I[\overline{t}\,]} \succ J[\overline{t}\,]$.*

This requirement means that if the inference engine is able to derive $J[\overline{x}]$ using $\overline{I[\overline{x}]}$ without any knowledge about the free metavariables $\overline{x}$, then a similar derivation must exist when instantiating the free metavariables with concrete terms. For example, if the inference engine can deduce a derivation for the identity function

$$(I_{\text{VAR}}\ I_{\text{ABS}}\ I_{\text{APP}}) \succ (\Gamma \vdash (\texttt{abs}\ x\ T\ x) : (\texttt{Fun}\ T\ T))$$

then a derivation must exist for any replacements of the free metavariables Γ, x, and T.[2]

Recall that our inference rules quantify bound metavariables, as is visible in the inference rule for lambda abstraction I_{ABS} shown in Section 3.1. SoundExt capitalizes the fact that inference rules can also contain free metavariables to install assumptions about specific metavariables. In contrast to bound metavariables, free metavariables in an inference rule may not be instantiated when applying the inference rule. For example, when deriving

$$(\forall \Gamma.\ \Gamma \vdash e : T) \succ \emptyset \vdash e : T$$

only the bound variable Γ gets instantiated to $\emptyset$ whereas e and T must match literally. Accordingly, we could not derive $\emptyset \vdash e_2 : T$ from the same inference rule, because e does not literally match e_2.

Finally, we require the inference engine to satisfy the cut rule:

Assumption 5 (Cut)**.** *If $\overline{I} \succ J_1$ and $\overline{I}\ J_1 \succ J_2$, then $\overline{I} \succ J_2$.*

We do not make any assumptions on decidability of the inference rules. Usually, the rules of a base system are in an algorithmic form to obtain a complete type checker but this is not required. Furthermore, inference rules of an extension may lead to an undecidable system, even if the base system is decidable. That is, we have no means to prevent nontermination of the type checker.

In our PLT Redex implementation, we do not use quantifiers in inference rules but implicitly quantify over all free variables. To encode non-unifiable metavariables, we wrap such metavariables in $(\texttt{symbol}\ x)$ nodes. Otherwise, our inference engine performs a simple proof-tree search and respects both metavariable substitution-invariance and the cut rule.

3.4 Extension soundness

Using the rewrite engine and the inference engine, we define a verification procedure for the soundness of extensions relative to a base system. The basic idea is to show that rewrite rules are type-preserving. We do so by (i) deriving an inference rule that admits exactly the programs generated by the rewrite rule but requires the

[2] Note that there is only a single syntactic category in SoundExt: terms t. As far as SoundExt or the inference engine are concerned, any term can be used to represent any object-language construct, such as a variable.

An extension $ext\ \overline{I}\ \overline{R}$ is sound with respect to a base system B if for all typing rules $I \in \overline{I}$ the following steps succeed:

Let $I = \forall \overline{x}.\ \overline{J[\overline{x}]} \Rightarrow (\Gamma[\overline{x}] \vdash e[\overline{x}] : T[\overline{x}])$.
Let $\overline{y}$ be fresh and distinct variables with $len\ \overline{y} = len\ \overline{x}$.

1. Perform one-step rewriting of rule's subject with extension's rewrite rules:
$$e[\overline{x}] \rightsquigarrow_{\overline{R}} e'[\overline{x}]$$
2. Show that derived rule $I_D = \forall \overline{x}.\ \overline{J[\overline{x}]} \Rightarrow (\Gamma[\overline{x}] \vdash e'[\overline{x}] : T[\overline{x}])$ is derivable in $B\ \overline{I}$:
$$B\ \overline{I}\ \overline{J[\overline{y}]} \succ (\Gamma[\overline{y}] \vdash e'[\overline{y}] : T[\overline{y}])$$

Figure 4. The SoundExt verification procedure.

original type, and (ii) verifying that this derived rule is derivable, that is, all programs it admits were already admitted by the original inference rules. Together, this shows that all programs generated by the rewrite rule are admitted by the original inference rules, and thus must be well-typed. The full verification procedure is shown in Figure 4.

In Step 1, we rewrite the subject of the inference rule I by applying the *rewrite* function. Since the subject of an inference rule typically includes metavariables, this amounts to a symbolic rewriting of the rule's subject. Due to Assumption 1 on the rewrite engine, the rewritten subject $e'[\overline{x}]$ captures all programs that can ever be generated by the rewrite rules $\overline{R}$ from programs admitted by I.

In Step 2, we define a derived inference rule I_D that uses the rewritten subject $e'[\overline{x}]$ but has the same premises, context, and object. The derived rule admits exactly those programs that can be generated by $\overline{R}$ from programs admitted by I. By showing that I_D is derivable in $B\ \overline{I}$, we ensure that generated programs have derivations in $B\ \overline{I}$ without I_D.

To verify the derivability of I_D, we instantiate its bound variables with fresh variables $\overline{y}$. We then install the premises of the derived rule as axioms $\overline{J[\overline{y}]}$ into the inference engine and try to derive the conclusion of the derived rule $\Gamma[\overline{y}] \vdash e'[\overline{y}] : T[\overline{y}]$. If this derivation succeeds, it means the rules from B and $\overline{I}$ prove that the premises of the derived rule entail the conclusion of the derived rule for any $\overline{y}$. Intuitively, we can use this derivation to eliminate any application of the derived rule I_D.

For example, for the *let* extension shown in Section 2, we prove the derivability of the derived rule T-Let' as follows:

$$(I_{\text{VAR}}\ I_{\text{ABS}}\ I_{\text{APP}}\ I_{\text{LET}}\ (\Gamma' \vdash e_1' : T_1')\ (\Gamma', x' : T_1' \vdash e_2' : T_2'))$$
$$\succ\ (\Gamma' \vdash (\texttt{app}\ (\texttt{abs}\ x'\ T_1'\ e_2')\ e_1') : T_2')$$

Note that the same unbound, fresh variables Γ', x', e_1', e_2', T_1', and T_2' appear in the axioms and the goal, but not freely in any of the other rules. Since the variables in the axioms are not quantified, the inference engine may only apply axioms to terms derived from the goal (this condition is part of Assumption 3). Note also that we permit the usage of an extension's own inference rules $\overline{I}$ in the derivability check. This enables extensions to desugar into recursive occurrences of the same extension without requiring the exact loop invariant as a premise of the inference rule.

Our PLT Redex implementation follows the verification procedure exactly, with the exception that instead of substituting fresh variables we "lock" metavariables in $(\texttt{symbol}\ x)$ nodes.

3.5 Metatheory

The goal of our verification procedure for extension soundness is to ensure that desugarings cannot generate code with type errors. The following is our main theorem:

Theorem 1 (Preservation). *Let $ext\ \overline{I}\ \overline{R}$ be a sound extension with respect to B. If $B\ \overline{I} \succ (\Gamma \vdash e : T)$, $e \rightsquigarrow^*_{\overline{R}} e'$, and $e' \in term\ B$, then $B \succ (\Gamma \vdash e' : T)$.*

That is, given a derivation for $\Gamma \vdash e : T$ in the extended system, we apply rewriting steps to the program e until it is desugared into a term of the base language. We show that the resulting base term is well-typed in the base system B and satisfies the judgment $\Gamma \vdash e' : T$.

Before turning to the proof of Theorem 1, we first prove a few important lemmas about the rewrite engine, the inference engine, and sound extensions.

Lemma 1. *If $e_1[\overline{x}] \rightsquigarrow_{\overline{R}} e_2[\overline{x}]$, then $e_1[\overline{t}] \rightsquigarrow_{\overline{R}} e_2[\overline{t}]$.*

Proof. Straightforward by induction on the derivation $e_1 \rightsquigarrow_{\overline{R}} e_2$, using Assumption 1. □

Lemma 2. *Let $e[\overline{x}]$ be a base-language term and $e_1 = e[\overline{t_1}]$. If $e_1 \rightsquigarrow_{\overline{R}} e_2$, then $e_2 = e[\overline{t_2}]$ where $t_1 \rightsquigarrow_{\overline{R}} t_2$ for exactly one $(t_1, t_2) \in \overline{(t_1, t_2)}$ and $t_1 = t_2$ for all others.*

Proof. By induction on the derivation $e_1 \rightsquigarrow_{\overline{R}} e_2$, using that *rewrite* fails for terms that start with a base-language constructor (Assumption 2) and that $e \rightsquigarrow_{\overline{R}} e$ preserves base-language constructors. □

The next lemma establishes the crucial property that a single rewrite step using a sound extension preserves types.

Lemma 3. *Let $ext\ \overline{I}\ \overline{R}$ be a sound extension with respect to B. If $B\ \overline{I} \succ (\Gamma \vdash e : T)$ and $e \rightsquigarrow_{\overline{R}} e'$, then $B\ \overline{I} \succ (\Gamma \vdash e' : T)$.*

Proof. By induction on the derivation $B\ \overline{I} \succ (\Gamma \vdash e : T)$.

Base case: The derivation consists of the application of an axiom

$$I_0 = \forall \overline{x}.\ \Gamma_0[\overline{x}] \vdash e_0[\overline{x}] : T_0[\overline{x}].$$

We have $e = e_0[\overline{t}]$, $\Gamma = \Gamma_0[\overline{t}]$, and $T = T_0[\overline{t}]$ for some substitute $\overline{t}$ of $\overline{x}$.
If $I_0 \in \overline{I}$, extension soundness entails $e_0[\overline{x}] \rightsquigarrow_{\overline{R}} e'_0[\overline{x}]$ and $B\ \overline{I} \succ (\Gamma_0[\overline{y}] \vdash e'_0[\overline{y}] : T_0[\overline{y}])$ for fresh $\overline{y}$. By Lemma 1 and $e_0[\overline{t}] = e$ we get $e'_0[\overline{t}] = e'$. By Assumption 4 we can substitute $\overline{t}$ for $\overline{y}$ and get $B\ \overline{I} \succ (\Gamma \vdash e' : T)$ as required.
If $I_0 \in B$, then $e_0[\overline{x}]$ is a base language term. By Lemma 2 we have $e' = e_0[\overline{t'}]$. Accordingly, we get a derivation of $B\ \overline{I} \succ (\Gamma \vdash e' : T)$ by instantiating I_0 with $\overline{x} = \overline{t'}$.

Step case: Assume the last rule applied in the derivation is

$$I_0 = \forall \overline{x}.\ \overline{J_0[\overline{x}]} \Rightarrow \Gamma_0[\overline{x}] \vdash e_0[\overline{x}] : T_0[\overline{x}].$$

We have $e = e_0[\overline{t}]$, $\Gamma = \Gamma_0[\overline{t}]$, and $T = T_0[\overline{t}]$ for some substitute $\overline{t}$ of $\overline{x}$, and $B\ \overline{I} \succ J_0[\overline{t}]$ for all $J_0[\overline{t}] \in \overline{J_0[\overline{t}]}$ (Assumption 3).
If $I_0 \in \overline{I}$, extension soundness entails $e_0[\overline{x}] \rightsquigarrow_{\overline{R}} e'_0[\overline{x}]$ and $B\ \overline{I}\ \overline{J_0[\overline{y}]} \succ (\Gamma_0[\overline{y}] \vdash e'_0[\overline{y}] : T_0[\overline{y}])$. By Lemma 1 and $e_0[\overline{t}] = e$ we get $e'_0[\overline{t}] = e'$. By Assumption 4 we can substitute $\overline{t}$ for $\overline{y}$ and get $B\ \overline{I}\ \overline{J_0[\overline{t}]} \succ (\Gamma \vdash e' : T)$. Repeated application of the cut rule (Assumption 5) yields the required $B\ \overline{I} \succ (\Gamma \vdash e' : T)$.
If $I_0 \in B$, then $e_0[\overline{x}]$ is a base language term. By Lemma 2 we have $e' = e_0[\overline{t'}]$ and $t \rightsquigarrow_{\overline{R}} t'$ for one $(t, t') \in \overline{(t, t')}$ and $t = t'$ for all others. By the induction hypothesis we get $B\ \overline{I} \succ J_0[\overline{t'}]$ since the extended syntax t is irrelevant in contexts and types and can be replaced by t. Accordingly, we get a derivation of $B\ \overline{I} \succ (\Gamma \vdash e' : T)$ by instantiating I_0 with $\overline{x} = \overline{t'}$. □

We can scale type preservation to the reflexive, transitive closure of the rewrite relation $\rightsquigarrow_{\overline{R}}$:

Lemma 4. *Let $ext\ \overline{I}\ \overline{R}$ be a sound extension with respect to B. If $B\ \overline{I} \succ (\Gamma \vdash e : T)$ and $e \rightsquigarrow^*_{\overline{R}} e'$, then $B\ \overline{I} \succ (\Gamma \vdash e' : T)$.*

Proof. Straightforward by induction on the derivation $e \rightsquigarrow^*_{\overline{R}} e'$, using Lemma 3. □

Finally, we can prove Theorem 1:

Proof of Theorem 1. By Lemma 4, we get $B\ \overline{I} \succ (\Gamma \vdash e' : T)$. Since we assume $e' \in term\ B$ and require rewrite rules to fail for pure base terms, the derivation tree of $\Gamma \vdash e' : T$ cannot contain an application of a rule from $\overline{I}$ because extension soundness requires a successful rewrite for a rule's subject. Accordingly, the derivation tree of $\Gamma \vdash e' : T$ only contains instantiations of rules from B, hence $B \succ (\Gamma \vdash e' : T)$ as required. □

In addition to our main preservation theorem, the verification procedure also ensures progress of desugarings:

Theorem 2 (Progress). *Let $ext\ \overline{I}\ \overline{R}$ be a sound extension with respect to B. If $B\ \overline{I} \succ (\Gamma \vdash e : T)$, then either $B \succ (\Gamma \vdash e : T)$ or there is an e' such that $e \rightsquigarrow_{\overline{R}} e'$.*

Proof. By induction on the derivation $B\ \overline{I} \succ (\Gamma \vdash e : T)$.

Base case: Either the axiom is from the base system B, or by Step 1 of extension soundness and Lemma 1 there is an e' with $e \rightsquigarrow_{\overline{R}} e'$.

Step case: If the last applied rule is from $\overline{I}$, Step 1 of extension soundness and Lemma 1 ensure there is an e' with $e \rightsquigarrow_{\overline{R}} e'$. Otherwise, assume the last applied rule is from the base system B. By the induction hypothesis all subderivations are either derivable in B or their subject can be desugared. If there is at least one subderivation of the latter kind, then the corresponding extended syntax must already be part of the current subject e because base rules cannot pattern match on extended syntax. Thus, by the definition of $\rightsquigarrow_{\overline{R}}$ the term e can be desugared. Otherwise all subderivations are derivable in B, and so is the current judgment. □

This concludes our correctness proof for the verification procedure of extension soundness employed by SoundExt. We have shown that our verification procedure guarantees well-typing of generated base-language programs.

3.6 Extension composition and overlapping definitions

As long as extensions are not syntactically overlapping, SoundExt supports *incremental extension* [6] (one extension desugars into code of another extension) and *extension unification* [6] (independent extensions can be unified into a single extension).

For incremental extension, we assume a sound extension $ext\ \overline{I_1}\ \overline{R_1}$ with respect to base system B. A second extension $ext\ \overline{I_2}\ \overline{R_2}$ can be defined on top of them by desugaring into the extended base system. We then require that $ext\ \overline{I_2}\ \overline{R_2}$ is a sound extension with respect to the extended base system $(B\ \overline{I_1})$. Since we desugar programs e from the double-extended language consecutively $e \rightsquigarrow^*_{\overline{R_2}} e' \rightsquigarrow^*_{\overline{R_1}} e''$, twice applying our soundness result from Theorem 1 proves that the final result e'' does not contain type errors if the original program e is well-typed.

For extension unification, we assume two extensions $ext\ \overline{I_1}\ \overline{R_1}$ and $ext\ \overline{I_2}\ \overline{R_2}$ both of which are sound with respect to the base system B. We can compose these extensions into a unified extension $ext\ \overline{I_1 I_2}\ \overline{R_1 R_2}$. The unified extension is sound with respect to the base system B, because (i) for every type rule there is a successful rewriting and (ii) the proof of derivability for a type rule remains valid in the unified extension. Accordingly, our verification procedure for extension soundness can be applied modularly to different extensions before composing them.

In case of a syntactic overlap, the composition of two sound extensions may be unsound if the type rule of one extension admits a term that is transformed by a desugaring of the other extension. To retain soundness, we have to cross-check all involved type rules for all potential desugarings, so that for any concrete rewriting the generated code is guaranteed to be free of type errors. This amounts to strengthening the contracts on desugarings by combining the expectations formulated in multiple type rules. If this cross-checking fails, the composition must fail. We have not implemented overlap detection in our PLT Redex implementation or SugarFomega. As alternative to the detection of overlaps and the reverification of soundness at composition time, we could restrict the syntactic flexibility of extensions (as in traditional macro systems) to guarantee unambiguous syntax [24].

3.7 Summary

We achieve type-sound language extensibility by requiring *small-step desugarings* that are applicable to the subject of corresponding type rules. This way, we can derive type rules that exactly admit those programs that can be generated from well-typed programs. By showing that these derived rules are admissible (by checking derivability), we ensure that the generated programs are well-typed themselves and do not require further type checking. In particular, we have shown that extension soundness entails that desugarings preserve types and do not get stuck.

4. SugarFomega

We have implemented a sound syntactically extensible programming language SugarFomega[3] by combining the base language System F_ω, with SugarJ-like syntactic extensibility, and SoundExt.

SugarJ [5, 8, 10] enables the syntactic extension of a base language like Java with arbitrary new syntax, given programs of that syntax can be desugared into the base language. SugarJ (and SugarFomega) employ the SDF2 syntax formalism [28] for definition of extended syntax and the Stratego rewrite language [30] for the definition of desugaring rules. SugarJ organizes language extensions in modules of the base language itself, so that regular module-import statements activate extensions locally by bringing the extended grammar and desugarings into the scope of the current module.

SugarJ also provides support for program analyses that annotate the input program with metadata. This information is used in error messages of the compiler as well as in our Eclipse-based extensible IDE [7], for example, to show type information in hover help. We employ the support for analyses to implement the F_ω type checker and the verification procedure for sound extensions.

4.1 The base language System F_ω

SugarFomega is based on System F_ω and primarily augments it with a simple module system that is amenable to SugarJ's module-based extension mechanism. We also add a few practical features: pair kinds, type synonyms, records, variants, higher-order iso-recursive types, and some primitive types. With the exception of higher-order recursive types and the module system, SugarFomega is fairly standard and all its components can be found in textbooks [22].

Modules and signatures. A SugarFomega module may import other modules and contains a sequence of value or type definitions that may be public. For example, we define a type synonym for polymorphic pairs, a swap function for pairs, and a private test expression that is not exported:

```
module Data.Pair
import Foo
public type Pair = \A::*. \B::*. {fst:A, snd:B}
public val  swap = \A::*. \B::*. \p:Pair A B.
                          {fst=p!snd, snd=p!fst}
val test = swap [Nat] [Bool] {fst=1, snd=false}
```

Kind judgments `~C |- ~T :: ~K`

```
~C |- ~T1 :: (~K => *) => ~K => *
~C |- ~T2 :: ~K
================================== K-Mu
~C |- mu (~T1, ~T2) :: *
```

Type judgments `~C |- ~e : ~T`

```
~C |- ~T :: *
~C |- ~T ~> mu (~T1, ~T2)
~C |- ~e : ~S
~C |- ~S ~> mu (~T1, ~T2)
~C |- ~T2 :: ~K
=================================== T-Unfold
~C |- unfold [~T] ~e :
      ~T1 (\A::~K. mu (~T1, A)) ~T2
```

Figure 5. Kind and type rule for higher-order iso-recursive types.

The definition of a module is valid if a signature is derivable, that is, if each type (value) definition is well-kinded (well-typed). The initial context for the derivation of a signature is build from the signatures of imported modules.

Higher-order recursive types. SugarFomega implements a form of higher-order iso-recursive types similar to Crary and Weirich [3]. Figure 5 shows the kind rule for our recursive type operator `mu` and the type rule for `unfold`, which performs a one-step unfolding of a recursive type. A recursive type is a pair `mu` (T_1, T_2) of types where T_2 is of kind K and turns the higher-kinded recursive type operator T_1 into a proper type.

For example, in SugarFomega, we can define a polymorphic list with the following type synonyms:

```
type LRec = \List::* => *. \A::*.
  <Nil: {}, Cons: {hd:A, tl:List A}>
type List = \A::*. mu (LRec, A)
```

The isomorphism between, for example, `List Nat` and its one-step unfolding is witnessed by `fold` and `unfold` according to their type rules:

```
                 mu (LRec, Nat)
unfold [List Nat]  ↓↑  fold [List Nat]
    <Nil: {}, Cons: {hd:Nat, tl:mu (LRec, Nat)}>
```

4.2 The SugarFomega type checker

To define the type system of F_ω, we implemented a domain-specific language for the declaration of inference rules:

$Premise_1$
...
$Premise_n$
========== $RuleName$
$Conclusion$

Our inference rules are layout-sensitive so that premises and conclusions can span multiple lines, given they adhere to the offside rule [9].

The conclusion of a rule as well as each premise is a judgment. Whereas our formalization of SoundExt in Section 3 was limited to type judgments, for System F_ω we generalized SoundExt to support multiple kinds of judgments. The most important judgments are:

[3] Implementation available online: http://sugarj.org/fomega

Γ	|- *defs*	==>	σ	Signature judgments
Γ	|- *e*	:	T	Type judgments
Γ	|- T	::	K	Kind judgments
Γ	|- T	~>	T'	Normalization judgments

For example, the kind and type rule for recursive types in Figure 5 are implemented in our language for inference rules, where metavariables are prefixed by a tilde ~. In fact, we implemented most of the F_ω type system through the declaration of inference rules.

We compile the inference rules to executable Stratego code that is called during the analysis phase of SugarFomega. The compiler has hard-wired knowledge about how to compile the different judgments. For example, our compiler makes the following common assumptions about input and output positions of judgments:

Input		Input		Output
Γ	|-	*defs*	==>	σ
Γ	|-	*e*	:	T
Γ	|-	T	::	K
Γ	|-	T	~>	T'

The code generated from different inference rules has a similar structure: First, we check that the rule's input matches the input expected by the conclusion. Second, we check the premises in order of appearance. Third, we compute the conclusion's output. For signature, kind, and type judgments, we store the output of a conclusion as annotations of the corresponding subject, so that we can reuse the signature, kind, or type during desugaring and in editor services such as hover help. Should an error occur, we annote them to the defective term instead of annotating a signature, kind, or type. Furthermore, note that the order of premises is significant: Before a metavariable can be used as input of a premise or as output of the conclusion, it must be introduced in an output position of a premise or as input of the conclusion.

Our compiler translates each rule into a certain Stratego strategy. For example, the compiler translates kind rules into definitions of `annotate-kind` and type rules translate into definitions of `annotate-type`. We eagerly normalize types and use Stratego's support for backtracking to explore all possible derivations (a compiler that produces *efficient* code for finding derivations is orthogonal to the work presented in this paper and left for future work).

We illustrate the compilation of inference rules by example of the SugarFomega type rule for *let* expressions (~ marks a metavariable, ~% marks a metavariable only for identifiers):

```
~C |-  ~e1  : ~T1                 // (P1)
~C |-  ~S  :: *                   // (P2)
~C |-  ~S  ~> ~U                  // (P3)
~C |-  ~T1 ~> ~U                  // (P4)
(~C;~%x:~S) |-  ~e2 : ~T2         // (P5)
====================================== T-Let
~C |- (let ~%x : ~S = ~e1 in ~e2) : ~T2
```

Figure 6 presents a simplified version of the Stratego code generated for `T-Let`:

- Line 2 matches the input of the conclusion of rule `T-Let` using abstract syntax. Only if the input is a *let* expression, the type derivation continues with an instantiation of rule `T-Let`.
- Lines 3 and 4 implement premise `(P1)`. The type of `e1` is computed and annotated by a recursive call. We require the successful typing of `e1` by retrieving its type into variable `T1` using `get-type`.
- Lines 5 to 8 implement premise `(P2)`. The kind of `S` is computed, annotated, and retrieved into a temporary variable `tmp1`. `(P2)` demands `S` to be of kind $*$, which we check using `kind-eq-star` in line 7. `kind-eq-star` returns a possibly empty list of error messages that we annotate to `S` in line 8.

```
1  annotate-type =
2      ?(C, node@Let(x, S, e1, e2))
3    ; <annotate-type> (C, e1)
4    ; <get-type> e1 => T1
5    ; <annotate-kind> (C, S)
6    ; <get-kind> S => tmp1
7    ; <kind-eq-star> tmp1 => msgs1
8    ; <add-context-errors> (msgs1, S)
9    ; <norm> (C, S) => U
10   ; <norm> (C, T1) => tmp2
11   ; <type-eq> (U, tmp2) => msgs2
12   ; <add-context-errors> (msgs2, T1)
13   ; <annotate-type> (CtxBindVar(C, x, S), e2)
14   ; <get-type> e2 => T2
15   ; <put-type> (T2, node)
```

Figure 6. Stratego code generated for `T-Let`.

- Lines 9 to 12 handle premises `(P3)` and `(P4)`. The normalization judgment of `(P3)` compiles into a call of the type-normalization strategy `norm`. During translation of `(P4)`, the compiler recognizes that the output `U` appears as output of a preceding judgment, namely `(P3)`. Therefore, the normal form of `T1` is stored in a temporary variable `tmp2`. The call of `type-eq` in line 11 checks that the types bound to `U` and `tmp2` indeed are equal (up to renaming of bound variables). `type-eq` returns a possibly empty list of error messages that we annotate to type `T1`.
- Lines 13 and 14 implement `(P5)`, similar to the translation of `(P1)` but with an enriched context that contains the binding `~%x:~S` represented by the term `CtxBindVar(C, x, S)`.
- Finally, line 15 annotates the resulting type to the *let* expression.

We use our domain-specific language for inference rules to implement the whole type system of System F_ω: kinding, typing, type normalization, and deriving module signatures. We provide SugarFomega programmers with the same language to define inference rules for language extensions.

4.3 Writing language extensions in SugarFomega

SugarFomega allows users to define language extensions in regular base-language modules. A SugarFomega extension takes the following form:

> **module** *Name*
> **syntax** { *SDF2 definitions* }
> **desugaring** *Strategy name* { *Stratego rewrite rules* }
> **typing** { *Typing rules* }

That is, a SugarFomega extension consists of an extended syntax, desugaring transformations from the extended syntax into the (possibly further extended) base language F_ω, and type rules for programs of the extended syntax. For example, Figure 7 displays the definition of a SugarFomega extension for *let* expressions.

- The **syntax** section adds a new production to the nonterminal `Expr` that is defined in the base grammar of SugarFomega. The extension declares that a *let* expression can be used whenever a `Expr` is expected. The annotation `{cons("Let")}` declares that a *let* expression is represented by an abstract syntax tree node of name `Let`.
- The **desugaring** section defines a Stratego rule `desugar-let` that implements the necessary rewriting. We use concrete syntax [29] for SugarFomega code in the declaration of rewrite rules. Like in type rules, a tilde ~ marks a metavariable. Often, it is useful to decompose a desugaring into multiple strategies. The identifier following the keyword **desugaring** names the entry point of desugaring that is called by the SugarFomega compiler.

```
module extensions.Let

syntax {
  context-free syntax
    "let" ID ":" Type "=" Expr "in" Expr -> Expr {cons("Let")}
}

desugaring desugar-let {
  desugar-let :
    |[ let ~%x : ~T = ~e1 in ~e2 ]| ->
    |[ (\ ~%x : ~T. ~e2) ~e1 ]|
}

typing {
  ~C |- ~e1  : ~T1
  ~C |- ~S  :: *
  ~C |- ~S  ~> ~U
  ~C |- ~T1 ~> ~U
  (~C; ~%x:~S) |- ~e2 : ~T2
  ====================================== T-Let
  ~C |- (let ~%x : ~S = ~e1 in ~e2) : ~T2
}
```

Figure 7. Declaration of a type-sound extension for *let* expressions.

- The `typing` section defines a type rule for *let* expressions as discussed in the previous subsections.

Since the language extension for *let* expressions is represented by a regular SugarFomega module, we can activate the extension by importing the module. The SugarFomega system then loads the grammar extensions, applies the desugarings to parsed code, and performs static analysis according to predefined and user-defined inference rules.

```
module test.Let
import extensions.Let

val test = let p : {x:Nat, y:Nat} = {x=1, y=2}
           in  p!x
```

4.4 Verifying type-soundness of extensions

SugarFomega verifies the soundness of each language extension using a modified version of SoundExt (Section 3) that supports all judgments required in the type system of System F_ω and knows about the input and output positions of judgments. Moreover, due to type-level abstraction in System F_ω, we require equivalent types everywhere we required syntactically equal types before. As usual, we check type equivalence by comparing the normal forms of types. Specifically, we modified the verification procedure for SugarFomega as follows:

- *Type rule*: Rewrite expression and assert equality of the normal forms of the expect and the actual type.
- *Kind rule*: Rewrite type and assert equality of the expect and the actual kind.
- *Signature rule*: Rewrite definitions and assert equality of the expected and the actual signature.
- *Type-normalization rule*: Rewrite input type and assert equality of the normal forms of the input and the output type.

We have not yet formally proved that these criterions entail type preservation. But we are very confident that they indeed do since we can in principle encode the different judgments into SoundExt's judgment form by auxiliary constructors.

Like in Section 3, we use the inference engine to verify the soundness of user-defined inference rules. Since we compile inference rules to Stratego, we use Stratego's support for dynamically scoped rewrite rules [2] to activate axioms dynamically. For example, the strategy `activate-dynamic-axiom` activates an axiom for a type judgment:

```
activate-dynamic-axiom =
    ?TypingJudgment(C, e, T)
  ; rules(Dynamic-Annotate-Type :+
           (C, e) -> <put-type> (T, e))
```

Given a type judgment, `activate-dynamic-axiom` extends the definition of `Dynamic-Annotate-Type` for the input `(C, e)`. For example, for the premise like `~C |- ~e1 : ~T1` from `T-Let`, `activate-dynamic-axiom` activates the following rule:

```
Dynamic-Annotate-Type :
  (C@Metavar("C"), e@Metavar("e1")) ->
  <put-type> (Metavar("T1"), e)
```

As required, this rule only accepts the specific term `Metavar("e1")`, and not any other expression. We hook `Dynamic-Annotate-Type` into the regular type checking routine `annotate-type` by extending it as follows:

```
annotate-type = Dynamic-Annotate-Type
```

That is, whenever a type judgment is checked, the type checker will consider `Dynamic-Annotate-Type`, too.

We show the Stratego code for verifying the soundness of a type rule in Figure 8. This implementation corresponds to the verification procedure of SoundExt with the above-mentioned modifications. In SugarFomega, the verification procedure acts as a static analysis for checking modules that define language extensions.

```
1  verify-context-rule =
2    ?TypingRule(premises, TypingJudgment(C, e, T))
3    if <desugar-one-step> e => e-des then
4      with-scoped-axioms(
5           <activate-dynamic-axioms> premises
6         ; <annotate-type> (C, e-des)
7         ; <get-type <+ !TyUnknown> e-des => U
8         ; <norm> (C, T) => T'
9         ; <norm> (C, U) => U'
10     )
11     ; <collect-all-errors> e-des => errs
12     ; if <not(is-empty)> errs then
13         !errs
14       else if <not(type-eq)> (T', U') then
15         !["Type mismatch"]
16       else
17         ![]
18       end end
19   else
20     !["Could not desugar conclusion"]
21   end
```

Figure 8. SugarFomega verification procedure for type rules.

- Strategy `verify-context-rule` gets a typing rule as input and produces a possibly empty list of error messages (lines 1 and 2).
- In line 3, `verify-context-rule` tries to desugar the expression `e` of the conclusion one step. If this fails, an error message is emitted and the verification fails (line 20).
- If the desugaring is successful, line 5 enables the premises of the type rule as additional axioms. To prevent that axioms are active outside the verification procedure, we scope them using the strategy `with-scoped-axioms` (line 4).
- While the additional axioms are active, we type check the desugared expression `des-e` (line 6). We retrieve the annotated type in line 7 or, if type checking fails, use `TyUnknown` instead.

- To make the expected and the actual type comparable, we normalize them in lines 8 and 9.
- Afterwards, we collect all errors that have occurred during type checking of `des-e` (line 11). If we find some errors, we return these errors and verification fails.
- Otherwise, we compare the normalized expected type `T'` and the normalized actual type `U'` (line 14). If they are not equal, we return an error message and verification fails.
- Otherwise, no errors are emitted and the verification succeeds.

We have implemented similar verification procedures for the other rules used in SugarFomega, in particular, kinding, type normalization, and deriving module signatures. As we demonstrate in the following section, SugarFomega permits users to integrate even sophisticated language features as language extensions, for which SugarFomega modularly, statically, and automatically verifies type-soundness.

5. Case studies

In the previous sections, we used *let* expressions as an exemplary language extensions that is easy to define and that SoundExt was able to prove sound. In the present section, we further demonstrate the applicability of SoundExt by extending SugarFomega with language extensions for monadic *do* blocks and algebraic data types.

5.1 Monadic *do* blocks

Monads enable programmers to abstract over different computational flavors, such as state-full computation or non-deterministic computation [20]. Due to this abstraction, it is possible to define combinators that are independent of concrete computational flavors. For example, the function `liftM2` lifts any pure function of type `A -> B -> C` into a monadic function `M A -> M B -> M C` for any monad `M`.

In SugarFomega, we can encode a monad as a type operator $M :: * \Rightarrow *$ with associated bind and return functions:

$$\begin{array}{lll} bind & : & \forall A :: *. \forall B :: *. M\ A \rightarrow (A \rightarrow M\ B) \rightarrow M\ B \\ return & : & \forall A :: *. A \rightarrow M\ A \end{array}$$

To support convenient programming with monads, we have developed a language extension of SugarFomega that introduces *do* notation similar to Haskell. We provide type rules for *do* blocks that detect type errors prior to desugaring. SugarFomega verifies the soundness of our extension to guarantee no type errors occur in desugared code.

Here is a simple *do* block as supported by our extension of SugarFomega:

```
do [T] {
    x:T1 <- e1
  ; y:T2 <- e2
  ; e3 }
```

A *do* block starts with a keyword **do**, followed by the result type of the computation that the *do* block represents. Inside a *do* block occurs a semicolon-separated list of computational statements, each of which may bind their result to a local variable. The last statement of a *do* block must be an expression that returns a value corresponding to the result type of the *do* block. Note that the type annotations in our encoding of *do* blocks are not strictly necessary; in Section 6 we discuss how to drop them while retaining automatically verifiable type-soundness.

As shown in Figure 9, we desugar a *do* block into an expression that is parameterized over a monad, that is, over a type operator `M` and functions `bind` and `return`. The first desugaring rule handles *do* blocks that only contain a final expression, whereas the second

```
desugaring desugar-do {
  desugar-do :
  |[ do [~T] { ~e } ]| ->
  |[ \M::*=>*.
     \bind: forall A::*. forall B::*.
              M A -> (A -> M B) -> M B.
     \return: forall A::*. A -> M A. ~e ]|

  desugar-do :
  |[ do [~T] { ~%x : ~S <- ~e1; ~stmts } ]| ->
  |[ \M::*=>*.
     \bind: forall A::*. forall B::*.
              M A -> (A -> M B) -> M B.
     \return: forall A::*. A -> M A.
     bind [~S] [~T] ~e1
       (\~%x:~S. do [~T] { ~stmts } [M] bind return) ]|
}
```

Figure 9. Desugaring rules for *do* blocks.

desugaring rule handles *do* blocks with multiple statements. In contrast to *let* expressions, the desugaring of *do* blocks requires recursion. We trigger recursion in the second desugaring rule by generating code that contains a residual *do* block, to which we propagate `M`, `bind`, and `return`.

SugarFomega only allows programmers to write programs that can be type checked before desugaring. Accordingly, we require type rules for *do* blocks. In Figure 10, we display the type rule for *do* blocks with multiple statements. The type of the conclusion clearly demonstrates our choice to implement *do* blocks as polymorphic functions. The premises `(P3)` and `(P7)` express the essential context conditions of *do* blocks:

- The right-hand side `~e1` of a monadic binding must be well-typed in a context that provides `bind` and `return`.
- The subsequent statements `~stmts` must be well-typed in the same context enriched by the bound variable `~%x`.

SugarFomega automatically verifies that these requirements are sufficient to guarantee that the desugared code is well-typed. For example, this allows us to define `liftM2` using *do* notation:

```
module MonadLift
import extensions.DoBlock
val liftM2 = \M::*=>*.
  \bind: forall A::*. forall B::*.
           M A -> (A -> M B) -> M B.
  \return: forall A::*. A -> M A.
  \A::*. \B::*. \C::*.
  \f: A -> B -> C. \m1: M A. \m2: M B.
    do [C] {
        x:A <- m1
      ; y:B <- m2
      ; return [C] (f x y)
    } [M] bind return
```

5.2 Algebraic data types

The type system of System F_ω is very flexible and expressive, but the encoding of tree-like data structures in terms of variants, records, and recursive types is cumbersome. To this end, we use SugarFomega to define a type-sound extension for algebraic data types like the following definition for polymorphic lists:

```
data List (A::*) = Nil {}
                 | Cons {hd: A, tl: List A}
```

This definition is desugared into a type synonym `List` and constructor functions `Nil` and `Cons` that type-normalize to the following definitions:

```
(~C; M::*=>*) |-  ~S :: *                                                                    // (P1)
(~C; M::*=>*) |-  ~T :: *                                                                    // (P2)
(~C; M::*=>*; bind: forall A::*. forall B::*. M A -> (A -> M B) -> M B                       // (P3)
            ; return: forall A::*. A -> M A)    |-    ~e1 : ~R1
(~C; M::*=>*) |-  ~R1 ~> M ~U1                                                               // (P4)
(~C; M::*=>*) |-  ~U1 :: *                                                                   // (P5)
(~C; M::*=>*) |-  ~S ~> ~U1                                                                  // (P6)
(~C; M::*=>*; bind: forall A::*. forall B::*. M A -> (A -> M B) -> M B                       // (P7)
            ; return: forall A::*. A -> M A; ~%x:~S)    |-    do [~T] { ~stmts } :
    forall M::*=>*. (forall A::*. forall B::*. M A -> (A -> M B) -> M B) -> (forall A::*. A -> M A) -> M ~T
============================================================================================================ T-DoCons
~C |- do [~T] { ~%x : ~S <- ~e1; ~stmts }
   : forall M::*=>*. (forall A::*. forall B::*. M A -> (A -> M B) -> M B) -> (forall A::*. A -> M A) -> M ~T
```

Figure 10. Typing rule for a *do* block with multiple statements.

```
type List = \A::*. mu (\List::*=>*. \A::*.
  <Nil:{}, Cons:{hd:A, tl:List A}>, A)

val Nil = \A::*. fold [List A]
  (<Nil={}> as <Nil:{}, Cons:{hd:A, tl:List A}>)

val Cons = \A::*. \hd:A. \tl:List A. fold [List A]
  (<Cons={hd=hd, tl=tl}> as
     <Nil:{}, Cons:{hd:A, tl:List A}>)
```

To achieve the desugaring of algebraic data types, we need to exercise two features of SugarFomega not discussed in detail before: *abstract intermediate program representations* for which no concrete syntax exists and *type-level language extensions*.

Abstract intermediate program representations. Since the verification procedure of SoundExt and SugarFomega require a rewriting to apply to the subject of a type rule, language extensions must be desugared in small-step fashion. For example, for *do* blocks the second desugaring created a residual *do* block, which is transformed in a later iteration of the fix-point desugaring. In a sense, we got lucky for *do* blocks, because the residual program could be described by concrete syntax.

More generally, and for algebraic data types in particular, it is not always possible to describe residual programs via concrete syntax (which users would be allowed to write, too). For this reason, SugarFomega allows desugaring transformations and inference rules to use abstract intermediate program representations instead of concrete syntax. Note that this was not a problem for SoundExt because we only used abstract syntax anyway.

An extension has to declare the abstract-syntax nodes it wants to use as part of the desugaring:

```
desugaring desugar-adt {
  signature constructors
    ADT-DCON:          ID * DataParams *
                       ID * Decls * DataCons -> Term
    ADT-DCON-FIELDS: Decls -> Term
    ADT-TABS:          DataParams * Expr -> Term
  ...
}
```

Afterwards, the extension can use these nodes in place of concrete syntax by prefixing them with `M~`. For example, we use an abstract intermediate node `ADT-TABS` to prefix the code generated for a constructor with the type parameters of the algebraic data type (a nested occurrence of `|[ ]|` escapes back to concrete syntax):

```
desugar-data :
  |[ M~ADT-TABS(|[]|, e) |] ->
  |[ ~e ]|

desugar-data :
  |[ M~ADT-TABS( |[ (~%X::~K) ~params ]| , e) ]| ->
  |[ \~%X::~K. M~ADT-TABS(params, e) ]|
```

```
~C |- ~e : ~T
======================================== T-ADT-TABS1
~C |- M~ADT-TABS(|[]|, e) : ~T

(~C; ~%X::~K) |- M~ADT-TABS(params, e) : ~T
============================================== T-ADT-TABS2
~C |- M~ADT-TABS(|[ (~%X::~K) ~params ]|, e)
   : forall ~%X::~K. ~T
```

In our case study for algebraic data types, we exclusively represent intermediate data-type fragments via abstract syntax. To this end, we employ 19 different abstract-syntax nodes for the generation of the type synonym and the constructor functions.

Type-level and kind-level language extensions. As described in Section 4.2 and 4.4, SugarFomega supports syntactic sugar at all levels: kinds, types, and expressions. However, an extension is only usable if there are inference rules that can be employed for the validation of a program using the extended syntax. For expression-level extensions, we have shown for *let* expressions and *do* blocks that type rules can provide the necessary validation. For type-level and kind-level extensions, other means are necessary.

For type-level extensions, there are two possibilities for the specification of valid usage patterns of extended types: using kind rules only or also adding type-normalization rules. These alternatives have an interesting consequence when using an abstract intermediate representation for extended types: The extended types can be introduced nominally or structurally. For example, consider the following kind rule that specifies the kind of the residual type `ADT-ABS`.

```
(~C;~%X::~K1) |- M~ADT-ABS(params, T) :: ~K2
============================================== K-ADT-ABS2
~C |- M~ADT-ABS(|[ (~%X::~K1) ~params ]|, T)
   :: ~K1 => ~K2
```

Since SugarFomega performs type checking prior to desugaring, this kind rule only applies to residual types `ADT-ABS`, and nothing else. Compare this with the following type-normalization rule that specifies to what the residual type `ADT-ABS` normalizes:

```
~C |- M~ADT-ABS(params, T) ~> ~T2
============================================ N-ADT-ABS2
~C |- M~ADT-ABS(|[ (~%X::~K) ~params ]|, T)
   ~> \~%X::~K. ~T2
```

Since type normalization happens every time two types are compared, this type-normalization rule permits the usage of `ADT-ABS` wherever a type `\~X::~K. ~T` is expected.

For our case study of algebraic data types, the difference is whether values of the generated type synonym can be defined only with the generated constructors (nominal) or with any expression of the right type (structural). Note that kind rules are required in most cases anyway, because during verification of type rules with kind-judgment premises, there is typically not enough information on types to perform type normalization.

For kind-level extensions, there is no such choice because there are no explicit sorts or super-kinds in SugarFomega. However, we added context-free kind normalization to permit the generation of kinds depending on the input program. For example, we use the following kind-normalization rule to permit the usage of the residual kind `ADT-CK` as a higher-order kind (used to describe the type arguments of an algebraic data-type constructor such as `List`):

```
M~ADT-CK(params) =::=> ~K2
================================= KN-ADT-PK2
M~ADT-CK(|[ (~%X::~K) ~params ]|)
=::=> ~K => ~K2
```

In our SugarFomega implementation of algebraic data types, we use kind rules, type-normalization rules, and kind-normalization rules. However, we found that our normalization rules always resemble the rewriting of the desugaring rules. As consequence, the verification is trivial because the desugaring of the normalization input yields the normalization output. Moreover, this is obvious boilerplate that we hope to remedy in a future version of our domain-specific language for inference engines.

Summary. Algebraic data types are by far the most sophisticated language extension we have implemented in SugarFomega. The whole extension comprises 19 abstract-syntax nodes, 34 desugaring rules, 4 module-signature derivation rules, 7 type rules, 13 kind rules, 21 type-normalization rules, and 4 kind-normalization rules.

6. Type reconstruction

As briefly mentioned before, quite a few of the type annotations we currently require are not necessary, because the defining expressions of the involved variables are statically available. For example, the language extension for *let* expressions (Figure 7) requires a type annotation for the bound variable, because such annotation is required in the desugared lambda abstraction. To reduce the number of required type annotations, we started to experiment with a *type-of* metalanguage construct that permits the reuse of an expression's type. For example, with the *type-of* construct, we can support *let* expressions without type annotations:

```
desugaring desugar-let {
  desugar-let :
    |[ let ~%x = ~e1 in ~e2 ]| ->
      |[ (\~%x:$(typeof ~e1). ~e2) ~e1 ]|
}
```

This desugaring is only applicable if `~e1` is well-typed, in which case the type of `~e1` is copied into the generated program. We are currently evaluating different alternatives for implementing the *type-of* construct, such that *type-of* is supported during the verification of extensions and while type checking user programs. Moreover, we are currently investigating how to support *type-of* constructs that are transitively generated, for example, by another extension that produces *let* expressions.

7. Related work

Most approaches for language extensibility have in common that type checking is only performed on the full expansion of the extended syntax, that is, after desugaring. There is no validation of transformation rules to ensure they produce well-typed code of the required type. Even in Typed Racket [27], a gradually typed Scheme dialect, macros are untyped and type checking operates on fully desugared core syntax. While some systems [4, 25] require the transformation itself to be a well-typed function, the employed program representations are not typed enough to make sufficient statements about the typing properties of the generated code. On the other hand, existing highly typed program representations as known from dependently typed languages such as Agda or from similar encodings in Haskell, have not yet been adopted by approaches for language extensibility.

Herman's λ_m-calculus [16] augments a Scheme-like macro system with signatures for macro definitions that describe their binding structure. These signatures allow to verify if a macro generates code that matches the signature. For example, this can be used to ensure that an argument bound by the macro must be used at a binding position in the generated code. The λ_m-calculus enables the definition of α-equivalence for unexpanded Scheme programs. However, guarantees are restricted to static scoping aspect of macros and do not scale to the static typing of terms.

MacroML [14] is an extension of the ML programming language with the possibility to define generative and binding macros in a statically typed setting. The semantics of a MacroML program is defined by a translation into the multi-stage programming language MetaML [26] and a type preservation result of this translation is proved. In contrast to MacroML, SoundExt allows desugarings to inspect and decompose user programs using pattern matching. Furthermore, MacroML macros that introduce new binding constructs have to be variations of predefined binding structures like lambda abstraction to unambiguously identify binding and bound occurrences of variables. In contrast, SoundExt allows type rules to freely specify extension-specific scoping of identifiers via the context in judgments. For example, a simple SugarFomega extension `openpair` could bring the components of a pair into the current scope by binding variables `fst` and `snd`. The corresponding type rule would clearly document the bound variables `fst` and `snd` and their scope. Such macro could not be defined in MacroML.

MetaHaskell [18] adds type-safe metaprogramming facilities with different object languages to Haskell. To turn a language into a MetaHaskell object language, a quasiquoter for the surface syntax, a type checker, and a unification procedure for object-language types have to be provided. The object language type checker is called by the MetaHaskell type checker to check embedded object programs. This technique only yields a type-safe type system if the object language's type checker is sound with respect to the dynamic semantics of the object language. In contrast to SoundExt, this condition is not checked mechanically but has to be manually verified.

Ziggurat [12, 13] is a metalanguage to extend other programming languages through Scheme-like macros and to attach static analyses like type checking or termination analysis to the new syntax. In Ziggurat, nodes of the syntax tree are represented as objects with a parsing and a rewrite function in an an object-oriented system called lazy delegation. Lazy delegation permits the implementation of static analyses explicitly for a node by implementing the corresponding method, or implicitly by delegating analysis to the objects generated during desugaring. However, static analyses themselves are not validated against desugarings and there is the danger that a malicious analysis of a subclass overrides a sound analysis of a super class.

Pluggable type systems [1] extend an existing type systems with additional constraints. Pluggable type systems may reject programs that, for example, do not comply to a certain design pattern or introduce new types. Implementations of pluggable type systems like JavaCOP [19] or the Checker Framework [21] provide infrastructure to implement type analyses and to integrate them into the semantic analysis phase of the compiler. The soundness of a pluggable type system is not verified mechanically, this is the implementer's responsibility. But JavaCOP has another interesting approach with respect to soundness: testing for soundness violations.

Their test harness supports the instrumentation of Java byte code with runtime checks to detect "stuck expressions" that the pluggable type system is supposed to prevent statically.

Roberson et al. [23] propose model checking to automatically prove the soundness of a type system for all program states of at most some finite size. Their technique is similar to ours: Identify well-typed intermediate programs, perform one step of reduction, and prove that the resulting program is also well-typed. However, the most important difference is that Roberson et al. inspect concrete program states and apply sophisticated pruning techniques to avoid state-space explosion, whereas SoundExt performs symbolic rewriting and equational reasoning.

Heeren et al. [15] propose an extensible type-inference mechanism in which libraries can define unification constraints. Since their system does not support syntactic extensibility, library functions are typeable in the base type system. Type-system extensions are verified sound by requiring that they only define specialized versions of base type rules. While less expressive, this approach is useful for defining library-specific error messages and we plan to integrate their mechanism into SugarFomega.

8. Conclusion and future work

We presented SoundExt, a formalism for syntactically extending a base language without affecting type soundness. In particular, SoundExt verifies language extension to guarantee that desugarings adhere to type preservation and progress. Accordingly, code generated from desugarings cannot contain type errors, which would break important abstraction barriers for programmers.

We applied SoundExt to the advanced base language System F_ω, resulting in SugarFomega, and successfully added nontrivial extensions for *do* blocks and algebraic data types in a type-sound way. In future work, we hope to use SoundExt to validate the desugarings and type rules of language extensions currently in use in compilers such as GHC, which will require solid support for type reconstruction and the generation of more efficient type checkers from inference rules.

References

[1] G. Bracha. Pluggable type systems. In *OOPSLA Workshop on Revival of Dynamic Languages*, 2004. Available at `http://bracha.org/pluggableTypesPosition.pdf`, accessed at Mar. 26 2013.

[2] M. Bravenboer, A. v. Dam, K. Olmos, and E. Visser. Program transformation with scoped dynamic rewrite rules. *Fundamenta Informaticae*, 69(1-2):123–178, 2006.

[3] K. Crary and S. Weirich. Flexible type analysis. In *Proceedings of International Conference on Functional Programming (ICFP)*, pages 233–248. ACM, 1999.

[4] D. de Rauglaudre. Camlp4 reference manual. `http://caml.inria.fr/pub/docs/manual-camlp4/index.html`, 2003. accessed Mar. 26 2013.

[5] S. Erdweg. *Extensible Languages for Flexible and Principled Domain Abstraction.* PhD thesis, Philipps-Universiät Marburg, 2013.

[6] S. Erdweg, P. G. Giarrusso, and T. Rendel. Language composition untangled. In *Proceedings of Workshop on Language Descriptions, Tools and Applications (LDTA)*, pages 7:1–7:8. ACM, 2012.

[7] S. Erdweg, L. C. L. Kats, T. Rendel, C. Kästner, K. Ostermann, and E. Visser. Growing a language environment with editor libraries. In *Proceedings of Conference on Generative Programming and Component Engineering (GPCE)*, pages 167–176. ACM, 2011.

[8] S. Erdweg, T. Rendel, C. Kästner, and K. Ostermann. SugarJ: Library-based syntactic language extensibility. In *Proceedings of Conference on Object-Oriented Programming, Systems, Languages, and Applications (OOPSLA)*, pages 391–406. ACM, 2011.

[9] S. Erdweg, T. Rendel, C. Kästner, and K. Ostermann. Layout-sensitive generalized parsing. In *Proceedings of Conference on Software Language Engineering (SLE)*, volume 7745 of *LNCS*, pages 244–263. Springer, 2012.

[10] S. Erdweg, F. Rieger, T. Rendel, and K. Ostermann. Layout-sensitive language extensibility with SugarHaskell. In *Proceedings of Haskell Symposium*, pages 149–160. ACM, 2012.

[11] M. Felleisen, R. B. Findler, and M. Flatt. *Semantics Engineering with PLT Redex.* MIT Press, 2009.

[12] D. Fisher and O. Shivers. Static analysis for syntax objects. In *Proceedings of International Conference on Functional Programming (ICFP)*, pages 111–121. ACM, 2006.

[13] D. Fisher and O. Shivers. Building language towers with Ziggurat. *Functional Programming*, 18(5-6):707–780, 2008.

[14] S. Ganz, A. Sabry, and W. Taha. Macros as multi-stage computations: Type-safe, generative, binding macros in MacroML. In *Proceedings of International Conference on Functional Programming (ICFP)*, pages 203–217. ACM, 2001.

[15] B. Heeren, J. Hage, and S. D. Swierstra. Scripting the type inference process. In *Proceedings of International Conference on Functional Programming (ICFP)*, pages 3–13. ACM, 2003.

[16] D. Herman. *A Theory of Typed Hygienic Macros.* PhD thesis, Northeastern University, Boston, Massachusetts, 2012.

[17] J. Łoś and R. Suszko. Remarks on sentential logics. *Indagationes Mathematicae*, 20:177–183, 1958.

[18] G. Mainland. Explicitly heterogeneous metaprogramming with MetaHaskell. In *Proceedings of International Conference on Functional Programming (ICFP)*, pages 311–322. ACM, 2012.

[19] S. Markstrum, D. Marino, M. Esquivel, T. Millstein, C. Andreae, and J. Noble. JavaCOP: Declarative pluggable types for Java. *Transactions on Programming Languages and Systems (TOPLAS)*, 32(2):4:1–4:37, 2010.

[20] E. Moggi. Notions of computation and monads. *Information and Computation*, 93(1):55–92, 1991.

[21] M. M. Papi, M. Ali, T. L. Correa, Jr., J. H. Perkins, and M. D. Ernst. Practical pluggable types for Java. In *Proceedings of International Symposium on Software Testing and Analysis (ISSTA)*, pages 201–212. ACM, 2008.

[22] B. C. Pierce. *Types and programming languages.* MIT press, 2002.

[23] M. Roberson, M. Harries, P. T. Darga, and C. Boyapati. Efficient software model checking of soundness of type systems. In *Proceedings of Conference on Object-Oriented Programming, Systems, Languages, and Applications (OOPSLA)*, pages 493–504. ACM, 2008.

[24] A. Schwerdfeger and E. Van Wyk. Verifiable composition of deterministic grammars. In *Proceedings of Conference on Programming Language Design and Implementation (PLDI)*, pages 199–210. ACM, 2009.

[25] T. Sheard and S. Peyton Jones. Template meta-programming for Haskell. In *Proceedings of Haskell Workshop*, pages 1–16. ACM, 2002.

[26] W. Taha and T. Sheard. MetaML and multi-stage programming with explicit annotations. *Theoretical Computer Science*, 248(1-2):211–242, 2000.

[27] S. Tobin-Hochstadt and M. Felleisen. Logical types for untyped languages. In *Proceedings of International Conference on Functional Programming (ICFP)*, pages 117–128. ACM, 2010.

[28] E. Visser. *Syntax Definition for Language Prototyping.* PhD thesis, University of Amsterdam, 1997.

[29] E. Visser. Meta-programming with concrete object syntax. In *Proceedings of Conference on Generative Programming and Component Engineering (GPCE)*, volume 2487 of *LNCS*, pages 299–315. Springer, 2002.

[30] E. Visser, Z.-E.-A. Benaissa, and A. P. Tolmach. Building program optimizers with rewriting strategies. In *Proceedings of International Conference on Functional Programming (ICFP)*, pages 13–26. ACM, 1998.

[31] A. K. Wright and M. Felleisen. A syntactic approach to type soundness. *Information and Computation*, 115(1):38–94, 1994.

A Nanopass Framework for Commercial Compiler Development

Andrew W. Keep
University of Utah
akeep@cs.utah.edu

R. Kent Dybvig
Cisco Systems Inc.
dyb@cisco.com

Abstract

Contemporary compilers must typically handle sophisticated high-level source languages, generate efficient code for multiple hardware architectures and operating systems, and support source-level debugging, profiling, and other program development tools. As a result, compilers tend to be among the most complex of software systems. Nanopass frameworks are designed to help manage this complexity. A nanopass compiler is comprised of many single-task passes with formally defined intermediate languages. The perceived downside of a nanopass compiler is that the extra passes will lead to substantially longer compilation times. To determine whether this is the case, we have created a plug replacement for the commercial Chez Scheme compiler, implemented using an updated nanopass framework, and we have compared the speed of the new compiler and the code it generates against the original compiler for a large set of benchmark programs. This paper describes the updated nanopass framework, the new compiler, and the results of our experiments. The compiler produces faster code than the original, averaging 15–27% depending on architecture and optimization level, due to a more sophisticated but slower register allocator and improvements to several optimizations. Compilation times average well within a factor of two of the original compiler, despite the slower register allocator and the replacement of five passes of the original 10 with over 50 nanopasses.

Categories and Subject Descriptors D.3.4 [*Programming Languages*]: Processors—Translator writing systems and compiler generators

General Terms Languages

Keywords Compiler; Nanopass; Scheme

1. Introduction

A compiler is typically structured as a series of passes, each analyzing source or intermediate code for an input program and possibly producing new intermediate code, with the final pass producing assembly or machine code for a target architecture. Historically, compilers employed no more than a few passes, because each pass involved reading source or intermediate code from cards, tape, or disk.

ICFP '13, September 25–27, 2013, Boston, MA, USA.

ACM 978-1-4503-2326-0/13/09...$15.00.
http://dx.doi.org/10.1145/2500365.2500618

Contemporary compilers, on the other hand, take advantage of large physical memories and virtual address spaces to keep intermediate representations in memory. At the same time, contemporary compilers are substantially more complex, having been called upon to handle larger, higher-level source languages, to generate efficient code for multiple hardware architectures and operating systems, to support automatic storage management, threading, and other runtime activities, and to support debugging, profiling, and other development tools. While it might be possible to support the additional complexity with the same small number of passes, it is no longer important or desirable to do so.

An attractive alternative is to separate a compiler into many, perhaps dozens, of single-task passes. This improves modularity, potentially making the compiler easier to maintain and extend. Constructing a compiler with many single-task passes, however, can require excessive boilerplate code to recur through unchanging forms, increasing compiler size and thus failing to decrease maintenance and extension overhead. If intermediate languages are not well specified, having many passes also increases the risk of errors due to inconsistencies among passes.

A nanopass framework is designed to address these challenges with a domain-specific language (DSL) that supports formally defined intermediate languages, a convenient pattern matching syntax implemented via inexpensive record dispatch, and automatic generation of boilerplate code. When a paper on the first nanopass framework was accepted for ICFP 2004 [20], however, the program committee required the authors to refocus the paper on education because they did not believe the nanopass methodology was suitable for commercial compilers. They were principally concerned with the compile-time overhead of repeated traversals. This concern was impossible to refute at the time because the prototype infrastructure and implementation were not mature enough to put to the test.

This paper describes a nanopass infrastructure that *is* suitable for developing commercial compilers. To establish the infrastructure's suitability for commercial compiler development, we set out to develop a compiler that is 100% compatible with the existing commercial Chez Scheme [5] compiler, produces code that is at least on par with the original compiler, and does so with compile times that are within a factor of two of the original compiler, despite our separate ambition to incorporate a new, slower register allocator. An extensive test suite, used to test the original compiler, is used to demonstrate the new compiler is compatible with the original, while a large set of benchmarks is used to establish its performance. On the benchmarks, the new compiler produces code that is 15–

```
(define-language Lsrc
  (terminals
    (uvar (x))
    (primitive (pr))
    (datum (d)))
  (Expr (e body)
    x
    (quote d)
    (if e0 e1 e2)
    (begin e* ... e)
    (lambda (x* ...) body)
    (let ([x* e*] ...) body)
    (letrec ([x* e*] ...) body)
    (set! x e)
    (pr e* ...)
    (call e e* ...)                   => (e e* ...)))
```

Figure 1. The `Lsrc` language

27% faster than the original compiler, depending on architecture and optimization level, with compile times that are well within the factor of two budget.

This paper is organized as follows. Section 2 describes the new nanopass framework and compares it with the original framework. Section 3 describes the differences between the new and original Chez Scheme compiler. Section 4 evaluates the run-time and compile-time performance of the new compiler against the original compiler. Section 5 presents related work, and Section 6 concludes.

2. The nanopass framework

A nanopass framework is a domain-specific language (DSL) for writing compilers. It provides two main syntactic forms: **`define-language`** for formally defining the intermediate-language grammars and **`define-pass`** for specifying passes that operate over these intermediate languages. Formally defining the intermediate languages allows the framework to fill in boilerplate code in passes, permits passes to check that output-language terms are well formed, and allows the framework to represent language terms as records internally while maintaining an S-expression pattern-matching and template-construction syntax.

The new nanopass framework builds on the prototype described by Sarkar et al. [20]. This section briefly describes the new framework and differences between this framework and the prototype. More information can be found in the first author's dissertation [14]. Examples are extracted from a student compiler used in a course on compiler implementation, since the Chez Scheme compiler is not open-source.

2.1 Defining languages

Languages definitions are similar to context-free grammars, in that they are composed of a set of terminals, a set of nonterminal symbols, a set of productions for each nonterminal, and a start symbol. An intermediate language definition for a simple variant of the Scheme programming language, post macro expansion, might look like `Lsrc` in Figure 1.

The `Lsrc` language consists of three terminals (listed in the **`terminals`** form) and a single nonterminal.

For each terminal, the compiler writer must supply a corresponding predicate. The framework adds a ? to the terminal name to determine the predicate name. In this case, the nanopass framework expects **`uvar?`**, **`primitive?`**, and **`datum?`** to be lexically visible where `Lsrc` is defined. Each terminal clause lists one or more meta-variables, used to refer to the terminal in nonterminal productions. For instance, `x` refers to a **`uvar`**.

```
(define-language L1
  (extends Lsrc)
  (terminals
    (- (datum (d)))
    (+ (constant (c))))
  (Expr (e body)
    (- (quote d))
    (+ (quote c))))
```

Figure 2. The `L1` language

The `Lsrc` language declares the nonterminal **`Expr`**. Nonterminals specify a name, a set of meta-variables, and a set of grammar productions. The **`Expr`** nonterminal has two meta-variables, **`e`** and **`body`**. These meta-variables, like the terminal meta-variables, are used to represent the nonterminal in a production.

Productions follow one of three forms: a single meta-variable, an S-expression that starts with a keyword, or an S-expression that does not start with a keyword (referred to as an *implicit* production). Productions cannot include keywords past the initial keyword.

The `x` production is the only single-meta-variable production and indicates that a **`uvar`** is an **`Expr`**. The only implicit S-expression production is **`(pr e* ...)`**, which specifies a primitive call with zero or more arguments. (The **`...`** following **`e*`** indicates that **`e*`** contains a list of **`Expr`**, the **`*`** suffix is used by convention to indicate plurality.) The **`(call e e* ...)`** production indicates a procedure call, and the **`call`** keyword differentiates it from a primitive call production. The **`=> (e e* ...)`** syntax indicates a *pretty* form for the production. The **`define-language`** form defines an unparser, and the unparser uses the pretty form when unparsing this production. The remaining productions correspond to the Scheme syntax that they represent.

2.2 Extending languages

The first pass of our student compiler is a simple expander that produces **`Lsrc`** language forms from S-expressions. The next pass expands complex quoted datum constants into code to construct these constants at load time.

The compiler writer could fully specify the output language, as we did with **`Lsrc`**. Fully specifying each language, however, results in verbose source code, particularly in a compiler with many intermediate languages. To avoid this, the framework supports a language extension form that succinctly describes only changes from one language to another. Figure 2 shows the output language.

The **`L1`** language removes the **`datum`** terminal and replaces it with the **`constant`** terminal. It also replaces the **`(quote d)`** production with a **`(quote c)`** production to indicate that only constants are allowed in the **`quote`** form.[1] The **`extends`** clause indicates a language extension form. Terminals are removed using the **`-`** clause and added using the **`+`** clause. Productions in a nonterminal are also removed using the **`-`** clause and added using the **`+`** clause.

2.3 Defining passes

The pass in Figure 3 converts an input program from the **`Lsrc`** intermediate language to the **`L1`** intermediate language. This pass

[1] If we failed to replace the `(quote d)` form, it would result in an error, since the `d` meta-variable is not bound in the new language.

```
(define-pass convert-complex-datum : Lsrc (x) -> L1 ()
  (definitions
    (define const-x* '())
    (define const-e* '())
    (define datum->expr
      (with-output-language (L1 Expr)
        (lambda (d)
          (cond
            [(pair? d) `(cons ,(datum->expr (car d))
                              ,(datum->expr (cdr d)))]
            [(vector? d)
             (let ([n (vector-length d)])
               (if (fxzero? n)
                   `(make-vector (quote 0))
                   (let ([t (unique-name 't)])
                     `(let ([,t (make-vector
                                  (quote ,n))])
                        (begin
                          ,(map (lambda (i v)
                                  `(vector-set! ,t
                                     (quote ,i)
                                     ,(datum->expr v)))
                                (iota n)
                                (vector->list d)) ...
                          ,t)))))]
            [else `(quote ,d)])))))
  (Expr : Expr (ir) -> Expr ()
    [(quote ,d) (guard (not (constant? d)))
     (let ([t (unique-name 't)])
       (set! const-x* (cons t const-x*))
       (set! const-e* (cons (datum->expr d) const-e*))
       t)])
  (let ([x (Expr x)])
    (if (null? const-x*)
        x
        `(let ([,const-x* ,const-e*] ...) ,x))))
```

Figure 3. The `convert-complex-datum` pass

removes the structured quoted datum by making the construction of the data explicit. To avoid constructing these constants more than once at run time, the pass also lifts datum creation to the start of the program.

A pass definition starts with a name and a signature. The signature specifies the input language (in this case, `Lsrc`) and list of formals (`x`) followed by the output language (`L1`) and a list of extra return expressions (`()`).

Following the name and signature, this pass specifies definitions for `const-x*`, `const-e*`, and `datum->expr` in the `definitions` clause. These definitions are scoped at the same level as the transformers in the pass. The `const-x*` and `const-e*` variables are initialized to null. The `const-x*` is extended with a new uvar and `const-e*` is extended with a new `Expr` each time a structured quoted datum is encountered. The `datum->expr` procedure recursively processes a structured quoted datum and produces the `L1 Expr` needed to construct it. Recursion terminates when a quoted constant is found.

Next, a transformer from the input nonterminal `Expr` to the output nonterminal `Expr` is defined. The transformer is named `Expr` and has a signature similar to that of the pass, with an input-language nonterminal and list of formals followed by the output-language nonterminal and list of extra-return-value expressions.

The transformer has a single clause that matches a quoted datum and uses a *guard* to ensure it is a pair or a vector. The `define-pass` macro autogenerates clauses matching the other input-language forms and producing equivalent output-language forms.

Each user-supplied clause consists of an input pattern, an optional `guard` clause, and one or more expressions that specify zero or more return values. The input pattern is derived from the productions specified in the input language. Pattern variables are unquoted, i.e., preceded by `,`. For instance, the clause for the `quote` production matches the pattern `(quote ,d)` and binds `d` to the `datum` specified by the `quote` form.

The output-language expression is constructed using a quasiquoted template. In the example, the quoted output-language expression is in the `datum->expr` procedure. Here, quasiquote, (`), is rebound to a form that constructs language forms based on the template, and unquote (,), is used to escape back into Scheme. The `,(datum->expr (car d))` thus puts the result of the recursive call to `datum->expr` into the output-language `(cons ,e0, e1)` form.

Following the `Expr` transformer is the body of the pass, which calls `Expr` to transform the `Lsrc Expr` term into an `L1 Expr` term and wraps the result in a `let` expression if any structured quoted datums are found in the program that is being compiled.

2.4 Comparison with the prototype nanopass framework

The prototype nanopass framework demonstrated that a nanopass framework is a viable approach to writing compilers, but only the first half of the student compiler was ever implemented using the framework. As such, the prototype framework has some rough edges that needed to be smoothed out in order to implement a replacement for the Chez Scheme compiler. The new nanopass framework focused on improvements in two areas, usability and performance.

On the usability side, the new nanopass framework introduces new features and improves error reporting. In the new framework, language definitions are no longer restricted to the top-level and can appear anywhere a Scheme definition can appear. Passes can be defined without an input language or output language, allowing a pass to take a non-language term as input or generate a non-language term as output. This allows passes to create general parsers, predicates, and code generators. Passes can also take additional arguments and return additional values, allowing information to flow through a pass without being encoded in the language term. Language terms can be constructed outside of a pass using the `with-output-language` form, as shown in Figure 3 and matched outside a pass using the `nanopass-case` form. The catamorphisms [17] syntax, used to recur on a sub-form of a language term in a pattern, supports passing extra arguments to transformers expecting more than one argument.

Error reporting has been improved, both to make messages easier to understand and to include source information for where the error occurred. Language definitions perform better checking, e.g., ensuring meta-variables are not repeated, removed productions existed in the base language, and the fields of a production are uniquely named.

On the performance side, the new nanopass framework uses an integer tag to perform pattern matching, which is slightly faster than the record dispatch previously used. In transformers, the order of clauses is respected, so that programmers can place clauses that are more likely to match first. The new framework also generates less code, so compiling a compiler generated with the nanopass framework is faster.

3. The new Chez Scheme compiler

Chez Scheme is a commercial Scheme compiler for R6RS Scheme with extensions, first released in 1985 [5] and under continuous development and improvement since. The compiler is written in Scheme and is comprised of 10 large, multipurpose passes. The compiler is almost absurdly fast, able to compile its own source code in roughly three seconds on contemporary hardware. The compiler is also designed to generate efficient code.

3.1 Workings of the existing Chez Scheme compiler

The compiler begins with a `syntax-case` expander, extended with a module system and R6RS libraries [6, 8, 12, 23]. The expander produces a simplified core language with `letrec`, `letrec*`, and `case-lambda` as binding forms, quoted constants, primitive references, procedure calls, variable references, and a handful of other forms. The first pass records source information used for debugging and profiling. The next pass places validity checks for variable references bound by `letrec` and `letrec*` [13, 24]. The next pass is the source optimizer [22] and can be run one or more times or not at all, depending on the options set in the compiler. A pass for handling `letrec` and `letrec*` [13, 24] is run at least once and is run after each run of the source optimizer. After this, either the interpreter is invoked to interpret the program or the back-end compiler is invoked to finish compilation and either execute the resulting code or write the machine code to the file system.

When the back-end compiler is invoked, the code is still in roughly the same form as the input language, although `letrec*` has been eliminated and `letrec` bindings bind only unassigned variables to `case-lambda` expressions. The compiler performs assignment conversion, closure conversion, various optimizations, and further code simplifications and replaces primitives in the source language with an internal set of simpler, although still higher level than assembly language, primitives. It also performs register allocation using a linear-scan style register allocator with a lazy register save and restore strategy [3], and generates code using destination-driven code generation [7].

The back end consists of five passes. The first pass, `cp1`, begins the process of closure conversion, recognizes loops, recognizes direct application of λ-expressions, begins handling multiple return value calls, sets up the foreign and foreign callable expressions, and converts primitive calls into a set of slightly lower-level inline calls. The next pass, `cpr0`, begins the register allocation process, determines the actual free variables of closures after performing closure optimization, performs assignment conversion, makes explicit all arguments to inlined primitives, and flags tail calls and loops. The register allocator reserves the architectural stack register, a Scheme frame pointer register, a thread context register pointer, and at least two temporary registers, depending on the target machine architecture, for use by the assembler. After this, the pass `cpr1` assigns variables to their initial register homes. The `cpr2` pass finishes register allocation, generating register saves and restores across non-tail calls and removing redundant register bindings. Finally, the `cp2` pass finishes compilation, converting the higher-level inlined primitives into a set of high-level instruction inlines that the assembler can convert into machine instructions for the target platform. Each of these back-end passes performs several optimizations in addition to those mentioned above, and some optimizations span multiple passes.

3.2 Workings of the new compiler

The new compiler starts with the same set of front-end passes, updated to use the nanopass framework.

The back end of the new compiler diverges significantly from that of the original compiler. Where the original compiler is structured as a set of multipurpose passes that each performs several tasks, the new compiler is organized as approximately 50 passes, with each pass completing primarily one task, using approximately 35 nanopass languages.

These passes implement most of the optimizations from the original compiler and improve on some, including support for implicit cross-library optimization, improvements to closure optimization [15], and improved handling of procedures that return multiple values.

The other big difference between the original compiler and the new compiler is the use of a graph-coloring register allocator. This change necessitated several other changes in the compiler, including the expansion of code into a near-assembly language form much earlier in the compiler, so that all of the temporaries that might be needed for the final code to conform to the operand requirements of the machine can be met. It also means that a full live analysis must be performed to compute the conflict graph needed by the register allocator. In the original compiler, the cost of the live analysis is largely avoided by tracking the liveness of registers, rather than the liveness of variables. Additionally, in the original compiler, primitive expansion is delayed until code generation at the cost of reserving two or more registers, depending on the target architecture.

The benefit of using a graph-coloring register allocator is that it packs spilled variables tighter on the frame, makes better use of registers, and generally produces more compact code. The new register allocator also uses move biasing to avoid frame-to-frame moves. This contributes to the generated code's faster run time, at the cost of substantially more compile-time overhead. Both the original and new compilers try to make good use of variable saves and restores around non-tail calls, allowing call-live variables to be accessed from a register, rather than from the frame. The original compiler follows a lazy-save strategy [3], while the new compiler attempts to get similar results by using a heuristic that estimates the cost of saving and restoring versus the cost of spilling to a frame location permanently. This is one place where the new compiler sometimes underperforms the original compiler.

Not all of the optimizations provided by the original compiler are provided by the new compiler. The most significant missing optimization is block allocation of closures. When several closures are created at the same time, a single allocation is performed to allocate the space for the entire group of closures. A more general block allocation optimization is planned for the new compiler but has not yet been implemented.

3.3 Ensuring compatibility

Over the course of Chez Scheme's development, an extensive suite of unit, functional, and regression tests has been developed to ensure that the compiler conforms to the relevant Scheme standards and documentation for Chez Scheme extensions. Chez Scheme is also bootstrapped, and the first test of the compiler is to compile itself and verify that code generated for the compiler is consistent with each run of the compiler. The new compiler passes all of these tests.

4. Evaluation of the new Chez Scheme compiler

4.1 Comparing the speed of generated code

We compare the performance of the original and new compilers on a set of benchmarks that includes the R6RS benchmarks [4]; a set of benchmarks, including some larger benchmarks, used to test the source optimizer; and a set of additional benchmarks used for performance regression testing.

The benchmark data was generated on an Intel Core i7-3960X with two CPUs, six cores per CPU, and 64 GB of RAM. The tests were conducted at both optimize level 2 (run-time type-checking enabled) and optimize level 3 (run-time type-checking disabled), using both the 32-bit and 64-bit instruction sets. Table 1 shows the average improvement in run time for benchmarks compiled with the new compiler over the original compiler. In the worst case, optimize level 3 with the 64-bit instruction set, the benchmarks still run 15.0% faster on average.

	x86 machine	x86_64 machine
Optimize Level 2	26.6%	22.0%
Optimize Level 3	22.3%	15.0%

Table 1. Average improvement in benchmark run times

Two of the benchmarks, `similix`, a self-applicable partial evaluator, and `softscheme`, a benchmark that performs soft typing, make use of the compiler during the run of the benchmark. This negatively affects the run time of these benchmarks and the overall average. Table 2 shows the normalized run time of these benchmarks on both the 32-bit and 64-bit versions of the compiler and at both optimization levels.

Opt. level	Machine type	Similix	Soft Scheme
2	x86	1.54	1.27
2	x86_64	1.41	1.32
3	x86	1.29	1.22
3	x86_64	1.39	1.24

Table 2. Normalized run times of `similix` and `softscheme`

Outside of these two outliers, the performance ranges on the 32-bit version between 0.417 and 1.05 at optimize level 2 and between 0.457 and 1.05 at optimize level 3. It ranges on the 64-bit version between 0.519 and 1.03 at optimize level 2 and between 0.489 and 1.14 at optimize level 3.

As discussed in Section 3.2, the new compiler contains several improvements over the original compiler, and each of these contributes to the better performance of the benchmarks. The biggest contributing factor, and the one that is consistent in all of the benchmarks, is the graph-coloring register allocator. The graph-coloring register allocator makes more efficient use of available registers, which is particularly helpful on the 32-bit Intel target, where only eight registers are available.

4.2 Comparing compilation speed

We set out with the goal of implementing a new compiler that ran within a factor of two of the original compiler. The extra compile-time budget was intended to allow the more expensive graph-coloring register allocator to be incorporated into the new compiler. Ideally, we would have created a nanopass compiler as near in function to old compiler as possible for apples-to-apples compile-time comparisons, but we did not have the resources to create two new compilers.

The two compilers were tested by compiling each benchmark five times and averaging compile times. The compile times are normalized, using the original compiler as a base. Table 3 presents the normalized numbers by machine type and optimization level. In the worst case (the 64-bit version at optimize level 2) the average compile time is a factor of 1.75 longer on the new compiler than on the original compiler. This time is well within our factor of two goal. Nevertheless, further tuning is still possible and will make the compile times for the new compiler even closer to those of the original compiler.

	x86 machine	x86_64 machine
Optimize Level 2	1.71	1.75
Optimize Level 3	1.64	1.71

Table 3. Normalized compile times of benchmarks

The compile time varies from one benchmark to another. On the 32-bit version, the normalized time ranges from a factor of 1.00 to 4.44 at optimize level 2 and 0.968 to 3.13 at optimize level 3. On the 64-bit version, normalized time ranges from a factor of 1.00 to 4.73 at optimize level 2 and 1.00 to 3.80 at optimize level 3.

It is natural to assume that the variance in compile times is related to the increased computational complexity of the graph-coloring register allocator; however, this does not seem to be the case. Figure 4 shows the normalized times versus the lines of expanded source code. The number of lines of expanded source code is determined by pretty printing the results of the expander run on each benchmark and then counting the number of line breaks. Overall, there does not seem to be a direct relationship between the number of lines of expanded code and the normalized compile time. An understanding of why this occurs might lead to overall improvements in compile time.

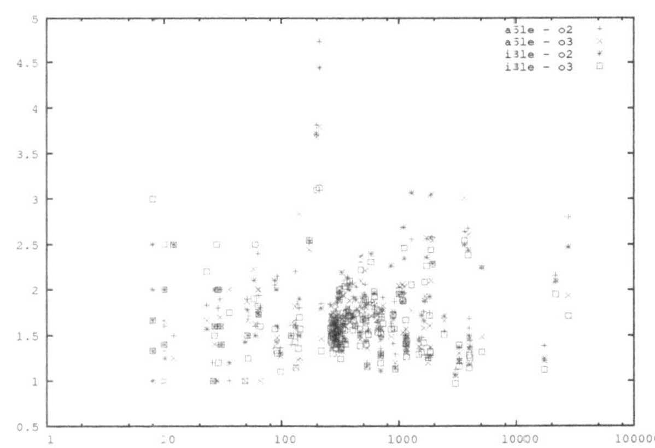

Figure 4. Normalized compile time vs. expanded source code size

5. Related work

Stratego/XT [2] is a DSL for writing source-to-source transformations. It provides a set of combinators for matching and rebuilding abstract syntax tree (AST) forms as well as strategies for performing different traversals of the AST. Pattern matching and AST construction in Stratego is different from that in the nanopass framework, because if construction of an AST fails, the next pattern will be tried, whereas the nanopass framework makes a committed (deterministic) choice with explicit guards for extra-grammatical checks, which simplifies debugging and improves compiler speed.

The JastAdd [9] system allows for the construction of modular and extensible compilers using Java's object-oriented class hierarchy, along with an external DSL to specify the AST and analysis and transformations on the AST. Each type of node in the AST has an associated class that encapsulates the transformations on the node type. Method dispatch and aspects are used with the visitor pattern to implement passes instead of pattern matching.

SableCC [11] is a system for building compilers and interpreters in Java. It provides a set of tools for writing the lexer and parser for the language and a method for defining multiple passes. Similar to JastAdd, it works on an AST represented by Java classes. Also similar to JastAdd, it uses the visitor pattern to implement the language transformations.

POET combines a transformation language and an empirical testing system to allow transformation to be tuned [26]. Although POET allows for some generic manipulation of an AST, it is largely focused on targeting specific regions of source code to be tuned. It can parse fragments of source code and operate on the AST fragment, preserving unparsed code across the transformation.

The ROSE [18] compiler infrastructure provides a C++ library for source-to-source transformation, along with front-ends and back-ends for both C/C++ and Fortran. Internally, ROSE represents source code using the ROSE Object-Oriented IR, with transformations written in C++. Although there is nothing specific that ties the ROSE transformation framework to C/C++ or Fortran, there are no tools to easily add new front-ends and back-ends, limiting the usefulness of ROSE for other languages.

The Rhodium framework takes a different approach from the other tools described here. Instead of using term rewriting, Rhodium bases transformations on data-flow equations and provides a framework for proving the soundness of transformations [16, 21]. The framework has also been extended to support inferring optimizations from the data-flow semantics defined by the compiler writer. The data-flow facts are defined over a C-like intermediate representation. This might be a good complement to the nanopass framework.

CodeBoost [1] is a more targeted tool. Although it was originally developed to support the Sophus numerical library, CodeBoost provides a simple way to write compiler transformations within C++ code. It is implemented using Stratego but provides an array of tools to make writing C++ code transformations easier.

The template-based metacompiler (Tm) [19] provides a macro language, similar to M4, for generating data structures and transformations that can be expanded in a language agnostic way. Tm provides tree-walker and analyzer templates and an existing C back-end for easier use.

Pavilion [25] is a DSL for writing analysis and optimization passes to improve the efficiency of generic programming in C++. The declarative language extends regular expressions with intersection and complement operators, variable quantification, path quantification, function definition, and native language access to Scheme to provide powerful matching during analysis and transformation.

Yoko [10] is a Haskell module for writing functions that transform an input type to a similar output type that requires only the interesting cases be specified, similar to how the nanopass framework operates over languages. The module builds on generic programming techniques to provide the `hcompos` function. The `hcompos` function takes the user-specified cases and autogenerates the necessary clauses to handle constructors from the input type not specified by the programmer, matching them with constructors of the output type with the same name.

6. Conclusion

The new Chez Scheme compiler demonstrates that a nanopass compiler can perform on par with a more traditionally structured compiler. Despite a more expensive register allocator and the replacement of the five back-end passes of the original 10 passes in the compiler with around 50 nanopasses, the new compiler still averages compile times that are within a factor of two of the original compiler. The new compiler also generates more efficient code, showing between a 15% and 26.6% improvement on a set of benchmarks, depending on the optimize level and the target architecture. The new nanopass framework made it easier to implement the new compiler and will make it easier to maintain and extend in the future.

Acknowledgments

Different parts of Keep's effort on this work were partially supported by the DARPA programs APAC and CRASH. Comments from Dan Friedman, Ryan Newton, and the anonymous reviewers led to several improvements in this papers presentation.

References

[1] O. S. Bagge, K. T. Kalleberg, M. Haveraaen, and E. Visser. Design of the CodeBoost transformation system for domain-specific optimisation of C++ programs. In D. Binkley and P. Tonella, editors, *Proc. 3rd International Workshop on Source Code Analysis and Manipulation*, SCAM '03, pages 65–75, Amsterdam, Sept. 2003. IEEE Computer Society Press. URL `http://www.codeboost.org/papers/codeboost-scam03.pdf`.

[2] M. Bravenboer, K. T. Kalleberg, R. Vermaas, and E. Visser. Stratego/XT 0.17. A language and toolset for program transformation. *Science of Computer Programming*, 72(1–2):52–70, June 2008. URL `http://dx.doi.org/10.1016/j.scico.2007.11.003`.

[3] R. G. Burger, O. Waddell, and R. K. Dybvig. Register allocation using lazy saves, eager restores, and greedy shuffling. In *Proc. ACM SIGPLAN 1995 Conference on Programming Language Design and Implementation*, PLDI '95, pages 130–138, New York, 1995. ACM. URL `http://doi.acm.org/10.1145/207110.207125`.

[4] W. D. Clinger. Description of benchmarks, 2008. URL `http://www.larcenists.org/benchmarksAboutR6.html`.

[5] R. K. Dybvig. *Chez Scheme Version 8 User's Guide*. Cadence Research Systems, 2009.

[6] R. K. Dybvig. *The Scheme Programming Language*. MIT Press, fourth edition, 2009.

[7] R. K. Dybvig, R. Hieb, and T. Butler. Destination-driven code generation. Technical Report TR302, Indiana University, February 1990.

[8] R. K. Dybvig, R. Hieb, and C. Bruggeman. Syntactic abstraction in Scheme. *LISP and Symbolic Computation*, 5(4):295–326, Dec. 1992. URL `http://dx.doi.org/10.1007/BF01806308`.

[9] T. Ekman and G. Hedin. The JastAdd system – modular extensible compiler construction. *Science of Computer Programming*, 69(1-3): 14–26, Dec. 2007. .

[10] N. Frisby, A. Gill, and P. Alexander. A pattern for almost homomorphic functions. In *ACM SIGPLAN Workshop on Generic Programming*, 09/2012 2012.

[11] E. Gagnon and L. Hendren. SableCC, an object-oriented compiler framework. In *Proc. 26th Conference on Technology of Object-Oriented Languages*, TOOLS '98, pages 140–154, 1998. .

[12] A. Ghuloum and R. K. Dybvig. Implicit phasing for R6RS libraries. In *Proc. 12th ACM SIGPLAN International Conference on Functional Programming*, pages 303–314, New York, 2007. ACM.

[13] A. Ghuloum and R. K. Dybvig. Fixing letrec (reloaded). In *Proc. 2009 Workshop on Scheme and Functional Programming*, Scheme '09, pages 57–65, 2009.

[14] A. W. Keep. *A Nanopass Framework for Commercial Compiler Development*. PhD thesis, Indiana University, Feb. 2013.

[15] A. W. Keep, A. Hearn, and R. K. Dybvig. Optimizing closures in O(0) time. In *Proc. 2012 Workshop on Scheme and Functional Programming*, Scheme '12, 2012.

[16] S. Lerner, T. Millstein, E. Rice, and C. Chambers. Automated soundness proofs for dataflow analyses and transformations via local rules. In *Proc. 32nd ACM SIGACT-SIGPLAN Symposium on Principles of Programming Languages*, POPL '05, pages 364–377, New York, 2005. ACM. URL `http://doi.acm.org/10.1145/1040305.1040335`.

[17] E. Meijer, M. M. Fokkinga, and R. Paterson. Functional programming with bananas, lenses, envelopes and barbed wire. In *Proc. 5th ACM Conference on Functional Programming Languages and Computer Architecture*, pages 124–144, London, UK, 1991. Springer-Verlag. ISBN 3-540-54396-1. URL `http://dl.acm.org/citation.cfm?id=645420.652535`.

[18] D. Quinlan, M. Schordan, Q. Yi, and B. R. de Supinski. Semantic-driven parallelization of loops operating on user-defined containers. In *Lecture Notes in Computer Science*, volume 2958/2004 of *Lecture Notes in Computer Science*, pages 524–538. Springer Berlin / Heidelberg, 2004.

[19] C. V. Reeuwijk. Tm: A code generator for recursive data structures. *Software: Practice and Experience*, 22(10):899–908, Oct. 1992. URL `http://dx.doi.org/10.1002/spe.4380221008`.

[20] D. Sarkar, O. Waddell, and R. K. Dybvig. A nanopass infrastructure for compiler education. In *Proc. 9th ACM SIGPLAN International Conference on Functional Programming*, ICFP '04, pages 201–212, New York, 2004. ACM. URL `http://doi.acm.org/10.1145/1016850.1016878`.

[21] E. R. Scherpelz, S. Lerner, and C. Chambers. Automatic inference of optimizer flow functions from semantic meanings. In *Proc. 2007 ACM SIGPLAN Conference on Programming Language Design and Implementation*, PLDI '07, pages 135–145, New York, 2007. ACM. URL `http://doi.acm.org/10.1145/1250734.1250750`.

[22] O. Waddell and R. K. Dybig. Fast and effective procedure inlining. In *Proc. 4th International Symposium on Static Analysis*, SAS '97, pages 35–52, London, 1997. Springer-Verlag.

[23] O. Waddell and R. K. Dybvig. Extending the scope of syntactic abstraction. In *Proc. 26th ACM SIGPLAN-SIGACT Symposium on Principles of Programming Languages*, POPL '99, pages 203–215, New York, 1999. ACM. URL `http://doi.acm.org/10.1145/292540.292559`.

[24] O. Waddell, D. Sarkar, and R. K. Dybvig. Fixing letrec: A faithful yet efficient implementation of Scheme's recursive binding construct. *Higher-order and Symbolic Computation*, 18(3/4):299–326, December 2005.

[25] J. J. Willcock. *A Language for Specifying Compiler Optimizations for Generic Software*. Doctoral dissertation, Indiana University, Bloomington, Indiana, USA, Dec. 2008.

[26] Q. Yi, K. Seymour, H. You, R. Vuduc, and D. Quinlan. POET: Parameterized optimizations for empirical tuning. Technical Report CS-TR-2006-006, University of Texas - San Antonio, 2006. URL `http://www.cs.utsa.edu/{~}qingyi/papers/poet-lang.pdf`.

Experience Report: Applying Random Testing to a Base Type Environment

Vincent St-Amour
PLT @ Northeastern University
stamourv@racket-lang.org

Neil Toronto
PLT @ Brigham Young University
ntoronto@racket-lang.org

Abstract

As programmers, programming in typed languages increases our confidence in the correctness of our programs. As type system designers, soundness proofs increase our confidence in the correctness of our type systems. There is more to typed languages than their typing rules, however. To be usable, a typed language needs to provide a well-furnished standard library and to specify types for its exports.

As software artifacts, these base type environments can rival typecheckers in complexity. Our experience with the Typed Racket base environment—which accounts for 31% of the code in the Typed Racket implementation—teaches us that writing type environments can be just as error-prone as writing typecheckers.

We report on our experience over the past two years of using random testing to increase our confidence in the correctness of the Typed Racket base environment.

Categories and Subject Descriptors D.2.5 [*Software Engineering*]: Testing and Debugging—Testing tools; D.3.3 [*Programming Languages*]: Language Constructs and Features

Keywords Random testing, Type environments, Numeric towers

1. Types as Specifications

Typecheckers prove claims about the run-time execution of programs. Programmers and compilers depend on the validity of these claims when they reason about programs. The correctness of these claims depends not only on the correctness of the underlying type system, but also on the correctness of the base type environment of the language. The type for any given primitive operation must be consistent with the operation's run-time behavior.

In languages with sophisticated type systems, types can encode precise specifications for primitive operations For example Alms (Tov and Pucella 2011) uses session types to encode mutual exclusion for lock operations, Vault (DeLine and Fähndrich 2001) uses typestate to encode protocols in the types of its networking primitives, and FISh (Jay 1999) uses shape types to encode the effect matrix operations have on matrix shapes. Such specifications can be subtle, making the encoding process error-prone.

ICFP'13, September 25–27, 2013, Boston, MA, USA.

ACM 978-1-4503-2326-0/13/09... $15.00.
http://dx.doi.org/10.1145/2500365.2500616

Typed Racket (Tobin-Hochstadt and Felleisen 2008) provides a rich numeric tower (St-Amour et al. 2012) similar to those provided by languages in the Lisp and Smalltalk families of languages, and it encodes precise type-based specifications for its numeric operations. The fine-grained types offered by the type system and the flexibility of the language's numeric operations result in large and complex specifications. Errors and oversights in these specifications have been a major source of bugs in Typed Racket.

The functional programming community has a successful history of using random testing (Claessen and Hughes 2000) to find bugs in programs ranging from undergraduate coursework (Page et al. 2008) to full-scale language models (Berghofer and Nipkow 2004; Klein et al. 2012; Klein et al. 2013). Inspired by these success stories, we decided to investigate whether random testing would help us detect bugs in the Typed Racket base environment—specifically in the implementation of its numeric tower. We report on our successful experience using PLT Redex (Felleisen et al. 2009) to build a random tester that we have been using for this task over the last two years.

The rest of the paper is organized as follows: section 2 provides background on the Typed Racket numeric tower, section 3 describes our random testing strategy, section 4 presents techniques we used to increase the effectiveness of our random tester, section 5 summarizes positive and negative aspects of our experiences and section 6 concludes.

2. The Typed Racket Numeric Tower

Typed Racket's approach to numeric types and operations—its *numeric tower* (St-Amour et al. 2012)—is inspired by those of untyped languages in the Lisp and Smalltalk families.

Numeric towers typically provide a deep hierarchy of numeric types including, in the case of Typed Racket, fixed-width and unbounded integer types, arbitrary-precision rational numbers, both single and double-precision floating-point numbers, and complex numbers. Numeric towers support generic and flexible numeric operations that accept numbers of any type, support *mixed-type arithmetic*—that is, programmers can freely mix and match numeric types such as `Integer` and `Float`—and always produce results with the most precise representation available.

In Typed Racket, the types of numeric operations include precise specifications of their flexible run-time behavior. Given the complexity of these behaviors, their specifications are often large and brittle.

The operations themselves are implemented in C as part of the Racket (Flatt and PLT 2010) runtime system and not in Typed Racket itself. This rules out the option of having the typechecker automatically infer—or even check—their types. The Typed Racket implementers must therefore manually assign types to each of them, a laborious and therefore error-prone process.

2.1 Specifications for Numeric Operations

In Typed Racket, numeric types can encode not only numeric *layers*—whether a number is an integer, a floating-point number, or a complex number—but also sign and range properties. For example, Typed Racket provides a `Positive-Float` type which only includes positive floating-point numbers and is a subtype of the more general `Float` type, which includes all floating-point numbers.

Types such as `Byte` and `Fixnum` impose range constraints on their members, the former including integers between 0 and 255 and the latter including all exact integers that can be represented in a tagged machine word. These types are related to each other via subtyping: `Byte` is a subtype of `Fixnum`, which is in turn a subtype of `Integer`—the type that contains all integers regardless of bit-width. Range-bounded types can be further partitioned by sign, to obtain for instance `Positive-Byte` or `Negative-Fixnum`.

Specifications for numeric operations—such as `+`, `round` and `sqrt`—can take advantage of the fine-grained distinctions encoded in these types to precisely describe the behavior of those operations. For example, the specification of the `sqrt` function expresses that the `Nonnegative-Real` type is closed under `sqrt`, but that it returns `Complex` numbers in the general case.

Types also encode the coercion rules that govern mixed-type arithmetic. For example, the specification of the `+` function expresses that the addition of an `Integer` and a `Float` returns a `Float`.

2.2 Encoding Specifications as Types

Typed Racket encodes specifications for numeric operations as ordered intersections of function types. That is, each property is individually encoded as a function type; all these properties are then intersected using Typed Racket's `case->` type constructor.

For example, the closure property of integers under addition is expressed using this function type,

```
[Integer Integer -> Integer]
```

the contagion rule for integer-float mixed-type arithmetic is expressed with these two function types

```
[Integer Float   -> Float]
[Float   Integer -> Float]
```

and sign preservation is encoded in these two function types

```
[Positive Positive -> Positive]
[Negative Negative -> Negative]
```

To build the type of `+` we intersect these properties, and all others that hold about addition:

```
(: + (case->
      [Zero     Zero     -> Zero]
      ...
      [Fixnum   Zero     -> Fixnum]
      [Zero     Fixnum   -> Fixnum]
      ...
      [Integer  Integer  -> Integer]
      ...
      [Integer  Float    -> Float]
      [Float    Integer  -> Float]
      [Float    Float    -> Float]
      ...
      [Positive Positive -> Positive]
      [Negative Negative -> Negative]
      ...))
```

Each side of a symmetric property needs to be encoded as a separate function type and, because of Typed Racket's checking rule for intersection types, additional function types are required for each case where two or more properties intersect. As a result, types for numeric primitives become large and complicated. For example, the type of `+` is an intersection type with 147 clauses while the type of $*$ has 209 clauses.

3. Random Testing Strategy

Types for numeric operations have been a significant source of bugs in Typed Racket. Of the 576 reported Typed Racket bugs, 63 (10.9%) can be traced back to the types of numeric operations, and 39 others (6.8%) can be traced back to other parts of the base type environment. Such bugs signal a mismatch between the type of an operation and the run-time behavior of the operation. Since we consider the run-time behavior of the numeric primitives to be the correct semantics, types need to be fixed when bugs are found.

The Typed Racket developers have spent time and effort manually testing the type environment,[1] but manual testing alone is insufficient. Handwritten tests often either test properties in isolation, or test combinations of a small number of properties together. Most combinations remain unexplored, including some in which properties combine to create interesting corner cases. We used random testing to improve the coverage of our test suite and find bugs before they cause problems in the real world.

3.1 Random Testing with PLT Redex

PLT Redex (Felleisen et al. 2009) is an embedded domain-specific language—built inside of Racket (Flatt and PLT 2010)—for defining and mechanizing executable language models. A typical modeling workflow with Redex is as follows. First, users define a grammar and a reduction semantics for their language. Then, they write functions that encode properties that they expect to hold about terms in their language, such as type soundness (Tobin-Hochstadt and Felleisen 2008) or determinism (Kuper and Newton 2012). Afterwards, they write test cases to check whether the property holds for specific terms.

Redex also provides support for random testing (Klein and Findler 2010), inspired by QuickCheck (Claessen and Hughes 2000). Redex's random testing facility, `redex-check`, takes as input a language grammar and a property expressed about terms in that language, generates random terms and checks whether the desired property holds. It has been previously used to find mistakes in nine ICFP 2009 papers (Klein et al. 2012) and to find bugs in a model of the Racket virtual machine (Klein et al. 2013).

3.2 Testing Type Preservation

We designed a language of arithmetic terms using Redex. The structure of the language is simple: it consists only of arithmetic expressions, with numbers at the leaves and arithmetic operations as the internal nodes. To detect discrepancies between types and run-time behavior, we test type preservation on randomly generated terms in this language. The process is as follows:

1. Our tester generates a random arithmetic expression.
2. It then invokes the Typed Racket typechecker on the expression.
3. If the expression is ill-typed, the tester rejects it and starts again with a new expression.
4. Otherwise, the tester asks the Typed Racket implementation to evaluate the expression.
5. It invokes the Typed Racket typechecker to typecheck the result.

If the type of the result is not a subtype of the type of the original expression, then the claim made by the typechecker does not hold

[1] The Typed Racket test suite has over 10,000 lines of handwritten tests.

and the tester has found a discrepancy. The result is unsound, almost always due to a bug in the type environment.

We encoded this preservation property as a Racket function which `redex-check` then applies to random terms.

3.3 Example: Floating-Point Underflow Bug

To illustrate this process, let us examine an example bug we found using random testing. Consider this excerpt from the type we originally assigned to Racket's hyperbolic sine function, `sinh`:

```
(: sinh (case->
         [Float-Zero     -> Float-Zero]
         [Positive-Float -> Positive-Float]
         [Negative-Float -> Negative-Float]
         ...))
```

Mathematically, the hyperbolic sine function maps zero to zero, positive reals to positive reals, and negative reals to negative reals. The above type encodes this mathematical statement.

Now consider the following randomly generated term:

```
(sinh 1.2535e-17)
```

Since `1.2535e-17` is of type `Positive-Float`, the entire expression should be of type `Positive-Float`, given the type of `sinh` above. However, the term evaluates to `0.0` which, in Typed Racket, is of type `Float-Zero`. The type `Float-Zero` is not a subtype of `Positive-Float`, which includes only *positive* floating-point numbers. Thus, the type fragment above does not accurately reflect the runtime behavior of `sinh`.

For values of x sufficiently close to zero, $\sinh(x)$ is too small to represent as a floating-point number, causing an underflow. We therefore need to correct the above type to account for this subtle corner case. This revised type fragment, taken from the current type of `sinh`, addresses this issue:

```
(: sinh (case->
         [Float-Zero     -> Float-Zero]
         [Positive-Float -> Nonnegative-Float]
         [Negative-Float -> Nonpositive-Float]
         ...))
```

4. Improving Random Test Case Generation

Since we applied random testing to a specific domain—numeric operations—we were able to leverage domain constraints to improve the quality of randomly generated test cases. With higher-quality test cases, we were able to find more bugs with fewer attempts than by using Redex's test case generation directly.

We improved the quality of test cases in two ways. First, we increased the probability of generating well-typed terms. Second, we used specialized random number generation to generate numeric corner cases with higher probability.

4.1 Generating Well-Typed Terms

Testing type preservation makes sense only for terms that are well-typed in the first place; our test infrastructure automatically rejects ill-typed terms. Therefore, to minimize wasting time on generating unusable terms, we engineered our grammar to generate well-typed terms with high probability.

When first designing our term grammar, a key design decision was to only allow trees of literal numbers and arithmetic operations as expressions. Variables and binders do not appear in the grammar, and thus cannot appear in the generated terms. This not only guarantees that the generated terms are closed, but it also rules out—by construction—terms that contain variables whose types are inconsistent between definition and use sites. Since we are interested in testing the types of numeric operations, there is no loss of generality; adding binders and variables would not uncover bugs that would not have been found otherwise.

Strategy	% of rejected terms (lower is better)
Baseline	57.6%
+ integer non-terminal	45.3%
+ float non-terminal	41.1%
+ integer and float non-terminals	1.6%

Figure 1: Percentage of rejected terms by generation strategy

That choice proved effective in practice. As the first row of figure 1 shows, only around half of the generated terms were ill-typed using our first attempt at a grammar.

Looking at the ratio of rejected terms does not tell the whole story, however. Most numeric operations in Typed Racket accept any kind of number as input—the `+` function accepts, e.g., integers and complex numbers alike. Other operations—which we call *type-limited* operations—accept inputs only from a portion of the numeric tower. For example, `modulo` accepts only integers, and `fl+` is a floating-point specific addition operation. By looking at a sample of rejected terms, we noticed that terms containing type-limited operations accounted for most of the rejections.

Those rejected terms most often featured subexpressions of type `Float` (or one of its subtypes) used as arguments to integer-specific functions. Because the inexactness of floating-point numbers is "contagious" for most operations, randomly generated terms are more likely to evaluate to floating-point numbers than to integers. Less common were rejected terms containing float-specific operations receiving integers or complex numbers as arguments.

Since terms containing type-limited operations were more likely to be rejected than other terms, type-limited operations were under-tested compared to other operations. Types of type-limited operations are not, on average, significantly simpler than types of other numeric operations; testing type-limited operations adequately is thus important.

While the types of numeric operations distinguish input types at a fine-grained level—e.g. they distinguish by sign, range, etc.—they all possess a *most general domain* that is a supertype of all its other domains. For example, while the `+` function distinguishes between the addition of two positive integer and the addition of two negative integers and assigns different types to the results of the two expressions, it accepts any value of type `Number`, which is a supertype of all its other valid input types.

The most general domains of the vast majority of type-limited operations belong to a small set of types: `Integer`, `Float` and `Real`. Furthermore, the most general domains of most type-limited operations are closed under those operations. Armed with these two observations, we refactored our arithmetic expression grammar so that it included an additional non-terminal for each of these types.

The productions for these non-terminals include literal numbers of that type, as well as type-limited operations with the appropriate most general domain. In addition, these non-terminals include productions for other, non-type-limited operations on which the non-terminal's type is closed. For example, to test the portion of the type of `+` that handles values of type `Integer` and its subtypes, we added productions that generate addition terms to the integer non-terminal. Figure 2 shows an abbreviated version of the resulting grammar. The `define-language` form takes the name of the language as its first argument, and each subsequent clause defines a non-terminal, in which the first element of the clause is the non-terminal's name and the remaining elements are productions.

```
(define-language tr-arith

  ; Float and its subtypes
  [F* (random-float) F]
  [F (* F* F*) (+ F* F*) (- F* F*) (/ F* F*)
     (max F* F*) (min F* F*) (abs F*)
     (floor F*) (ceiling F*)
     (truncate F*) (round F*)
     (cos F*) (sin F*) (tan F*)
     ...
     ; float-specific operations
     (fl+ F* F*) (fl- F* F*)
     (fl* F* F*) (fl/ F* F*)
     (flmin F* F*) (flmax F* F*) (flabs F*)
     ...]

  ; Integer and its subtypes
  [I* (random-integer) I]
  [I (* I* I*) (+ I* I*) (- I* I*)
     (max I* I*) (min I* I*) (abs I*)
     ...
     ; integer-specific operations
     (modulo I* I*) (remainder I* I*)
     (quotient I* I*) (gcd I* I*) (lcm I* I*)
     ...]

  ; any numeric type
  [E* (random-number) E F I]
  [E (* E* E*) (+ E* E*) (- E* E*) (/ E* E*)
     (max E* E*) (min E* E*) (abs E*)
     (floor E*) (ceiling E*)
     (truncate E*) (round E*)
     (sqrt E*) (log E*) (exp E*)
     (cos E*) (sin E*) (tan E*)
     ...])
```

Figure 2: Abbreviated grammar for Typed Racket arithmetic expressions

This grammar refactoring significantly lowered the term rejection rate. Figure 1 shows the impact of the additional non-terminals on the rejection rate. In turn, this refactoring increased the amount of testing of type-limited operations.

4.2 Generating Numeric Corner Cases

In addition to reducing the ratio of rejected test cases, we were also interested in increasing the ratio of bugs found per test case. Most of the bugs we had found in Typed Racket's numeric types were related to *numeric corner cases*, that is, cases where the usual rules governing the behavior of numeric operations do not apply. Corner cases lead to counter-intuitive behavior, which we—as type environment designers—often overlook and forget to encode as part of numeric types.

Based on our corpus of numeric tower-related bugs, we identified three main sources of corner cases: mixed-type arithmetic, *special values* and *representation limitations*. A key observation is that corner cases are not uniformly distributed across the entire numeric tower. To increase the likelihood that individual test cases would trigger a bug, we engineered random number generation to generate these three cases on a regular basis, while still adequately testing the common cases.

4.2.1 Mixed-type arithmetic

Mixed-type arithmetic exercises the coercion and contagion rules of numeric primitives described in section 2.2. These rules are quite complex and not always intuitive, which makes the portions of numeric types that deal with mixed-type arithmetic especially error-prone.

To trigger mixed-type arithmetic, the random generator we use for real numbers picks a numeric layer at random, then calls the relevant layer-specific generator. Specifically, the `random-integer->random-real` function, shown in figure 3, takes as argument a random integer provided by the Redex random test generator and returns a random real number from a random layer.

Using this technique, random terms generated for the "any numeric type" non-terminal are highly likely to feature mixed-type arithmetic. Furthermore, the "any numeric type" expressions can have subexpressions drawn from type-limited expressions, which also introduces mixed-type arithmetic.

4.2.2 Special values

When it comes to special values, such as the floating-point infinities, NaN and the floating-point zeroes, numeric primitives deal with these as special cases, usually mirrored by special cases in numeric types.

Integer `0` is also often handled as a special case. For example, `0` is the null element of multiplication, and causes the `*` function to ignore all coercion and contagion rules. Instead it returns `0` directly, and that must be reflected in the type.

To ensure an adequate representation of special values, we allocate portions of the random distributions specifically to them. As the last three conditional clauses in figure 4 show, NaN and each of the two floating-point infinities are generated with probability 0.05 when generating floating-point numbers. The floating-point zeroes are similarly special-cased. Special values in other layers—such as integer `0`, and the single-precision floating-point special values—are handled similarly.

4.2.3 Representation Limitations

Because of limitations of numeric representations, properties that we expect to hold about mathematical functions may not hold of their implementations in the standard library. Since we rely heavily on our intuition about mathematical functions when assigning types and often overlook the specifics of numeric representations, such limitations are a frequent source of bugs.

Bugs due to overlooking floating-point underflow—as discussed in section 3.3—are examples of bugs due to representation limitations. Other examples include floating-point overflow and automatic fixnum to bignum promotion when integer values exceed a certain range.

To ensure that these cases are exercised, we reserve part of the distribution for values that are near representation boundaries—e.g. extremely small or extremely large floating-point numbers or integers just small enough to be represented as fixnums. Figure 4 also shows the generation of floating-point numbers in these ranges.

To quantify the effectiveness of these reserved portions of the distribution, we attempted to trigger the underflow bug discussed in section 3.3 by generating random applications of the `sinh` function. Without these reserved portions of our distribution, we generated five million random terms and none of them triggered the bug. With those reserved portions, we executed 10 test runs. For each run, the bug was always triggered within 29 attempts, with 7 attempts being neccessary on average.

```
(define (random-integer->random-real i)
  (define r (random))
  ; probability 0.25 each
  (cond
   [(< r 0.25)
    i] ; random integer
   [(< r 0.5)
    (random-integer->random-rational i)]
   [(< r 0.75)
    (random-integer->random-flonum i)]
   [else ; single-precision flonum
    (random-integer->random-single i)]))
```

Figure 3: Allocation of random numbers to layers

```
(define (random-integer->random-flonum i)
  (define r (random))
  (cond

    ; 0.25: laplace-distributed with scale i
    [(< r 0.25) (random-laplace (abs i))]

    ; 0.25: uniform bits
    [(< r 0.5)  (random-uniform-flonum)]

    ; 0.35: very small or very large
    [(< r 0.85)
     (define r (random))
     (cond [(< r 0.5)
            (define x (ordinal->flonum i))
            (if (= x 0.0)
                ; special case: float zeroes
                (if (< (random) 0.5) 0.0 -0.0)
                x)]
           [(< r 0.75)
            (flstep -inf.0 (abs i))]
           [else
            (flstep +inf.0 (- (abs i)))])]

    ; 0.05 each: +nan.0, +inf.0, -inf.0
    [(< r 0.9)   +nan.0]
    [(< r 0.95)  +inf.0]
    [else        -inf.0]))
```

Figure 4: Random generation of floating-point numbers

5. Lessons Learned

Randomly testing the Typed Racket base environment has been a success. We achieved our goal of automatically finding bugs in the Typed Racket environment. Based on our experience, we recommend using Redex-based random testing to typed language implementers looking to test their type environments.

This section provides some details on positive and negative aspects of our experience.

5.1 What Worked

Random testing shined for some aspects of our project. Of them, the following should be of general interest to other typed language implementers.

Finding bugs Our random tester successfully found a large number of bugs. These bugs had not been found through manual testing, which suggests that random testing and manual testing complement each other.

Some of the bugs uncovered by random testing had already been reported by users (but had not been fixed yet). Our random checker created test cases that were often more useful as starting points for the debugging phase than user-provided test cases. Randomly generated terms tended to be small compared to user-provided test cases, which were often complete functions. Furthermore, random test cases included numeric operations only which again narrowed down debugging significantly.

Testing the full implementation Our random tester calls out to the Typed Racket implementation directly both to typecheck terms and to evaluate them. Redex can call arbitrary Racket code, which made this workflow convenient. Being able to test the actual Typed Racket implementation, rather than testing a separate model, was key to effectively finding bugs.

Confidence when refactoring The Typed Racket numeric tower is in constant evolution. We need to assign new types when new primitives are added to the Racket runtime, and we constantly revise the design of Typed Racket's numeric tower to improve its usability. The addition of a random tester makes us much more confident when refactoring the numeric tower. We follow each change to numeric types with a round of random testing, in addition to manual testing.

For example, in July 2012, the first author undertook a major change in the design of the numeric tower: for usability reasons, we decided to include NaN as a valid value to all non-singleton floating-point types. This refactoring required changing the majority of the types of float-specific operations, and of many generic operations as well—several days of work. Without a random tester, the chances of introducing subtle bugs and not detecting them would have made such a refactoring terrifying. In the end, we may even have decided against it, and left the usability issue unaddressed.

With random testing as part of the development cycle, however, the refactoring was a success. We implemented a first version of the new types, ran the random checker, fixed the bugs it found, and repeated the process. When short test runs stopped revealing bugs, we let the checker run overnight. Eventually, we trusted our refactoring and released it. So far, no bug has been reported that could be traced to it.

Low effort required Writing the first version of the random tester took the first author, who had no previous experience with Redex, about two hours. That initial effort resulted in a working random generator that successfully found bugs. Racket's extensive `math` library made our subsequent experimentation with random distributions—described in section 4—easy.

Continuous integration Our random tester is run every time a change is committed to the Racket code base. DrDr,[2] Racket's continuous integration system, runs one thousand random test cases on every change, in addition to running the manually written Typed Racket test suite. Random testing accounts for about a minute and a half of this process.

In general, continuous integration is useful to detect regressions. When combined with random testing, it also increases test coverage by running new random test cases every time a change is made.

[2] `drdr.racket-lang.org`

5.2 What Could Have Worked Better

While we were developing our random tester, we encountered three limitations of Redex. None were show-stoppers—we successfully worked around them—but they nonetheless slowed us down.

Type system integration We needed to manually adjust our grammar to produce well-typed terms as often as possible. In doing so, we manually encoded aspects of the Typed Racket type system as part of our grammar. Changes to the type system may accidentally cause an increase of the test case rejection rate and require manual changes to the grammar. Had Redex been able to use our type system to guide its random generation, this effort would not have been necessary.

Default random number generation Redex provides a random number generator as part of its random testing support. It generates numbers from the full range of Racket's numeric types—including fractions and complex numbers—which made it a good starting point. Due to its inability to generate corner cases sufficiently often, however, we eventually replaced it with our own custom random number generator.

Test case reduction While randomly generated test cases were usually smaller than user-provided test cases, they were often larger than necessary. Often, only one or two of a test case's operations would be relevant to the exposed bug. Therefore, the first step of our response to failing test cases is to find which part of the term triggers the bug and isolate it. Had Redex provided test case reduction, our debugging cycle would have been significantly shorter.

6. Conclusion

Based on our experience with Typed Racket over the last two years, we have found that random testing is an effective technique for increasing confidence in a language's base type environment.

With only a small amount of effort, we were able to implement a basic random tester and uncover bugs. With a modest amount of additional work, we were able to increase the effectiveness of our tester significantly. As a result of those efforts, the Typed Racket base type environment is now much more robust than it was two years ago.

Acknowledgments We thank Casey Klein and Robby Findler for suggesting that we use random testing to find bugs in the Typed Racket numeric tower. This work has been supported by the NSERC.

Bibliography

Stefan Berghofer and Tobias Nipkow. Random testing in Isabelle/HOL. In *Proc. Conf. on Software Engineering and Formal Methods*, pp. 230–239, 2004.

Koen Claessen and John Hughes. QuickCheck: a lightweight tool for random testing of Haskell programs. In *Proc. International Conf. on Functional Programming*, pp. 268–279, 2000.

Robert DeLine and Manuel Fähndrich. Enforcing high-level protocols in low-level software. In *Proc. Conf. on Programming Language Design and Implementation*, pp. 59–69, 2001.

Matthias Felleisen, Robert Bruce Findler, and Matthew Flatt. *Semantics Engineering with PLT Redex*. MIT Press, 2009.

Matthew Flatt and PLT. Reference: Racket. PLT Inc., PLT-TR-2010-1, 2010. `http://racket-lang.org/tr1/`

C. Barry Jay. Programming in FISh. *International Journal on Software Tools for Technology Transfer* 2(3), pp. 307–315, 1999.

Casey Klein, John Clements, Christos Dimoulas, Carl Eastlund, Matthias Felleisen, Matthew Flatt, Jay McCarthy, Jon Rafkind, Sam Tobin-Hochstadt, and Robert Bruce Findler. Run your research: on the effectiveness of lightweight mechanization. In *Proc. Symp. on Principles of Programming Languages*, pp. 285–296, 2012.

Casey Klein and Robert Bruce Findler. Randomized testing in PLT Redex. In *Proc. Works. Scheme and Functional Programming*, pp. 26–36, 2010.

Casey Klein, Matthew Flatt, and Robert Bruce Findler. The Racket virtual machine and randomized testing. *Higher-Order and Symbolic Computation*, 2013.

Lindsey Kuper and Ryan Newton. A lattice-theoretical approach to deterministic parallelism with shared state. Indiana University, TR702, 2012.

Rex Page, Carl Eastlund, and Matthias Felleisen. Functional programming and theorem proving for undergraduates: a progress report. In *Proc. Works. Functional and Declarative Programming in Education*, pp. 21–30, 2008.

Vincent St-Amour, Sam Tobin-Hochstadt, Matthew Flatt, and Matthias Felleisen. Typing the numeric tower. In *Proc. Practical Aspects of Declarative Languages*, pp. 289–303, 2012.

Sam Tobin-Hochstadt and Matthias Felleisen. The design and implementation of Typed Scheme. In *Proc. Symp. on Principles of Programming Languages*, pp. 395–406, 2008.

Jesse A. Tov and Riccardo Pucella. Practical affine types. In *Proc. Symp. on Principles of Programming Languages*, pp. 447–458, 2011.

Experience Report: Functional Programming of mHealth Applications

Christian L Petersen Matthias Görges Dustin Dunsmuir J Mark Ansermino Guy A Dumont
University of British Columbia, Vancouver, BC, Canada
{cpetersen mgorges ddunsmuir}@cw.bc.ca anserminos@yahoo.ca guyd@ece.ubc.ca

Abstract

A modular framework for the development of medical applications that promotes deterministic, robust and correct code is presented. The system is based on the portable Gambit Scheme programming language and provides a flexible cross-platform environment for developing graphical applications on mobile devices as well as medical instrumentation interfaces running on embedded platforms. Real world applications of this framework for mobile diagnostics, telemonitoring and automated drug infusions are reported.

The source code for the core framework is open source and available at: `https://github.com/part-cw/lambdanative`.

Categories and Subject Descriptors D.1.1 [*Programming Techniques*]: Applicative (Functional) Programming; D.2.3 [*General*]: Coding Tools and Techniques; D.3.2 [*Programming Languages*]: Language Classifications - Applicative (Functional) Languages

Keywords functional programming, Scheme, application programming, medical systems, cross-platform development

1. Introduction

The Pediatric Anesthesia Research Team (PART) at the University of British Columbia is a multidisciplinary research team conducting clinical research to improve the safety and outcomes of children both in the hospital and at home. In recent years the team has increased its focus on technology innovation, and is currently developing a range of new diagnostic and monitoring solutions for low cost mobile and embedded applications. As this technology is developed in-house with very limited resources, a new software development framework promoting robust efficient code, extensive testing and debugging facilities, fast development and flexible cross-platform deployment was required.

The team has four code developers on staff; one programmer, two physicists and one engineer, with diverse coding backgrounds. The typical application development process involves a much larger diverse group of clinicians, nurses, community healthcare workers, engineers, graphic designers and research assistants.

Traditionally, biomedical research teams write graphical software applications in Matlab, Visual Basic and LabView. These prototyping languages are not a good fit for robust performance-oriented platform-independent coding. On the other hand, performance-critical applications are traditionally written in C, the ubiquitous system language that is available on virtually all platforms. C is however a very low level language and vulnerable to common null pointer dereferences.

We first discovered Scheme as an extension language to C, and the ability to automatically generate C applications from Scheme was a natural next step. Functional languages, such as Scheme, offer an attractive alternative to conventional languages, especially when combined with a C compilation backend. In this paper we describe a Scheme based software development solution using the Gambit-C Scheme to C compiler [1, 2]. Scheme is a mature language originally developed at MIT over the period 1975-1980, and is standardized on the official IEEE standard 1178-1990 [3] and the Revised Reports on the Algorithmic Language Scheme [4]. It features an exceptionally simple homoiconic syntax based on s-expressions.

The primary goal in the design of the framework was to strike a balance between productivity, correct programming and performance. The brevity and simplicity of Scheme code promotes productivity and correctness, which is essential for mission critical medical applications. At the same time, the C backend allows compilation of high-performance binaries. Many diagnostic medical devices require low-level access to relatively high bandwidth sensors, and tight integration between Scheme and C is essential to facilitate this in real time.

The framework currently contains many distinct applications ranging from medical device servers running on embedded systems, over graphical interfaces running on medical flat panel PCs, to mobile applications for iPhone and Android. In this paper we examine three examples of these applications and discuss their implementation.

2. Concept

The application model adopted herein relies on the fact that modern operating systems share many core features. For example, iOS requires applications to be developed in Objective C. However, much of the underlying core operating system (Darwin) is written in C, and can readily be addressed though the standard UNIX and POSIX application programming interfaces. The same holds true for the Android operating system, which requires applications to be developed in Java, while the underlying operating system (Linux) is C based. Another common denominator between most modern computing platforms is the presence of an accelerated OpenGL or OpenGL ES graphics engine [5]. This provides an efficient universal mechanism for graphical user interfaces to function regardless of the underlying operating system.

It is thus possible to construct a cross-platform program that, while meeting the minimum requirements of the host operating system, performs the bulk of its operations through a universal C

ICFP'13 September 25–27 2013, Boston, MA, USA
Copyright is held by the owner/author(s). Publication rights licensed to ACM.
ACM 978-1-4503-2326-0/13/09... $15.00
http://dx.doi.org/10.1145/2500365.2500615

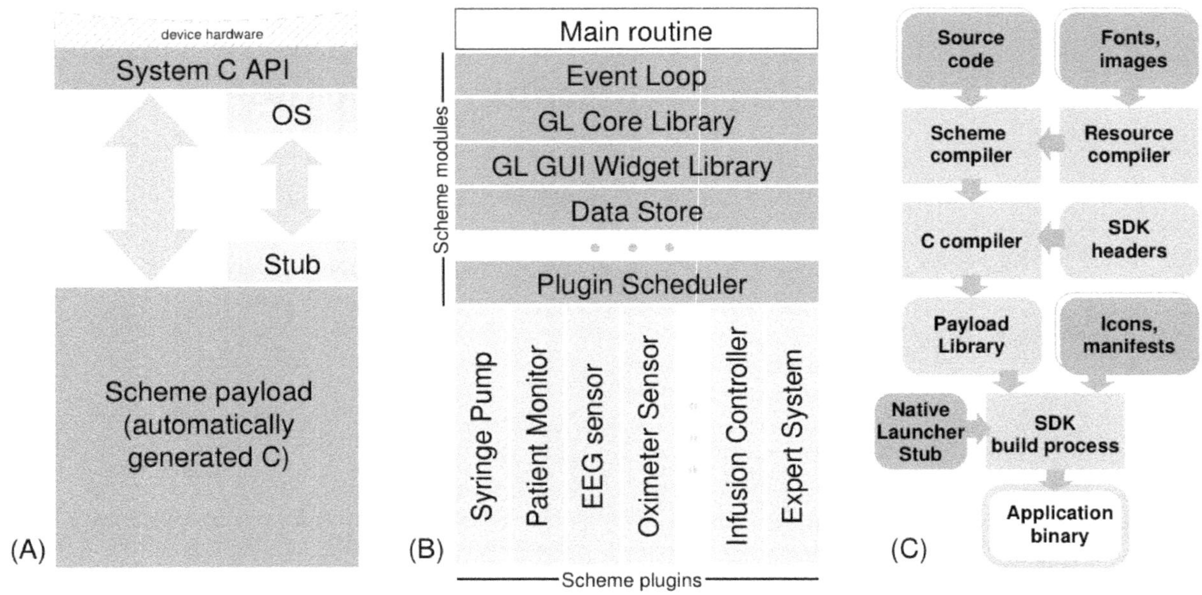

Figure 1. (A) Schematic of the portable application concept. (B) Application structure. (C) Compilation flow diagram.

application interface. This is illustrated in Fig 1(A). The application consists of a payload written in Scheme which is compiled to a native binary using the Gambit Scheme-to-C compiler and the C (cross-)compiler available for the target platform. A small stub shared between all applications in the framework manages the operating system specific application requirements, launches the program, and relays events to the payload.

The advantage of this approach is that a single code base can be deployed unchanged to a wide range of platforms, and run with a high level of performance suitable for IO and computationally intensive applications. Support for a new platform is simply a matter of writing another stub to launch the application on the platform and tie into its operating system event system. The framework has successfully been used to build applications for iOS, Android, Mac OS X, Linux, Windows, OpenBSD, and NetBSD.

The disadvantage of the approach is that a Native Development Kit with a C cross-compiler is required to build the payload. While all modern operating systems have this compiler available, some vendors may choose to withhold access to the compiler. In addition, user interface elements integrated into to the host operating system are not readily available to the payload. To overcome the interface limitations we have developed a widget based graphics engine entirely in Scheme, which provides a flexible platform-independent front end to the host OpenGL or OpenGL ES Graphics Processing Unit (GPU).

3. Structure

The applications are structured in a modular fashion to maximize code reuse between applications. This is illustrated in Fig 1 (B). Each application consists of a main routine that references modules in a common code repository shared by all applications in the framework. The four main modules shared by most applications are `eventloop`, `glcore`, `glgui` and `store`.

The `eventloop` module is responsible for feeding user and operating system events such as touch screen presses and redraw triggers to the payload application. It also relays sensor information such as battery level and device orientation to the application.

The graphics engine consists of a minimal Scheme wrapper around the OpenGL and OpenGL ES functions in `glcore` and a Scheme based graphical user interface in `glgui`. `glgui` implements a full widget system with buttons, labels, boxes, scrollable lists, keypads, images, containers, modal dialogs etc. and is easily expandable with more widget types. Each widget type consists of a hash table holding widget properties, a procedure for drawing the current representation of the widget and a procedure for handling input events. Widgets are associated with gui hash tables, and multiple gui tables can be displayed on screen at the same time. This allows simple grouping of widgets to support different screen configurations. The system also supports rotation and scaling to accommodate different screen geometries, resolutions and device orientation events.

`store` is a generic data store implemented as a hash table with support for data timeouts and categories. Data stores are used throughout the applications as a convenient way to organize data. For example in the telemonitoring application described below, patient data is grouped in individual data stores based on the network address of the patient monitors from which the data originates.

The framework also includes support for a plugin structure built around the `scheduler` module. The scheduler drives the sequential execution of plugins based on their type (four types are supported; input, algorithm, decision support and output). Plugins are instantiated against a data store, and multiple instances are allowed. For example, this allows multiple syringe pump drivers and infusion controllers to be instantiated for different drugs. This functionality is used in the closed-loop anesthesia controller described later.

The stub (in Fig. 1 (A) and (C)) which ties the Scheme payload into the operating system is a small piece of code in the native language of each platform, and is responsible for opening an OpenGL window and relaying rendering and user events to the payload event loop. The rendering itself is accomplished through direct calls to OpenGL in `glcore`.

4. Development and debugging

The framework is designed to be independent of an Integrated Development Environment (IDE), allowing developers to choose their

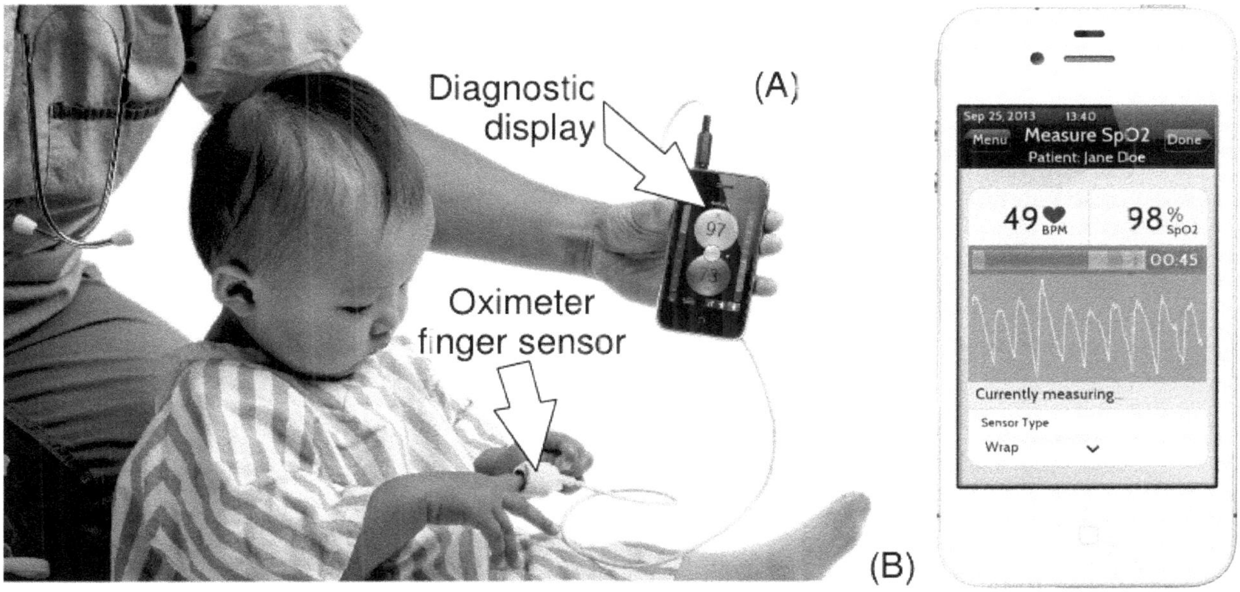

Figure 2. (A) Elements of the phone oximeter. (B) Screen shot showing a PIERS phone oximeter measurement in progress.

most productive environment. Developers are currently working with diverse software development environments ranging from the Eclipse IDE to the Vi editor on both Mac OS X and Linux.

The application framework incorporates a simple file based logging system that can be used for fault finding. Exceptions triggered in the Scheme payload will result in a message about the fault written to the log. Applications built in debug mode include source code file and line number information, allowing easy identification of the problem code. Faults on the C side can similarly be tracked down by compiling in debug mode and using a platform specific stack analysis tool like `ndk-stack` for Android.

A simple unit test system is used to test integrity of algorithmic components such as the encryption and compression communication routines, and a `lint`-like static analyzer [6] is available to find structural problems within the code, such as shadowed declarations and use of reserved keywords.

The built-in Scheme interpreter and equivalence of data and code provide unique ways to investigate and debug the state of the live running system. For example, a console application can be used to test a new code module interactively, prior to deployment in the final applications.

Profiling is accomplished by using Gambit-C's internal ability to capture thread continuations and provide information about file names and line numbers to build statistical information about bottle necks in the source code.

An automated smoke test script is used to periodically build and run all applications in the framework and verify that the binaries are runnable. This catches compatibility problems when making changes to the common code base of the framework.

For application verification we have developed systematic test suites. For example, an automated test including 100 simulated patients is used to verify the integrity of the the drug delivery controller described later. These tests run in real-time, using the built-in interpreter to script the inputs to the applications.

The everyday development and training within the programming team takes place in a flat structure, where code is reviewed and bugs resolved by drawing on the individual knowledge of each developer about particular portions of the code. The somewhat simplistic debugging tools have not limited us so far. The most elusive bugs were unexpected number types at the foreign function interface which caused type conversion problems in the C API calls.

5. Compilation

The compilation flow diagram is shown in Fig 1 (C). The basic idea is to build a single static library containing all of the Scheme payload, and link this library to a small launcher stub in the native language of the target platform (Objective C on iOS and OS X, Java on Android etc).

The payload is compiled using the standard automake tool chain. First the Scheme source files are converted to C using the Gambit-C `gsc` compiler. Next, resources such as images and fonts are processed into Scheme data with custom resource compilation tools and likewise compiled to C with `gsc`. Finally, the resulting intermediate C source files are compiled to object files using the target platform (cross-)compiler against the SDK provided header files. The resulting object files are assembled into a single static payload library.

Compilation of the application binary is complicated by the platform vendors requirement for specific tools. For example, iPhone applications must be built with XCode to satisfy the stringent code signing requirements for app store submissions. For this reason a CMake script is used to automatically generate an XCode project and `xcodebuild` is used to link the payload to the application stub and generate a valid application binary. Similarly the unconventional linking done in the Android build chain requires automating the use of the Android NDK `ant` based build system. The framework also automatically handles the manifests and icon graphics needed for the SDK driven builds on the different platforms.

6. Applications

The following sections describe three representative examples of the framework applications. Most of the applications are research tools used for human trials, and have been used to collect clinical data from more than 10,000 subjects in Canada, France, India, Uganda, Bangladesh, and South Africa, in more than 10 separate clinical studies.

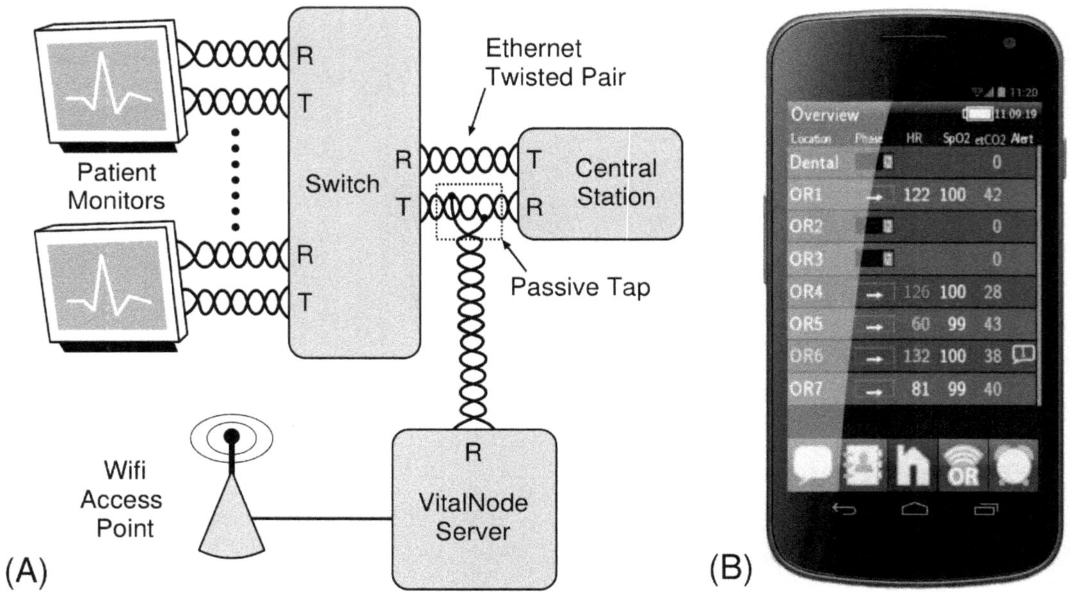

Figure 3. (A) Schematic of the VitalNode server accessing a patient monitor network through a passive tap. (B) telePORT application overview screen showing real time vital signs from a hospitals operating room theatres.

Almost all our application code is functional style Scheme (R5RS) without macros. The code repository contains 317,829 lines of Scheme, including comments and auto-generated code. There are 58 modules, 30 plugins and 77 applications. The only other languages used are C and shell script for supporting tools.

Current applications are deployed on embedded platforms, medical grade flat panel displays, netbooks, and smartphones running iOS and Android. The applications have no noticeable performance problems with respect to garbage collection, memory leaks, footprint etc. Our telemonitoring server described below has uptimes of over a year running on embedded hardware, and our mobile applications run on devices with only 128Mb RAM.

Any device used for diagnostic purposes in humans requires regulatory approval. Health Canada and regional ethics boards have approved the use of our devices for clinical research. The use of Scheme did not directly impact the regulatory process, which is focused on documentation and hazard analysis/mitigation.

7. Use case: The Phone Oximeter

A pulse oximeter is a noninvasive sensor that measures the oxygen concentration of blood. This is a critically important tool for continuous monitoring of oxygen saturation (SpO_2) in the operating room (OR), and is also a good predictor of disease severity and treatment response in a wide range of diseases such as pneumonia in children [7]. The Phone Oximeter is an inexpensive and portable pulse oximeter that runs on a mobile phone [8], as shown in Fig 2 (A). This device is targeted at users in low and middle income countries with little or no availability of conventional pulse oximetry equipment.

For research, we are designing mobile phone applications to record and store accurate spot-checks of a patients SpO_2 using the Phone Oximeter. Fig 2 (B) shows the measurement screen of one of our newest such applications, Pre-Eclampsia Integrated Estimate of RiSk (PIERS), which is described later in this section. This screen displays a photoplethysmogram, as well as heart rate (HR) and SpO_2 trends.

PhoneOxR [9] and its sequel PhoneOxR2 are Phone Oximeter applications used to collect accurate SpO_2 and HR values for patients admitted to studies on post discharge mortality, newborn and early childhood sepsis, and respiratory distress in Uganda, Bangladesh, and India respectively.

Our first goal with these applications was to ensure the accuracy of data used within the research studies. Changes in data quality reflected in a Signal Quality Index (SQI) result in prominent colour changes on the display. A horizontal progress bar shows the SQI colour over time, to promote the collection of good data, as seen in Fig. 2 (B). The percent of the recording that was good quality, as well as the median HR and SpO_2 trend values calculated from only green (high quality) sections of the recording are displayed at the end of the recording.

For each study subject, these applications create patient records, which include the median HR and SpO_2 as calculated above. A survey component allows entry of patient details such as demographics and medical history for each patient. The data is stored locally in an encrypted database and whenever network access is available the data is sent to a secure Research Electronic Data Capture (REDCap) [10] server via the REDCap application programming interface.

The PIERS application Fig 2 (B) represents the next step in our Phone Oximeter applications as it provides an interface for collecting not just SpO_2 but also the details of signs, symptoms, medical history, and medications taken over multiple visits with a patient.

This information is the input to a decision tree, which includes the miniPIERS predictive model, to assess the risk of pre-eclampsia and provide a recommendation, such as urgent transport to the hospital. The miniPIERS model is similar to the fullPIERS model [11], but it excludes the use of laboratory tests so that it can be used in community and primary health care facilities where these test are not possible. This application is designed to be used by midwives in local clinics and a simplified version of the application is being constructed to be used by community health care workers in their regular visits to pregnant women's homes. This application has undergone multiple iterations of usability testing and the simplified

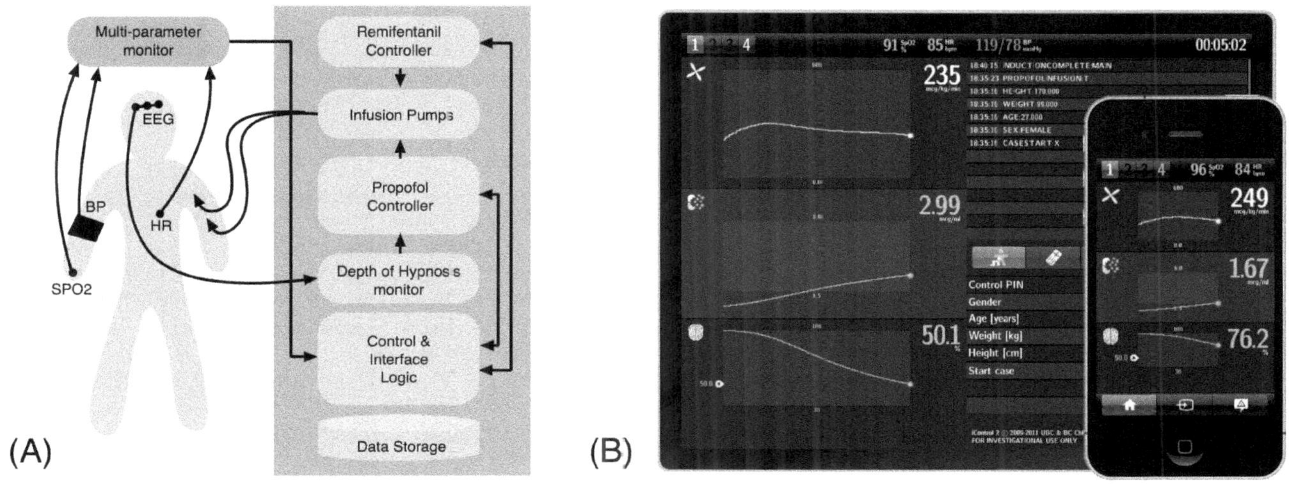

Figure 4. (A) Schematic of the iControl system for automated drug administration during general intravenous anesthesia. (B) The iControl interface running on platforms with different screen sizes.

version will be used in a multi-site study in India, Nigeria, Pakistan and Mozambique in the near future.

8. Use case: The telePORT monitoring and messaging device

Conventional physiological monitors in multi-bed environments such as operating rooms (OR) and intensive care units (ICU) are connected to central monitoring stations. However, these central stations are immobile and have limited proprietary interfaces. In order to make better use of collected patient data, we have developed a data access node and accompanying wireless real-time display of multi-bed patient data for mobile phones, which operates independently of the commercial patient monitor network.

We use an intrinsically safe method for extracting physiological trends and waveforms from patient monitoring networks by means of a passive network tap [12]. The tap is inserted into the central monitor network, Fig. 3 (A), and an exact copy of the network traffic is analyzed in real time with no impact on the network itself. Data collected from the tap is analyzed by a VitalNode server, developed in the application framework. This server runs on a Soekris 5501 embedded computer, and uses the PCAP (Packet CAPture) [13] application programming interface interfaced to a Scheme based parser plugin. Our parser understands raw network packages from Philips IntelliVue MP70 and Datex-Ohmeda S/5 monitors and stores continuous waveforms and vital sign trends from the monitors. This data is then fed through a forward chaining inference engine decision support plugin in the framework to generate trend based alerts. This approach allows wireless and wired access to encrypted physiological data, from all beds of the entire OR, ICU or ward to which the system is connected, as well as secure message exchange between users of the system.

telePORTs purpose is to improve information exchange, and simplify communication between anesthesia team members [14]. The telePORT interface is shown in Fig 3 (B). It runs on a mobile phone and polls user- and system generated messages, vital signs trends, and waveforms securely over the hospitals wifi network from the VitalNode server. It then supports the users work though five components: A) an overview screen, which provides the user with basic information about their subscribed monitoring locations, such as the anesthetic phase and three vital sign values. If additional detail is required access to waveforms and trends is provided. B) a messaging screen, which works as a combination of person-to-person chat system, and a system to receive requests for help through a button pressed on the patient monitor in an OR, C) a phonebook screen, which lists frequently used phone extension and pager numbers; and provides editing capabilities on the device, D) a room subscription screen, where room monitoring locations are subscribed to and where subscriptions can be delegated to other users, and E) a reminder screen, which allow the user to set up time- and anesthetic phase-based reminders. telePORT has been used in our department continuously for the last year with highly favourable reviews by its users. Based on this success, we are currently in the progress of developing a mobile monitoring, information exchange, and team communication solution for nurses, respiratory therapists and physicians in the ICU.

9. Use case: The iControl anesthesia controller

Today, intravenous anesthesia is typically delivered by a manually adjusted continuous infusion; a syringe pump is programmed to deliver a fixed volume per unit time, usually calculated on a weight basis with dosage based on a historical population average. Due to the high inter-patient variability, it is difficult to predict a manual infusion rate that will accurately produce the desired target brain concentration of the drug. Too little drug will mean that the patient will move or wake up, and too much drug will result in prolonged recovery and an increase in side effects such as cardiovascular or respiratory depression.

An automated anesthetic drug delivery system that offers a continuously adjusted rate of intravenous drug administration has advantages over traditional static (weight based) infusion, including greater hemodynamic and respiratory stability, more stable depth of anesthesia, the ability to predict recovery, and a lower total dose of drug administered.

iControl is such a closed-loop solution that delivers drugs based on feedback from electroencephalography (EEG) derived measurements of depth of hypnosis, as shown schematically in Fig 4 (A). Closed-loop control technology is used extensively in many fields such as the aviation and nuclear industry, but has yet to make a significant impact in anesthesia (or medicine in general). One of the main reasons for this is the natural concern about safety of closed-loop systems in medical applications.

The iControl system was designed and implemented using rigorous validation requirements of high-risk medical instrumentation, including a detailed user and system requirements specification, hazard analysis, and system design specification. The system underwent usability studies and extensive manual and automated system tests prior to being approved for clinical trials by Health Canada.

iControl is implemented as a client-server system. The server resides on a Soekris 5501 embedded computer running Linux or OpenBSD. The server has several sub-processes that use the framework plugin structure to feed data from syringe pumps and patient monitors to a patient specific data store. A controller plugin instantiated on the patient store calculates the new infusion rates and instructs the pump plugins to update the devices. The server communicates with a client interface through the same encrypted communication scheme as used by the telePORT application.

The iControl client interface is shown in Fig 4 (B). It features a real time display of current infusion rates, estimated brain concentrations of the delivered drugs, measured depth of hypnosis, and target depth of hypnosis.

The system is controlled through a simple touch screen based input system that is designed to provide a consistent and safe interface. The user interface screen layout automatically reconfigures based on the size of the display. The primary system console client runs on a medical grade flat panel PC (Windows XP embedded), mounted on a mobile medical cart together with pumps, EEG monitor and the embedded controller. Remote monitoring is possible over wifi by running the iControl interface application on a mobile phone or tablet. Multiple clients can run against the server simultaneously.

iControl has successfully been used to automate hypnotic drug (propofol) delivery in adults [15] and children [16, 17] , and is currently used in a study on adults controlling both hypnotic and analgesic drug (remifentanil) delivery concurrently.

10. Conclusions

A modular framework for cross-platform development of robust medical applications has been developed and used for deployment of diverse applications ranging from mission-critical embedded drug delivery systems to diagnostic and monitoring apps on iPhone and Android smart phones.

The use of Scheme and the extensive reuse of code between applications have enabled efficient development cycles with minimal resource requirements and a very small code base. The ability to deploy applications on a wide range of different platforms has proven to provide great flexibility and offers a way to easily port the system to new platforms if the need arises. The possibility of developing on a platform other than the target platform also provides greater productivity as it allows developers to work with the platform and development tools they prefer.

The biggest challenge encountered has been the learning curve associated with the Scheme language, and the lack of knowledge of functional programming in the engineering and the medical community from which we normally recruit. Unfamiliar syntax appears to be the biggest barrier. Use of a more familiar C or Java like in-fix notation, for example as provided by the Gambit-C internal "six" notation, may overcome this problem, and provide a robust cross-platform development system that can benefit from the strength of functional programming while being disseminated to the programming community at large.

A. Source code

The source code for the core framework, including simple demonstrator applications, is open source and available for download at: `https://github.com/part-cw/lambdanative`.

References

[1] Gambit Scheme programming language, `http://gambitscheme.org`

[2] Feeley M, Miller JS, Guillermo JR, Wilson JA. Compiling higher-order languages into fully tail-recursive portable C. Technical Report 1078, département d'informatique et r.o., Université de Montréal (1997)

[3] IEEE Standard for the Scheme Programming Language, IEEE 1178-1990, ISBN: 1559371250

[4] The Revised^6 Report on the Algorithmic Language Scheme, `http://www.r6rs.org`

[5] Kilgard MJ, Akeley K. Modern OpenGL: its design and evolution. SIGGRAPH Asia '08, p. 13 (2008)

[6] Johnson S. Lint, a C program checker. Computer Science Technical Report 65, Bell Laboratories, December 1977

[7] Neuman MI, Monuteaux MC, Scully KJ, Bachur RG. Prediction of Pneumonia in a Pediatric Emergency Department. Pediatrics, 2011; 128:2 p. 246-53

[8] Karlen W, Hudson J, Lim J, Petersen C, Anand R, Dumont GA, Ansermino JM. The Phone Oximeter. IEEE Engineering in Medicine and Biology Society Unconference, Boston, USA, August 30, 2011

[9] Dunsmuir D, Petersen C, Karlen W, Lim J, Dumont GA, Ansermino JM. The Phone Oximeter for Mobile Spot-Check. Society for Technology in Anesthesia 2012 Annual Meeting, Palm Beach, FL, USA, January 18-21, 2012

[10] Harris PA, Taylor R, Thielke R, Payne J, Gonzalez N, Conde JG. Research electronic data capture (REDCap) - A metadata-driven methodology and workflow process for providing translational research informatics support. J Biomed Inform. 2009, 42(2), p. 377-81

[11] von Dadelszen P, Payne B, Li J, Ansermino JM, Broughton-Pipkin F, Cote AM, Douglas JM, Gruslin A, Hutcheon JA, Joseph KS, Kyle PM, Lee T, Loughna P, Menzies JM, Merialdi M, Millman AL, Moore MP, Moutquin JM, Ouellet AB, Smith GN, Walker JJ, Walley KR, Walters BN, Widmer M, Lee SK, Russell JA, Magee LA. Predicting adverse maternal outcomes in pre-eclampsia: the fullPIERS (Pre-eclampsia Integrated Estimate of RiSk) model - development and validation. Lancet, 2011, 377 (9761), p. 219-227

[12] Görges M, Petersen C, Ansermino JM, Capturing vital signs for research in a multi-bed monitoring environment. Anesth Analg, 2011, 113 (2S Suppl), p. 42

[13] McCanne S, Jacobson V. The BSD Packet Filter: A New Architecture for User-level Packet Capture. Proc. of the USENIX Winter 1993 Conference p. 2

[14] Görges M, Ansermino JM. Development of a Mobile Monitoring and Communications Solution for Anesthesia Team Members. Anesth Analg, 2011, 112 (5S Suppl), p. S207

[15] Dumont G, Liu N, Petersen C, Chazot T, Fischler M. Closed-Loop Administration of Propofol Guided by the NeuroSense: Clinical Evaluation Using Robust Proportional-Integral-Derivative Design. American Society of Anesthesiologists (ASA) Annual Meeting 2011

[16] van Heusden K, Dumont GA, Soltesz K, Petersen C, West N, Ansermino JM. Clinical evaluation of closed-loop controlled propofol infusion in children. World Congress of Anesthesiologists, Buenos Aries, Argentina, March 25-30, 2012

[17] West N, Dumont GA, van Heusden K, Khosravi S, Petersen C, Ansermino JM. The administration of closed-loop control of anesthesia for gastrointestinal endoscopic investigations in children. Society for Pediatric Anesthesia AAP Pediatric Anesthesiology Annual Meeting, Tampa, FL, USA, February 23-26, 2012

Hoare-Style Reasoning with (Algebraic) Continuations

Germán Andrés Delbianco
IMDEA Software Institute
Universidad Politécnica de Madrid
german.delbianco@imdea.org

Aleksandar Nanevski
IMDEA Software Institute
aleks.nanevski@imdea.org

Abstract

Continuations are programming abstractions that allow for manipulating the "future" of a computation. Amongst their many applications, they enable implementing unstructured program flow through higher-order control operators such as callcc. In this paper we develop a Hoare-style logic for the verification of programs with higher-order control, in the presence of dynamic state. This is done by designing a dependent type theory with first class callcc and abort operators, where pre- and postconditions of programs are tracked through types. Our operators are algebraic in the sense of Plotkin and Power, and Jaskelioff, to reduce the annotation burden and enable verification by symbolic evaluation. We illustrate working with the logic by verifying a number of characteristic examples.

Categories and Subject Descriptors D.3.3 [*Language Constructs and Features*]: Control structures; F.3.1 [*Logics and Meanings of Programs*]: Specifying and Verifying and Reasoning about Programs—Logic of programs, Pre- and post-conditions; F.3.3 [*Studies of Program Constructs*]: [Control Primitives]

General Terms Languages, Verification

Keywords Continuations, Hoare Logic, Dependent Types, callcc

1. Introduction

Continuations are powerful abstractions that model the "future of a computation" [36]. They have a ubiquitous presence in programming languages: they allow for a family of program transformation techniques in the style of many CPS transformations [11], they underlie the denotational semantics of programs with jumps [16, 42], they give computational content to classical proofs [20], they have been used to structure computational effects [17, 21] and also to design compilation techniques. Moreover, certain programming languages provide first-class control operators which manipulate continuations, e.g. the variants of **callcc** in Scheme, ML and Haskell, or the related $\mathcal{C}$ and $\mathcal{F}$ control operators [15, 14].

The ability to manipulate "the future" makes these operators more powerful than plain **goto**-like instructions, but it also hinders the formal reasoning about programs. Although the state of the art concerning formal reasoning about continuations is vast, it has focused predominantly (with notable exceptions discussed below) on the semantic modelling of higher-order control operators and CPS transformations [15, 20, 11, 47], and verification of programs directly in the semantic model [41, 13].

In contrast, in this paper we are interested in developing a Hoare-style logic in which one can systematically specify and verify full functional correctness of programs with higher-order jumps, in the presence of dynamic mutable state and the ability to capture continuations and return them as results of computations, potentially encapsulated into closures.

The ability to capture and return continuations makes our task more difficult when compared to the previous work on Hoare logics for first-order jumps (i.e. **goto**'s) in high-level languages [9, 25, 2] and low-level machine code [38, 46, 23]. In particular, the higher order nature of **callcc** entails the need for a Hoare logic capable of reasoning about (potentially higher-order) functions. It also makes it somewhat more difficult to design the specification methodology, i.e. decide on just what kind of information should the proof developer provide in the form of annotations when specifying a program involving **callcc**, and how should that information relate the context in which the continuation is captured to the context in which it is invoked.

The presence of dynamic state significantly complicates matters, and differentiates our work from recent Hoare-style logics for higher-order jumps [5, 10]. From the semantic point of view, supporting dynamic state requires building a model in which executing a continuation does not roll back the mutable state to the point at which the continuation is captured. From the specification point of view, it requires reconciling **callcc** with Separation logic [31, 37]. In this paper, we accomplish the task in a novel manner, combining Separation *assertion* logic with large footprint semantics and large footprint inference rules for verification in the style of symbolic evaluation.

More concretely, our contribution in this paper is the development of $\mathsf{HTT_{cc}}$, a framework for Hoare-style reasoning with higher-order programs, control effects and mutable, dynamic state. To the best of our knowledge, this is the first formal system for reasoning about such combination of features. We define a dependent type-theory with first class continuations which uses monadic types indexed by pre- and postconditions as our specifications in the style of Separation logic. This has been done before for a language with state, e.g. in *Hoare Type Theory* (HTT) [29, 30], but now we extend the approach to a language with continuations. In particular, we rely on *dependent records* (i.e. iterated Σ-types) as an essential tool for specification of programs which "capture the continuation" in a closure that is later invoked.

In order to make specification and verification in $\mathsf{HTT_{cc}}$ more palatable, we focus on a specific choice of control operators which are *algebraic* in the sense of Plotkin and Power [33, 34] and Jaskelioff [22]; that is. the control operators commute with sequential composition. We argue that the algebraic control operators are less burdensome for verification than the non-algebraic alternatives, be-

ICFP '13, September 25–27, 2013, Boston, MA, USA.

ACM 978-1-4503-2326-0/13/09... $15.00.
http://dx.doi.org/10.1145/2500365.2500593

1. $\{x \mapsto v\}$

2. $c \leftarrow$ **callcc** f.

$$\textbf{ret}\ (\textbf{abort}\ f\ (x\ :=\ !x + 1\,;\ \textbf{ret}\ (\textbf{ret}\ ())));$$

3. $\{x \mapsto v \curlywedge \{x \mapsto v + 1\}\,c\,\{\bot\} \curlyvee$
   $x \mapsto v + 2 \curlywedge \{x \mapsto v + 3\}\,c\,\{x \mapsto v + 3\}\}$

4. $x\ :=\ !x + 1\,;$

5. $\{x \mapsto v + 1 \curlywedge \{x \mapsto v + 1\}\,c\,\{\bot\} \curlyvee$
   $x \mapsto v + 3 \curlywedge \{x \mapsto v + 3\}\,c\,\{x \mapsto v + 3\}\}$

6. c

7. $\{x \mapsto v + 3\}$

Figure 1. An idealised proof outline for **inc3**.

cause in practice they require less annotations to be manually provided by the user. In particular, the algebraic **callcc** typically requires manual description of only the jumping behaviour of the code, whereas, in our experience, the non-algebraic variants require manual description of both the jumping and the normal termination of the **callcc** block.

To test our design in practice, we have implemented $\mathsf{HTT_{cc}}$ as a shallow embedding in the Calculus of Inductive Constructions (CIC), as realised in Coq [27, 6] and Ssreflect [19]. We have mechanised its denotational semantics and soundness proofs and used the framework to verify a survey of standard examples which cover the usual continuation idioms. A subset of the examples is presented in Section 6. All of our Coq code is available on-line [12].

2. Overview

The language of $\mathsf{HTT_{cc}}$ uses monads, as in Haskell, to separate the purely functional and the imperative fragment of the language. In addition to capturing continuations via **callcc** and jumping to them via **abort**, the imperative fragment supports recursion (which we consider a side effect), and heap-mutating commands such as allocation, deallocation, reading from and writing into heap locations. We use **ret** v for a monadic command returning a value v, and $x \leftarrow e_1; e_2$ for monadic bind (i.e. a sequential composition), which first executes e_1, then binds the return result to x before executing e_2. We abbreviate with $e_1; e_2$ when $x \notin \mathsf{FV}(e_2)$. As customary with monadic languages, we assume that a command is evaluated only upon being bound in a sequential composition. Until then, the command's execution is suspended.

2.1 Algebraicity

As our **callcc** and **abort** are non-standard, we briefly illustrate them by example. Figure 1 shows an *informal* proof outline—in a style of partial correctness Hoare logic or Separation logic—for a function **inc3**, which uses a backward jump to increment the value of pointer x by 3. Our actual syntax for **inc3**, and the manual assertions needed for its specification, will be introduced in Section 2.3. We first discuss the behaviour of the function, and then return to the proof outline.

In the first command (line 2), **inc3** captures the continuation, which, at that point, is $\lambda c.\ x\ :=\ !x + 1;\ c$, corresponding to the code in lines $4 - 6$, with the variable c abstracted. The continuation is encapsulated inside a *continuation object* f, which may be viewed as a label for jumps. Next, the body of **callcc** is executed, and the suspended command **abort** $f\,(x\ :=\ !\,x + 1;$ **ret** (**ret** ())) is bound to c.[1] The program continues by incrementing x (line 4), after which c follows (line 6). Execution of c causes a jump to the continuation encapsulated inside f. However, before the control is passed to the continuation, the second argument of **abort**—$x\ :=\ !\,x+1$; **ret** (**ret** ())— is executed. Thus, x is incremented again, and **ret** () is passed as the argument c to the continuation encapsulated inside f. Passing the control to the continuation corresponds to a backward jump to line 4. Thus, x is incremented once again, followed by execution of c. Since the latter variable is now bound to **ret** (), its execution falls through and **inc3** returns (), after having incremented x three times.

The non-standard aspect of our control operators is that **abort** allows executing arbitrary side-effectful command—in the above case $x\ :=\ !\,x + 1$—as part of performing the jump. This is different from the customary **callcc** and **throw** [28, 48, 49], as the latter only passes a *value* upon a jump. We refer to this side-effectful command as *finalisation* code, as it is executed immediately before the jump, thus ending the normal control flow. Obviously, **throw** can be mimicked by **abort** by using a trivial finalisation code which immediately returns. Dually, **abort** $f\ e$ can be implemented by sequential composition which executes e, followed by **throw**ing the obtained value to f.

However, choosing **abort** as a primitive, awards special status to the finalisation code, which makes the control operators *algebraic* [22, 33, 34]. More concretely, **callcc** commutes with sequential composition, a property we use in Section 4 to formulate a methodology for Hoare-style specification and verification by symbolic evaluation. We illustrate how the commutation arises by the following equations, which can be derived from Jaskelioff [22].

$$x \leftarrow (\textbf{callcc}\,f.\,e_1); e_2 = \textbf{callcc}\,g.x \leftarrow [(g \triangleright x.\,e_2)/f]e_1;\ e_2 \quad (1)$$

$$\textbf{abort}\ (g \triangleright x.e_2)\ e_1 = \textbf{abort}\ g\ (x \leftarrow e_1;\ e_2) \quad (2)$$

$$\textit{where}\quad g \triangleright x.\,e_2 \triangleq \lambda t.\ g\ (x \leftarrow t; e_2)$$

Consider equation (1). The continuation captured inside f on the left side of the equation includes e_2. On the right side, **callcc** has been commuted out of the scope of x, and thus e_2 cannot be part of the continuation captured inside g. To induce that the expressions on the two sides of equality behave the same, jumps to g on the right side must be *preceded* by an execution of e_2. Because our primitives provide for finalisation code, we could enforce such a discipline by using e_2 as finalisation code for every **abort** to g. This is achieved by uniformly substituting f in e_1 with a new continuation object $g \triangleright x.e_2$. The new object is engineered so that aborting to it object behaves like aborting to g with the finalisation code extended by e_2, as captured in equation (2). Thus, execution of e_2 precedes the jumps to g, just as required.

2.2 Proof outline

As customary in Separation Logic, heaps are finite maps from the type **ptr** of pointers (isomorphic to $\mathbb{N}$) to values. The predicate $x \mapsto v$ holds only of a singleton heap with a pointer x, storing the value v. We use $\curlywedge$, $\curlyvee$, for point-wise conjunction and disjunction of heap *predicates*, and $\top$ and $\bot$ for the always true and always false predicate, respectively. In subsequent examples, we will also use separating conjunction $P * Q$, which holds of a heap h if h can be split into disjoint parts satisfying predicates P and Q, respectively. We will also use the predicate $\mathsf{this}\ h$, which holds only of heaps equal to h. We write $P\ h$ or alternatively, $h \in P$, when the predicate P holds of the heap h. We retain $\wedge$, $\vee$, True and False for the customary propositional (i.e., non-separation) connectives.

Referring to Figure 1, the line 1 states that the program starts with the initial heap containing a pointer x storing the integer v (though we omit the type annotations). $\mathsf{HTT_{cc}}$ uses *large footprint*

[1] As usual with monads, the binding strips the outer **ret**.

annotations which describe the full heap in which the program runs, rather than just a subheap that the program needs (in contrast to the *small footprint* annotations from Separation logic). Thereby, the proof outline in Figure 1 describes the behaviour of **inc3** when the heap contains *exactly* the pointer x storing v, but no other pointers. For now, we restrict ourselves to this simple case in order to focus on algebraicity, but we explain in Section 3 how to generalise the annotations of **inc3** to cover larger heaps.

Going back to Figure 1, at line 3, after the continuation is captured in line 2, the current heap is unchanged, but the program variable c is bound to the command **abort** f (**ret** (**ret** ( ))), which itself has to be specified. The Hoare triple $\{x \mapsto v+1\}\ c\ \{\bot\}$ indicates that c should be executed only after x is incremented (precondition $x \mapsto v+1$), and that the execution of c causes a jump (postcondition $\bot$). This behaviour precisely corresponds to the intended use for c in line 6. However, as c in line 6 executes a backward jump, the assertion in line 3 has to describe the state right after the jump, but before the program proceeds with executing line 4 for the second time. This is the role of the second disjunct in line 2. It shows that the program point is reached for the second time with x incremented twice. As described in Section 2.1, at that point c is bound to **ret** ( ), and can be specified by $\{x \mapsto v+3\}\ c\ \{x \mapsto v+3\}$ to indicate that this second instance of c will be executed after x is incremented once more (precondition $x \mapsto v+3$). The second execution of c does not jump, but falls through with the heap unchanged (postcondition $x \mapsto v+3$).

After x is incremented in line 4, the assertion in line 5 accounts for the change in the heap: compared to line 3, the value of x is incremented in both disjuncts, while the specifications for c remain unchanged. Now, command c is safe to execute in line 6, because the heap in both disjuncts satisfies the respective preconditions for c. The program terminates satisfying $x \mapsto v+3$ (line 7), which is a disjunction of the postcondition of c from line 5.

2.3 Proof annotations as dependent types

The crucial point in the proof outline for **inc3** is deciding on the specifications for c in line 3, which indicate the intended use of c in the rest of the program (i.e., c is executed when x stores $v+1$ and $v+3$, jumping in the first case, and falling through in the second). Such specifications depend on the structure of the rest of the program, and cannot be gleaned solely from the body of **callcc** in line 2. In this paper, we adopt the approach that such information is provided by the programmer in the form of annotations. This is similar to the way loop invariants often have to be provided when verifying structured programs. In $\mathsf{HTT}_{\mathbf{cc}}$, we use *type annotations* for this purpose. However, because the annotations clearly depend on run-time values (e.g., the contents of the pointer x in Figure 1), we have to use *dependent types*.

In particular, $\mathsf{HTT}_{\mathbf{cc}}$ features two type constructors which we use to provide annotations for side-effectful programs and for continuation objects. Intuitively, the type $\mathsf{SK}^*\ \{P\}\ A\ \{Q\}$ classifies programs with precondition P, postcondition Q and return value of type A. The type $\mathsf{Kont}^*\ \{R\}\{P\}\ A\ \{Q\}$ classifies continuation objects. R describes what holds when the continuation is captured by **callcc**, and is refered to as the *initial condition*. Precondition P describes what must hold of the heap when **abort**ing to the continuation object; thus immediately before the finalisation code is executed. postcondition Q describes the heap and the value obtained after the execution of the finalisation code, but before the actual jump. In both types, the assertions R, P and Q may depend on program values. Additionally, Q may depend on the dedicated variable $r{:}A$, naming the return value.

We employ the notation $[v_1{:}A_1, \ldots, v_n{:}A_n].\ \mathsf{SK}^*\ \{P\}\ A\ \{Q\}$, often omitting the types A_i, to specify that $v_1, \ldots, v_n$ are variables that may scope through P and Q (and similarly for R, P and Q

$$
\begin{aligned}
&\mathbf{inc3}\,(x{:}\mathsf{ptr}) : [v].\ \mathsf{SK}^*\ \{x \mapsto v\}\,(\,)\,\{x \mapsto v+3\} \triangleq\\
&\quad \mathbf{do}\ \ c \leftarrow \mathbf{callcc}_j\\
&\qquad\quad f : [v].\ \mathsf{Kont}^*\ \{j \in x \mapsto v\}\,\{x \mapsto v+1\}\ \Sigma{\bullet}\mathsf{SK}\,(\,)\\
&\qquad\qquad\qquad\qquad \{r.\ x \mapsto v+2\ \curlywedge\\
&\qquad\qquad\qquad\qquad\ \ \mathsf{spec}\,r \sqsubseteq (x \mapsto v+3, x \mapsto v+3)^*\}.\\
&\qquad\quad \mathbf{do}\,(\mathbf{ret}\ [\mathbf{abort}\ f\ \ (x := \ !x+1;\ \mathbf{ret}\ [\mathbf{ret}\ (\,)]])])\\
&\qquad\quad : [v].\ \mathsf{SK}^*\ \ \{x \mapsto v \curlywedge j \in x \mapsto v\}\ \Sigma{\bullet}\mathsf{SK}\,(\,)\\
&\qquad\qquad\qquad\qquad \{r.\ x \mapsto v \curlywedge \mathsf{spec}\,r \sqsubseteq (x \mapsto v+1, \bot)^*\};\\
&\quad x := \ !x+1;\\
&\quad \mathbf{cmd}\ c.
\end{aligned}
$$

Figure 2. Specification of **inc3** via type annotations.

in Kont^* types). In Hoare logic terminology, such variables are known as *logical*; they may appear in assertions, but not in the code. In first-order Hoare logics, logical variables have global scope and are used to relate the initial and ending states of a computation. In our setting, the scope of logical variables is *local* to the type in which they are bound. This is required in any Hoare logic for a language with procedures and recursion [24] such as $\mathsf{HTT}_{\mathbf{cc}}$, where a logical variable used in the specification of a recursive procedure, may have to be instantiated differently to satisfy the preconditions of different recursive calls.

Additionally, we employ a *dependent record type* $\Sigma{\bullet}\mathsf{SK}\ A$, which packages a precondition and a postcondition together with a computation, and thus abstracts existentially over them. In other words, a value of type $\Sigma{\bullet}\mathsf{SK}\ A$ is a *structure* of the form $[P, Q, e]$, where $e\ :\ \mathsf{SK}^*\ \{P\}\ A\ \{Q\}$. As we show subsequently, values of this type will be used whenever we "nest" the monadic types, i.e. build computations that return other computations, which may potentially capture continuations. Given $c\ :\ \Sigma{\bullet}\mathsf{SK}\ A$, we will use $\mathsf{spec}\ c$ and $\mathbf{cmd}\ c$ to project the components when necessary:

$$
\begin{aligned}
\mathsf{spec}\ &: [P, Q, e] \mapsto (P, Q)\\
\mathbf{cmd}\ &: [P, Q, e] \mapsto e
\end{aligned}
$$

We will abuse the notation and write $[e]$ instead of $[(P, Q), e]$, as the Hoare triple type of e—and hence its P and Q components—can usually be inferred, as we describe in Section 4. We will also use the symbol $\sqsubseteq$ to denote the usual Hoare ordering (i.e., pre-strengthening/post-weakening) on pairs (P, Q).

We now present in Figure 2 the fully annotated version of **inc3**, as it is written in $\mathsf{HTT}_{\mathbf{cc}}$. Apart from the obvious typing annotations and the explicit use of the aforementioned constructors and projections for $\Sigma{\bullet}\mathsf{SK}\,(\,)$, there are additional syntactic elements that did not appear in Figure 1. We use the expression $\mathbf{do}\ e\ :\ \mathsf{SK}^*\ \{P\}\ A\ \{Q\}$ (potentially with logical variables) whenever we want to explicitly ascribe the specification (P, Q) to e, rather than use the tightest specification that the system infers for e. Such ascription will entail a proof obligation that (P, Q) is valid for e, as we explain in Section 4. When the type ascription is explicitly bound to a variable x, we write $x : \mathsf{SK}^*\ \{P\}\ A\ \{Q\} \triangleq \mathbf{do}\ e$.

We also make explicit that **callcc** captures the *current heap*, in addition to the current continuation, through the *heap* variable j that is bound by **callcc** and which we declare as an index (e.g., $\mathbf{callcc}_j$). The variable j scopes over the whole **callcc** body, including the type of the continuation object f. However, it is introduced strictly for purposes of specification, and we shall use it only in the annotations, but not in the executable code over which it scopes. The role of j is to relate the values of the various logical variables in its scope. In Figure 2, e.g., the assertion $j \in x \mapsto v$ appears in the type of the continuation object f and in the type of the body of **callcc**, thus implying that the (distinct) logical variables named v in the two types, in fact denote the same value – that stored in x at the entry to **callcc**. In Figure 1 we used a single *global* logical variable v for this purpose, but, as explained, global logical variables do not scale to Hoare-style reasoning about procedural languages.

Figure 2 uses the constructor $[\_]$ twice. Once around $c_1 =$ **abort** $f\,(x\ :=\ !x + 1\,;\ \mathbf{ret}\,[\mathbf{ret}\,(\,)])$ and again around $c_2 =$ **ret** $(\,)$, which is embedded inside c_1. As explained in Section 2.1 at different points of execution, both c_1 and c_2 are assigned to the variable c, and thus, all three must have the same type. Because the Hoare types of c_1 and c_2 actually differ in the pre- and postconditions, we employ $[\_]$ to abstract over the whole specifications, coercing c_1 and c_2 to Σ•SK( ). The individual specifications of c_1 and c_2 are then re-established using the spec r projection in other program annotations.

For example, $[c_1]$ is the return value of **callcc**. The explicitly ascribed SK* type states that $\mathsf{spec}\,r \sqsubseteq (x \mapsto v + 1, \bot)^*$, exposing that c_1 performs a jump and should be executed only when x is incremented once.[2] On the other hand, $[c_2]$ is the value of the finalisation code of the **abort** to f in c_1. Hence, the variable r in the postcondition of f's type stands for $[c_2]$, and the formula $\mathsf{spec}\,r \sqsubseteq (x \mapsto v + 3, x \mapsto v + 3)^*$ in f's postcondition exposes that c_2 does not change the state, but should be executed only when x is incremented by 3. The types of f and the **callcc** body in Figure 2 explicitly provide the required information about the intended uses of the code bound to c at various execution points. Indeed, the postconditions of these two types are essentially the two disjuncts from line 3, Figure 1, with the formulas involving spec r replacing the Hoare triples over c. In this sense, the spec projection out of the record type Σ•SK represents Hoare triples when they are *nested*, i.e. used within the assertions of other Hoare triples.

It is important, however, that the two disjuncts in line 3, Figure 1 are specified in two different places in **inc3** from Figure 2. In particular, the type of f provides the disjunct describing what happens when f is jumped to, whereas the inner type ascription provides the disjunct describing the normal return value of the **callcc** block. This pattern whereby f specifies only the jumping behaviour is characteristic of the algebraic **callcc** operator. On the other hand, as we shall see in Section 6, the annotations describing the non-jumping behaviour in the body of **callcc** can often be inferred (though in the case of **inc3** we had to explicitly ascribe them because the return value nests a jump). In the non-algebraic case, in our experience, f has to *always* be manually annotated with the full disjunction of the jumping and non-jumping cases, resulting in larger and more cumbersome annotations and proofs.

3. Notation, logical variables, large footprint

While logical variables are very useful in specifications, they are somewhat inconvenient to work with in the meta theory. The main hindrance is that premises of inference rules may contain Hoare triples with differing contexts of logical variables, which have to coalesce in some way into a logical context of the Hoare triple in the conclusion. Typically, simple conjoining of contexts is not what is wanted, as some sharing of variables is desired. But then, it becomes problematic how to specify just exactly which variables should be shared in the conclusion, and which should not. To circumvent the issue, in this section we introduce SK and Kont types which do not use logical variables at all, and show how SK* and Kont* types with logical variables from Section 2, become merely notational abbreviations.

[2] The reader can ignore the operation $(-)^*$ for now; it will be defined in Section 3.

As a first step, we introduce the type SK $A\ (P,\ Q)$ of effectful computations where P is a precondition over heaps, as discussed in the previous section, but Q is a *binary* postcondition, ranging over the ending result of the program (of type A) and the initial and ending heaps, much as in VDM-style specifications [7, 30]. We use CIC-style notation to classify logical propositions by the type Prop, and represent predicates as functions into Prop.

Definition 1 (A-specs). *Given P : preT and Q : postT A an A-specification, or A-spec, is a pair (P, Q) : specT A with:*

$$\begin{aligned}\mathsf{pre}\mathbf{T} &\triangleq \mathsf{heap} \to \mathsf{Prop}\\ \mathsf{post}\mathbf{T}\,A &\triangleq A \to \mathsf{heap} \to \mathsf{heap} \to \mathsf{Prop}\\ \mathsf{spec}\mathbf{T}\,A &\triangleq \mathsf{pre}\mathbf{T}\ \times \mathsf{post}\mathbf{T}\,A\end{aligned}$$

The notation $[\Delta]$. SK* $\{P\}\,A\,\{Q\}$ from Section 2, with unary $\{P\}$ and $\{Q\}$ is an abbreviation, as we illustrate next.

Example 2. The type $[v]$. SK* $\{x \mapsto v\}\,(\,)\,\{x \mapsto v+3\}$ of **inc3** from Figure 2, is an abbreviation of the specification:

$$\begin{aligned}&\mathsf{SK}\,(\,)\,(\lambda i.\,\exists v.\, i \in x \mapsto v,\\ &\qquad \lambda\, r\, i\, m.\,\forall v.\, i \in x \mapsto v \to m \in x \mapsto v + 3)\end{aligned}$$

The SK type introduces an explicit quantification over v in the precondition to guarantee that **inc3** is safe to execute in the heap containing (only) the pointer x. The universal quantification in the postcondition expresses that upon termination, the value pointed to by x is incremented by 3. To express this property, the precondition $x \mapsto v$ has to be repeated as part of an implication in the binary postcondition, which is obviously cumbersome, thus motivating the following notation, generalising to a context Δ.[3]

Definition 3 (SK*). *Given a type A, P : preT, Q : postT A the type notation $[\Delta]$. SK* $\{P\}\,A\,\{Q\}$ is defined as:*

$$[\Delta].\ \mathsf{SK}^*\ \{P\}\,A\,\{Q\}\ \triangleq\ \mathsf{SK}\,A\,(P, Q)^*_\Delta$$

where $(P, Q)^*_\Delta$ is the A-spec defined as follows:

$$(P, Q)^*_\Delta \triangleq (\lambda\, i.\ \exists\Delta.\, i \in P,\ \lambda\, r\, i\, m.\ \forall\Delta.\, i \in P \to m \in Q)$$

The second step is to introduce the type Kont $A\ R\ Q$ of continuation objects. R:preT is the initial condition, describing the heap at the point of a jump. Q:postT A is a binary postcondition relating the initial heap with the ending heap and value of the finalisation code. The Kont type will always be in scope of a variable j denoting the heap at the point of continuation capture (the index of **callcc** in Figure 2); thus R and Q may depend on j as well.

We next show how the the type Kont* from Section 2, is a notation over Kont, but first we need to generalise somewhat. As the following example illustrates, the Kont* types actually require *two* different kinds of logical variables.

Example 4. Consider a continuation object which is captured when the heap $j = x \mapsto v$, can be jumped to only when x is incremented by *some* p, and whose finalisation code increments p further by 1. The scenario uses the program variable x and two logical variables, v and p. However, v and p clearly have different nature; v is implicitly universally quantified, while quantification over p is existential when describing the precondition for the jump, and universal in the description of the finalisation code. Thus, we put v and p into two different contexts, and describe the continuation object by the type

$$[v], \langle p\rangle.\ \mathsf{Kont}^*\ \{j \in x \mapsto v\}\{x \mapsto v + p\}\,A\,\{x \mapsto v + p + 1\}$$

We refer to the two kinds of variables and contexts as *box* and *diamond* variables and contexts, respectively. In Figure 2 we only

[3] The notation also explains the operator $(-)^*$ (with the empty context Δ), that was used in Figure 2.

used the box contexts, and in general, when the diamond context is empty, we simply omit it. However, diamond context is not always empty, as we will illustrate in the **ping–pong** program in Section 6.2.

Definition 5 (Kont*). *Let* Δ *and* Γ *be contexts of logical variables, and* j *be a distinguished heap variable, possibly occurring freely in* $R : \mathsf{pre}\mathbf{T}$, $P : \mathsf{pre}\mathbf{T}$ *and* $Q : \mathsf{post}\mathbf{T}\,A$. *Then the notation* $[\Delta], \langle\Gamma\rangle.\,\mathsf{Kont}^*\,\{R\}\{P\}\,A\,\{Q\}$, *is an abbreviation for the following* Kont *type without logical variable contexts.*

$$[\Delta], \langle\Gamma\rangle.\,\mathsf{Kont}^*\,\{R\}\{P\}\,A\,\{Q\} \triangleq$$
$$\mathsf{Kont}\,A\ \ (\lambda\, i.\,\forall\Delta.\,R \to \exists\Gamma.\,i \in P)$$
$$(\lambda\, r\, m\, i.\,\forall\Delta.\,R \to \forall\Gamma.\,i \in P \to m \in Q)$$

All the variables in Δ *are universally quantified in the notation, whereas the variables in* Γ *are existentially quantified in the initial condition, and universally in the postcondition.*

We close the section by revisiting the issue of large footprint annotations. In Section 2, **inc3** could execute only in a heap with *exactly* the pointer x, and no others. We now explain how to specify **inc3** to admit execution in the presence of additional pointers. We will use a (box) logical variable of type heap, to describe the sub-heaps that *do not* contain x. For example, the more general annotation for **inc3** is given below.

$$\mathbf{inc3}\,(x{:}\mathsf{ptr}) : [v, h].\,\mathsf{SK}^*\ \ \{x \mapsto v * \mathsf{this}\,h\}()$$
$$\{x \mapsto v + 3 * \mathsf{this}\,h\} \triangleq$$

$$\mathbf{do}\ c \leftarrow \mathbf{callcc}_j$$
$$f : [v, h].\,\mathsf{Kont}^*\{j \in x \mapsto v * \mathsf{this}\,h\}$$
$$\{x \mapsto v + 1 * \mathsf{this}\,h\}\Sigma\text{•}\mathsf{SK}\,()$$
$$\{r.\,x \mapsto v + 2 * \mathsf{this}\,h$$
$$\curlywedge\ \mathsf{spec}\,r \sqsubseteq (x \mapsto v + 3 * \mathsf{this}\,h,$$
$$x \mapsto v + 3 * \mathsf{this}\,h)^*\}.$$
$$\mathbf{do}\,(\mathbf{ret}\ [\mathbf{abort}\ f\ \ (x := \ !x + 1;\ \mathbf{ret}\ [\mathbf{ret}\ ()])])$$
$$: [v, h].\,\mathsf{SK}^*\,\{x \mapsto v * \mathsf{this}\,h \curlywedge j \in x \mapsto v * \mathsf{this}\,h\}$$
$$\Sigma\text{•}\mathsf{SK}\,()$$
$$\{r.\,x \mapsto v * \mathsf{this}\,h$$
$$\curlywedge\ \mathsf{spec}\,r \sqsubseteq (x \mapsto v + 1 * \mathsf{this}\,h, \bot)^*\};$$
$$x := \ !x + 1;$$
$$\mathbf{cmd}\ c.$$

The annotations introduce a logical variable h, the assertions this h, and separating conjunction $*$, to name the part of the heap disjoint from the pointer x. The occurrence of the same this h in both the pre- and postcondition of **inc3**, specifies that **inc3** keeps this part of the heap invariant. Moreover, h is local to the Hoare triples in which it appears (unlike in first-order Hoare or Separation logic, where logical variables are global). Thus, a specification of **inc3** can be extended to a larger heap merely by instantiating h, rather than by means of a dedicated *frame rule* as in Separation logic. Because of the repeated occurrences of this h in the assertions, this style of annotation is a bit more verbose than in Separation logic, where the invariance of residual heaps is implicit. However, in practice, the extra logical variable did not affect our proofs. We discuss in Section 7 the reasons for needing large footprints, and some alternative designs.

4. Inference rules

We develop the semantics of $\mathsf{HTT_{cc}}$ using the Calculus of Inductive Constructions (CIC) as the meta logic. The choice provides us directly with a method to prototype $\mathsf{HTT_{cc}}$ as a shallow embedding in Coq, thus inheriting a number of useful constructs, such as

$$\mathbf{ret} : \Pi v{:}A.\,[h].\,\mathsf{SK}^*\ \{\mathsf{this}\,h\}\ A\ \{r.\ \mathsf{this}\,h \curlywedge r = v\}$$
$$\mathbf{alloc} : \Pi v{:}A.\,[h].\,\mathsf{SK}^*\ \{\mathsf{this}\,h\}\ \mathsf{ptr}\ \{r.\ r \mapsto v * \mathsf{this}\,h\}$$
$$\mathbf{dealloc} : \Pi x{:}\mathsf{ptr}.\,[B, v{:}B, h].\,\mathsf{SK}^*\,\{x \mapsto v * \mathsf{this}\,h\}\ ()\ \{\mathsf{this}\,h\}$$
$$\mathbf{:=} : \Pi x{:}\mathsf{ptr}.\,\Pi v{:}A.\,[B, w{:}B, h].\,\mathsf{SK}^*\ \ \{x \mapsto w * \mathsf{this}\,h\}\ ()$$
$$\{x \mapsto v * \mathsf{this}\,h\}$$
$$\mathbf{!} : \Pi x{:}\mathsf{ptr}.\,[v{:}A, h].\,\mathsf{SK}^*\ \ \{x \mapsto v * \mathsf{this}\,h\}\ A$$
$$\{r.\ x \mapsto v * \mathsf{this}\,h \curlywedge r = v\}$$

Figure 3. $\mathsf{HTT_{cc}}$ typing assignment for primitive commands.

dependent Π and Σ types, which we have already used in Section 2. For the sake of brevity, we omit the treatment of such standard constructs (it can be found in [27, 6]), and freely assume the standard typing rules and the various syntactic categories of CIC, such as, e.g., variable contexts. We only present our *impure* monadic extensions: the typing rules for the SK and Kont types, and related terms. In Section 5, we develop the semantic model for $\mathsf{HTT_{cc}}$, which we mechanised in Coq, to show the soundness of the extension.

The specific rules of $\mathsf{HTT_{cc}}$ are of two distinct kinds. The first kind consists of *typing rules*, which serve to infer the default program specifications (weakest precondition for memory safety, and strongest postcondition wrt. that precondition). The inference is important in practice because it minimises the amount of annotations that the user has to provide manually. The second kind consists of *structural lemmas* that formalise the reasoning about Hoare-ordering of specifications. As illustrated in Figure 2, such reasoning is needed in several situations: (1) We may explicitly need to ascribe a custom specification to a program, and this requires a proof that the default specification can be pre-weakened and post-strengthened into a desired one, and (2) We may use the relation $\sqsubseteq$, to explicitly declare that a $[-]$-abstracted command satisfies a predetermined specification. The two kinds of rules are discussed in Sections 4.1 and 4.2, respectively.

4.1 Typing rules

From here on, we use s and variants to range over specifications (P, Q), with pre s and post s projecting out the components.

Bind rule in Figure 4 perhaps best exemplifies the inference nature of our typing rules. Given programs e_1 and e_2 with specification s_1 and s_2, respectively, the rule infers the tightest specification for the sequential composition $x \leftarrow e_1; e_2$ as follows. Because the execution of the compositions starts with e_1, the inferred precondition must require that pre s_1 holds of the initial heap i. After e_1 terminates with an intermediate value x and heap h satisfying post $s_1\,x\,i\,h$, it must be that pre $(s_2\,x)\,h$ so that e_2 is safe to run. The inferred postcondition declares the existence of an intermediate value x, and and a heap obtained after e_1 but before e_2, as per relational composition post $s_1\,x \circ$ post $(s_2\,x)\,r$.

Bind, as well as the other rules in Figure 4, use SK and Kont types *without* logical variable contexts, which is why we introduced such types in Section 3 in the first place. Omitting logical variables facilitates specification inference, as it circumvents the issue of reconciling potentially different contexts of logical variables that may appear in the type for e_1 and the type for e_2.

Abort rule infers a precondition that has a dual role The first conjunct $R\,i$ ensures that the continuation object f is **aborted** to only in heaps i for which the initial condition R is satisfied. The second conjunct $s \sqsubseteq (R \curlywedge \mathsf{this}\,i, Q)$ ensures that e is an appropriate finalisation code for f; that is, the specification s of e can be weakened into a precondition R and postcondition Q, as required by the type of f. Additionally, this i allows the proof of the weakening to

$$\frac{\Gamma \vdash e_1 : \mathsf{SK}\ A\ s_1 \qquad \Gamma, x : A \vdash e_2 : \mathsf{SK}\ B\ (s_2\ x)}{\Gamma \vdash x \leftarrow e_1; e_2 : \mathsf{SK}\ B\ (\lambda i.\, \mathsf{pre}\ s_1\ i \wedge \forall x\, h.\, \mathsf{post}\ s_1\ x\ i\ h \rightarrow \mathsf{pre}\ (s_2\ x)\ h, \lambda r\, i\, m.\ \exists x.(\mathsf{post}\ s_1\ x \circ \mathsf{post}\ (s_2\ x)\ r)\ i\ m)}\ \textsc{Bind}$$

$$\frac{\Gamma, j : \mathsf{heap},\ f : \mathsf{Kont}\, A\, (R\, j)\, (Q\, j) \vdash e : \mathsf{SK}\ A\ (s\, j)}{\Gamma \vdash \mathbf{callcc}_j\ f\,.\, e : \mathsf{SK}\ A\ (\lambda i.\ \mathsf{pre}\, (s\, i)\, i,\ \lambda r\, i\, m.\ \mathsf{post}\, (s\, i)\, r\, i\, m \vee (R \circ Q\, i\, r)\, i\, m)}\ \textsc{CallCC}$$

$$\frac{\Gamma \vdash f : \mathsf{Kont}\, A\, R\, Q \qquad \Gamma \vdash e : \mathsf{SK}\ A\ s}{\Gamma \vdash \mathbf{abort}_B\ f\ e : \mathsf{SK}\ B\ (\lambda i.\ R\, i \wedge\ s \sqsubseteq (R \curlywedge \mathsf{this}\, i, Q),\ \lambda r\, i\, m.\ \mathsf{False})}\ \textsc{Abort}$$

$$\frac{\Gamma \vdash e_1 : \mathsf{SK}\ A\ s_1 \quad s_1 \sqsubseteq s_2}{\Gamma \vdash \mathbf{do}\ e_1 : \mathsf{SK}\ A\ s_2}\ \textsc{Do} \qquad \frac{\Gamma \vdash e : \mathsf{bool} \qquad \Gamma \vdash e_1 : \mathsf{SK}\ A\ s_1 \qquad \Gamma \vdash e_2 : \mathsf{SK}\ A\ s_2}{\Gamma \vdash \mathbf{if}\ e\ \mathbf{then}\ e_1\ \mathbf{else}\ e_2 : \mathsf{SK}\ A\ (\mathsf{if}\ e\ \mathsf{then}\ s_1\ \mathsf{else}\ s_2)}\ \textsc{If}$$

$$\frac{\Gamma \vdash f : (\Pi x{:}A.\, \mathsf{SK}\ (B\, x)\ (s\, x)) \rightarrow \Pi x{:}A.\, \mathsf{SK}\ (B\, x)\ (s\, x)}{\Gamma \vdash \mathbf{fix}\, f : \Pi x{:}A.\, \mathsf{SK}\ (B\, x)\ (s\, x)}\ \textsc{Fix}$$

Figure 4. $\mathsf{HTT_{cc}}$ typing rules for specification inference.

exploit the knowledge that the heap in which the finalisation code executes is exactly i. The exact definition of $\sqsubseteq$ will be given in Section 4.2. Because **abort** does not return any values, its return type B is arbitrary and can be supplied by the user. We omit annotating this type in examples as it can be usually inferred from the context.

CALLCC rule in Figure 4, infers the specification for **callcc** $f.\,e$. The premise of the rule introduces the heap variable j, which, as illustrated in Section 2, provides a common point for f and e to "synchronise" on, thereby fixing the values of various logical variables in relation to j. In the conclusion of the rule, j will be instantiated with the initial heap of **callcc**; that is, with the heap at the point of continuation capture.

The specification of f allows aborting to f only in heaps satisfying $R\,j$. After f's finalisation code terminates, the resulting heap and value satisfy $Q\,j$. If e has a specification s, then the tightest specification of **callcc** $f.\,e$ can be inferred as follows. Because the execution of the whole command starts with e, the inferred precondition has to be derived out of e's precondition $\mathsf{pre}\,(s\,j)$. The unknown j is instantiated with the actual initial heap, to obtain the tightest precondition $\lambda\, i.\ \mathsf{pre}\,(s\, i)\, i$. The postcondition is a disjunction expressing that e may produce two different outcomes: it either aborts to f, or it does not. The left disjunct $\mathsf{post}\,(s\,i)\,r\,i\,m$ describes the non-aborting case; it simply equals the postcondition of e with j instantiated by i. In those cases when e actually aborts, the disjunct will be False, as it embeds the postcondition of the ABORT rule. The right disjunct is a relational composition $(R \circ Q\,i\,r)\,i\,m$ which describes the aborting case, as follows. In the aborting case, there exists a heap—call it h—that is current at the point of **abort**. Due to the specification of f, R must relate i and h. Additionally, m and r are obtained after the finalisation code of f is executed at h, and thus $Q\,i\,r$ must relate h and m as well.

The annotations specifying the continuation object (R and Q) appear in a negative position in the premise of CALLCC, and cannot be inferred automatically. In contrast, the specification s for e is generated by e's typing derivation. The property that *only* the aborting case has to be specified manually, differentiates the algebraic **callcc** from the standard, non-algebraic alternatives. A detailed comparison is presented in Section 7.

Other rules The rule DO implements a type ascription, requiring a proof that the specification s_1 can be weakened into s_2, as in the usual Hoare logic rule of consequence. The IF rule uses the type-level conditional, available in CIC, to compute the specification of a program-level conditional out of the types of the components. The FIX rule implements the usual typing for recursive procedures, requiring that an SK type be established for the procedure body, under a hypothesis that the recursive calls satisfy the same type. The primitive stateful commands have standard Separation logic specifications (Figure 3), except that they are extended to the large footprint idiom by naming the unused heap with the logical variable h.

Additional notation In the rest of the paper, we will use explicit names for the derived specifications in Figure 4. For example, we write $\mathsf{callcc\_s}\ R\ Q\ s$ for $(\lambda i.\ \mathsf{pre}\,(s\, i)\, i, \lambda\, r\, i\, m.\ \mathsf{post}\,(s\, i)\, r\, i\, m \vee (R \circ Q\, i\, r)\, i\, m)$, $\mathsf{abort\_s}\ R\ Q\ s$ for $(\lambda i.\ R\ i \wedge s \sqsubseteq (R \curlywedge \mathsf{this}\, i, Q), \lambda\, r\, i\, m.\ \mathsf{False})$, and similarly for $\mathsf{bind\_s}$, $\mathsf{read\_s}$, etc.

4.2 Structural lemmas and symbolic evaluation

The Hoare ordering on two specifications s_1 and s_2 is defined as:

$$s_1 \sqsubseteq s_2 \triangleq \forall i.\ \mathsf{pre}\ s_2\ i \rightarrow \mathsf{verify}\ i\ s_1\ (\lambda\, r{:}A\, m.\ \mathsf{post}\ s_2\ y\ i\ m)$$

where for any $\kappa : A \rightarrow \mathsf{heap} \rightarrow \mathsf{prop}$:

$$\mathsf{verify}\ i\ s\ \kappa \triangleq \mathsf{pre}\ s\ i \wedge \forall\, r\, m.\ \mathsf{post}\ s\ r\ i\ m \rightarrow \kappa\ r\ m$$

The definition of $s_1 \sqsubseteq s_2$ states that $\mathsf{pre}\ s_1$ weakens into $\mathsf{pre}\ s_2$ and $\mathsf{post}\ s_2$ strengthens into $\mathsf{post}\ s_1$, as in the Hoare logic rule of consequence. It is split into two stages in order to exploit the hypothetical reasoning of CIC and Coq. In practice, the hypothesis $\mathsf{pre}\ s_2\ i$ will always move into the hypothesis context of Coq, leaving verify to describe the remaining proof goal.

The $\mathsf{HTT_{cc}}$ proof obligations arise directly from the side condition about Hoare ordering in the rule DO in Figure 4, when the user wants to ascribe a desired specification to a program. In the practical work with $\mathsf{HTT_{cc}}$, the proof obligations are discharged by applying a number of carefully crafted lemmas about verify that implement verification by *symbolic evaluation.* We illustrate the process here, and discuss the relationship to algebraicity of control operators in Section 4.3.

For instance, let e_1 and e_2 be computations with specifications s_1 and $s_2\ x$, respectively. The inferred specification for $x \leftarrow e_1; e_2$ is $\mathsf{bind\_s}\ s_1\ s_2$. An $\mathsf{HTT_{cc}}$ proof obligation establishing that in some heap i, the execution of the sequential composition produces a heap and a value satisfying κ, will have the form:

$$\mathsf{verify}\ i\ (\mathsf{bind\_s}\ s_1\ s_2)\ \kappa$$

The idea of symbolic evaluation is to discharge such a goal as follows. It suffices to show that verifying a composite B-spec $(\mathsf{bind\_s}\ s_1\ s_2)$ can be reduced to verifying s_1 against a κ', where κ' itself involves verifying s_2 against κ. The process is iterated as long as s_2 contains sequential compositions, and can be seen as a sequence of applications of the following lemmas in $\mathsf{HTT_{cc}}$:

$$\begin{aligned}\text{STEP} &: \mathsf{verify}\ i\ s_1 (\lambda\, y\, m.\ \mathsf{verify}\ m\ (s_2\ y)\ \kappa) \to \\ &\quad \mathsf{verify}\ i\ (\mathsf{bind\_s}\ s_1\ s_2)\ \kappa \\ \text{VALDO} &: \mathsf{pre}\ s\ i \to (\forall x\, i\, m.\ \mathsf{post}\ s\, x\, i\, m \to \kappa\, x\, m) \to \\ &\quad \mathsf{verify}\ i\ s\ \kappa\end{aligned}$$

The STEP lemma implements the iterative step, and VALDO lemma applies in the end, when there are no outstanding sequential compositions to be stepped through.

The VALDO lemma may be specialised to streamline the symbolic evaluation for specific commands. For example, let f : $\mathsf{Kont}\,A\,R\,Q$ and e : $\mathsf{SK}\,A\,s$. The inferred spec for **abort** f e is $\mathsf{abort\_s}\ R\ Q\ s = (\lambda\, i.\ R\, i \wedge s \sqsubseteq (R, Q), \lambda\, r\, i\, m.\ \mathsf{False})$. Taking this spec for s in VALDO, after some simplification, we obtain:

$$\begin{aligned}\text{VALABORT} &: R\, i \to \mathsf{verify}\ i\ s\ (\lambda r.\, \lambda m.\, Q\, r\, i\, m) \to \\ &\quad \mathsf{verify}\ i\ (\mathsf{abort\_s}\ R\ Q\ s)\ \kappa\end{aligned}$$

In other words, to verify **abort** to f, we need to show that R holds of the current heap, and that the supplied finalisation code satisfies Q after running in i.

In case $e_1 = \mathbf{callcc}_j\ f.\ e$, the inferred spec is $\mathsf{callcc\_s}\ R\ Q\ s = (\lambda\, i.\ \mathsf{pre}\,(s\, i)\, i, \lambda\, r\, i\, m.\ \mathsf{post}\,(s\, i)\, r\, i\, m \vee (R \circ Q\, i\, r)\ i\, m)$, for some j and f : $\mathsf{Kont}\,A\,(R\ j)\,(Q\ j)$ and e : $\mathsf{SK}\ A\ (s\ j)$. Taking this spec for s, and after some rearrangement of the disjunction in the postcondition of $\mathsf{callcc\_s}$, VALDO can be specialised into the following lemma.

$$\begin{aligned}\text{VALCC} &: \mathsf{verify}\, i\ (s\ i)\ \kappa \to \\ &\quad (\forall r{:}A\, m.\ (R \circ (Q\, i\, r))\, i\, m \to \kappa\, r\, m) \to \\ &\quad \mathsf{verify}\, i\ (\mathsf{callcc\_s}\ R\, Q\, s)\ \kappa\end{aligned}$$

The first hypothesis corresponds to the case when e does not abort. In that case, the goal reduces to verifying $(s\ i)$ against κ. The second hypothesis corresponds to the aborting case. In that case e produces an ending heap m and value x satisfying $(R \circ (Q\ i))\, x\, i\, m$; that is e first reaches an aborting heap out of i (predicate R), and then executes the finalisation code $(Q\ i)$. Then we just need to prove that κ holds after the execution of the finalisation code.

Specialised symbolic execution lemmas can be proved for all other primitive commands. Furthermore, because verify is an ordinary logical definition, users can establish such lemmas for their own programs as well, directly in the logic.

Example 6. We can implement the usual **throw** command, as an **abort** with an immediately-returning finalisation code. Given f : $\mathsf{Kont}\,A\,R\,Q$ and a value $v{:}A$, we define:

$$\mathbf{throw}\ g\ v \triangleq \mathbf{abort}\ f\ (\mathbf{ret}\ v)$$

The inferred specification $\mathsf{throw\_s}\ R\ Q\ v = \mathsf{abort\_s}\ R\ Q\ (\mathsf{ret\_s}\ v)$ can be proved to satisfy a streamlined version of VALABORT, which exploits the trivial nature of the finalisation code to simplify one of the hypotheses.

$$\text{VALTHROW} : R\, i \to Q\, v\, i\, i \to \mathsf{verify}\ i\ (\mathsf{throw\_s}\ R\ Q\ v)\ \kappa$$

4.3 Algebraicity at the level of specifications

In this section, we show that the algebraicity property of **callcc** can be expressed as a lemma over specifications, similar to the symbolic evaluation lemmas from the previous section. This lemma, which we call ALGCC, expresses that we can commute the specification forms $\mathsf{bind\_s}$ and $\mathsf{callcc\_s}$, thus lifting to the level of specifications the algebraicity equation (1) from Section 2. However, stating the ALGCC lemma requires generalising somewhat the definition of $\mathsf{callcc\_s}\ R\, Q\, s_1$. We first introduce the generalised definition, which we rename $\mathsf{algcc\_s}\ R\, s_0\, s_1$, and then describe the intuition behind it.

Consider a program of the form $x \leftarrow (\mathbf{callcc}_j\ f.\ e_1); e_2$, where f : $\mathsf{Kont}\,A\,(R\ j)\,(Q\ j)$, e_1 : $\mathsf{SK}\ A\ (s_1\ j)$, and $x{:}A \vdash e_2$: $\mathsf{SK}\ B\ (s_2 x)$. Then, side-by-side, the two definitions look like:

$$\begin{aligned}\mathsf{callcc\_s}\ R\, Q\, s_1 &= (\lambda\, i.\ \mathsf{pre}\ (s_1\ i)\ i \\ &\qquad \lambda\, r\, i\, m.\ \mathsf{post}\ (s_1\ i)\, r\, i\, m \vee (R \circ Q\, i\, r)\ i\, m) \\ \mathsf{algcc\_s}\ R\, s_0\, s_1 &= (\lambda\, i.\ \mathsf{pre}\ (s_1\ i)\ i \wedge \forall h. R\, i\, h \to \mathsf{pre}\ (s_0\ i)\ h, \\ &\qquad \lambda\, r\, i\, m.\ \mathsf{post}\ (s_1\ i)\, r\, i\, m \\ &\qquad\quad \vee (R \circ \mathsf{post}\ (s_0\ i)\ r)\ i\, m)\end{aligned}$$

The main difference is that where $\mathsf{callcc\_s}$ uses only the postcondition Q (abstracting over j) to specify the finalisation code, $\mathsf{algcc\_s}$ takes a full specification s_0 (also abstracting over j), which includes a precondition as well. In $\mathsf{callcc\_s}$, the precondition for the finalisation code is assumed to be the trivially true heap predicate, and we can prove the equation

$$\mathsf{callcc\_s}\ R\, Q\, s_1 = \mathsf{algcc\_s}\ R\, (\lambda\, j.\, (\top, Q\ j))\, s_1.$$

Intuitively, $\mathsf{callcc\_s}$ could use the trivial precondition for the finalisation code, because R already describes what holds of the heap at the point of abort, and this is the same heap in which the finalisation code executes. However, the main property of algebraic commutation is that it changes the finalisation code by extending it with e_2, though it does not change the point of **abort**ing. The new definition $\mathsf{algcc\_s}$ thus divorces R and $\mathsf{pre}\ s_0$, so that the algebraicity lemma can express that R remains fixed, while $\mathsf{pre}\ s_0$ changes. The changes to $\mathsf{pre}\ s_0$ cannot be arbitrary, however, as the finalisation code always executes in a heap in which **abort** is called. Thus, the precondition of $\mathsf{algcc\_s}$ includes a conjunct that R implies $\mathsf{pre}\ s_0$ for every initial heap i, and aborting heap h.

We can now state the algebraicity lemma for **callcc**, with the omitted proof included in our Coq files.

$$\begin{aligned}\text{ALGCC} &: \mathsf{verify}\, i\ (\mathsf{bind\_s}\ (\mathsf{algcc\_s}\ R\, s_0\, s_1)\ s_2)\ \kappa \quad \leftrightarrow \\ &\quad \mathsf{verify}\, i\ (\mathsf{algcc\_s}\ R\ (\lambda\, j.\ \mathsf{bind\_s}\ (s_0\ j)\ s_2) \\ &\qquad (\lambda\, j.\ \mathsf{bind\_s}\ (s_1\ j)\ s_2))\ \kappa\end{aligned}$$

5. Denotational semantics

In this section we present the semantics of $\mathsf{HTT_{cc}}$ as a shallow embedding into CIC. That is, we provide a semantic interpretation function $[\![-]\!]$ that maps $\mathsf{HTT_{cc}}$ types SK and Kont into types defined in CIC, but acts as identity on all the other types inherited from CIC, such as nat or heap. Similarly, the interpretation of terms maps the monadic constructs such as **callcc**, **abort**, etc., into CIC-terms, while acting as an identity on all the other terms inherited from CIC. The interpretation extends homomorphically to variable contexts as well.

5.1 Semantics of types

As customary in the case of control operators, our denotational semantics is parameterised wrt. the type X of return results for the continuations. We further require that X is a *complete lattice*, thus providing us with means to model the fixed point combinator in CIC, using the Knaster-Tarski theorem.

Definition 7. *Given a type A, and predicates P : $\mathsf{pre}\mathbf{T}$ and Q : $\mathsf{post}\mathbf{T}\ A$, the types $\mathsf{SK}\ A\ (P, Q)$ and $\mathsf{Kont}\ A\ P\ Q$ are interpreted as follows.*

$$\begin{aligned}&[\![\mathsf{SK}\ A\ (P, Q)\,]\!] \triangleq \\ &\quad \Pi i{:}\mathsf{heap}.\ [\![P]\!]\ i \to (\Pi r{:}[\![A]\!].\ \Pi m{:}\mathsf{heap}.\ [\![Q]\!]\ r\, i\, m \to X) \to X \\ &[\![\mathsf{Kont}\ A\ P\ Q]\!] \triangleq [\![\mathsf{SK}\ A\ (P, Q)]\!] \to \Pi j{:}\mathsf{heap}.\ [\![P]\!]\ j \to X\end{aligned}$$

A computation of SK type takes a heap i satisfying the precondition P, and a *continuation* requiring the postcondition Q as a precondition. Intuitively, the continuation applies to the ending value and heap of the computation, to produce a result in X. As the latter type is a complete lattice, the possible results include divergence, denoted by the bottom element of the lattice. We don't model the faulting behaviour such as type or memory errors (e.g., de-referencing a dangling pointer), but instead rely on the proofs of $[\![P]\!]\,i$ and $[\![Q]\!]\,r\,i\,m$ to statically ensure that a computation executes only in heaps and continuations for which such errors do not occur. In this sense, well-typed (i.e., well-specified) computations in $\mathsf{HTT_{cc}}$ do not fault, as usual for type systems and for *fault-avoiding* Hoare logics such as Separation logic.

A further useful intuition about our model may be gained if one erases the dependencies on P and Q in Definition 7. This results in the following informal equations:

$$\begin{aligned}[\![\mathsf{SK}\,A]\!] &= \mathsf{heap} \to ([\![A]\!] \to \mathsf{heap} \to X) \to X\\ [\![\mathsf{Kont}\,A]\!] &= [\![\mathsf{SK}\,A]\!] \to \mathsf{heap} \to X\end{aligned}$$

The first equation shows that the $\mathsf{SK}\,A$ type is essentially the standard *state-passing continuation monad*. The second equation shows that a continuation object semantically requires two arguments: an explicit finalisation code (the $\mathsf{SK}\,A$ type), and a heap. Of course, the finalisation code is explicitly provided by the program as an argument of abort. Importantly, the heap argument is *implicitly* supplied by the denotation of **abort** as the heap current at the point of **abort**ing to f.

Of course, the parametrisation with finalisation code is what makes our control operators algebraic, and is directly inspired by Jaskelioff [22]. On the other hand, the further heap argument makes the $\mathsf{Kont}\,A$ type implement *non-rollbacking* continuations. In contrast, the algebraic **callcc** presented by Jaskelioff for a state and continuations monad does roll-back the state to the one captured together with the current continuation.

5.2 Semantics of computations

For the sake of brevity, we present only the denotational semantics of the control operators **callcc** and **abort**. Moreover, we illustrate only the simplified setting where the dependencies on P and Q are erased from the types (as in the above informal equations), and the dependencies on the proofs of $[\![P]\!]\,i$ and $[\![Q]\!]\,r\,i\,m$ are erased from the terms. The full dependency-respecting denotations for all the monadic commands from Figures 4 and 3 are implemented in the companion Coq files.

Definition 8 (**callcc** $f.\,e$)**.** *Given* $f : [\![Kont\,A]\!]$ *and* $e : [\![\mathsf{SK}\,A]\!]$, *the denotation of* **callcc** $f.\,e$ *of type* $[\![\mathsf{SK}\,A]\!]$ *is defined as:* [4]

$$\begin{aligned}[\![\mathbf{callcc}]\!] &: ([\![\mathsf{Kont}A]\!] \to [\![\mathsf{SK}\,A]\!]) \to [\![\mathsf{SK}\,A]\!]\\ [\![\mathbf{callcc}\,f.\,e]\!] &\triangleq \lambda i : \mathsf{heap}.\,\lambda k : [\![A]\!] \to \mathsf{heap} \to X.\\ &\qquad [\lambda c : [\![\mathsf{SK}\,A]\!].\,\lambda h : \mathsf{heap}.\,c\;h\;k/f][\![e]\!]\;i\;k\end{aligned}$$

Intuitively, executing **callcc** $f.\,e$ corresponds to applying the denotation to the initial (i.e., captured) heap i and continuation k. The body e is executed using the same heap and continuation. However, first the variable $f : [\![\mathsf{Kont}\,A]\!]$ is bound to a continuation object that, when supplied the finalisation code c and a heap h that is current at the point of aborting to f, executes c in h passing the control (i.e., jumping) to k.

Definition 9 ($\mathbf{abort}_B\ f\ e$)**.** *Given* $f : [\![\mathsf{Kont}\,A]\!]$ *and* $e : [\![\mathsf{SK}\,A]\!]$, *the denotation of* $\mathbf{abort}_B\ f\ e$ *of type* $[\![\mathsf{SK}\,B]\!]$ *is given by:*

$$\begin{aligned}[\![\mathbf{abort}_B]\!] &: [\![\mathsf{Kont}\,A]\!] \to [\![\mathsf{SK}\,A]\!] \to [\![\mathsf{SK}\,B]\!]\\ [\![\mathbf{abort}_B\ f\ e]\!] &\triangleq \lambda i : \mathsf{heap}.\,\lambda k : [\![B]\!] \to \mathsf{heap} \to X.\ [\![f]\!]\ [\![e]\!]\ i\end{aligned}$$

Theorem 10 (Soundness)**.** *If* $\Gamma \vdash e : A$ *then* $[\![\Gamma]\!] \vdash_{CIC} [\![e]\!] : [\![A]\!]$.

Proof. The proof is by induction on the structure of e. The interesting cases are when e is one of the monadic commands (correspondingly, when A is an SK type), as in all other cases the semantic function is trivial. When e is a monadic command, the soundness proof for the command is intertwined with the definition of the denotation of e. For example, in the case of $e = \mathbf{callcc}_j\ f.\,e$ the denotation will involve parametrization on the proofs of $[\![P]\!]\,i$ and $[\![Q]\!]\,r\,i\,m$, for the appropriate P and Q, that we have simplified away in our discussion. Such proof parameters are used in the denotations to build larger proofs on-the-fly, as necessary to make the various sub-terms of the denotation typecheck, until ultimately the whole denotation term typechecks wrt. the specification given in Figure 4. Similar considerations apply for other monadic terms as well. One exception is the fixed point construct **fix** f, whose soundness is proved by an appeal to Knaster-Tarski theorem over the monotone completion of f. The Knaster-Tarski theorem applies because $[\![ST\,A\,(P,Q)]\!]$ is a complete lattice, being defined as a function space into a complete lattice X. We have mechanised all the steps of the proof in our Coq files. □

[4] Omitting the index j to **callcc**, which may only appear in the erased dependencies.

```
rember-up-to-last (x : A) (xs : list A) :
   [h]. SK* {this h} (list A) {r. this h ⅄ r = rember x xs [ ]} ≜
  do (callcc_j
        exit : [h]. Kont* {j ∈ this h}
                          {if x ∈ xs then this h else ⊥}
                          (list A)
                          {r. this h ⅄ r = rember x xs [ ]}.
        fix (λ f : remberT. λ ys : list A.
              if ys is y :: ys' then
                   zs ← f ys';
                   if x == y then throw exit zs
                   else ret (y::zs)
              else ret [ ]) xs)
where

 remberT ≜ Πys : list A.
   SK* {this j ⅄ ∃ps. xs = ps++ys} (list A)
       {r. this j ⅄ r ∈ remberP x ys [ ]}

 remberP x xs acc ≜  if xs is y :: ys' then
                          if x == y then ∅
                          else remberP x ys' (acc++[y])
                     else {ps | ps = acc}
```

Figure 5. rember-up-to-last in $\mathsf{HTT_{cc}}$.

6. A short verification survey

We present the verification of two examples exhibiting non-trivial patterns for programming with continuations. The first example, rember-up-to-last, illustrates *downwards or exit* continuations, whereby a jump is used to escape early from a recursive call, whilst discarding suspended computations. The second example, ping–pong, illustrates *upwards* continuations or *unstructured* loop, where the executions of a captured continuation are interleaved with user code, thereby mimicking the cooperating behaviour of (a simplified version of) coroutines. In the companion files [12], we verify other examples as well, such as escaping from infinite loops and using continuations to implement error handlers.

```
rember (x : A) (xs acc : list A) : list A ≜
        if xs is y::ys' then
              if x == y then rember x ys' [ ]
              else rember x ys' (acc++[y])
        else acc.
```

Figure 6. Purely functional rember.

6.1 rember-up-to-last

Let A be a type supporting decidable equality; i.e., there exists a function $==: A \to A \to \mathsf{bool}$. Given $x : A$ and a list $xs : \mathsf{list}\, A$, rember-up-to-last $x\, xs$, returns the ending segment of xs after the last occurrence of x; if x does not occur in xs, the whole xs is returned [18, p. 55]. For example, if $xs = [23, 16, 42, 4, 42, 8, 15, 16]$, then rember-up-to-last $4\ xs = [42, 8, 15, 16]$, rember-up-to-last $16\ xs = [\,]$ and rember-up-to-last $42\, xs = [8, 15, 16]$. However, rember-up-to-last $7\ xs = xs$.

Figure 5 implements rember-up-to-last in $\mathsf{HTT_{cc}}$, following the ML implementation by Thielecke [47]. For simplicity, we use purely-functional lists instead of imperative, singly- or doubly-linked lists. The implementation works as follows. In line 2, it captures the continuation with **callcc**. Then, it recurses over the input list xs, searching for x (lines 3–5), rebuilding the input list on the way back (line 7). If x is found (line 6), it jumps out of the loop, by **throw**ing to the captured continuation (Example 5). The returned value zs is the list rebuilt so far, while the outstanding iterations of the loop intended to further rebuild the list, are cancelled.

We also develop a purely-functional version rember (Figure 6) by induction on xs. rember does not use **callcc**, but instead relies on *tail recursion* and the accumulator acc to keep track of the currently rebuilt list. Of course, the implementation with jumps is preferable from the efficiency standpoint, but we require the pure rember in order to *specify* rember-up-to-last.

We now analyse the type annotations in Figure 5. Those for rember-up-to-last (line 1) are quite intuitive. The function can run in an arbitrary heap h (this h in the precondition). It leaves the heap unchanged (this h in the postcondition), and the return result r is the same as running the tail-recursive rember with the empty initial accumulator. The continuation object $exit$ (line 2) is specified as follows. The initial condition exposes that the captured heap j equals h. A jump to exit may occur only when the precondition is satisfied; in this case, only when $x \in xs$. The postcondition states that the heap is unchanged, and the return value equals running rember, as expected.

The most interesting annotations is the *loop invariant* remberT provided as the type of the recursive function f. The precondition states that f is only ever applied to the tail ys of xs; hence xs can be partitioned as $ps{+\!\!+}ys$. The partitioning is made explicit in the precondition, as it will be required when proving that we are throwing the correct ending segment in line 6. In the postcondition, remberT has to state that f produces the correct result. Importantly, however, it cannot use the helper function rember! rember requires an accumulator argument, but as f itself *is not* tail recursive, it is not clear which value to supply for the accumulator. Unlike in the specifications of rember-up-to-last and exit, it's incorrect to use $[\,]$, as that does not reflect the looping behaviour. It's also incorrect to existentially abstract over the accumulator, as that produces too weak a property which then does not imply the postcondition of rember-up-to-last, where the accumulator is $[\,]$.

The workaround is to define a helper function remberP, which is similar to rember, but records when the jumps in f appear, as

```
1. {∃h. this h}
2. do ( callcc_j exit .
3. {∃h. this h ∧ j = h}
4. {this j ∧ xs = [ ]++xs}
5.   fix (λ f ys.
6. {∃ps. this j ∧ xs = ps++ys}
7.              if ys is y :: ys' then
8. {∃ps. this j ∧ xs = ps++(y:: ys')}
9.                   zs ← f ys';
10. {∃ps. this j ∧ xs = ps++(y:: ys') ∧ zs ∈ remberP x ys' [ ]}
11.                  if x == y then
12. {∃ps. this j ∧ xs = ps++(x::ys') ∧ zs ∈ remberP x ys' [ ]}
13. {this j ∧ x ∈ xs ∧ zs = rember x xs [ ]}
14.                       throw exit zs
15. {⊥}
16.                  else ret (y::zs)
17. ∃ps. this j ∧ xs = ps++(y:: ys')
              ∧ y::zs ∈ rememberP x (y::ys') [ ]}
18.             else ret [ ]
19. {∃ps. this j ∧ xs = ps ∧ [ ] ∈ remberP x [ ] [ ]}
20.                          ) xs)
21. {this j ∧ r ∈ remberP x xs [ ]}
22. {∃h. this h ∧ (r ∈ remberP x xs [ ] ∨
                  (x ∈ xs ∧ r = rember x xs [ ]))}
23. {∃h. this h ∧ r = rember x xs [ ]}
```

Figure 7. Proof outline for rember-up-to-last $x\ xs$.

follows. remberP returns either an empty *set* of values, to signalise a jump, or a singleton set, with the correct value, in the non-jumping case. More precisely, we have the following lemma:

$$\mathsf{rmb\_rmbP} : r \in \mathsf{remberP}\ x\ xs\ acc \to r = \mathsf{rember}\ x\ xs\ acc.$$

Then, the loop invariant remberT can assert that the return value r is always in the set defined by remberP. In the case of a jump, this property is evidently false, since the set is empty. But, in such a case, the program behaviour is described by the annotation on exit anyway, and the loop invariant need not bother describing it again.

Figure 7 presents a proof outline for rember-up-to-last $x\ xs$. The trivially true assertion $\exists h.\, \mathsf{this}\, h$ in line 1 corresponds to unfolding the notation for the type SK^* with a precondition this h, and a logical variable h. In line 3, the current heap h is captured into the variable j, corresponding to substituting h for j in the rule BNDCC, Section 4. In the proof outline, we cannot represent the substitution because j appears in the rest of the code, so instead we equate j with h in the assertion. Line 6 starts the verification of the loop; it shows that the precondition of the loop invariant remberT holds; the heap is unchanged wrt. the captured heap, and there exists a partition $xs = ps{+\!\!+}ys$. One critical point in the proof is Line 13, where we need to establish $zs = \mathsf{rember}\ x\ xs\ [\,]$, which is the precondition for **throw**. This property can be proved out of the partitioning $xs = ps{+\!\!+}(x :: ys')$ and $zs \in \mathsf{remberP}\ x\ ys'\ [\,]$ available in Line 12, by using rmb_rmbP and additional two helper lemmas (though we elide the derivation here):

rmb_cat :

$$\text{rember } x\ (ps +\!\!+ ys)\ acc = \text{rember } ys\ (\text{rember } x\ acc\ ps)$$

$$\text{rmb\_in} : \text{rember } x\ xs\ acc = \text{if } x \in xs \text{ then rember } x\ xs\ [\,] \text{ else } (acc +\!\!+ xs)$$

Another critical point is line 17, where we need to prove $y :: zs \in$ remberP $x\ (y :: ys')\ [\,]$, required to establish the postcondition of the loop. The property is proved out of $zs \in$ remberP $x\ ys'\ [\,]$ available in line 10, after unfolding the definition of remberP once, and using the following lemma about remberP:

$$zs \in \text{remberP } x\ ys\ acc \to y{::}zs \in \text{remberP } x\ ys\ (y{::}acc).$$

Line 19 describes what holds in the else branch of the main conditional in the loop, and line 21 establishes that the loop invariant holds at the end of the loop. Line 21 is a common weakening of lines 15, 17 and 19. Line 22 includes a disjunction, showing that the line can be reached by a normal termination of the loop (line 21), or by a jump to exit. Line 23 is obtained out of line 22 by applying rmb_rmbP, and establishes the specified postcondition of rember-up-to-last.

6.2 Ping-Pong cooperation

In Section 2 we presented **inc3**, which used a closure to capture a continuation and execute it twice. Here, we generalise the idea to n calls to **abort**, thus iterating n times the captured continuation. The result is an interleaving between the captured continuation and the finalisation code in the closure, which creates a cooperation pattern resembling that of coroutines [47] – albeit one without the full power of coroutine *fork* or *yield* operations, which further require storing continuations into the heap [40, 35]. Unlike **inc3**, where both the captured continuation and the finalisation code executed the same code, we will have different computations for the captured continuation, ping, and for the finalisation code in the closure, pong, and use the pre- and postconditions to show that these are interleaved in the evaluation of ping–pong. Since our motivation is to verify the cooperation pattern, rather than ping and pong *per se*, we give a trivial implementation for the latter functions: ping$\triangleq$ incr x and pong$\triangleq$ incr y, where:

$$\text{incr } z : [v\ h].\,\text{SK}^*\ \{z \mapsto v * \text{this } h\}\ (\,)\ \{z \mapsto v + 1 * \text{this } h\}$$
$$\triangleq \mathbf{do}\ (v \leftarrow\ !x;\ x := v + 1)$$

Figure 8 presents ping–pong, whose structure is close to that of **inc3**. In line 2, **callcc** captures the continuation corresponding to the rest of the program $\lambda c.$ ping; **cmd** c and binds it to the continuation object k. The body of **callcc** returns a function f defined recursively on n. If n is non-zero (line 5), f returns a closure which aborts to the captured continuation with the finalisation code consisting of pong followed by the recursive call to f. In the zero case, f returns the computation pong. The result of this recursive function is bound to c in the sequel. When $n > 0$, c will be bound to a closure with n calls to **abort** nested in the finalisation code:

$$\underbrace{[\mathbf{abort}\ k\ (\text{pong}; \mathbf{ret}\ [\mathbf{abort}\ k\ (\cdots\ \mathbf{abort}\ k}_{n \text{ calls to } \mathbf{abort}\ k}(\mathbf{ret}\ [\text{pong}]))])]$$

After **callcc**, ping is evaluated to increment x, and then c is evaluated. If $n = 0$, and thus c is bound to [pong], the value at y is incremented an the function terminates. If $n > 0$, the *outermost* **abort** in the closure above is executed, thus running pong as the finalisation code and passing the rest of the nested computations in the closure, bound to c, to the captured continuation. This results in a backward jump to line 7. The loop continues until the closure is consumed in full and the function terminates. As a result ping and pong are interleaved $n + 1$ times.

```
1. ping–pong (n : nat) :
     [v w h]. SK* {x ↦ v ∗ y ↦ w ∗ this h}()
                  {x ↦ v + n + 1 ∗ y ↦ w + n + 1 ∗ this h} ≜
2.   do (c ← callcc_j
           k : [v w h]⟨p⟩.
            Kont* {j ∈ x ↦ v ∗ y ↦ w ∗ this h}
                  {if n ≠ 0 then
                     x ↦ v + p + 1 ∗ y ↦ w + p ∗ this h
                   else ⊥} Σ•SK ()
                  {r. x ↦ v + p + 1
                     ∗ y ↦ w + p + 1 ∗ this h
                     ⋏ spec r ⊑ (x ↦ v + p + 2 ∗
                                 y ↦ w + p + 1 ∗ this h,
                                 if p + 1 = n then
                                   x ↦ v + n + 1 ∗
                                   y ↦ w + n + 1 ∗ this h
                                 else ⊥)*}.
3.            fix (λ f : pingpongT. λ z : nat.
4.               if z is Suc z' then
5.                  ret [abort k (pong; (f z'))]
6.               else ret [pong]) n;
7.       ping;
8.       cmd c).
```

where

```
pingpongT ≜ Πz : nat.
  [v w p h]. SK* {x ↦ v + p ∗ y ↦ w + p ∗ this h
                  ⋏ j ∈ x ↦ v ∗ this h ∗ y ↦ w ⋏ z ≤ n
                  ⋏ p + z = n} Σ•SK ()
                 {r. x ↦ v + p ∗ y ↦ v + p ∗ this h
                   ⋏ spec r ⊑ (x ↦ v + p + 1 ∗ y ↦ v + p
                               ∗ this h,
                               if p = n then
                                 x ↦ v + n + 1 ∗
                                 y ↦ w + n + 1 ∗ this h
                               else ⊥)*}
```

Figure 8. ping–pong cooperation.

This behaviour is reflected in the type of ping–pong: when the function is executed in a heap containing at least the pointers x and y storing some natural number, the result after $n + 1$ executions of ping and pong is a heap with the same shape, where the values of x and y are both incremented $n + 1$ times.

The type invariant pingpongT describes the specification of the loop that defines the closure f described above: on each iteration of the recursive call, we insert calls to pong deeper into the closure, which will execute after the corresponding ping. Then, we make explicit that on each recursive call, the values stored in the heap have been incremented appropriately. We introduce a (box) logical variable p to account for this fact: when the recursive call to f occurs, p calls to ping and p calls to pong have occurred. The recursive call produces a closure whose spec we define using $\sqsubseteq$. The closure should be run in a heap after the $(p + 1)$-execution of ping. As for the postcondition, If $p \neq n$, then the closure's head is a call to **abort**, line 5, and the postcondition is $\bot$. If $p = n$, i.e. this is the last iteration of f, then the closure corresponds to the one in line 6, entailing that this is the last execution of the loop, if $n > 0$

or that there was no loop at all otherwise. Hence, the final heap of the closure results $x \mapsto v + n + 1 * y \mapsto w + n + 1 * \mathsf{this}\, h$.

Unlike the case of **inc3**, the continuation object k here is aborted to more than once. As a result, the precondition in Kont^* has to accommodate for the changes in the state in each of the different jumping points. This is solved by using a (diamond) logical variable p, which allows us to discriminate the changes of each particular jumping point wrt. the captured heap j. The precondition in k states that the calls to **abort** occur when $n > 0$. Then, the heap at each jumping point should reflect the effect of $p + 1$ executions of ping and p executions of **pong**. The postcondition states that the finalisation code performs $p + 1$ execution of pong, and that it returns a closure which, again, is meant to run after the next ping. The postcondition in the closure is similar to the one in pingpongT, albeit the current iteration being $p + 1$ rather than p, as one ping has already executed.

In an online Appendix [12], we present a detailed proof outline for ping–pong. The Coq script can be found in the source files.

7. Discussion and related work

***Reasoning with non-algebraic* callcc** To understand the difference in specification and reasoning between algebraic and non-algebraic control operators, we have repeated our formal development for a non-algebraic set of operators, which we also make available online [12]. As a basis, we gave control operators a more familiar type for *non-parameterised* continuation monads [49]:

$$\mathsf{callcc} : ((A \to \mathsf{SK}\, B) \to \mathsf{SK}\, A) \to \mathsf{SK}\, A$$
$$\mathsf{throw} : (A \to \mathsf{SK}\, B) \to A \to \mathsf{SK}\, B$$

Continuation objects are ordinary side-effectful functions of type $A \to \mathsf{SK}\, B$, which do not make provisions for finalisation code, and are thus not algebraic [22]. The same remark applies to the type given to the $\mathcal{C}$-operator in [48], which is a different, but closely related control operator [15, 14].

We managed to soundly parameterise the monad with Hoare-style assertions using the following typing rules.

$$\frac{j, f : \Pi x{:}A.\ \mathsf{SK}\, B\, (S\, x\, j, \lambda\, r\, i\, m.\, \mathsf{False}) \vdash e : \mathsf{SK}\, A\, (P\, j, Q\, j) \quad \forall j.\, (P\, j, Q\, j) \sqsubseteq (\lambda\, i.\, j = i \wedge R\, i, S)}{\vdash \mathbf{callcc}_j\ f.\, e : \mathsf{SK}\, A\, (R, S)}$$

$$\frac{\vdash f : \Pi x{:}A.\ \mathsf{SK}\, B\, (R, \lambda\, r\, i\, m.\, \mathsf{False}) \qquad \vdash e : A}{\vdash \mathbf{throw}\, f\, e : \mathsf{SK}\, B\, (R, \lambda\, r\, i\, m.\, \mathsf{False})}$$

The intuition for the **callcc** rule is that the user must provide the ending specification pair (R, S). The (binary) postcondition S for the whole command is used as a precondition for the continuation object f, after S is first instantiated with the value x that is passed to f, and the captured heap j. The rule has a side condition requiring that the specification $(P\, j, Q\, j)$ inferred for the body e, can be weakened into the desired (R, S), under the knowledge that the captured heap j equals the initial heap i

The requirement that the specification (R, S) has to be provided by hand, practically differentiates the algebraic and non-algebraic operators. In the non-algebraic **callcc**, the specification is monolithic, and the postcondition S is usually a disjunction whose cases specify both the jumping and the non-jumping behaviour of the code. The algebraic **callcc** separates the two cases; the jumping is manually specified in the type of f, but the non-jumping specification can often be inferred by the typing rules from the structure of e, say, if e is straight line code, or by using the invariants provided with the loops in e, otherwise. Our examples rember-up-to-last and ping–pong illustrate the point, whereby e's specification directly corresponds to the supplied loop invariants. In the non-algebraic case, specifying these two examples incurs an overhead that the same annotation has to be provided twice; once as the loop invariant, and again as part of the specification of **callcc**.

Small vs. large footprints The need for large footprints and explicit naming of residual heaps arises in $\mathsf{HTT_{cc}}$ due to the control operators. The $\mathsf{HTT_{cc}}$ typing rule for ABORT, requires first discharging a precondition that the heap i at the point of the jump is related by the initial condition R to the heap j at the point of continuation capture. R is an ordinary predicate on heaps, rather than a Hoare triple. Thus, the usual idea of Separation logic, whereby a Hoare triple leaves the unused parts of a program implicitly unchanged, does not directly apply, and we have to name the unused parts in i and j in order to explicitly state their equality.

We have considered an alternative whereby the denotational semantics of control operators may automatically determine the unused part of the heap, by subtracting out of the current heap the portion described by the assertions. However, for this to work, the assertions would have to be *precise*, i.e., uniquely determine the portion to be subtracted. But then, the precision of each used assertion has to be formally proved. Thus, we opted for slightly increasing the specification burden by introducing explicit $\mathsf{this}\, h$ predicates, as a trade-off for not having to prove precision of assertions.

Despite the slight overhead of large footprints, we have not found them too problematic in practice. The naming of the residual heaps is intuitive and can be done systematically. Moreover, the logical variables used in the naming are *local* to the Hoare triple. This makes a big difference from ordinary first-order Hoare or Separation logic, where the global nature of logical variables makes such a naming scheme—and correspondingly, the use of large footprints—a complete non-starter. But mostly, it is the presence of separating conjunction $*$, which makes $\mathsf{HTT_{cc}}$ capable of reasoning about heap disjointness with the same ease inherent in Separation logic, irrespective of whether the annotations describe full or partial heaps.

Specification-only variables and implicit constructions Our **callcc** primitive is indexed by a specification-only variable j, which binds the heap at the point of continuation capture. j should be used only in the assertions and proofs, but not in the executable parts of the **callcc** block. Unfortunately, Coq (and consequently $\mathsf{HTT_{cc}}$) does not currently provide any means for enforcing this syntactic distinction. Declaring variables such as j as specification-only *is* natively supported by Coq*, an extension of Coq based on the *Implicit Calculus of Constructions* [3]. In the future, we plan to explore embedding $\mathsf{HTT_{cc}}$ into Coq*, to make use of this feature.

***Higher-order heaps and semantic models for* callcc** Dreyer et al. [13] and Støvring and Lassen [41] develop semantics models and methods for equational reasoning in such models, for programs with continuations and mutable store. A specific focus in both works is on higher-order heaps [26, 50, 39]; that is, the ability to store computations (and continuations as a special case) into the heap. $\mathsf{HTT_{cc}}$'s model is much simpler in this particular respect. While it allows programs that return continuations, and closures encapsulating continuations, it does not allow programs that store side-effectful computations into the heap. The reason is that we defined SK and Kont types *in terms of* heap, rather than *mutually recursively with* heap, as required for stored computations. In the future, we will develop a model for $\mathsf{HTT_{cc}}$ with stored computations. We plan to build on the model for HTT by Svendsen et al. [43], which includes higher-order heaps, but no control operators. Our ultimate aim is to implement proper coroutines, following Reppy [35, cp. 10], and use them to verify concurrency primitives. Moreover, our inference of weakest pre- and strongest postconditions by the rules presented in Figure 4 is also in the spirit of *characteristic formulae* [32, 1, 8].

Hoare logics for higher-order control Crolard and Polonowski [10] have recently developed a Hoare logic for control operators, in which specifications are carried out in types. While in this respect, the approach is similar to $\mathsf{HTT_{cc}}$ from the high-level point of view, there is a number of differences. For example, Crolard and Polonowski only consider mutable stack variables with block scope, but no pointers or aliasing. Procedures are not allowed to contain free variables, and type dependencies contain first-order data only, such as natural numbers. In contrast, in $\mathsf{HTT_{cc}}$, we allow the full expressiveness of CIC, including Σ-types over specifications, which, as we illustrated, is required for specifying closures that return captured continuations. Berger [5] presents a first-order Hoare logic for **callcc** in an otherwise purely functional language. One of the main features of the logic is the polarity distinction between the types of programs that perform jumps ('jumping-to') and the types of labels for jumps ('being-jumped-to'). From the point of view of reasoning, the logic allows nesting Hoare triples inside the assertions. This is necessary for specifying closures with captured continuations, and achieves the same effect as Σ-types over specifications in our dependently-typed setting.

Hoare reasoning through dependent types Related systems that employ Hoare-style specification via types are HTT [30] and F^* [44]. HTT is a direct precursor of $\mathsf{HTT_{cc}}$, but does not include the control operators. It uses an embedding of (small footprint) Separation logic via monads into Coq to formulate annotations and discharge verification conditions. A similar idea of Hoare monads in Coq, without control operators, has also been considered by Swierstra [45]. F^* specifies computations using a somewhat different monad from the above work. Instead of postconditions ranging over the input and output heaps, F^* considers predicate transformers ranging over *sets* of input and output heaps. F^* does not include a separate form of preconditions to specify safety; thus, its Hoare logic is not fault-avoiding as is $\mathsf{HTT_{cc}}$, or other systems based on Separation logic. F^* relies on Z3 for automatic discharge of verification conditions. In order to facilitate automation, its assertion logic is a first-order fragment supported by Z3. F^* does not consider **callcc**, or other abstractions required by it, such as Σ-types over specifications.

CPS translation CPS translation in the case of dependent types has been studied by Barthe and Uustalu [4] who show the impossibility of CPS-translating dependent inductive and Σ-types. As $\mathsf{HTT_{cc}}$ essentially relies on Σ-types to encode nested Hoare triples – as inhabitants of the Σ•SK type – it seems impossible to present $\mathsf{HTT_{cc}}$ as a CPS translation into a **callcc**-free fragment of $\mathsf{HTT_{cc}}$.

8. Conclusions

In this paper, we have presented $\mathsf{HTT_{cc}}$, a higher-order type theory for verification of programs with **callcc** control operators. $\mathsf{HTT_{cc}}$ supports mutable state in the style of Separation logic, and, to the best of our knowledge, is the first Hoare logic or type theory to support the combination of higher-order functions, mutable state and control operators. The support for mutable state comes with a twist, however. While our assertion logic embeds separating conjunction $*$, we used large footprint specification style, which we found necessary to relate heaps captured with the continuation to heaps at the point of a jump. We use *algebraic* control operators, initially introduced by Jaskelioff [22], which we here adapt to non-rollbackable state. We argue that in practice, the algebraic operators require less manual program annotations, than the non-algebraic variants. We have implemented $\mathsf{HTT_{cc}}$ as an embedding in Coq, and verified a number of characteristic example programs that use **callcc** [12].

Acknowledgements We thank the anonymous referees for their helpful feedback and comments on the paper. We also thank Mauro Jaskelioff for the fruitful discussions about algebraic effects.

This research was partially supported by the Spanish MINECO projects TIN2010-20639 Paran10 and TIN2012-39391-C04-01 Strongsoft, AMAROUT grant PCOFUND-GA-2008-229599, and Ramon y Cajal grant RYC-2010-0743.

References

[1] ACETO, L., AND INGÓLFSDÓTTIR, A. Characteristic formulae: From automata to logic. *Bulletin of the EATCS 91* (2007).

[2] ARBIB, M. A., AND ALAGIC, S. Proof rules for gotos. *Acta Inf. 11* (1979).

[3] BARRAS, B., AND BERNARDO, B. The implicit calculus of constructions as a programming language with dependent types. In *FoSSaCS* (2008).

[4] BARTHE, G., AND UUSTALU, T. CPS translating inductive and coinductive types. In *PEPM* (2002).

[5] BERGER, M. Program logics for sequential higher-order control. In *FSEN* (2009).

[6] BERTOT, Y., AND CASTÉRAN, P. *Interactive Theorem Proving and Program Development. Coq'Art: The Calculus of Inductive Constructions*. 2004.

[7] BJØRNER, D., AND JONES, C. B., Eds. *The Vienna Development Method: The Meta-Language* (1978), vol. 61 of *LNCS*.

[8] CHARGUÉRAUD, A. *Characteristic Formulae for Mechanized Program Verification*. PhD thesis, Université Paris-Diderot, 2010.

[9] CLINT, M., AND HOARE, C. A. R. Program proving: Jumps and functions. *Acta Inf. 1* (1972).

[10] CROLARD, T., AND POLONOWSKI, E. Deriving a Floyd-Hoare logic for non-local jumps from a formulæ-as-types notion of control. *J. Log. Algebr. Program. 81*, 3 (2012).

[11] DANVY, O., AND FILINSKI, A. Representing control: A study of the CPS transformation. *MSCS 2*, 4 (1992).

[12] DELBIANCO, G. A., AND NANEVSKI, A. Supporting material. http://software.imdea.org/~germand/HTTcc, March 2013.

[13] DREYER, D., NEIS, G., AND BIRKEDAL, L. The impact of higher-order state and control effects on local relational reasoning. In *ICFP* (2010).

[14] FELLEISEN, M., FRIEDMAN, D. P., DUBA, B., AND MERRILL, J. Beyond Continuations. Tech. Rep. 216, Indiana University, 1987.

[15] FELLEISEN, M., FRIEDMAN, D. P., KOHLBECKER, E. E., AND DUBA, B. F. Reasoning with continuations. In *LICS* (1986).

[16] FELLEISEN, M., WAND, M., FRIEDMAN, D., AND DUBA, B. Abstract continuations: a mathematical semantics for handling full jumps. In *LISP and functional programming* (1988).

[17] FILINSKI, A. Representing monads. In *POPL* (1994).

[18] FRIEDMAN, D. P., AND FELLEISEN, M. *The Seasoned Schemer*. 1996.

[19] GONTHIER, G., MAHBOUBI, A., AND TASSI, E. A Small Scale Reflection Extension for the Coq system. Tech. Rep. 6455, INRIA, 2008.

[20] GRIFFIN, T. A formulae-as-types notion of control. In *POPL* (1990).

[21] HYLAND, M., LEVY, P. B., PLOTKIN, G. D., AND POWER, J. Combining algebraic effects with continuations. *TCS 375*, 1-3 (2007).

[22] JASKELIOFF, M. Modular monad transformers. In *ESOP* (2009).

[23] JENSEN, J. B., BENTON, N., AND KENNEDY, A. High-level separation logic for low-level code. In *POPL* (2013).

[24] KLEYMANN, T. Hoare logic and auxiliary variables. *Formal Aspects of Computing 11* (1999).

[25] KOWALTOWSKI, T. Axiomatic approach to side effects and general jumps. *Acta Inf. 7* (1977).

[26] KRISHNASWAMI, N. R. *Verifying Higher-Order Imperative Programs with Higher-Order Separation Logic*. PhD thesis, Carnegie Mellon University, 2011.

[27] THE COQ DEVELOPMENT TEAM. *The Coq proof assistant reference manual*. TypiCal Project, 2012. Version 8.4.

[28] MOGGI, E. Computational lambda-calculus and monads. In *LICS* (1989).

[29] NANEVSKI, A., MORRISETT, J. G., AND BIRKEDAL, L. Hoare type theory, polymorphism and separation. *JFP 18*, 5-6 (2008).

[30] NANEVSKI, A., VAFEIADIS, V., AND BERDINE, J. Structuring the verification of heap-manipulating programs. In *POPL* (2010).

[31] O'HEARN, P. W., REYNOLDS, J. C., AND YANG, H. Local reasoning about programs that alter data structures. In *CSL* (2001).

[32] PARK, D. M. R. Concurrency and automata on infinite sequences. In *Theoretical Computer Science* (1981).

[33] PLOTKIN, G. D., AND POWER, A. J. Computational effects and operations: An overview. *ENTCS 73* (2004).

[34] PLOTKIN, G. D., AND POWER, J. Algebraic operations and generic effects. *Applied Categorical Structures 11*, 1 (2003).

[35] REPPY, J. H. *Concurrent Programming in ML*. Cambridge University Press, Cambridge, England, 1999.

[36] REYNOLDS, J. C. The discoveries of continuations. *LISP and Symbolic Computation 6*, 3-4 (1993).

[37] REYNOLDS, J. C. Separation logic: A logic for shared mutable data structures. In *LICS* (2002).

[38] SAABAS, A., AND UUSTALU, T. A compositional natural semantics and Hoare logic for low-level languages. *TCS 373*, 3 (2007).

[39] SCHWINGHAMMER, J., BIRKEDAL, L., REUS, B., AND YANG, H. Nested Hoare triples and frame rules for higher-order store. *LMCS 7*, 3 (2011).

[40] SPRINGER, G., AND FRIEDMAN, D. P. *Scheme and the Art of Programming*. MIT Press and McGraw-Hill, 1989

[41] STØVRING, K., AND LASSEN, S. B. A complete, co-inductive syntactic theory of sequential control and state. In *POPL* (2007).

[42] STRACHEY, C., AND WADSWORTH, C. P. Continuations: A mathematical semantics for handling full jumps. *HOSC 13*, 1/2 (2000).

[43] SVENDSEN, K., BIRKEDAL, L., AND NANEVSKI, A. Partiality, state and dependent types. In *TLCA* (2011).

[44] SWAMY, N., WEINBERGER, J., SCHLESINGER, C., CHEN, J., AND LIVSHITS, B. Verifying higher-order programs with the Dijkstra monad. In *PLDI* (2013).

[45] SWIERSTRA, W. A hoare logic for the state monad. TPHOLs '09.

[46] TAN, G., AND APPEL, A. W. A compositional logic for control flow. In *VMCAI* (2006).

[47] THIELECKE, H. *Categorical Structure of Continuation Passing Style*. PhD thesis, University of Edimburgh, 1997.

[48] THIELECKE, H. Control effects as a modality. *JFP 19*, 1 (2009).

[49] WADLER, P. Monads and composable continuations. *LISP and Symbolic Computation 7*, 1 (1994).

[50] YOSHIDA, N., HONDA, K., AND BERGER, M. Logical reasoning for higher-order functions with local state. *LMCS 4*, 4 (2008).

Unifying Refinement and Hoare-Style Reasoning in a Logic for Higher-Order Concurrency

Aaron Turon
MPI-SWS
turon@mpi-sws.org

Derek Dreyer
MPI-SWS
dreyer@mpi-sws.org

Lars Birkedal
Aarhus University
birkedal@cs.au.dk

Abstract

Modular programming and modular verification go hand in hand, but most existing logics for concurrency ignore two crucial forms of modularity: *higher-order functions*, which are essential for building reusable components, and *granularity abstraction*, a key technique for hiding the intricacies of fine-grained concurrent data structures from the clients of those data structures. In this paper, we present CaReSL, the first logic to support the use of granularity abstraction for modular verification of higher-order concurrent programs. After motivating the features of CaReSL through a variety of illustrative examples, we demonstrate its effectiveness by using it to tackle a significant case study: the first formal proof of (partial) correctness for Hendler *et al.*'s "flat combining" algorithm.

Categories and Subject Descriptors D.3.1 [*Programming Languages*]: Formal Definitions and Theory; F.3.1 [*Logics and Meanings of Programs*]: Specifying and Verifying and Reasoning about Programs

Keywords Contextual refinement; higher-order functions; fine-grained concurrency; separation logic; Kripke logical relations.

1. Introduction

Over the past decade, a number of Hoare logics have been developed to cope with the complexities of concurrent programming [20, 32, 7, 3, 18, 4, 27]. Unsurprisingly, the name of the game in these logics is improving support for *modular* reasoning along a variety of dimensions. Concurrent Abstract Predicates (CAP) [3], for example, utilizes a deft combination of *separation logic* [26] (for spatially-modular reasoning about resources and ownership), *rely-guarantee* [15] (for thread-modular reasoning in the presence of interference), and *abstract predicates* [21] (for hiding invariants about a module's private data structures from its clients).

At the same time, of course, the importance of modularity is not restricted to verification. Programmers use modularity in the *design* of their concurrent programs, precisely to enable reasoning about individual program components in relative isolation. And indeed, certain aspects of advanced concurrency logics, such as their aforementioned use of abstract predicates, are geared toward building proofs that reflect the data abstraction inherent in well-designed programs.

ICFP '13, September 25–27, 2013, Boston, MA, USA.

ACM 978-1-4503-2326-0/13/09... $15.00.
http://dx.doi.org/10.1145/2500365.2500600

We contend, however, that existing concurrency logics are not exploiting the modular design of sophisticated concurrent programs to full effect. In particular, we observe that there are two crucial dimensions of modular concurrent programming that existing logics provide no way to leverage in the construction of proofs: namely, **higher-order functions** and **granularity abstraction**.

Higher-order concurrency Higher-order functional abstraction is of course one of the most basic hammers in the modern programmer's toolkit for writing reusable and modular code. Moreover, a number of concurrent programming patterns rely on it: work stealing [2], Concurrent ML-style events [25], concurrent iterators [16], parallel evaluation strategies [29], and monadic approaches to concurrent programming [10], just to name a few.

Yet, verification of higher-order concurrent programs remains a largely unexplored topic. To our knowledge, only a few existing logics can handle higher-order concurrent programs [27, 17, 14], but these logics are limited in other ways—in particular, they do not presently support verification of "fine-grained" concurrent ADTs. This leads us directly to the second limitation we observe of the state of the art, concerning granularity abstraction.

Granularity abstraction via contextual refinement An easy way to adapt a sequential mutable data structure for concurrent access is to employ *coarse-grained* synchronization: use a single global lock, and instrument each of the operations on the data structure so that they acquire the lock before they begin and release it after they complete. On the other hand, more sophisticated implementations of concurrent data structures employ *fine-grained* synchronization: they protect different parts of a data structure with different locks, or avoid locking altogether, so that threads can access disjoint pieces of the data structure in parallel.

There may seem at first glance to be a fundamental trade-off here. Fine-grained synchronization enables parallelism, but makes the data structures that use it very tricky to reason about directly, due to their complex internal coordination between threads. Coarse-grained synchronization sequentializes access to the data structure, which is bad for parallelism but perfect for client-side reasoning, since it enables clients to reason about concurrent accesses as if each operation takes effect atomically.

Fortunately, modular programming comes to the rescue. In particular, so long as tricky uses of fine-grained synchronization are confined to the hidden state of a carefully crafted ADT, it is possible to prove that the fine-grained implementation of the ADT is a *contextual refinement* of some coarse-grained implementation. Contextual refinement means that, assuming clients only access the ADT through its abstract interface (so that the state really is hidden), every behavior that clients can observe of the fine-grained implementation is also observable of the coarse-grained one. Thus, clients can pretend, for the purpose of simplifying their own verification, that they are using the coarse-grained version, yet be sure that their code will still be correct when linked with the more efficient fine-grained version. This is what we call *granularity abstraction*. (Note: granularity abstraction is similar to *atomicity abstraction* [19], but is more general in that, as we will see in the iterator example later in this section, it applies even if the target of the abstraction is only *somewhat* coarse-grained.)

To illustrate this point more concretely, let us consider a simple motivating example of reasoning about Treiber's stack [28]. (We will in fact use this very example as part of a larger case study later in the paper.) Treiber's stack is a fine-grained implementation of a concurrent stack ADT. Instead of requiring concurrently executing push and pop operations to contend for a global lock on the whole stack (as a coarse-grained implementation would), Treiber's implementation allows them to race to access the head of the stack using compare-and-set (CAS). (The implementation of Treiber's stack is shown in Figure 9, and discussed in detail in §3.3.)

Now, the reader may expect that stacks should admit a canonical, principal specification (spec, for short), perhaps something like the following "precise" spec which tracks the exact contents s of the stack using the abstract predicate $\mathsf{Con}(s)$:

$$\{\mathsf{Con}(s)\}\ \mathsf{push}(x)\ \{\mathsf{Con}(x :: s)\}$$
$$\{\mathsf{Con}(s)\}\ \mathsf{pop}()\ \{\mathsf{ret}.\ (\mathsf{ret} = \mathsf{none} \wedge s = \mathsf{nil} \wedge \mathsf{Con}(s)) \vee (\exists x, s'. \mathsf{ret} = \mathsf{some}(x) \wedge s = x :: s' \wedge \mathsf{Con}(s'))\}$$

The trouble with using this spec in a concurrent setting is that knowledge about the exact contents of the stack is not stable under interference from other threads. As a result, some concurrency logics prohibit this spec altogether. Others permit the spec, but force the $\mathsf{Con}(s)$ predicate to be treated as a resource that only one thread can own at a time, thus effectively preventing any concurrent access to the stack and defeating the point of using Treiber's stack in the first place!

We want instead to capture the idea that the client threads of a data structure interact with it according to some (application-specific) protocol. Take, for example, the following "per-item" spec, which abstracts away from the LIFO nature of the stack and instead imposes an item-level protocol:

$$\forall x.\ \{p(x)\}\ \mathsf{push}(x)\ \{\mathbf{true}\}$$
$$\wedge\quad \{\mathbf{true}\}\ \mathsf{pop}()\ \{\mathsf{ret}.\ \mathsf{ret} = \mathsf{none} \vee (\exists x.\ \mathsf{ret} = \mathsf{some}(x) \wedge p(x))\}$$

Given an arbitrary predicate p of the client's choice, this per-item spec asserts that the stack contains only elements that satisfy the predicate p. It is pleasantly simple, and sufficient for the purposes of the case study we present later in the paper. It should be clear, however, that this "per-item" spec is far from a canonical or principal specification of stacks: the same spec would also be satisfied, for instance, by queues.

This brings us to our key point: different clients have different needs, and so we may want to verify the stack ADT against a range of different Hoare-style specs, but we do not want to have to re-verify *Treiber's implementation* each time. Ideally, we would like to modularly decompose the proof effort into two parts:

1. Prove that Treiber's implementation is a contextual refinement of a coarse-grained, lock-based implementation, which serves as a simple *reference implementation* of the stack ADT.
2. Use Hoare-style reasoning to verify that this reference implementation satisfies the various specs of interest to clients.

This decomposition engenders a clean separation of concerns, confining the difficulty of reasoning about Treiber's particular implementation[1] to the proof of refinement, and simplifying the verification of the stack ADT against different client specs.

The story we have just told is, *in principle*, nothing new. The ability to prove granularity abstraction via contextual refinement has been accepted in the concurrency literature as a useful correctness criterion for tricky concurrent data structures, precisely because of the modular decomposition of proof effort that it ought to facilitate [13, 8, 9]. Unfortunately, despite the utility of such a modular decomposition in theory, *no existing concurrency logic* actually supports it in practice. In particular, very few systems support proofs of contextual refinement at all, and those few that do support refinement proofs—such as the recent work of Liang and Feng [18]—do not provide a means of composing refinement with client-side Hoare-style verification in a unified logic.

Granularity abstraction for higher-order functions Although supporting granularity abstraction is already a challenge for first-order concurrent programs, it becomes even more interesting for higher-order concurrent programs.

Suppose, for instance, we wished to add a higher-order iterator, iter, to the concurrent stack ADT. (Such concurrent iterators are already commonplace [16].) Adding iter to Treiber's implementation is trivial: iter(f) will (without acquiring any lock) just read the current head pointer of the stack and apply f to each element of the stack accessible from it. But how do we specify the behavior of this iterator? What reference implementation should we use in proving granularity abstraction? Unlike for push and pop, it does not make sense for the reference implementation of iter(f) to be "maximally" coarse-grained (*i.e.,* to execute entirely within a critical section) because that will not correspond to the reality of the implementation we just described. In particular, the Treiber implementation does *not* freeze modifications to the stack while f is being applied to each element, so it does not contextually refine the maximally coarse-grained implementation of iteration.

Rather, what the Treiber iterator guarantees is that f will be applied to all the elements that were accessible from some node that was the head of the stack *at some point in time*. A clean way to specify this behavior is via a reference implementation that (1) acquires the lock, (2) takes a "snapshot" (*i.e.,* makes a copy) of the stack, (3) releases the lock, and (4) iterates f over the snapshot. (For the code of this reference implementation, see Figure 9.) What makes this reference implementation so intriguing is that it is only *somewhat* coarse-grained, yet as we will show later in the paper, it is nonetheless quite useful as a target for granularity abstraction.

This example demonstrates the flexibility of refinement, a flexibility which has not heretofore been tested, since no one has previously applied granularity abstraction to higher-order ADTs.

CaReSL: A logic for higher-order concurrency

In this paper, we present CaReSL (pronounced "carousel"), the first logic to support the use of granularity abstraction for modular verification of higher-order concurrent programs.

In providing both refinement and Hoare-style reasoning, CaReSL builds on ideas from two distinct lines of research:

- *Kripke logical relations* [22, 1, 5]. Logical relations are a fundamental technique for proving refinement in languages with *e.g.,* higher-order functions, polymorphism, and recursive types. Logical relations explain observable behavior in terms of the logical interpretation of each type. For example, two functions of type $\tau \to \tau'$ are logically related if giving them related inputs of type τ *implies* that they will produce related results of type τ'. *Kripke* logical relations are defined relative to a "possible world" that describes the relationship between the internal, hidden state of a program and that of its spec.
- *Concurrent separation logics* [20, 32, 3]. Separation logic is a reimagining of Hoare logic in which assertions are understood relative to some *portion* of the heap, with the separating conjunction $P * Q$ dividing up the heap between assertions P and Q. The motivation for separation is *local* reasoning: pre- and post-conditions need only mention the relevant portion of the

[1] Treiber's stack is actually one of the easiest fine-grained data structures to reason about, but our general line of argument applies equally well to more sophisticated implementations, such as the HSY elimination stack [12].

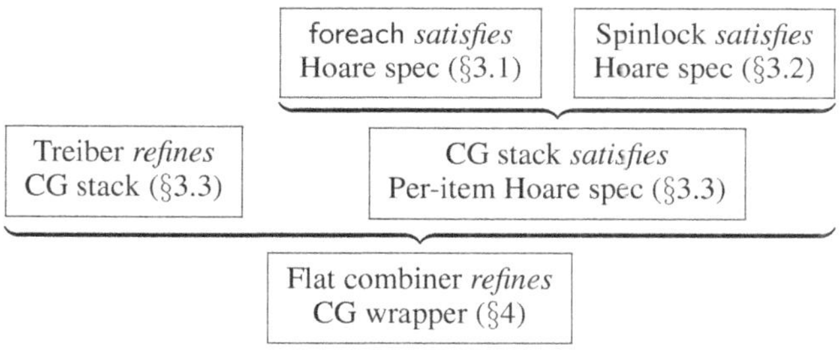

Figure 1. The structure of the case study—and paper

heap, and the rest of the heap can be presumed invariant. Most concurrent separation logics also add some form of protocols (*e.g.*, rely-guarantee), which facilitate compositional reasoning by constraining the potential interference between threads operating concurrently on some *shared* portion of the heap.

Rather than a combination of these approaches, CaReSL is an attempt to unify them. So, for example, the logic does *not* include refinement as a primitive notion. Instead, refinement is derived from Hoare-style reasoning: to prove that e refines e', one merely proves a particular Hoare triple about e, allowing the tools of concurrent separation logic to be exploited in the proof of logical relatedness. In the other direction, CaReSL is a modal logic with the possible worlds of Kripke logical relations, which can in turn be used to express the shared-state protocols of concurrent separation logics. The unification yields surprising new techniques, such as the use of modal *necessity* ($\Box$) to hide resources that an ADT's client would otherwise have to thread through their reasoning (§3.2).[2]

The semantics of CaReSL is derived directly from the model of Turon *et al.* [31], who presented the first formal proofs of refinement for fine-grained data structures in an ML-like setting (although they did not use it to reason about higher-order examples). Compared with Turon *et al.*'s work, which was purely semantic, CaReSL provides a *syntactic* theory for carrying out refinement proofs at a much higher level of abstraction. This proof theory, in turn, is inspired by Dreyer *et al.*'s LADR [5], a modal logic for reasoning about contextual equivalence of (sequential) stateful ML programs. CaReSL exemplifies how the key ideas of LADR are just as relevant to—and arguably even more compelling when adapted to—the concurrent setting.

To demonstrate the effectiveness of CaReSL, we use it to tackle a significant case study: namely, the first formal proof of (partial) correctness for Hendler *et al.*'s "flat combining" algorithm [11]. Flat combining provides a generic way to turn a sequential ADT into a relatively efficient concurrent one, by having certain threads perform—in one fell swoop—the combined actions requested by a whole bunch of other threads. The flat combining algorithm is interesting not only because it itself is a rather sophisticated higher-order function, but also because it is modularly assembled from other higher-order components, including a fine-grained stack with concurrent iterator. We therefore take the opportunity to verify flat combining in a modular way that mirrors the modular structure of its implementation.

Figure 1 illustrates the high-level structure of our proof, which involves an intertwined application of refinement and Hoare-style verification. For example, we prove that Treiber's stack refines the coarse-grained (CG) reference implementation of stacks; we then use Hoare-style reasoning to prove that the reference implementation satisfies the per-item spec; and finally we rely on the per-item spec in the proof that the flat combining algorithm refines an even higher-level abstraction. Every component of the case study involves higher-order code and therefore higher-order specifications.

[2] Previously, such hiding required the subtle *anti-frame* rule [24].

Syntax

Val $\quad v ::= () \mid \mathbf{true} \mid \mathbf{false} \mid (v, v) \mid \mathbf{inj}_i\ v \mid \mathbf{rec}\ f(x).e \mid \Lambda.e \mid \ell$

Exp $\quad e ::= v \mid \mathbf{if}\ e\ \mathbf{then}\ e\ \mathbf{else}\ e \mid e\ e \mid e\ \_ \mid (e, e) \mid \mathbf{prj}_i\ e \mid \mathbf{inj}_i\ e$
$\quad\mid \mathsf{case}(e, \mathbf{inj}_1\ x \Rightarrow e, \mathbf{inj}_2\ y \Rightarrow e) \mid \mathbf{new}\ e \mid \mathbf{get}\ e \mid e := e$
$\quad\mid \mathbf{CAS}(e, e, e) \mid \mathbf{newLcl} \mid \mathbf{getLcl}(e) \mid \mathbf{setLcl}(e, e) \mid \mathbf{fork}\ e$

CType $\quad \sigma ::= \mathbf{B} \mid \mathbf{ref}\ \tau \mid \mathbf{refLcl}\ \tau \mid \mu\alpha.\sigma$

Type $\quad \tau ::= \sigma \mid \mathbf{1} \mid \alpha \mid \tau \times \tau \mid \tau + \tau \mid \mu\alpha.\tau \mid \forall\alpha.\tau \mid \tau \to \tau$

ECtx $\quad K ::= [\,] \mid \mathbf{if}\ K\ \mathbf{then}\ e\ \mathbf{else}\ e \mid K\ e \mid v\ K \mid \cdots$

Typing contexts

$$\Delta ::= \cdot \mid \Delta, \alpha \qquad \Gamma ::= \cdot \mid \Gamma, x : \tau \qquad \Omega ::= \Delta; \Gamma$$

Well-typed expressions $\quad \boxed{\Delta; \Gamma \vdash e : \tau}$

$$\frac{\Omega \vdash e : \mathbf{ref}\ \sigma \qquad \Omega \vdash e_o : \sigma \qquad \Omega \vdash e_n : \sigma}{\Omega \vdash \mathbf{CAS}(e, e_o, e_n) : \mathbf{B}} \qquad \frac{\Omega \vdash e : \forall\alpha.\tau}{\Omega \vdash e\ \_ : \tau[\tau'/\alpha]}$$

Machine configurations

TLV $\quad L \in \mathbb{N} \xrightarrow{\text{fin}} \text{Value} \qquad$ TPool $\quad \mathcal{E} \in \mathbb{N} \xrightarrow{\text{fin}} \text{Expression}$

Heaps $\quad h \in \mathbb{N} \xrightarrow{\text{fin}} (\text{Val} \cup \text{TLV}) \qquad$ Config $\quad \varsigma ::= h; \mathcal{E}$

Thread-local lookup $\quad \lfloor L \rfloor(i) \triangleq \begin{cases} \mathsf{none} & i \notin \text{dom}(L) \\ \mathsf{some}(L(i)) & \text{otherwise} \end{cases}$

Pure reduction $\quad \boxed{e \overset{\text{pure}}{\to} e'}$

$$(\mathbf{rec}\ f(x).e)\ v \overset{\text{pure}}{\to} e[\mathbf{rec}\ f(x).e/f, v/x] \qquad (\Lambda.e)\ \_ \overset{\text{pure}}{\to} e$$

Per-thread reduction $\quad \boxed{h; e \overset{i}{\to} h'; e'}$

$$\begin{array}{rcll} h; e & \overset{i}{\to} & h; e' & \text{when } e \overset{\text{pure}}{\to} e' \\ h; \mathbf{newLcl} & \overset{i}{\to} & h \uplus [\ell \mapsto \emptyset]; \ell & \\ h \uplus [\ell \mapsto L]; \mathbf{setLcl}(\ell, v) & \overset{i}{\to} & h \uplus [\ell \mapsto L[i := v]]; () & \\ h; \mathbf{getLcl}(\ell) & \overset{i}{\to} & h; v & \text{when } h(\ell) = L,\ \lfloor L \rfloor(i) = v \\ h; \mathbf{CAS}(\ell, v_o, v_n) & \overset{i}{\to} & h; \mathbf{false} & \text{when } h(\ell) \neq v_o \\ h \uplus [\ell \mapsto v_o]; \mathbf{CAS}(\ell, v_o, v_n) & \overset{i}{\to} & h \uplus [\ell \mapsto v_n]; \mathbf{true} & \end{array}$$

General reduction $\quad \boxed{h; \mathcal{E} \to h'; \mathcal{E}'}$

$$\frac{h; e \overset{i}{\to} h'; e'}{h; \mathcal{E} \uplus [i \mapsto K[e]] \to h'; \mathcal{E} \uplus [i \mapsto K[e']]}$$

$$h; \mathcal{E} \uplus [i \mapsto K[\mathbf{fork}\ e]] \to h; \mathcal{E} \uplus [i \mapsto K[()]] \uplus [j \mapsto e]$$

Figure 2. The calculus: $F^{\mu!}$ with **fork**, **CAS**, and thread-local refs

2. The programming model

The programming language for our program logic is sketched in Figure 2; the full details are in the appendix [30]. It has a standard core: the polymorphic lambda calculus with sums, products, references, and equi-recursive types. We elide all type annotations in terms, but polymorphism is nevertheless introduced and eliminated by explicit type abstraction ($\Lambda.e$) and application ($e\ \_$). To this standard core, we add concurrency (through a **fork** construct), atomic compare-and-set (**CAS**) and thread-local references (type **refLcl** τ).

While normal references provide shared state through which threads can communicate, thread-local references allow multiple threads to access disjoint values in memory (a different one for each thread) using a common location. Formally, each thread-local reference has an associated *thread ID-indexed* table L, which is initially empty. Thus for **refLcl** τ, the **getLcl** operation returns an "option" of type $1+\tau$, reflecting whether the thread-local reference has been initialized for the thread that invoked it.[3] Thread-local references are commonly used when a single data structure needs mutable, thread-local storage for an unbounded number of threads; the flat combining algorithm presented in §4 embodies this technique.

We define a small-step, call-by-value operational semantics, using evaluation contexts K to specify a left-to-right evaluation order within each thread. The $\overset{\text{pure}}{\to}$ relation gives the reductions that do not interact with the heap, while $\overset{i}{\to}$ gives general, single-thread reductions for the thread with ID i. These reductions are then lifted to general reduction $\to$ of *machine configurations* ς, which consist of a heap h together with an ID-indexed pool $\mathcal{E}$ of threads.

The type system imposes two important restrictions. First, recursive types $\mu\alpha.\tau$ must be *guarded*, meaning that all free occurrences of α in τ must appear under a non-μ type constructor. Second, because **CAS** exposes physical equality comparison of word-sized values at the hardware level, it can only be applied to references of *comparable type* σ, which we take to be base types and locations.

If $\Omega \vdash e_I : \tau$ and $\Omega \vdash e_S : \tau$, we say e_I *contextually refines* e_S, written $\Omega \models e_I \preceq e_S : \tau$, if, for every pair of thread IDs i and j,

$$\begin{aligned}\forall C : (\Omega,\tau) \rightsquigarrow (\emptyset, \mathbf{B}).\ \forall n.\forall \mathcal{E}_I.\ & \emptyset; [i \mapsto C[e_I]] \to^* h_I; [i \mapsto v] \uplus \mathcal{E}_I \\ \implies \exists \mathcal{E}_S.\ & \emptyset; [j \mapsto C[e_S]] \to^* h_S; [j \mapsto v] \uplus \mathcal{E}_S\end{aligned}$$

where $C : (\Omega,\tau) \rightsquigarrow (\Omega',\tau')$ is the standard typing judgment for contexts (guaranteeing that $\Omega \vdash e : \tau$ implies $\Omega' \vdash C[e] : \tau'$). This definition resembles the standard one for sequential languages, but take note that only the termination behavior of the main thread is observed; as with most languages in practice, we assume that once the main thread has finished, any forked threads are aborted.

3. CaReSL

While CaReSL ultimately provides mixed refinement and Hoare-style reasoning about higher-order concurrent programs, it is easiest to understand by first considering less powerful "sublogics", and then gradually incorporating more powerful features:

- We begin with a core logic that provides separation-logic reasoning for sequential (but higher-order) programs (§3.1). In this core logic, both Hoare triples and heap assertions live in a single syntactic class: they are propositions. Thus propositions include *e.g.,* implications between Hoare triples, which are ubiquitous when reasoning about higher-order code. Propositions also include first- and second-order quantification, guarded recursion, separating conjunction, and modal necessitation—all standard concepts whose interplay we explain in §3.1.
- We then add concurrency, leading to a concurrent separation logic for higher-order programs (§3.2). The new concept needed to deal with concurrency is that of a *protocol* governing some shared region of the heap. We express protocols through transition systems whose states provide an abstraction of the heap region's actual state. Threads can gain or lose *roles* in the protocol, which determine the transitions those (and other) threads are permitted to take. Traditional rely/guarantee reasoning can be recovered as a particular, restricted way of using protocols.
- Finally, we show how to reason about refinement, yielding a **C**oncurrent **a**nd **Re**fined **S**eparation **L**ogic (**CaReSL**) for higher-order programs (§3.3). As explained in the introduction, CaReSL does not simply add refinement as a primitive notion on top of a concurrent separation logic. Instead, CaReSL treats refinement as a derived notion, expressed as a particular Hoare-style specification. In order to do so, however, CaReSL does require one further extension: the notion of "spec resources", first introduced by Turon *et al.* [31], which allow pieces of a program configuration (heap and threads) to be manipulated as logical resources within Hoare-style proofs.

[3] Throughout, we let $\mathsf{none} \triangleq \mathbf{inj}_1\ ()$ and $\mathsf{some}(e) \triangleq \mathbf{inj}_2\ e$.

While CaReSL is the main contribution of the paper, its sublogics are of independent interest. We explain them by way of idiomatic higher-order examples, each of which serves as a component of the case study in §4.

3.1 Core logic: Sequential higher-order programs

To motivate the basic ingredients of core CaReSL, we begin with the quintessential higher-order stateful combinator, foreach:

$$\mathsf{foreach} : \forall\alpha.(\alpha \to \mathbf{1}) \to \mathsf{list}(\alpha) \to \mathbf{1} \qquad \mathsf{list}(\alpha) \triangleq \mu\beta.\mathbf{1} + (\alpha \times \beta)$$

$$\begin{aligned}\mathsf{foreach} \triangleq \Lambda.\ \lambda f.\ \mathbf{rec}\ \mathsf{loop}(l).\ \mathbf{case}\ l\ \mathbf{of}\ & \mathsf{none} \Rightarrow () \\ \mid\ & \mathsf{some}(x,n) \Rightarrow f(x);\ \mathsf{loop}(n)\end{aligned}$$

A specification of foreach should explain that foreach $f\ l$ "lifts" the imperative behavior of f (which works on elements) to l (a list of elements). But to do so, it needs to *quantify* over the unknown behavior of an unknown function in a way that can be lifted to lists.

One possibility is to characterize f by means of a Hoare triple, while ultimately quantifying over the pre- and post-conditions of that triple. Suppose that $p(x)$ and $q(x)$ are predicates on values x, and that r is an arbitrary proposition, such that

$$\forall x.\ \{p(x) * r\}\ f(x)\ \{q(x) * r\}$$

The idea is that when f is applied to an element x of the list, it may assume both that $p(x)$ holds and that an invariant r holds of a disjoint portion of the heap. If $f(x)$ transforms $p(x)$ to $q(x)$ while maintaining the invariant, then foreach lifts that behavior to an entire list—regardless of what the predicates actually are. To capture the assumption that $p(x)$ holds of each element of a list l, we need something like the following recursive predicate:[4]

$$\mathrm{Map}_p(l) \triangleq l = \mathsf{none} \vee (\exists x, n.\ l = \mathsf{some}(x,n) * p(x) * \mathrm{Map}_p(n))$$

Note that, thanks to the use of the separating conjunction $*$, for each x in l there is a *disjoint region* of the heap satisfying $p(x)$.

These ideas lead to the following spec for foreach:

$$\begin{aligned}&\forall p, q, r.\ \forall f.\ (\forall x.\{p(x) * r\}\ f(x)\ \{q(x) * r\}) \\ &\quad \Rightarrow \forall l.\ \left\{\mathrm{Map}_p(l) * r\right\}\ \mathsf{foreach}\ \_\ f\ l\ \left\{\mathrm{Map}_q(l) * r\right\}\end{aligned}$$

Formalizing this sketch will require a logic with a number of basic features: we need to be able to mix Hoare triples with other kinds of connectives (*e.g.,* implication), to quantify over both values (*e.g.,* f and x) and predicates (*e.g.,* p and q), and to define recursive predicates (*e.g.,* Map). With these goals in mind, we now explore CaReSL's design more systematically.

Syntax Figure 3 presents core CaReSL—the fragment of the logic appropriate for reasoning about sequential, higher-order code. CaReSL is a multi-sorted second-order logic, meaning that its syntax is stratified into the following three layers.

First, there are *terms* M, N, which come in a variety of *sorts* Σ, including the values and expressions of the language, as well as thread-local storage (with operations $\lfloor - \rfloor$, $\uplus$ and $:=$). The judgment $\mathcal{X} \vdash M : \Sigma$ gives the sort of a term (where $\mathcal{X}$ is a variable context giving the sorts of term and predicate variables).

Second, there are *propositions* P, Q, R, which include the connectives of multi-sorted first-order logic (*e.g.,* $\forall X \in \Sigma.P$) and second-order logic (*e.g.,* $\exists p \in \mathbb{P}(\Sigma).P$) with their standard meanings. The judgment $\mathcal{X} \vdash P : \mathbb{B}$ asserts that the proposition P is well-sorted.

Third, there are *predicates* φ, ψ, which are just propositions parameterized by a term: a predicate of sort $\mathbb{P}(\Sigma)$ can be introduced by $(X \in \Sigma).P$, which binds an unknown term X of sort Σ in P,

[4] Throughout, names of functions and types are written in lower case sans-serif, while predicate names are Capitalized Serif.

Syntax

Terms $M ::= X \mid (M, M) \mid n \mid e \mid M \uplus M \mid \lfloor M \rfloor(M) \mid M[M := M]$

Sorts $\Sigma ::= \mathbf{1} \mid \Sigma \times \Sigma \mid \mathsf{Nat} \mid \mathsf{Val} \mid \mathsf{Exp} \mid \mathsf{AtomicExp} \mid \mathsf{LclStorage}$

Preds $\varphi ::= p \mid (X \in \Sigma).P \mid \mu p \in \mathbb{P}(\Sigma).\varphi$

Propositions P ::=

$\mathsf{True} \mid P \Rightarrow P \mid P \wedge P \mid P \vee P \mid \exists X \in \Sigma.P \mid \forall X \in \Sigma.P \mid \triangleright P \mid$
$\varphi(M) \mid \exists p \in \mathbb{P}(\Sigma).P \mid \forall p \in \mathbb{P}(\Sigma).P \mid P * P \mid M \hookrightarrow_{\mathrm{I}} M \mid A$

Necessary ("always") propositions A ::=

$\Box P \mid M \overset{\text{pure}}{\to} M \mid M{=}M \mid (\!|P|\!)\ M \Rrightarrow_{\mathrm{IS}} M\ (\!|\varphi|\!) \mid \{P\}\ M \Rrightarrow M\ \{\varphi\}$

Contexts

$\mathcal{X} ::= \cdot \mid \mathcal{X}, X : \Sigma \mid \mathcal{X}, p : \mathbb{P}(\Sigma) \qquad \mathcal{P} ::= \cdot \mid \mathcal{P}, P \qquad \mathcal{C} ::= \mathcal{X}; \mathcal{P}$

Well-sorted terms $\boxed{\mathcal{X} \vdash M : \Sigma}$

$$\frac{}{\mathcal{X}, X : \Sigma \vdash X : \Sigma} \qquad \frac{\mathcal{X} \vdash M : \mathsf{LclStorage} \quad \mathcal{X} \vdash N : \mathsf{Nat}}{\mathcal{X} \vdash \lfloor M \rfloor(N) : \mathsf{Val}} \qquad \ldots$$

Well-sorted props. $\boxed{\mathcal{X} \vdash P : \mathbb{B}}$ ***Well-sorted preds.*** $\boxed{\mathcal{X} \vdash \varphi : \mathbb{P}(\Sigma)}$

Figure 3. Core CaReSL: Syntax

and eliminated by $\varphi(M)$ (also written $M \in \varphi$) which substitutes M for the parameter of φ. Because sorts include unit and products, predicates can express *relations* of arbitrary arity. The judgment $\mathcal{X} \vdash \varphi : \mathbb{P}(\Sigma)$ asserts that φ is a well-sorted predicate over terms of sort Σ.

In general, term variables are written X. But to avoid cluttering our rules and proofs with sort annotations, we use variables x, y, z for sort Val and i, j, k, ℓ for sort Nat. We abuse notation, writing *e.g.*, v, e or L to stand for a term of sort Val, Exp or LclStorage, respectively.

In addition to this standard logical setup, CaReSL adopts key connectives from separation logic. In general, these connectives will refer to a variety of "resources" that will be introduced as we go along. In *core* CaReSL, however, the only resource is the heap. The *points-to* assertion $\ell \hookrightarrow_{\mathrm{I}} v$ holds of any heap containing a location ℓ that points to the value v. (Ignore the I subscript for now; we will return to it in §3.3). The *separating conjunction* $P * Q$ holds if the currently-owned resources (here, a portion of the heap) can be split into two disjoint parts satisfying P and Q respectively.

While the truth of some propositions (*e.g.*, $\ell \hookrightarrow_{\mathrm{I}} v$) is *contingent* on the presence of certain resources, others (*e.g.*, $M = N$) are *necessary*: if they hold, they do so regardless of the currently-owned resources, and therefore will continue to hold in any future state. (Such propositions are called "pure" in separation logic parlance.) The syntactic subcategory A of necessary propositions includes claims about term equality, about the operational semantics ($M \overset{\text{pure}}{\to} N$), and Hoare triples. Arbitrary propositions can be made necessary via the $\Box$ ("always") modality, where $\Box P$ holds if P holds for all possible resources. As we will see shortly, necessary propositions play by special rules: they can move freely through Hoare triples and separating conjunctions.

Ultimately, CaReSL distinguishes between triples about general expressions e and those about *atomic* expressions a (which execute in a single step). Since this distinction is motivated by concurrency, we postpone its explanation to §3.2. We include the distinction syntactically in core CaReSL, but it can be safely ignored for now.

Atomic expressions a have the following grammar:

$\mathbf{new}\ v \mid \mathbf{get}\ v \mid v := v \mid \mathbf{CAS}(v, v, v) \mid \mathbf{newLcl} \mid \mathbf{getLcl}(v) \mid \mathbf{setLcl}(v, v)$

The propositions for atomic triples[5] $(\!|P|\!)\ i \Rrightarrow_{\mathrm{IS}} a\ (\!|\varphi|\!)$ and general triples $\{P\}\ i \Rrightarrow e\ \{\varphi\}$ are both parameterized by a *thread ID* i; the expression may access thread-local storage, in which case its behavior is ID-dependent. (When the thread ID doesn't matter, we write $\{P\}\ e\ \{\varphi\}$ as short for $\forall i.\ \{P\}\ i \Rrightarrow e\ \{\varphi\}$.) In addition, since we are working with an expression language (as opposed to a command language), postconditions are *predicates* over the return value of the expression, rather than simply propositions about the final state of the heap. But when an expression returns unit, we often abuse notation and write a proposition instead.

[5] Again, ignore the IS subscript until §3.3.

Logical axioms and rules

$$\frac{\mathcal{X}; A \vdash P}{\mathcal{X}; \mathcal{P}, A \vdash \Box P}\ \Box\mathrm{I} \qquad \frac{\mathcal{C} \vdash P}{\mathcal{C} \vdash \triangleright P}\ \textsc{Mono} \qquad \frac{\mathcal{C}, \triangleright P \vdash P}{\mathcal{C} \vdash P}\ \textsc{Löb}$$

$$\begin{array}{rcl} \Box(P \Rightarrow Q) & \Rightarrow & \Box P \Rightarrow \Box Q \\ A & \Rightarrow & \Box A \\ \Box P & \Rightarrow & P \end{array} \qquad \begin{array}{c} A * P \Leftrightarrow A \wedge P \\ \mathsf{True} * P \Leftrightarrow P \\ \triangleright(P * Q) \Leftrightarrow \triangleright P * \triangleright Q \end{array}$$

$$\frac{\mathcal{C}, p : \mathbb{P}(\Sigma) \vdash P}{\mathcal{C} \vdash \forall p \in \mathbb{P}(\Sigma).\ P}\ \forall_2\mathrm{I} \qquad \begin{array}{c} M \in (X \in \Sigma).P \Leftrightarrow P[M/X] \\ M \in (\mu p.\varphi) \Leftrightarrow M \in \varphi[\mu p.\varphi/p] \end{array}$$

Figure 4. Core CaReSL: Selected logical axioms and rules

In order to support recursive assertions, the logic includes *guarded recursion* ($\mu p \in \mathbb{P}(\Sigma).\ P$), which entails the following tradeoff. On the one hand, guarded recursion allows occurrences of the recursive predicate p to appear negatively, which is crucial for modelling recursive types (§3.3) but is usually prohibited for lack of monotonicity. On the other hand, the recursion is "guarded" in that references to p in P must appear under the $\triangleright$ modality. A proposition $\triangleright Q$ represents the present knowledge that Q holds *later*, *i.e.*, after at least one step of computation. Guarded recursion supports a coinductive style of reasoning: to prove P one can assume $\triangleright P$, but this assumption is only useful after at least one step of computation. As we explain in §5, our use of guarded recursion descends from a line of work on *step-indexed* logical relations, but the interaction with Hoare triples is a novelty of CaReSL.

Proof rules The main judgment of CaReSL is written $\mathcal{C} \vdash P$, where $\mathcal{C} = \mathcal{X}; \mathcal{P}$ is a *combined* context of annotated term/predicate variables $\mathcal{X}$ and propositional assumptions $\mathcal{P}$. The meaning is the usual one: for any way of instantiating the variables in $\mathcal{X}$, if the hypotheses $\mathcal{P}$ are true for a given resource (*i.e.*, for the moment, a given heap), then P is true of the same resource. We implicitly assume $\mathcal{X} \vdash Q : \mathbb{B}$ for every proposition Q in $\mathcal{P}$ and likewise that $\mathcal{X} \vdash P : \mathbb{B}$ holds.

A few basic logical axioms and proof rules for core CaReSL are shown in Figure 4. Axioms hold in an arbitrary well-sorted context. The axioms include all the standard ones for a multi-sorted second-order logic (we show only $\forall_2$I), as well as several characterizing separating conjunction and the $\Box$ and $\triangleright$ modalities. We'll just mention the highlights:

- Because True is a unit for separating conjunction (and every proposition implies True), propositions are *affine*: we can "throw away" resources, because $(P * Q) \Rightarrow (\mathsf{True} * Q) \Rightarrow Q$.
- The two conjunctions $*$ and $\wedge$ are identical if at least one of their operands is a necessary proposition. Consequently, necessary propositions can be "freely copied": $A \Rightarrow A * A$
- The Löb rule provides a coinductive reasoning principle: to prove P, you may assume P—but only under the $\triangleright$ modality, which guards use of the assumption until at least one step of computation has taken place. On the other hand, Mono says that any proposition can be *weakened* to one that is guarded. (Both Mono and Löb are inherited from LADR [5].) We will momentarily see how $\triangleright$ is eliminated in Hoare-style reasoning.
- The $\triangleright$ modality distributes over $*$, as it does with most other connectives, except implication and recursion.

Atomic Hoare logic (where IS ::= I | S as explained in §3.3)

$$
\begin{array}{ll}
\llparenthesis \mathrm{True} \rrparenthesis\ i \Mapsto_{\mathrm{IS}} \textsf{new}\ v & \llparenthesis \mathsf{ret}.\ \mathsf{ret} \hookrightarrow_{\mathrm{IS}} v \rrparenthesis \\
\llparenthesis v \hookrightarrow_{\mathrm{IS}} v' \rrparenthesis\ i \Mapsto_{\mathrm{IS}} \textsf{get}\ v & \llparenthesis \mathsf{ret}.\ \mathsf{ret} = v' * v \hookrightarrow_{\mathrm{IS}} v' \rrparenthesis \\
\llparenthesis v \hookrightarrow_{\mathrm{IS}} - \rrparenthesis\ i \Mapsto_{\mathrm{IS}} v\ :=\ v' & \llparenthesis \mathsf{ret}.\ \mathsf{ret} = () * v \hookrightarrow_{\mathrm{IS}} v' \rrparenthesis \\
\llparenthesis \mathrm{True} \rrparenthesis\ i \Mapsto_{\mathrm{IS}} \textsf{newLcl} & \llparenthesis \mathsf{ret}.\ \mathsf{ret} \hookrightarrow_{\mathrm{IS}} \emptyset \rrparenthesis \\
\llparenthesis v \hookrightarrow_{\mathrm{IS}} L \rrparenthesis\ i \Mapsto_{\mathrm{IS}} \textsf{getLcl}(v) & \llparenthesis \mathsf{ret}.\ \mathsf{ret} = \lfloor L \rfloor (i) * v \hookrightarrow_{\mathrm{IS}} L \rrparenthesis \\
\llparenthesis v \hookrightarrow_{\mathrm{IS}} L \rrparenthesis\ i \Mapsto_{\mathrm{IS}} \textsf{setLcl}(v, v') & \llparenthesis \mathsf{ret}.\ \mathsf{ret} = () * v \hookrightarrow_{\mathrm{IS}} L[i := v'] \rrparenthesis \\
\llparenthesis v \hookrightarrow_{\mathrm{IS}} v' \rrparenthesis\ i \Mapsto_{\mathrm{IS}} & \llparenthesis \mathsf{ret}.\ (v' = v_o * \mathsf{ret} = \textsf{true} * v \hookrightarrow_{\mathrm{IS}} v_n) \\
\qquad \textsf{CAS}(v, v_o, v_n) & \quad \vee\ (v' \neq v_o * \mathsf{ret} = \textsf{false} * v \hookrightarrow_{\mathrm{IS}} v') \rrparenthesis
\end{array}
$$

$$
\frac{\mathcal{X}; P \vdash P' \qquad \mathcal{X}; \mathcal{P} \vdash \llparenthesis P' \rrparenthesis\ i \Mapsto_{\mathrm{IS}} a\ \llparenthesis x.\ Q' \rrparenthesis \qquad \mathcal{X}, x; Q' \vdash Q}{\mathcal{X}; \mathcal{P} \vdash \llparenthesis P \rrparenthesis\ i \Mapsto_{\mathrm{IS}} a\ \llparenthesis x.\ Q \rrparenthesis}\ \textsc{ACsq}
$$

$$
\frac{\mathcal{C} \vdash \llparenthesis P \rrparenthesis\ i \Mapsto_{\mathrm{IS}} a\ \llparenthesis x.\ Q \rrparenthesis}{\mathcal{C} \vdash \llparenthesis P * R \rrparenthesis\ i \Mapsto_{\mathrm{IS}} a\ \llparenthesis x.\ Q * R \rrparenthesis}\ \textsc{AFrame}
$$

(ADisj, AEx elided)

General Hoare logic

$$
\frac{\mathcal{C} \vdash \llparenthesis P \rrparenthesis\ i \Mapsto_{\mathrm{I}} a\ \llparenthesis Q \rrparenthesis}{\mathcal{C} \vdash \{\triangleright P\}\ i \Mapsto a\ \{Q\}}\ \textsc{Private}
\qquad
\frac{\mathcal{C} \vdash e \stackrel{\mathrm{pure}}{\to} e' \quad \mathcal{C} \vdash \{P\}\ i \Mapsto e'\ \{\varphi\}}{\mathcal{C} \vdash \{\triangleright P\}\ i \Mapsto e\ \{\varphi\}}\ \textsc{Pure}
$$

$$
\frac{\mathcal{C} \vdash \{P\}\ i \Mapsto e\ \{x.\ Q\} \qquad \mathcal{C}, x \vdash \{Q\}\ i \Mapsto K[x]\ \{R\}}{\mathcal{C} \vdash \{P\}\ i \Mapsto K[e]\ \{R\}}\ \textsc{Bind}
$$

$$
\mathcal{C} \vdash \{\mathrm{True}\}\ i \Mapsto v\ \{x.\ x = v\}\ \textsc{Ret}
$$

(Csq, Frame, Disj, Ex elided)

$$
\frac{\mathcal{C} \vdash A \quad \mathcal{C} \vdash \{P * A\}\ i \Mapsto e\ \{\varphi\}}{\mathcal{C} \vdash \{P\}\ i \Mapsto e\ \{\varphi\}}\ \textsc{AIn}
\qquad
\frac{\mathcal{C}, A \vdash \{P\}\ i \Mapsto e\ \{\varphi\}}{\mathcal{C} \vdash \{P * A\}\ i \Mapsto e\ \{\varphi\}}\ \textsc{AOut}
$$

Derivable rules

$$
\frac{\mathcal{C}, f, \forall x. \{\triangleright P\}\ i \Mapsto f\ x\ \{\varphi\} \vdash \forall x.\ \{P\}\ i \Mapsto e\ \{\varphi\}}{\mathcal{C} \vdash \forall x.\ \{\triangleright P\}\ i \Mapsto (\textbf{rec}\ f(x).e)\ x\ \{\varphi\}}\ \textsc{Rec}
$$

$$
\frac{\begin{array}{c}\mathcal{C} \vdash \{P\}\ i \Mapsto e\ \{x.\ \exists y.\ (x = \textsf{inj}_1\ y * \triangleright Q_1) \vee (x = \textsf{inj}_2\ y * \triangleright Q_2)\} \\ \forall k \in \{1, 2\} :\ \mathcal{C}, x, y \vdash \{x = \textsf{inj}_k\ y * Q_k\}\ i \Mapsto e_k\ \{\varphi\}\end{array}}{\mathcal{C} \vdash \{P\}\ i \Mapsto \textsf{case}(e, \textsf{inj}_1\ y \Rightarrow e_1, \textsf{inj}_2\ y \Rightarrow e_2)\ \{\varphi\}}
$$

Figure 5. Core CaReSL: Hoare logic

The rules for atomic triples (Figure 5) are formulated in the standard style of separation logic. They transcribe the operational semantics of atomic expressions, mentioning only the part of the heap relevant to the expression. Atomic Hoare logic supports the usual rules—consequence, framing, disjunction, $\exists$-elimination—with one important exception: it does not support a sequencing rule, since a sequence of atomic expressions is not atomic.

All atomic expressions take exactly one step to execute, and in so doing allow us to peel off a layer of the $\triangleright$ modality. To cut down on clutter, the precondition in an atomic triple is *implicitly* understood as being under one $\triangleright$ modality. The rule Private, which lifts an atomic triple to a general one, makes this implicit assumption explicit. (In core CaReSL, *all* resources are private; §3.2 adds shared resources.) To handle pure reduction steps (like β-reduction), the Pure rule appeals directly to the operational semantics using the necessary proposition $e \stackrel{\mathrm{pure}}{\to} e'$. The rest of the rules for general Hoare triples are mostly standard; we show only the nonstandard rules in Figure 5.

In an expression language, the monadic nature of Hoare logic becomes visible: the Bind rule replaces the usual rule of sequencing, while Ret is used to inject a value into a Hoare triple.

We also have a rule allowing necessary propositions to move freely from the proof context into preconditions (AIn), and vice versa (AOut). In general, any contingent assumptions like $x \hookrightarrow_{\mathrm{I}} 3$ need to be given explicitly in the precondition of a Hoare triple, because the truth of such statements can change over time; the triple says that it is only usable at times when its precondition holds. But in the specific case of necessary propositions, we can do better: we know that if such a proposition happens to be true now, it will be true forever, and so it does not need to be given explicitly in the precondition. As we will see in §3.2, these rules will allow us to completely hide pieces of state that are known to always obey a certain protocol.

Finally, using Löb and Pure, together with standard Hoare rules, we can derive specialized rules for constructs like recursive functions and pattern matching—the two derived rules in Figure 5.

***Verifying* foreach** Having seen core CaReSL in detail, we can now return to the foreach example. First, we need to rewrite our sketch of the specification more formally. The Map predicate needs to employ guarded recursion:

$$
\begin{array}{l}
\mathrm{Map}_{\varphi} \triangleq \mu m \in \mathbb{P}(\mathrm{Val}).\ (l \in \mathrm{Val}). \\
\qquad l = \mathsf{none} \vee (\exists x, n.\ l = \mathsf{some}(x, n) * \varphi(x) * \triangleright m(n))
\end{array}
$$

while the foreach spec should be annotated with sorts:

$$
\begin{array}{l}
\forall p, q \in \mathbb{P}(\mathrm{Val}). \forall r \in \mathbb{P}(\mathbf{1}).\ \forall f.\ (\forall x. \{p(x) * r\}\ f(x)\ \{q(x) * r\}) \\
\quad \Rightarrow \quad \forall l.\ \left\{\mathrm{Map}_p(l) * r\right\}\ \mathsf{foreach}\ \_\ f\ l\ \left\{\mathrm{Map}_q(l) * r\right\}
\end{array}
$$

To prove foreach correct, we use a kind of Hoare "proof outline", annotating each program point with a proposition:

$\mathsf{foreach} \triangleq \Lambda.\ \lambda f.\ \textbf{rec}\ \mathsf{loop}(l).$

Prop context:	**Variables:** $f, i, p, q, r, l, \mathsf{loop}$
$\forall x.\ \{p(x) * r\}\ i \Mapsto f(x)\ \{q(x) * r\}$	
$\forall n.\ \left\{\triangleright(\mathrm{Map}_p(n) * r)\right\}\ i \Mapsto \mathsf{loop}\ n\ \left\{\mathrm{Map}_q(n) * r\right\}$	

$$
\begin{array}{l}
\{\mathrm{Map}_p(l) * r\} \\
\textbf{case}\ l\ \textbf{of}\ \mathsf{none} \Rightarrow \{l = \mathsf{none} * \mathrm{Map}_p(l) * r\}\ ()\ \{\mathrm{Map}_q(l) * r\} \\
\qquad \mid \mathsf{some}(x, n) \Rightarrow \{l = \mathsf{some}(x, n) * \mathrm{Map}_p(l) * r\} \\
\qquad\qquad \{l = \mathsf{some}(x, n) * p(x) * \triangleright\mathrm{Map}_p(n) * r\} \\
\qquad\qquad f(x); \\
\qquad\qquad \{l = \mathsf{some}(x, n) * q(x) * \triangleright\mathrm{Map}_p(n) * r\} \\
\qquad\qquad \mathsf{loop}(n) \\
\qquad\qquad \{l = \mathsf{some}(x, n) * q(x) * \mathrm{Map}_q(n) * r\} \\
\qquad\qquad \{\mathrm{Map}_q(l) * r\}
\end{array}
$$

Proof outlines implicitly apply the Hoare logic rule corresponding to each language construct: for recursive functions and pattern matching we use the derived rules shown earlier; for an atomic expression we use the corresponding axiom; when going under a Λ or λx we use the Pure rule and prove a triple about the function as applied to _ or x respectively. The frame rule is applied implicitly as needed, while uses of consequence are shown by writing a sequence of assertions (each one implying the next). We do not explicitly write the thread ID in a proof outline, but it is always clear from context (and, for our examples, always the variable i).

We supplement traditional proof outlines with boxed *context assertions* spelling out an extension to both the variable context $\mathcal{X}$ and proposition context $\mathcal{P}$. Extending the context with new variables introduces a universal quantification (using *e.g.,* the rule $\forall_2$I in Figure 4), while adding propositions introduces an implication. We use the AIn rule implicitly to bring necessary consequences of the proof context into the Hoare-style outline.

The proof for foreach is quite straightforward: the initial case analysis on the input list allows us to expand the definition of the Map predicate, which for the nonempty case gives us the necessary knowledge to execute f on an element of the list; note the heavy use of the frame rule to add invariant propositions. The use of $\triangleright$ in Map is neatly dispatched by the use of the Rec rule for foreach.

3.2 Adding concurrency: Protocols for shared state

To reason about concurrency, we need to reason about the protocols governing shared (and often hidden) state. Take, for example, the following higher-order spinlock:

$$
\begin{aligned}
\mathsf{tryAcq} &\triangleq \lambda x.\ \mathbf{CAS}(x, \mathbf{false}, \mathbf{true})\\
\mathsf{acq} &\triangleq \mathbf{rec}\ \mathsf{loop}(x).\ \mathbf{if}\ \mathsf{tryAcq}(x)\ \mathbf{then}\ ()\ \mathbf{else}\ \mathsf{oop}(x)\\
\mathsf{rel} &\triangleq \lambda x.\ x := \mathbf{false}
\end{aligned}
$$

$$
\begin{aligned}
\mathsf{mkSync} &: \mathbf{1} \to \forall\alpha.\forall\beta.(\alpha \to \beta) \to (\alpha \to \beta)\\
\mathsf{mkSync} &\triangleq \lambda().\ \mathbf{let}\ \mathsf{lock} = \mathbf{new}\ \mathbf{false}\ \mathbf{in}\\
&\qquad \Lambda.\Lambda.\lambda f.\lambda x.\ \mathsf{acq}(\mathsf{lock});\ \mathbf{let}\ z = f(x)\ \mathbf{in}\ \mathsf{rel}(\mathsf{lock});\ z
\end{aligned}
$$

Each invocation of mkSync creates a new *wrapper* that closes over a fresh, hidden lock. The wrapper can then be used to add simple synchronization to an arbitrary function. There are, of course, a variety of ways to use synchronization, but a particularly common one is to protect access to some shared resource characterized by an invariant p—an idea that leads to the following specification:

$$\forall p \in \mathbb{P}(\mathbf{1}).\ \{p\}\ \mathsf{mkSync}\ ()\ \left\{s.\ \mathsf{Syncer}_p(s)\right\}$$

$$\textit{where}\ \mathsf{Syncer}_p \triangleq (s \in \mathrm{Val}).\ \Box\forall f, x, q, r.\ \ \{p * q\}\ f\ x\ \{z.\ p * r(z)\} \Rightarrow \{q\}\ s\ \_\ f\ x\ \{z.\ r(z)\}$$

The spec says that when mkSync() is executed, the client can choose some invariant resource p, giving up control over the resource in exchange for a synchronization wrapper s. When s is later applied to a function f, it provides f with exclusive access to the resource p (seemingly out of thin air), which f can use however it pleases, so long as the invariant is reestablished on completion.

Intuitively, the reason that mkSync satisfies its specification is that the lock itself is *hidden*: all access to it is mediated through the wrapper s, which the client can only apply to invariant-preserving functions. Hiding enables mkSync to maintain an internal *protocol* in which, whenever the lock is free, the invariant p holds. To express this protocol, as well as the more sophisticated protocols needed for fine-grained concurrency (§3.3, §4), CaReSL provides a syntactic account of the semantic protocols of Turon *et al.* [31].

Protocols A protocol π governs a shared resource abstractly, by means of a set of protocol states (S) equipped with a transition relation ($\rightsquigarrow$). Each state $s \in S$ has an associated proposition $\varphi(s)$ giving its concrete interpretation in terms of *e.g.,* heap resources. The idea is then that any thread is allowed to update the shared resource, so long as at each atomic step those concrete updates correspond to a permitted abstract transition.

In general, although all threads must abide by a given protocol, not all of them play the same role within it. For example, a protocol governing a lock might have two states, Locked and Unlocked, with transitions in both directions, but we usually want to allow only the thread that acquired the lock to be allowed to release it (as is the case in the mkSync example). To allow threads to take on or relinquish roles dynamically, protocols employ *tokens* that individual threads may own. By taking a transition, a thread may "earn" a token from the protocol; conversely, certain transitions require a thread to "pay" by giving up a previously-earned token. For the locking protocol, we use a single token *Lock*:

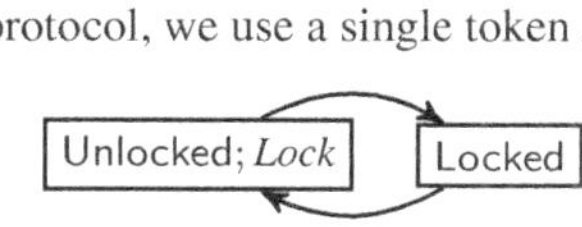

In the Unlocked state, the protocol itself owns the *Lock*, which we show by annotating the state with the token. A thread that transitions from Unlocked to Locked then earns (takes ownership of) the *Lock*. Conversely, to transition back to the Unlocked state, a thread must transfer the *Lock* back to the protocol—a move only possible for the thread that owns the *Lock*.

Formally, a protocol $\pi = (S, \rightsquigarrow, \mathcal{T}, \varphi)$ is given by a transition system (S and $\rightsquigarrow$), a function $\mathcal{T}$ giving the set of tokens owned by the protocol at each state, and a predicate φ on states giving their interpretations. To be able to talk about states and tokens in the logic, we add sorts State and TokSet, for which we will use the metavariables s and T respectively; see Figure 6. We leave the grammar of terms for these sorts open-ended, implicitly extending it as needed for particular transition systems.[6] Thus, we can give an interpretation $\mathsf{LockInterp}_p$ for the lock protocol that is appropriate for an instance of mkSync protecting an invariant p:

$$\mathsf{LockInterp}_p \triangleq (s \in \mathrm{State}).\ s = \mathsf{Locked} \lor (s = \mathsf{Unlocked} * p)$$

Protocols

$$\text{Protocol}\ \ \pi ::= (S, \rightsquigarrow, \mathcal{T}, \varphi)\quad \text{where}\quad S \subseteq \text{State},\ \ \rightsquigarrow\ \subseteq S \times S,\ \ \mathcal{T} \in S \to \text{TokSet},\ \ \varphi\ \text{token-pure}$$

$$
\begin{aligned}
(s; T) \rightsquigarrow_\pi (s'; T') &\triangleq s\ (\pi.\rightsquigarrow)\ s' \land \pi.\mathcal{T}(s) \uplus T = \pi.\mathcal{T}(s') \uplus T'\\
\text{frame}_\pi(s; T) &\triangleq (s;\ \text{AllTokens} - (\pi.\mathcal{T}(s) \uplus T))
\end{aligned}
$$

$$
\begin{aligned}
(s; T)\ \sqsubseteq^{\text{guar}}_{\mathcal{T}}\ (s'; T') &\triangleq (s; T) \rightsquigarrow^*_\pi (s'; T')\\
(s; T)\ \sqsubseteq^{\text{rely}}_{\mathcal{T}}\ (s'; T') &\triangleq \text{frame}_\pi(s; T) \rightsquigarrow^*_\pi \text{frame}_\pi(s'; T')
\end{aligned}
$$

Syntax

$$
\begin{aligned}
&\text{Sort} && \Sigma ::= \cdots \mid \text{State} \mid \text{TokSet}\\
&\text{Prop} && P := \cdots \mid \boxed{M}^{M}_{\pi} \mid \textit{Tid}(M)\\
&\text{AbProp} && A ::= \cdots \mid M \sqsubseteq^{\text{rely}}_\pi M \mid M \sqsubseteq^{\text{guar}}_\pi M \mid \text{TokPure}(P)
\end{aligned}
$$

Hoare logic (*where* $\pi[\![b]\!] \triangleq \exists s.b = (s, -) \land \pi.\varphi(s)$)

$$\frac{\mathcal{C} \vdash \{P\}\ i \Rrightarrow e\ \{x.\ Q * \pi[\![b]\!]\}}{\mathcal{C} \vdash \{P\}\ i \Rrightarrow e\ \left\{x.\ Q * \exists n.\ \boxed{b}^{n}_{\pi}\right\}}\ \textsc{NewIsl}$$

$$\frac{\mathcal{C} \vdash \forall b \overset{\text{rely}}{\sqsupseteq_\pi} b_0.\ (\!|\pi[\![b]\!] * P|\!)\ i \Rrightarrow_{\mathrm{I}} a\ (\!|x.\ \exists b' \overset{\text{guar}}{\sqsupseteq_\pi} b.\ \pi[\![b']\!] * Q|\!)}{\mathcal{C} \vdash \left\{\boxed{b_0}^{n}_{\pi} * \triangleright P\right\}\ i \Rrightarrow a\ \left\{x.\ \exists b'.\ \boxed{b'}^{n}_{\pi} * Q\right\}}\ \textsc{UpdIsl}$$

$$\frac{\mathcal{C} \vdash \{P * \textit{Tid}(j)\}\ j \Rrightarrow e\ \{\mathsf{ret}.\ \mathsf{ret} = ()\}}{\mathcal{C} \vdash \{P\}\ i \Rrightarrow \mathbf{fork}\ e\ \{\mathsf{ret}.\ \mathsf{ret} = ()\}}\ \textsc{Fork}$$

Logical axioms and rules

$$\boxed{s_1; T_1}^{n}_{\pi} * \boxed{s_2; T_2}^{n}_{\pi} \Leftrightarrow \qquad \textsc{SplitIsl}$$
$$\exists s.\ \boxed{s; T_1 \uplus T_2}^{n}_{\pi} \land (s; T_1) \overset{\text{rely}}{\sqsupseteq_\pi} (s_1; T_1) \land (s; T_2) \overset{\text{rely}}{\sqsupseteq_\pi} (s_2; T_2)$$

Figure 6. CaReSL: Incorporating concurrency and protocols

The combination of transition systems and tokens gives rise to *token-sensitive transitions*. A transition from state/tokens $(s; T)$ to state/tokens $(s'; T')$ is permitted by π, written $(s; T) \rightsquigarrow_\pi (s'; T')$, so long as the *law of token conservation* holds: the disjoint union of the thread's tokens and the protocols tokens $T \uplus \pi.\mathcal{T}(s)$ before the transition must be the same as the disjoint union $T' \uplus \pi.\mathcal{T}(s')$ afterwards.[7] Token-sensitive transitions constrain both what a thread can do (the *guarantee* moves $\sqsubseteq^{\text{guar}}_\pi$ enabled by its tokens) and what its environment can do (the *rely* moves $\sqsubseteq^{\text{rely}}_\pi$ enabled by the tokens owned by other threads). See Figure 6.

Island assertions In CaReSL, all resources are either privately owned by a thread, or else governed by a shared protocol. When a heap assertion like $x \hookrightarrow_{\mathrm{I}} 3$ appears in the pre- or postcondition of a triple, it is understood as asserting private ownership over the corresponding portion of the heap; no other thread is allowed to access it. Thus the rules of core CaReSL are immediately sound in a concurrent setting: there is no interference to account for.

To talk about shared resources, CaReSL includes *island assertions* $\boxed{b}^{n}_{\pi}$ (similar to region assertions in RGSep/CAP). As the name suggests, each island is an independent region of the heap governed by its own laws (the protocol π). The number n is the "name" of the island, which is used to distinguish between multiple islands with the same protocol; we often leave off the name when

[6] To be completely formal, we could allow each transition system to come equipped with its own explicit grammar of states and tokens.

[7] We use notation like $\pi.\mathcal{T}$ to extract named components from a tuple.

it is existentially quantified. The term b (of sort State $\times$ TokSet) asserts private ownership of a set of tokens,[8] and acts as a "rely-lower bound" on the state of the protocol: the current state of the protocol is some $b' \sqsupseteq_{\pi}^{\text{rely}} b$. Thus, in CaReSL *every assertion about shared resources is automatically stable under interference.*

While a thread's island assertions cannot be invalidated by a change its environment makes, they *can* be invalidated by a change the thread itself makes. For example, if a thread owns *Lock* in Locked state of the mkSync protocol, the environment cannot change the state at all—but the thread itself can move to the Unlocked state. There is, however, a special class of island assertions which are "completely" stable, *i.e.,* that act as necessary propositions: island assertions that do not claim any tokens. To understand why, consider that when no tokens are owned, the $\sqsubseteq_{\pi}^{\text{rely}}$ relation *degenerates* to the underlying transition system of the protocol, which means it contains all possible moves that any thread can make. Formally, we have $\boxed{(M;\emptyset)}_{\pi}^{n} \Rightarrow \Box\,\boxed{(M;\emptyset)}_{\pi}^{n}$.

When island assertions *do* claim ownership over tokens (a form of resource), they can be meaningfully combined by separating conjunction; see the SPLITISL rule in Figure 6, which takes into account the fact that the assertions give only rely-lower bounds.[9]

There are two Hoare logic rules for working with islands (Figure 6). The rule NEWISL creates a new island starting with an initial state and token set bound b; the resources necessary to satisfy the protocol's initial state must be present as private resources, and afterwards will be shared. (The shorthand $\pi[\![b]\!]$ just gives the interpretation at the state in b.) Once an island is established, the only way to access the shared resources it governs is through the UPDISL rule, which can only be applied to an *atomic* expression. Starting from an initial bound b_0, the atomic expression a might be (instantaneously) executed in any rely-reachable b; for each such state, the expression is granted exclusive access to the shared resource, but in its single atomic step, it must make a guarantee move in the protocol. This rule reveals the important semantic difference between atomic and general triples: through the UPDISL rule, atomic triples gain access to the concrete resources owned by shared islands, while general triples only have access to island assertions.

Thread creation In a protocol, threads gain and lose roles (tokens) by making deliberate moves within the protocol. But there is also a role that every thread plays *automatically*: the role of being a thread with a certain ID. To support protocols that use thread IDs (such as the one in §4), CaReSL builds in a proposition $\mathit{Tid}(j)$ that asserts the existence of a thread j, and acts as an *uncopyable* resource: $\mathit{Tid}(j) * \mathit{Tid}(j) \Leftrightarrow$ False. The resource is introduced by the FORK rule, which also allows the parent thread to transfer an arbitrary P to the newly-forked thread. (The parent can keep resources for itself via the FRAME rule.) The trivial postconditions in FORK may seem alarming, but they reflect the fact that the language has no **join** mechanism: the *only* form of communication between threads is shared state, mediated by a shared protocol.

***Verifying* mkSync** The interpretations $\pi.\varphi(s)$ of protocol states in CaReSL inherit a limitation from their semantic treatment by Turon *et al.* [31]: they must be token-pure, *i.e.,* they cannot assert ownership of island tokens. The necessary proposition TokPure(P) can be used to assert that, for example, an unknown proposition is token-pure and thus safe to use in an interpretation, and we need such a restriction on p in mkSync:

$$\forall p \in \mathbb{P}(\mathbf{1}).\ \mathrm{TokPure}(p) \Rightarrow \{p\}\ i \Mapsto \mathsf{mkSync}\ ()\ \left\{s.\ \mathsf{Syncer}_p(s)\right\}$$
$$\textit{where}\ \ \mathsf{Syncer}_p \triangleq (s \in \mathrm{Val}).\ \Box\forall f, x, q, r.\ \{p * q\}\ f\ x\ \{z.\ p * r(z)\} \Rightarrow \{q\}\ s\ \_\ \_\ f\ x\ \{z.\ r(z)\}$$

The hidden protocol $\mathrm{LockProt}_p$ for mkSync just puts together the pieces we have already seen:

$$\mathrm{LockProt}_p \triangleq (\{\mathsf{Locked}, \mathsf{Unlocked}\}, \rightsquigarrow, \mathcal{T}, \mathrm{LockInterp}_p)$$

where $\rightsquigarrow$ and $\mathcal{T}$ are given by the transition system for locking shown above.

The high-level proof outline for mkSync is straightforward:

$\lambda().$ **Prop context:** TokPure(p) **Variables:** p

$\{p\}$ **let** lock = **new false** $\{p * \mathsf{lock} \hookrightarrow_{\text{I}} \textbf{false}\}$

$\{\exists n.\ \boxed{\mathsf{Unlocked};\emptyset}_{\mathrm{LockProt}_p}^{n}\}$

$\Lambda.\Lambda.\lambda f.\lambda x.$

Prop context: $\Box\,\boxed{\mathsf{Unlocked};\emptyset}_{\mathrm{LockProt}_p}$ $\{p * q\}\ f\ x\ \{z.\ p * r(z)\}$ **Variables:** f, x, q, r

$\{q\}$	$\{\boxed{\mathsf{Unlocked};\emptyset}_{\mathrm{LockProt}_p} * q\}$
acq(lock);	$\{\boxed{\mathsf{Locked};\mathit{Lock}}_{\mathrm{LockProt}_p} * p * q\}$
let $z = f(x)$	$\{\boxed{\mathsf{Locked};\mathit{Lock}}_{\mathrm{LockProt}_p} * p * r(z)\}$
rel(lock);	$\{\boxed{\mathsf{Unlocked};\emptyset}_{\mathrm{LockProt}_p} * r(z)\}$
z	$\{z.\ r(z)\}$

After allocating the hidden lock, we move it into a fresh island using NEWISL, and then move that island assertion (wrapped with $\Box$) into the proof context (using AOUT) before reasoning about the returned wrapper function. In this way the protocol is completely hidden from the client, yet available to the closure we return to the client—mirroring the fact that lock is hidden from the client but available in the closure. Since the spec $\mathsf{Syncer}_p(s)$ is a necessary proposition, the client may move the spec into its proof context, and thus freely use the synchronization wrapper s without threading *any* assertion about it through its proof. (Previous logics, like CAP, require at least that the client thread through an abstract predicate standing for the lock.)

When verifying the closure, we begin with a precondition q of the client's choice, but then apply AIN to load the hidden island assertion into the precondition. The subsequent lines use the locking protocol to acquire the resource p, execute the client's function f, and then return p to the protocol. The tokens in the island assertions, which say what the *thread* owns at each point, complement those (in $\pi.\mathcal{T}$) labelling the corresponding states in the protocol.

The triples for acq and rel must ultimately be proved by appeal to the UPDISL rule. For acq, the *bound* on the protocol is just (Unlocked; $\emptyset$), which means that the *actual* state might be either Locked or Unlocked. The **CAS** within acq will return:

- **true** if successful; the state must have been Unlocked. We make a guarantee move to (Locked; *Lock*), gaining the token.
- **false** if it fails; the state must have been Locked. We do not change the state, and the acq function retries by calling loop.

On the other hand, for rel, the bound (Locked; *Lock*) means that the protocol *must* be in state Locked: the environment cannot move to Unlocked because it does not own *Lock*. But since rel *does* own *Lock*, it can simply update the lock to **false**, corresponding to a guarantee move to the Unlocked state in the protocol.

3.3 Adding refinement: Reasoning about specification code

At this point, we have seen the fragment of CaReSL providing Hoare-style specs and proofs for higher-order concurrent programs, as exemplified (in a simple way) by the mkSync example. This section explains the other major component of the logic: higher-order granularity abstraction, exemplified (in a simple way) by the Treiber stack with iterator.

[8] An island assertion is only satisfied if the asserted token set is disjoint from the tokens owned by the protocol at the asserted state.

[9] We assume that terms M include disjoint union on token sets.

Syntax

$$\Sigma ::= \cdots \mid \text{EvalCtx} \qquad P ::= \cdots \mid M \hookrightarrow_{\mathrm{S}} M \mid M \Mapsto_{\mathrm{S}} M$$
$$M ::= \cdots \mid K \mid M[M] \qquad A ::= \cdots \mid P \rightarrow_{\mathrm{S}} F \mid M \bowtie M$$

Spec rewriting

$$\frac{\mathcal{C} \vdash e \overset{\text{pure}}{\rightarrow} e'}{\mathcal{C} \vdash (P * j \Mapsto_{\mathrm{S}} K[e]) \rightarrow_{\mathrm{S}} (P * j \Mapsto_{\mathrm{S}} K[e'])}\ \text{SPURE}$$

$$\frac{\mathcal{C} \vdash (\!|P|\!)\ j \Mapsto_{\mathrm{S}} a\ (\!|x.\ Q|\!)}{\mathcal{C} \vdash (P * j \Mapsto_{\mathrm{S}} K[a]) \rightarrow_{\mathrm{S}} (\exists x.\ Q * j \Mapsto_{\mathrm{S}} K[x])}\ \text{SPRIM}$$

$$\mathcal{C} \vdash (j \Mapsto_{\mathrm{S}} K[\textbf{fork}\ e]) \rightarrow_{\mathrm{S}} (j \Mapsto_{\mathrm{S}} K[()] * k \Mapsto_{\mathrm{S}} e)\ \text{SFORK}$$

Hoare logic (AEXECSPEC elided)

$$\frac{\mathcal{C} \vdash \{P\}\ i \Mapsto e\ \{x.\ Q\} \qquad \mathcal{C} \vdash Q \rightarrow_{\mathrm{S}} R}{\mathcal{C} \vdash \{P\}\ i \Mapsto e\ \{x.\ R\}}\ \text{EXECSPEC}$$

$$\frac{\mathcal{C}, j \bowtie j' \vdash \{P * \mathit{Tid}(j) * j' \Mapsto_{\mathrm{S}} e_{\mathrm{S}}\}\ j \Mapsto e_{\mathrm{I}}\ \{x.\ x = ()\}}{\mathcal{C} \vdash \{P * i' \Mapsto_{\mathrm{S}} K[\textbf{fork}\ e_{\mathrm{S}}]\}\ i \Mapsto \textbf{fork}\ e_{\mathrm{I}}\ \{i' \Mapsto_{\mathrm{S}} K[()]\}}\ \text{FORKS}$$

Figure 7. CaReSL: Incorporating spec resources

Spec resources While it is possible to formulate a relational version of Hoare logic (with Hoare *quadruples* [33]), or to develop special-purpose logics for refinement [5], our goal with CaReSL is to support *both* standard Hoare-style reasoning and refinement reasoning in a single unified logic. In particular, we want a treatment of refinement that re-uses as much Hoare-style reasoning as possible. To this end, we adapt the idea of *specification resources*, first proposed by Turon *et al.* [31] as a way of proving refinement when threads engage in "cooperation" (a point we return to in §4). We will show how spec resources make it possible to state and prove refinements as an *entirely* derived concept on top of the Hoare logic we have already built up, in particular allowing protocols and triples to serve double-duty when reasoning about spec code.

To prove that e_{I} refines e_{S}, one must (intuitively) show that every behavior observable of e_{I} is observable of e_{S} as well. Our strategy is to encode these proof obligations into certain Hoare triples about the execution of e_{I}, but with pre- and postconditions instrumented with pieces of the corresponding spec state—both heap and code—which we treat as resources in CaReSL. These spec resources are entirely a fiction of the logic: they do not reflect anything about the *physical* state of e_{I}, but they must be used through logical rules that enforce the operational semantics for e_{S}.

There are two basic spec resource assertions: the *(spec) points-to* assertion $\ell \hookrightarrow_{\mathrm{S}} v$, which claims ownership of a fragment of the spec heap containing a location ℓ that points to the value v, and the *spec thread* assertion $i \Mapsto_{\mathrm{S}} e$, which claims ownership of a spec thread with ID i executing expression e. The separating conjunction $P * Q$ works in the usual way with these resources, dividing up the spec heap and thread pool between the propositions P and Q. We also add a final sort, EvalCtx, and terms K and $M[N]$ for expressing and combining them, which makes it possible to *abstract* over the evaluation context for some spec thread. (By convention, the variable κ is always of sort EvalCtx.)

In addition, CaReSL provides a necessary proposition $P \rightarrow_{\mathrm{S}} Q$, which says that the spec resources owned by P can, according to the operational semantics, take a step to those owned by Q. All other resources must be left invariant. The rule SPURE lifts the pure stepping relation from the operational semantics directly. The rule SPRIM, on the other hand, *re-uses* atomic triples to support reasoning about atomic spec expressions. (The subscript IS in the laws of atomic triples allows them to be used in *either* implementation mode I or spec mode S.) The EXECSPEC Hoare rule (and identical AEXECSPEC rule for atomic triples) allows the specification to be

Relating expressions

$$(e_{\mathrm{I}}, e_{\mathrm{S}}) \downarrow \varphi \triangleq \forall (i \bowtie j), \kappa.$$
$$\{\mathit{Tid}(i) * j \Mapsto_{\mathrm{S}} \kappa[e_{\mathrm{S}}]\}\ i \Mapsto e_{\mathrm{I}}\ \{x_{\mathrm{I}}.\ \exists x_{\mathrm{S}}.\ \varphi(x_{\mathrm{I}}, x_{\mathrm{S}}) * \mathit{Tid}(i) * j \Mapsto_{\mathrm{S}} \kappa[x_{\mathrm{S}}]\}$$

Relating values

$$[\![\mathbf{1}]\!] \triangleq (x_{\mathrm{I}}, x_{\mathrm{S}}).\ x_{\mathrm{I}} = x_{\mathrm{S}} = () \qquad [\![\mu\alpha.\tau]\!] \triangleq \mu\alpha.[\![\tau]\!]$$
$$[\![\mathbf{B}]\!] \triangleq (x_{\mathrm{I}}, x_{\mathrm{S}}).\ (x_{\mathrm{I}} = x_{\mathrm{S}} = \textbf{true}) \vee (x_{\mathrm{I}} = x_{\mathrm{S}} = \textbf{false}) \qquad [\![\alpha]\!] \triangleq \alpha$$

$$[\![\tau_1 \times \tau_2]\!] \triangleq (x_{\mathrm{I}}, x_{\mathrm{S}}).\ (\textbf{prj}_1\ x_{\mathrm{I}}, \textbf{prj}_1\ x_{\mathrm{S}}) \downarrow [\![\tau_1]\!] \wedge (\textbf{prj}_2\ x_{\mathrm{I}}, \textbf{prj}_2\ x_{\mathrm{S}}) \downarrow [\![\tau_2]\!]$$
$$[\![\tau_1 + \tau_2]\!] \triangleq (x_{\mathrm{I}}, x_{\mathrm{S}}).\ (\triangleright\exists (y_{\mathrm{I}}, y_{\mathrm{S}}) \in [\![\tau_1]\!].\ x_{\mathrm{I}} = \textbf{inj}_1\ y_{\mathrm{I}} \wedge x_{\mathrm{S}} = \textbf{inj}_1\ y_{\mathrm{S}})$$
$$\vee\ (\triangleright\exists (y_{\mathrm{I}}, y_{\mathrm{S}}) \in [\![\tau_2]\!].\ x_{\mathrm{I}} = \textbf{inj}_2\ y_{\mathrm{I}} \wedge x_{\mathrm{S}} = \textbf{inj}_2\ y_{\mathrm{S}})$$
$$[\![\tau \rightarrow \tau']\!] \triangleq (x_{\mathrm{I}}, x_{\mathrm{S}}).\ \Box\forall y_{\mathrm{I}}, y_{\mathrm{S}}.(\triangleright(y_{\mathrm{I}}, y_{\mathrm{S}}) \in [\![\tau]\!]) \Rightarrow (x_{\mathrm{I}}\ y_{\mathrm{I}}, x_{\mathrm{S}}\ y_{\mathrm{S}}) \downarrow [\![\tau']\!]$$
$$[\![\forall\alpha.\tau]\!] \triangleq (x_{\mathrm{I}}, x_{\mathrm{S}}).\ \Box\forall\alpha.\text{Type}(\alpha) \Rightarrow (x_{\mathrm{I}}\ \_, x_{\mathrm{S}}\ \_) \downarrow [\![\tau]\!]$$
$$[\![\textbf{ref}\ \tau]\!] \triangleq (x_{\mathrm{I}}, x_{\mathrm{S}}).\ \text{Inv}(\exists (y_{\mathrm{I}}, y_{\mathrm{S}}) \in [\![\tau]\!].\ x_{\mathrm{I}} \hookrightarrow_{\mathrm{I}} y_{\mathrm{I}} * x_{\mathrm{S}} \hookrightarrow_{\mathrm{S}} y_{\mathrm{S}})$$
$$[\![\textbf{refLcl}\ \tau]\!] \triangleq (x_{\mathrm{I}}, x_{\mathrm{S}}).\ \text{Inv}\begin{pmatrix}\exists L_{\mathrm{I}}, L_{\mathrm{S}}.\ x_{\mathrm{I}} \hookrightarrow_{\mathrm{I}} L_{\mathrm{I}} * x_{\mathrm{S}} \hookrightarrow_{\mathrm{S}} L_{\mathrm{S}} * \\ \forall (i \bowtie j).\ (\lfloor L_{\mathrm{I}} \rfloor(i), \lfloor L_{\mathrm{S}} \rfloor(j)) \in [\![\mathbf{1} + \tau]\!]\end{pmatrix}$$

Invariant protocols $\text{Inv}(P) \triangleq \exists n.\ \boxed{0; \emptyset}^{n}_{(\{0\}, \emptyset, [0 \mapsto \emptyset], (s).P)}$

Type interpretations $\text{Type}(\varphi) \triangleq \Box\forall (x_{\mathrm{I}}, x_{\mathrm{S}}) \in \varphi.\ \Box(x_{\mathrm{I}}, x_{\mathrm{S}}) \in \varphi$

Logical relatedness* (i.e., *refinement)

$$\overline{\alpha}; \overline{x : \tau} \vdash e_{\mathrm{I}} \preceq e_{\mathrm{S}} : \tau \triangleq$$
$$\overline{\alpha}, \overline{x_{\mathrm{I}}, x_{\mathrm{S}}}; \overline{\text{Type}(\alpha)}, \overline{(x_{\mathrm{I}}, x_{\mathrm{S}}) \in [\![\tau]\!]} \vdash (e_{\mathrm{I}}\overline{[x_{\mathrm{I}}/x]}, e_{\mathrm{S}}\overline{[x_{\mathrm{S}}/x]}) \downarrow [\![\tau]\!]$$

Figure 8. Encoding refinement in CaReSL

"executed" within any postcondition, *i.e.,* at any point in a proof. Since EXECSPEC can be applied repeatedly, a single step of some implementation code—*e.g.,* an atomic expression—can correspond to an arbitrary number of spec steps.

Putting these pieces together, a triple like

$$\{j \Mapsto_{\mathrm{S}} e_{\mathrm{S}}\}\ i \Mapsto e_{\mathrm{I}}\ \{x_{\mathrm{I}}.\ \exists x_{\mathrm{S}}.\ j \Mapsto_{\mathrm{S}} x_{\mathrm{S}} * \varphi(x_{\mathrm{I}}, x_{\mathrm{S}})\}$$

says that if e_{I} produces some value x_{I}, then e_{S} can be executed to produce some value x_{S} such that $\varphi(x_{\mathrm{I}}, x_{\mathrm{S}})$ holds—exactly the kind of observational claim we set out to make.

Encoding refinement To give a full account of refinement, we also need to ensure that updates to public reference cells by the implementation are matched in lock-step by updates by the spec, which we will do by imposing a protocol governing public reference cells. And to account for thread-local references, we must also track a *correspondence* between implementation and specification thread IDs, which allows us to state invariants connecting the storage on either side. The (necessary) assertion $i \bowtie j$ asserts that the implementation thread i and spec thread j belong to the bijective correspondence, *i.e.,* $(i \bowtie j) \wedge (i' \bowtie j') \Rightarrow (i = i' \Leftrightarrow j = j')$. Correspondences are introduced using the rule FORKS, a variant of FORK that jointly creates fresh implementation and spec threads.

And that's all: using these ingredients, we can *encode* refinement by simply writing down a particular predicate in CaReSL.

The encoded predicate expresses a logical relation—a variant of the relation given semantically by Turon *et al.* [31]—following the approach first laid out by Plotkin and Abadi [23] We define the relation in stages (see Figure 8).

First, we have the proposition $(e_{\mathrm{I}}, e_{\mathrm{S}}) \downarrow \varphi$, which is a more general version of the triple we suggested above: it includes assumptions about thread IDs, and permits compositional reasoning about specs by quantifying over an unknown evaluation context κ. The expressions do not begin with private ownership of any heap resources because, when proving refinement, we must assume that any pre-existing state is shared with the context. As we will see in a moment, this shared state is governed by an extremely liberal protocol; all we can assume about the context is that it is well-typed.

Second, we have the binary predicate $[\![\tau]\!]$, which is satisfied by $(v_{\mathrm{I}}, v_{\mathrm{S}})$ when the observations a context can make of v_{I} can

```
stackS  :  ∀α. (α → 1) × (1 → (1 + α)) × ((α → 1) → 1)
stackS  ≜  Λ. let sync = mkSync(), hdS = new (none)
  let push = λx. hdS := some(x, get hdS)
  let pop  = λ(). case get hdS of none          ⇒ none
                                | some(x, n) ⇒ hdS := n; some(x)
  let snap = sync _ _ (λ().get hdS)
  let iter  = λf. foreach _ f (snap())
  in (sync _ _ push, sync _ _ pop, iter)

stackI ≜ Λ. let hdI = new nil                      where nil ≜ new none,
  let push = rec try(x).                           cons e ≜ new some(e)
    let c = get hdI, n = cons(x, c)
    in if CAS(hdI, c, n) then () else try(x),
  let pop = rec try().
    let c = get hdI in case get c of
        none ⇒ none
      | some(d, n) ⇒ if CAS(hdI, c, n) then some(d) else try()
  let iter = λf.  let rec loop(c) = case get c of
                     none ⇒ ()   |   some(d, n) ⇒ f(d); loop(n)
                  in loop(get hdI)
  in (push, pop, iter)
```

Figure 9. Coarse- and fine-grained stacks, with iterators

also be made of v_S—the heart of the logical relation. It is defined by induction on the structure of τ, since the ways a value can be observed depend on its type:

For **ground types**, the context can observe the exact value, so only equal values are in the interpretation.

For **product types**, the context can project both sides of the product, so two values are related iff each of their projections are related; similarly for **sums**. The context can observe **functions** only by applying them, so one function is related to another iff, when applied to related values, they produce related results.

Recursive and **polymorphic** types are interpreted via guarded recursion and second-order quantification, respectively; we pun type variables α, β as predicate variables, which are implicitly assumed to be of sort $\mathbb{P}(\text{Val} \times \text{Val})$, and for quantification explicitly required to satisfy Type(α). These two constraints guarantee that the relation $[\![\tau]\!]$ is a resource-insensitive, binary predicate on values. The resource-insensitivity reflects the fact that refinement between values must hold in an arbitrary context of observation/usage—including contexts that freely copy the values in question—which means that we can assume nothing about privately-owned resources.

The context can interact with values of **reference type** by either reading from or writing to them at any time. Thus, references assert the existence of a simple *invariant* protocol with a single state, whose interpretation says that related locations must continuously point to related values. For **thread-local references**, the statement is qualified by indexing the storage table by related thread IDs.

The uses of $\triangleright$ throughout are necessary to ensure that recursive predicate variables α only occur in guarded positions. Note that island assertions are implicitly guarded, as are uses of $(e_I, e_S) \downarrow \varphi$ where e_I is not a value, because any α mentioned therein will not be interpreted until after a step of computation.

Finally, e_I is *logically related* to e_S at some context Ω and type τ if $\Omega \vdash e_I \preceq e_S : \tau$, which is shorthand for a use of the $\mathcal{C} \vdash P$ judgment of CaReSL. The proof context closes all type variables α with arbitrary type interpretations and all term variables x with *pairs* of term variables related at the appropriate types. Thus, a term with a free variable of type **ref** τ will gain access in its proof context to a shared invariant protocol governing the corresponding location. The protocol in turn forces updates to the reference in the implementation to occur in lock-step with those in the spec. *Private* references, *i.e.*, those allocated *within* the implementation or spec, face no such requirement—unless or until they are exposed.

Treiber's stack, with an iterator We now sketch a simple refinement proof. Figure 9 gives two stack implementations. The first, stack_S, is a coarse-grained reference implementation (which we think of as a specification). Its representation includes a mutable reference hd_S to an immutable list, as well as a synchronization wrapper sync provided by mkSync. The exported functions to push and pop from the stack simply wrap the corresponding updates to hd_S with synchronization. But the iterator is *not* fully synchronized: it takes an atomic snapshot of the stack, then calls its argument f on each element of the snapshot without holding any locks. So by the time f is called, the contents of the stack may have changed.

The second implementation, stack_I, is Treiber's stack supplemented with an iterator. Treiber's stack [28] is one of the simplest lock-free data structures—a kind of "Hello World" for concurrent program logics. Like stack_S, Treiber's stack maintains a reference hd_I to a list that it uses to represent the stack. Instead of using a lock, however, it updates hd_I directly (and atomically) using **CAS**, which requires the contents of hd_I to have a *comparable* type, *i.e.*, to be testable for pointer equality. Thus hd_I is of type **ref** clist(α), where $\mathsf{clist}(\alpha) \triangleq \mu\beta.\ \mathbf{ref}\ (\mathbf{1} + (\alpha \times \beta))$. The push and pop functions employ *optimistic concurrency*: instead of acquiring a lock to inform other threads that they are going to make a change, they just take a snapshot of the current hd_I, compute a new value, and use **CAS** to install the new value if the identity of the hd_I has not changed. Intuitively, this strategy works because if the hd_I's identity has not changed, then *nothing* about the stack has changed: *all* mutation is performed by identity-changing updates to hd_I. The iterator simply walks over the stack's contents starting from a (possibly stale!) snapshot of hd_I.

To prove that stack_I refines stack_S, we begin as follows:

$\mathsf{stack}_I \triangleq \Lambda.$ | **Prop context:** Type(α), $i \bowtie j$ **Variables:** α, i, j, κ |

$$\{j \Rightarrow_S \kappa[\mathsf{stack}_S\ \_]\}\ \ \mathbf{let}\ \mathsf{hd}_I = \mathbf{new}\ \mathsf{nil}$$
$$\{j \Rightarrow_S \kappa[\mathsf{stack}_S\ \_] * \exists x.\ \mathsf{hd}_I \hookrightarrow_I x * x \hookrightarrow_I \mathsf{none}\} \qquad (\textsc{ExecSpec})$$
$$\left\{\begin{array}{l}\exists\ \mathsf{hd}_S, \mathsf{lock}.\ \mathsf{hd}_S \hookrightarrow_S \mathsf{none} * \mathsf{lock} \hookrightarrow_S \mathbf{false} * j \Rightarrow_S \kappa[\mathsf{stack}'_S] * \\ \quad \exists x.\ \mathsf{hd}_I \hookrightarrow_I x * x \hookrightarrow_I \mathsf{none}\end{array}\right\}$$

We have executed the "preambles" of both the implementation and spec—the code that allocates their respective hidden state. (Let stack'_S denote the rest of the spec code after the **let**-binding of sync and hd_S.) At this point, we will use NEWISL to move *all* of this state into a hidden island, with a protocol that we can use when proving refinement for each exported function.

The states s of the protocol are maps $\text{Loc} \stackrel{\text{fin}}{\rightharpoonup} \text{Val}$ which simply record the identity and contents of every node added to stack_I. The transition relation $s \rightsquigarrow s' \triangleq s \subseteq s'$ captures the idea that, once a node has appeared in the stack, its contents never change. There are no tokens. We interpret a state s as follows:

$$\varphi \triangleq (s).\ \mathsf{lock} \hookrightarrow_S \mathbf{false} * \mathop{\LARGE\ast}_{\ell \in \mathrm{dom}(s)} \ell \hookrightarrow_I s(\ell)$$
$$* \ \exists x_I, x_S.\ \mathsf{hd}_I \hookrightarrow_I x_I * \mathsf{hd}_S \hookrightarrow_S x_S * \mathrm{Link}(s, x_I, x_S)$$

Because the lock is protected by the protocol, we can only execute the exported spec functions with AEXECSPEC, as part of an application of UPDISL; by stipulating $\mathsf{lock} \hookrightarrow_S \mathbf{false}$, the interpretation furthermore requires that we run the spec in "big steps", starting and ending in unlocked states. It also says that the implementation and spec stack contents are *linked*, in the following sense:

$$\mathrm{Link} \triangleq \mu p.\ (s, x_I, x_S).\ \exists x'_I, s'.\ s = [x_I \mapsto x'_I] \uplus s' *$$
$$(x'_I = \mathsf{none} * x_S = \mathsf{none}) \vee \left(\begin{array}{l}\exists y_I, z_I.\ x'_I = \mathsf{some}(y_I, z_I) * \\ \exists y_S, z_S.\ x_S = \mathsf{some}(y_S, z_S) * \\ (y_I, y_S) \in \alpha * \triangleright p(s', z_I, z_S)\end{array}\right)$$

Linking requires that the stack state s contain an entire linked list starting from hd_I, and that each element of the list be related (at type α) to the corresponding element of the list in hd_S. *But it does so without mentioning the heap at all!* This is the key: it means that $\mathrm{Link}(s, x_I, x_S) \Rightarrow \Box\mathrm{Link}(s, x_I, x_S)$, so the Link assertion can be freely copied in the proof for iter when the traversal begins. Since the abstract state s of the stack can only grow, all of the nodes mentioned in this "snapshot" of Link are guaranteed to still be available in the region of the heap governed by the protocol, with their original values, as traversal proceeds—even if, in the meantime, the nodes are no longer reachable from hd_I.

The full proof outlines are available in the appendix [30].

Combining refinement and Hoare-style reasoning Suppose a client of Treiber's stack wishes to use it only in a weak way, via a "per-item" spec similar to the one suggested in the introduction:

$$\mathrm{PerItem} \triangleq (e \in \mathrm{Expr}).\ \forall p, q \in \mathbb{P}(\mathrm{Val}).$$
$$(\forall x.\ \mathrm{TokPure}(p(x)) \land (p(x) \Rrightarrow \Box q(x))) \Rightarrow$$
$$\{\mathrm{True}\}\ e\ \{\mathsf{obj}.\ \mathsf{obj} = (\mathsf{add}, \mathsf{rem}, \mathsf{iter}) \land \Box P\}, \quad \textit{where}$$

$$P \triangleq \forall x.\ \{p(x)\}\ \mathsf{add}(x)\ \{\mathsf{ret}.\ \mathsf{ret} = ()\}$$
$$\land\ \{\mathrm{True}\}\ \mathsf{rem}()\ \{\mathsf{ret}.\ \mathsf{ret} = \mathsf{none} \lor (\exists x.\ \mathsf{ret} = \mathsf{some}(x) * p(\mathsf{ret}))\}$$
$$\land\ \forall f, r.\ (\forall x.\ \{q(x) * r\}\ f(x)\ \{r\}) \Rightarrow \{r\}\ \mathsf{iter}(f)\ \{r\}$$

This "per-item" spec associates a resource p with each element of the stack, which is transferred to and from the data structure when adding or removing elements. If, in addition, each per-item resource entails some permanent knowledge $\Box q$, then that knowledge can be safely assumed by a function concurrently iterating over the stack, even if the resources originally supporting it have been consumed. As we will see in the case study (§4), this spec for iteration is useful for associating permanent, token-free knowledge about some other protocol with each item that appears in the stack.

While the per-item spec could in principle be applied directly to Treiber's stack (*i.e.,* we could prove PerItem($\mathsf{stack}_\mathrm{I}$ _)), doing so would repeat much of the verification we just performed. On the other hand, proving PerItem($\mathsf{stack}_\mathrm{S}$ _) is nearly trivial: we just instantiate the spinlock spec given in §3.2 with the representation invariant $\mathrm{Rep}_p \triangleq \exists l.\ \mathsf{hd}_\mathrm{S} \hookrightarrow_\mathrm{I} l * \mathrm{Map}_p(l)$. To verify iter, we need only observe that $\mathrm{Map}_p(l) \Rrightarrow \Box\mathrm{Map}_q(l)$, *i.e.,* the snapshot of the stack provides a list of necessarily true associated facts. (The details are in the appendix [30].) By mixing refinement and Hoare logic, we can thus significantly modularize our verification effort.

3.4 Soundness

The model theory of CaReSL is based directly on the semantic model of Turon *et al.* [31], with minor adjustments to accommodate the assertions $\mathit{Tid}(i)$ and $i \bowtie j$ necessary for reasoning about thread-local storage. (Since this paper is focused on the complementary aim of giving a syntactic proof theory, we do not delve into the model here; it can be found in full in the appendix [30]).

Soundness for CaReSL encompasses two theorems. **First**, that $\mathcal{C} \vdash P$ implies $\mathcal{C} \models P$, where the latter is the semantic entailment relation of the model. Proving this theorem requires validating, in particular, the key Hoare logic rules, which we do in the appendix; these proofs resemble the proofs of key lemmas supporting Turon *et al.*'s model. **Second**, that $\cdot \vdash (\Omega \vdash e_\mathrm{I} \preceq e_\mathrm{S} : \tau)$ implies $\Omega \models e_\mathrm{I} \preceq e_\mathrm{S} : \tau$, *i.e.,* that the logical relation is sound for contextual refinement. Again, this proof follows the soundness proof of Turon *et al.*, except that we can carry it out at a much higher level of abstraction using CaReSL's proof rules.

4. Case study: Flat combining

Using CaReSL's combination of Hoare-style and refinement reasoning, we can verify higher-order concurrent algorithms in layers of abstraction—and this section shows how to do it.

We study the recent *flat combining* construction of Hendler *et al.* [11], which takes an arbitrary sequential data structure and transforms it into a concurrent one in which all operations appear to take effect atomically. One can do so by merely wrapping each operation with synchronization on a global lock—indeed, this is

```
flatS ≜ mkSync()   :   [∀α. ∀β. (α → β) → (α → β)]

flatI ≜ Λ[α]. Λ[β]. λf : [α → β].      (Annotated with types for clarity)
  let lock : [ref B] = new (false)
  let lclOps : [refLcl op] = newLcl            (where op ≜ ref (α + β))
  let (add, _, iter) = stackI [op]
  let install : [α → op] = λ req. case getLcl(lclOps)
    of some(o) ⇒ o := inj1 req; o
     | none ⇒ let o = new (inj1 req) in setLcl(lclOps, o); add(o); o
  let doOp : [op → 1] = λo. case get(o)
    of inj1 req ⇒ o := inj2 f(req)
     | inj2 res ⇒ ()
  in λx : [α]. let o = install(x)
               let rec loop() = case get(o)
                 of inj1 _  ⇒ if not(get lock) and tryAcq(lock) then
                                 iter doOp; rel(lock); loop()
                               else loop()
                  | inj2 res ⇒ res
               in oop()
```

Figure 10. Flat combining: Spec and implementation

what our *spec* does—but flat combining takes a cache-friendly approach intended for hard-to-parallelize data structures.

The basic idea is to allow concurrent threads to advertise, through a lock-free side channel, their intent to perform an operation on the data structure. One of the threads then becomes the *combiner*: it locks the data structure and services the requests of all the other threads, one at a time (though new requests may be published concurrently with the combiner's execution). The algorithm exhibits relatively good cache behavior for two reasons: (1) most of the time, operations do not need to execute *any* **CAS**es to complete and (2) the combining thread enjoys good cache locality when executing the operations of the sequential data structure. In practice, flat combining yields remarkably strong performance, even when compared against completely lock-free data structures.

The algorithm and its spec The flat combining algorithm was originally given as informal prose, so our first task is to formalize its implementation and find an appropriate spec, while making its higher-order structure explicit. We do so in Figure 10.

We model an "arbitrary sequential data structure" as a closure f of some type $\alpha \to \beta$, where α represents the input to an operation to be performed, β represents the result, and calling the function performs the operation by imperatively updating some state hidden within the closure. In other words, $\alpha \to \beta$ represents the type of an *object*. The goal of flat combining, then, is to wrap this object with (cache-efficient) synchronization. Its spec, flat_S, simply uses mkSync to provide generic synchronization via global locking.

Our flat combining implementation flat_I uses three data structures to control synchronization.[10] First, it uses a global lock to ensure that only one thread at a time acts as the combiner. Second, it uses a Treiber's stack to enable threads to *enroll* in the data structure. To enroll, a thread inserts an *operation record* of type **ref** $(\alpha + \beta)$, by which it can both advertise requests (of type α) and then await the results (of type β). The combiner performs these requests by iterating over the stack: for each record containing an $\mathbf{inj}_1$ req, it applies f to req, obtaining result res and updating the record to $\mathbf{inj}_2$ res. Finally, the thread-local reference lclOps allows threads to re-use their operation record once they have enrolled. Note that operation records can be added to the stack or reset from β to α at *any* time—even when the combiner holds the lock.

[10] This implementation simplifies Hendler *et al.*'s description in three respects: it uses a stack rather than a queue, operation records are never de-enrolled, and the combiner does not coalesce multiple operations into a single step. The first simplification makes little difference, because ultimately we give a modular proof using our per-item spec, which could be applied to a queue as well. The other two need only minor changes to the protocol.

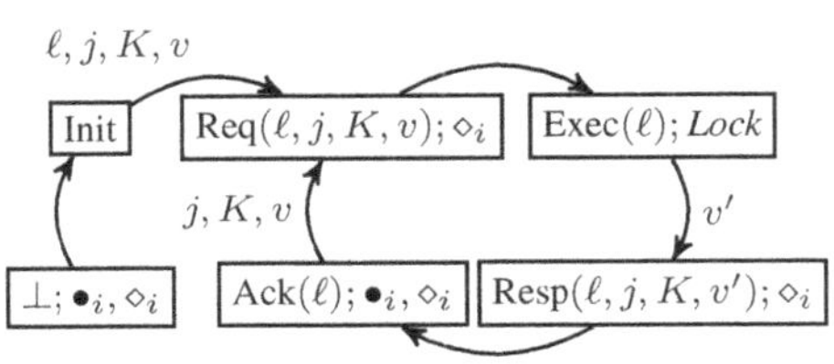

$$\begin{aligned}
[\![\text{Init}]\!]_i^L &\triangleq \mathit{Tid}(i) \\
[\![\text{Req}(\ell, j, \kappa, x_\text{I})]\!]_i^L &\triangleq L(i) = \ell * \ell \hookrightarrow_\text{I} \mathbf{inj}_1\ x_\text{I} * \mathit{Tid}(i) * \exists x_\text{S}.\ (x_\text{I}, x_\text{S}) \in \alpha * j \Rrightarrow_\text{S} \kappa[f'_\text{S}\ x_\text{S}] \\
[\![\text{Exec}(\ell)]\!]_i^L &\triangleq L(i) = \ell * \ell \hookrightarrow_\text{I} \mathbf{inj}_1\ - * \mathit{Tid}(i) \\
[\![\text{Resp}(\ell, j, \kappa, y_\text{I})]\!]_i^L &\triangleq L(i) = \ell * \ell \hookrightarrow_\text{I} \mathbf{inj}_2\ y_\text{I} * \mathit{Tid}(i) * \exists y_\text{S}.\ (y_\text{I}, y_\text{S}) \in \beta * j \Rrightarrow_\text{S} \kappa[y_\text{S}] \\
[\![\text{Ack}(\ell)]\!]_i^L &\triangleq L(i) = \ell * \ell \hookrightarrow_\text{I} \mathbf{inj}_2\ -
\end{aligned}$$

where $f'_\text{S} \triangleq \lambda x.\ \mathsf{acq}(\mathsf{lock}_\text{S}); \mathbf{let}\ r = f_\text{S}(x)\ \mathbf{in}\ \mathsf{rel}(\mathsf{lock}_\text{S});\ r$

Figure 11. The protocol for the operation record of thread i

Unfortunately, if we set out to prove the refinement

$$\cdot \vdash \mathsf{flat}_\text{I} \preceq \mathsf{flat}_\text{S} : \forall\alpha.\ \forall\beta.\ (\alpha \to \beta) \to (\alpha \to \beta)$$

we will run headlong into a problem: it does not hold! To wit: let

$$\begin{aligned} C \ \triangleq\ & \mathbf{let}\ r = \mathbf{newLcl},\ f = [\ ]\ \_\ \_\ (\lambda().\ \mathbf{getLcl}(r)) \\ & \mathbf{in}\ \mathbf{fork}\ (\mathbf{setLcl}(r, \mathbf{true});\ f());\quad \mathbf{setLcl}(r, \mathbf{false});\ f() \end{aligned}$$

When this context is applied to flat_S, it always returns $\mathsf{some}(\mathbf{false})$, because the final $f()$ is always executed on the thread whose local r is **false**. But when applied to flat_I, it can also return $\mathsf{some}(\mathbf{true})$: the forked thread might act as the combiner, performing *both* applications of f and thus using its own thread-local value for r.

The crux of the problem is that thread-local storage allows functions to observe the identity of the thread executing them. We need to rule out this kind of side effect. We do so by unrolling the definition of refinement for functions, and simply removing access to ID-related knowledge, leading to a *qualified refinement*:

$$\begin{aligned} & \forall\alpha, \beta, f_\text{I}, f_\text{S}. \\ & \quad \text{Type}(\alpha) \wedge \text{Type}(\beta) \wedge \Box(\forall(x_\text{I}, x_\text{S}) \in \alpha.\ (f_\text{I}\ x_\text{I}, f_\text{S}\ x_\text{S}) \downarrow^{\text{pure}} \beta) \\ & \quad \Rightarrow\ \cdot \vdash \mathsf{flat}_\text{I}\ \_\ \_\ f_\text{I} \preceq \mathsf{flat}_\text{S}\ \_\ \_\ f_\text{S} : \alpha \to \beta \end{aligned}$$

$$\begin{aligned} \text{where } (e_\text{I}, e_\text{S}) \downarrow^{\text{pure}} \varphi \ \triangleq\ & \forall i, j, \kappa. \\ & \{j \Rrightarrow_\text{S} \kappa[e_\text{S}]\}\ i \Rrightarrow e_\text{I}\ \{x_\text{I}.\ \exists x_\text{S}.\ \varphi(x_\text{I}, x_\text{S}) * j \Rrightarrow_\text{S} \kappa[x_\text{S}]\} \end{aligned}$$

This "pure" notion of related expressions embodies a semantic version of purity in a type-and-effect system where the only effect is "uses thread-local storage". It coincides *exactly* with the expression relation in Turon *et al.* [31], where thread-local storage was not present. It is easy to prove, using CaReSL, that for any well-typed $f : \tau \to \tau'$ that does not use thread-local storage (*i.e.,* an "effect-free" f) we have $\Box\forall(x_\text{I}, x_\text{S}) \in [\![\tau]\!].\ (f\ x_\text{I}, f\ x_\text{S}) \downarrow^{\text{pure}} [\![\tau']\!]$.

The protocol To prove the qualified refinement, we need to formulate a protocol characterizing the algorithm. We do so by giving a local protocol governing the operation record of each thread, and then tying these local protocols together into a single global one. Figure 11 gives the local protocol for a thread with ID i, where the states have the following informal meanings:

$\perp$	thread i has not yet created its operation record
Init	thread i is creating its operation record
Req	thread i has requested an operation be performed
Exec	the combiner is executing thread i's operation
Resp	thread i's operation has been completed
Ack	thread i has acknowledged the completion

The cycle in the protocol reflects that, once thread i has enrolled an operation record, it can reuse that record indefinitely. The labels on transitions signify *branching* on the values of the listed variables. Note that, while ℓ (the location of the operation record) is chosen arbitrarily during initialization, it must remain fixed thereafter.

Movement through the local protocol encompasses two roles: that of thread i, and that of the combiner. The protocol guarantees: (1) when thread i begins execution of the flat combining algorithm, the current state is either $\perp$ or Ack, meaning that either there is no operation record associated with the thread, or that the associated record is ready to be re-used; (2) only thread i can move to or from Init and Ack; and (3) only the combiner can move to or from Exec.

To fully understand how these constraints are enforced, we must take into account both the tokens and the state interpretations of the protocol. The tokens include $\bullet_i$ and $\diamond_i$ (one for each thread i, used only in i's local protocol) and a single global token *Lock* representing ownership of the combiner's lock.

The interpretations $[\![-]\!]_i^L$ of the non-$\perp$ states are shown in the figure; the parameter L represents the contents of lclOps. With the exception of $\perp$ and Ack, all states assert ownership of $\mathit{Tid}(i)$. On the other hand, when thread i begins executing the algorithm, *it* will have ownership of $\mathit{Tid}(i)$ (recall the definition of refinement, §3.3). Thus, thread i can assume that the protocol is in state $\perp$ or Ack—and only thread i can take a step away from these states. For thread i to take such a step, it must "prove" that it *is* thread i by giving up $\mathit{Tid}(i)$, but in return it gains the token $\bullet_i$ as a "receipt" that can later be traded back for $\mathit{Tid}(i)$ by moving (back) to Ack. All told, the ownership of $\mathit{Tid}(i)$ and the corresponding token $\bullet_i$ account for the first two of the guarantees listed above.

The third guarantee is achieved using a similar strategy: to move to the Exec state, the combiner must "prove" that it holds the lock by temporarily giving up the (global) *Lock* token, but it receives the (local) token $\diamond_i$ as a receipt. Subsequently, only the combiner can move to Resp, making the opposite trade.

After initialization, each state also asserts that the location ℓ of the operation record for thread i both corresponds to $L(i)$ and points to an appropriate sum injection (depending on the state).

A final aspect of the local protocol is capturing the *cooperation* inherent in flat combining: the combiner executes code on behalf of other threads. Cooperation is difficult for compositional refinement techniques to handle, because such techniques usually require proving that for *each piece* of implementation code the corresponding piece of spec code behaves the same way—and thus they typically provide no way to account for the *mismatch* between implementation and spec that cooperation entails. While our definition of refinement (§3.3) likewise imposes a one-to-one relationship between implementation and spec code in its pre- and post-conditions, our treatment of spec code as a resource allows ownership to be transferred to other threads *during* the execution of the implementation.

Thus, the Req and Resp states of our protocol assert *shared* ownership of i's spec code (running in spec thread j). In moving from Req to Exec the combiner thread must take ownership of the spec code $\kappa[f'_\text{S}\ x_\text{S}]$; and to subsequently move to Resp, the combiner must actually evaluate this code on thread i's behalf until $f'_\text{S}\ x_\text{S}$ reaches a value y_S. Subsequently, when moving to the Ack state, thread i regains ownership of both $\mathit{Tid}(i)$ *and* its spec code, by giving up its "receipt" token, $\bullet_i$.

The global transition system is then a *product construction*:

State space	$\left\{ (S, s) \;\middle|\; \begin{array}{l} S \in \mathbb{N} \overset{\text{fin}}{\rightharpoonup} \text{OpState},\quad s \in \text{LockState}, \\ \text{at most one } S(i) \text{ or } s \text{ owns } \mathit{Lock} \end{array} \right\}$
Transitions	$(S, s) \leadsto (S', s') \ \triangleq\ s \leadsto^?_{\text{lock}} s' \wedge \forall i.\ S(i) \leadsto^?_i S'(i)$
Owned tokens	$\mathcal{T}(S, s) \ \triangleq\ \mathcal{T}_{\text{lock}}(s) \cup \bigcup_i \mathcal{T}_i(S(i))$

A global state includes a collection S of local states from the operation record protocol (Figure 11), one for each thread ID. In giving the state space, we pun the $\perp$ state with an "undefined" input to a partial function—and thus, we require that only a finite number of threads i have a non-$\bot$ state in S. Global states also have a single state s drawn from the standard locking protocol (§3.2), reflecting the state of the global lock. The global *Lock* token is *shared* amongst all of the combined protocols: in a valid global state, at most one of the local states $S(i)$ or s may claim the *Lock* token. A transition in the global protocol allows each local protocol to make at most one transition. Finally, the tokens owned in a global state are just the union of all the tokens claimed by the local states.

Recall that in the refinement proof for Treiber's stack (§3.3), the spec lock is treated continuously as a protocol-owned resource with value **false**, capturing the atomicity of the implementation code: if an implementation step coincides with *any* spec steps, it must coincide with an entire critical section's worth, going from unlocked to unlocked spec states in big steps. The combiner implementation, by contrast, is executing a function f_I that is not necessarily atomic; all we know is that f_I refines f_S. We must therefore allow the spec lock to be held for multiple implementation steps, which we do by interpreting lock states as follows:

$$\begin{aligned} [\![\mathsf{Unlocked}]\!] &\triangleq \mathsf{lock} \hookrightarrow_\mathrm{I} \mathbf{false} * \mathsf{lock}_\mathrm{S} \hookrightarrow_\mathrm{S} \mathbf{false} \\ [\![\mathsf{Locked}]\!] &\triangleq \mathsf{lock} \hookrightarrow_\mathrm{I} \mathbf{true} \end{aligned}$$

In short, the combiner gains private ownership of both the *Lock* token and the spec lock itself (*i.e.,* the internal lock used by mkSync; see f'_S in Figure 11) when it acquires the implementation lock.

Finally, we lift these local interpretations to interpret global states via the following predicate:

$$(S, s).\ [\![s]\!] * \exists L.\ \mathsf{lclOps} \hookrightarrow_\mathrm{I} L * \mathop{\ast}_{i \in \mathrm{dom}(S)} [\![S(i)]\!]^L_i$$

The proof We close with a high-level view of the proof itself; details, as usual, are in the appendix. Unrolling the statement of qualified refinement, we need to prove

$$\{\mathit{Tid}(i) * j \Rrightarrow_\mathrm{S} K[\mathsf{flat}_\mathrm{S}\ \_\ \_\ f_\mathrm{S}]\}\quad i \Rrightarrow \mathsf{flat}_\mathrm{I}\ \_\ \_\ f_\mathrm{I}$$
$$\{x_\mathrm{I}.\ \exists x_\mathrm{S}.\ (x_\mathrm{I}, x_\mathrm{S}) \in [\![\alpha \to \beta]\!] * \mathit{Tid}(i) * j \Rrightarrow_\mathrm{S} K[x_\mathrm{S}]\}$$

under the assumptions

$$i \bowtie j,\ \ \mathrm{Type}(\alpha),\ \ \mathrm{Type}(\beta),\ \ \Box(\forall (x_\mathrm{I}, x_\mathrm{S}) \in \alpha.(f_\mathrm{I}\ x_\mathrm{I}, f_\mathrm{S}\ x_\mathrm{S}) \downarrow^{\mathrm{pure}} \beta)$$

The proof begins in much the same way as the refinement proof for Treiber's stack (§3.3): we execute the **let**-bound expressions that allocate the hidden state in both the implementation and spec, *i.e.,*

$$\mathsf{lock} \hookrightarrow_\mathrm{I} \mathbf{false} * \mathsf{lclOps} \hookrightarrow_\mathrm{I} \emptyset * \exists\ \mathsf{lock}_\mathrm{S}.\ j \Rrightarrow_\mathrm{S} K[f'_\mathrm{S}] * \mathsf{lock}_\mathrm{S} \hookrightarrow_\mathrm{S} \mathbf{false}$$

where lock_S is the lock allocated by mkSync and f'_S is as in Figure 11. These resources are precisely what we need to apply NEWISL for our global protocol, moving them from private to shared ownership. Letting π be the global protocol defined above, we can claim $\Box\ \boxed{(\emptyset, \mathsf{Unlocked}); \emptyset}^n_\pi$, *i.e.,* permanent knowledge that the global protocol exists. We must then, in the context of this island and our previous assumptions, show that the closure returned by flat_I refines the one returned by flat_S, *i.e.,* f'_S, at type $\alpha \to \beta$.

We first verify a version $\mathsf{flat}'_\mathrm{I}$ of the flat combining algorithm that is identical to the one in Figure 10, except that it uses the coarse-grained stack, allowing us to use the per-item spec of §3.3. We instantiate the per-item spec using the same predicate Op for per-item resources and iteration knowledge (p and q, respectively, in the per-item spec): $\mathrm{Op} \triangleq (\ell).\ \exists k.\ \boxed{[k \mapsto \mathrm{Req}(\ell, -, -, -)]}^n_\pi$.[11] This is a *local* assertion about the global protocol, in that the states of threads other than k can be in any rely-future state of $\bot$, *i.e.,* any state whatsoever. The Op predicate just claims that location ℓ is an initialized operation record for *some* thread. By the per-item spec, all locations inserted into the stack must satisfy this property—and since we have $\mathrm{Op}(\ell) \Rightarrow \Box\mathrm{Op}(\ell)$, the property can be assumed even when iterating over stale elements of the stack. Operation records are created via install, whose specification consumes $\mathit{Tid}(i)$ and associated spec resources in exchange for the "receipt" $\bullet_i$:

$$\{\mathit{Tid}(i) * j \Rrightarrow_\mathrm{S} K[f'_\mathrm{S}\ x_\mathrm{S}]\}\ i \Rrightarrow \mathsf{install}\ x \left\{o.\ \boxed{[i \mapsto \mathrm{Req}(o, j, K, x)]; \bullet_i}^n_\pi\right\}$$

[11] We leave off the locking state when it is Unlocked.

for any $(x, x_\mathrm{S}) \in \alpha$ (*i.e.,* for any related arguments). The combiner actually performs operations via doOp,

$$\{\mathrm{Op}(o) * P\}\ \mathsf{doOp}\ o\ \{P\} \quad \text{where} \quad P \triangleq \boxed{\emptyset; \mathit{Lock}}^n_\pi * \mathsf{lock}_\mathrm{S} \hookrightarrow_\mathrm{S} \mathbf{false}$$

which assumes that the given location o is a valid operation record, and that the invoking thread owns the *Lock* token as well as the spec lock. The shape of the spec for doOp exactly matches that required for iteration in the per-item spec (§3.3), with P serving as the loop invariant, thus allowing us to deduce $\{P\}$ iter doOp $\{P\}$. These auxiliary specs make it straightforward to prove refinement for the closures returned by $\mathsf{flat}'_\mathrm{I}$ (with coarse-grained stack) and flat_S.

Finally, suppose we plug the combiner into a client context C that provides a suitable argument f. The above proof (together with soundness, §3.4) allows us to deduce $\models C[\mathsf{flat}'_\mathrm{I}] \preceq C[\mathsf{flat}_\mathrm{S}] : \tau$. Likewise, refinement for Treiber's stack allows us to deduce $\models C[\mathsf{flat}_\mathrm{I}] \preceq C[\mathsf{flat}'_\mathrm{I}] : \tau$. Since refinement is *transitive*, we can compose these together to conclude $\models C[\mathsf{flat}_\mathrm{I}] \preceq C[\mathsf{flat}_\mathrm{S}] : \tau$.[12]

5. Related work

In many respects, CaReSL builds directly on the semantic foundation that we and colleagues laid in our prior work [31]. There, we developed a relational Kripke model of a language very similar to the one considered here, and showed how granularity abstraction for several sophisticated (but structurally simple) fine-grained data structures could be established by direct appeal to the model. The present work is a natural continuation of that work. First, we provide a *logic* that greatly simplifies reasoning compared to working with the model; such a proof theory is essential for scaling the verification method to large examples. Second, we use our logic not just to prove granularity abstraction results in isolation (as we did before), but also to facilitate the modular verification of a higher-order, structurally complex program. Along the way, we also extend our prior model to handle thread-local storage.

The logic itself draws inspiration from LADR [5], which in turn provided a proof theory for reasoning about a *sequential* relational Kripke model (ADR [1]). Aside from incorporating concurrency, CaReSL offers a deeper unification of refinement and Hoare logic by treating refinement as a mode of use of Hoare logic.

Higher-order functions and concurrency While there has been stunning progress in logics for concurrency over the last decade, very few of these logics meaningfully support *higher-order* programming, and among those that do, none supports reasoning about fine-grained synchronization or granularity abstraction.

The logic that comes closest is *higher-order concurrent abstract predicates* (HOCAP), first proposed for reasoning about first-order code [4] (the "higher-order" refers to the logic of predicates) and very recently applied to higher-order code as well [27]. HOCAP, like its predecessor CAP [3], accounts for concurrency by way of "shared region" assertions that constrain the possible updates to a shared resource. Our island assertions resemble shared region assertions—indeed, we have adopted notation suggesting as much—but work at a higher level of abstraction (*i.e.,* protocol states), separating *knowledge* bounding the state of the protocol (treated as a copyable assertion) from the *rights* to change the state (treated as a linear resource: tokens); see [31] for a more detailed comparison. Because CAP lacks granularity abstraction, it is difficult to give a single "principal" specification for a data structure. Instead, one gives specialized specs (like the per-item spec for stacks) reflecting particular usages envisioned for a client—which means new client scenarios necessitate new proofs. HOCAP attempts to

[12] We are appealing to *semantic* refinement here to take advantage of transitivity. This reasoning can be internalized in CaReSL by adding a proposition for semantic refinement and axioms for refinement soundness and transitivity, but there is little to be gained from doing so.

address this shortcoming by explicitly quantifying over the way a client uses a data structure, but (1) this introduces the potential for a problematic circularity, which clients must explicitly prove does not arise, and (2) it is not clear how to scale the approach to handle *cooperation* between threads (as in the flat combiner).

Other concurrency logics that support higher-order functions—such as Hobor *et al.*'s extension of concurrent separation logic [14], or the very recent *Subjective Concurrent Separation Logic* [17]—support only reasoning about simple lock-based synchronization, and do not enable the kinds of refinement proofs we have presented.

Granularity abstraction Herlihy and Wing's seminal notion of *linearizability* [13] has long been held as the gold standard of correctness for concurrent data structures, but as Filipović *et al.* argue [8], what clients of these data structures *really* want is a contextual refinement property. Filipović *et al.* go on to show that, under certain (strong) assumptions about a programming language, linearizability implies contextual refinement for that language. More recently, Gotsman and Yang generalized both linearizability and Filipović *et al.*'s result (the so-called *abstraction theorem*) to include potential ownership transfer of memory between concurrent data structures and their clients in a first-order setting [9]. While in principle proofs of linearizability can be composed with these results to support granularity abstraction, no existing logic has provided support for doing so. We found it simpler to work with refinement directly (in particular, to *encode* it directly into a Hoare logic), rather than reasoning about linearizability. CaReSL enables clients to layer ownership-transferring protocols *on top* of a coarse-grained reference implementation, *after* applying granularity abstraction, as we showed with the per-item spec (§3.3).

The only Hoare logic we are aware of that can (formally) prove refinement results is Liang and Feng's new logic [18] (extending LRG [7]), which is inspired by the use of ghost state in Vafeiadis's thesis [32]. The logic is powerful enough to deal with a range of sophisticated, fine-grained concurrent algorithms, but it is limited to *first-order* code. In addition, the specifications used in refinement are not reference implementations, but are instead essentially atomic Hoare triples. While such specifications are appealingly abstract, they present two limitations: (1) they do not model the more general notion of granularity abstraction (supporting only *atomicity* abstraction, as we explained in footnote 1) and (2) they do not support the kind of transitive composition of proofs that we used in our case study. As a result, it is unclear how to use the logic to build modular proofs layering Hoare logic and refinement.

A radically different approach to atomicity abstraction is Lipton's method of *reduction* [19], which is based on showing that an atomic step *commutes* with all concurrent activity, and can therefore be coalesced into a larger atomic block with *e.g.,* code that is sequenced after it. Elmas *et al.* developed a logic for proving linearizability via a combination of reduction and abstraction [6], which in some ways resembles our interleaved application of refinement and Hoare-style reasoning, but with a rather different way of *proving* refinement. It is limited, however, to first-order code and atomicity refinement, and like HOCAP it is not powerful enough to handle fine-grained algorithms that employ cooperation. Moreover, it does not allow linearizability proofs to be composed transitively.

Acknowledgments We would like to thank David Swasey for his careful reading of both the paper and its appendix. This work was partially funded by the EC FET project ADVENT.

References

[1] A. Ahmed, D. Dreyer, and A. Rossberg. State-dependent representation independence. In *POPL*, 2009.

[2] R. D. Blumofe, C. F. Joerg, B. C. Kuszmaul, C. E. Leiserson, K. H. Randall, and Y. Zhou. Cilk: An efficient multithreaded runtime system. *JPDC*, 37(1):55–69, Aug. 1996.

[3] T. Dinsdale-Young, M. Dodds, P. Gardner, M. Parkinson, and V. Vafeiadis. Concurrent abstract predicates. In *ECOOP*, 2010.

[4] M. Dodds, S. Jagannathan, and M. Parkinson. Modular reasoning for deterministic parallelism. In *POPL*, 2011.

[5] D. Dreyer, G. Neis, A. Rossberg, and L. Birkedal. A relational modal logic for higher-order stateful ADTs. In *POPL*, 2010.

[6] T. Elmas, S. Qadeer, A. Sezgin, O. Subasi, and S. Tasiran. Simplifying linearizability proofs with reduction and abstraction. In *TACAS*, 2010.

[7] X. Feng. Local rely-guarantee reasoning. In *POPL*, 2009.

[8] I. Filipović, P. O'Hearn, N. Rinetzky, and H. Yang. Abstraction for concurrent objects. *Theoretical Computer Science*, 411, 2010.

[9] A. Gotsman and H. Yang. Linearizability with ownership transfer. In *CONCUR*, 2012.

[10] T. Harris, S. Marlow, S. Peyton-Jones, and M. Herlihy. Composable memory transactions. In *PPOPP*, 2005.

[11] D. Hendler, I. Incze, N. Shavit, and M. Tzafrir. Flat combining and the synchronization-parallelism tradeoff. In *SPAA*, 2010.

[12] D. Hendler, N. Shavit, and L. Yerushalmi. A scalable lock-free stack algorithm. In *SPAA*, 2004.

[13] M. P. Herlihy and J. M. Wing. Linearizability: a correctness condition for concurrent objects. *TOPLAS*, 12(3):463–492, 1990.

[14] A. Hobor, A. W. Appel, and F. Z. Nardelli. Oracle semantics for concurrent separation logic. In *ESOP*, 2008.

[15] C. B. Jones. Tentative steps toward a development method for interfering programs. *TOPLAS*, 5(4):596–619, 1983.

[16] D. Lea. The java.util.concurrent ConcurrentHashMap.

[17] R. Ley-Wild and A. Nanevski. Subjective auxiliary state for coarse-grained concurrency. In *POPL*, 2013.

[18] H. Liang and X. Feng. Modular verification of linearizability with non-fixed linearization points. In *PLDI*, 2013.

[19] R. J. Lipton. Reduction: a method of proving properties of parallel programs. *Commun. ACM*, 18(12):717–721, 1975.

[20] P. W. O'Hearn. Resources, concurrency, and local reasoning. *Theor. Comput. Sci.*, 375(1-3):271–307, 2007.

[21] M. Parkinson and G. Bierman. Separation logic and abstraction. In *POPL*, 2005.

[22] A. M. Pitts and I. Stark. Operational reasoning for functions with local state. In *HOOTS*, 1998.

[23] G. Plotkin and M. Abadi. A logic for parametric polymorphism. In *TLCA*, 1993.

[24] F. Pottier. Hiding local state in direct style: a higher-order anti-frame rule. In *LICS*, 2008.

[25] J. H. Reppy. *Higher-order concurrency*. PhD thesis, Cornell University, 1992.

[26] J. C. Reynolds. Separation logic: A logic for shared mutable data structures. In *LICS*, 2002.

[27] K. Svendsen, L. Birkedal, and M. Parkinson. Modular reasoning about separation of concurrent data structures. In *ESOP*, 2013.

[28] R. Treiber. Systems programming: coping with parallelism. Technical report, Almaden Research Center, 1986.

[29] P. W. Trinder, K. Hammond, H.-W. Loidl, and S. L. Peyton Jones. Algorithm + strategy = parallelism. *JFP*, 8(1):23–60, Jan. 1998.

[30] A. Turon, D. Dreyer, and L. Birkedal. Unifying refinement and Hoare-style reasoning in a logic for higher-order concurrency: Appendix. `http://www.mpi-sws.org/~turon/caresl/appendix.pdf`.

[31] A. Turon, J. Thamsborg, A. Ahmed, L. Birkedal, and D. Dreyer. Logical relations for fine-grained concurrency. In *POPL*, 2013.

[32] V. Vafeiadis. *Modular fine-grained concurrency verification*. PhD thesis, University of Cambridge, 2008.

[33] H. Yang. Relational separation logic. *TCS*, 375(1-3):308–334, 2007.

The Bedrock Structured Programming System

Combining Generative Metaprogramming and Hoare Logic in an Extensible Program Verifier

Adam Chlipala
MIT CSAIL
adamc@csail.mit.edu

Abstract

We report on the design and implementation of an extensible programming language and its intrinsic support for formal verification. Our language is targeted at low-level programming of infrastructure like operating systems and runtime systems. It is based on a cross-platform core combining characteristics of assembly languages and compiler intermediate languages. From this foundation, we take literally the saying that C is a "macro assembly language": we introduce an expressive notion of *certified low-level macros*, sufficient to build up the usual features of C and beyond as macros with no special support in the core. Furthermore, our macros have integrated support for strongest postcondition calculation and verification condition generation, so that we can provide a high-productivity formal verification environment within Coq for programs composed from any combination of macros. Our macro interface is expressive enough to support features that low-level programs usually only access through external tools with no formal guarantees, such as declarative parsing or SQL-inspired querying. The abstraction level of these macros only imposes a *compile-time* cost, via the execution of functional Coq programs that compute programs in our intermediate language; but the *run-time* cost is not substantially greater than for more conventional C code. We describe our experiences constructing a full C-like language stack using macros, with some experiments on the verifiability and performance of individual programs running on that stack.

Categories and Subject Descriptors F.3.1 [*Logics and meanings of programs*]: Mechanical verification; D.3.4 [*Programming Languages*]: Compilers

Keywords generative metaprogramming; interactive proof assistants; low-level programming languages; functional programming

1. Introduction

A fundamental tension in programming language design is between performance and abstraction. Closer to the high-performance end of the spectrum, we have languages like C, which are often used to implement low-level infrastructure that many applications depend on. Examples include operating systems and runtime systems, which today are almost exclusively written in C and its close relatives.

ICFP '13, September 25–27, 2013, Boston, MA, USA.
ACM 978-1-4503-2326-0/13/09.
http://dx.doi.org/10.1145/2500365.2500592

Need we always choose between performance and abstraction? One approach to retaining both is *metaprogramming*, from basic cases of textual macro substitution as in the C preprocessor, to sophisticated code generators like Yacc. Here we employ abstractions that in a sense are *compile-time only*, running programs that generate programs in C or other low-level languages. As a result, we incur no run-time cost to abstraction.

Unfortunately, code generation is hard to get right. The C preprocessor's textual substitution mechanism allows for all sorts of scoping errors in macro definitions. There exist widely used alternatives, like the macro systems of Lisp/Scheme, OCaml (Camlp4), and Haskell (Template Haskell), which can enforce "hygiene" requirements on lexical scoping in macro definitions.

The functional programming community knows well the advantages of code generation with languages like Haskell and ML as *metalanguages* for *embedded domain-specific languages (DSLs)*. That is, one represents the programs of some object language, like C or CUDA, as data within the metalanguage, making it possible to compute programs of the object language *at compile time* using all of the abstraction features of the metalanguage.

There is a tower of static assurance levels for this kind of generative metaprogramming. Tools like Yacc receive little static assurance from their implementation languages, as they output source code as strings that the implementation language does not analyze. Conventional macro systems, from primitive token substitution in C to hygienic Scheme macros, can provide stronger *lexical* guarantees. Next in the tower are languages that allow for *static typing* of macros, guaranteeing that any of their applications produce both scope-safe and type-safe object-language code. Languages in this category include MetaML [30] and MacroML [13], for *homogeneous* metaprogramming where the meta and object languages are the same; and MetaHaskell [22], for *heterogeneous* metaprogramming where meta and object languages are different (e.g., Haskell and CUDA). Our contribution in this paper is to continue higher up this tower of static guarantees: we support separate static checking of macros to guarantee that *they always produce functionally correct object-language code*.

The programming language and associated verification tools will need to provide a *proof rule* for each macro. A naive proof rule just expands macro applications using their definitions, providing no abstraction benefit. We could ask instead that *macro definitions include proof rules*, and that the verification system requires programmers to *prove that their macro definitions respect the associated proof rules*. In effect, we have a macro system supporting modularity in the style of well-designed functions, classes, or libraries, with clear separation between implementation and interface.

In this paper, we report on our experiences building such a macro system for a low-level language, intended as a replacement for C in the systems programming domain. This macro system is part of the Bedrock library for the Coq proof assistant, which provides an integrated environment for program implementation, specification, and verification. A prior publication [8] introduced Bedrock's support for proof automation, implementing example programs using an earlier version of our macro system but not describing it in detail. Since that paper was written, the macro system has evolved, and we have used it to implement more interesting examples. We now present its design and implementation in detail, along with the higher-level language design principle that motivates it.

Our metalanguage is Gallina, the functional programming language in Coq's logic. Our object language is a tiny compiler intermediate language. We build up the usual features of C via unprivileged macros, and then we go further and implement features like *declarative parsing* and *declarative querying of data structures* as macros rather than ad-hoc external tools like Yacc and MySQL.

To support productive formal verification, we tag each macro with a *proof rule*. To be more precise, each macro contains a *predicate transformer*, which evolves a logical assertion to reflect the effects of a program statement; and a *verification condition generator*, which outputs proof obligations associated with a use of the macro. These are some of the standard tools of highly automated program verification, and requiring them of all macros lets us build a generic verification environment that supports automated proofs about programs built with macros drawn from diverse sources. We call the central abstraction **certified low-level macros**.

Our implementations and proofs have much in common with compiler verification. For instance, CompCert [21] is a C compiler implemented in Coq with a proof that it preserves program semantics. Each of our macro implementations looks like one case of the CompCert compiler, dealing with a specific source language syntax construct, paired with the corresponding correctness proof cases. A specific program may draw upon several macros implemented by different programmers, who never considered how their macros might interact. The proof approach from CompCert does not extend straightforwardly to this setting, since each CompCert subproof refers to one or more *simulation* relations between the programs of different fixed languages. It is not apparent how such an approach could be extended to verify compilation rules for extensible languages. For instance, in that conventional setting, function pointers may be specified informally as "points to the code our compiler would generate from the corresponding source-level function body," an explanation that does not adapt naturally to the case of an extensible compiler. We would rather not verify handling of function pointers relative to a particular set of available macros.

The key selling point of compile-time metaprogramming is *performance*. Programmers will come up with different code constructs that mimic those available in higher-level programming languages, but implemented in a way that facilitates case-specific optimization and in general promotes performance. We are able to attach specifications to such macros in a way that makes reasoning about use of a macro more like reasoning about a function call than reasoning directly about low-level code after macro expansion.

At a high level, then, our contribution can be viewed alternatively as *an extensible programming language* or *an extensible Hoare-logic program verifier*. We present **the first low-level language with a notion of macros that cleanly separates interface and implementation, to such an extent as to enable mostly automated correctness verification without macro expansion**. We prove correctness theorems within a framework for *modular verification*, where we can verify libraries separately and then link together their correctness theorems into whole-program correctness theorems, without revisiting details of code implementation or proof. This modularity holds even in the presence of a mutable heap that may hold callable code pointers, thanks to the XCAP [26] program logic that sits at the base of our framework.

Constants	c	::=	[width-32 bitvectors]
Code labels	ℓ	::=	...
Registers	r	::=	$\mathsf{Sp} \mid \mathsf{Rp} \mid \mathsf{Rv}$
Addresses	a	::=	$r \mid c \mid r + c$
Lvalues	L	::=	$r \mid [a]_8 \mid [a]_{32}$
Rvalues	R	::=	$L \mid c \mid \ell$
Binops	o	::=	$+ \mid - \mid \times$
Tests	t	::=	$= \mid \neq \mid < \mid \leq$
Instructions	i	::=	$L \leftarrow R \mid L \leftarrow R \; o \; R$
Jumps	j	::=	$\mathsf{goto}\ R \mid \mathsf{if}\ (R\ t\ R)\ \mathsf{then}\ \ell\ \mathsf{else}\ \ell$
Specs	S	::=	...
Blocks	B	::=	$\ell : \{S\}\ i^*; j$
Modules	M	::=	B^*

Figure 1. Syntax of the Bedrock IL

The remaining sections of this paper will walk through the steps of building our stack of macros. We begin with a tiny assembly-like language and proceed to introduce our notion of certified low-level macros for it, build macros for basic C-like constructs, add support for local variables and function calls, and culminate in the high-level macros for declarative parsing and querying. Next we evaluate the effectiveness of our platform in terms of program verifiability and run-time performance, and we finish with a comparison to related work.

Source code to both the Bedrock library and our example programs is available in the latest Bedrock source distribution at:

`http://plv.csail.mit.edu/bedrock/`

2. The Bedrock IL

The lowest layer of Bedrock is a simple intermediate language inspired by common assembly languages. This Bedrock IL is easy to compile to those "real" languages, using only localized replacement of IL concepts with assembly language constructs. A single verification result applies to all target architectures. So far, we have built a compiler to AMD64 assembly (currently unverified), and we expect it will be easy to implement sound translations to other popular architectures like ARM and 32-bit x86.

Figure 1 gives the full syntax of the Bedrock IL. There are small finite sets of registers, addressing modes (for both 8-bit and 32-bit memory accesses), and forms of lvalues and rvalues (borrowing C terminology). Straightline instructions do assignment or arithmetic, and jump instructions do unconditional branching or branching based on the result of an arithmetic comparison. A standalone code module is a set of basic blocks, each with a code label and a specification.

Bedrock is based on the XCAP program logic [26] of Ni and Shao, and block specifications use the XCAP assertion language, which supports a limited form of higher-order logic tailored to reasoning about first-class code pointers. A module is *correct* when every one of its blocks satisfies two conditions:

- *Progress*: When control enters the block in a machine state satisfying the spec, control continues safely at least until the end of the block.

- *Preservation*: When control enters the block in a machine state satisfying the spec and exits the block by jumping to some other block, the spec of the new block is satisfied.

In this way, we can construct an inductive proof of infinite safe execution, giving us *memory safety*. Further, we may also treat each block spec as an *assertion*, so that we verify absence of assertion failures, giving us *functional correctness*. XCAP supports separate verification and linking of modules, via mechanisms that we will not go into here, but we do want to emphasize that XCAP supports *modular verification*, where libraries can be verified separately in a way that permits composition of their correctness theorems to conclude whole-program theorems. It is not trivial to design a framework that permits such modular proof rules in the presence of a mutable higher-order heap, where code from one module might find in the heap a pointer to code from another module written and verified independently. Building on XCAP enables us to realize this level of modularity without doing much explicit extra work.

What does it mean for a Bedrock IL program to be *safe*? There are two sorts of bad instruction executions that violate safety. First, a jump to a nonexistent code label is illegal. Second, a Bedrock IL program is restricted to read or write only memory addresses allowed by a configurable *memory policy*.

These informal notions are codified in a conventional Coq operational semantics. We support sound compilation to a variety of assembly languages by considering machine states to contain a read-only component describing the byte ordering of words in memory, with enough expressiveness to describe little-endian, big-endian, and other orders. As a result, we can work with a trivial "array of bytes" memory model, rather than the more complex memory model used in, e.g., the informal ANSI C semantics and the closely related formal semantics of CompCert [21]. The simplistic memory model we adopt makes it difficult to reason about many standard program transformations and optimizations, but we still achieve reasonable performance with an optimizer-free implementation (see Section 6).

There is a great benefit to starting from a language with such a simple semantics. Our final platform is *foundational*, in the sense that we produce formal proofs that can be checked and audited with relatively small trusted code bases. We need to trust the Coq proof checker and its dependencies, which can be made small compared to program verifiers in general. Beyond that, we must make sure that the statement of the theorem we prove matches our informal notion of program safety or correctness. The theorems that come out of our system are stated only in terms of the Bedrock IL operational semantics, which is quite small and easy to audit. Most importantly in the context of this paper, the final theorem statements are independent of any details of our macro system.

A final foundational theorem will be of the form "if execution begins at code address ℓ_1 in a state satisfying the spec of ℓ_1, then if execution ever reaches code address ℓ_2, the spec of ℓ_2 will be satisfied." In the sections that follow, we will introduce convenient notations not just for programs, but also for specifications; for instance, see the notation for specifying functions with local variables in Section 4. If such a notation appears in a final correctness theorem, then its definition must be considered part of the trusted base. However, we are able to prove final theorems that reduce our notations to simpler concepts. For instance, while we may verify the `main()` function of a program against a precondition-postcondition-style specification inspired by separation logic [28], the final theorem statement need only say that `main()` requires "all memory addresses between 0 and N are allowed by the memory access policy." We prove that the latter implies the former, and so a final audit of a verified program need only ensure that the latter is accurate.

```
Definition appendS : spec := SPEC("x", "y") reserving 2
  Al ls1, Al ls2,
  PRE[V] sll ls1 (V "x") * sll ls2 (V "y")
  POST[R] sll (ls1 ++ ls2) R.

bfunction "append"("x", "y", "r", "tmp") [appendS]
  If ("x" = 0) {
    Return "y"
  } else {
    "r" ← "x";;
    "tmp" ←* "x" + 4;;
    [Al p1, Al x, Al ls1, Al ls2,
      PRE[V] ⌈ V "x" ≠ $0 ⌉ * ⌈ V "tmp" = p1 ⌉ * V "x" ↦ x
        * (V "x" ^+ $4) ↦ p1 * sll ls1 p1 * sll ls2 (V "y")
      POST[R] ⌈ R = V "r" ⌉ * sll (x :: ls1 ++ ls2) (V "x") ]
    While ("tmp" ≠ 0) {
      "x" ← "tmp";;
      "tmp" ←* "x" + 4
    };;

    "x" + 4 *← "y";;
    Return "r"
  }
end
```

Figure 2. Bedrock implementation of destructive list append

3. Certified Low-Level Macros

Bedrock's structured programming system uses macros to present a C-like view of the Bedrock IL. Figure 2 shows an example, a destructive linked-list append function, beginning with its formal specification, whose explanation we put off until later. The body of the implementation uses standard control flow constructs like `if` and `while` to group together sequences of operations on local variables, which are named with string literals to appease Coq's lexer. (In this paper, we never use a string literal for its more conventional purpose in C-like code, so it is safe to assume that literals indicate object-language identifiers.) A token $\leftarrow *$ indicates a memory read operation, while $*\leftarrow$ indicates a write. A *loop invariant* appears within square brackets. We will have a bit more to say later about the language of specifications and invariants, though it is not our focus in this paper, as our architecture applies to other specification languages, too.

For now, the take-away message from Figure 2 is that it denotes *a Coq program for computing an assembly program*, in the style of heterogeneous generative metaprogramming. None of the control flow constructs are built into the language, but rather they use macros that any Bedrock programmer can define without modifying the library. We also want to prove that the computed assembly program is correct. Programming, compilation, and proving are all done completely within the normal Coq environment.

We will introduce our central concept of macro in two stages. First we introduce the aspects needed to support compilation of programs, and then we add the features to support verification.

3.1 The Code Generation Part of a Macro

In our setting, a macro stands for a *statement* in the sense of C-like languages. To make sense of this concept, we must impose a notion of *structured programs* on top of the freeform control flow of the Bedrock IL.

Figure 3 summarizes such an interface. The fundamental task of a macro is to *mutate a program by appending new basic blocks to it*. Successive blocks are assigned successive numeric labels. To run a macro, it must be passed one input: the *exit label* of the block its statement should jump to when finished. This label will have

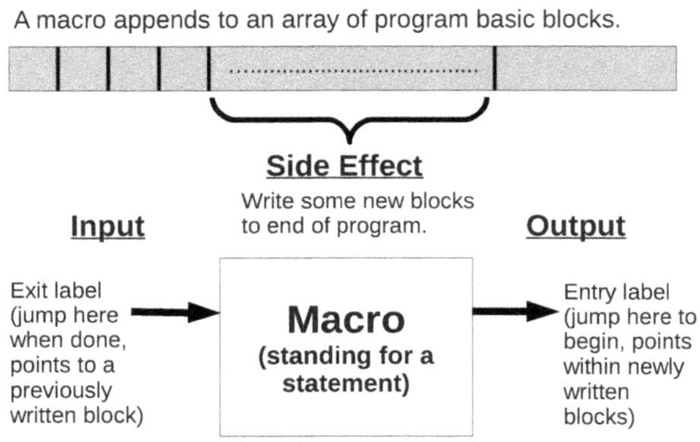

Figure 3. The interface of a low-level macro

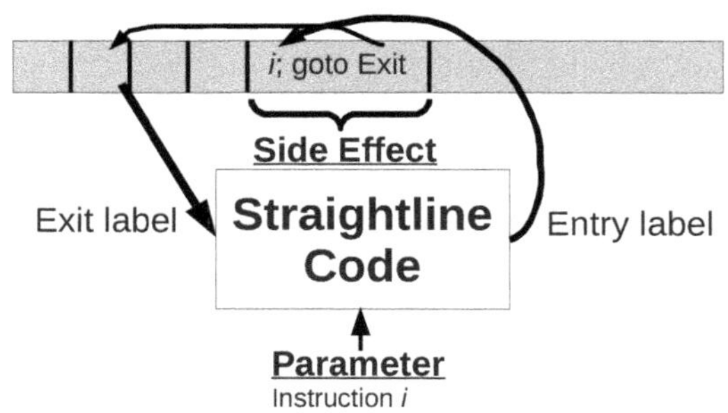

Figure 4. Sketch of macro for single straightline instructions

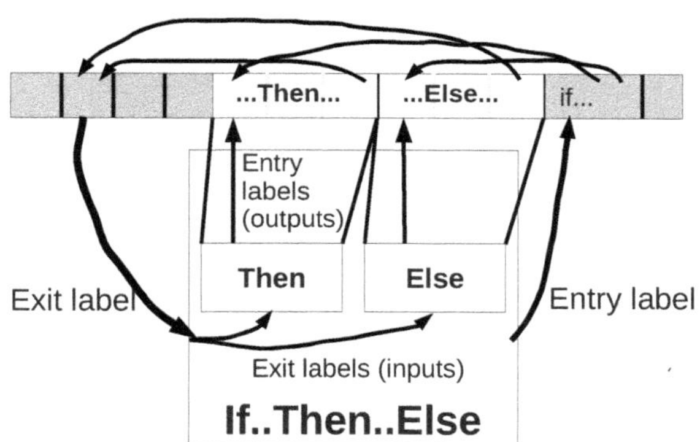

Figure 5. Sketch of macro for if..then..else

been allocated previously by other macros. A macro runs by not only creating new basic blocks, but also returning one more value: an *entry label* within the freshly generated code blocks. A macro's statement is run by jumping to the entry label.

Consider the very basic example of a macro for converting a straightline IL instruction into a statement. Figure 4 sketches a simple implementation. Macros are implemented as functional programs in Coq's logic, so it is natural to think of them as *statement combinators*. The straightline code combinator takes an instruction i as its parameter. When run, the macro allocates a single block, consisting of i followed by a direct jump to the exit label. The output entry label points to the new block.

A more involved example is the if..then..else macro, as sketched in Figure 5. While Bedrock IL includes a standard conditional jump

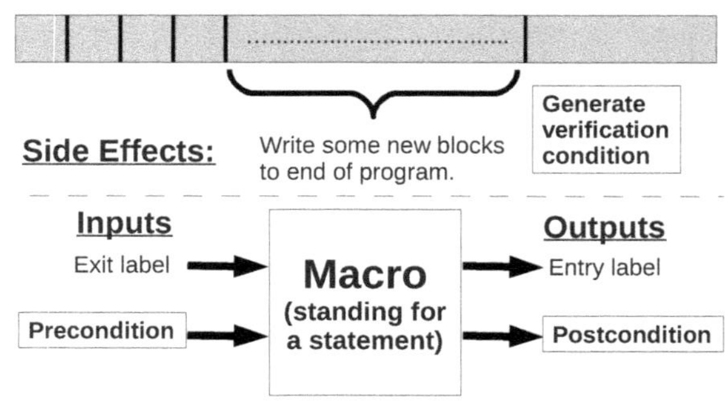

Figure 6. The interface of a certified low-level macro

instruction, we would rather program in terms of a higher-level statement combinator that hides details of code block label allocation. The if..then..else combinator takes three arguments: a *test expression*, suitable as an argument to Bedrock IL's low-level conditional jump; a *then statement*, to run when the test passes; and an *else statement*, to run when the test fails. The two statement parameters will generally be constructed with further macro applications, and the if..then..else combinator should work correctly regardless of the details of the two statements.

An instance of the if..then..else combinator works as follows:

- The macro is passed an *exit label* as input. The same label is passed along unchanged as the *exit label* inputs to the *then* and *else* statements. That is, regardless of which way the test expression evaluates, the statement we jump to should exit the if..then..else upon completion.
- Each of the *then* and *else* macros generates some code blocks to represent itself, outputting an *entry label* for each. The if..then..else macro adds one more code block, a conditional jump using the test expression, jumping to the *entry label* of either the *then* or *else* case, depending on how the test evaluates.
- Finally, the overall macro outputs the address of the conditional test as its own *entry label*.

The working of the macro is broadly similar to standard compilation strategies. To support an expressive macro system, it is crucial to choose a macro interface compatible with a wide range of compilation rules. Many other such architectures are possible. For instance, Benton et al. [2] use an intermediate language with explicitly scoped local labels. The verification support of our approach ought to adapt straightforwardly to many such compilation schemes, since in a sense verification considers only a macro's *interface* and not its *implementation*.

It is worth mentioning one mundane aspect of macro implementation, which is registering concrete parsing notations for macros. We rely on Coq's extensible parser for this purpose. For instance, here is the notation we introduce for calls to the if..then..else combinator `If_`:

```
Notation "'If' c { b1 } 'else' { b2 }" := (If_ c b1 b2)
  (no associativity, at level 95, c at level 0) : SP_scope.
```

All of the standard control-flow constructs of C-like languages are straightforward to encode in our macro system, but, before we consider more examples, we back up to extend the macro interface for verification support.

3.2 Verification Support

Figure 6 gives the expanded interface of *certified* low-level macros, where we add the ingredients needed to build a formal verification environment that supports automated proofs about programs that use macros drawn from diverse sources. At a high level, the addition is this: We previously defined a macro as a **compilation rule**. Verification support involves also including a **predicate transformer** (closely related to the idea of a *strongest postcondition* calculator) and a **verification condition generator**.

The **predicate transformer** of a macro maps a *precondition* to a *postcondition*. Both sorts of conditions are logical predicates over Bedrock IL machine states; that is, they can be represented as functions typed like `state` → `Prop`, returning logical propositions given machine states as input. The precondition describes the machine state on entry to a statement, and the postcondition describes the machine state when control exits the statement. The postcondition is computed as a function, or *transformation*, of the precondition, leading to the name *predicate transformer*. At a high level, the predicate transformer of a macro answers the question *what does this macro do?*

A macro also includes a **verification condition generator**, which given a precondition outputs a logical formula (a verification condition) that the programmer must prove. If the verification condition is false, the statement may not work as expected. At a high level, the verification condition generator answers the question *which uses of this macro are safe and functionally correct?*

More formally, we define the verification part of a macro with:

$$\begin{array}{rcl} \text{Predicates} & \mathbb{P} & = & \mathsf{state} \rightarrow \mathsf{Prop} \\ \text{Predicate transformers} & \mathbb{T} & = & \mathbb{P} \rightarrow \mathbb{P} \\ \text{Verification condition generators} & \mathbb{C} & = & \mathbb{P} \rightarrow \mathsf{Prop} \\ \text{Verification parts of macros} & \mathbb{V} & = & \mathbb{T} \times \mathbb{C} \end{array}$$

At a high level, the intent of these definitions is as follows: Consider a macro definition $M(x_1, \ldots, x_n) = E$, expanding an M invocation into some more primitive statement E. Let the associated predicate transformer be $T \in \mathbb{T}$ and the verification condition generator be $C \in \mathbb{C}$. Client code sees the following Hoare-logic proof rule for a macro invocation with a particular precondition $P \in \mathbb{P}$:

$$\{P \wedge C(P)\} M(e_1, \ldots, e_n) \{T(P)\}$$

The formal version of this notation is complicated by the need to deal with *sets of IL basic blocks*, rather than the usual structured statements. To give an intuition for those details, we return to extended versions of our previous example macros. First, consider the straightline code macro with instruction parameter i. When called with precondition P, the macro produces:

- **Verification condition:** $\forall s.\ P(s) \Rightarrow \exists s'.\ s \stackrel{i}{\longrightarrow} s'$
- **Postcondition:** $\lambda s.\ \exists s'.\ P(s') \wedge s' \stackrel{i}{\longrightarrow} s$

Preconditions and postconditions are predicates, or functions from machine states to logical propositions, so we often notate them as anonymous λ functions. The judgment $s \stackrel{i}{\longrightarrow} s'$ asserts that running instruction i transforms state s into state s'. Instruction executions that would violate Bedrock IL safety do not belong to this relation.

Thus, the verification condition expresses the idea that the precondition implies safety of executing the instruction i. The postcondition is actually the *strongest postcondition* for this particular macro, denoting exactly the set of states that could be reached by running i in a state satisfying P. In general, macros need to expose *sound* postconditions, which include all possible states upon statement exit, but macros need not always return *strongest* postconditions. Indeed, the chance to return weaker postconditions is essential for supporting separation of interface and implementation in macros, where some details of macro implementation are hidden in specifications that are easier to reason about than strongest postconditions.

Consider now the if..then..else macro, where the parameters are a conditional test e, a *then* statement with predicate transformer T_1 and verification condition generator C_1, and an *else* statement with predicate transformer T_0 and verification condition generator C_0. If the overall precondition is P, the macro produces:

- **Verification condition:** $\left(\bigwedge_{b\in\{0,1\}} C_b(\lambda s.\ P(s) \wedge s \stackrel{e}{\longrightarrow} b)\right)$ $\wedge\ (\forall s.\ P(s) \Rightarrow \exists b.\ s \stackrel{e}{\longrightarrow} b)$
- **Postcondition:** $\lambda s'.\ \bigvee_{b\in\{0,1\}} T_b(\lambda s.\ P(s) \wedge s \stackrel{e}{\longrightarrow} b)(s')$

We write $s \stackrel{e}{\longrightarrow} b$ to indicate that conditional test e evaluates to Boolean value $b \in \{0, 1\}$ in state s. The overall verification condition is the conjunction of the two sub-statements' verification conditions, plus the requirement that the precondition imply safety of evaluating the conditional test. The overall postcondition is a disjunction of the sub-statements' postconditions. In each case, we pass off extended preconditions that combine the original precondition P with information on the outcome of the test e.

We have decided that a macro constitutes a *parsing rule*, a *compilation rule*, a *predicate transformer*, and a *verification condition generator*. The last crucial ingredient is a *proof that all of the above agree with each other in an appropriately sound way*. That is, we package macros with *dependently typed records* that contain not just functions but also machine-checked proofs about those functions. Such a thing is easy to do in Coq, as shown by our definition of macros below. (These definitions actually occur in a Coq *section* that introduces parameters describing the code's assumptions about its own module and others, but we omit such details here to simplify the presentation.)

Note that this code incorporates a few optimizations, including representing verification conditions as *lists of propositions* instead of single propositions, to allow conjunction of verification conditions without creating arbitrarily bushy conjunction trees; and *staging* of macros in a manner similar to currying, so that programs may be verified without the need to generate code for them. We write `Prop` for the type of logical propositions, or standalone facts; and `assert` for the type of predicates over machine states, or functions from states to `Prop`.

```
(* Delayed code generation part of macro output *)
Record codeGen (Precondition : assert) (Base Exit : N)
     (Postcondition : assert) (VerifCond : list Prop) := {
  Entry : N;
  Blocks : list (assert * block);

  PreconditionOk : ∃ bl, nth_error Blocks (nat_of_N Entry)
    = Some (Precondition, bl);

  BlocksOk : vcs VerifCond
    → Exit < Base
    → List.Forall (fun p ⇒ blockOk
      (imps Blocks Base Exit Postcondition) (fst p) (snd p))
      Blocks
}.

(* Immediate verification part of macro output *)
Record codeOut (Precondition : assert) := {
  Postcondition : assert;
  VerifCond : list Prop;
  Generate : ∀ Base Exit : N,
    codeGen Precondition Base Exit Postcondition VerifCond
}.

(* Overall type of a macro, a dependent function type *)
Definition cmd := ∀ cin : assert, codeOut cin.
```

We will explain these definitions in reverse. A macro, of type `cmd`, has a *dependent function type*, where the return type of the function is allowed to mention the *value* of the actual parameter. In this case, the formal parameter `cin` is the input precondition, and we return a value of a type `codeOut cin` specialized to the precondition. Where our earlier less formal definitions treated predicate transformers and verification condition generators as independent functions over preconditions, here we instead make the whole macro a function on preconditions.

A `codeOut` record contains the computed postcondition and verification condition, as well as `Generate`, a function that we call if we wish to do code generation, too.

A `codeGen` record contains the output of code generation. While our earlier sketches refer to generation of new code blocks as an imperative process, we implement generation in Coq via returning lists of *new* blocks only. Furthermore, a `Generate` function is passed not only the `Exit` label for a statement, but also `Base`, the address that will be given to the first new code block returned by this macro. In general, the nth block in the output will have label `Base` $+\ n$. It is important to fix the labeling convention to allow the macro to create internal jumps in its code blocks.

Specifically, the `codeGen` record includes the `Entry` label of the statement and the list of its new `Blocks`. Additionally, proofs of two *theorems* must be packaged in the same dependent record. The `PreconditionOk` theorem asserts that the requested precondition really has been assigned as the spec of the statement's entry block. The `BlocksOk` theorem asserts that every block in `Blocks` is correct according to the rules of XCAP.

This latter statement uses a predicate `blockOk` that can be thought of as a judgment $\Gamma \vdash B$, asserting the correctness of basic block B under the assumptions in Γ, a finite map from code labels to assumed preconditions for their associated blocks. Here we build Γ with a function `imps`, which constructs a finite map containing (a) the `Exit` label with spec `Postcondition`, (b) the macro's `Blocks` themselves with their associated specs, and (c) any label-spec pairs for other modules that are listed explicitly as imports. We also note that `BlocksOk` takes as premises (a) the truth of the verification condition and (b) an assertion that the `Exit` label is less than the `Base` label, so that the macro knows it will not accidentally generate a block with the same address as the exit block it should jump to.

The new components of certified macros are very similar to conventional logical manipulations in program verification tools and verified compilers. The power of the idea comes from formalizing the requirements on statements with a precise, open interface. We have proved a Coq theorem that any statement satisfying the `cmd` interface is compiled into a valid XCAP module, when its verification condition holds and it is started in a state satisfying the claimed precondition. This notion of module validity follows XCAP's modular verification approach, so that it is possible to link such theorems together to produce theorems about larger composite modules, without revisiting module internals.

We close out this section with more examples of combinators for conventional C-like control constructs, before turning in the following sections to local variables, calling conventions, and higher-level notations not commonly supported in C-like languages.

3.3 More Examples

Certified low-level macros are compatible with classic Hoare-logic proof rules that require the programmer to provide *invariants*. For instance, consider a macro for a while loop, with conditional test e, *loop invariant* I, and a body statement that has predicate transformer T and verification condition generator C. The macro's logical outputs then mirror standard proof rules, where P again stands for the precondition passed into the macro.

- **Verification condition:** $C(\lambda s.\ I(s) \land s \xrightarrow{e} 1)$
  $\land\ (\forall s.\ P(s) \Rightarrow I(s))$
  $\land\ (\forall s.\ I(s) \Rightarrow \exists b.\ s \xrightarrow{e} b)$
  $\land\ (\forall s.\ T(\lambda s'.\ I(s') \land s' \xrightarrow{e} 1)(s) \Rightarrow I(s))$
- **Postcondition:** $\lambda s.\ I(s) \land s \xrightarrow{e} 0$

The respective verification conditions are the conditions of the loop body, an implication from loop precondition to loop invariant, an implication from loop invariant to safety of conditional test, and an implication from loop body postcondition to loop invariant. The overall loop postcondition is the conjunction of the loop invariant with the failure of the conditional test.

It is also possible to write macros for function calls, where the crucial challenge is to reason about the passing of a return pointer as first-class data. The macro must allocate a new block whose address will be passed as return pointer. We follow the convention that a function receives its return pointer in Bedrock IL register Rp. The compilation part of a function-call macro may simply use its own exit label as the return pointer.

Since there is no succinct logical counterpart to $\xrightarrow{i}$ for expressing the effect of a whole function call, we ask the programmer to provide an invariant I, characterizing the machine state after the function call returns. To state the logical outputs of the function-call macro, we use the XCAP notation $\{P\}p$ to indicate that machine word p is the address of a basic block whose spec is implied by condition P. As is usual at the assembly level, our programs are effectively in continuation-passing style, so it is natural to reason about first-class return pointers with *Hoare doubles* (preconditions only) rather than the more common *Hoare triples* (preconditions and postconditions).

As usual, below let P stand for the precondition passed into the function-call macro. Additionally, let Q be the spec of the function being called, which is in precondition-only form just as for return pointers.

- **Verification condition:**
  $\forall s, p, s'.\ P(s) \land s \xrightarrow{\mathsf{Rp} \leftarrow p} s' \land \{I\}p \Rightarrow Q(s')$
- **Postcondition:** I

The verification condition is stated in terms of the assignment of an arbitrary code pointer p to the return pointer register Rp, subject to the constraint that invariant I is a valid spec for p's basic block. The invariant I itself is used as the call's postcondition.

A complete calling convention also deals with function arguments and local variables. Further, the reader may be worried about the readability of complex specs in continuation-passing style with Hoare doubles. The next section addresses both concerns, describing how we use more macros and other notational conventions to present a more normal perspective on C-like functions.

4. Local Variables and Calling Conventions

Figure 2 contained a specification in a conventional precondition-and-postcondition style, hiding the complexities of continuation-passing-style reasoning. As another example, here is Coq code for a spec we might write for an in-place linked list reversal function. The predicate `sll` stands for "singly linked list," and its parameters are a functional list and a pointer to the root of a matching linked list in memory.

```
SPEC("l") reserving 5
  Al L,
  PRE[V] sll L (V "l")
  POST[R] sll (rev L) R
```

In order, the four lines of such a spec may be thought of as:

1. A *header* giving the function's formal arguments, plus how many free additional stack slots it requires (`reserving` clause)
2. Universal quantifiers for *specification variables* (similar to *ghost variables*) that may be mentioned in both precondition and postcondition
3. A *precondition*, introducing a local name `V` for a function assigning values to actual arguments
4. A *postcondition*, introducing a local name `R` for the function return value

A more compact notation, closer to usual Hoare logic conventions but with explicit use of functions to handle binding of `V` and `R`, might be:

$$\forall L.\ \{\lambda V.\ \mathsf{sll}(L, V(l))\} f(l, 5) \{\lambda V, R.\ \mathsf{sll}(\mathsf{rev}(L), R)\}$$

A mechanical translation produces a continuation-passing style version of this spec, where we only need to assign a precondition. As is usual with this sort of translation, *universal* quantifiers scoped over both precondition and postcondition turn into *existential* quantifiers appearing within the precondition; and calling-convention registers appear explicitly, where Rp holds the return pointer and Rv the function return value.

$$\{\exists L, V.\ \mathsf{sll}(L, V(l)) \wedge \{\mathsf{sll}(\mathsf{rev}(L), \mathsf{Rv})\}\mathsf{Rp}\} f(l, 5)$$

In this specification, the call stack is still treated implicitly. We must eventually be explicit about *call stack as data structure* to bridge the semantic gap to the Bedrock IL. Here is the final version of the specification, using a predicate locals to represent a call stack frame. Register Sp holds the stack pointer.

$$\{\exists L, V.\ \mathsf{locals}(\{l\}, V, 5, \mathsf{Sp}) * \mathsf{sll}(L, V(l)) \\ \wedge \{\exists V'.\ \mathsf{locals}(\{l\}, V', 5, \mathsf{Sp}) * \mathsf{sll}(\mathsf{rev}(L), \mathsf{Rv})\}\mathsf{Rp}\} f$$

Here locals is just another abstract predicate [27] like sll. A fact $\mathsf{locals}(D, V, n, v)$ says that a stack frame with domain D and variable values V is located at address v, and it has at least n more free stack slots remaining. The overall list-reverse spec above indicates that the stack frame must be present with some variable values V at call time, and the separating conjunction $*$ expresses that the call stack and the input linked list must occupy disjoint memory. A nested Hoare double ascribes a precondition to the return pointer Rp. This "postcondition" is the same as the function "precondition" except that (1) local variable values are allowed to change to some arbitrary V' and (2) the linked list has been reversed.

In general, a traditional function spec looks like $\forall \vec{x}.\ \{P\} f(\vec{y}, n) \{Q\}$, where P is a function over V, and Q is a function over V and R. The desugaring of this spec into a low-level XCAP precondition is:

$$\{\exists \vec{x}, V.\ \mathsf{locals}(\vec{y}, V, n, \mathsf{Sp}) * P(V) \\ \wedge \{\exists V'.\ \mathsf{locals}(\vec{y}, V', n, \mathsf{Sp}) * Q(V, \mathsf{Rv})\}\mathsf{Rp}\} f$$

To do code generation and computation of verification conditions and postconditions, a macro now needs to know the local variable set $\vec{y}$ and the reserved stack slot count n. Therefore, we add these two values as additional parameters to each macro. We do not update any of the logical components of macros; local variables are instead handled in a more traditional macro expansion style, without any new hiding of implementation from interface. For instance, a statement that reads a local variable will be compiled to refer directly to the concrete offset of that variable from the stack pointer, with verification conditions that reveal the compilation details directly. We have extended Bedrock's separation logic proof automation to reason properly about the interaction of such stack pointer indirection and the locals predicate.

5. Higher-Level Notations

Certified low-level macros do not merely encode strongest postcondition calculators, to declare the effects of statements. Instead, macro authors have the freedom to expose weaker postconditions, just as the author of a conventional function may choose a weaker postcondition to enforce data abstraction or another form of information hiding. Conventional Hoare logics have a *rule of consequence* facilitating this sort of hiding in a straightforward way, where one may conclude $\{P\}c\{Q\}$ from $\{P'\}c\{Q'\}$, given $P \Rightarrow P'$ and $Q' \Rightarrow Q$.

We have implemented a simple *wrapper* combinator for macros, embodying the rule of consequence. A programmer uses preexisting macros to implement a chunk of code, taking advantage of the associated proof automation to simplify verification of that chunk. Then the chunk may be *wrapped* with a new predicate transformer and verification condition generator, if appropriate conditions are proved. In particular, say that the original statement has transformer T' and generator C', and the wrapper is introducing new transformer T and generator C. The conditions that make the wrapping sound are:

- $\forall P.\ C(P) \Rightarrow C'(P)$
- $\forall P, s.\ C(P) \wedge T'(P)(s) \Rightarrow T(P)(s)$

These conditions are a direct reinterpretation of the rule of consequence, and they are feasible to prove for a variety of higher-level notations that construct the underlying statements programmatically, via recursive functions over macro parameters. In the rest of this section, we give a motivating example for two higher-level macros and then describe their implementations.

5.1 A Motivating Example

Figure 7 shows an example program that uses higher-level macros. The program is a simple idealization of a network server processing queries over a database. We deal not with network IO, but rather just with decoding and processing requests and encoding the results in memory. We say that the database is an array of machine integers, as is the packet of encoded query requests. The output of the server is stored in a linked list.

The lefthand column of the figure gives the program implementation. Our program declares a module `m`, which imports function `malloc` from module `malloc`, with *specification* `mallocS`. Next, we define function `main`, beginning with its list of local variables, including formal arguments.

The main body of the function is a loop over all requests contained in the request array `cmd`. We take advantage of two high-level macros to make our implementation more declarative.

First, we use a *parsing* syntax similar to ML-style pattern matching, via the `Match` macro. Its arguments name an array, its length (`Size` clause), and a local variable storing our current index within the array (`Position` clause). A `Match` has a sequence of cases consisting of patterns and bodies. A pattern is a sequence of items that are either constants, to indicate that a specific machine word value must be found in the corresponding array position; or a variable name (string literal), to indicate that any machine word may appear in the position. All variables are assigned the appropriate values from the array before executing the body of a matching pattern.

The other high-level macro is for *declarative querying* of arrays, chosen as a simple example illustrating many of the same challenges applicable to more expressive SQL-style querying. The `For` macro takes as arguments a loop variable to store an array index, another variable to store the value found at that index (`Holding` clause), the array to query (`in` clause), the length of that array (`Size` clause), and a filter condition choosing which array cells to

Figure 7. Implementation, specification, and verification of our main case study program

```
(* Program implementation *)
Definition m := bimport [[ "malloc"!"malloc" @ [mallocS] ]]
  bmodule "m" {{
    bfunction "main"("cmd", "cmdLen", "data", "dataLen",
                "output", "position", "posn", "lower", "upper",
                "index", "value", "res", "node") [mainS]
      "output" ← 0;;
      "position" ← 0;;
      [(* ... invariant omitted ... *)]
      While ("position" < "cmdLen") {
        Match "cmd" Size "cmdLen" Position "position" {
          (* ValueIsGe *)
          Case (0 ++ "posn" ++ "lower")
            "res" ← 0;;
            [(* ... invariant omitted ... *)]
            For "index" Holding "value" in "data"
              Size "dataLen"
              Where ((Index = "posn") && (Value ≥ "lower")) {
                "res" ← 1
            };;
            "node" ← Call "malloc"!"malloc"(0)
            [(* ... invariant omitted ... *)];;
            "node" *← "res";;
            "node" + 4 *← "output";;
            "output" ← "node"
          end;;

          (* MaxInRange *)
          Case (1 ++ "lower" ++ "upper")
            "res" ← 0;;
            [(* ... invariant omitted ... *)]
            For "index" Holding "value" in "data"
              Size "dataLen"
              Where (("lower" ≤ Value) && (Value ≤ "upper")
                    && (Value ≥ "res")) {
                "res" ← "value"
            };;
            "node" ← Call "malloc"!"malloc"(0)
            [(* ... invariant omitted ... *)];;
            "node" *← "res";;
            "node" + 4 *← "output";;
            "output" ← "node"
          end;;

          (* CollectBelow *)
          Case (2 ++ "lower" ++ "upper")
            [(* ... invariant omitted ... *)]
            For "index" Holding "value" in "data"
              Size "dataLen"
              Where ((Index ≥ "lower")
                    && (Value ≤ "upper")) {
              "node" ← Call "malloc"!"malloc"(0)
              [(* ... invariant omitted ... *)];;
              "node" *← "value";;
              "node" + 4 *← "output";;
              "output" ← "node"
            }
          end
        } Default {
          Fail (* Impossible: the match was exhaustive. *)
        }
      };;

      Return "output"
    end
  }}.
```

```
(* Requests that the server may receive.
 * (W is the type of machine words.) *)
Inductive req :=
| ValueIsGe (index valueLowerBound : W)
(* Test if the value stored at this array index is
 * at least as large as this value. *)

| MaxInRange (lowerBound upperBound : W)
(* Find the maximum value within the given
 * range of values. *)

| CollectBelow (indexLowerBound valueUpperBound : W)
(* Collect a list of all values satisfying
 * the given bounds on index and value. *).

(* Representation of requests as lists of words. *)
Definition encode (r : req) : list W :=
  match r with
    | ValueIsGe a b ⇒ $0 :: a :: b :: nil
    | MaxInRange a b ⇒ $1 :: a :: b :: nil
    | CollectBelow a b ⇒ $2 :: a :: b :: nil
  end.

(* Representation of sequences of requests *)
Fixpoint encodeAll (rs : list req) : list W :=
  match rs with
    | nil ⇒ nil
    | r :: rs' ⇒ encode r ++ encodeAll rs'
  end.

(* Omitted here: some helper functions *)

(* Compute the proper response to a request,
 * as transformation on a list of output values. *)
Definition response (data acc : list W) (r : req) : list W :=
  match r with
    | ValueIsGe index lower ⇒
      valueIsGe data index lower :: acc
    | MaxInRange lower upper ⇒
      maxInRange lower upper data :: acc
    | CollectBelow lower upper ⇒
      collectBelow upper (skipn (wordToNat lower) data) acc
  end.

(* Proper response to a request sequence *)
Definition responseAll (data : list W) (rs : list req)
                       (acc : list W) : list W :=
  fold_left (response data) rs acc.

(* Specification of the server main() function *)
Definition mainS := SPEC("cmd", "cmdLen", "data", "dataLen")
  reserving 15 Al r, Al d,
  PRE[V] array (encodeAll r) (V "cmd") * array d (V "data")
    * mallocHeap
    * ⌈ V "cmdLen" = length (encodeAll r) ⌉
    * ⌈ V "dataLen" = length d ⌉
    * ⌈ goodSize (length (encodeAll r) + 3) ⌉
  POST[R] array (encodeAll r) (V "cmd") * array d (V "data")
    * mallocHeap * sll (responseAll d r nil) R.

(* Omitted: lemmas and tactics about lists *)

(* Correctness theorem *)
Theorem ok : moduleOk m.
Proof.
  vcgen; abstract (parse0; for0; post; evaluate hints;
    repeat (parse1 finish; use_match);
    multi_ex; sep hints; finish).
Qed.
```

visit in the loop (`Where` clause). The key property of `For` is that *it performs compile-time analysis of the `Where` condition to optimize query execution.* If the `Where` condition implies a known value for the array index, the "loop" only visits that cell. If the condition implies a lower bound on array indices, the loop skips the earlier indices. *The proof rule of the `For` macro hides the details of which optimizations are used,* allowing verification to proceed only in terms of high-level logical concepts.

The righthand column of Figure 7 excerpts the specification and correctness proof for the program. The specification follows the Bedrock style of *using pure functional programs as specifications for low-level programs.* In particular, we define functional datatypes to represent requests to the server, and we write functional programs to map requests to their network encodings and their appropriate responses. The three different kinds of queries are represented with capitalized datatype constructors (e.g., `ValueIsGe`) and specified with pure mathematical functions in lowercase (e.g., `valueIsGe`).

The specification `mainS` applies to our `main` function, giving its list of formal arguments, the arrays `cmd` and `data` plus their lengths. Two universal quantifiers ("`Al`") bind names to the purely functional versions of `cmd` and `data`, respectively.

The precondition (`PRE`) clause binds a local function `V` that may be used to access the actual parameter values (e.g., `V "cmd"` as the value of `cmd`). The first three $*$-separated formulas here say, respectively, that there are regions with an array pointed to by parameter `cmd` and storing an encoding of the queries, an array pointed to by parameter `data` and storing an encoding of the database, and finally the internal data structures of the `malloc` library. Further subformulas use the lifting operator $\lceil\ \rceil$, for lifting normal Coq propositions into separation logic formulas. We require that `cmdLen` and `dataLen` store the lengths of the proper arrays, and we require that adding 3 to the query array length does not overflow a 32-bit word (which the `goodSize` predicate formalizes).

A postcondition (`POST`) binds the local variable `R` to stand for the return value. Here we assert that the same two arrays remain in memory unchanged, the `malloc` library state is intact, and the return value is the root of a linked list.

Finally, the program is proved to meet its spec with a short sequences of Coq tactics. Some of them, like `vcgen` and `sep`, come from the Bedrock library. Others, like `parse0` and `for0`, come from the libraries providing the `Match` and `For` macros. In this way, macro authors can also provide reusable procedures for discharging the sorts of verification conditions that their macros generate, while leaving the programmer full flexibility to apply other proof techniques instead.

Some details are omitted in the figure. The `main` implementation includes 7 invariants, predicates over intermediate program states that guide verification condition generation. Together these invariants take up 72 lines of code. We also omit 350 lines of lemma statements and proof script, setting up the key arguments behind the program's correctness. Crucially, *these lemmas are only about properties of lists*, our functional models of arrays and imperative linked lists; we need do no manual proving work specific to program syntax, program states, or memories.

This program uses at least 7 different macros, at varying levels of abstraction from statement sequencing to declarative querying, but the verification is independent of macro implementation details. The level of proof automation used here also means that small changes to the program often require little manual adaptation of proofs. Nonetheless, in the end we get a *foundational* theorem, stated in terms of a simple assembly-level operational semantics and with a proof checked by the normal Coq proof checker. Furthermore, the example program runs only about 25% more slowly than a conventional C program for the same task, as compared to an OCaml implementation we built at a similar level of abstraction, which runs in about 400% of the time of the C program. We return to performance details in Section 6.

5.2 Parsing Arrays of Machine Words

Consider now the general interface of the parsing macro from Figure 7. Its simplest form is as follows:

```
Match array Size size Position pos {
  Case pattern bodyStmt end
} Default { defaultStmt }
```

Here the challenge is giving the macro a strong enough interface without revealing its internal workings. We intentionally set out to hide the details of array access, but programmers should still be able to prove reasonable correctness theorems about programs that use this macro. One concrete challenge is which precondition we choose as the input to *bodyStmt*, a sub-statement that is run when pattern-matching succeeds. We do not want to mention the exact sequence of instructions executed between the start of the `Match` and that point. If we did, the programmer would need to reason about memory safety and semantics of a sequence of array accesses, on *every* invocation of the macro.

The alternate approach that we take here is to construct a *bodyStmt* precondition *in terms of a simpler instruction sequence, different from the one actually executed, but with the same effect.* The instruction sequence is written in terms of the *functional model* of the array, a Coq list.

For instance, the pattern 0 ++ `"posn"` ++ `"lower"` from Figure 7 matches an array span starting with constant 0 and followed by any two other values, such that those two values are bound to names `posn` and `lower` before running *bodyStmt*. Let L be a mathematical list asserted to describe the contents of the array. The semantics of the example match may now be expressed with, first, an assertion that $L = a, b, c, \ldots$ for fresh variables a, b, and c; and second, this instruction sequence:

$$\mathsf{assume}(a = 0); \texttt{posn} \leftarrow b; \texttt{lower} \leftarrow c$$

We express exactly the intent of the pattern, without exposing any details of array access. Instruction sequences like the above are handled trivially by Bedrock's proof automation, without imposing memory safety proof obligations on the programmer. It is easy to code a recursive Coq function to translate a pattern into such a sequence of instructions.

The postcondition of the `Match` macro is just the disjunction of the postconditions for *bodyStmt* and *defaultStmt*, when they are passed preconditions constructed using the encoding technique above. The verification conditions include some administrative facts about variables: all program variables mentioned are declared as local variables, and the variables *array* and *pos* are not also used within patterns. The verification conditions of *bodyStmt* and *defaultStmt* are also inherited. Finally, one new verification condition asserts that the overall precondition for the `Match` implies that there exists an array at the address specified by *array*, where *pos* is a valid index into that array, and adding the length of the pattern to *pos* does not overflow a 32-bit word.

5.3 Declarative Querying of Arrays

Figure 7 demonstrated the `For` macro, which loops over exactly those cells of an array that satisfy a filter condition. The macro implementation analyzes the syntax of the condition to perform optimizations. Such a process is a simplified version of what goes on in an SQL query planner. The interface of the `For` macro should hide the details of the optimizations that are performed.

Our complete implementation uses a form of loop invariant that is similar to the one introduced by Tuerk [31], where an invariant includes both a precondition and a postcondition to simplify application of the separation logic frame rule. However, we will present here a simplified version with only a conventional loop invariant. There the general form of a `For` invocation is:

```
[After prefix PRE[V] invariant]
For index Holding value in array Size len Where condition
  { bodyStmt }
```

The *condition* may refer both to local variables and to the special variables `Index` and `Value` for the current array index and cell value, respectively. Our current implementation performs two optimizations: When *condition* is a conjunction where one conjunct is `Index` $= i$, then the "loop" need only visit cell i. When *condition* is a conjunction where one conjunct is `Index` $\geq i$, then the loop may begin at i rather than 0. The optimizer correctly handles cases where i is a local variable.

As in the previous subsection, here we have the challenge of assigning `For` a specification that does not reveal too much about its inner workings. Ideally, programmers who use `For` will only be faced with proof obligations about mathematical lists, not arrays or the details of compiling complex Boolean tests. This time, we use the conventional idea of a *loop invariant*, but modified to expose a list-level view of the action.

The schematic `For` invocation above includes a loop invariant, where an `After` clause introduces a local name *prefix* for the list of array cell values that have already been visited. In the course of a naive complete loop through the array, *prefix* progresses from the empty list to the full value list. However, optimizations may lead to some loop iterations being skipped, though such details should be hidden in the interface of `For`.

We are now ready to sketch what that interface is. The postcondition is simply that there exists an array in memory pointed to by *array*, such that the loop invariant holds for the full array contents. Verification conditions include both administrative requirements on variable names and the inherited verification condition of *bodyStmt*. The more interesting conditions are:

1. The loop invariant is independent of the values of *index* and *value*, which will often be changed without calling the loop body to *fast forward* past indices that the optimizer determines cannot match the filter condition. (Note that the invariant may still depend on the *functional list* of array cells already visited, just not on the values of local variables used incidentally to track progress in visiting cells.)
2. The precondition implies the loop invariant.
3. When the loop invariant holds for an array value prefix L, and when the filter condition will reject the next value if it equals v, then the loop invariant also holds for prefix L, v. This condition is crucial to justify the soundness of fast forwarding.
4. The postcondition of *bodyStmt* implies the loop invariant, where *bodyStmt* is passed a suitably high-level precondition expressed in terms of mathematical lists and the loop invariant.

6. Evaluation

Together, the core macro system definitions and all of the macros we have built on top of them take up about 4000 lines of Coq code within the Bedrock library.

We have built a few tactics to lower the cost of macro implementation, but our primary interest has been in the effort required to implement and verify individual programs, like the example of Figure 7. An important part of evaluation is the run-time performance of programs, since we motivated certified low-level macros with the possibility to combine the high performance of low-level languages with the abstractions of high-level languages. To gather some rough evidence that our implementation succeeds in this respect, we ran an experiment with four different implementations of the same "server" example[1]:

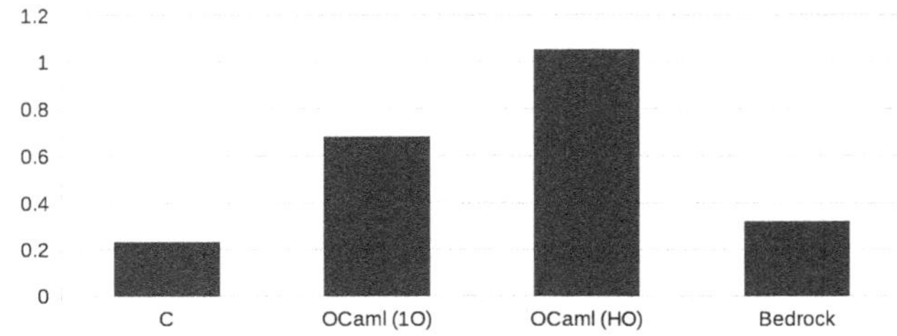

Figure 8. Running time (in seconds) of the four different implementations of the server example, running the same randomly generated workload of 200 queries on an array of 100,000 elements

1. A conventional C program (50 lines) not taking advantage of metaprogramming. This is our baseline of high performance.
2. A first-order (later abbreviated 1O) OCaml program (36 lines), with no variant types (beyond linked lists) or first-class functions. This is our baseline of the cost of switching to a popular high-level language.
3. A higher-order (later abbreviated HO) OCaml program (106 lines, including reusable library code), taking advantage of idioms like parser combinators and embedded interpreters for ASTs. This version illustrates the cost of employing nice abstractions that can be type checked in isolation, which is not the case for abstractions embodied as Camlp4 macros.
4. The Bedrock implementation from Figure 7 (50 lines, compiled to 561 lines of assembly with the Bedrock `malloc` library linked in), which is the only one of the implementations that we verified as correct.

Figure 8 shows the results of running all four compiled programs on a particular random workload chosen to be large enough for performance differences to show. These experiments were run on a 2.4 GHz Intel Xeon processor with 12 GB of RAM, using GCC 4.4.5 and OCaml 3.12.1. They show the first-order OCaml program running in roughly 300% of the time of the C program, with the higher-order OCaml program running in roughly 500% of the C program's time. In contrast, the Bedrock program runs in about 125% of the time of the C program. We replicated the experiment on a 4.2 GHz AMD FX processor with 16 GB of RAM, where the performance difference between C and Bedrock was within the granularity of measurement, and the first- and higher-order OCaml programs ran respectively in about 300% and 350% of the time for the C and Bedrock programs. It is worth pointing out that Bedrock is the only language implementation used here that does not yet have an optimizer, whereas we used the default optimization options of each other compiler, `gcc` and the `ocamlopt` native-code OCaml compiler.

We experimented with verifying programs for several months before generating any executable assembly code. The first program we actually executed was iterative factorial, and the second was the server program in Figure 7. Both worked correctly on the first try, providing at least some small testament to the debugging power of our verification environment.

We have verified a few other substantial case studies, as detailed in Figure 9, breaking down their lines of code into relevant categories. The case studies include some classic functions over imper-

[1] In directory `examples/comparison` of the Bedrock distribution

File	Program	Invar.	Tactics	Other	Overh.
Server	50	79	167	239	9.7
LinkedList	42	26	27	31	2.0
Malloc	43	16	112	94	5.2
ListSet	50	31	23	46	2.0
TreeSet	108	40	25	45	1.0
Queue	53	22	80	93	3.7
Memoize	26	13	56	50	4.6

Figure 9. Case study verifications, with data on annotation burden, in lines of code

ative linked lists, the `malloc` library, implementations of a single finite set abstract data type interface with both unsorted lists and binary search trees, an implementation of the bag abstract data type using a queue, and an implementation of an abstract data type of memoized functions, where a closure stored in memory contains both a function pointer and an associated 1-element memo table. All case studies are built up from certified low-level macros, where our running example Server uses the most advanced macros.

In Figure 9, the *program* column counts lines of executable code; *invar.* refers to function specs, loop invariants, and post-function call invariants; *tactics* refers to literal proofs of theorems as well as reusable tactic functions and hints; and *other* collects the remaining lines, which are mostly helper function definitions and lemma statements. We omit lines of code that are duplicated between Coq modules and their interfaces.

The final column of Figure 9 gives the verification *overhead*, or ratio of verification code to executable code. The more basic examples range from overheads of 1.0 to 5.2, which compare reasonably well to common ratios in Coq developments, such as the overhead of about 7 in the original CompCert paper [21]. The overhead is slightly below 10 for our server example, which involves a fair amount of program-specific correctness reasoning.

We should also point out that the code size statistics from the original Bedrock paper [8] can also be taken as evidence for the effectiveness of the macro system presented in this paper, which is a moderate evolution of the macro system used previously and never presented in detail before.

The main weakness of our present implementation is the running time of automated proof search and proof checking. On the machines used in the experiments, the server example runs for about an hour finding and checking proofs. The other case studies take less time, but still have running times measured in minutes, at best. We do not view this as a huge obstacle from a scientific perspective, as much opportunity remains to take advantage of parallelism. The Server example generates about 100 independent verification conditions, each of which could be discharged on a different processor core, dropping the total verification time for the example to a few minutes. We need only wait for Coq to support forking processes to handle disjoint subgoals of a single proof.

7. Related Work

The original Bedrock paper [8] used a simpler macro system but did not report on its details. Compared to that macro system, our new one from this paper is distinguished by including a calling convention supporting named local variables, as well as the implementation and verification of high-level macros like our parsing and querying examples.

Benton et al. [2] report on a system for formal verification of assembly programs in Coq using higher-order separation logic. Based on an intermediate language with scoped local labels, they define a few macros of moderate complexity, like while loop and function call (the latter handling only storing the return pointer to a register, not stack frame management). Proofs are largely manual with interspersed use of automation tactics, leading to about 10 lines of proof per line of assembly code, as opposed to an about even ratio between the two in our most complicated macro-based example. Their work explores an interesting alternate separation logic featuring a novel higher-order frame rule. We expect that an approach like ours in this paper could be adapted to the formalism of Benton et al. and many others, as our respective projects deal mostly with orthogonal concerns.

Work by Myreen et al. [24, 25] has demonstrated another mechanized separation logic suitable for reasoning about realistic assembly languages. The FLINT project has produced XCAP [26], the assembly-level program logic we adopt in this work, as well as several other logics targeting interesting aspects of assembly program behavior [5, 10–12, 23]. Other related work with mechanized separation logic has gone on at the level of C programs, as in Appel et al.'s Verified Software Toolchain [1]. Mechanized proofs in these logics have been long and manual, and previously no macro system had been demonstrated for them at the level of this paper's most sophisticated examples.

The L4.verified kernel verification project [20] employs a tool [15] for verified translation of C code into functional programs in higher-order logic, applying optimizations that choose simpler types for functions that use fewer varieties of side effect. In a sense, their tool reverses the action of the Bedrock macro system, providing similar foundational guarantees for the fixed C language. In contrast, our work makes it possible for programmers to add their own new language constructs, including higher-level macros like our declarative array querying that are unlikely to be reconstructible automatically from C code.

Macros have been most studied in the context of Lisp and Scheme. Notable in that area is work by Herman and Wand [17], which shows how to assign macros interfaces sufficient to guarantee *hygiene*, or lack of undesirable variable capture, without the need to expand macro definitions to check program validity. Our work also assigns interfaces to macros, for low-level rather than high-level code, and facilitating formal verification of functional correctness rather than just proper use of binding constructs.

In the functional programming world, the use of *embedded domain-specific languages* is already quite popular, for supporting safe code generation to low-level languages via high-level functional programs. For instance, the Harpy Haskell library [14] supports generation of x86 assembly code. Recent tools like Meta-Haskell [22] allow generation of programs in low-level languages like C, CUDA, and assembly, where Haskell-level type checking guarantees that code generators will never output type-incorrect programs. Our work in this paper can be viewed as starting from the same foundation of type-safe metaprogramming and expanding it to support verification of functional correctness.

Extensible C variants like xtc [16] and xoc [9] allow the programmer to specify new statement forms and static checking disciplines. These systems can provide much nicer syntax than what we have available within Coq, and there is room for such features to migrate to proof assistants. The key disadvantage of existing extensible compilers is that they provide no foundational guarantees; custom static analysis disciplines do not have clear semantics, so these languages are not compatible with foundational verification of functional correctness.

Safe "systems languages" include low-level languages like Cyclone [19] and various higher-level languages with features targeted at systems programming. Some are known for their use in particular operating systems projects, such as Modula-3 in SPIN [4] and Sing# in Singularity [18]. None of these languages are extensible, and none give foundational safety or functional correctness guarantees.

Tools like Smallfoot [3] and Space Invader [6, 32] apply separation logic to check memory safety of low-level programs automatically. Other systems, including TVLA [29] and XISA [7], can verify memory safety or even functional correctness using other formalisms for data structure invariants. These tools apply to fixed programming languages with no modular macro systems.

8. Conclusion

We have presented *certified low-level macros*, a technique supporting metaprogramming for low-level software, where programs may be verified formally without looking inside the definitions of macros. Rather, macros export formal interfaces that include predicate transformers and verification condition generators. We have demonstrated how to build up a C-like language stack, starting from a simple intermediate language and culminating in high-level notation for tasks like parsing and declarative querying that are usually supported via ad-hoc external tools. Concrete programs have mostly automated Coq proofs, generating foundational results with statements independent of our macro system; and the performance of our compiled programs is competitive with C programs.

One direction for future research is optimization of the programs that result from macro expansion. As these programs are in a form more like conventional assembly language than conventional compiler intermediate languages, it is not obvious how to do sound optimization. We plan to investigate how we might take advantage of the verified preconditions associated with all basic blocks, to recover semantic information and perhaps allow optimizations that are too difficult to implement with traditional dataflow analysis.

Acknowledgments

The author would like to thank Gregory Malecha and Thomas Braibant, for work on Bedrock proof automation that is used in the case studies from this paper; as well as Thomas Braibant, Ryan Kavanagh, Antonis Stampoulis, and Peng Wang, for their feedback on drafts of this paper.

This material is based on research sponsored by DARPA under agreement number FA8750-12-2-0293. The U.S. Government is authorized to reproduce and distribute reprints for Governmental purposes notwithstanding any copyright notation thereon. The views and conclusions contained herein are those of the authors and should not be interpreted as necessarily representing the official policies or endorsements, either expressed or implied, of DARPA or the U.S. Government.

References

[1] A. W. Appel. Verified software toolchain. In *Proc. ESOP*, volume 6602 of *LNCS*, pages 1–17. Springer-Verlag, 2011.

[2] N. Benton, J. B. Jensen, and A. Kennedy. High-level separation logic for low-level code. In *Proc. POPL*, pages 301–314. ACM, 2013.

[3] J. Berdine, C. Calcagno, and P. W. O'Hearn. Smallfoot: Modular automatic assertion checking with separation logic. In *Proc. FMCO*, volume 4111 of *LNCS*, pages 115–137. Springer-Verlag, 2005.

[4] B. N. Bershad, S. Savage, P. Pardyak, E. G. Sirer, M. E. Fiuczynski, D. Becker, C. Chambers, and S. Eggers. Extensibility, safety and performance in the SPIN operating system. In *Proc. SOSP*, pages 267–283. ACM, 1995.

[5] H. Cai, Z. Shao, and A. Vaynberg. Certified self-modifying code. In *Proc. PLDI*, pages 66–77. ACM, 2007.

[6] C. Calcagno, D. Distefano, P. O'Hearn, and H. Yang. Compositional shape analysis by means of bi-abduction. In *Proc. POPL*, pages 289–300. ACM, 2009.

[7] B.-Y. E. Chang and X. Rival. Relational inductive shape analysis. In *Proc. POPL*, pages 247–260. ACM, 2008.

[8] A. Chlipala. Mostly-automated verification of low-level programs in computational separation logic. In *Proc. PLDI*, pages 234–245. ACM, 2011.

[9] R. Cox, T. Bergan, A. T. Clements, F. Kaashoek, and E. Kohler. Xoc, an extension-oriented compiler for systems programming. In *Proc. ASPLOS*, pages 244–254. ACM, 2008.

[10] X. Feng and Z. Shao. Modular verification of concurrent assembly code with dynamic thread creation and termination. In *Proc. ICFP*, pages 254–267. ACM, 2005.

[11] X. Feng, Z. Shao, A. Vaynberg, S. Xiang, and Z. Ni. Modular verification of assembly code with stack-based control abstractions. In *Proc. PLDI*, pages 401–414. ACM, 2006.

[12] X. Feng, Z. Shao, Y. Dong, and Y. Guo. Certifying low-level programs with hardware interrupts and preemptive threads. In *Proc. PLDI*, pages 170–182. ACM, 2008.

[13] S. E. Ganz, A. Sabry, and W. Taha. Macros as multi-stage computations: type-safe, generative, binding macros in MacroML. In *Proc. ICFP*, pages 74–85. ACM, 2001.

[14] M. Grabmüller and D. Kleeblatt. Harpy: Run-time code generation in Haskell. In *Proc. Haskell Workshop*, page 94. ACM, 2007.

[15] D. Greenaway, J. Andronick, and G. Klein. Bridging the gap: Automatic verified abstraction of C. In *Proc. ITP*, volume 7406 of *LNCS*, pages 99–115. Springer-Verlag, 2012.

[16] R. Grimm. Better extensibility through modular syntax. In *Proc. PLDI*, pages 38–51. ACM, 2006.

[17] D. Herman and M. Wand. A theory of hygienic macros. In *Proc. ESOP*, volume 4960 of *LNCS*, pages 48–62. Springer-Verlag, 2008.

[18] G. C. Hunt and J. R. Larus. Singularity: Rethinking the software stack. *ACM SIGOPS Operating Systems Review*, 41(2):37–49, 2007.

[19] T. Jim, J. G. Morrisett, D. Grossman, M. W. Hicks, J. Cheney, and Y. Wang. Cyclone: A safe dialect of C. In *Proc. USENIX ATC*, pages 275–288. USENIX Association, 2002.

[20] G. Klein, K. Elphinstone, G. Heiser, J. Andronick, D. Cock, P. Derrin, D. Elkaduwe, K. Engelhardt, R. Kolanski, M. Norrish, T. Sewell, H. Tuch, and S. Winwood. seL4: Formal verification of an OS kernel. In *Proc. SOSP*, pages 207–220. ACM, 2009.

[21] X. Leroy. Formal certification of a compiler back-end or: programming a compiler with a proof assistant. In *Proc. POPL*, pages 42–54. ACM, 2006.

[22] G. Mainland. Explicitly heterogeneous metaprogramming with MetaHaskell. In *Proc. ICFP*, pages 311–322. ACM, 2012.

[23] A. McCreight, Z. Shao, C. Lin, and L. Li. A general framework for certifying garbage collectors and their mutators. In *Proc. PLDI*, pages 468–479. ACM, 2007.

[24] M. O. Myreen. Verified just-in-time compiler on x86. In *Proc. POPL*, pages 107–118. ACM, 2010.

[25] M. O. Myreen and M. J. C. Gordon. Hoare logic for realistically modelled machine code. In *Proc. TACAS*, volume 4424 of *LNCS*, pages 568–582. Springer-Verlag, 2007.

[26] Z. Ni and Z. Shao. Certified assembly programming with embedded code pointers. In *Proc. POPL*, pages 320–333. ACM, 2006.

[27] M. Parkinson and G. Bierman. Separation logic and abstraction. In *Proc. POPL*, pages 247–258. ACM, 2005.

[28] J. C. Reynolds. Separation logic: A logic for shared mutable data structures. In *Proc. LICS*, pages 55–74. IEEE Computer Society, 2002.

[29] M. Sagiv, T. Reps, and R. Wilhelm. Parametric shape analysis via 3-valued logic. *TOPLAS*, 24(3):217–298, May 2002.

[30] W. Taha and T. Sheard. Multi-stage programming with explicit annotations. In *Proc. PEPM*, pages 203–217. ACM, 1997.

[31] T. Tuerk. Local reasoning about while-loops. In *Proc. VSTTE Theory Workshop*, 2010.

[32] H. Yang, O. Lee, J. Berdine, C. Calcagno, B. Cook, D. Distefano, and P. O'Hearn. Scalable shape analysis for systems code. In *Proc. CAV*, volume 5123 of *LNCS*, pages 385–398. Springer-Verlag, 2008.

A Practical Theory of Language-Integrated Query

James Cheney
The University of Edinburgh
jcheney@inf.ed.ac.uk

Sam Lindley
University of Strathclyde
Sam.Lindley@ed.ac.uk

Philip Wadler
The University of Edinburgh
wadler@inf.ed.ac.uk

Abstract

Language-integrated query is receiving renewed attention, in part because of its support through Microsoft's LINQ framework. We present a practical theory of language-integrated query based on quotation and normalisation of quoted terms. Our technique supports join queries, abstraction over values and predicates, composition of queries, dynamic generation of queries, and queries with nested intermediate data. Higher-order features prove useful even for constructing first-order queries. We prove a theorem characterising when a host query is guaranteed to generate a single SQL query. We present experimental results confirming our technique works, even in situations where Microsoft's LINQ framework either fails to produce an SQL query or, in one case, produces an avalanche of SQL queries.

Categories and Subject Descriptors D.1.1 [*Applicative (Functional) Programming*]; D.3.1 [*Formal Definitions and Theory*]; D.3.2 [*Language Classifications*]: Applicative (functional) languages; D.3.3 [*Language Constructs and Features*]; H.2.3 [*Languages*]: Query languages

Keywords lambda calculus; LINQ; F#; SQL; quotation; anti-quotation

1. Introduction

What is the difference between theory and practice?
In theory there is no difference, but in practice there is.[1]

A quarter-century ago, Copeland and Maier (1984) decried the "impedance mismatch" between database and conventional programming models, and Atkinson and Buneman (1987) spoke of "The need for a *uniform* language" (their emphasis), and observed that "Databases and programming languages have developed almost independently of one another for the past twenty years." Smooth integration of database queries with programming languages, also known as *language-integrated query*, remains an open problem. Language-integrated query is receiving renewed attention, in part because of its support through Microsoft's LINQ framework (Meijer et al. 2006; Syme 2006).

[1] Attributed variously to Yogi Berra, William T. Harbaugh, Karl Marx, Chuck Reid, and Jan L. A. van de Snepscheut.

ICFP '13, September 25–27, 2013, Boston, MA, USA.

ACM 978-1-4503-2326-0/13/09... $15.00.
http://dx.doi.org/10.1145/2500365.2500586

The problem is simple: two languages are more than twice as difficult to use as one language. The host and query languages often use different notations for the same thing, and convenient abstractions such as higher-order functions and nesting may not be available in the query language. Interfacing between the two adds to the mental burden on the programmer and leads to complex code, bugs, and security holes such as SQL injection attacks. Wrapper libraries, such as JDBC, provide raw access to high-performance SQL, but the resulting code is difficult to maintain. Object-relational mapping frameworks, such as Hibernate, provide an object-oriented view of the data that makes code easier to maintain but sacrifices performance (Goldschmidt et al. 2008); and workarounds to recover performance, such as framework-specific query languages, reintroduce the drawbacks of the two-language approach.

We present a practical theory of language-integrated query, consisting of a theoretical model, T-LINQ, and a practical implementation, P-LINQ. Our approach is based on quotation and normalisation of quoted terms. Our approach can be used in off-the-shelf languages, such as F#, fits with existing frameworks, such as Microsoft LINQ, and does not require specialised type systems of the kind found in Ur (Chlipala 2010) or our own work on Links (Cooper et al. 2007; Cooper 2009). In this paper we focus on SQL queries, although we believe the techniques adapt to other targets, such as XQuery, and may even be applicable to DSLs for domains other than query.

Microsoft LINQ was released as a part of .NET Framework 3.5 in November 2007, and LINQ continues to evolve with new releases. LINQ operators construct queries in a host language, and LINQ providers translate these into a target language, such as SQL, XQuery, or GPU code. In this paper we focus on Microsoft's LINQ to SQL provider, which targets Microsoft SQL Server. There are variants of LINQ for C#, Visual Basic, and F#, among others. T-LINQ and P-LINQ correspond to LINQ for F#. Similar techniques may apply to C#, though it requires some tricks to support anti-quotation (Petricek 2007b). A few details of F# 3.0 hinder smooth integration with P-LINQ, and we are working with Microsoft to enable its wider use.

Our formal theory T-LINQ is similar in scope, power, and translation technique to NRC (Buneman et al. 1994; Wong 1996) and to our own previous work on Links (Cooper et al. 2007; Cooper 2009). NRC is a special-purpose, first-order query language, and does not address integration into a general-purpose language. Links supports higher-order queries and addresses integration, but requires a special-purpose type-and-effect system. Our achievement here is to transpose most of the benefits of Links for language-integrated querying to a widely-used practical language.

We had previously argued that Links offered significant benefits over LINQ. A precise comparison was difficult because LINQ, like many practical systems, is large and not precisely defined. To explore the relationship between Links and LINQ, we formulated a core calculus capturing essential features of LINQ. In the course of formulating T-LINQ, we realised that many of the benefits of

Links can in fact be achieved in LINQ, and we are pleased to offer P-LINQ as a widely-available alternative.

Through a series of examples, we show how our technique supports join queries, abstraction over values and predicates, composition of queries, dynamic generation of queries, and queries containing intermediate nested data. We believe our series of examples distills an important set of features, and may be of independent interest. Among other things, these examples demonstrate the value of higher-order functions and nesting in queries, even when the target query language, in this case SQL, is first-order and does not support nested data.

We require that each query in the host language generate exactly one SQL query. Alluding to twin perils Odysseus sought to skirt when navigating the straits of Medina, we seek to avoid *Scylla and Charybdis*. Scylla stands for the case where the system fails to generate a query, signalling an error. Charybdis stands for the case where the system generates multiple queries, hindering efficiency. The overhead of accessing a database is high, and to a first approximation cost is proportional to the number of queries. We particularly want to avoid a query avalanche, in the sense of Grust et al. (2010), where a single host query generates a number of SQL queries proportional to the size of the data.

Current LINQ implementations may founder on either of these perils. Scylla: many of our examples fail under either F# 2.0 or F# 3.0, and different examples fail in the two different systems. Charybdis: one of our examples causes a query avalanche in F# 3.0. In Grust et al. (2010) avalanches are caused by queries with nested results; interestingly, the avalanche is caused by a query with flat results, but with nested intermediate structure. The documentation for F# LINQ does not explain when host queries may fail or when multiple SQL queries may be generated; trial and error is required to determine what does or does not work.

Our work avoids these perils. For T-LINQ, we prove the Scylla and Charybdis theorem, characterising when a host query is guaranteed to generate a single SQL query. All our examples are easily seen to satisfy the characterisation in the theorem, and indeed our theory yields the same SQL query for each that one would write by hand. For P-LINQ, we verify that its run time on our examples is comparable to that of F# 2.0 and F# 3.0, in the cases where those systems generate a query, and significantly faster in the one case where F# 3.0 generates an avalanche—indeed, arbitrarily faster as the size of the data grows.

Our theory models only a fraction of the features of LINQ, but our practice applies to its entirety. T-LINQ supports queries formed from comprehensions, union, and existence tests, but excludes sorting, grouping, and aggregation; extending it to these other features is important future work. However, P-LINQ supports all features of LINQ, and we validate its coverage and performance, showing it has comparable runtime to F# 3.0 for all 62 database queries listed in the F# 3.0 documentation.

The language features we require are lambda abstraction, records and lists, comprehension notation, and quotation and anti-quotation. Quotation and anti-quotation first appear in Lisp, and are also found in Scheme, Racket, Haskell (via Template Haskell), OCaml (via Camlp4), and F#. Quotation comes in two forms, *closed* and *open*; in the former, quoted terms must contain no free quoted variables. All languages with quotation support closed quotation, while only some support open quotation; in particular, F# only supports closed quotation. Our approach requires only closed quotation.

We observe that one should abstract when possible in the quoted language rather than the host language, as this enables composition while restricting to closed quotation. Though it seems obvious in retrospect, that one should abstract when possible in the quoted language came as a surprise to us; previously, we had assumed one should abstract when possible in the host language, as is done when using open quotation.

people

name	age
"Alex"	60
"Bert"	55
"Cora"	33
"Drew"	31
"Edna"	21
"Fred"	60

couples

her	him
"Alex"	"Bert"
"Cora"	"Drew"
"Edna"	"Fred"

Figure 1. People as a Database

Many embedded domain specific languages (EDSLs) build expression trees as constructs of the host language. For instance, in Nikola (Mainland and Morrisett 2010) or Feldspar (Axelsson et al. 2010; Axelsson and Svenningsson 2012), addition is overloaded so that $a + b$ denotes either an integer (of type **int**) or a quotation of an expression that yields an integer (of type Expr< **int** >), depending on whether a and b denote either the former or latter. For technical reasons, overloading does not apply to all operations, so users have the minor inconvenience of writing $a < b$ as $a \; .<. \; b$ and **if** a **then** b **else** c as $a \; ? \; (b, c)$. In our case, quotation avoids this inconvenience, allowing terms in the embedded language to use identical syntax to the host language. It is common for EDSLs to reuse the type system of the host language as the type system of the embedded language—here we have, in effect, extended the same idea to syntax.

The contributions of this paper are:

- We introduce our technique, and through a series of examples show how it supports join queries, abstraction over values and predicates, composition of queries, dynamic generation of queries, and nesting of intermediate data. We also present a larger example of translation from XPath to SQL, which illustrates the power resulting from combining higher-order queries with language integration. (Sections 2, 3, and 4).
- We develop our theoretical model, T-LINQ, and prove standard results, including a theorem that normalisation always succeeds in translating any T-LINQ query to SQL. (Section 5.)
- We observe that one should abstract when possible in the quoted language rather than the host language, in order to support composition in the presence of closed quotation, and we show how closed quotation can simulate open quotation. (Section 6 and 7.)
- We describe our practical implementation, P-LINQ, and present experimental results confirming our technique works in practice. We observe that F# 2.0 or F# 3.0 fail on key examples where we succeed; that when F# 2.0 or F# 3.0 succeed our performance is comparable; that when F# 3.0 avalanches our performance is arbitrarily better as the problem size grows; and that we handle with comparable performance all 62 database query examples in the F# 3.0 documentation. (Sections 8 and 9.)
- We discuss related work, and summarise our results in the form of a recipe that may apply to a wide variety of domain-specific languages. (Sections 10 and 11.)

Our implementation, examples, and experimental data are available online in the ACM Digital Library.

2. Fundamentals

We consider a simplified programming language, based loosely on F# (Syme et al. 2012), featuring records and list comprehensions.

```
{people =
   [{name = "Alex" ; age = 60};
    {name = "Bert" ; age = 55};
    {name = "Cora" ; age = 33};
    {name = "Drew"; age = 31};
    {name = "Edna"; age = 21};
    {name = "Fred" ; age = 60}];
 couples =
   [{her = "Alex" ; him = "Bert" };
    {her = "Cora" ; him = "Drew" };
    {her = "Edna"; him = "Fred" }]}
```

Figure 2. People as Data

We review the relationship between comprehensions and database queries and then introduce the use of quotation to construct queries.

2.1 Comprehensions and Queries

For purposes of illustration, we consider a simple database containing two tables, shown in Figure 1. The first table, people, has columns for name and age, and the second table, couples, has columns for her and him. (Schema update will be required once equal marriage legislation passes in Scotland.) Here is an SQL query that finds the name of every woman that is older than her mate, paired with the difference in ages.

```
select w.name as name, w.age − m.age as diff
from couples as c, people as w, people as m
where c.her = w.name and c.him = m.name and
      w.age > m.age
```

It returns the following table:

name	diff
"Alex"	5
"Cora"	2

Assuming the people table is indexed with name as a key, this query can be answered in time $O(|\mathsf{couples}|)$.

The database is represented in T-LINQ as a record of tables, where each table is represented as a list of rows, and each row is represented as a record of scalars.

```
type DB = {people : {name : string; age : int} list;
           couples : {her : string; him : string} list}
```

Following F#, we use lists to represent tables, and will not consider the order of their elements as significant. We follow the notational conventions of F#, writing lists in square brackets and records in curly braces.

Our language includes a construct that takes the name of the database and returns its content as a data structure.

```
let db′ : DB = database("People")
```

If "People" is the name of the database in Figure 1, then db′ is bound to the value shown in Figure 2. We stick a prime on the name to warn that this is too naive: typically, the database will be too large to read into main memory. We consider a feasible alternative in the next section.

Many programming languages provide a comprehension notation offering operations over lists analogous to those provided by SQL over tables (Trinder and Wadler 1989; Buneman et al. 1994). F# also supports a form of comprehension notation called *computation expressions* (Petricek and Syme 2012). T-LINQ follows this approach, so the previous query can be written as follows.

```
let differences′ : {name : string; diff : int} list =
  for c in db′.couples do
  for w in db′.people do
  for m in db′.people do
  if c.her = w.name && c.him = m.name &&
     w.age > m.age then
  yield {name : w.name; diff : w.age − m.age}
```

Evaluating differences′ returns the value

```
[{name = "Alex"; diff = 5}; {name = "Cora"; diff = 2}]
```

which corresponds to the table returned by the previous SQL query. Again, we stick a prime on the name to warn that this technique is too naive: typically, in-memory evaluation of a comprehension does not take advantage of indexing, and so requires time $O(|\mathsf{couples}| \cdot |\mathsf{people}|^2)$. We consider a feasible alternative in the next section.

Here we use three constructs, similar to those supported in the sequence expressions of F#. The term **for** x **in** M **do** N binds x to each value in the list M and computes the list N, concatenating the results; in mathematical notation, we write $\biguplus\{N \mid x \in M\}$; note that x is free in M but bound in N. The term **if** L **then** M evaluates boolean L and returns list M if it is true and the empty list otherwise. The term **yield** M returns a singleton list containing the value of M.

Many languages support similar notation, including Haskell, Python, C#, and F#. The T-LINQ term

for x **in** L **do for** y **in** M **do if** P **then yield** N

is equivalent to the mathematical notation

$$\{N \mid x \in L,\ y \in M,\ P\}$$

or the F# sequence expression

seq {**for** x **in** L **do for** y **in** M **do if** P **then yield** N}.

The last is identical to T-LINQ, save it is preceded by the keyword **seq** and surrounded by braces.

2.2 Query via Quotation

T-LINQ allows programmers to access databases using a notation nearly identical to the naive approach of the previous section, but generating efficient queries in SQL. The recipe for conversion is as follows. First, we wrap the reference to the database inside quotation brackets, `<@ ··· @>`.

```
let db : Expr< DB > = <@ database("People") @>
```

Next, we wrap the query inside quotation brackets, `<@ ··· @>`, and wrap occurrences of any externally bound variable, such as db, in anti-quotation brackets, `(% ··· )`.

```
let differences : Expr< {name : string; diff : int} list > =
  <@ for c in (%db).couples do
     for w in (%db).people do
     for m in (%db).people do
     if c.her = w.name && c.him = m.name &&
        w.age > m.age then
     yield {name : w.name; diff : w.age − m.age} @>
```

Finally, to get the answer we evaluate the term

$$\textbf{run}(\mathsf{differences}) \qquad (1)$$

Evaluating (1) takes the quoted expression, normalises it, translates the normalised expression to SQL, evaluates the SQL query on the database, and imports the resulting table as a data structure. In this case, the quoted expression is already in normal form, and it translates into the SQL in the previous section, and so returns the table and answer seen previously. We drop the warning primes, because the answer is computed feasibly by access to the database.

The notation `<@ ··· @>` indicates quotation, which views an expression of type A as a data structure of type Expr< A > that represents the expression as an abstract syntax tree. The notation `(% ··· )` indicates anti-quotation, which splices a value of type Expr< A > into a quoted expression at a point expecting a quoted term of type A. Database access, indicated by the keyword **database**, denotes the value of the database viewed as a record of tables, where each table is a list of rows, and each row is a record of scalars. Database access is only permitted within quotation, as its use outside quotation would require reading the entire database into main memory, which is in general infeasible. Query evaluation, indicated by the keyword **run**, takes an expression of type Expr< A >, normalises it, translates the normalised expression to SQL, evaluates the SQL query on the database, and imports the result as a data structure of type A.

Some restrictions are required on the abstract syntax tree in a **run** expression in order to ensure that it may be successfully translated to SQL. First, all database literals within a given query must refer to a single database on which the query is to be evaluated. Second, the return type must be a *flat relation type*, that is, a list of records with fields of scalar type. Third, the expression must not contain operations that cannot be converted to SQL, such as recursion. (Technically, SQL supports some forms of recursion, such as transitive closure, but current LINQ systems do not.) Fourth, we restrict our attention to queries built from sequence comprehensions, emptiness tests, and sequence union. In T-LINQ, these restrictions are statically checked (in the case of the first restriction, by only supporting one database); in P-LINQ, these restrictions are dynamically checked.

T-LINQ captures the essence of query processing in Microsoft LINQ, particularly as it is expressed in F#. However, the details of Microsoft LINQ are more complicated, involving three types Expression<A>, IEnumerable<A> and IQueryable<A> that play overlapping roles, together with implicit type-based coercions including a type-based approach to quotation in C# and Visual Basic, plus special additional query notations in C#, Visual Basic, and F# 3.0. We relate our model to the pragmatics of LINQ in Section 8.

2.3 Abstracting over Values

Our quoted language supports abstraction. Here is a query that finds the names of all people with ages in a given range, inclusive of the lower bound but exclusive of the upper bound.

```
type Names = {name : string} list
let range : Expr< (int, int) → Names > =
  <@ fun(a, b) → for w in (%db).people do
                   if a ≤ w.age && w.age < b then
                   yield {name : w.name} @>
```

We insist that the answer type always corresponds to a table, so here we return a list of records with a name field, rather than just a list of strings.

Here we have abstracted in the quoted language rather than the host language. As we shall see, this is essential to being able to reuse queries flexibly in constructing other queries. As we explain in Section 6, we recommend abstracting in the quoted language rather that the host language whenever possible, because it supports composition.

Here we use the usual F# notation for function abstraction. Function applications inside queries normalise by beta reduction:

$$(\textbf{fun}(\overline{x}) \rightarrow N)(\overline{M}) \leadsto N[\overline{x := M}],$$

where $N[\overline{x := M}]$ denotes the capture-avoiding substitution of terms $\overline{M}$ for variables $\overline{x}$ in term N.

We form a specific query by instantiating the parameters:

```
run(<@ (%range)(30,40) @>)                                    (2)
```

Evaluating (2) finds everyone in their thirties:

```
[{name = "Cora"}; {name = "Drew"}]
```

In this case, the term passed to **run** is not quite in normal form: it requires one step of beta-reduction, substituting the actuals 30 and 40 for the formals a and b.

More generally, we can instantiate arbitrary values by use of the **lift** operator, which lifts a value of some base type O into a quoted expression of type Expr< O >.

```
let a = 30
let b = 40
run(<@ (%range)(lift(a), lift(b)) @>)
```

This returns the same value as the previous query.

2.4 Abstracting over a Predicate

In general, we may abstract over an arbitrary predicate.

```
let satisfies : Expr< (int → bool) → Names > =
  <@ fun(p) → for w in (%db).people do
              if p(w.age) then
              yield {name : w.name} @>
```

A predicate over ages is denoted by a function from integers to booleans. We form a specific query by instantiating the predicate:

```
run(<@ (%satisfies)(fun(x) → 30 ≤ x && x < 40) @>)            (3)
```

Evaluating (3) yields the same query as (2). In this case, the term passed to **run** requires two steps of beta-reduction to normalise. The first step replaces p by the function, and enables the second step, which replaces x by w.age.

We can instantiate the query with any predicate, so long as it only contains operators available in SQL:

```
run(<@ (%satisfies)(fun(x) → x mod 2 = 0) @>)                 (4)
```

Evaluating (4) finds everyone whose age is even. It would not work if, say, the predicate invoked recursion.

2.5 Composing Queries

Uniformly defining queries as quotations makes it easy to compose queries. Say that given two names, we wish to find the names of everyone at least as old as the first but no older than the second. To express this concisely, we define an auxiliary query that finds a person's age.

```
let getAge : Expr< string → int list > =
  <@ fun(s) → for u in (%db).people do
              if u.name = s then yield u.age @>
```

If names are keys, this will return at most one age. It returns a list of integers, not a list of records, so it is not suitable for use as a query on its own, but may be used inside other queries. We may now form our query by composing two uses of the auxiliary getAge with the query range.

```
let compose : Expr< (string, string) → Names > =
  <@ fun(s, t) → for a in (%getAge)(s) do
                 for b in (%getAge)(t) do
                 (%range)(a, b) @>
```

We form a specific query by instantiating the parameters.

```
run(<@ (%compose)("Edna", "Bert") @>)                         (5)
```

Evaluating (5) yields the value:

```
[{name = "Cora"}; {name = "Drew"}; {name = "Edna"}]
```

Unlike the previous examples, normalisation of this query requires rules other than beta-reduction; it is described in detail in Section 5.4.

2.6 Dynamically Generated Queries

We now consider dynamically generated queries. The following algebraic datatype represents predicates over integers as abstract syntax trees.

```
type Predicate =
  | Above of int
  | Below of int
  | And of Predicate × Predicate
  | Or of Predicate × Predicate
  | Not of Predicate
```

We take Above(a) to denote all ages greater than or equal to a, and Below(a) to denote all ages strictly less than a, so each is the negation of the other.

For instance, the following trees both specify predicates that select everyone in their thirties:

```
let t0 : Predicate = And(Above(30), Below(40))
let t1 : Predicate = Not(Or(Below(30), Above(40)))
```

Given a tree representing a predicate we can compute the quotation of a function representing the predicate. We make use of the **lift** operator, which lifts a value of some base type O into a quoted expression of type Expr< O >. The definition is straightforward.

```
let rec P(t : Predicate) : Expr< int → bool > =
  match t with
  | Above(a)→ <@ fun(x) → (%lift(a)) ≤ x @>
  | Below(a)→ <@ fun(x) → x < (%lift(a)) @>
  | And(t, u)→ <@ fun(x) → (%P(t))(x) && (%P(u))(x) @>
  | Or(t, u)  → <@ fun(x) → (%P(t))(x) || (%P(u))(x) @>
  | Not(t)    → <@ fun(x) → not((%P(t))(x)) @>
```

For instance, P(t_0) returns

```
<@ fun(x) → (fun(x) → 30 ≤ x)(x) &&
            (fun(x) → x < 40)(x) @>
```

Applying normalisation to the above simplifies it to

```
<@ fun(x) → 30 ≤ x && x < 40 @>.
```

Note how normalisation enables modular construction of a dynamic query.

We can combine P with the previously defined satisfies to find all people that satisfy a given predicate:

```
run(<@ (%satisfies)(%P(t0)) @>)                    (6)
```

Evaluating (6) yields the same query as (2) and (3). We may also instantiate to a different predicate:

```
run(<@ (%satisfies)(%P(t1)) @>)                    (7)
```

Evaluating (7) yields the same answer as (6), though it normalises to a slightly different term, where the test 30 ≤ w.age && w.age < 40 is replaced by **not**(w.age < 30 || 40 ≤ w.age).

This series of examples illustrates our key result: including abstraction in the quoted language and normalising quoted terms supports abstraction over values, abstraction over predicates, composition of queries, and dynamic generation of queries.

3. Nesting

We now consider nested data, and show further advantages of the use of normalisation before execution of a query.

```
{departments =
   [{dpt = "Product"}; {dpt = "Quality"};
    {dpt = "Research"}; {dpt = "Sales"}];
 employees =
   [{dpt = "Product"; emp = "Alex"};
    {dpt = "Product"; emp = "Bert"};
    {dpt = "Research"; emp = "Cora"};
    {dpt = "Research"; emp = "Drew"};
    {dpt = "Research"; emp = "Edna"};
    {dpt = "Sales"; emp = "Fred"}];
 tasks =
   [{emp = "Alex"; tsk = "build"};
    {emp = "Bert"; tsk = "build"};
    {emp = "Cora"; tsk = "abstract"};
    {emp = "Cora"; tsk = "build"};
    {emp = "Cora"; tsk = "design"};
    {emp = "Drew"; tsk = "abstract"};
    {emp = "Drew"; tsk = "design"};
    {emp = "Edna"; tsk = "abstract"};
    {emp = "Edna"; tsk = "call"};
    {emp = "Edna"; tsk = "design"};
    {emp = "Fred"; tsk = "call"}]}
```

Figure 3. Organisation as Flat Data

For purposes of illustration, we consider a simplified database representing an organisation, with tables listing departments, employees belonging to each department, and tasks performed by each employee. Its type is Org, defined as follows.

```
type Org = {departments : {dpt : string} list;
            employees :   {dpt : string; emp : string} list;
            tasks :       {emp : string; tsk : string} list }
```

We bind a variable to a reference to the relevant database.

```
let org : Expr< Org > = <@ database("Org") @>
```

The corresponding data is shown in Figure 3.

The following parameterised query finds departments where *every* employee can perform a given task u.

```
let expertise' : Expr< string → {dpt : string} list > =
  <@ fun(u) →
       for d in (%org).departments do
       if not(exists(
         for e in (%org).employees do
         if d.dpt = e.dpt && not(exists(
           for t in (%org).tasks do
           if e.emp = t.emp && t.tsk = u then yield { })
         )) then yield { })
       )) then yield {dpt = d.dpt} @>
```

Evaluating

```
run(<@ (%expertise')("abstract") @>)               (8)
```

finds departments where every employee can abstract:

```
[{dpt = "Quality"}; {dpt = "Research"}]
```

There are no employees in the Quality department, so it will be contained in the result of this query regardless of the task specified.

Query expertise′ works as follows. The innermost **for** yields an empty record for each task t performed by employee e that is equal to u; the resulting list is empty if employee e cannot perform task u. The middle **for** yields an empty record for each employee e in department d that cannot perform task u; the resulting list is empty if every employee in department d can perform task u. Therefore,

```
[{dpt = "Product"; employees =
  [{emp = "Alex"; tasks = ["build"]}
   {emp = "Bert"; tasks = ["build"]}]};
 {dpt = "Quality"; employees = []};
 {dpt = "Research"; employees =
  [{emp = "Cora"; tasks = ["abstract"; "build"; "design"]};
   {emp = "Drew"; tasks = ["abstract"; "design"]};
   {emp = "Edna"; tasks = ["abstract"; "call"; "design"]}]};
 {dpt = "Sales"; employees =
  [{emp = "Fred"; tasks = ["call"]}]}]
```

Figure 4. Organisation as Nested Data

the outermost **for** yields departments where every employee can perform task u. We stick a prime on the name to warn that the query is hard to read. Using nested intermediate data structures will help us formulate a more readable equivalent.

3.1 Nested Structures

An alternative way to represent an organisation uses nesting, where each department record contains a list of employees and each employee record contains a list of tasks:

```
type NestedOrg =
  {dpt : string; employees :
    {emp : string; tasks : string list} list} list
```

We convert the first representation into the second as follows:

```
let nestedOrg : Expr< NestedOrg > =
  <@ for d in (%org).departments do
     yield {dpt = d.dpt; employees =
              for e in (%org).employees do
              if d.dpt = e.dpt then
              yield {emp = e.emp; tasks =
                       for t in (%org).tasks do
                       if e.emp = t.emp then
                       yield t.tsk}} @>
```

If org is bound to the data in Figure 3, then nestedOrg is bound to the data in Figure 4. We cannot write **run**(nestedOrg) to compute this value directly, because **run** requires an argument that is flat, and the type of nestedOrg is nested. However, it can be convenient to use nestedOrg to formulate other queries, as we now show.

3.2 A Query over a Nested Structure

For convenience, we define several higher-order queries. The first takes a predicate and a list and returns **true** if the predicate holds for *any* item in the list.

```
let any : Expr< (A list, A → bool) → bool > =
  <@ fun(xs, p) →
       exists(for x in xs do if p(x) then yield { }) @>
```

The second takes a predicate and a list and returns **true** if the predicate holds for *all* items in the list. It is defined in terms of any using De Morgan duality.

```
let all : Expr< (A list, A → bool) → bool > =
  <@ fun(xs, p) →
       not((%any)(xs, fun(x) → not(p(x)))) @>
```

The third takes a value and a list and returns **true** if the value appears in the list. It is also defined in terms of any.

```
let contains : Expr< (A list, A) → bool > =
  <@ fun(xs, u) → (%any)(xs, fun(x) → x = u) @>
```

All three of these resemble well-known operators from functional programming, and similar operators with the same names are provided in Microsoft's LINQ framework. We define all three as quotations, so that they may be used in queries.

We define a query equivalent to expertise′ as follows:

```
let expertise : Expr< string → {dpt : string} list > =
  <@ fun(u) →
       for d in (%nestedOrg)
       if (%all)(d.employees,
            fun(e) → (%contains)(e.tasks, u) then
       yield {dpt = d.dpt} @>
```

Evaluating

```
run(<@ (%expertise)("abstract") @>)        (9)
```

yields the same query as the previous example, (8).

In order for this to work, normalisation must not only perform beta-reduction, but also perform various reductions on sequence expressions that are well known from the literature on conservativity results. The complete set of reductions that we require is discussed in Section 5.

4. From XPath to SQL

So far, all of our examples (except satisfies) could have been written in a higher-order variant of SQL, implemented using normalisation; they do not illustrate the full power of our approach. We now consider the problem of dynamic generation of SQL queries that simulate XPath queries over XML data represented as relations. This requires not only support for higher-order queries within SQL, but also the capability to construct queries dynamically using recursion and other host language features.

We represent tree-structured XML in a relation using "stretched" pre-order and post-order indexes; see, for example, Grust et al. (2004, sec. 4.2). Each node of the tree corresponds to a row in a table xml with schema:

```
type Node =
  {id : int, parent : int, name : string, pre : int, post : int}
```

The id field uniquely identifies each node; the parent field refers to the identifier of the node's parent (or -1 for the root node); the name field stores the element tag name; and the pre and post fields store the position of the opening and closing brackets of the node in its serialisation. For example, Figure 5 shows an XML tree and its tabular representation.

The datatypes Axis and Path, defined below, represent the abstract syntax of a fragment of XPath.

```
type Axis =                  type Path =
  | Self                       | Seq of Path × Path
  | Child                      | Axis of Axis
  | Descendant                 | Name of string
  | DescendantOrSelf           | Filter of Path
  | Following
  | FollowingSibling
  | Rev of Axis
```

The Axis datatype defines the primitive forward axes and Rev to reverse the axes (the reverse of child is parent, the reverse of descendant is ancestor, and so on). The Path datatype defines Seq to concatenate two paths, Axis to define an axis step, Name to test whether an element's name is equal to a given string, and Filter to test whether a path expression is satisfiable from a given node.

Figure 6 gives the complete code of an evaluator for this fragment of XPath, which generates one SQL query per XPath query. The functions axis and path are defined by case analysis over the datatypes Axis and Path, respectively; they yield predicates that

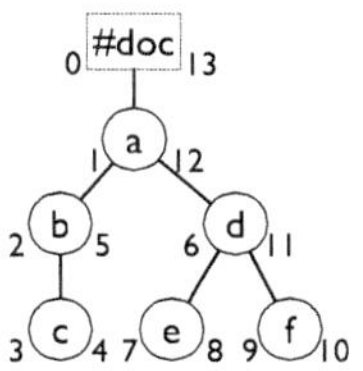

xml

id	parent	name	pre	post
0	-1	"#doc"	0	13
1	0	"a"	1	12
2	1	"b"	2	5
3	2	"c"	3	4
4	1	"d"	6	11
5	4	"e"	7	8
6	4	"f"	9	10

Figure 5. XML Tree and Tabular Representation

```
let rec axis(ax : Axis) : Expr< (Node, Node) → bool > =
  match ax with
  | Self → <@ fun(s, t) → s.id = t.id @>
  | Child → <@ fun(s, t) → s.id = t.parent @>
  | Descendant → <@ fun(s, t) →
      s.pre < t.pre && t.post < s.post @>
  | DescendantOrSelf → <@ fun(s, t) →
      s.pre ≤ t.pre && t.post ≤ s.post @>
  | Following → <@ fun(s, t) → s.post < t.pre @>
  | FollowingSibling → <@ fun(s, t) →
      s.post < t.pre && s.parent = t.parent @>
  | Rev(axis) → <@ fun(s, t) → (%axis(ax))(t, s) @>
let rec path(p : Path) : Expr< (Node, Node) → bool > =
  match p with
  | Seq(p, q) → <@ fun(s, u) → (%any)((%db).xml,
      fun(t) → (%path(p))(s, t) && (%path(q))(t, u)) @>
  | Axis(ax) → axis(ax)
  | Name(name) → <@ fun(s, t) →
      s.id = t.id && s.name = name @>
  | Filter(p) → <@ fun(s, t) → s.id = t.id &&
      (%any)((%db).xml, fun(u) → (%path(p))(s, u)) @>
let xpath(p : Path) : Expr< int list > =
  <@ for root in (%db).xml do
     for s in (%db).xml do
     if root.parent = -1 && (%path(p))(root, s) then
     yield s.id @>
```

Figure 6. An Evaluator for XPath

hold when two nodes are related by the given axis or path. The function xpath translates a Path p to a query expression that returns each node in the table that matches p, starting from the root.

In our tests we consider the following example paths.

$$\mathsf{xp}_0 = \texttt{/*/*} \tag{10}$$
$$\mathsf{xp}_1 = \texttt{//*/parent::*} \tag{11}$$
$$\mathsf{xp}_2 = \texttt{//*[following-sibling::d]} \tag{12}$$
$$\mathsf{xp}_3 = \texttt{//f[ancestor::*/preceding::b]} \tag{13}$$

Translation of XPath to Path is straightforward; for example, xp_0 is `Seq(Axis(Child), Axis(Child))`. The four queries yield the results `[2,4]`, `[1,2,4]`, `[2]`, and `[6]`, respectively on the example data in Figure 5.

While this is a small fragment of XPath, there is no obstacle to adding other features such as attributes, boolean operations on filters, or tests on text data.

5. Core Language

In this section we give a formal account of T-LINQ as a lambda calculus with comprehension, quotation, and constructs to access a database and run queries. Queries are constructed by quotation, and—crucially!—the quoted term is normalised as part of the process of issuing a query.

In practice, host and quoted languages are usually identical, but this is a design choice. In T-LINQ, there are small, but important, differences between the host and quoted languages.

(base)	O	$::=$	**int** | **bool** | **string**
(type)	A, B	$::=$	$O \mid A \to B \mid \{\overline{\ell : A}\} \mid A$ **list** | Expr< A >
(table)	T	$::=$	$\{\overline{\ell : O}\}$ **list**
(env't)	Γ, Δ	$::=$	$\cdot \mid \Gamma, x : A$
(term)	L, M, N	$::=$	$c \mid op(\overline{M})$ | **lift** M | x | **fun**$(x) \to N$
		|	$L\ M$ | **rec** $f(x) \to N$ | $\{\overline{\ell = M}\}$ | $L.\ell$
		|	**yield** M | `[]` | M `@` N | **for** x **in** M **do** N
		|	**exists** M | **if** L **then** M | **run** M
		|	<@ M @> | **database**(db) | (%M)

Figure 7. Syntax of T-LINQ

5.1 Typing Rules

The syntax of types and terms is given in Figure 7 and the typing rules are given in Figure 8. There are two typing judgements, one for host terms and one for quoted terms. Judgement $\Gamma \vdash M : A$ states that host term M has type A in type environment Γ, and judgement $\Gamma; \Delta \vdash M : A$ states that quoted term M has type A in host type environment Γ and quoted type environment Δ. For simplicity, we assume that all queries are on a single database db; in practice, we check dynamically that each query refers to a single database. We assume a signature Σ that maps each constant c, each primitive operator op, and the database db to its type.

Most of the typing rules are standard, and mirrored across both judgements; we list here the rules that differ. Recursion is only available in a host term (REC); other operations available to the host but not the database may be modelled similarly. The database is only available in a quoted term (DATABASE). A term of base type O can be lifted to a quoted term of type Expr< O > (LIFT). A quoted term of table type T can be evaluated as a query (RUN). The rule for quoting requires the quoted type environment to be empty, ensuring quoted terms are closed (QUOTE). The rule for splicing is the only place the host type environment Γ is referenced in the typing rules for quoted terms (ANTIQUOTE).

5.2 Operational Semantics

The syntax of values and evaluation contexts is given in Figure 9. Values are standard, save that we add values <@ Q @>, where Q is a *quotation value*, a quoted term in which all anti-quotes have been resolved. We write $[\overline{V}]$ to abbreviate **yield** V_1 @ $\cdots$ @**yield** V_n @ `[]`. The semantics is parameterised by an interpretation δ for each primitive operation op, and an interpretation Ω for the database db, both of which respect types: if $\Sigma(op) = \overline{O} \to O$ and $\vdash \overline{V : O}$ and $V = \delta(op, \overline{V})$ then $\vdash V : O$, and $\vdash \Omega(\mathsf{db}) : \Sigma(\mathsf{db})$.

Reduction $M \longrightarrow N$ is the relation in Figure 10. We write $\longrightarrow^*$ for the reflexive and transitive closure of $\longrightarrow$. The rules are standard apart from those for quotation and query evaluation. All of the rules are interpreted relative to a fixed database; the *eval* function evaluates the query against this database. Evaluation contexts $\mathcal{E}$ enforce left-to-right call-by-value evaluation, and quotation contexts $\mathcal{Q}$ are contexts over quoted terms that have no anti-quotation to the left of the hole. Rule (lift) converts a constant into a quoted constant, and rule (splice) resolves an anti-quote once its body has been evaluated to a quotation. Rule (run) evaluates a quotation value Q by first *normalising* Q to yield an equivalent SQL query $S = norm(Q)$, and then *evaluating* S on the database to yield the

$$\boxed{\Gamma \vdash M : A}$$

$$\textsc{Const}\ \frac{\Sigma(c) = A}{\Gamma \vdash c : A} \qquad \textsc{Op}\ \frac{\Sigma(op) = (\overline{O}) \to O \qquad \overline{\Gamma \vdash M : O}}{\Gamma \vdash op(\overline{M}) : O} \qquad \textsc{Lift}\ \frac{\Gamma \vdash M : O}{\Gamma \vdash \mathbf{lift}\ M : \mathsf{Expr}\text{<}O\text{>}} \qquad \textsc{Var}\ \frac{x : A \in \Gamma}{\Gamma \vdash x : A} \qquad \textsc{Fun}\ \frac{\Gamma, x : A \vdash N : B}{\Gamma \vdash \mathbf{fun}(x) \to N : A \to B}$$

$$\textsc{App}\ \frac{\Gamma \vdash L : A \to B \qquad \Gamma \vdash M : A}{\Gamma \vdash L\ M : B} \qquad \textsc{Rec}\ \frac{\Gamma, f : A \to B, x : A \vdash N : B}{\Gamma \vdash \mathbf{rec}\ f(x) \to N : A \to B} \qquad \textsc{Record}\ \frac{\overline{\Gamma \vdash M : A}}{\Gamma \vdash \{\overline{\ell = M}\} : \{\overline{\ell : A}\}} \qquad \textsc{Project}\ \frac{\Gamma \vdash L : \{\overline{\ell : A}\}}{\Gamma \vdash L.\ell_i : A_i}$$

$$\textsc{Singleton}\ \frac{\Gamma \vdash M : A}{\Gamma \vdash \mathbf{yield}\ M : A\ \mathbf{list}} \qquad \textsc{Empty}\ \frac{}{\Gamma \vdash \texttt{[]} : A\ \mathbf{list}} \qquad \textsc{Union}\ \frac{\Gamma \vdash M : A\ \mathbf{list} \qquad \Gamma \vdash N : A\ \mathbf{list}}{\Gamma \vdash M\ \texttt{@}\ N : A\ \mathbf{list}} \qquad \textsc{For}\ \frac{\Gamma \vdash M : A\ \mathbf{list} \qquad \Gamma, x : A \vdash N : B\ \mathbf{list}}{\Gamma \vdash \mathbf{for}\ x\ \mathbf{in}\ M\ \mathbf{do}\ N : B\ \mathbf{list}}$$

$$\textsc{Exists}\ \frac{\Gamma \vdash M : A\ \mathbf{list}}{\Gamma \vdash \mathbf{exists}\ M : \mathbf{bool}} \qquad \textsc{If}\ \frac{\Gamma \vdash L : \mathbf{bool} \qquad \Gamma \vdash M : A\ \mathbf{list}}{\Gamma \vdash \mathbf{if}\ L\ \mathbf{then}\ M : A\ \mathbf{list}} \qquad \textsc{Run}\ \frac{\Gamma \vdash M : \mathsf{Expr}\text{<}T\text{>}}{\Gamma \vdash \mathbf{run}\ M : T} \qquad \textsc{Quote}\ \frac{\Gamma; \cdot \vdash M : A}{\Gamma \vdash \texttt{<@}\ M\ \texttt{@>} : \mathsf{Expr}\text{<}A\text{>}}$$

$$\boxed{\Gamma; \Delta \vdash M : A}$$

$$\textsc{ConstQ}\ \frac{\Sigma(c) = A}{\Gamma; \Delta \vdash c : A} \qquad \textsc{OpQ}\ \frac{\Sigma(op) = (\overline{O}) \to O \qquad \overline{\Gamma; \Delta \vdash M : O}}{\Gamma; \Delta \vdash op(\overline{M}) : O} \qquad \textsc{VarQ}\ \frac{x : A \in \Delta}{\Gamma; \Delta \vdash x : A} \qquad \textsc{FunQ}\ \frac{\Gamma; \Delta, x : A \vdash N : B}{\Gamma; \Delta \vdash \mathbf{fun}(x) \to N : A \to B}$$

$$\textsc{AppQ}\ \frac{\Gamma; \Delta \vdash L : A \to B \qquad \Gamma; \Delta \vdash M : A}{\Gamma; \Delta \vdash L\ M : B} \qquad \textsc{RecordQ}\ \frac{\overline{\Gamma; \Delta \vdash M : A}}{\Gamma; \Delta \vdash \{\overline{\ell = M}\} : \{\overline{\ell : A}\}} \qquad \textsc{ProjectQ}\ \frac{\Gamma; \Delta \vdash L : \{\overline{\ell : A}\}}{\Gamma; \Delta \vdash L.\ell_i : A_i} \qquad \textsc{SingletonQ}\ \frac{\Gamma; \Delta \vdash M : A}{\Gamma; \Delta \vdash \mathbf{yield}\ M : A\ \mathbf{list}}$$

$$\textsc{EmptyQ}\ \frac{}{\Gamma; \Delta \vdash \texttt{[]} : A\ \mathbf{list}} \qquad \textsc{UnionQ}\ \frac{\Gamma; \Delta \vdash M : A\ \mathbf{list} \qquad \Gamma; \Delta \vdash N : A\ \mathbf{list}}{\Gamma; \Delta \vdash M\ \texttt{@}\ N : A\ \mathbf{list}} \qquad \textsc{ForQ}\ \frac{\Gamma; \Delta \vdash M : A\ \mathbf{list} \qquad \Gamma; \Delta, x : A \vdash N : B\ \mathbf{list}}{\Gamma; \Delta \vdash \mathbf{for}\ x\ \mathbf{in}\ M\ \mathbf{do}\ N : B\ \mathbf{list}}$$

$$\textsc{ExistsQ}\ \frac{\Gamma; \Delta \vdash M : A\ \mathbf{list}}{\Gamma; \Delta \vdash \mathbf{exists}\ M : \mathbf{bool}} \qquad \textsc{IfQ}\ \frac{\Gamma; \Delta \vdash L : \mathbf{bool} \qquad \Gamma; \Delta \vdash M : A\ \mathbf{list}}{\Gamma; \Delta \vdash \mathbf{if}\ L\ \mathbf{then}\ M : A\ \mathbf{list}} \qquad \textsc{Database}\ \frac{\Sigma(\mathsf{db}) = \{\overline{\ell : T}\}}{\Gamma; \Delta \vdash \mathbf{database}(\mathsf{db}) : \{\overline{\ell : T}\}} \qquad \textsc{Antiquote}\ \frac{\Gamma \vdash M : \mathsf{Expr}\text{<}A\text{>}}{\Gamma; \Delta \vdash (\texttt{\%}M) : A}$$

Figure 8. Typing Rules for T-LINQ

value $V = eval(\Omega, S)$. Define $eval(\Omega, Q) = V$ when $\Omega(Q) \longrightarrow^* V$, where $\Omega(Q)$ replaces each occurrence of **database**(db) in Q by $\Omega(\mathsf{db})$. The following section defines $norm(Q)$, and shows that normalisation preserves types and meaning: if $\cdot; \cdot \vdash Q : T$ and $S = norm(Q)$ then $\vdash S : T$ and $eval(\Omega, S) = eval(\Omega, Q)$.

It is straightforward to show that type soundness holds, via the usual method of preservation and progress.

PROPOSITION 1. *If* $\Gamma \vdash M : A$ *and* $M \longrightarrow N$ *then* $\Gamma \vdash N : A$. *If* $\Gamma \vdash M : A$ *then either* M *is a value or* $M \longrightarrow N$ *for some* N.

5.3 Query Normalisation

In this section we establish the Scylla and Charybdis theorem: Every quoted term of flat type can be normalised to a term that is isomorphic to a single SQL query.

Query normalisation is central to our technique. Similar techniques go back to Wong (1996), and the work here is based directly on Cooper (2009) and Lindley and Cheney (2012). The query normalisation function $norm$ is based on two reduction relations, symbolic reduction, $P \rightsquigarrow Q$, and *ad-hoc* reduction, $P \hookrightarrow Q$. We write $\rightsquigarrow^*$ and $\hookrightarrow^*$ for the reflexive and transitive closure of $\rightsquigarrow$ and $\hookrightarrow$ respectively. Define $norm(P) = R$ when $P \rightsquigarrow^* Q$ and $Q \hookrightarrow^* R$, where Q and R are in normal form with respect to $\rightsquigarrow$ and $\hookrightarrow$, respectively.

Symbolic reduction $P \rightsquigarrow Q$ is the compatible closure of the rules in Figure 11. The rules are straightforward, including beta-reduction for functions, records, and booleans, plus the usual laws for monads with sums (Trinder 1991). Terms in normal form under this relation satisfy the subformula property: with the exception of predicates (such as $<$ or **exists**), the type of a subterm must be a subformula of either the type of a free variable or of the type of the term (Prawitz 1965). Hence, symbolic reduction eliminates nesting from a term that returns a value of table type.

Ad-hoc reduction, $P \hookrightarrow Q$, is the compatible closure of the rules in Figure 12. These reductions account for the lack of uniformity in SQL. Rule (for-@), which hoists a union out of a comprehension body, is the only rule that is not sound for a list semantics, since it changes the order in which elements are generated.

Rewriting preserves types and meaning.

PROPOSITION 2. *If* $\vdash P : A$ *and* $P \rightsquigarrow Q$ *or* $P \hookrightarrow Q$ *then* $\vdash Q : A$ *and* $eval(\Omega, P) = eval(\Omega, Q)$.

The normal form of a query is easy to compute because rewrites may be applied in any order and rewriting always terminates.

$$
\begin{array}{lll}
\text{(value)} & & \\
V, W & ::= & c \mid \mathbf{fun}(x) \to M \mid \mathbf{rec}\, f(x) \to M \mid \{\overline{\ell = V}\} \\
& \mid & [\overline{V}] \mid \texttt{<@}\, Q\, \texttt{@>} \\
\text{(quotation value)} & & \\
P, Q, R & ::= & c \mid op(\overline{Q}) \mid \mathbf{lift}\ Q \mid x \mid \mathbf{fun}(x) \to R \mid P\ Q \\
& \mid & \{\overline{\ell = Q}\} \mid P.\ell \mid \mathbf{yield}\ Q \mid \texttt{[]} \mid Q\ \texttt{@}\ R \\
& \mid & \mathbf{for}\ x\ \mathbf{in}\ Q\ \mathbf{do}\ R \mid \mathbf{exists}\ Q \mid \mathbf{if}\ P\ \mathbf{then}\ Q \\
& \mid & \mathbf{database}(\mathsf{db}) \\
\text{(evaluation context)} & & \\
\mathcal{E} & ::= & [\,] \mid op(\overline{V}, \mathcal{E}, \overline{M}) \mid \mathbf{lift}\ \mathcal{E} \mid \mathcal{E}\ M \mid V\ \mathcal{E} \\
& \mid & \{\overline{\ell = V}, \ell' = \mathcal{E}, \overline{\ell'' = M}\} \mid \mathcal{E}.\ell \mid \mathbf{yield}\ \mathcal{E} \\
& \mid & \mathcal{E}\ \texttt{@}\ M \mid V\ \texttt{@}\ \mathcal{E} \mid \mathbf{for}\ x\ \mathbf{in}\ \mathcal{E}\ \mathbf{do}\ N \mid \mathbf{exists}\ \mathcal{E} \\
& \mid & \mathbf{if}\ \mathcal{E}\ \mathbf{then}\ M \mid \mathbf{run}\ \mathcal{E} \mid \texttt{<@}\ \mathcal{Q}[(\texttt{\%}\mathcal{E})]\ \texttt{@>} \\
\text{(quotation context)} & & \\
\mathcal{Q} & ::= & [\,] \mid op(\overline{Q}, \mathcal{Q}, \overline{M}) \mid \mathbf{lift}\ \mathcal{Q} \mid \mathbf{fun}(x) \to \mathcal{Q} \\
& \mid & \mathcal{Q}\ M \mid Q\ \mathcal{Q} \mid \{\overline{\ell = Q}, \ell' = \mathcal{Q}, \overline{\ell' = M}\} \\
& \mid & \mathcal{Q}.\ell \mid \mathbf{yield}\ \mathcal{Q} \mid \mathcal{Q}\ \texttt{@}\ M \mid Q\ \texttt{@}\ \mathcal{Q} \\
& \mid & \mathbf{for}\ x\ \mathbf{in}\ \mathcal{Q}\ \mathbf{do}\ N \mid \mathbf{for}\ x\ \mathbf{in}\ Q\ \mathbf{do}\ \mathcal{Q} \\
& \mid & \mathbf{exists}\ \mathcal{Q} \mid \mathbf{if}\ \mathcal{Q}\ \mathbf{then}\ M \mid \mathbf{if}\ Q\ \mathbf{then}\ \mathcal{Q} \mid \mathbf{run}\ \mathcal{Q}
\end{array}
$$

Figure 9. Values and Evaluation Contexts

$$
\begin{array}{rcll}
op(\overline{V}) & \longrightarrow & \delta(op, \overline{V}) & \\
(\mathbf{fun}(x) \to N)\ V & \longrightarrow & N[x := V] & \\
(\mathbf{rec}\ f(x) \to N)\ V & \longrightarrow & M[f := \mathbf{rec}\ f(x) \to N, x := V] & \\
\{\overline{\ell = V}\}.\ell_i & \longrightarrow & V_i & \\
\mathbf{if\ true\ then}\ M & \longrightarrow & M & \\
\mathbf{if\ false\ then}\ M & \longrightarrow & \texttt{[]} & \\
\mathbf{for}\ x\ \mathbf{in\ yield}\ V\ \mathbf{do}\ M & \longrightarrow & M[x := V] & \\
\mathbf{for}\ x\ \mathbf{in}\ \texttt{[]}\ \mathbf{do}\ N & \longrightarrow & \texttt{[]} & \\
\mathbf{for}\ x\ \mathbf{in}\ L\ \texttt{@}\ M\ \mathbf{do}\ N & \longrightarrow & & \\
& & (\mathbf{for}\ x\ \mathbf{in}\ L\ \mathbf{do}\ N)\ \texttt{@}\ (\mathbf{for}\ x\ \mathbf{in}\ M\ \mathbf{do}\ N) & \\
\mathbf{exists}\ \texttt{[]} & \longrightarrow & \mathbf{false} & \\
\mathbf{exists}\ [\overline{V}] & \longrightarrow & \mathbf{true}, \quad |\overline{V}| > 0 & \\
\mathbf{run}\ \texttt{<@}\ Q\ \texttt{@>} & \longrightarrow & eval(norm(Q)) & \text{(run)} \\
\mathbf{lift}\ c & \longrightarrow & \texttt{<@}\ c\ \texttt{@>} & \text{(lift)} \\
\texttt{<@}\ \mathcal{Q}[(\texttt{\%<@}\ Q\ \texttt{@>})]\ \texttt{@>} & \longrightarrow & \texttt{<@}\ \mathcal{Q}[Q]\ \texttt{@>} & \text{(splice)}
\end{array}
$$

$$
\frac{M \longrightarrow N}{\mathcal{E}[M] \longrightarrow \mathcal{E}[N]}
$$

Figure 10. Operational Semantics for T-LINQ

PROPOSITION 3. *Both $\leadsto$ and $\hookrightarrow$ are confluent and strongly normalising for typed terms.*

The proof is straightforward. Factoring into two relations makes the strong normalisation proof easier than in Cooper (2009).

The grammar of normalised terms, given in Figure 13, is essentially isomorphic to a subset of SQL. The correspondence is not quite exact, because the SQL standard has no notation for empty records, and lacks constructs for an empty table or to access a table or table variable directly (the first constructs of S, X, and Y, respectively); but these idiosyncrasies are easy to work around, and are handled already by LINQ. It is straightforward to establish that if Q is a closed term of table type T, then its normalisation exists and matches the grammar of S.

PROPOSITION 4 (Scylla and Charybdis). *If $\vdash Q : T$ then there exists an S such that $S = norm(Q)$.*

$$
\begin{array}{rcll}
(\mathbf{fun}(x) \to R)\ Q & \leadsto & R[x := Q] & \\
\{\overline{\ell = Q}\}.\ell_i & \leadsto & Q_i & \\
\mathbf{for}\ x\ \mathbf{in}\ (\mathbf{yield}\ Q)\ \mathbf{do}\ R & \leadsto & R[x := Q] & \text{(for-yld)} \\
\mathbf{for}\ y\ \mathbf{in}\ (\mathbf{for}\ x\ \mathbf{in}\ P\ \mathbf{do}\ Q)\ \mathbf{do}\ R & \leadsto & & \\
& & \mathbf{for}\ x\ \mathbf{in}\ P\ \mathbf{do}\ (\mathbf{for}\ y\ \mathbf{in}\ Q\ \mathbf{do}\ R) & \text{(for-for)} \\
\mathbf{for}\ x\ \mathbf{in}\ (\mathbf{if}\ P\ \mathbf{then}\ Q)\ \mathbf{do}\ R & \leadsto & & \\
& & \mathbf{if}\ P\ \mathbf{then}\ (\mathbf{for}\ x\ \mathbf{in}\ Q\ \mathbf{do}\ R) & \text{(for-if)} \\
\mathbf{for}\ x\ \mathbf{in}\ \texttt{[]}\ \mathbf{do}\ N & \leadsto & \texttt{[]} & \\
\mathbf{for}\ x\ \mathbf{in}\ (P\ \texttt{@}\ Q)\ \mathbf{do}\ R & \leadsto & & \\
& & (\mathbf{for}\ x\ \mathbf{in}\ P\ \mathbf{do}\ R)\ \texttt{@}\ (\mathbf{for}\ x\ \mathbf{in}\ Q\ \mathbf{do}\ R) & \\
\mathbf{if\ true\ then}\ Q & \leadsto & Q & \\
\mathbf{if\ false\ then}\ Q & \leadsto & \texttt{[]} &
\end{array}
$$

Figure 11. Normalisation Stage 1: symbolic reduction

$$
\begin{array}{rcll}
\mathbf{for}\ x\ \mathbf{in}\ P\ \mathbf{do}\ (Q\ \texttt{@}\ R) & \hookrightarrow & & \text{(for-@)} \\
& & (\mathbf{for}\ x\ \mathbf{in}\ P\ \mathbf{do}\ Q)\ \texttt{@}\ (\mathbf{for}\ x\ \mathbf{in}\ P\ \mathbf{do}\ R) & \\
\mathbf{for}\ x\ \mathbf{in}\ P\ \mathbf{do}\ \texttt{[]} & \hookrightarrow & \texttt{[]} & \\
\mathbf{if}\ P\ \mathbf{then}\ (Q\ \texttt{@}\ R) & \hookrightarrow & (\mathbf{if}\ P\ \mathbf{then}\ Q)\ \texttt{@}\ (\mathbf{if}\ P\ \mathbf{then}\ R) & \\
\mathbf{if}\ P\ \mathbf{then}\ \texttt{[]} & \hookrightarrow & \texttt{[]} & \\
\mathbf{if}\ P\ \mathbf{then}\ (\mathbf{if}\ Q\ \mathbf{then}\ R) & \hookrightarrow & \mathbf{if}\ (P\ \texttt{\&\&}\ Q)\ \mathbf{then}\ R & \text{(if-if)} \\
\mathbf{if}\ P\ \mathbf{then}\ (\mathbf{for}\ x\ \mathbf{in}\ Q\ \mathbf{do}\ R) & \hookrightarrow & \mathbf{for}\ x\ \mathbf{in}\ Q\ \mathbf{do}\ (\mathbf{if}\ P\ \mathbf{then}\ R) & \\
& & & \text{(if-for)}
\end{array}
$$

Figure 12. Normalisation Stage 2: *ad-hoc* reduction

$$
\begin{array}{lll}
\text{(SQL query)} & S & ::= \texttt{[]} \mid X \mid X_1\ \texttt{@}\ X_2 \\
\text{(collection)} & X & ::= \mathbf{database}(\mathsf{db}) \mid \mathbf{yield}\ Y \mid \mathbf{if}\ Z\ \mathbf{then\ yield}\ Y \\
& & \quad \mid \mathbf{for}\ x\ \mathbf{in\ database}(\mathsf{db}).\ell\ \mathbf{do}\ X \\
\text{(record)} & Y & ::= x \mid \{\overline{\ell = Z}\} \\
\text{(base)} & Z & ::= c \mid x.\ell \mid op(\overline{X}) \mid \mathbf{exists}\ S
\end{array}
$$

Figure 13. Syntax of Normalised Terms

5.4 An Example

As an example of normalisation, we consider evaluation of query (5) from Section 2.5.

```
run(<@ (%compose)("Edna", "Bert") @>)
```

After splicing, the quotation becomes:

```
(fun(s, t) →
  for a in (fun(s) →
              for u in database("People").people do
              if u.name = s then yield u.age) (s) do
  for b in (fun(s) →
              for u in database("People").people do
              if u.name = s then yield u.age) (t) do
  (fun(a, b) →
    for w in database("People").people do
    if a ≤ w.age && w.age < b then
    yield {name : w.name}) (a, b))
("Edna", "Bert")
```

For stage 1 (Figure 11), applying four beta-reductions yields:

```
for a in (for u in database("People").people do
          if u.name = "Edna" then yield u.age) do
for b in (for u in database("People").people do
          if u.name = "Bert" then yield u.age) do
for w in database("People").people do
if a ≤ w.age && w.age < b then
yield {name : w.name}
```

Continuing stage 1, applying each of rules (for-for), (for-if), and (for-yld) twice, and renaming to avoid capture, yields:

```
for u in database("People").people do
if u.name = "Edna" then
for v in database("People").people do
if v.name = "Bert" then
for w in database("People").people do
if u.age ≤ w.age && w.age < v.age then
yield {name : w.name}
```

For stage 2 (Figure 12), applying rule (if-for) thrice and rule (if-if) twice yields:

```
for u in database("People").people do
for v in database("People").people do
for w in database("People").people do
if u.name = "Edna" && v.name = "Bert" &&
  u.age ≤ w.age && w.age < v.age then
yield {name : w.name}
```

This is in normal form, and easily converted to SQL. Running it yields the answer given previously.

6. Quoted Language vs. Host Language

We write in a style where we abstract in the quoted language whenever possible. As we shall see, this is essential if several functions are to be composed into a single query, as in Section 2.5. We abstract in the host language only when we need a feature not present in the quoted language, such as recursion, as used to construct dynamic queries in Sections 2.6 and 4.

Another style, which might at first appear appealing, is to always abstract in the host language. For instance, one might redefine range from Section 2.3 as follows.

```
let range'(a : Expr<int>, b : Expr<int>) : Expr<Names> =
  <@ for w in (%db).people do
    if (%a) ≤ w.age && w.age < (%b) then
    yield {name : w.name} @>
```

(Or one might define a variant where a and b have type **int** and lifting is used, which raises similar issues.) Before, we wrote an invocation like this:

```
run(<@ (%range)(30,40) @>).
```

Now, we write an invocation like this:

```
run(range'(<@ 30 @>, <@ 40 @>)).
```

The latter may be slightly more efficient, as it directly yields a quotation in normal form, and no beta-reduction is required. For this reason, we had originally assumed that one should abstract in the host language, but late in the process of writing this paper we realised this is a mistake. We stick a prime on the name to warn that this form of definition hinders composition.

Let's see what goes wrong with composition. In Section 2.5 we used range to define compose. Attempting a revision using range′ yields the following.

```
let compose' : Expr<(string, string) → Names> =
  <@ fun(s, t) → for a in (%getAge)(s) do
                 for b in (%getAge)(t) do
                 (%range'(<@ a @>, <@ b @>)) @>
```

Warning: the above is not legal in F# (or T-LINQ)! Previously, all the quotations we saw were *closed*, since every quoted variable is bound within the quotation; but the two quotations <@ a @> and <@ b @> passed to range′ are *open*, since they contain free quoted variables. In this case, the variables become bound after splicing into the surrounding quotation, but, in general, open quotations come with no guarantee that free variables meet their binding occurrences. For this reason, open quotations are illegal in F# and in T-LINQ, and there is no easy way to use range′ to define compose′.

Typing closed quotation is straightforward in current languages, and is supported in F# or in any language with GADTs (Cheney and Hinze 2003). In contrast, open quotation in a typed language requires some form of specialised type system; experimental languages that support open quotation include MetaML (Taha and Sheard 2000) or Ur (Chlipala 2010), and a recent experimental feature in GHC supports MetaML typing rules for quotations. We sketch a simple type system that supports open quotation in Section 7, and show how closed quotation can simulate that form of open quotation, which suggests how closed quotation may be adequate for situations where one might have thought open quotation was required.

While open quotation avoids the cost of some beta-reductions, it does not avoid the need for the other normalisation rules discussed in Section 5.3. Further, the cost of normalising a quoted term is low compared to the cost of evaluating the resulting SQL query against the database, as demonstrated in Section 9. Thus, we believe closed quotation and normalisation provide a practical alternative to more elaborate systems that support open quotation.

7. Open Quotation

Section 6 discussed the difference between closed and open quotation. T-LINQ and P-LINQ, like F#, support only closed quotation. Here we generalise T-LINQ to support a form of open quotation, and we show how this form may be simulated by closed quotation. Choi et al. (2011) give a similar result. Our formalisation of open quotation is not as powerful as that found in systems such as MetaML or Ur, but the translation is suggestive of why closed quotation may be adequate for dealing with cases (such as composition of queries or dynamic generation of queries) that one may previously have thought required open quotation.

For the extension, we add a type environment to the type of quoted terms, generalising $\mathsf{Expr}{<}A{>}$ to $\mathsf{Expr}{<}\Delta; A{>}$, where Δ specifies the types of the free variables in the quoted term. Only four typing rules need to change.

LIFT
$$\frac{\Gamma \vdash M : O}{\Gamma \vdash \mathbf{lift}(M) : \mathsf{Expr}{<}\cdot; O{>}}$$

RUN
$$\frac{\Gamma \vdash M : \mathsf{Expr}{<}\cdot; T{>}}{\Gamma \vdash \mathbf{run}\, M : T}$$

QUOTE
$$\frac{\Gamma; \Delta \vdash M : A}{\Gamma \vdash \texttt{<@}\, M\, \texttt{@>}_\Delta : \mathsf{Expr}{<}\Delta; A{>}}$$

ANTIQUOTE
$$\frac{\Gamma \vdash M : \mathsf{Expr}{<}\Delta; A{>}}{\Gamma; \Delta \vdash (\%M)_\Delta : A}$$

In order to allow syntax-directed typechecking, we add type environment annotations to quotation and antiquotation expressions.

To simulate the extended language in the original, we represent an open quotation of type $\mathsf{Expr}{<}\Delta; A{>}$ by a closed quotation of type $\mathsf{Expr}{<}\Delta \to A{>}$, explicitly abstracting over each of the free variables in the quoted type environment. We specify translations of types, host terms, and query terms from the extended language back into the original language. There is only one case of interest for each translation.

$$\begin{aligned}
[\![\mathsf{Expr}{<}\Delta; A{>}]\!] &= \mathsf{Expr}{<}[\![\Delta]\!] \to [\![A]\!]{>} \\
[\![\texttt{<@}\, M\, \texttt{@>}_\Delta]\!] &= \texttt{<@}\, \mathbf{fun}(\Delta) \to [\![M]\!]\, \texttt{@>} \\
[\![(\%M)_\Delta]\!] &= (\%M)\ \Delta
\end{aligned}$$

All of the other cases are defined homomorphically. Here Δ on the right-hand side stands in the first line for a tuple of the types in the environment; in the second line for a tuple of the bindings in the environment, over which the translation is abstracted; and in the third line for a tuple of the variables in the environment, to which the translation is applied. All tuples must be consistently ordered, say alphabetically on the names of the variables in Δ.

PROPOSITION 5. *The translation preserves types, and the extended language is simulated by the original language.*

- *If* $\Gamma \vdash M : A$ *then* $[\![\Gamma]\!] \vdash [\![M]\!]$.
- *If* $\Gamma; \Delta \vdash M : A$ *then* $[\![\Gamma]\!]; [\![\Delta]\!] \vdash [\![M]\!] : [\![A]\!]$.
- *If* $\Gamma \vdash M : A$ *and* $M \longrightarrow N$ *then* $[\![M]\!] \longrightarrow [\![N]\!]$.
- *If* $\Gamma; \Delta \vdash M : A$ *and* $M \longrightarrow N$ *then* $[\![M]\!] \longrightarrow [\![N]\!]$.

8. Comparison to Microsoft LINQ

T-LINQ abstracts from several distracting issues in the implementation of Microsoft LINQ for C#, Visual Basic, and F#.

Microsoft's LINQ library includes interfaces IEnumerable<A> and IQueryable<A> that provide standard query operators including selection, join, filtering, grouping, sorting, and aggregation. These query operators are defined to act both on sequences and on quotations that yield sequences. LINQ query expressions in C# or Visual Basic are translated to code that calls the methods in these interfaces. For example, a C# LINQ query

from x **in** e **where** p(x) **select** f(x)

translates to the sequence of calls

e.Where(x ⇒ p(x)).Select(x ⇒ f(x))

Depending on the context, lambda-abstractions in C# and Visual Basic are treated either as functions or as quoted functions.

Any external data source that can implement some of the query operations can be connected to LINQ using a *query provider*. Implementing a query provider can be difficult, in part because of the overhead of dealing with the Expression<A> type. Eini (2011) characterises the experience of writing a custom query provider as "doom, gloom with just a tad of despair". Microsoft supplies a LINQ to SQL query provider for SQL Server. Microsoft's query provider is proprietary, so its behaviour is a black box, but it does appear to perform some beta-reduction and other normalisation.

As we have already described, F# supports LINQ using syntactic sugar for comprehensions (called *computation expressions* (Petricek and Syme 2012)), quotations, and reflection. In the F# PowerPack library made available for F# 2.0, some LINQ capabilities are supported by a translator from the F# Expr< A > type to the LINQ Expression<A> type. This implementation has some bugs and limitations, for instance, it fails to translate arguments of **exists** in the test of a conditional.

F# 3.0 supports LINQ through an improved translation based on computation expressions (Petricek and Syme 2012). In F# 3.0, one can simply write **query**$\{e\}$ to indicate that a computation expression e should be interpreted as a query; the standard library class QueryBuilder translates e to a C# LINQ expression and evaluates it. This implementation also has some bugs and limitations, for instance, it forbids some uses of splicing, and does not correctly process some queries that start with a conditional.

9. Implementation and Results

To validate our design, we implemented a pre-processor that takes any quoted F# sequence expression over the standard query operators and normalises it as described in Section 5.3. In theory, our normaliser could be followed by either the F# 2.0 or F# 3.0 backend, but the bugs noted in the previous section prevent some of our sample queries from working with each. The F# 2.0 PowerPack is distributed as a separate library and easy to modify, while the F# 3.0 backend is built-in and difficult to modify. Hence, for most of our experiments, we opted to use F# 2.0 LINQ syntax and a modified version of the F# 2.0 backend with our pre-processor. To experiment with grouping, aggregation and other operations that are only supported in F# 3.0, we have also developed a prototype that provides subclasses of the F# 3.0 QueryBuilder library class, along with variants of the **query**$\{\cdots\}$ keyword, that perform normalisation before calling F# 3.0's LINQ implementation. The QueryBuilder implementation employs some subtle tricks to support type-directed dispatch so that **query**$\{\cdots\}$ works for both in-memory and external database calls. Unfortunately, these tricks make it difficult to smoothly override the QueryBuilder class to provide drop-in compatible behaviour; in our implementation, we provide different variants of the query keyword for use in different contexts. This limitation could easily be overcome by a change to the F# 3.0 QueryBuilder class, and we are discussing this possibility with Microsoft. We use the term P-LINQ to refer to both implementations, and specify the back-end F# LINQ implementation used when it is relevant.

Example	F# 2.0	F# 3.0	P-LINQ	*norm*
differences (1)	17.6	20.6	18.1	0.5
range (2)	×	5.6	2.9	0.3
satisfies (3)	2.6	×	2.9	0.3
satisfies (4)	4.4	×	4.6	0.3
compose (5)	×	×	4.0	0.8
P(t_0) (6)	2.8	×	3.3	0.3
P(t_1) (7)	2.7	×	3.0	0.3
expertise′ (8)	7.2*	9.2	8.0*	0.6
expertise (9)	×	66.7[av]	8.3*	0.9
xp_0 (10)	×	8.3	7.9	1.9
xp_1 (11)	×	14.7	13.4	1.1
xp_2 (12)	×	17.9	20.7*	2.2
xp_3 (13)	×	3744.9	3768.6*	4.4

All times in milliseconds. × marks failures.
* marks cases requiring modified F# 2.0 PowerPack library.
[av] marks the case where a query avalanche occurs.
$|$people$| = 10000$, $|$couples$| = 5000$, $|$employees$| = 5000$, $|$tasks$| = 4931$, $|$xml$| = 6527$

Table 1. Experimental Results.

All experiments were run on a Dell OptiPlex 790 with Intel Core i5-2400 CPU at 3.10 GHz, 4GB RAM and a 7200 RPM hard drive with 8MB cache, and using Microsoft .NET 4.0 runtime, Visual Studio 2012 v11.0.50727.1, and SQL Server 2012, all running on the same machine to avoid any network-related latency. All reported times are the medians of 21 trials. All source code for the examples, the data, and the modified F# 2.0 PowerPack library is available online (Cheney et al. 2012).

Table 1 summarises our experimental results. We wrote and ran versions of each example using the F# 2.0 PowerPack LINQ library, the F# 3.0 LINQ library, and P-LINQ (using the F# 2.0 backend). We randomly generated data for the couples and organisation databases, and used an existing repository of XML data, with sizes as listed in the table. Each entry in the table either indicates that the query failed (×), or gives the total time in milliseconds for successful evaluation, including time to generate the SQL query (or queries, in the case of an avalanche), to evaluate the query, and to construct a value from the result. For P-LINQ, the total includes time to normalise the quoted expression; this is also shown separately in the column labelled *norm*.

F# 2.0 failed on seven examples, and F# 3.0 failed on five, though each succeeds on examples on which the other fails. The modified PowerPack library was required in one case by F# 2.0 and in four cases by P-LINQ. F# 3.0 generated an avalanche of SQL queries for query (9); this example query involves nested intermediate data but its result is flat, in contrast to cases of avalanche

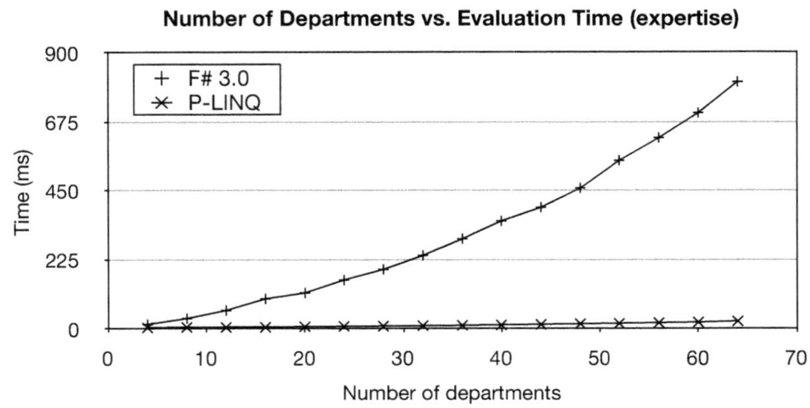

Figure 14. Query avalanche results. Each department is of size 100, with each employee assigned 0, 1, or 2 tasks at random.

Q#	F# 3.0	P-LINQ	*norm*
Q1	2.0	2.4	0.3
Q2	1.5	1.7	0.2
Q5	1.7	2.1	0.3
Q6	1.7	2.1	0.3
Q7	1.5	1.8	0.2
Q8	2.3	2.4	0.2
Q9	2.3	2.7	0.3
Q10	1.4	1.7	0.2
Q11	1.4	1.7	0.2
Q12	4.4	4.9	0.4
Q13	2.5	2.9	0.4
Q14	2.5	2.9	0.3
Q15	3.5	4.0	0.5
Q16	3.5	4.0	0.5
Q17	6.2	6.7	0.4
Q18	1.5	1.8	0.2
Q19	1.5	1.8	0.2
Q20	1.5	1.8	0.2
Q21	1.6	1.9	0.3
Q22	1.6	1.9	0.3
Q23	1.6	1.9	0.3

Q#	F# 3.0	P-LINQ	*norm*
Q24	1.8	2.0	0.3
Q25	1.4	1.6	0.2
Q27	1.8	2.1	0.2
Q29	1.5	1.7	0.2
Q30	1.8	2.0	0.2
Q32	2.7	3.1	0.3
Q33	2.8	3.1	0.3
Q34	3.1	3.6	0.5
Q35	3.1	3.6	0.4
Q36	2.2	2.4	0.2
Q37	1.3	1.6	0.2
Q38	4.2	4.9	0.6
Q39	4.2	4.7	0.4
Q40	4.1	4.6	0.4
Q41	6.3	7.3	0.6
Q42	4.7	5.5	0.5
Q43	7.2	6.9	0.7
Q44	5.4	6.2	0.7
Q45	2.2	2.6	0.3
Q46	2.3	2.7	0.4
Q47	2.1	2.5	0.3

Q#	F# 3.0	P-LINQ	*norm*
Q48	2.1	2.5	0.3
Q49	2.4	2.7	0.3
Q50	2.2	2.5	0.3
Q51	2.0	2.4	0.3
Q52	6.1	5.9	0.4
Q53	11.9	11.2	0.6
Q54	4.4	4.8	0.4
Q55	5.2	5.6	0.4
Q56	4.6	5.1	0.5
Q57	2.5	2.9	0.4
Q58	2.5	2.9	0.4
Q59	3.1	3.6	0.5
Q60	3.6	4.4	0.7
Q61	5.8	6.3	0.3
Q62	5.4	5.9	0.2
Q63	3.4	3.8	0.4
Q64	4.3	4.9	0.6
Q65	10.2	10.1	0.4
Q66	8.9	8.7	0.6
Q67	14.7	13.1	1.1

Table 2. Comparison of F# 3.0 and P-LINQ (using F# 3.0 as a back-end) on the 62 example database queries in the F# 3.0 documentation (Microsoft 2013). There are 67 examples in total; five query expressions (Q3, Q4, Q26, Q28, Q31) are excluded because they execute on in-memory lists rather than generate SQL.

reported by Grust et al. (2010), all of which return nested results. As guaranteed by Proposition 4, translation for P-LINQ always succeeds and never generates avalanches for queries with flat results.

Generally, normalisation time is dwarfed by query evaluation time, in some cases by several orders of magnitude. The F# type Expr< A > maintains information irrelevant to our application, so we elected to normalise by converting the F# type Expr< A > to our own custom representation, normalising that, and converting back to Expr< A >. Profiling suggests most of the time in our normaliser is spent converting to our custom representation. The only way to traverse Expr< A > expressions in F# is through active pattern matching, which appears to be expensive.

To evaluate the impact of query avalanches, we reran query (9) with F# 3.0 and P-LINQ with varying numbers of departments, ranging from 4 to 64. For F# 3.0, the number of queries performed is $d+1$ where d is the number of departments. The results are shown in Figure 14. Both approaches scale roughly linearly in the number of departments (and hence, total data size); we summarise the results in terms of the average time s to process each department. The value of s for F# 3.0 is 12.8 milliseconds per department, while that for P-LINQ is 0.3. These results confirm that P-LINQ's normalisation can reap significant savings by avoiding query avalanches.

T-LINQ does not include constructs such as sorting, grouping, or aggregation, which are important in practical use of LINQ. We have designed P-LINQ so that it rewrites any subterm it recognises, and carries through other constructs unchanged. Our results suggest this is a practical alternative: we tested this prototype on all 62 of the example database queries on the F# 3.0 Query Expressions documentation page (Microsoft 2013). (There are also five tests that do not generate SQL queries, which we excluded from the experiments.) All of these queries are concrete, that is, none involves abstraction, and they are evaluated on a small database of about 30 records. The results are shown in Table 2. We summarise the results in terms of the ratio r of P-LINQ to F# 3.0 evaluation time. The geometric mean of r over all tests is 1.13 (so on average P-LINQ is 13% slower), and the minimum and maximum values of r over all tests is 0.89 and 1.24, respectively (so at best P-LINQ is 11% faster and at worst 24% slower). All the translations succeeded, suggesting that normalisation does not interfere with F# 3.0's support for additional query operators. These results demonstrate that the overhead of normalisation is modest, even for small data sets, and occasionally normalisation improves query time, even for concrete queries.

At present, F# 3.0 does not allow overriding the default query builder, so we cannot yet provide our implementation as a drop-in replacement. We are discussing with the Microsoft F# team how best to make our techniques available in a future version of F#.

10. Related Work

LINQ has attracted considerable commercial interest, but has not been extensively documented in the research literature. Meijer et al. (2006) and Meijer (2011) give overviews of the foundations of LINQ. Syme (2006) presents an early version of F#'s quotation and reflection capabilities, illustrated via applications to LINQ, GPU code generation, and runtime F# code generation. Bierman et al. (2007) present a formalisation of several extensions to C#, including LINQ. Eini (2011) identifies obstacles to implementing LINQ providers for non-SQL databases. Beckman (2012) advocates LINQ as an interface to cloud computing platforms. Petricek and Syme (2012) and Syme et al. (2012) describe F# 3.0's sequence expressions and the related computation builder mechanism. Use of LINQ for abstraction over values and predicates and dynamic generation of queries has been discussed in blogs and online forums, such as Petricek (2007b,a), but has not, to our knowledge, previously been modelled formally.

Type-safe quotation and meta-programming is an active research area. Davies and Pfenning (2001) introduce a calculus $\lambda^{\Box}$ for closed multistage programming based on a modal logic, where each stage uses the same language. T-LINQ can be viewed as a variant with just two stages, each using a slightly different language. Rhiger (2012) presents a calculus for multistage programming with open quotations, noting that closed quotation leads to less efficient code due to administrative redexes. In our setting, such administrative redexes have negligible cost because we normalisation time is dominated by query execution time. Choi et al. (2011) present a translation from open to closed quotation similar to ours, aimed at supporting translation-based static analysis for staged computation. Van den Bussche et al. (2005) present a meta-querying system for SQL, but does not consider type safety or language integration.

Integrating queries into a general-purpose language is also an active research area. Ohori and Ueno (2011) introduces SML#, which offers direct support for SQL queries, including a type system that guarantees each query accesses only a single database. It does not normalise queries. Chlipala (2010) introduces Ur/Web, which uses open quotations with a sophisticated type system. It also does not normalise queries. Ur/Web can express most of the queries given here, though it relies on subqueries to express query composition, and it cannot express the nested query (9) of Section 3.2 (Adam Chlipala, personal communication, January 2013). Budiu et al. (2013) present a general framework for composing compilers based on LCF-style tactics, and apply this methodology to a subset of LINQ in C# called μLINQ. It would be interesting to see whether this approach can be used for T-LINQ.

Grust et al. (2009, 2010) describe Ferry, a functional query language that, like our work, supports higher-order functions and nested data, but goes beyond our work in also supporting queries that return nested results. The Ferry team have implemented several LINQ query providers, as well as interfacing Ferry with Links (Ulrich 2011) and Haskell (Giorgidze et al. 2010). Henglein and Larsen (2010) consider efficient in-memory evaluation of query-like constructs using lazy evaluation and generic discrimination. These approaches employ complementary techniques to our normalisation-based approach; combining our results with these systems appears possible, and should be explored in future work.

In our case the host language and quoted language are taken to be identical, but that is a design choice. An approach where host and quoted languages differ is described by Mainland (2012).

We indicate quotations syntactically (with `<@ ··· @>`). An alternative approach is to indicate quotation by type declaration, as is done in C# and with Lightweight Modular Staging in Scala (Rompf and Odersky 2012). Another alternative is not to support quotation in the language but to use an embedded DSL to construct parse trees, an approach taken in Nikola (Mainland and Morrisett 2010) and Feldspar (Axelsson et al. 2010; Axelsson and Svenningsson 2012). We intend to team with Feldspar researchers to compare their approach with ours.

11. Conclusion

We presented a simple theory of language-integrated query based on quotation and normalisation. Through a series of examples, we demonstrated that our technique supports abstraction over values and predicates, composition of queries, dynamic generation of queries, and queries with nested intermediate data; and that higher-order features proved useful even for dynamic generation of first-order queries. We developed a formal theory, T-LINQ, and proved that normalisation always succeeds in translating any query of flat relation type to SQL. We presented an implementation in F# called P-LINQ, and experimental results confirming our technique works in practice as predicted. We observed that for several of our examples, Microsoft's LINQ framework either fails to produce an SQL query or produces an avalanche of SQL queries.

In essence, we have supplied a recipe for using a host language to generate code in a target language. The recipe involves three languages: the host language (in our case, F#), the target language (in our case, SQL), and a quoted language (in our case, essentially F# again).

- The host language should support quotation and anti-quotation of terms in the quoted language: in our case, we use F# quotation.
- The quoted language may need to add constructs not in the host language (so it is as expressive as the target language), and omit some constructs in the host language (so it is not more expressive than the target language after normalisation): in our case, the quoted language adds the **database** construct but omits recursion.
- The quoted language should at least support lambda abstraction and typing: support for lambda abstraction means it is sufficient to support closed quotations, which in turn makes it easier to support typing.
- Finally—and most importantly—one must identify an adequate normalisation procedure. Normalisation should at least perform beta-reduction: thus the quoted language may exploit the expressiveness of lambda abstraction even if the target language is first order. Normalisation may perform operations other than beta-reduction: in our case, additional rewrite rules support translation into SQL.

Applying the recipe to other domains is an important area for future work.

To conclude, let's compare the theoretical and practical aspects of our work. Regarding the host and quoted languages, the recipe above makes clear they may differ in theory, and this is the case in T-LINQ; in practice, they tend to be the same, and this is the case in P-LINQ. Regarding coverage, T-LINQ differs from full LINQ, and extending it to cover sorting, grouping, and aggregation remains important work for tomorrow. Meanwhile, P-LINQ supports the same features as LINQ, and it can be put to work today.

Our opening adage acknowledges that theory can fall short of the needs of practice. In contrast, our experience confirms that practice benefits from a judicious dose of theory, even when that theory is incomplete. We propose a reversal of the opening platitude.

What is the difference between theory and practice?
In theory there is a difference, but in practice there isn't.

Acknowledgments

We are grateful to Nada Amin, James McKinna, Tomas Petricek, Simon Peyton Jones, Tiark Rompf, and Don Syme for comments on this work. The second author would like to thank Conor McBride for the craic. This work is supported in part by a Google Research Award (Lindley), EPSRC grants EP/J014591/1 (Lindley) and EP/K034413/1 (Lindley, Wadler), and a Royal Society University Research Fellowship (Cheney).

References

M. P. Atkinson and O. P. Buneman. Types and persistence in database programming languages. *ACM Comput. Surv.*, 19(2):105–170, 1987.

E. Axelsson and J. Svenningsson. Combining deep and shallow embedding for EDSL. In *TFP*, 2012.

E. Axelsson, K. Claessen, M. Sheeran, J. Svenningsson, D. Engdal, and A. Persson. The design and implementation of Feldspar—an embedded language for digital signal processing. In J. Hage and M. T. Morazán, editors, *IFL*, volume 6647 of *LNCS*, pages 121–136. Springer, 2010.

B. Beckman. Why LINQ matters: cloud composability guaranteed. *Commun. ACM*, 55(4):38–44, Apr. 2012.

G. M. Bierman, E. Meijer, and M. Torgersen. Lost in translation: formalizing proposed extensions to C#. In *OOPSLA*, pages 479–498. ACM, 2007.

M. Budiu, J. Galenson, and G. D. Plotkin. The compiler forest. In *ESOP*, number 7792 in LNCS, pages 21–40. Springer-Verlag, 2013.

P. Buneman, L. Libkin, D. Suciu, V. Tannen, and L. Wong. Comprehension syntax. *SIGMOD Record*, 23:87–96, 1994.

J. Cheney and R. Hinze. First-class phantom types. Computer and Information Science Technical Report TR2003-1901, Cornell University, 2003.

J. Cheney, S. Lindley, and P. Wadler. A practical theory of language-integrated query (code supplement), 2012. `http://homepages.inf.ed.ac.uk/jcheney/linq`.

A. J. Chlipala. Ur: statically-typed metaprogramming with type-level record computation. In *PLDI*, pages 122–133. ACM, 2010.

W. Choi, B. Aktemur, K. Yi, and M. Tatsuta. Static analysis of multi-staged programs via unstaging translation. In *POPL*, pages 81–92. ACM, 2011.

E. Cooper. The script-writer's dream: How to write great SQL in your own language, and be sure it will succeed. In *DBPL*, number 5708 in LNCS, pages 36–51. Springer-Verlag, 2009.

E. Cooper, S. Lindley, P. Wadler, and J. Yallop. Links: web programming without tiers. In *FMCO*, volume 4709 of *LNCS*, pages 266–296, 2007.

G. Copeland and D. Maier. Making Smalltalk a database system. *SIGMOD Rec.*, 14(2):316–325, 1984.

R. Davies and F. Pfenning. A modal analysis of staged computation. *J. ACM*, 48(3):555–604, 2001.

O. Eini. The pain of implementing LINQ providers. *Commun. ACM*, 54(8): 55–61, 2011.

G. Giorgidze, T. Grust, T. Schreiber, and J. Weijers. Haskell boards the Ferry - database-supported program execution for Haskell. In *IFL*, number 6647 in LNCS, pages 1–18. Springer-Verlag, 2010.

T. Goldschmidt, R. Reussner, and J. Winzen. A case study evaluation of maintainability and performance of persistency techniques. In *ICSE*, pages 401–410. ACM, 2008.

T. Grust, M. van Keulen, and J. Teubner. Accelerating XPath evaluation in any RDBMS. *ACM Trans. Database Syst.*, 29:91–131, 2004.

T. Grust, M. Mayr, J. Rittinger, and T. Schreiber. Ferry: Database-supported program execution. In *SIGMOD*, pages 1063–1066. ACM, 2009.

T. Grust, J. Rittinger, and T. Schreiber. Avalanche-safe LINQ compilation. *PVLDB*, 3(1):162–172, 2010.

F. Henglein and K. F. Larsen. Generic multiset programming with discrimination-based joins and symbolic cartesian products. *Higher-Order and Symbolic Computation*, 23(3):337–370, 2010.

S. Lindley and J. Cheney. Row-based effect types for database integration. In *TLDI*, pages 91–102. ACM, 2012.

G. Mainland. Explicitly heterogeneous metaprogramming with MetaHaskell. In P. Thiemann and R. B. Findler, editors, *ICFP*, pages 311–322. ACM, 2012. ISBN 978-1-4503-1054-3.

G. Mainland and G. Morrisett. Nikola: embedding compiled GPU functions in haskell. In J. Gibbons, editor, *Haskell Symposium*, pages 67–78. ACM, 2010. ISBN 978-1-4503-0252-4.

E. Meijer. The world according to LINQ. *Commun. ACM*, 54(10):45–51, Oct. 2011.

E. Meijer, B. Beckman, and G. M. Bierman. LINQ: reconciling object, relations and XML in the .NET framework. In *SIGMOD*, page 706. ACM, 2006.

Microsoft. Query expressions (F# 3.0 documentation), 2013. `http://msdn.microsoft.com/en-us/library/vstudio/-hh225374.aspx`, accessed March 18, 2013.

A. Ohori and K. Ueno. Making Standard ML a practical database programming language. In *ICFP*, pages 307–319. ACM, 2011.

T. Petricek. Building LINQ queries at runtime in (F#), 2007a. `http://tomasp.net/blog/dynamic-flinq.aspx`.

T. Petricek. Building LINQ queries at runtime in (C#), 2007b. `http://tomasp.net/blog/dynamic-linq-queries.aspx`.

T. Petricek and D. Syme. Syntax Matters: Writing abstract computations in F#. Pre-proceedings of TFP, 2012. `http://www.cl.cam.ac.uk/~tp322/drafts/notations.pdf`.

D. Prawitz. *Natural Deduction: A Proof-Theoretical Study*. Almqvist and Wiksell, Stockholm, 1965.

M. Rhiger. Staged computation with staged lexical scope. In *ESOP*, number 7211 in LNCS, pages 559–578. Springer-Verlag, 2012.

T. Rompf and M. Odersky. Lightweight modular staging: a pragmatic approach to runtime code generation and compiled dsls. *Commun. ACM*, 55(6):121–130, 2012.

D. Syme. Leveraging .NET meta-programming components from F#: integrated queries and interoperable heterogeneous execution. In *ML Workshop*, pages 43–54. ACM, 2006.

D. Syme, A. Granicz, and A. Cisternino. *Expert F# 3.0*. Apress, 2012. ISBN 978-1-4302-4650-3.

W. Taha and T. Sheard. MetaML and multi-stage programming with explicit annotations. *Theor. Comput. Sci.*, 248(1-2):211–242, 2000.

P. Trinder. Comprehensions, a query notation for DBPLs. In *Proceedings of 3rd International Workshop on Database Programming Languages*, pages 49–62. Morgan Kaufmann, 1991.

P. Trinder and P. Wadler. Improving list comprehension database queries. In *TENCON '89.*, 1989.

A. Ulrich. A Ferry-based query backend for the Links programming language. Master's thesis, University of Tübingen, 2011.

J. Van den Bussche, S. Vansummeren, and G. Vossen. Towards practical meta-querying. *Inf. Syst.*, 30(4):317–332, 2005.

L. Wong. Normal forms and conservative extension properties for query languages over collection types. *J. Comput. Syst. Sci.*, 52(3):495–505, 1996.

Calculating Threesomes, with Blame

Ronald Garcia
University of British Columbia
rxg@cs.ubc.ca

Abstract

Coercions and threesomes both enable a language to combine static and dynamic types while avoiding cast-based space leaks. Coercion calculi elegantly specify space-efficient cast behavior, even when augmented with blame tracking, but implementing their semantics directly is difficult. Threesomes, on the other hand, have a straightforward recursive implementation, but endowing them with blame tracking is challenging. In this paper, we show that you can use that elegant spec to produce that straightforward implementation: we use the coercion calculus to derive threesomes with blame. In particular, we construct novel threesome calculi for blame tracking strategies that detect errors earlier, catch more errors, and reflect an intuitive conception of safe and unsafe casts based on traditional subtyping.

Categories and Subject Descriptors D.3.1 [*Software*]: Programming Languages—Formal Definitions and Theory

General Terms Languages, Theory

Keywords casts, space efficiency, threesomes, coercions, labeled types

1. Introduction

Plenty of research has gone into designing languages that integrate static and dynamic typing. This paper extends existing work on effectively implementing such languages and exposes connections between two ways of specifying them.

A popular approach in this area is to extend a language with a dynamic type and use casts to mediate between static and dynamic code. Here we focus on $\lambda^{\langle T \rangle}$, a family of languages based on the lambda calculus extended with a dynamic type $\star$ and explicit casts between types (see Fig. 1). The language was introduced by Siek and Taha (2006), but since then a variety of semantics have been developed for it.

Herman et al. (2007) observed that *higher-order* casts—casts between function types—cause space leaks in programs (Sec. 3). To avoid this hazard, they used *coercions* (Henglein 1994), a low-level representation for sequences of casts, to accumulate higher-order casts in a compact form. Siek and Wadler (2010) prevent these same space leaks using *threesomes*, a special pairing of casts that can represent any sequence of standard casts.

ICFP '13, September 25–27, 2013, Boston, MA, USA.

http://dx.doi.org/10.1145/2500365.2500603

Coercions and threesomes both prevent space leaks, but they have different strengths and weaknesses. Coercion calculi describe space-efficient casts in a way that is easy to understand, and it is straightforward to extend them with support for blame tracking, but implementing them directly is difficult (Sec. 3.4). Threesomes, on the other hand, have a straightforward recursive implementation, but endowing them with blame tracking was a subtle and opaque process (Sec. 3.1.1). Moreover, the Threesome Calculus (Siek and Wadler 2010) supports only one blame tracking strategy, but other blame tracking strategies have been developed on top of coercions with useful properties like catching earlier errors and admitting a traditional notion of subtyping to characterize safe casts (Siek et al. 2009). We desire an effective implementation approach for these other strategies. This paper addresses this problem with the following **contributions**:

- We develop three new threesome calculi that correspond to blame tracking strategies identified by Siek et al. (2009). These calculi lay groundwork for effectively implementing languages with these other strategies, thereby supporting earlier error detection and an intuitive conception of safe and unsafe casts based on traditional subtyping (Secs. 5–6).
- To produce these results, we first revisit the coercion- and threesome-based variants of the Blame Calculus (Siek and Wadler 2010; Siek et al. 2009; Wadler and Findler 2009). These calculi were developed independently and proven to correspond after the fact. Here, we start from the coercion calculus and transform it into a threesome calculus in small, easily verified steps (Sec. 4). This reconstruction provides our strategy for developing new threesomes, but it also clearly shows that coercions and threesomes are two alternative representations of the same concept, one more suited to specification and the other to implementation.

2. Related Work

Henglein (1994) introduced the *Coercion Calculus* and used it to develop a core theory of dynamic typing that adds a dynamic type to $\lambda^{\rightarrow}$. In this model, all programs are typeable and their semantics are given by translation to an internal language with coercions to mediate between types.

Siek and Taha (2006) introduced the concept of *gradual typing*, whereby a program explicitly combines static and dynamic typing using a notion of *type consistency*. In contrast to Henglein (1994), some programs (deemed "type-inconsistent") are rejected statically. Well-typed programs are given meaning by translation to $\lambda^{\langle T \rangle}$, which was directly given operational semantics.

Herman et al. (2007) observed that gradually-typed programs could exhibit space leaks that are not visible in the surface language, including leaks on tail calls. They give an equivalent semantics for programs using the coercion calculus and prove that it is space efficient.

Matthews and Findler (2009) introduced and explored abstract semantics for programming systems involving multiple interoperating languages; in parallel, Tobin-Hochstadt and Felleisen (2006) developed a framework for interlanguage migration, whereby dynamically typed modules may coexist with statically-typed modules. These works use blame to establish type soundness theorems that extend Milner's conception of type safety in light of dynamic typing: only dynamically typed modules can go wrong.

Wadler and Findler (2009) adapted the results of the above work on multi-language semantics and inter-language migration to the context of languages like $\lambda^{\langle T \rangle}$ that freely mix dynamic and static types throughout. Their *Blame Calculus* adds blame labels (Findler and Felleisen 2002) to casts and satisfies a soundness theorem that ensures that only the dynamic part of a program can be blamed for runtime type errors.

Siek et al. (2009) introduced a family of related semantics for $\lambda^{\langle T \rangle}$ based on coercions. Four variants of the coercion calculus explore two axes of cast behavior: how aggressively or lazily type inconsistencies are detected, and whether blame tracking strategies will blame casts between types that satisfy the traditional subtyping relation.

Finally, Siek and Wadler (2010) introduce threesomes as an alternative approach to implementing space-efficient casts.

This paper builds on these works by constructing threesome calculi for all of the language semantics captured by Siek et al. (2009). In doing so, it answers affirmatively the open question whether the full design space could be given threesome semantics, it clarifies the relationship between the Threesome Calculus and its corresponding coercion calculus, and it lays groundwork for extending threesomes to more fully-featured language designs.

3. Background: Casts, Threesomes, and Coercions

In this section we discuss the background material that underlies this work. Most everything in this section is prior work, though the presentation of Lazy UD in this section veers slightly from prior work in ways that make the development herein more convenient. We have proven that the system here is equivalent to the original, but it's not worth dwelling on.

The $\lambda^{\langle T \rangle}$ language (Fig. 1) extends the lambda calculus with a dynamic type $\star$, and a runtime *cast expression* $\langle T_2 \Leftarrow T_1 \rangle^l\, e$, which attempts to coerce the value of expression e from type T_1 to type T_2. If it succeeds, then computation proceeds with the value at the new type; if it fails, then a *cast error* uses the label l to pinpoint blame. By convention, casts always associate to the right, so $\langle T_3 \Leftarrow T_2 \rangle^{l_2} \langle T_2 \Leftarrow T_1 \rangle^{l_1}\, e$ means $\langle T_3 \Leftarrow T_2 \rangle^{l_2} (\langle T_2 \Leftarrow T_1 \rangle^{l_1}\, e)$.

Basic casts are straightforward. For instance, we can cast numbers to and from $\star$:

$$\langle \texttt{Int} \Leftarrow \star \rangle^{l_2} \langle \star \Leftarrow \texttt{Int} \rangle^{l_1}\, 42 \longrightarrow^* 42$$

but projecting a $\star$-wrapped integer to the wrong type fails:

$$\langle \texttt{Bool} \Leftarrow \star \rangle^{l_2} \langle \star \Leftarrow \texttt{Int} \rangle^{l_1}\, 42 \longrightarrow^* \textbf{blame}\ l_2$$

The label on the *projection* l_2 from $\star$ to `Bool` is used to report failure. Languages like $\lambda^{\langle T \rangle}$ also support higher-order casts on function-typed objects. Their meaning is dictated by the structure of the relevant types. As a basic example, consider the expression:

$$f \equiv \langle \star \to \texttt{Bool} \Leftarrow \star \to \star \rangle^{l_2}\, \lambda x : \star . \langle \star \Leftarrow \texttt{Int} \rangle^{l_1}\, 42$$

The function inside of the l_2 cast can never successfully behave as $\star \to$ `Bool`, but we cannot know this without analyzing the body of the function. To detect such errors without analyzing functions, higher-order casts adopt the strategy of delaying resolution of the cast, and carry its blame label so that failure can be detected when the function is used (Findler and Felleisen 2002). The cast splits when the casted function is applied, and its pieces are resolved using the first-order strategy:

$$\begin{aligned}
& f\ (\langle \star \Leftarrow \texttt{Int} \rangle^{l_3}\, 7) \\
\longrightarrow\ & \langle \texttt{Bool} \Leftarrow \star \rangle^{l_2} ((\lambda x : \star . \langle \star \Leftarrow \texttt{Int} \rangle^{l_1}\, 42) \\
& \qquad \langle \star \Leftarrow \star \rangle^{l_2} \langle \star \Leftarrow \texttt{Int} \rangle^{l_3}\, 7) \\
\longrightarrow\ & \langle \texttt{Bool} \Leftarrow \star \rangle^{l_2} ((\lambda x : \star . \langle \star \Leftarrow \texttt{Int} \rangle^{l_1}\, 42)\ \langle \star \Leftarrow \texttt{Int} \rangle^{l_3}\, 7) \\
\longrightarrow\ & \langle \texttt{Bool} \Leftarrow \star \rangle^{l_2} \langle \star \Leftarrow \texttt{Int} \rangle^{l_1}\, 42 \\
\longrightarrow\ & \textbf{blame}\ l_2 .
\end{aligned}$$

Space Efficiency: As Herman et al. (2007) observe, delayed higher-order casts can lead to undesirable space consumption, both by accumulating casts around values as well as on the control stack. To demonstrate the first, they present the following example.

```
let rec even(n : Int, k : Dyn→Bool) : Bool =
  if (n = 0) then k(⟨⋆⇐Bool⟩^l1 True)
  else odd(n - 1, ⟨Bool → Bool⇐⋆ → Bool⟩^l2 k)
and odd(n : Int, k : Bool→Bool) : Bool =
  if (n = 0) then k(False)
  else even(n - 1, ⟨⋆ → Bool⇐Bool → Bool⟩^l3 k)
```

Whenever `even` or `odd` is called at non-zero value, another wrapper is placed around the function k. Despite these functions being tail recursive, a trace of this routine shows the accumulating casts.

```
even(3,k) ⟶*
 odd(2,⟨Bool → Bool⇐⋆ → Bool⟩^l2 k) ⟶*
even(1,⟨⋆ → Bool⇐Bool → Bool⟩^l3
       ⟨Bool → Bool⇐⋆ → Bool⟩^l2 k) ⟶*
odd(0,⟨Bool → Bool⇐⋆ → Bool⟩^l2
       ⟨⋆ → Bool⇐Bool → Bool⟩^l3
       ⟨Bool → Bool⇐⋆ → Bool⟩^l2 k) ⟶ ...
```

Casts can also accumulate on the runtime stack and break proper tail recursion.

Blame Tracking Strategies: Wadler and Findler (2009) adapted the notion of blame tracking from higher-order contracts to higher-order casts. Later, Siek et al. (2009) observed that various calculi detect cast failures differently for the same expressions. Their design space for casts varies its cast detection strategies along two dimensions.

First, some cast calculi detect failures more aggressively than others. Take for example the following expression:

$$\langle \texttt{Bool} \to \texttt{Int} \Leftarrow \star \to \star \rangle^{l_2} \langle \star \to \star \Leftarrow \texttt{Int} \to \texttt{Int} \rangle^{l_1} (\lambda x : \texttt{Int}.\ x)$$

The top-level type constructors of both casts are consistent, but the inner types marked in gray, `Int` and `Bool`, conflict. According to the design space, a *lazy* blame tracking strategy evaluates this expression without error: an error is reported later, though, if the function is ever applied. An *eager* strategy, however, reports an error immediately.

Second, when a failure does occur, the part of the source program that is identified as the culprit depends on the blame strategy in place. The Blame Calculus was designed to enable a statically-typed language to interact with a dynamically typed counterpart. It uses casts to mediate between the two, and blame is allocated according to the philosophy that "well-typed programs can't be blamed." Alternatively, the $\star$ type has also been used to express fine-grained combination of dynamic and static typing within a single language, as in gradual typing (Siek and Taha 2006). When a failure happens in this model, the concern is with which specific location in the unified source program failed. This correlates with the failure of a particular cast that was injected when the program was compiled.

Syntax

$x \in$ Variables, $k \in$ Constants, $B \in$ BaseTypes, $l \in$ Labels

atomic types	P	$::=$	$B \mid \star$
types	T	$::=$	$P \mid T \to T$
expressions	e	$::=$	$k \mid x \mid \lambda x : T.\ e \mid e\ e \mid \langle T \Leftarrow T \rangle^l\ e$

$\boxed{\Gamma \vdash e : T}$ **Well-typed Expressions**

$$\ldots \quad \frac{\Gamma \vdash e : T_1}{\Gamma \vdash \langle T_2 \Leftarrow T_1 \rangle^l\ e : T_2}$$

Figure 1. The $\lambda^{\langle T \rangle}$ Calculus

This difference in strategy manifests in the cast calculus. Take the following expression:

$$\begin{array}{l}(\lambda y : \star.\langle \star \to \texttt{Int} \Leftarrow \star \rangle^{l_3}\ y)\\ \quad(\langle \star \Leftarrow \texttt{Bool} \to \texttt{Bool} \rangle^{l_2}\ \lambda x : \texttt{Bool}.\ x)\\ \quad\quad(\langle \star \Leftarrow \texttt{Int} \rangle^{l_1}\ 1)\end{array}$$

It fails with blame under both strategies, but blame is assigned quite differently. The Blame Calculus *blames the context around the l_2 cast*, i.e.,

$$((\lambda y.: \star.\langle \star \to \texttt{Int} \Leftarrow \star \rangle^{l_3}\ y)\ \square)\ \langle \star \Leftarrow \texttt{Int} \rangle^{l_1}\ 1$$

because on considering the two types in the l_2 cast, $\star$ is more dynamic than $\texttt{Bool} \to \texttt{Bool}$. The failure is attributed to the code on the more dynamic side of the l_2 cast: its surrounding context. In general, when neither type in a cast is definitively more static than the other, the direction blamed for a failure depends on the particular expressions involved.[1]

The strategy associated with gradual typing, on the other hand *blames the l_3 cast*. In this model, the $\star$ type is viewed as a universal supertype to which any other type can safely be "upcast."[2] Thus the l_3 cast is a "downcast" that tries to extract more type information from a dynamically typed value, but fails. This model, which we call the "D" model, never blames upcasts. For comparison, we call the model of the Blame Calculus "UD", since it blames with respect to both upcasts and downcasts.

Siek et al. (2009) present 4 coercion-based calculi—named Lazy UD, Lazy D, Eager UD, and Eager D—that exhibit these different points in the design space of casts while supporting space-efficiency. The Lazy UD variant corresponds directly to the Blame Calculus of Wadler and Findler (2009), which was specified in terms of casts rather than coercions, and subject to the space leaks identified by (Herman et al. 2007).

3.1 Introduction to Threesomes

In this subsection, we give a high-level intuition for how threesomes work. In Sec. 4, we derive a fully detailed semantics for a threesome calculus, so we defer some details until then.

Threesomes represent any sequence of casts as exactly two casts, a cast $\langle T_2 \Leftarrow T_1 \rangle$ from a less *precise* type T_1 to a more precise type T_2 followed by a cast $\langle T_3 \Leftarrow T_2 \rangle$ to a less precise type T_3. The middle type T_2 captures all the type information carried by the sequence of casts it represents. This representation detects cast failures exactly when traditional casts would. For succinctness, such threesomes are written $\langle T_3 \overset{T_2}{\Longleftarrow} T_1 \rangle$.

The precision relation is formalized as a (partial) ordering of types $<:_n$:

$$\frac{}{\bot <:_n T} \qquad \frac{}{B <:_n B} \qquad \frac{}{T <:_n \star}$$

$$\frac{T_1 <:_n T_3 \quad T_2 <:_n T_4}{T_1 \to T_2 <:_n T_3 \to T_4}$$

[1] Sec. 3.1 gives a precise characterization of "more static."

[2] This model is orthogonal to, and compatible with, languages that already support subtyping. See Sec. 4.5.

Precision amounts to replacing the dynamic part of a type with a non-dynamic type, or introducing a type inconsistency to reflect conflicting information. Wadler and Findler call this relation *naïve subtyping* because it corresponds to the classic misguided definition of subtyping for functions, covariant in the domain types, with $\star$ as the top (least precise) type and $\bot$ as the bottom (most precise) type.

This partial order induces a *greatest lower bound* $\&$ on types, which is used to implement threesomes. To ensure that $\&$ is well defined, the "type" $\bot$ is used to represent type inconsistencies. The definition of $\&$ is as follows:

$$\begin{aligned}\star \,\&\, T = T \,\&\, \star &= T\\ B \,\&\, B &= B\\ (T_1 \to T_2) \,\&\, (T_3 \to T_4) &= (T_1 \,\&\, T_3) \to (T_2 \,\&\, T_4)\\ T_1 \,\&\, T_2 &= \bot \text{ if } T_1 \# T_2\end{aligned}$$

This definition appeals to *shallow inconsistency* $\#$, which is when two non-$\star$ types have different *leading type constructors* $\lceil T \rceil$:

$$T_1 \# T_2 \text{ iff } \lceil T_1 \rceil \neq \lceil T_2 \rceil \quad \text{where } \lceil B \rceil = B \text{ and } \lceil T_1 \to T_2 \rceil = \star \to \star.$$

Formally, the greatest lower bound compares the structure of two types, and when a $\star$ in one type meets a static type in the other, the static type is the used. For example, $(\texttt{Bool} \to \star)\ \&\ (\star \to \texttt{Int}) = (\texttt{Bool} \to \texttt{Int})$, and so the cast $\langle \texttt{Bool} \to \star \Leftarrow \star \to \texttt{Int} \rangle$ translates to the $\langle \texttt{Bool} \to \star \overset{\texttt{Bool} \to \texttt{Int}}{\Longleftarrow} \star \to \texttt{Int} \rangle$ threesome. The $\bot$ type is the greatest lower bound of any two shallowly inconsistent types.

Any sequence of threesomes can be represented as a single threesome by taking the innermost and outermost types of the sequence as the new outer types, and taking the greatest lower bound of all the middle types as the new middle type, and thereby summarizing all the type information from the casts. Since $(\texttt{Bool} \to \texttt{Int})\ \&\ (\texttt{Bool} \to \bot) = (\texttt{Bool} \to \bot)$, for instance, the following pair of threesomes reduces to a single threesome:

$$\begin{array}{l}\langle \texttt{Bool} \to \star \overset{\texttt{Bool} \to \texttt{Int}}{\Longleftarrow} \star \to \texttt{Int} \rangle \langle \star \to \texttt{Int} \overset{\texttt{Bool} \to \bot}{\Longleftarrow} \texttt{Bool} \to \star \rangle f\\ \longrightarrow \langle \texttt{Bool} \to \star \overset{\texttt{Bool} \to \bot}{\Longleftarrow} \texttt{Bool} \to \star \rangle f.\end{array}$$

If we consider the even-odd example again, and ignore blame for now, we can compile its casts to threesomes. Then the earlier execution trace demonstrates the space savings of threesomes:

$$\begin{array}{l}\texttt{even(3,k)} \longrightarrow^*\\ \texttt{odd(2,}\langle \texttt{Bool} \to \texttt{Bool} \overset{\texttt{Bool} \to \texttt{Bool}}{\Longleftarrow} \star \to \texttt{Bool} \rangle\texttt{k)} \longrightarrow^*\\ \texttt{even(1,}\langle \star \to \texttt{Bool} \overset{\texttt{Bool} \to \texttt{Bool}}{\Longleftarrow} \star \to \texttt{Bool} \rangle\texttt{k)} \longrightarrow^*\\ \texttt{odd(0,}\langle \texttt{Bool} \to \texttt{Bool} \overset{\texttt{Bool} \to \texttt{Bool}}{\Longleftarrow} \star \to \texttt{Bool} \rangle\texttt{k)} \longrightarrow \ldots\end{array}$$

Rather than accumulating like casts, threesomes reduce to a single equivalent threesome at each step.

3.1.1 Adding Blame to Threesomes is Subtle

Threesomes are easy to implement, since $\&$ is a simple recursive function, and threesomes without blame are easy to understand. However, threesomes become somewhat mystifying when they are enhanced with blame tracking. To support blame tracking, Siek and Wadler (2010) sprinkle blame labels throughout the structure of the middle types, now calling them *labeled types*, and extend composition to propagate those labels. Developing the annotation strategy was a subtle and time-consuming process (Siek 2011b), involving trial and error.[3] One is hard-pressed to recognize the blame strategy as encoded in the labeling of the types or the structure of the composition operation.

Syntax

atomic types	P	$::=$	$B \mid \star$
types	T	$::=$	$P \mid T \to T$
dynables	G	$::=$	$B \mid \star \to \star$
coercions	c	$::=$	$\iota_P \mid G! \mid G?^l \mid c \to c \mid c \circ c \mid \mathtt{Fail}^l$
wrappers	o	$::=$	$G! \mid u \to u \mid G! \circ (u \to u)$
failures	f	$::=$	$\mathtt{Fail}^l$
canonicals	u	$::=$	$\iota_P \mid \mathtt{Fail}^l \mid G! \mid u \to u \mid G! \circ (u \to u)$
		$\mid$	$G?^l \mid \mathtt{Fail}^l \circ G?^l \mid G! \circ G?^l \mid (u \to u) \circ G?^l$
		$\mid$	$G! \circ (u \to u) \circ G?^l$

$\boxed{\vdash c : T_2 \Leftarrow T_1}$ **Well-typed Coercions**

$$\frac{}{\vdash \iota_P : P \Leftarrow P} \qquad \frac{}{\vdash B?^l : B \Leftarrow \star}$$

$$\frac{}{\vdash (\star \to \star)?^l : (\star \to \star) \Leftarrow \star}$$

$$\frac{}{\vdash B! : \star \Leftarrow B} \qquad \frac{}{\vdash (\star \to \star)! : \star \Leftarrow (\star \to \star)} \qquad \frac{}{\vdash \mathtt{Fail}^l : T_2 \Leftarrow T_1}$$

$$\frac{\vdash c_1 : T_2 \Leftarrow T_1 \quad \vdash c_2 : T_4 \Leftarrow T_3}{\vdash c_1 \to c_2 : T_1 \to T_4 \Leftarrow T_2 \to T_3} \qquad \frac{\vdash c_2 : T_3 \Leftarrow T_2 \quad \vdash c_1 : T_2 \Leftarrow T_1}{\vdash c_2 \circ c_1 : T_3 \Leftarrow T_1}$$

$\boxed{c \longrightarrow c}$ **Notions of Reduction**

(1) $\iota_P \circ c \longrightarrow c$

(2) $c \circ \iota_P \longrightarrow c$

(3) $B?^l \circ B! \longrightarrow \iota_B$

(4) $(\star \to \star)?^l \circ (\star \to \star)! \longrightarrow (\iota_\star \to \iota_\star)$

(5) $(c_1 \to c_2) \circ (c_3 \to c_4) \longrightarrow (c_3 \circ c_1) \to (c_2 \circ c_4)$

(6) $\mathtt{Fail}^l \circ c \longrightarrow \mathtt{Fail}^l$ if $c \equiv G!$ or $c \equiv (c_1 \to c_2)$

(7) $c \circ \mathtt{Fail}^l \longrightarrow \mathtt{Fail}^l$

(8) $G_1?^l \circ G_2! \longrightarrow \mathtt{Fail}^l$ if $G_1 \# G_2$

$\boxed{\langle\!\langle T \Leftarrow T \rangle\!\rangle^l = c}$ **Cast Translation**

$$\langle\!\langle P \Leftarrow P \rangle\!\rangle^l = \iota_P \qquad \langle\!\langle \star \Leftarrow B \rangle\!\rangle^l = B! \qquad \langle\!\langle B \Leftarrow \star \rangle\!\rangle^l = B?^l$$

$$\langle\!\langle \star \Leftarrow (T_3 \to T_4) \rangle\!\rangle^l = (\star \to \star)! \circ (\langle\!\langle T_3 \Leftarrow \star \rangle\!\rangle^{\bar{l}} \to \langle\!\langle \star \Leftarrow T_4 \rangle\!\rangle^l)$$

$$\langle\!\langle (T_1 \to T_2) \Leftarrow \star \rangle\!\rangle^l = (\langle\!\langle \star \Leftarrow T_1 \rangle\!\rangle^{\bar{l}} \to \langle\!\langle T_2 \Leftarrow \star \rangle\!\rangle^l) \circ (\star \to \star)?^l$$

$$\langle\!\langle T_1 \to T_2 \Leftarrow T_3 \to T_4 \rangle\!\rangle^l = \langle\!\langle T_3 \Leftarrow T_1 \rangle\!\rangle^{\bar{l}} \to \langle\!\langle T_2 \Leftarrow T_4 \rangle\!\rangle^l$$

$$\langle\!\langle T_1 \Leftarrow T_2 \rangle\!\rangle^l = \mathtt{Fail}^l \quad \text{if } T_1 \# T_2$$

Figure 2. Lazy UD Coercion Calculus

3.2 Lazy UD Coercions, In Detail

Armed with a general understanding of threesomes, we now turn attention to coercions. Since this is the starting point for our work, we immediately explain them in detail. Fig. 2 presents the Lazy UD Coercion Calculus. Coercions are expressions in a small language that characterizes type casts. Identity coercions ι_P behave as no-ops. Injection coercions $G!$ cast values of type G to the $\star$ type. Projection coercions $G?^l$ do the opposite, casting values from $\star$ to G, or blaming the l label if they fail. Failure coercions $\mathtt{Fail}^l$ report failure and indicate which label is to blame. Arrow coercions $c \to c$ represent coercions between two function types. Sequences of coercions are composed using the $\circ$ operator. Coercion expressions are identified up to associativity of composition.

Under the UD model, a cast failure reports a blame label, which indicates which cast to consider, as well as a *polarity*, which indicates whether the term inside the cast or its surrounding context is to blame for the failure. To implement this behavior, each blame label attached to a coercion is endowed with a polarity during compilation from casts to coercions. Source-language casts are deemed to have positive polarity, but polarity reverses when compiling the domain of any cast between function types. The result is that coercions that lie to the left of an odd number of coercion arrows have negative polarity; the rest have positive polarity. An inversion operation $\bar{l}$ on labels reverses their polarity. This operation is involutive, meaning $\bar{\bar{l}} = l$.

Coercions are typed according to the type of input they admit and the output type they produce. Note that for arrow coercions, typing is contravariant in their domains. From here on, we only consider well-typed coercions.

To characterize coercion reduction, we first isolate some varieties of legal coercions. The canonical coercions u are the normal forms of coercions with respect to coercion reduction. The wrappers o represent delayed (sequences of) casts wrapped around simple program values. Failure coercions f are used in the coercion-based lambda calculus to indicate when casting a value has failed.

Coercion reduction is the compatible closure of the notions of reduction $c \longrightarrow c$; for simplicity we use the same notation for both.

Type casts are translated to coercions using the $\langle\!\langle T \Leftarrow T \rangle\!\rangle^l$ function. For example, the paired casts

$$\langle \star \to \mathtt{Bool} \Leftarrow \mathtt{Bool} \to \mathtt{Bool} \rangle^{l_3} \langle \mathtt{Bool} \to \mathtt{Bool} \Leftarrow \star \to \mathtt{Bool} \rangle^{l_2}$$

compile and reduce to the well-typed coercion expression

$$\vdash (\mathtt{Bool}! \circ \mathtt{Bool}?^{l_3}) \to \iota_{\mathtt{Bool}} : (\star \to \mathtt{Bool}) \Leftarrow (\star \to \mathtt{Bool}).$$

3.2.1 Properties of Coercion Reduction

In this subsection we state some of the classic properties of the coercion calculus. Though these have been proven previously, we prove them again to account for the changes from Henglein (1994) (specifically the introduction of blame, and the removal of non-atomic ι_T coercions). These properties of the coercion calculus are used in the development to follow.[4]

Proposition 1. *Coercion reduction $\longrightarrow$ preserves typing.*

Proof. By cases on reduction. □

Proposition 2 (Siek (2011a)). *$\longrightarrow$ is strongly normalizing.*

Proof. Consider as a size metric the lexicographic order on 1) the size of the coercion (raw number of non-ι_P nodes) and 2) the number of function coercions. Then coercion reduction decreases that metric. □

Proposition 3. *c is normal iff c is a u.*

Proof. The only-if part is proven by induction on the typing judgment $\vdash c : T_2 \Leftarrow T_1$. The only interesting case is $c_1 \circ c_2$ which can be proven by cases, using the induction hypothesis to deduce that $c_1 = u_1$ and $c_2 = u_2$.

The if part is proven by induction on the structure of u. □

Proposition 4. *Coercion reduction $\longrightarrow$ is confluent.*

Proof. Since reduction is normalizing, we need only confirm that critical pairs converge. Among the reduction rules, two pairs of rules overlap with each other completely:

1. $\iota_P \circ c$ and $c \circ \iota_P$;
2. $\iota_P \circ c$ and $c \circ \mathtt{Fail}^l$;

Also, five redex pairs $c_1 \circ c_2$ and $c_2 \circ c_3$ interact because $\circ$ is associative:

[3] e.g. "We initially tried to label bottom types with a single label ... . However, that approach fails to capture the correct blame tracking behavior." (Siek and Wadler 2010)

[4] We have proven all of these except for confluence for all four coercion calculi discussed in this paper. Confluence does not hold for the eager calculi.

Syntax

expressions	e	::=	$k \mid x \mid \lambda x : T.\ e \mid e\ e \mid \langle u \rangle e \mid \textbf{blame}\ l$
simple values	s	::=	$k \mid \lambda x : T.\ e$
values	v	::=	$s \mid \langle o \rangle s$
canonicals	w	::=	$v \mid \textbf{blame}\ l$
cast-free contexts	F	::=	$\square \mid E[\square\ e] \mid E[v\ \square]$
evaluation contexts	E	::=	$F \mid F[\langle u \rangle \square]$

$\boxed{\Gamma \vdash e : T}$ **Well-typed Expressions**

$$\ldots \quad \frac{\Gamma \vdash e : T_1 \quad \vdash u : T_2 \Leftarrow T_1}{\Gamma \vdash \langle u \rangle e : T_2}$$

$\boxed{\mathcal{C}^{\langle c \rangle}[\![\cdot]\!] : \lambda^{\langle T \rangle} \to \lambda^{\langle c \rangle}}$ **Program Translation**

$$\ldots$$
$$\mathcal{C}^{\langle c \rangle}[\![\langle T_2 \Leftarrow T_1 \rangle^l\ t]\!] = \langle \langle\!\langle T_2 \Leftarrow T_1 \rangle\!\rangle^l \rangle \mathcal{C}^{\langle c \rangle}[\![t]\!]$$

$\boxed{e \longrightarrow e}$ **Notions of Reduction**

(9) $(\lambda x : T.e)\ v \longrightarrow [v/x]\,e$

(10) $(\langle u_1 \to u_2 \rangle s)\ v \longrightarrow \langle u_2 \rangle (s\ (\langle u_1 \rangle v))$

(11) $\langle u_1 \rangle \langle u_2 \rangle e \longrightarrow_c \langle u_3 \rangle e$ if $(u_1 \circ u_2) \longrightarrow^* u_3$

(12) $\langle \iota_B \rangle s \longrightarrow_c s$

(13) $\langle f \rangle s \longrightarrow_c \textbf{blame}\ l$

$\boxed{e \longmapsto e}$ **Standard Reduction**

$$\frac{e_1 \longrightarrow e_2}{E[e_1] \longmapsto E[e_2]} \qquad \frac{e_1 \longrightarrow_c e_2}{F[e_1] \longmapsto F[e_2]}$$

$$\frac{}{E[\textbf{blame}\ l] \longmapsto \textbf{blame}\ l}\ E \neq \square$$

Figure 3. The $\lambda^{\langle c \rangle}$ Calculus

1. $\iota_P \circ c_2 \circ c_3$;
2. $c_1 \circ c_2 \circ \iota_P$;
3. $c_1 \circ c_2 \circ \texttt{Fail}^l$;
4. $\texttt{Fail}^l \circ (c_{11} \to c_{12}) \circ (c_{21} \to c_{22})$; and
5. $(c_{11} \to c_{12}) \circ (c_{21} \to c_{22}) \circ (c_{31} \to c_{32})$.

In each case, reduction converges. □

3.3 The $\lambda^{\langle c \rangle}$ Calculus

To use the coercion calculus, we translate $\lambda^{\langle T \rangle}$ programs to $\lambda^{\langle c \rangle}$, the simply-typed lambda calculus with coercions, presented in Fig. 3 (Siek et al. 2009). Its syntax differs from $\lambda^{\langle T \rangle}$ only in that cast expressions are replaced with normal coercion expressions $\langle u \rangle e$. The translation from $\lambda^{\langle T \rangle}$ to $\lambda^{\langle c \rangle}$ is simple: The $\mathcal{C}^{\langle c \rangle}[\![t]\!]$ function translates t by replacing each cast $\langle T_1 \Leftarrow T_2 \rangle^l$ with its corresponding coercion $\langle\!\langle T_1 \Leftarrow T_2 \rangle\!\rangle^l$.

The $\lambda^{\langle c \rangle}$ notions of reduction are split into *plain reductions* $e \longrightarrow e$ and *coercion reductions* $e \longrightarrow_c e$. Rule 12 is specialized to ι_B, because there are no simple values s of type $\star$. Rule 11 appeals to coercion calculus reduction to compose and normalize two sequential coercions.To ensure that coercions are compressed on the stack, coercion reductions $\longrightarrow_c$ can only happen in a context with no immediately pending coercion. Plain reductions $\longrightarrow$, on the other hand, can happen in any evaluation context. If a coercion fails, a program results in blame. In general, $\lambda^{\langle c \rangle}$ is parameterized over the definition and semantics of the coercion calculus. By changing the coercion language, we can switch the blame-tracking strategy.

Proposition 5. *The $\lambda^{\langle c \rangle}$ calculus is type safe.*

Proposition 6 ((Siek et al. 2009))**.** *The $\lambda^{\langle c \rangle}$ calculus is space efficient.*

Proposition 7 ((Siek et al. 2009))**.** *The $\lambda^{\langle c \rangle}$ calculus with Lazy UD coercions corresponds to the Blame Calculus.*

If we consider the even-odd example again, we can compile its casts to coercions and see the space savings in the resulting trace:

$$\texttt{even(3,k)} \longrightarrow^* \texttt{odd(2,}\langle B! \to \iota \rangle\texttt{k)} \longrightarrow^*$$
$$\texttt{even(1,}\langle B! \circ B?^{l_3} \to \iota \rangle\texttt{k)} \longrightarrow^* \texttt{odd(0,}\langle B! \to \iota \rangle\texttt{k)} \longrightarrow \ldots$$

This sequence of coercions repeats for larger numbers.

3.4 Implementing Coercions is Hard

Coercions cleanly and elegantly specify space-efficient cast semantics, which is one reason they were used to characterize the design space of casts in (Siek et al. 2009). However, they are difficult to implement directly for two reasons. First, coercions are defined *up to associativity*, which can make some redexes harder to find, and can interfere with developing a deterministic reduction strategy. Second, some coercion compositions remain *inert*, meaning that they do not reduce, but composing with another coercion may warrant a reduction. These two properties interact with each other in troublesome ways. Consider the coercion expression $((\star \to \star)?^l \circ ((\star \to \star)! \circ (c_1 \to c_2))) \circ (c_3 \to c_4)$. The subexpression $(\star \to \star)! \circ (c_1 \to c_2)$ is inert, so it does not reduce. However, the coercions $(\star \to \star)?^l$ and $(\star \to \star)!$ could reduce if composed directly, but in order to do so, the compositions must be reassociated first. The result, $\iota_\star \to \iota_\star$, could then compose with $c_1 \to c_2$. Meanwhile, the two arrow coercions $c_1 \to c_2$ and $c_3 \to c_4$ could also reduce, but are also blocked by how they are associated. One might try to devise an ad hoc reassociation scheme or represent a sequence of coercions as lists, but it would necessarily involve pairwise comparisons, bidirectional search, and splicing into the middle of complex coercion expressions. In short, it remains a challenge to design a redex search and reduction strategy that is complete in the face of inert compositions and associativity, yet simple enough to reason about and implement correctly. We do exactly this in the next section.

4. Threesomes for Lazy UD

This section presents a way to transform Lazy UD coercions into Lazy UD Threesomes using small, easily verified steps. The strategy we apply and explain here is used later to produce similar results for other coercion calculi.

4.1 Composing normal coercions as a function

Our strategy begins by focusing specifically on normal coercions u. Recall that coercions reduction is both confluent and strongly normalizing. These two properties ensure there exists, in theory, a well-defined composition function for normal coercions.

Definition 1 (Normal Composition)**.** *Let* $\text{NORMC}^{T_2 \Leftarrow T_1}$ *be the set of well-typed normal coercions* $\vdash u : T_2 \Leftarrow T_1$*. Then define the* normal composition *function*

$$\odot : \text{NORMC}^{T_3 \Leftarrow T_2} \times \text{NORMC}^{T_2 \Leftarrow T_1} \to \text{NORMC}^{T_3 \Leftarrow T_1}$$

as follows:

$$u_1 \odot u_2 = u_3 \quad \textit{iff} \quad (u_1 \circ u_2) \longrightarrow^* u_3.$$

Using this definition, we can restate rule 11 of $\lambda^{\langle c \rangle}$ as follows:

(11) $\langle u_1 \rangle \langle u_2 \rangle e \longrightarrow_c \langle u_1 \odot u_2 \rangle e$

This rephrasing does not resolve our issues with the coercion calculus, because $\odot$ is defined in terms of nondeterministic coercion reduction, the source of our troubles. We address this next.

Syntax

dynables	G	$::=$	$B \mid \star \to \star$
supercoercions	$\ddot{c}$	$::=$	$\mathtt{Fail}^l \mid \mathtt{Fail}^{lGl} \mid G! \mid G?^l \mid G!?^l \mid \iota_P$
		$\mid$	$\ddot{c} \to \ddot{c} \mid \ddot{c} \mathrel{!\!\to} \ddot{c} \mid \ddot{c} \to ?^l\, \ddot{c} \mid \ddot{c} \mathrel{!\!\to} ?^l\, \ddot{c}$
wrappers	$\ddot{o}$	$::=$	$G! \mid \ddot{c} \to \ddot{c} \mid \ddot{c} \mathrel{!\!\to} \ddot{c}$
failures	$\ddot{f}$	$::=$	$\mathtt{Fail}^l$

$\boxed{\vdash^{\mathcal{S}} \ddot{c} : T \Leftarrow T}$ **Well-typed Supercoercion**

$$\ldots \quad \frac{}{\vdash^{\mathcal{S}} \mathtt{Fail}^{l_1 G l_2} : T \Leftarrow \star} \qquad \frac{}{\vdash^{\mathcal{S}} G!?^l : \star \Leftarrow \star}$$

$$\frac{\vdash^{\mathcal{S}} \ddot{c}_1 : T_2 \Leftarrow \star \quad \vdash^{\mathcal{S}} \ddot{c}_2 : \star \Leftarrow T_3}{\vdash^{\mathcal{S}} \ddot{c}_1 \mathrel{!\!\to} \ddot{c}_2 : \star \Leftarrow T_2 \to T_3} \qquad \frac{\vdash^{\mathcal{S}} \ddot{c}_1 : \star \Leftarrow T_1 \quad \vdash^{\mathcal{S}} \ddot{c}_2 : T_4 \Leftarrow \star}{\vdash^{\mathcal{S}} \ddot{c}_1 \to ?^l\, \ddot{c}_2 : T_1 \to T_4 \Leftarrow \star}$$

$$\frac{\vdash^{\mathcal{S}} \ddot{c}_1 : \star \Leftarrow \star \quad \vdash^{\mathcal{S}} \ddot{c}_2 : \star \Leftarrow \star}{\vdash^{\mathcal{S}} \ddot{c}_1 \mathrel{!\!\to} ?^l\, \ddot{c}_2 : \star \Leftarrow \star}$$

$\boxed{\mathcal{N}[\![\ddot{c}]\!] = c}$ **Supercoercion Meaning**

$$\begin{aligned}
\mathcal{N}[\![\iota_P]\!] &= \iota_P \\
\mathcal{N}[\![\mathtt{Fail}^l]\!] &= \mathtt{Fail}^l \\
\mathcal{N}[\![\mathtt{Fail}^{l_1 G l_2}]\!] &= \mathtt{Fail}^{l_1} \circ G?^{l_2} \\
\mathcal{N}[\![G!]\!] &= G! \\
\mathcal{N}[\![G?^l]\!] &= G?^l \\
\mathcal{N}[\![G!?^l]\!] &= G! \circ G?^l \\
\mathcal{N}[\![\ddot{c}_1 \to \ddot{c}_2]\!] &= \mathcal{N}[\![\ddot{c}_1]\!] \to \mathcal{N}[\![\ddot{c}_2]\!] \\
\mathcal{N}[\![\ddot{c}_1 \mathrel{!\!\to} \ddot{c}_2]\!] &= (\star \to \star)! \circ (\mathcal{N}[\![\ddot{c}_1]\!] \to \mathcal{N}[\![\ddot{c}_2]\!]) \\
\mathcal{N}[\![\ddot{c}_1 \to ?^l\, \ddot{c}_2]\!] &= (\mathcal{N}[\![\ddot{c}_1]\!] \to \mathcal{N}[\![\ddot{c}_2]\!]) \circ (\star \to \star)?^l \\
\mathcal{N}[\![\ddot{c}_1 \mathrel{!\!\to} ?^l\, \ddot{c}_2]\!] &= (\star \to \star)! \circ (\mathcal{N}[\![\ddot{c}_1]\!] \to \mathcal{N}[\![\ddot{c}_2]\!]) \circ (\star \to \star)?^l
\end{aligned}$$

Figure 4. LazyUD Supercoercions

4.2 Supercoercions

Our next step toward a simple implementation is to replace the set of normal coercion expressions $u \in$ NORMC with a new set of composition-free coercions $\ddot{c} \in$ SUPERC, one for each form that a normal coercion can take (Fig. 4). We call them *supercoercions*, since a single supercoercion may stand for the composition of several traditional coercions.

We define the meaning of our supercoercions in terms of the normal coercions by giving a bijective mapping.

Proposition 8. *$\mathcal{N}[\![\cdot]\!]$ is one-to-one and onto.*

Supercoercions correspond directly to normal coercions according to the (reversible) mapping $\mathcal{N}[\![\cdot]\!]$. The types for supercoercions correspond to normal coercion types, so both $\mathcal{N}[\![\cdot]\!]$ and $\mathcal{N}^{-1}[\![\cdot]\!]$ preserve typing.

Proposition 9. $\vdash^{\mathcal{S}} \ddot{c} : T_2 \Leftarrow T_1$ *iff* $\vdash \mathcal{N}[\![\ddot{c}]\!] : T_2 \Leftarrow T_1$.

Proof. By induction on derivations for each direction. □

Composing supercoercions We define composition of supercoercions in terms of composition $\odot$ of normal coercions.

Definition 2. *The function*

$$\bullet : \text{SUPERC}^{T_3 \Leftarrow T_2} \times \text{SUPERC}^{T_2 \Leftarrow T_1} \to \text{SUPERC}^{T_3 \Leftarrow T_1}$$

is defined as follows: $\ddot{c}_1 \bullet \ddot{c}_2 = \mathcal{N}^{-1}[\![\mathcal{N}[\![\ddot{c}_1]\!] \odot \mathcal{N}[\![\ddot{c}_2]\!]]\!]$.

Since $\odot$, $\mathcal{N}^{-1}[\![\cdot]\!]$, and $\mathcal{N}[\![\cdot]\!]$ are well-defined, so is $\bullet$, but it is still defined in terms of normal coercion composition. However, starting from this abstract definition, we can calculate a new recursive definition over the structure of supercoercions.

To produce our equations, we rely on the fact that normal arrow coercions compose in a syntax-directed way.

Proposition 10.
$(u_1 \to u_2) \odot (u_3 \to u_4) = (u_3 \odot u_1) \to (u_2 \odot u_4)$

Proof. Straightforward calculation. □

Now, using Def. 2 and Prop. 10, we calculate a recursive definition of $\bullet$. Here is one example case:

$$\begin{aligned}
&(\ddot{c}_1 \to ?^l\, \ddot{c}_2) \bullet (\ddot{c}_3 \mathrel{!\!\to} \ddot{c}_4) \\
&= \mathcal{N}^{-1}[\![\mathcal{N}[\![(\ddot{c}_1 \to ?^l\, \ddot{c}_2)]\!] \odot \mathcal{N}[\![(\ddot{c}_3 \mathrel{!\!\to} \ddot{c}_4)]\!]]\!] \\
&= \mathcal{N}^{-1}[\![((\mathcal{N}[\![\ddot{c}_1]\!] \to \mathcal{N}[\![\ddot{c}_2]\!]) \circ (\star \to \star)?^l) \odot \\
&\qquad ((\star \to \star)! \circ (\mathcal{N}[\![\ddot{c}_3]\!] \to \mathcal{N}[\![\ddot{c}_4]\!]))]\!]
\end{aligned}$$

but by reduction,

$$\begin{aligned}
&(\mathcal{N}[\![\ddot{c}_1]\!] \to \mathcal{N}[\![\ddot{c}_2]\!]) \circ (\star \to \star)?^l \circ (\star \to \star)! \circ (\mathcal{N}[\![\ddot{c}_3]\!] \to \mathcal{N}[\![\ddot{c}_4]\!]) \\
&\longrightarrow^* (\mathcal{N}[\![\ddot{c}_1]\!] \to \mathcal{N}[\![\ddot{c}_2]\!]) \circ (\mathcal{N}[\![\ddot{c}_3]\!] \to \mathcal{N}[\![\ddot{c}_4]\!]) \\
&\longrightarrow^* (\mathcal{N}[\![\ddot{c}_3]\!] \odot \mathcal{N}[\![\ddot{c}_1]\!]) \to (\mathcal{N}[\![\ddot{c}_2]\!] \odot \mathcal{N}[\![\ddot{c}_4]\!]) \quad \text{(by Prop. 10)},
\end{aligned}$$

so,

$$\begin{aligned}
&\mathcal{N}^{-1}[\![(\mathcal{N}[\![\ddot{c}_3]\!] \odot \mathcal{N}[\![\ddot{c}_1]\!]) \to (\mathcal{N}[\![\ddot{c}_2]\!] \odot \mathcal{N}[\![\ddot{c}_4]\!])]\!] \\
&= \mathcal{N}^{-1}[\![(\mathcal{N}[\![\ddot{c}_3]\!] \odot \mathcal{N}[\![\ddot{c}_1]\!])]\!] \to \mathcal{N}^{-1}[\![(\mathcal{N}[\![\ddot{c}_2]\!] \odot \mathcal{N}[\![\ddot{c}_4]\!])]\!] \\
&= (\ddot{c}_3 \bullet \ddot{c}_1) \to (\ddot{c}_2 \bullet \ddot{c}_4)
\end{aligned}$$

so we have

$$(\ddot{c}_1 \to ?^l\, \ddot{c}_2) \bullet (\ddot{c}_3 \mathrel{!\!\to} \ddot{c}_4) = (\ddot{c}_3 \bullet \ddot{c}_1) \to (\ddot{c}_2 \bullet \ddot{c}_4).$$

We calculate new equations for all pairs of compatible supercoercions to get the full recursive definition.[5]

Supercoercions can be used to normalize *arbitrary* coercion expressions. To see this, recall that each atomic coercion is also a supercoercion, so we can compose them using $\bullet$. Combining this with the translation from normal arrow coercions, we get a translation from non-normal coercions to supercoercions:

$$\begin{aligned}
\ddot{\mathcal{C}}[\![c]\!] &= c \text{ if } c \text{ is atomic;} \\
\ddot{\mathcal{C}}[\![c_1 \circ c_2]\!] &= \ddot{\mathcal{C}}[\![c_1]\!] \bullet \ddot{\mathcal{C}}[\![c_2]\!]; \\
\ddot{\mathcal{C}}[\![c_1 \to c_2]\!] &= \ddot{\mathcal{C}}[\![c_1]\!] \to \ddot{\mathcal{C}}[\![c_2]\!]
\end{aligned}$$

For example, the problematic coercion from Sec. 3.4 translates directly to its corresponding supercoercion (assuming $\ddot{\mathcal{C}}[\![c_i]\!] = \ddot{c}_i$):

$$\begin{aligned}
&((\ast \to \ast)?^l \bullet ((\star \to \star)! \bullet (\ddot{c}_1 \to \ddot{c}_2))) \bullet (\ddot{c}_3 \to \ddot{c}_4) \\
&= ((\ast \to \ast)?^l \bullet (\ddot{c}_1 \mathrel{!\!\to} \ddot{c}_2)) \bullet (\ddot{c}_3 \to \ddot{c}_4) \\
&= (\ddot{c}_1 \to \ddot{c}_2) \bullet (\ddot{c}_3 \to \ddot{c}_4) \\
&= (\ddot{c}_3 \bullet \ddot{c}_1) \to (\ddot{c}_2 \bullet \ddot{c}_4)
\end{aligned}$$

Then, since we can always map supercoercions back to normal coercions, we immediately see that $c_1 \odot c_2 = \mathcal{N}[\![\ddot{\mathcal{C}}[\![c_1 \circ c_2]\!]]\!]$, that is, $\mathcal{N}[\![\ddot{\mathcal{C}}[\![\cdot]\!]]\!]$ implements a recursive normalizer for traditional coercions, overcoming our troubles with associativity and inertness.

4.3 $\lambda^{\langle \ddot{c} \rangle}$: A Supercoercion-based calculus

Since supercoercions are isomorphic to normal coercions, we can skip the back-and-forth translation steps and instead define a direct implementation semantics for $\lambda^{\langle c \rangle}$: simply replace normal coercions u with supercoercions $\ddot{c}$ and the normal composition $\odot$ with $\bullet$. The resulting calculus $\lambda^{\langle \ddot{c} \rangle}$, presented in Fig. 5, is a deterministic calculus with an easy-to-implement composition operator. like $\lambda^{\langle c \rangle}$, this calculus is parameterized on the definition of supercoercions.

Proposition 11. *Consider the compatible extension of $\mathcal{N}^{-1}[\![\cdot]\!]$ over $\lambda^{\langle c \rangle}$ terms. If t is a $\lambda^{\langle c \rangle}$ term, then*

$$\lambda^{\langle c \rangle} \vdash t \longrightarrow^* w \textit{ iff } \lambda^{\langle \ddot{c} \rangle} \vdash \mathcal{N}^{-1}[\![t]\!] \longrightarrow^* \mathcal{N}^{-1}[\![w]\!].$$

Proof. By a straightforward bisimulation. □

To complete our implementation, we compile $\lambda^{\langle T \rangle}$ terms to $\lambda^{\langle \ddot{c} \rangle}$ terms using the $\mathcal{C}^{\langle \ddot{c} \rangle}[\![\cdot]\!]$ function.

[5] We formalized and checked completeness of our definition using Twelf. Its equations are correct by construction.

Syntax

expressions	e	$::=$	$k \mid x \mid \lambda x : T.\ e \mid e\ e \mid \langle \ddot{c} \rangle e \mid$ **blame** l
simple values	s	$::=$	$k \mid \lambda x : T.\ e$
values	v	$::=$	$s \mid \langle \ddot{o} \rangle s$
canonicals	w	$::=$	$v \mid$ **blame** l
cast-free contexts	F	$::=$	$\square \mid E[\square\ e] \mid E[v\ \square]$
evaluation contexts	E	$::=$	$F \mid F[\langle \ddot{c} \rangle \square]$

$\boxed{\Gamma \vdash^{\mathcal{S}} e : T}$ **Well-typed Expressions**

$$\ldots \quad \frac{\Gamma \vdash^{\mathcal{S}} e : T_1 \qquad \vdash^{\mathcal{S}} \ddot{c} : T_2 \Leftarrow T_1}{\Gamma \vdash^{\mathcal{S}} \langle \ddot{c} \rangle e : T_2}$$

$\boxed{\mathcal{C}^{\langle \ddot{c} \rangle}[\![\cdot]\!] : \lambda^{\langle T \rangle} \to \lambda^{\langle \ddot{c} \rangle}}$ **Program Translation**

$$\ldots$$
$$\mathcal{C}^{\langle \ddot{c} \rangle}[\![\langle T_2 \Leftarrow T_1 \rangle^l\ t]\!] = \langle \mathcal{N}^{-1}[\![\langle\!\langle T_2 \Leftarrow T_1 \rangle\!\rangle^l]\!] \rangle \mathcal{C}^{\langle \ddot{c} \rangle}[\![t]\!]$$

$\boxed{e \longrightarrow e}$ **Notions of Reduction**

(9') $(\lambda x : T.e)\ v \longrightarrow [v/x]\, e$

(10') $(\langle \ddot{c}_1 \to \ddot{c}_2 \rangle s)\ v \longrightarrow \langle \ddot{c}_2 \rangle (s\ (\langle \ddot{c}_1 \rangle v))$

(11') $\langle \ddot{c}_1 \rangle \langle \ddot{c}_2 \rangle e \longrightarrow_c \langle \ddot{c}_1 \bullet \ddot{c}_2 \rangle e$

(12') $\langle \iota_B \rangle s \longrightarrow_c s$

(13') $\langle \ddot{f} \rangle s \longrightarrow_c$ **blame** l

Figure 5. The $\lambda^{\langle \ddot{c} \rangle}$ Calculus

4.4 Simplification: from Supercoercions to Threesomes

Supercoercions, while effective, are not particularly succinct. They consist of 11 forms, including the original coercions. Furthermore, supercoercion composition is defined with 60 equations. Intuitively, this happens because coercion computation was already defined for coercions and now the additional supercoercions must repeat the same computations for each possible normal form. For example, consider two composition equations:

$$(\ddot{c}_1 \to \ddot{c}_2) \bullet (\ddot{c}_3 \to \ddot{c}_4) = (\ddot{c}_3 \bullet \ddot{c}_1) \to (\ddot{c}_2 \bullet \ddot{c}_4)$$
$$(\ddot{c}_1 \to ?^l\, \ddot{c}_2) \bullet (\ddot{c}_3 \,!\!\to \ddot{c}_4) = (\ddot{c}_3 \bullet \ddot{c}_1) \to (\ddot{c}_2 \bullet \ddot{c}_4)$$

The derivations for both equations involved composing arrow coercions, so each internalizes that reduction step. This computation appears as part of different equations because several different normal form coercions contain an arrow coercion component within them. We would like to find a representation for normal coercions that removes this computational redundancy, and in fact we do. To address this blow-up, we apply correctness-preserving transformations to refine our large but correct system into a streamlined and equivalent counterpart. To our delight, the resulting system is in fact nearly exactly the Threesomes of (Siek and Wadler 2010).

4.4.1 Primitive arrow coercions are redundant

In the following two analogous equations,

$$B?^l \bullet B! = \iota_B \qquad (\star \to \star)?^l \bullet (\star \to \star)! = \iota_\star \to \iota_\star$$

the equation for base types produces a single ι_B, while the rule for arrows creates a complex arrow coercion. However, this complex coercion behaves as if it were a primitive identity coercion $\iota_{\star\to\star}$.

Other primitive coercion equations reveal similar correspondences. For example, consider these two equations:

$$B!?^l \bullet B! = B! \qquad (\star \to \star)!?^l \bullet (\star \to \star)! = \iota_\star \,!\!\to \iota_\star$$

They have corresponding primitive left-hand sides, but the result of composing primitive arrow compositions is a complex arrow composition. In this case, one would expect that the $\iota_\star \,!\!\to \iota_\star$ coercion behaves as if it were the primitive $(\star \to \star)!$ coercion, and indeed it does. For instance, if we substitute for $(\star \to \star)!$ on the left side of the above equation, then the definition of $\bullet$ gives

$$(\star \to \star)!?^l \bullet (\iota_\star \,!\!\to \iota_\star) = \iota_\star \,!\!\to \iota_\star$$

This correspondence generalizes to all primitive arrow coercions.

Proposition 12. *Let $\mathcal{S}_1[\![\ddot{c}]\!]$ be defined by*

$$\mathcal{S}_1[\![(\star \to \star)!]\!] = \iota_\star \,!\!\to \iota_\star \qquad \mathcal{S}_1[\![(\star \to \star)?^l]\!] = \iota_\star \to ?^l\, \iota_\star$$
$$\mathcal{S}_1[\![(\star \to \star)!?^l]\!] = \iota_\star \,!\!\to ?^l\, \iota_\star \qquad \mathcal{S}_1[\![\ddot{c}]\!] = \ddot{c} \quad \textit{otherwise}.$$

Then $\mathcal{S}_1[\![\ddot{c}_1 \bullet \ddot{c}_2]\!] = \mathcal{S}_1[\![\ddot{c}_1]\!] \bullet \mathcal{S}_1[\![\ddot{c}_2]\!]$.

This means that the primitive arrow supercoercions are redundant and can be discarded. This simplification is safe because it preserves failure supercoercions $\texttt{Fail}^l$.

We produce a new translation $\mathcal{S} = \mathcal{S}_1 \circ \mathcal{N}^{-1}$ from normal coercions to supercoercions. This mapping is not bijective though, e.g. $\mathcal{N}[\![\mathcal{S}[\![(\star \to \star)?^l]\!]]\!] = \mathcal{N}[\![\iota_\star \to ?^l\, \iota_\star]\!] = (\star \to \star)?^l \circ (\iota_\star \to \iota_\star)$.

4.4.2 Merge primitive coercions into type-polymorphic counterparts

Consider again the base type equations from the last subsection:

$$B?^l \bullet B! = \iota_B \qquad B!?^l \bullet B! = B!$$

They are examples of redundancy in supercoercions: the derivations for both equations involve reducing the coercion $B?^l \circ B!$ (recall that $\mathcal{N}[\![B!?^l]\!] = B! \circ B?^l$). Surprisingly, we can factor away this redundancy; doing so depends on the internal structure and the types of the base type coercions.

The base type coercions can be grouped based on their behavior and syntactic structure. The supercoercions $B!$ and ι_B both coerce from a source type B, and perform safe coercions that will not cause blame, so they have no blame label. Consider them group 1. On the other hand, $B?^l$ and $B!?^l$ both coerce from source type $\star$, and perform a possibly unsafe coercion, so they each carry a blame label. Consider them group 2. Now, looking back at both equations, each is an instance of composing a supercoercion from group 2 with one from group 1 to get another from group 1. Within these groups, the members can be differentiated based on their types: for group 1, $\vdash B! : \star \Leftarrow B$ but $\vdash \iota_B : B \Leftarrow B$; for group 2, $\vdash B?^l : B \Leftarrow \star$ but $\vdash B!?^l : \star \Leftarrow \star$.

In fact, these four uni-typed coercions can be replaced with two "polymorphic" coercions, one for each group, so long as the type of the context where they are used is known. We define two coercions based on the indices from their group: B, and B^l. Each can be typed according to two typing rules:

$$\vdash B : \star \Leftarrow B \qquad \vdash B^l : \star \Leftarrow \star$$
$$\vdash B : B \Leftarrow B \qquad \vdash B^l : B \Leftarrow \star$$

We can then define a new set of supercoercions $\ddot{c}'$ by replacing the old base type supercoercions with these new ones. We define the meaning of the polymorphic supercoercions in terms of the original supercoercions. Since the typings of the new supercoercions matter, however, we first define a translation $\mathcal{S}_{\mathcal{D}}[\![\cdot]\!]$ that yields type derivations $\mathcal{D}$ rather than simply supercoercions. Since the source supercoercions are uni-typed, the translation is unambiguous. The definition is the compatible extension of the following equations:

$$\mathcal{S}_{\mathcal{D}}[\![B!]\!] = \overline{\vdash B : \star \Leftarrow B} \qquad \mathcal{S}_{\mathcal{D}}[\![B!?^l]\!] = \overline{\vdash B^l : \star \Leftarrow \star}$$
$$\mathcal{S}_{\mathcal{D}}[\![\iota_B]\!] = \overline{\vdash B : B \Leftarrow B} \qquad \mathcal{S}_{\mathcal{D}}[\![B?^l]\!] = \overline{\vdash B^l : B \Leftarrow \star}.$$

Proposition 13. *$\mathcal{S}_{\mathcal{D}}[\![\cdot]\!]$ is bijective and preserves typing.*

This translation retains a one-to-one correspondence between typing derivations for supercoercions, but there are fewer target supercoercions than source supercoercions. Ultimately we want to exploit that simplification, so we define the translation $\mathcal{S}_2[\![\ddot{c}]\!] = |\mathcal{S}_{\mathcal{D}}[\![\ddot{c}]\!]|$ from supercoercions to polymorphic supercoercions, where $|\mathcal{D}|$ extracts a supercoercion from its type derivation.

This gives us the translation that we want and, somewhat surprisingly, composition on the resulting polymorphic coercions is well-defined.

Proposition 14. *The equation $\mathcal{S}_2[\![\ddot{c}_1]\!] \bullet_2 \mathcal{S}_2[\![\ddot{c}_2]\!] = \mathcal{S}_2[\![\ddot{c}_1 \bullet \ddot{c}_2]\!]$ defines a function $\bullet_2$ on the polymorphic supercoercions $\ddot{c}'$.*

Proof. By simultaneous induction on $\ddot{c}_1$ and $\ddot{c}_2$. □

This result means that we can replace the base type supercoercions with polymorphic counterparts and still get a well-defined notion of composition that preserves failure $\texttt{Fail}^l$. We take this as our notion of supercoercions and drop the primes and subscripts.

This polymorphic simplification can also be applied to arrow coercions. By doing so, we can combine $\ddot{c} \to \ddot{c}$ and $\ddot{c} \mathrel{!\!\to} \ddot{c}$ as a single coercion $\ddot{c} \to \ddot{c}$ and replace $\ddot{c} \to ?^l\ \ddot{c}$ and $\ddot{c} \mathrel{!\!\to} ?^l\ \ddot{c}$ with the single coercion $\ddot{c} \to^l \ddot{c}$. This transformation is subject to the same correctness criteria as above and similarly decreases the number of supercoercions and the number of composition equations.

4.4.3 Introduce Optional Data and Coalesce

With a slight change of representation, we can merge the two base type coercions, B, and B^l, into one. First, we produce a new form of coercion which features *optional* labels p, where ϵ indicates the absence of a label. Now we can merge both base type coercions into one coercion of the form B^p. Similarly, we can merge arrow casts into the form $\ddot{c} \to^p \ddot{c}$. We can now refer to atomic and arrow coercions uniformly as an optionally labeled type constructor Q^p, standing for either an atomic coercion B^p or an arrow coercion $\ddot{c} \to^p \ddot{c}$. At this point we are close to uncovering our labeled types. In direct analogy with leading type constructors $\lceil T \rceil$, we define $\lceil Q^p \rceil$ to yield Q^p's leading constructor; similarly we define coercion inconsistency $Q_1^p \# Q_2^p$ to hold when two coercions have incompatible top-level constructors.

Introducing optional labels further simplifies our definition of composition. For example, the four equations: $B \bullet B = B$, $B \bullet B^l = B^l$, $B^l \bullet B = B$, and $B^{l_1} \bullet B^{l_2} = B^{l_2}$ become one equation: $B^{p_1} \bullet B^{p_2} = B^{p_2}$. Notice that the function need not even inspect p_2: it simply copies it over to the result. The same thing happens with arrow coercions.

Using the same strategy, we merge the $\texttt{Fail}^l$ and $\texttt{Fail}^{lGl}$ forms by making the G and l pair into an optional annotation H. We call it a *projector* since it represents an optional projection before a failure cast. Finally, we define a helper function $[\cdot]$ that interprets a labeled type Q^p into a projector H. This completes our simplification process, yielding the labeled types and composition operator of Fig. 6.

We define $\mathcal{S}[\![\cdot]\!]$ to be the transformation from coercions to labeled types that results from composing the supercoercion translation $\mathcal{N}^{-1}[\![\cdot]\!]$ and transformations $\mathcal{S}_i[\![\cdot]\!]$ corresponding to each step of simplification.[6]

The resulting labeled types closely mirror those of Siek and Wadler (2010), but for a few cosmetic differences:

1. In general $\ddot{c}$ corresponds directly to labeled types P;
2. Our $\iota_\star$ corresponds to the labeled type $*$;
3. The B^p and $\ddot{c} \to^p \ddot{c}$ coercions are the same;
4. $\texttt{Fail}^{lH}$ corresponds to $\bot^{lGp}$, with H playing the role of Gp. In the original Threesomes, only the label p was optional. Our derivation reveals, however, that G is only needed if an actual label is present.

[6] For brevity, we omit $\mathcal{S}_i[\![\cdot]\!]$ definitions for polymorphic arrows and optional data.

Syntax

dynables	G	$::=$	$B \mid \star \to \star$
optional labels	p	$::=$	$\epsilon \mid l$
failure projectors	H	$::=$	$\epsilon \mid Gl$
labeled constructors	Q^p	$::=$	$B^p \mid \ddot{c} \to^p \ddot{c}$
labeled types	$\ddot{c}$	$::=$	$\iota_\star \mid \texttt{Fail}^{lH} \mid Q^p$
wrappers	$\ddot{o}$	$::=$	$B^\epsilon \mid \ddot{c} \to^\epsilon \ddot{c}$
failures	$\ddot{f}$	$::=$	$\texttt{Fail}^l$

$\boxed{\ddot{c} \bullet \ddot{c} = \ddot{c}}$ **Composition**

$$\begin{aligned}
\iota_\star \bullet \ddot{c} = \ddot{c} \bullet \iota_\star &= \ddot{c} \\
B^{p1} \bullet B^{p2} &= B^{p2} \\
(\ddot{c}_1 \to^{p1} \ddot{c}_2) \bullet (\ddot{c}_3 \to^{p2} \ddot{c}_4) &= (\ddot{c}_3 \bullet \ddot{c}_1) \to^{p2} (\ddot{c}_2 \bullet \ddot{c}_4) \\
Q_1^{l_1} \bullet Q_2^{p2} &= \texttt{Fail}^{l_1 [Q_2^{p2}]} \text{ if } Q_1 \# Q_2 \\
\ddot{c} \bullet \texttt{Fail}^{l_1 H} &= \texttt{Fail}^{l_1 H} \\
\texttt{Fail}^l \bullet Q^p &= \texttt{Fail}^{l [Q^p]} \\
\texttt{Fail}^{l_1 G l_2} \bullet Q^{p3} &= \texttt{Fail}^{l_1 [Q^{p3}]} \text{ if } \lceil Q \rceil = G \\
\texttt{Fail}^{l_1 G l_2} \bullet Q^{p} &= \texttt{Fail}^{l_2 [Q^{p}]} \text{ if } \lceil Q \rceil \neq G
\end{aligned}$$

$\boxed{[Q^p] = H}$ **Failure Projector**

$$\begin{aligned}
[Q^\epsilon] &= \epsilon \\
[B^l] &= Bl \\
[\ddot{c}_1 \to^l \ddot{c}_2] &= (\star \to \star)l
\end{aligned}$$

$\boxed{\lceil Q^p \rceil = G}$ **Type Constructor**

$$\begin{aligned}
\lceil B^p \rceil &= B \\
\lceil \ddot{c}_1 \to^p \ddot{c}_2 \rceil &= (\star \to \star).
\end{aligned}$$

$\boxed{\langle\!\langle \star \Leftarrow \star \rangle\!\rangle^l}$ **Cast Translation**

$$\langle\!\langle \star \Leftarrow \star \rangle\!\rangle^l = \iota_\star \qquad \langle\!\langle \star \Leftarrow B \rangle\!\rangle^l = B^\epsilon \qquad \langle\!\langle B \Leftarrow B \rangle\!\rangle^l = B^\epsilon$$
$$\langle\!\langle B \Leftarrow \star \rangle\!\rangle^l = B^l \qquad \langle\!\langle T_1 \Leftarrow T_2 \rangle\!\rangle^l = \texttt{Fail}^{l\epsilon} \text{ if } T_1 \# T_2$$
$$\langle\!\langle \star \Leftarrow T_1 \to T_2 \rangle\!\rangle^l = \langle\!\langle T_1 \Leftarrow \star \rangle\!\rangle^{\bar{l}} \to^\epsilon \langle\!\langle \star \Leftarrow T_2 \rangle\!\rangle^l$$
$$\langle\!\langle T_1 \to T_2 \Leftarrow \star \rangle\!\rangle^l = \langle\!\langle \star \Leftarrow T_1 \rangle\!\rangle^{\bar{l}} \to^l \langle\!\langle T_2 \Leftarrow \star \rangle\!\rangle^l$$
$$\langle\!\langle T_1 \to T_2 \Leftarrow T_3 \to T_4 \rangle\!\rangle^l = \langle\!\langle T_3 \Leftarrow T_1 \rangle\!\rangle^{\bar{l}} \to^\epsilon \langle\!\langle T_2 \Leftarrow T_4 \rangle\!\rangle^l$$

Figure 6. Lazy UD Labeled Types

Cast translation is defined by composing the original cast-to-coercions translation $\langle\!\langle T \Leftarrow T \rangle\!\rangle^l$ with $\mathcal{S}[\![\cdot]\!]$. We explicitly calculated this direct definition, but it exactly mirrors that in (Siek and Wadler 2010). Now, if we consider our running example from even-odd, the casts $\langle \star \to \texttt{Bool} \Leftarrow \texttt{Bool} \to \texttt{Bool} \rangle^{l_3} \langle \texttt{Bool} \to \texttt{Bool} \Leftarrow \star \to \texttt{Bool} \rangle^{l_2}$ compile and compose to the labeled type $\texttt{Bool}^{l_3} \to \texttt{Bool}^\epsilon$.

4.4.4 From $\lambda^{\langle \ddot{c} \rangle}$ to the Threesome Calculus $\lambda^{\mathcal{T}}$

Just as we replaced normal coercions in $\lambda^{\langle c \rangle}$ with supercoercions to produce $\lambda^{\langle \ddot{c} \rangle}$, so can we now replace supercoercions with labeled types. However, there is a catch. Consider rule (12') of $\lambda^{\langle \ddot{c} \rangle}$. The ι_B supercoercion corresponds to the labeled type B^ϵ, but so does the $B!$ supercoercion. To disambiguate these two possible situations, we can use the type information for the labeled type. We replace the supercoercions $\ddot{c}$ in $\lambda^{\langle \ddot{c} \rangle}$ with *threesomes* $\langle T_2 \overset{\ddot{c}}{\Longleftarrow} T_1 \rangle$, where $\vdash \ddot{c} : T_2 \Leftarrow T_1$, resulting in the Threesome Calculus of Siek and Wadler (2010). To compile casts to threesomes, we produce the corresponding labeled type and attach the source and target types:

$$\mathcal{T}[\![\langle T_2 \Leftarrow T_1 \rangle^l]\!] = \langle T_2 \overset{\langle\!\langle T_2 \Leftarrow T_1 \rangle\!\rangle^l}{\Longleftarrow} T_1 \rangle.$$

Proposition 15. *Consider the compatible extension of $\mathcal{T}[\![\cdot]\!]$ over $\lambda^{\langle c \rangle}$ terms. If t is a $\lambda^{\langle c \rangle}$ term, then*

$$\lambda^{\langle c \rangle} \vdash t \longrightarrow^* w \textit{ iff } \lambda^{\mathcal{T}} \vdash \mathcal{T}[\![t]\!] \longrightarrow^* \mathcal{T}[\![w]\!].$$

Proof. By a straightforward bisimulation. □

Syntax

expressions	e	$::=$	$k \mid x \mid \lambda x : T.\ e \mid e\ e \mid \langle T_2 \overset{\ddot{c}}{\Longleftarrow} T_1 \rangle e$
		$\mid$	$\textbf{blame}\ l$
simple values	s	$::=$	$k \mid \lambda x : T.\ e$
values	v	$::=$	$s \mid \langle T_2 \overset{\ddot{c}}{\Longleftarrow} T_1 \rangle s$
canonicals	w	$::=$	$v \mid \textbf{blame}\ l$
cast-free contexts	F	$::=$	$\square \mid E[\square\ e] \quad E[v\ \square]$
evaluation contexts	E	$::=$	$F \mid F\left[\langle T_2 \overset{\ddot{c}}{\Longleftarrow} T_1 \rangle \square\right]$

$\boxed{\Gamma \vdash^{S} e : T}$ **Well-typed Expressions**

$$\ldots \qquad \frac{\Gamma \vdash^{S} e : T_1 \qquad \vdash^{S} \ddot{c} : T_2 \Leftarrow T_1}{\Gamma \vdash^{S} \langle T_2 \overset{\ddot{c}}{\Longleftarrow} T_1 \rangle e \quad T_2}$$

$\boxed{\mathcal{C}^{\mathcal{T}}[\![\cdot]\!] : \lambda^{\langle T \rangle} \to \lambda^{\mathcal{T}}}$ **Program Translation**

$$\ldots$$

$$\mathcal{C}^{\mathcal{T}}[\![\langle T_2 \Leftarrow T_1 \rangle^{l}\ t]\!] = \langle \mathcal{T}[\![\langle\!\langle T_2 \Leftarrow T_1 \rangle\!\rangle^{l}]\!] \rangle \mathcal{C}^{\mathcal{T}}[\![t]\!]$$

$\boxed{e \longrightarrow e}$ **Notions of Reduction**

(9'') $$(\lambda x : T.e)\ v \longrightarrow [v/x]\, e$$

(10'')

$$(\langle T_1 \to T_2 \overset{\ddot{c}_1 \to^{\epsilon} \ddot{c}_2}{\Longleftarrow} T_3 \to T_4 \rangle s)\ v \longrightarrow \langle T_2 \overset{\ddot{c}_2}{\Longleftarrow} T_4 \rangle (s\ (\langle T_3 \overset{\ddot{c}_1}{\Longleftarrow} T_1 \rangle v))$$

(11'') $$\langle T_3 \overset{\ddot{c}_1}{\Longleftarrow} T_2 \rangle \langle T_2 \overset{\ddot{c}_2}{\Longleftarrow} T_1 \rangle e \longrightarrow_c \langle T_3 \overset{\ddot{c}_1 \bullet \ddot{c}_2}{\Longleftarrow} T_1 \rangle e$$

(12'') $$\langle B \overset{B^{\epsilon}}{\Longleftarrow} B \rangle s \longrightarrow_c s$$

(13'') $$\langle T_2 \overset{\ddot{f}}{\Longleftarrow} T_1 \rangle s \longrightarrow_c \textbf{blame}\ l$$

Figure 7. The Threesome Calculus ($\lambda^{\mathcal{T}}$)

Re-constructing the Threesome Calculus sheds new light on the relationship between Lazy UD coercions and threesomes, but the key benefit of this process is that it gave us a strategy for developing new threesomes corresponding to alternative blame tracking strategies.

4.5 Extensions

The development presented here focuses on the particulars of the Blame Calculus, but our results extend to more developed languages. We briefly discuss some examples next.

Other Type Constructors In addition to function types, Henglein (1994) specifies coercions for arbitrary type constructors $tc(T_1, \ldots, T_n)$. Each type constructor induces three new coercions:

$$\frac{\vdash c_1 : T_{11} \Leftarrow T_{12} \qquad \ldots \vdash c_n : T_{n1} \Leftarrow T_{n2}}{\vdash tc(c_1, \ldots, c_n) : tc(T_{11}, \ldots, T_{n1}) \Leftarrow tc(T_{12}, \ldots, T_{n2})}$$

$$\frac{}{\vdash tc(\star, \ldots, \star)! : \star \Leftarrow tc(\star, \ldots, \star)}$$

$$\frac{}{\vdash tc(\star, \ldots, \star)?^{l} : tc(\star, \ldots, \star) \Leftarrow \star}$$

as well as two new coercion reduction rules:

$$tc(\star, \ldots, \star)?^{l} \circ tc(\star, \ldots, \star)! \longrightarrow tc(\iota_\star, \ldots, \iota_\star)$$

$$tc(c_{11}, \ldots, c_{1n}) \circ tc(c_{21}, \ldots, c_{2n}) \longrightarrow tc(c_{11} \circ c_{21}, \ldots, c_{1n} \circ c_{2n})$$

The tc type constructor is added to the set of dynables G, which means that rule (8) also accounts for cases like $tc?^{l} \circ B!$. Finally, casts between tc and $\star$ are translated much like function types:

$$\langle\!\langle tc(T_1, \ldots, T_n) \Leftarrow \star \rangle\!\rangle^{l} =$$
$$\langle\!\langle tc(T_1, \ldots, T_n) \Leftarrow tc(\star, \ldots, \star) \rangle\!\rangle^{l} \circ \langle\!\langle tc(\star, \ldots, \star) \Leftarrow \star \rangle\!\rangle^{l}$$
$$\langle\!\langle tc(T_{11}, \ldots, T_{1n}) \Leftarrow tc(T_{21}, \ldots, T_{2n}) \rangle\!\rangle^{l} =$$
$$tc(\langle\!\langle T_{11} \Leftarrow T_{21} \rangle\!\rangle^{l}, \ldots, \langle\!\langle T_{1n} \Leftarrow T_{2n} \rangle\!\rangle^{l})$$

Props. 4 and 2 are easily extended to establish confluence and strong normalization for the resulting system, and just like Prop 10 shows for function coercions, all type-constructor coercions compose in a syntax-directed way.

Proposition 16. $tc(u_{11}, \ldots, u_{1n}) \odot tc(u_{21}, \ldots, u_{2n}) = tc(u_{11} \odot u_{21}, \ldots, u_{1n} \odot u_{2n})$.

Using Prop. 16, we can derive supercoercions and simplify them to threesomes. Finally, the corresponding lambda calculus would have been extended to describe how wrapped values are treated. For instance, to extend the lambda calculus with pairs and pair coercions $c \times c$, we also add reduction rules for projecting coerced values. These translate directly to $\lambda^{\langle T \rangle}$ rules:

$$fst\ \langle \ddot{c}_1 \times \ddot{c}_2 \rangle v \longrightarrow \langle \ddot{c}_1 \rangle (fst\ v)$$
$$snd\ \langle \ddot{c}_1 \times \ddot{c}_2 \rangle v \longrightarrow \langle \ddot{c}_2 \rangle (snd\ v)$$

Subtyping The languages discussed here use "subtyping" relations to characterize which casts are safe, but these relations are orthogonal to subtyping as a programming language feature. In fact, a programming language with a priori support for subtyping can be easily extended to support dynamic types. To do so, $\star$ is added as above, and its only subtype is itself: $\star <: \star$. Then, issues of subtyping and issues of casting are kept orthogonal. For instance, in a language with record types, each record is treated as its own type constructor and coercions extend as in the last section. Siek and Taha (2007) analyze the combination of structural subtyping and dynamic types in more detail. Their $\mathbf{Ob}^{\langle\cdot\rangle}_{<:}$ language uses (space-inefficient) casts to combine structural subtyping and dynamic types in exactly this way.

Alternative Blame Strategies In this section, we systematically reconstructed an existing artifact. While interesting in its own right, the biggest payoff is that we can use the same process to produce new artifacts. Next, we use this approach to produce three new threesome calculi for three alternate blame strategies.

5. Lazy D Threesomes

The Lazy D blame strategy retains the laziness of the Blame Calculus (i.e., Lazy UD), but distributes blame in a manner that's consistent with the traditional notion of subtyping, treating $\star$ as the top of the subtype hierarchy. In this section we develop threesomes that implement the Lazy D strategy. To get a Lazy D threesome calculus, simply replace the Lazy UD labeled types in $\lambda^{\mathcal{T}}$ with their Lazy D counterparts.

The Lazy D coercion calculus extends the Lazy UD calculus by adding primitive injections and projections at every type:

$$G ::= B \mid T \to T$$

Under Lazy D, a cast between any arbitrary function type and $\star$ translates to a primitive coercion:

$$\langle\!\langle \star \Leftarrow T_1 \to T_2 \rangle\!\rangle^{l} = (T_1 \to T_2)! \qquad \langle\!\langle T_1 \to T_2 \Leftarrow \star \rangle\!\rangle^{l} = (T_1 \to T_2)?^{l}$$

Under Lazy UD, such casts translated to complex coercions. In addition, D-style blame labels do not need polarity: blame is ascribed to the particular cast that failed, so the identity of the blame label suffices. The reduction rules for Lazy D must address how complex injections interact with complex projections. This is handled by the following reduction rule:

$$T_1?^{l} \circ T_2! \longrightarrow \langle\!\langle T_1 \Leftarrow T_2 \rangle\!\rangle^{l}$$

This rule subsumes the Lazy UD rules 3, 4, and 8—all of the Lazy UD rules that involve injections composed with projections. For Lazy D, however, this rule must be stated in this general format because there are an unbounded number of concrete instances.

Taking the above differences into account, we can define a set of Lazy D supercoercions that denote normal Lazy D coercion expressions. The main difference with the Lazy D calculus is that primitive injections $G!$ and projections $G?^l$ are indexed by arbitrary types. One side effect of this is that normal arrow coercions like $(c_1 \to c_2) \circ G?^l$ must track the particular type G associated with the leading projection. This difference manifests in the syntax of supercoercions as well as the associated meaning function $\mathcal{N}$:

$$\mathcal{N}[\![\ddot{c}_1 \to^{?(T_1\to T_2)l} \ddot{c}_2]\!] = (\mathcal{N}[\![\ddot{c}_1]\!] \to \mathcal{N}[\![\ddot{c}_2]\!]) \circ (T_1 \to T_2)?^l$$
$$\mathcal{N}[\![\ddot{c}_1 \;{}^{T_1\to T_2 !}{\to}\; \ddot{c}_2]\!] = (T_1 \to T_2)! \circ (\mathcal{N}[\![\ddot{c}_1]\!] \to \mathcal{N}[\![\ddot{c}_2]\!])$$
$$\mathcal{N}[\![\ddot{c}_1 \;{}^{T_1\to T_2 !}{\to}^{?(T_3\to T_4)l}\; \ddot{c}_2]\!] =$$
$$(T_1 \to T_2)! \circ (\mathcal{N}[\![\ddot{c}_1]\!] \to \mathcal{N}[\![\ddot{c}_2]\!]) \circ (T_3 \to T_4)?^l$$

The type indices on arrow supercoercions correspond to leading projections and trailing injections between arrow types and $\star$. Now that any arrow type can be immediately projected to or injected from $\star$, we must keep track of which type is specifically intended. This affects how blame propagates among coercions.

Using the same calculational technique as in Sec 4.2, we define Lazy D supercoercion composition. The directly calculated composition function for Lazy D is more complex than that for Lazy UD because of the intervening type projections and injections that must be compiled and combined for arrow coercions. For example,

$$(\ddot{c}_1 \to^{?(T_1\to T_2)l} \ddot{c}_2) \bullet (\ddot{c}_3 \;{}^{T_3\to T_4 !}{\to}\; \ddot{c}_4) =$$
$$(\ddot{c}_3 \bullet \langle\!\langle T_3 \Leftarrow T_1\rangle\!\rangle^l \bullet \ddot{c}_1) \to (\ddot{c}_2 \bullet \langle\!\langle T_2 \Leftarrow T_4\rangle\!\rangle^l \bullet \ddot{c}_4)$$

Lazy D composition must appeal to cast translation as part of its definition.

Given a set of supercoercions and composition, we apply the same simplification techniques to arrive at a set of labeled types. Only a few details differ, primarily with respect to eradicating primitive arrows, and merging the different forms of complex arrow coercions. Here we focus on the key differences.

As with Lazy UD (cf. Sec. 4.4.1), primitive arrow coercions can be replaced with complex arrow coercions, but here they become more complex. We can deduce the structure of the correspondence by specializing the corresponding reduction rule:

$$(T_1 \to T_2)?^l \circ (T_1 \to T_2)! \longrightarrow \langle\!\langle T_1 \Leftarrow T_1\rangle\!\rangle^l \to \langle\!\langle T_2 \Leftarrow T_2\rangle\!\rangle^l$$

Much like in the case of UD, the resulting coercion behaves like a primitive identity coercion $\iota_{T_1\to T_2}$ and this observation motivates an analogous simplification. We can define a function $\mathcal{I}(T)$ that constructs identity coercions for arbitrary types:

$$\mathcal{I}(P) = \iota_P$$
$$\mathcal{I}(T_1 \to T_2) = \mathcal{I}(T_1) \to \mathcal{I}(T_2)$$

Note that $\mathcal{I}(T) = \langle\!\langle T \Leftarrow T\rangle\!\rangle^l$ for arbitrary label l. Given this, we can define a simplification.

Proposition 17. *Let $\mathcal{S}_1[\![\ddot{c}]\!]$ be defined by*

$$\mathcal{S}_1[\![(T_1 \to T_2)!]\!] = \mathcal{I}(T_1) \;{}^{T_1\to T_2 !}{\to}\; \mathcal{I}(T_2)$$
$$\mathcal{S}_1[\![(T_1 \to T_2)?^l]\!] = \mathcal{I}(T_1) \to^{?(T_1\to T_2)l} \mathcal{I}(T_2)$$
$$\mathcal{S}_1[\![(T_1 \to T_2)!?^l]\!] = \mathcal{I}(T_1) \;{}^{T_1\to T_2 !}{\to}^{?(T_1\to T_2)l}\; \mathcal{I}(T_2)$$
$$\mathcal{S}_1[\![\ddot{c}]\!] = \ddot{c} \quad \textit{otherwise.}$$

Then $\mathcal{S}_1[\![\ddot{c}_1 \bullet \ddot{c}_2]\!] = \mathcal{S}_1[\![\ddot{c}_1]\!] \bullet \mathcal{S}_1[\![\ddot{c}_2]\!]$.

As with Lazy UD, this change makes some supercoercions larger, but these forms often arise at runtime as casts interact anyway, so the size benefit of the original form is short-lived. Furthermore, casts retain the same asymptotic space bound at run-time, bounded by the size of the types that appear in the program. Thus, the resulting supercoercions are still space-efficient.

Syntax

dynables	G	$::=$	$B \mid T \to T$
optional labels	p	$::=$	$\epsilon \mid l$
projectors	H	$::=$	$\epsilon \mid Gl$
injectors	S	$::=$	$\epsilon \mid T \to T$
labeled constructor	Q	$::=$	$B^p \mid \ddot{c} \;{}^{S}{\to}^{H}\; \ddot{c}$
labeled types	$\ddot{c}$	$::=$	$\iota_\star \mid \texttt{Fail}^{lH} \mid Q$
wrappers	$\ddot{o}$	$::=$	$B^\epsilon \mid \ddot{c} \;{}^{S}{\to}^{\epsilon}\; \ddot{c}$
failures	$\ddot{f}$	$::=$	$\texttt{Fail}^l$

$\boxed{\ddot{c} \bullet \ddot{c} = \ddot{c}}$ **Composition**

$$\iota_\star \bullet \ddot{c} = \ddot{c} \bullet \iota_\star = \ddot{c}$$
$$B^{p1} \bullet B^{p2} = B^{p2}$$
$$(\ddot{c}_1 \;{}^{S}{\to}^{\epsilon}\; \ddot{c}_2) \bullet (\ddot{c}_3 \;{}^{\epsilon}{\to}^{H}\; \ddot{c}_4) = (\ddot{c}_3 \bullet \ddot{c}_1) \;{}^{S}{\to}^{H}\; (\ddot{c}_2 \bullet \ddot{c}_4)$$
$$(\ddot{c}_1 \;{}^{S}{\to}^{(T_1\to T_2)l_1}\; \ddot{c}_2) \bullet (\ddot{c}_3 \;{}^{T_3\to T_4}{\to}^{H}\; \ddot{c}_4) =$$
$$(\ddot{c}_3 \bullet \langle\!\langle T_3 \Leftarrow T_1\rangle\!\rangle^{l_1} \bullet \ddot{c}_1) \;{}^{S}{\to}^{H}\; (\ddot{c}_2 \bullet \langle\!\langle T_2 \Leftarrow T_4\rangle\!\rangle^{l_1} \bullet \ddot{c}_4)$$
$$Q_1 \bullet Q_2 = \texttt{Fail}^{l[Q_2]} \text{ if } Q_1 \# Q_2,\ [Q_1] = Gl$$
$$\ddot{c} \bullet \texttt{Fail}^{lH} = \texttt{Fail}^{lH}$$
$$\texttt{Fail}^{l\epsilon} \bullet Q = \texttt{Fail}^{l[Q]}$$
$$\texttt{Fail}^{l_1 G_1 l_2} \bullet Q = \texttt{Fail}^{l_1 [Q]} \text{ if } \lceil G_1 \rceil = \lceil Q \rceil$$
$$\texttt{Fail}^{l_1 G_1 l_2} \bullet Q = \texttt{Fail}^{l_2 [Q]} \text{ if } \lceil G_1 \rceil \neq \lceil Q \rceil$$

$\boxed{[Q] = H}$ **Projector**

$$[B^\epsilon] = \epsilon$$
$$[B^l] = Bl$$
$$[c_1 \;{}^{S}{\to}^{\epsilon}\; c_2] = \epsilon$$
$$[c_1 \;{}^{S}{\to}^{Gl}\; c_2] = Gl$$

$\boxed{\begin{array}{l}\lceil Q \rceil = G \\ \lceil T \rceil = G\end{array}}$ **Type Constructor**

$$\lceil B^p \rceil = B$$
$$\lceil c_1 \;{}^{S}{\to}^{H}\; c_2 \rceil = (\star \to \star)$$
$$\lceil B \rceil = B$$
$$\lceil T_1 \to T_2 \rceil = (\star \to \star)$$

$\boxed{\langle\!\langle \star \Leftarrow \star \rangle\!\rangle^l}$ **Cast Translation**

...

$$\langle\!\langle \star \Leftarrow T_1 \to T_2\rangle\!\rangle^l = \langle\!\langle T_1 \Leftarrow T_1\rangle\!\rangle^l \;{}^{T_1\to T_2}{\to}^{\epsilon}\; \langle\!\langle T_2 \Leftarrow T_2\rangle\!\rangle^l$$
$$\langle\!\langle T_1 \to T_2 \Leftarrow \star\rangle\!\rangle^l = \langle\!\langle T_1 \Leftarrow T_1\rangle\!\rangle^l \;{}^{\epsilon}{\to}^{(T_1\to T_2)^l}\; \langle\!\langle T_2 \Leftarrow T_2\rangle\!\rangle^l$$
$$\langle\!\langle T_1 \to T_2 \Leftarrow T_3 \to T_4\rangle\!\rangle^l = \langle\!\langle T_3 \Leftarrow T_1\rangle\!\rangle^l \to^{\epsilon} \langle\!\langle T_2 \Leftarrow T_4\rangle\!\rangle^l$$

Figure 8. Lazy D Labeled Types

Under Lazy D, merging arrows leads to two different optional labels: *projectors* H, which represent a possible projection from $\star$, and *injectors* S, which represent a possible injection to $\star$. H is analogous to the optional label for Lazy UD failure coercions, and is used similarly in Lazy D.

Once again, we merge the two `Fail` supercoercions as $\texttt{Fail}^{lH}$, and introduce Lazy D analogues of $[\cdot]$ and $\lceil\cdot\rceil$ to unify the definition of composition. The projector function $\lceil\cdot\rceil$ is more complex to account for projector indices on arrow coercions.

Fig. 8 presents the corresponding Lazy D labeled types. When used to instantiate $\lambda^{\mathcal{T}}$, they satisfy the equivalent of Prop. 15.

To demonstrate the difference between D and UD cast compilation, consider the cast $\langle \texttt{Bool} \to \texttt{Bool} \Leftarrow \star\rangle^l$. It compiles to the Lazy D labeled type $\texttt{Bool} \to^{?(\texttt{Bool}\to\texttt{Bool})l} \texttt{Bool}$. Since Lazy UD is just Lazy D with restricted dynables, we can interpret the Lazy UD counterpart of this cast as being equivalent to $\texttt{Bool} \to^{?(\star\to\star)l} \texttt{Bool}$. These two labeled types propagate blame quite differently.

The Lazy D supercoercions are more complex than their Lazy UD counterparts. This is a side-effect of Lazy D's larger space of coercions. In fact, if we restrict G to only B and $\star \to \star$, it is easy to check that the equations relate directly to those for Lazy UD.

6. Eager Threesomes

As discussed in Sec. 3, eager coercion calculi differ from lazy variants in that they detect and report some cast failures earlier. In particular, an arrow coercion $c_1 \to c_2$ cannot be in normal form and have any of its leaves be a $\mathtt{Fail}^l$ cast. Such failures percolate upwards. For instance, under Lazy UD, $\mathtt{Fail}^l \to \iota_\star$ was normal. That is no longer the case.

To support eager checking, the grammar for normal coercions must change.

$$
\begin{array}{llcl}
\text{wrappers} & o & ::= & G! \mid m \to m \mid G! \circ (m \to m) \\
\text{failures} & f & ::= & \mathtt{Fail}^l \mid \mathtt{Fail}^l \circ (m \to m) \\
\text{normal values} & m & ::= & \iota_P \mid o \mid \mathtt{Fail}^l \circ (m \to m) \mid G?^l \\
 & & \mid & o \circ G?^l \mid f \circ G?^l \\
\text{normal coercions} & u & ::= & \mathtt{Fail}^l \mid m
\end{array}
$$

To characterize the normal eager coercions, we differentiate between normal coercions at the toplevel and *normal values* m, which can safely appear under an arrow. In particular, $\mathtt{Fail}^l$ by itself cannot appear under an arrow.

During reduction, definitive failures percolate upwards based on two new rules:

$$(\mathtt{Fail}^l \to c) \longrightarrow \mathtt{Fail}^l \qquad (m \to \mathtt{Fail}^l) \longrightarrow \mathtt{Fail}^l$$

To ensure that the inner failures of complex expressions take precedence, arrow coercions can only be combined if the subcoercions are known to not be failures.

$$(m_1 \to m_2) \circ (m_3 \to m_4) \longrightarrow (m_3 \circ m_1) \to (m_2 \circ m_4)$$

Otherwise, a coercion like $(\mathtt{Fail}^{l_1} \to c_1) \circ (\mathtt{Fail}^{l_2} \to c_2)$ could reduce to either $\mathtt{Fail}^{l_2}$ or $\mathtt{Fail}^{l_1}$, depending on reduction order. Furthermore, we restrict rule 6 from the Lazy UD coercion calculus to ensure that a failing coercion never consumes an arrow coercion to its right:

$$\mathtt{Fail}^l \circ G! \longrightarrow \mathtt{Fail}^l$$

Without this restriction, a coercion like

$$\mathtt{Fail}^{l_1} \circ (\star \to \mathtt{Int}?^{l_2}) \circ (\star \to \mathtt{Bool}!)$$

could reduce to either $\mathtt{Fail}^{l_1}$ or $\mathtt{Fail}^{l_2}$.

Finally, to support eager blame tracking we introduce $\mathtt{Fail}^l \circ (m_1 \to m_2)$ as an additional form of failure f. Since the coercion calculus can no longer reduce $\mathtt{Fail}^l \circ (m_1 \to m_2)$, it is up to $\lambda^{\langle c \rangle}$ to detect it.

As with the lazy variants, these calculi are strongly normalizing, but in contrast confluence does *not* hold. This means that the eager coercion calculi does not independently specify a deterministic strategy for casts. However, the derivation of labeled types, in concert with the space-efficient evaluation semantics, amounts to imposing an order of evaluation on eager coercions.

Because of the new reduction rules, complex arrow coercions interact with composition differently. To capture this difference, we define an operation $\widehat{\to}$ that combines normal coercions according to whether either is a failure.

$$
\begin{aligned}
m \mathbin{\widehat{\to}} m &= m \to m \\
\mathtt{Fail}^l \mathbin{\widehat{\to}} u &= \mathtt{Fail}^l \\
m \mathbin{\widehat{\to}} \mathtt{Fail}^l &= \mathtt{Fail}^l
\end{aligned}
$$

Armed with this, we can succinctly characterize how eager arrow coercions compose.

6.1 Eager D and Eager UD Threesomes

Applying our calculational approach to the eager calculi largely follows the same pattern as for the lazy calculi. As with the normal eager coercions, non-failure supercoercion values $\ddot{m}$ must be differentiated from the full set of supercoercions $\ddot{c}$. Thus, the simple arrow supercoercions have the form $\ddot{m} \to \ddot{m}$. To represent the notion of a failure coercion followed by an arrow coercion, Eager D extends the Lazy D supercoercions with two failure arrow supercoercions, whose interpretations are as follows:

$$\mathcal{N}[\![\ddot{m}_1 \overset{\mathtt{F}^l}{\to} \ddot{m}_2]\!] = \mathtt{Fail}^l \circ \mathcal{N}[\![\ddot{m}_1 \to \ddot{m}_2]\!]$$

$$\mathcal{N}[\![\ddot{m}_1 \overset{\mathtt{F}^{l_1}}{\to} ?^{(T_1 \to T_2)l_2} \ddot{m}_2]\!] = \mathtt{Fail}^{l_1} \circ (\mathcal{N}[\![\ddot{m}_1 \to \ddot{m}_2]\!] \circ (T_1 \to T_2)?^{l_2})$$

Syntax

$$
\begin{array}{llcl}
\text{dynables} & G & ::= & B \mid T \to T \\
\text{optional labels} & p & ::= & \epsilon \mid l \\
\text{projectors} & H & ::= & \epsilon \mid Gl \\
\text{injectors} & S & ::= & \epsilon \mid T \to T \mid l \\
\text{labeled types} & \ddot{c} & ::= & \iota_\star \mid \mathtt{Fail}^{lH} \mid B^p \mid \ddot{m} \ {}^{S}\!\!\to^{H} \ddot{m} \\
\text{values} & \ddot{m} & ::= & \iota_\star \mid B^p \mid \ddot{m} \ {}^{S}\!\!\to^{H} \ddot{m} \\
\text{wrappers} & \ddot{o} & ::= & B^\epsilon \mid \ddot{m} \ {}^{\epsilon}\!\!\to^{\epsilon} \ddot{m} \mid \ddot{m} \ {}^{T \to T}\!\!\to^{\epsilon} \ddot{m} \\
\text{failures} & \ddot{f} & ::= & \mathtt{Fail}^l \mid \ddot{m}_1 \ {}^{l}\!\!\to^{\epsilon} \ddot{m}_2
\end{array}
$$

$\boxed{\ddot{c} \bullet \ddot{c} = \ddot{c}}$ **Composition**

$$
\begin{aligned}
\iota_\star \bullet \ddot{c} = \ddot{c} \bullet \iota_\star &= \ddot{c} \\
B^{p1} \bullet B^{p2} &= B^{p2} \\
B_1^{l_1} \bullet B_2^{p2} &= \mathtt{Fail}^{l_1 [B_2^{p2}]} \text{ if } B_1 \neq B_2 \\
B^{l_1} \bullet (\ddot{m}_1 \ {}^{T_1 \to T_2}\!\!\to^{H} \ddot{m}_2) &= \ddot{m}_1 \ {}^{l_1}\!\!\to^{H} \ddot{m}_2 \\
(\ddot{m}_1 \ {}^{S}\!\!\to^{Gl_1} \ddot{m}_2) \bullet B^{p2} &= \mathtt{Fail}^{l_1 [B^{p2}]} \\
\ddot{c} \bullet \mathtt{Fail}^{lH} &= \mathtt{Fail}^{lH} \\
\ddot{c} \bullet (\ddot{m}_1 \ {}^{l_1}\!\!\to^{H} \ddot{m}_2) &= \ddot{m}_1 \ {}^{l_1}\!\!\to^{H} \ddot{m}_2 \\
\mathtt{Fail}^l \bullet B^p &= \mathtt{Fail}^{l[B^p]} \\
\mathtt{Fail}^{l_1 B l_2} \bullet B^p &= \mathtt{Fail}^{l_1 [B^p]} \\
\mathtt{Fail}^{l_1 B_1 l_2} \bullet B_2^p &= \mathtt{Fail}^{l_2 [B_2^p]} \text{ if } B_1 \neq B_2 \\
\mathtt{Fail}^{l_1 B l_2} \bullet (\ddot{m}_1 \ {}^{T_1 \to T_2}\!\!\to^{H} \ddot{m}_2) &= \ddot{m}_1 \ {}^{l_2}\!\!\to^{H} \ddot{m}_2 \\
\mathtt{Fail}^l \bullet (\ddot{m}_1 \ {}^{\epsilon}\!\!\to^{H} \ddot{m}_2) &= \ddot{m}_1 \ {}^{l}\!\!\to^{H} \ddot{m}_2 \\
\mathtt{Fail}^l \bullet (\ddot{m}_1 \ {}^{T_1 \to T_2}\!\!\to^{H} \ddot{m}_2) &= \ddot{m}_1 \ {}^{l}\!\!\to^{H} \ddot{m}_2 \\
(\ddot{m}_1 \ {}^{S}\!\!\to^{\epsilon} \ddot{m}_2) \bullet (\ddot{m}_3 \ {}^{\epsilon}\!\!\to^{H} \ddot{m}_4) &= (\ddot{m}_3 \bullet \ddot{m}_1) \ {}^{S}\widehat{\to}^{H} (\ddot{m}_2 \bullet \ddot{m}_4) \\
(\ddot{m}_1 \ {}^{S}\!\!\to^{(T_1 \to T_2)l} \ddot{m}_2) \bullet (\ddot{m}_3 \ {}^{T_3 \to T_4}\!\!\to^{H} \ddot{m}_4) &= \\
(\ddot{m}_3 \bullet (\langle\!\langle T_3 \Leftarrow T_1 \rangle\!\rangle^l \bullet \ddot{m}_1)) \ {}^{S}\widehat{\to}^{H} &((\ddot{m}_2 \bullet \langle\!\langle T_2 \Leftarrow T_4 \rangle\!\rangle^l) \bullet \ddot{m}_4)
\end{aligned}
$$

$\boxed{[B^p] = H}$ **Projector**

$$
\begin{aligned}
[B^\epsilon] &= \epsilon \\
[B^l] &= Bl
\end{aligned}
$$

$\boxed{\ddot{c} \ {}^{S}\widehat{\to}^{H} \ddot{c}}$ **Arrow Constructor**

$$
\begin{aligned}
\ddot{m}_1 \ {}^{S}\widehat{\to}^{H} \ddot{m}_2 &= \ddot{m}_1 \ {}^{S}\!\!\to^{H} \ddot{m}_2 \\
\mathtt{Fail}^l \ {}^{S}\widehat{\to}^{\epsilon} \ddot{c}_2 &= \mathtt{Fail}^l \\
\ddot{m}_1 \ {}^{S}\widehat{\to}^{\epsilon} \mathtt{Fail}^l &= \mathtt{Fail}^l \\
\mathtt{Fail}^{l_1} \ {}^{S}\widehat{\to}^{(T_1 \to T_2)l_2} \ddot{c}_2 &= \\
\ddot{m}_1 \ {}^{S}\widehat{\to}^{(T_1 \to T_2)l_2} \mathtt{Fail}^{l_1} &= \\
\mathcal{I}(T_1) \ {}^{l_1}\!\!\to^{(T_1 \to T_2)l_2} \mathcal{I}(T_2)
\end{aligned}
$$

$\boxed{\langle\!\langle \star \Leftarrow \star \rangle\!\rangle^l}$ **Cast Translation**

$$\ldots$$

$$
\begin{aligned}
\langle\!\langle \star \Leftarrow T_1 \to T_2 \rangle\!\rangle^l &= \langle\!\langle T_1 \Leftarrow T_1 \rangle\!\rangle^l \ {}^{T_1 \to T_2}\widehat{\to}^{\epsilon} \langle\!\langle T_2 \Leftarrow T_2 \rangle\!\rangle^l \\
\langle\!\langle T_1 \to T_2 \Leftarrow \star \rangle\!\rangle^l &= \langle\!\langle T_1 \Leftarrow T_1 \rangle\!\rangle^l \ {}^{\epsilon}\widehat{\to}^{(T_1 \to T_2)^l} \langle\!\langle T_2 \Leftarrow T_2 \rangle\!\rangle^l \\
\langle\!\langle T_1 \to T_2 \Leftarrow T_3 \to T_4 \rangle\!\rangle^l &= \langle\!\langle T_3 \Leftarrow T_1 \rangle\!\rangle^l \ \widehat{\to}^{\epsilon} \langle\!\langle T_2 \Leftarrow T_4 \rangle\!\rangle^l
\end{aligned}
$$

Figure 9. Eager D Labeled Types

Composition for Eager D supercoercions introduces a number of new equations that characterize failure arrow supercoercions. These feed into the definition of Eager D labeled types.

Simplifying Eager D supercoercions involves two twists compared to Lazy D. First, $\mathtt{Fail}^{l_1 (T_1 \to T_2) l_2}$ coercions can be replaced by failure arrows $\mathcal{I}(T_1) \overset{\mathtt{F}^{l_1}}{\to} ?^{(T_1 \to T_2)l_2} \mathcal{I}(T_2)$. Furthermore, the downcast label S on arrow types adds an extra blame label component for representing failure arrows and several equations account

Syntax

dynables	G	$::=$	$B \mid \star \rightarrow \star$
optional labels	p	$::=$	$\epsilon \mid l$
failure projectors	H	$::=$	$\epsilon \mid Bl$
labeled types	$\ddot{c}$	$::=$	$\iota_\star \mid \mathtt{Fail}^{lH} \mid B^p \mid \ddot{m} \;{}^{p}\!\!\rightarrow^{p} \ddot{m}$
values	$\ddot{m}$	$::=$	$\iota_\star \mid B^p \mid \ddot{m} \;{}^{p}\!\!\rightarrow^{p} \ddot{m}$
wrappers	$\ddot{o}$	$::=$	$B^\epsilon \mid \ddot{c} \;{}^{\epsilon}\!\!\rightarrow^{\epsilon} \ddot{c}$
failures	$\ddot{f}$	$::=$	$\mathtt{Fail}^l \mid \ddot{m}_1 \;{}^{l}\!\!\rightarrow^{\epsilon} \ddot{m}_2$

$\boxed{\ddot{c} \bullet \ddot{c} = \ddot{c}}$ **Composition**

$$
\begin{aligned}
\iota_\star \bullet \ddot{c} = \ddot{c} \bullet \iota_\star &= \ddot{c} \\
B^{p_1} \bullet B^{p_2} &= B^{p_2} \\
(\ddot{m}_1 \;{}^{p_1}\!\!\rightarrow^{p_2} \ddot{m}_2) \bullet (\ddot{m}_3 \;{}^{\epsilon}\!\!\rightarrow^{p_3} \ddot{m}_4) &= (\ddot{m}_3 \bullet \ddot{m}_1) \;{}^{p_1}\widehat{\rightarrow}^{p_3} (\ddot{m}_2 \bullet \ddot{m}_4) \\
B_1^l \bullet B_2^p &= \mathtt{Fail}^{l[B_2^p]} \text{ if } B_1 \neq B_2 \\
B^l \bullet (\ddot{m}_1 \;{}^{p_1}\!\!\rightarrow^{p_2} \ddot{m}_2) &= (\ddot{m}_1 \;{}^{l}\!\!\rightarrow^{p_2} \ddot{m}_2) \\
(\ddot{m}_1 \;{}^{p_1}\!\!\rightarrow^{l} \ddot{m}_2) \bullet B^{p_2} &= \mathtt{Fail}^{l[B^{p_2}]} \\
\ddot{c} \bullet \mathtt{Fail}^{lH} &= \mathtt{Fail}^{lH} \\
\ddot{c} \bullet (\ddot{m}_1 \;{}^{l}\!\!\rightarrow^{p} \ddot{m}_2) &= \ddot{m}_1 \;{}^{l}\!\!\rightarrow^{p} \ddot{m}_2 \\
\mathtt{Fail}^l \bullet B^p &= \mathtt{Fail}^{l[B^p]} \\
\mathtt{Fail}^l \bullet (\ddot{m}_1 \;{}^{\epsilon}\!\!\rightarrow^{p} \ddot{m}_2) &= \ddot{m}_1 \;{}^{l}\!\!\rightarrow^{p} \ddot{m}_2 \\
\mathtt{Fail}^{l_1 B l_2} \bullet B^p &= \mathtt{Fail}^{l_1[B^p]} \\
\mathtt{Fail}^{l_1 B_1 l_2} \bullet B_2^p &= \mathtt{Fail}^{l_2[B_2^p]} \text{ if } B_1 \neq B_2 \\
\mathtt{Fail}^{l_1 B l_2} \bullet (\ddot{m}_1 \;{}^{\epsilon}\!\!\rightarrow^{p} \ddot{m}_2) &= \ddot{m}_1 \;{}^{l_2}\!\!\rightarrow^{p} \ddot{m}_2
\end{aligned}
$$

$\boxed{[B^p] = H}$ **Failure Projector**

$$[B^\epsilon] = \epsilon$$

$$\left[B^l\right] = Bl$$

$\boxed{\ddot{c} \;{}^{p}\widehat{\rightarrow}^{p}\; \ddot{c}}$ **Arrow Constructor**

$$
\begin{aligned}
\ddot{m}_1 \;{}^{p_1}\widehat{\rightarrow}^{p_2} \ddot{m}_2 &= \ddot{m}_1 \;{}^{p_1}\!\!\rightarrow^{p_2} \ddot{m}_2 \\
\mathtt{Fail}^l \;{}^{p}\widehat{\rightarrow}^{\epsilon} \ddot{c}_2 &= \\
\ddot{m}_1 \;{}^{p}\widehat{\rightarrow}^{\epsilon} \mathtt{Fail}^l &= \mathtt{Fail}^l \\
\mathtt{Fail}^{l_1} \;{}^{p}\widehat{\rightarrow}^{l_2} \ddot{c}_2 &= \\
\ddot{m}_1 \;{}^{p}\widehat{\rightarrow}^{l_2} \mathtt{Fail}^{l_1} &= \iota_\star \;{}^{l_1}\!\!\rightarrow^{l_2} \iota_\star
\end{aligned}
$$

$\boxed{\langle\!\langle \star \Leftarrow \star \rangle\!\rangle^l}$ **Cast Translation**

...

$$
\begin{aligned}
\langle\!\langle \star \Leftarrow T_1 \rightarrow T_2 \rangle\!\rangle^l &= \langle\!\langle T_1 \Leftarrow \star \rangle\!\rangle^{\bar{l}} \;\widehat{\rightarrow}^{\epsilon}\; \langle\!\langle \star \Leftarrow T_2 \rangle\!\rangle^l \\
\langle\!\langle T_1 \rightarrow T_2 \Leftarrow \star \rangle\!\rangle^l &= \langle\!\langle \star \Leftarrow T_1 \rangle\!\rangle^{\bar{l}} \;\widehat{\rightarrow}^{l}\; \langle\!\langle T_2 \Leftarrow \star \rangle\!\rangle^l \\
\langle\!\langle T_1 \rightarrow T_2 \Leftarrow T_3 \rightarrow T_4 \rangle\!\rangle^l &= \langle\!\langle T_3 \Leftarrow T_1 \rangle\!\rangle^{\bar{l}} \;\widehat{\rightarrow}^{\epsilon}\; \langle\!\langle T_2 \Leftarrow T_4 \rangle\!\rangle^l
\end{aligned}
$$

Figure 10. Eager UD Labeled Types

for failure arrows. Fig. 9 presents the Eager D labeled types. Compilation of casts for Eager D is the same as for Lazy D except that the arrow constructors $\widehat{\rightarrow}$ must be used to percolate failures upwards.

Finally, we add $\ddot{c}_1 \;{}^{l}\!\!\rightarrow^{\epsilon} \ddot{c}_2$ as an additional failure coercion f so that $\lambda^{\mathcal{T}}$ can detect it as a failure. This corresponds to the analogous addition to the coercion calculus.

Having computed Eager D labeled types, the Eager UD variant can be easily computed by restricting the projectable types G to base types B and $(\star \rightarrow \star)$. This restriction removes the need for type annotations on arrow coercions, leading to a much simpler form. Fig. 10 presents the Eager UD labeled types. Compilation of casts for Eager UD is the same as for Lazy UD except for the use of arrow constructors to propagate failures. Note that Eager UD blame labels are polarized.

7. Discussion

The primary contributions of this paper are novel threesome semantics for coercion calculi, each of which supports desirable properties, like catching more errors sooner and a blame strategy based on traditional subtyping. It was previously unknown whether the labeling protocol for threesomes could be adapted to capture D-style blame tracking or the Eager variant of UD. This paper answers that question affirmatively.

The eager threesome calculi in particular point to some significant benefits to our approach. Composing eager labeled types no longer corresponds to the greatest lower bound of the two types, i.e., $\bot \& (T_1 \rightarrow T_2) = \bot$ does not apply for eager threesomes. This suggests that the original approach of experimenting with labels on threesomes without blame might have led to troubles. On the other hand, each of the three new threesome calculi were quicker to develop than the Lazy UD reconstruction once it was completed.

In addition to new threesome-based semantics, the paper offers a fresh perspective on the original labeled types and Threesome Calculus. Labeled types were developed from scratch, starting from the concept of threesomes without blame, and adding blame labels later. We construct the same concept, but do so from a different starting point, normal coercions, and proceed by stepwise refinement, maintaining correctness at each step. This process reveals that threesomes with blame can be viewed as a streamlined implementation strategy for coercions, and exposes some of the rich structure contained in the original system.

If such languages are to have practical impact, they will need to be scaled beyond the basic lambda calculus to support more types (e.g., parametric polymorphism (Ahmed et al. 2011)). As another step toward full-fledged implementations, we will endeavor to extend our threesome calculi with these features, first extending coercion calculi to support them.

8. Acknowledgements

We thank Jeremy Siek and Éric Tanter for motivating this work and enlightening discussions about this topic. We also thank Philip Wadler and anonymous reviewers for their helpful comments.

References

Amal Ahmed, Robert Bruce Findler, Jeremy Siek, and Philip Wadler. Blame for all. In *Proc. Symposium on Principles of Programming Languages*, POPL '11, pages 201–214, New York, NY, USA, 2011. ACM.

Robert Bruce Findler and Matthias Felleisen. Contracts for higher-order functions. In *Int. Conf. on Functional Programming*, October 2002.

Fritz Henglein. Dynamic typing: syntax and proof theory. *Science of Computer Programming*, 22(3):197–230, June 1994.

David Herman, Aaron Tomb, and Cormac Flanagan. Space-efficient gradual typing. In *Trends in Functional Prog.*, page XXVIII, April 2007.

Jacob Matthews and Robert Bruce Findler. Operational semantics for multi-language programs. *ACM Trans. Program. Lang. Syst.*, 31(3):12:1–12:44, April 2009.

Jeremy Siek. Strong normalization for coercion calculi. Unpublished Manuscript, 2011a.

Jeremy Siek, 2011b. Private Correspondence.

Jeremy Siek and Walid Taha. Gradual typing for functional languages. In *Proc. Scheme and Functional Programming Workshop*, September 2006.

Jeremy Siek and Walid Taha. Gradual typing for objects. In *Proc. European Conference on Object-Oriented Programming*, ECOOP '07, pages 2–27, Berlin, 2007. Springer-Verlag.

Jeremy Siek and Philip Wadler. Threesomes, with and without blame. In *Proc. Symposium on Principles of Programming Languages*, POPL '10, pages 365–376, New York, NY, USA, 2010. ACM.

Jeremy Siek, Ronald Garcia, and Walid Taha. Exploring the design space of higher-order casts. In *Proc. European Symposium on Programming Languages*, ESOP '09, pages 17–31, Berlin, 2009. Springer-Verlag.

Sam Tobin-Hochstadt and Matthias Felleisen. Interlanguage migration: from scripts to programs. In *Companion to Symposium on Object-oriented Programming Systems, Languages, and Applications*, OOPSLA '06, pages 964–974, New York, 2006. ACM.

Philip Wadler and Robert Bruce Findler. Well-typed programs can't be blamed. In *Proc. European Symposium on Programming Languages*, ESOP '09, pages 1–16, Berlin, 2009. Springer-Verlag.

Complete and Easy Bidirectional Typechecking for Higher-Rank Polymorphism

Joshua Dunfield   Neelakantan R. Krishnaswami

Max Planck Institute for Software Systems
Kaiserslautern and Saarbrücken, Germany
{joshua,neelk}@mpi-sws.org

Abstract

Bidirectional typechecking, in which terms either synthesize a type or are checked against a known type, has become popular for its scalability (unlike Damas-Milner type inference, bidirectional typing remains decidable even for very expressive type systems), its error reporting, and its relative ease of implementation. Following design principles from proof theory, bidirectional typing can be applied to many type constructs. The principles underlying a bidirectional approach to polymorphism, however, are less obvious. We give a declarative, bidirectional account of higher-rank polymorphism, grounded in proof theory; this calculus enjoys many properties such as η-reduction and predictability of annotations. We give an algorithm for implementing the declarative system; our algorithm is remarkably simple and well-behaved, despite being both sound and complete.

Categories and Subject Descriptors D.3.3 [*Programming Languages*]: Language Constructs and Features—polymorphism

Keywords bidirectional typechecking, higher-rank polymorphism

1. Introduction

Bidirectional typechecking (Pierce and Turner 2000) has become one of the most popular techniques for implementing typecheckers in new languages. This technique has been used for dependent types (Coquand 1996; Abel et al. 2008; Löh et al. 2008; Asperti et al. 2012); subtyping (Pierce and Turner 2000); intersection, union, indexed and refinement types (Xi 1998; Davies and Pfenning 2000; Dunfield and Pfenning 2004); termination checking (Abel 2004); higher-rank polymorphism (Peyton Jones et al. 2007; Dunfield 2009); refinement types for LF (Lovas 2010); contextual modal types (Pientka 2008); compiler intermediate representations (Chlipala et al. 2005); and object-oriented languages including C$^\sharp$ (Bierman et al. 2007) and Scala (Odersky et al. 2001). As can be seen, it scales well to advanced type systems; moreover, it is easy to implement, and yields relatively high-quality error messages (Peyton Jones et al. 2007).

ICFP '13, September 25–27, 2013, Boston, MA, USA.

ACM 978-1-4503-2326-0/13/09... $15.00.
http://dx.doi.org/10.1145/2500365.2500582

However, the theoretical foundation of bidirectional typechecking has lagged behind its application. As shown by Watkins et al. (2004), bidirectional typechecking can be understood in terms of the normalization of intuitionistic type theory, in which normal forms correspond to the checking mode of bidirectional typechecking, and neutral (or atomic) terms correspond to the synthesis mode. This enables a proof of the elegant property that type annotations are only necessary at reducible expressions, and that normal forms need no annotations at all. The benefit of the proof-theoretic view is that it gives a simple and easy-to-understand declarative account of where type annotations are necessary, without reference to the details of the typechecking algorithm.

While the proof-theoretic account of bidirectional typechecking has been scaled up as far as type refinements and intersection and union types (Pfenning 2008), as yet there has been no completely satisfactory account of how to extend the proof-theoretic approach to handle polymorphism. This is especially vexing, since the ability of bidirectional *algorithms* to gracefully accommodate polymorphism (even higher-rank polymorphism) has been one of their chief attractions.

In this paper, we extend the proof-theoretic account of bidirectional typechecking to full higher-rank polymorphism (i.e., predicative System F), and consequently show that bidirectional typechecking is not merely sound with respect to the declarative semantics, but also that it is *complete*. Better still, the algorithm we give for doing so is extraordinarily *simple*.

First, as a specification of type checking, we give a declarative bidirectional type system which guesses all quantifier instantiations. This calculus is a small but significant contribution of this paper, since it possesses desirable properties, such as the preservation of typability under η-reduction, that are missing from the type assignment version of System F. Furthermore, we can use the bidirectional character of our declarative calculus to show a number of refactoring theorems, enabling us to precisely characterize what sorts of substitutions (and reverse substitutions) preserve typability, where type annotations are needed, and when programmers may safely delete type annotations.

Then, we give a bidirectional algorithm that always finds corresponding instantiations. As a consequence of completeness, we can show that our algorithm never needs explicit type applications, and that type annotations are only required for polymorphic, reducible expressions—which, in practice, means that only let-bindings of functions at polymorphic type need type annotations; no other expressions need annotations.

Our algorithm is both simple to understand and simple to implement. The key data structure is an ordered context containing all bindings, including type variables, term variables, and existential variables denoting partial type information. By maintaining order, we are able to easily manage scope information, which is particu-

$$\text{Terms} \quad e \quad ::= \quad x \mid () \mid \lambda x.\, e \mid e\, e \mid (e : A)$$

Figure 1. Source expressions

Types	A, B, C	$::=$	$1 \mid \alpha \mid \forall\alpha.\, A \mid A \to B$
Monotypes	τ, σ	$::=$	$1 \mid \alpha \mid \tau \to \sigma$
Contexts	Ψ	$::=$	$\cdot \mid \Psi, \alpha \mid \Psi, x : A$

Figure 2. Syntax of declarative types and contexts

larly important in higher-rank systems, where different quantifiers may be instantiated with different sets of free variables. Furthermore, ordered contexts admit a notion of *extension* or *information increase*, which organizes and simplifies the soundness and completeness proofs of the algorithmic system with respect to the declarative one.

Contributions. We make the following contributions:

- We give a declarative, bidirectional account of higher-rank polymorphism, grounded strongly in proof theory. This calculus has important properties (such as η-reduction) that the type assignment variant of System F lacks, yet is sound and complete (up to βη-equivalence) with respect to System F.

  As a result, we can explain where type annotations are needed, where they may be deleted, and why important code transformations are sound, all without reference to the implementation.
- We give a very simple algorithm for implementing the declarative system. Our algorithm does not need any data structure more sophisticated than a list, but can still solve all of the problems which arise in typechecking higher-rank polymorphism without any need for search or backtracking.
- We prove that our algorithm is both *sound* and *complete* with respect to our declarative specification of typing. This proof is cleanly structured around *context extension*, a relational notion of information increase, corresponding to the intuition that our algorithm progressively resolves type constraints.

  As a result of completeness, programmers may safely "pay no attention to the implementor behind the curtain", and ignore all the algorithmic details of unification and type inference: the algorithm does exactly what the declarative specification says, no more and no less.

Lemmas and proofs. Proofs of the main results, as well as statements of all lemmas (and their proofs), can be found in the appendix, available from `www.cs.cmu.edu/~joshuad/bidir/`.

2. Declarative Type System

In order to show that our algorithm is sound and complete, we need to give a declarative type system to serve as the specification for our algorithm. Surprisingly, it turns out that finding the correct declarative system to use as a specification is itself an interesting problem!

Much work on type inference for higher-rank polymorphism takes the type assignment variant of System F as a specification of type inference. Unfortunately, under these rules typing is not stable under η-reductions. For example, suppose f is a variable of type $1 \to \forall\alpha.\, \alpha$. Then the term $\lambda x.\, f\, x$ can be ascribed the type $1 \to 1$, since the polymorphic quantifier can be instantiated to 1 between the f and the x. But the η-reduct f cannot be ascribed the type $1 \to 1$, because the quantifier cannot be instantiated until after f has been applied. This is especially unfortunate in pure languages like Haskell, where the η law is a valid program equality.

Therefore, we do not use the type assignment version of System F as our declarative specification of type checking and inference.

$\boxed{\Psi \vdash A}$ Under context Ψ, type A is well-formed

$$\frac{\alpha \in \Psi}{\Psi \vdash \alpha}\ \text{DeclUvarWF} \qquad \frac{}{\Psi \vdash 1}\ \text{DeclUnitWF}$$

$$\frac{\Psi \vdash A \qquad \Psi \vdash B}{\Psi \vdash A \to B}\ \text{DeclArrowWF} \qquad \frac{\Psi, \alpha \vdash A}{\Psi \vdash \forall\alpha.\, A}\ \text{DeclForallWF}$$

$\boxed{\Psi \vdash A \leq B}$ Under context Ψ, type A is a subtype of B

$$\frac{\alpha \in \Psi}{\Psi \vdash \alpha \leq \alpha}\ {\leq}\text{Var} \qquad \frac{}{\Psi \vdash 1 \leq 1}\ {\leq}\text{Unit}$$

$$\frac{\Psi \vdash B_1 \leq A_1 \qquad \Psi \vdash A_2 \leq B_2}{\Psi \vdash A_1 \to A_2 \leq B_1 \to B_2}\ {\leq}{\to}$$

$$\frac{\Psi \vdash \tau \qquad \Psi \vdash [\tau/\alpha]A \leq B}{\Psi \vdash \forall\alpha.\, A \leq B}\ {\leq}\forall\text{L} \qquad \frac{\Psi, \beta \vdash A \leq B}{\Psi \vdash A \leq \forall\beta.\, B}\ {\leq}\forall\text{R}$$

Figure 3. Well-formedness of types and subtyping in the declarative system

Instead, we give a declarative, bidirectional system as the specification. Traditionally, bidirectional systems are given in terms of a *checking* judgment $\Psi \vdash e \Leftarrow A$, which takes a type A as input and ensures that the term e *checks against* that type, and a *synthesis* judgment $\Psi \vdash e \Rightarrow A$, which takes a term e and *produces* a type A. This two-judgment formulation is satisfactory for simple types, but breaks down in the presence of polymorphism.

The essential problem is as follows: the standard bidirectional rule for checking applications $e_1\ e_2$ in non-polymorphic systems is to synthesize type $A \to B$ for e_1, and then check e_2 against A, returning B as the type. With polymorphism, however, we may have an application $e_1\ e_2$ in which e_1 synthesizes a term of polymorphic type (e.g., $\forall\alpha.\, \alpha \to \alpha$). Furthermore, we do not know *a priori* how many quantifiers we need to instantiate.

To solve this problem, we turn to *focalization* (Andreoli 1992), the proof-theoretic foundation of bidirectional typechecking. In focused sequent calculi, it is natural to give terms in *spine form* (Cervesato and Pfenning 2003; Simmons 2012), sequences of applications to a head. So we view every application as really being a spine consisting of a series of type applications followed by a term application, and introduce an *application judgment* $\Psi \vdash A \bullet e \Rrightarrow C$, which says that if a term of type A is applied to argument e, the result has type C. Consequently, quantifiers will be instantiated exactly when needed to reveal a function type.

The application judgment lets us suppress explicit type applications, but to get the η law, we need more. Recall the example with $f : 1 \to \forall\alpha.\, \alpha$. In η-reducing $\lambda x.\, f\, x$ to f, we reduce the number of applications in the term. That is, we no longer have a syntactic position at which we can (implicitly) instantiate polymorphic quantifiers. To handle this, we follow Odersky and Läufer (1996) in modeling type instantiation using *subtyping*, where subtyping is defined as a "more-polymorphic-than" relation that guesses type instantiations arbitrarily deeply within types. As a result, $1 \to \forall\alpha.\, \alpha$ is a subtype of $1 \to 1$, and the η law holds.

Happily, subtyping *does* fit naturally into bidirectional systems (Davies and Pfenning 2000; Dunfield 2007; Lovas 2010), so we can give a declarative, bidirectional type system that guesses type instantiations, but is otherwise entirely syntax-directed. In particular, subsumption is confined to a single rule (which switches from checking to synthesis), and our use of an application judgment determines when to instantiate quantifiers. The resulting system is very well-behaved, and ensures that the expected typability results (such as typability being preserved by η-reductions) continue to hold. Furthermore, our declarative formulation makes it clear that

$\boxed{\Psi \vdash e \Leftarrow A}$ Under context Ψ, e checks against input type A

$\boxed{\Psi \vdash e \Rightarrow A}$ Under context Ψ, e synthesizes output type A

$\boxed{\Psi \vdash A \bullet e \Rightarrow\!\!\!\Rightarrow C}$ Under context Ψ, applying a function of type A to e synthesizes type C

$$\frac{(x:A) \in \Psi}{\Psi \vdash x \Rightarrow A}\,\text{DeclVar} \qquad \frac{\Psi \vdash e \Rightarrow A \quad \Psi \vdash A \leq B}{\Psi \vdash e \Leftarrow B}\,\text{DeclSub} \qquad \frac{\Psi \vdash A \quad \Psi \vdash e \Leftarrow A}{\Psi \vdash (e:A) \Rightarrow A}\,\text{DeclAnno}$$

$$\frac{}{\Psi \vdash () \Leftarrow 1}\,\text{Decl1I} \qquad \frac{}{\Psi \vdash () \Rightarrow 1}\,\text{Decl1I}{\Rightarrow} \qquad \frac{\Psi, \alpha \vdash e \Leftarrow A}{\Psi \vdash e \Leftarrow \forall\alpha.\, A}\,\text{Decl}\forall\text{I} \qquad \frac{\Psi \vdash \tau \quad \Psi \vdash [\tau/\alpha]A \bullet e \Rightarrow\!\!\!\Rightarrow C}{\Psi \vdash \forall\alpha.\, A \bullet e \Rightarrow\!\!\!\Rightarrow C}\,\text{Decl}\forall\text{App}$$

$$\frac{\Psi, x:A \vdash e \Leftarrow B}{\Psi \vdash \lambda x.\, e \Leftarrow A \to B}\,\text{Decl}{\to}\text{I} \qquad \frac{\Psi \vdash \sigma \to \tau \quad \Psi, x:\sigma \vdash e \Leftarrow \tau}{\Psi \vdash \lambda x.\, e \Rightarrow \sigma \to \tau}\,\text{Decl}{\to}\text{I}{\Rightarrow} \qquad \frac{\Psi \vdash e_1 \Rightarrow A \quad \Psi \vdash A \bullet e_2 \Rightarrow\!\!\!\Rightarrow C}{\Psi \vdash e_1\, e_2 \Rightarrow C}\,\text{Decl}{\to}\text{E}$$

$$\frac{\Psi \vdash e \Leftarrow A}{\Psi \vdash A \to C \bullet e \Rightarrow\!\!\!\Rightarrow C}\,\text{Decl}{\to}\text{App}$$

Figure 4. Declarative typing

the fundamental algorithmic problem in extending bidirectional typechecking to polymorphism is precisely the problem of figuring out what the missing type applications are.

Preserving the η-rule for functions comes at a cost. The subtyping relation induced by instantiation is undecidable for *impredicative* polymorphism (Tiuryn and Urzyczyn 1996; Chrząszcz 1998). Since we want a complete typechecking algorithm, we consequently restrict our system to predicative polymorphism, where polymorphic quantifiers can be instantiated only with monomorphic types. We discuss alternatives in Section 9.

2.1 Typing in Detail

Language overview. In Figure 1, we give the grammar for our language. We have a unit term $()$, variables x, lambda-abstraction $\lambda x.\, e$, application $e_1\, e_2$, and type annotation $(e : A)$. We write A, B, C for types (Figure 2): types are the unit type 1, type variables α, universal quantification $\forall\alpha.\, A$, and functions $A \to B$. Monotypes τ and σ are the same, less the universal quantifier. Contexts Ψ are lists of type variable declarations, and term variables $x : A$, with the expected well-formedness condition. (We give a single-context formulation mixing type and term hypotheses to simplify the presentation.)

Checking, synthesis, and application. Our type system has three main judgments, given in Figure 4. The checking judgment $\Psi \vdash e \Leftarrow A$ asserts that e checks against the type A in the context Ψ. The synthesis judgment $\Psi \vdash e \Rightarrow A$ says that we can synthesize the type A for e in the context Ψ. Finally, an *application judgment* $\Psi \vdash A \bullet e \Rightarrow\!\!\!\Rightarrow C$ says that if a (possibly polymorphic) function of type A is applied to argument e, then the whole application synthesizes C for the whole application.

As is standard in the proof-theoretic presentations of bidirectional typechecking, each of the introduction forms in our calculus has a corresponding checking rule. The Decl1I rule says that $()$ checks against the unit type 1. The Decl→I rule says that $\lambda x.\, e$ checks against the function type $A \to B$ if e checks against B with the additional hypothesis that x has type A. The Decl∀I rule says that e has type $\forall\alpha.\, A$ if e has type A in a context extended with a fresh α.[1] Sums, products and recursive types can be added similarly (we leave them out for simplicity). Rule DeclSub mediates between synthesis and checking: it says that e can be checked against B, if e synthesizes A and A is a subtype of B (that is, A is at least as polymorphic as B).

As expected, we can infer a type for a variable (the DeclVar rule) just by looking it up in the context. Likewise, the DeclAnno rule says that we can synthesize a type A for a term with a type annotation $(e : A)$ just by returning that type (after checking that the term does actually check against A).

Application is a little more complex: we have to eliminate universals until we reach an arrow type. To do this, we use an application judgment $\Psi \vdash A \bullet e \Rightarrow\!\!\!\Rightarrow C$, which says that if we apply a term of type A to an argument e, we get something of type C. This judgment works by guessing instantiations of polymorphic quantifiers in rule Decl∀App. Once we have instantiated enough quantifiers to expose an arrow $A \to C$, we check e against A and return C in rule Decl→App.

In the following example, where we are applying some function polymorphic in α, Decl∀App instantiates the outer quantifier (to the unit type 1; we elide the premise $\Psi \vdash 1$), but leaves the inner quantifier over β alone.

$$\dfrac{\dfrac{\Psi \vdash x \Leftarrow (\forall\beta.\, \beta\to\beta)}{\Psi \vdash (\forall\beta.\, \beta\to\beta) \to 1 \to 1 \bullet x \Rightarrow\!\!\!\Rightarrow 1 \to 1}\,\text{Decl}{\to}\text{App}}{\Psi \vdash \big(\forall\alpha.\, (\forall\beta.\, \beta\to\beta) \to \alpha \to \alpha\big) \bullet x \Rightarrow\!\!\!\Rightarrow 1 \to 1}\,\text{Decl}\forall\text{App}$$

In the minimal proof-theoretic formulation of bidirectionality (Davies and Pfenning 2000; Dunfield and Pfenning 2004), introduction forms are checked and elimination forms synthesize, full stop. Even $()$ cannot synthesize its type! Actual bidirectional typecheckers tend to take a more liberal view, adding synthesis rules for at least some introduction forms. To show that our system can accommodate these kinds of extensions, we add the Decl1I⇒ and Decl→I⇒ rules, which synthesize a unit type for $()$ and a monomorphic function type for lambda expressions $\lambda x.\, e$. We examine other variations, including a purist bidirectional no-inference alternative, and a liberal Damas-Milner alternative, in Section 8.

Instantiating types. We express the fact that one type is a polymorphic generalization of another by means of the subtyping judgment given in Figure 3. One important aspect of the judgment is that types are compared relative to a context of free variables. This simplifies our rules, by letting us eliminate the awkward side conditions on sets of free variables that plague many presentations. Most of the subtyping judgment is typical: it proceeds structurally on types, with a contravariant twist for the arrow; all the real ac-

[1] Note that we do not require an explicit type abstraction operation. As a result, an implementation needs to use some technique like scoped type variables (Peyton Jones and Shields 2004) to mention bound type variables in annotations. This point does not matter to the abstract syntax, though.

tion is contained within the two subtyping rules for the universal quantifier.

The left rule, $\leq\forall L$, says that a type $\forall\alpha. A$ is a subtype of B, if some instance $[\tau/\alpha]A$ is a subtype of B. This is what makes these rules only a declarative specification: $\leq\forall L$ guesses the instantiation τ "out of thin air", and so the rules do not directly yield an algorithm.

The right rule $\leq\forall R$ is a little more subtle. It says that A is a subtype of $\forall\beta. B$ if we can show that A is a subtype of B in a context extended with β. There are two intuitions for this rule, one semantic, the other proof-theoretic. The semantic intuition is that since $\forall\beta. B$ is a subtype of $[\tau/\beta]B$ for any τ, we need A to be a subtype of $[\tau/\beta]B$ for any τ. Then, if we can show that A is a subtype of B, with a free variable β, we can appeal to a substitution principle for subtyping to conclude that for all τ, type A is a subtype of $[\tau/\beta]B$.

The proof-theoretic intuition is simpler. The rules $\leq\forall L$ and $\leq\forall R$ are just the left and right rules for universal quantification in the sequent calculus. Type inference is a form of theorem proving, and our subtype relation gives some of the inference rules a theorem prover may use. Following good proof-theoretic hygiene enables us to leave the reflexivity and transitivity rules out of the subtype relation, since they are admissible properties (in sequent calculus terms, they are the identity and cut-admissibility properties). The absence of these rules (particularly, the absence of transitivity), in turn, simplifies a number of proofs. In fact, the rules are practically syntax-directed: the only exception is when both types are quantifiers, and either $\leq\forall L$ or $\leq\forall R$ could be tried. Since $\leq\forall R$ is invertible, however, in practice one can apply it eagerly.

Let-generalization. In many accounts of type inference, let-bindings are treated specially. For example, traditional Damas-Milner type inference only does polymorphic generalization at let-bindings. Instead, we have sought to avoid a special treatment of let-bindings. In logical terms, let-bindings internalize the cut rule, and so special treatment puts the cut-elimination property of the calculus at risk—that is, typability may not be preserved when a let-binding is substituted away. To make let-generalization safe, additional properties like the principal types property are needed, a property endangered by rich type system features like higher-rank polymorphism, refinement types (Dunfield 2007) and GADTs (Vytiniotis et al. 2010).

To emphasize this point, we have omitted let-binding from our formal development. But since cut is admissible—i.e., the substitution theorem holds—restoring let-bindings is easy, as long as they get no special treatment incompatible with substitution. For example, the standard bidirectional rule for let-bindings is suitable:

$$\frac{\Psi \vdash e \Rightarrow A \qquad \Psi, x : A \vdash e' \Leftarrow C}{\Psi \vdash \mathsf{let}\ x = e\ \mathsf{in}\ e' \Leftarrow C}$$

Note the absence of generalization in this rule.

2.2 Bidirectional Typing and Type Assignment System F

Since our declarative specification is (quite consciously) not the usual type-assignment presentation of System F, a natural question is to ask what the relationship is. Luckily, the two systems are quite closely related: we can show that if a term is well-typed in our type assignment system, it is always possible to add type annotations to make the term well-typed in the bidirectional system; conversely, if the bidirectional system types a term, then some $\beta\eta$-equal term is well-typed under the type assignment system.

We formalize these properties with the following theorems, taking $|e|$ to be the erasure of all type annotations from a term. We give the rules for our type assignment System F in Figure 5.

$\boxed{\Psi \vdash e : A}$ Under context Ψ, e has type A

$$\frac{(x : A) \in \Psi}{\Psi \vdash x : A}\ \mathsf{AVar} \qquad \frac{}{\Psi \vdash () : 1}\ \mathsf{AUnit}$$

$$\frac{\Psi, x : A \vdash e : B}{\Psi \vdash \lambda x.\, e : A \to B}\ \mathsf{A{\to}I} \qquad \frac{\Psi \vdash e_1 : A \to B \qquad \Psi \vdash e_2 : A}{\Psi \vdash e_1\ e_2 : B}\ \mathsf{A{\to}E}$$

$$\frac{\Psi, \alpha \vdash e : A}{\Psi \vdash e : \forall\alpha.\, A}\ \mathsf{A\forall I} \qquad \frac{\Psi \vdash e : \forall\alpha.\, A \qquad \Psi \vdash \tau}{\Psi \vdash e : [\tau/\alpha]A}\ \mathsf{A\forall E}$$

Figure 5. Type assignment rules for predicative System F

Theorem 1 (Completeness of Bidirectional Typing)**.** *If* $\Psi \vdash e : A$ *then there exists* e' *such that* $\Psi \vdash e' \Rightarrow A$ *and* $|e'| = e$.

Theorem 2 (Soundness of Bidirectional Typing)**.** *If* $\Psi \vdash e \Leftarrow A$ *then there exists* e' *such that* $\Psi \vdash e' : A$ *and* $e' =_{\beta\eta} |e|$.

Note that in the soundness theorem, the equality is up to β and η. We may need to η-expand bidirectionally-typed terms to make them typecheck under the type assignment system, and within the proof of soundness, we β-reduce identity coercions.

2.3 Robustness of Typing

Type annotations are an essential part of the bidirectional approach: they mediate between type checking and type synthesis. However, we want to relieve programmers from having to write redundant type annotations, and even more importantly, enable programmers to easily predict where type annotations are needed.

Since our declarative system is bidirectional, the basic property is that type annotations are required only at redexes. Additionally, these typing rules can infer (actually, guess) all monomorphic types, so the answer to the question of where annotations are needed is: only on bindings of polymorphic type.[2] Where bidirectional typing really stands out is in its robustness under substitution. We can freely substitute and "unsubstitute" terms:

Theorem 3 (Substitution)**.** *Assume* $\Psi \vdash e \Rightarrow A$.

- *If* $\Psi, x : A \vdash e' \Leftarrow C$ *then* $\Psi \vdash [e/x]e' \Leftarrow C$.
- *If* $\Psi, x : A \vdash e' \Rightarrow C$ *then* $\Psi \vdash [e/x]e' \Rightarrow C$.

Theorem 4 (Inverse Substitution)**.** *Assume* $\Psi \vdash e \Leftarrow A$.

- *If* $\Psi \vdash [(e : A)/x]e' \Leftarrow C$ *then* $\Psi, x : A \vdash e' \Leftarrow C$.
- *If* $\Psi \vdash [(e : A)/x]e' \Rightarrow C$ *then* $\Psi, x : A \vdash e' \Rightarrow C$.

Substitution is stated in terms of synthesizing expressions, since any checking term can be turned into a synthesizing term by adding an annotation. Dually, inverse substitution allows extracting any checking term into a let-binding with a type annotation.[3] However, doing so indiscriminately can lead to a term with many redundant annotations, and so we also characterize when annotations can safely be removed:

Theorem 5 (Annotation Removal)**.** *We have that:*

- *If* $\Psi \vdash \big((\lambda x.\, e) : A\big) \Leftarrow C$ *then* $\Psi \vdash \lambda x.\, e \Leftarrow C$.
- *If* $\Psi \vdash (() : A) \Leftarrow C$ *then* $\Psi \vdash () \Leftarrow C$.
- *If* $\Psi \vdash e_1\ (e_2 : A) \Rightarrow C$ *then* $\Psi \vdash e_1\ e_2 \Rightarrow C$.
- *If* $\Psi \vdash (x : A) \Rightarrow A$ *then* $\Psi \vdash x \Rightarrow B$ *and* $\Psi \vdash B \leq A$.

[2] The number of annotations can be reduced still further; see Section 8 for how to infer the types of all terms typable under Damas-Milner.

[3] The generalization of Theorem 4 to any synthesizing term—not just $(e : A)$—does not hold. For example, given $e = \lambda y.\, y$ and $e' = x$ and $\Psi \vdash \lambda y.\, y \Rightarrow 1 \to 1$ and $\Psi \vdash \lambda y.\, y \Leftarrow C_1 \to C_2$, we cannot derive $\Psi, x : 1 \to 1 \vdash x \Leftarrow C_1 \to C_2$ unless C_1 and C_2 happen to be 1.

Types	A, B, C	$::=$	$1 \mid \alpha \mid \hat{\alpha} \mid \forall\alpha.\, A \mid A \to B$
Monotypes	τ, σ	$::=$	$1 \mid \alpha \mid \hat{\alpha} \mid \tau \to \sigma$
Contexts	Γ, Δ, Θ	$::=$	$\cdot \mid \Gamma, \alpha \mid \Gamma, x : A$ $\mid \Gamma, \hat{\alpha} \mid \Gamma, \hat{\alpha} = \tau \mid \Gamma, \blacktriangleright_{\hat{\alpha}}$
Complete Contexts	Ω	$::=$	$\cdot \mid \Omega, \alpha \mid \Omega, x : A$ $\mid \Omega, \hat{\alpha} = \tau \quad \Omega, \blacktriangleright_{\hat{\alpha}}$

Figure 6. Syntax of types, monotypes, and contexts in the algorithmic system

- *If* $\Psi \vdash ((e_1\, e_2) : A) \Rightarrow A$ *then* $\Psi \vdash e_1\, e_2 \Rightarrow B$ *and* $\Psi \vdash B \leq A$.
- *If* $\Psi \vdash ((e : B) : A) \Rightarrow A$ *then* $\Psi \vdash (e : B) \Rightarrow B$ *and* $\Psi \vdash B \leq A$.
- *If* $\Psi \vdash ((\lambda x.\, e) : \sigma \to \tau) \Rightarrow \sigma \to \tau$ *then* $\Psi \vdash \lambda x.\, e \Rightarrow \sigma \to \tau$.

We can also show that the expected η-laws hold:

Theorem 6 (Soundness of Eta)**.**
If $\Psi \vdash \lambda x.\, e\, x \Leftarrow A$ *and* $x \notin FV(e)$, *then* $\Psi \vdash e \Leftarrow A$.

3. Algorithmic Type System

Our declarative bidirectional system is a fine specification of how typing should behave, but it enjoys guessing entirely too much: the typing rules Decl∀App and Decl→I⇒ could only be implemented with the help of an oracle. The declarative subtyping rule ≤∀L has the same problem.

The first step in building our *algorithmic* bidirectional system will be to modify the three oracular rules so that, instead of guessing a type, they defer the choice by creating an existential type variable, to be solved later. However, our existential variables are not exactly unification variables; they are organized into *ordered algorithmic contexts* (Section 3.1), which define the variables' scope and controls the free variables of their solutions.

The algorithmic type system consists of subtyping rules (Figure 9, discussed in Section 3.2), instantiation rules (Figure 10, discussed in Section 3.3), and typing rules (Figure 11, discussed in Section 3.4). All of the rules manipulate the contexts in a way consistent with *context extension*, a metatheoretic notion described in Section 4; context extension is key in stating and proving decidability, soundness and completeness.

3.1 Algorithmic Contexts

A notion of (ordered) algorithmic context is central to our approach. Like declarative contexts Ψ, algorithmic contexts Γ (see Figure 6; we also use the letters Δ and Θ) contain declarations of universal type variables α and term variable typings $x : A$. Unlike declarative contexts, algorithmic contexts also contain declarations of existential type variables $\hat{\alpha}$, which are either unsolved (and we simply write $\hat{\alpha}$) or solved to some monotype ($\hat{\alpha} = \tau$). Finally, for scoping reasons that will become clear when we examine the rules, algorithmic contexts also include a *marker* $\blacktriangleright_{\hat{\alpha}}$.

Complete contexts Ω are the same as contexts, except that they cannot have unsolved variables.

The well-formedness rules for contexts (Figure 7, bottom) do not only prohibit duplicate declarations, but also enforce order: if $\Gamma = (\Gamma_L, x : A, \Gamma_R)$, the type A must be well-formed under Γ_L; it cannot refer to variables α or $\hat{\alpha}$ in Γ_R. Similarly, if $\Gamma = (\Gamma_L, \hat{\alpha} = \tau, \Gamma_R)$, the solution type τ must be well-formed under Γ_L. Consequently, circularity is ruled out: $(\hat{\alpha} = \hat{\beta}, \hat{\beta} = \hat{\alpha})$ is not well-formed.

$\boxed{\Gamma \vdash A}$ Under context Γ, type A is well-formed

$$\frac{}{\Gamma[\alpha] \vdash \alpha}\ \mathsf{UvarWF} \qquad \frac{}{\Gamma \vdash 1}\ \mathsf{UnitWF}$$

$$\frac{\Gamma \vdash A \qquad \Gamma \vdash B}{\Gamma \vdash A \to B}\ \mathsf{ArrowWF} \qquad \frac{\Gamma, \alpha \vdash A}{\Gamma \vdash \forall\alpha.\, A}\ \mathsf{ForallWF}$$

$$\frac{}{\Gamma[\hat{\alpha}] \vdash \hat{\alpha}}\ \mathsf{EvarWF} \qquad \frac{}{\Gamma[\hat{\alpha} = \tau] \vdash \hat{\alpha}}\ \mathsf{SolvedEvarWF}$$

$\boxed{\Gamma\ ctx}$ Algorithmic context Γ is well-formed

$$\frac{}{\cdot\ ctx}\ \mathsf{EmptyCtx} \qquad \frac{\Gamma\ ctx \qquad \alpha \notin \mathsf{dom}(\Gamma)}{\Gamma, \alpha\ ctx}\ \mathsf{UvarCtx}$$

$$\frac{\Gamma\ ctx \qquad x \notin \mathsf{dom}(\Gamma) \qquad \Gamma \vdash A}{\Gamma, x : A\ ctx}\ \mathsf{VarCtx}$$

$$\frac{\Gamma\ ctx \qquad \hat{\alpha} \notin \mathsf{dom}(\Gamma)}{\Gamma, \hat{\alpha}\ ctx}\ \mathsf{EvarCtx}$$

$$\frac{\Gamma\ ctx \qquad \hat{\alpha} \notin \mathsf{dom}(\Gamma) \qquad \Gamma \vdash \tau}{\Gamma, \hat{\alpha} = \tau\ ctx}\ \mathsf{SolvedEvarCtx}$$

$$\frac{\Gamma\ ctx \qquad \blacktriangleright_{\hat{\alpha}} \notin \Gamma \qquad \hat{\alpha} \notin \mathsf{dom}(\Gamma)}{\Gamma, \blacktriangleright_{\hat{\alpha}}\ ctx}\ \mathsf{MarkerCtx}$$

Figure 7. Well-formedness of types and contexts in the algorithmic system

$$\begin{array}{lcl}
[\Gamma]\alpha & = & \alpha \\
[\Gamma]1 & = & 1 \\
[\Gamma[\hat{\alpha} = \tau]]\hat{\alpha} & = & [\Gamma[\hat{\alpha} = \tau]]\tau \\
[\Gamma[\hat{\alpha}]]\hat{\alpha} & = & \hat{\alpha} \\
[\Gamma](A \to B) & = & ([\Gamma]A) \to ([\Gamma]B) \\
[\Gamma](\forall\alpha.\, A) & = & \forall\alpha.\, [\Gamma]A
\end{array}$$

Figure 8. Applying a context, as a substitution, to a type

Contexts as substitutions on types. An algorithmic context can be viewed as a substitution for its solved existential variables. For example, $\hat{\alpha} = 1, \hat{\beta} = \hat{\alpha} \to 1$ can be applied as if it were the substitution $1/\hat{\alpha}, (\hat{\alpha}\to 1)/\hat{\beta}$ (applied right to left), or the simultaneous substitution $1/\hat{\alpha}, (1\to 1)/\hat{\beta}$. We write $[\Gamma]A$ for Γ applied as a substitution to type A; this operation is defined in Figure 8.

Complete contexts. Complete contexts Ω (Figure 6) have no unsolved variables. Therefore, applying such a context to a type A (provided it is well-formed: $\Omega \vdash A$) yields a type $[\Omega]A$ with no existentials. Complete contexts are essential for stating and proving soundness and completeness, but are not explicitly distinguished in any of our rules.

Hole notation. Since we will manipulate contexts not only by appending declarations (as in the declarative system) but by inserting and replacing declarations in the middle, a notation for contexts with a hole is useful:

$$\Gamma = \Gamma_0[\Theta] \quad \text{means } \Gamma \text{ has the form } (\Gamma_L, \Theta, \Gamma_R)$$

For example, if $\Gamma = \Gamma_0[\hat{\beta}] = (\hat{\alpha}, \hat{\beta}, x : \hat{\beta})$, then $\Gamma_0[\hat{\beta} = \hat{\alpha}] = (\hat{\alpha}, \hat{\beta} = \hat{\alpha}, x : \hat{\beta})$. Since this notation is concise, we use it even in rules that do not replace declarations, such as the rules for type well-formedness in Figure 7.

Occasionally, we also need contexts with *two* ordered holes:

$$\Gamma = \Gamma_0[\Theta_1][\Theta_2] \quad \text{means } \Gamma \text{ has the form } (\Gamma_L, \Theta_1, \Gamma_M, \Theta_2, \Gamma_R)$$

Input and output contexts. Our declarative system used a subtyping judgment and three typing judgments: checking, synthesis, and application. Our algorithmic system includes similar judgment forms, except that we replace the declarative context Ψ with an algorithmic context Γ (the *input context*), and add an *output* context Δ written after a backwards turnstile: $\Gamma \vdash A <: B \dashv \Delta$ for subtyping, $\Gamma \vdash e \Leftarrow A \dashv \Delta$ for checking, and so on. Unsolved existential variables get solved when they are compared against a type. For example, $\hat{\alpha} <: \beta$ would lead to replacing the unsolved declaration $\hat{\alpha}$ with $\hat{\alpha} = \beta$ in the context (provided β is declared to the left of $\hat{\alpha}$). Input contexts thus evolve into output contexts that are "more solved".

The differences between the declarative and algorithmic systems, particularly manipulations of existential variables, are most prominent in the subtyping rules, so we discuss those first.

3.2 Algorithmic Subtyping

The first four subtyping rules in Figure 9 do not directly manipulate the context, but do illustrate how contexts are propagated.

Rules $<:$Var and $<:$Unit are reflexive rules; neither involves existential variables, so the output context in the conclusion is the same as the input context Γ. Rule $<:$Exvar concludes that any unsolved existential variable is a subtype of itself, but this gives no clue as to how to solve that existential, so the output context is similarly unchanged.

Rule $<:\rightarrow$ is a bit more interesting: it has two premises, where the first premise has an output context Θ, which is used as the input context to the second (subtyping) premise; the second premise has output context Δ, which is the output of the conclusion.[4] Note that in $<:\rightarrow$'s second premise, we do not simply check that $A_2 <: B_2$, but apply the first premise's output Θ to those types:

$$\Theta \vdash [\Theta]A_2 <: [\Theta]B_2 \dashv \Delta$$

This maintains a general invariant: whenever we try to derive $\Gamma \vdash A <: B \dashv \Delta$, the types A and B are already fully applied under Γ. That is, they contain no existential variables already solved in Γ. On balance, this invariant simplifies the system: the extra applications of Θ in $<:\rightarrow$ avoid the need for extra rules for replacing solved variables with their solutions.

All the rules discussed so far have been natural extensions of the declarative rules, with $<:$Exvar being a logical way to extend reflexivity to types containing existentials. Rule $<:\forall$L diverges significantly from the corresponding declarative rule $\leq\forall$L. Instead of replacing the type variable α with a guessed τ, rule $<:\forall$L replaces α with a new existential variable $\hat{\alpha}$, which it adds to the premise's input context: $\Gamma, \blacktriangleright_{\hat{\alpha}}, \hat{\alpha} \vdash [\hat{\alpha}/\alpha]A <: B \dashv \Delta, \blacktriangleright_{\hat{\alpha}}, \Theta$. The peculiar-looking $\blacktriangleright_{\hat{\alpha}}$ is a *scope marker*, pronounced "marker $\hat{\alpha}$", which will delineate existentials created by *articulation* (the step of solving $\hat{\alpha}$ to $\hat{\alpha}_1 \rightarrow \hat{\alpha}_2$, discussed in the next subsection). The output context $(\Delta, \blacktriangleright_{\hat{\alpha}}, \Theta)$ allows for some additional (existential) variables to appear after $\blacktriangleright_{\hat{\alpha}}$, in a trailing context Θ. These existential variables could mention $\hat{\alpha}$, or (if they appear between $\blacktriangleright_{\hat{\alpha}}$ and $\hat{\alpha}$) could be mentioned *by* $\hat{\alpha}$; since $\hat{\alpha}$ goes out of scope in the conclusion, we drop such "trailing existentials" from the concluding output context, which is simply Δ.[5]

Rule $<:\forall$R is fairly close to the declarative version, but for scoping reasons similar to $<:\forall$L, it also drops Θ, the part of the context to the right of the universal type variable α. (Articulation makes no sense for universal variables, so α can act as its own marker.)

The last two rules are essential: they derive subtypings with an unsolved existential on one side, and an arbitrary type on the other. Rule $<:$InstantiateL derives $\hat{\alpha} <: A$, and $<:$InstantiateR derives $A <: \hat{\alpha}$. These rules do not directly change the output context; they just do an "occurs check" $\hat{\alpha} \notin FV(A)$ to avoid circularity, and leave all the real work to the instantiation judgment.

3.3 Instantiation

Two almost-symmetric judgments instantiate unsolved existential variables: $\Gamma \vdash \hat{\alpha} :\leqq A \dashv \Delta$ and $\Gamma \vdash A \leqq: \hat{\alpha} \dashv \Delta$. The symbol $:\leqq$ suggests assignment of the variable to its left, but also subtyping: the subtyping rule $<:$InstantiateL moves from instantiation $\hat{\alpha} :\leqq A$, read "instantiate $\hat{\alpha}$ to a subtype of A", to subtyping $\hat{\alpha} <: A$. The symmetric judgment $A \leqq: \hat{\alpha}$ can be read "instantiate $\hat{\alpha}$ to a supertype of A".

The first instantiation rule in Figure 10, InstLSolve, sets $\hat{\alpha}$ to τ in the output context: its conclusion is $\Gamma, \hat{\alpha}, \Gamma' \vdash \hat{\alpha} :\leqq \tau \dashv \Gamma, \hat{\alpha} = \tau, \Gamma'$. The premise $\Gamma \vdash \tau$ checks that the monotype τ is well-formed under the prefix context Γ. To check the soundness of this rule, we can take the conclusion $\hat{\alpha} :\leqq \tau$, substitute our new solution for $\hat{\alpha}$, and check that the resulting subtyping makes sense. Since $[\Gamma, \hat{\alpha} = \tau, \Gamma']\hat{\alpha} = \tau$, we ask whether $\tau <: \tau$ makes sense, and of course it does through reflexivity.

Rule InstLArr can be applied when the type A in $\hat{\alpha} :\leqq A$ has the form $A_1 \rightarrow A_2$. It follows that $\hat{\alpha}$'s solution must have the form $\cdots \rightarrow \cdots$, so we "articulate" $\hat{\alpha}$, giving it the solution $\hat{\alpha}_1 \rightarrow \hat{\alpha}_2$ where the $\hat{\alpha}_k$ are fresh existentials. We insert their declarations just before $\hat{\alpha}$—they must be to the left of $\hat{\alpha}$ so they can be mentioned in its solution, but they must be close enough to $\hat{\alpha}$ that they appear to the *right* of the marker $\blacktriangleright_{\hat{\alpha}}$ introduced by $<:\forall$L. Note that the first premise $A_1 \leqq: \hat{\alpha}_1$ switches to the other instantiation judgment. Also, the second premise $\Theta \vdash \hat{\alpha}_2 :\leqq [\Theta]A_2 \dashv \Delta$ applies Θ to A_2, to apply any solutions found in the first premise.

The other rules are somewhat subtle. Rule InstLReach derives

$$\Gamma[\hat{\alpha}][\hat{\beta}] \vdash \hat{\alpha} :\leqq \hat{\beta} \dashv \Gamma[\hat{\alpha}][\hat{\beta} = \hat{\alpha}]$$

where, as explained in Section 3.1, $\Gamma[\hat{\alpha}][\hat{\beta}]$ denotes a context where some unsolved existential variable $\hat{\alpha}$ is declared to the left of $\hat{\beta}$. In this situation, we cannot use InstLSolve to set $\hat{\alpha}$ to $\hat{\beta}$ because $\hat{\beta}$ is not well-formed under the part of the context to the left of $\hat{\alpha}$. Instead, we set $\hat{\beta}$ to $\hat{\alpha}$.

Rule InstLAllR is the instantiation version of $<:\forall$R. Since our polymorphism is predicative, we can't assign $\forall\beta.\ B$ to $\hat{\alpha}$, but we can decompose the quantifier in the same way that subtyping does.

The rules for the second judgment $A \leqq: \hat{\alpha}$ are similar: InstRSolve, InstRReach and InstRArr are direct analogues of the first three $\hat{\alpha} :\leqq A$ rules, and InstRAllL is the instantiation version of $<:\forall$L.

Example. The interplay between instantiation and quantifiers is delicate. For example, consider the problem of instantiating $\hat{\beta}$ to a supertype of $\forall\alpha.\ \alpha$. In this case, the type $\forall\alpha.\ \alpha$ is so polymorphic that it places no constraints at all on $\hat{\beta}$. Therefore, it seems we are at risk of being forced to make a necessarily incomplete choice—but the instantiation judgment's ability to "change its mind" about which variable to instantiate saves the day:

[4] Rule $<:\rightarrow$ enforces that the function domains B_1, A_1 are compared first: Θ is an input to the second premise. But this is an arbitrary choice; the system would behave the same if we chose to check the codomains first.

[5] In our setting, it is safe to drop trailing existentials that are unsolved: such variables are unconstrained, and we can treat them as having been instantiated to any well-formed type, such as 1. In a dependently typed setting, we would need to check that at least one solution exists.

$\boxed{\Gamma \vdash A <: B \dashv \Delta}$ Under input context Γ, type A is a subtype of B, with output context Δ

$$\frac{}{\Gamma[\alpha] \vdash \alpha <: \alpha \dashv \Gamma[\alpha]}\ {<:}\mathsf{Var} \qquad \frac{}{\Gamma \vdash 1 <: 1 \dashv \Gamma}\ {<:}\mathsf{Unit} \qquad \frac{}{\Gamma[\hat\alpha] \vdash \hat\alpha <: \hat\alpha \dashv \Gamma[\hat\alpha]}\ {<:}\mathsf{Exvar}$$

$$\frac{\Gamma \vdash B_1 <: A_1 \dashv \Theta \qquad \Theta \vdash [\Theta]A_2 <: [\Theta]B_2 \dashv \Delta}{\Gamma \vdash A_1 \to A_2 <: B_1 \to B_2 \dashv \Delta}\ {<:}{\to}$$

$$\frac{\Gamma, \blacktriangleright_{\hat\alpha}, \hat\alpha \vdash [\hat\alpha/\alpha]A <: B \dashv \Delta, \blacktriangleright_{\hat\alpha}, \Theta}{\Gamma \vdash \forall\alpha.\, A <: B \dashv \Delta}\ {<:}\forall\mathsf{L} \qquad \frac{\Gamma, \alpha \vdash A <: B \dashv \Delta, \alpha, \Theta}{\Gamma \vdash A <: \forall\alpha.\, B \dashv \Delta}\ {<:}\forall\mathsf{R}$$

$$\frac{\hat\alpha \notin FV(A) \qquad \Gamma[\hat\alpha] \vdash \hat\alpha \mathrel{:\leqq} A \dashv \Delta}{\Gamma[\hat\alpha] \vdash \hat\alpha <: A \dashv \Delta}\ {<:}\mathsf{InstantiateL} \qquad \frac{\hat\alpha \notin FV(A) \qquad \Gamma[\hat\alpha] \vdash A \mathrel{\leqq:} \hat\alpha \dashv \Delta}{\Gamma[\hat\alpha] \vdash A <: \hat\alpha \dashv \Delta}\ {<:}\mathsf{InstantiateR}$$

Figure 9. Algorithmic subtyping

$\boxed{\Gamma \vdash \hat\alpha \mathrel{:\leqq} A \dashv \Delta}$ Under input context Γ, instantiate $\hat\alpha$ such that $\hat\alpha <: A$, with output context Δ

$$\frac{\Gamma \vdash \tau}{\Gamma, \hat\alpha, \Gamma' \vdash \hat\alpha \mathrel{:\leqq} \tau \dashv \Gamma, \hat\alpha = \tau, \Gamma'}\ \mathsf{InstLSolve} \qquad \frac{}{\Gamma[\hat\alpha][\hat\beta] \vdash \hat\alpha \mathrel{:\leqq} \hat\beta \dashv \Gamma[\hat\alpha][\hat\beta = \hat\alpha]}\ \mathsf{InstLReach}$$

$$\frac{\Gamma[\hat\alpha_2, \hat\alpha_1, \hat\alpha = \hat\alpha_1 \to \hat\alpha_2] \vdash A_1 \mathrel{\leqq:} \hat\alpha_1 \dashv \Theta \qquad \Theta \vdash \hat\alpha_2 \mathrel{:\leqq} [\Theta]A_2 \dashv \Delta}{\Gamma[\hat\alpha] \vdash \hat\alpha \mathrel{:\leqq} A_1 \to A_2 \dashv \Delta}\ \mathsf{InstLArr} \qquad \frac{\Gamma[\hat\alpha], \beta \vdash \hat\alpha \mathrel{:\leqq} B \dashv \Delta, \beta, \Delta'}{\Gamma[\hat\alpha] \vdash \hat\alpha \mathrel{:\leqq} \forall\beta.\, B \dashv \Delta}\ \mathsf{InstLAllR}$$

$\boxed{\Gamma \vdash A \mathrel{\leqq:} \hat\alpha \dashv \Delta}$ Under input context Γ, instantiate $\hat\alpha$ such that $A <: \hat\alpha$, with output context Δ

$$\frac{\Gamma \vdash \tau}{\Gamma, \hat\alpha, \Gamma' \vdash \tau \mathrel{\leqq:} \hat\alpha \dashv \Gamma, \hat\alpha = \tau, \Gamma'}\ \mathsf{nstRSolve} \qquad \frac{}{\Gamma[\hat\alpha][\hat\beta] \vdash \hat\beta \mathrel{\leqq:} \hat\alpha \dashv \Gamma[\hat\alpha][\hat\beta = \hat\alpha]}\ \mathsf{InstRReach}$$

$$\frac{\Gamma[\hat\alpha_2, \hat\alpha_1, \hat\alpha = \hat\alpha_1 \to \hat\alpha_2] \vdash \hat\alpha_1 \mathrel{:\leqq} A_1 \dashv \Theta \qquad \Theta \vdash [\Theta]A_2 \mathrel{\leqq:} \hat\alpha_2 \dashv \Delta}{\Gamma[\hat\alpha] \vdash A_1 \to A_2 \mathrel{\leqq:} \hat\alpha \dashv \Delta}\ \mathsf{InstRArr} \qquad \frac{\Gamma[\hat\alpha], \blacktriangleright_{\hat\beta}, \hat\beta \vdash [\hat\beta/\beta]B \mathrel{\leqq:} \hat\alpha \dashv \Delta, \blacktriangleright_{\hat\beta}, \Delta'}{\Gamma[\hat\alpha] \vdash \forall\beta.\, B \mathrel{\leqq:} \hat\alpha \dashv \Delta}\ \mathsf{InstRAllL}$$

Figure 10. Instantiation

$\boxed{\Gamma \vdash e \Leftarrow A \dashv \Delta}$ Under input context Γ, e checks against input type A, with output context Δ

$\boxed{\Gamma \vdash e \Rightarrow A \dashv \Delta}$ Under input context Γ, e synthesizes output type A, with output context Δ

$\boxed{\Gamma \vdash A \bullet e \mathrel{\Rightarrow\!\!\!\Rightarrow} C \dashv \Delta}$ Under input context Γ, applying a function of type A to e synthesizes type C, with output context Δ

$$\frac{(x : A) \in \Gamma}{\Gamma \vdash x \Rightarrow A \dashv \Gamma}\ \mathsf{Var} \qquad \frac{\Gamma \vdash e \Rightarrow A \dashv \Theta \qquad \Theta \vdash [\Theta]A <: [\Theta]B \dashv \Delta}{\Gamma \vdash e \Leftarrow B \dashv \Delta}\ \mathsf{Sub} \qquad \frac{\Gamma \vdash A \qquad \Gamma \vdash e \Leftarrow A \dashv \Delta}{\Gamma \vdash (e : A) \Rightarrow A \dashv \Delta}\ \mathsf{Anno}$$

$$\frac{}{\Gamma \vdash () \Leftarrow 1 \dashv \Gamma}\ 1\mathsf{I} \qquad \frac{}{\Gamma \vdash () \Rightarrow 1 \dashv \Gamma}\ 1\mathsf{I}{\Rightarrow} \qquad \frac{\Gamma, \alpha \vdash e \Leftarrow A \dashv \Delta, \alpha, \Theta}{\Gamma \vdash e \Leftarrow \forall\alpha.\, A \dashv \Delta}\ \forall\mathsf{I} \qquad \frac{\Gamma, \hat\alpha \vdash [\hat\alpha/\alpha]A \bullet e \mathrel{\Rightarrow\!\!\!\Rightarrow} C \dashv \Delta}{\Gamma \vdash \forall\alpha.\, A \bullet e \mathrel{\Rightarrow\!\!\!\Rightarrow} C \dashv \Delta}\ \forall\mathsf{App}$$

$$\frac{\Gamma, x : A \vdash e \Leftarrow B \dashv \Delta, x : A, \Theta}{\Gamma \vdash \lambda x.\, e \Leftarrow A \to B \dashv \Delta}\ {\to}\mathsf{I} \qquad \frac{\Gamma, \hat\alpha, \hat\beta, x : \hat\alpha \vdash e \Leftarrow \hat\beta \dashv \Delta, x : \hat\alpha, \Theta}{\Gamma \vdash \lambda x.\, e \Rightarrow \hat\alpha \to \hat\beta \dashv \Delta}\ {\to}\mathsf{I}{\Rightarrow} \qquad \frac{\Gamma \vdash e_1 \Rightarrow A \dashv \Theta \qquad \Theta \vdash [\Theta]A \bullet e_2 \mathrel{\Rightarrow\!\!\!\Rightarrow} C \dashv \Delta}{\Gamma \vdash e_1\, e_2 \Rightarrow C \dashv \Delta}\ {\to}\mathsf{E}$$

$$\frac{\Gamma[\hat\alpha_2, \hat\alpha_1, \hat\alpha = \hat\alpha_1 \to \hat\alpha_2] \vdash e \Leftarrow \hat\alpha_1 \dashv \Delta}{\Gamma[\hat\alpha] \vdash \hat\alpha \bullet e \mathrel{\Rightarrow\!\!\!\Rightarrow} \hat\alpha_2 \dashv \Delta}\ \hat\alpha\mathsf{App} \qquad \frac{\Gamma \vdash e \Leftarrow A \dashv \Delta}{\Gamma \vdash A \to C \bullet e \mathrel{\Rightarrow\!\!\!\Rightarrow} C \dashv \Delta}\ {\to}\mathsf{App}$$

Figure 11. Algorithmic typing

$$\frac{\dfrac{}{\Gamma[\hat\beta], \blacktriangleright_{\hat\alpha}, \hat\alpha \vdash \hat\alpha :\leq= \hat\beta \dashv \Gamma[\hat\beta], \blacktriangleright_{\hat\alpha}, \hat\alpha = \hat\beta}\ \mathsf{InstRReach}}{\Gamma[\hat\beta] \vdash \forall\alpha.\,\alpha :\leq= \hat\beta \dashv \Gamma[\hat\beta]}\ \mathsf{InstRAllL}$$

Here, we introduce a new variable $\hat\alpha$ to go under the universal quantifier; then, instantiation applies InstRReach to set $\hat\alpha$, not $\hat\beta$. Hence, $\hat\beta$ is, correctly, *not constrained* by this subtyping problem.

Thus, instantiation does not necessarily solve *any* existential variable. However, instantiation to any monotype τ will solve an existential variable—that is, for input context Γ and output Δ, we have $\mathsf{unsolved}(\Delta) < \mathsf{unsolved}(\Gamma)$. This will be critical for decidability of subtyping (Section 5.2).

Another example. In Figure 12 we show a derivation that uses quantifier instantiation (InstRAllL), articulation (InstRArr) and "reaching" (InstLReach), as well as InstRSolve. In the output context $\Delta = \Gamma[\hat\beta_2, \hat\beta_1{=}\hat\beta_2, \hat\alpha{=}\hat\beta_1{\rightarrow}\hat\beta_2]$ note that $\hat\alpha$ is solved to $\hat\beta_1 \rightarrow \hat\beta_2$, and $\hat\beta_2$ is solved to $\hat\beta_1$. Thus, $[\Delta]\hat\alpha = \hat\beta_1{\rightarrow}\hat\beta_1$, which is a monomorphic approximation of $\forall\beta.\beta{\rightarrow}\beta$.

3.4 Algorithmic Typing

We now turn to the typing rules in Figure 11. Many of these rules follow the declarative rules, with extra context machinery. Rule Var uses an assumption $x : A$ without generating any new information, so the output context in its conclusion $\Gamma \vdash x \Rightarrow A \dashv \Gamma$ is just the input context. Rule Sub's first premise has an output context Θ, used as the input context to the second (subtyping) premise, which has output context Δ, the output of the conclusion. Rule Anno does not directly change the context, but the derivation of its premise might include the use of some rule that does, so we propagate the premise's output context Δ to the conclusion.

Unit and $\forall$. In the second row of typing rules, 1I and 1I$\Rightarrow$ generate no new information and simply propagate the input context.

$\forall$I is more interesting: Like the declarative rule Decl$\forall$I, it adds a universal type variable α to the (input) context. The output context of the premise $\Gamma, \alpha \vdash e \Leftarrow A \dashv \Delta, \alpha, \Theta$ allows for some additional (existential) variables to appear after α, in a trailing context Θ. These existential variables could depend on α; since α goes out of scope in the conclusion, we must drop them from the concluding output context, which is just Δ: the part of the premise's output context that cannot depend on α.

The application-judgment rule $\forall$App serves a similar purpose to the subtyping rule $<:\forall$L, but does *not* place a marker before $\hat\alpha$: the variable $\hat\alpha$ may appear in the output type C, so $\hat\alpha$ must survive in the output context Δ.

Functions. In the third row of typing rules, rule $\rightarrow$I follows the same scheme: the declarations Θ following $x : A$ are dropped in the conclusion's output context.

Rule $\rightarrow$I$\Rightarrow$ corresponds to Decl$\rightarrow$I$\Rightarrow$, one of the guessing rules, so we create new existential variables $\hat\alpha$ (for the function domain) and $\hat\beta$ (for the codomain) and check the function body against $\hat\beta$. As in $\forall$App, we do not place a marker before $\hat\alpha$, because $\hat\alpha$ and $\hat\beta$ appear in the output type ($\lambda x.\, e \Rightarrow \hat\alpha \rightarrow \hat\beta$).

Rule $\rightarrow$E is the expected analogue of Decl$\rightarrow$E; like other rules with two premises, it applies the intermediate context Θ.

On the last row of typing rules, $\hat\alpha$App derives $\hat\alpha \bullet e \Rightarrow\!\!\Rightarrow \hat\alpha_2$ where $\hat\alpha$ is unsolved in the input context. Here we have an application judgment, which is supposed to synthesize a type for an application $e_1\ e$ where e_1 has type $\hat\alpha$. We know that e_1 should have function type; similarly to InstLArr/InstRArr, we introduce $\hat\alpha_1$ and $\hat\alpha_2$ and add $\hat\alpha = \hat\alpha_1{\rightarrow}\hat\alpha_2$ to the context. (Rule $\hat\alpha$App is the only algorithmic typing rule that does not correspond to a declarative rule.)

Finally, rule $\rightarrow$App is analogous to Decl$\rightarrow$App.

4. Context Extension

We motivated the algorithmic rules by saying that they evolved input contexts to output contexts that were "more solved". To state and prove the metatheoretic results of decidability, soundness and completeness (Sections 5–7), we introduce a context extension judgment $\Gamma \longrightarrow \Delta$. This judgment captures a notion of information increase from an input context Γ to an output context Δ, and relates algorithmic contexts Γ and Δ to completely solved extensions Ω, which correspond—via the context application described in Section 4.1—to declarative contexts Ψ.

The judgment $\Gamma \longrightarrow \Delta$ is read "Γ is extended by Δ" (or Δ extends Γ). Another reading is that Δ carries at least as much information as Γ. A third reading is that $\Gamma \longrightarrow \Delta$ means that Γ is *entailed by* Δ: all positive information derivable from Γ (say, that existential variable $\hat\alpha$ is in scope) can also be derived from Δ (which may have more information, say, that $\hat\alpha$ is equal to a particular type). This reading is realized by several key lemmas; for instance, extension preserves well-formedness: if $\Gamma \vdash A$ and $\Gamma \longrightarrow \Delta$, then $\Delta \vdash A$.

The rules deriving the context extension judgment (Figure 13) say that the empty context extends the empty context ($\longrightarrow$ID); a term variable typing $x : A'$ extends $x : A$ if applying the extending context Δ to A and A' yields the same type ($\longrightarrow$Var); universal type variables must match ($\longrightarrow$Uvar); scope markers must match ($\longrightarrow$Marker); and, existential variables may:

- appear unsolved in both contexts ($\longrightarrow$Unsolved),
- appear solved in both contexts, if applying the extending context Δ makes the solutions τ and τ' equal ($\longrightarrow$Solved),
- get solved by the extending context ($\longrightarrow$Solve),
- be added by the extending context, either without a solution ($\longrightarrow$Add) or with a solution ($\longrightarrow$AddSolved);

Extension does *not* allow solutions to disappear: information must increase. It *does* allow solutions to change, but only if the change preserves or increases information. The extension

$$(\hat\alpha, \hat\beta = \hat\alpha) \longrightarrow (\hat\alpha = 1, \hat\beta = \hat\alpha)$$

directly increases information about $\hat\alpha$, and indirectly increases information about $\hat\beta$. Perhaps more interestingly, the extension

$$\underbrace{(\hat\alpha = 1, \hat\beta = \hat\alpha)}_{\Delta} \longrightarrow \underbrace{(\hat\alpha = 1, \hat\beta = 1)}_{\Omega}$$

also holds: while the solution of $\hat\beta$ in Ω is different, in the sense that Ω contains $\hat\beta = 1$ while Δ contains $\hat\beta = \hat\alpha$, applying Ω to the two solutions gives the same thing: applying Ω to Δ's solution of $\hat\beta$ gives $[\Omega]\hat\alpha = [\Omega]1 = 1$, while applying Ω to Ω's own solution for $\hat\beta$ also gives 1, because $[\Omega]1 = 1$.

Extension is quite rigid, however, in two senses. First, if a declaration appears in Γ, it appears in all extensions of Γ. Second, *extension preserves order*. For example, if $\hat\beta$ is declared after $\hat\alpha$ in Γ, then $\hat\beta$ will also be declared after $\hat\alpha$ in every extension of Γ. This holds for every variety of declaration. This rigidity aids in enforcing type variable scoping and dependencies, which are nontrivial in a setting with higher-rank polymorphism.

This combination of rigidity (in demanding that the order of declarations be preserved) with flexibility (in how existential type variable solutions are expressed) manages to satisfy scoping and dependency relations *and* give enough room to maneuver in the algorithm and metatheory.

4.1 Context Application

A complete context Ω (Figure 6) has no unsolved variables, so applying it to a (well-formed) type yields a type $[\Omega]A$ with no existen-

$$\dfrac{\dfrac{\dfrac{\overbrace{\Gamma', \blacktriangleright_{\hat\beta}}^{\text{context to the left of }\hat\beta} \vdash \hat\beta_1}{\Gamma', \blacktriangleright_{\hat\beta}, \hat\beta \vdash \hat\beta_2 :\leqq \hat\beta \dashv \Gamma', \blacktriangleright_{\hat\beta}, \hat\beta=\hat\beta_1}\,\mathsf{InstLReach} \qquad \dfrac{\overbrace{\ldots, \hat\beta_2}^{\text{context to the left of }\hat\beta_1} \vdash \hat\beta_2}{\Gamma', \blacktriangleright_{\hat\beta}, \hat\beta=\hat\beta_1 \vdash \hat\beta_2 \leqq: \hat\beta_1 \dashv \Delta, \blacktriangleright_{\hat\beta}, \hat\beta=\hat\beta_1}\,\mathsf{InstRSolve}}{\Gamma[\hat\alpha], \blacktriangleright_{\hat\beta}, \hat\beta \vdash \hat\beta \to \hat\beta \leqq: \hat\alpha \dashv \Delta, \blacktriangleright_{\hat\beta}, \hat\beta=\hat\beta_1}\,\mathsf{InstRArr}}{\Gamma[\hat\alpha] \vdash (\forall\beta.\, \beta \to \beta) \leqq: \hat\alpha \dashv \Delta}\,\mathsf{InstRAllL}$$

$$\Delta = \Gamma[\hat\beta_2, \hat\beta_1 = \hat\beta_2, \hat\alpha = \hat\beta_1 \to \hat\beta_2] \qquad \Gamma' = \Gamma[\hat\beta_2, \hat\beta_1, \hat\alpha = \hat\beta_1 \to \hat\beta_2]$$

Figure 12. Example of instantiation

$\boxed{\Gamma \longrightarrow \Delta}$ Γ is extended by Δ

$$\dfrac{}{\cdot \longrightarrow \cdot}\,{\longrightarrow}\mathsf{ID} \qquad \dfrac{\Gamma \longrightarrow \Delta \quad [\Delta]A = [\Delta]A'}{\Gamma, x : A \longrightarrow \Delta, x : A'}\,{\longrightarrow}\mathsf{Var} \qquad \dfrac{\Gamma \longrightarrow \Delta}{\Gamma, \alpha \longrightarrow \Delta, \alpha}\,{\longrightarrow}\mathsf{Uvar}$$

$$\dfrac{\Gamma \longrightarrow \Delta}{\Gamma, \hat\alpha \longrightarrow \Delta, \hat\alpha}\,{\longrightarrow}\mathsf{Unsolved} \qquad \dfrac{\Gamma \longrightarrow \Delta \quad [\Delta]\tau = [\Delta]\tau'}{\Gamma, \hat\alpha = \tau \longrightarrow \Delta, \hat\alpha = \tau'}\,{\longrightarrow}\mathsf{Solved} \qquad \dfrac{\Gamma \longrightarrow \Delta}{\Gamma, \hat\alpha \longrightarrow \Delta, \hat\alpha = \tau}\,{\longrightarrow}\mathsf{Solve} \qquad \dfrac{\Gamma \longrightarrow \Delta}{\Gamma \longrightarrow \Delta, \hat\alpha}\,{\longrightarrow}\mathsf{Add}$$

$$\dfrac{\Gamma \longrightarrow \Delta}{\Gamma \longrightarrow \Delta, \hat\alpha = \tau}\,{\longrightarrow}\mathsf{AddSolved} \qquad \dfrac{\Gamma \longrightarrow \Delta}{\Gamma, \blacktriangleright_{\hat\alpha} \longrightarrow \Delta, \blacktriangleright_{\hat\alpha}}\,{\longrightarrow}\mathsf{Marker}$$

Figure 13. Context extension

$$\begin{array}{lcll}
[\cdot]\cdot & = & \cdot & \\
[\Omega, x : A](\Gamma, x : A_\Gamma) & = & [\Omega]\Gamma,\ x : [\Omega]A & \text{if } [\Omega]A = [\Omega]A_\Gamma \\
[\Omega, \alpha](\Gamma, \alpha) & = & [\Omega]\Gamma,\ \alpha & \\
[\Omega, \hat\alpha = \tau](\Gamma, \hat\alpha) & = & [\Omega]\Gamma & \\
[\Omega, \hat\alpha = \tau](\Gamma, \hat\alpha = \tau_\Gamma) & = & [\Omega]\Gamma & \text{if } [\Omega]\tau = [\Omega]\tau_\Gamma \\
[\Omega, \hat\alpha = \tau]\Gamma & = & [\Omega]\Gamma & \text{if } \hat\alpha \notin \mathsf{dom}(\Gamma) \\
[\Omega, \blacktriangleright_{\hat\alpha}](\Gamma, \blacktriangleright_{\hat\alpha}) & = & [\Omega]\Gamma &
\end{array}$$

Figure 14. Applying a complete context Ω to a context

tials. Such a type is well-formed under a *declarative* context—with just α and $x : A$ declarations—obtained by dropping all the existential declarations and applying Ω to declarations $x : A$ (to yield $x : [\Omega]A$). We can think of this context as the result of applying Ω to itself: $[\Omega]\Omega$.

More generally, we can apply Ω to any context Γ that it extends. This operation of context application $[\Omega]\Gamma$ is given in Figure 14. The application $[\Omega]\Gamma$ is defined if and only if $\Gamma \longrightarrow \Omega$, and applying Ω to any such Γ yields the same declarative context $[\Omega]\Omega$:

Lemma (Stability of Complete Contexts). *If* $\Gamma \longrightarrow \Omega$ *then* $[\Omega]\Gamma = [\Omega]\Omega$.

5. Decidability

Our algorithmic type system is decidable. Since the typing rules (Figure 11) depend on the subtyping rules (Figure 9), which in turn depend on the instantiation rules (Figure 10), showing that the typing judgments (checking, synthesis and application) are decidable requires that we show that the instantiation and subtyping judgments are decidable.

5.1 Decidability of Instantiation

As discussed in Section 3.3, deriving $\Gamma \vdash \hat\alpha :\leqq A \dashv \Delta$ does not necessarily instantiate any existential variable (unless A is a monotype). However, the instantiation rules do preserve the size of (substituted) types:

Lemma (Instantiation Size Preservation).
If $\Gamma = (\Gamma_0, \hat\alpha, \Gamma_1)$ *and* $\Gamma \vdash \hat\alpha :\leqq A \dashv \Delta$ *or* $\Gamma \vdash A \leqq: \hat\alpha \dashv \Delta$, *and* $\Gamma \vdash B$ *and* $\hat\alpha \notin FV([\Gamma]B)$, *then* $|[\Gamma]B| = |[\Delta]B|$, *where* $|C|$ *is the plain size of* C.

Using this lemma, we can show that the type A in the instantiation judgment always get smaller, even in rule $\mathsf{InstLArr}$: the second premise applies the intermediate context Θ to A_2, but the lemma tells us that this application cannot make A_2 larger, and A_2 is smaller than the conclusion's type ($A_1 \to A_2$).

Now we can prove decidability of instantiation, assuming that $\hat\alpha$ is unsolved in the input context Γ, that A is well-formed under Γ, that A is fully applied ($[\Gamma]A = A$), and that $\hat\alpha$ does not occur in A. These conditions are guaranteed when instantiation is invoked, because the typing rule Sub applies the input substitution, and the subtyping rules apply the substitution where needed—in exactly one place: the second premise of $<:\to$. The proof is based on the (substituted) types in the premises being smaller than the (substituted) type in the conclusion.

Theorem 7 (Decidability of Instantiation).
If $\Gamma = \Gamma_0[\hat\alpha]$ *and* $\Gamma \vdash A$ *such that* $[\Gamma]A = A$ *and* $\hat\alpha \notin FV(A)$, *then:*

(1) Either there exists Δ *such that* $\Gamma_0[\hat\alpha] \vdash \hat\alpha :\leqq A \dashv \Delta$, *or not.*

(2) Either there exists Δ *such that* $\Gamma_0[\hat\alpha] \vdash A \leqq: \hat\alpha \dashv \Delta$, *or not.*

5.2 Decidability of Algorithmic Subtyping

To prove decidability of the subtyping system in Figure 9, measure judgments $\Gamma \vdash A <: B \dashv \Delta$ lexicographically by

(S1) the number of $\forall$ quantifiers in A and B;

(S2) $|\mathsf{unsolved}(\Gamma)|$, the number of unsolved existentials in Γ;

(S3) $|\Gamma \vdash A| + |\Gamma \vdash B|$.

Part (S3) uses *contextual size*, which penalizes solved variables (*):

Definition (Contextual Size).

$$\begin{array}{lcll}
|\Gamma \vdash \alpha| & = & 1 & \\
|\Gamma[\hat\alpha] \vdash \hat\alpha| & = & 1 & \\
|\Gamma[\hat\alpha = \tau] \vdash \hat\alpha| & = & 1 + |\Gamma[\hat\alpha = \tau] \vdash \tau| & (*) \\
|\Gamma \vdash \forall\alpha.\, A| & = & 1 + |\Gamma, \alpha \vdash A| & \\
|\Gamma \vdash A \to B| & = & 1 + |\Gamma \vdash A| + |\Gamma \vdash B| &
\end{array}$$

For example, if $\Gamma = (\beta, \hat\alpha = \beta)$ then $|\Gamma \vdash \hat\alpha| = 1 + |\Gamma \vdash \beta| = 1 + 1 = 2$, whereas the plain size of $\hat\alpha$ is simply 1.

The connection between (S1) and (S2) may be clarified by examining rule $<:\rightarrow$, whose conclusion says that $A_1 \rightarrow A_2$ is a subtype of $B_1 \rightarrow B_2$. If A_2 or B_2 is polymorphic, then the first premise on $A_1 \rightarrow A_2$ is smaller by (S1). Otherwise, the first premise has the same input context as the conclusion, so it has the same (S2), but is smaller by (S3). If B_1 or A_1 is polymorphic, then the second premise is smaller by (S1). Otherwise, we use the property that instantiating a monotype always solves an existential:

Lemma (Monotypes Solve Variables). *If* $\Gamma \vdash \hat{\alpha} :\leqq \tau \dashv \Delta$ *or* $\Gamma \vdash \tau \leqq: \hat{\alpha} \dashv \Delta$, *then if* $[\Gamma]\tau = \tau$ *and* $\hat{\alpha} \notin FV([\Gamma]\tau)$, *we have* $|\mathsf{unsolved}(\Gamma)| = |\mathsf{unsolved}(\Delta)| + 1$

A couple of other lemmas are worth mentioning: subtyping on two monotypes cannot increase the number of unsolved existentials, and applying a substitution Γ to a type does not increase the type's size with respect to Γ.

Lemma (Monotype Monotonicity).
If $\Gamma \vdash \tau_1 <: \tau_2 \dashv \Delta$ *then* $|\mathsf{unsolved}(\Delta)| \leq |\mathsf{unsolved}(\Gamma)|$.

Lemma (Substitution Decreases Size).
If $\Gamma \vdash A$ *then* $|\Gamma \vdash [\Gamma]A| \leq |\Gamma \vdash A|$.

Theorem 8 (Decidability of Subtyping).
Given a context Γ *and types* A, B *such that* $\Gamma \vdash A$ *and* $\Gamma \vdash B$ *and* $[\Gamma]A = A$ *and* $[\Gamma]B = B$, *it is decidable whether there exists* Δ *such that* $\Gamma \vdash A <: B \dashv \Delta$.

5.3 Decidability of Algorithmic Typing

Theorem 9 (Decidability of Typing).

(i) Synthesis: *Given a context* Γ *and a term* e, *it is decidable whether there exist a type* A *and a context* Δ *such that* $\Gamma \vdash e \Rightarrow A \dashv \Delta$.

(ii) Checking: *Given a context* Γ, *a term* e, *and a type* B *such that* $\Gamma \vdash B$, *it is decidable whether there is a context* Δ *such that* $\Gamma \vdash e \Leftarrow B \dashv \Delta$.

(iii) Application: *Given a context* Γ, *a term* e, *and a type* A *such that* $\Gamma \vdash A$, *it is decidable whether there exist a type* C *and a context* Δ *such that* $\Gamma \vdash A \bullet e \Rrightarrow C \dashv \Delta$.

The following induction measure suffices to prove decidability:

$$\left\langle e, \begin{array}{ll} \Rightarrow & \\ \Leftarrow, & |\Gamma \vdash B| \\ \Rrightarrow, & |\Gamma \vdash A| \end{array} \right\rangle$$

where $\langle \ldots \rangle$ denotes lexicographic order, and where (when comparing two judgments typing the same term e) the synthesis judgment (top line) is considered smaller than the checking judgment (second line), which in turn is considered smaller than the application judgment (bottom line). That is, $\Rightarrow \prec \Leftarrow \prec \Rrightarrow$. In Sub, this makes the synthesis premise smaller than the checking conclusion; in $\rightarrow$App and $\hat{\alpha}$App, this makes the checking premise smaller than the application conclusion.

Since we have no explicit introduction form for polymorphism, the rule $\forall$I has the same term e in its premise and conclusion, and both the premise and conclusion are the same kind of judgment (checking). The rule $\forall$App is similar (with application judgments in premise and conclusion). Therefore, given two judgments on the same term, and that are both checking judgments or both application judgments, we use the size of the input type expression—which *does* get smaller in $\forall$I and $\forall$App.

6. Soundness

We want the algorithmic specifications of subtyping and typing to be sound with respect to the declarative specifications. Roughly, given a derivation of an algorithmic judgment with input context Γ and output context Δ, and some complete context Ω that extends Δ (which therefore extends Γ), applying Ω throughout the given algorithmic judgment should yield a derivable declarative judgment. Let's make that rough outline concrete for instantiation, showing that the action of the instantiation rules is consistent with declarative subtyping:

Theorem 10 (Instantiation Soundness).
Given $\Delta \longrightarrow \Omega$ *and* $[\Gamma]B = B$ *and* $\hat{\alpha} \notin FV(B)$:

(1) If $\Gamma \vdash \hat{\alpha} :\leqq B \dashv \Delta$ *then* $[\Omega]\Delta \vdash [\Omega]\hat{\alpha} \leq [\Omega]B$.

(2) If $\Gamma \vdash B \leqq: \hat{\alpha} \dashv \Delta$ *then* $[\Omega]\Delta \vdash [\Omega]B \leq [\Omega]\hat{\alpha}$.

Note that the declarative derivation is under $[\Omega]\Delta$, which is Ω applied to the algorithmic output context Δ.

With instantiation soundness, we can prove the expected soundness property for subtyping:

Theorem 11 (Soundness of Algorithmic Subtyping).
If $\Gamma \vdash A <: B \dashv \Delta$ *where* $[\Gamma]A = A$ *and* $[\Gamma]B = B$ *and* $\Delta \longrightarrow \Omega$ *then* $[\Omega]\Delta \vdash [\Omega]A \leq [\Omega]B$.

Finally, knowing that subtyping is sound, we can prove that typing is sound:

Theorem 12 (Soundness of Algorithmic Typing). *Given* $\Delta \longrightarrow \Omega$:

(i) If $\Gamma \vdash e \Leftarrow A \dashv \Delta$ *then* $[\Omega]\Delta \vdash e \Leftarrow [\Omega]A$.

(ii) If $\Gamma \vdash e \Rightarrow A \dashv \Delta$ *then* $[\Omega]\Delta \vdash e \Rightarrow [\Omega]A$.

(iii) If $\Gamma \vdash A \bullet e \Rrightarrow C \dashv \Delta$ *then* $[\Omega]\Delta \vdash [\Omega]A \bullet e \Rrightarrow [\Omega]C$.

The proofs need several lemmas, including this one:

Lemma (Typing Extension).
If $\Gamma \vdash e \Leftarrow A \dashv \Delta$ *or* $\Gamma \vdash e \Rightarrow A \dashv \Delta$ *or* $\Gamma \vdash A \bullet e \Rrightarrow C \dashv \Delta$ *then* $\Gamma \longrightarrow \Delta$.

7. Completeness

Completeness of the algorithmic system is something like soundness in reverse: given a declarative derivation of $[\Omega]\Gamma \vdash [\Omega] \cdots$, we want to get an algorithmic derivation of $\Gamma \vdash \cdots \dashv \Delta$.

For soundness, the output context Δ such that $\Delta \longrightarrow \Omega$ was given; $\Gamma \longrightarrow \Omega$ followed from Typing Extension (the above lemma) and transitivity of extension. For completeness, only Γ is given, so we have $\Gamma \longrightarrow \Omega$ in the antecedent. Then we might expect to show, along with $\Gamma \vdash \cdots \dashv \Delta$, that $\Delta \longrightarrow \Omega$. But this is not general enough: the algorithmic rules generate fresh existential variables, so Δ may have existentials that are not found in Γ, nor in Ω. In completeness, we are given a declarative derivation, which contains no existentials; the completeness proof must build up the completing context Ω along with the algorithmic derivation. Thus, completeness will produce an Ω' which extends both the given Ω and the output context of the algorithmic derivation: $\Omega \longrightarrow \Omega'$ and $\Delta \longrightarrow \Omega'$. (By transitivity, we also get $\Gamma \longrightarrow \Omega'$.)

As with soundness, we have three main completeness results, for instantiation, subtyping and typing.

Theorem 13 (Instantiation Completeness). *Given* $\Gamma \longrightarrow \Omega$ *and* $A = [\Gamma]A$ *and* $\hat{\alpha} \in \mathsf{unsolved}(\Gamma)$ *and* $\hat{\alpha} \notin FV(A)$:

(1) If $[\Omega]\Gamma \vdash [\Omega]\hat{\alpha} \leq [\Omega]A$ *then there are* Δ, Ω' *such that* $\Omega \longrightarrow \Omega'$ *and* $\Delta \longrightarrow \Omega'$ *and* $\Gamma \vdash \hat{\alpha} :\leqq A \dashv \Delta$.

(2) If $[\Omega]\Gamma \vdash [\Omega]A \leq [\Omega]\hat{\alpha}$ *then there are* Δ, Ω' *such that* $\Omega \longrightarrow \Omega'$ *and* $\Delta \longrightarrow \Omega'$ *and* $\Gamma \vdash A \leqq: \hat{\alpha} \dashv \Delta$.

Theorem 14 (Generalized Completeness of Subtyping).
If $\Gamma \longrightarrow \Omega$ *and* $\Gamma \vdash A$ *and* $\Gamma \vdash B$ *and* $[\Omega]\Gamma \vdash [\Omega]A \leq [\Omega]B$ *then there exist* Δ *and* Ω' *such that* $\Delta \longrightarrow \Omega'$ *and* $\Omega \longrightarrow \Omega'$ *and* $\Gamma \vdash [\Gamma]A <: [\Gamma]B \dashv \Delta$.

Theorem 15 (Completeness of Algorithmic Typing).
Given $\Gamma \longrightarrow \Omega$ *and* $\Gamma \vdash A$:

(i) *If* $[\Omega]\Gamma \vdash e \Leftarrow [\Omega]A$
then there exist Δ *and* Ω'
such that $\Delta \longrightarrow \Omega'$ *and* $\Omega \longrightarrow \Omega'$ *and* $\Gamma \vdash e \Leftarrow [\Gamma]A \dashv \Delta$.

(ii) *If* $[\Omega]\Gamma \vdash e \Rightarrow A$
then there exist Δ, Ω', *and* A'
such that $\Delta \longrightarrow \Omega'$ *and* $\Omega \longrightarrow \Omega'$ *and* $\Gamma \vdash e \Rightarrow A' \dashv \Delta$
and $A = [\Omega']A'$.

(iii) *If* $[\Omega]\Gamma \vdash [\Omega]A \bullet e \Rightarrow\!\!\!\Rightarrow C$
then there exist Δ, Ω', *and* C'
such that $\Delta \longrightarrow \Omega'$ *and* $\Omega \longrightarrow \Omega'$
and $\Gamma \vdash [\Gamma]A \bullet e \Rightarrow\!\!\!\Rightarrow C' \dashv \Delta$ *and* $C = [\Omega']C'$.

8. Design Variations

The rules we give infer monomorphic types, but require annotations for all polymorphic bindings. In this section, we consider alternatives to this choice.

Eliminating type inference. To eliminate type inference from the declarative system, it suffices to drop the Decl$\rightarrow$I$\Rightarrow$ and Decl1I$\Rightarrow$ rules. The corresponding alterations to the algorithmic system are a little more delicate: simply deleting the $\rightarrow$I$\Rightarrow$ and 1I$\Rightarrow$ rules breaks completeness. To see why, suppose that we have a variable f of type $\forall\alpha.\ \alpha \rightarrow \alpha$, and consider the application f (). Our algorithm will introduce a new existential variable $\hat\alpha$ for α, and then check () against $\hat\alpha$. Without the 1I$\Rightarrow$ rule, typechecking will fail. To restore completeness, we need to modify these two rules. Instead of being *synthesis* rules, we will change them to *checking* rules that check values against an unknown existential variable.

$$\frac{}{\Gamma[\hat\alpha] \vdash () \Leftarrow \hat\alpha \dashv \Gamma[\hat\alpha = 1]}\ 1\text{I}\hat\alpha$$

$$\frac{\Gamma[\hat\alpha_2, \hat\alpha_1, \hat\alpha = \hat\alpha_1 \rightarrow \hat\alpha_2], x : \hat\alpha_1 \vdash e \Leftarrow \hat\alpha_2 \dashv \Delta, x : \hat\alpha_1, \Delta'}{\Gamma[\hat\alpha] \vdash \lambda x.\, e \Leftarrow \hat\alpha \dashv \Delta}\ \rightarrow\text{I}\hat\alpha$$

With these two rules replacing 1I$\Rightarrow$ and $\rightarrow$I$\Rightarrow$, we have a complete algorithm for the no-inference bidirectional system.

Full Damas-Milner type inference. Another alternative is to increase the amount of type inference done. For instance, a natural question is whether we can extend the bidirectional approach to subsume the inference done by the algorithm of Damas and Milner (1982). This appears feasible: we can alter the $\rightarrow$I$\Rightarrow$ rule to support ML-style type inference.

$$\frac{\begin{array}{c}\Gamma, \blacktriangleright_{\hat\alpha}, \hat\alpha, \hat\beta, x : \hat\alpha \vdash e \Leftarrow \hat\beta \dashv \Delta, \blacktriangleright_{\hat\alpha}, \Delta' \\ \tau = [\Delta'](\hat\alpha \rightarrow \hat\beta) \qquad \vec{\hat\alpha} = \mathsf{unsolved}(\Delta')\end{array}}{\Gamma \vdash \lambda x.\, e \Rightarrow \forall\vec\alpha.\ [\vec\alpha/\vec{\hat\alpha}]\tau \dashv \Delta}\ \rightarrow\text{I}{\Rightarrow}'$$

In this rule, we introduce a marker $\blacktriangleright_{\hat\alpha}$ into the context, and then check the function body against the type $\hat\beta$. Then, our output type substitutes away all the solved existential variables to the right of the marker $\blacktriangleright_{\hat\alpha}$, and generalizes over all of the unsolved variables to the right of the marker. Using an ordered context gives precise control over the scope of the existential variables, making it easy to express polymorphic generalization.

The above is only a sketch; we have not defined the corresponding declarative system, nor proved completeness.

9. Related Work and Discussion

9.1 Type Inference for System F

Because type inference for System F is undecidable (Wells 1999), designing type inference algorithms for first-class polymorphism inherently involves navigating a variety of design tradeoffs. As a result, there have been a wide variety of proposals for extending type systems beyond the Damas-Milner "sweet spot". The main tradeoff appears to be a "two-out-of-three" choice: language designers can keep any two of: (1) the η-law for functions, (2) impredicative instantiation, and (3) the standard type language of System F.

As discussed in Section 2, for typability under η-reductions, it is necessary for subtyping to instantiate deeply: that is, we must allow instantiation of quantifiers to the right of an arrow. However, Tiuryn and Urzyczyn (1996) and Chrząszcz (1998) showed that the subtyping relation for impredicative System F is undecidable. As a result, if we want η *and* a complete algorithm, then either the polymorphic instantiations must be predicative, or a different language of types must be used.

Figure 15 summarizes the different choices made by the designers of this and related systems.

Impredicativity and the η-law. The designers of $\mathsf{ML^F}$ (Le Botlan and Rémy 2003; Rémy and Yakobowski 2008; Le Botlan and Rémy 2009) chose to use a different language of types, one with a form of bounded quantification. This increases the expressivity of types enough to ensure principal types, which means that (1) required annotations are few and predictable, and (2) their system is very robust in the face of program transformations, including η. However, the richness of the $\mathsf{ML^F}$ type structure requires a sophisticated metatheory and correspondingly intricate implementation techniques.

Impredicativity and System F types. Much of the other work on higher-rank polymorphism avoids changing the language of types.

The HML system of Leijen (2009) and the FPH system of Vytiniotis et al. (2008) both retain the type language of (impredicative) System F. Each of these systems gives as a specification a slightly different extension to the declarative Damas-Milner type system, and handle the issue of inference in slightly different ways. HML is essentially a restriction of $\mathsf{ML^F}$, in which the external language of types is limited to System F, but which uses the technology of $\mathsf{ML^F}$ internally, as part of type inference. FPH, on the other hand, extends and generalizes work on boxy types (Vytiniotis et al. 2006) to control type inference. The differences in expressive power between these two systems are subtle—roughly speaking, FPH requires slightly more annotations, but has a less complicated specification. However, in both systems, the same heuristic guidance to the programmer applies: place explicit annotations on binders with fancy types.

The η-law and System F types. Peyton Jones et al. (2007) developed an approach for typechecking higher-rank predicative polymorphism that is closely related to ours. They define a bidirectional declarative system similar to our own, but which lacks an application judgment. This complicates the presentation of their system, forcing them to introduce an additional grammatical category of types beyond monotypes and polytypes, and requires many rules to carry an additional subtyping premise. Next, they enrich the subtyping rules of Odersky and Läufer (1996) with the distributivity axiom of Mitchell (1988), which we rejected on ideological grounds: it is a valid coercion, but is not orthogonal (it is a single rule mixing two different type connectives) and does not correspond to a rule in the sequent calculus. They do not prove the soundness and completeness of their Haskell reference implementation, but it appears to implement behavior close to our application judgment.

History of our approach. Several of the ideas used in the present paper descend from Dunfield (2009), an approach to first-class polymorphism (including impredicativity) also based on ordered contexts with existential variables instantiated via subtyping. In

System	η-laws?	Impredicative?	System F type language?
$\mathsf{ML^F}$	yes	yes	no
FPH	no	yes	yes
HML	no	yes	yes
Peyton Jones et al. (2007)	yes	no	yes
This paper	yes	no	yes

Figure 15. Comparison of type inference algorithms

fact, the present work began as an attempt to extend Dunfield (2009) with type-level computation. During that attempt, we found several shortcomings and problems. The most serious is that the decidability and completeness arguments were not valid. These problems may be fixable, but instead we started over, reusing several of the high-level ideas in different technical forms.

9.2 Other Type Systems

Pierce and Turner (2000) developed bidirectional typechecking for rich subtyping, with specific techniques for instantiating polymorphism within function application (hence, *local* type inference). Their declarative specification is more complex than ours, and their algorithm depends on computing approximations of upper and lower bounds on types. *Colored local type inference* (Odersky et al. 2001) allows different *parts* of type expressions to be propagated in different directions. Our approach gets a similar effect by manipulating type expressions with existential variables.

9.3 Our Algorithm

One of our main contributions is our new algorithm for type inference, which is remarkable in its simplicity. Three key ideas underpin our algorithm.

Ordered contexts. We move away from the traditional "bag of constraints" model of type inference, and instead embed existential variables and their values directly into an ordered context. Thus, straightforward scoping rules control the free variables of the types each existential variable may be instantiated with, without any need for model-theoretic techniques like skolemization, which fit awkwardly into a type-theoretic discipline. Using an ordered context permits handling quantifiers in a manner resembling the level-based generalization mechanism of Rémy (1992), used also in $\mathsf{ML^F}$ (Le Botlan and Rémy 2009).

The instantiation judgment. The original inspiration for instantiation comes from the "greedy" algorithm of Cardelli (1993), which eagerly uses type information to solve existential constraints. In that setting—a language with rather ambitious subtyping—the greedy algorithm was incomplete: consider a function of type $\forall\alpha.\ \alpha \to \alpha \to \alpha$ applied to a *Cat* and an *Animal*; the cat will be checked against an existential $\hat{\alpha}$, which instantiates $\hat{\alpha}$ to *Cat*, but checking the second argument, *Animal* <: *Cat*, fails. (Reversing the order of arguments makes typing succeed!)

In our setting, where subtyping represents the specialization order induced by quantifier instantiation, it is possible to get a complete algorithm, by slightly relaxing the pure greedy strategy. Rather than eagerly setting constraints, we first look under quantifiers (in the InstLAllR and InstRAllL rules) to see if there is a feasible monotype instantiation, and we also use the the InstLReach and InstRReach to set the "wrong" existential variable in case we need to equate an existential variable with one to its right in the context. Looking under quantifiers seems forced by our restriction to predicative polymorphism, and "reaching" seems forced by our use of an ordered context, but the combination of these mechanisms fortuitously enables our algorithm to find good upper and lower monomorphic approximations of polymorphic types.

This is surprising, since it is quite contrary to the implementation strategy of $\mathsf{ML^F}$ (also used by HML and FPH). There, the language of type constraints supports bounds on fully quantified types, and the algorithm incrementally refines these constraints. In contrast, we only ever create equational constraints on existentials (bounds are not needed), and once we have a solution for an existential, our algorithm never needs to revisit its decision.

Distinguishing instantiation as a separate judgment is new in this paper, and beneficial: Dunfield (2009) baked instantiation into the subtyping rules, resulting in a system whose direct implementation required substantial backtracking—over a set of rules including arbitrary application of substitutions. We, instead, maintain an invariant in subtyping and instantiation that the types are always fully applied with respect to an input context, obviating the need for explicit rules to apply substitutions.

Context extension. Finally, we introduce a context-extension judgment as the central invariant in our correctness proofs. This permits us to state many properties important to our algorithm abstractly, without reference to the details of our algorithm.

We are not the only ones to study context-based approaches to type inference. Recently, Gundry et al. (2010) recast the classic Damas-Milner algorithm, which manipulates unstructured sets of equality constraints, as structured constraint solving under ordered contexts. A (semantic) notion of information increase is central to their development, as (syntactic) context extension is to ours. While their formulation supports only ML-style prenex polymorphism, the ultimate goal is a foundation for type inference for dependent types. To some extent, both our algorithm and theirs can be understood in terms of the proof system of Miller (1992) for mixed-prefix unification. We each restrict the unification problem, and then give a proof search algorithm to solve the type inference problem.

Acknowledgments

Thanks to the anonymous ICFP reviewers for their comments, which have (we hope) led to a more correct paper.

References

Andreas Abel. Termination checking with types. *RAIRO—Theoretical Informatics and Applications*, 38(4):277–319, 2004. Special Issue: Fixed Points in Computer Science (FICS'03).

Andreas Abel, Thierry Coquand, and Peter Dybjer. Verifying a semantic βη-conversion test for Martin-Löf type theory. In *Mathematics of Program Construction (MPC'08)*, volume 5133 of *LNCS*, pages 29–56, 2008.

Jean-Marc Andreoli. Logic programming with focusing proofs in linear logic. *J. Logic and Computation*, 2(3):297–347, 1992.

Andrea Asperti, Wilmer Ricciotti, Claudio Sacerdoti Coen, and Enrico Tassi. A bi-directional refinement algorithm for the calculus of (co)inductive constructions. *Logical Methods in Computer Science*, 8(1), 2012.

Gavin M. Bierman, Erik Meijer, and Mads Torgersen. Lost in translation: formalizing proposed extensions to C♯. In *OOPSLA*, 2007.

Luca Cardelli. An implementation of $F_{<:}$. Research report 97, DEC/Compaq Systems Research Center, February 1993.

Iliano Cervesato and Frank Pfenning. A linear spine calculus. *J. Logic and Computation*, 13(5):639–688, 2003.

Adam Chlipala, Leaf Petersen, and Robert Harper. Strict bidirectional type checking. In *Workshop on Types in Language Design and Impl. (TLDI '05)*, pages 71–78, 2005.

Jacek Chrząszcz. Polymorphic subtyping without distributivity. In *Mathematical Foundations of Computer Science*, volume 1450 of *LNCS*, pages 346–355. Springer, 1998.

Thierry Coquand. An algorithm for type-checking dependent types. *Science of Computer Programming*, 26(1–3):167–177, 1996.

Luis Damas and Robin Milner. Principal type-schemes for functional programs. In *POPL*, pages 207–212. ACM, 1982.

Rowan Davies and Frank Pfenning. Intersection types and computational effects. In *ICFP*, pages 198–208, 2000.

Joshua Dunfield. *A Unified System of Type Refinements*. PhD thesis, Carnegie Mellon University, 2007. CMU-CS-07-129.

Joshua Dunfield. Greedy bidirectional polymorphism. In *ML Workshop*, pages 15–26, 2009. `http://www.cs.cmu.edu/~joshuad/papers/poly/`.

Joshua Dunfield and Frank Pfenning. Tridirectional typechecking. In *POPL*, pages 281–292, January 2004.

Adam Gundry, Conor McBride, and James McKinna. Type inference in context. In *Mathematically Structured Functional Programming (MSFP)*, 2010.

Didier Le Botlan and Didier Rémy. $\mathsf{ML^F}$: raising ML to the power of System F. In *ICFP*, pages 27–38, 2003.

Didier Le Botlan and Didier Rémy. Recasting $\mathsf{ML^F}$. *Information and Computation*, 207:726–785, 2009.

Daan Leijen. Flexible types: robust type inference for first-class polymorphism. In *POPL*, pages 66–77, 2009.

Andres Löh, Conor McBride, and Wouter Swierstra. A tutorial implementation of a dependently typed lambda calculus. Unpublished draft, `http://people.cs.uu.nl/andres/LambdaPi/index.html`, 2008.

William Lovas. *Refinement Types for Logical Frameworks*. PhD thesis, Carnegie Mellon University, 2010. CMU-CS-10-138.

Dale Miller. Unification under a mixed prefix. *J. Symbolic Computation*, 14:321–358, 1992.

John C. Mitchell. Polymorphic type inference and containment. *Information and Computation*, 76:211–249, 1988.

Martin Odersky and Konstantin Läufer. Putting type annotations to work. In *POPL*, 1996.

Martin Odersky, Matthias Zenger, and Christoph Zenger. Colored local type inference. In *POPL*, pages 41–53, 2001.

Simon Peyton Jones and Mark Shields. Lexically scoped type variables. Technical report, Microsoft Research, 2004.

Simon Peyton Jones, Dimitrios Vytiniotis, Stephanie Weirich, and Mark Shields. Practical type inference for arbitrary-rank types. *J. Functional Programming*, 17(1):1–82, 2007.

Frank Pfenning. Church and Curry: Combining intrinsic and extrinsic typing. In *Reasoning in Simple Type Theory: Festschrift in Honor of Peter B. Andrews on His 70th Birthday*. College Publications, 2008.

Brigitte Pientka. A type-theoretic foundation for programming with higher-order abstract syntax and first-class substitutions. In *POPL*, pages 371–382, 2008.

Benjamin C. Pierce and David N. Turner. Local type inference. *ACM Trans. Prog. Lang. Sys.*, 22:1–44, 2000.

Didier Rémy. Extension of ML type system with a sorted equational theory on types. Research Report 1766, INRIA, 1992.

Didier Rémy and Boris Yakobowski. From ML to $\mathsf{ML^F}$: graphic type constraints with efficient type inference. In *ICFP*, pages 63–74, 2008.

Robert J. Simmons. Structural focalization. arXiv:`1109.6273v4 [cs.LO]`, 2012.

Jerzy Tiuryn and Paweł Urzyczyn. The subtyping problem for second-order types is undecidable. In *LICS*, 1996.

Dimitrios Vytiniotis, Stephanie Weirich, and Simon L. Peyton Jones. Boxy types: inference for higher-rank types and impredicativity. In *ICFP*, pages 251–262, 2006.

Dimitrios Vytiniotis, Stephanie Weirich, and Simon L. Peyton Jones. FPH: First-class polymorphism for Haskell. In *ICFP*, pages 295–306, 2008.

Dimitrios Vytiniotis, Simon Peyton Jones, and Tom Schrijvers. Let should not be generalised. In *Workshop on Types in Language Design and Impl. (TLDI '10)*, pages 39–50, 2010.

Kevin Watkins, Iliano Cervesato, Frank Pfenning, and David Walker. A concurrent logical framework: The propositional fragment. In *Types for Proofs and Programs*, pages 355–377. Springer-Verlag LNCS 3085, 2004.

J. B. Wells. Typability and type checking in System F are equivalent and undecidable. *Annals of Pure and Applied Logic*, 98: 111–156, 1999.

Hongwei Xi. *Dependent Types in Practical Programming*. PhD thesis, Carnegie Mellon University, 1998.

Optimizing Abstract Abstract Machines

J. Ian Johnson
Northeastern University
ianj@ccs.neu.edu

Nicholas Labich
Northeastern University
labichn@ccs.neu.edu

Matthew Might
University of Utah
might@cs.utah.edu

David Van Horn
Northeastern University
dvanhorn@ccs.neu.edu

Abstract

The technique of *abstracting abstract machines* (AAM) provides a systematic approach for deriving computable approximations of evaluators that are easily proved sound. This article contributes a complementary step-by-step process for subsequently going from a naive analyzer derived under the AAM approach to an efficient and correct implementation. The end result of the process is a two to three order-of-magnitude improvement over the systematically derived analyzer, making it competitive with hand-optimized implementations that compute fundamentally less precise results.

Categories and Subject Descriptors F.3.2 [*Semantics of Programming Languages*]: Program analysis

Keywords abstract machines; abstract interpretation

1. Introduction

Program analysis provides sound predictive models of program behavior, but in order for such models to be effective, they must be efficiently computable and correct. Past approaches to designing program analyses have often featured abstractions that are far removed from the original language semantics, requiring ingenuity in their construction and effort in their verification. The *abstracting abstract machines* (AAM) approach [30, 32] to deriving program analyses provides an alternative: a systematic way of transforming a programming language semantics in the form of an abstract machine into a family of abstract interpreters. It thus reduces the burden of constructing and verifying the soundness of an abstract interpreter.

By taking a machine-oriented view of computation, AAM makes it possible to design, verify, and implement program analyzers for realistic language features typically considered difficult to model. The approach was originally applied to features such as higher-order functions, stack inspection, exceptions, laziness, first-class continuations, and garbage collection. It has since been used to verify actor-[8] and thread-based [20] parallelism and behavioral

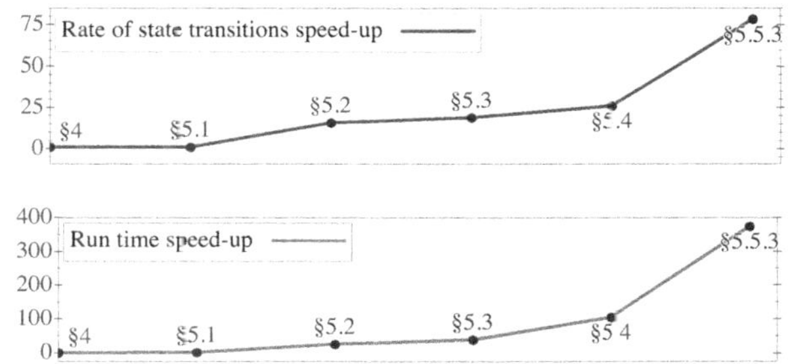

Figure 1. Factor improvements over the baseline analyzer for the Vardoulakis and Shivers benchmark in terms of the rate of state transitions and total analysis time. (Bigger is better.) Each point is marked with the section that introduces the optimization.

contracts [29]; it has been used to model Coq [24], Dalvik [23], Erlang [9], JavaScript [31], and Racket [29].

The primary strength of the approach is that abstract interpreters can be easily derived through a small number of steps from existing machine models. Since the relationships between abstract machines and higher-level semantic models—such as definitional interpreters [27], structured operational semantics [26], and reduction semantics [12]—are well understood [6], it is possible to navigate from these high-level semantic models to sound program analyzers in a systematic way. Moreover, since these analyses so closely resemble a language's interpreter (a) implementing an analysis requires little more than implementing an interpreter, (b) a single implementation can serve as both an interpreter and analyzer, and (c) verifying the correctness of the implementation is straightforward.

Unfortunately, the AAM approach yields analyzers with poor performance relative to hand-optimized analyzers. Our work takes aim squarely at this "efficiency gap," and narrows it in an equally systematic way through a number of simple steps, many of which are inspired by run-time implementation techniques such as laziness and compilation to avoid interpretative overhead. Each of these steps is proven correct, so the end result is an implementation that is trustworthy and efficient.

In this article, we develop a systematic approach to deriving a practical implementation of an abstract-machine-based analyzer using mostly semantic means rather than tricky engineering. Our goal is to empower programming language implementers and researchers to explore and convincingly exhibit their ideas with a low barrier to entry. The optimizations we describe are widely applicable and apparently effective to scale far beyond the size of pro-

ICFP '13, September 25–27, Boston, MA, USA..

ACM 978-1-4503-2326-0/13/09... $15.00.
http://dx.doi.org/10.1145/2500365.2500604

grams typically considered in the recent literature on flow analysis for functional languages.

2. At a glance

We start with a quick review of the AAM approach to develop an analysis framework and then apply our step-by-step optimization techniques in the simplified setting of a core functional language. This allows us to explicate the optimizations with a minimal amount of inessential technical overhead. Following that, we scale this approach up to an analyzer for a realistic untyped, higher-order imperative language with a number of interesting features and then measure improvements across a suite of benchmarks.

At each step during the initial presentation and development, we evaluated the implementation on a set of benchmarks. The highlighted benchmark in figure 1 is from Vardoulakis and Shivers [33] that tests distributivity of multiplication over addition on Church numerals. For the step-by-step development, this benchmark is particularly informative:

1. it can be written in most modern programming languages,
2. it was designed to stress an analyzer's ability to deal with complicated environment and control structure arising from the use of higher-order functions to encode arithmetic, and
3. its improvement is about median in the benchmark suite considered in section 6, and thus it serves as a good sanity check for each of the optimization techniques considered.

We start, in section 3, by developing an abstract interpreter according to the AAM approach. In the initial abstraction, each state carries a store (what is called per-state store variance). The space of stores is exponential in size; without further abstraction, the analysis is exponential and thus cannot analyze the example in a reasonable amount of time. In section 4, we perform a further abstraction by widening the store. The resulting analyzer sacrifices precision for speed and is able to analyze the example in about 1 minute. This step is described by Van Horn and Might [32, §3.5–6] and is necessary to make even small examples feasible. We therefore take a widened interpreter as the baseline for our evaluation.

Section 5 gives a series of simple abstractions and implementation techniques that, in total, speed up the analysis by nearly a factor of 500, dropping the analysis time to a fraction of a second. Figure 1 shows the step-wise improvement of the analysis time for this example.

The AAM approach, in essence, does the following: it takes a machine-based view of computation and turns it into a *finitary approximation* by bounding the size of the store. With a limited address space, the store must map addresses to *sets* of values. Store updates are interpreted as joins, and store dereferences are interpreted by non-deterministic choice of an element from a set. The result of analyzing a program is a finite directed graph where nodes in the graph are (abstract) machine states and edges denote machine transitions between states.

The techniques we propose for optimizing analysis fall into the following categories:

1. generate fewer states by avoiding the eager exploration of non-deterministic choices that will later collapse into a single join point. We accomplish this by applying lazy evaluation techniques so that non-determinism is evaluated *by need.*
2. generate fewer states by avoiding unnecessary, intermediate states of a computation. We accomplish this by applying compilation techniques from functional languages to avoid interpretive overhead in the machine transition system.

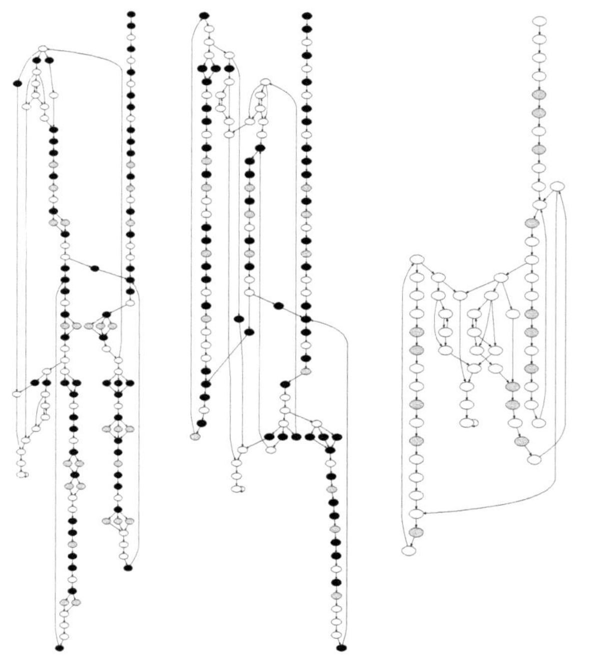

(a) Baseline (b) Lazy (c) Compiled (& lazy)

Figure 2. Example state graphs for Earl et. al. program. Gray states follow variable references, `ev` states are black, and all others are white. Part (a) shows the baseline analyzer result. It has long "corridor" transitions and "diamond" subgraphs that fan-out from nondeterminism and fan-in from joins. Part (b) shows the result of performing nondeterminism lazily and thus avoids many of the diamond subgraphs. Part (c) shows the result of abstract compilation that removes interpretive overhead in the form of intermediate states, thus minimizing the corridor transitions. The end result is a more compact abstraction of the program that can be generated faster.

3. generate states faster. We accomplish this by better algorithm design in the fixed-point computation we use to generate state graphs.

Figure 2 shows the effect of (1) and (2) for the small motivating example in Earl, et al. [10]. By generating significantly fewer states at a significantly faster rate, we are able to achieve large performance improvements in terms of both time and space.

Section 6 describes the evaluation of each optimization technique applied to an implementation supporting a more realistic set of features, including mutation, first-class control, compound data, a full numeric tower and many more forms of primitive data and operations. We evaluate this implementation against a set of benchmark programs drawn from the literature. For all benchmarks, the optimized analyzer outperforms the baseline by at least a factor of two to three orders of magnitude.

Section 7 relates this work to the literature and section 8 concludes.

3. Abstract interpretation of ISWIM

In this section, we give a brief review of the AAM approach by defining a sound analytic framework for a core higher-order functional language: Landin's ISWIM [16]. In the subsequent sections, we will explore optimizations for the analyzer in this simplified set-

$$
\begin{array}{llcl}
\text{Expressions} & e & = & \mathtt{var}^{\ell}(x) \\
 & & | & \mathtt{lit}^{\ell}(l) \\
 & & | & \mathtt{lam}^{\ell}(x, e) \\
 & & | & \mathtt{app}^{\ell}(e, e) \\
 & & | & \mathtt{if}^{\ell}(e, e, e) \\
\text{Variables} & x & = & \mathtt{x} \mid \mathtt{y} \mid \ldots \\
\text{Literals} & l & = & z \mid b \mid o \\
\text{Integers} & z & = & \mathtt{0} \mid \mathtt{1} \mid \mathtt{-1} \mid \ldots \\
\text{Booleans} & b & = & \mathtt{tt} \mid \mathtt{ff} \\
\text{Operations} & o & = & \mathtt{zero?} \mid \mathtt{add1} \mid \mathtt{sub1} \mid \ldots
\end{array}
$$

Figure 3. Syntax of ISWIM

$$
\begin{array}{llcl}
\text{Values} & v, u & = & \mathtt{clos}\ (x, e, \rho) \mid l \mid \kappa \\
\text{States} & \varsigma & = & \mathtt{ev}^t(e, \rho, \sigma, \kappa) \\
 & & | & \mathtt{co}\ (\kappa, v, \sigma) \\
 & & | & \mathtt{ap}^t(v, v, \sigma, \kappa) \\
\text{Continuations} & \kappa & = & \mathtt{halt} \\
 & & | & \mathtt{fun}\ (v, a_\kappa) \\
 & & | & \mathtt{arg}\ (e, \rho, a_\kappa) \\
 & & | & \mathtt{ifk}\ (e, e, \rho, a_\kappa) \\
\text{Addresses} & a & \in & \mathit{Addr} \\
\text{Times} & t & \in & \mathit{Time} \\
\text{Environments} & \rho & \in & \mathit{Var} \rightharpoonup \mathit{Addr} \\
\text{Stores} & \sigma & \in & \mathit{Addr} \rightharpoonup \wp(\mathit{Value})
\end{array}
$$

Figure 4. Abstract machine components

$$
\mathit{traces}(e) = \{\mathtt{ev}^{t_0}(e, \varnothing, \varnothing, \mathtt{halt}) \longmapsto\!\!\!\!\rightarrow \varsigma\} \text{ where}
$$

$$
\begin{array}{rcl}
\multicolumn{3}{c}{\varsigma \longmapsto \varsigma' \text{ defined to be the following}} \\
\multicolumn{3}{c}{\text{let } t' = \mathit{tick}(\varsigma)} \\
\mathtt{ev}\ (\mathtt{var}\ (x), \rho, \sigma, \kappa) & \longmapsto & \mathtt{co}\ (\kappa, v, \sigma) \text{ if } v \in \sigma(\rho(x)) \\
\mathtt{ev}\ (\mathtt{lit}\ (l), \rho, \sigma, \kappa) & \longmapsto & \mathtt{co}\ (\kappa, l, \sigma) \\
\mathtt{ev}^t(\mathtt{lam}\ (x, e), \rho, \sigma, \kappa) & \longmapsto & \mathtt{co}\ (\kappa, \mathtt{clos}\ (x, e, \rho), \sigma) \\
\mathtt{ev}^t(\mathtt{app}^{\ell}(e_0, e_1), \rho, \sigma, \kappa) & \longmapsto & \mathtt{ev}^{t'}(e_0, \rho, \sigma', \mathtt{arg}^t_{\ell}(e_1, \rho, a_\kappa)) \\
 & & \text{where } a_\kappa = \mathit{allockont}^t_{\ell}(\sigma, \kappa) \\
 & & \quad \sigma' = \sigma \sqcup [a_\kappa \mapsto \{\kappa\}] \\
\mathtt{ev}^t(\mathtt{if}^{\ell}(e_0, e_1, e_2), \rho, \sigma, \kappa) & \longmapsto & \mathtt{ev}^{t'}(e_0, \rho, \sigma', \mathtt{ifk}^t(e_1, e_2, \rho, a_\kappa)) \\
 & & \text{where } a_\kappa = \mathit{allockont}^t_{\ell}(\sigma, \kappa) \\
 & & \quad \sigma' = \sigma \sqcup [a_\kappa \mapsto \{\kappa\}] \\
\mathtt{co}\ (\mathtt{arg}^t_{\ell}(e, \rho, a_\kappa), v, \sigma) & \longmapsto & \mathtt{ev}^t(e, \rho, \sigma, \mathtt{fun}^t_{\ell}(v, a_\kappa)) \\
\mathtt{co}\ (\mathtt{fun}^t_{\ell}(u, a_\kappa), v, \sigma) & \longmapsto & \mathtt{ap}^t_{\ell}(u, v, \kappa, \sigma) \text{ if } \kappa \in \sigma(a_\kappa) \\
\mathtt{co}\ (\mathtt{ifk}^t(e_0, e_1, \rho, a_\kappa), \mathtt{tt}, \sigma) & \longmapsto & \mathtt{ev}^{t'}(e_0, \rho, \sigma, \kappa) \text{ if } \kappa \in \sigma(a_\kappa) \\
\mathtt{co}\ (\mathtt{ifk}^t(e_0, e_1, \rho, a_\kappa), \mathtt{ff}, \sigma) & \longmapsto & \mathtt{ev}^{t'}(e_1, \rho, \sigma, \kappa) \text{ if } \kappa \in \sigma(a_\kappa) \\
\mathtt{ap}^t_{\ell}(\mathtt{clos}\ (x, e, \rho), v, \sigma, \kappa) & \longmapsto & \mathtt{ev}^{t'}(e, \rho', \sigma', \kappa) \\
 & & \text{where } a = \mathit{alloc}(\varsigma) \\
 & & \quad \rho' = \rho[x \mapsto a] \\
 & & \quad \sigma' = \sigma \sqcup [a \mapsto \{v\}] \\
\mathtt{ap}^t_{\ell}(o, v, \sigma, \kappa) & \longmapsto & \mathtt{co}\ (\kappa, v', \sigma) \text{ if } v' \in \Delta(o, v)
\end{array}
$$

Figure 5. Abstract abstract machine for ISWIM

ting, but scaling these techniques to realistic languages is straightforward and has been done for the analyzer evaluated in section 6.

ISWIM is a family of programming languages parameterized by a set of base values and operations. To make things concrete, we consider a member of the ISWIM family with integers, booleans, and a few operations. Figure 3 defines the syntax of ISWIM. It includes variables, literals (either integers, booleans, or operations), λ-expressions for defining procedures, procedure applications, and conditionals. Expressions carry a label, ℓ, which is drawn from an unspecified set and denotes the source location of the expression; labels are used to disambiguate distinct, but syntactically identical pieces of syntax. We omit the label annotation in contexts where it is irrelevant.

The semantics is defined in terms of a machine model. The machine components are defined in figure 4; figure 5 defines the transition relation (unmentioned components stay the same). The evaluation of a program is defined as its set of traces that arise from iterating the machine transition relation. The *traces* function produces the set of all proofs of reachability for any state ς from the injection of program e (from which one could extract a string of states). The machine is a very slight variation on a standard abstract machine for ISWIM in "eval, continue, apply" form [6]. It can be systematically derived from a definitional interpreter through a continuation-passing style transformation and defunctionalization, or from a structural operational semantics using the refocusing construction of Danvy and Nielsen [7].

Compared with the standard machine semantics, this definition is different in the following ways, which make it abstractable as a program analyzer:

- the store maps addresses to *sets* of values, [1] not single values,
- continuations are heap-allocated, not stack-allocated,
- there are "timestamps" ($t \in \mathit{Time}$) and syntax labels (ℓ) threaded through the computation, and
- the machine is implicitly parameterized by the functions *alloc*, *allockont*, *tick*, Δ, and spaces *Addr*, *Time* (and initial $t_0 \in \mathit{Time}$).

Concrete interpretation To characterize concrete interpretation, set the implicit parameters of the relation given in figure 5 as follows:

$$\mathit{alloc}(\varsigma) = a \text{ where } a \notin \text{ the } \sigma \text{ within } \varsigma$$

$$\mathit{allockont}^t_{\ell}(\sigma, \kappa) = a_\kappa \text{ where } a_\kappa \notin \sigma$$

These functions appear to ignore ℓ and t, but they can be used to determinize the choice of fresh addresses. The $\sqcup$ on stores in the figure is a point-wise lifting of $\cup$: $\sigma \sqcup \sigma' = \lambda a.\sigma(a) \cup \sigma'(a)$. The resulting relation is non-deterministic in its choice of addresses, however it must always choose a fresh address when allocating a continuation or variable binding. If we consider machine states equivalent up to consistent renaming and fix an allocation scheme, this relation defines a deterministic machine (the relation is really a function).

The interpretation of primitive operations is defined by setting Δ as follows:

$$z + 1 \in \Delta(\mathtt{add1}, z) \qquad z - 1 \in \Delta(\mathtt{sub1}, z)$$

$$\mathtt{tt} \in \Delta(\mathtt{zero?}, \mathtt{0}) \qquad \mathtt{ff} \in \Delta(\mathtt{zero?}, z) \text{ if } z \neq \mathtt{0}$$

Abstract interpretation To characterize abstract interpretation, set the implicit parameters just as above, but drop the $a \notin \sigma$ condition. The Δ relation takes some care to not make the analysis run forever; a simple instantiation is a flat abstraction where arithmetic operations return an abstract top element $\mathtt{Z}$, and $\mathtt{zero?}$ returns both $\mathtt{tt}$ and $\mathtt{ff}$ on $\mathtt{Z}$. This family of interpreters is also non-deterministic in choices of addresses, but it is free to choose addresses that are already in use. Consequently, the machines may be non-deterministic when multiple values reside in a store location.

[1] More generally, we can have stores map to any domain that forms a Galois connection with sets of values, enabling Δ to produce elaborate abstractions of base values (e.g., interval or octagon abstractions). We use sets of values for a simpler exposition.

It is important to recognize from this definition that *any* allocation strategy is a sound abstract interpretation [21]. In particular, concrete interpretation is a kind of abstract interpretation. So is an interpretation that allocates a single cell into which all bindings and continuations are stored. The former is an abstract interpretation with uncomputable reachability and gives only the ground truth of a program's behavior; the latter is an abstract interpretation that is easy to compute but gives little information. Useful program analyses lay somewhere in between and can be characterized by their choice of address representation and allocation strategy. Uniform k-CFA [25], presented next, is one such analysis.

Uniform k-CFA To characterize uniform k-CFA, set the allocation strategy as follows, for a fixed constant k:

$$\begin{aligned}
\mathit{Time} &= \mathit{Label}^* \\
t_0 &= \epsilon \\
\mathit{alloc}(\mathtt{ap}^t_\ell(\mathtt{clos}\ (x, e, \rho), v, \sigma, \kappa)) &= x\lfloor \ell t \rfloor_k \\
\mathit{allockont}^t_\ell(\sigma, \kappa) &= \ell t \\
\mathit{tick}(\mathtt{ev}^t(e, \rho, \sigma, \kappa)) &= t \\
\mathit{tick}(\mathtt{co}\ (\mathtt{arg}^t(e, \rho, a_\kappa), v, \sigma)) &= t \\
\mathit{tick}(\mathtt{ap}^t_\ell(u, v, \kappa)) &= \lfloor \ell t \rfloor_k \\
\lfloor t \rfloor_0 = \lfloor \epsilon \rfloor_k &= t_0 \\
\lfloor \ell t \rfloor_{k+1} &= \ell \lfloor t \rfloor_k
\end{aligned}$$

The $\lfloor \cdot \rfloor_k$ notation denotes the truncation of a list of symbols to the leftmost k symbols.

All that remains is the interpretation of primitives. For abstract interpretation, we set Δ to the function that returns Z on all inputs—a symbolic value we interpret as denoting the set of all integers.

At this point, we have abstracted the original machine to one which has a finite state space for any given program, and thus forms the basis of a sound, computable program analyzer for ISWIM.

4. From machine semantics to baseline analyzer

The uniform k-CFA allocation strategy would make *traces* in figure 5 a computable abstraction of possible executions, but one that is too inefficient to run, even on small examples. Through this section, we explain a succession of approximations to reach a more appropriate baseline analysis. We ground this path by first formulating the analysis in terms of a classic fixed-point computation.

4.1 Static analysis as fixed-point computation

Conceptually, the AAM approach calls for computing an analysis as a graph exploration: (1) start with an initial state, and (2) compute the transitive closure of the transition relation from that state. All visited states are potentially reachable in the concrete, and all paths through the graph are possible traces of execution.

We can cast this exploration process in terms of a fixed-point calculation. Given the initial state ς_0 and the transition relation $\longmapsto$, we define the global transfer function:

$$F_{\varsigma_0} : \wp(\mathit{State}) \times \wp(\mathit{State} \times \mathit{State}) \to \wp(\mathit{State}) \times \wp(\mathit{State} \times \mathit{State}).$$

Internally, this global transfer function computes the successors of all supplied states, and then includes the initial state:

$$\begin{aligned}
F_{\varsigma_0}(V, E) &= (\{\varsigma_0\} \cup V', E') \\
E' &= \{(\varsigma, \varsigma') \mid \varsigma \in V \text{ and } \varsigma \longmapsto \varsigma'\} \\
V' &= \{\varsigma' \mid (\varsigma, \varsigma') \in E'\}
\end{aligned}$$

Then, the evaluator for the analysis computes the least fixed-point of the global transfer function: $\mathit{eval}(e) = \mathrm{lfp}(F_{\varsigma_0})$, where $\varsigma_0 = \mathtt{ev}^{t_0}(e, \varnothing, \varnothing, \mathtt{halt})$.

The possible traces of execution tell us the most about a program, so we take $\mathit{traces}(e)$ to be the (regular) set of paths through the computed graph. We elide the construction of the set of edges in this paper.

To conduct this naive exploration on the Vardoulakis and Shivers example would require considerable time. Even though the state space is finite, it is exponential in the size of the program. Even with $k = 0$, there are exponentially many stores in the AAM framework.

In the next subsection, we fix this with store widening to reach polynomial (albeit of high degree) complexity. This widening effectively lifts the store out of individual states to create a single, global shared store for all.

4.2 Store widening

A common technique to accelerate convergence in flow analyses is to share a common, global store. Formally, we can cast this optimization as a second abstraction or as the application of a widening operator [2] during the fixed-point iteration. In the ISWIM language, such a widening makes 0-CFA quartic in the size of the program. Thus, complexity drops from intractable exponentiality to a merely daunting polynomial.

Since we can cast this optimization as a widening, there is no need to change the transition relation itself. Rather, what changes is the structure of the fixed-point iteration. In each pass, the algorithm will collect all newly produced stores and join them together. Then, before each transition, it installs this joined store into current state.

To describe this process, AAM defined a transformation of the reduction relation so that it operates on a pair of a set of contexts (C) and a store (σ). A context includes all non-store components, *e.g.*, the expression, the environment and the stack. The transformed relation, $\widehat{\longmapsto}$, is

$$\begin{aligned}
&(C, \sigma) \mathrel{\widehat{\longmapsto}} (C', \sigma'), \\
&\text{where } C' = \{c' \mid \mathit{wn}(c, \sigma) \longmapsto \mathit{wn}(c', \sigma^c), c \in C\} \\
&\qquad \sigma' = \bigsqcup \{\sigma^c \mid \mathit{wn}(c, \sigma) \longmapsto \mathit{wn}(c', \sigma^c), c \in C\} \\
&\qquad \mathit{wn} : \mathit{Context} \times \mathit{Store} \to \mathit{State} \\
&\mathit{wn}(\mathtt{ev}\ (e, \rho, \kappa), \sigma) = \mathtt{ev}\ (e, \rho, \sigma, \kappa) \\
&\mathit{wn}(\mathtt{co}\ (v, \kappa), \sigma) = \mathtt{co}\ (v, \kappa, \sigma) \\
&\mathit{wn}(\mathtt{ap}\ (u, v, \kappa), \sigma) = \mathtt{ap}\ (u, v, \sigma, \kappa)
\end{aligned}$$

To retain soundness, this store grows monotonically as the least upper bound of all occurring stores.

4.3 Store-allocate all values

The final approximation we make to get to our baseline is to store-allocate all values that appear, so that any non-machine state that contains a value instead contains an address to a value. The AAM approach stops at the previous optimization. However, the funcontinuation stores a value, and this makes the space of continuations quadratic rather than linear in the size of the program, for a monovariant analysis like 0-CFA. Having the space of continuations grow linearly with the size of the program will drop the overall complexity to cubic (as expected). We also need to allocate an address for the argument position in an apstate.

To achieve this linearity for continuations, we allocate an address for the value position when we create the continuation. This address and the tail address are both determined by the label of the application point, so the space becomes linear and the overall complexity drops to cubic. This is a critical abstraction in languages with n-ary functions, since otherwise the continuation space grows

[2] Technically, we would have to copy the value of the global store to all states being stepped to fit the formal definition of a widening, but this representation is order-isomorphic to that.

super-exponentially ($\mathcal{O}(n^n)$). We extend the semantics to additionally allocate an address for the function value when creating the `fun` continuation. The continuation has to contain this address to remember where to retrieve values from in the store.

The new evaluation rules follow, where $t' = tick(\varsigma)$:

$$\begin{aligned}\mathtt{co}^t(\mathtt{arg}\ (e, \rho, a_\kappa), v, \sigma) &\longmapsto \mathtt{ev}^{t'}(e, \rho, \sigma', \mathtt{fun}\ (a, a_\kappa))\\ \text{where } a &= alloc(\varsigma)\\ \sigma' &= \sigma \sqcup [a \mapsto \{v\}]\end{aligned}$$

Now instead of storing the evaluated function in the continuation frame itself, we indirect it through the store for further control on complexity and precision:

$$\begin{aligned}\mathtt{co}^t(\mathtt{fun}\ (a, a_\kappa), v, \sigma) &\longmapsto \mathtt{ap}_\ell^{t'}(u, a, \kappa, \sigma')\\ \text{if } \kappa &\in \sigma(a_\kappa), u \in \sigma(a)\\ \text{where } a &= alloc(\varsigma)\\ \sigma' &= \sigma \sqcup [a \mapsto \{v\}]\end{aligned}$$

Associated with this indirection, we now apply all functions stored in the address. This nondeterminism is necessary in order to continue with evaluation.

5. Implementation techniques

In this section, we discuss the optimizations for abstract interpreters that yield our ultimate performance gains. We have two broad categories of these optimizations: (1) pragmatic improvement, (2) transition elimination. The pragmatic improvements reduce overhead and trade space for time by utilizing:

1. timestamped stores;
2. store deltas; and
3. imperative, pre-allocated data structures.

The transition-elimination optimizations reduce the overall number of transitions made by the analyzer by performing:

4. frontier-based semantics;
5. lazy non-determinism; and
6. abstract compilation.

All pragmatic improvements are precision preserving (form complete abstractions), but the semantic changes are not in some cases, for reasons we will describe. We did not observe the precision differences in our evaluation.

We apply the frontier-based semantics combined with timestamped stores as our first step. The move to the imperative will be made last in order to show the effectiveness of these techniques in the purely functional realm.

5.1 Timestamped frontier

The semantics given for store widening in section 4.2, while simple, is wasteful. It also does not model what typical implementations do. It causes all states found so far to step each iteration, even if they are not revisited. This has negative performance *and* precision consequences (changes to the store can travel back in time in straight-line code). We instead use a frontier-based semantics that corresponds to the classic worklist algorithms for analysis. The difference is that the store is not modified in-place, but updated after all frontier states have been processed. This has implications for the analysis' precision and determinism. Specifically, higher precision, and it is deterministic even if set iteration is not.

The state space changes from a store and set of contexts to a set of seen abstract states (context plus store), S, a set of contexts to step (the frontier), F, and a store to step those contexts with, σ:

$$(S, F, \sigma) \;\widehat{\longmapsto}\; (S \cup S', F', \sigma')$$

We constantly see more states, so S is always growing. The frontier, which is what remains to be done, changes. Let's start with the result of stepping all the contexts in F paired with the current store (call it I for intermediate):

$$I = \{(c', \sigma') \mid wn(c, \sigma) \longmapsto wn(c', \sigma'), c \in F\}$$

The next store is the least upper bound of all the stores in I:

$$\sigma' = \bigsqcup \{\sigma \mid (\_, \sigma) \in I\}$$

The next frontier is exactly the states that we found from stepping the last frontier, but have not seen before. They must be *states*, so we pair the contexts with the next store:

$$F' = \{c \mid (c, \_) \in I, (c, \sigma') \notin S\}$$

Finally, we add what we know we had not yet seen to the seen set:

$$S' = \{(c, \sigma') \mid c \in F'\}$$

To inject a program e into this machine, we start off knowing we have seen the first state, and that we need to process the first state:

$$\begin{aligned}inject(e) &= (\{(c_0, \bot)\}, \{c_0\}, \bot)\\ \text{where } c_0 &= \mathtt{ev}\ (e, \bot, \mathtt{halt})\end{aligned}$$

Notice that now S has several copies of the abstract store in it. As it is, this semantics is much less efficient (but still more precise) than the previously proposed semantics because membership checks have to compare entire stores. Checking equality is expensive because the stores within each state are large, and nearly every entry must be checked against every other due to high similarities amongst stores.

And, there is a better way. Shivers' original work on k-CFA was susceptible to the same problem, and he suggested three complementary optimizations: (1) make the store global; (2) update the store imperatively; and (3) associate every change in the store with a version number – its timestamp. Then, put timestamps in states where previously there were stores. Given two states, the analysis can now compare their stores just by comparing their timestamps – a constant-time operation.

There are two subtle losses of precision in Shivers' original timestamp technique that we can fix.

1. In our semantics, the store does not change until the entire frontier has been explored. This avoids cross-branch pollution which would otherwise happen in Shivers' semantics, e.g., when one branch writes to address a and another branch reads from address a.
2. The common implementation strategy for timestamps destructively updates each state's timestamp. This loses *temporal* information about the contexts a state is visited in, and in what order. Our semantics has a drop-in replacement of timestamps for stores in the seen set ($\hat{S}$), so we do not experience precision loss.

$$\Sigma \in Store^* \qquad \hat{S} \subseteq \mathbb{N} \times Context \qquad F \subseteq Context$$

$$(\hat{S}, F, \sigma, \Sigma, t) \widehat{\longmapsto}^T (\hat{S} \cup \hat{S}', F', \sigma', \Sigma', t')$$
$$\text{where } I = \{(c', \sigma^c) \mid wn(c, \sigma) \longmapsto wn(c', \sigma^c), c \in F\}$$
$$\sigma' = \bigsqcup \{\sigma^c \mid (\_, \sigma^c) \in I\}$$
$$(t', \Sigma') = \begin{cases} (t+1, \sigma'\Sigma') & \text{if } \sigma' \neq \sigma \\ (t, \Sigma) & \text{otherwise} \end{cases}$$
$$F' = \{c \mid (c, \_) \in I, (c, t') \notin \hat{S}\}$$
$$\hat{S}' = \{(c, t') \mid c \in F'\}$$
$$inject(e) = (\{(c_0, 0)\}, \{c_0\}, \bot, \bot{:}\epsilon, 0)$$
$$\text{where } c_0 = \texttt{ev}\ (e, \bot, \texttt{halt})$$

The observation Shivers made was that the store is increasing monotonically, so all stores throughout execution will be totally ordered (form a chain). This observation allows you to replace stores with pointers into this chain. We keep the stores around in Σ to achieve a complete abstraction. This corresponds to the temporal information about the execution's effect on the store.

Note also that F is only populated with states that have not been seen at the resulting store. This is what produces the more precise abstraction than the baseline widening.

The general fixed-point combinator we showed above can be specialized to this semantics, as well. In fact, $\widehat{\longmapsto}^T$ is a functional relation, so we can get the least fixed-point of it directly.

Lemma 1. $\widehat{\longmapsto}$ *maintains the invariant that all stores in* S *are totally ordered and* σ *is an upper bound of the stores in* S.

Lemma 2. $\widehat{\longmapsto}^T$ *maintains the invariant that* Σ *is in order with respect to* $\sqsupset$ *and* $\sigma = hd(\Sigma)$.

Theorem 1. $\widehat{\longmapsto}^T$ *is a complete abstraction of* $\widehat{\longmapsto}$.

The proof follows from the order isomorphism that, in one direction, sorts all the stores in S to form Σ, and translates stores in S to their distance from the end of Σ (their timestamp). In the other direction, timestamps in $\hat{S}$ are replaced by the stores they point to in Σ.

5.2 Locally log-based store deltas

The above technique requires joining entire (large) stores together. Additionally, there is still a comparison of stores, which we established is expensive. Not every step will modify all addresses of the store, so joining entire stores is wasteful in terms of memory and time. We can instead log store changes and replay the change log on the full store after all steps have completed, noting when there is an actual change. This uses far fewer join and comparison operations, leading to less overhead, and is precision-preserving.

We represent change logs as $\xi \in \mathit{Store\Delta} = (\mathit{Addr} \times \mathcal{P}(\mathit{Storeable}))^*$. Each $\sigma \sqcup [a \mapsto vs]$ becomes a log addition $(a, vs){:}\xi$, where ξ begins empty (ϵ) for each step. Applying the changes to the full store is straightforward:

$$replay : (\mathit{Store\Delta} \times \mathit{Store}) \to (\mathit{Store} \times \mathit{Boolean})$$
$$replay([(a_i, vs_i), \ldots], \sigma) = (\sigma', \delta?(vs_i, \sigma(a_i)) \vee \ldots)$$
$$\text{where } \sigma' = \sigma \sqcup [a_i \mapsto vs_i] \sqcup \ldots$$
$$\delta?(vs, vs') = vs' \stackrel{?}{=} vs \sqcup vs'$$

We change the semantics slightly to add to the change log rather than produce an entire modified store. The transition relation is identical except for the addition of this change log. We maintain the invariant that lookups will never rely on the change log, so we can use the originally supplied store unmodified.

A taste of the changes to the reduction relation is as follows:

$$\longmapsto_{\sigma\xi} \subseteq (\mathit{Context} \times \mathit{Store}) \times (\mathit{Context} \times \mathit{Store\Delta})$$

$$(\texttt{ap}^t_\ell(\texttt{clos}\ (x, e, \rho), a, \kappa), \sigma) \longmapsto_{\sigma\xi} (\texttt{ev}^{t'}(e, \rho', \kappa), (a', \sigma(a)){:}\epsilon)$$
$$\text{where } a' = alloc(\varsigma)$$
$$\rho' = \rho[x \mapsto a']$$

We lift $\longmapsto_{\sigma\xi}$ to accommodate for the asymmetry in the input and output, and change the frontier-based semantics in the following way:

$$(\hat{S}, F, \sigma, \Sigma, t) \widehat{\longmapsto}_{\sigma\xi} (\hat{S} \cup \hat{S}', F', \sigma', \Sigma', t')$$
$$\text{where } I = \{(c', \xi) \mid (c, \sigma) \longmapsto_{\sigma\xi} (c', \xi)\}$$
$$(\sigma', \Delta?) = replay(appendall(\{\xi \mid (\_, \xi) \in I\}), \sigma)$$
$$(t', \Sigma') = \begin{cases} (t+1, \sigma\Sigma) & \text{if } \Delta? \\ (t, \Sigma) & \text{otherwise} \end{cases}$$
$$F' = \{c \mid (c, \_) \in I, (c, t') \notin \hat{S}\}$$
$$\hat{S}' = \{(c, t') \mid c \in F'\}$$
$$appendall(\varnothing) = \epsilon$$
$$appendall(\{\xi\} \cup \Xi) = append(\xi, appendall(\Xi))$$

Here *appendall* combines change logs across all non-deterministic steps for a state to later be replayed. The order the combination happens in doesn't matter, because join is associative and commutative.

Lemma 3. $(c, \sigma) \longmapsto_{\sigma\xi} (c', \xi)$ *iff* $wn(c, \sigma) \longmapsto wn(c', replay(\xi, \sigma))$

By cases on $\longmapsto_{\sigma\xi}$ and $\longmapsto$.

Lemma 4 ($\Delta?$ means change)**.** *Let* $replay(\xi, \sigma) = (\sigma', \Delta?)$. $\sigma' \neq \sigma$ *iff* $\Delta?$.

By induction on ξ.

Theorem 2. $\widehat{\longmapsto}_{\sigma\xi}$ *is a complete abstraction of* $\widehat{\longmapsto}^T$.

Follows from previous lemma and that join is associative and commutative.

5.3 Lazy non-determinism

Tracing the execution of the analysis reveals an immediate shortcoming: there is a high degree of branching and merging in the exploration. Surveying this branching has no benefit for precision. For example, in a function application, `(f x y)`, where `f`, `x` and `y` each have several values each argument evaluation induces n-way branching, only to be ultimately joined back together in their respective application positions. Transition patterns of this shape litter the state-graph:

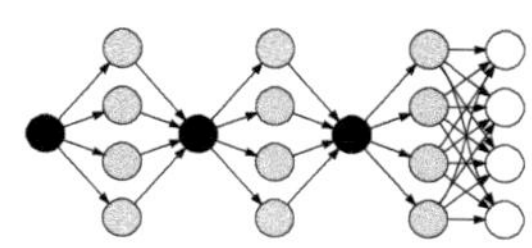

To avoid the spurious forking and joining, we *delay* the non-determinism until and unless it is needed in *strict contexts* (such as the guard of an `if`, a called procedure, or a numerical primitive application). Doing so collapses these forks and joins into a linear sequence of states:

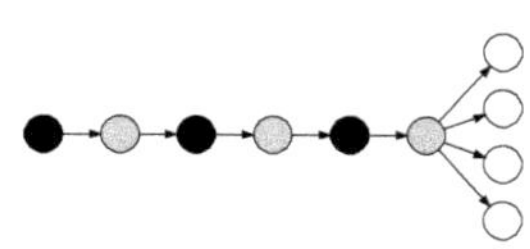

This shift does not change the concrete semantics of the language to be lazy. Rather, it abstracts over transitions that the original non-deterministic semantics steps through. We say the abstraction is *lazy* because it delays splitting on the values in an address until they are *needed* in the semantics. It does not change the execution order that leads to the values that are stored in the address.

We introduce a new kind of value, $\texttt{addr}\ (a)$, that represents a delayed non-deterministic choice of a value from $\sigma(a)$. The following rules highlight the changes to the semantics:

$$\begin{aligned}
&\mathit{force} : \mathit{Store} \times \mathit{Value} \to \mathcal{P}(\mathit{Value})\\
&\mathit{force}(\sigma, \texttt{addr}\ (a)) = \sigma(a)\\
&\mathit{force}(\sigma, v) = \{v\}\\
&\texttt{ev}\ (\texttt{var}\ (x), \rho, \kappa, \sigma) \longmapsto_{\mathcal{L}} \texttt{co}\ (\kappa, \texttt{addr}\ (\rho(x)), \sigma)\\
&\texttt{co}\ (\texttt{arg}^t_\ell(e, \rho, a_\kappa), v, \sigma) \longmapsto_{\mathcal{L}} \texttt{ev}^{t'}(e, \rho, \sigma', \texttt{fun}^t_\ell(a_f, a_\kappa))\\
&\quad \text{where } a_f = \mathit{alloc}(\varsigma)\\
&\quad\quad \sigma' = \sigma \sqcup [a \mapsto \mathit{force}(\sigma\ v)]\\
&\texttt{co}\ (\texttt{ifk}^t(e_0, e_1, \rho, a_\kappa), v, \sigma) \longmapsto_{\mathcal{L}} \texttt{ev}^{t'}(e_0, \rho, \sigma, \kappa)\\
&\quad \text{if } \kappa \in \sigma(a_\kappa), \texttt{tt} \in \mathit{force}(\sigma, v)
\end{aligned}$$

Since `if` guards are in strict position, we must force the value to determine which branch to to take. The middle rule uses *force* only to combine with values in the store - it does not introduce needless non-determinism.

We have two choices for how to implement lazy non-determinism.

Option 1: Lose precision; simplify implementation This semantics introduces a subtle precision difference over the baseline. Consider a configuration where a reference to a variable and a binding of a variable will happen in one step, since store widening leads to stepping several states in one big "step." With laziness, the reference will mean the original binding(s) of the variable *or* the new binding, because the actual store lookup is delayed one step (i.e. laziness is administrative).

Option 2: Regain precision; complicate implementation The administrative nature of laziness means that we could remove the loss in precision by storing the result of the lookup in a value representing a delayed nondeterministic choice. This is a more common choice in 0CFA implementations we have seen, but it interferes with the next optimization due to the invariant from store deltas we have that lookups must not depend on the change log.

Theorem 3 (Soundness). *If $\varsigma \longmapsto \varsigma'$ and $\varsigma \sqsubseteq \hat{\varsigma}$ then there exists a $\hat{\varsigma}'$ such that $\hat{\varsigma} \longmapsto_{\mathcal{L}} \hat{\varsigma}'$ and $\varsigma' \sqsubseteq \hat{\varsigma}'$*

Here $\sqsubseteq$ is straightforward — the left-hand side store must be contained in the right-hand-side store, and if values occur in the states, the left-hand-side value must be in the forced corresponding right-hand-side value. The proof is by cases on $\varsigma \longmapsto \varsigma'$.

5.4 Abstract compilation

The prior optimization saved time by doing the same amount of reasoning as before but in fewer transitions. We can exploit the same idea—same reasoning, fewer transitions—with abstract compilation. Abstract compilation transforms complex expressions whose *abstract* evaluation is deterministic into "abstract bytecodes." The abstract interpreter then does in one transition what previously took many. Refer back to figure 2 to see the effect of abstract compilation. In short, abstract compilation eliminates unnecessary allocation, deallocation and branching. The technique is precision preserving without store widening. We discuss the precision differences with store widening at the end of the section.

The compilation step converts expressions into functions that expect the other components of the `ev` state. Its definition in figure 6 shows close similarity to the rules for interpreting `ev` states. The next step is to change reduction rules that create `ev` states to instead call these functions. Figure 7 shows the modified reduction relation. The only change from the previous semantics is that `ev` state construction is replaced by calling the compiled expression. For notational coherence, we write $\lambda^t(\mathit{args}\ldots)$ for $\lambda(\mathit{args}\ldots, t)$ and $k^t(\mathit{args}\ldots)$ for $k(\mathit{args}\ldots, t)$.

$$\begin{aligned}
&[\![_]\!] : \mathit{Expr} \to \mathit{Store}\\
&\quad \to \mathit{Env} \times \mathit{Store}\Delta \times \mathit{Kont} \times \mathit{Time}\\
&\quad \to \mathit{State}\\
&t' = \mathit{tick}(\ell, \rho, \sigma, t)\\
&[\![\texttt{var}\ (x)]\!]_\sigma = \lambda^t(\rho, \xi, \kappa).\texttt{co}\ (\kappa, \texttt{addr}\ (\rho(x))), \xi\\
&[\![\texttt{lit}\ (l)]\!]_\sigma = \lambda^t(\rho, \xi, \kappa).\texttt{co}\ (\kappa, l), \xi\\
&[\![\texttt{lam}\ (x, e)]\!]_\sigma = \lambda^t(\rho, \xi, \kappa).\texttt{co}\ (\kappa, \texttt{clos}\ (x, [\![e]\!], \rho)), \xi\\
&[\![\texttt{app}^\ell(e_0, e_1)]\!]_\sigma = \lambda^t(\rho, \xi, \kappa).[\![e_0]\!]^{t'}(\rho, \xi', \texttt{arg}^t_\ell([\![e_1]\!], \rho, a_\kappa))\\
&\quad \text{where } a_\kappa = \mathit{allockont}^t_\ell(\sigma, \kappa)\\
&\quad\quad \xi' = (a_\kappa, \{\kappa\}){:}\xi\\
&[\![\texttt{if}^\ell(e_0, e_1, e_2)]\!]_\sigma = \lambda^t(\rho, \xi, \kappa).[\![e_0]\!]^{t'}(\rho, \xi', \texttt{ifk}^t([\![e_1]\!], [\![e_2]\!], \rho, a_\kappa))\\
&\quad \text{where } a_\kappa = \mathit{allockont}^t_\ell(\sigma, \kappa)\\
&\quad\quad \xi' = (a_\kappa, \{\kappa\}){:}\xi
\end{aligned}$$

Figure 6. Abstract compilation

$$\begin{aligned}
&\mathit{traces}(e) = \{\mathit{inject}([\![e]\!]^{t_0}_\bot(\bot, \epsilon, \texttt{halt})) \longmapsto\!\!\!\!\to \varsigma\} \text{ where}\\
&\mathit{inject}(c, \xi) = \mathit{wn}(c, \mathit{replay}(\xi, \bot))\\
&\mathit{wn}(c, \sigma) \longmapsto \mathit{wn}(c', \sigma') \iff c\ [\![\longmapsto]\!]_\sigma\ c', \xi\\
&\xi \text{ is such that } \mathit{replay}(\xi, \sigma) = \sigma'\\[1ex]
&\texttt{co}\ (\texttt{arg}^t_\ell(k, \rho, a_\kappa), v)\ [\![\longmapsto]\!]_\sigma\ k^t(\sigma)(\rho, \xi, \texttt{fun}^t_\ell(a_f, a_\kappa))\\
&\quad \text{where } a_f = \mathit{alloc}(\varsigma)\\
&\quad\quad \xi = (a_f, \mathit{force}(\sigma, v)){:}\epsilon\\
&\texttt{co}\ (\texttt{fun}^t_\ell(a_f, a_\kappa), v)\ [\![\longmapsto]\!]_\sigma\ \texttt{ap}^t_\ell(u, a, \kappa), (a, \mathit{force}(\sigma, v)){:}\epsilon\\
&\quad \text{if } u \in \sigma(a_f), \kappa \in \sigma(a_\kappa)\\
&\texttt{co}\ (\texttt{ifk}^t(k_0, k_1, \rho, a_\kappa), \texttt{tt})\ [\![\longmapsto]\!]_\sigma\ k^t_0(\sigma)(\rho, \epsilon, \kappa) \text{ if } \kappa \in \sigma(a_\kappa)\\
&\texttt{co}\ (\texttt{ifk}^t(k_0, k_1, \rho, a_\kappa), \texttt{ff})\ [\![\longmapsto]\!]_\sigma\ k^t_1(\sigma)(\rho, \epsilon, \kappa) \text{ if } \kappa \in \sigma(a_\kappa)\\[1ex]
&\texttt{ap}^t_\ell(\texttt{clos}\ (x, k, \rho), a, \kappa)\ [\![\longmapsto]\!]_\sigma\ k^{t'}(\sigma)(\rho', \xi, \kappa)\\
&\quad \text{where } \rho' = \rho[x \mapsto a]\\
&\quad\quad \xi = (a, \sigma(a)){:}\epsilon\\
&\texttt{ap}\ (o, a, \kappa)\ [\![\longmapsto]\!]_\sigma\ \texttt{co}\ (\kappa, u), \epsilon\\
&\quad \text{where } v \in \sigma(a), u \in \Delta(o, v)
\end{aligned}$$

Figure 7. Abstract abstract machine for compiled ISWIM

Correctness The correctness of abstract compilation seems obvious, but it has never before been rigorously proved. What constitutes correctness in the case of dropped states, anyway? Applying an abstract bytecode's function does many "steps" in one go, at the end of which, the two semantics line up again (modulo representation of expressions). This constitutes the use of a notion of stuttering. We provide a formal analysis of abstract compilation *without* store widening with a proof of a stuttering bisimulation [3] between this semantics and lazy non-determinism without widening to show precision preservation.

The number of transitions that can occur in succession from an abstract bytecode is roughly bounded by the amount of expression nesting in the program. We can use the expression containment order to prove stuttering bisimulation with a well-founded equivalence bisimulation (WEB) [?]. WEBs are equivalent to the notion of a stuttering bisimulation, but are more amenable to mechanization since they also only require reasoning over one step of the reduction relation. The trick is in defining a well-founded ordering that determines when the two semantics will match up again, what Manolios calls the pair of functions *erankt* and *erankl* (but we don't need *erankl* since the uncompiled semantics doesn't stutter).

We define a refinement, r, from non-compiled to compiled states (built structurally) by "committing" all the actions of an `ev` state (defined similarly to $[\![\_]\!]$, but immediately applies the functions), and subsequently changing all expressions with their compiled variants. Since WEBs are for single transition systems, a WEB refinement is over the disjoint union of our two semantics, and the equivalence relation we use is just that a state is related to its refined state (and itself). Call this relation B.

Before we prove this setup is indeed a WEB, we need one lemma that applying an abstract bytecode's function is equal to refining the corresponding `ev` state:

Lemma 5 (Compile/commit). *Let* $c, \xi' = [\![e]\!]^t_{r(\sigma)}(\rho, \xi, r(\kappa))$. *Let* $wn(c', \sigma') = r(\mathtt{ev}^t(e, \rho, \sigma, \kappa))$. $wn(c, replay(\xi', \sigma)) = wn(c', replay(\xi, \sigma'))$.

The proof is by induction on e.

Theorem 4 (Precision preservation). *B is a WEB on* $\longmapsto_{\mathcal{L}} \uplus \longmapsto$

The proof follows by cases on $\longmapsto_{\mathcal{L}} \uplus \longmapsto$ with the WEB *witness* being the well-order on expressions (with a $\bot$ element), and the following *erankt*, *erankl* functions:

$$\begin{aligned} erankt(\mathtt{ev}^t(e, \rho, \sigma, \kappa)) &= e \\ erankt(\varsigma) &= \bot \quad \text{otherwise} \\ erankl(s, s') &= 0 \end{aligned}$$

All cases are either simple steps or appeals to the well-order on *erankt*'s range. The other rank function, *erankl* is unnecessary, so we just make it the constant 0 function. The $[\![\longmapsto]\!]$ cases are trivial.

Wide store and abstract compilation It is possible for different stores to occur between the different semantics because abstract compilation can change the order in which the store is changed (across steps). This is the case because some "corridor" expressions may compile down to change the store before some others, meaning there is no stuttering relationship with the wide lazy semantics. Although there is a difference pre- and post- abstract compilation, the result is still deterministic in contrast to Shivers' technique. The soundness is in tact since we can add store-widening the correct unwidened semantics with an easy correctness proof. Call $[\![\widehat{\longmapsto}]\!]$ the result of the widening operator from the previous section on $[\![\longmapsto]\!]$.

5.5 Imperative, pre-allocated data structures

Thus far, we have made our optimizations in a purely functional manner. For the final push for performance, we need to dip into the imperative. In this section, we show an alternative representation of the store and seen set that are more space-efficient and are amenable to destructive updates by adhering to a history for each address.

The following transfer function has several components that can be destructively updated, and intermediate sets can be elided by adding to global sets. In fact, the log of store deltas can be removed as well, by updating the store in-place, and on lookup, using the first value timestamped $\leq$ the current timestamp. We start with the purely functional view.

5.5.1 Pure setup for imperative implementation

The store maps to a stack of timestamped sets of abstract values. Throughout this section, we will be taking the parameter t to be the "current time," or the length of the store chain at the beginning of the step.

$$\sigma \in Store = Addr \to ValStack$$
$$V \in ValStack = (\mathbb{N} \times \wp(Storeable))^*$$

To allow imperative store updates, we maintain an invariant that we never look up values tagged at a time in the future:

$$lookup(V, t) = \begin{cases} vs & \text{if } V = (t', vs){:}V', t' \leq t \\ vs' & \text{if } V = (t', vs){:}(t'', vs'){:}V', t' > t \end{cases}$$

To construct this value stack, we have a time-parameterized join operation that also tracks changes to the store. If joining with a time in the future, we just add to it. Otherwise, we're making a change for the future ($t+1$), but only if there is an actual change.

$$\begin{aligned} \sigma \sqcup_t [a \mapsto vs] &= \sigma[a \mapsto V], \Delta? \\ &\text{where } (V, \Delta?) = \sigma(a) \sqcup_t vs \\ \epsilon \sqcup_t vs &= (t, vs), \mathtt{tt} \\ (t', vs){:}V \sqcup_t vs' &= (t', vs \sqcup vs'){:}V, \delta?(vs, vs') \text{ if } t' > t \\ V \sqcup_t vs &= (t+1, vs^*){:}V, \mathtt{tt} \text{ if } vs_t \neq vs^* \\ &\quad \text{where } vs_t = lookup(\sigma(a), t) \\ &\quad\quad vs^* = vs \sqcup vs_t \\ V \sqcup_t vs &= V, \mathtt{ff} \text{ otherwise} \end{aligned}$$

For the purposes of space, we reuse the $[\![\longmapsto]\!]$ semantics, although the *replay* of the produced ξ objects should be in-place, and the *lookup* function should be using this single-threaded store. Because the store has all the temporal information baked into it, we rephrase the core semantics in terms of a transfer function. The least fixed-point of this function gives a more compact representation of the reduction relation of the previous section.

$$\begin{aligned} System &= (\widehat{State} \to \mathbb{N}^*) \times \wp(\widehat{State}) \times Store \times \mathbb{N} \\ \mathcal{F} &: System \to System \\ \mathcal{F}(\hat{S}, F, \sigma, t) &= (\hat{S}', F', \sigma', t') \\ &\text{where } I = \{(c', \xi) \mid c \in F, c\, [\![\longmapsto]\!]_{\sigma^*}\, c', \xi\} \\ \sigma^* &= \lambda a.lookup(\sigma(a), t) \\ (\sigma', \Delta?) &= replay(appendall(\{\xi \mid (\_, \xi) \in I\}), \sigma) \\ t' &= \begin{cases} t+1 & \text{if } \Delta? \\ t & \text{otherwise} \end{cases} \\ F' &= \{c \mid (c, \_) \in I, \Delta? \vee \hat{S}(c) \neq t{:}\_\} \\ \hat{S}' &= \lambda c. \begin{cases} t'{:}\hat{S}(c) & \text{if } c \in F' \\ \hat{S}(c) & \text{otherwise} \end{cases} \end{aligned}$$

We prove semantic equivalence with the previous semantics with a lock-step bisimulation with the stack of stores abstraction, which follow from equational reasoning from the following lemmas:

Lemma 6. *Stores of value stacks completely abstract stacks of stores.*

This depends on some well-formedness conditions about the order of the stacks. The store of value stacks can be translated to a stack of stores by taking successive "snapshots" of the store at different timestamps from the max timestamp it holds down to 0. Vice versa, we replay the changes across adjacent stores in the stack.

We apply a similar construction to the different representation of seen states in order to get the final result:

Theorem 5. *$\mathcal{F}$ is a complete abstraction of $[\![\widehat{\longmapsto}]\!]$.*

5.5.2 Pure to imperative

The intermediate data structures of the above transfer function can all be streamlined into globals that are destructively updated. In particular, there are 5 globals:

1. $\hat{S}$: the *seen* set, though made a map for faster membership tests and updates.
2. F: the *frontier* set, which must be persisent or copied for the iteration through the set to be correct.
3. σ: the store, which represents all stores that occur in the machine semantics.
4. t: the timestamp, or length of the store chain.
5. $\Delta?$: whether the store changed when stepping states in F.

The reduction relation would then instead of building store deltas, update the global store. We would also not view it as a general relation, but a function that adds all next states to F if they have not already been seen. At the end of iterating through F, $\hat{S}$ is updated with the new states at the next timestamp. There is no cross-step store poisoning since the lookup is restricted to the current step's time, which points to the same value throughout the step.

5.5.3 Pre-allocating the store

Internally, the algorithm at this stage uses hash tables to model the store to allow arbitrary address representations. But, such a dynamic structure isn't necessary when we know the structure of the store in advance.In a monovariant allocation strategy, the domain of the store is bounded by the number of expressions in the program. If we label each expression with a unique natural, the analysis can index directly into the store without a hash or a collision. Even for polyvariant analyses, it is possible to compute the maximum number of addresses and similarly pre-allocate either the spine of the store or (if memory is no concern) the entire store.

6. Evaluation

We have implemented, optimized, and evaluated an analysis framework supporting higher-order functions, state, first-class control, compound data, and a large number of primitive kinds of data and operations such as floating point, complex, and exact rational arithmetic. The analysis is evaluated against a suite of Scheme benchmarks drawn from the literature. [3] For each benchmark, we collect analysis times, peak memory usage (as determined by Racket's GC statistics), and the rate of states-per-second explored by the analysis for each of the optimizations discussed in section 5 cumulatively applied. The analysis is stopped after consuming 30 minutes of time or 1 gigabyte of space [4]. When presenting *relative* numbers, we use the timeout limits as a lower bound on the actual time required (i.e., one minute versus timeout is at least 30 times faster) thus giving a conservative estimate of improvements.

For those benchmarks that did complete on the baseline, the optimized analyzer outperformed the baseline by a factor of two to three orders of magnitude.

We use the following set of benchmarks:

Program	LOC	Time (sec)		Space (MB)		Speed $\frac{state}{sec}$	
nucleic	3492	m	66.9	m	238	44	9K
matrix	747	t	3.4	294	114	68	87K
nbody	1435	t	22.9	361	171	67	57K
earley	667	1.1K	0.4	409	114	252	95K
maze	681	t	2.6	332	114	55	118K
church	42	44.9	0.1	86	114	714	56K
lattice	214	348.5	0.2	231	114	382	104K
boyer	642	m	13.4	m	130	39	39K
mbrotZ	69	373.6	0.1	295	114	540	63K

Figure 8. Overview performance comparison between baseline and optimized analyzer (entries of t mean timeout, and m mean out of memory)

1. **nucleic**: a floating-point intensive application taken from molecular biology that has been used widely in benchmarking functional language implementations [13] and analyses (e.g. [14, 34]). It is a constraint satisfaction algorithm used to determine the three-dimensional structure of nucleic acids.
2. **matrix** tests whether a matrix is maximal among all matrices of the same dimension obtainable by simple reordering of rows and columns and negation of any subset of rows and columns. It is written in continuation-passing style (used in [14, 34]).
3. **nbody**: implementation [35] of the Greengard multipole algorithm for computing gravitational forces on point masses distributed uniformly in a cube (used in [14, 34]).
4. **earley**: Earley's parsing algorithm, applied to a 15-symbol input according to a simple ambiguous grammar. A real program, applied to small data whose exponential behavior leads to a peak heap size of half a gigabyte or more during concrete execution.
5. **maze**: generates a random maze using Scheme's `call/cc` operation and finds a path solving the maze (used in [14, 34]).
6. **church**: tests distributivity of multiplication over addition for Church numerals (introduced by [33]).
7. **lattice**: enumerates the order-preserving maps between two finite lattices (used in [14, 34]).
8. **boyer**: a term-rewriting theorem prover (used in [14, 34]).
9. **mbrotZ**: generates Mandelbrot fractal using complex numbers.
10. **graphs**: counts the number of directed graphs with a distinguished root and k vertices, each having out-degree at most 2. It is written in a continuation-passing style and makes extensive use of higher-order procedures—it creates closures almost as often as it performs non-tail procedure calls (used by [14, 34]).

Figure 8 gives an overview of the benchmark results in terms of absolute time, space, and speed between the baseline and most optimized analyzer. Figure 9 plots the factors of improvement over the baseline for each optimization step.

To determine the impact of each section's technique on precision, we evaluated a singleton variable analysis to find opportunities to inline constants and closed functions. We found no change in the results across all implementations, including Shivers' timestamp approximation—from an empirical point of view, these techniques are precision preserving despite the theoretical loss of precision.

Our step-wise optimizations strictly produce better analysis times with no observed loss of precision. The final result is a systematically derived and verified implementation that operates within a small factor performance loss compared to a hand-

[3] Source code of the implementation and benchmark suite available at `https://github.com/dvanhorn/oaam`

[4] All benchmarks are calculated as an average of 5 runs, done in parallel (each isolated to a core), on an 12-core, 64-bit Intel Xeon machine running at 2.40GHz with 12Gb of memory.

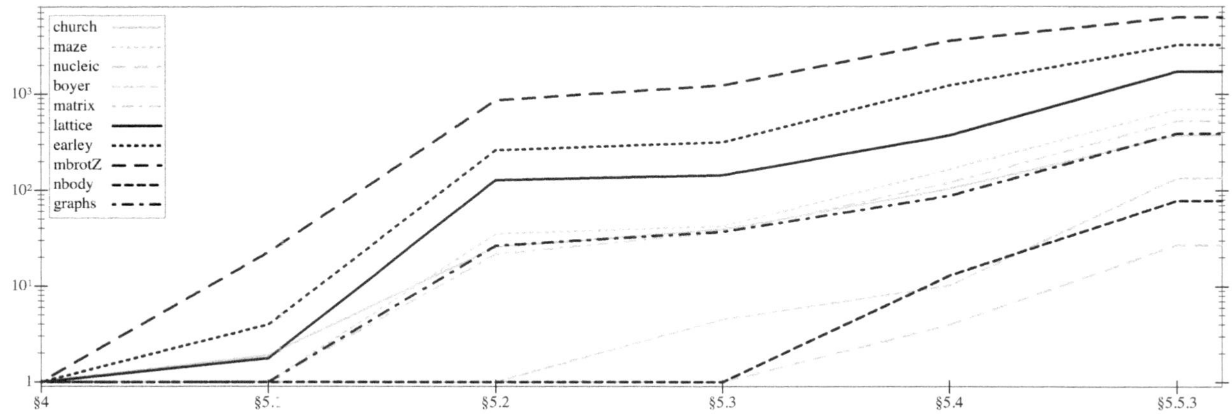

(a) Total analysis time speed-up (baseline / optimized)

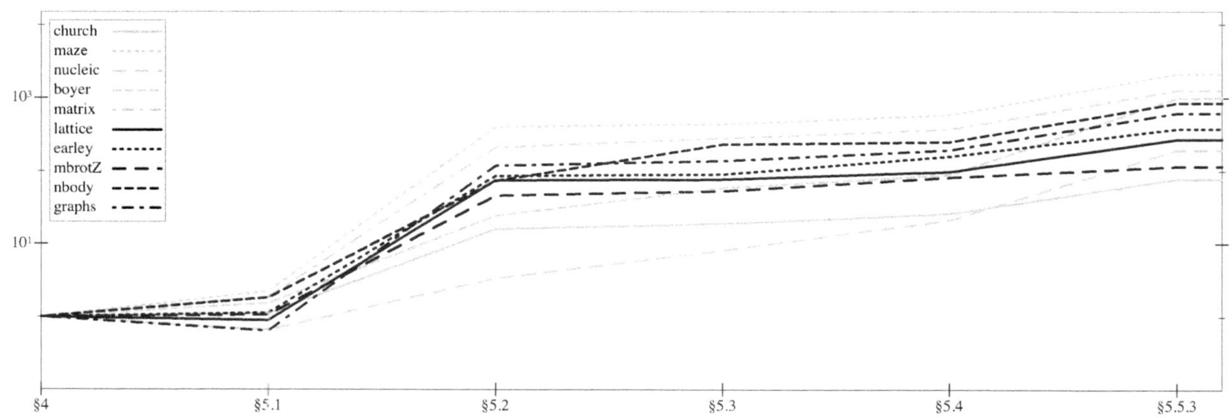

(b) Rate of state transitions speed-up (optimized / baseline)

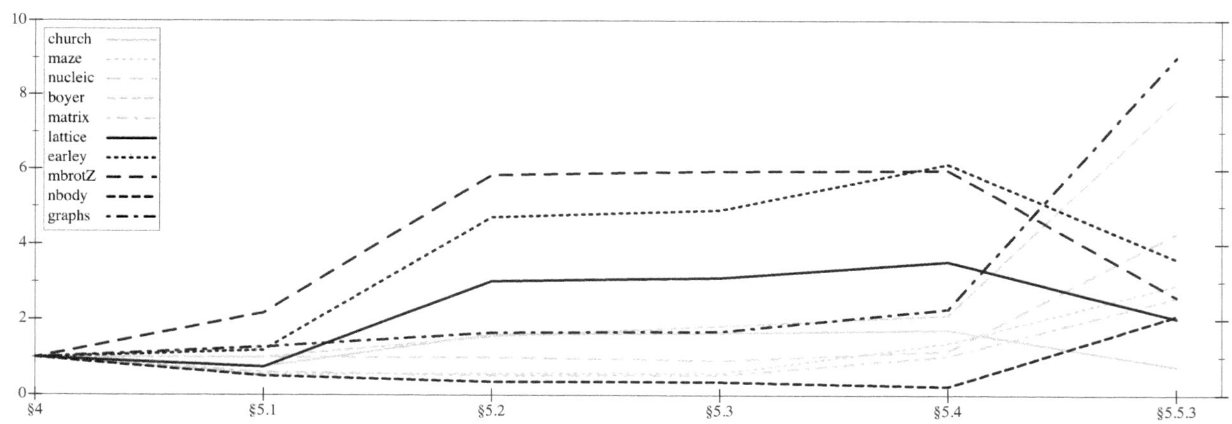

(c) Peak memory usage improvement (baseline / optimized)

Figure 9. Factors of improvement over baseline for each step of optimization (bigger is better).

optimized, unverified implementation. Moreover, much of the performance gains are achieved with purely functional methods, which allow the use of these methods in rewriting tools and others with restricted input languages. Peak memory usage is often considerably improved by the end of the optimization steps, but the effect of mutation has unexpected consequence on the analyzers memory consumption, likely due to a larger-than-necessary preallocated store.

Comparison with other flow analysis implementations The analysis considered here computes results similar to Earl, et al.'s 0-CFA implementation [10], which times out on the Vardculakis and Shivers benchmark because it does not widen the store as described for our baseline evaluator. So even though it offers a fair point of comparison, a more thorough evaluation is probably uninformative as the other benchmarks are likely to timeout as well (and it would require significant effort to extend their implementation with the features needed to analyze our benchmark suite). That implementation is evaluated against much smaller benchmarks: the largest program is 30 lines.

Vardoulakis and Shivers evaluate their CFA2 analyzer [33] against a variant of 0-CFA defined in their framework and the example we draw on is the largest benchmark Vardoulakis and Shivers consider. More work would be required to scale the analyzer to the set of features required by our benchmarks.

The only analyzer we were able to find that proved capable of analyzing the full suite of benchmarks considered here was the Polymorphic splitting system of Wright and Jagannathan [34]. [5] Unfortunately, these analyses compute an inherently different and incomparable form of analysis via a global acceptability judgment. Consequently, we have omitted a complete comparison with these implementations. The AAM approach provides more precision in terms of temporal-ordering of program states, which comes at a cost that can be avoided in constraint-based approaches. Consequently implementation techniques cannot be "ported" between these two approaches. However, our optimized implementation is within an order of magnitude of the performance of Wright and Jaganathan's analyzer. Although we would like to improve this to be more competitive, the optimized AAM approach still has many strengths to recommend it in terms of precision, ease of implementation and verification, and rapid design. We can get closer to their performance by relying on the representation of addresses and the behavior of $alloc$ to pre-allocate most data structures and split the abstract store out into parts that are more quickly accessed and updated. Our semantic optimizations can still be applied to an analysis that does abstract garbage collection [22], whereas the polymorphic splitting implementation is tied strongly to a single-threaded store.

7. Related work

Abstracting Abstract Machines This work clearly closely follows Van Horn and Might's original papers on abstracting abstract machines [30, 32], which in turn is one piece of the large body of research on flow analysis for higher-order languages (see Midtgaard [19] for a thorough survey). The AAM approach sits at the confluence of two major lines of research: (1) the study of abstract machines [17] and their systematic construction [27], and (2) the theory of abstract interpretation [4, 5].

Frameworks for flow analysis of higher-order programs Besides the original AAM work, the analysis most similar to that presented in section 3 is the infinitary control-flow analysis of Nielson and Nielson [25] and the unified treatment of flow analysis by Jagannathan and Weeks [15]. Both are parameterized in such a way that in the limit, the analysis is equivalent to an interpreter for the language, just as is the case here. What is different is that both give a constraint-based formulation of the abstract semantics rather than a finite machine model.

Abstract compilation Boucher and Feeley [1] introduced the idea of abstract compilation, which used closure generation [11] to improve the performance of control flow analysis. We have adapted the closure generation technique from compositional evaluators to abstract machines and applied it to similar effect.

Constraint-based program analysis for higher-order languages Constraint-based program analyses (e.g. [18, 25, 28, 34]) typically compute sets of abstract values for each program point. These values approximate values arising at run-time for each program point. Value sets are computed as the least solution to a set of (inclusion or equality) constraints. The constraints must be designed and proved as a sound approximation of the semantics. Efficient implementations of these kinds of analyses often take the form of worklist-based graph algorithms for constraint solving, and are thus quite different from the interpreter implementation. The approach thus requires effort in constraint system design and implementation, and the resulting system require verification effort to prove the constraint system is sound and that the implementation is correct.

This effort increases substantially as the complexity of the analyzed language increases. Both the work of maintaining the concrete semantics and constraint system (and the relations between them) must be scaled simultaneously. However, constraint systems, which have been extensively studied in their own right, enjoy efficient implementation techniques and can be expressed in declarative logic languages that are heavily optimized [2]. Consequently, constraint-based analyses can be computed quickly. For example, Jagannathan and Wright's polymorphic splitting implementation [34] analyses the Vardoulakis and Shivers benchmark about 5.5 times faster than the fastest implementation considered here. These analyses compute very different things, so the performance comparison is not apples-to-apples.

The AAM approach, and the state transition graphs it generates, encodes temporal properties not found in classical constraint-based analyses for higher-order programs. Such analyses (ultimately) compute judgments on program terms and contexts, e.g., at expression e, variable x may have value v. The judgments do not relate the order in which expressions and context may be evaluated in a program, e.g., it has nothing to say with regard to question like, "Do we always evaluate e_1 before e_2?"The state transition graphs can answer these kinds of queries, but evaluation demonstrated this does not come for free.

8. Conclusion

Abstract machines are not only a good model for rapid analysis development, they can be systematically developed into efficient algorithms that can be proved correct. We view the primary contribution of this work as a systematic path that eases the design, verification, and implementation of analyses using the abstracting abstract machine approach to within a factor of performant constraint-based analyses.

Acknowledgments We thank Suresh Jagannathan for providing source code to the polymorphic splitting analyzer [34] and Ilya Sergey for the introspective pushdown analyzer [10]. We thank Sam Tobin-Hochstadt for encouragement and feedback—he was the first to prompt us to look into how to make effective implementations of the AAM approach. We thank Vincent St-Amour and Mitchell Wand for feedback on early drafts and Greg Morrisett and Matthias Felleisen for discussions. We thank our anonymous reviewers for their detailed comments. This material is based on re-

[5] This is not a coincidence; these papers set a high standard for evaluation, which we consciously aimed to approach.

search sponsored by DARPA under the programs Automated Program Analysis for Cybersecurity (FA8750-12-2-0106) and Clean-Slate Resilient Adaptive Hosts (CRASH). The U.S. Government is authorized to reproduce and distribute reprints for Governmental purposes notwithstanding any copyright notation thereon.

References

[1] Dominique Boucher and Marc Feeley. Abstract compilation: A new implementation paradigm for static analysis. In Tibor Gyimóthy, editor, *Compiler Construction: 6th International Conference, CC'96 Linköping, Sweden, April 2426, 1996 Proceedings*, pages 192–207, 1996.

[2] Martin Bravenboer and Yannis Smaragdakis. Strictly declarative specification of sophisticated points-to analyses. In *OOPSLA '09: Proceedings of the 24th annual ACM SIGPLAN Conference on Object-Oriented Programming, Systems, Languages, and Applications*, 2009.

[3] M. C. Browne, E. M. Clarke, and O. Grümberg. Characterizing finite kripke structures in propositional temporal logic. *Theor. Comput. Sci.*, 59(1-2):115–131, 1988.

[4] Patrick Cousot and Radhia Cousot. Abstract interpretation: a unified lattice model for static analysis of programs by construction or approximation of fixpoints. In *POPL '77: Proceedings of the 4th ACM SIGACT-SIGPLAN Symposium on Principles of Programming Languages*, pages 238–252. ACM, 1977.

[5] Patrick Cousot and Radhia Cousot. Systematic design of program analysis frameworks. In *Proceedings of the 6th ACM SIGACT-SIGPLAN Symposium on Principles of Programming Languages*, POPL '79, pages 269–282. ACM, 1979.

[6] Olivier Danvy. *An Analytical Approach to Program as Data Objects*. DSc thesis, Department of Computer Science, Aarhus University, 2006.

[7] Olivier Danvy and Lasse R. Nielsen. Refocusing in reduction semantics. Research Report BRICS RS-04-26, Department of Computer Science, Aarhus University, 2004.

[8] E. D'Osualdo, J. Kochems, and C.-H. L. Ong. Automatic verification of Erlang-style concurrency. Technical report, University of Oxford DCS Technical Report, 2012. `http://mjolnir.cs.ox.ac.uk/soter/papers/erlang-verif.pdf`.

[9] E. D'Osualdo, J. Kochems, and C.-H. L. Ong. Soter: An automatic safety verifier for Erlang. Technical report, University of Oxford DCS Technical Report, 2012. `http://mjolnir.cs.ox.ac.uk/soter/papers/soter-demo.pdf`.

[10] Christopher Earl, Ilya Sergey, Matthew Might, and David Van Horn. Introspective pushdown analysis of higher-order programs. In *Proceedings of the 17th ACM SIGPLAN International Conference on Functional Programming*, ICFP '12, pages 177–188. ACM, 2012.

[11] Marc Feeley and Guy Lapalme. Using closures for code generation. *Comput. Lang.*, 12(1):47–66, 1987.

[12] Matthias Felleisen, Robert B. Findler, and Matthew Flatt. *Semantics Engineering with PLT Redex*. MIT Press, 2009.

[13] Pieter H. Hartel, Marc Feeley, Martin Alt, Lennart Augustsson, Peter Baumann, Marcel Beemster, Emmanuel Chailloux, Christine H. Flood, Wolfgang Grieskamp, John H. G. Van Groningen, Kevin Hammond, Bogumil Hausman, Melody Y. Ivory, Richard E. Jones, Jasper Kamperman, Peter Lee, Xavier Leroy, Rafael D. Lins, Sandra Loosemore, Niklas Röjemo, Manuel Serrano, Jean P. Talpin, Jon Thackray, Stephen Thomas, Pum Walters, Pierre Weis, and Peter Wentworth. Benchmarking implementations of functional languages with "pseudoknot", a float-intensive benchmark. *Journal of Functional Programming*, 6(04):621–655, 1996.

[14] Suresh Jagannathan, Peter Thiemann, Stephen Weeks, and Andrew Wright. Single and loving it: must-alias analysis for higher-order languages. In *POPL '98: Proceedings of the 25th ACM SIGPLAN-SIGACT Symposium on Principles of Programming Languages*, pages 329–341. ACM, 1998.

[15] Suresh Jagannathan and Stephen Weeks. A unified treatment of flow analysis in higher-order languages. In *POPL '95: Proceedings of the 22nd ACM SIGPLAN-SIGACT Symposium on Principles of Programming Languages*, pages 393–407. ACM Press, 1995.

[16] P. J. Landin. The next 700 programming languages. *Commun. ACM*, 9(3):157–166, 1966.

[17] Peter J. Landin. The mechanical evaluation of expressions. *The Computer Journal*, 6(4):308–320, 1964.

[18] Philippe Meunier, Robert B. Findler, and Matthias Felleisen. Modular set-based analysis from contracts. In *POPL '06: Conference record of the 33rd ACM SIGPLAN-SIGACT Symposium on Principles of Programming Languages*, pages 218–231. ACM, 2006.

[19] Jan Midtgaard. Control-flow analysis of functional programs. *ACM Computing Surveys*, 2011.

[20] Matthew Might and David Van Horn. A family of abstract interpretations for static analysis of concurrent Higher-Order programs. In Eran Yahav, editor, *Static Analysis*, volume 6887 of *Lecture Notes in Computer Science*, pages 180–197. Springer Berlin Heidelberg, 2011.

[21] Matthew Might and Panagiotis Manolios. A posteriori soundness for non-deterministic abstract interpretations. In *Proceedings of the 10th International Conference on Verification, Model Checking, and Abstract Interpretation*, VMCAI '09, pages 260–274. Springer-Verlag, 2009.

[22] Matthew Might and Olin Shivers. Improving flow analyses via ΓCFA: Abstract garbage collection and counting. In *Proceedings of the 11th ACM International Conference on Functional Programming (ICFP 2006)*, pages 13–25, 2006.

[23] Matthew Might and David Van Horn. Scalable and precise abstractions of programs for trustworthy software. Technical report, 2012.

[24] Greg Morrisett. Harvard university course cs252r: Advanced functional language compilation. `http://www.eecs.harvard.edu/~greg/cs252rfa12/`.

[25] Flemming Nielson and Hanne R. Nielson. Infinitary control flow analysis: a collecting semantics for closure analysis. In *POPL '97: Proceedings of the 24th ACM SIGPLAN-SIGACT Symposium on Principles of Programming Languages*, pages 332–345. ACM Press, 1997.

[26] G. D. Plotkin. A structural approach to operational semantics. Technical Report DAIMI FN-19, 1981.

[27] John C. Reynolds. Definitional interpreters for Higher-Order programming languages. *Higher-Order and Symbolic Computation*, 11(4):363–397, 1998.

[28] Paul A. Steckler and Mitchell Wand. Lightweight closure conversion. *ACM Trans. Program. Lang. Syst.*, 19(1):48–86, 1997.

[29] Sam Tobin-Hochstadt and David Van Horn. Higher-order symbolic execution via contracts. In *Proceedings of the ACM International Conference on Object Oriented Programming Systems Languages and Applications*, OOPSLA '12, pages 537–554. ACM, 2012.

[30] David Van Horn and Matthew Might. Abstracting abstract machines: a systematic approach to higher-order program analysis. *Communications of the ACM*, 54:101–109, 2011.

[31] David Van Horn and Matthew Might. An analytic framework for JavaScript. *CoRR*, abs/1109.4467, 2011.

[32] David Van Horn and Matthew Might. Systematic abstraction of abstract machines. *Journal of Functional Programming*, 22(Special Issue 4-5):705–746, 2012.

[33] Dimitrios Vardoulakis and Olin Shivers. CFA2: a Context-Free approach to Control-Flow analysis. *Logical Methods in Computer Science*, 7(2), 2011.

[34] Andrew K. Wright and Suresh Jagannathan. Polymorphic splitting: an effective polyvariant flow analysis. *ACM Trans. Program. Lang. Syst.*, 20(1):166–207, 1998.

[35] Feng Zhao. An O(N) algorithm for Three-Dimensional N-Body simulations. Master's thesis, MIT, 1987.

Testing Noninterference, Quickly

Cătălin Hriţcu[1] John Hughes[2] Benjamin C. Pierce[1] Antal Spector-Zabusky[1] Dimitrios Vytiniotis[3]
Arthur Azevedo de Amorim[1] Leonidas Lampropoulos[1]

[1]University of Pennsylvania [2]Chalmers University [3]Microsoft Research

Abstract

Information-flow control mechanisms are difficult to design and labor intensive to prove correct. To reduce the time wasted on proof attempts doomed to fail due to broken definitions, we advocate modern random testing techniques for finding counterexamples during the design process. We show how to use QuickCheck, a property-based random-testing tool, to guide the design of a simple information-flow abstract machine. We find that both sophisticated strategies for generating well-distributed random programs and readily falsifiable formulations of noninterference properties are critically important. We propose several approaches and evaluate their effectiveness on a collection of injected bugs of varying subtlety. We also present an effective technique for shrinking large counterexamples to minimal, easily comprehensible ones. Taken together, our best methods enable us to quickly and automatically generate simple counterexamples for all these bugs.

Categories and Subject Descriptors D.2.5 [*Testing and Debugging*]: Testing tools (e.g., data generators, coverage testing); D.4.6 [*Security and Protection*]: Information flow controls

General Terms Security, Languages, Design

Keywords random testing; security; design; dynamic information-flow control; noninterference; abstract machine; QuickCheck

1. Introduction

Secure information-flow control (IFC) is nearly impossible to achieve by careful design alone. The mechanisms involved are intricate and easy to get wrong: static type systems must impose numerous constraints that interact with other typing rules in subtle ways, while dynamic mechanisms must appropriately propagate taints and raise security exceptions when necessary. This intricacy makes it hard to be confident in the correctness of such mechanisms without detailed proofs; however, carrying out these proofs while designing the mechanisms can be an exercise in frustration, with a great deal of time spent attempting to verify broken definitions! The question we address in this paper is: Can we use modern *testing* techniques to discover bugs in IFC enforcement mechanisms quickly and effectively? If so, then we can use testing to catch most errors during the design phase, postponing proof attempts until we are reasonably confident that the design is correct.

ICFP '13, September 25–27, 2013, Boston, MA, USA.

ACM 978-1-4503-2326-0/13/09... $15.00.
http://dx.doi.org/10.1145/2500365.2500574

To answer this question, we take as a case study the task of extending a simple abstract stack-and-pointer machine to track dynamic information flow and enforce termination-insensitive noninterference [23]. Although our machine is simple, this exercise is both nontrivial and novel. While simpler notions of dynamic *taint tracking* are well studied for both high- and low-level languages, it has only recently been shown [1, 24] that dynamic checks are capable of soundly enforcing strong security properties. Moreover, sound dynamic IFC has been studied only in the context of lambda-calculi [1, 16, 25] and While programs [24]; the unstructured control flow of a low-level machine poses additional challenges. (Testing of static IFC mechanisms is left as future work.)

We show how QuickCheck [9], a popular property-based testing tool, can be used to formulate and test noninterference properties of our abstract machine, quickly find a variety of missing-taint and missing-exception bugs, and incrementally guide the design of a correct version of the machine. One significant challenge is that both the strategy for generating random programs and the precise formulation of the noninterference property have a dramatic impact on the time required to discover bugs; we benchmark several variations of each to identify the most effective choices. In particular, we observe that checking the unwinding conditions [14] of our noninterference property can be much more effective than directly testing the original property.

Our results should be of interest both to researchers in language-based security, who can now add random testing to their tools for debugging subtle enforcement mechanisms; and to the random-testing community, where our techniques for generating and shrinking random programs may be useful for checking other properties of abstract machines. Our primary contributions are: (1) a demonstration of the effectiveness of random testing for discovering counterexamples to noninterference in a low-level information-flow machine; (2) a range of program generation strategies for finding such counterexamples; (3) an empirical comparison of how effective combinations of these strategies and formulations of noninterference are in finding counterexamples; and (4) an effective methodology for shrinking large counterexamples to smaller, more readable ones. Our information-flow abstract machine, while simple, is also novel, and may be a useful artifact for further research.

2. Basic IFC

We begin by introducing the core of our abstract machine. In §5 we will extend this simple core with control flow (jumps and procedure calls), but the presence of pointers already raises opportunities for some subtle mistakes in information-flow control.

We write $[]$ for the empty list and $x : s$ for the list whose first element is x and whose tail is s; we also write $[x_0, x_1, \ldots, x_n]$ for the list $x_0 : x_1 : \cdots : x_n : []$. If l is a list and $0 \leq j < |l|$, then $l(j)$ selects the jth element of l and $l\{j \mapsto x\}$ produces the list that is like l except that the jth element is replaced by x.

Bare machine Our basic machine (without information-flow labels) has seven instructions:

$$\textit{Instr} ::= \textit{Push}\ x \mid \textit{Pop} \mid \textit{Load} \mid \textit{Store} \mid \textit{Add} \mid \textit{Noop} \mid \textit{Halt}$$

The x argument to *Push* is an integer (an immediate constant).

A machine state S is a 4-tuple consisting of a program counter pc (an integer), a stack s (a list of integers), a memory m (another list of integers), and an instruction memory i (a list of instructions), written $\boxed{pc \mid s \mid m \mid i}$. Often, i will be fixed in some context and we will write just $\boxed{pc \mid s \mid m}$ for the varying parts of the machine state.

The single-step reduction relation on machine states, written $S \Rightarrow S'$, is straightforward to define; we elide it here, for brevity. (It is included in a longer version of the paper, available from `http://www.crash-safe.org/node/24`.) This relation is a partial function: it is deterministic, but some machine states don't step to anything. Such a stuck machine state is said to be *halted* if $i(pc) = \textit{Halt}$ and *failed* in all other cases (e.g., if the machine is trying to execute an *Add* with an empty stack, or if the pc points outside the bounds of the instruction memory). We write $\Rightarrow^*$ for the reflexive, transitive closure of $\Rightarrow$. When $S \Rightarrow^* S'$ and S' is a halted state, we write $S \Downarrow S'$.

Machine with labeled data In a (fine-grained) dynamic IFC system [1, 16, 24, 25] security levels (called labels) are attached to runtime values and propagated during execution, enforcing the constraint that information derived from secret data does not leak to untrusted processes or to the public network. Each value is protected by an individual IFC label representing a security level (e.g., secret or public). We now add labeled data to our simple stack machine. Instead of bare integers, the basic data items in the instruction and data memories and the stack are now *values* of the form $x@L$, where x is an integer and L is either $\bot$ (public) or $\top$ (secret). We order labels by $\bot \sqsubseteq \top$and write $L_1 \vee L_2$ for the *join* (least upper bound) of L_1 and L_2. When v is a value, we write $\mathcal{L}_v$ for v's label part and $v@L$ for the value obtained by joining L to $\mathcal{L}_v$—i.e., $(x@L_1)@L_2 = x@(L_1 \vee L_2)$.

The instructions are exactly the same except that the immediate argument to *Push* becomes a value. Machine states have the same shape as the basic machine, with the stack and memory now being lists of values. The set of *initial* states of this machine, *Init*, contains states of the form $\boxed{0 \mid [\,] \mid m_0 \mid i}$, where m_0 can be of any length and contains only $0@\bot$. We use *Halted* to denote the set of halted states of the machine.

Noninterference (EENI) We define what it means for this basic IFC machine to be "secure" using a standard notion of termination-insensitive noninterference [1, 16, 23]; we call it *end-to-end noninterference* (or *EENI*) to distinguish it from the stronger notions we will introduce in §6. The main idea of EENI is to directly encode the intuition that secret inputs should not influence public outputs. By secret inputs we mean values labeled $\top$ in the initial state; because of the form of our initial states, such values can appear only in instruction memories. By secret outputs we mean values labeled $\top$ in a halted state. More precisely, EENI states that for any two executions starting from initial states that are *indistinguishable to a low observer* (or just *indistinguishable*) and ending in halted states H_1 and H_2, the final states H_1 and H_2 are also indistinguishable. Intuitively, two states are indistinguishable if they differ only in values labeled $\top$. To make this formal, we define an equivalence relation on states compositionally from equivalence relations over their components.

2.1 Definition: Two values $x_1@L_1$ and $x_2@L_2$ are said to be *indistinguishable*, written $x_1@L_1 \approx x_2@L_2$, if either $L_1 = L_2 = \top$ or else $x_1 = x_2$ and $L_1 = L_2 = \bot$. Two instructions i_1 and i_2 are indistinguishable if they are the same instruction, or if $i_1 = \textit{Push}\ v_1$, and $i_2 = \textit{Push}\ v_2$, and $v_1 \approx v_2$. Two lists (memories, stacks, or instruction memories) l_1 and l_2 are indistinguishable if they have the same length and $l_1(x) \approx l_2(x)$ for all x such that $0 \le x < |l_1|$.

For machine states we have a choice as to how much of the state we want to consider observable; we choose (somewhat arbitrarily) that the observer can only see the data and instruction memories, but not the stack or the pc. (Other choices would give the observer either somewhat more power—e.g., we could make the stack and pc observable—or somewhat less—e.g., we could restrict the observer to some designated region of "I/O memory," or extend the architecture with I/O instructions and only observe the traces of inputs and outputs.)

2.2 Definition: Machine states $S_1 = \boxed{pc_1 \mid s_1 \mid m_1 \mid i_1}$ and $S_2 = \boxed{pc_2 \mid s_2 \mid m_2 \mid i_2}$ are *indistinguishable with respect to memories*, written $S_1 \approx_{mem} S_2$, if $m_1 \approx m_2$ and $i_1 \approx i_2$.

2.3 Definition: A machine semantics is *end-to-end noninterfering* with respect to some sets of states *Start* and *End* and an indistinguishability relation $\approx$, written $\text{EENI}_{\textit{Start},\textit{End},\approx}$, if for any $S_1, S_2 \in \textit{Start}$ and $H_1, H_2 \in \textit{End}$ such that $S_1 \approx S_2$ and such that $S_1 \Downarrow H_1$ and $S_2 \Downarrow H_2$, we have $H_1 \approx H_2$.

We take $\text{EENI}_{\textit{Init},\textit{Halted},\approx_{mem}}$ as our baseline security property; i.e., we only consider executions starting in initial states and ending in halted states, and we use indistinguishability with respect to memories. The EENI definition above is, however, more general, and we will consider other instantiations of it later.

Information-flow rules Our next task is to enrich the rules for the step function to take information-flow labels into account. For most of the rules, there are multiple plausible ways to do this, and some opportunities for subtle mistakes even with these few instructions. To illustrate the design methodology we hope to support, we first propose a naive set of rules and then use QuickCheck-generated counterexamples to identify and help repair mistakes until no more can be found.

$$\frac{i(pc) = \textit{Noop}}{\boxed{pc \mid s \mid m} \Rightarrow \boxed{pc{+}1 \mid s \mid m}} \quad (\textsc{Noop})$$

$$\frac{i(pc) = \textit{Push}\ v}{\boxed{pc \mid s \mid m} \Rightarrow \boxed{pc{+}1 \mid v : s \mid m}} \quad (\textsc{Push})$$

$$\frac{i(pc) = \textit{Pop}}{\boxed{pc \mid v : s \mid m} \Rightarrow \boxed{pc{+}1 \mid s \mid m}} \quad (\textsc{Pop})$$

$$\frac{i(pc) = \textit{Load}}{\boxed{pc \mid x@L_x : s \mid m} \Rightarrow \boxed{pc{+}1 \mid m(x) : s \mid m}} \quad (\textsc{Load}^*)$$

$$\frac{i(pc) = \textit{Store}}{\boxed{pc \mid x@L_x : v : s \mid m} \Rightarrow \boxed{pc{+}1 \mid s \mid m\{x \mapsto v\}}} \quad (\textsc{Store}^*\textsc{ab})$$

$$\frac{i(pc) = \textit{Add}}{\boxed{pc \mid x@L_x : y@L_y : s \mid m} \Rightarrow \boxed{pc{+}1 \mid (x{+}y)@\bot : s \mid m}} \quad (\textsc{Add}^*)$$

The NOOP rule is the same as in the unlabeled machine. In the PUSH and POP rules, we simply change the relevant integers to be labeled values; luckily, this obvious adaptation happens to be correct. But now our luck runs out: the simple changes that we've made in the other rules will all turn out to be wrong. (We include a star in the names of incorrect rules to indicate this. The rule STORE*AB actually contains *two* bugs, which we refer to as A and B; we will discuss them separately later.) Fortunately, QuickCheck can rapidly pinpoint the problems, as we will see.

Figure 1 shows the first counterexample that QuickCheck gives us when we present it with the step function defined by the six rules above and ask it to try to invalidate the EENI property. (The LaTeX source for all the figures was generated automatically by our QuickCheck testing infrastructure.) The first line of the figure is the counterexample itself: a pair of four-instruction programs, differing only in the constant argument of the second *Push*. The first program pushes $0@\top$, while the second pushes $1@\top$, and these two values are indistinguishable. We display the two programs, and the other parts of the two machine states, in a "merged" format. Pieces of data that are the same between the two machines are written just once; at any place where the two machines differ, the value of the first machine is written above the value of the second machine, separated by a horizontal line. The rest of the figure shows what happens when we run this program. On the first step, the pc starts out at 0; the memory, which has two locations, starts out as $[0@\bot, 0@\bot]$; the stack starts out empty; and the next instruction to be executed ($i(pc)$) is *Push* $1@\bot$. On the next step, this value has been pushed on the stack and the next instruction is either *Push* $0@\top$ or *Push* $1@\top$; one or the other of these values is pushed on the stack. On the next, we *Store* the second stack element ($1@\bot$) into the location pointed to by the first (either $0@\top$ or $1@\top$), so that now the memory contains $1@\bot$ in either location 0 or location 1 (the other location remains unchanged, and contains $0@\bot$). At this point, both machines halt. This pair of execution sequences shows that EENI fails: in the initial state, the two programs are indistinguishable to a low observer (their only difference is labeled $\top$), but in the final states the memories contain different values at the same location, both of which are labeled $\bot$.

Thinking about this counterexample, it soon becomes apparent what went wrong with the *Store* instruction: since pointers labeled $\top$ are allowed to vary between the two runs, it is not safe to store a low value through a high pointer. One simple but draconian fix is simply to stop the machine if it tries to perform such a store (i.e., we could add the side-condition $L_x = \bot$ to the rule). A more permissive option is to allow the store to take place, but require it to taint the stored value with the label on the pointer:

$$\frac{i(pc) = Store}{pc \;\; x@L_x : y@L_y : s \;\; m \;\Rightarrow\; pc{+}1 \;\; s \;\; m\{x \mapsto y@(L_x \vee L_y)\}} \qquad (\text{STORE*B})$$

Unfortunately, QuickCheck's next counterexample (Figure 2) shows that this rule is still not quite good enough. This counterexample is quite similar to the first one, but it illustrates a more subtle point: our definition of noninterference allows the observer to distinguish between final memory states that differ only in their *labels*.[1] Since the STORE*B rule taints the label of the stored value with the label of the pointer, the fact that the *Store* changes different locations is visible in the fact that a label changes from $\bot$ to $\top$ on a different memory location in each run. To avoid this issue, we adopt the "no sensitive upgrades" rule [1, 28], which demands that the label on the current contents of a memory location being stored into are above the label of the pointer used for the store —i.e., it is illegal to overwrite a low value via a high pointer (and trying to do so terminates the machine). Adding this side condition brings us to a correct version of the STORE rule.

$$\frac{i(pc) = Store \qquad L_x \sqsubseteq \mathcal{L}_{m(x)}}{pc \;\; x@L_x : y@L_y : s \;\; m \;\Rightarrow\; pc{+}1 \;\; s \;\; m\{x \mapsto y@(L_x \vee L_y)\}} \qquad (\text{STORE})$$

[1] See the first clause of Definition 2.1. One might imagine that this could be fixed easily by changing the definition so that labels are not observable—i.e., $x@\bot \approx x@\top$ for any x. Sadly, this is known not to work [22]. (QuickCheck can also find a counterexample; see §A).

$i = \left[\; Push\ 1@\bot, Push\ \frac{0}{1}@\top, Store, Halt \;\right]$

pc	m	s	$i(pc)$
0	$[0@\bot, 0@\bot]$	$[\,]$	*Push* $1@\bot$
1	$[0@\bot, 0@\bot]$	$[1@\bot]$	*Push* $\frac{0}{1}@\top$
2	$[0@\bot, 0@\bot]$	$\left[\frac{0}{1}@\top, 1@\bot\right]$	*Store*
3	$\left[\frac{1}{0}@\bot, \frac{0}{1}@\bot\right]$	$[\,]$	*Halt*

Figure 1. Counterexample to STORE*AB

$i = \left[\; Push\ 0@\bot, Push\ \frac{0}{1}@\top, Store, Halt \;\right]$

pc	m	s	$i(pc)$
0	$[0@\bot, 0@\bot]$	$[\,]$	*Push* $0@\bot$
1	$[0@\bot, 0@\bot]$	$[0@\bot]$	*Push* $\frac{0}{1}@\top$
2	$[0@\bot, 0@\bot]$	$\left[\frac{0}{1}@\top, 0@\bot\right]$	*Store*
3	$\left[0@\frac{\top}{\bot}, 0@\frac{\bot}{\top}\right]$	$[\,]$	*Halt*

Figure 2. Counterexample to STORE*B

$i = \left[\; Push\ \frac{0}{1}@\top, Push\ 0@\bot, Add, Push\ 0@\bot, Store, Halt \;\right]$

Figure 3. Counterexample to ADD*

$i = \left[\; Push\ 0@\bot, Push\ 1@\bot, Push\ 0@\bot, Store, Push\ \frac{0}{1}@\top, Load, Store, Halt \;\right]$

Figure 4. Counterexample to LOAD*

The next counterexample found by QuickCheck (Figure 3) points out a straightforward problem in the ADD* rule: adding $0@\bot$ to $0@\top$ yields $0@\bot$. (We elide the detailed execution trace for this example and most of the ones that we will see later, for brevity. They can be found in the long version.) The problem is that the taints on the arguments to *Add* are not propagated to its result. The *Store* is needed in order to make the difference observable. The easy (and standard) fix is to use the join of the argument labels as the label of the result:

$$\frac{i(pc) = Add}{pc \;\; x@L_x : y@L_y : s \;\; m \;\Rightarrow\; pc{+}1 \;\; (x{+}y)@(L_x \vee L_y) : s \;\; m} \qquad (\text{ADD})$$

The final counterexample (Figure 4) alerts us to the fact that the LOAD* rule contains a similar mistake to the original STORE*AB rule: loading a low value through a high pointer should taint the loaded value. The program in Figure 4 is a little longer than the one in Figure 1 because it needs to do a little work at the beginning to set up a memory state containing two different low values. It then pushes a high address pointing to one or the other of those cells onto the stack; loads (different, low addresses) through that pointer; and finally stores $0@\bot$ to the resulting address in memory and halts. In this case, we can make the same change to LOAD* as we did to STORE*AB: we taint the loaded value with the join of its label and the address's label. This time (unlike the case of *Store*, where the fact that we were changing the memory gave us additional opportunities for bugs), this change gives us the correct rule for *Load*,

$$\frac{i(pc) = \mathit{Load}}{\boxed{pc \;\; x@L_x : s \;\; m} \Rightarrow \boxed{pc{+}1 \;\; m(x)@L_x : s \;\; m}} \quad \text{(LOAD)}$$

and QuickCheck is unable to find any further counterexamples.

More bugs The original IFC version of the step rules illustrate one set of mistakes that we might plausibly have made, but there are more possible mistakes:

$$\frac{i(pc) = \mathit{Push}\ x@L}{\boxed{pc \;\; s \;\; m} \Rightarrow \boxed{pc{+}1 \;\; x@\bot : s \;\; m}} \quad \text{(PUSH*)}$$

$$\frac{i(pc) = \mathit{Store}}{\boxed{pc \;\; x@L_x : y@L_y : s \;\; m} \Rightarrow \boxed{pc{+}1 \;\; s \;\; m\{x \mapsto y@\bot\}}} \quad \text{(STORE*C)}$$

Although it is unlikely that we'd write these rather silly rules by accident, it is worth including them in our experiments because they can be invalidated by short counterexamples and thus provide useful data points for less effective testing strategies.

We will also gather statistics for a partially fixed but still wrong rule for *Store*, in which the no-sensitive-upgrades check is performed but the result is not properly tainted:

$$\frac{i(pc) = \mathit{Store} \qquad L_x \sqsubseteq \mathcal{L}_{m(x)}}{\boxed{pc \;\; x@L_x : v : s \;\; m} \Rightarrow \boxed{pc{+}1 \;\; s \;\; m\{x \mapsto v\}}} \quad \text{(STORE*A)}$$

3. QuickCheck

We test noninterference using QuickCheck [9], a tool that tests properties expressed in Haskell. Often, QuickCheck is used to test properties that should hold for all inhabitants of a certain type. QuickCheck repeatedly generates random values of the desired type, instantiates the property with them, and checks it directly by evaluating it to a boolean. This process continues until either a counterexample is found or a specified timeout is reached. QuickCheck supplies default test data generators for many standard types. Additionally, the user can supply custom generators for their own types. In order to test EENI, for example, we needed to define custom generators for values, instructions, and machine states (each of which depends on the previous generator: machine states contain instructions, some of which contain values). The effectiveness of testing (i.e., mean time to discover bugs) depends on the sophistication of these generators, a topic we explore in detail in §4.

QuickCheck properties may also be guarded by *preconditions*; EENI is an example of why this is necessary, as it only applies to pairs of indistinguishable initial machine states that both successfully execute to halted states. Testing a property with a precondition proceeds similarly: a sequence of random values are generated and tested, up to a user-specified maximum. The difference is that if there is a precondition, it is instantiated with the random value first. If the precondition does not hold, this random value is summarily discarded. If the precondition does hold, then the rest of the property is checked just as before. Although preconditions are very useful, too high a proportion of discards can lead to slow testing or a badly skewed distribution of test cases (since some kinds of test case may be discarded much more often than others). To help diagnose such problems, QuickCheck can collect statistics about the tests it tried.

When a test fails, the failing test case is often large, containing many irrelevant details. QuickCheck then tries to *shrink* the test case, by searching for a similar but smaller test case that also fails. To do this, it greedily explores a number of "shrinking candidates": modifications of the original failing test case that are "smaller" in some sense. The property is tested for each of these, and as soon as a failure is found, that candidate becomes the starting point for a new shrinking search (and the other candidates are discarded). Eventually this process terminates in a failing test case that is *locally minimal*: none of its shrinking candidates fails. This failing case is then reported to the user. It is often very much smaller than the original randomly generated test case, and it is thus easy to use it to diagnose the failure because it (hopefully) contains no irrelevant details. Just like generation strategies, shrinking strategies are type dependent; they are defined by QuickCheck for standard types, and by the user for other types. We discuss the custom shrinking strategies we use for machine states in §7.

4. Test Generation Strategies

We are ready now to begin exploring ways to generate potential counterexamples. At the outset, we need to address one fundamental issue. Noninterference properties quantify over a *pair* of indistinguishable starting states: $\forall S_1, S_2 \in \mathit{Start}.\ S_1 \approx S_2 \implies \ldots$. This is a very strong precondition, which is unlikely to be satisfied for independently generated states. Instead, we generate *indistinguishable pairs* of states together. The first state is generated randomly using one of the techniques described later in this section. The second is obtained by randomly varying the "high parts" of the first. We refer to the second state as the *variation* of the first. The resulting pair thus satisfies indistinguishability by construction. Note that we have not compromised completeness: by generating a random state and randomly varying we still guarantee that it is possible to generate all pairs of indistinguishable states. Naturally, the resulting distributions will depend on the specifics of the generation and variation methods used, as we shall see.

Since EENI considers only executions that start at initial states, we only need to randomly generate the contents of the instruction memory (the program that the machine executes) together with the *size* of the data memory (in initial states, the contents of the memory are fixed and the stack is guaranteed to be empty).

Figure 5 offers an empirical comparison of all the generation strategies described in this section. For a given test-generation strategy, we inject bugs one at a time into the machine definition and measure the time spent on average until that bug is found (*mean time to failure*, or MTTF). Tests were run one at a time on seven identical machines, each with 4× 2.4 GHz Intel processors and 11.7 GB of RAM; they were running Fedora 16 and GHC 7.4.2, and using QuickCheck 2.5.1.1. We run each test for 5 minutes (300 seconds) or until 4000 counterexamples are found, whichever comes first.

Naive instruction generation The simplest way to generate programs is by choosing a sequence of instructions *independently* and *uniformly*. We generate individual instructions by selecting an instruction type uniformly (i.e., *Noop*, *Push*, etc.) and then filling in its fields using QuickCheck's built-in generators. Labels are also chosen uniformly. We then build the instruction memory by sampling a number (currently a random number between 20 and 50) of instructions from this generator.

The first column of Figure 5 shows how this strategy performs on the bugs from §2. Disappointingly, but perhaps not too surpris-

Generation strategy	NAIVE	WEIGHTED	SEQUENCE	SEQUENCE	BYEXEC
Smart integers?	NO	NO	NO	YES	YES
ADD*	83247.01	5344.26	561.58	30.05	0.87
PUSH*	3552.54	309.20	0.21	0.07	0.01
LOAD*	—	—	73115.63	2258.93	4.03
STORE*A	—	—	38036.22	32227.10	1233.51
STORE*B	47365.97	1713.72	0.85	0.12	0.25
STORE*C	7660.07	426.11	0.41	0.31	0.02
MTTF arithmetic mean	—	—	**18619.15**	**5752.76**	**206.45**
MTTF geometric mean	—	—	**69.73**	**13.33**	**0.77**
Average tests / second	24129	11466	8541	7915	3284
Average discard rate	79%	62%	65%	59%	4%

Figure 5. Comparison of generation strategies for the basic machine. The first part of the table shows the mean time to find a failing test case (MTTF) in milliseconds for each bug. The second part lists the arithmetic and geometric mean for the MTTF over all bugs. The third part shows the number of tests per second and the proportion of test cases that were discarded because they did not satisfy some precondition.

Average number of execution steps: 0.47.
74% stack underflow, 21% halt, and 4% load or store out of range.

Figure 6. Execution statistics for naive instruction generation. Executions fail early, and the main reason for failure is stack underflow.

Average number of execution steps: 2.69.
38% halt, 35% stack underflow, and 25% load or store out of range.

Figure 7. Execution statistics when generating instructions with a weighted distribution. The main reason for failure is now *Halt*, followed by stack underflow.

Average number of execution steps: 3.86.
37% halt, 28% load or store out of range, 20% stack underflow, and 13% sensitive upgrade.

Figure 8. Execution statistics when generating sequences of instructions. Out-of-range addresses are now the biggest reason for termination.

Average number of execution steps: 4.22.
41% halt, 21% stack underflow, 21% load or store out of range, and 15% sensitive upgrade.

Figure 9. Execution statistics when using smart integers with sequences of instructions. The percentage of address out of range errors has halved.

ingly, naive instruction generation can only find four of the six bugs within 5 minutes. How can we do better?

One obvious weakness is that the discard rate is quite high, indicating that one or both machines often fail to reach a halted state. By asking QuickCheck to collect statistics on the execution traces of test cases (Figure 6), we can also see a second problem: the average execution length is only 0.46 steps! Such short runs are not useful for finding counterexamples to EENI (at a minimum, any counterexample must include a *Store* instruction to put bad values into the memory and a *Halt* so that the run terminates, plus whatever other instructions are needed to produce the bad values). So our next step is to vary the distribution of instructions so as to generate programs that run for longer and thus have a chance to get into more interesting states.

Weighted distribution on instructions Figure 6 shows that by far the most common reason for early termination is a stack underflow. After a bit of thought, this makes perfect sense: the stack is initially empty, so if the first instruction that we generate is anything but a *Push*, *Halt*, or *Noop*, we will fail immediately. Instead of a uniform distribution on instructions, we can do better by increasing the weights of *Push* and *Halt*—*Push* to reduce the number of stack underflows, and *Halt* because each execution must reach a halted state to satisfy EENI's precondition. The results after this change shown in the second column of Figure 5. Although this strategy still performs badly for the LOAD* and STORE*A bugs, there is a significant improvement on both discard rates and the MTTF. Run length is also better, averaging 2.71 steps. As Figure 7 shows, executing *Halt* is now the main reason for termination, with stack underflows and out-of-range accesses close behind.

Generating useful instruction sequences more often To further reduce stack underflows we can generate *sequences* of instructions that make sense together. For instance, instead of generating single *Store* instructions, we can additionally generate sequences of the form $[Push\ a, Store]$ (where a is a valid address), and similarly for other instructions that use stack elements. The results are shown in the third column of Figure 5. With sequence generation we can now find all bugs, faster than before. Programs run for slightly longer (3.87). As expected, stack underflows are less common than before (Figure 8) and out-of-range addresses are now the second biggest reason for termination.

Smart integers: generating addresses more often To reduce the number of errors caused by out-of-range addresses, we can give preference to *valid* memory addresses, i.e., integers within memory bounds, when generating values. We do this not only when generating the state of the first machine, but also when *varying* it, since both machines need to halt successfully in order to satisfy the precondition of EENI. Column four of Figure 5 shows the results after making this improvement to the previous generator. We see an improvement on the MTTF. The average run length is now 4.23 steps, and the percentage of address-out-of-range errors is decreased.

Generation by execution We can go even further. In addition to weighted distributions, sequences, and smart integers, we try to generate instructions that *do not cause a crash*. In general (for more interesting machines) deciding whether an arbitrary instruction sequence causes a crash is undecidable. In particular we cannot know in advance all possible states in which an instruction will be executed. We can only make a guess—a very accurate one for this simple machine. This leads us to the following *generation by execu-*

Average execution steps: 11.60 (generated) / 11.26 (variation). 95% halt / halt, 3% halt / load or store out of range, and 1% halt / sensitive upgrade.

Figure 10. Execution statistics for generation by execution, broken down for the variations.

$$i = \left[\begin{array}{l} \mathit{Push}\ \tfrac{2}{5}@\top, \mathit{Jump}, \mathit{Push}\ 1@\bot, \mathit{Push}\ 0@\bot, \mathit{Store}, \\ \mathit{Halt} \end{array}\right]$$

Figure 11. Counterexample to JUMP*AB: A textbook example of an implicit flow

tion strategy: We generate a single instruction or a small sequence of instructions, as before, except that now we restrict generation to instructions that do not cause the machine to crash in the current state. When we find one, we execute it to reach a new state and then repeat the process to generate further instructions. We continue until we have generated a reasonably sized instruction stream (currently, randomly chosen between 20–50 instructions). We discuss how this idea generalizes to machines with nontrivial control flow in §5.

As we generate more instructions, we make sure to increase the probability of generating a *Halt* instruction, to reduce the chances of the machine running off the end of the instruction stream. As a result, (i) we maintain low discard ratios for EENI since we increase the probability that executions finish with a *Halt* instruction, and (ii) we avoid extremely long executions whose long time to generate and run could be more fruitfully used for other test cases.

The MTTF (last column of Figure 5) is now significantly lower than in any previous generation method, although this strategy runs fewer tests per second than the previous ones (because both test case generation and execution take longer). Figure 10 shows that 94% of the pairs both successfully halt, which is in line with the very low discard rate of Figure 5, and that programs run for much longer. Happily, varying a machine that successfully halts has a high probability of generating a machine that also halts.

5. Control Flow

Up to this point, we've seen how varying the program generation strategy can make orders-of-magnitude difference in the speed at which counterexamples are found for a very simple—almost trivial—information-flow machine. Now we are ready to make the machine more interesting and see how these techniques perform on the new bugs that arise, as well as how their performance changes on the bugs we've already seen. In this section, we add *Jump*, *Call*, and *Return* instructions—and, with them, the possibility that information can leak via the program's control flow.

Jumps, implicit flows, and the pc ***label*** We first add a new *Jump* instruction that takes the first element from the stack and sets the pc to that address:

$$\frac{i(pc) = \mathit{Jump}}{\boxed{pc \mid x@L_x : s \mid m} \Rightarrow \boxed{x \mid s \mid m}} \qquad (\text{JUMP*AB})$$

(The jump target may be an invalid address. In this case, the machine will be stuck on the next instruction.)

Note that this rule simply ignores the label on the jump target on the stack. This is unsound, and QuickCheck easily finds the counterexample in Figure 11—a textbook case of an *implicit flow* [23]. A secret is used as the target of a jump, which causes the instructions that are executed afterwards to differ between the two machines; one of the machines halts immediately, whereas the other one does a *Store* to a low location and only then halts, causing the final memories to be distinguishable.

$$i = \left[\begin{array}{l} \mathit{Push}\ 1@\bot, \mathit{Push}\ \tfrac{4}{6}@\top, \mathit{Jump}, \mathit{Halt}, \mathit{Push}\ 0@\bot, \\ \mathit{Store}, \mathit{Push}\ 3@\bot, \mathit{Jump} \end{array}\right]$$

pc	m	s	$i(pc)$
$0@\bot$	$[0@\bot]$	$[\,]$	*Push* $1@\bot$
$1@\bot$	$[0@\bot]$	$[1@\bot]$	*Push* $\frac{4}{6}@\top$
$2@\bot$	$[0@\bot]$	$[\frac{4}{6}@\top, 1@\bot]$	*Jump*
Machine 1 continues...			
$4@\top$	$[0@\bot]$	$[1@\bot]$	*Push* $0@\bot$
$5@\top$	$[0@\bot]$	$[0@\bot, 1@\bot]$	*Store*
$6@\top$	$[1@\bot]$	$[\,]$	*Push* $3@\bot$
$7@\top$	$[1@\bot]$	$[3@\bot]$	*Jump*
$3@\bot$	$[1@\bot]$	$[\,]$	*Halt*
Machine 2 continues...			
$6@\top$	$[0@\bot]$	$[1@\bot]$	*Push* $3@\bot$
$7@\top$	$[0@\bot]$	$[3@\bot, 1@\bot]$	*Jump*
$3@\bot$	$[0@\bot]$	$[1@\bot]$	*Halt*

Figure 12. Counterexample to JUMP*B: *Jump* should not lower the pc label

The standard way to prevent implicit flows is to label the pc—i.e., to make it a value, not a bare integer. Initial states have $pc = 0@\bot$, and after a jump to a secret address the label of the pc becomes $\top$:

$$\frac{i(pc) = \mathit{Jump}}{\boxed{pc \mid x@L_x : s \mid m} \Rightarrow \boxed{x@L_x \mid s \mid m}} \qquad (\text{JUMP*B})$$

While the pc is high, the two machines may be executing different instructions, and so we cannot expect the machine states to correspond. We therefore extend the definition of $\approx_{mem}$ so that *all* high machine states are deemed equivalent. (We call a state "high" if the pc is labeled $\top$, and "low" otherwise.)

5.1 Definition: Machine states $S_1 = \boxed{pc_1 \mid s_1 \mid m_1 \mid i_1}$ and $S_2 = \boxed{pc_2 \mid s_2 \mid m_2 \mid i_2}$ are indistinguishable with respect to memories, written $S_1 \approx_{mem} S_2$, if either $\mathcal{L}_{pc_1} = \mathcal{L}_{pc_2} = \top$ or else $\mathcal{L}_{pc_1} = \mathcal{L}_{pc_2} = \bot$ and $m_1 \approx m_2$ and $i_1 \approx i_2$.

The JUMP*B rule is still wrong, however, since it not only raises the pc label when jumping to a high address but also lowers it when jumping to a low address. The counterexample in Figure 12 illustrates that the latter behavior is problematic. The fix is to label the pc after a jump with the *join* of the current pc label and the label of the target address.

$$\frac{i(pc) = \mathit{Jump}}{\boxed{pc \mid x@L_x : s \mid m} \Rightarrow \boxed{x@(L_x \vee \mathcal{L}_{pc}) \mid s \mid m}} \qquad (\text{JUMP})$$

With this rule for jumps QuickCheck no longer finds any counterexamples. Some readers may find this odd: In order to fully address implicit flows, it is usually necessary to modify the rules for memory stores to handle the case where the pc is labeled high [1, 22]. The current machine doesn't require this, but the reason is subtle: here, the pc can go from $\bot$ to $\top$ when we jump to a secret address, but it never goes from $\top$ to $\bot$! It doesn't matter what the machine does when the pc is high, because none of its actions will ever be observable—all high machine states are indistinguishable.

To make things more interesting, we need to enrich the machine with some mechanism that allows the pc to safely return to $\bot$ after it has become $\top$. One way to achieve this is to add *Call* and *Return* instructions, a task we turn to next.

Restoring the pc label with calls and returns IFC systems (both static and dynamic) generally rely on control flow *merge points* (i.e., post-dominators of the branch point in the control flow graph where the control was tainted by a secret) to detect when the influence of secrets on control flow is no longer relevant and the pc label can safely be restored. Control flow merge points are, however, much more evident for structured control features such as conditionals than they are for jumps. Moreover, since we are doing purely dynamic IFC we cannot distinguish between safe uses of jumps and unsafe ones (e.g., the one in Figure 12). So we keep jumps as they are (only raising the pc label) and add support for structured programming and restoring the pc label in the form of *Call* and *Return* instructions, which are of course useful in their own right.

To support these instructions, we need some way of representing stack frames. We choose a straightforward representation, in which each stack element can now be either a value (as before) or a *return address*, marked R, recording the pc (including its label!) from which the corresponding *Call* was made. We also extend the indistinguishability relation on stack elements so that return addresses are only equivalent to other return addresses and $\mathsf{R}(x_1@L_1) \approx \mathsf{R}(x_2@L_2)$ if either $L_1 = L_2 = \top$ or else $x_1 = x_2$ and $L_1 = L_2 = \bot$ (this is the same as for values).[2]

We also need a way to pass arguments to and return results from a called procedure. For this, we annotate the *Call* and *Return* instructions with an integer indicating how many stack values should be passed or returned (0 or 1 in the case of *Return*). Formally, *Call* n expects an address $x@L_x$ followed by n values on the stack. It sets the pc to x, labels this new pc by the join of L_x and the current pc label (as we did for *Jump*—we're eliding the step of getting this bit wrong at first and letting QuickCheck find a counterexample), and adds the return address frame to the stack *under* the n arguments.

$$\frac{i(pc) = \textit{Call}\ n \qquad L = L_x \vee L_{pc}}{\begin{array}{l} x_{pc}@L_{pc} \ \ x@L_x : v_1 : \ldots : v_n : s \ \ m \ \Rightarrow \\ x@L \ \ v_1 : \ldots : v_n : \mathsf{R}(x_{pc}{+}1@L_{pc}) : s \ \ m \end{array}} \quad (\textsc{Call*b})$$

Return n' traverses the stack until it finds the first return address and jumps to it. Moreover it restores the pc label to the label stored in that R entry, and preserves the first n' elements on the stack as return values, discarding all other elements in this stack frame.

$$\frac{i(pc) = \textit{Return}\ n' \qquad n' \in \{0,1\} \qquad k \geq n'}{\begin{array}{l} pc \ \ v_1 : \ldots : v_k : \mathsf{R}(x@L_x) : s \ \ m \ \Rightarrow \\ x@L_x \ \ v_1 : \ldots : v_{n'} : s \ \ m \end{array}} \quad (\textsc{Return*ab})$$

Finally, we observe that we cannot expect the current EENI instantiation to hold for this changed machine, since now one machine can halt in a high state while the other can continue, return to a low state, and only then halt. Since we cannot equate high and low states (see §A), we need to change the EENI instance we use to $\text{EENI}_{\textit{Init},\textit{Halted}\cap\textit{Low},\approx_{mem}}$, where *Low* denotes the set of states with $pc = \bot$. Thus, we only consider executions that end in a low halting state.

After these changes, we can turn QuickCheck loose and start finding more bugs. The first one, listed in Figure 13, is essentially another instance of the implicit flow bug, which is not surprising given the discussion at the end of the previous subsection. We need to change the rule for *Store* so that the new memory contents are tainted with the current pc label. This eliminates the current counterexample; QuickCheck then finds a very similar one in which the *labels* of values in the memories differ between the two machines. The usual way to prevent this problem is to extend the no-sensitive-upgrades check so that low-labeled data cannot be overwritten in a high context [1, 28]. This leads to the correct rule for stores:

$$\frac{i(pc) = \textit{Store} \qquad \mathcal{L}_{pc} \vee L_x \sqsubseteq \mathcal{L}_{m(x)}}{\begin{array}{l} pc \ \ x@L_x : y@L_y : s \ \ m \ \Rightarrow \\ pc{+}1 \ \ s \ \ m\{x \mapsto y@(L_x \vee L_y \vee \mathcal{L}_{pc})\} \end{array}} \quad (\textsc{Store})$$

The next counterexample found by QuickCheck (Figure 14) shows that returning values from a high context to a low one is unsound if we do not label those values as secrets. To fix this, we taint all the returned values with the pre-return pc label.

$$\frac{i(pc) = \textit{Return}\ n' \qquad n' \in \{0,1\} \qquad k \geq n'}{\begin{array}{l} pc \ \ v_1 : \ldots : v_k : \mathsf{R}(x@L_x) : s \ \ m \ \Rightarrow \\ x@L_x \ \ v_1@\mathcal{L}_{pc} : \ldots : v_{n'}@\mathcal{L}_{pc} : s \ \ m \end{array}} \quad (\textsc{Return*b})$$

The next counterexample, listed in Figure 15, shows (maybe somewhat surprisingly) that it is unsound to specify the number of results to return in the *Return* instruction, because then the number of results returned may depend on secret flows of control. To restore soundness, we need to pre-declare at each *Call* whether the corresponding *Return* will return a value—i.e., the *Call* instruction should be annotated with *two* integers, one for parameters and the other for results; accordingly, each stack frame should include not only a return address but also a number of return values. These changes lead us to the correct rules:

$$\frac{i(pc) = \textit{Call}\ n\ n' \qquad n' \in \{0,1\} \qquad L = L_x \vee L_{pc}}{\begin{array}{l} x_{pc}@L_{pc} \ \ x@L_x : v_1 : \ldots : v_n : s \ \ m \ \Rightarrow \\ x@L \ \ v_1 : \ldots : v_n : \mathsf{R}(x_{pc}{+}1, n')@L_{pc} : s \ \ m \end{array}} \quad (\textsc{Call})$$

$$\frac{i(pc) = \textit{Return} \qquad k \geq n'}{\begin{array}{l} pc \ \ v_1 : \ldots : v_k : \mathsf{R}(x, n')@L_x : s \ \ m \ \Rightarrow \\ x@L_x \ \ v_1@\mathcal{L}_{pc} : \ldots : v_{n'}@\mathcal{L}_{pc} : s \ \ m \end{array}} \quad (\textsc{Return})$$

$$i = \left[\begin{array}{l} \textit{Push}\ \tfrac{3}{6}@\top, \textit{Call}\ 0, \textit{Halt}, \textit{Push}\ 1@\bot, \textit{Push}\ 0@\bot, \\ \textit{Store}, \textit{Return}\ 0 \end{array}\right]$$

Figure 13. Counterexample to old STORE rule in the presence of *Call* and *Return*: Raising pc label is not enough to prevent implicit flows. Once we have a mechanism (like *Return*) for restoring the pc label, we need to be more careful about stores in high contexts.

$$i = \left[\begin{array}{l} \textit{Push}\ 1@\bot, \textit{Push}\ \tfrac{7}{6}@\top, \textit{Call}\ 1, \textit{Push}\ 0@\bot, \textit{Store}, \\ \textit{Halt}, \textit{Push}\ 0@\bot, \textit{Return}\ 1 \end{array}\right]$$

Figure 14. Counterexample to RETURN*AB: *Return* needs to taint the returned values.

$$i = \left[\begin{array}{l} \textit{Push}\ 0@\bot, \textit{Push}\ \tfrac{6}{7}@\top, \textit{Call}\ 0, \textit{Push}\ 0@\bot, \textit{Store}, \\ \textit{Halt}, \textit{Return}\ 0, \textit{Push}\ 0@\bot, \textit{Return}\ 1 \end{array}\right]$$

Figure 15. Counterexample to CALL*B and RETURN*B: It is unsound to choose how many results to return on *Return*.

[2] High return addresses and high values need to be distinguishable to a low observer, as we discovered when QuickCheck generated an unexpected counterexample (which we list in §A).

$$i = \left[\begin{array}{l} \textit{Push } 5@\bot, \textit{Call } 0\ 1, \textit{Push } 0@\bot, \textit{Store}, \textit{Halt}, \\ \textit{Push } 0@\bot, \textit{Push } \tfrac{8}{9}@\top, \textit{Call } 0\ 0, \textit{Pop}, \textit{Push } 0@\bot, \\ \textit{Return} \end{array}\right]$$

Figure 16. Counterexample to POP*: It is unsound not to protect the call stack.

The final counterexample found by QuickCheck is quite a bit longer (see Figure 16). It shows that we cannot allow instructions like *Pop* to remove return addresses from the stack, as does the following broken rule (we use e to denote an arbitrary stack entry):

$$\frac{i(pc) = \textit{Pop}}{\boxed{pc \mid e : s \mid m} \Rightarrow \boxed{pc{+}1 \mid s \mid m}} \quad (\text{POP*})$$

To protect the call frames on the stack, we change this rule to only pop values (all the other rules can already only operate on values).

$$\frac{i(pc) = \textit{Pop}}{\boxed{pc \mid v : s \mid m} \Rightarrow \boxed{pc{+}1 \mid s \mid m}} \quad (\text{POP})$$

Generation by execution and control flow Generation by execution is still applicable in the presence of interesting control flow but we have to make small modifications to the original algorithm. We still generate a single instruction or sequence that does not crash, as before, and we execute to compute a new state. However, unlike before, while executing this newly generated sequence of instructions, it is possible to "land" in a position in the instruction stream where we have already generated an instruction. (e.g. via a backward jump): If this happens then we keep executing the already generated instructions. If the machine stops (or we reach a loop-avoiding cutoff) then we stop the process and return the so-far generated instruction stream. If there are no more instructions to execute then we go on to generate more instructions. There is one more possibility though: the machine may *crashes* while executing an already generated instruction. To address this issue, we make sure that we never generate an instruction that causes the machine to crash in *a number of steps*. We refer to this number of steps as the *lookahead* parameter and in our experiments we use a lookahead of just 2 steps. If we cannot generate such an instruction, we retry with a smaller lookahead, until we succeed.

Since it now becomes possible to generate instruction streams that cause the machine to crash in some number of steps, one might be worried about the discard ratio for EENI. However, the ever increasing probability of generating a *Halt* (discussed in §4) counterbalances this issue.

Finding the bugs We experimentally evaluated the effectiveness of testing for this new version of the machine, by adding the bugs discussed in this section to the ones applicable for the previous machine. The results of generation by execution with lookahead for this machine are shown in the first column of Figure 17. As we can see, all old bugs are still found relatively fast. It takes slightly longer to find them when compared to the previous machine, but this is to be expected: when we extend the machine, we are also increasing the state space to be explored. The new control-flow-specific bugs are all found, with the exception of POP*. Discard rates are much higher compared to generation by execution in Figure 5, for two reasons. First, control flow can cause loops, so we discard machines that run for more than 50 steps without halting.[3] Second, as described previously, generation by execution in the presence of control flow is much less accurate.

[3] Detailed profiling revealed that 18% of the pairs of machines both loop, and loopy machines push the average number of execution steps to 22.

Alternative generation strategies Generation by execution has proved to be simple to implement and effective in finding bugs. Even this method, however, required some tuning, driven by experimental evaluation. For instance, our first implementations did not involve increasing probabilities of *Halt* instructions. We also experimented with different lookahead values. Larger lookaheads introduce significant overheads in generation as every generated instruction costs many steps of execution, and the payoff of lower discard rates was not worth the increased generation cost.

We have also explored (and dismissed) several other generation strategies, and we outline two of these below:

- *Generation by forward execution.* Generation by execution fills in the instruction stream in patches, due to generated jumps. It is hence possible for the instruction stream to contain "holes" with *Noop* instructions. An alternative strategy is to generate instructions in a forward style only: if we generate a branch then we *save* the current state along with the branch target, but keep generating instructions as if the branch was not taken. If we ever reach the target of the branch we may use the saved state as a potentially more accurate state that we can use to generate more instructions. This strategy delivered similar results as generation by execution, but due to its more complicated nature we dismissed it and used the basic design instead.
- *Variational generation by execution.* In this design, we first generate a machine with generation by execution. We then *vary* the machine and run generation by execution for the resulting machine, in the hope that we can fill in the holes in the originally generated instruction stream with instructions from a variational execution. As before, we did not find that the results justified the generation overheads and complexity of this strategy.

6. Strengthening the Tested Property

The last few counterexamples in §5 are fairly long and quite difficult for QuickCheck to find, even with the best test-generation strategy. In this section we explore a different approach: strengthening the *property* we are testing so that counterexamples become shorter and easier to find. Figure 17 summarizes the variants of noninterference that we consider and how they affect test performance.

Making entire low states observable Every counterexample that we've seen involves pushing an address, executing a *Store* instruction, and halting. These steps are all necessary because of the choice we made in §2 to ignore the stack when defining indistinguishability on machine states. A counterexample that leaks a secret onto the stack must continue by storing it into memory; similarly, a counterexample that leaks a secret into the pc must execute *Store* at least twice. This suggests that we can get shorter counterexamples by redefining indistinguishability as follows:

6.1 Definition: Machine states $S_1 = \boxed{pc_1 \mid s_1 \mid m_1 \mid i_1}$ and $S_2 = \boxed{pc_2 \mid s_2 \mid m_2 \mid i_2}$ are indistinguishable with respect to entire low states, written $S_1 \approx_{low} S_2$, if either $\mathcal{L}_{pc_1} = \mathcal{L}_{pc_2} = \top$ or else $\mathcal{L}_{pc_1} = \mathcal{L}_{pc_2} = \bot$, $m_1 \approx m_2$, $i_1 \approx i_2$, $s_1 \approx s_2$, and $pc_1 \approx pc_2$.

We now strengthen $\text{EENI}_{\mathit{Init},\mathit{Halted}\cap\mathit{Low},\approx_{mem}}$, the property we have been testing, to $\text{EENI}_{\mathit{Init},\mathit{Halted}\cap\mathit{Low},\approx_{low}}$; this is stronger because $\approx_{mem}$ and $\approx_{low}$ agree on initial states, while for halted states $\approx_{low} \subset \approx_{mem}$. Indeed, for this stronger property, QuickCheck finds bugs faster (compare the first two columns of Figure 17).

Quasi-initial states Many counterexamples begin by pushing values onto the stack and storing values into memory. This is necessary because each test starts with an empty stack and low, zeroed memory. We can make counterexamples easier to find by allowing the two machines to start with arbitrary (indistinguishable)

Tested property	EENI	EENI	EENI	LLNI	SSNI	SSNI
Starting states	*Init*	*Init*	*QInit*	*QInit*	*All*	*All*
Equivalence relation	$\approx_{mem}$	$\approx_{low}$	$\approx_{low}$	$\approx_{low}$	$\approx_{full}$	$\approx_{full}$
Generation strategy	BYEXEC2	BYEXEC2	BYEXEC2	BYEXEC2	NAIVE	TINYSSNI
ADD*	37.07	2.38	1.38	0.36	0.24	0.11
PUSH*	0.22	0.02	0.02	0.01	1.06	0.06
LOAD*	155.07	37.50	5.73	1.14	3.25	0.61
STORE*A	20018.67	18658.56	124.78	84.08	289.63	16.32
STORE*B	13.02	12.87	16.10	5.25	31.11	0.33
STORE*C	0.35	0.34	0.33	0.08	0.73	0.03
JUMP*A	48.84	7.58	5.26	0.08	1.45	0.09
JUMP*B	2421.99	158.36	104.62	2.80	16.88	0.49
STORE*D	13289.39	12295.65	873.79	232.19	8.77	1.13
STORE*E	1047.56	1129.48	717.72	177.75	2.26	0.29
CALL*A	3919.08	174.66	115.15	5.97	31.71	0.62
RETURN*A	12804.51	4698.17	1490.80	337.74	1110.09	3.10
CALL*B+RETURN*B	69081.50	6940.67	1811.66	396.37	1194.30	4.56
POP*	—	51753.13	16107.22	1828.56	30.68	0.42
MTTF arithmetic mean	—	**6847.81**	**1526.75**	**219.46**	**194.44**	**2.01**
MTTF geometric mean	—	**135.76**	**46.48**	**7.69**	**12.87**	**0.47**
Average tests / second	2795	2797	2391	1224	8490	18407
Average discard rate	65%	65%	69%	0%	40%	9%

Figure 17. Experiments for control flow machine. MTTF given in milliseconds.

stacks and memories; we call such states *quasi-initial*. Formally, the set *QInit* of quasi-initial states contains all states of the form $\boxed{0@\bot \mid s \mid m \mid i}$, for arbitrary s, m, and i.

The advantage of generating more varied start states is that parts of the state space may be difficult to reach by running generated code from an initial state; for example, to get two return addresses on the stack, we must successfully execute two *Call* instructions. Thus, bugs that are only manifested in these hard-to-reach states may be discovered very slowly or not at all. Generating "intermediate" states directly gives us better control over their distribution, which can help eliminate such blind spots in testing. The disadvantage of this approach is that a quasi-initial state may not be *reachable* from any initial state, so in principle QuickCheck may report spurious counterexamples that cannot actually arise in a real execution. For example, a quasi-initial state may have a non-zero value in memory, even though the program contains no *Store* instruction that could have written it. In general, we could address such problems by carefully formulating the important invariants of reachable states and ensuring that we generate quasi-initial states satisfying them. In practice, though, we have not encountered any spurious counterexamples for our machine, even with quasi-initial states.

Instantiating EENI with *QInit*, we obtain a stronger property $\text{EENI}_{\mathit{QInit},\mathit{Halted}\cap\mathit{Low},\approx_{low}}$ (stronger because $\mathit{Init} \subset \mathit{QInit}$) that does indeed find bugs faster, as column 3 of Figure 17 shows.

LLNI: Low-lockstep noninterference While making the full state observable and starting from quasi-initial states significantly improves EENI, we can get even better results by moving to a yet stronger noninterference property. The intuition is that EENI generates machines and runs them for a long time, but it only compares the final states, and only when both machines successfully halt; these preconditions lead to rather large discard rates. Why not compare *intermediate* states as well, and report a bug as soon as intermediate states are distinguishable? While the pc is high, the two machines may be executing different instructions, so their states will naturally differ; we therefore ignore these states and require only that low execution states are pointwise indistinguishable. We call this new property *low-lockstep noninterference* (or *LLNI*).

The function *trace* S computes the (possibly infinite) list of states obtained by executing our machine starting from state S. This is a function because our machine is deterministic.

6.2 Definition: $\mathit{trace}\ S = \begin{cases} [S] & \text{if } S \text{ is stuck} \\ S : \mathit{trace}\ S' & \text{if } S \Rightarrow S' \end{cases}$

While, in practice, we test LLNI over finite prefixes of traces, the definition below is also valid for potentially infinite traces.

6.3 Definition: A machine semantics is *low-lockstep noninterfering* with respect to the indistinguishability relation $\approx$ (written $\text{LLNI}_{\approx}$) if, for any quasi-initial states S_1 and S_2 with $S_1 \approx S_2$, we have $\mathit{trace}\ S_1 \approx^* \mathit{trace}\ S_2$, where $\approx^*$ is defined coinductively by the following rules:

$$\frac{S_1, S_2 \in \mathit{Low} \quad S_1 \approx S_2 \quad t_1 \approx^* t_2}{(S_1 : t_1) \approx^* (S_2 : t_2)} \quad \text{(LOW LOCKSTEP)}$$

$$\frac{S_1 \notin \mathit{Low} \quad t_1 \approx^* t_2}{(S_1 : t_1) \approx^* t_2} \quad \text{(HIGH FILTER)}$$

$$\frac{}{[\,] \approx^* [\,]} \quad \text{(LOCKSTEP END)}$$

$$\frac{S_1 \notin \mathit{Low}}{[S_1] \approx^* t_2} \quad \text{(HIGH END)}$$

$$\frac{S_1 \in \mathit{Low} \quad S_1 \notin \mathit{Halted} \quad S_1 \approx S_2}{[S_1] \approx^* (S_2 : t_2)} \quad \text{(LOW ERROR END)}$$

$$\frac{t_1 \approx^* t_2}{t_2 \approx^* t_1} \quad \text{(SYMMETRY)}$$

The rule LOW LOCKSTEP requires low states in the two traces to be pointwise indistinguishable, while HIGH FILTER (together with SYMMETRY) simply filters out high states from either trace. The remaining rules are about termination: because we are working with termination-insensitive noninterference, we allow one of the traces to continue (maybe forever) even if the other has terminated in a state that is not low (HIGH END) or not halted (LOW ERROR END).

Additionally, we allow the two traces to terminate simultaneously (LOCKSTEP END). We implement these rules in Haskell as a recursive predicate over lazy lists.

In general, LLNI implies EENI, but not vice versa. However, the correct version of our machine does satisfy LLNI, and we have not observed any cases where QuickChecking a buggy machine with LLNI finds a bug that is not also a bug with regard to EENI. Testing LLNI instead of EENI leads to significant improvement in the bug detection rate for all bugs, as the results in the fourth column Figure 17 show. In these experiments no generated machine states are discarded, since LLNI applies to both successful (halting) executions and failing or infinite executions. The generation strategies described in §4 also apply to LLNI without much change; also, as for EENI, generation by execution (with lookahead of 2 steps) performs better than the more basic strategies, so we don't consider those for LLNI.

SSNI: Single-step noninterference Until now, we have focused on using sophisticated (and potentially slow) techniques for generating long-running machine states, and then checking equivalence for low halting states (EENI) or at every low step (LLNI). An alternative is to define a stronger property that talks about *all* possible single steps of execution starting from two indistinguishable states.

Proofs of noninterference usually go by induction on a pair of execution traces; to preserve the corresponding invariant, the proof needs to consider how each execution step affects the indistinguishability relation. This gives rise to properties known as "unwinding conditions" [14]; the corresponding conditions for our machine form a property we call *single-step noninterference* (*SSNI*).

We start by observing that LLNI implies that, if two low states are indistinguishable and each takes a step to another low state, then the resulting states are also indistinguishable. However, this alone is not a strong enough invariant to guarantee the indistinguishability of whole traces. In particular, if the two machines perform a *Return* from a high state to a low state, we would need to conclude that the two low states are equivalent without knowing anything about the original high states. This indicates that, for SSNI, we can no longer consider all high states indistinguishable. The indistinguishability relation on high states needs to be strong enough to ensure that when both machines return to low states, those low states are also indistinguishable. Moreover, we need to ensure that if one of the machines takes a step from a high state to another high state, then the old and new high states are equivalent. The following definition captures all these constraints formally; we write S^L for a machine state whose *pc* label is L.

6.4 Definition: A machine semantics is *single-step noninterfering* with respect to the indistinguishability relation $\approx$ (written $\text{SSNI}_{\approx}$) if the following four conditions are all satisfied:

1. For all low states $S_1^\perp$ and $S_2^\perp$, if $S_1^\perp \approx S_2^\perp$, $S_1^\perp \Rightarrow S_1$, and $S_2^\perp \Rightarrow S_2$, then $S_1 \approx S_2$;
2. For all high states $S^\top$ with $S^\top \Rightarrow S_\star^\top$, we have $S^\top \approx S_\star^\top$;
3. For all high states $S_1^\top$ and $S_2^\top$, if $S_1^\top \approx S_2^\top$, $S_1^\top \Rightarrow S_1^\perp$, $S_2^\top \Rightarrow S_2^\perp$, and states $S_1^\perp$ and $S_2^\perp$ are low, then $S_1^\perp \approx S_2^\perp$;
4. For all low states $S_1^\perp$ and $S_2^\perp$, if $S_1^\perp \approx S_2^\perp$ and $S_1^\perp$ is halted, then $S_2^\perp$ is stuck.

Note that SSNI talks about completely arbitrary states, not just (quasi-)initial ones.

The definition of SSNI is parametric in the indistinguishability relation used, and it can take some work to find the right relation. As discussed above, $\approx_{low}$ is too weak and QuickCheck can easily find counterexamples to condition 3, e.g., by choosing two indistinguishable machine states with $i = [\textit{Return}]$, $pc = 0@\top$, and $s = \left[\mathsf{R}(\frac{0}{1}, 0)@\perp\right]$; after a single step the two machines have distinguishable pcs $0@\perp$ and $1@\perp$, respectively. On the other hand, treating high states exactly like low states in the indistinguishability relation is too strong. In this case QuickCheck finds counterexamples to condition 2, e.g., a single machine state with $i = [\ \textit{Pop}\ ]$, $pc = 0@\top$, and $s = [0@\perp]$ steps to a state with $s = []$, which would not be considered indistinguishable. These counterexamples show that indistinguishable high states can have different pcs and can have completely different stack frames at the top of the stack. So all we can require for two high states to be equivalent is that their memories and instruction memories agree and that the parts of the stacks below the topmost low return address are equivalent. This is strong enough to ensure condition 3.

6.5 Definition: Machine states $S_1 = \boxed{pc_1 \mid s_1 \mid m_1 \mid i_1}$ and $S_2 = \boxed{pc_2 \mid s_2 \mid m_2 \mid i_2}$ are *indistinguishable with respect to whole machine states*, written $S_1 \approx_{full} S_2$, if $m_1 \approx m_2$, $i_1 \approx i_2$, $\mathcal{L}_{pc_1} = \mathcal{L}_{pc_2}$, and additionally

- if $\mathcal{L}_{pc_1} = \perp$ then $s_1 \approx s_2$ and $pc_1 \approx pc_2$, and
- if $\mathcal{L}_{pc_1} = \top$ then *cropStack* $s_1 \approx$ *cropStack* s_2.

The *cropStack* helper function takes a stack and removes elements from the top until it reaches the first low return address (or until all elements are removed).

The fifth column of Figure 17 shows that, even with arbitrary starting states generated completely naively, $\text{SSNI}_{\approx_{full}}$ performs very well. If we tweak the weights a bit and additionally observe that since we only execute the generated machine for only one step, we can begin with very small states (e.g., the instruction memory can be of size 2), then we can find all bugs very quickly. As the last column of Figure 17 illustrates, each bug is found in under 20 milliseconds. (This last optimization is a bit risky, since we need to make sure that these very small states are still large enough to exercise all bugs we might have—e.g., an instruction memory of size 1 is not enough to exhibit the CALL*B+RETURN*B bug using SSNI.) Compared to other properties, QuickCheck executes many more tests per second with SSNI for both generation strategies.

Discussion In this section we have seen that strengthening the noninterference property is a very effective way of improving the effectiveness of random testing our IFC machine. It is not without costs, though. Changing the security property required some expertise and, in the case of LLNI and SSNI, manual proofs showing that the new property implies EENI, the baseline security property. In the case of SSNI we used additional invariants of our machine (captured by $\approx_{full}$) and finding these invariants would probably constitute the most creative part of doing a full security proof. While we could use the counterexamples provided by QuickCheck to guide our search for the right invariants, we expect that for more realistic machines the process of interpreting the counterexamples and manually refining the invariants will be significantly harder than for our very simple machine.

The potential users of our techniques will have to choose a point in the continuum between testing and proving that best matches the characteristics of their practical application. At one end, we present ways of testing the original EENI property without changing it in any way, by putting all the smarts in clever generation strategies. At the other end, one can imagine using random testing just as the first step towards a full proof of a stronger property such as SSNI. For our simple machine, Azevedo de Amorim et al. [2] did in fact prove recently in Coq that SSNI holds, and did not find any bugs that had escaped our testing. Moreover, we proved in Coq that for any deterministic machine and for any indistinguishability relation that is an equivalence, SSNI implies LLNI and LLNI implies EENI.

7. Shrinking Strategies

The counterexamples presented in this paper are not the initial randomly generated tests; they are the result of QuickCheck shrinking these to minimal examples. For example, randomly generated counterexamples to EENI for the PUSH* bug usually consist of 20–40 instructions; the minimal counterexample uses just four. In this section we describe the shrinking strategies we used.

Shrinking labeled values, instructions, and stack elements By default, QuickCheck already implements a shrinking strategy for integers. For labels, we shrink $\top$ to $\bot$, because we prefer to see counterexamples in which labels are only $\top$ if this is essential to the failure. Values are shrunk by shrinking either the label or the contents. (If we need to shrink *both* the label and the contents, then this is achieved in two separate shrinking steps.)

We allow any instruction to shrink to *Noop*, which preserves a counterexample if the instruction was unnecessary; or to *Halt*, which preserves a counterexample if the bug had already manifested by the time that instruction was reached. To avoid an infinite shrinking loop, we do not shrink *Noop* at all, while *Halt* can shrink only to *Noop*. Instructions of the form *Push* a are also shrunk by shrinking a. Finally, instructions of the form *Call* a r are also shrunk by shrinking a or r, or by being replaced with *Jump*.

For quasi-initial or arbitrary states the stack contains a mixture of values and return addresses, which are shrunk pointwise.

Machine states Machine states contain an instruction memory, a data memory, a stack, and the initial pc, the first three of which can be shrunk. We allow any element of the memories or the stack to be shrunk by the methods above; additionally, shrinking may *remove* elements from any of the three.

We allow shrinking to remove arbitrary elements of the data memory or the stack, but in the case of the data memory we first try to remove the last value. This is because removing other elements changes all subsequent memory addresses, likely invalidating the counterexample and thus rendering the shrinking step unsuccessful.

In the case of the instruction memory, we only try to remove *Noop* instructions, since removing other instructions is likely to change the stack or the control flow fairly drastically, and thus risks invalidating a counterexample. Other instructions can still be removed in two stages, by first shrinking them to a *Noop*.

Variations One difficulty that arises when shrinking noninterference counterexamples is that the test cases must be pairs of *indistinguishable* machines. Shrinking each machine state independently will most likely yield distinguishable pairs, which are invalid test cases, since they fail to satisfy the precondition of the property we are testing. In order to shrink effectively, we need to shrink both states of a variation *simultaneously*, and in the same way.

For instance, if we shrink one machine state by deleting a *Noop* in the middle of its instruction memory, then we must delete the same instruction in the corresponding variation. Similarly, if a particular element gets shrunk in a memory location, then the same location should be shrunk in the other state of the variation, and only in ways that produce indistinguishable states. We have implemented all of the shrinking strategies described above as operations on *pairs* of indistinguishable states, and ensured that they generate only shrinking candidates that are also indistinguishable.

When we use the full state equivalence $\approx_{full}$, we can shrink stacks slightly differently: we only need to synchronize shrinking steps on the *low* parts of the stacks. Since the equivalence relation ignores the high half of the stacks, we are free to shrink those parts of the two states independently, provided that high return addresses don't get transformed into low ones.

Optimizing shrinking We applied a number of optimizations to make the shrinking process faster and more effective. One way we sped up shrinking was by turning on QuickCheck's "smart shrinking," which optimizes the order in which shrinking candidates are tried. If a counterexample a can be shrunk to any b_i, but the first k of these are not counterexamples, then it is likely that the first k shrinking candidates for b_{k+1} will not be counterexamples either, because a and b_{k+1} are likely to be similar in structure and so to have similar lists of shrinking candidates. Smart shrinking just changes the order in which these candidates are tried: it defers the first k shrinking candidates for b_{k+1} until after more likely ones have been tried This sped up shrinking dramatically in our tests.

We also observed that many reported counterexamples contained *Noop* instructions—in some cases many of them—even though we implemented *Noop* removal as a shrinking step. On examining these counterexamples, we discovered that they could not be shrunk because removing a *Noop* changes the addresses of subsequent instructions, at least one of which was the target of a *Jump* or *Call* instruction. So to preserve the behavior of the counterexample, we needed to remove the *Noop* instruction *and adjust the target of a control transfer* in the same shrinking step. Since control transfer targets are taken off the stack, and such values can be generated during the test in many different ways, we simply allowed *Noop* removal to be combined with any other shrinking step—which might, for example, decrement any value on the initial stack, or any value stored in the initial memory, or any constant in a *Push* instruction. This combined shrinking step was much more effective in removing unnecessary *Noop*s.

Occasionally, we observed shrunk counterexamples containing two or more unnecessary *Noop*s, but where removing just one *Noop* led to a non-counterexample. We therefore used QuickCheck's *double shrinking* which allows a counterexample to shrink in two steps to another counterexample, even if the intermediate value is not a counterexample. With this technique, QuickCheck could remove all unnecessary *Noop*s, albeit at a cost in shrinking time.

We also observed that some reported test cases contained unnecessary *sequences* of instructions, which could be elided together, but not one by one. We added a shrinking step that can replace any two instructions by *Noop*s simultaneously (and thus, thanks to double shrinking, up to four), which solved this problem.

With this combination of methods, almost all counterexamples we found shrink to minimal examples, from which no instruction, stack element, or memory element could be removed without invalidating the counterexample.

8. Related Work

Generating random inputs for testing is a large research area, but the particular sub-area of testing language implementations by generating random *programs* is less well studied. PLT Redex [18] is a domain-specific language for defining operational semantics within PLT Scheme, which includes a property-based random testing framework inspired by QuickCheck. This framework uses a formalized language definition to automatically generate simple test-cases. To generate better test cases, however, Klein et al. find that the generation strategy needs to be tuned for the particular language; this agrees with our observation that fine-tuned strategies are required to obtain the best results. They argue that the effort required to find bugs using PLT Redex is less than the effort required for a formal proof of correctness, and that random testing is sometimes viable in cases where full proof seems infeasible.

CSmith [27] is a C compiler testing tool that generates random C programs, avoiding ones whose behavior is undefined by the C99 standard. When generating programs, CSmith does not attempt to model the current state of the machine; instead, it chooses program fragments that are correct with respect to some static safety analysis (including type-, pointer-, array-, and initializer-safety, etc.). We found that modeling the actual state of our (much simpler) machine to check that generated programs were hopefully well-formed, as in our generation by execution strategy, made our test-case generation far more effective at finding noninterference bugs. In order to get smaller counterexamples, Regehr et al. present C-Reduce [21], a tool for reducing test-case C programs such as those produced by CSmith. They note that conventional shrinking methods usually introduce test cases with undefined behavior; thus, they put a great deal of effort and domain specific knowledge into shrinking well-defined programs only to programs that remain well-defined. To do this, they use a variety of search techniques to find better reduction steps and to couple smaller ones together. Our use of QuickCheck's *double shrinking* is similar to their simultaneous reductions, although we observed no need in our setting for more sophisticated searching methods than the greedy one that is guaranteed to produce a local minimum. Regehr et al.'s work on reduction is partly based on Zeller and Hildebrandt's formalization of the delta debugging algorithm *ddmin* [29], a non-domain-specific algorithm for simplifying and isolating failure-inducing program inputs with an extension of binary search. In our work, as in Regehr et al.'s, domain-specific knowledge is crucial for successful shrinking.

Another relevant example of testing programs by generating random input is Randoop [19], which generates random sequences of calls to Java APIs. Noting that many generated sequences crash after only a few calls, before any interesting bugs are discovered, Randoop performs *feedback directed* random testing, in which previously found sequences that did not crash are randomly extended. This enables Randoop to generate tests that run much longer before crashing, which are much more effective at revealing bugs. Our generation by execution strategy is similar in spirit, and likewise results in a substantial improvement in bug detection rates.

A state-machine modeling library for (an Erlang version of) QuickCheck has been developed by Quviq [17]. It generates sequences of API calls to a stateful system satisfying preconditions formulated in terms of a model of the system state, associating a (model) state transition function with each API call. API call generators also use the model state to avoid generating calls whose preconditions cannot be satisfied. Our generation-by-execution strategy works in a similar way for straightline code.

A powerful and widely used approach to testing is symbolic execution—in particular, *concolic testing* and related dynamic symbolic execution techniques [8]. The idea is to mix symbolic and concrete execution in order to achieve higher code coverage. The choice of which concrete executions to generate is guided by a constraint solver and path conditions obtained from the symbolic executions. Originating with DART [13] and PathCrawler [26], a variety of tools and methods have appeared. We wondered whether dynamic symbolic execution could be used instead of random testing for finding noninterference bugs. As a first step, we implemented a simulator for a version of our abstract machine in C and tested it with KLEE [7], a state-of-the-art symbolic execution tool. Using KLEE out of the box and without any expert knowledge in the area, we attempted to invalidate various assertions of noninterference. Unfortunately, we were only able to find a counterexample for PUSH*, the simplest possible bug, in addition to a few implementation errors (e.g., out-of-bound pointers for invalid machine configurations). The main problem seems to be that the state space we need to explore is too large, so we don't cover enough of it to reach the particular IFC-violating configurations.

In interactive theorem provers, automatically generating counterexamples for false conjectures can prevent wasting time and effort on proof attempts doomed to fail. Dybjer [10] propose a QuickCheck-like tool for the Agda/Alfa proof assistant. Berghofer and Nipkow [3] proposed a QuickCheck-like tool for Isabelle/HOL. This was recently extended by Bulwahn [5] to also support exhaustive and narrowing-based symbolic testing. Moreover, Bulwahn's tool uses Horn clause data flow analysis to automatically devise generators that only produce data that satisfies the precondition of the tested conjecture [6]. Eastlund [11] implemented DoubleCheck, an adaption of QuickCheck for ACL2. Chamarthi et al. [20] later proposed a more advanced counterexample finding tool for ACL2s, which uses the full power of the theorem prover and libraries to simplify conjectures so that they are easier to falsify. While all these tools are general and only require the statement of the conjecture to be in a special form (e.g., executable specification), so they could in principle be applied to test noninterference, our experience with QuickCheck suggests that for the best results one has to incorporate domain knowledge about the machine and the property being tested. We hope to compare our work against these tools in the future and provide experimental evidence for this intuition.

On the dynamic IFC side Birgisson et al. [4] have a good overview of related work. Our correct rule for *Store* is called the *no-sensitive-upgrades* policy in the literature and was first proposed by Zdancewic [28] and later adapted to the purely dynamic IFC setting by Austin and Flanagan [1]. Hedin and Sabelfeld [15] improve the precision of the no-sensitive-upgrades policy by explicit *upgrade annotations*, which raise the level of a location before branching on secrets. They apply their technique to a core calculus of JavaScript that includes objects, higher-order functions, exceptions, and dynamic code evaluation. Birgisson et al. [4] show that random testing with QuickCheck can be used to infer upgrade instructions in this setting. The main idea is that whenever a random test causes the program to be stopped by the IFC monitor because it attempts a sensitive upgrade, the program can be rewritten by introducing an upgrade annotation that prevents the upgrade from being deemed sensitive on the next run of the program.

9. Conclusions and Outlook

We have shown how random testing can be used to discover counterexamples to noninterference in a simple information-flow machine and how to shrink counterexamples discovered in this way to simpler, more comprehensible ones. The techniques we present bring many orders of magnitude improvement in the rate at which bugs are found, and for the hardest-to-find bugs (to EENI) the minimal counterexamples are 10-15 instructions long – well beyond the scope of naive exhaustive testing. Even if we ultimately care about full security proofs [2], using random testing should greatly speed the initial design process and allow us to concentrate more of our energy on proving things that are correct or nearly correct.

What crucially remains to be seen is whether our results will scale up to more realistic settings. We are actively pursuing this question in the context of CRASH/SAFE, an ambitious hardware–software co-design effort underway at Penn, Harvard, Northeastern, and BAE Systems, with IFC as a key feature at all levels, from hardware to application code. The design involves a number of abstract machines, all much more complex than the stack machine we have studied here. We hope to use random testing both for checking noninterference properties of individual abstract machines and for checking that the code running on lower-level abstract machines correctly implements the higher-level abstractions.

Just how well do our methods need to perform to find bugs effectively in these machines? The true answer is anybody's guess, but for a very rough estimate we might guess there will be around 10× as many instructions on a real SAFE machine, that each instruction might be on average 3× more complex, and that several cross-cutting features will induce additional complexity factors—e.g., "public labels" [16] (?2×), dynamic memory allocation (?2×), a "fat pointer" memory model (?2×), a more complex lattice of labels (?2×), and dynamic principal generation (?2×). Combining these, we could be finding bugs more than 1000× more slowly. If this calculation is in the right ballpark, then EENI is nowhere near fast enough: even for our stack machine, it can take several minutes to find some bugs. Between LLNI and SSNI, on the other hand, there is a tradeoff (discussed in §6) between the overhead of finding good invariants for SSNI and the increased bug-finding rate once this is done. Both approaches seem potentially useful (and potentially fast enough), perhaps at different points in the design process. In particular, checking SSNI may help find invariants that will also be needed for a formal proof.

Preliminary experiments on testing a more complex register machine with some of the extra features enumerated above show that most of our techniques scale directly to the new setting with only minor modifications. For this more complex machine, EENI is (as expected) impractical for finding non-trivial IFC bugs. LLNI variants, on the other hand, uncovered a plethora of (truly accidental) bugs in our initial implementation, and also aided in the discovery of increasingly strong invariants. So far we have been unable to come up with a correct SSNI invariant; however, we have been using the testing framework to hone in on a correct formulation.

We expect that our techniques are flexible enough to be applied to checking other relational properties of programs (i.e., properties of pairs of related runs)—in particular, the many variants and generalizations of noninterference. Beyond noninterference properties, preliminary experiments with checking correspondence between concrete and abstract versions of our current stack machine suggest that many of our techniques can also be adapted for this purpose. For example, the generate-by-execution strategy and many of the shrinking tricks apply just as well to single programs as to pairs of related programs. This gives us hope that they may be useful for checking yet further properties of abstract machines.

Acknowledgments We thank the participants in the discussion at the IFIP WG 2.8 Storulvån meeting that originated this work: Ulf Norell, Rishiyur S. Nikhil, Michał Pałka, Nick Smallbone, and Meng Wang. We also thank Johannes Borgström, Cristian Cadar, Delphine Demange, Matthias Felleisen, Robby Findler, Alex Groce, Casey Klein, Ben Karel, Scott Moore, Michał Pałka, John Regehr, Howard Reubenstein, Alejandro Russo, Deian Stefan, Greg Sullivan, and Andrew Tolmach, for providing feedback on a draft, and the members of the CRASH/SAFE team and Manolis Papadakis for fruitful discussions. This material is based upon work supported by the DARPA CRASH program through the US Air Force Research Laboratory (AFRL) under Contract No. FA8650-10-C-7090. The views expressed are those of the authors and do not reflect the official policy or position of the Department of Defense or the U.S. Government. The work is also partially funded under the Swedish Foundation for Strategic Research grant RAWFP.

References

[1] T. H. Austin and C. Flanagan. Efficient purely-dynamic information flow analysis. In *Workshop on Programming Languages and Analysis for Security (PLAS)*, PLAS. 2009.

[2] A. Azevedo de Amorim, N. Collins, A. DeHon, D. Demange, C. Hriţcu, D. Pichardie, B. C. Pierce, R. Pollack, and A. Tolmach. A verified information-flow architecture. Under submission, July 2013.

[3] S. Berghofer and T. Nipkow. Random testing in Isabelle/HOL. In *2nd International Conference on Software Engineering and Formal Methods (SEFM)*. 2004.

[4] A. Birgisson, D. Hedin, and A. Sabelfeld. Boosting the permissiveness of dynamic information-flow tracking by testing. In *17th European Symposium on Research in Computer Security*, ESORICS. 2012.

[5] L. Bulwahn. The new Quickcheck for Isabelle - random, exhaustive and symbolic testing under one roof. In *2nd International Conference on Certified Programs and Proofs (CPP)*, volume 7679 of *Lecture Notes in Computer Science*. 2012.

[6] L. Bulwahn. Smart testing of functional programs in Isabelle. In *18th International Conference on Logic for Programming, Artificial Intelligence, and Reasoning (LPAR)*, volume 7180 of *Lecture Notes in Computer Science*. 2012.

[7] C. Cadar, D. Dunbar, and D. Engler. KLEE: unassisted and automatic generation of high-coverage tests for complex systems programs. In *8th USENIX conference on Operating systems design and implementation*, OSDI. 2008.

[8] C. Cadar, P. Godefroid, S. Khurshid, C. S. Păsăreanu, K. Sen, N. Tillmann, and W. Visser. Symbolic execution for software testing in practice: preliminary assessment. In *33rd International Conference on Software Engineering*, ICSE '11. 2011.

[9] K. Claessen and J. Hughes. QuickCheck: a lightweight tool for random testing of Haskell programs. In *5th ACM SIGPLAN International Conference on Functional Programming*, ICFP. 2000.

[10] P. Dybjer, Q. Haiyan, and M. Takeyama. Combining testing and proving in dependent type theory. In *16th International Conference on Theorem Proving in Higher Order Logics (TPHOLs)*, volume 2758 of *Lecture Notes in Computer Science*. 2003.

[11] C. Eastlund. Doublecheck your theorems. In *ACL2*. 2009.

[12] J. S. Fenton. Memoryless subsystems. *The Computer Journal*, 17(2):143–147, 1974.

[13] P. Godefroid, N. Klarlund, and K. Sen. DART: directed automated random testing. In *ACM SIGPLAN Conference on Programming Language Design and Implementation*, PLDI. 2005.

[14] J. A. Goguen and J. Meseguer. Unwinding and inference control. In *IEEE Symposium on Security and Privacy*, 1984.

[15] D. Hedin and A. Sabelfeld. Information-flow security for a core of JavaScript. In *25th IEEE Computer Security Foundations Symposium (CSF)*, CSF. 2012.

[16] C. Hriţcu, M. Greenberg, B. Karel, B. C. Pierce, and G. Morrisett. All your IFCException are belong to us. In *34th IEEE Symposium on Security and Privacy*. May 2013.

[17] J. Hughes. QuickCheck testing for fun and profit. In *9th International Symposium on Practical Aspects of Declarative Languages (PADL)*, volume 4354 of *Lecture Notes in Computer Science*. 2007.

[18] C. Klein, J. Clements, C. Dimoulas, C. Eastlund, M. Felleisen, M. Flatt, J. A. McCarthy, J. Rafkind, S. Tobin-Hochstadt, and R. B. Findler. Run your research: On the effectiveness of lightweight mechanization. In *Principles of Programming Languages (POPL)*, 2012.

[19] C. Pacheco and M. D. Ernst. Randoop: feedback-directed random testing for Java. In *22nd ACM SIGPLAN Conference on Object-Oriented Programming Systems And Applications*, OOPSLA. 2007.

[20] H. Raju Chamarthi, P. Dillinger, M. Kaufmann, and P. Manolios. Integrating testing and interactive theorem proving. In *ACL2*, 2011.

[21] J. Regehr, Y. Chen, P. Cuoq, E. Eide, C. Ellison, and X. Yang. Test-case reduction for C compiler bugs. In *33rd ACM SIGPLAN conference on Programming Language Design and Implementation*. ACM, 2012.

[22] A. Russo and A. Sabelfeld. Dynamic vs. static flow-sensitive security analysis. In *23rd Computer Security Foundations Symposium (CSF)*, CSF. 2010.

[23] A. Sabelfeld and A. Myers. Language-based information-flow security. *IEEE Journal on Selected Areas in Communications*, 21(1):5–19, January 2003.

[24] A. Sabelfeld and A. Russo. From dynamic to static and back: Riding the roller coaster of information-flow control research. In *Ershov Memorial Conference*. 2009.

[25] D. Stefan, A. Russo, J. C. Mitchell, and D. Mazières. Flexible dynamic information flow control in Haskell. In *4th Symposium on Haskell*. 2011.

[26] N. Williams, B. Marre, and P. Mouy. On-the-fly generation of K-path tests for C functions. In *19th IEEE International Conference on Automated Software Engineering*, ASE. 2004.

[27] X. Yang, Y. Chen, E. Eide, and J. Regehr. Finding and understanding bugs in C compilers. In *ACM SIGPLAN Conference on Programming Language Design and Implementation*, PLDI. 2011.

[28] S. A. Zdancewic. *Programming Languages for Information Security*. PhD thesis, Cornell University, August 2002.

$$i = \left[\begin{array}{l} \textit{Push}\ 1@\bot, \textit{Push}\ 0@\top, \textit{Push}\ 1@\bot, \textit{Store}, \textit{Push}\ \frac{1@\top}{0@\bot}, \\ \textit{Store}, \textit{Halt} \end{array}\right]$$

pc	m	s	$i(pc)$
$0@\bot$	$[0@\bot, 0@\bot]$	$[]$	*Push* $1@\bot$
$1@\bot$	$[0@\bot, 0@\bot]$	$[1@\bot]$	*Push* $0@\top$
$2@\bot$	$[0@\bot, 0@\bot]$	$[0@\top, 1@\bot]$	*Push* $1@\bot$
$3@\bot$	$[0@\bot, 0@\bot]$	$[1@\bot, 0@\top, 1@\bot]$	*Store*
$4@\bot$	$[0@\bot, 0@\top]$	$[1@\bot]$	*Push* $\frac{1@\top}{0@\bot}$
$5@\bot$	$[0@\bot, 0@\top]$	$\left[\frac{1@\top}{0@\bot}, 1@\bot\right]$	*Store*
$6@\bot$	$\left[\frac{0}{1}@\bot, \frac{1}{0}@\top\right]$	$[]$	*Halt*

Figure 18. A counterexample showing that it is wrong to make high atoms be equivalent to all other atoms.

[29] A. Zeller and R. Hildebrandt. Simplifying and isolating failure-inducing input. *IEEE Transactions on Software Engineering*, 28(2):183–200, 2002.

A. Varying the Indistinguishability Relation

Labels need to be observable As seen in §2, our definition of indistinguishability of values (Definition 2.1) allows the observer to distinguish between final memory states that differ only in their *labels*. One might imagine changing the definition of indistinguishability so that labels are not observable. There are at least two ways one can imagine doing this; however, both are wrong. First, one could try defining indistinguishability of atoms so that $x@\bot \approx y@\top$ for any x and y. QuickCheck easily finds a counterexample to this (Figure 18). Second, one could try refining this so that only $x@\bot \approx x@\top$, i.e., a high atom is equivalent with a low one only when the payloads are equal. QuickCheck also disproves this alternative (Figure 19), and the counterexample produced by QuickCheck illustrates how, even with the correct rules, a difference in the labels of two atoms can be turned into a difference in the values of two atoms. This counterexample is reminiscent of a well-known "flow-sensitivity attack" (Figure 1 in [22]; attributed to [12]).

Weakening EENI when adding calls and returns The counterexample in Figure 20 shows that once we have a way to restore the pc label, we can no longer expect all pairs of halting states to be indistinguishable in EENI. In particular, as the counterexample shows, one machine can halt in a high state, while the other can return to low, and only then halt. Since our indistinguishability relation only equates states with the same pc label, these two halting states are distinguishable. The solution we use in §5 is to weaken the EENI instance, by considering only ending states that are both halting and low (i.e., we change to $\mathrm{EENI}_{\mathit{Init},\mathit{Halted}\cap\mathit{Low},\approx_{mem}}$).

Indistinguishability for stack elements when adding calls and returns In §5 we defined the indistinguishability relation on stack elements so that return addresses are only equivalent to other return addresses and (as for values) $\mathsf{R}(x_1@L_1) \approx \mathsf{R}(x_2@L_2)$ if either $L_1 = L_2 = \top$ or $x_1 = x_2$ and $L_1 = L_2 = \bot$. If instead we considered high return addresses and high values to be indistinguishable, QuickCheck would find a counterexample. This counterexample requires quasi-initial states (and $\approx_{low}$) and is listed in Figure 21. The first machine performs only one *Return* that throws away two elements from the stack and then halts. The second machine returns twice: the first time to the same *Return*, unwinding the stack and raising the pc; and the second time to the *Halt* instruction, labeling the return value high in the process. The final states are distinguishable because the elements on the stack have different labels. As we saw earlier, such a counterexample can be extended to one in which values also differ.

$$i = \left[\begin{array}{l} \textit{Push}\ 1@\bot, \textit{Push}\ 0@\frac{\top}{\bot}, \textit{Push}\ 0@\bot, \textit{Store}, \textit{Push}\ \frac{7}{9}@\top, \\ \textit{Call}\ 1\ 0, \textit{Halt}, \textit{Push}\ 0@\bot, \textit{Store}, \textit{Return} \end{array}\right]$$

pc	m	s	$i(pc)$
$0@\bot$	$[0@\bot]$	$[]$	*Push* $1@\bot$
$1@\bot$	$[0@\bot]$	$[1@\bot]$	*Push* $0@\frac{\top}{\bot}$
$2@\bot$	$[0@\bot]$	$\left[0@\frac{\top}{\bot}, 1@\bot\right]$	*Push* $0@\bot$
$3@\bot$	$[0@\bot]$	$\left[0@\bot, 0@\frac{\top}{\bot}, 1@\bot\right]$	*Store*
$4@\bot$	$\left[0@\frac{\top}{\bot}\right]$	$[1@\bot]$	*Push* $\frac{7}{9}@\top$
$5@\bot$	$\left[0@\frac{\top}{\bot}\right]$	$\left[\frac{7}{9}@\top, 1@\bot\right]$	*Call* 1 0
Machine 1 continues...			
$7@\top$	$[0@\top]$	$[1@\bot, \mathsf{R}(6,0)@\bot]$	*Push* $0@\bot$
$8@\top$	$[0@\top]$	$[0@\bot, 1@\bot, \mathsf{R}(6,0)@\bot]$	*Store*
$9@\top$	$[1@\top]$	$[\mathsf{R}(6,0)@\bot]$	*Return*
$6@\bot$	$[1@\top]$	$[]$	*Halt*
Machine 2 continues...			
$9@\top$	$[0@\bot]$	$[1@\bot, \mathsf{R}(6,0)@\bot]$	*Return*
$6@\bot$	$[0@\bot]$	$[]$	*Halt*

Figure 19. A counterexample showing that it is also wrong to make high atoms equivalent to low atoms with the same payload.

$$i = \left[\ \textit{Push}\ \frac{2}{3}@\top, \textit{Call}\ 0\ 0, \textit{Halt}, \textit{Return}\ \right]$$

pc	m	s	$i(pc)$
$0@\bot$	$[]$	$[]$	*Push* $\frac{2}{3}@\top$
$1@\bot$	$[]$	$\left[\frac{2}{3}@\top\right]$	*Call* 0 0
Machine 1 continues...			
$2@\top$	$[]$	$[\mathsf{R}(2,0)@\bot]$	*Halt*
Machine 2 continues...			
$3@\top$	$[]$	$[\mathsf{R}(2,0)@\bot]$	*Return*
$2@\bot$	$[]$	$[]$	*Halt*

Figure 20. A counterexample justifying the change to $\mathrm{EENI}_{\mathit{Init},\mathit{Halted}\cap\mathit{Low},\approx_{mem}}$ in §5.

$$i = [\ \textit{Return}, \textit{Halt}\ ]$$

pc	m	s	$i(pc)$
$0@\bot$	$[]$	$\left[0@\bot, \frac{0@\top}{\mathsf{R}(0,0)@\top}, 0@\bot, \mathsf{R}(1,1)@\bot\right]$	*Return*
Machine 1 continues...			
$1@\bot$	$[]$	$[0@\bot]$	*Halt*
Machine 2 continues...			
$0@\top$	$[]$	$[0@\bot, \mathsf{R}(1,1)@\bot]$	*Return*
$1@\bot$	$[]$	$[0@\top]$	*Halt*

Figure 21. A counterexample that motivates the indistinguishability of stack elements for the machine with calls and returns.

Author Index

www.ingramcontent.com/pod-product-compliance
Ingram Content Group UK Ltd.
Pitfield, Milton Keynes, MK11 3LW, UK
UKHW051413290926
15471UKWH00009B/1588

9 781450 323260